A RAGE TO LIVE

Also by Mary S. Lovell

Straight on till Morning: The Biography of Beryl Markham
The Sound of Wings: The Biography of Amelia Earhart
Cast No Shadow: The Spy who changed the course of World War II
A Scandalous Life: The Biography of Jane Digby
The Splendid Outcast: The African Short Stories of Beryl Markham

MARY S. LOVELL

A RAGE TO LIVE

A biography of Richard and Isabel
BURTON

Wise wretch! With pleasure too refined to please,
With too much spirit to be e'er at ease,
With too much quickness ever to be taught;
With too much thinking to have common thought,
You purchase pain with all that joy can give,
And die of nothing but a rage to live . . .

Alexander Pope

W·W·NORTON

NEW YORK · LONDON

For information about permission to reproduce selections from this book,
write to Permissions, W. W. Norton & Company, Inc.,
500 Fifth Avenue, New York, NY 10110.

Composition and manufacturing by the Haddon Craftsmen, Inc.

Library of Congress Cataloging-in-Publication Data

Lovell, Mary S.
    A rage to live : a biography of Richard and Isabel Burton / Mary
S. Lovell. — 1st American ed.
        p.   cm.
    Includes bibliographical references (p.   ) and index.
    ISBN 0-393-04672-9
    1. Burton, Richard Francis, Sir, 1821–1890. 2. Burton, Richard
Francis, Sir, 1821–1890—Marriage. 3. Explorers' spouses—Great
Britain—Biography. 4. Explorers—Great Britain—Biography.
5. Scholars—Great Britain—Biography. 6. Burton, Isabel, Lady,
1831–1896.   I. Title.
G246.B8L68   1998
910′.92′241—dc21
[B]   98-29886
                                                                    CIP

W. W. Norton & Company, Inc., 500 Fifth Avenue, New York, NY 10110
http://www.wwnorton.com

W. W. Norton & Company Ltd., 10 Coptic Street, London WC1A 1PU

2 3 4 5 6 7 8 9 0

This book is dedicated with my thanks to

Quentin Keynes

who has always been fascinated with
Richard Burton's story. Despite the fact
that twenty-four hours in a day are barely
sufficient to allow him to deal with his
own interests, he has been unstinting in his
help and encouragement to me.

CONTENTS

Author's Note

Burton often used archaic words, he also invented words (e.g. 'unfriends'), and he spelled foreign place-names and expressions phonetically, and inconsistently. The forenames of associates suffered; one called Huseyn might be spelled Hoseyn, Hosayn, Husayn and Huseyn in a single work. Even in his book titles, variances occur; for example he spelled Sind (in present-day Pakistan) variously as Sindh, Scinde and Scindh (see Bibliography). Place-names in Africa received similar treatment. As a general rule, throughout this book I have used present-day spellings in the run of text, but have retained the original spelling in quoted extracts.

Also, where I felt it would enhance readability, I have taken the liberty of adding punctuation to some extracts from original manuscripts. I have not included square brackets to indicate these additions, i.e. [,] or can[']t, feeling this would be unnecessarily intrusive.

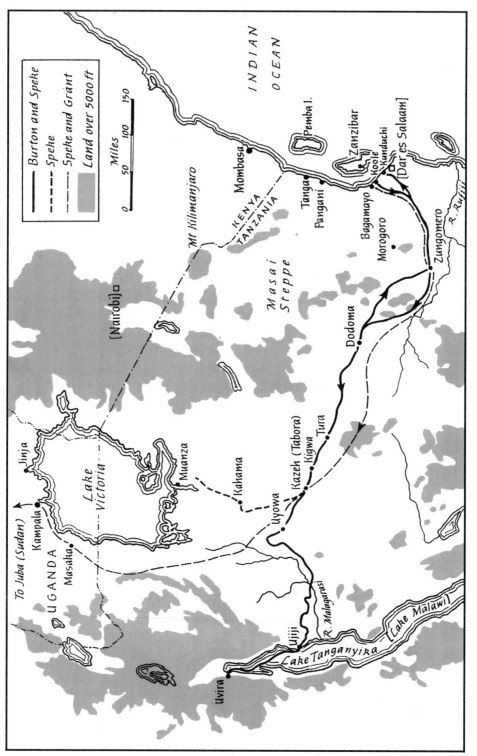

Burton's East African Journeys, 1857–9

Richard Francis Burton 1821–1890

*He was one of those men in whom nature runs riot; she endows him
with not one or two but twenty different talents, all of them far beyond
the average, and then withholds the one ingredient that might have
brought them to perfection – a sense of balance and direction . . .
Burton never entirely went on an expedition to reach a goal; he was
also out to explore himself in new surroundings. This is why his books
are greater than his journeys and why the man is greater than his
career. The mystery of Central Africa died when the country was
explored, but Burton lives on as a splendid and provoking enigma.*
Alan Moorehead

Isabel Arundell Burton 1831–1896

*I can see Mrs Burton now, a stylishly dressed woman – my childish
idea of a princess – talking, talking, talking . . . [she] was of medium
height, dark haired, bright complexioned, and very animated in her
manner . . . [her] stream of eloquence never seemed to be
exhausted . . . she waved her hand eloquently and her eyes flashed.*
Laura Friswell

INTRODUCTION

After Richard Burton's death his widow Isabel burned all his unpublished manuscripts, diaries and papers, in a conflagration which lasted days . . .

That, at least, is the generally accepted story. It is how Isabel Burton has been depicted in history, and a score of biographies written in the century since the deaths of Richard and Isabel have only served to bolster this charge of literary vandalism. In fact, a number of collections both private and institutional throughout the world containing large tranches of Burton papers (many used in this book have never previously been published or used) prove that such burning as took place was neither so complete, nor the *mindless* act, of which she has been so often accused. Rather, the surviving Burton papers – scattered though they are – probably constitute one of the largest collections of papers of any individual to come down to us from that age of diary burners.

In writing this biography the biggest single problem was caused by the overwhelming amount of surviving material; what to edit so that Burton researchers and collectors (of whom there are an astonishing number) are informed of newly discovered information, without cheating the reader new to Burton's story by over-condensing already known facts. Well-known anecdotes contained in earlier biographies had to be edited out to make way for more important new material.

The first draft of the manuscript for this book consisted of over a thousand pages and 280,000 words. Cuts had to be made, but even to reach the draft stage I had jettisoned perhaps a third of my research.

I was vaguely aware of the accepted version of the destruction of Burton papers when, in 1992, I was researching a biography of Jane Digby (the Victorian aristocrat who became matriarch of a Bedouin tribe). The Burtons had been close friends of Jane during their time in Damascus and, as always in my biographical research, my first discipline was to seek out papers and diaries of the contemporaries of my subjects. This took me to the Wiltshire Record Office at Trowbridge where, I had ascertained, the Arundell papers were lodged. Knowing that Isabel was a member of the Arundell family of Wardour Castle in Wiltshire, I hoped that there might be some clues among the surviving papers of her relatives; letters from her, perhaps, from Damascus. I was agreeably surprised to be advised by the archivist, Mr Stephen Hobbs, that the Records Office had 'seven boxes of unclassified material belonging to Isabel Burton' (see Appendix 1) and set about unpacking them with alacrity.

Although there was very little about Jane Digby in the boxes, there was a great deal of fascinating Burton material; letters, notes, family photograph albums, manuscripts, journals and cuttings albums – and I realised instantly that most of it had not been included in the two most recent biographies I had read about the Burtons. I surmised that the biographers concerned had not found the Trowbridge collection. Later, as I researched further, I came to realise that no biographers had ever found this material. It was unknown to published writers and researchers on Burton and was, in fact, important enough to form the base of a new biography. My publishers agreed. When I was finally able to start working full-time on the Burton book I began, as usual, with a plan of campaign. No biographer can afford to ignore the existing bibliography, but I was determined that this would not be yet another rehash of the previous biographies. Rather, I would examine, and take photocopies where possible, of all existing original papers and documents that the Burtons and their connections had left and work from those, reading all the known collections of Burton materials and seeking out hitherto unknown ones. And though I could not go to the places where Richard Burton had lived in India, Pakistan and South America, I could visit, and was familiar with, all the other places associated with the story of this extraordinary couple; East Africa, Syria and the Middle East, the United States and various European cities including Trieste where they lived until Burton's death in 1890.

My research has resulted in the discovery of numerous new primary documents which answer many of the questions that have perplexed Burton scholars until now. Not all, but many. For example, previous biographers without the benefit of the Trowbridge papers (and only one had limited use of the treasure trove that forms the Quentin Keynes collection, to which I was given unreserved access), maintain that Burton's marriage was a disaster. In fact, as we shall see it was a mutual joy and highly beneficial to him. I found additional previously unknown caches of letters and papers, such as those in the fascinating archives of Zanzibar which, like the above, have never been examined by Burton researchers.

Disregarding this new material, the last two major biographies of Richard Burton are first-class studies. Fawn Brodie's brilliant and perceptive synopsis of Burton's work on *One Thousand and One Nights* could hardly be improved upon. Frank McLynn's analysis of his academic prowess is that of one scholar writing of another.[1] Yet lacking historical evidence, both authors relied heavily on post-Freudian psychoanalysis to speculate upon Burton's motives and explain his general behaviour, and his relationship with Isabel. Although in no way wishing to undermine either of these excellent books, I felt deeply uneasy about this methodology when it was used, *without supporting historical evidence*, to reinforce personal theory, to establish fundamental characteristics in Burton, and particularly to deduce his sexual inclinations. In effect, the persons asking the questions were also providing the answers, a century after the subject's death, by extracting highly selective quotes, often from the subject's fictional writings, and in at least one important case using incorrect data (see pp. 343–345).

In this way both writers reached the conclusion that Burton was either a crypto-homosexual, or a bisexual. Part of the reasoning used by both was the fact that Burton liked to have about him younger men such as John Hanning Speke, Charles Tyrwhitt Drake, Vincent Lovett Cameron and Foster Fitzgerald Arbuthnot. But this completely ignores the fact that some of his closest friends in life – Richard Monkton Milnes, Henry Murray, Walter Scott and George Bird, to name a few – were many years older, and also that he was equally friendly with contemporaries such as John Steinhaueser and Alfred B. Richards. In short, Burton drew friends, quite normally, across the generations and from both sexes. It is demonstrably untrue to say, as one of these writers did, that Burton was a misogynist with no women friends.

I am not a trained psychologist and I do not automatically reject psychology as a biographical tool (though I confess to a sinking feeling when I see phrases such as 'he was tortured by sexual guilt' in any biography). But psychoanalysis is not an exact science, even when the subject is alive and able to answer in person. The charge of homosexuality has no power to shock as we approach the end of the twentieth century. Society has learned tolerance in the century since the persecution of Oscar Wilde, but in the present climate it is not enough for the subject of a biography to be simply extraordinary. There is a disturbing trend towards imposing some fashionable psychiatric spin to increase readership. My research has unearthed a great deal of previously unpublished material which demonstrates that Burton was heterosexual, and that prior to his successful marriage he had a number of heterosexual affairs; that he had a number of close platonic women friends such as the novelist, Ouida, and Lallah Bird (a member of the Bohemian set), with both of whom he maintained a lively and affectionate correspondence from his youth until his death; and that he loved Isabel in the romantic sense.

Burton was a questioner, a polymath who searched with intellectual curiosity for explanations in multi-disciplines; so I do not rule out sexual experimentation by him. He regarded all aspects of sex – sexual behaviour, sexual love, sexual pleasures and preferences – as an important subject for anthropological study during his entire life, even after he became (as I suspect) impotent in middle age. And like the ancient Greeks he read and often quoted, particularly Ovid, he felt no sense of shame about this interest which he recognised as a primary instinct in humans. I am absolutely certain, however, that there is no historical evidence to support the theory that Burton was homosexual. The burden of *proof* is on those who imply the reverse. It is not good enough to point to the few chapters he wrote on homosexual practices as conclusive evidence, when the bulk of his erotic works concentrates on heterosexual activities, and on several occasions in his *private* correspondence he referred to homosexuality as a perversion.

My best guess after four years' work, three of those years spent in full-time research, is that as a young unattached Army officer Richard was initially amused and normally excited by the 'naughty' pornographic element of the erotica he found in India and Arabia. But the authoritative scholarship in his learned and now famous translations of the *Kama Sutra*, *The Perfumed Garden* and *The Arabian Nights* betrays a far more complex interest than that of a man enjoying a few chuckles with his cronies over a piece of forbidden literature.

He was a many-faceted man who combined the unlikely qualities of both daring adventurer and scholar. A near genius, he never attained the destiny which might have been his because he never learned to discipline the massive intellect that enabled him, for example, to learn 29 languages and a dozen additional dialects, many so fluently that he could fool native speakers into believing he had been born in their country. He had a teacher's love of passing on knowledge and his books are a cornucopia of information, though they are not easy reading. However, his natural inquisitiveness makes them comprehensive repositories of knowledge on diverse subjects. He dropped out of Oxford University after little more than a year's tuition and thereafter his acquisition of knowledge was self-acquired, yet his papers and books demonstrate his ability to debate obscure subjects and themes at intensive levels of comprehension, even with men who had dedicated their lives to their specific study. He once ended a letter on Shakespeare's endless ability, to a correspondent who was an eminent Shakespeare scholar, with the phrase 'each man makes his own Shakespeare'.[2]

By the same standard, each biographer makes their own Burton by a unique perception of an amount of material too substantial to utilise in full. There is enough information on Burton in his own published works, private papers and the publications and papers of other writers to expand probably a dozen of the chapters in this book into books in their own right. And Burton crammed so much living into his three-score years and – almost – ten that each one could potentially merit publication.

But even a life packed with incident and adventure was insufficient to ensure really lasting celebrity. A young relative of mine was recently overheard telling a friend that I was 'writing a book about Richard Burton'.

'But,' he finished apologetically, 'it's not the *famous* one.'

1

A GIPSY CHILDHOOD
1821–1840

Richard Burton began his autobiography, 'Autobiographers generally begin too late. Elderly gentlemen of eminence sit down to compose memories and describe with fond minuteness babyhood, childhood, and boyhood and drop the pen before reaching adolescence . . .'[1] Fortunately Burton did not drop his pen until he had reached the prime of his life. Because most of his early papers perished in a warehouse fire he is virtually the only authority for much of what is known about his early years, and although some of the salient facts can be verified by diligent research we must take his word (and, sometimes, a pinch of salt) for the more colourful anecdotes.

Even so, when he started dictating his autobiography to his wife, en route to India in 1876,[2] he began with a surprising error. He stated that his birthplace was his grandparents' home, Barham House, Barham Wood, near Elstree in Hertfordshire. In fact he was born in Torquay, Devon at 9.30 p.m. on the evening of 19 March 1821. One would assume that he had never been told where he was born but for the fact that in his application for entry to Trinity College, Oxford, at the age of 19 he wrote his birthplace as 'Torquay'.[3] He was the first child of Captain Joseph Netterville Burton and his wife Martha, and by the date of the child's baptism six months later the young family had moved to Barham House to live with his mother's parents Richard and Sarah Baker.[4] At the parents' request the officiating clergyman made a note of Richard's birth and birthplace alongside the baptismal entry.[5]

The forces of destiny were at work early in the child's life, for it seems that a quarrel between the King and Queen of England was, ultimately, partially responsible for the peripatetic style of life that Richard's parents subsequently adopted, and the restless, roving traits this engendered in their son.

Captain Joseph Burton was half Irish. In appearance he was considered very handsome with a high 'Roman' profile, swarthy colouring, black hair and piercing black eyes. He was the third son, one of twelve children[6] of a Protestant clergyman who had migrated from Westmorland, in the north of England, to Ireland and combined his ecclesiastic duties with those of a local squire in Tuam, County Galway. Joseph's mother, also the child of a clergyman, was said to be the great-granddaughter of King Louis XIV by his mistress the Countess of Montmorency, and had inherited 'unmistakable Bourbon features'.[7] Life in Ireland was inexpensive so the family was comfortably circumstanced, but Joseph – like his brothers – was nevertheless obliged to earn a living. Being 'gently born', however, there were only two acceptable options open to him: to purchase a commission in the Army, which could prove expensive, or to follow his father into the church.

His dilemma was resolved easily enough when King George III's Army recruiting in Ireland offered free commissions to gentlemen who could bring with them a number of men willing to take the King's shilling. The 17-year-old Joseph rounded up several dozen youths from his father's estate who were happy to accompany the young master for the sheer adventure of it. In a short time the adventure wore off and the young men of Tuam found their way back to the soil, but by then Joseph Burton had been commissioned and posted to Sicily where he saw service in 1802 under Sir John Moore and was promoted to second-lieutenant in 1807. A decade or so later he distinguished himself in the taking of Genoa[8] and the year 1815 found him still a Captain, but with the 'local rank' of Major, the senior officer of the small British garrison at Genoa in Italy.

At this point in Joseph Burton's military career fate intervened in the ample form of Her Royal Highness Princess Caroline, the discarded wife of the Prince Regent. In April and May 1815 at the time of the visit to Genoa of the Princess, Captain Burton little imagined how large an influence she would have, albeit indirectly, on his future life. For him and his fellow officers she was the wife of the heir to the throne, and as such was owed all the loyalty and respect due to that position. She in turn showed great kindness to the British officers, welcoming their visits to her residence about half a mile outside the city in the respectable suburbs. Her cheerful condescension was much appreciated, and it would be fair to say that she won their affection and admiration during her brief visit.[9]

With Napoleon safely confined in St Helena and the peace concluded, Joseph returned home to Ireland where he found the family estate in dire condition following the death of his father. Having obtained his mother's permission, he called in the tenants who had paid no 'rint' for a considerable time and impressed upon them that he would be calling personally to collect all rents and arrears. Thereafter he was shot at on a regular basis as he rode around the estate, but he collected no rents. It did not take him long to decide that a bucolic existence in Ireland was no substitute for the glories of Italy. He had grown away from his numerous brothers and sisters, and the damp climate aggravated his asthma. He therefore returned to his regiment, the 36th Foot, in Nottinghamshire. The asthma continued to bother him and he was placed on extended sick leave.

At one of the parties or balls, invitations for which were inevitably showered upon unmarried officers, Joseph met Martha Baker, one of three heiress daughters of a wealthy Hertfordshire squire. They married in early 1820 at much the same time as King George III died following his record reign of 59 years. The new monarch, George IV, had no intention of sharing his throne with his separated wife whom he abhorred and, as a consequence, in May or June of that year the hapless Joseph, scarcely returned from his honeymoon in the Lake District, was summoned by the secret committee whose task it was to gather evidence of adultery by Princess (now Queen) Caroline, and ordered to provide testimony against her to enable the King to obtain a divorce.

Joseph could probably recall very little, if any, of the Princess's said-to-be scandalous behaviour in Italy which, in fact, was rather more a breach of good taste than impropriety. Her chief indiscretion in Genoa appears to have consisted of being drawn through the streets in an illuminated phaeton constructed in the shape of a conch shell. It was decorated with mother-of-pearl, and drawn by two tiny piebald ponies led by a child dressed as a pink Cupid. Inside, the Princess reclined: 'a vast woman of fiftyish, short, round, and high in colour, wrapped in a gauzy *décolleté* gown with a pink bodice. The pink feathers of her head-dress floated in the wind, and a short white skirt came to scarcely past her knees, leaving on view fat pink legs.'[10]

George IV is said to have blanched at the sheer vulgarity of it, and blushed at the impression conveyed in Europe of the British royal family, made a laughing-stock by the unfortunate Princess who was now Queen. But having tolerated the often licentious and expensive vulgarity of the King in his days as Regent, His Majesty's level-headed subjects were not so easily persuaded that the Queen's sins were sufficiently offensive to merit her being set aside. Captain Joseph Netterville Burton, like the majority of the British gentry, took the Queen's side, not least because she had shown kindness to the men of his garrison five years earlier. Therefore, when asked, he declined to act as witness for the prosecution.

Little is known of Joseph's career apart from the standard terse notes in his Army record.[11] Richard Burton tells us that his father was a keen duellist 'and shot one brother-officer twice, nursing him tenderly each time afterwards'. The offence on each occasion had been 'saying something unpleasant' and though the first affair of honour resulted in Joseph merely 'winging' his man, an Irishman, at the second meeting the unfortunate opponent was crippled for life.[12] Neither of these affairs of honour is mentioned in his Army record. Before being summoned by the War Office on the King's business Joseph had been offered the post of aide-de-camp to Lord William Bentinck, Governor General of India, with all the prospects of promotion that such a position entailed. Joseph, however, laid all such prospects on the line when he 'flatly refused' to give evidence about his Queen, though ordered to do so by the Commander-in-Chief (Lord Wellington) who was acting for the King. The unfortunate result of his abjuration was that he was requested to stand down from active service and placed indefinitely 'on half-pay'.[13]

The couple's first child, Richard Francis, was born in March of the following year. At the time the Burtons were living in Torquay, then a 'delightful & romantic watering place' of some 2,000 people which had, a contemporary guide book informs, 'become a fashionable resort for invalids'.[14] Tor Church records a large number of Bakers in its registers, and it is probable that the couple were staying with relatives of Martha so that Joseph could take advantage of the mild spring of the West Country and the benefits of the spa to relieve his asthma. Coincidentally, Richard was born within cannon-shot of the birthplaces of two men with whom he would be often compared; the Elizabethan scholar/adventurers Walter Raleigh and Francis Drake.

It was Richard Burton's belief that his parents had gone to live abroad when he was only a few months old, and this sits oddly with his 'first memory' of being 'brought down after dinner at Barham House to eat white currants, seated upon the knee of a tall man with yellow hair and blue eyes', a description which fits his grandfather Baker.[15] In fact, family documents reveal that Richard was five years old when Joseph Burton took his family to Europe for health reasons.[16] By then two further children had been born: Maria Katherine Elizabeth in 1823, and Edward Joseph in July 1824. Joseph's elder brother Francis had married Martha's younger sister Sarah, and Richard Baker was clearly wary of his two Burton sons-in-law. When he died of a heart attack, it was found that he had sensibly left his daughters' considerable inheritances tied up in trusts providing them with a lifetime income but no access to the capital. However, the old man doted on young Richard and indeed was said to have been on his way to his solicitors to change his will in the child's favour when he collapsed and died. It was probably the English weather, as well as the size of their income, which provoked the Burtons' move to the softer climate of Southern Europe, for Joseph's asthma had worsened and he found the English winters intolerable. In 1825[17] the family settled in the heart of France at Tours where there was a sizeable English community, surprising considering the recent conflict between the two countries.

Joseph and Martha Burton leased the Chateau de Beauséjour. It was a rambling old mansion on a hill on the right bank of the Loire, surrounded by pastures and vineyards and commanding a splendid view of the surrounding countryside. Here the young Burtons flourished despite the fact that their English nurse could not stand living among foreigners and quickly returned home, leaving her charges to a succession of Frenchwomen. Their childhood was the usual mixture of schoolroom, dogs and horses. They slept in a nursery at the top of the house and recalled being 'hustled out of our little cots, and taken to the drawing room' in the frequent violent storms of the hot summers, and playing with their Noah's ark and the carved wooden animals. Summer holidays were spent at St Malo and other seaside resorts in Brittany.

On his own admission, Richard's father loved Richard 'more than any other being on earth'.[18] He also considered his bright son an infant prodigy, and Richard was therefore provided with the best education that could be procured by a private tutor. That he began learning his alphabet, multiplication tables and prayers at a very tender age is not very surprising, but that he began Latin at three and Greek at four is perhaps more unusual. He also began what he calls 'the study of Arms' almost as soon as he could walk, so that guns and fencing – particularly the latter – became lifelong passions.

When Richard was six, Maria four and Edward three, their education at home came to an end and, with their bundles of books tied with leather straps, they were taken in a small carriage each day to a school in the nearby town. Richard hated it, which is at odds with his insatiable and lifelong desire to acquire knowledge and his ability to absorb information quickly and easily. His antipathy was due to the school's headmaster, Mr Gilchrist, whom Richard describes as 'brutal . . . he caned his pupils to the utmost.'[19] Richard attended this school for three years from the age of six, and fifty years later he was still able to recall with clarity Mr Gilchrist's relish when he administered the cane to his small charges. Noticeably, for the remainder of his life Richard characteristically rebelled against any form of authority.[20] The school at least widened his curriculum, and in addition to the lessons begun at home Richard showed an early aptitude for French and drawing but no accomplishment in music or dancing. He seemed rather proud of this fact, as though he considered the latter pursuits unmanly.

The Burtons' life at Tours was punctuated by regular visits from members of the family. Aunt Georgina (youngest of the three Baker sisters) was a great favourite; she eventually married Robert Bagshawe, Member of Parliament for Harwich. Grandmama Burton, with her 'unmistakable' Bourbon looks and her feisty Irish nature, was seemingly tolerated rather than loved. Richard tells the story of how this woman was once alone at home but for a young maid when the house was broken into by thieves. She went upstairs, opened the barrel of gunpowder, loaded her pistol and went down to confront the intruders who rapidly decamped. When she asked the 'raw Irish' maid what had become of her candle in the confusion, the girl replied she had left it 'on the barrel of black salt, upstairs'. The intrepid Grandmother Burton had then to go up and carefully rescue the candle before it blew the house to smithereens.

It was Grandmother Baker, however, who was in residence when in 1832[21] Joseph decided to return to live in England with the intention of sending his boys to the 'right' schools. The Burtons had already moved from the old chateau on the hillside into the town of Tours for the convenience of being close to the day school, and Richard recalled in his autobiography that he and his brother became members of a 'gang' of small Anglo-French ruffians who broke windows, fought with street urchins and purloined their fathers' guns to shoot at church monuments and weather-vanes. Clearly it was time for a move.

The disposable chattels were duly auctioned and the remaining possessions – together with the six members of the family, a maid and various pet dogs – were decanted into the huge old-fashioned yellow-bodied travelling coach for the long and tedious journey back to England. It was bad enough that the postilion, 'wearing seven-league boots', was content to make a steady five miles an hour along the boring, arrow-straight, poplar-lined, unpaved roads; but things worsened as they reached Paris for, hearing that cholera was raging, Grandmama Baker insisted on stuffing the children's noses full of camphor whenever they neared a town. Such inns as they found were unwholesome and expensive and the journey was exhausting to all concerned. Richard still recalled its awfulness as an old man, though the family must have made the same journey on several occasions to reach the summer holiday destinations he described so cheerfully. At last they reached Dieppe and after a short interval spent enjoying the familiar sandy beaches (while Richard's mother recovered from the rigours of travel), they sailed for England.

Bored and fractious, the children were determined from the outset to dislike their native land. The family's coach was harnessed to teams of hirelings and Richard and Edward amused themselves by poking the horses with a long stick until discovered by the postboys, when they were sentenced to ride inside. Here they were reduced to making uncomplimentary comparisons between their home in France and the land of their birth. Even Brighton – then the brightest hub of Society outside London – was condemned as 'full of smoke . . . with air unfit for breathing . . . small . . . prim . . . melancholy'. The beach, unlike Dieppe's firm golden sands, was 'shingle'; the sea 'grey and heaving'. The food was 'revolting' after the cuisine of France, the standard of milk and bread came in for particular aversion and the wine was

'like medicine' after the excellent Bordeaux to which their juvenile
palates had already become accustomed. After the clear warm skies of
mid-France, the weather, naturally, was execrable. Some deep part of
Richard would always reject England, even though he always referred
to it as 'home'.

After a short time the family settled in Richmond so that the boys
could be 'prepped' for a major public school. Joseph had his sights set
on Eton or Harrow and, ultimately, Oxford or Cambridge for his
sons. A family friend recommended a suitable preparatory school at
Richmond Green and a house was duly found. Again, Richard's memories conflict with strict reality. He writes:

> After sundry attempts at housing themselves in the tiny doll-rooms
> in the stuffy village, they at last found a house, so-called by cour-
> tesy, in 'Maids of Honour Row' between the River and the Green,
> a house with a strip of garden fronting it, which a sparrow could
> hop across in thirty seconds.[22]

Far from being the mean residence of Richard's memory, Maids of
Honour Row proves, in fact, to have been one of the more desirable
residences in the town. A tall, smart and elegantly designed terrace a
stone's throw from one of the attractive broad country reaches of the
Thames, it also had the advantage of overlooking the school which
faced them across Richmond Green. It lacked the generous open
views of the chateau at Tours, of course, Richard's yardstick for a
home, and it was clearly this and the loss of freedom that relegated it
to a place of derision in his memory.

Certainly, the freedom that the two boys had previously enjoyed
was drastically curtailed at the preparatory school, which had
undoubtedly been one of Captain Burton's intentions. Richard
loathed it and claimed the school to be a 'horror of horrors', though
probably it was no better or worse than any other of its day. It was
run by the Reverend Charles Delafosse, a 'bluff and portly man, with
dark hair and short whiskers, whose grand aquiline nose took a
prodigious deal of snuff'. It was, said Richard, 'a kind of Dotheboys
Hall' to which gentlemen were content to send their sons and pay
£100 a year plus extras for the same education that could be obtained
on the Continent for £20.

Whatever the academic merits of the school might have been,

Richard's chief memories were of constant fist fights; 'at one time I had 32 affairs of honour to settle,' he wrote. His father's predilection for duelling appears to have been handed down, and Richard may have been unpopular because he fought like a French alley-cat 'with knees and feet as well as his fists'; hardly the fighting technique of an embryo English gentleman. He was beaten, he claims, 'like a shotten herring', to the extent that his bruises attracted the attention of maid-servants who bathed the boys on Saturday nights. 'Drat the boy,' one said, unsympathetically, 'what has he been doing? He's all black and blue.'[23] When one considers all the elements here, Richard's intense hatred of the school, his fights and reports of hard beatings, his sister's description that 'he was a thin, dark little boy, with small features and large black eyes . . . proud, sensitive, shy and nervous', allied to the fact that he was somehow 'different' – he spoke French fluently and soaked up learning like a sponge – it is probable that he was the victim of serious bullying.

It comes as no surprise to learn of the boys' delight when, a year later, after several pupils had died of measles, the school was temporarily closed and the two boys were sent to stay with their Aunt Georgina to whom they related the whole horror of the nightmare establishment. She was quite prepared to listen, especially when the already 'cadaverously' thin Richard himself became ill with measles. She brought the boys' claims to the attention of their parents and Captain Burton, who had felt the sacrifice of living in England worth-while only inasmuch as his sons were reaping an educational benefit from it, decided to return to France.

Pausing only to allow Richard to convalesce, to engage a governess for Maria and a male tutor for Richard and Edward, the family and its small entourage embarked for Boulogne. We do not know how Mrs Burton or Maria felt about this second migration, but Captain Burton was happy to return to the forests of France with all the boar hunting and shooting he could wish and the fine southern climate; and Richard and Edward were delirious with joy at the thought of never returning to Delafosse's establishment. The older Richard, how-ever, when dictating his autobiography, recognised that the move had been a bad one and had irrevocably cast his lot in life as an outsider.

Any young man making his way in Victorian England needed the background of a recognised school and the grounding in public school precepts and mores, plus a 'network' of fellow-pupils who knew him and his background, and recognised him as one of themselves. It follows that this would be even more important if the young man concerned was without substantial means. Though he claimed the credit for persuading his father to return to France, Richard also blamed him for not sticking by his earlier decision to have his sons educated in England. Had Joseph insisted that the boys stuck out their time with Delafosse and went to Eton as planned, Richard felt, he would have been spared much heartache in later life.

> . . . future soldiers and statesmen must be prepared by Eton and Cambridge . . . the more English they are, even to the cut of their hair, the better. In consequence of being brought up abroad, we never thoroughly understood English society, nor did society understand us. And . . . it is a *real* advantage to belong to some parish. It is a great thing, when you have won a battle, or explored Central Africa, to be welcomed home by some little corner of the Great World, which takes a pride in your exploits, because they reflect honour upon itself. In the contrary condition you are a waif, a stray; you are a blaze of light without a focus.[24]

But at the time, in the late summer of 1833, Richard could not see ahead. At 12 years old he felt only delight and relief at the return to France which was 'home' to him. The family settled at Blois, 40 miles or so from their former residence, in an expatriate community so similar to that at Tours that Richard thought it not worth describing, and in yet another large country house on a hillside overlooking the Loire.

Here, in a room set aside as 'the schoolroom', Mr Du Pré, an Oxford undergraduate, attempted to instil the Classics as well as the standard subjects in daily sessions of six or seven hours. He also taught them swimming. A Frenchman was called in to perfect the boys' French; besides which there was a dancing master who imparted a comprehensive teaching of all the dances a young man would need in a ballroom, and a fencing master who alone of their teachers captured the wholehearted attention of his pupils. So much did Richard and Edward enjoy fencing that all their spare time was given over to perfecting their techniques. Familiarity bred contempt and they began to fence without face masks until Richard in a bold thrust forced his foil into Edward's open mouth, nearly destroying the soft palate. The

accident distressed Richard a good deal. The two boys were inseparable friends; they formed an alliance, so to speak, against the
grown-ups.

After a year of this, life at Blois began to pall for the Burton parents. Martha as well as Joseph suffered from asthma, and possibly life
in the rich farmland of Central France stimulated undiagnosed
bronchial allergies. Captain Burton began to talk of taking the family
to live in Italy. It appears that Mrs Burton was not wholly in favour
of this scheme, for Grandmother Baker (who was paying a visit at the
time) was heard by the younger Burtons to exclaim to her son-in-law
'You'll kill your wife, Sir!' This interesting conversation included her
assertions that Captain Burton wished to return to Italy because during his days in Sicily there had been a young woman who still received
a regular allowance from him, 'to keep off claims' as Richard delicately phrased it in his autobiography.

Joseph Burton had long tolerated his mother-in-law's interference
in his marriage and the barely concealed allusions to the fact that it
was Martha's inheritance which supported the Burton family. He
believed that given access to her capital he could have made their fortune on the stock market, and it rankled that it was tied up in trust
out of his reach. He attempted many disastrous entrepreneurial
schemes during Richard's childhood, always blaming his failures on
an inadequacy of project funding. But Grandmama Baker had gone
too far this time. She was packed off to England and Captain Burton
pulled the old yellow travelling chariot out of its stall, sold up once
again, and set off southwards.

The journey was long, punctuated by attacks of asthma by both
invalids, and though the discomforts of travel were equal to their
previous treks Richard was less inclined to dwell on these and wrote
instead of the places they saw and stayed at on their route. Lyons,
Avignon, Provence, Marseilles, the voyage to Leghorn (Livorno) in
Italy, and their ultimate destination, Pisa.

'Nothing could be shadier than the English Colony at Pisa,'
Richard recalled in his autobiography. As well as respectable invalids
and widows eking out an existence in genteel poverty, it included a
large number of officers like Joseph, some on half-pay for heaven only
knew what transgressions, ladies fallen from grace, and a generous
sprinkling of 'black sheep' remittance men. Education went on as
before, with the added subjects of Italian and – another horror –

violin lessons. Edward showed great ability in the latter and could eventually, it was felt, have earned his living as a professional musician had he ever needed to do so. Richard on the other hand was a frustrated and poor student of music; eventually he lost his temper and broke the violin over the music master's head, which put an end to the misery of both student and instructor. But Richard did not always get his own way. When he learned that his sons had taken liberties with some guns they had purchased with money bullied from their sister Maria, Captain Burton returned the weapons to the shop to the impotent fury of the two sturdy teenagers.

In the following year the family went trekking again: Sienna, Perugia, Florence, Rome and Naples. Here they leased a villa on the Chiaja overlooking the Bay of Naples for the following winter, before sailing across the bay to Sorrento where they spent the summer of Richard's dreams in a large house, the grounds of which included small sheltered bays of the yellowest of sand, the bluest of warm waters and smugglers' caves. There were boating trips to Ischia, to Capri with its romantic Blue Grotto, Salerno and its splendid ruin, the temples of Paestum 'more splendid still'. Here the two boys indulged in their first bout of heavy drinking, and went cock-fighting. To pass the long evenings Richard learned to play chess blindfolded. Before long he could play four games simultaneously, with four different partners, and win all of them; a feat which he maintained as a sort of 'party trick' all his life. A party trick it may have been, but it provides a useful measure of the intellectual capacity of Richard Burton, both as a 14-year-old and in old age.[25]

When the summer was over the family returned to Naples and settled in for the winter. It was a lively place and a good base for excursions to Herculaneum, Pompeii and Vesuvius. Further subjects were added to the school curriculum here. Signor Caraccioli, celebrated for his marine painting, was hired to teach the children oil painting. Richard was an apt pupil, and he also learned from the artist the knack of caricature. The well-known fencing-master Cavalli, who taught according to the old Neapolitan school, was also engaged. This was fencing stripped of all the flourish and elegance of the newer French school, but Richard noted that in any duel between a Neapolitan and a Frenchman the former was sure to win. The two boys therefore worked hard at this subject, devoting four hours a day to perfecting their skills.

By now, the brothers would be more accurately described as youths. Allowing for some confusion in Richard's recollection of dates, he was about 16 or 17 and Edward 14. In recalling the pranks he once called 'wild for strictly brought up Protestant boys', Richard reluctantly admitted 40 years on that 'they would be nothing now'. These escapades included what he called 'orgies' in the local brothel. But the term should not be taken too literally, since throughout his life Burton frequently used the expression in his correspondence to describe stag drinking sessions or lively parties. Nevertheless it is reasonable to assume, reading between the lines of his autobiography, that he was initiated into his first sexual experience at this time. Some unfortunate correspondence, which contained 'declarations of pure love' by the Burton brothers and passages of 'debauchery' by two sirens of the brothel, was discovered by his mother in Richard's bed chamber. An almighty row followed in which Captain Burton and Mr Du Pré climbed the stairs to administer what they considered a fitting punishment – horsewhipping. The boys escaped and climbed up the chimney to the roof, where they sat and refused to come down until their parents' anger turned to anxiety and it was agreed they could descend without punishment.

Nevertheless, the escapade was looked upon as so serious that the family at once packed and left Naples, indeed shook the dust of Italy off their shoes and set off by steamer for Marseilles and Pau where the next year was spent adding yet further subjects to the curriculum. A mathematics teacher who was also 'something of a philosopher' was employed to cram specialist knowledge where Mr Du Pré's expertise ended. The Bearnais dialect, a mixture of French, Spanish and Provençal *patois* learned on the streets was *extra curricula*. But the brothers were already almost beyond the schoolroom. In their spare time they took instruction in boxing from their father's Irish groom with the declared intention of thrashing the hapless Mr Du Pré who reported a steady catalogue of the boys' misdeeds to their father. They also took to smoking and drinking. After one heavy drinking session they staggered home and managed to convince their mother that they were ill. Their father was not so easily taken in; after examining one son he curtly informed her, 'the beast's in liquor' and turned on his heel. Mrs Burton burst into tears.

The incident provoked the family's move to Argélès, which provided an opportunity for Richard and Edward to become infatuated with the pretty daughters of a neighbour. The elder girl was already engaged to a rich planter and shed no tears when they were parted, but the other three of the foursome were heartbroken. The parting was brought about when, at the onset of winter, Captain Burton's asthma worsened and a decision was made to return, yet again, to Pisa. Here Richard had his first serious love-affair with 'Signorina Caterina P——'. In a poem written years afterwards Richard wrote that Caterina's eyes 'Redoubtable artilleries . . . struck my tender heart/ But little came of that amour/ I was a pauper, she was poor/ And so we met to part'.[26] Caterina, the elder daughter of their land-lady, was 'tall, slim and dark, with the palest possible complexion'. Her younger sister, Antonia, 'could not boast the same classical features'.[27] 'I fell in love with the elder,' Richard recalled, 'and Edward with the latter. Proposals of marriage were made and accepted . . . but a serious obstacle occurred in . . . getting the ceremony performed.' The relationship was going along nicely until Edward ended up in gaol after a drunken brawl, a nasty incident which precipitated yet another move for the Burton family. 'The adieux of Caterina and Antonia were heart-rending.' The lovers agreed to keep in touch by letter, and so they did for a short time.[28]

The last home that the Burtons enjoyed together as a family was at Lucca, a spa town inland from Pisa. Again there was a sizeable community of black-sheep English and semi-permanent invalids to provide the society which the older Burtons enjoyed. During all those troublesome years of their sons' teenage escapades it must not be thought that they were merely stay-at-home, worried parents. They were often out in society; Captain Burton took pains to cultivate acquaintanceship with anybody of influence passing through town, particularly if they might one day be of assistance to his teenage boys. By now he had made the remarkable decision that the behaviour of his sons, clearly beyond his control, fitted them for a career in the church.

Richard and Edward continued to get into scrapes which included girls, drinking and even, on one occasion, the sampling of opium. One long-term friend whom Richard met at this time was Louis Desanges. Desanges' chief talent as a teenager appeared to lie in a splendid counter-tenor voice, but later he migrated to France and became a celebrated war artist. The atmosphere in the Burton household had now become one of continuous noisy strife as Captain Burton ineffectively attempted to maintain authority over his two unruly sons. Mrs Burton was almost continuously in tears. At last their father (who shortly afterwards retired with the rank of Lieutenant Colonel) admitted defeat; the time had come to divide and rule.

He decided that the boys would be sent to England, and after some appropriate cramming Richard would go to Oxford and Edward to Cambridge with the aim of them both making a career in the church. Richard, suffering from a form of teenage eczema, was sent in the care of Mr Du Pré to a sulphur spa in Switzerland for six weeks prior to setting out for England. Captain Burton took Edward directly to England, and it was some months before the brothers met again at the Hampstead home of their Grandmother Baker and 'the Aunts' – Georgina, and Sarah (recently widowed after the death of Francis Burton). Sarah was accompanied by her two pretty daughters, Sarah and Elizabeth Burton, and though they were first cousins this did not prevent an immediate attraction between Richard and Elizabeth. Richard, it seems, fell in and out of love with remarkable frequency.

The return to England marked the end of Richard's childhood. After a short time the brothers, still comparing England unfavourably against their European 'home', were sent to their respective destinations and Joseph Burton returned, no doubt with a sigh of relief, to his wife and daughter in Italy. The family's time together in the future would be very limited, and tame after the recent tumultuous years. Despite his lack of success as a disciplinarian Joseph Burton, who was a devoted father, had done his best by his intelligent and irrepressible sons. Their education, while unconventional, gave them a thorough grounding in a wider range of subjects than their contemporaries at public school would have received. They had grown up with a large measure of independence, and through their extensive travels (which appear to have left Richard with a fevered restlessness) enjoyed a range of experiences denied to those formally educated in England.

Unfortunately, these advantages also served to set them apart from their fellows. It was the beginning of Richard Burton's life as an outsider.

2

UNDERGRADUATE
TO GRIFFIN
1840—1842

Richard was 19 when he went up to Trinity College, Oxford, for the Michaelmas term in the autumn of 1840. By then he was fully grown and described as 'standing about five feet eleven, his broad deep chest and square shoulders reduce his apparent height very considerably, and the illusion is intensified by hands and feet of Oriental small-ness.'[1] He had well-defined features, prominent cheekbones, dark 'penetrating' eyes, a determined mouth, black hair and in appearance was said to resemble his 'handsome Roman-looking' father. The neat entry in the Admissions Register at Trinity, in Richard's own hand, is written in Latin.[2]

He was accepted on condition that he lodged, during his freshman year, as a 'resident pupil' with Dr William Greenhill on The Broad.[3] Greenhill (himself a Trinity graduate), was a physician at the Radcliffe Infirmary and church-warden at St Mary's, and his wife was the daughter of Dr Arnold (of Rugby School). This suited Richard, the Greenhills' home seemed always filled with erudite people and entertaining discussion and even after he moved into rooms at Trinity in September 1841,[4] he was a regular visitor to the couple's welcoming parlour.

Richard's lack of formal education manifested itself in gaucheness. Almost his first act at Oxford was to challenge a passing senior student to a duel because the man had hooted in derision at the long and drooping Italianate moustachios affected by Richard. His famous sensitivities were stung and he knew exactly how to deal with such an insult. In the best courtly traditions of his Continental upbringing he bowed politely, handed over his card and issued a challenge to his tormentor to settle the matter honourably with his own choice of weapons. Duelling had been outlawed for many decades in England by 1840, so it is hardly surprising that the offender was taken aback by such remarkable behaviour; indeed the man in question probably dined out on the story for the rest of his life. It was explained to Richard how matters stood and he felt, he said, half quoting Napoleon, as though he had come to live among a nation of grocers.

A year later when he moved to rooms in College, he was warned by a well-meaning College Porter of the torments normally inflicted on new residents (although he was by then no longer a freshman) and advised to lock and bar his door. Belligerently, Richard did the opposite. Having plunged his poker into the heart of the fire to provide a forbidding weapon, he threw open his door as a challenge and eagerly awaited all-comers. His neighbours immediately recognised that here was a man not to be trifled with, but perhaps not to be liked either. At all stages of his career he was apt to cover uncertainty with a display of aggressive bravura to which others reacted variously with fear, irritation and dislike.

For all his widely acquired knowledge, and despite the fact that in his parents' home he would have been exposed to a totally English lifestyle, Richard had missed out on a vital part of formal English education: the ethos of play-up-and-play-the-game; submission to the system – even those unpleasant customs such as 'fagging' and 'bumping'; give and take; take your punishment like a good chap and maintain – especially in extremis – a stiff upper lip. Experience of these customs made one part of the establishment club. There must have been other students at that time who had been educated at home privately; it was not a unique situation. But there was something within Richard that prevented him identifying himself with the mass of his contemporaries. He recognised in later life that it would have been tactful to be more submissive and less brash, that he should have tried to integrate, but at Oxford he was what he was. Different.

This is not to say that he was friendless. Far from it. He mixed with a knot of men from several colleges[5] and was often the ringleader in high-spirited student pranks against both tutors and fellow undergraduates. Each day he attended a few lectures and tutorials, but this took (depending on which version of his memoirs one reads) only a small proportion of his time;[6] the rest he spent enjoying those activities that most attracted him. Although an able horseman, he could not afford to keep a horse of his own and refused to ride a 'miserable hireling', so he took up rowing (he was an oar in the college Torpid),[7] fencing 'the great solace of my life', and single-stick practice.[8] It was through fencing in the salle-d'armes at Oxford that he made the acquaintance of an Exeter College man, Alfred Bate Richards, who became a firm friend.[9] A.B. Richards – who would achieve fame as the youthful editor of the Morning Advertiser – was upwards of six foot, broad and muscular; even Richard declined to box with him, though he was his superior with the sword.

Among other pleasures of his days at Oxford recalled by Richard were long walks which 'somehow or other always ended at Bagley Wood, where a pretty gipsy girl (Selina), dressed in silks and satins, sat in state to receive the shillings and the homage of undergraduates'. The description 'homage' is likely to be a euphemism. The road to Bagley Wood was then a well-known haunt of local prostitutes plying for trade. In his first book, Oxford Unmasked, Alfred B. Richards explains that the visits of undergraduates to the area were for a purpose 'too delicate for us to investigate'. Richard admits, however, that he spent a good deal of his time at Oxford 'squiring dames', as well as hiding from his tailor.[10] Debt was an almost universal problem among undergraduates.

In a man destined for the church, Richard's self-confessed near-ignorance of the Anglican creed and articles of faith was lamentable. Early-morning chapel was compulsory for undergraduates, but Richard voluntarily attended the stirring 4-o'clock sermons at the University Church of St Mary the Virgin on the High Street. These were delivered by the Vicar, John Henry Newman, leader of the controversial Oxford Movement. The subjects that interested Newman most during Richard's time at Oxford were the Anglican Church's attitude to Roman Catholicism, and Monophysitism (the theory that Christ was primarily divine with human attributes).[11]

Newman eventually found his own hard-won route to spiritual conviction, shaking the Church of England to its roots by resigning his incumbency of St Mary's in 1846 to convert to Roman Catholicism (and ultimately to become a cardinal), but he was still searching when his famous sermons were packing St Mary's every afternoon in 1840. It is clearly from Newman that Richard formed the opinions (quoted by his wife in the *Life*) that Roman Catholicism was the only possible alternative to atheism. It was the controversial aspect of the sermons which first drew Richard, but it was Newman himself, and his academically developed opinions, that held Richard's attention throughout his time at University. And, though he differed in opinion from Newman (Richard's religious views will be discussed later), the experience undoubtedly provided the kernel of Richard's lifelong search for a personal gnosis, and there was no man at Oxford he held in greater respect.

Although he was ostensibly studying with a view to entering the church, Richard was not a regular church-goer from choice and he preferred on Sundays to visit Abingdon, then the nearest railway station to Oxford, where one could hire and drive a tandem. This awkward driving rig where one horse is attached to a pole in front of the other (rather than side by side) had only one real merit; it was forbidden to undergraduates, presumably because of the inherent difficulties and consequent danger. He also 'managed to hunt out [a] work on falconry and studied its pages with . . . interest' and began a study of the occult, especially the mystical values supposedly attached to numbers. He had a lifelong fascination with the possibility of unknown influences, talismans, potions and magical power.

At the Greenhills', Richard met the Arabist, Señor Don Pascual de Gayangos. Dr Greenhill had studied languages – Greek, Latin, French and Arabic – and hoped thereby to 'restore the fragments of Greek medicine that are preserved in the Arab language'.[12] It was undoubtedly his admiration of Greenhill, and the multi-lingual discussions between his mentor and de Gayangos that stimulated Richard's desire to learn Arabic. There was no Arab tutoring at Oxford, and he began studying Arabic alone by 'attacking' an Arabic grammar from Greenhill's library. He used his own method of learning a new language, tried and tested as he travelled around Europe during his childhood, and since he is celebrated for the number of languages he eventually learned, his system is worth recording.

> I got a simple grammar and vocabulary, marked out the forms and words which I knew were absolutely necessary, and learned them by heart by carrying them in my pocket and looking over them at spare moments during the day. I never worked more than a quarter

of an hour at a time, for after that the lesson lost its freshness. After learning some 300 words, easily done in a week, I stumbled through some easy book-work . . . and underlined every word that I wished to recollect . . . If I came across a new sound like the Arabic *Ghayn* I trained my tongue to it by repeating it so many thousand times a day . . .

Then, when he believed he had 'the neck of the language . . . broken', he went on to teach himself how to form Arabic characters. No doubt he took pleasure in demonstrating his quick ability to Greenhill and de Gayangos, but his pride was cut to the quick when the Spaniard burst out laughing at his demonstration of the alphabet for he wrote it as a European from left to right, instead of from right to left.[13] Richard was never one to take ridicule gracefully, but on this occasion he bit his tongue and accepted it because he was keen to learn.

Richard and Edward spent the Christmas vacation at their Grandmother Baker's house in London. 'A man who dances, who dresses decently and is tolerably well introduced,' wrote Richard, 'rarely wants invitations to balls in London and I found some occupation for my evenings. But I sadly wanted a club . . .' Lacking one, he and Edward found their way into gaming halls but at least they did not lose money. At home 'the Aunts' made a point of inviting interesting guests for the benefit of the two brothers. On one occasion this consisted of a Mrs White, wife of the Colonel of the 3rd Dragoons, and her three strapping sons who were about to leave for an Army career in India. The Afghan War had broken out in 1838 and the most ambitious young men of the British middle classes were making their way to India in the hope of making a name for themselves. The conversation with the White brothers fired Richard and Edward with enthusiasm and, said Richard, 'gave me the first idea of going there'.[14]

All too soon, it seemed, Hilary Term began and Richard was back in Oxford. Term started badly. 'I had made a name for fastness . . . and now a reaction had set in. They laughed at me, at my first lecture, because I spoke in Roman Latin – real Latin – I did not know the English Latin, only known in England.'[15] In his autobiography he attributed his lack of success at Oxford largely to the fact that during his *viva voce* he boldly argued with his Latin examiners regarding correct pronunciation, and could not resist noting that some years later *his* method of pronunciation had become the received style in universities.

For the first two terms of the year, he said, 'I worked regularly 12 hours a day [and] failed in everything, chiefly I flattered myself because Latin hexameters and Greek iambics had not entered into the lists of my studies . . .'[16] He tried, at his father's insistence, for two scholarships and won neither. At the time his unaccustomed lack of success depressed him and led him to lower his aims; he decided that he was more likely to achieve a second rather than a first-class degree. 'Men who may rely upon first classes are bred to it from childhood . . . as dogs and cats are trained. They must not waste time and memory upon foreign tongues . . .' he said with an air of self-justification.[17]

The long summer vacation of 1841 was spent with his parents and siblings in Weisbaden, where Richard and Edward spent a good deal of time perfecting their fencing technique and attempting to gain admission to one of the famed Heidelberg fencing brigades. They offered to take on all-comers without, they stipulated, the heavy protective clothing habitually worn there. However, when the high standard of Richard's fencing was reported no one came forward to take up the challenge.

But Richard had also been giving some thought to his future career and took the opportunity for a heart-to-heart discussion with his father about this, pleading to be allowed to buy a commission in the Army or to emigrate to Australia or Canada. He said he was prepared to join the Swiss Guards at Naples, the Austrian Service, or even the Foreign Legion, so desperate was he to avoid being coerced into a career in the church. Edward backed him up, he too was unhappy with both Cambridge and with the career mapped out for him. Captain Burton, however, was adamant. They *would* return to University, they *would* attempt to win scholarships and they *would* go into the church. Given Richard's intellectual ability, if not at that stage any proven academic achievement, this dislike of University is puzzling until one recalls that he had never happily accepted the traditions of formal education. He found the regime at Oxford too fixed in its orbit for his thought processes, he was already too self-reliant.

The brothers duly returned to their respective colleges, but with an ill will and a determination to get themselves rusticated. They hoped that the disgrace of being sent down for a few months would be sufficient to put an end to any thought of a career in the church, agreeing that rustication was preferable to expulsion since the latter might

imply ungentlemanly behaviour. Richard set about his plan by holding noisy parties and being deliberately provocative. One method he
employed to irritate was to distribute a series of unflattering caricatures of dons and tutors, decorated with equally unflattering
epigrams. He had used this ploy successfully to upset Mr Du Pré on
several occasions, and had found the ones which caused most offence
were those showing a sketch of the tombstone of his victim, with a
suitably insulting rhyming epitaph. At Oxford some found their way
into print, and as he made no attempt to hide his authorship it
advanced his plan. But rustication was a serious business and the
dons were inclined, wherever possible, to regard youthful high spirits
with tolerance. By the Christmas vacation Richard realised that he
needed a bolder scheme.

The ideal opportunity arose when a celebrated steeplechaser,
'Oliver the Irishman', came to the area in the spring of 1842 for an
open race. Many undergraduates thought they stood a chance across
country against the great man, and the University authorities placed
the races off-limits and called an important lecture for the same hour
that the chase was to be run. Undoubtedly, as with the tandems, the
restriction had its roots in the potential dangers and not – as the disappointed undergraduates opined – pure officiousness. Steeplechasing
in those days was a mad dash across open countryside on hunters,
leaping whatever obstacle came in the way, riding from one highly visible point on the landscape (usually a church steeple) to another.
Richard conspicuously missed the lecture, arranging for a forbidden
tandem to wait for him behind Worcester College to convey him and
a few friends to the races. The event was duly enjoyed – probably had
he owned a horse Richard would have participated rather than merely
watched from his cart – and afterwards he returned in high spirits to
await his penance.

Summoned to an interview, it looked for a time as though his
scheme might backfire and the miscreants be let off with yet another
caution. Richard could not allow this to happen. He stepped forward and boldly argued that there was no moral turpitude in
attending a race meeting. In banning their attendance, he said, the
University had treated undergraduates like schoolboys, and he threw
in a few well-worn phrases such as 'trust begets trust' as added irri-
tants. The result was that while his fellow culprits were merely sent
down for the remainder of term, Richard was recommended not to

return from his rustication. This was rather more punishment than he had planned and, 'stung by a sense of injustice', he said he hoped the Council would, in that case, return the 'caution money' deposited by his father. At the insulting inference that the college authorities might 'lose' the money in the college coffers there was, he recalled, 'a general rise of dignities, as if my violent expulsion from the room was intended. I made them my lowest and most courtly bow, Austrian fashion, which bends the body almost double, wished them all happiness for the future, and retired from the scene.'[18] As a matter of record the 'caution money' of £30 was returned to his father in April 1842, a month after Richard was sent down.[19]

Richard's departure from Oxford with his co-conspirators (who were safe in the knowledge that they would be returning the following term) was a gesture of defiance typical of him. A tandem-driven dog-cart was driven up to the doors of Trinity. It was probably an unfortunate accident that caused the plunging leader to steer the shaft horse (and thus the wheels of the laden cart) across the Master's prized flower-beds as they turned out of the gates into Broad Street. Some dons enjoying a peaceful game of bowls stopped in astonishment at this outrage. Ignoring them and blowing kisses to the shop-girls of Oxford, Richard bowled out of town to the merry notes of a coaching horn blown by one of his 'companions in misfortune'.

His triumphant nonchalance masked the seeds of suspicion that the act was not perhaps, a wise move. Later he would freely acknowledge its foolishness, while his friend and fellow-undergraduate Alfred Bate Richards would write that 'none of us saw the treasure we had among us'.[20] Richard would return several times to his *Alma Mater* in the future, and there would be no hard feelings, but he was up at Oxford only five terms and the opportunity of channelling his great intellect into disciplined processes was lost to the academic community for ever.

To his doting aunts, to whom he referred as 'the family harem', it was easy for Richard to spin the smooth story that he had been allowed to leave early for the Easter vacation as a reward for achieving a double first. They had no difficulty in believing him; he had been such a clever child and teenager that academic achievement was a foregone conclusion. They sprang a celebration dinner party and to Richard's chagrin proudly announced the reason. They were appropriately startled when one of the guests grinned at Richard with immediate understanding. 'Rusticated, eh?' said the Judas at the table. His aunts were not *that* slow; they made enquiries and Richard found himself in deep trouble. But when the resulting family furore settled Richard had achieved what he had set out to accomplish, with only a little help from world events.

Shortly before he was sent down there was a massive tragedy in Afghanistan, a country made sullen and indignant by British occupation. A combination of Governor General Lord Auckland's insensate policies concerning the roles of the former rulers, and the ill-equipped and poorly protected British occupation force under the command of General Elphinstone (a man weakened by illness and fatigue) led to a successful attack by the Emirs on the garrison at Kabul. Before the fighting began a column of 16,000 people – British and Indian troops, wives, children, nannies, grooms, cooks, servants and assorted hangers-on – set out in the snow through the high passes towards the safety of Jalalabad.[21]

> . . . without supplies with scanty transport, amid snow and ice, over high passes and jagged rocks and through deep narrow valleys, harried day and night by vengeful tribesmen and falling easy victim to the gun and the knife of the relentless and treacherous enemy. Of all their number only one solitary being [Dr William Brydon] reached a refuge from his pursuers.[22]

The Afghans attacked the column, Dr Brydon reported, slaughtering the troops and plundering the animals and equipment. 'Nor were the unarmed and helpless camp followers spared. Soon the snow was crimson with blood.'[23] Many simply froze to death as they struggled along, snow-blind and lost in the appalling weather conditions of winter in the mountains. It took Dr Brydon a week to reach Jalalabad, the sole survivor of the thousands who had set out. It was the worst disaster suffered by the British in India, including the Mutiny of 1857.[24] When Dr Brydon's story of the massacre reached London an outraged public clamoured for retaliation, fearing that the defeat, if unavenged, would affect 'discipline in the Indian army . . . the stability of British rule and our credit for justice among the nations of Asia'.[25]

With all possibility of academic glory gone, and having firmly demonstrated the fact that he was unsuited to a life in the church, in fact in disgrace and 'fit for nothing but to be shot at for sixpence a day [by] those Afghans (how I blessed their name)',[26] Richard begged to be allowed to be part of the force being mustered to 'teach the Afghans a lesson'. Given the political climate of the day his father, a loyal military man, could hardly refuse. And having capitulated, he bombarded Richard with advice on how to succeed in a military environment.

Richard would have preferred a crack regiment; several of his many cousins served in Cavalry or Guards regiments. Instead he joined the British East India Company's Army where he was commissioned as an ensign. He stated in his autobiography that the choice of regiment was a direct result of his father's refusal to testify against the late Queen Caroline; implying that nothing else was available to him. But even a junior commission in a good regiment could cost thousands of pounds, and it was likely that his long-suffering father could not afford a better commission. Edward, having been set an example by Richard, also contrived somehow to get himself sent down and followed his brother via an Army posting to Ceylon.

According to the files of the East India Company, no money changed hands for Richard's commission in the Bombay Infantry (most of the men killed in the Afghan massacre were from the Bombay Presidency), and if it did it was a highly illicit transaction. A family friend, Joseph Maitland, recommended Richard to John Lock, a Director of the Honourable East India Company. Directors of the Company received a number of cadet nominations a year, but were forbidden to sell them.[27] Richard implied in his autobiography that Joseph Maitland had sold his recommendation to Captain Burton for 'about £500', but in 19-year-old Richard's petition for cadetship he wrote 'No' to the question, 'Do you believe any person has received or is about to receive any pecuniary consideration . . . on account of your nomination?'[28] And his Aunt Georgina, who acted as his guardian for the appropriate certificates, swore that 'no monies had been paid'. Both parties signed to the effect that if any money was found to have changed hands Richard would be subject to dismissal from the Company's service. But then he also swore 'in duty bound' to pray regularly.

The East India Company had begun as a trading organisation in the eighteenth century. Growing rapidly it obtained the right to keep a force of guards to defend its properties and staff. By the mid-nineteenth century, due largely to the lucrative opium trade with

China, the Company's interests had flourished.[29] In the process it had acquired huge tracts of property and the old security force had become a full-scale army. While nominally subject to the regular British Army regulations, in practice the Company's Army came under the direct control of the Directors of the East India Company (E.I.C.) who sat in 'Courts'. These Directors were immensely powerful and dominated the subcontinent from the three centres (called Presidencies) of Bombay, Madras and Bengal. The Court at the London headquarters in Leadenhall Street comprised twenty-four Directors who commanded the entire machine. Not for nothing were these men regarded as 'the Kings of Leadenhall Street', for they were as powerful as monarchs. Sir Charles Napier referred to them as 'ephemeral sovereigns' and Lord Wellesley as 'ignominious tyrants of the East'.[30] They were totally heedless of the culture they found and overran in India, appropriating sacred buildings for their own secular use. They once considered demolishing the Taj Mahal for its materials.[31]

Richard claimed in his autobiography that he spent the spring and early summer frivolously, but it is evident that he did not fritter away his time for he gave up boxing and fencing to learn Hindustani with an old Scot named Duncan Forbes, a faculty member of Kings College, London, who 'had spent a year or so in Bombay, and upon the strength of it was perfect master of Oriental languages . . . he spoke all his Eastern languages with the broadest Scotch accent . . .'[32]

To the customary tropical kit, much of which would prove useless, Richard added two unusual items. The first was a wig; growing up in hot climates, he said, had taught him the value of shaving his head to keep cool, and the wig was for social occasions. The second was a bull-terrier bitch called Pepper, bought during his period at University and of which he was extremely fond. Thus equipped and in high spirits, he boarded the barque *John Knox* for the four-month journey round Africa, via the Cape, to India, and sailed down the Thames on 18 June 1842. He always cried at partings, but his tears were for his aunts, not the country of his birth in which he always felt an alien.

It did not take him long to conclude that he was superior to the score of fellow-cadets in education and class, writing them off as 'Yahoos' who spent most of their time firing their pistols. Understandable perhaps, he said, for, 'were not all these young gentlemen going out to be Commanders-in-Chief?' But where his fellows sought amusements to while away the tedious hours of the long passage, Richard spent the greater part of his time working on his Hindustani with three Indian crew members. He found some time for recreation: teaching his brother-officers to fence, single-stick practice with one of the ship's officers, regular gymnastics to keep himself fit, and swimming in a sail draped over the side of the ship to foil any sharks. Invited by the ship's Captain (whose inability to keep adequate discipline Richard deplored) to a boxing match, Richard knocked the older man 'into a cocked hat'.

He was impressed with the view of the Cape and fascinated at the long Antarctic waves 'miles in length' in those land-free waters which rolled by 'in lines as regular as those of soldiers marching over a plain',[33] but he saw nothing of the East African coast which would later become of such importance to him. As soon as they rounded the tip of Africa the Captain set a course for the west coast of India. They reached their destination after dark on the evening of 27 October. All day long the expectant passengers, primed by the scent which seamen call the smell of land and landsmen call the smell of the sea, had craned to catch the first glimpse of the Indian coast.

Dawn revealed the low, sun-bleached profile of Bombay, then part of a chain of islands (later linked to form a peninsula). It compared unfavourably with Richard's childhood memories of the breathtaking Bay of Naples and with what he had read of Bombay's towers gleaming brightly against the dark blue sea. The only tower he could see was the spire of the Anglican Cathedral 'sploched and corroded as if by gangrene'. But even worse disillusion was in store. Shortly afterwards the Government pilot arrived on board:

> . . . excited questions were put to him, 'What was he doing in Afghanistan? What of the war?' At his answer all hopes fell to zero. Lord Ellenborough had succeeded Lord Auckland. The avenging army had returned through the Khaybar Pass. The Campaign was finished . . . and there was no chance of becoming Commander-in-Chief within the year.[34]

Richard shook off the crashing disappointment philosophically. After all, he reasoned, he had sought travel and adventure and here he was in the most cosmopolitan city in the East.

There was no docking facility and the passengers – the newly arrived cadets who were known in India as 'Griffins' or 'Griffs' – were taken in a 'shore boat' and landed at the Appolo Bunder, fondly regarded by generations of British travellers as the 'Gateway to India'. Richard, determined to avoid being lumped together with the grow-ing number of Victorians who published travel diaries full of breathless uncritical descriptions, rarely enthused in his travel writ-ings. To him the great gateway was merely 'a shabby doorway in the dingy old fortifications'[35] which had been left behind by the Portuguese in 1661 when the island of Bombay was ceded to King Charles II on his marriage, as part of the dowry of the Princess Catherine of Braganza.[36]

Having taken in the most immediate sights of Bombay which he found 'marvelously picturesque', with its noisy, colourful crowds of people from every part of the East, yet disappointingly squalid, Richard parted from those friends he had made on the voyage and made his way to the British hotel at the Fort. Because it was run by an Englishman he blithely assumed it would maintain at least rudimen-tary standards, and after almost five months at sea in cramped, hot quarters he was eagerly anticipating the usual amenities of civilisation. He was appalled to find the hotel . . .

> an abomination. Its teas and curries haunted the sensorium of memory for the rest of man's natural life. The rooms were loose boxes, and at night intoxicated acquaintances stood upon chairs and amused themselves by looking over the thin cloth walls.[37]

On the following day Richard reported himself for duty at the Presidency. A few days later – not surprising given his description of his quarters – he contracted the inevitable 'seasoning sickness' (diar-rhoea) of a new visitor to the East. 'Sick with rage' over the lack of privacy and squalor of his accommodation, he reported to the Fort Surgeon, Dr J.W. 'Paddy' Ryan, who arranged for Richard to move into the Sanatorium, a collection of small bungalows overlooking Back Bay which were cleaner and offered more privacy than the hotel. Nevertheless they were hovels in which 'an Englishman tolerably well off would hardly kennel his dogs', and he had to share his two rooms with the permanent residents: lizards, and bandicoot rats that ran across his body at night and snuffled at him with 'damp, uncomfort-able snouts'. Dr Ryan cautioned Richard that the only way to survive

India was to take several glasses of good port daily – advice that Richard steadfastly adhered to throughout his time there.

At the Fort Richard immediately sought out the Parsee broker known as 'the General' who made his living by being able to supply new arrivals with any item they had forgotten or found indispensable, from a needle to a buggy, or even a loan. Realising the inadequacy of his former language teachers Richard was desperate for tuition. Within days he was introduced to and had hired Dosabhai Sohrabji, also a Parsee, as his *munshi* (teacher). The old man, widely regarded as the best language teacher in Bombay, taught Hindustani, Gujerati, and a brand of Persian as spoken in India. Richard took to him immediately; he lapped up one-to-one teaching. He also hired a *mubid*, or priest, whose white cap and coat indicated that he had 'coached many generations of *griffs*', and with these two mentors Richard threw himself into learning the Hindustani language with the passionate enthusiasm that became so characteristic whenever he set himself a task. One tutor took over when the first one tired; later they described Richard as 'a man who could learn languages running'.[38]

Apart from study, he had quickly recognised, there was little else for him to do to pass the time. The only part of the day cool enough for pleasurable riding was dawn or dusk. During the following weeks, while he was being 'salted' (acclimatised), he spent some time wandering around the city trying out his Hindustani, his knowledge of which was improving rapidly. In the Bhindi Bazaar, the heart of Bombay, his senses were assaulted by the bright colours and heat, the variety of new sounds, the swarming crowds, the strange, spicy and sometimes unpleasant smells, the sheer vivacity of life that swirled around him. For all his expressed disgust at the squalor of India – or rather the dirt, disease and poverty of Bombay at this point – it is obvious from his writings that he revelled in the experience.

Captain Cleland, master of the *John Knox* had a sister who lived in Bombay and it was she who introduced Richard to 'what passed in Bombay for Society', at which he stood 'aghast'. It was, he said, a middle-class society suddenly elevated to the top of the tree, and which had 'lost its head accordingly'; men whose parents at home were 'small tradesmen . . . found themselves ruling districts and commanding Regiments, riding in carriages . . . and earning more in a month than their parents earned in a year'.[39] Ability did not appear to be an essential asset for office, Richard noted sourly, all it took to obtain the highest positions in this petty, snobbish and bigoted colonial community was a connection with one of the 'Kings of Leadenhall Street'. British customs such as 'tiffin' (a heavy lunch eaten at 2 p.m.) and the accepted social niceties of Anglo-Indian life, most intended to bring a touch of 'home' to the expatriates, he rejected as ridiculous, tiresome and inappropriate to the climate.

He was not averse to attending social functions, for besides the welcome though sparse female company ('thirty two cavaliers to three dames', he said) there was always a chance he might meet a senior officer who could be a useful connection in the future. In general, though, he was bored by the lengthy and substantial dinners, and startled by the coy husband-catching stratagems of the young women of 'the fishing fleet' and their chaperones. It is clear that he quickly became as much an outsider in India as he had formerly been at Oxford.

Within a few weeks, one of the 'rackety' fellow inmates of the Sanatorium had introduced Richard to the girls in the local brothel in the Bhindi Bazaar[40] where 'dark young persons in gaudy dress, mock jewels and hair japaned with cocoa-nut oil'[41] sat or stood in the door-way of houses offering their services to male passers-by; but about this society and this episode, said Burton as he dictated his memoirs to his wife, 'the less said . . . the better'.[42] Sexual curiosity and experimentation was common among British expatriates in the East, just as it was for those making the Grand Tour of Europe. The mere fact of being away from family and society, and the resulting lack of moral censorship, offered countless opportunities for exotic indulgence. Richard had lost his virginity as a teenager in Italy and was thereafter an enthusiastic exponent of the art of love-making.

Shortly after his arrival at Bombay, he had been advised that he was posted to the 18th Bombay Native Infantry (not the 14th as he had believed when he set out from England). On 14 November he was advised he was to be based at Baroda in Gujerat in the north-west of India, and six weeks after his arrival at Bombay he received his marching orders and set out to join his regiment.[43]

By now, he had realised that his situation in India was not an enviable one. Though subject to both the East India Company's rules and the Queen's Regulations, service in the former's army was considered inferior to that of the latter. The officers in the Queen's service regarded the Company's army as a second-rate service little more than a policing force staffed by the lower middle classes, and treated its officers accordingly. This was bad enough, but Company officers were unable, except in exceptional circumstances, to rise to high ranks. Richard's natural arrogance and sense of superiority bristled at the pettiness engendered by this form of class distinction, which ran through local society as well as through the two armies, and also at the unfairness – for it was an indisputable fact that the Company's army had seen as much, if not more, military action on the subcontinent.

He was also shaken by his first sight of sepoys, the native soldiers who served under the British in India. He described them as sloppy, scruffy individuals with unkempt hair and greasy ill-fitting uniforms that were a travesty of the British scarlet. These were the men he was to command. With no prospect of war in which to win his laurels, his life in the Company's army stretched before him; an endless round of military duties in camp, punctuated by leaves to Bombay where for the most part any society he was likely to encounter was, to him, stultifyingly banal. He saw quite clearly that if he was content to live as other officers he could enjoy the easy, pleasant life of the ruling class in India, a round of polite social diversions and *shikar*, or sport. 'But,' he said, 'some are vain enough to want more, and of these fools was I.' He was more trapped than he had been at Oxford, and it was in this mood that he consciously or unconsciously sought a project to keep himself sane.

Since the moment of his arrival in the subcontinent he had been fascinated by the diversity and richness of India's national cultures. Judging by the writings of his contemporaries, the intensity of his interest was unusual. Though he was undeniably a child of the society that believed God was an Englishman – he fully subscribed to the belief that the British were superior – he had never acquired a sentimental love for England as 'home'. This alone set him apart, but nor did he regard the inhabitants of the subcontinent as merely 'uncivilised natives', and he was scornful as he noted that many of his brother-officers regarded the 'natives (very often far better than themselves) as faggots ready for burning . . .'[44] There was not a subaltern, he said sardonically 'who did not consider himself perfectly capable of governing a million Hindus'.[45]

While he himself had been appalled at his first sight of a sepoy in his shabby travesty of regimental dress, Richard soon concluded that the same man 'in his national dress was uncommonly picturesque, with his long hair let down, his light jacket of white cotton, his salmon-coloured waistcloth falling to his ankles in graceful folds, and his feet in slippers of bright cloth somewhat like the *pieds d'ours* of the mediaeval man-at-arms'.[46] And as to their character, he was to conclude, 'They are stout hearts and true, these fellows . . . and you may . . . rely upon their faith and loyalty.'[47]

Richard's writings on India are sprinkled throughout with references to the squalor and unwholesomeness of life there; he never overcame his disgust with the dirt and misery of its teeming cities, but he was fascinated with its social anthropology and ethnology. He wanted to know more. The small amount of Hindustani he had learned, spoken at first haltingly and then with increasing confidence, had already stood him in good stead but in the babble of languages (there are more than 200 languages and dialects spoken in India) it gave him access to only a small part of the community. In order to study the cultures of India in any depth he would need half-a-dozen or more languages, at least, and by the time he set out from Bombay he already had this objective in his sights. He also believed that linguistic proficiency could provide him with a route to promotion in the absence of military action. He was looking forward to his trip to Baroda, and to seeing the real India. Bombay with its centuries of European domination was more garrison than town, he thought.

Just as the quarrel between George IV and Caroline of Brunswick had a fateful effect on Richard's childhood, the results of this seemingly innocuous resolution made by the hopeful 21-year-old subaltern would also have life-altering effects.

3

THE SUBALTERN
1843–1845

Richard set out from Bombay sailing northwards aboard a native *pattimar* – an unimposing long, low boat with a high stern containing a small stuffy cabin. In the centre of the deck was a space for the travellers' horses to be tethered. Most of the remaining deck space was taken up by three mast-like poles which carried the lateen sails. The entire vessel was 'strung together' with coir rope and leather bindings, and was inhabited by an interesting variety of insects and vermin.

He had already acquired a retinue of servants among whom were a valet, a bearer, a *syce* (groom) and his two *munshis*. These were headed by a handsome young Goanese called Salvador Soares who acted as major-domo. 'At that time a subaltern never had less than a dozen servants,'[1] said Richard, lightly revealing what he dismissed as a relatively simple lifestyle. In addition he had purchased a horse, rejecting the so-called Arabs offered in the horse market (showy but ill-broken half-breeds shipped over from the Persian Gulf, he said), in favour of one of the small native 'Kattiwar' horses. It was a bright dun with black points, vicious but as full of spirit as a thoroughbred. As with his bull terrier bitch (more bull than terrier, he said) Richard admired aggression as long as it could be channelled. The Kattiwar was fast on the turn and could be steered by the legs only, leaving hands free for combat.

During the two weeks' voyage to the Gulf of Cambay, Richard made a point of landing each evening to look at the country and 'eat the air'. He passed the days sitting on the cramped deck sheltering from the fierce sun under an awning watching the coast drift by, studying Hindustani and sometimes making notes of his observations. His journal would eventually form the basis for his first book – though that was some years ahead; at present he was simply a 21-year-old man absorbing new experiences, enjoying his comparative liberty, looking forward to a new life and relishing his first taste of being in command of his party.

His retinue and luggage was landed on a mud bank known as the Tankaria-Bunder from which point four days, making 12–15 miles a day, would take him to his regiment just outside Baroda. Unexpectedly impressed by the tranquil beauty and lush green countryside of Gujerat in winter, he was also charmed at the little villages of thatched huts to which each evening the grazing herds returned as the villagers prepared their suppers. He made notes of the 'sounds and smells peculiarly Indian'; the sharp bark of a monkey, the yelps of pariah dogs. Peacocks sitting high in the oak trees screamed at the red disk of the setting sun veiled in drifts of blue smoke from the numerous cooking fires fuelled by dried cow dung which emitted a pervasive and evocative, but not unpleasant, aroma when mixed with the scent of spices and coconut oil. He had hired several native carts to transport his effects and at night a mattress spread out under one of these provided him with accommodation. It was comfortable enough, he said, for young limbs and strong nerves. The moon was so bright that its silver light lay on the emerald green of Gujerat as if frost were lying. 'How lovely are these Oriental nights,' he wrote.[2]

He could not help comparing the apparent affluence of the villages under native rule with the wretchedness of those under British collectors. Later, after he made a nuisance of himself by insisting on explanations, the differences were clarified for him. Under British collectors, taxes were set and had to be paid whether or not the resident had had a good year. The Gaikwar collector, on the other hand, varied his taxes according to the harvest, and thus the natives preferred their own rulers. However, the British system had two things in its favour; there was no torture when payments could not be made, and if a householder had a windfall he was not compelled to hand it over.

After four days he arrived at Baroda and was directed to the ubiquitous Travellers Bungalow, a rudimentary inn with the barest of comforts. But as soon as his presence was made known he was called upon by a reception committee of seven brother officers; only half of those shown in the Company's staff lists were stationed at Baroda, the other half being quartered at Mhow on the borders of the neighbouring Presidency of Bengal. For better or worse, these men were to be his companions for many years: Major Houghton James, then commanding the 18th Bombay Native Infantry (B.N.I.); Captain Frederick Westbrooke, second-in-command; Lieutenant Andrew MacDonald who was married (and therefore a 'sober' man); Lieut. Adjutant Henry Cracroft; Lieut. 'Jas' John Combe; Ensign Stanley Raikes and Assistant Surgeon Frederick S. Arnott M.D.[3]

He obviously made a reasonable first impression for he was borne back to the camp in great good humour. There Assistant Surgeon Arnott arranged his accommodation and that evening he was introduced to the Regimental Mess – then consisting of eight members including himself. Its 'large cool hall and *punkahs*, its clean napery and bright silver, its servants each standing behind his master's chair, and the cheroots and hookahs which appeared with the disappearance of the table-cloth' came as a pleasant surprise to him. It was the first suggestion of clean, well-ordered and comfortable living arrangements that he had seen since leaving England. His brother-officers, copious beer drinkers to a man in common with most British officers, were surprised that the latest addition to their ranks drank no beer but 'adhered manfully to a couple of glasses of Port', as recommended by Dr Paddy Ryan. Richard had decided that if port cured fever it might also prevent a fever developing, and years later would credit his survival of the white man's grave of West Africa to his practice of drinking only port wine.

However, the subaltern's bungalow allotted to him was more in keeping with what he had come to expect in India. It was a shabby thatched cottage, 'not unlike a cowshed', sited among similar buildings housing unmarried officers in an area often referred to as the 'chummeries'. Here he installed his 'slender household' and settled down to the daily routine. His duties consisted of a certain amount of daily drilling of the 'jolly Greens', the regimental tag for the B.N.I. sepoys who wore green jackets rather than scarlet, and interpreting at court-martials of dreary length.[4] Richard used all his free time profitably studying languages. He went about this with such enthusiasm that 'two munshis barely sufficed for me', but it was not long before he acquired a form of additional tutoring.

White women (referred to as *bibis* by Indian servants) were at that time a comparative rarity in India, and the few who were to be seen outside the Presidencies were accompanying their husbands. Richard was scornful of those bachelors who spent their time 'peacocking', that is dressing in full uniform to go calling at the prescribed time, 11 a.m. in 'the heat of the day', on the wives of officers. It was a natural consequence that fit and healthy young males turned to the *bubu* (Indian woman) for female companionship. Burton called them 'morganatic wives'. On his arrival at the Corps, Richard found that virtually every officer was 'more or less provided with one of these helpmates',[5] and freely admitted to losing no time in following the example of the older men. His *bubu* mistress was only the first of several Indian women with whom he lived and he did not divulge her name. 'These irregular unions,' he wrote, 'were mostly temporary under agreement to cease when the regiment left the station.'[6]

A major advantage to Richard – besides the obvious one – was that such a partner was a 'walking dictionary':

> all but indispensable to the student and she teaches him not only Hindostani grammar, but the syntaxes of native Life. She keeps house for him, never allowing him to save money, or, if possible, to waste it. She keeps the servants in order. She has an infallible recipe to prevent maternity, especially if her tenure depends on such compact. She looks after him in sickness, and is one of the best nurses, and, as it is not good for man to live alone, she makes him a manner of a home.[7]

A serious disadvantage was that by the time Richard arrived in India the 'half-marriage' arrangements which had worked happily for many years had, he said, begun to be viewed with disapproval by senior Staff Officers 'doubtless at the instance of their wives'. Certainly Richard's involvement was, on at least one later occasion, harmful to his prospects. He was discreet about the relationships in his autobiographical writings, but his poetry is more revealing:

> I loved – yes, I! Ah, let me tell
> The fatal charms by which I fell!
> Her form the tam'risk's waving shoot,
> Her breast the cocoa's youngling fruit.

Her eyes were jetty, jet her hair,
O'ershading face like lotus fair;
Her lips were rubies, guarding flowers
Of jasmine dewed with vernal showers . . .[8]

At first Richard worked hard at drilling his sepoys for although the Afghan War was technically over, skirmishes such as that fought by Charles Napier 'the Conqueror of Scinde'* at Meeanee and Dubba in February 1843, suggested that the Army might yet be called upon. When this did not happen, Richard – ambitious and keen for advancement – experienced an aggrieved sense of frustration. Eventually, though, he fell into the normal routine of the Cantonment which began at sunrise on the parade ground followed by bathing and breakfast. He then studied with his *munshi* until 9 a.m., when there was a formal breakfast in the mess. After this most men went to the billiard-room and some went visiting. Richard invariably skipped tiffin, settling for a snack of biscuits and a glass of port so that he could work at his language study for the entire day until he went for a constitutional ride just before sunset. After this there was Mess Dinner at 7 o'clock, followed by a game of whist and 'a stroll home under the marvellous Gujerat skies'.[9]

Occasionally he rode into Baroda with one or two of his brother-officers. It was a shabby walled city with a population of 150,000, pleasantly situated on a bank of the Vishwamitra River. The outings made a welcome change from the dull routine of his days, and he was always eager for any new sight or experience, but he also saw and felt the hot-eyed hostility of the citizens to the white sahibs. There was the inevitable 'red light' district patronised by the British; in Burton's day 'all the tenements, which ran to three or four stories in height, had balconies where the Muslim courtesans would sit idly singing, composing poetry . . . chatting to friends, calling to people on the street, serving cool sherbets and sweets to their admirers':

The floors of the apartments were spread with rich carpets and covered with clean white sheets; the balcony tiles were sprinkled

---

* Scinde; also sometimes spelled Scind or Scindh by Burton. The accepted present-day spelling is Sindh and this is the one used throughout in this book, except in quoting extracts when the original spelling is copied.

with fresh water and the parapets lined with fragrant clay water
pots smelling of new earth. Then there were the flowers. Flowers
garland everything, the doorways and rafters, the cots and piles of
cushions, and the women wore them in their hair and draped their
lovers especially with the *mogra*, the flower known as *ráth-kí-rání*,
'Queen of the Night', which would be spread on beds when the
couple united, to be crushed in moments of passion. Over all wafted
the sweet smell of the hookahs, and incense, opium and hemp.[10]

Despite the animosity of the masses, the British were on good terms
with the ruler of the area, the Prince or Gaikwar,[11] who sometimes
entertained the officers. Richard was not averse to field sports – how
could he be, growing up with a father and brother whose chief interests lay in that direction and when field sports were the major
occupation of the English gentleman? But he was uneasy about some
of the 'sport' the Prince showed them: 'A fight between two elephants
with cut tusks, or a caged tiger and buffalo – the last being generally
the winner – or a wrangle between two fierce stallions.' The cock-
fighting, however, Richard enjoyed immensely. He admired the bold
aggression of the huge birds who would attack anything (even
humans), and shortly afterwards he purchased his own bird, *Bhujang*
(the dragon) who was the victor in many fights. Richard also enjoyed
the occasional hunting picnic on elephants. The jungles inland of the
city swarmed with game and – always interested in the scientific
aspect of venery as opposed to killing with guns – he was interested to
see the Prince's cheetahs, hunting leopards or falcons at work.

Within three months of his move to Baroda, Richard's teachers
considered him ready to take the regimental examination in
Hindustani. He therefore applied for and was granted 2 months'
leave to travel to Bombay to be examined. His previous experience of
accommodation had soured him to hotel life in Bombay, so with the
help of the old Parsee General he hired a tent and camped outside the
city with his servants. The examination consisted of reading from several printed books in the native language, translating some letters,
making a short address and conversing with the examiners. The
examining *munshi* was a rival to Richard's tutor, Dosabhai, and was
therefore not inclined to let Richard off lightly. However, his Service
Record reveals that on 5 May Richard passed the examination easily,
coming first of 11 candidates – which led, several months later, to an

appointment in General Orders as Interpreter to his Corps with an increase to his salary of 30 rupees a month.[12] Before leaving Bombay to return to Baroda he laid in a store of books on the Gujerati language.

During the following months Richard experienced the full horror of the monsoon season at Baroda when the parade-ground lay under a sheet of water. Regimental duties were suspended and the air was so laden with flying insects that it was dangerous even to open one's mouth; food and drink had to be covered between mouthfuls. Rain fell as though it was being continuously emptied out of buckets, a man could not travel between his tent and the mess without becoming soaked. It was airless, hot and oppressive, and the men fell into a depressive *ennui*. In what must have been a huge test of will-power Richard worked even harder – 12 hours a day – on his studies.

But these did not consist solely of the new language, for which he had added a new teacher to his team of instructors. Under this man, a *Nágar Bráhmin* or 'Snake Priest', called Hím Chand, Richard also investigated the practice of Hinduism:

> I carefully read . . . the publications of the Asiatic Society, questioning my teachers, and committing to writing page after page of notes, and eventually my Hindu teacher officially allowed me to wear the *Janeo* (Brahminical thread).[13]

While not denying that he must have gone through some of the rites of *sufism*, some writers claim that there are ambiguities in his account of how he achieved such high status in the *Nágar Bráhmin* sect.[14] Certainly it would have involved a far more intensive study than Richard details in his autobiography; even the ceremony of initiation, called *upanaya*, would have taken a week of preparation involving periods of fasting, praying and purification and ritual cleansings of the body. When all ceremonies were completed he would have been dressed in a cotton cloth that fell from the waist, the upper torso left bare for anointing with precious oils. His head would have been shaved except for the Brahminical tuft. And as a climax he would have been handed the sacred cord which is the sign that he has been 'twice born'.[15] As a Bráhmin he was bound to say the specific prayers or mantras known only to the members of the sect, which were thought to have mystical powers. Living as he did, in 'the chummery',[16] it would have been difficult for him to keep such activities secret, but apparently he did not even try to do so. He seems to have had a naïve confidence that everyone would view his interest as academically as he did.

Instead his activities drew clucks of disapproval from some brother-officers. Miscegenation, or 'going native', was almost the equivalent of a white woman consorting with a non-white man. It was not only viewed as sickening and disgraceful but it 'let the side down'. But so fascinated was Richard by his studies that he did not see the potential harm his interest might cause him, even when he began to be referred to as 'the White Nigger' – jokingly by his friends, sneeringly by those less affectionate. Or if he did see, he chose to ignore it. The term 'nigger' was not necessarily a pejorative one, then; it was a noun in common use and one often used by Richard himself to describe natives whom he liked. Nor was Richard unpopular, or at least not universally so, but his brother-officers were surprised at his relentless drive to learn about the native culture, unsure about him because he was so obviously different. Learning a language was one thing, but what sort of man would work twelve hours a day at it, spending all his time talking in foreign languages with natives, when he could be joining in the regular regimental activities with his own kind?

Richard compounded this divergence when he abandoned the Anglican chapel and began attending Roman Catholic services held by a black Goan priest for the few Catholic servants about the garrison. Roman Catholics had only been free to practise their religion in England since 1829 when the Act of Catholic Emancipation was passed. There was still a great fear, suspicion and distrust of them by the Establishment. This alone was enough to make the faith interesting to Richard as a project for study and, as he had sworn to pray regularly on his induction into the Company's service and had to be seen to pray somewhere, he made the little Goan his spiritual parent. In fact, as he betrays in *Scinde*, his chief reason was to further his knowledge of the Portuguese language. Nor had he forgotten Newman's sermons, and he welcomed the opportunity to study the Roman Catholic religion in detail, just as – later – he did that of Islam. Whether he took his interest as far as a service of baptism is a matter for speculation.

The appeal of ethnic cultures for Richard should not be misconstrued. It was ethnology as a branch of science that held him fascinated, not some premature 'political correctness'. He was voracious in his search for knowledge of Oriental practices, and his easy facility for learning languages was the key which would unlock the store of knowledge to which he aspired. He was a child of the mid-nineteenth century and just as racially prejudiced as his contemporaries, just as arrogantly sure of the superiority of the British (and of Burton in particular), just as certain that the British were justified in the plunder of India. He was ever capable of a well-aimed kick at a lazy servant and boasted of the 'well deserved beatings' that he administered.

Even at this early stage in his life he was a driven man, channelling his inner tension into a restless search for knowledge. Present-day teachers in India are 'astounded' by the quantity of his detailed intimate and often recondite knowledge of every aspect of society in Sindh. 'How,' asks one, 'could Burton contrive to acquire [this] within hardly five years residence in Sindh?'[17]

In September 1843 he again appeared before the examination board, this time tested in the Gujerati language. Again he was placed first of the entry, this time beating into second place Lieutenant Christopher Palmer Rigby who, until Richard's arrival, had been the best linguist in the Presidency. Richard was granted an extension of leave in the city until 10 November when he heard that his regiment had received orders to march to Sindh. At this welcome news he hastily returned to Baroda to take part in the preparations for the move to the British garrison at Karachi.

On 1 January 1844 Richard and his men boarded the steamer *Semiramis* which he described as the ship from hell;[18] however, it led to a meeting with a man who would become one of his closest friends in India. Captain Walter Scott of the Bombay Engineers was making his way, following a recent promotion, to Sindh where he was to head a survey of the canal system on the instruction of Sir Charles Napier.

Scott, besides being an able engineer, was a nephew of Sir Walter Scott the writer and poet, and a devotee of books on history and romance. Among his favourites were Hollinshead and Froissart, books that Richard was familiar with. Furthermore, Scott's reading on the voyage was a book on the canal system of the Po valley in Italy. It was good news to him to meet someone who not only knew the area and could aid him with Italian translation, but who was as well-read in his favourite subjects as himself and who, furthermore, could quote tracts of Sir Walter Scott's works from memory. By the end of the journey the two had become fast friends.

After four days they had their first sight of Karachi which was, said Richard, small and primitive. It was the only working port in Sindh, though at that time it had few pretensions to that description:

> . . . surrounded by a tall wall . . . topped with fancy crenelles and perpendicularly striped, with . . . holes down which the besieged could pour hot oil, or boiling water. Streets there were none; every house looked like a small fort and they almost met over the narrow lanes that formed the only thoroughfares. The bazaar, [was] a long line of miserable shops covered over with rude matting . . . Nothing could exceed the filthiness of the town; sewers there were none . . . There was no sign of barracks, and two race-courses were laid out before anyone thought of church or chapel. Yet Karachi showed abundant signs of life. Sir Charles Napier thoroughly believed in its future, and loudly proclaimed that it would take the wind out of Bombay sails.[19]

Sir Charles Napier, who had conquered and annexed Sindh in the previous year – and was known to Victorian schoolboys chiefly for his (probably apocryphal) one-word report of the victory: 'Peccavi' – Latin for 'I have sinned' (I have Sindh)[20] – had made Karachi his temporary base. The town was already 'swarming with troops' when the 18th B.N.I. and Richard arrived, but after a month of discomfort the unit was ordered to make its base at Gharra, half a day's ride away but within sound of the evening gun. There were no buildings there, the barracks was a tented camp on a sandstone plateau. Frequent sandstorms, a daytime temperature of 125°F and relentless dust made life difficult and uncomfortable.

Unlike some of the older officers, Burton had no money to build a house. His monthly salary was 180 rupees (the equivalent in current-day values would be £6,500 a year)[21] and every rupee he could spare after paying his mess bills went towards new books and tuition. He was therefore compelled to live for months in a single-poled tent pitched under a milk-bush hedge. In order to make it tolerable in the hottest hours of the day, he used to cover his table with a wet cloth and sit underneath it. It was a miserable few months. He had his studies to take his mind off physical discomfort, but the difficulties of working in such conditions were immense; despite the wet cloth the gritty dust got into his eyes, which felt as though cayenne pepper had been sprinkled in them, and it frequently took up to two and a half hours to cover four pages of paper 'as the pen becomes clogged and the paper covered every few minutes' so that he ended up with 'a neat little cake of Indus mud and Scinde sand moulded in the form of the paper'.[22]

At the first mutterings of a move to Sindh he had informally taken up the Sindhi language, but he was formally studying Maráthá under the regimental *pandit* and on 25 October 1844 he was duly examined by the language board, as usual coming first of the half-dozen entrants.[23]

By now he was qualified as Regimental Interpreter in the three major native languages, Hindustani, Gujerati and Maráthá. He already spoke and wrote a rudimentary Arabic dating from the interest he developed at Oxford, which was a useful 'lingua franca' in the bazaars, and in November 1844 he began to study that most elegant of Oriental languages, Persian, because it would provide access to a rich source of Oriental manuscripts and Eastern culture. Only one man in the Bombay Army rivalled Burton for his linguistic skills. Lieut. Christopher Rigby of the 16th B.N.I., who had been longer in India, was still marginally ahead at this point, having already qualified in Persian. Richard's zealous study had already brought him to the attention of his superiors; in his annual report he was regarded as a keen officer who had learned his duties well and was attentive to his responsibilities.[24] It is difficult to believe that Rigby's minor defeat by Burton in the Gujerati language exam, and Burton's rising star in the field of linguistics, were the sole causes of Rigby's lifelong bitter enmity towards Burton, yet the ill-feeling between them certainly began at this time and there seems to be no other explanation.

To Richard's pleasure, he found on his return that he had been transferred to Walter Scott's team as Assistant Surveyor, at Scott's personal request. 'A Staff appointment,' said Richard, 'has the effect of doing away with one's bad opinion of any place.' The most important books on hydrodynamics were written in Italian and it was on the grounds that his fluency in that language would be useful, Richard hints, that permission was granted. To this smooth explanation of his transfer into the Survey Department must also be added the historical knowledge that, like the infamous 'Passport Control Office' in the present century, the bona-fide Indian Army 'Survey Department' provided a convenient cover for undercover intelligence agents during the British occupation of India, or 'The Great Game', as it came to be called.[25] He threw himself into learning the use of the basic surveying instruments – compass, theodolite and spirit level – and on 10 December 1844, with six camels and a work party, he set off southwards for the Guni River. With blistering temperatures during the day falling to below freezing at night it was not always pleasurable work, but he learned on the job and apparently made such a success of his first project that he was commended for his Survey Report. Scott's own report reveals that Richard 'levelled' 152 miles of canals during the cold weather of 1844–45.[26]

His life was not unremitting work, however, for he was able to indulge in some sporting activities. Certainly he spent some of his days hawking, a sport that had interested him as a boy in France and which would become the subject of one of his first books. His descriptions provide a picture of Richard as a fairly stereotypical British officer, surrounded by his native servants, a *sahib* at ease with the Indian élite. And there is no doubt that though Richard constantly challenged authority he was very much part of that Colonial life which he later affected to dislike. This is an evening in December 1844, 'very like the close of a fine May day in England', a blushing 'rosy-red' scene:

> We, that is my friend Ibrhaim Khan Talpoor, with . . . his secretary and I supported by Hari Chand were passing the last of an active day, spent among the marshes, in our red arm chairs under the spreading . . . trees of the Amir's village. Behind us the modest encampment, a tent or two, half a dozen canvas sheds tenanted by Government surveying assistants, horses picketed in their night clothes [rugs], camels at the squat; Pepper the terrier looking more spiteful than ever because tied up and motley groups of syces, beaters and camel-drivers . . . conspicuous among them stood Antonio [my] Portuguese butler . . .[27]

On Christmas Day, unexpectedly, Richard suffered from homesickness. Imagining the joyous carolling of church bells and groaning tables of roast beef and plum pudding, he returned from 'a disconsolate stroll' to an ill-lit tent and a dinner of 'a boiled barn-door, with a *biftek* of goat'. He missed his family a good deal.[28] Edward was now in the Bengal Army and stationed in Ceylon. Their young sister Maria was about to be married to Henry Stisted, who was also an officer in the Indian Army. Stisted had completed his ten-year statutory period of service and was currently in England enjoying his three years of paid leave.

The 18th B.N.I. had moved to Hyderabad by the time Richard completed his canal project in February 1845, but he was not obliged to follow them. He was based in Karachi at the headquarters of the Survey Team with four brother-officers: Lieutenants Blagrave, Maclagan, Venrenin and Price. From somewhere he found the money to build himself a bungalow to house his *ménage*. A short time later a young woman called Núr Ján was installed there.

During the initial period of his time in India, Richard clearly learned a great deal from his mistresses. In his early books he was far more conversant with the intimate details of an Indian woman's underclothes than one would expect of a young bachelor, describing them with obvious first-hand knowledge of fastenings and even the time it took (twenty minutes) to properly fold the wide *sutthan* (pantaloons) to fit tightly around the ankles. He was critical of the tight and restrictive undergarments (such as stays) of European women, which he felt were unhealthy.[29] Though he does not say so in the follow passage, there are sufficient clues in the surrounding text to suggest to the careful reader that it is a description of his paramour:

Her long fine jetty hair, perfumed with jessamine [is banded] over a well-arched forehead . . . Behind the [hair] is collected into one large tail, which . . . hangs down below the waist, and – chief of many charms – never belonged to any other person; it is plaited with lines of red silk . . . and when the head is well shaped, no coiffure can be prettier than this. Her eyes are large and full of fire, black and white as an onyx stone, of almond shape, with long drooping lashes, undeniably beautiful. I do not know exactly whether to approve the Kajal [Khol] which encircles the gems . . . However I dare not condemn it . . . The nose is straight and the thin nostrils are delicately turned. You perhaps do not, I do, admire their burden . . . a gold flower . . . the mouth is well formed and . . . sensual.[30]

Many years later, when Richard came to write his famous erotic books he was just as confident in his descriptions of the love-making and sexual needs of Indian women, detailing among other facts their extraordinary vaginal muscular control; in fact, he said mischievously, 'a woman can knead every muscle and at times catch a mosquito between her toes. I knew an officer in India whose mistress hurt his feelings by so doing at a critical time when he attributed her movement to pleasure.'[31] He was fully aware of the time and care needed by a man to stimulate his mate to orgasm. 'A woman [must] be prepared for intercourse if she is to derive satisfaction from it,' he wrote. He was possibly unique among his English contemporaries in his conviction that a successful marriage or partnership required the woman to enjoy the sexual act as well as the man.[32]

> Moslems and Easterns in general study, and intelligently study, the art and mystery of satisfying the physical woman . . . I have noticed among Barbarians the system of 'making men', that is, of teaching lads first arrived at puberty the nice conduct of the *instrumentum paratum plantandis civibus*; a branch of the knowledge-tree which our modern education grossly neglects, thereby entailing untold miseries upon individuals, families and generations.[33]

As with all his research he took the study of sex seriously, even experimenting with so-called 'soft' recreational drugs such as 'bhang' (hashish) to gauge their enhancement of sexual pleasure and physical endurance, and making notes about the experience.

He enjoyed life at Karachi. The days were filled with work; planning and mapping the surveys and more importantly, in Richard's case, practising latitudes and longitudes until his right eye became comparatively short-sighted; experience that would stand him in good stead in the future. His evenings were not dull, for he had integrated well with the existing Survey Team and shortly after his arrival they organised their own Mess. It was in a bungalow in the Survey Office compound and rapidly became renowned for the lively behaviour of its patrons. His quarters, described obliquely but minutely, were in direct contrast to the 'white stucco pile' of the staff officer, and the small neat, carefully curtained homes of the married field-officers. Richard's bungalow, jealously trellised around with bamboo fencing and 'showing manifest traces of the bubu' was in the unmarried officers' compound called 'Subaltern Hall' where young officers 'chummed' together in bachelor squalor:

> . . . the fine head of an Arab peeping out of his loose box is the only sign of life about the place . . . the fences are broken down by being leapt over, the garden destroyed by being galloped over . . . piled close by shattered chests, old torn fly-tents, legless chairs and other pieces of furniture which have suffered from the wars within . . .

In various books of Richard's there are descriptions of the bachelor life the junior officers enjoyed. There were outings to the *nautch*, to watch dancing girls, occasions that varied from innocent cultural displays to highly erotic entertainment. His early books hint archly about immoral activities, and in his later works he would make it clear that there was no type of sex that could not be acquired at a price in India, but much of the recreation these young men enjoyed was that of overgrown, bored schoolboys. It was harmless and puerile. Watching women bathing in the Indus through binoculars, or what Richard called 'larking' with his friends, Lieutenants Waterton, Rivers-White and Beresford. There were visits to *fakirs*, and sallies to the nearby swamp with their quarrelsome terriers. There, they would attract the huge alligators – up to twenty foot long – with a hook baited with a chicken head. By means of a wire noose twist dropped over the snout so that the jaws were muzzled, and with the aid of a sharply pronged fork, they would then proceed to ride the beast:

> . . . just as the steed is plunging into his own element, the jockey springs actively up, leaps on one side, avoids a terrible lash from the serrated tail and again escapes better than he deserves. Poor devils of alligators – how they must ponder upon and confabulate about the good times that were! Once, jolly as monks or rectors, with nothing in the world to do but to eat, drink, sleep, waddle and be respected; now pelted at, fished for, bullied and besieged . . . poor devils![34]

But as usual most of his spare time was spent studying, Sindi and Persian. Yet another tutor was enrolled, an unusual one this time. *Mirza* (scholar) Mohammed Hosayn of Shiraz was a brother of the

Prince Agha Khan Mahallati. Hosayn and Richard became close friends and the *Mirza* even introduced his somewhat superior pupil to his family, possibly at Richard's suggestion. Richard also became acquainted at this time with two Persian scholars. The first, holder of the rank Khan Bahádur, was *Mirza* Ali Akhbar who had been *munshi* to Sir Charles Napier but owed his promotion to gallant behaviour on the battlefield. Ali Akhbar still worked for Napier, but he lived outside the camp in a bungalow which he shared with another first-rate Persian scholar, *Mirza* Dáud. Richard began to spend more and more of his time with these two men, often in the company of Mohammed Hosayn, so it was hardly surprising that the sinister sobriquet of 'White Nigger' emerged again.

Initially the term was probably used facetiously by his friends when he refused to join them in some lark, but the enemies that Richard made throughout his life, such as C.P. Rigby (who will resurface in a later chapter), did not apply it as an endearment. It is reasonably safe to assume that Richard's Indian mistress was in situ in the Karachi house at this time, for when his game-cock *Bhujang* died and Richard buried the bird in a small grave outside his bungalow, word went round the regiment that it was the grave of a baby. Richard heard of this rumour and thought it so ludicrous that it merited no denial.

However, others who heard the rumour believed it and it helped to form the basis of a questionable moral reputation that would haunt Richard for the rest of his life.

4

MIRZA ABDULLAH
1845–1846

As his studies progressed it could have only been a natural progression, completely within character, for Richard to try to pass himself off as an Asian to test his command of languages.

Portraits of Richard Burton in his twenties and thirties illustrate perfectly the descriptions of him by his contemporaries: exotic; foreign; gypsy-looking; dark; swarthy; etc. His high cheekbones, dark – almost black – eyes, hair and moustache lent themselves perfectly to such a plan, and may even have suggested it. He needed only a little walnut juice or henna to darken his face and hands, and an appropriate national costume to effect the transformation to his adopted persona. The addition of some kohl around the eyes was optional and sometimes he added a long flowing wig and false beard.

Other factors undoubtedly played some part in this plan, however. As well as the inherent danger from internal sources in the form of possible uprisings under the old rulers, the British lived in constant fear of Russian penetration of the Indian border. As a result, an informal intelligence organisation had burgeoned within the Survey Office. By the time Richard went to India the Survey Office had been sending suitable British officers, in disguise, among the native population for some years. As early as 1830, Lieut. Arthur Conolly of the 6th Bengal Native Light Cavalry travelled in disguise as a merchant to 'reconnoitre the military and political no-man's land between Caucasus and the Khyber' to provide information for Lord Ellenborough. It was

Conolly who coined the term 'The Great Game' to describe the intelligence service in India.[1] Conolly's cover was penetrated on several
occasions, the most dangerous when he was taken seriously ill and
nursed to health by some monks. He wrote a book about his experiences (omitting his most sensitive findings) in 1834, which was so well
known in London that all young subalterns leaving for India when
Richard did must have read it. Conolly eventually came to grief and
was beheaded in Bokhara in 1842.[2]

Nor was Conolly alone. Lieut. Alexander Burnes became a hero for
his similar adventures in 1831; he too died a hero's death, hacked to
death by a fanatical mob in 1841 after his true identity was discovered. Lieut. Eldred Pottinger went successfully into Afghanistan in
1837 (his disguise only penetrated once, by a friendly contact of
Conolly's), to return safely and become the model for the hero of a
best-selling romantic novel *The Hero of Herat*. He died of natural
causes, a fever, at the age of 32.[3] These men, and a few others forming an élite group of no more than half a dozen, had operated the
Great Game before Napier conquered Sindh. They were all good linguists, and all were able – to a greater or lesser degree – to live and
travel as natives among native peoples.

> A succession of young Indian Army officers, political agents,
> explorers and surveyors were to criss-cross immense areas of
> Central Asia, mapping the passes and deserts, tracing rivers to their
> source, noting strategic features, observing which routes were nego-
> tiable by artillery, studying the languages and customs of the tribes,
> and seeking to win the confidence and friendship of their rulers.
> They kept their ears open for gossip – which ruler was going to war
> with whom . . . By this way or that, what they learned eventually
> found its way back to their superiors, who in turn passed it on to
> theirs. The Great Game had begun . . .[4]

Precise information about Intelligence operations by British officers
under Napier is limited. It is known that he used 'native agents' as
infiltrators, but the little Richard revealed about his personal activities
in disguise is so similar to the published accounts of Conolly, Burnes
and Pottinger *et al* that it is impossible to conclude anything other
than that, primarily because of his special linguistic abilities, Richard
was recruited specifically to provide similar information. One of

Richard's oldest friends referred fleetingly in a biographical sketch to the fact that,

> Burton used to . . . collect information for Sir Charles Napier . . . not a little useful to local Government . . . he arrived at secrets which were quite out of the reach of his brother officers and surveyors . . . Captain MacMurdo [later, General Sir William MacMurdo, head of Napier's Intelligence Section] . . . frequently consulted his journals . . .[5]

After discussions with his three mentors Richard decided it would be a mistake to adopt the identity of a local man, for despite his fluency his accent inevitably contained inflections that could have led to exposure. The sad fates of Conolly and company a few years earlier must have been much in the minds of his Intelligence masters as in Richard's. As a result 'Mirza Abdullah the Bushiri' came into being; a half-Iranian, half-Arab traveller in fine linens and jewellery who hailed from Bushire, in the Persian Gulf. *Mirza* Abdullah probably made his first appearance in the early summer of 1845 and the advantages of the disguise were immediately apparent, for Richard found that peasants no longer ran away as he rode through fields, village girls did not vanish into huts as he approached, beggars no longer plagued him and even the cur dogs did not bark at him.[6]

His dress was simple:

> a muslin *pirhan*, or shirt with hanging arms, and skirts like a blouse buttoned around your neck . . . a pair of blue silk *shalwars* or drawers, wide enough, without exaggeration, for a young married couple and the baby . . . tight around the ankles and gathered in with plaits around the waist . . . [The] coat is a long white cotton garment . . . then a pair of yellow leather papooshes [slippers], worked with silk flowers, a shawl by way of a girdle and in it a small Persian knife, with ivory handle and a watered blade . . .[7]

He covered his shaven head with a cotton skull-cap around which was wound twelve yards of muslin; he recalled that it took him many months to learn how to tie this turban properly. A colourful cloak for cold weather, and a pair of soft yellow boots to the knee for riding, completed the wardrobe except for a gold signet ring of an unusual snake-head design,[8] a spear and a couple of pistols tucked in his belt.

Richard realised that a knowledge of the language, and ethnic dress, alone would not make him an insider in a foreign country, and that he had to penetrate the social veneer shown to foreigners if he was to glean the real day-to-day motivations of a subject people. He was carefully non-judgmental so that he might be regarded as a confidant. He rehearsed Abdullah's mannerisms to ensure that they became second nature; caressing his beard with his right hand – never the left, swearing by his beard when he wished to be emphatic, aware that such an oath pledged his honour.[9] He learned to walk with one hand on his hip and the other grasping his spear, to sit Turkish fashion and to remain still for a decent space of time lest his observers should think he had no dignity. His mentors had told him that he might – if musically inclined – hum a little in a low voice but he must never whistle, a purely European trait which Indians interpreted as the way in which the British communicated with the devil. He knew he must be correct in every minor detail of custom and behaviour if he was not to be detected.

Obviously, he needed transport of some kind. For example, a Bushire traveller would not ride a horse that was clearly groomed and clipped at a military establishment. Sometimes he rode a borrowed native horse, but he found a camel more appropriate to his disguise. Richard's first experience of riding a camel was a disaster. Having confidently borrowed a likely-looking animal from the Corps, he was naïvely unaware that the animal he chose was not a riding camel but a baggage animal. He took it away to practise riding it in secret. Once he had succeeded in mounting the 'roaring and yelling beast', a difficult process in itself, it continuously attempted to bite the boot of its rider. After several hours of truculence, alternately refusing to move and attempting to dislodge his rider by rushing under a low thorn tree, the camel bolted out of control 'in a canter which felt exactly like the pace of horse taking a five-barred gate at every stride'. Eventually the animal came to a halt in a muddy swamp where he fell on his side and its dazed rider was able to struggle free. 'I did not mount that animal again,' Richard wrote succinctly.[10] A more suitable camel was found and before long he was riding to and from the Fort in native dress with total confidence: 'I . . . frequently passed my Commanding Officer in the Gateway of Fort Hyderabad without his recognising me.'[11]

It was an audacious disguise, for there was nothing discreet about *Mirza* Abdullah the Bushiri; he was a well-to-do young merchant with a high profile. As he rode into villages crowds gathered to see him, and sat and talked freely with him; he to pass on the news and they about their concerns and hopes, their loves and hates, their fears and, not least, of their *ferengi* (foreign) masters. And sometimes, Richard wrote:

> When the Mirza arrived in a strange town, his first step was to secure a house in or near the bazaar for the purpose of evening *conversazioni*. Now and then he rented a shop, and furnished it with clammy dates, viscid molasses, tobacco, ginger, rancid oil, and strong-smelling sweetmeats: and wonderful tales Fame told about these establishments. Yet somehow or other, though they were more crowded than a first-rate milliners rooms in town, they throve not in a pecuniary point of view; the cause of which was, I believe, that the polite Mirza was in the habit of giving the heaviest possible weight for their money to all the ladies, particularly the pretty ones . . .[12]

Given his charismatic confidence and youthful good looks, he probably cut a dashing figure. So it is perhaps not surprising that he found himself welcomed into harems by 'fast and fashionable dames' to display his stock of muslins, linens and calicoes. A number of women were physically attracted to him and he even received proposals from the fathers of some. If a husband appeared full of outraged indignation that a strange young man had gained admittance to the heart of his home, *Mirza* Abdullah would swiftly untie his canvas roll of jewellery knowing that his exit would be insisted upon only over the dead bodies of the women of the household. He revelled in the 'gup' (gossip) exchanged in this arena as much as his female customers.

He often spent an evening playing chess with elders and, as he became bolder, Richard – as *Mirza* Abdullah – sometimes joined students in the Mosque during the evenings to debate tenets of faith with the *Mullah* under the dim light of an oil lamp. He also patronised an inn where hemp and opium were sold; freely admitting to taking both and even detailing their effect on him. '. . . Of course the more habituated a man becomes to the use of drugs,' he said, 'the more pleasurable he finds the excitement it produces . . .' and '. . . opium taken in moderation is not a whit more injurious to a man than alcohol'. However, he deprecated the taking of drugs to evade reality.[13] He visited the local marriage 'match-makers' to swap welters of gossip on local domestic scandals, and as he insinuated himself deeper into native society he began to learn a great deal about its sexual mores. He even gate-crashed private parties, secure in the conviction that a clean turban and good manners were a universal passport.

It was at this time, he relates in his autobiography, that he first began to learn about the divergent sexual activities that he wrote about many years later in the controversial Terminal Essay to his *1001 Nights*. In fact he never fully detailed his observations or adventures. Primarily, he was bound by the rules of his Army service not to do so, and – so he stated – he doubted whether anyone would believe him.[14]

Erotic adventures aside, it does not take much imagination to work out the type of raw information, obtained by Richard on such forays, which would have been of interest to his Commanders. Sindh was an occupied country whose people did not bear the British yoke lightly. At the time of Richard's masquerades, Napier – nicknamed 'The Devil's Brother' – was constantly on the alert for possible uprisings under the leadership of native princes.[15] His Intelligence chief MacMurdo used an extensive network of Indian agents to gather information,[16] but undoubtedly would have regarded the word and interpretation of a British officer as more reliable. Another obvious advantage of using a British 'plant' was the ability to start any rumours that Napier wished disseminated among the population. As a trader Richard was expected to be – indeed was welcomed as – a catalyst for gossip, stories and rumours, and he gathered and spread these freely as he went about. Ironically, when he posed as a native Richard was as much an outsider among his ethnic friends as he was among Europeans.

Richard provided few details of his work in his books, but that he was in prolonged close contact with Napier's Intelligence machine for at least two years is beyond doubt. One of his *munshis*, the Persian scholar *Mirza* Ali Akhbar Khan Bahá, is known to have been an agent in the pay of the British.[17] Previously, Ali Akhbar had been *munshi* to Napier himself, and was prominent in covert activities prior to the battles, two years earlier, of Meeanee and Dubba. In his autobiography Richard hinted at the type of Intelligence work which helped Napier to victory on those occasions, details of which he learned from Ali Akhbar. Two official reports were published about the encounters, Richard said, but a third would be needed to tell the story of how the victories were really achieved:

> . . . nor can we expect a public document to do so; how the mulatto who had been in charge of the Amir's guns had been persuaded to fire high, and how the Talpur traitor who commanded the cavalry, openly drew off his men and showed the shameless example of flight. When the day shall come to publish details concerning disbursements of 'Secret Service Money in India' the public will learn strange things.[18]

Sir Charles Napier was already a seasoned campaigner of 60 when he was sent to India. His appearance was impressive; he had the lined face of an old warrior with keen hawklike eyes and 'a nose like an eagle's beak'. He had a complete disregard for his personal comfort, but was assiduous regarding the needs of those under his command. He delighted in Rabelaisian *bon mots* in the Mess, rarely missed a regimental or brigade parade. Though he was a hard task-master he was liked by the junior officers, and worshipped as a hero by the common soldiers, in fact by all 'who did not thwart or oppose him'.[19] He waged a fierce and continuous battle with the government over outmoded policies, and was undiplomatically outspoken.

It is difficult to know how close could have been the relationship between the most senior officer in the Province and a lowly ensign. The exchanges between them, subsequently quoted by Richard's wife, imply that Napier regarded Richard as a smart young officer who did not prevaricate. Napier had tried and failed to learn Hindustani, and was reduced to speaking to his men through interpreters. He always said he would give 10,000 rupees to be able to address the sepoys personally. On one occasion when inspecting a newly built bridge he asked Richard how many bricks it contained, knowing this to be an impossible question. Richard answered calmly without hesitating, '229,010, Sir Charles', at which the great man turned away and smiled. At a Grand Review arranged to impress local Emirs he instructed Richard, 'Lieut. Burton, be pleased to inform these gentlemen that I propose to form these men in line, then to break into echelon by the right, and to form a square on the centre battalion . . .' It took him several minutes to complete the long technical instruction. There were no words by which Richard could convey such a complicated message in the dialect spoken by the audience but he

heard Napier out, saluted smartly and said, 'Yes, Sir.' He then turned
to the audience and addressed them:

> 'Oh, Chiefs! Our Great Man is going to show you the way we
> fight, and you must be attentive to the rules.' He then touched his
> cap to Sir Charles.
> 'Have you explained all?' he asked
> 'Everything, Sir,' answered Richard.
> 'A most concentrated language that must be,' said Sir Charles riding
> off . . .[20]

Richard was firmly in Napier's camp in the quarrel which developed
between the old Commander and Major James Outram, dividing the
Army in Western India into two factions. Long before Napier
appeared in north-west India, Outram had made recommendations
on the course of action that should be adopted there regarding the
Emirs; but when Napier reached the same conclusions and moreover
acted successfully upon them, Outram – no doubt aggrieved that
someone else had reaped the glory he felt should have been his own –
became Napier's strongest critic. While on leave in England Outram
allied himself with the powerful 'Kings of Leadenhall Street', against
whom Napier had long set his face.

Richard instinctively sided with Napier though he thought the
General's hot temper led him, sometimes, to act impetuously and
make mistakes. For example, said Richard, Napier bowed to opinion
at home and liberated all the slaves brought over from Africa ('turned
them out to starve,' was Richard's cynical response). Nevertheless
within a year of conquering Sindh, Napier had made the province
safer than any other part of India and he began tackling the social
problems. He banned many accepted practices such as that of *suti*,
and the less well-known about *badi* – whereby a poor man could
ensure his family's future by accepting payment to hang in place of a
convicted rich man. Napier's social reforms led to what must be
Richard's most bizarre military duty.

The establishment of brothels near a military camp is inevitable.
But when it was reported to Napier, in 1845 or 1846* that the town
of Karachi with its poor native population of 2,000 was able to sup-

---

*The precise date is unknown. Richard did not pass his Sindi language test until
September 1848, but it is clear that he had been able to merge with the native
community from a date much earlier than this.

port, besides its rash of conventional bordellos, three others where not women but boys and eunuchs were for hire, he had to act. Even today when homosexual relationships between consenting adults are accepted, an establishment offering young boys as prostitutes would not be regarded lightly. To Victorian society there was little to choose between the criminal offences of the homosexual or the pedophile since each was regarded as unspeakable. Since Karachi was within a mile of the military cantonment, as well as checking the veracity of the report Napier undoubtedly wanted to be sure that none of his men were involved, but investigation would require the greatest discretion.

At the time Richard was the only British officer who could speak Sindhi and, he said in his autobiography, he was able to walk into a bazaar, correctly identify the castes and know the manners, customs, religions and superstitions of each. It appears that Napier himself was involved in the decision to send Richard on this delicate mission – the only one which Richard ever detailed. He wrote that he undertook the task 'on express condition' that his report would remain confidential to Napier's administration and would 'not be forwarded to the Bombay Government, from whom supporters of the Conqueror's policy could expect scant favour, mercy or justice'.

Accompanied by a Munshi, Mirza Mohammed Hosayn of Shiraz, and habited as a merchant, Mirza Abdullah the Bushiri, I passed many an evening in the townlet, visited all the porneia and obtained the fullest details which were despatched to Government House . . .[21]

His account of what he saw in these establishments was perhaps more enthusiastically detailed than was required. He had been asked to 'make a few enquiries and report back'. His own sexual curiosity, his desire to examine sexual matters 'scientifically', coupled with a natural fascination with the erotic, his knack of acute observation and the desire to record minutely everything he observed, got the better of his judgement. Napier was, apparently, particularly arrested by Richard's explanation that a boy prostitute commanded double the price of a eunuch because 'the scrotum of the unmutilated boy could be used as a kind of bridle for directing [his] movements . . .'[22] Richard does not say in his autobiography whether he observed any British officers among the clients of the brothels, but it appears not for elsewhere[23] he stated that he knew of 'only one case of sodomy' in his regiment during his service at Karachi. This involved two sepoys of different castes and ended in tragedy.

From several obscure references in Richard and Isabel Burton's writings, it is clear that Richard's work as an undercover agent continued throughout 1845, and we have information of other *personae* adopted by him:

> He was sent out amongst the wild tribes of the hills and plains to collect information for Sir Charles. He did not go as a British Officer . . . a tattered, dirty looking dervish would wander on foot, lodge in mosques, where he was venerated as a saintly man, mix with the strangest company, join the Beloch and the Brahui tribes (Indo-Scythians) about whom nothing then was known. . . . Sometimes he worked with the men in native dress, 'Jats', and Camel Men at levelling canals.[24]

No further *precise* details of what Richard Burton's Intelligence work entailed have ever surfaced, and the entertaining but unsubstantiated particulars provided by a recent biographer[25] about his activities as an agent appear to be based on an imaginative mixture of conjecture and Rudyard Kipling's character, Strickland. On this subject, however, it is worth noting that Isabel Burton – who heard all Richard's stories and anecdotes and knew far more about the matter than she ever wrote – believed that Kipling had based Strickland on Richard Burton and his 'secret service' experiences in India.[26] Kipling was not born until 1865, and it is certain that he drew on a wider range of experiences than Richard's alone for his fascinating canon of *Boys Own* adventure stories. However, many scholars agree that Richard's career cannot be ruled out as a source of inspiration to Kipling.

During his trips Richard had of necessity to leave his bull-terrier bitch, Pepper, behind as the dog's presence would obviously betray his cover. On one of these missions the dog became ill and, to Richard's anger and distress, was allowed by her carer to die for the want of a few pence worth of drugs. It is not Isabel's only mention of pet animals at this time. Richard's language studies continued unabated, and his interest in the science of the spoken word led him to conduct an interesting experiment with some pet monkeys. Curious as to whether primates used some form of speech to communicate, he gathered together forty monkeys of various ages and species and installed them in his house in an attempt to compile a vocabulary of 'monkey language'. He learned to imitate their sounds, repeating them over and over, and believed they understood some of them. Each monkey had a name, Isabel explained:

> . . . he had his doctor, his chaplain, his secretary, his aide-de-camp, his agent, and one tiny one, a very pretty, small, silky looking monkey, he used to call his wife and put pearls in her ears. His great amusement was to keep a kind of refectory for them, where they all sat down on chairs at mealtimes, and the servants waited on them and each had its bowl and plate, with the food and drink proper for them. He sat at the head of the table, and the pretty little monkey sat by him in a high baby's chair . . .[27]

He had a list of about sixty words before the experiment was concluded, but unfortunately the results were lost in a fire (in 1860) in which almost all of his early papers perished. To his contemporaries such an experiment – not unusual in the late twentieth century – was regarded as whimsical and bizarre.

What of Richard's emotional life in his mid-twenties? Although he wrote many descriptive passages of women in general, and describes a number of women in particular, one stands out from the others. The apparent importance to Richard of this woman was promulgated after his death by a niece (his sister Maria's daughter), Georgiana Stisted, who speciously claimed that her uncle's reference to 'a Persian Princess' concealed the love of his life. Richard's description of this girl certainly confirms his physical attraction. She was, he said, 'one of the prettiest girls ever seen . . . with features carved in marble like a Greek's, the noble, thoughtful Italian brow, eyes deep and lustrous as an Andalusian's, and the airy, graceful, kind of figure with which Mohammed, according to our poets, peopled his man's paradise'.[28]

He related the anecdote in one of his first books, *Scind*, and repeated it word-for-word thirty years later in *Scinde Revisited*,* telling how he saw the anonymous girl at an evening encampment as she was being escorted, highly chaperoned, 'to her father's house, near Kurrachee'.[29] The following morning, he wrote, 'a small slave

---

* See earlier notes on Burton's spelling of Sindh.

boy of some twelve summers kept hanging around at the entrance of
the tent trying to evade all eyes but mine'. It transpired that the boy,
whose name was Lallu, was in the service of the beautiful girl. Burton
gave the child a rupee to go and spend in the bazaar while he wrote
a flowery *billet doux* ('the correct thing at this stage of an *affaire de
coeur*') to the boy's mistress, addressing her as, 'the rosebud of my
heart . . . the fine linen of my soul'. Lallu duly promised to put the
letter discreetly into the hand of his mistress and report back that
afternoon.

When the boy returned some hours later it was with a verbal
message that his mistress was unwell, and wished to know whether
her admirer had any medical knowledge and might send her a restorative elixir. Knowing, apparently precisely, what might appeal to her,
Burton immediately proceeded to brew up a warmed distillation of
gin and glucose, lightly perfumed with a drop of eau-de-cologne,
which he sent back hopefully.

Before there was any further opportunity for liaison, the Persians
began to strike camp. Litters were hoisted on to the backs of camels
and, shortly, accompanied by her attendants the girl emerged from her
tent, modestly enveloped in her flowing robes and wearing the
burqua. She lightly mounted her kneeling camel and seated herself in
her litter before turning her veiled face towards Richard. He heard a
tiny giggle. She leaned over and whispered something to the slave girl
seated beside her and the two girls giggled merrily together. Then she
drew the litter curtains and the camels began to move away.[30] There
is no epilogue and he never mentioned the girl again, except to repeat
the story of the encampment, word-for-word, in *Scinde Revisited*
some thirty years later.

Fifteen years after that, Richard's niece, Georgiana Stisted, would
insist that there was more to the relationship than this passing encounter; she claimed that her uncle confided in his sister (Georgiana's
mother) that the girl was a serious attachment. And there is some
circumstantial evidence to support a stronger association than the
brief meeting he wrote about, for embedded in Richard's story are
clues to the girl's identity. He says Lallu served the girl 'in the house
of a great *Sardar* (noble), the A***a Khan'.[31] Surely this can be none
other than the Agha Khan Mahallati, the older brother of Richard's
close friend and mentor, *Mirza* Mohammed Hosayn? In other words,
a house which Richard elsewhere describes in some detail as being

one where he was frequently received, and with whose male inhabitants he was on very friendly terms. He hunted and dined with them.

The Agha Khan had been 'cultivated' by Napier; he was awarded an annual pension of £2,000 and granted the noble title of 'Highness' for services rendered. He was important to the British, and it is probable that Richard was asked to report what transpired during his visits. We know he had no love for the Agha Khan; on his return to England he wrote that 'the Agha Khan . . . has done much to injure [his] tribe by his rapacity and ill-judged extortion.'[32] As he passed to and from the house of the Agha Khan, it is not inconceivable that Richard caught further glimpses of the girl who was the niece of one of his closest friends; 'a pretty woman when she wishes,' he wrote confidently, 'will always let you see something under the veil.'[33] But any deeper relationship such as the one suggested by Georgiana seems out of the question. As head of the Isma'ílí Shia sect, the Prince Imán Agha Khan had the status of royalty. His fabled wealth stemmed from the tributes of the faithful, topped up by the previously-mentioned annual pension of £2,000 (worth £64,320 today)[34] from the British in appreciation of his support in Sindh. A high-born girl of this family would never have been available to a penniless British officer, though with Richard's record one cannot entirely rule out an illicit relationship.

Georgiana's version of the story of the romance, apparently learned from her mother, tells us that Richard met the girl during one of his 'rambles'.

> Her personal charms . . . inspired him with a feeling little short of idolatry . . . never had he so loved before, never did he so love again . . . She worshipped him in return; but such rapture was not to last. He would have married her and brought her home to his family, for she was as good as she was beautiful [but she was] snatched from him in the bright flower of her youth, and the brightest hours of their joy-dream. Her untimely end proved a bitter and enduring sorrow . . . Years after when he told the story, his sister perceived with ready intuition that he could hardly bear to speak of that awful parting, even the gentlest sympathy hurt like a touch on an open wound. From the day of the death of his best beloved he became subject to fits of melancholy . . .[35]

It is clear that Richard did not tell his sister a great deal; merely that he

had once loved an Oriental girl (that she was also a Princess was crucial to Georgiana's romantic ideal) and that she had died before the
romance could flourish. The Stisteds assumed that the girl Richard
wrote of in *Scinde* and *Scinde Revisited* was the same girl he spoke of
to his sister. With its tragic ending the womenfolk of Richard's family
could view the relationship equably, for they were never forced to confront the inevitable trauma of his bringing home a black wife. But their
rejection of the aristocratic Englishwoman Richard eventually chose as
his wife simply because she was a Roman Catholic, leads to the suspicion that such a match would never have found favour with them.

A fragment of an unpublished poem in one of Richard's notebooks
has been quoted by recent biographers[36] to lend weight to the 'Persian
Girl' story. In fact it has no more substance than Georgiana Stisted's
romantic concoction. With a watermark of 1847, and the first entries
dating from about that time (the handwriting style compares with
that in dated manuscripts), this notebook contains poetry written by
Richard over a period of some years. It is certainly tempting to read
the poem in question – over 400 lines of epic love, passion and violence – as being autobiographical:

> . . . And her breath would fall on my glowing cheek
>   with sweet perfume
> Of the Chaman's breeze when a thousand flowers
>   of fragrance bloom.
> And the rounded forms of her youthful charms
> Voluptuous heaved in my circling arms
> Little I thought that the hand of death
> So soon would stay that fragrant breath
> Or that those locks with their beauteous wave
> So soon would be pent in the darksome grave
> Or that soft warm hand that glorious head
>   Be pillowed on the grave's cold stone
> Leaving my hapless self to tread
>   Life's weary ways alone, alone . . . [37]

However, thanks to Mr Quentin Keynes I have been able to transcribe
the entire poem from the original manuscript for the first time, and
the theory that it is autobiographical seems doubtful. Related by an
old man, it tells the story of an incident which occurred in his youth,

concerning his only love, a beautiful girl named Shireen ('Shireen, Shireen . . . I breathed that sound of love'). The lovers often met secretly by moonlight in a grassy bower on the banks of the Bandamír river in Persia. One night, instead of the 'lines of her white robed form' treading softly towards the trysting place he sees three men carrying a white bundle. He watches as the men begin to dig a hole and the mood of the poem abruptly changes from one of calm seren- ity, with mild breezes, nightbirds trilling and perfumed blossoms floating on sparkling waters, to a sinister darkness. 'Lightning flashed, thunder rolled and the greenwood groaned and the nightwind moaned . . .' as he recognises the bundle to be that of the shrouded body of Shireen. She has been poisoned (we are not told how he knows this) and her murderers are digging her grave.

Anger and a need for vengeance gave the storyteller a superhuman strength; he rapidly despatched two of the men with a single stroke of his sword each. The remaining man was the real villain and he was not allowed to die so easily. The two fought:

> . . . our ringing blades sang thro' the midnight air
> He was brave and bold, methinks, that Lord
> And wielded a not unskilled sword

The end is a foregone conclusion. The storyteller defeats his oppo- nent, exults over his death throes and removes Shireen's body so that she does not lie among her assassins:

> My footsteps strayed towards the bower
> Where in happier days we used to meet
> I placed her limbs on that leafy seat
> And kneeling raised the winding sheet
> To snatch one long last parting glance
> At that brow of angelic radiance
> Once more these burning lips to press
> To her soft cheek, her waving tress
> Whose curls so oft in fond caress
> Loosed from the binding fillet rolled
> Over my bosom their musky fold . . .

After burying Shireen (a name still prevalent in modern-day Iran and

Pakistan) the storyteller became 'a solitary man', a traveller who wandered the earth from icy hill to desert shore, and always thinking of his beautiful lost, and only, love.

Richard was certainly not an old man when he penned this, nor had he visited Persia or other places mentioned in the poem, so it cannot be literally autobiographical. Much of his poetry, like that in his published *Kasìdah*, drew on the rich mythology of Asia and the Arab world. He was fascinated, too, with story-telling as an art in itself. Towards the end of his life he would achieve lasting fame for bringing the unexpurgated tales of the *Arabian Nights* to an English-speaking audience, but even in his earliest non-fiction works he could not resist repeating some of the tales of love, chivalry and revenge that he learned as he imbibed new languages and cultures. What has not been previously noted about the Shireen manuscript is the fact that he has numbered the lines in pencil (the poem is written in ink) at approximately every tenth line, a technique he often used when trans-lating foreign works, duplicating the numbers in both the original and his translation to assist him in comparing like with like. Furthermore, throughout the work there are lines (within verses that otherwise scan and read rapidly) left blank or partially completed. We know, from his published writings, that to further his study of the Persian language Richard read and translated works of Persian poets, partic-ularly Saadi. Although I have not been able to verify it, I think it possible that the Shireen poem is an incomplete translation of Saadi's epic poem of thirty years of wandering.[38]

This does not affect Richard's anecdote; the beautiful girl from the house of the Agha Khan undoubtedly existed, and may or may not have been the girl of whom Richard spoke briefly to his sister, for there is some surviving evidence in his own handwriting to support a relationship of sorts. In the same notebook as the Shireen poem, writ-ten in faded pencil is a newly discovered and transcribed poem called 'Past Loves' which is indisputably autobiographical since it mentions by name several women with whom he was known to be involved; 'One,' he says, 'was the flower of Isfahan/A princess and a courte-san . . .' (see complete poem in Appendix 2).

There were other women in his life in India. Richard delighted in the company of women and his early books are full of lengthy descriptions of their temperaments, artifices, clothes and habits, betraying an intimate observation and indicating that he was still falling in and out of love on a regular basis. He worshipped at the shrine of youth and beauty; was repelled, with a young man's horror and cruelty, by age and ugliness. He dissected the behaviour and character of the women he met in much the same way that he examined, academically, the subjects of other numerous interests. Although he was disgusted by the squalid surroundings at Larkhana, famed for its *nautch* dancing girls, he delighted in the lithe grace of the beautiful *prima donna* 'Moonbeam' and her even more beautiful younger sister, Núr Ján (who, as we shall see, became Richard's mistress).[39]

Then there is the curious story of the kidnapped nun, related in *Goa* through Salvador, Richard's Portuguese butler. Surely, the unnamed lieutenant described by him could only be Richard (who had just heard he was to be promoted to the rank of second-lieutenant):

> . . . my master Lieut.——, of the —— Regt. [was] a very clever gentleman who knew everything. He could talk to each man of a multitude in his own language, and all of them would appear equally surprised by, and delighted with him. Besides, his faith was every man's faith. In a certain Mussulmanee country he married a girl and divorced her a week afterward. Moreover, he chanted the Koran, and the circumcised dogs considered him something of a saint . . .[40]

The phrase 'married a girl and divorced her after a week' is something of a puzzle, for it fits no known Burton episode, but there are other clues as to the identity of the lieutenant embedded in the story which tells how – speaking Portuguese – he obtained the confidence of the prioress of a convent by pretending his young sister wished to enter such an establishment. He was introduced to several young nuns and their Latin professor, 'a very pretty white girl, with large black eyes, a modest smile and a darling of a figure'. Naturally the two fell in love. 'As soon as I saw that Latin professor's face,' Salvador said, 'I understood the whole nature and disposition of the affair.' During the few occasions the would-be lovers were able to talk, an understanding was reached to the effect that, somehow, she would be 'rescued'. In common with all the residents of the convent the girl was closely chaperoned, but the lieutenant hit on a way of communicating with her. He sent a case of cognac to the prioress and a nosegay of jessamine blossoms to the Latin professor. Concealed in the blossoms was a note to the effect that she should be prepared to leave that night. Salvador watched his master, whose 'face – as usual when he went on such expeditions – was blackened . . . I never saw an English gentleman look more like a Mussulman thief.'[41]

Accompanied by Khudadad, an Afghan servant (Richard's Afghan servant was called Allahad), the lieutenant entered the convent by means of an illicitly obtained key and the judicious use of the point of his knife in the lock of a grating. Silently the men made their way to the cloisters where the Latin teacher slept. 'But my master, in the hurry of the moment, took the wrong turning, and found himself in the chamber of the sub-prioress, whose sleeping form was instantly raised, embraced and borne off in triumph by the exulting Khudadad . . .'

> My officer lingered for a few minutes to ascertain that all was right. He then crept out of the room, closed the door outside, passed through the garden, carefully locked the gate whose key he threw away, and ran towards the place where he had appointed to meet Khudadad and his lovely burden. But imagine his horror and disgust when, instead of the expected large black eyes and the pretty rosebud of a mouth, a pair of rolling yellow balls rolled fearfully in his face, and two big black lips, at first shut with terror, began to shout and scream and abuse him with all their might.

Rejecting Khudadad's suggestion that they should cut the woman's throat, and having thrown away the key, there was little the lieutenant could do except tie and gag the old nun and leave her to be found, meanwhile making good an escape. After that the doors and windows of the convent were barred and protected as though a thousand prisoners lived there. There was no further mention of the Latin professor, but one shudders to think what her fate might have been were she suspected of colluding with the kidnappers.

Because of the manner in which the story is told, one is tempted to dismiss it as yet another of Burton's fables. Yet there is some evidence that the extraordinary adventure did happen, and that Richard was indeed the lieutenant described by Salvador, for in her biography of him (see Chapters 34 and 35), his wife wrote about their visit to Goa in 1876:

We drove once to a large village called Ribander for the purpose of seeing the Convent of Misericordia. Here are kept under strict surveillance . . . seventy orphan girls, educated by the nuns, and who, when grown up, remain in the house until they receive an offer of marriage . . . [in *Goa and the Blue Mountains*] Richard gives an amusing account of his visit to this convent when he was a young lieutenant thirty years before.[42]

And finally, during this period there is a girl known in previous biographies as 'fair Margaret of Clifton' who, states a previous biographer,[43] Richard 'loved and courted, wooed in vain'. Clifton was a British resort outside Karachi and Richard knew it well during his time there. Fair Margaret is the only European girl that Richard mentioned by name in India and here, unquestionably, had he been interested, he would have been competing for her favours with his brother-officers. However, the poem (again having been fully transcribed by the author for the first time) reveals not the lament of a heart-broken young man but a rollicking satire about the unsuccessful love affair of one of Richard's brother-officers, his friend Lieutenant Henry Bateman. This hugely entertaining poem in which Richard plays with styles and cadences is full of high-spirited fun,

> . . . Ever since that hallowed hour
> Chained their souls with mystic power
> Careless of the wind and shower
> Want of fortune dot and dower
> Ma's cross word and pa's look sour
> Brother's brows that grimly lower . . .
> Every day when work was o'er
> Bateman sought his Margaret's bower
> > And there
> > The pair
> > Sat sighing
> > Wooing
> > Cooing
> > Dying
> > Crying
> > O my love
> > O my dove

In fact they stopped at nothing save
The sin of – reader, don't look grave . . .[44]

As far as his official Service Record is concerned, Richard continued working in the Survey Department under the command of Captain Walter Scott on an ambitious project to drain and protect an area of marsh along the Indus river, considered important by Napier, possibly as important as gathering intelligence.[45] The first attempt was unsuccessful, and when Scott reported that their tidal barrier had been breached by a flood tide Sir Charles replied suggesting they construct a dyke similar to that used in Dymchurch, Kent. By way of comfort for Scott's disappointment the General reminded him that the river Thames had

> . . . *pissed* on Brunel twice or thrice. Now the Indus has only offered you that indignity *once* and you may now treat him as the Emperor Tiberius treated his guests which my modesty prevents my telling you . . . let me know a few lines daily how things go on for I am very anxious indeed. I began the work without sanction and I expect to be blown up as well as the bund![46]

Richard appears to have worked on this project until he was granted leave to travel to Bombay on 15 October for his examination in Persian. This time he passed first out of 30 candidates. A month later he and Captain Scott started out for a Survey Tour of Northern Sindh via Gharra and Jarak to Kotri, and then crossed to Hyderabad where Richard's own Corps were based and finally to Sakhur.

The expedition marked the end of a year which Richard described as his 'pleasant careless life' in Karachi. His Service Record at this point was a glowing record of a good officer, who was attentive and hard-working.[47] The trip itself was a pleasant diversion and Richard was never happier than when travelling and being exposed to new sights. They spent Christmas at Hyderabad where the hospitality offered them by the officers of the 18th B.N.I. was generous and 'very jolly'. Richard was in high spirits, which led to one of his practical jokes. He attempted (and succeeded to a degree) to hoax an archaeological team excavating a site nearby which they believed ('absurdly', said Richard) to be the camp of Alexander. He constructed a fake grammar purporting to be that of the mythical 'lost tribes of Israel' (which Scott refused to allow him to use) and laid a contemporary jar embossed with 'Etruscian' figures in a prominent position for discovery. For a few weeks it was hailed as a remarkable find and Richard enjoyed the team's gullibility. One wonders how, some years later when he himself developed a keen interest in archaeology, he would have reacted to a similar trick being perpetrated on him.

While this trip was in progress, exciting things were happening on the wider canvas of Anglo-Indian history. Richard had heard rumours in the bazaars, of course, but it was not until January 1846 that there was any confirmation of the start of what came to be called the Great Sikh War which added the Punjab to the British territories. By mid-December 1845 Napier and Simpson had already begun to assemble the units of the Bombay army into 'the largest force of Europeans ever assembled in India' after the Sikhs crossed the agreed boundary of their territory.[48] Scott did not receive the news until a month later in a letter from Napier's aide-de-camp:

> The General says you may allow as many of your assistants as you can spare to join their regiments, if going on service; with the understanding that they must resign their appointments [in the Survey Department] and will not be reappointed.[49]

Despite his contentment working on Scott's team, Richard – who had just been gazetted a lieutenant[50] – was 'wild to go . . . I was miserable that anything should take place in India without my being in the thick of the fight.'[51] Scott was reluctant to send in Richard's resignation from the Survey Department but was eventually prevailed upon to do so, for distinguishing behaviour in battle was far and away the shortest route to promotion. Richard immediately applied formally for permission to march, but Napier had already left Karachi. When permission was refused, Richard assumed that the decision had been made by one of Napier's A.D.C.s and returned to Scott at Sakkur plotting how to get himself to the scene of the action. In fact the refusal was by direct order of the Acting Regimental C.O., General Sir James Simpson.

Some of Richard's former 'chums' in the Karachi bungalow had marched with the 18th from Karachi in December, and had already seen action in the first wave of fighting. One, Lieut. J.L. Blagrave, wrote to Richard, 'I wish you could have seen it, it was a beautiful sight and at first just like a glorious Grand Review. We got the order . . . to be ready at 3 a.m. to move against them and by sunrise we were all lined up behind the artillery . . .' A long and detailed account of the advance and the capture of guns, positions and standards followed, until they reached the banks of a river . . .

> when for a moment or two there was slight confusion for we had come on so fast that we had got between a large body of flying enemy and the ford, but we faced both ways and cleared the field. The carnage in the river was awful, hundreds falling every minute . . . their letters state their loss at 20,000 but even – say – 10,000 which I don't think beyond the mark considering the numbers that fell in their determination to escape, and the numbers drowned . . . I wish you could have seen the engagement, it was the finest and most exciting sight I have ever seen though there were one or two cases that made my blood curdle – fellows being shot who had thrown down their arms. I saved one but was wrong . . . for he afterwards escaped . . . picked up a musket and commenced fighting . . . your friend Rivers White is now in my Corps . . . he bids me send his salams and tells me to say that he has at last earned and won a medal . . .[52]

It is not difficult to imagine how this letter affected Richard, already frustrated by his orders to stay with the Survey Team. When fate intervened yet again in his life, he grasped the opportunity heedless of how it might be regarded by his superiors. A routine memo arrived from the Survey H.Q. in Bengal stating that all Assistant Surveyors must provide independent sureties for the expensive government equipment in their possession. Richard replied immediately that he could find no one willing to act as guarantor for him. This was a clear coded message that he wanted out of the Survey Department in order to join his Corps for the coming battle, and in the prevailing climate was sympathetically received at H.Q. His resignation was accepted and he was told to rejoin his Corps forthwith. General Simpson, not privy to low-level administrative decisions taken in Bengal, only learned of the circumnavigation of his orders after the event. On 23 February the Hyderabad section of the 18th B.N.I. Corps marched 'merrily' from Rohri and Richard, spoiling for the fight, was with them.

They were expected to make 50 miles a day, and this almost super-human feat, Richard states, could only be accomplished by doping the camels with *bhang*. He does not explain how the men withstood the pace.[53] After nearly three weeks the 'model army of 13,000' reached Bahádwalpur. But the 18th B.N.I. arrived only to be given the crushing order to retire. There was nothing to do but rest and begin the return journey. The morale of men marching fast with a clear purpose can withstand the inevitable discomforts of physical exertion under a broiling sun; to the dispirited returning army, the discomforts and deprivations were less tolerable. When the 'Jolly Greens' arrived back at Gharra the prevailing mood was one of soured tempers and quick irritability.

Richard subsequently wrote that this was the period in his life upon which he reflected with least satisfaction. He does not elaborate greatly, but he refers inexplicably to domestic unpleasantness involving 'a young person, Núr Ján'. All we are told about this affair was written thirty years later by Richard in his *Scinde Revisited* when he visits his former home: 'How small and mean are the dimensions, which loom so large in the pictures stored within the brain. There I temporarily buried the young person when the police-master gave orders to search the house.'[54] Clearly he had confided in his wife at that time about the matter, for she confirmed in a footnote to this memory that it had been 'a very romantic affair'.[55] Why the police had been called we do not know; there are several possibilities.

From the snippets of information left by Richard about Núr Ján, there is no way of knowing how long she lived with him as his mistress. What we do know is that Richard met her at a *nautch* organised by Harí Chand, a senior aide to the Agha Khan. Richard had met Harí Chand during his first days at Karachi, and the *Bráhmin* had played a major role in Richard's study of his sect. He often crops up in Richard's trio of books on Sindh and it is clear that Richard distrusted and disliked him. Chand, he says, was a cunning and dishonest man who boasted openly of his numerous sexual conquests, especially of European women. It was Chand who secured the services of the troupe of dancers from the town of Larkhana to entertain his friends.[56] The troop's chief attraction was its *prima donna*, the famous and beautiful dancer Mahtab ('the Moonbeam') with her lovely 'perfect oval' face, doe-like eyes and the gloss of youth on her hair and fine skin. But it was Núr Ján ('Radiant Light'), the youngest and prettiest of the dancers, with whom Richard fell in love. In his poem 'Past Loves', he called her 'fair Núr Ján, the Venus of Bolochistan'.[57]

A dancer purchased as a child and trained from childhood was a valuable commodity. As such it is unlikely that Núr Ján was free to roam at will or freely make the decision to become the live-in mistress of a British officer. Harí Chand was no doubt responsible for her safe return to Larkhana, and if he discovered that the girl was living with Richard it was doubtless he who sent the police to recover her. Did Richard bury her under some straw when the police came to search his house? Or was she killed, poisoned perhaps, as punishment for running away with Richard? There is a fascinating possibility that she was the girl whom Salvador referred to when he confided that his Lieutenant had once 'married for a week and then divorced'. Certainly, Núr Ján has an equal claim with the Persian princess to have been the girl Richard claimed to have 'loved and lost' when he confided in his sister, but he could hardly have told his family that he considered bringing home a *nautch* dancing girl. Importantly, in his poem about his former loves he dismisses the Persian princess as 'most charming'; it was little Núr Ján who, he says, 'was most to my mind'.[58]

Whatever is the truth, Núr Ján disappeared at this point from Richard's life. And although he would later confide the details of the 'very romantic affair' concerning Núr Ján to his wife,[59] his remark in the Terminal Essay of *Arabian Nights*, that 'while thousands of Europeans have cohabited for years with, and had families by, "native women" they are never loved by them – at least I never heard of a case,' appears to rule out the mutual passion Georgiana Stisted promulgated for her uncle and his 'Persian Princess', or for that matter with Núr Ján.

Perhaps it was just as well. General Sir James Simpson abhorred the practice of the *bubu*, and in a letter written to Napier only weeks before Richard and Núr Ján's relationship finished, he determined to end it.

Hyderabad
30th Dec 1845

Dear Sir Charles,
   . . . I hope you will allow me a day or two to look around for an

A.D.C. I had better have *none* than one who will be useless to the Service and to myself. There is one here who would suit me, but he has that disgraceful encumbrance of a black woman . . . and I think a Registered Officer who shows such a bad example to the Native Officer does not deserve any favour shown him. Nearly every officer in the 18th [Bombay Native Infantry] is similarly circumstanced, and in this respect I never saw a Corps so bedevilled. I hope to break some of these disgraceful liaisons when they move! . . .[60]

One incident which adversely affected Richard's military career occurred shortly after the return of the Corps from their arduous march. Richard had not lost his ability to throw off caricatures adorned with a few pithy lines of doggerel verse, and was amusing his brother-officers one evening with this talent when the acting C.O. of the Corps, Colonel Henry Corsellis, arrived in the Mess. Born in India of English parentage, Corsellis was a bluff, impatient sort of man who believed he knew more about his native country than anyone – better, most certainly, than an upstart 'white nigger' – and there was no love lost between him and Richard. When Corsellis curtly asked why he had not been included in his library of caricatures, Richard – knowing that he was 'in for a row' anyway over the way in which he had left the Survey Team without proper permission – sneeringly obliged by sketching a tombstone, engraved upon it the name of his subject and underneath wrote a pithy, derisive couplet. The procedure, which in the past had nettled his old tutor Du Pré and the dons at Oxford, also worked with Corsellis. One of Richard's surviving notebooks contains the reason for the senior officer's displeasure.[61]

> Here lies the body of Colonel Corsellis
> The rest of the fellow, I fancy, in hell is.[62]

It seems reasonably mild, if a little disrespectful, but it was all that was needed to fan the embers of dislike which had been glowing between the two men and Richard states, without further elaboration, that afterwards they 'went at it hammer and tongues'. Corsellis subsequently reported him for insubordinate behaviour.

A short time later Richard's house, constructed of sun-dried mud bricks, became so thoroughly soaked by the monsoon rains that the fabric returned to its original viscous state and disintegrated. Richard was sitting in what he facetiously called his 'drawing room' reading aloud to his *munshi* when the roof collapsed and a ton of mud fell on them. The *munshi* escaped unhurt, but Richard suffered a badly injured leg. He felt they were lucky to get off so lightly, but his description of the incident confirms that when this happened he was living there alone, and there is no further mention of any live-in mistresses.

He had only two pleasant memories of that unhappy spring of 1846. First, he met and became friends with Lieut. John Frederick Steinhaueser who would play an important role in his life, and second, the sick leave granted as the result of his injured leg was spent in the home of his Afghan *munshi* on 'the banks of the beautiful Phuleli [river], seated upon a felt rug spread beneath a shadowy tamarind tree, with beds of sweet-smelling *rayhan* (basil) round'.[63] In this peaceful setting he spent his days reading and watching the colourful throng of passengers crossing the river on a nearby ferry while his friend and tutor Mohammed Hosayn taught him the soft strains of the mysterious, philosophical *Hafiz*.

5

INDIAN SUMMER
1846–1849

The summer of 1846 found Richard still at odds with the world. He had lost his mistress; his friend, Mohammed Hosayn, was about to return to Persia;[1] he was irritated by the injury to his leg, and his career was on hold. Despite all his hard work his life was not moving in any positive direction. He had applied to rejoin the Survey Team but this had been refused, for he was in disfavour on the twin counts of his having rejoined his regiment to march on the Sikhs in direct contravention of an order, and of insubordinate behaviour to his Commanding Officer. All his former eagerness turned to disgust.

Captain Walter Scott was increasingly concerned for his younger friend, now known among his contemporaries as 'Ruffian Dick'. He recognised Richard's mood of frustration and was anxious that he should not ruin his career by a further act of impulsive wilfulness. Knowing how close Richard was to his father, Scott wrote to Joseph Burton in Italy for guidance, but the reply took some months to arrive for the Burtons were spending the summer in London that year:

> 7 Cumberland St
> Portman Sq. London
> 7th July 1846
>
> My dear Sir,
>   I have received your very kind letter of the 19th April . . . it is much to be regretted that my beloved son has met with the

disapprobation of the best General of the day and I also regret that
he has been removed from under your command, for I always valued
your sound advice and disinterested friendship . . . However Richard
only acted up to the instructions I repeatedly gave him, namely,
'never to tolerate a situation which might possibly prevent his seeing
service, especially until he might have made a good name for himself
in the field of battle'. For my part I am perfectly convinced that he
never intended to disobey Sir Charles's orders, so far the reverse that
he imagined nothing could raise him so high in the estimation of the
General *sans peure et sans lâche*, as distinguishing himself in actions
which I am sure Richard intended to do if an opportunity offered.

From what I can learn my son tendered his resignation in due
form to General Sympson [sic] the then *Commander of the Forces
in Scinde* which the General accepted, in consequence of which my
son did not think that he was acting in disobedience of orders as Sir
Charles had refused the Command of the Army to the General officer that permitted Richard to join the 18th.

Had the army of Scinde seen service in the battles of the Sutley
etc. and the officers returned, some with medals some with promotions; might they not say to my son 'you have remained behind
surveying, and pocketing rupees whilst we were risking our lives,
and gaining laurels in the field of battle'. How could he avoid these
imputations but by acting as he did? Tho' his life is dearer to me
than that of any other being in existence, I hope he will always risk
it whenever his reputation as a soldier, or his patriotism as an
Englishman may be in question.

I am very anxious that Richard may pass his examination in the
Persian language in the course of this year as it may possibly bring
him into notice in Bombay, for I think it would be advisable for him
to pay visits to persons of rank etc to whom he has letters of introduction. Sir Thos McMahon offered me a situation for Richard in
the irregular Cavalry for which the latter ought to feel very grateful.
I did not accept the General's kind offer lest Richard should be
removed from his studies . . . [I hope to have] an opportunity of
shewing my gratitude for the essential service you have rendered to
my son. Believe me to remain

> Yours very sincerely,
> Jos. Burton[2]

By the time Scott received this reply Richard was again in sick quarters. The summer of 1846 was unusually hot and sticky and there was a severe outbreak of cholera. The Army suffered badly and some 800 soldiers died of the illness. Napier lost his favourite nephew and A.D.C., John Napier, in the epidemic, as well as a grand-niece. There was hardly a man in the 18th B.N.I. Regiment who did not suffer from recurrent fevers and diarrhoea. Scott made a further attempt to have Richard transferred to his command by appealing directly to Napier but the response was negative

19th August [1846]

Private

My dear Scott,
    The General says he is sorry that he cannot appoint Burton *at present* to the survey, because he is under a cloud, which has not yet been cleared up. He has been behaving rather bumptiously to his Commanding Officer, and the matter is not yet settled. Until it is, it is impossible for the General to give him an appointment. It is a great pity, for he evidently would be very useful to you. Perhaps it may come right in time.

Yrs sincerely
Wm Napier[3]
[ADC to Sir Charles Napier]

The fresh rejection provoked an almost predictable reaction of belligerence. 'Existence . . . in India is precarious,' Richard stated, 'who can tell how soon a fever or a bullet may send him to the jackals? Consequently we are, perhaps, a little over anxious to "live while we may".'[4] The following weeks marked an important turning point in Richard Burton's life. For the past year or so, under the influence of Scott and in anticipation of advancement, it had appeared that he might be conforming. But in 1846 he appears to have decided that regular service in the Company was unrewarding, or at least he did not have the patience to wait until reward seemed likely.

    A satirical (unpublished) work written by Richard at this time called *Anglo-Indian Glossary*[5] provides pertinent clues as to his sense of disillusionment. Four years of unremitting work and linguistic

achievement had advanced his career no faster than those officers
who idled away their free time on the polo field or on tiger shoots.
The following extracts are typical:

> **Aide de Camp.** An officer nearly connected to some Major General
> whose duty it is to wait upon the M. General's wife, pick up the
> daughter's pocket handkerchiefs and make himself generally useful
> in a large establishment.

> **Arrest.** The most grateful hours of retirement and literary ease
> which the writer of these pages has ever enjoyed.

> **Colonel** . . . An individual whose distinctive marks are brass spurs
> and a gilt scabbard. He generally speaking would make your for-
> tune could you buy him at your price and sell him at his own
> valuation of himself.

> **Interpreter** . . . An officer who is called upon at least once a month
> to make himself ridiculous by screaming out before 1,000 Sepoys
> some debased dialect which in his boasting minutes he terms Urdu
> or Hindust[ani]. He has also to be present at all Court M. where the
> Subalterns who have not passed in the language look greedily for-
> ward to his breaking down or not understanding some phrase . . .

> **Leave.** The great aim of a Military Man's existence . . .

Perhaps the most personally revealing of his depressingly negative
definitions in this work is his recommended procedure (by far the
longest and detailed passage) for 'obtaining Sick Leave'. Given what
we know about his life at this time, it is reasonable to assume that he
was recording first-hand experience. Just as some years earlier he
had set his mind to be rusticated from University in order to join the
Army, now his objective was extended leave of absence and he set
about achieving his aim in a similarly single-minded fashion.

First, he adopted a general air of wretchedness, and though he
appeared daily at Inspection he was seen elsewhere only rarely and
never at Mess. He visited the office of the Garrison Surgeon, 'supported by two strong Negroes', and swore he never drank when his
daily quota was half a dozen bottles and that he did not smoke when

his daily ration was 12 Manillas. He posted a sentinel near his door so that any visitor invariably found him on his bed, and made a point of ostentatiously wishing the Assistant Surgeon good night at 8 p.m. He began to vow deep affection for the Corps, declaring that his prospects would be ruined by leaving it.

His rooms were allowed to assume the uncared-for appearance of a semi-invalid, with sloppy cups and flabby toast left on the table. In reality he continued to consume suppers of lobster salad, oysters, curry, port wine and ice cream secretly. By day his rooms were darkened and he failed to light his lamp at night. Occasionally he took emetics and sent a 'well-instructed servant' to rouse the doctor at 2 a.m. He even wrote a new will and begged the doctor to act as executor.[6]

There is little doubt that earlier in the same year Richard had been genuinely ill. The apparent lack of improvement in his condition by early September 1846 was, however, more likely due to his dramatic skills than cholera. He was sent to Bombay for treatment and convinced the Surgeon General there that he was not capable of active service. His Service Record reveals that in January 1847 he was 'granted leave for 2 years to proceed to the Neilgherry Hills on SCGO' (sick leave).[7] Richard exulted that after the strait-jacket of military routine ahead of him lay 'the delightful prospect of two quiet years' during which he could call his life his own again and might lie in bed half the day if he wished.[8]

For someone so apparently ill, he displayed a remarkable ability to organise a semi-expedition. He showed no desire to lie in bed half the day, indeed he lost no time in engaging a teacher to coach him in Arabic, and hiring a *pattimar* called 'Joy of the Ocean'. Then, with his horse and a small retinue of servants he set out on his journey to Ootacamund in the highlands of Nilgiris, or 'Blue Mountains of Coimbatore', via Goa. It was not the most direct route, but he especially wished to visit Goa in the furtherance of his study of Portuguese. He had recently become interested in the works of the poet Luis Vaz de Camões (called by Richard 'Camoens') who had lived in Goa three centuries earlier. The poet's romantic epic *Os Lusiadas* was to fascinate Richard for decades, just as did the tales of the *Arabian Nights*.

Richard did not spend long at Goa; less than six weeks later he was in Ootacamund, or 'Ooty' as it has been affectionately known by generations of English visitors. However it was enough to research his first book (published four years later), *Goa and the Blue Mountains*, an eclectic mix of material from a description of old Goa, its streets, its ruins, churches, monasteries and convents, to an account of its history and people. In it he was intolerant and critical, but this was normal; nowhere in all his vast travels was Richard ever destined to find a place that met with lasting unqualified approval.

Throughout his time in India, Richard had made a point of visiting the libraries of bibliophiles and collectors. While in Bombay he haunted the library of the Court of Directors which housed a large collection of largely untranslated ancient Oriental manuscripts.[9] His time in Goa was no exception; in the pages of *Goa and the Blue Mountains* he mentions visiting four such libraries. Whenever possible he copied out or purchased manuscripts, and already possessed the foundations of a substantial collection. When he had exhausted Goa and its environs he set out for the 4-day cruise down the coast to Punány where he left the boat for the 10-day overland ride.

By the end of March 1847, having sent back most of his servants and ordered his baggage to follow him, Richard and his reduced ménage reached the highlands. The journey was not without its excitements. One night he woke to find half a dozen intruders in his room, naked except for a coating of grease to prevent easy capture.[10] One man came close to Richard's bed and held a long, sharp knife close to his jugular. Since an officer of his own regiment had recently been critically wounded in an identical attack in the same vicinity a few weeks earlier, Richard 'judged it inexpedient in the extreme to excite him by any display of activity' so he closed his eyes and pretended deep sleep until the intruders left with a candlestick they believed, incorrectly, to be silver.[11]

As usual Richard was careful to forearm future travellers with correct information. Thus he would dismiss a waterfall, highly recommended by current guide books, as 'only needing water' to make it worth the couple of hours' detour, and a famous river as 'a muddy ditch'. But even he thought the Blue Mountains an adequate repayment for the effort of the journey, for the air was blessedly cool and damp and he began to 'look down upon the steamy plains below with a sense of acute enjoyment'. A daisy on a roadside bank, the first he had seen since leaving England, lifted his spirits. A hotel run by an Englishman provided the joy of an excellent dinner, a comfortable sitting room and a clean bed. His appetite returned, he could walk for hours whereas at sea level an hour had been exhausting to him.

It was too much to hope that Richard would continue to be so satisfied with his lot. Initially he fell in with the round of dinners, balls, soirées, horse-racing and other social activities that the British organised in Ooty to make their colonial sojourn a tolerably enjoyable one. He especially appreciated the determination to banish military 'shop' despite the large number of officers present in the town. He rode out to view and make extensive notes on the surrounding country, its inhabitants, its flora and fauna. But these pleasures palled when the weather changed with the coming of the rains and the seasonal visitors returned to the plains. Ootacamund out of season was simply a dull provincial town with little or nothing to recommend it.

News came up from his regiment that was not welcomed by Richard. Sir Charles Napier had resigned the Governorship of Sindh and was returning to Europe on extended leave. General Simpson had already left. Any progress that Richard had made in forging personal relationships with his Commanders, a procedure strongly recommended by his father, had now been lost. To add to his growing despondency, Richard suffered an attack of 'rheumatic ophthalmia' which intermittently affected his ability to work on his current study projects, Arabic, Persian, Telugu and Toda (a local tribe). Soon he began to feel what seemed strongly like confinement in Ootacamund, as keenly as he had previously felt that of the military regimen, and he became depressed and morose. There were 104 officers on sick leave in Ooty at the time and only a handful of unattached women. '. . . you have promised to ride with Miss A——, who will assuredly confer the honour of her company upon your enemy Mr B—— if you keep her waiting five minutes.'[12] His sour comments that the women disdained 'anyone below the rank of field officer' suggest that he had little success with the opposite sex in Ooty. People who had initially befriended him began to look coldly upon him after dinners where he drank too freely and exercised his cynical and all-too-often barbed wit.[13]

By August he was ready to sacrifice the remainder of his sick leave; anything to escape the boredom of Ooty with its lack of good society, access to books and the company of learned *munshis*. He blamed his eye problems on the damp, cold weather and thought these would clear up if he returned to lower and warmer altitudes. But what seems to have precipitated the final decision was the death of his tough little horse in a bad fall on slippery clay.[14] The horse had been with him from the first days of his arrival in India when he had been so full of enthusiasm for the life before him. He advised the Officer-in-Charge at Ooty that he was fit for duty, fully aware that a return at that moment involved all the discomforts of a lumpy voyage by steamer up the north-west Indian coast against strong monsoon head winds.

On 1 September he rode down from the hills to Ghat, and twelve days later reached Calicut where he did some further research into his study of Camoens before embarking on the S.S. *Seaforth*. The notes he made in the town, the site of one of the most remarkable sections of *The Lusiads*, would be filed away and later used for a book. A month later in Bombay, after some difficulty in getting a place on the examination course, he passed first of thirty entrants in the Persian examination. He now equalled his rival, C.P. Rigby, in proficiency in native languages, and the Court of Directors had little hesitation in recommending a reward to Richard in the shape of an honorarium of 1,000 rupees, the same sum received by Rigby in the previous year.[15]

After a few weeks Richard was – to his relief – appointed to the Survey Department again and received orders to return to Sindh. The journey was not without its exciting moments. As the vessel approached Karachi in the rough seas and howling wind, the passengers discovered that the Captain and crew were roaring drunk and incapable of safely bringing the vessel into the tricky port with its myriad mud-banks. They therefore insisted on Richard assuming command. He ordered the ship out to sea until the following morning when the wind had eased and they were able to land safely.[16]

His eye problems did not abate as he had assumed, and the glaring sun in which the survey was carried out made it impossible for him to work on a regular basis. An ointment with a mercury base recommended for application to his eyes only increased the complaint, which in fact would continue to afflict him for some years. It made him miserable when his comrades had to perform his share of the allotted tasks and even his language programme was affected, but in the periods when the pain and irritation was reduced he worked at his Arabic and Sindi studies. He had also completed, during that year, his first full translation, 'Akhlak i Hindi' or 'Pilpay's Fables'. It was a forerunner of his most famous work on Oriental folk-lore.[17]

His Annual Inspection Report for January 1848 was still complimentary: 'evinces a zeal for the service; regularity, and attention to his
duties highly creditable, and is well acquainted as far as his experience
has allowed him to progress.'[18] He had been in India six years at this
point. But the *joie de vivre* had gone out of his life and had been
replaced by depression and a resentment of his lot.

It was at this time, while genuinely incapacitated and with time to
think and dream, that he conceived the idea for his great Arabian
adventure. It was impossible to live in the East without being aware
of the great annual Islamic pilgrimage, the *Haj*, to the birthplace of
the Prophet. Richard was fascinated with the accounts he had read of
the few Europeans who had made the *Haj* and written of their adventure: Ludovico de Bartema in 1503, Joseph Pitts of Exeter in 1680,
the Catelonian Badia (alias Ali Bey el Abbasi) in 1807, Giovanni
Finati in 1811 and the famous Swiss traveller Burkhardt in 1814. But
they had not gone as born believers; Bartema travelled as a Mameluke
in the days when Mamelukes were Christian slaves to the Turks, Pitts
was a captive carried there by his Algerian master, Badia's political
position was known to the authorities, and Finati was an Albanian
soldier. Even the great Burkhardt had revealed himself as a European
to the Pasha, and although his account was the most detailed so far he
was a sick man when he reached Medinah and had not visited all the
holy sites. And still, even after the latest adventures by the young
Finn, George Wallin, whose travels in Arabia during 1845 and 1848
were the subject of so much excitement in the Royal Geographical
Society (and whose *Journal* Richard had read), *still*, no European, no
infidel, had ever entered Mecca as 'one of the people'.[19]

The more he thought of it the more the notion took shape as a
credible project. There were plenty of hearsay descriptions written of
the rites and ceremonies of the *Haj*, Richard noted, but no descriptions of the practical day-to-day experiences of an ordinary pilgrim.
Supposing he, with his proven flair for disguise and his linguistic
abilities, were to make such a journey disguised as a true-born
believer? He would be a 'made man' for surely, he reasoned, there was
a best-selling book in it. Real success would hang not so much on
reaching the Holy Places as on doing so undetected. But there was
also a very real danger that were he to be discovered he might be
killed, as Conolly had been in Afghanistan when detected.

It was not unusual for officers to obtain paid leave for explorations

which advanced the Company's knowledge of the lands bordering its
territories. A commission in the Army in India was the passport to
adventure for a number of young men, contemporaries of Burton's
such as Grant and Speke who received full pay and expenses while
carrying out explorations, nominally on behalf of the Company.
Indeed, during his time in India Richard met many of the geographers
and explorers who would become household names a decade or so
later.

A positive direction had been lacking in Richard's life for some time
and, having set a course, he fixed on it with typical tenacity. Through
the half-Bedouin Sheikh Hashim, an Arabic teacher whom Richard
had brought with him from Bombay, he not only improved his knowledge of the language but learned to recite a quarter of the Koran
from memory:

> I devoted all my time and energy; not forgetting a sympathetic
> study of Sufism, the *Gnosticism of Al-Islam* which would raise me
> high above the rank of a mere Moslem. I conscientiously went
> through the *chillá*, or quarantine of fasting and other exercises,
> which, by-the-by, proved rather over-exciting to the brain. At times,
> when over-strung, I relieved my nerves with a course of Sikh reli-
> gion and literature . . . as I had already been invested by a strict
> Hindu with the *Janeo* or 'Brahminical thread' my experience of
> Eastern faiths became phenomenal, and I became a Master-Sufi.[20]

The creed appealed to him; especially the codes, clues and mystic
revelations that were revealed only to the secret circle of initiates.
Similarly he studied, and remained deeply affected by, the creed of
Zoroaster, the east Persian prophet (c.628–55) who preached a form
of dualism in which good and evil are in perpetual conflict. It has
often been said, even recently, that at heart Richard was a Muslim;
that he accepted the Muslim faith and lived by it throughout his life.
My conclusion is that this is to exaggerate reality. Burton investigated Islam thoroughly, as he did Catholicism and other forms of
Christian religion; he was to spend his life searching with an open
mind for a truth that he could wholeheartedly embrace; whether or
not he found it is discussed later. Meanwhile, he saw no difficulty in
embracing Islam and the creed of Sufism as part of his research;
indeed he actively enjoyed the complex rituals which encompassed a

sort of brotherhood with fellow worshippers. But he regarded his observance of Islam as the means to an end rather than a statement of faith. Indeed he regarded Sufism as 'the Eastern parent of Free-Masonry'; an organisation to which most of his brother-officers and, for a time, Richard himself belonged.[21] Had his aim been to penetrate the Vatican he would just as willingly have trained as a priest to achieve it. The magnetism of Islam for him lay in the diverse cultures of the peoples; and in outwardly accepting the faith he gained the ability to move in and out of these worlds as an observer with intimate understanding.

One of Burton's oldest friends, A.B. Richards, was responsible for revealing to the world in 1864 the fact that part of his preparations for the *Haj* involved circumcision.[22] Certainly, it would have been foolish to attempt such a venture without this definitive mark of the devout Muslim. He had to anticipate the possibility of a serious illness requiring total nursing, and he knew that Arthur Conolly's disguise had been penetrated during such circumstances in 1830.* Were Richard to be discovered to be an uncircumcised man, and therefore not what he purported to be, his chances of survival among fanatics in Mecca were small.

His own operation is not mentioned in any of Richard's published works, but he quoted an earlier traveller in Arabia on the subject of circumcision, 'I look upon the safety of their journey as almost impossible, unless they have previously submitted to the rite.'[23] This advice was 'correct' said Burton, 'the danger is doubled by non-compliance with the custom.'[24] Elsewhere in *Pilgrimage*, Burton stated that the 'external' evidence of a Muslim was 'absolutely inde-spensible . . . in bigoted Moslem countries it is considered sine qua non.'

We do not know where the operation was performed. If it occurred in India while Richard was taking his Islamic studies beyond the ordinary level, there is a very likely candidate as surgeon, for at the time he was sharing a bungalow with Dr Stocks, the Assistant Surgeon to the garrison and a keen amateur botanist. Stocks could have performed the circumcision, but equally it might have been done ritually as part of an initiation ceremony. We know that Richard was

*See p. 83 and previous chapter.

stoical under physical pain. Some years later he had surgery to remove
a large cyst on his back. The operation was performed without any
painkilling relief and a witness* recorded how Burton spent the time
smoking a cigar, chatting, and occasionally asking his surgeon to
hurry up and get his work over with.[25]

Recognising that he needed the approval, sanction and financial
support of the Government at Bombay to underwrite a trip of the type
he planned, Richard did not neglect his military duties despite his
indisposition. When his weak eyes made it impossible to contribute
anything of value to the Survey Team, he devoted his time to producing two lengthy reports for the Court of Directors on Sindh and its
people, in collaboration with his friend Dr John Ellerton Stocks. Here
and elsewhere he included warnings that an Indian uprising was
almost inevitable; the 'hot eyed hostility' he had noticed when he
first arrived in the subcontinent had escalated. His warnings were not
only inevitably ignored but were regarded as insubordinate.[26] Two
further papers[27] were accepted and published by the Royal Asiatic
Society in Bombay. He also spent time among the Jats, or Camel
Men, of the Survey Department, producing a grammar and vocabulary of their language, and attempted to relate their origins to those of
gipsies. 'The more sluggish became my sight,' he wrote, 'the more
active became my brain, which could be satisfied only with twelve to
fourteen hours a day of alchemy, mnemonics, "Mantih" or Eastern
logic, Arabic, Sindi and Panjabi . . .'[28]

Despite his heavy work-load Walter Abraham, a botanical
draughtsman employed by Stocks since 1847 to help him in his work,
recalled Richard as a 'jovial' companion, who attracted to his bungalow 'all the learned men in Karachi'. He wrote of Richard's
linguistic fluency, confirming that even close friends were fooled by
his disguises.[29]

> . . . I was often [a] witness to this . . . he was on special duty, which
> in his case meant to perfect himself for some political duty by mas-
> tering the language of the country [Sindi] . . . a stranger who did not
> see him and heard him speaking would fancy he heard a native. His
> domestic servants were a Portuguese with whom he spoke

*His wife Isabel.

Portuguese and Goanese, an African, a Persian, and a Sindi or Beloochee. These spoke their mother tongues to [him] as he was engaged in his studies with Munshis who relieved each other every two hours from 10 to 4 daily . . .

His hair was dressed à la Persian – long and shaved from the forehead to the top of his head . . . when he went out for a ride he wore a wig . . . his complexion was also thorough Persian so that nature obviously intended him for the work he . . . so successfully performed. I was witness to his first essay in disguising himself as a poor Persian and taking in his friend Mr Moonshee Ali Ackbar [who] was seated one evening . . . in front of his bungalow . . . with a lot of his friends enjoying the evening breeze . . . Richard, disguised as a Persian traveller, approached them and after the usual compliments enquired for the rest-house, and as a matter of course gave a long rigmarole account of his travels and of people the moonshee knew and thus excited his curiosity.[30]

A long conversation followed and when it ended Richard walked away. From a short distance he called out in his own voice if his friend 'did not know him'. The *munshi* was totally perplexed as to where the voice of his friend Lieut. Burton had come from. The incident ended in much laughter, but it illustrates the power of Richard's acting ability.

As 1848 drew to a close he had sat and passed examinations in Sindi and Punjabe, and was declared qualified to transact public business in both languages. His 'opthalmia' still caused him pain and bouts of blindness but he had his Holy Grail before him, and a great deal of preparatory work was necessary to enable him to succeed in such a highly dangerous venture. Even so he set this ambition aside when the Sikh Wars broke out afresh and a force headed by General Auchmuty was sent to deal with the matter. Burton told his cousin Sarah Burton in a letter dated 14th November 1848:

. . . A furious affair has broken out in Mooltan and the Punjab and I have applied to the General commanding to go with him on his personal staff. A few days more will decide the business – and I am not a little anxious about it, for though still suffering a little from my old complaint, Ophthalmia, yet these opportunities are too far between to be lost.[31]

Richard applied for the post of Interpreter on the Commander's personal staff and he must have felt reasonably confident of success. This was just the sort of opportunity for which he had worked and studied. He now spoke at least six native languages fluently and was proficient in two others. No one could touch him in ethnic knowledge. He was therefore devastated to be told that the appointment had been awarded to a man of junior rank and with a single language, Hindustani (the first that Richard had learned), to his credit. Richard immediately assumed that this man had some high-placed connection; it was not the first time he had come up against 'interest' and been defeated, he said sourly.

It is possible, of course, that it was his health problems which had affected his selection. The effects of seven years' hard work in an adverse climate and condition had taken their inevitable toll and Richard suffered from constant racking fevers. He had lost weight due to his frequent fasts while undergoing instruction in Islamic rites, his eyes were red and swollen, causing him constant pain and irritation. But he subsequently learned from a friend who worked in the Secretariat at Bombay of another reason for his being passed over, and with hindsight he chose to believe this version.

When Sir Charles Napier resigned the Governorship of Sindh he was replaced not by a soldier but by a Civilian Commissioner Mr R.K. Pringle, an employee of the Honourable East India Company who became the Administrator of the province. Napier had kept his promise to Richard; the Intelligence reports submitted on the subject of the male brothels in Karachi had not been sent to Bombay. But nor were they removed and destroyed by his staff when Sir Charles left for Europe in the spring of 1847. Pringle was a far cry from the Rabelaisian soldier and Richard's report was found and read with shock and revulsion.[32] It was subsequently sent to Bombay with a firm recommendation that Lieutenant Burton be dismissed from the Service.

Many Burton scholars have searched for this report without success. Lacking any evidence, recent biographers have inferred that it contained information damaging to Richard because it detailed his intimate personal involvement in the proceedings (this will be discussed in a later chapter). It was no doubt in view of the fact that he had undertaken the task under orders from Sir Charles Napier that Richard was not dismissed, but nevertheless, given the apparent enthusiasm with which he had completed the Karachi brothel assignment, no one at Bombay felt inclined to favour him. The word went round that he was a bounder, and though few actually knew what lay behind his acknowledged besmirched reputation, the consequences reverberated for the remainder of his life.[33]

Richard knew nothing of this long-term effect at the time. He felt only the depression of defeat; the rejection 'broke my heart', he wrote many years later. He had no need to pretend to be ill when he decided that it was a waste of his life to remain in active service in India, and he immediately applied for home leave on the grounds of ill-health. 'Sick, sorry and almost in tears of rage I bad adieu to my friends and comrades,' he recalled.[34] At Bombay the Medical Board found his condition so serious that it was feared he would not survive the passage home. Clearly he was uncertain himself, for he even wrote a short note of farewell to his family.[35] With a personal servant, Mohammed Allahdad, he was loaded, virtually insensible, aboard the brig *Eliza*. A few weeks of fresh ocean breezes and care restored him, and by the time he reached England he was enjoying reasonable health again.

On his arrival in India in 1842 Richard had been a green youth whose sole experience of life outside his family circle had been a short spell at University. It had been an important phase in his development, for when he departed India for Europe in March 1849 aged 28 he was a man in his prime who had experienced much and learned much, about himself as well as his chosen fields of study, and had developed complex characteristics. He was undoubtedly a leader, but his undeniable effort and achievement in India which had gone unrewarded led to a ferocious cynicism, and a lifelong grievance that would eventually amount almost to paranoia. Coupled with his inability to submit to authority, this made him a difficult man to place in any of the spheres in which he later chose to serve. His strongly developed sense of humour could be alternately boyishly attractive, cynically clever, or caustically sardonic.

But his sense of humour often helped him to survive difficult situations. He was loyal to his friends and generally commanded loyalty in return. He was interested in and felt passionately about everything;

in his books he admired, he disapproved, he hated, he loved, he judged, he scoffed, he delighted, he scorned. But he never ignored; always there is a sense of his intense involvement with life and his eagerness to embrace all that it has to offer. His personal relationships were equally extreme. His close friends cherished the relationship, but he made enemies with an alarming facility and those often developed a lifelong hatred of him.

Burton had not yet finished with India; indeed he would remain an officer on the payroll of the British East India Company for a further thirteen years, but he would never again serve actively in the subcontinent.

6

MISS ARUNDELL
1831–1852

Isabella Arundell was born on a Sunday, she tells us in her autobiography, 'at ten minutes to 9 a.m., March 20th, 1831 at 4 Great Cumberland Place near the Marble Arch'.[1] She was very precise about such details for she had a lifelong interest in astrology.

Her father was Henry Raymond Arundell, favourite nephew of the 10th Baron Arundell of Wardour, and Isabella was the first child of his second marriage; the first having ended in 1828 when his bride of a year, the former Mary Isabel Constable – daughter of Sir Thomas Clifford Constable, Bart. of Chudleigh in Devon – died giving birth to a son, Theodore.

Isabella's mother was Eliza Gerard, daughter of Sir John Gerard, Bart. of Garswood, Lancashire and sister to the 1st Baron Gerard. Eliza had been the 'best friend' of Henry Arundell's first wife and was also related through marriage to the Arundells. She was a devout and rather severe woman who took her role as a Catholic wife and mother very seriously.

Baby Isabella was thus the scion of two of the great families of England. The Arundells are a branch of England's foremost Catholic family whose ancestors came to England with the Conqueror, and about whom the (not strictly accurate) old couplet tells us:

> Since William rose and Harold fell,
> There have been Earls at Arundel.[2]

The Arundells of Wardour, however, trace their lineage to Roger de Arundell who is mentioned in the Domesday Book as having estates in the West Country. Wardour Castle came into the family during the reign of Henry VII (a kinsman through marriage) but Thomas, the first Lord Arundell of Wardour and Chancellor to Queen Catherine Howard, was executed on Tower Hill on a trumped-up charge of conspiracy.[3]

The maternal line, the Gerard family, was equally important in British history, springing from the Dukes of Leinster and Earls of Plymouth. Gerard predecessors suffered greatly in defence of their sovereigns; one was tortured for his support of Mary Queen of Scots; another liquidated his estates in the cause of King Charles I.[4]

So Isabella was justifiably proud of her heritage, spending her childhood in the rambling great house of Wardour in Wiltshire where her parents occupied a wing, and her imagination fed on the rich lore of her ancestors. Her role model was the famous Lady Blanche Arundell whose husband raised a regiment at his own expense and went off to fight in support of King Charles I. Alone at Wardour with only a handful of servants, Lady Blanche defended the castle against a force of hundreds of Roundhead troops who besieged it for nine days. Eventually, out of supplies, she had no alternative but to hand over her home under honourable terms which were promptly broken by the Parliamentarians. When Lord Arundell returned the couple chose to blow up the castle rather than leave it in the hands of the King's enemy. In 1770 a vast Palladian mansion, also called Wardour Castle, was built near the ruins of the ancient Castle in the 700-acre park. It was here, amidst ornate plasterwork and gilded magnificence, that Isabella grew up.[5]

As a baby her face had the intelligent, curious expression of a kitten; from that time until her death she was universally known to her closest friends and family as 'Puss', and though at school she was known by her baptismal name, Isabella,[6] she disliked it and later chose to shorten it to Isabel. Her family enjoyed a uniquely privileged lifestyle as the Georgian era gave way to the Victorian age. Theirs was a life of house-parties, visiting nobility, scores of servants. However, it was a strict life for the Arundell children who were attended by nannies, nursemaids and governesses in the nurseries on the top floor. Plain food, long walks, regular habits, politeness, cleanliness and godliness were the bench-marks of a good upbringing.

Isabel's main contact with her parents was in the afternoon after luncheon, when she and her elder half-brother Theodore were dressed formally – she, typically in white muslin and blue satin ribbons, he in a 'Lord Fauntleroy' green velvet suit with a lace-frilled collar – and taken downstairs. 'We were not allowed to speak unless spoken to; we were not allowed to ask for anything unless it was given to us. We kissed our father and mother's hands, and asked their blessing before going upstairs and we stood upright by the side of them all the time we were in the room,' Isabel recalled.[7] Occasionally they were taken for a drive in the park with their mother in a dark green carriage, the coachman and footman both bewigged and dressed in the dark green and gold Arundell livery. The house had its own huge chapel in the west wing, and the kitchen was so vast that young ladies of the Arundell household 'had their first riding lessons around the kitchen table'.[8]

Henry Arundell Esquire was small, fair, boyish-looking and spent most of his time – in common with the majority of men in his social strata – hunting and shooting. As the grandson of a previous Lord Arundell he had spent his entire life, prior to his second marriage, at Wardour. He was a valued member of the extended Arundell family, and he was a contented man even though – due to the English law of primogeniture – his income was modest. But with his second marriage his responsibilities grew, and his inherited income was insufficient to meet the needs of his steadily burgeoning family. After the death of his first cousin Lord James Everard Arundell, who had also been his best friend, Henry decided to move to London to improve his fortunes.

The family lived at 14 Montagu Place, near Bryanston Square, where little Isabella's earliest memories were of the watchman passing along the street under her window intoning, 'Past one o'clock, and a cloudy morning . . .' Winters were spent in hunting boxes in the Shires.[9] Henry had not been educated to make money, but his familiarity with the wine cellars of Wardour enabled him to recognise a good vintage. With a partner he set up as a wine merchant in Mayfair and in time the business became highly successful, enabling him to purchase a small country house, Furze Hall, at Ingatestone, Essex. The family let the London house and moved to Essex in 1841. Being 'in trade' was socially unacceptable, so Henry's laudable entrepreneurialism was kept a close family secret.

At an unknown point in Isabel's early childhood she contracted malignant typhus, and was actually certified dead by two doctors who were attending her on the occasion. Mrs Arundell's grief at the death of her eldest child was so violent that a priest was sent for to give her consolation. Isabel's lifelong fear of being buried alive is undoubtedly rooted in this incident. The priest . . .

> happened to be the famous . . . Jesuit and theologian, old Father Randal Lythegoe. He consoled my mother for some time, then he knelt down and prayed for me, and then he got up and put on his stole. 'What are you going to do, Father?' said my mother. 'I am going to give her Extreme Unction,' he said. 'But you can't; she has been dead several hours.' 'I don't care about that,' he said. 'I am going to risk it.' He did so and about two hours after he was gone I opened my eyes, and gradually came to.[10]

When she was ten Isabel was sent to a convent boarding school some twenty miles from Furze Hall. New Hall – still regarded as the leading Roman Catholic girls' school in England – was run by the Canonesses of the Holy Sepulchre, a Flemish order of nuns, and had become popular after the Catholic Emancipation Act in 1829. The fees and extras for each girl amounted to more than the average worker's annual wage, so it is safe to say it was an élite establishment. Many Arundell girls attended New Hall, and the school register shows that Miss Isabella Arundell arrived there for the first time on 3 June 1841, 'she is to take the common lessons, and to learn Music and Dancing . . . she has not been to Confession; she abstains one day a week . . . she is to take wine when she abstains.'[11] The 'young lady boarders' were taught:

> reading and writing; the English, French and Italian languages, by principles; sacred and profane history; arithmetic; double-entry book-keeping; the art of letter-writing for all occasions; household budgeting and book-keeping; the difference in weights and measures in different countries; heraldry; geography; the use of globes and the sphere; the principles of natural history suitable for persons of the sex; embroidery and all kinds of needlework; the art of drawing and painting flowers etc.[12]

There is no surviving record of her specific academic achievements or disappointments; the major occurrences in Isabel's school life were when she made her first Communion in December 1841 and caught measles in April 1843. The account books of her 'extras' perhaps convey more of her youthful personal life with her purchases of velvet bonnets and ribbons, and muslin pinafores. There were fur-lined gloves for winter, soft kid gloves for summer, silk gloves for dancing. Besides there were hair combs, books and regular use of a carriage. Henry Arundell had an 'arrangement' with the nuns. He supplied them with wines and sherry and although some of Isabel's fees were settled in 'gold and banknotes', more often they were settled in kind and the bills marked 'Paid by credit for sherry and wine' or 'Paid by Pipe of Port'. The nuns sound like a jolly bunch, for a 'pipe' equalled two hogsheads or 126 gallons; but of course it is possible that the wines were kept for visitors.[13]

They were also kind and gentle, and Isabel (still known as 'Miss Isabella' at that time) was happy there. She was a bright, intelligent, observant girl, but the nuns were educating potential wives and mothers, not university students, and the Latin Isabel learned was sufficient for her to understand Mass and Catholic studies rather than the Classics.[14] The family regularly visited their grand relations; at Wardour they had their own apartment. At Garswood, the Gerard country seat in Lancashire where her mother had grown up, they were also warmly welcomed. But 'home' to Isabel was Furze Hall, a straggling unpretentious old white farm-house romantically swathed in roses, honeysuckle and ivy, with stables and kennels where the entire family could indulge their passion for horses and dogs.[15] It lay quietly in an undulating, well-wooded landscape where the children (Henry and Eliza were to have eleven children) were free to play and wander safely. In the winter holidays there was skating, and sliding and sledges. In the long hot summers Isabel often escaped into a contented solitude.

Though she loved her family passionately, and would always be unusually close to them, she enjoyed her own company and was content to wander alone in the woods or ride her 'fat little pony', with her dog 'Sikh' running at its heels, across the fields to find a quiet spot where she could lose herself in a favourite book; 'I was very enthusiastic about gipsies, Bedawin Arabs and everything Eastern and mystic, and especially about a wild and lawless life,' she recalled.[16]

She was an obedient girl in general; but in one matter she regularly disobeyed her parents. Stoneymoore Wood, behind the Viper Inn at Mill Green, was the site of an annual summer encampment of a band of gipsies and Isabel was drawn there like a file to a magnet.[17] Mr and Mrs Arundell had strictly forbidden their children to associate with gipsies, and in respect of the tinkers and basket-vendors who travelled the lanes Isabel obeyed the instruction. But the 'real' gipsies delighted her, especially one matriarch whose name was Hagar Burton (Burton being, coincidentally, one of the famous surnames of the ancient gipsy families): 'a tall, slender, handsome, distinguished, refined woman who had much influence in her tribe . . . many an hour did I pass with her . . . she used to call me "Daisy".'[18]

There is a strange tale about this woman, and were it not for the fact that Richard Burton later confirmed having seen the document mentioned,[19] one would be tempted to wonder whether Isabel had invented or imagined the incident. As the tribe were about to leave the area Isabel went to say goodbye. She was presented with a straw fly-catcher (which she kept all her life), and Hagar cast Isabel's horoscope which she wrote in Romany and gave to her after translating it:

> You will cross the sea, and be in the same town as your destiny and know it not. Every obstacle will rise up against you, and such a combination of circumstances, that it will require all your courage, energy and intelligence to meet them. Your life will be like one swimming against big waves; but . . . you will always win . . . You will bear the name of our tribe, and be right proud of it. You will be as we are, but far greater than we. Your life is all wandering, change, and adventure. One soul in two bodies in life or death, never long apart. Show this to the man you take for your husband. Hagar Burton.[20]

Hagar told Isabel that she would have many suitors but would wait for years for the one to whom she was destined, that the name of the tribe (Burton) would cause her many a sorrowful and humiliating hour, but when those who had sought 'him' in his heyday fell away with his youth and strength 'you shall remain bright and purified to him as the morning star . . .' she forecast. Isabel was about 15 at this time, suffering from puppy fat and all the *gauche* uncertainty of ado-lescence. She was tall, about 5 foot 7 inches, her fair, clear skin tanned too easily in an age when white skin was fashionable, and she had a too-determined chin. Yet Hagar had given her a dream of her destiny and so she was comforted by some 'good points': fine eyes, large and dark blue, a mane of thick, lustrous, soft golden-brown hair and an aquiline nose. Her speaking voice was said to be particularly sweet, remaining so even in old age.[21]

She was 16 during her last year at New Hall, and among the usual 'extras', items of books and mending and shoe repairs, is the exciting evidence of Isabel's approaching womanhood: stockings, garters and stays. This final bill for extras, totalling £21.6.0, was marked 'Pd by Pipe of Port' as many of the former ones had been, but in the hundreds of thousands of words written by Isabel during her lifetime she never once referred to her father's occupation, though it had provided her education as well as that of three sisters.

Eighteen months later, in 1849, the family sold their Essex home and returned to their house in Montagu Place. Isabel made her début at a ball at Almack's Assembly Rooms, the exclusive haunt of the upper classes, in the spring of the following year. She was presented to the Queen by a kinswoman, the Duchess of Norfolk, the senior woman among the great clan of once-puissant Catholic nobility; the 'old families' who had clung to the 'old religion' into which it was assumed Isabel would marry. The patronage of the Duchess bestowed instant *cachet* upon Isabel and guaranteed her 'Almack vouchers' and invitations to the most select parties and soirées. Isabel never forgot her first ball:

> I wore white tarlatan [a filmy muslin] over white silk, and the first skirt was looped up . . . with a blush rose. My hair which was very abundant, was tressed in an indescribable fashion by Alexandre, and decked with blush roses . . . We arrived at Almack's at about eleven. The scene was dazzlingly brilliant . . . the grand staircase and ante chamber were decked with garlands and festoons of white and gold muslin and ribbons. The blaze of lights, the odour of flowers, the perfumes, the diamonds, and the magnificent dresses of the cream of British aristocracy smote upon my senses; all was new to me and all was sweet. Julian's band played . . .[22]

Isabel's family had been absent from London for many seasons but 'the world of the gentle by birth and breeding', said Isabel, was small and generous. 'We were there by right to assume our position in the circle . . . [and] everyone had a hearty welcome for my people.' There was some good natured chaff about the Arundells having buried themselves in the country for too long. Her mother, Isabel marvelled, was quite changed. Not only was Mrs Arundell looking young and fashionable but instead of frightening young men away as she did in the country, she 'seemed to attract them, engage them in conversation'. Isabel was at once taken up. Her mother had told her she would be a success if she got four dances;

> but I was engaged seven or eight deep soon after I entered the ballroom, and had more partners than I could dance with in one night . . . mother was delighted with me . . . I was very much confused at the amount of staring (I did not know that every new girl was stared at on her first appearance); and one may think how vain and credulous I was, when I overheard some one telling my mother that I had been quoted as the new beauty at his club. Fancy, poor ugly me.[23]

The next months were a whirl of excitement to a girl so strictly educated and protected; the parties, the balls, the soirées, the ballet, the opera. Her first opera featured Jenny Lind and Gardoni singing the leads in *La Sonnambula*. '. . . When the music commenced I forgot I was on earth,' Isabel wrote in her teenage diary. She was a gifted musician herself, at least she could entertain a drawing room of guests and provide her listeners with pleasure; she played the piano and the guitar and had a good contralto voice.[24] Then there was shopping, riding in Rotten Row at the fashionable hour between 5 and 6 p.m., home to dress for dinner followed by parties and balls – two or three a night. Her 'favourite men joined us in walks and rides, came into our opera-box, and barred all the waltzes . . . This lasted every day and night from March till the end of July . . . I was dancing mad,' she recalled.[25]

The point of all this gaiety was, of course, marriage. Almack's, founded during the Regency for the specific purpose of introductions between the 'right sort of people', was still the most exigent marriage market in the Western world.[26] But Isabel, captivated by the sheer joy of it all, was equally capable of standing back and observing this new world into which she had been plunged. She identified and was amused by the penniless bachelors of good name hanging out for an

heiress, the roués looking for freshness, naïve girls flattered by a practised compliment, desperate girls determined to find a husband, any
husband. Many of the men Isabel dismissed as 'animated tailor's
dummies . . . I have seen dukes' daughters gladly accept men that I
would have turned up my nose at,' she wrote gleefully.[27] Isabel had
already written a portrait of her ideal man into her diary, but despite
a surplus of dancing partners no man so far met her criteria.
Nevertheless, she vowed she would have such a man or no one.

> My ideal is about six feet in height; he has not an ounce of fat on
> him; he has broad and muscular shoulders, a powerful deep chest;
> he is a Hercules of manly strength. He has black hair, a brown
> complexion, a clever forehead, sagacious eyebrows, large, black,
> wondrous eyes . . . with long dark lashes. He is a soldier and a *man*.
> He is accustomed to command and to be obeyed. He frowns on the
> ordinary affairs of life, but his face always lights up for me. In his
> dress he never adopts the fopperies of the day but his clothes suit
> him – they are made for him not he for them . . . my ideal of hap-
> piness is to be to such a man wife, comrade, friend – everything to
> him, to sacrifice all for him . . . such a man only will I wed . . . but
> if I find such a man, and afterwards discover he is not for me then
> I will never marry . . . I will become a sister of charity of St Vincent
> de Paul.[28]

Such a resolution removed any air of desperation so evident in other
girls and may have accounted for her popularity. Certainly, as Hagar
Burton had predicted, she did not lack suitors. When one young man
showed her his written assessments of the crop of débutantes, she saw
her own name: 'Isabel Arundell, eighteen, beauty, talent and goodness; original. Chief fault £0.0s.0d.'[29] Lack of dowry was certainly a
disadvantage, yet her family background and important connections
were significant, and she might well have attracted an eligible husband for those alone. She had developed into a striking young
woman, with a queenly manner and a Junoesque build; her large
sparkling eyes, thick long golden hair and fair colouring were
bonuses. But for a heavy jawline she would have been a beauty. Even
so, it was said by her contemporaries that 'no portrait ever did justice
to her' and that 'when she was in any company you could look at no
one else.'[30] To her mother's disappointment no good Catholic man

came forward to claim Isabel, or at least no one to whom Isabel gave any encouragement.

It cost a great deal to launch a girl creditably in society, and there was little Blanche's début to consider in a few years' time. That summer Henry Arundell decided that a couple of years living economically in France might be financially expedient. Besides, their latest child, baby Raymond Everard, was sickly; a change of air for him, sea-bathing for the children, and French masters to finish Isabel's education were added advantages. The fifteen-hour 'fresh' Channel crossing was Isabel's first journey from England and while the rest of her family concentrated on retaining their breakfast, Isabel, who was to prove a robust sailor, sat on deck and hopefully recalled Hagar Burton's prophecy that she would 'cross the sea' and be in the same town as her destiny. They had leased a house in the Haute Ville at Boulogne for an indefinite period, a barn of a place and as badly equipped as only inexpensive rented accommodation can be. Isabel, who longed to travel, had expected the comforts of Brighton and the romance of Naples; she was intensely disappointed with dreary Boulogne after the glitter of a London Season.

When she forgot to be fashionably dejected by the lack of smartness, the dirty-looking sea and 'poisonous-looking smelling mud of the harbour' where the tide always seemed to be out, she began to take notice and to enjoy the novelty of new surroundings. As usual it was people rather than scenery that interested her most, and just as the gipsies in Stoneymore Wood had once attracted so now did the *poissardes* or fisher-women of Boulogne. Of Spanish and Flemish extraction, they kept themselves apart from the burghers of the town, she noticed, and had their own *patois* and moral code, never marrying out of their own colony. They were tall, brown and handsome and wore a colourful dress in bright primary colours with snowy-white kerchiefs. The men went out to sea fishing and the women worked at shrimping, making tackle, marketing and cleaning the fishing boats between trips. And as with the gipsies there was a matriarchal figure of the clan, known as Queen Carolina, with whom Isabel made friends. There was a younger element of 'Billingsgate' girls whose behaviour and language was rough and coarse, who used to call rude remarks and sing vulgar songs at Isabel as she walked through them, but she chose to ignore them. In fact she was forbidden to walk out unchaperoned so, as with Hagar, these visits to Carolina had to be made covertly, without her parents' knowledge.

Although there were a number of English families living in Boulogne, few were considered superior enough by the Arundells to be admitted into their circle of acquaintances. Generally there was the same mix of half-pay officers, impecunious widows, respectable invalids that the Burtons knew so well from their travels. Only half a dozen families, most of them Catholic and 'the *crème*' of society, were considered suitable to associate with the Arundells. Nevertheless, Isabel recalled, 'the two winters we were there were gay, there was a sort of *laisser aller* about the place and the summers were very pleasant.' Their mother was very strict with her children, but this did not prevent Isabel and 15-year-old Blanche (also a New Hall student) from regularly helping themselves to their father's cigars which they smoked in the attic, splashing on perfume afterwards to disguise any tell-tale aromas. Isabel recalled that it was boredom that drove her to this misdemeanour, for apart from French lessons, an occasional dance and the childish company of her siblings – Blanche 15, Renfric 14, Rudy 11, Henry 10, 'Dilly' 9, Emma 7, and baby Raymond (three children had died in infancy) – there was little to do unless her father relented and took her with him when he went rough shooting for rabbits with his eldest son Theo.[31] The cigar-smoking eventually ended when her father noticed the shortages in his stock and a servant was suspected. Isabel was never apprehended, but later she would become a confirmed smoker.

Their mother took them for daily walking exercise, usually up the main thoroughfare and beside the stone Ramparts of the town, a mile-long esplanade with shady trees and good views out over the sea. This was the fashionable 'lounge' for the daily *promenade* in fine weather and most of the socialising that went on in Boulogne took place there. Here was where the fashion-conscious displayed new finery, where social engagements were issued and contracted, where discreet flirtations occurred, and it was the only place where Isabel and Blanche were allowed to walk without a chaperone. It was here, without warning, when Isabel was at her most bored and restless, that the pivotal event of her life occurred. She was with Blanche when walking towards her came the embodiment of her 'ideal man'.

He was five feet eleven inches in height, very broad, thin and

muscular; he had very dark hair; black, clearly defined, sagacious
eyebrows; a brown weather-beaten complexion: straight Arab features; a determined-looking mouth and chin, nearly covered by an
enormous black moustache . . . but the most remarkable part of his
appearance was two large, black, flashing eyes with long lashes
that pierced one through and through . . . when he smiled, he
smiled as though it hurt him . . . he was dressed in a black, short,
shaggy coat, and shouldered a short thick stick as if he were on
guard.[32]

Their eyes met, and held, and she believed the impact on him must
have been as strong as it was on her, for she thought she saw him start
slightly. For Isabel it was as though his eyes saw through to her soul.
'I was completely magnetised,' she said, 'and when we had got a little
distance away, I turned to my sister, and whispered to her, "That
man will marry me."'[33]

With what impatience Isabel must have waited for her walk the next
day! And he was there again. The difficulty was that with no one to
introduce them they could not be seen to speak. She did not even
know his name. And he knew better than to risk her reputation by
directly approaching her. Nevertheless he was clearly attracted by
Isabel, for he followed them for a way and then pointedly walked to a
wall in their vision and chalked a message. Isabel went up to see what
he had written and read the words, 'May I speak to you?' Taking up
the chalk he had left there, Isabel wrote back, 'No; mother will be
angry.'[34] Richard was either flirting outrageously, which is unlikely
given the mores of the times and Isabel's virginal status, or else he was
genuinely attracted and wished to take the chance meeting further.

The extraordinary little scene must have been witnessed by someone; perhaps Blanche ratted on her elder sister, for Mrs Arundell did
find out and she *was* angry. Isabel had broken the social code and
shown herself unworthy of trust; from that day the rules governing
their walks were reinforced. There would be no further unchaperoned
outings, and hours spent at French and music lessons were increased.

The destiny predicted by Hagar was not, however, to be so easily
subverted. Shortly after this incident, in the spring of 1851 a cousin of
Isabel's father, Mrs Buckley, arrived at Boulogne with her daughter
Louisa[35] and, as they were socially acceptable, Isabel was allowed to
join them for walks. The Buckleys, however, being less aristocratic

than the Arundells, were quickly absorbed into the wider social circle of English expatriates among whose number was the family of Captain and Mrs Joseph Burton.

One day, only shortly after the Buckleys' arrival, Isabel was walking with her mother when they came upon Mrs Buckley and her party. The 'ideal man' was among them and to Isabel's agony was openly flirting with pretty Louisa. However, at least it led to a formal introduction and she learned that his name was Richard Burton. Immediately, Hagar Burton's prediction – 'you will bear the name of our tribe' – flashed across her mind and she was completely unsettled. Eventually she judged it safe to look up at him and found he was looking at her with those dark, compelling eyes. 'Again I thrilled through and through,' she recalled. 'He must have thought me very stupid, for I hardly spoke a word during that brief meeting.'

She was too shy to attempt attracting his attention, convinced that she was too ugly to interest him, and seeing his interest in the bright and chatty Louisa who was clearly not as strictly controlled as Miss Arundell. But whenever she saw him at the Ramparts Isabel would make an excuse to extend her walk so that she could watch him. Sometimes she caught the sound of his deep voice, 'so soft and sweet that I remained spellbound'. On one occasion Louisa asked Richard to write something for Isabel, the custom then being for young men to write a poem or clever saying which young ladies stuck into an album. Richard contributed a motto in Arabic characters. But the lovelorn Isabel did not paste it into her book, instead she wore it 'next to her heart'. Much later she learned that it read '*Sháwir hunna wa khálif hunn*a', and was amused at the translation, 'Consult women and do the contrary.'

One day the Buckleys gave a party and dance for a large number of people. Not all of the guests were of the calibre that Mrs Arundell insisted upon, and unusually Isabel was allowed to attend:

> . . . there was Richard like a star among rushlights! That was a night of nights; he waltzed with me once, and spoke to me several times, and I kept my sash where he put his arm around my waist to waltz, and my gloves, which his hands had clasped. I never wore them again.[36]

Poor Isabel. Richard truly was the man of her dreams; not only in

appearance and temperament, but fresh from India he personified a
life that she longed for, for herself, in her wildest imaginings; a life of
Oriental travel and 'lawless' adventure. But he was unreachable, for
even had he been truly interested her mother would never permit him
to court her. He belonged to the 'upper middle-classes' and was outside their *milieu*. So she wallowed in self-pity, miserably confiding in
her diary that if only Providence had blessed her with the man she
loved, 'what a different being I might be.'

Throughout the summer she saw him occasionally at parties, confident among the ladies, telling his stories about India, talking of the
books he was writing. The anecdotes of his experiences, and his evident ambition to succeed in life, set him so far apart from her that she
felt unable even to approach him and contented herself with surreptitiously observing him whenever she thought he would not notice.

When 2-year-old Raymond Everard died at the beginning of 1852,
the Arundell family went into deep mourning. No social visits, no outings or gaiety of any sort were allowed. It was almost a relief to
Isabel not to have to watch Richard paying attention to other girls,
and to have an acceptable reason for heartfelt misery. And then came
a *coup d'état* in which there were some isolated attacks on the English
residents. Their windows were broken and Isabel's shaggy little terrier,
Sikh, was killed by rioters. The Arundells decided that it was time to
return to England.

On 9 May 1852 they departed from Boulogne on the cross-
Channel paddle steamer. Isabel had agonised over whether to seek out
Richard and say goodbye, but she thought he was so uninterested,
that his life was so far apart from hers and that it was so unlikely they
would ever meet again, that it was a waste of effort. 'To see him
would be only to give myself more pain, and therefore I did not.' She
sat on deck and watched the town slide away. 'It contained all I
wanted and who I thought I should see no more. I was sad at heart;
but proud of the way in which I had behaved . . . though I would
rather have had love and happiness, I felt that I was as gold tried in
the fire.'[37]

Two years of economy appear to have assisted the Arundell fortunes, for when the mourning period was over they took their place
in Society again, comfortably if not ostentatiously, in preparation for
Blanche's début in the following year. Isabel, 21 by this time, did not
lack her own small court of admirers but, despite the hints of her

mother about love growing from friendship, she showed no interest in anyone. Her diary was her constant friend and to it she confided her innermost thoughts:

> They say it is time I married (perhaps it is); but it is never time to marry any man one does not love, because such a deed can never be undone. Richard may be a delusion of my brain. But how dull is reality! With all to make me happy I pine and hanker for him . . . as if I were not complete. Is it wrong to want someone to love more than one's mother and father? . . . One always pictures the 'proper man' . . . living on his estate, whence as his lady, one might rise to be a leader of Almack's. But I am much mistaken if I do not deserve a better fate. I could not live like a vegetable in the country. I cannot picture myself in a white apron, with a bunch of keys, scolding my maids, counting eggs . . . And I should not like to marry a country squire, nor a lawyer (I hear the parchments crackle now), nor a parson, nor a clerk in a London office. God help me! A dry crust, privations, pain, danger for him I love would be better . . . how worthless should I be to any other man but Richard Burton.[38]

As the elder daughter of a large family, Isabel had plenty of allotted domestic duties to keep her occupied and her unrequited secret commitment had steadied her. Outwardly she appeared to conform to Society's rules; in reality she was a mere observer, politely distant to admirers. When she visited her grand relatives at Arundell Castle and at Garswood near Newton-le-Willow, Lancashire, she was a popular guest for her liveliness and musical ability. Her obsession for Richard Burton changed her reading habits for ever. In the months that followed the visit to Boulogne she began to read everything she could about India, and it was not long before this intelligent but inadequately educated woman began to reason desperately that there *must* be more to life than was on offer for the conventional Victorian female:

> . . . we women simply are born, marry and die. Who misses us? Why should we not have some useful, active life? Why, with spirits, brains and energies, are women to exist upon worsted work and household accounts? It makes me sick, and I will not do it.[39]

She assumed Richard remained at Boulogne until he returned to his regiment; she can have heard nothing of him except for the publication in his absence of three books which she bought and pored over until she almost knew them by heart. It was to be more than a year before any news came of him. By then it appeared he had become a national hero – and was even further out of her reach.

7

FLIRTATIONS
1849–1853

When Richard arrived in London from India aboard the *Eliza* in the summer of 1849, he went straight to his Aunt Georgina's home and roused the household in the small hours of the morning.[1] It is an indication of the closeness of the Burton family that he did this on a number of occasions throughout his life and was always received joyously. He then spent a short time with the orphaned daughters of his late Aunt Sarah.

It may be recalled that Sarah, the middle sister of the Baker trio, had married Joseph Burton's younger brother Francis, who died some years before Sarah herself expired in 1848. The principal attraction of this visit for Richard was his cousin Eliza Burton, who had always interested him and with whom he had been in correspondence during his time in India. Eliza was the first of two girls to whom he proposed marriage within a year. She was 'lively, amiable, well-dowered', and it was a mutual attraction which apparently had the approval of Richard's immediate family. Unfortunately, Eliza's trustees did not see it in the same light; she was the co-heiress of the trust her grandfather had set up for her mother and was thus very comfortably placed. Richard's lack of prospects made him ineligible as her suitor. Eliza 'believed herself in love with Richard'; she languished for a while and eventually married a rich landowner near Ludlow in Shropshire.[2]

Richard's closest family – his parents, his sister Maria and her two

small daughters Georgiana ('Georgie') and Maria ('Minnie') Stisted –
were in Pisa, and after a few weeks during which he was not only
rejected by his cousin but visited publishers and doctors, and got
himself elected to a London club (the East India United Services
Club), he set off for Italy. The only family member missing from the
reunion was Edward, who was still serving in Ceylon. The temperate
autumn climate of Italy was a joy to Richard after the discomforts of
the tropics, but relaxation was alien to him; his immediate plans were
to publish his books, and he spent his time assembling his copious
notes. More long-term he had his Arabian expedition in view, but that
depended on his obtaining the necessary sponsorship. And there was,
too, the thought that if the Company would not back his proposals
for an expedition to Arabia he might resign his commission, return to
Oxford and obtain his degree.[3] A few months later Richard escorted
his sister and her two little girls back to England. Allahdad, who was
missing his home and had developed a violent dislike of Italians, had
become more of a liability than an asset by this time and sailed for
Bombay as soon as they returned to London.

During the early months of 1850 Richard settled down to work on
the first of his books, *Goa and the Blue Mountains*, at his sister's
rented house in Dover. When he visited London he stayed at his club
and quickly became acquainted with some interesting men-about-
town such as Captain the Hon. Henry A. Murray, who was to become
a close friend.[4] On the recommendation of his doctor, John Scott,
Richard was a frequent visitor to the spa towns of Leamington and
Malvern, the waters being considered efficacious for his eye troubles. In April Maria received double-edged news from India,
simultaneously rejoicing that her husband Henry had been promoted
to the rank of Lieutenant-Colonel and grieving the improbability of
his being granted imminent home leave. Unlike Richard, Henry
Stisted had the happy knack of being in the right place at the right
time; he had served in Afghanistan, taking part in the storming of
Ghuznee, the capture of Khelat and the occupation of Kabul. He was
to enjoy an illustrious military career.

By November Richard had finished the manuscript of *Goa and the
Blue Mountains* and delivered it to his publishers, and *Sindh and the
Races that Inhabit the Valley of the Indus* which he submitted to the
Directors of the East India Company, requesting permission to publish
and dedicate it to the Court of Directors.[5] Technically he did not need

their permission to publish, but the move was an astute one. The book on the ethnology and topography of Sindh was clearly not aimed at the popular or circulating library market. Any potential readership was in India. Immediately he was advised that the request had been approved, Richard wrote expressing a hope that the Court would extend their patronage to purchase 150 copies of the book. They complied and informed him that they were, in fact, willing to subscribe to a further 50 copies.[6] This book, still widely regarded as the best textbook on many aspects of Scindi ethnology,[7] is still in print and used in schools in Pakistan.

Having completed a third book, *Scinde*, a quirky semi-autobio-graphical tour of Sindh in which his own adventures (such as the sighting of the Persian Girl) are related to a mythical fellow-traveller Mr John Bull, Richard decided during the winter of 1850–51, to spend some time in Boulogne with the intention of attending the famed fencing school of Monsieur Constantin.[8] Fencing was still Richard's favourite pastime and he wished to refine some of the new movements he had invented; the '*une-deux*' and the '*manchette*', (cut-ting the sword arm of the opponent). For these he subsequently earned the coveted *Brevet de pointe*, and for the excellence of his swordsmanship he became a *Maître d'Armes*. A friend confirmed his extraordinary ability in a bout with a celebrated swordsman of the French Hussars:

> . . . it was a sight to see Burton with his eagle eye keenly fixed on his adversary, shortly followed by a very rapid swing of his arm and a sharp stroke downwards when the Frenchman was disarmed. He did this seven times in succession, when [his opponent] declined any further contest, saying his wrist was nearly dislocated by the force with which the Englishman struck his weapon. The spectators . . . were astonished at Burton who, with the exception of a prod in the neck, was otherwise untouched.[9]

But Richard had spent too many lonely years in India. He found it easy to cope with solitude during his adventures and when he was working, but equally he was a man who needed an audience and enjoyed company, actively seeking it when not employed. Also he genuinely missed his family who were always uncritical and affec-tionate. It did not take much to persuade his sister to bring her two children to Boulogne to join him. Maria told her daughter that Richard was a sweet-tempered man to live with and that the only occasion she ever saw him angry during their time together at Boulogne was when the two small nieces were allowed by their nurse to venture too close to the edge of the quay which lacked a safety rail.[10] As soon as the weather improved, his parents, to whom he had also written that he was lonely, ventured north from Italy to join them in Boulogne. Richard moved from his small apartment at 36 rue des Pipots to the house rented by the Burton family at No. 1 rue d'Aumont, in Boulogne's *Haute Ville*.[11]

There Richard worked on the various proof editions of his first three books and the ms. of a fourth, *Falconry in the Valley of the Indus*, as well as his fencing. His output was extraordinary; in under two years he produced four books totalling over 1,500 published pages of text, as well as specialist papers. Although Isabel saw him about the town at this time he did not, she says, 'lead the life that was led by the general colony at Boulogne. He had a little set of men friends, knew some of the French, had a great many flirtations, one very serious one . . .'[12] Georgiana Stisted confirms this; 'that he had a great many *affaires de coeur* is no secret',[13] and she also mentions a serious flirtation calling it 'a very evanescent one, which like the last [Eliza Burton] soon came to an untimely end'.[14] In fact the object of his most serious attentions at this time was another Elizabeth and another family connection. This young woman, Elizabeth Stisted, was the sister of Maria's husband Henry. It is likely that she spent a good deal of time with Maria to keep her company during Henry's prolonged absences and that she joined her sister-in-law in Boulogne that summer just as *Goa and the Blue Mountains*, the first of Richard's books to be published, was finished proofing and about to be printed. The enamoured Richard dedicated it to her:

> To Miss Elizabeth Stisted
> This little work, Which owes its existence to her
> Friendly suggestions, is dedicated,
> in token of gratitude and affection
> by the Author

That *Goa* owed its existence to Miss Stisted is doubtful since it was already in preparation during his time in India. But Richard needed a 'respectable' reason for dedicating the book to an unmarried woman and, indeed, he may well have consulted her on one or two matters. Little is known about the relationship except that, again, he proposed marriage and was, again, rejected on the grounds of lack of prospects.

In her biography of Richard Burton, Georgiana was careful not to identify by name these two aunts of hers, both named Elizabeth, who fell in love with Burton and to whom he proposed, since there were only two acceptable reasons for Victorian women of good families to have their names in print; their marriage and their death. Georgiana was convinced, however, that either of them would have made her uncle an ideal wife and that the sole reason for the rejections was pecuniary. It is certain that Elizabeth Stisted was still in Richard's thoughts some two years after they parted and he even found a way to mention her, respectably, in the text of what was perhaps his greatest travel book, *Personal Narrative of a Pilgrimage to Al-Madinah and Meccah.** He need not have done, for he did not provide any provenance for other items in his luggage, but he could not resist:

> . . . I had also a substantial housewife, the gift of a kind relative, Miss Elizabeth Stisted; it was a roll of canvas, carefully soiled, and garnished with needles and thread, cobblers wax, buttons and other articles . . .[15]

Prior to his marriage in 1861 Elizabeth Stisted was the only woman, indeed the only 'relative' (she was not, strictly speaking, a relative of Richard's, of course) who was mentioned in the text of his books by name, and in combination with the 'affectionate' dedication to Goa it is reasonable to assume she was the most serious of those youthful love affairs about which we know.[16] I believe it was Elizabeth Stisted of whom he wrote in his poem 'Past Loves':**

> Next was a little girl who stole
> Most artlessly my heart and soul
>   And has she not them yet?

---

* Referred to as the *Pilgrimage* for the remainder of this book.
**See full text in Appendix 2.

> Here again poverty and pride
> Combined to drive me from her side
> And so to part we met.

The other relationship about which we know anything at all was his flirtation with Louisa Buckley, Isabel's cousin. Isabel was very jealous of this relationship which continued, platonically, even after Louisa married Captain Wm. Segrave. Georgiana Stisted also refers to her; 'with comical imprudence, considering the state of his finances, he had again fallen in love, this time with a pretty but penniless girl of eighteen, whose mother was unpleasantly outspoken about his daring, with his prospects, to propose to *her* daughter'.[17]

What we can infer from these relationships is that Richard was not averse to marrying at this point, despite the fact that he saw marriage as a curtailment to further adventures and travel.[18] Impecuniosity was not, however, his only disadvantage as far as the protective mothers of virtuous young women were concerned. He had a dubious reputation. He was flirtatious (by his own admission he had relationships with 'dozens' of women and some he fancied himself in love with). But that was not necessarily held to be a bad thing in a bachelor, and as his niece said, 'women fell in love with him by the score.'[19]

One girl who did so – all we know of her is that her name was Louise, nicknamed 'Thing Divine' (but she must not be confused with Louisa Buckley Segrave) – enjoyed a brief flirtation with Richard until he met her mother, a large woman who dressed 'loudly'. It dawned on him that young Louise might grow up to resemble her mother, and his ardour cooled rapidly. When the mother demanded to know what his intentions were towards her daughter, Richard responded unchivalrously, 'Strictly dishonourable, Ma'am,' and was shown the door. The incident resurfaced years later in a poem:

> I, too, am there, with 'Thing Divine',
> Bending before the marble shrine . . .
> When sudden on my raptured sight
> Falls deadly and disarming blight . . .
> An apparition grim – I saw
> The middle-aged British mother-in-law!

The pink silk hood her head was on
Did make a triste comparison
With blossomed brow and green-grey eyes,
And cheeks bespread with vinous dyes,
And mouth and nose – all, all, in fine,
Caricature of 'Thing Divine'.

Full low the Doppleganger's dress
Of moire and tulle, in last distress
To decorate the massive charms
Displayed to manhood's shrinking arms
Large loomed her waist 'spite pinching stays,
As man-o'-war in bye-gone days . . .[20]

Reports began to filter through the community at Boulogne (perhaps through letters from India) that 'something was known about him'. No one knew what it was, but 'it was not quite nice'. Richard did not help himself. With his quirky sense of humour it amused him to tell stories against himself, and his versions of adventures in India were strong meat for English drawing rooms. If company bored him he would take out a book and begin to read it, or leave the room abruptly. Yet he was very indignant when he noticed that numbers of the English contingent in Boulogne began to cross the road at his approach, making it obvious that they were deliberately avoiding him. And he was 'ruefully surprised' on hearing that an elderly woman had declared 'she would not and could not sit in the room with that fellow Burton'.[21] Mrs Arundell, who held herself and her girls above the general run of English people in Boulogne anyway, heard these reports and formed a long-term opinion of Richard as a highly unsuitable man.

Isabel need not have worried unduly about leaving Richard to the temptations of her cousin Louisa and other women. She did not know it, but he returned to England shortly after she did, with his intentions and ambitions now firmly directed towards achieving fame and fortune. He had already overrun his two years' sick leave and an extension of six months. Yet he needed further time to organise his planned adventure. He was examined by Dr Scott, who certified that Richard was still suffering the disabling effects of:

ophthalmia . . . coupled with functional derangement of digestive organs, and further that the chronic affection of the testicle from which he has long suffered is not entirely removed.[22]

The doctor obligingly stated that Lieutenant Burton would be well advised to avoid the forthcoming hot season in India; he therefore recommended a further six months' extension of leave. Six months later the ophthalmia had improved, but there was a return of the urethral stricture from which he had suffered in the previous year together with a painful swelling of the left testicle. 'For the perfect cure of both these affections,' Dr Scott wrote, a further six months' extension was 'absolutely necessary for Lieut. Burton's restoration to health.'[23] This was approved on 27 October.[24] Richard's genito-urinary infection, later diagnosed as orchitis, dated from 'an attack of mumps, raging neuralgia and an internal inflammation'[25] in Boulogne in 1851, which subsequently flared up during any period of low immunity for the remainder of his life.[26]

Despite impaired health Richard had used the interim summer months of 1852 to advantage. Apart from the completion of his fourth book, *Falconry in the Valley of the Indus*, which included a short, reasonably sensible autobiography in its postscript,[27] he had achieved introductions to leading members of the Royal Geographical Society: Sir Roderick Murchison, Dr Norton Shaw, General Monteith, Colonel William Sykes and Colonel P. Yorke among others. Monteith and Sykes were retired officers of the East India Company, Sykes had become a Director and later became the Deputy Chairman; both were impressed with Richard's scientific approach to research. Murchison had been the youngest member of the founding committee of the Society in 1830 and was its *éminence grise* by 1852. All would be immensely influential in his life over the next years.

Through General Monteith Richard offered his services to the Society, having learned that they had a sum of £200 available for an exploration of Arabia. This money had originally been provided in 1846 by the East India Company for the Rev. Thomas Brockman's proposed exploration of the Hadramaut. Brockman died of fever in Oman before he could undertake the expedition and eventually the money was offered to the brilliant Finnish explorer and Arabist, Dr George August Wallin,[28] to undertake a similar venture. Wallin refused it in 1851 on the grounds that it was inadequate, stating that he needed £400 at least.[29] But the R.G.S. had no additional funds to offer, and by 1852 Wallin had still not made his expedition.

Richard wrote to Wallin explaining his plans and asking for information, but the letter was returned long after Richard's expedition was over with the message that Professor Wallin had died. In any case, Richard had already made his intentions known to the Royal Geographical Society committee; these were, he said, the removal of 'that opprobrium to modern adventure, the huge white blot which in our maps still notes the Eastern and Central regions of Arabia'.[30] The R.G.S., eager to see Arabia explored, took the bait.

In November Richard returned to Boulogne. Also at Boulogne in that month was Colonel Sir James Outram, who was on his way to London to attend the funeral of the Duke of Wellington. Richard had always openly sided with Napier in the feud between the two men, but he still hoped for, and got, a fair-minded sponsorship from Outram whom he respected greatly.[31] Outram had left India, having been forced to resign from his post as British Resident (Political) at Baroda because of a report he had submitted regarding bribery and corruption in the Company which had caused great offence. At such a time it is doubtful that his word carried a great deal of weight with the Directors, but Richard would not necessarily have known this and he needed the Company to sanction a further 3 years' leave on full pay to enable him to successfully carry out his proposed exploration. From Bolougne he wrote to the R.G.S., the brevity of his letter indicating that it was in answer to a request:

Hotel de Paris
Boulogne
[Rec'd 3rd November 1852]

I propose to explore the country extending from Muskat to Aden, specifically Shak'r and Hazramaut. I wish particularly to trace the ancient cities of Himyar, and to travel as far inland as circumstances will permit.

R. Burton Lt.
Bombay Army[32]

This abrupt note contains no mention of any intention to visit Mecca

and Medina, but he already had this in mind on 18 July when he
visited a maker of crystals and mirrors, Frederick Hockley, at his
workshop in Croydon, accompanied by his friend Captain Henry
Murray. '[He] was then contemplating his pilgrimage to Medina and
Mecca . . .' Hockley stated. 'I had the pleasure of giving to him a
small, oval, mounted crystal [and] . . . a black mirror.'[33] Richard's
letter to the Court of Directors a few days later was more detailed but
still made no mention of his real plans, merely that he was interested
in making himself useful to the promotion of science at the end of his
furlough in April when he would be returning to India. He thought
this could best be done by exploring en route . . .

> that part of Arabia which extends from Muscat to Aden, including
> the provinces of Shayr and Shakr, Haddramaut – the Region of
> Frankincense and the Himyaritic land of ancient fame. The meagre
> details which I have gathered from various sources lead me to sup-
> pose that the long belt of mountains which links the coast, is
> intersected by rich and fertile valleys which support large and pow-
> erful tribes.

Should the Directors grant him permission to explore this interesting
region, he went on, he would use his best endeavours to make as
accurate a survey of it as circumstances permitted. And he added the
sweetener he hoped would most appeal to their commercial instincts:

> I would also ascertain the nature and extent of its resources, and
> attempt to remove the obstructions which the ignorance or apathy
> of the natives may have opposed to the establishment of direct
> commercial relations with the Western Coast of our Indian
> Empire . . .[34]

But although the R.G.S. Council members were in favour of Richard's
proposed expedition, the East India Company was not. In the first
edition of his book on the journey to Mecca and Medina (Richard
was still employed by the Company when it was published) he tactfully explained this lack of enthusiasm as being due to the nature of
the journey and the unwillingness of the Directors to place one of
their officers in certain danger. This is borne out by a note made by
Murchison in the files at the Royal Geographical Society. But in a

second edition of *A Personal Narrative* published in 1879, when the East India Company no longer existed, Richard claimed that there was another reason for their lack of support. In 1851, besides submitting his book on the ethnology and topography of Sindh to the Court of Directors, Richard had apparently written 'certain remarks upon the subject of Anglo-India misrule' including predictions of native insurrection. It was these remarks (later vindicated by the Indian Mutiny), Richard believed, that caused the Directors to withhold their sanction.[35]

These volunteered comments were not well received, and now, when he needed the support of the 'Kings of Leadenhall Street' – '[they] much disliking,' said Richard, 'my impolitic habit of telling political truths' – were not disposed to look kindly on an impetuous fire-eater, no matter how tempting he made the bait.[36] This is startlingly similar to his claims that he was denied advancement in India because of his reporting style. Whatever the truth behind it, the Directors replied to Roderick Murchison on 20 January 1853:

> Sir, I have laid before the Court of Directors . . . your letter of 22nd December stating on the part of the Royal Geographical Society a favourable opinion of . . . Lt. Burton who is desirous of exploring the Eastern Portions of Arabia and expressing a hope that the Court will empower that officer to undertake a proposed Expedition . . . [The Directors regret they] are unable to give their sanction . . .[37]

It is not known whether Outram played any part in these discussions. Certainly he must have had some fellow-feeling for Richard, if Richard's claims about Outram's own ill-received report are true. It was possibly out of consideration for his emissaries that, although Richard's request to be allowed to explore Arabia was refused, he was granted an extension of furlough in order to visit 'on his way to India' Egypt and the south-eastern parts of Arabia for the purpose of pursuing his Arabic studies, in particular to master the Egyptian accent.[38] Richard was disappointed but decided to continue virtually as planned, merely curtailing the scale of his explorations to suit the reduced time available, facing whatever consequences arose. He dashed off a letter to Norton Shaw (Assistant Secretary of the Royal Geographical Society), advising the grant of leave, hoping that it was sufficient to retain the sponsorship of the R.G.S., '[I] abandon myself to you and Providence,' he wrote impetuously.[39]

Although he had not admitted to the East India Company his plan to visit Mecca and Medina, he had told them that he thought his disguise as a 'petty trader and physician' would render him safe 'even in the midst of Mecca'.[40] He certainly discussed penetrating the sacred cities with members of the Royal Geographical Society, for the Expedition Committee met on 7 February to consider it as a project worthy of support. Richard subsequently attended and outlined to this Committee his plans which involved, according to the Committee minutes, joining 'the Egyptian Caravan for Cairo, and to penetrate via Medinah and Meccah, through the province of Hadramaut to the southern coast of Arabia'. As a result the Committee resolved to support the expedition to the extent of the £200 in its coffers, in two stages of £100, having amended the plan only to accommodate Richard's wish to join the Damascus Caravan travelling from Medina to Mecca, rather than take the Egyptian one to Medina only.[41] One member who had not been present wrote to Shaw afterwards to say that he was sorry to hear that 'Lt. Burton talks of Mecca and Medina. It is difficult to enter them without great hazard, and if detected by a *kafir*, who would answer for his life or escape from Arabia?'[42]

There is no doubt that visiting the Holy Cities was a clear departure from his written intentions to the Company of the previous November. Perhaps the reason lay in the fact that he believed permission would not be readily given for a trip which guaranteed physical danger without any obvious commercial rewards. But since he had, in effect, no brief from the Company except permission to improve his Arabic, he was travelling on behalf of the R.G.S. in a civilian capacity rather than as an officer. However, because several Directors were also members of the R.G.S. Council, the details of his mission were known about. Just to make sure that he understood the position Richard was firmly informed in writing, on two occasions, that the extension of leave granted to him was finite and that if he failed to reach his Presidency 'on or before 30th March 1854' he would 'be out of the service under the terms of the Statute of 33 George III Chapter 52, Section 70'.[43]

Norton Shaw, having availed himself of some of Richard's incredibly detailed knowledge of the topography of India, was firmly behind him, describing him as 'a very clever India Officer'.[44] Shaw was one of the few men privy to the audaciousness of Richard's full plan, which at that stage was to travel to Arabia disguised as 'Shayk Abdullah bin Yusef el Farangi' (Abdullah, son of Joseph the foreigner). In Alexandria he was to stay with John Wingfield Larking, British Consul-General in Egypt, while he metamorphosed into 'El Makim el Najee'.[45] At no point did he intend to be seen in Western dress and secrecy was of the utmost importance. No word must leak out to blow his cover and no detail that might betray him as an infidel could be overlooked. As discussed earlier, a short biographical sketch written by A.B. Richards and published in 1864, stated that as part of his preparations Richard had himself circumcised.[46]

Recent biographers have queried the actual dangers that would have attached to detection, but there were several incidents in the mid-nineteenth century when infidels were killed after having been detected in holy places. Whether or not he was actually justified in his fears, Richard genuinely believed – given what he had learned in India about the *Haj* – that discovery of his true identity would lead to execution. In short, the success of his unique plan to go as 'one of the people' hinged on his not being detected as a European. He spent time with Mr and Mrs Larking in London, going over the arrangements.[47]

When he was not working at his language and practical preparations for the 'Pilgrimage', or relaxing with Henry Murray at his bachelor's rooms at No. D4 the Albany in Piccadilly among like-minded men such as Richard Monckton Milnes (both of these were much older men than he, and played a major role in his life), or the much younger Foster Fitzgerald Arbuthnot,[48] Richard was to be found at the Royal Asiatic Society's library (later he asked permission to be allowed to take a few books home so he could spend longer working on them) or the Royal Geographical Society's rooms at Whitehall Place.[49] Here he made friends with leading geographers of the day such as Francis Galton, a Fellow of the R.G.S. who had travelled extensively in South Africa and was the author of a book on the subject.[50]

At the end of March Richard visited his family in Bath for the final time before his departure. He had a psychological horror of saying goodbyes and inevitably became highly emotional, his hands growing cold and shaking and his eyes filling with tears, according to his family.[51] He had consequently developed the habit of slipping away without telling anyone he was leaving, and his parting remark to them on this occasion was his usual, 'Adieu, sans adieu.' Before he left, however, he gave his sister the unusual gold ring he had worn as *Mirza* Abdullah in India as a keepsake. It was 'a gold, scaly serpent with a large diamond in its flat head'. After his departure, his mother found a letter he had left for her in which he told her about his planned expedition and left instructions about what should be done with his 'small stock of valuables' should he come to harm.[52] The ring he had given Maria caused great drama in the family, for it was later stolen from her while she was staying with her cousin Miss Eliza Burton and never found.[53]

On 3 April the first phase of the complicated plan was put into effect. At his lodgings in London Richard again transformed himself by means of a shaven head, false beard and Oriental clothing, into Sheikh Abdullah, a Persian scholar who spoke little English. Accompanied by a friend and brother-officer, Captain Henry Grindley of the Bengal Cavalry, acting as Abdullah's interpreter, he travelled to Southampton. Had Lieutenant Burton boarded the ship and Sheikh Abdullah disembarked, no matter how good the disguise, someone – a crew member – would have noticed and who knew what harm might be done at the outset? Once Richard had boarded the P. & O. steamer S.S. *Bengal*, Grindley's part in the plan ended and he returned to London. But Richard was not completely alone. Also in on the secret was fellow-passenger John Larking, who was returning with his wife to their home in Alexandria. The *Bengal* weighed anchor on the following morning, giving Richard exactly eleven months in which to achieve his aims.

8

THE PILGRIM
1853

The two-week voyage to Alexandria was uneventful and Richard used the time to grow his own beard and 'get into character', for it was more than three years since he had lived publicly as Abdullah. 'It was not exactly pleasant,' Richard said, 'to speak broken English the whole way and rigorously refuse . . . the pleasure of addressing the opposite sex. But under the circumstances it was necessary.'[1] There were no hitches, no passenger openly queried Abdullah's identity, although a rich Turk who had met Richard previously

> . . . was struck with the regularity and earnestness with which a certain poorly-dressed Arab performed his devotions, and watching him rather narrowly suddenly recognised his friend . . . Burton. A burst of laughter followed; but Burton seeing his disguise penetrated, merely made a quick sign of silence, and went on with his prayers. Turâbi took the hint but subsequently they had many a chat in private.[2]

Despite this small hitch, by the time he disembarked Richard had begun to feel more confident in his alternative persona.

The plan unfolded nicely.[3] It had already been decided that before he set off for Cairo Richard would stay with the Larkings in the role of *munshi*. At Alexandria, Larking's father-in-law John Thurburn (the latter had once provided the Arabian traveller Burkhardt with similar hospitality), met the ship and conveyed his daughter and the two men to Larking's villa on the banks of the Mahmudiyah canal. Here Richard was given as lodgings a small detached 'pavilion . . . among white myrtle blossoms, and . . . rosy oleander flowers with the almond smell', where he could lodge, for the most part unobserved by the Larkings' servants and visitors, while he made the final preparations for his pilgrimage. He spent a month revising the Koran and perfecting his Muslim prayers (partially forgotten through lack of practice), doctoring local inhabitants (his character had some knowledge as a physician to account for his carrying medical supplies) with simple remedies, and making himself ready.

As time went on Richard began to feel that *Mirza* Abdullah was too grand a character for a rootless traveller, so he swapped his new-looking *jubbah* – a long outer garment worn by scholars and professional men – for a worn and mended homespun brown robe. A wandering dervish with a knowledge of magic and horoscopes, and rudimentary doctoring, Richard decided, would be a better cover.

> No character in the Moslem world is so proper for disguise as that of *darwaysh*. It is assumed by all ranks, ages and creeds; by the nobleman who had been disgraced at court, and by the peasant who is too idle to till the ground; . . . He may pray or not, marry or remain single, as he pleases, be respectable in cloth of frieze [or] cloth of gold, and no one asks him – the charactered vagabond – Why he comes here? or Wherefore he goes there? He may wend his way on foot alone, or ride his Arab mare followed by a dozen servants; he is equally feared without weapons, as swaggering through the streets armed to the teeth. The more haughty and offensive he is to people, the more they respect him; a decided advantage to the traveller of choleric temperament.[4]

By far the longest time was spent obtaining the necessary passport and paperwork that would permit travel and the carrying of a weapon for self-protection. Here John Larking could offer no assistance and no privileges; it was necessary that the dervish, Abdullah, visit the various officials in person. Richard spent days squatting on his heels in the burning sun, in apparently humble patience, waiting for British and Turkish civil servants to attend to his requests. The Turks sometimes drove him off with rude oaths and kicks when the bureau closed without warning, and he had to work at keeping his temper. At length he was driven to bribing a minor official with *bakshish* to further the progress of his application. The British were hardly better, treating him with casual arrogance and charging five shillings for a certificate declaring him to be an Anglo-Indian subject under their protection. In the light of England's revenue from India of £70 million, Richard thought this charge on poor Indian travellers shameful. 'Oh the meanness of our magnificence! the littleness of our greatness!' he wrote.[5]

At last he was ready. His equipment was impressively limited for a hazardous journey of some months' duration: a rag containing a soft wood stick well-chewed at one end (for cleaning teeth), a piece of soap and a comb.; two changes of clothing including one good one for 'critical' occasions, a goatskin water-bag, a cotton pillow, a blanket, and a sheet which would do duty both as a tent and a mosquito curtain. These items were stowed in two locally made saddlebags. He also had a Persian rug, rolled up round a bright yellow umbrella/parasol purchased in the bazaar, while a small gaily painted wooden box, 'capable of withstanding falls from a camel twice a day', contained the tools of a doctor, basic drugs, ointments and cotton dressings. Hidden away in his clothing were his surveying instruments; a sextant, a 'copper cased watch' with Arabic numerals, and compass.

He carried a dagger and a brass ink-stand and pen-holder, which were stuck into his belt. In his pocket was a 'mighty rosary which on occasion might have been converted into a weapon of defence'. Small coins and some silver were contained in a cotton purse in the pocket of his robe, but £25 in gold was stowed away in a substantial leather money-belt fastened securely beneath his clothing. The final personal item was Elizabeth Stisted's 'canvas housewife . . . most useful in lands . . . where the sight of a man darning his coat or patching his slippers teems with pleasing ideas of humility'.[6]

At the end of May he was ready to set out for Cairo. He parted from his friend John Larking, who humorously dismissed any tendency towards sentiment in their parting by irreverently suggesting he should administer a *bastinado* to induce in Richard a sense of 'true Oriental feeling'.[7] No matter what he had said and written for the sake of expediency before his departure, Richard had a clear primary object in his own mind of what he wished to accomplish. He wished to visit the two most sacred places of Islam, Medina and Mecca, and to cross the 'unknown Arabian peninsula in a direct line from either

Al-Madínah to Maskat, or diagonally from Meccah to Makallah on the Indian Ocean'.[8]

What he hoped to gain as a result of such a journey or journeys, apart from the sheer adventure and sense of achievement, was new information. Whether any market for well-bred horses could be opened up between central Arabia and India, for example. To map the great unexplored 'Empty Quarter'. To try to prove Colonel Sykes' pet theory that there must exist certain physiological differences among the various tribes of Arabs which would disprove their common origin.[9]

Afterwards, Richard's adoption of Eastern disguise offended some who suggested it was a totally unnecessary affectation since anyone who went to the Turkish authorities and professed to be a convert could join the *Haj*. In such a case, it was pointed out, he would have been excused had he made any mistakes in the elaborate Muslim ritual, and he would not have been in danger of his life. But this kind of *Haj* had already been done. Richard felt that only by travelling as a born Muslim could he obtain truly accurate information. He knew, from his experiences in India as Abdullah, the difference between the way an insider was treated by the native community, and the veneer of acceptance offered to those – even those invited as friends – who were outsiders. He wanted to know how a genuine pilgrim felt, and to reach the sacrosanct heart of Islam, so he chose the path of a true-born believer. Besides, he said,

> my spirit could not bend to own myself a *renegade* – to be pointed at and shunned and catechised, an object of suspicion to the many and of contempt to all. Moreover it would have obstructed the aim of my wandering. The convert is always watched . . . and men do not willingly give information to a 'new Moslem', especially a Frank; they suspect his conversion to be feigned or forced, look upon him as a spy, and let him see as little of life as possible. Firmly as my heart was set on travelling in Arabia, by Heaven! I would have given up the project rather than purchase a doubtful and partial success at such a price.[10]

The journey to Cairo took three scorching days. Richard, in character, had taken a third-class passage (deck accommodation), the sun burned him all day and dews soaked him all night, reminding him of his days in Sindh. During the voyage he made a friend, *Haji* Wali, with whom he stayed in a *caravanserai* in Cairo (and in fact corresponded with him for many years afterwards). Since it was Ramadan the two men fasted and prayed together and, amazingly, Richard ended up confiding his plans. Perhaps his companion penetrated the disguise, at any rate it was at *Haji* Wali's suggestion that 'Abdullah' subtly changed his identity again, to that of a Pathan[11] born in India of Afghan parents, educated in Rangoon, and now a wanderer. Certainly, Richard spoke all the languages to make this story believable, Hindustani, Persian and Arabic; and again, the hybrid nature of the new character would explain minor lapses. It was vital to be word perfect in his cover at all times for the customary first greeting between men, in the bazaar, on a camel, in a mosque was, 'What news? What is thy name? Whence comest thou?' They expected answers.

Richard could never have undertaken this exploit without the experience and knowledge he had gained in India. He laid aside his dervish gown with its wide blue pantaloons and short shirt, and Abdullah Khan wearing an enormous sprigged muslin turban and the dress he had been so familiar with in India, made his entrance. Now he stuck two pistols in his sash, twirled his moustachios in indication of suppressed anger, and every action, from the grunt on drinking a glass of water to the personal hygiene of a devout Muslim, was practised and perfected.

He remained in Cairo a month, during which he purchased two camels and the requisite provisions: tea, coffee, loaf sugar, rice, dates, biscuits, oil, vinegar, tobacco, lanterns, cooking pots, three large water-skins for desert travel and a small bell-shaped tent. For protection he purchased two pistols, and he had a leather merchant make a unique holder for his *Hamail*, the pocket Koran carried by pilgrims to denote their holy undertaking. It is generally carried in an embroidered crimson velvet or red morocco case, slung by red silk cords over the left shoulder to hang down by the right side. Richard's carrying case looked ordinary enough but he had had it specially made so that in addition to housing his Koran it provided three hidden compartments. One housed his watch and compass, the second some ready money, and the third carried pencils, penknife and paper torn into small slips which he could conceal in the palm of his hand for scribbling notes or making sketches which he would later copy into his diary, a thin volume which could be carried in his breast pocket. He also made some dubious new acquaintances, and engaged in some amusing escapades with them which resulted in his being arrested at least once and thrown into prison overnight. He set himself up as a doctor, at which he enjoyed unlooked-for success, and finally found it convenient to leave the city after a drunken party with an Albanian captain scandalised respectable neighbours.

One camel Richard appropriated for himself. The other carried his luggage and his 'Mecca boy', Mohammed el-Basyúni, a beardless 18-year-old, 'chocolate-brown, with high features and a bold profile'. Short in stature and with a decided tendency to corpulence, Mohammed could read a little, write his name, and was profoundly knowledgeable upon Mecca, the *Haj* and prayers. He had been to Constantinople with a homebound pilgrim and was now returning to his widowed mother in Mecca. Richard met him when he purchased from Mohammed the mandatory set of pilgrim clothes called '*Al-Ihram*'.[12] The youth saw a way of being paid for making his journey home and proposed himself as Richard's travelling companion. Richard was amused by the boy's cocky self-confidence, but also recognised how useful he might be to him, so he hired him in addition to his other servant, a small Indian youth called Nur.

Having sent his servants and luggage on ahead, Richard set out alone from Cairo at 3 p.m. one afternoon towards Suez, an 80-mile ride across the desert which he intended to accomplish in 30 hours under 'forced march' conditions to ascertain how much damage four years of soft living in Europe had done to his powers of endurance. 'There are few better tests,' he wrote feelingly, 'than an eighty mile ride in mid-summer, on a bad wooden saddle, borne by a worse dromedary, across the Suez Desert . . .'[13] Discomfort or no, he enjoyed it. Spiritually he grew in the desert; his senses quickened, and he felt a 'keen animal enjoyment' simply in existing. 'Once your tastes have conformed to the tranquillity of such travel,' he wrote, 'you . . . suffer real pain in return-ing to the turmoil of civilisation.'[14] Real pain came too, after his arrival in Suez after dark on the following day when aching in every limb, with large raw areas where skin had been rubbed off, badly sunburned and physically exhausted, he was forced to spread his rug on a bare floor in an otherwise empty room. 'Lamenting the effects of four years' domi-cile in Europe, and equally disquieted in mind about the fate of my goods and chattels I fell into an uncomfortable sleep.'[15]

In the morning, refreshed and reunited with his belongings, he was introduced by Mohammed to a party of four Medina-bound travellers with whom he threw in his lot. They were Omar Effendi, a Circassian; Saad, his black 'pure African' servant who was nicknamed 'Al Jinni' (the Demon); Sheikh Hamid el Samman, who was morally 'no better than he should be' but who had a residence in Medina which would be useful, Richard thought, when they arrived there; and Salih Shakkar, a lanky 16-year-old boy with the ideas and composure of a 46-year-old man. Each of his travelling companions approached Richard independently, within the space of a few hours, to ask for a loan. 'Seeing that their company would be an advantage, I hearkened favourably to the honeyed request for a few crowns,' he said, though he was astute enough to take material items as pawns to ensure repayment.

Immediately he became favoured in the party as a man of some substance. He was given precedence at meals, his opinion was sought on all matters needing decision, and in short Richard, alias Abdullah, suddenly found himself a person of consequence. This apparent adoption of him caused him to be over-confident and led to his cover being questioned. Thrown into close quarters with the men, he had not objected when

> . . . they looked at my clothes, overhauled my medicine chest, and criticised my pistols; they sneered at my copper-cased watch and remembered having seen a compass at Constantinople. Therefore I imagined they would think little about a sextant. This was a mistake. The boy Mohammed, I afterwards learned,[16] waited only my leaving the room to declare that the would-be Hadji was one of the Infidels from India, and a council sat to discuss the case. Fortunately for me, Omar Effendi had looked over a letter which I had written that morning, and he had at various times received categorical replies to certain questions in high theology. He felt himself justified in declaring *ex cathedra*, the boy Mohammed's position perfectly untenable . . .[17]

Mohammed, clearly a bright boy, was severely castigated by his companions for impugning the character of the pious Abdullah and the matter was allowed to drop. But Richard had seen the expressions of the men when they saw the sextant, realised the potential danger in carrying it and disposed of it. For the next few days he prayed, ostentatiously, five times a day. It was an object lesson, learned early in the trip not to relax his guard, although as it transpired Mohammed never entirely lost his innate suspicions about his employer.

The party sailed from Suez on 8 July – 'a fierce July day' – bound for Yambu. The vessel, a *sambuk* of fifty tons, was a two masted hulk with wedge-like bows, a poop deck and a single lateen sail. She had no means of reefing, no compass, no log, no sounding lines, no spare ropes and no charts. The crew consisted of six boys. Built to take 60 passengers, she was overcrowded to the point of capsize with a jabbering rabble of almost a hundred excitable, excited and anxious pilgrims who had to fight, literally, for space to sleep. Richard wrote that he cast a wistful look at the British flag floating over the Consulate as they slipped anchor for the 600-mile voyage, a distance 'doubled', he said, 'by detours'.[18]

Having appropriated their space on the poop deck, an area 10 ft by 8 ft intended to accommodate 18 passengers and for which luxury they had paid an additional fee, Richard and his companions found themselves defending it with clubs and swords against a force of twenty or more desperate men swarming up from the deckless hold armed with staves. The fighting was at its height when Richard spotted a large earthenware jar full of drinking water; this massive item weighing, he thought, in excess of 100 lb, he rolled down upon the attackers with a mighty push and the bruising, cuts from shards and surprise engendered by a severe soaking brought a speedy end to the fracas.[19] Even so the voyage was an exercise in cramped endurance, enlivened by occasional incidents which Richard found interesting or amusing, but otherwise his diary consisted of descriptions of coastline and brassy skies, and the inevitable discomforts of living on a crowded open deck with no facilities whatsoever. Stricken with diarrhoea, he mourned the fact that his medical chest with its stock of opium was stowed in the hold where he could not reach it. The ship anchored every couple of nights so that the passengers could wade ashore to bathe, find fresh water and cook hot food. On one of these shore trips Richard stepped on a poisonous spiny sea urchin, and by the time he landed at Yambu he could not put his foot to the ground. The pain and swelling lasted over a month. Running aground was commonplace; that they made their destination safely seemed something of a miracle to Richard and his fellow passengers.

After 14 days of purgatory they arrived at the port of Yambu, in El Hijaz, 130 miles south-west of Medina. Yambu's charm lay not in its architecture or site but in refreshing baths, fresh sweet drinking water and the availability of camels for hire. The desert road to the Holy City lay through mountain passes where a band of murderous Bedouin robbers preyed on pilgrims and travellers alike. They were led by an aged chieftain called Saad, popularly known as 'the Old Man of the Mountains', who was locked in a lifelong blood-feud with the Sheríf of Mecca who had slain Saad's nephew. As retaliation he had threatened, Richard was told, 'to cut the throat of every hen venturing into his passes'. The pilgrims joined up with an armed escort for the journey, but the Bedouins lay in wait and the travellers were driven back under heavy fire.

In the following week three or four caravans arrived at Yambu and combined to make the journey together. Richard's party joined them. By now, on the advice of friendly fellow-travellers, he had adopted the dress of an Arab to avoid paying extra tolls as they travelled. He invested in a full-length tight-sleeved cotton shirt, worn under an *abba*, a short-sleeved cloak of dark green woven in fine wool. On his head he wore a small skull cap covered by a colourful *keffiyeh*, a square of brightly striped material folded in a triangle placed over the head and secured at the crown with an *agal*. The ends of the head-dress could be worn loose or looped into the *agal*, or – in storms – drawn across the face as protection.

Richard was at the height of his physical prowess: young, fit, powerful, and dressed in the graceful splendour of a reasonably prosperous Arab, he cut a considerable dash. His badly swollen foot, however, made it expedient for him to travel in a *shugduf*, a tented seat carried by a camel normally used by women but regarded as acceptable for an invalid. Apart from the extra comfort the canopy provided a modicum of privacy which Richard used to write and sketch surreptitiously as they travelled. He had as an object lesson here the fate of the German traveller Adolphe von Wrede who in 1843, disguised as a Bedouin called Abd el Hud, was discovered making sketches in the Hadramaut and accused of being an English spy. Not only was von Wrede lucky to escape with his life, Richard wrote, but 'had the mortification to see his sketch-books, the labour of months, summarily appropriated and destroyed by the Arabs'.[20] In the dreaded 'Pilgrim's Pass' they were attacked, as they expected to be;

Richard, along with his fellow-travellers, could only blaze away hopefully at the attackers ensconced high in the mountains on either side
of the pass, hoping to shroud himself in smoke. Twelve of the pilgrims
were killed in the skirmish, as well as numerous camels and donkeys.

For the next 36 hours they travelled without stopping, harried day
and night by snipers, and on the second morning as the sun rose
Richard was suffering intense pain from his poisoned foot as well as
from inevitable tiredness. Half an hour after dawn they passed
through a lane with dark lava rocks banked high on either side of
them. This opened up into a sudden and unexpected view of the city
of Medina spread out beneath them; 'It was like a vision in the
Arabian Nights,' Richard wrote. 'We halted our camels as if by word
of command. All dismounted, in imitation of the pious of old, and sat
down, jaded and hungry as we were, to feast our eyes . . .'[21] The
panoramic view of buildings, gardens and orchards was all the more
striking after the desolation and danger of the past few days. 'I now
understood the . . . phrase in the Moslem ritual,' he continued, '"And
when the Pilgrim's eyes shall fall upon the trees of el Medinah,* let
him raise his voice and bless the prophet with the choicest of blessings."'[22]

Richard was invited to the house of Sheikh Hamid, to refresh himself and take breakfast before visiting the Holy Place. It was the fact
that Hamid lived in Medina which had induced Richard, whilst in
Suez, to encourage the acquaintance by making a small loan; just as
he had taken Mohammed as a servant principally because the youth
lived with his mother in Mecca. He saw that their friendship would
provide a respectable cover and base for him in those cities. After they
had performed the requisite religious ablution the party mounted
donkeys and set out for the mosque. The site of the Prophet's tomb**
Masjid el Nabawhi was originally a small graveyard shaded by date
trees. The 400-year-old mosque on the site when Richard visited was
of stone and 420 ft by 340 ft. A covered porch, not unlike the cloister
of a monastery, ran round the courtyard. The tomb, held in a
detached tower some 55 ft square situated in the south-eastern corner

---

*Burton spelled proper names phonetically; e.g. Medina/Medinah;
Mecca/Meccah; Muscat/Maskat; Hajji/Hadji.
**Burton put this at c.569–632 AD.

of the building, was capped with the mighty green dome which was the dominant feature of the city.

Entering the garden of the mosque the pilgrims turned towards Mecca and prayed, recited two chapters of the Koran, and gave alms to the poor in gratitude for being allowed to complete the journey in safety. Then they were allowed to stand by the windows of the tomb chamber and recite a complicated ritual of blessings. Richard felt he was being carefully watched and he thought that as he had been taught to pray by Hosayn in India, it was possible that he retained some traces of Sh'ia in his devotions. They 'probably suspected I was an Ajami or Persian, and these heretics have often attempted to defile the tombs', he surmised. Later he learned that several Shi'ite Muslims had been killed in recent years by hot-headed Sunni fanatics who regarded all Persians as heretics.[23] He had been wise to change Abdullah's nationality from a Persian to a Pathan, and apparently he passed inspection for – after all the prayers were said – he was allowed to look upon the tomb of the Prophet. In the dim lamp-light he was able to see nothing but the covering: 'a curtain of handsome silk and cotton brocade, green with white letters worked into it. The exact place of Mohammed's tomb . . . is distinguished by a large pearl rosary and the celebrated . . . constellation of pearls . . . suspended breast high to the curtain . . . described [as a] "brilliant star set in diamonds and pearls" placed in the dark that a man's eye may be able to endure its splendours . . .'

Richard spent a month there, exploring, asking questions, taking notes and making surreptitious sketches on scraps of paper which he folded small and hid in tins in his medical chest. Noting the strong seams of quartz and granite, he even panned for gold with some limited success; all his life Richard would harbour dreams of finding gold. Ever the scientist and doubter, classicist and historian, he read all he could find on the historical life of the Prophet and concluded that the site believed to be the Prophet's tomb was of doubtful provenance. This was completely in character. Years later he would cast similar doubts on the authenticity of the site said to be that of Christ's tomb at Jerusalem.

The cause of his lengthy sojourn in Medina was the wait for the great Damascus Caravan due to halt there on its way to Mecca. At some point shortly after his arrival in Medina he had made the important decision that it was not possible to cross the Arabian peninsula from there, as he had originally hoped. It had clearly still been an option when he arrived at Medina, for in a paper to the R.G.S. he revealed that he had investigated this plan: 'At El Medinah I heard a tradition that in days of yore a high road ran from the city, passing through this wild region to Hadramaut. It had, however, been deserted for ages, and my informants considered me demented when I talked of travelling by it.'[24]

In his formal account of the journey, *A Personal Narrative*, he adds that the quarrel between the Russians and Turks, which was at a simmering point at this stage but would erupt later in the Crimea, 'had extended its excitement even into the bowels of Arabia' and was a causal factor in his decision that 'to travel eastward according to my original intention was impossible'.[25] He had discussed travelling with the Beni Harb tribe of Bedouins, but having got to know them subsequently rejected this plan on the grounds that they were a particularly quarrelsome bunch who might easily get him killed in a tribal dispute over a mare, or some equally petty cause. The chief obstacle, however, was the limitation on his time which 'would not admit of my starting as a Bedouin across the desert. No guide would accompany me before the month of September and it would have been impossible for me to have reached Muscat before June or July next.'[26] However, there was one further possible way of crossing Arabia. At Mecca, he hoped, there might be a Pilgrim Caravan from Muscat on the east coast which he could join for its return journey.

But the pure romance of the *Haj* – the pilgrimage to Mecca – was a powerful lure in itself. His journey to the Prophet's tomb at Medina was not a pilgrimage but a *ziyarat*, a visitation or pious act. But a man who has travelled to the birthplace of the Prophet, and fulfilled all the necessary obligations, earned the title *Hajji* for life, and was entitled to wear the green turban that universally denoted the status of a *Hajji* throughout Islam. Such a dignity, Burton reasoned, would be useful in any future expeditions he might make in Arabia.[27]

When the Damascus Caravan, with upwards of 50,000 weary pilgrims, arrived on 28 August, Richard was ready. He had patched up his water-skins, hired two camels and laid in a store of provisions for the 10-day trek, 250 miles across desert. The old Bedouin from whom he hired the camels gave him lots of advice, warning him especially against the Bedouin brotherhood of camel men, 'wild men' who infiltrated the Caravan with the sole intention of robbing the pilgrims.[28]

It was wise, he told Richard, to eat salt with such men once a day, for under the Bedouin code they could not then do him any injury.

In the early morning of Wednesday 31 August 1853, at the sound of the signal gun announcing the departure of the Caravan, Richard parted from his friends and embraced his host Sheikh Hamid, who had taken a great deal of trouble to ensure his former travelling companion was properly equipped for his journey. Accompanied by Nur and Mohammed, he cantered their camels to catch up with the moving mass headed into the desert on the Darb el Sharki or eastern route to Mecca. The Sheríf had wished to take the shorter coastal route, but the path lay through the mountains and since negotiations with Saad had been unsuccessful, the longer and far more arduous trek across the Nejd desert was forced upon the pilgrims. The news, delivered in shocked tones on the eve of the departure by his host, made Richard whoop with delight, for the few Europeans who had previously travelled to Mecca had all taken the other road. Even so, his feelings must have been a mixture of excitement and apprehension as he fell into marching pace in the column; already he had achieved a good part of his plan. Often now, he wrote, he was so much Abdullah that he almost forgot he was English.

To be part of such a striking assembly as it dragged its colourful length across the open desert under a pitiless blue sky was an amazing experience. The heat alone made it a test of physical endurance for man and beast. Energy was sapped further by filmy sprays of sand blasted across the face by the strong desert winds – the *simoon* – like 'the flaming breath of a lion', said Richard. 'The upseething atmosphere, the heat-reek, the dancing of the air upon the baked surface of bright yellow soil . . . blurs the giant figures of camels which, at a distance, appear strings of gigantic birds.' By far the greatest problem was water, for wells were few and far between. Animals other than camels required the bulk of water that was carried, and rationing was essential; 'the only remedy is to be patient and not talk. The first two hours gives you the mastery,' Richard wrote. 'If you drink you cannot stop.'[29]

There were many classes of pilgrim; the poorest trudged on foot with the coffee, tobacco and sherbet sellers, and the country folk driving flocks of sheep and goats to be sold en route. Next in the social structure came humble souls on donkeys and asses. Women rode on carpet-covered boxes tied to the sides of beasts, or, if more affluent, in *shugduf* panniers with elaborate awnings like miniature tents. The very rich were carried in splendid scarlet litters, with their prancing thoroughbred horses led beside them.

> . . . Respectable men mount dromedaries, or blood camels, known for their small size, fine limbs, and their large deer-like eyes; their saddles show crimson sheep-skins . . . girthed over fine saddle bags, whose long tassels of bright worsted hang almost to the ground. Irregular soldiers have picturesquely equipped steeds. Here and there rides some old Arab Shaykh, preceded by his varlets performing a war dance . . . firing their guns in the air . . . brandishing their bared swords, leaping frantically with part-coloured rags floating in the air and tossing high their long spears.[30]

Once they saw a huge yellow lion, majestically sitting watching the Caravan from a high cliff, but generally there was no life except for scavenger birds. The mortality rate of the poorer classes of pilgrims was appalling; often an entire Caravan returned to Damascus more than decimated from diseases such as cholera or typhoid.[31] Exhaustion, sun and heatstroke, and thirst also took an inevitable toll, and there was always the threat of attack by desert marauders. The dead, and those so close to death that they were unable to travel further, were wrapped in their Mecca shroud, prayed over and buried in a shallow sand trench along the way. Pilgrims dying en route were accorded martyrdom in Paradise and the same spiritual status as those who reached Mecca; despite this Richard shuddered to think of those not quite dead who were left behind knowing that vultures would not wait until they had expired. Animals fared no better and dropped by the score, over-burdened, exhausted, under-watered, providing rich pickings for vultures.

Within a two-day march (47 miles) of Mecca they halted at an oasis called Zaribah. Here they ceremonially exchanged their everyday dress for the clean *Ihrám* and between prayers they shaved, trimmed beards and pared nails (for the last time until after their objective had been achieved), and bathed.[32] They set off again, everyone calling out the loud pilgrim cry '*Labbayk*' ('Here am I') as often as he or she could do so.

The most hazardous section of the trip now lay before them, the pass known as 'Valley Perilous'. They entered the ill-famed place knowing they would be attacked by the brigand Utajbah tribe, for no Caravan had ever gone through peacefully. The women became silent, and even the pious shouts of the men gradually died away so that in that quiet place only the occasional isolated stifled cry of '*Labbayk*' was heard above the shuffling of thousands of feet and the grunts of camels.

> The cause soon became apparent. A small curl of blue smoke on the summit of the right-hand precipice suddenly caught my eye, and simultaneously with the echoing crack of the matchlock, a dromedary in front of me, shot through the heart rolled on the sands . . . Ensued terrible confusion. Women screamed . . . and men vociferated, each one striving with might and main to urge his animal beyond the place of death. But the road was narrow . . . vehicles and animals were soon jammed into a solid immovable mass, while at every shot a cold shudder ran through the huge body. Our guard, the irregular horsemen, about one thousand in number, pushed up and down . . . shouting to and ordering one another . . . No one seemed to whisper 'Crown the heights.'
>
> Presently two or three hundred Wahabis [from the Shammar] . . . sprang from their bareback camels, with their elf locks tossing in the wind, and the flaming matches of their guns casting a lurid light over their wild features. Led by the Sheríf Zayd, a brave Meccan noble . . . they swarmed up the steep, and the robbers, after receiving a few shots retired to fire upon our rear . . .[33]

The enforced halt now became a headlong flight. Boxes and belongings that were improperly secured fell from galloping beasts on to the shingle and were left, along with the dead, for the waiting looters. Camel carcasses would provide a feast for the tribe. Through the night the grim crowds hurried onwards between the looming black cliffs, their way lit by burning tar-brands. At dawn they emerged from the Valley Perilous into the open skies and sunlit peace of Wady Laymun (Valley of Limes). Here a wide babbling stream that cooled the air ran through orchards of pomegranates and other fruit trees, providing an amazing and tranquil contrast to the night of fear. In a heady atmosphere of relief the pilgrims rested before embarking on the final march. By sunset that evening everyone was filled with eager anticipation as eyes strained for the first sight of Mecca. But it was

not until 1 a.m. that the cries went up, and the entire Caravan burst
into loud thankful cries of 'Labbayk'. 'With a heartfelt "Alhamdu
Lillah",' Richard wrote, 'I looked from my litter and saw under the
chandelier of the Southern Cross the dim outlines of a large city, a
shade darker than the surrounding plain . . . There it is at last, the
bourne of long and weary travel, realising the plans and hopes of
many and many a year!'[34]

At dawn next day Richard and Mohammed performed the cere-
monial ablutions and walked swiftly to the Great Temple of Mecca
where, in the middle of the massive colonnaded plaza, stood the far-
famed *Kaabah* towards which every Muslim turns in daily prayer:

> . . . The scene is one of the wildest excitement . . . men prostrate
> themselves on the pavement . . . shedding floods of tears and pour-
> ing forth frenzied ejaculations. [Even] the most careless . . . never
> contemplate it for the first time without fear and awe.[35]

The huge stone building, measured in paces by Richard as he cir-
cumambulated it seven times (as required), was roughly 40 ft by 35 ft
and (he estimated) about 45 ft high. It was covered by a 'veil', a curtain of dull black material with Koranic verses woven into it in
shining black. A door curtain of gold thread on red silk matched the
bright band of material running around the building at two thirds of
its height. The Black Stone, kissed by all pilgrims, was fixed into the
wall in the south-eastern corner at between 4–5 ft high in a silver
mount. Believed once to have been pure white and become black by
reason of man's sins, the sacred stone was worn as smooth as polished
glass by centuries of caresses. Richard, examining it closely as he
kissed and rubbed his hands and forehead against it, thought it was
most likely 'a common aerolite'.*

The only entrance into the *Kaabah* was a narrow door, 7 ft off the
ground, into which a favoured few were hoisted in men's arms. After
days of ritual and prayer conducted in unbearable heat, barefooted on
hot stone, bare-headed and bare-shouldered in searing sun, and
thanks to the boy Mohammed, Richard managed to get into the
Kaabah. With mixed feelings he was lifted up and manhandled in

---

*Meteorite.

through the door. Looking round at the windowless walls and the door guarded by fanatics, he felt a sensation, 'akin to that of trapped rat' in the highly charged atmosphere of religious fervour. An official, the keeper of the silver padlock of the *Kaabah*, sat with him and enquired his name, nation and other particulars:

> A blunder, a hasty action, a misjudged word, a prayer or a bow, not strictly the right shibboleth, and my bones would have whitened the desert sand. This did not, however, prevent my carefully observing the scene during our long prayer, and making a rough plan with a pencil upon my white *ihram*. . .[36]

This penetration by Richard of the holiest place in Mecca must be regarded as the apogee of his adventure. The week that followed was packed with ritual, ceremony and personal incident. There was the 'stoning of the devil' where pilgrims symbolically pelt a rock set in a wall outside the town, with 'seven stones washed in seven waters'. For Richard this day almost proved disastrous when he was thrown by his donkey and landed under a rearing and bucking dromedary. Only by quick thinking – he pulled out his dagger and jabbed at the camel's belly until it moved off – did he escape injury. Then there was the six-hour walk to Mount Arafat, the visitation to which actually conferred the state of *Hajji*. Here his recollections mainly centre on a pretty girl of about 18 with whom he enjoyed an eye-to-eye flirtation. He called her 'Flirtilla' and described her as having citron-coloured skin, a voluptuous figure and – when she drew aside her veil coquettishly – a charmingly dimpled mouth, but he lost her in the crowd. There was, too, the awful 'day of sacrifice' when each pilgrim offers an animal. The smell of death and blood as thousands of sheep and goats were sacrificially slaughtered and left in the hot sun to bleed to death appalled him. He suspected that this ceremony was the root cause of the diseases which so often attacked the home-going Caravan.

By the end of 'Holy Week' Richard had satisfied all requirements of the pilgrimage, had called at all the sacred stopping places, all the mosques, had received his testimony. He was now entitled to call himself *Hajji* and don the green turban. He had met leading families and been declared by them 'Verily, a good young man.'[37] He had been summoned to dine with the *Zemzemi*, 'a person of great importance, being the guardian of some dames of high degree between Cairo and

Constantinople'.[38] This dinner is not, however, recalled because of the importance of the guest of honour, but for the dessert. In his book Richard described the sweet squares of *Raha*, made of 'a thin jelly', powdered, flavoured and scented. As a result he is widely credited by the confectionery industry as being the man who first brought 'Turkish Delight' to Europe.[39]

His discovery that there had been no Pilgrim Caravan from the East Coast for some years – pilgrims from Muscat were obliged to visit Hijaz by sea via Jeddah – was a disappointment.[40] But realising that he had accomplished everything that could be accomplished, he was suddenly overwhelmed by a longing to leave Mecca and return to the safety of Cairo. He became careless; Mohammed spotted him sketching at the opening of his *shugduf* and cried out that he would get them killed. Richard laughed and told him to look the other way and distract any busybodies.

He hired camels, sent his heavy luggage on ahead, and with Mohammed and Nur joined a caravan of donkeys to the coast. Two days later they reached Jeddah. The sight of the sea and the British flag over the Consulate acted upon him like a tonic. He found a room overlooking the harbour, ordered it swept, sprinkled with water and laid with rugs. He slept that night as he had not been able to do for months.

On the following day, because he had run out of money, it was necessary to cash the final draft provided by the R.G.S. The Arab dragoman at the British Consulate was reluctant to admit the travel-stained Afghan. Leaving Richard at the door, he went off to take advice and shortly Richard heard an English voice saying: 'Let the dirty nigger wait.' The past months had taught him patience if nothing else. He waited. Eventually the Vice-Consul, Mr Charles Cole, rose from his sick-bed to see him. Adopting a humble posture, Richard handed Cole a scrawled note which read: 'Don't recognise me; I am Dick Burton but I am not safe yet . . .' Cole could have seen few enough English travellers; such an introduction must have had a sensational effect on him. Richard visited the Consulate in secret several times during his stay in Jeddah and was always grateful for the consideration and great hospitality extended by Cole.

A few days later he booked his passage on a steamer bound for Egypt and took Mohammed and Nur aboard while he stowed his belongings. Soon afterwards he became aware of a new coolness in

Mohammed's attitude to him. Richard wished to remain in disguise until the steamer left Jeddah, but the reduction of physical danger must have blunted his performance. Something he said or did while they were on the steamer exposed his cover, for a bitter Mohammed later told Nur, 'Now I understood, your master is a sahib from India; he hath laughed at our beards.'[41]

Richard never worked out what gave him away. Perhaps Mohammed glimpsed Richard's Western clothes in his luggage. Perhaps it was simply that he had booked a first-class passage; on a British ship a first-class cabin would never have been allocated to 'a native'. Nevertheless it is some indication of Richard's mastery of disguise, for during his pilgrimage he was always in Mohammed's close company. And although the youth recognised that something was not right, his suspicions about Richard did not crystallise until after the venture was over. Soon afterwards Mohammed returned to Mecca, adequately rewarded but still cool, and on 26 September Richard sailed for Suez, mentally and physically exhausted from the physical rigours and mental stress of his adventure.

Once the S.S. *Dwarka* was under way Richard shed his disguise. Shaved, bathed and rested, he joined the passengers in Western clothes as Lieutenant Burton. So different was his appearance that none of the pilgrims on the ship recognised him as their former companion. Abdullah the Afghan was assumed to have departed Jeddah by some other means. As he sailed up the Red Sea, one of his few British fellow-passengers was William Strickland, a priest who – by a quirk of fate – happened to be a cousin of Isabel Arundell. Each time Strickland took out his prayer book Richard pointedly read from the Koran. By the end of the voyage the two men had become good friends.[42]

9

DREAMS OF AFRICA
1853–1854

When Richard sailed for Egypt it was with the intention of resting before making a second attempt to traverse Arabia, this time 'via Muwylah'. Six months of unused leave still remained to him, making a short exploration just feasible, but the heat and stress had taken a physical toll that surprised him[1] and by the time he arrived at Suez he had already abandoned the plan. He reported briefly to Norton Shaw, through the East India Company overland mail, advising his successful penetration of the core of Islam and explaining, 'My health has suffered a little from the hardships . . . upon the way. I cannot, therefore, exactly say when I shall be ready to make a second attempt.'[2]

In Cairo he assumed Arab garb so that Edward Lear and Thomas Seddon could paint him as 'the Pilgrim', and again when some fellow-officers from Sindh arrived at Shepheard's Hotel en route from Bombay to London. One of the men present would later recall:

As they sat talking and smoking, there passed repeatedly in front of them an Arab in his loose flowing robes, with head proudly erect, and the peculiar swinging stride of those sons of the desert. As he strode backwards and forwards he drew nearer and nearer to the little knot of officers till at last, as he swept by, the flying folds of his burnous brushed against one of the officers. 'Damn that nigger's impudence!' said the officer; 'if he does that again I'll kick him.' To his surprise the dignified Arab halted, wheeled round, and exclaimed, 'Well, damn it, Hawkins, that's a nice way to welcome a fellow after two years' absence.' 'By God, it's Ruffian Dick,' cried Hawkins . . .[3]

It was several weeks before Richard, alias 'Ruffian Dick'[4] – a cognomen he carried throughout his years of service in the Indian Army – next wrote to Norton Shaw, and in his letter he mentions an intriguing rumour he had heard. It would subsequently affect the direction of his entire life.

Private

Oct 53
[Recd 30 Oct]

My dear Shaw,

I hope the Soc. won't think badly of my not having written before. Couldn't. Besides, having nothing whatever to say I thought it best to say nothing. You will find 'Darb el Sharki' a most interesting route I believe & the watershed carefully considered. My direction, British Hotel, Cairo. Would the Soc. like me to go from Akabah to the Dead Sea?

Don't be astonished at the coin going sharp. At Cairo I lived for nothing – but the Hijaz is awfully expensive. As a pauper you can take no notes, and the better you travel the more you see and hear. A single camel from Medinah to Mecca [cost] £3! So old Wallin was right . . .[5]

I hear that the Geographical has been speaking about an expedition to Zanzibar. *Dhak'ilak*, as the Arabs say – 'I take refuge with you.' I shall strain every nerve to command it, or rather get the command – and if you will assist me I'm a made man . . . I will write to you next mail as I'm in an awful hurry. Mail starts instanter. Many kind wishes to you. Pray acknowledge my gratitude to the Soc. Adieu. If you see Murray or Parkyns kindest remembrances.

Yrs
R. Burton

PS. Could you get my arrival in Egypt reported in some London papers. Just to warn my friends that travel is safe.[6]

The tone of this letter conveys Richard's high spirits. He was lionised by the British in Cairo, and in London reports of his daring expedition placed his name on every man's lips.[7] In fact the Mecca journey was probably one of Richard's two greatest successes in the field of pure adventure, inasmuch as it placed him within the select group of men who penetrated and were totally accepted by people of an alien culture.[8]

Though he professed to dislike fuss, Richard loved an audience appreciative of his abilities. This grew from the openly expressed admiration of his family at his childhood precocity. He lapped up praise as his due; many of his letters and books – even his humour – seem deliberately calculated to invite approbation and esteem. But to be of value to him, such admiration had to be on his terms. He had to know that he had done well enough to deserve praise. Previous biographers have queried why, at this crucial moment, Richard did not return to London to capitalise on his achievement and reap the popularity that would inevitably have resulted from a society dedicated to opening new frontiers and making heroes. There are several obvious reasons. First, by Richard's own standards he did not regard his mission as being wholly successful (he had not crossed Arabia). Second, it was more than probable that he could not return to England under the terms of his furlough (he was supposed to be in the Middle East on his way to India, after all). And third, he was too ill with dysentery to travel anywhere.

But it is his reference to Zanzibar that stands out in the above letter. His information was obtained from Dr John Ellerton Stocks, his friend from Karachi who had stopped over at Shepheard's Hotel en route to London, where he intended to resurrect interest in his long-proposed botanic exploration of the Somalia coast. Their discussions caught Richard's imagination. In 1853 the east coast of Africa was still unexplored, the only penetration having been made by a few dedicated missionaries, but the Royal Geographical Society had been agitating since May 1849 'for the release of one or two competent officers from the East India Company's army to undertake a systematic exploration' of both Somalia and East Africa.[9]

Richard knew of Stock's plans, and his own interest had been enhanced by campfire gossip during his pilgrimage. There he had heard scarcely believable stories of the interior of Africa where, Arab slave traders claimed, there was a system of vast inland seas, and mountains of eternal snows sitting on the equator. What is more, these stories were now being given some substance by returning missionaries. It occurred to Richard that he could expand the expedition proposals made by Stocks. When he next wrote to Norton Shaw from Shepheard's Hotel, Cairo on 16 November 1853, it was a long and important letter containing a great deal of information about Richard's health, aspirations, concerns and moral attitude, he also mentioned the intriguing rumours about East Africa which, at this point, even he seemed reluctant to believe:

My dear Shaw,
    I've been laid up since writing to you – the usual dysentery which welcomes one on return from a hard trip. I won't say it was aggravated by my disgust at my failure in crossing the Peninsula but, joking apart, the 'physic' of a successful man differs wildly from that of the poor devil who has failed . . . Krapf[10] [has] just arrived from Zanzibar with discoveries about source of White Nile, Kilimanjaro & Mts of Moon which remind one of a 'de Lunatico'. I have not seen him but don't intend to miss the spectacle, especially to pump what really has been done and what remains to be done . . .
    The Bombay Govt, a short time before this, sanctioned an expedition to the Somali Coast or rather country. But Carter (the *Palinurus* Doctor) not relishing the chance of losing his cod – that misguided people are in the habit of cutting them off and hanging them as ornaments round their arms – preferred not to explore the interior.[11] Now I shall be ready next season to explore the interior, if leave can be procured . . . my wish is to attack (scientifically) Zanzibar & if I can only get pay from Govt for a few good men to accompany me (one to survey, another for physics and botany) I doubt not of our grand success. My health will probably come round in the winter as I'm already better and stronger. The month of March must see me in India & I'm ready to start for it immediately after the hot season. Want one summer for Amharic & the vulgar tongue.
    I'm working at the sketches etc which I made at Mecca and Medinah, there are artists here who can assist but none in India. So notes go on slowly especially as writing works one's brain & brain works one's belly. I am preparing a paper for the society which they

shall receive in the spring. I only hope that they understand the reason of my silence.

About Zanzibar I have plenty of sound practical reasons why a mission there is highly advisable. A scientific mission of course. It is one of the headquarters of slavery – the Americans are quietly but surely carrying off the commerce of the country – and it has very great resources quite undeveloped. As a native I found out a spy of old Mohamet Ali[12] who let me into all kinds of secrets about the country and wanted me to accompany him. I should have done so if I had not been bound for Arabia. You will ask why I now prefer Zanzibar to Arabia. Because I have now tried both sides of Arabia and see no practical results. Travelling is a joy there and nothing would delight me more than leave for 3 or 4 years to the Eastern Coast. But nothing except more discoveries of desert valleys & tribes would come of it. No horses, no spices and scant credit, as von Wrede's book – a ridiculous affair if reports here speak truly of how he collected it – will take the maidenhead of the subject. Dr Stocks tells me that at Bombay they will not oppose me, but that no one will lend a helping hand. Consequently they will require some force from without.

Anent [Dr. J. Ellerton] Stocks. I gave him a note to you and if you draw him out you will collect information about a part of Beluchistan completely unknown. The fellow writes well but is modest – shameful defect! I intended him to accompany me to Zanzibar and I verily believe he would still do it. Above all things he's an excellent chap, but a mad bitch. Very mad.

. . . I'm living in the house with Galeazzo Visconti, the revolutionist, and a young fellow called Sankey a traveller in Barbary. It – the house – is a precious scene of depravity; showing what Cairo can do at a pinch and beating the Arabian Nights all to chalks! That too when the Pasha has positively forbidden fornication! . . . We've an American Missionary woman at the hotel who proposes authorship. 'Tis to be hoped she won't write as she conversationalises. As I'm still dressed nigger fashion and called the Hadji, she funks me a few. But at dinner I catch her gimlet eyes and see the case will open, and consequently, oh Shaw!, wonderful are the tastes of Yemen which are conveyed to her 'sensorium' . . .

Pray excuse garrulity and believe me,

Ever yours
Shayk Abdullah[13]

Soon afterwards Richard had an opportunity to speak to the man who could give him first-hand information about Africa's interior. His meeting in Cairo with the African traveller and missionary, Dr Johann Ludwig Krapf, stoked up his growing enthusiasm for Africa. But it was a relevant passage in *Ptolemy* which ended his desire to explore Arabia, and caused him to transfer his attention to Africa. It read:

> Then concerning the navigation between the Aromata Promontory, [the place of seven ships generally supposed to be north of Kilwa], a Mariner of Tyre declares that a certain Diogenes, one of those sailing to India . . . when near Aromata and having the Troglodytic region on the right [some of the Somalis were cave-dwellers], reached, after twenty-five days march, the lakes whence the Nile flows and of which point Rhapta is a little more to the south.[14]

Given what Krapf had told him, and the stories he had heard from Arab traders, Richard wrote that this remarkable passage, with its confident statement, 'the Lakes whence the Nile flows', struck him like a revelation. 'It was the *mot de l'enigme*, the way to make the egg stand upright, the rending of the veil of Isis . . .'[15] For 3,000 years explorers had tried following the Nile upstream to trace the source. In a flash Richard saw a way of making history, and at the same time stultifying the old Eastern proverb, *'Facilius sit Nili caput invenire'* ('It would be easier to discover the source of the Nile').

In his next letter to Shaw, dated 16 December, Richard explained that he was still in Cairo and still suffering from the dysentery which stubbornly persisted, but that he had not wasted the time for he was working on his paper for the R.G.S. which he hoped to get to them in May. This manuscript also, ultimately, provided the base for his famous book on his *haj*. Meanwhile, letters from home brought news of the publication of his book *A Complete System of Bayonet Exercise* in London, which had been well reviewed even though it had not necessarily found favour with military chiefs since it implied, inevitably, some criticism of accepted methods of training.[16]

He told Shaw that he had lost almost three months due to illness and time was no longer on his side for further explorations in Arabia. 'If the Society wishes I will reapply for leave to Arabia . . . but Zanzibar appears to be the field.'[17] Shaw should make a point of meeting Krapf who was on his way to England, but, Richard wrote, 'he is, I hope, only my John the Baptist.' Meanwhile, by a fortunate circumstance Lord Elphinstone[18] passed through Cairo on his way to Bombay, to take up his post there as Governor. His father Mount-stuart Elphinstone[19] had been a friend of Richard's father, indeed he had been best man at Joseph Burton's wedding. It was rela-tively easy, therefore, for Richard to gain an audience with him to discuss the hints he had already made to Shaw about exploring East Africa.

By the time Shaw received the letter, Richard was on his way back to Bombay, having left Cairo on 16 January bound for Suez. He trav-elled with two men in whose company he spent a good deal of time in Cairo: the 'half-blind' traveller Charles Didier and his English companion/secretary the Abbé James Hamilton, who had also been stricken with dysentery necessitating a halt in their travels.[20] From Suez, Didier and Hamilton hired a vessel bound for Jeddah while Richard embarked on a steamer to Aden. There he spent two weeks as the guest of his old friend John Steinhaueser – nicknamed by his friends for some inexplicable reason 'Styggins' – who had recently been appointed Civil Surgeon at the Aden garrison.[21]

Steinhaueser, who had a Swiss father and English mother, was edu-cated at Harrow and Oxford, and went out to India in December 1845. He met Richard in the following year when he was posted to the 18th B.N.I. at Karachi for a time before being sent on to Hyderabad. He studied Hindustani and, like Richard, had been intro-duced to some of the tales from the *Arabian Nights* in the process. Richard's lengthy love affair with the fables of the *Arabian Nights* cer-tainly began in India, but it is probably during these weeks in Aden, while he was en route to Bombay, that he and Steinhaueser decided to collaborate on an English translation. At the time there was no seri-ous plan to publish the bawdy stories; they read and translated them, aloud, for amusement during the long hot evenings. They enjoyed a mutual fantasy of a semi-retired future in the south of France near Canebière, which Richard regarded as 'a bit of Africa in Europe . . . For years, my greatest friend, Dr Steinhaueser and myself indulged in visions of a country cottage, where we would pass our days in ham-mocks . . . and never admit books or papers, pens or ink, letters or telegrams. This retreat was intended to be a rest . . . in order to pre-pare for senility.'[22]

What of Isabel Arundell all this time? She was living the life of a

dutiful unmarried daughter and, when the news about Richard's success broke, was helping to prepare her younger sister, Blanche, for her
début.[23] When details reached her, either from newspaper reports
placed by the R.G.S. or possibly through general gossip, she was
elated for him. In her diary she recorded:

> Richard has just come back with flying colours from Mecca; but
> instead of coming home, he has gone to Bombay to rejoin his regi-
> ment. I glory in his glory . . . but I am alone and unloved. Love can
> illuminate the dark roof of poverty, and can lighten the fetters of a
> slave; the most miserable position of humanity is tolerable with its
> support, the most splendid irksome without . . . if I could but go
> through life trusting one faithful heart . . . There is no joy for me;
> the lustre of life is gone. How swiftly my sorrow followed my joy!
> I can laugh, dance, sing as others do, but there is a dull gnawing
> always at my heart.[24]

Isabel was 22 years old in the spring of 1854. Recognising her daughter's fascination with the East (though doubtless not the source of her
interest) her mother gave her a copy of Disraeli's *Tancred* as a birthday gift.[25] It became one of Isabel's favourite books.

Richard reported for duty in good time on 21 February.[26] His first
priority after doing so was to complete his paper on the pilgrimage for
the R.G.S.[27] After that he concentrated his energies on obtaining permission to lead an expedition to Africa. He knew that not only had
the R.G.S. long advocated an exploration of Somalia and East Africa,
but that questions had been asked in the House of Commons as to
why this objective had not yet been achieved.[28] In 1850 and again in
1851, proposals were made by Dr Henry Carter and Dr John Ellerton
Stocks (both good friends of Richard's prior to his departure from
India in 1849), to do so. These plans had plenty of support but the
R.G.S. rejected them because, although much valuable information
might be gained by skirting the coast, the proposed ventures did not
'fulfil the primary and great object of the . . . Geographical Society
which . . . is to have the interior explored'.[29] It was generally con-
ceded that the expedition lacked an able, adventurous, suitably
experienced young man as leader. With his much-vaunted success in
Arabia and the support of the Committee of the R.G.S., Richard had
high hopes of being that man. Certainly, he had no desire to stay in

India where, despite his achievements, he was still surprisingly unpopular.

One Burton researcher suggests that Richard 'was disliked because he was both a man of action and "too clever by half" – a daunting combination. Add to this his youthful arrogance and intolerance; his weird habit of going native and his unsettling skill with local languages, and young run-of-the-mill Englishmen of the time would have found him uncomfortable company. The English (not the Scots or Welsh) have always mistrusted cleverness, whereas on the continent, where Burton was brought up, intellect has always been admired and cherished. His companions must have been as puzzling to him as he was to them.'[30] It seems scarcely credible, now, that Richard's general unpopularity was due to his propensity for 'going native' and airing his views that the customs of the British in India were ridiculous and inappropriate. But even Isabel, who turned a blind eye to any failings in Richard, confirmed the point in her memoir, saying 'he did not stay long at Bombay after he rejoined his Regiment. He was not popular in it, and he disliked the routine . . .'[31] There was no room in the Indian Army for non-conformists.

However, Richard did have support in India among some powerful men, Elphinstone for one; and also James Grant Lumsden, a senior Member of Council of the Bombay Government with whom Richard had become acquainted on the ship between Aden and Bombay. Richard was still travelling as an Arab, wearing the robes and green turban of an accredited *Hajji*, with an African servant called Salmin and an Arab butler. Lumsden noticed him one day and remarked to a companion 'what a clever face that Arab has', whereupon Richard turned and addressed him in English.[32] Lumsden invited Richard to stay at his house 'Belair' in Bombay, 'on the Mazagoon side of the island' and Richard accepted the offer of luxurious accommodation with alacrity.[33] Here he worked on the manuscript of his three-volume work *A Personal Narrative of a Pilgrimage to Meccah and Medinah*, using an Indian clerk to make a 'fair copy' of his draft for the publisher.[34]

A month later an official letter was forwarded with a warm recommendation from the Bombay Council that Richard lead an exploratory expedition to Somalia, accompanied by Dr Stocks, and Lieutenant G.E. Herne of the 1st Bombay European Regiment of Fusiliers.[35] To enable him to prepare for the expedition while he awaited formal acceptance by the Court of Directors in London (which seems to have been regarded as a mere formality in India), he was transferred temporarily from the 18th B.N.I. into the Political Department and allowed to return to Aden with a grant of £1,000.[36] In London at a meeting of the Royal Geographical Society, Richard's paper on his *Haj* captivated the audience.[37]

In Aden, while he waited for the official letter of permission to arrive, Richard applied to be formally examined in Arabic and began working at the Somali language, aided by a grammar written by his old rival C.P. Rigby,[38] and acquiring as much information as he could about the geography and anthropology of the country. His unpopularity in Bombay followed him to Aden, where he was received coldly by many staff officers whose 'active jealousy . . . thwarted all my projects'.[39] He read the official reports of the few British officers who had already attempted to visit Somalia[40] and trawled for new information among native sources in the port; Arab and Somali traders, prostitutes, native fishermen. In particular he wished to visit Harar, the 'forbidden' walled capital city of Ethiopia, which was said to be built of stone. At the time no European even knew the precise position of the city, despite the fact that it lay only 10 days by camel from the coast, due to a native superstition that the entrance of the first Christian in Harar would precipitate its downfall. Richard also felt strongly that Berbera, on the Horn of Africa, was potentially a far better situation for a British base than Aden, on the grounds of climate, water and other vital supplies, as well as easier access to the Red Sea.

When the long-awaited official permission finally arrived it was somewhat disappointing. It noted and approved Richard's plan to visit Harar and survey the coast around Berbera before travelling south to Zanzibar for the start of 'his more important expedition westward'. It accepted the Bombay Government's recommendations that the officers should proceed, with full pay, expedition expenses of 500 rupees a month, the free supply of surveying equipment, and free transport in Navy vessels. But the period of furlough granted to accomplish its objectives was limited to only one year. Furthermore, because of the death of a member of a previous survey expedition, the sanction was conditional:

Lt. Burton must be positively enjoined not to incur any immoderate

risks . . . he should carefully feel his way and not proceed unless he
has reasonable grounds in believing that his life, and that of his associates, will not be seriously endangered . . . [This expedition] is to be
considered not official but undertaken by Lt. Burton as a private
traveller, the Government giving no more protection to him than
they would do to any individual totally unconnected with the Service.
Lt. Burton seems eminently qualified to conduct such an expedition
which requires not only peculiar attainments, but the combination of
energy and perseverance with prudence and discretion . . .[41]

Meanwhile two further occurrences swung Richard's fate on its
hinges. Shortly after his arrival in Aden he was stunned to receive
news that John Ellerton Stocks had died of a cerebral haemorrhage in
London. Richard was deeply attached to his closest friends, and was
always emotionally affected when any of them died. But Stocks' death
also affected the expedition. He had been a knowledgeable and enthusiastic botanist and was, as a well-qualified medical practitioner,
irreplaceable in the team. Herne was the botanic acolyte of Stocks,
but he had nothing approaching the knowledge of the older man;
Herne's value to Richard lay in his surveying, knowledge of the new
science of photography, and mechanical engineering. Still, there was
nothing for it, Herne would have to take over as team botanist, and
Lieut. William Stroyan of the Indian Navy, 'one of the best
astronomers and surveyors . . . in the Indian Navy', was recruited as
third man.[42] The formal primary objective of the expedition now
became geographic rather than botanic.

The second piece of news was that James Outram, now Brigadier-
General Outram, had been posted to the troubled British port of
Aden as the Political Resident, which effectively placed Richard under
Outram's command. As Burton later wrote in an unpublished memoir
of Outram, he had met his new Commander socially only a short time
previously: 'we met at times in Bombay at James Grant Lumsden's
house . . .'[43] But Richard recalled that when 51-year-old Outram
(gracefully called by his old rival Napier 'the Bayard of India') arrived
to take up his post in Aden,

he was in bad health, hardly left the house and looked a weary old
man with yellow skin and a bloated nose like a nutmeg grater . . .
[he was] hipped and disgusted. His temper had become savage

rather than fiery as in his youth. It was reported that when tiger
hunting he and his brother Francis, who suicided himself in 1829,
quarrelled so violently that they exchanged rifle shots . . . he would
brook no rival.[44]

Outram and Burton had never been able to agree on Charles Napier's
policies in Sindh, and, said Richard,

> . . . Nor personally did Outram and I agree. In his youth he had
> formed a plan of exploring East Central Africa and I believe he had
> submitted [plans] to the Government, but when he came to
> Command he was unwilling to incur the responsibility of allowing
> an officer to carry out what he had proposed. His excuse was the
> imminent risk of life and the trouble that a murder would cause.
> And here, considered personally, he was right. But I found it hard to
> be opposed by a man who had himself proposed to do the same
> thing . . .[45]

The fierceness of Outram's opposition is strange when only a short
time earlier (November 1852) he had joined the R.G.S. in backing
Richard's initial proposals. It was almost certainly a genuine concern
for the younger man which caused his change of heart.

Little was known about Harar, but that knowledge – from explorers who had attempted to reach the city and failed – indicated a
barbaric, aggressive and bloodthirsty regime. The reigning prince,
Aboo Bekr, even imprisoned his brothers and members of his family
in dungeons in his palace. Throughout the period of preparation for
the expedition, Outram did everything he could to place obstacles in
Richard's path on the grounds that the proposals had no scientific
value and the expedition was merely a wild adventure, with potentially fatal consequences, by a set of reckless young men.[46] It was
generally felt that there was limited danger involved in *coastal* explorations of Somalia, but several expeditions to Harar and the interior
had been attempted since Dr Krapf's abortive mission in 1841.
Lieutenants Barker and Christopher of the Indian Navy, M. Rochel
d'Hericourt and Dr Beke had all begun, and been forced to abandon,

---

* Burton lists these, and other authorities on the area, in *First Footsteps*: Vol i.
p.xxviii.

expeditions to Harar.* Outram felt so strongly about the dangers that he asked Dr Buist, Editor of the *Bombay Times*, to write unfavourably about Richard's expedition,[47] as confirmed by Buist's hindsight editorial in May of the following year. 'In August last, Col. Outram, then only a fortnight in office . . . pointed out to us most emphatically the extreme unwisdom of the so-called Somali Expedition and the tragedy that . . . was almost certain to follow the wild adventure of a set of reckless young men.'[48]

Recognising the formidable nature of his adversary, and in an attempt to reduce opposition, Richard agreed to three amendments to his plans which, ultimately, would prove disastrous. First, he agreed to postpone the expedition into the interior of Africa until the end of the famous Somali coastal trading event called the 'Berbera Fair' in April of the following year (1855), so that the members of the expedition could travel part of the way within one of the larger caravans returning homewards. Second, he reversed his original intention 'to march in a body using Berbera as a base of operations westwards to Harar, and thence in a South-easterly direction to Zanzibar'. He split the group, giving each member an individual project and 'as a thrust at the pessimists and the faint-hearted, he decided to travel alone to "the forbidden city" of Harar, the religious capital of Ethiopia'.[49] Third, and most significant, he agreed to take an extra team member in the capacity of Assistant Surveyor and Collector of Zoological Specimens.[50] 'I have the honour to assure you that to the best of my judgment,' he wrote to Outram, 'Lt. Speke's presence is likely to be useful to the Expedition, and that I should wish him to accompany it provided he is placed under my orders.'[51]

John Hanning Speke was the son of a Somerset squire. He was 27 years old, 6 years younger than Richard, at the time of their first meeting in late September 1854.[52] He was 6 ft tall, slender, with blue eyes and tawny fair hair; an archetypal English officer in appearance. Speke had sought out Richard Burton at Outram's suggestion and asked to join the expedition, saying that 'being tired of life he had come to be killed in Africa', a remark which Richard took to be 'a whimsical affectation'.[53] He noticed that Speke was 'full of energy and life . . . a highly nervous temperament, a token of endurance, and long wiry, but not muscular limbs, that could cover the ground at a swinging pace'.[54] He had some limited experience in surveying having mapped the territory over which he had hunted in Tibet, but he spoke no languages other than limited Hindustani. His place on the expedition was somewhat superfluous, for both Herne and Stroyan were far more experienced men. But Speke was desperate to get to Africa for shooting and Richard, whose own hopes had so often been blocked by authority, felt a great sympathy; ' . . . he did not even know the names of the coastal towns. I saw him engage as protectors or *abbans* any Somali donkey boys who could speak English. I saw that he was going to lose his money and his "leave" and his life. Why should I have cared? I do not know . . . I applied officially for him and thus saved his furlough and his money by putting him on full service.'[55]

Speke has been described as he was at that time, in an excellent biography. His 'self-confidence was absolute, his charm and unrestrained enthusiasm a delight . . . the outstanding quality was . . . an innocence and with innocence, utter contentment.' However, admits his biographer, 'though Speke's plans to visit Africa were made with characteristic care, they were founded on sadly inadequate information.'[56] Like other writers, Speke's biographer believes that there was an initial mutual attraction between Burton and Speke, based on Speke's fascination with the charismatic successful adventurer and Burton's lifelong enjoyment of a 'younger brother' figure at his heels.

Speke applied to join the Indian Army at the age of 17 and was accepted a year later in 1844. He served in the 46th Regiment of Bengal Native Infantry for the requisite ten years, earning service medals in several skirmishes including the Multan campaign (which had caused Richard so much anguish when his application to participate was turned down in 1849). By 1854 Speke was entitled to a three-year furlough, which he had decided to spend partly visiting his family in England and partly indulging in his favourite pastime, shooting and hunting. He had already spent a great deal of time, whenever he could get leave in fact, doing just this in India and Tibet, as a satisfactory alternative to 'wasting my time and running into debt' like many of his fellow subalterns. As a result he had a huge collection of stuffed and mounted fauna which was to form the basis of a personal museum at his family home, Jordans, near Ilminster in Somerset. 'There are now but few animals,' he boasted confidently, 'to be found in either India, Tibet or the Himalaya Mountains, specimens of which have not fallen victims to my gun.'[57]

Before returning to England he had decided to spend some time shooting in Africa, intending that the specimens and trophies to be 'bagged' in that unexplored country would help to create a unique gallery of exotic fauna. In Speke, shooting as a sport amounted almost to a mania, but it must be regarded in the light of the times. Speke was unusually passionate, but he was far from unique among his contemporaries. The majority of upper and middle-class Englishmen regarded hunting and shooting as a *raison d'être*; Speke was merely more dedicated than most. Surviving letters between Speke and his close friends James Augustus Grant (whom he met in 1847) and Captain Hay, the Assistant Commissioner at Fort Kagna, are full of references to guns, kills and 'letting fly' at tigers, wild pigs, jackals, bears and deer. These men were fully fledged 'insiders' who wallowed happily in all aspects of the Raj and its panoply of tiffin, polo, pig-sticking, military parades and scores of inexpensive natives as servants. That is to say, they were the norm.[58]

It was Richard who was unusual. He had grown up in a hunting household; both his father and brother Edward were rabid hunters, and he was tolerant of their fixation without ever catching the bug himself. Richard occasionally joined a shoot in India, but he was never enthusiastic about killing animals after an occasion when he accidentally shot a monkey and to his great distress its screams and sobs sounded exactly like those of a wounded child. Since then he rarely shot an animal other than 'for the pot' or in self-protection, and was a very careful and accurate shot. This attitude did not however apply to game birds, or birds regarded as 'vermin' such as crows, which he shot happily.[59]

In Speke's books, written after he and Burton became enemies in 1859, he claimed it had *always* been his intention to cross Somalia and proceed to the 'Lunae Montes . . . the range delineated on Ptolemy's map, nowadays better known as the Mountains of the Moon'. In this region, he claimed, he had proposed to do some serious hunting of 'species of animals hitherto unknown', while at the same time surveying the country.[60] But this statement is not supported by letters written by Speke at the time he met Richard. Exploration and surveying then played very minor parts in his plans; primarily he wanted to hunt and neither the interior of Somalia, the Mountains of the Moon nor the Nile were ever mentioned by him. Furthermore, Speke had suffered from 'ophthalmic attacks in childhood, which rendered reading a painful task'.[61] On his own admission he abandoned his books in favour of 'bird nesting' and country pursuits, so that though he had received an adequate education it was a limited one.[62] He was neither intellectual nor a classicist, and it is doubtful that he had ever read Ptolemy before he met Richard. In short, as we shall see, these latter claims were a fiction invented by Speke to justify (to himself, as much as his readers) his subsequent behaviour.

At their first meeting Richard explained the basis of his proposed explorations; his conversations with Krapf, his interpretations of Ptolemy, the stories of the Arabs. Later, he stated categorically that when they first met, Speke 'had never thought of the Nile, and he was astonished at my views, which he deemed impractical. He had no qualifications for the excursion he proposed to himself, except that of being a good sportsman. He was ignorant of the native races in Africa, he had brought with him almost £400 worth of cheap and useless guns and revolvers . . . which the Africans would have rejected with disdain . . .'[63] It was certainly hunting and guns that formed the main topic of most of Speke's surviving correspondence, such as the following letter giving his contemporary reaction to his first meeting with Richard:

Aden 10th October 1854

My Dear Hay,

I don't remember . . . whether I told you of my trip to Thibet . . . I got the finest Yak (bull) there ever shot and have sent it together [with] some other specimens to the French exhibition to be finally deposited . . . at my house in England.

I . . . came away here prepared for a shooting trip of two years but on arrival I found a party going into the same country on Gov't account that was approved by old Outram here, and he of course sticking to his old opinion objected to my going as he said the risk of life could not be compensated for by any discoveries that could be made. So I sat down and talked with the Captain of the expedition, Burton, who went in disguise to Mekka, that done there was very little difficulty in getting myself sent on duty to go with them. So now, instead of a three year furlough, I am on unlimited duty, clearing all pay and allowances and doing what I of all things most desired . . .

J.H. Speke[64]

Speke's letters to Captain James Grant[65] tell the same story; he writes of 'going across to Somalia' to hunt, but mentions no intention of striking inland for exploration purposes. Colonel Outram, he told Grant, was absolutely set against his going (Outram therefore was consistent, and not merely opposed to Richard *per se*). Outram claimed that the Somalis had such a wild, inhospitable nature that it meant certain death to a European to set foot there, so much so, Speke wrote, 'that I thought all was up . . . but I have managed to square myself with the party going on Gov't account.'[66]

> Burton goes on 20th to Harrur . . . a place hitherto hermetically sealed. Of course he goes in disguise and cannot return until March next. I go on the 15th to Bundur . . . strike southwest and make a tour of 600 miles collecting specimens of Zoo-ology and mapping my route, while the other two squat on their haunches at Berbera and make notes till we join them . . .[67]

Speke was, as can be seen by his letters, eager – indeed he was very gratified – at having been allowed to join the expedition. Richard had no extra funding to support another member of the team; the £1,000 promised by the Bombay Government was to be paid in quarterly instalments, and the first £250 had already been expended on equipment. So it was an act of kindness on his part. Speke happily agreed to cover his own expenses and purchase some much-needed supplies when Richard confidently predicted that if they were successful they could rely on all expedition costs being met. Speke was to be, he wrote, 'a Jack-of-all-trades, assisting everybody, looking after the interests of the men, portioning out their rations, setting the guards, and collecting specimens of natural history'.[68]

Almost the last thing Richard did prior to leaving Aden was to be examined in Arabic by Lieut. Robert Lambert Playfair.[69] Playfair was Personal and Political Assistant to Outram, and a friend of C.P. Rigby and Brigadier Coghlan (Outram's successor). None of these men liked Richard. Playfair initially asked the distinguished Arabist, Professor George Percy Badger, to preside at Richard's examination, as he had recently done for Playfair's own test. Badger declined, for having been warned by Playfair that Richard could be 'very vindictive' he was unwilling to incur animosity.[70] Playfair therefore conducted the tests himself, sending the papers to Badger afterwards. 'After looking them over,' Badger told Richard many years later, 'I sent them back to him with a note eulogising your attainments and . . . remarking on the absurdity of the Bombay Committee being made to judge your proficiency inasmuch as I did not believe that any of them possessed a tithe of the knowledge of Arabic you did.'[71]

Despite Badger's plaudits, and in what can only be attributed to the jealousy that Richard always claimed Playfair felt, Playfair recommended to the Bombay Committee that Richard be failed in the examination. This petty act was monstrous in view of the time Richard had recently spent living with significant success as an Arab among Arabs. However, Playfair had his way, and Richard was duly 'plucked' (failed) in Arabic.

Richard knew nothing of this at the time. Having already spent far too long in Aden, where he found the atmosphere stultifying, he was eager to be away from the dull routine of meaningless parades and the pretentious, insular society. It was scarcely possible to address a woman twice without the entire camp assuming an 'affair' was in progress, he commented sourly, 'a pleasant predicament for those who really love women's society'.[72]

At the first possible moment, he left Aden for the siren-like attractions of Africa's mysterious interior.

10

DISASTER IN
THE HORN OF AFRICA
1854–1855

Speke was reluctant to sit about in Aden until Richard's expected return in March, nor did he wish to join the Survey Team of Herne and Stroyan 'squatting on the beach' at Berbera. Richard suggested he sail to Kurayat, on a specific mission. He was to travel into the coastal mountain region, 'to trace the celebrated Wady Nogal [in the north-east of Somalia], noting its watershed . . . to purchase horses and camels for the future use of the Expedition, and to collect specimens of the reddish earth, which according to older African travellers, denotes the presence of gold dust'.[1] Richard himself recruited some of Speke's men, including an *abban* (guide/interpreter) called Samuntar who came from Bunder Goray, a small harbour roughly half-way between Berbera and the most easterly point of the Somali coast. He seemed, therefore, ideally placed to act as guide and interpreter for Speke, whose only knowledge of languages other than English was a limited amount of Hindustani. Unfortunately, Samuntar knew no English; he spoke Arabic and also 'a smattering of Hindustani'. This placed Speke in a somewhat unenviable position but presumably he accepted the situation; he was not known for docility and he was no worse off than had he recruited a Somali donkey boy off the wharf at Aden, which had been his original intention.

A week after Speke left Aden, Richard departed on 29 October 1854, once again in the guise of his alter ego *Hajji* Abdullah. His destination was the port of Zayla in Somalia, which was under the rule of Chief Sharmarkay, a British sympathiser who had once entertained Krapf. He landed to the well-remembered sounds of Islam. 'Again the melodious chant of the Muezzin,' he wrote, 'no evening bell can compare with it for solemnity and beauty – and in the neighbouring mosque the loudly intoned . . . "Allaho Akbar", far superior to any organ, rang in my ear . . . I fell asleep feeling once more at home.'[2] He was delayed in the port for 26 days, enjoyable 'days of sleep, and pipes, and coffee', which he spent preparing for his march to Harar and mingling with the multi-ethnic but wholly Islamic population.

The long delay in his setting off was due to a war which had broken out between the Governor of Zayla (Al *Hajji* Sharmarky) and the Sultan of Harar over the murder of Sharmarkay's adopted son. The result was that the Sultan had expelled all strangers from the city of Harar and the access route between the city and the coast – the Isa Somal, normally used by traders and slave caravans – was closed. Also smallpox was said to be raging in the interior and terrified inhabitants en route were reported to be preventing travellers from entering their villages.

It was not smallpox that Richard contracted during this period, however, but syphilis.[3] That he was captivated by the Somali women is evident by his descriptions in *First Footsteps*; with their lustrous hair plaited and twined with flowers, their 'long big eyes, broad brows . . . rich brown complexions and round faces, they greatly resemble the stony beauties of Egypt . . . One of their peculiar charms is a soft, low and plaintive voice . . . Always an excellent thing in a woman, here it has an undefinable charm. I have often lain awake for hours listening to the conversations . . . [sounding] in my ears rather like music than mere utterance.'[4]

Two women are specifically mentioned by him in his account of his visit to Zayla in *First Footsteps in East Africa*; both were daughters of Sharmarkay by different mothers. The first was a young, long-haired daughter of an Indian woman who was 'much admired . . . she coquettes by combing, dancing, singing and slapping slave-girls whenever an adorer may be looking'; second, 'a matron of Abyssinian descent, as her skin, scarcely darker than a gypsy's . . . and her gaudily fringed dress, denote . . . she passes her day superintending the slave-girls and weaving mats . . . We soon made acquaintance . . .'[5]

'There are no harlots in Somaliland,' he wrote, 'but there are plenty of wives who, because of the inactivity of their husbands, prostitute their bodies without scruple. The man makes his intention clear by nods and smiles and shameless finger gestures. If the woman smiles, Venus rejoices . . .' However, the Somalis placed great value on virginity in unmarried women; 'in cases of scandal the [bride's] tribe revenges its honour upon the man.'[6] It therefore seems more likely that the woman who infected Richard was either the second, the 'matron', or one of Sharmarkay's numerous slave-girls, for as an honoured guest these were made available to Richard.

So well did he integrate within the general community that he sometimes led the prayers in the mosque.[7] Most days he received visitors; Arabs, Somalis, Persians and Indians flocked to the house Sharmarkay had provided for him. Over coffee and pipes he often entertained them with the best-known poems and stories from *The Arabian Nights*. All across the Orient the storyteller is a welcome guest at any fireside, and Richard's bawdy renderings were greeted rapturously wherever he went. Commenting on the *Arabian Nights*, some thirty years before his published translation, on its contrasts of 'genuine pearls of wisdom' and 'ribald obscenity', he said:

> The most familiar of books in England, next to the Bible, it is one of the least known, the reason being that about one-fifth is utterly unfit for translation; and the most sanguine Orientalist would not dare to render literally more than three-quarters of the remainder.[8]

In addition to storytelling *Hajji* Abdullah drew horoscopes, read palms and could perform a few simple magic tricks. No wonder the inhabitants could not keep away from the house of this fascinating young visitor. By 2 p.m. each afternoon there would come a loud clamour at the door; if he was slow to answer he would be humorously accused of hiding a Christian inside. After a while even Mohammed Sharmarkay – elder son of the old chief, an educated patrician man of about 30 – began calling to discuss books and theology, and to play a form of draughts called *Shahh*. But Richard's occupations were not all cerebral; often he went on excursions with the tribesmen, or joined them in spear practice, and though he could not match the Somalis' (still) unequalled ability to jump, he wrote, 'I soon acquired the reputation of being the strongest man in Zayla; this is perhaps the easiest way of winning respect from a barbarous people, who honour body, and degrade mind to mere cunning.'[9]

As travelling companions Richard hired Mohammed Mahmud, a member of the Hamal tribe, Gulad, a Somali from Berbera (both men had served in the police force at Aden), and Abdi Abokr – a Somali whose name quaintly translated to 'End of Time'. 'End of Time' was an illiterate 'hedge priest'; he had little knowledge of Islamic theology but he could recite part of the Koran. Despite the fact that Richard was initially amused by 'End of Time' and his polite fund of quotations for every occasion, it was Governor Sharmarkay's assurance that he regarded the 40-year-old Abokr as an adopted son, and that he was consequently in possession of many 'state secrets', which guaranteed him a place in Richard's guard.

Towards the end of November Richard lost patience with the tales of smallpox and of murdering brigands on the road, suspecting that they were the mere devices of his hospitable host to prevent him from travelling. Old Sharmarkay could not understand Richard's urge to travel to Harar, but it is clear he knew *Hajji* Abdullah was, for all his understanding of Islam, at least allied to the English, for he told Richard, 'If the English wish to take Harar, let them send me 500 soldiers; if not, I can give you all information concerning it.' But seeing Richard's determination he began to offer constructive help, in the hope, Richard thought, of deriving some benefit from the expedition. Camels and fine riding mules were procured. An *abban* called Raghi, of the Isa tribe, two plump women cooks aged about 30 nicknamed Sheherazad and Dunyazad (after the sisters in *The Arabian Nights*), a one-eyed lad called Yusuf, a number of nameless porters and fifty baggage donkeys swelled the entourage. On parting Sharmarkay provided his guest with a *firman* as passport, and letters of introduction which would ensure a friendly reception in villages along the route.[10]

In Somalia, *Hajji* Abdullah was once again a well-to-do merchant; he rode a grandly accoutred white mule and his person bristled with revolvers. He was, said Richard, 'a grave and reverend Signor, with rosary in hand and Koran on lips . . . he talks at dreary length about Holy Places, writes a pretty hand, has read and can recite much poetry . . . and feels equally at home whether sultan or slave sit upon his counter. He has a wife and children at home . . .'[11] Sheherazad, however, who had once visited Aden, was vaguely suspicious of his credentials, refusing ever to meet his eye.

His book, *First Footsteps in East Africa*, is his day-to-day journal of this journey, with sage and often humorous comments added. For many Burton scholars it is the most entertaining of all his works. He records the inevitable difficulties of travel during the dry season, heat, lack of water and fresh grass for the animals, the pleasures of the journey such as breathtaking scenery, the conversations with people he met, the weather. His observations of the country, its peoples, languages, customs and geology are so acute and fresh that over a century later his book is still being used as a standard work. 'First Footsteps,' writes the modern anthropologist Dr I.M. Lewis, 'remains the best general description of northern Somali society . . .'[12] The African trait of telling a visitor what is most likely to make the visitor happy, regardless of the truth (e.g. a point on the map predicted as several hours' march might in fact be one of several days), only gradually dawned on Richard. Equally their love of scare-mongering; for instance, he was often warned that his pale skin would be flayed off him in Harar.

As always in his travels, he took particular notice of women; old women were usually described in unflattering terms (Burton was, after all, only 33 at this time) but he always had an eye for a pretty face; 'the first really pretty face seen by me in the Somali country,' he says, appreciatively describing one girl's rich nut-brown skin and special grace of movement, her full lips and eyes of jet and pearl, her svelte figure and long neck. 'As a tribute to her prettiness I gave her some cloth, tobacco and . . . salt; her husband stood by and though the preference was marked he displayed neither anger nor jealousy.'[13] Almost uniquely in early books by Europeans on Africa, his references to wildlife and hunting are few. He joined an unsuccessful elephant hunt (elephants were great destroyers of crops), and wrote of the methods used to kill the animals with distaste; he shot at a lion to scare it off, and killed gazelles to feed his people. Frequent, oblique references to his feverish ill health over Christmas and through early January (which he blames on colic due to bad water at the coast), and to the rough and ready cauterising treatments offered by his *abban* lead one to suspect, with the knowledge of hindsight, that the early stages of syphilis were causing him some discomfort. After eight years' military service in India it is unlikely that he would not have recognised the symptoms. It is probable that he treated himself with the mercury pills he always carried in his medical chest for his recurrent ophthalmia.[14]

As he neared Harar his companions, plainly frightened, begged to be left behind. At the last moment Richard decided to abandon his oriental disguise and enter Harar as an Englishman to prevent being mistaken for a Turk because of his white skin. Englishmen, he reasoned, were an unknown quantity in Africa, but the Turks were known, feared and hated. He wrote a letter of introduction to the Emir in English, forging the signature of the Political Officer at Aden, and another to Lieutenant Herne containing all his notes which he 'entrusted to End of Time in case of accident'. Then, accompanied by only two of his guards he went on through the thickly forested valleys where everyone they met prophesied that they were 'dead men'. He had his first sight of the hilltop city of grey stone from two miles away. As a spectacle he thought it was something of 'a disappointment; nothing conspicuous appeared but two grey minarets of rude shape: many would have grudged exposing three lives to win so paltry a prize. But of all who have attempted, none have ever succeeded in entering that pile of stone.'[15]

He approached the gates with a cool, swaggering air that he was far from feeling, and demanded admittance. After a lengthy delay he was shown into the throne-room of the Emir; 'I walked into a vast hall, a hundred feet long, between two rows of Galla spear men . . . they were large [and] half-naked . . . standing like statues with fierce movable eyes, each one holding, with its butt end on the ground, a huge spear with a head the size of a shovel . . . I had a six-shooter concealed in my waist-belt, and determined at the first show of excitement to run up to the Amir and put it to his head, if it were necessary, to save my own life . . .'[16] The 'bigoted prince whose least word was death' was a thin and anaemic young man of about 25 with slightly bulging eyes. He was grandly dressed in crimson flowing robes edged with white fur and a white turban wound round a conical crimson cap, and resembled, thought Richard, a small Indian Rajah. Surrounding him was his court, and more of the sinister-looking royal guard.

Richard extended a confident greeting: a loud 'Peace be upon ye!' in Arabic. Whereupon the young man extended his hand, 'bony and yellow as a kite's claw, [and] snapped his thumb and middle finger. Two chamberlains stepping forward, held my forearms, and assisted me to bend low over the finger, which however I did not kiss, being naturally averse to performing that operation upon any but a woman's hand.'[17] To Richard's relief his subsequent diplomatic enquiries after the Sultan's health and a polite speech about the changes of Political Agents in Arabia were well received and His Highness smiled graciously.

Following the audience, Richard and his two servants were shown to a room in the Emir's second palace which they were told to regard as their home while in Harar, and fed before being taken for a detailed inquisition by the Treasurer about the purpose of their visit. Richard managed to turn the conversation to the possible establishment of friendly commercial relations between England and Harar, and left the meeting feeling reasonably confident that his forged credentials had been accepted. When they returned to their room, however, he found that his servant's weapons had been confiscated and taken to 'a safe place', which led him to believe that his position was not so secure as he had formerly supposed. The unease this generated was compounded by the knowledge that he was closely watched the entire time he was in the palace. This meant he was never able to write or sketch but, recalling the old belief that a Christian would be the cause of the downfall of the city, he proceeded with extreme caution. Only when he walked outside the city walls could he put pen to paper.

His anthropological studies were not affected by the ban on writing. He was particularly fascinated to learn, whether from first- or second-hand knowledge is not divulged, that among the Galla women the vaginal muscles were abnormally developed. 'A woman can exert them as to cause pain to a man, and, when sitting on his thighs, she can induce the orgasm without moving any other part of her person,' he wrote. His research into religions and theology was also furthered while in the city. At a reading and discussion of the Koran one day he was able to explain a theological point that had escaped the elders. Their approbation led to a further interview with the Emir.

Richard was in Harar for ten days, the last six of which were spent trying to obtain permission to leave, between interminable interviews with ministers. On one notable occasion he was allowed to examine the Sultan's antiquarian library ('the only truly valuable MS in the place was a fine old copy of the Koran'), on another the Sultan's *mullah* cast Richard's horoscope.[18] Each day brought a fresh excuse to detain them, and each day the trio became more and more anxious. Richard wrote of living in acute fear of his life and those of his servants; an indicator that he was a brave man rather than a fearless one, an important difference. Finally, after promising to send a British physician to the Emir who was suffering from a bronchial infection, they were given leave to depart:

> Long before dawn . . . the mules were saddled, bridled and charged with our scanty luggage. After a hasty breakfast we . . . mounted and pricked through the desert streets. Suddenly my weakness and sickness left me – so potent a drug is joy! – we passed the gates loudly salaming to the warders . . . a weight of care and anxiety fell from me like a cloak of lead.[19]

They hurried away from the city hardly daring to believe they would not be pursued,* and their arrival in the first village was the signal for loud rejoicing, word having been passed along that they had been killed. They pushed on but as soon as they reached the safety of the Girhi mountains Richard called a halt and made camp. He wanted to make maximum use of the information he had acquired before he forgot any of it. He gathered a small team around him: a banished citizen of Harar, an old Bedouin, and Ali Shar, a poet renowned for his wit and eloquence.

> . . . his linguistic sagacity enabled me to perform a feat of no ordinary difficulty, that of drawing out a grammatical sketch of the language . . . Our hours were spent in unremitting toil; we began at sunrise, the hut was ever crowded with Bedouin critics, and it was late at night before the manuscript was laid by. On the evening of the third day my literati started upon their feet, and shook my hand, declaring that I knew as much as they did . . .[20]

From this labour Richard produced a Harari grammar and vocabulary. He also concluded that the people of Harar were a distinct race with a unique language. Essentially, he stated, they were successful producers and traders of coffee, tobacco and saffron and fine-woven

---

* The old tradition that Harar's prosperity depended on the exclusion of infidels, and that the city would fall with the entry of the first European, soon proved correct. After Burton's visit it was no longer regarded as a 'forbidden city' and within a generation it had been occupied by the Egyptians and made an open city.

cloth, which were much sought after along the coasts and in Arabia.[21]

Richard determined to halve the journey time and return to the coast at Berbera in two weeks instead of four. It was a tedious, hot trek, fraught with encounters with difficult tribesmen demanding material tokens of friendship. His party were often outnumbered, but he found that a single shot over their hosts' heads helped to even the imbalance; even so, he had to part with many gifts of cloth, beads and vital supplies. There was almost no water along the route – sometimes they went 24 hours without drink and Richard, sucking pebbles, said he would have traded years of his life for a mouthful of liquid. Never before, or again, would he suffer so much from thirst; 'probably it was in consequence,' he wrote, 'of being at the time in weak health so soon after Mecca.'[22] He was also concerned for the starving, thirsty and reluctant animals who were so thin that huge sores formed under their loads. They had to be driven every step of the way, often at the point of a spear in the flanks, across stony plains between arid mountains that would have taxed even fit beasts. At night there was a constant and real threat of attack by lions.

The worst section came almost at the end of the journey when they had not been near a village for 36 hours because all the local tribes were blood enemies of the people of Zayla (and therefore Richard's entourage). The party were almost, to a man, ready to die of dehydration within hours,

> The short twilight of the tropics was drawing in, I looked up and saw a *katta* or sand grouse, with its pigeon-like flight, making for the nearer hills. These birds must drink at least once a day, and generally towards evening when they are safe to carry water in their bills to their young. I cried out 'See the *katta*!' All revived at once, took heart, and followed the bird, which suddenly plunged down about a hundred yards away, showing us a charming spring, a little shaft of water about two feet in diameter, in margin of green. We jumped from our saddles, and man and beast plunged their heads into the water and drank till they could drink no more. I have never since shot a *katta*.[23]

When the exhausted group arrived safely at the camp of Stroyan and Herne at the beginning of February after a trek of some two weeks, news of the distance travelled in the last five days amazed the local people almost as much as Richard's safe return from Harar. Some doubted he had actually been there. His first act was to see that the animals were washed in the sea, their wounds dressed with cold-water bandages and that they were copiously fed. Then he slept.

Stroyan and Herne had spent a month conscientiously making expedition notes and buying up a few animals. They had not been lonely, the annual Berbera Fair having attracted some 20,000 human visitors (and almost as many animals), who came on foot and by every kind of craft from all parts of the Indian Ocean. There was no Chief in overall charge, and no common language, although many traders spoke a bastardised Arabic/Swahili. The inevitable consequence was constant quarrels and fights invariably settled by the knife or spear. In the Babel of languages, Richard was peculiarly at home and under normal circumstances would have been a long-term visitor, questioning and gossiping, trading information. But he spent only a few days wandering among the visitors and viewing the local sites that Herne and Stroyan believed would be suitable for European settlement. He was anxious to return to Aden to report his success and re-equip for the major expedition that lay ahead. He now knew it would be necessary to obtain a longer period of leave for the entire team, and this was a priority for him. He was also physically unwell; he had been low since Christmas and the physical hardship of the past months would not have facilitated any recovery, still less the irritations he inevitably endured from the secondary stage of syphilis. Leaving Stroyan and Herne at Berbera he sailed for Aden, reaching the camp on 9 February, four months after his departure.

He had every reason to be pleased with himself at this point, and he was.[24] He had achieved his objective in a shorter time than anticipated, within his budget, with no casualties and no equipment losses. His journals were crammed with scientific, geographic and ethnologic information on a country previously unknown to the authorities (and, incidentally, sufficient material for a book), he had produced a vocabulary of an unknown language, and he had braved an awesome African taboo.[25]

Recalling Outram's displeasure at Richard's original plan that his party should travel disguised as Arabs – a feeling shared by Speke, on whose fair-haired, lanky frame the disguise was scarcely believable, added to which he did not speak Arabic – it was especially good to be able to report that he had been received as an English envoy at Harar.

But Outram had already returned to India. His replacement was Colonel Coghlan, who became leader of the small coterie that regarded Richard in anything but friendly terms. Richard was irritated by the pettiness of these men, but he regarded them as insignificant, believing that support for him in the R.G.S. and by the Bombay Council was virtually assured by his recent success. He was wrong to underestimate them, however.

He was disappointed to learn that Speke had sent a report of a failure in his mission, for all other objectives, so far, had been met. A further irritation was that there had been no notice in General Orders of the results of his examination in Arabic taken before he left for Zayla. With no knowledge of Playfair's perfidy, and assuming without question that he had passed, Richard wrote to Colonel Coghlan confidently pointing out the lacuna, requesting that this latest qualification be duly entered in his record and the appropriate increase added to his salary.[26] He would not learn the true facts surrounding this affair for some time.

Speke returned to Aden on 20 February depressed at his lack of success and blaming everything and everyone but himself. Richard was sympathetic; in a postscript to his lengthy report on the Harar trip written for the *Bombay Gazette*, he wrote generously of Speke stating that he had succeeded in reaching the plateau 'above the Ghauts', but that the rascality of his *abban* and wars between the tribes had prevented him from penetrating far inland. However, 'he has brought back a fine collection of fauna, some of which I believe must be new to science . . .'[27]

Burton completely misread Speke's character. He had no way of knowing at that point that Speke habitually blamed his failures on others and always returned from trips with stories of how he had been cheated or let down by someone in the group. In fact, though he had an appealing charm of manner, Speke was an arrogant man with an overweening vanity and pettiness. The choice of guide, made by Burton, was certainly unfortunate, for Samuntar was in considerable debt and bled the expedition resources to meet the demands of his creditors. But the causes of Speke's failure were compound: a complete lack of understanding of the native peoples; his inability to speak the language (he could not even understand the orders being given to his porters and staff by his interpreter); and weak leadership. He had no natural sympathy for Islamic culture and referred to the

Africans in his letters as 'creatures' or savages. Samuntar would never have been able to defraud or trick Richard in the same way but, in Speke's defence, Richard as the expedition leader should have recognised that the younger man would be placed in an impossible position if he could not communicate.

Having realised he could not achieve his expedition objectives, Speke had vented his anger through his gun and made up for the lack of success in other fields by a mighty tally of 'specimens'. Everything that moved fell victim, from the tiniest birds, rock hyraxes, klip springers and snakes to antelope, hyenas, bustards and ostriches. Even so he was not satisfied; he abhorred the fact that the rhino had been wiped out by local hunters, robbing him of an opportunity to kill one himself, and that he was not able to kill an elephant by hamstringing as the natives did. He mourned his inability to shoot 'a singular canine looking animal' that had wandered into his camp one evening. Richard would eventually learn the hard way about Speke's true character; meantime he defended his assistant surveyor staunchly in an official report to Lieut. Playfair:

> Lt. Speke . . . has reported to me in the strongest terms the bad conduct of Mohammed Samuntar his Abban . . . Lt. Speke has been plundered, threatened, detained and impeded from entering the country he was directed to explore . . .[28]

On Richard's recommendation, Samuntar was tried for fraud, with Speke and his two favourite servants appearing as enthusiastic witnesses for the prosecution. Found guilty and 'appropriately chastised' as a warning to others, Samuntar was fined 200 rupees, imprisoned for two months and banished from Aden. Later Richard would learn that this caused a good deal of resentment in Somalia, where it was felt that Samuntar had only behaved as all *abbans* did; food and supplies in acceptable amounts being regarded as 'perks of the job'.

Letters awaiting his return brought Richard family news. His mother had died on 18 December while he was on the road to Harar; his brother Edward had at last returned on furlough and was staying at Boulogne with their father, sister and nieces. Richard hardly mentioned his mother in his memoirs, though his niece recalled Richard and her mother often speaking of Mrs Martha Burton with great admiration and affection.[29] There are several illuminating references in his books; 'nice to be able to feel proud of one's parents,' he said on one occasion, and there was a pathetic allusion to 'the gaps' he found in his family when he returned home in 1855. That he loved his mother, as he loved all his family, is beyond question. His Aunt Georgina reported a story of him as a boy rolling on the floor howling with rage because his mother had had to walk, when other women could afford a carriage.

Writing to the Royal Geographical Society on the requisite black-edged paper of the bereaved, Richard summarised his previous trip; 'by next mail you shall receive a paper,' he promised:

> My success at Harar has emboldened me and I have applied for a 2nd year's leave. The Court of Directors will not, I think, refuse it, especially if it be at all backed up by the Roy. Geog. Soc. My plans (public) are now to march southward to the Webbe, Shebagli and Ganana. Privately and *entre nous*, I want to settle the question of Krapf and 'eternal snows'. There is little doubt of the White Nile being thereabouts. And you will hear with pleasure that there is an open route through Africa, to the Atlantic. I heard about it at Harar . . .[30]

His chief difficulties, he believed, lay in the Galla country where the 'penis cutting people' dwelt. However, 'we march as masters with 20 guns and horses etc, so that by day we need not fear hosts.'

Speke, meanwhile, was writing letters too; to his family and friends. His letter to James Grant, with whom his name will be ever linked in history, even at this stage – only days before he departed on what was to be a major exploration of the territory – made no mention of a desire to visit the 'Mountains of the Moon' or search for the Nile. This is particularly relevant in view of the fact that later he would claim that these were his long-held ambitions. Three-quarters of the letter is about guns and shooting, and the remainder gossip about his recent trip.

By 25 March Richard's preparations were complete and he was ready to depart for Berbera where the Fair was breaking up. Recalling his own difficulty in buying animals at Zayla, he despatched Speke to the African coast north of Berbera to buy as many camels as he could and march them the short distance along the coast to join Herne and Stroyan. This time Speke was accompanied by a tried and tested *abban*, Mohammed Gooled, known as 'el Balyuz' (the ambassador), who had been recruited for the expedition by Lieut. Dansey, the Assistant Political Agent at Aden. Richard then requested a passage for himself and his party aboard the British Navy vessel *Mahi* which was about to leave for Mussowah, and papers empowering him to enforce the British determination to end the slave caravans of the Turkish *Porte*.[31]

'If I had "let well alone", I should have done well,' Richard wrote with hindsight. At this point he had reached a pinnacle, with notable success in his explorations of Arabia and Somalia. Though a number of his future ventures would be even more noteworthy, they would all be blighted in some manner. But he could not have known this and when, on 7 April 1855, Richard returned to Berbera, he was confident in his arrangements, his provisions, himself. Over-confident, in fact.

Speke, having purchased 26 camels to add to the 30 animals already purchased by Herne and Stroyan, arrived safely at Berbera as planned. He wrote of his astonishment at the size of the caravans coming and going from the Fair, and at the sight of hundreds of slaves being driven in chain gangs.[32]

The Captain of the British Navy gunboat, *Mahi*, had orders to relieve *Elphinstone* on blockade duties elsewhere in the Red Sea and could not, as Richard had hoped, remain with them until the expedition was ready to depart. But he saw Richard's camp safely established, and diplomatic exchanges made with the local chiefs, before he sailed. The camp, on a rocky ridge of a beach within sound of gunshot of the harbour, and three-quarters of a mile from the town of Berbera, was organised according to British Army convention. The three 'Rowtie' tents of the officers were erected in a short row behind the camel ranks, and in front of the horse and mule lines. Speke's tent was on the left (nearest the sea), Stroyan's on the right. A larger tent occupied by Burton and Herne was sited between these two, about a dozen paces from each. The space between the tents was filled with the heavy expedition baggage and used by the three *abbans* as sleeping quarters. Two armed sentries patrolled the camp all night, regularly checked, for the first few days, by one or other of the officers. After a week of uneventful nights it was agreed between Burton and Speke (who was responsible for security) that these checks were unnecessary and that they should get a full quota of sleep in readiness for the hardships to come.

On the 9th the first wind and rain of the monsoon season saw mats stripped from tent frames, camels loaded and thousands of travellers departing from Berbera on their homeward journey. By the following day a few camel carcasses, the burned-out remains of numerous camp fires, some straggler tribes and a handful of vessels anchored in the creek were all that was left of the host. Richard met officials of the caravan departing from the Fair towards Ogaden who – seeing the string of 56 camels, lines of mules and horses, and armed sentries of Richard's expedition – were anxious that his party should join them for the added safety of both groups. Richard was only too happy to join forces but he felt obliged to wait for the arrival of another British ship, promised within about a week. It should bring essential surveying equipment, which had been sent from Bombay but had still not arrived in Aden when the *Mahi* sailed. Furthermore, it would also bring the mid-April mail from England, in which Richard undoubtedly hoped to hear news from his bereaved family, as well as reaction to his letter to Norton Shaw at the R.G.S.

On 15 April, unwilling to wait any longer, the Ogaden Caravan departed. Travelling with it were a large number of Richard's porters and guides, the plan being that Richard and the remaining members of the expedition would follow them, fast and light, as soon as the supplies and mail had been received and catch them up. All the vessels left the harbour and the English camp was the only sign of life on the otherwise deserted coastline. Three days later a native trading craft, a *bugalow*, bound for its home port of Aynterad, arrived from Aden; it carried an unimportant letter from Aden, but none of the items for which Richard was waiting. The captain did not intend stopping at Berbera and indeed did not enter the harbour but kedged off the headland, ready to sail during the night. Ten Somalis disembarked and applied to Richard to join his expedition as far as Ogaden. He engaged four of them – all he could afford to feed within his budget.

That evening, the 18th, Richard invited the ship's captain, Yusuf, and his crew to supper. He could not have known that this hospitality would save his life and that of two of his three companions. A deposition made by Richard a few days later describes an incident which occurred during supper and was to have far-reaching effects.

At sunset he heard musket fire behind the tents. Three men from the same tribe as the *abban* Balyuz had arrived and the guards, suspecting a foraying party, had fired over their heads. Richard ordered Speke to reprimand them sharply, ordering them to reserve their fire until they were certain of attack when they were to fire 'into . . . not above' the attackers. Then, suspicious about the sudden appearance of the strangers, Richard asked Balyuz to enquire what their business was.

> The reply was so plausible that it completely deceived even Balyooz [sic], one of the acutest of the Somal . . . [They said] the Haji Sharmarkay of Zayla was waiting at Siyarro (a port not 20 miles east of Berbera) with four vessels, [for] a favourable opportunity of seizing Berbera and of erecting a fort there. Our visitors swore by the oath of divorce – the most solemn a Somali knows – that seeing a bugalow visiting the port at such an unusual season they had come down to ascertain if it brought Sharmarkay's men and materials for building.[33]

Scoffing at the suggestion that their arrival should give rise to apprehension – after all they belonged to the *abban*'s own tribe, '[they] not only deceived us,' Richard wrote, 'but deceived even their own fellow countrymen. Accordingly, the usual two sentries were posted for the night, and the usual orders issued.'

He was either unaware, or chose to disbelieve, what most of the native members of the expedition afterwards claimed to have known. That rumours had been spreading along the coast all winter that the presence of the British officers signified two things; one, that the British intended to suppress the slave trade (which was of immense importance to the Somalis), and two, that the British either wished to take Somalia for themselves, or hand Berbera over to their ally Sharmarkay who had long wished to take the town into his coastal fiefdom. It was whispered, therefore, that the British Expedition must not be allowed to reach the Ogaden country.

It is surprising that Richard, who prided himself on knowing the mind of the peoples among whom he travelled, did not sense, or hear of, the antagonism that existed. His brushes with danger in Arabia and Harar where he was constantly testing himself, and from which he had emerged unscathed, seem to have given him an illusion of invulnerability, making him careless of the potential hazards. Almost certainly, had the expedition left with the Ogaden Caravan as originally planned, the disaster that subsequently befell them would have been averted.

Balyuz, when asked about the matter some weeks later, said that he had told Lieut. Burton that he did not believe the story told by the three men (whom he described as 'spies'); 'I . . . recommended eight or nine additional men be set to watch that night. Mr Burton spoke to Sheikh Ahmed, his head servant, in Persian and in consequence I do not know [what was decided].'[34] Another man, Said (one of the two sentries), stated that he had asked Richard for some more ammunition as he had only two rounds remaining of the five Richard had issued him. When asked where the other three rounds had gone, he explained that he had used one firing at a mark for target practise, and the rest when the three horsemen came. 'Mr Burton told me never to mind as there was no fear.'[35] Stroyan's *abban* testified that he had told Lieut. Burton on several occasions of his concern and that he was afraid to remain at the camp. 'Mr Burton replied that he feared no one and bid me go to . . . my tribe . . . I told Mr Burton on at least three distinct occasions that he would be attacked, as the tribes had left and plunderers were always about at the termination of the fair. Mr Burton said that if a thousand attacked him he had no fear. He said, "Solitude will not eat you."'[36]

After his supper guests had returned to their ship, too overcome with hospitality to sail until the following morning, Richard and his three companions retired to their tents. Between 2 and 3 a.m. they were awakened by the sound of shouts and gunfire; simultaneously Balyuz rushed into the tent declaring that they were under attack and handed Richard a gun that he found tied to the table. Richard was not unduly alarmed for, as he said in his deposition, 'such incidents are but too common in the countries through which I have travelled.' Seeing Herne had his Colt revolver in his hand, Richard asked him to leave by the rear of the tent and take some of the men to investigate the disturbance. Meanwhile, finding that the gun Balyuz had thrust at him was unloaded, he drew his sabre 'and prepared for work', calling out as he did so to waken Speke and Stroyan. Speke joined him in the main tent almost immediately, his tent having been attacked and beaten down with clubs, and a barrage of stones and other missiles. Herne quickly returned; he had shot two of the enemy and his gun was empty. They were overwhelmed, he said, their attackers numbering between two and three hundred.

At first Richard had judged it best to stand and defend the main tent, fending off intruders, but after hearing Herne's report, and when the tent itself came under siege with screams and shouts 'intending to terrify', he gave the command to escape; 'the tent had been almost beaten down . . . had we been entangled in its folds, like mice in a trap, we would have been speared with unpleasant facility.'

> I . . . sallied out, closely followed by Herne, with Speke in the rear. The prospect was not agreeable. About twenty men were kneeling and crouching at the tent entrance, whilst many [others] . . . stood further off, or ran about shouting the war-cry, or with shouts and blows drove away our camels. Among the enemy were many of our attendants . . . After breaking through the mob at the tent entrance, [believing] I saw the form of Stroyan lying upon the sand, I cut my way with my sabre towards it [under attack from dozens of Somali clubs], whilst Balyuz – who was violently pushing me out of the affray – rendered the strokes of my sabre uncertain . . . I mistook him in the dark and turned to cut him down; he cried out in alarm. The well known voice stopped me, and that instant's hesitation allowed a spearman to step forward and leave a javelin in my mouth and retire . . .[37]

The barbed spearhead of the javelin, thrust with the precision and power of a warrior who had hunted and fought with such a weapon all his life, entered Richard's left cheek travelling in a downwards direction. It pierced the roof of his mouth, transfixing the top jaw to the lower, dislodged some back teeth, and punched an exit through the right cheek.

In an agony magnified by the unbalanced weight of the huge weapon upon which his head was, so to speak, impaled, Richard somehow stumbled to cover where some of his servants were hiding beyond the fighting. They ran off, fearing that Richard would draw the enemy to them, but the faithful Balyuz followed and led him to where he thought Speke, Herne and Stroyan had taken refuge. Finding the others were not there, Balyuz went off to search for them; soon afterwards Richard met one of his men, Golab, and by gestures and grunts attempted to instruct him to see if the Aynterad bugalow was still anchored and, if so, to ask the Captain to aid them by bringing his ship into the main harbour. He knew that Captain Yusuf's plan had been to sail with the dawn land-breeze. 'At that point,' he said afterwards, 'our lives hung by a thread. Had the vessel departed as . . .

intended, nothing could have saved us.' Richard could not remove the barbed spearhead, and spent the remaining two hours until daybreak alternately stumbling about in search of his companions, and 'resting' when totally overcome by pain and faintness caused by loss of blood. By the first light of dawn he could just make out the bugalow making sail, apparently to leave the harbour. With his last remaining strength he lumbered to the spit at the head of the creek, and signalled frantically. Fortunately he was spotted by Captain Yusuf. He was taken on to the vessel where he persuaded the crew to arm themselves and return to the scene of the attack to seek his companions. Soon Herne appeared, and closely following him, the badly wounded Speke. Finally, the body of Stroyan was carried aboard, with injuries described by Richard.

> A spear had traversed his heart, another had pierced his abdomen, and a frightful gash, apparently of a sword, had opened the upper part of his forehead: the body had been bruised with war clubs and the thighs showed marks of violence after death. This is the severest blow of all that occurred to us; we had lived together like brothers. Lt. Stroyan was a universal favourite . . .[38]

A member of the crew removed the javelin from Richard's face, severing the wooden shaft at the hilt of the weapon, before pulling the metal spearhead out through Richard's right cheek. Presently Yusuf and his landing party returned 'reporting that the enemy had fled, carrying off all our cloth, tobacco, swords and other weapons. The rice, part of the dates, our books and broken boxes together with injured instruments and other articles remained on the ground', Richard stated in his report. 'I spent that day at Berbera bringing off our property and firing guns to recall our servants who had run away. In the evening unable to bring off any more kit I ordered the remainder to be set on fire . . .'[39]

Richard's Official Report of the events of 19 April 1855 is now archived with the India Office records and is accompanied by the signed statements of Speke and Herne. Several versions of the incident were later written and published by the men involved, but these 'on-the-spot' testimonies have an immediacy lacking in the subsequent well thought-out statements, and are especially interesting in view of the fact that Speke would later change many aspects of the testimony he made and signed within 48 hours of the fatal incident.

I . . . was awoke about 3 a.m. on the morning of the 19th instant [April 1855] by hearing Lieut. Burton crying out to Lieut. Stroyan 'get up, old fellow'. Almost at the same instant I heard the report of three discharges from firearms, as if fired in a volley . . . Conceiving it to be nothing but . . . a false alarm, I remained in my tent. Immediately after I heard, as it were, a beating of clubs on my tent . . . and a shuffling of feet outside. On this I ran across to Lieut. Burton's tent and asked him if there was 'any shooting', meaning were we attacked. He replied 'I rather think that there is'.

I then took my revolver and went outside the tent, receiving a smart blow on the knee from a stone . . . I soon saw 2 heads peeping over our ammunition boxes about 7 or 8 yards to my left, but I did not fire at them not being certain of my shot. Shortly after I saw another 2 Somalis bent down or crouching along, advancing with their shields before their bodies and their spears ready poised in their hands either to throw or strike. I fired my pistol and apparently wounded a man as he staggered back . . . I fired twice at these men . . . I then rushed amongst them and found that the pistol a Deane and Adams [five shot] would no longer revolve. Whilst holding it within two yards of a man's head I received a wound on my shoulder from either a spear or knife and a smart blow on my lungs from a club, which took away my breath, and felled me to the earth and whilst down, two or three men jumped on me and pinioned my hands behind my back and then led me away a prisoner . . .

[Later] a Somali approached me and whisking a sword round him, pretended to strike me, as if with the intention of killing me . . . He acted this twice and then left me to join in the plunder. He was succeeded by a man with a spear who commenced spearing me. Once I caught his spear but he pulled a club out of his girdle and gave me such a violent blow that it quite paralysed my arm, and caused me to drop the spear. He tried to spear my heart but I caught it with my hand which was severely cut on the back, he speared me also on the right shoulder and in the left thigh and then paused a little and came round to my right side and passed his spear sharply through my right thigh. Seeing that he was determined to kill me, I jumped up with a menacing look at the man, which caused him to fall back a little. I seized the opportunity of his being thrown off his guard and ran towards the sea and looking round I saw that he had cast his spear at me which I managed to avoid and picking my way amongst the Somalis who flung a shower of 12 to 15 spears at me . . . I ran till I found out that I was not pursued, and then lay down under a sand hill exhausted from loss of blood.[40]

When he regained his strength Speke made his way to the town of Berbera and presently 'met some of our party coming to meet me . . . By the assistance of these people I managed to hobble down to the vessel about 3 miles away at the head of the reef, the entrance to the harbour . . .'

Herne's statement confirmed that he, too, had been woken by Burton who told him they were about to be attacked. He immediately rose, armed himself with his revolver, and went out of the rear of the tent to investigate. He estimated the attacking party at 'about 200 men'. Almost immediately a group of men rushed him. Backing towards the tent he tripped over a guy rope which caused his revolver to go off. As he tried to rise a man raised his club to strike him and he fired at and wounded his attacker. Gaining entry through the rear of the tent he found Burton and Speke defending the front entrance. He shot and wounded a man who followed him into the tent.

After this I endeavoured to find my powder horn, but not being very successful endeavoured to find some spears that used always to be tied to the pole of the tent . . . but these had been taken away. I made another attempt to find the powder horn, when I observed men entering in rear of the Rowtie which was evidently being let down upon us. You [Burton] signalled us to make a dash through them which I did . . . When we reached the sand below, I saw you attacking a man who gave you a wound in the mouth . . . I having nothing but what I thought at the time an unloaded pistol and as they did not attempt to renew the attack I fell back. In so doing I came across a body of 10 or 12 men who made way for me and allowed me to pass . . .

Herne also hid among the sand dunes until dawn when he met up with Balyuz and the two men began a search for the rest of the party until they met up with crew members of the bugalow. In Herne's opinion 'the attack which occurred was an accident not to be avoided by any of the ordinary methods of prudence. Two sentries had been duly posted, one in front, the other in rear and the men had been specially ordered not to fire over the heads of their enemies. Had any of the guard or Somalis stood, we should have resisted the attack but under such overpowering numbers we had no chance.'

There were small inconsistencies in the formal statements given by the various witnesses concerning times and precise position, but this is normal, every witness viewing an incident from his own vantage point and having a personal agenda. However, the *main* points of Richard's account of what happened after the initial attack were agreed by everyone.

When the three surviving officers reached Aden in the early morning of 22 April, three days after the attack, two of them were in a sorry state. Herne had only superficial cuts and bruises, but the other two had to be carried to a nearby hotel at Steamer Point. Richard's good friend Dr John Steinhaueser was the Resident Civil Surgeon, but he was absent and it was the Acting Civil Surgeon who was on duty. Speke, who had departed Aden only a month earlier looking fair, tanned and fit, appeared the worst injured. He was 'a miserable-looking cripple . . . emaciated from loss of blood'. The muscle tissues damaged by spear thrusts racked and twisted his limbs with contraction 'into indescribable positions'; his body was a mass of livid contusions and gaping wounds. He had a high fever and in those pre-antibiotic days septicaemia was a significant danger in the tropics. 'This gentleman,' wrote the doctor, 'received eleven wounds chiefly from spears, the most serious is the right thigh . . .' [41]

Lieutenant Dansey at once offered a room in his house so that Speke could be nursed in comfort. Colonel William Coghlan, who had succeeded Outram, sat at Speke's bedside with tears in his eyes until the patient was well enough to be shipped home three weeks later to convalesce. The doctor gravely suggested that a three-year leave was needed to recover completely. A month after arriving in England Speke's wounds 'closed up like cuts in an India rubber ball . . . I never felt the least inconvenience.' He then volunteered for service in the Crimea.

Long-term, Richard's wounds were in fact the more severe of the two, leaving him with permanent damage and facial scarring. Eating and drinking were made extremely difficult because of the open wounds in his mouth and damaged jaw and teeth. He also had a fever. Furthermore, he had been physically unwell for some months and the root of this was immediately apparent to the doctor, who was responsible for an entire garrison of men of a sexually active age. 'On my arrival,' he reported,

> . . . I found Lieutenant Burton with a spear wound which piercing the cheek removed two of the molar teeth and divided the roof of the mouth; the spear entered on the left side of the face and came out on the right. Lieutenant Burton's wound is a serious one, and as he has recently suffered from secondary syphilis must immediately proceed to Europe as it would not be proper to allow him to remain in Aden during the approaching hot weather.[42]

Fortunately for Richard, Dr John Steinhaueser, who was Registrar for Aden as well as its Senior Medical Officer,[43] soon returned and he invited Richard to move in with him to be cared for until he was fit enough to ship home. This was some time after Speke left, for in addition to his immediate problems Richard's lowered immunity laid him wide open to an attack of whooping-cough that was raging in Aden.[44]

While Richard convalesced in Steinhaueser's agreeable company, a group of men he would later describe as his 'unfriends' – Coghlan, Playfair, Rigby and Anderson – were already plotting how they could bring him down.

11

WITH BEATSON'S HORSE
IN THE CRIMEA
1855–1856

The dossier on 'The Somali Expedition', kept open for two years, eventually comprised hundreds of papers containing statements, opinions and recommendations.[1] It was useless for Richard to counter the claims that he had not adequately protected the camp by pointing out that had he been able to post twenty armed guards that night they could not have resisted a surprise attack by 200–300 armed natives attacking under cover of darkness in their own territory. Useless to say, when told that he should have expected an attack, that Herne and Stroyan had lived on the site in complete safety for six months; that the ease with which the British could blockade Berbera as punishment for any incidents had led them all to believe they were safe there; that their delay in leaving was caused by the non-arrival of important equipment which had not been sent as promised; that it was originally intended that the *Mahi* would be able to stand by until they departed; or that had he not listened to Outram the expedition would have departed months earlier.

These were all valid, irrefutable points, but they fell on ears unwilling to hear. It was generally held by Playfair, Coghlan *et al* that inadequate leadership had invited the attack. Their motives seem inexplicable. Richard put it down to professional jealousy; many officers would have liked to lead expeditions, to 'make their name', he said. But the men concerned all became reasonably well known to their peers after distinguished careers. What could have made Richard such an object of dislike to them?[2] That the enmity existed is patent. Extant correspondence between Coghlan and Playfair, and Anderson and the Bombay Government about the 'Somali Expedition' makes grim reading, not only for its grisly accounts of the attack on the British by the Somalis but for the clear prejudice against Richard. Speke's biographer suggested that 'Burton's swashbuckling character and spirit of reckless adventure provided a convenient target for the many in authority who envied his ability or had perhaps already felt the rough edge of his tongue.'[3]

No Commanding Officer likes to see an incident 'on his patch' and Brigadier Coghlan was especially critical. 'The reasons adduced by Lieutenant Burton are inconsistent,' he wrote, after reading the testimonies of the guards and servants of the expedition and taking statements from local tribal chiefs. Although he did not give full credence to the statements of these men, he stated, he was inclined to believe them. Several Africans claimed to have warned Richard to increase the guard on the evening of the attack and requested fresh supplies of ammunition, explaining that their supplies had been exhausted by firing at birds during the previous day. Richard had refused to re-supply them, they stated, so that when attacked they could not defend. The most damning indictment would appear to have been Balyuz's statement; after all, he was a tried and trusted servant of the British and the senior African advisor to the expedition. But the remark hidden in the statement of Richard's personal servant reveals what was probably the real reason why Richard had ignored Balyuz's warnings: '. . . Balyuz told Mr Burton that the Somalis of the party had had recourse to necromancy and [through this] had discovered that a body of men would come to attack us . . .'[4] It was hardly surprising that Richard chose to ignore Balyuz's warning given that it was based on supposed messages from the dead.

In his lengthy summary, Coghlan referred to the 'false security in which the Expedition indulged . . . had the surprise occurred farther inland it is probable that not a single member of the expedition would have returned to tell the tale . . . It may seem harsh to criticise the conduct of these officers who, to the grief of their wounds and loss of their property, must add the total failure of their long-cherished scheme; but I cannot refrain from observing that their whole proceeding is marked by a want of caution and vigilance . . . [this was] a treacherous assault which common prudence and forethought might have prevented . . .'[5] The maximum possible damage was caused when these comments were read in Bombay at the same time as Richard's application to be allowed a year's leave of absence to 'continue the researches in the Somali country, together with a request . . . [for] the local rank of Major'. The reply was almost a foregone conclusion;

> The disaster . . . reported in Brigadier Coghlan's letter to the Secretary of 23rd April renders it in our opinion inexpedient to entertain any application for its further prosecution.[6]

The decision to write this curt letter was not a unanimous one, as is evidenced by a note pencilled on the bottom of the file copy by one of the Directors. 'Unless further notice is intended in the Secret Department, this seems to me to be a very meagre despatch. Ought we not to notice Lieutenant Burton's illness and incapacity, . . . [and] the favourable opinion presently entertained of him? . . .'

By this time Richard was on his way to England and a blizzard of correspondence winged its way between Bombay, Aden and London without his involvement. Months later, Coghlan and Playfair each visited Somalia. Coghlan organised a naval blockade of the port of Berbera as a 'punishment' and demonstration of British power and disapproval. Playfair, sent with a goodly armed escort to investigate, 'extracted a solemn promise' from the chiefs about their future behaviour. An Official Inquiry into the affair commended Playfair for his judgment, ability and tact in his handling of the matter, and Coghlan for the blockade, a measure which Richard recommended in his first report of the incident. Richard, however, was 'severely censured'.[7] Only then did he become aware of the nature of the campaign against him. On James Grant Lumsden's strong recommendation, Richard appealed to the Court of Directors stating his case in the strongest terms. Lumsden himself formally protested that Coghlan seemed to have taken the evidence of the tribal elders as fact, to the prejudice of Lieut. Burton. 'The extreme carelessness evinced in the utter disregard of a solemn warning, as stated, appears highly improbable,' he countered in defence of his friend. Had Burton been so guilty of the 'obstinate neglect' of his duties, why had the surviving members of the expedition not spoken up?[8] Coghlan rejected inferred charges of undue prejudice, and blustered, 'I have no desire to damage Lt.

Burton in the estimation of the Government . . . I have been at pains to elicit the truth . . .'[9]

The carefully worded reply to Coghlan's protest proves that Richard still had some support in high places from those not wholly convinced that he was as blameworthy as the Staff Officers at Aden would have it; 'His Lordship in Council is satisfied that you could have had no wish to prejudice Lt. Burton . . . but in your letter dated the 26th November last, you certainly accuse Lieutenant Burton, in very positive terms, of culpable carelessness . . . While you do this on the authority of the elders of the [tribes] you do not appear to have required any officer of the Expedition to reply to their state-ments . . .'[10] Herne was questioned again and backed up Richard's statement, and confirmed that he knew nothing of the warnings that the sentries claimed to have given Richard.[11]

The matter rumbled on, chiefly because of the commercial poten-tial of Somalia. Although he had previously rejected Richard's evaluation of the port as an ideal place to establish a British Agency, following his own visit there Coghlan did a U-turn. Without acknowl-edging Richard's report, he recommended Berbera to the Bombay Government as an optimal site, being the 'Emporium of the trade of North Eastern Africa'. He did not trust the French, he warned, and because of Berbera's proximity to Aden, it was not in Britain's com-mercial interests to allow another nation to secure the area. But throughout his correspondence he stressed that the tribal chiefs had no ability to repay the members of Burton's expedition for the plun-dered animals and equipment. And he insisted that because of their disregard for their own safety those officers 'had no claim to com-pensation for the loss of their property'.[12] This provoked a protest from the Captain of the *Mahi*. During the blockade of Berbera he learned that a man of some importance in the Esa Moosa tribe – his name was Rage – had sold much of the plunder, 'yet,' he pointed out, 'his name does not appear in the list of those being investigated for the offences . . .'[13]

The overall impression from reading the whole of this voluminous correspondence is that though Richard's leadership was eventually vindicated in the minds of the Bombay Government, nothing was done to counteract the damage done to his reputation in the interim, probably because no one would take responsibility for making a deci-sion to repay the significant financial losses suffered by the officers.

Government equipment (valued at 5,500 rupees) comprised less than half the total losses, estimated at 13,800* rupees:

Speke	4,100 rupees
Herne	500
Stroyan	1,750
Burton	1,950

Richard spent the early part of the summer of 1855 in London recovering from his wounds with the help of 'a clever surgeon and a skilled dentist',[14] and working on his book *First Footsteps in Africa* which he dedicated to Lumsden.[15] The conventional treatment for venereal disease was mercury, which left the patient at a low ebb. Richard would have been advised, if he did not already know, that once the secondary stage had cleared up he would remain infectious for three years, and must abstain from sexual intercourse during that time. What happened after three years could not be prognosticated with any certainty. His health would be normal and he could resume sexual activities. The tertiary stage could erupt years or many decades later, attacking the heart or brain with fatal results; madness was the symptom most sufferers of syphilis feared. On the other hand, a patient might die of old age in his bed without ever developing tertiary symptoms.

His arrival in London in May 1855 had not gone unnoticed, for not only was it reported in the newspapers, but he wrote several long letters to *The Times*. Shortly after his return to London his three-volume work, *Personal Narrative of a Pilgrimage to Meccah and El-Medinah*, was published and sold well. He ought to have been lionised as a hero, and to a limited extent he was fêted, but a rumour sprang up which clung to him throughout his life and detracted from his reputation as a man to be admired. The story went round the clubs, and was apparently believed, that Burton had been observed by his Arab boy standing up to urinate (rather than squatting as the Arabs do); and that, thus detected as an infidel, he had killed the youth to save himself. Richard disclaimed this allegation of murder all

---

* 13,800 'Company Rupees' equalled £1,390 in 1855 values. Present-day conversion approximates to £47,260.

his life, but nothing he said ever dispelled the rumour and it was still being quoted in many of his obituaries 40 years later. Richard's exaggerated care and minute observation of Islamic customs and behaviour, alone, made the charge a ridiculous one. But as a close woman friend said, Richard enjoyed telling incredible stories with a grave expression; the rapt attention and discomfort of his listeners provided him with amusement and he seemed to take a delight 'in being thought by people in general a devil incarnate'.

> 'Did you really shoot that Arab boy,' I asked him once; for the killing of the Arab boy was always being cast up against him.
>   'Oh yes,' he answered. 'Why not? Do you suppose one can live in these countries as one lives in Pall Mall and Piccadilly?' And he laughed.[16]

In more serious conversations he utterly rejected the charge, as another friend testified:

> I felt that I knew him well enough to venture upon a few questions regarding his Mekkah pilgrimage, and first of all [especially] the current belief that he had killed a man who discovered or suspected that he was an unbeliever!
>   The story was that he had been seen by the other man outside his tent while supposing that he was free from all observation. He told me there was no truth in the story. He knew very well that the alleged incident was widely regarded as fact and he gave me to understand that he had never cared to contend it, but was only amazed by its persistence.[17]

In 1855 the notice of Richard's arrival and his letters, in fact every item that touched his life, was cut out and pasted into Isabel Arundell's scrapbook, each piece annotated and commented upon by her in her strong, clear handwriting.[18] Still besotted, she either was too shy to attempt to make contact with him or feared rejection, but that she monitored his progress closely is evident from a diary entry in the spring of 1855:

> We have got the news of Richard's magnificent ride to Harar, his staying ten days in Harar, of his wonderful ride back, his most daring

expedition, and then we heard of the dreadful attack by the natives in his tent, and how Stroyan was killed, Herne untouched, Speke with eleven wounds, and Richard with a lance through his jaw. They escaped in a native dhow to Aden and it was doubtful whether Richard would recover. Doubtless this is the danger alluded to by the clairvoyant, and the cause of my horrible dreams concerning him about the time it happened. I hope to Heaven he will not go back![19]

Her reference to a clairvoyant would, doubtless, have found favour with Richard. He, too, had consulted clairvoyants and fortune-tellers all his life; even at Oxford one of his first actions had been to have his horoscope cast. An earlier entry in Isabel's diary discloses more about her own life. Newspaper accounts of the war in the Crimea, detailing the twin scourges of cholera and malaria which claimed as many victims as the enemy, and the horrors and inhumane treatment meted out to the sick and wounded, had been appearing almost since the British occupied Balaclava on 27 October 1854. '. . . the manner in which [the sick] are treated is worthy only of the savages of Dahome!' thundered a despatch from Lord Russell in *The Times*. 'Here the French are greatly our superiors. Their medical arrangements are extremely good, their surgeons more numerous and they have the Sisters of Charity . . .' A letter in the following day's edition asked, 'Why have we no Sisters of Charity?' Sidney Herbert, 'Secretary-at-War', having taken note of the seething anger of the public, on his own responsibility invited the virtually unknown Florence Nightingale to take a party of nurses out to Scutari, with the Government's sanction and at their expense. Her sickening reports of the wounded – lying naked, emaciated, filthy, not only without pain relief but without even the most basic human needs – moved the national conscience.[20] Isabel, now 24 – intelligent, bored, trapped in a vacuous life – was in a fever to help, as she confided to her journal:

It has been an awful winter in the Crimea. I have given up reading the *Times*; it makes me so miserable and one is so impotent. I have made three struggles to be allowed to join Florence Nightingale. How I envy the women who are allowed to go out as nurses! I have written again and again to Florence Nightingale; but the superintendent has answered me that I am too young and inexperienced, and will not do.[21]

Though a single woman herself, Nightingale preferred married women as nurses. She saw that most young unmarried women, though ardent, were not up to the rigours of Scutari. Isabel was disappointed but undeterred; she determined to do something for the war effort.

She called together a number of her best friends for a meeting in March 1855. Her memoranda book records the first meeting of these women.[22] Two of them were known to Richard, Louisa Buckley (now Mrs Segrave) and Prudence Cooper; the others were daughters of leading Catholic families. Prevented from going to the Crimea, the group decided sensibly to do what they could in London to ease the lot of the poorest families of men serving at the front. They would wear a 'uniform' of sorts to denote membership: a scarlet sash with a diamond star rosette at meetings, and a silver whistle. The latter item was considered essential in consideration of the poor areas in which they were likely to work; it was to summon help should they need it. Initially they decided to call the organisation 'The Whistle Club', but this was later changed to 'The Stella Club' on Isabel's recommendation. As organiser she carefully noted the items she was empowered to purchase on behalf of the members: 'flag; stamped paper, seal'.[23]

It would be easy to dismiss the efforts of these young women, with their dashing scarlet and costly bejewelled insignias, as facile. But given their *milieu*, their privileged home life and sheltered existence, their aim not simply to raise money but to personally take assistance into the heaving slums and stews of Victorian London was laudable. At a time when many women of their class felt they were 'doing their bit' by handing out white feathers (symbol of cowardice) to young men out of uniform, the objective of Isabel's group was at least constructive; to provide succour to the destitute families of soldiers in the Crimea, just as – had they been given the opportunity – they would have helped the soldiers themselves at the front. They each subscribed what they could personally afford and each was responsible for acquiring a number of donations. By dint of persuasion and bullying, Isabel collected a hundred guineas, 'in shillings and sixpences', in ten days and eventually there were 150 members of the club, all collecting and working for the cause. They began a clothing collection, and with their first funds purchased the equipment for a soup kitchen. She wrote:

. . . I cannot attempt to describe the scenes of misery we saw . . . I know now the misery of London . . . My beat contained one hundred women of all creeds and situations and about two hundred children. I spared no time or exertion . . . I read and wrote their letters, visited the sick and dying . . . In many cellars, garrets and courts policemen warned me not to enter, but I always said to them . . . 'I go to take the women something; they will not hurt me; but I should be glad if you waited outside in case I do not come out'.[24]

Isabel found a ready sympathy, and gratitude, among the slum dwellers for her work; the only sour note came from women of her own class who objected to the fact that she provided the same assistance for 'fallen women' as for soldiers' wives. A picture begins to emerge of Isabel as a young woman with significant organisational ability and a fearless nature. She was not a rebel, however, and would never have done anything likely to distress her parents.

By mid-June the wounds to Richard's palate had recovered sufficiently to enable him to read his paper on Harar at one of the Royal Geographical Society's famous Monday-evening lectures.[25] He had done a significant amount of preparation, and the lukewarm public reception of his account of the expedition was a major disappointment to him. He thought his success at Harar would overshadow the Berbera incident, and was relying on an enthusiastic reception to provide impetus to his plans for a future expedition to Africa. It was not that the Fellows of the R.G.S. found Richard's Harar paper uninteresting; they discussed it at length. But the world outside the R.G.S., like Isabel and her friends, was entirely wrapped up in news of the Crimean War. So there was no enthusiastic reception of his adventures and achievement.[26]

Joseph Burton, now widowed and in frail health, was still living in Bath and Richard had been visiting his father at weekends whenever possible. Maria was living quietly in Boulogne, and while Richard was preparing his R.G.S. lecture their brother Edward arrived there to spend some time while en route to London. Within days of delivering his lecture Richard was also in Boulogne paying a short visit with his siblings. Fearing from what they had heard that he might be badly disfigured, Maria and Edward were relieved at his appearance. The largest visible wound, on Richard's left cheek, had almost healed, leaving a long, livid scar which pulled at and puckered the skin under his lower left eyelid – endowing him, for the rest of his life, with a slightly sinister expression. But that apart 'he looked what he was', a healthy, tanned, powerfully built young officer 'in the prime of manhood'.[27] His thick dark hair, waved at the temples, was fashionably cut and parted in the middle, and he wore a neatly trimmed moustache.

There was much to talk about. During a decade of being parted, dissimilarities in the brothers had become obvious. Edward, regarded by his superiors as a fine soldier, was full of military 'shop'. He loved Army life and had almost as many hunting stories as Speke. He was the crack shot of his regiment, and 'many were the elephants, tigers, cheetah and smaller game that fell before his redoubtable gun' in Ceylon.[28] Richard, who viewed Army service as a passport to greater things and not an end in itself, wanted to discuss the Crimean War and the chances of gaining promotion. Visiting Maria and 'Ned', as he called him, was not his sole reason for being in France. He had already submitted an application to the East India Company, to be transferred to service in the Crimea. Having obtained some letters of introduction he was on his way to Marseilles, bound for Balaclava via Constantinople, on one of the French *Messageries Impériale* ships. He was not content to wait on conventional channels of communication, having heard how other Indian Army officers had fared by doing so.

Lord Raglan, Commander-in-Chief of the British Army in the Crimea, had served on Wellington's staff as a young man but had had no experience of leading men into battle before assuming command in the Crimea at the age of 65. Richard described him as 'a good ordinary man, placed by the folly of his friends in extraordinary circumstances'. Raglan believed that wars could and should be fought in a gentlemanly fashion, commanded by aristocracy and, moreover, that all senior ranks should also be held by members of the ruling classes. He positively encouraged the sale of commissions at outlandish prices affordable only by the very rich, and refused to allow experienced soldiers whom he regarded as 'not the right sort' to have any involvement in strategic decision-making. Prejudice against Indian Army officers ran high in the British Army anyway; under Raglan this feeling reached an apogee and they were discouraged even from applying to join the British Expeditionary Force. This disastrous policy resulted in Indian Army officers with years of experience in Cavalry regiments, many of whom had distinguished themselves in action under Napier – the very men needed – being passed over in favour of men such as Lord Cardigan and Lord Lucan. The few former Indian Army officers who were given senior rank found themselves side-lined into the Turkish Contingent.

Richard felt that the best way to take advantage of the war, and hopefully to better his circumstances, was to make his own way out to Staff H.Q. at Balaclava and apply in person. Edward agreed to join him after a period for rest and visiting their father. As usual Richard found the parting difficult. It would have been harder still had he known that he would never see Edward in full health again. Next time he saw Ned, the bright young man would be a brain-damaged mute.

Richard arrived in the Crimea after an entertaining voyage during which he met some friends who would come into his story later: Dr Nicora, Percy Smythe, Lieut. Frederick Wingfield. But he was too late, most of the important engagements of the Crimean War had already been fought; only Sebastopol remained, though Richard could not have known that. Raglan died on 28 June 1855, the day that Richard arrived in Balaclava.[29] The interregnum Commander-in-Chief was none other than Richard's old Commander, General Sir James Simpson (called by his friend Napier 'Jimmy Dismal'). Hearing this news, Richard was reasonably confident that he would be sympathetically received.

Simpson had passed pensionable age and having inherited a hot seat was unsure and indecisive. He could not personally offer Richard a post but suggested he contact Robert Vivian, an old India Army campaigner, who had been placed in charge of the Turkish forces.[30] To Richard's gratification this led to the offer of a command under General Beatson, whom Richard had met while both were on leave in 1852 at Boulogne.

Beatson was a peppery man in his late fifties, with grey hair, bluff face and portly figure. He rode English thoroughbreds as chargers and cut a distinctive and effective figure. Having served for 35 years with distinction in the Bengal Army, he was one of the first on the scene when the Crimean War began; 'he went to Head-quarters at once,' Richard wrote, 'and, for the mere fun of the thing, joined in the heavy cavalry charge.' Subsequently, Beatson was invited to organise an Irregular Cavalry Corps, which he called 'Beatson's Horse', consisting of some 4,000 'Bashi-Bazouks', to be independent of the Turkish Contingent of 12,000 Regulars reporting to General Vivian.

Richard had first come across these Bedouin mercenaries, the 'Bazoukas' as they were known to the British, in the Hejaz during his *Haj*. They were, he said, 'wild men from Syria & Albania, fierce . . . and caring little for life'.[31]

All the British officers who served with the Turkish forces wore ostentatious uniforms in order to maintain the respect of the men under their command, and Richard was no exception; 'I was in the gorgeous Bashi-Bazouk uniform, blazing with gold,' he said. Beatson's jacket was said to be so stiff with gold embroidery that it could stand up of its own accord. Most of the officers engaged by Beatson were much to Richard's taste – Lieut.-Colonel Sankey, for example, whom he had first met in Egypt after his *Haj*, and with whom he had visited the pyramids in the company of Lord Elphinstone; but there were also some black sheep such as Lieut.-Colonel O'Reilly, who would become infamous in Syria a decade or so later.

Once again, however, Richard found himself down-wind of the Establishment in the military unit in which he served. He had a warm letter of introduction to Lord Stratford[32] (from Robert Bagshawe M.P., who had married Aunt Georgina). Stratford was a useful contact, but he was very much in sympathy with the late Lord Raglan's pejorative views of irregular troops. The Bashi-Bazouks, in particular, were an anathema to him, and he and Colonel Beatson were constantly at loggerheads. Knowing this, Richard, whose duties included the sending and receiving of official dispatches, was appalled at Beatson's lack of basic diplomacy in his dealings with Lord Stratford. He gave as an example a despatch in which Beatson invited the Ambassador to accept his views or fight a duel; 'pistols for two and coffee for one' as Richard put it. 'I took it out,' he said, 'but my General did not thank me for it.'

As the winter set in Richard tired of drilling his men daily in bayonet practice and acting as staff secretary to Beatson, and when he thought he saw 'the way to a grand success' he moved impulsively. The walled Turkish town of Kars, occupied by the Russians, had been under siege for months, subjecting its unfortunate residents to famine, cholera and snipers. Various half-hearted attempts were made to break the siege, and Richard heard that the reason Lieut.-Colonel Hussey-Vivian had been unable to act appropriately was a lack of transport. In a spirit of elation he worked out a strategy for the relief of the town and called on Lord Stratford to explain his proposal. He had, he reported, '2,640 sabres in perfect readiness to march', and moreover, he had the necessary logistical support. He was totally bewildered at the outrage with which his plan was received. Stratford bellowed at him in a fury, 'You are the most impudent man in the Bombay army, Sir!' Knowing the Ambassador's reputation for sudden flares of rage, Richard kept his own temper. Within minutes Stratford had subsided and calmly told Richard without further explanation that the plan could not be entertained, adding politely, 'Of course you'll dine with us today?'

Many months later, when he learned that Kars was always intended by the British as a sacrificial pawn in the overall allied strategy concerning Sebastopol, Richard understood Lord Stratford's pique that 'a mere Captain of the Bashi-Bazouks had madly attempted to arrest the course of *haute politique*'. Stratford knew that Richard was not a fool and must have also known about his undercover work in India, for by way of consolation he asked Richard if he was interested in travelling to the remote city of Daghestan in the Caucasus Mountains to make contact with the Muslim leader Shamyl. It was an Intelligence mission fraught with danger. Shamyl was a charismatic holy man, an *Imam*, who led an army of fierce mountain tribesmen in an attenuated David and Goliath *jihad* against the domination of the infidel Czar. Undoubtedly it was in British interests to support Shamyl; his harrying guerrilla tactics in the mountains had accounted for countless Russian troops and resources which otherwise would have been employed in the Crimea, and it was due to him that the ultimate Russian conquest of the mountains took so long.

Richard was surprised at the request, for reports of Shamyl were unpleasant. He had recently been accused of flogging some Russian women whom he had taken prisoner, an act Richard considered an unspeakable atrocity. 'I could not understand how Lord Stratford who had an unmitigated horror of all Russian cruelties, and who always expressed it in the rawest terms, could ally himself with such a ruffian,' he wrote. Nevertheless, he consulted his two acquaintances, Lord Alison and Percy Smythe (later Lord Strangford), who both agreed that though the mission involved a long ride through Russian territory it might be accomplished, and he could rely on plenty of information about the territory, and also contacts, for the harems in Constantinople were filled with patriotic Circassian women who would gladly give assistance to anyone working against the Russians.

Richard seriously considered accepting and went to see Lord Stratford in Constantinople. Querying what he was to tell Shamyl when asked the purpose of his visit, Lord Stratford replied blithely, 'Oh, say that you are sent to report to *me*.' Richard pointed out logically that Shamyl would naturally expect some promises of aid in the form of money, arms and possibly troops. Without such a motive for the visit the leader would undoubtedly recognise Richard as having been sent simply to spy, in which case his 'chances of returning to Constantinople would be uncommonly small'. But Stratford would not offer any practical support and Richard sensibly rejected the scheme as ill-thought-out.

When he returned from Constantinople to his Corps he found an astonishing situation; following a squabble, the Bashi-Bazouks were under seige by their own side.

On the morning of 26th September we were astounded to see the Turkish Regulars drawn out in array against us, infantry supported by the guns, which were pointed at our camp, and patrols of cavalry patrolling the rear. Three War-steamers commanded the main entrance of the town and the enemy's outposts were established within three hundred yards of the 1st Regiment of Beatson's Horse . . . the inhabitants had closed their shops, and the British Consulate was deserted. The steamer *Redpole* was sent off in hottest haste to Constantinople with a report that a trifling squabble . . . had ended in deadly conflict, and that the most terrible consequences were likely to ensue.

Not without effort, Beatson curbed the fiery inclination of Bashi-Bazouks to reply to this insult; the Turkish Regulars were peacefully drawn off, and calm was eventually restored without a shot being fired.

Meanwhile, H.B.M. Consul of Balaclava, Mr Consul Calvert, aboard the *Redpole*, carried an exaggerated account of the incident, describing it as a 'furore of mutiny'.[33] An order came from Headquarters relieving Beatson of his command and, not surprisingly, Richard was implicated. Beatson, who had fallen from his horse, was unwell when this news was delivered so Richard, acting as Chief of Staff, rounded up several officers and called upon the relief Commanding Officer to lay the true facts before him. He was not believed. Exaggerated and inaccurate reports of undisciplined behaviour by the Bashi-Bazouks had been widely circulated throughout the British Army, and even reported in the press: 'The Bashi Bazouks, commanded by General Beatson, were displaying all the violence and rapacity of their class, little, if at all, restrained by the presence of their English officers . . .'[34]

In protest against what they saw as an injustice, Richard and his group resigned. 'It was this proceeding, I suppose,' said Richard, 'which afterwards gave rise to a report that I had done my best to cause a mutiny.'[35] He left the Crimea on 18 October with Beatson, and in doing so missed his brother's arrival there by about ten days. Finding that there was no future for him in the Crimea, Edward Burton travelled on to Ceylon.

As soon as he arrived in London, Beatson initiated civil proceedings against the men who, he charged, had conspired to make his position untenable. It would be another four years before the case came to court. Richard loyally supported his chief, a quixotic gesture for although he liked Beatson, he considered the older man's methods undisciplined.

Richard's small part in the matter was exaggerated in a report by H.B.M. Consul, Mr Skene, whose real target was Beatson. Skene had exchanged some hot words when Beatson first arrived in the Dardanelles after Skene was refused a lucrative contract to supply horses.[36] Recognising Lord Stratford's predisposition against the Irregulars, Skene wrote a report that he knew would be accepted. To bolster his case he stated that not only had Richard incited all the officers of the former Beatson's Horse to 'mutiny', by resigning rather than serve under another Commander, but that Richard had kept the order replacing Beatson secret 'for three whole weeks unknown to anyone but General Beatson'.[37]

Again, Richard's reputation suffered. He was lumped together with the more disreputable officers such as O'Reilly in collective recollections of Beatson's Horse, and it was left to those who knew better – such as Percy Smythe – to defend his reputation when possible. Smythe (later, Lord Strangford) was an unusual eccentric who would find his own fame. So shortsighted that in order to read he held the paper to his nose, he was, with one possible exception (Professor Palmer, who comes into the story in a later chapter) the most accomplished multi-linguist that Richard ever met. 'He seemed to take in a language through every pore, and to have time for all its niceties and eccentricities; for instance he could speak Persian like a Shirázi, and also with the hideous drawl of a Hindostani.'[38] His eccentricities and untidy dress often led people to underestimate him, but he was a shrewd man and he liked Richard. When, after Richard's departure several lurid stories went round about him – one in particular reporting that he had been caught in a Turkish *harem* and castrated – Smythe demanded to know the source, and the originator turned out to be Burton's former brother-officer in the Bashi-Bazouks, Lieutenant O'Reilly.

Described by many contemporaries as 'an unmitigated scoundrel whose life has been sullied by every species of vice',[39] O'Reilly's reputation was already poor when Richard knew him. Later, he was involved in the armed robbery of the Post Office at Alexandria, he attempted (unsuccessfully) to swindle a Greek heiress out of her inheritance, and committed dozens of crimes in Syria. The brief time they had served together in Beatson's Horse enabled O'Reilly to embroider his mischievous stories about Richard with enough accurate characteristics to give them a verisimilitude. He was given to intimating that he and Richard had undertaken various raffish episodes together, explaining, 'I and Burton are great scamps.' Percy Smythe did his best, in his mild way, to scotch these stories, saying, 'No, that won't do, O'Reilly is a real scamp, but Burton is only wild.'[40] However, like the story that he had killed the man in Arabia, the tale that Richard had been caught and castrated was widely spread and believed in England.

On his arrival in London, Richard wrote some letters in *The Times* about the situation in the Crimea, and as a consequence was again approached regarding an Intelligence mission. This time it was a cause he believed in wholeheartedly: to assist the Circassians to attack Georgia. He had support from two influential men, Lord Palmerston and Henry Rawlinson, but diplomatic agreements between Russia and France overran the proposals. Isabel saw his contributions in *The Times* and wrote in her diary, 'Richard has come home, and is in town. God be praised!'[41] Her resolute love for him, stemming from that single glance on the Ramparts of Boulogne, had persisted for five years. Despite numerous introductions to, and the attentions of, many eligible young men she never met anyone else who fitted her image of the perfect man for her. She felt 'a personal shame and wounded pride' in this unrequited love of hers, but felt powerless to overcome it, even though she recognised that it was making a misery of what should have been the best years of her life.[42] But even had she felt able to overcome her personal reticence sufficiently to drop Richard a short polite note welcoming him back (just permissible by virtue of their introduction), how could she do so when his name was held in such disrepute by the stricter elements of society? One contemporary wrote that, 'Pious mothers loathed Burton's name, and even men of the world mentioned it apologetically.'[43] At the very least he was regarded as a rough diamond, a hard-living soldier of fortune, and as such he was not for the likes of Miss Arundell.

Ever since he had entered the Army Richard had worked almost unceasingly to better himself in his chosen career. Had he been more tractable and/or better connected, inevitably his record would have led to rapid promotion. But despite everything he had done – and he had *actively* pursued success and glory – nothing had come of his efforts. His exacting work in India had been overshadowed by the reaction to his secret report on homosexuality; his journey to Mecca was dimmed by the specious rumours that he had killed a man; his expedition to Harar was partially eclipsed by the fiasco at Berbera. True, he was recognised as 'a personality', and fame might ultimately lead to the sort of success where he could make a decent living doing what he wanted to do, but his reputation both professionally and socially was muddied. His savings, the little money he had earned from his books and saved from his Army pay had been invested in his last mission and lost at Berbera. The Lieut.-Colonelcy bestowed by Beatson, although actually entered in Richard's Army Service Record, was subsequently expunged without ever being gazetted, and the news that he had been made Captain in the Indian Army provided none of the satisfaction it would have done a year earlier. It is hardly surprising that he was disillusioned, yet the Indian Army still provided the only route to the success he sought, and his lone travels in Somalia had strengthened his wish to explore the African interior.

He spent those early months of 1856 in the company of men like Francis Galton, Admiral Sir George Back, Norton Shaw, Sir Roderick Murchison and other Committee members of the Royal Geographical Society, where the word of the day was Africa and talk of 'the source of the Nile' had reached the proportions of a search for the Holy

Grail.[44] Richard saturated himself with everything known or written about Africa, with the reports from the missionaries Rebmann and Krapf and with the verbal statements of Arab traders and Somalis of the great lake or lakes in the interior. He was convinced not only of the existence of a lake system, but that in conjunction with the reports of snow-capped mountains, the source of the Nile must lie thereabouts. Murchison clearly agreed for he went on record, stating that the man who 'shall first lay down the true position of these equatorial snowy mountains and who shall satisfy us that they throw off the waters of the White Nile will be justly considered among the greatest benefactors of this age of geographical science'. Confident now that this was where his destiny lay, Richard actively encouraged the growing demands for exploration, for there was no one else except Livingstone (who had just travelled up to the Equator through Central Africa from the Cape) so supremely fitted to undertake such a quest as himself.

Galton, a man who had already travelled extensively and written about his wanderings, had planned to make this expedition himself, but his marriage and lack of good health conspired against him. He therefore threw his support behind Burton, though his memoir makes it clear he did not know quite what to make of him. He had known Richard since before his *Haj* and saw him often during 1856, sometimes at the R.G.S. rooms, other times at the Athenaeum Club or the Royal Asiatic Library, but mostly at Henry Murray's apartment in the Albany. Murray, one of Richard's closest friends for some years, an excellent and popular host, brought together a great variety of men of diverse interests.[45]

One of the men whom Richard first met at Murray's apartment was Laurence Oliphant. An acquaintance rather than close friend, Oliphant subsequently became a man of pivotal importance in Richard's life. His family connections on the board of the East India Company and his position as secretary to Lord Elgin, as well as being an interesting personality in his own right, recommended him to Richard. When Oliphant suggested that Richard should write to John Blackwood in Edinburgh with a view to getting an account of his travels published in *Blackwood's Magazine*, and offered a letter of introduction, Richard was pleased to accept.

In early April Richard wrote formally to Norton Shaw requesting . . .

that the Royal Geographic Society . . . afford me their powerful aid in carrying out my original project of penetrating into East Africa . . . Lately Colonel Sykes, Deputy Chairman of the Hon. EIC informed me that the plan might be revived by a recommendation from the R.G.S. . . . I am prepared to start alone & if judged necessary disguised as an Arab merchant. Should however the R.G.S. incline towards an expedition, with the idea that a virgin country of such extent as the line proposed could scarcely be investigated by a single traveller, I should be happy to place before them a detailed scheme for operations in the interior combined with a survey . . . of the coast . . .[46]

Three days later the Expedition Committee met to discuss his letter and resolved that

. . . not less on the ground of geographical discovery, than for the probable commercial . . . and political advantages, and the establishment of amicable intercourse with the various tribes . . . to make the request of H.M. Government and that of the East India Company, of an Expedition from Zanzibar . . . to ascertain in the first instance the limits of the Inland Sea known to exist, to record such geographical facts as may be desirable, to determine the exportable products of the country and ethnology of the tribes. In addition . . . the Expedition may lead to the solution of that great geographical problem, the determination of the head source of the White Nile.[47]

Richard was notified that he had the full support of the R.G.S. and within a week submitted his plans. He set out the dual objectives of the expedition: first, to ascertain the limits of the 'inland sea', and second, to determine the exportable produce and ethnology of the tribes (and this is important in view of what eventually occurred). Noting in passing that Zanzibar, 'a country mentioned in the Periplus[48] & by Pliny, subjugated by the Portuguese, visited successively by English, French & Americans, and [despite] having diplomatic relations with those powers, is almost geographically blank,' he proceeded to detail his proposals. He would sail for Bombay in the autumn, equip and recruit African aides, and sail with the first of the North-East monsoons for Zanzibar, from where he

would set out for the East African mainland as soon as the rains
were over:

> The RGS would doubtless not be contented with a mere explo-
> ration of the U[jiji] Lakes. It is generally believed that the sources of
> the White Nile are to be found among the mass of mountains lying
> between 1° S. & 1° N. latitude, & 32° & 36° E. longitude.
> Moreover, the routes of Arab caravans who in 18 months have
> crossed Africa returning from Beneguela to Mozambique, *force
> upon us the feasibility of extensive exploration*. These two are sep-
> arate and distinct objects. They would, however, be greatly
> facilitated by a preparatory exped. to the U. Lakes as the informa-
> tion there procured by an intelligent eyewitness would serve for the
> better guidance of his successors. The increased attention now paid
> by Europe to E. Africa, renders in my humble opinion, another
> exertion on our part necessary. The prospects warrant . . . our
> believing that a line of steamers will soon be established from the
> Cape of G. Hope to Aden, passing by Mauritius and Zanzibar as
> the key of the E. coast . . .

He goes on to allay the fears, expressed by some members of the
Society, for his personal safety:

> I have already had the honour to record my willingness to proceed
> alone to E. Africa. Yet it would scarcely be wise to stake success
> upon a single life when 2 or 3 travellers would at all times be safer
> & in case of accident more likely to preserve the results of their
> labours. I should therefore propose as my companion, Lt Speke of
> the Bombay Army. If aided with a sergeant or non-commissioned
> officer for the purpose of assisting us in observations & surveys we
> should be enabled to perform a more perfect work.[49]

Like Richard, Speke had been attached to the Turkish Contingent
under General Vivian, had seen little active service, and had emerged
as a Captain. During a period of leave in Constantinople he met
Laurence Oliphant, who was there with his father; their mutual
acquaintance with Burton was sufficient introduction. Speke mentioned his desire to revisit Africa and search for the source of the
Nile. 'Of course he is dying to go back and try again, but he is going

to take a turn at Sebastopol first,' Oliphant wrote to his mother.[50]

Speke's surviving correspondence, however, shows that if he did have a serious ambition in the spring of 1856 to return to Africa, he subjugated it in favour of one which seemed more achievable to him, given his personal experiences; a lengthy hunting expedition in the Caucasus Mountains with a friend, Edmund Smythe, whom he described as 'an old and notorious Himalayan sportsman'.[51] Although Speke was not a member of the R.G.S., recalling what he had learned from Richard he wrote to Norton Shaw from Constantinople to ask if the Society could assist them in obtaining passports to travel into Russian territory. Shaw replied that because of the Crimean War it was next to impossible to get passports and advised him in the strongest terms to drop the project. He added the information that Captain Burton was at that very moment organising a major expedition into the heart of Central Africa. Shaw must have communicated Speke's request to Richard, for in the same post to Speke was a letter from Richard inviting him to join his expedition. Speke, who had undoubtedly been filled with visions of Africa by Richard, accepted, dropping his plans with Smythe immediately in order to return to London.[52]

Since Speke would later make certain claims about his position in the expedition, it is worth pausing briefly in the narrative here to stress that he had neither the knowledge, experience nor breadth of education (bearing in mind Richard's extensive research and his understanding of languages), to have planned and led an expedition to the unknown 'interior' of Africa at that point. He was not a geographer or explorer in any sense of the word. He did not – at the time – even belong to those organisations such as the Royal Geographical Society who were pursuing and funding explorations. He had no access to the relevant technical papers that were being published, contemporaneously, by those organisations in which the latest theories and findings (including Richard's) were openly discussed.

Speke was by nature a hunter, who had learned enough about surveying and tracking to enable him to make reasonably successful trips into the Himalayas accompanied by native interpreters. His sole mission in Africa had been a failure, unless one counts the numbers of animals slaughtered. He did not meet his mission objectives, and demonstrated that he was unable to command Africans. In short, no committee would have entertained an application from Speke to lead an expedition. And, since it should be noted somewhere, the responsibility to post sentries and ensure adequate security at Berbera had been Speke's. Richard, as Commander, quite correctly took the ultimate blame for this failure, but with hindsight it might be thought that his chief mistake lay in appointing Speke to the task in the first place.

Richard, who was an articulate speaker and raconteur, a man of mesmeric charisma who was already known to the public, had openly shared his sources and research about Africa with his companions on the previous expedition. He loved to air his knowledge with anyone who would listen to him including the Bombay Government, the Expedition Committee of the R.G.S. and his private correspondents. As far back as 1853 he had been openly stating the foundations for his convictions about the Great Central Lake, or – as he latterly suspected – the lake system; about the unlikely glacier on the Equator; and about the probable source of the Nile.

We have a description by Speke of evenings spent at Berbera around the camp fire where these facts were the topics under discussion.[53] That is, Burton's knowledge of the writings of the Greek-Egyptian geographer, Claudius Ptolemaeus ('Ptolemy'), Pliny and other writers of antiquity, together with his conversations and correspondence with the missionaries Krapf, Erhardt and Rebmann. He also told of the learned papers made available to him by the R.G.S. and Royal Asiatic Society, written by men such as James Macqueen of the Indian Navy in 1845; and, not least, his conversations *in their own languages* with Arab traders during his Arabian adventure, and with various Africans in Somalia, about personal observations and rumour concerning these geographical features. It is inconceivable that as they sat together around the camp fire every evening, drinking coffee and smoking, discussing the matter which so engrossed every Victorian geographer, *the very matter upon which they were actually engaged*, Richard did not elaborate in the greatest detail. And it would have been a poor individual, especially given the confident spirit of exploration engendered by Victorian society, who could resist the lure.

Speke was, indeed, fascinated by Burton's narratives. So much so that in time he came to believe that they were *his own*; that he, Speke, had been their 'onlie begetter'. He later stated, and possibly convinced himself, that he had first heard of the supposed position of a

Great Lake (from which conversation, he claimed to have concluded that it was the probable source of the Nile) from some Somalis he met at Kurrum during his failed mission in the Horn of Africa in 1854. By the time he wrote this, he had clearly forgotten that he had not been able to converse with the Somalis during that journey; indeed, that he had used his inability to understand them as the primary defence for the failure of his mission.

Eventually Speke would come to believe that the scholarship, the formation of the theory and the drive to explore Africa's core, 'to rip Africa open' as he put it, had been his own. He cited a learned paper in Volume III (1801) of the *Asiatic Researches* as evidence of the scholarship which led to the formation of his theory.[54] In fact, he would hardly acknowledge that Richard Burton played any part in the matter at all and came to believe that he had been the real Commander of the expedition. It was unfortunate for him, therefore, that the paper upon which he claimed to have based his theory was discovered, shortly after the appearance of his book, to be an elaborate hoax based on forged documents.[55] But in 1856 these things were all in the distant future.

12

SECRET ENGAGEMENT
1856

The Expedition Committee of the R.G.S. comprised many supporters of Richard's: Francis Galton, Richard Monckton Milnes, Sir Roderick Murchison, John Arrowsmith and Colonel Sykes. Following an anxious request from Richard at the end of May for formal confirmation of their sanction so that he could begin the four months' work of preparing and equipping the expedition,[1] and further pressure applied by the Arctic explorer Admiral Sir George Back who had heavily supported Richard throughout the discussions, the Committee met in early June. The result of their meeting was set out as a recommendation to the East India Company stating the expedition objectives:

> The object of the proposed Expedition is to penetrate into the interior of Equatorial Africa from the East Coast in the Direction of the Lake, to ascertain the nature and the drainage generally of this part of the continent together with its other natural features, the position of its inhabited places, the character of its people, their resources and condition and the best means of establishing intercourse with them. The discovery of the Lake, and the parting of the rivers flowing into the East Coast on the one hand and towards the North and West on the other would naturally lead in the direction of the long-sought sources of the Nile, which have never before been attempted to be reached from this quarter. The attempt to solve this problem alone would suffice to attract the attention of the world to the proposed expedition.

To carry out this important objective the Council places great dependence on the experience and energy of Captain Burton . . . the qualities of this Officer and explorer were laid before the Hon Court by the council of the RGS in a communication dated Dec 22 1852. Since that time Captn Burton's memorable journey to Mecca and Medinah, and his bold expedition to the African city of Harar, have fully sustained the opinion then expressed . . . the expedition has already received the support of Her Majesty's Government to the extent of £1000.[2]

At one point Richard had considered making the search for the source of the Nile the expedition objective, but the German explorer Heinrich Barth (famous for his journey to Timbuktu) cautioned him about doing so, telling him firmly, 'no prudent man would *pledge* himself to discover the source of the Nile.'[3] The declared mission objective therefore was to locate and map the lakes, with any additional discoveries to be regarded as a bonus.

While waiting for Speke's arrival in London, Richard contacted several likely candidates for the third man position; Erhardt and Rebmann were obvious contenders. He also wrote to his friend, John Steinhaueser, who expressed a keen interest in joining him as a fourth man. Several additional candidates had applied through the R.G.S.; only one was considered suitable, and Richard wrote to Shaw requesting him to ask this man to join the party. 'If he cannot be with us I leave you to find a good honest John Bull who does not fear niggers . . . I've ordered a metallic boat from America,' he said breezily.[4]

As well as male candidates there were two female applicants. The first, 59-year-old Madame Ida Pfeiffer, had already achieved some public recognition by travelling alone through the near Middle East, Peru and the Celebes Sea – usually, according to her memoir published in 1851, swindled by sea captains, cheated by camel-drivers and exhausted by guides. She loved every moment of it. She had been raised as a boy by her misogynist father and, having brought up a family and outlived the much older husband she had been forced to marry, now wished to devote the remainder of her life to adventurous travel. Mrs Pfeiffer haunted Richard's waking hours, writing innumerable letters, following him wherever he went, pleading with him at every turn to allow her to join his expedition. Even when he disappeared, with relieved exasperation, into the safety of his (gentlemen only) club, she sent in notes from the door which were presented to him by grinning page-boys who adopted cheeky knowing looks as they told him, 'A lady wants to see you, sir!'[5] He did not escape her attentions until he left for Africa. Mrs Pfeiffer eventually set off alone for Madagascar in 1858. There, unfortunately, she contracted a fever which proved fatal.[6]

The second woman, unnamed in a letter to Richard's publishers, was a 'lady sportsman domiciled on the Himalayas after the death of her husband (an officer in the Indian army)'. She wrote to Richard listing her qualifications, her shooting ability and willingness to oversee domestic arrangements, cooking, needlework and so on. She ended her letter with the words: '. . . You need not think there could be any scandal about it because I am a grandmother.' Richard always claimed he had responded (somewhat ungallantly), 'Madam, had you not said you were a grandmother I might have consented.'[7]

When John Speke (called 'Jack' by Richard and other close friends) arrived back in London, he went as Richard's guest to the R.G.S. where he was shown, displayed on the walls, a map drawn up by Rebmann and Erhardt in the previous year. It showed a huge lake of indeterminate shape, 'like a huge slug' said some. Speke remarked later that everyone who saw 'The Slug Map' laughed in disbelief at the idea of a lake of such proportions – 300 miles wide and 800 in length, 'A single sheet of water . . . quite equal in size to, if not larger than, the great salt Caspian.'[8] In the 'Notice' appended to this map in January 1856, Erhardt had stated:

> The last point to the west in the Masai country is Burgenei; at the foot of the . . . mountains the country becomes arid, and the soil stony, mixed with sulphur and full of hot springs until one reaches Burgenei. A caravan of about twenty men left this spot and proceeded west in search of ivory, and came at the end of eight days, after a deal of trouble, to a large lake, on the shores of which dwelt the Wanyamwezi. It stretched to the north, south and west beyond the horizon . . .[9]

Although not convinced of the total accuracy of Erhardt's information (which Erhardt gathered from traders shortly before he left Mombasa in November 1855), Richard not only believed in the existence of the lake but suspected, from what he had been told at Harar, that there was not one but several lakes which were possible feeders for the fabled 'springs' of the Nile.[10] However, the existence of the lake or lakes was by no means regarded as a foregone conclusion by the geographers, and the debates on the matter were frequent and furious.

Official sanction of the expedition was eventually received from the East India Company, but with the somewhat disappointing news that instead of contributing £1,000 towards costs (as Colonel Sykes had virtually promised) the Directors had granted Richard two years' leave on full pay and allowances 'without prejudice to his position as a Regimental Officer' as their contribution. Permission for Speke to accompany him was refused. The Government in India had finally recognised the simmering resentment harboured by the subjugated inhabitants of India for the British (something Richard had identified and warned about on several occasions prior to leaving India in 1849). In the summer of 1856 they were diligently increasing military forces, ordering that no extensions of leave would be considered, and no officer in the Indian Army might be placed on duty out of India.

Speke was deeply disappointed having, in his own words, 'sacrificed' his Caucasian shooting expedition to accompany Richard (notwithstanding that he would have found it equally difficult to gain permission for that venture). Richard was not so easily squashed. He told Speke that if he would accompany him to Bombay he felt sure he could talk Lord Elphinstone and J.G. Lumsden into releasing him to join the officially supported expedition. Regarding Speke's other concern, his expenses, Richard was equally dismissive; both men still expected some reimbursement from the Company for their losses at Berbera. And when Richard took Speke to meet the President of the R.G.S., he – Sir Roderick Murchison – told Speke that if they succeeded in their aim they need not consider money. After all, identifying the source of the Nile was potentially the greatest discovery since that of the North American continent. In order to fund his trip to Bombay and the purchase of equipment, however, Richard gave Speke a personal cheque as a loan.[11]

Richard now began his preparations in earnest and a surviving indication of his minute care is a somewhat surprising detail; illuminated, sealed and signed letters written by Cardinal Wiseman to the Catholic missionaries in East Africa and to the British Consul at Zanzibar, Colonel Atkins Hamerton. Although Colonel Hamerton was asked through official channels to afford the expedition all the assistance in his power, Richard had discovered that Hamerton was a Roman Catholic and believed a letter of introduction from Wiseman might guarantee a more informal and personal commitment. Richard Monckton Milnes, Burton's strongest supporter, numbered Wiseman among his closest friends and it is probably through him (rather than Isabel Arundell, as has been generally assumed) that Richard made this contact.[12]

London June 28th 1856

Dear Sir,

Allow me to introduce to you Captain Burton, the bearer of this note, who is employed by the Government to make an expedition to Africa, at the head of a little band of adventurers. Captain Burton has been highly spoken of in the papers here and I have been asked to give him this introduction to you as a Catholic officer.

I am, dear Sir,
Yours sincerely in Christ
N. Card. Wiseman[13]

Among the welter of preparations for the expedition there were several important occurrences in Richard's personal life. First, news was received from Ceylon that Edward Burton had been seriously injured. While on an elephant hunt in the spring of 1856 he was set upon by Singalese villagers – Buddhists – who, furious at Edward's slaughter of animals that they revered as sacred, beat him senseless with a battery of stones and clubs. This was obviously of great concern to the emotionally close Burton family, but they were reassured to hear that Edward appeared to be making a good recovery.[14] Second, Richard had fallen in love again.

During that spring of 1856 Isabel Arundell had been pleasantly occupied in a full London Season when Blanche, the sister next to her in age, made her début. Both women were much courted and admired even though Isabel, at 24, was in some danger of being considered 'on the shelf'. But she had none of the desperation of women who felt obliged to marry simply to avoid spinsterhood, and there was still only one man in her life. This obsession was a cause of much anguish to her. The two sisters attended the Royal Ascot meeting in June and, as they queued to enter the Royal Enclosure, Isabel was charmed to see her childhood friend, the gipsy matriarch Hagar Burton, among the gaily dressed crowds. Leaning out of her carriage, Isabel shook hands and the woman asked, 'Are you Daisy Burton yet?' Isabel shook her head, replying ruefully that she wished she were.

> [Hagar's] face lit up. 'Patience;' she said, 'it is just coming.' She waved her hand, for at that moment she was rudely thrust from the carriage. I never saw her again.[15]

During a visit to the annual Regatta at Cowes at the end of July, the event which marks the end of the English summer social Season, Blanche was introduced to Mr John Smyth Piggott at the Royal Yacht Squadron Ball. Although he was more than twice her age, and had a mistress of many years' standing in Paris, Smyth Piggott was considered highly eligible, having several large estates in Somerset near Weston-Super-Mare of which he was Lord of the Manor. Not least, he was a Roman Catholic.[16] Blanche was Isabel's closest confidante at that time, and having seen what unrequited love had done for her elder sister, she had no wish to emulate her apparently permanent spinsterhood. Shortly after the Arundell girls returned to London, and to her mother's delight, Blanche accepted Smyth Piggott's proposal, settling for what would become a deeply unsatisfactory marriage. The wedding was planned for the following year.

Richard Burton had also been in town throughout that spring Season; Isabel heard of him from time to time but the two had not met. So although the gipsy's words were comforting, she had no reason to pin any hopes on them. However two months later, in the middle of August,[17] when Isabel and Blanche were taking their customary walk near their home in Hyde Park's Botanical Gardens, Isabel suddenly saw Richard walking towards her with her pretty cousin Louisa Segrave on his arm. Recalling that in Boulogne Richard and Louisa had enjoyed a semi-serious attachment, the sight must have been like a knife to Isabel's emotions, even though Louisa was then safely and happily married to a naval Captain. Isabel would always be jealous of her smaller, pretty and plump, fair cousin. The four stopped and shook hands and chatted.

It was the first time Isabel had seen Richard since the well-publicised incident at Berbera, and she must have examined his appearance with some anxiety. The well-cut velvet-collared frock-coat he adopted in town could not hide his muscular fitness. He wore his thick black hair in a fashionable style, and sported a moustache with long ends that drooped either side of his mouth. Isabel did not recount her reactions to his facial scarring in her autobiography, merely saying, 'all the old Boulogne memories and feelings returned to me'; the inference is that the scarring was not too disfiguring. When Richard asked her if she came to the Gardens often she replied that she generally came each day between 11 and 1 o'clock in hot weather, to read and study. In answer to his query on the subject of her study, she showed him her well-thumbed copy of *Tancred* and he 'explained' parts of it that she had not understood.

Isabel recalled that they chatted for about an hour, and when she rose to leave he gave her the same penetrating stare with which he had transfixed her attention at Boulogne. She pretended to look away, yet she felt his eyes boring into her as she said goodbye to her cousin, pretending nonchalance. As they walked away, the sisters heard Richard say to their cousin that Isabel had grown very charming since he had seen her as a schoolgirl at Boulogne. Louisa, who spent a great deal of her free time with Isabel, and with her had been one of the founder members of the now defunct Stella Club,[18] glanced back and uttered a mischievous cousinly, 'Ugh!' At home Isabel gazed at herself in the looking glass; trembling with anguish, she thought she looked 'a fright'.[19]

The best surviving portraits of Isabel at this time confirm descriptions of her contemporaries that she was 'handsome and fascinating'.[20] Even those who disliked her paid tribute to Isabel's scintillating personality and her 'presence'. She was also musically gifted. It was an age when all women of her class were educated to perform at parties and soirées; as Mr Rochester told Jane Eyre, 'all young ladies say they can play "a little".' But Isabel's talent was apparently better than average; she was always in demand to perform, had a rich contralto voice, and accompanied herself on the piano and guitar. Her repertoire ran to several hundred pieces of music and she was a lively performer.[21]

On the following morning Isabel and Blanche went to the gardens again as usual. Richard was sitting in the place where they had met on the previous day, alone this time, and obviously waiting for them. He was composing some poetry to show his friend Richard Monckton Milnes and when he saw the Arundell sisters approaching he rose and walked towards them, smiling, charming, saying he hoped Isabel wouldn't chalk up 'Mother will be angry' as she had at Boulogne. He was there again on the following day, and on the days after that. As they began to know each other better and she aired her knowledge of his travels, her own constant study of the East and her wish to travel, and he told her his plans for his forthcoming expedition, Isabel sensed his manner towards her change.

'This went on for a fortnight. I trod on air,' Isabel wrote. What Blanche (technically her elder sister's chaperone during these meetings) was doing during these long and increasingly intimate daily talks is unknown. Certainly she could not have been in the immediate vicinity when at the end of that magical two weeks Richard, who was about to leave for a short trip to Germany, stole his arm around Isabel's waist and nuzzled her cheek and asked if she would be prepared '. . . to give up civilisation? And if I could get the Consulate of Damascus will you marry me and go and live there?' Isabel was so overcome with mixed emotions that she could not find her voice, and Richard, probably misinterpreting her silence, continued, 'Do not give me an answer now, because it will mean a very serious step for you . . . giving up your people and all that you are used to, and living the sort of life that Lady Hester Stanhope led. I see the capabilities in you, but you must think it over.'[22] Finding Isabel still silent, Richard thought he had offended her. 'Forgive me,' he said, drawing back, 'I ought not to have asked so much.'

At last she was able to speak. The heartache with which she had lived for so many years was coated with the balm of his words and the face she lifted to his was radiant. 'I do not want to think it over,' she told him quietly. 'I have been thinking it over for six years, ever since I first saw you at Boulogne. I have prayed for you every morning and night, I have followed your career minutely, I have read every word you ever wrote, and I would rather have a crust and a tent with you than be Queen of all the world.' And she gave him her answer, 'Yes, YES!'[23]

In her partially completed autobiography Isabel chose to 'pass over the next few minutes', saying only that 'all that has been written or said on the subject of the first kiss is trash compared to the reality.' After a while Richard warned her, 'Your people will not give you to me.' They both knew that on at least three counts – his financial prospects, his religion, and his reputation – he was absolutely ineligible. Isabel, who must have considered this often during the past six years, replied fearlessly, 'I know that, but I belong to myself – I give myself away.' This was a bold statement given the times in which she lived and her affectionate deference to her parents. Of age she might be, but women of Isabel's class were financially dependent and did not contract their own marriages without parental sanction. The alternative to obtaining consent, a runaway marriage, was out of the question. The Queen had made it plain that she considered marriages of this nature abhorrent and would not 'receive' women who were party to such a union. Social ostracism for Isabel would end Richard's plans to seek a position in the Foreign Office after his return from Africa. But these considerations needed no discussion by the lovers; they were well known to them. Richard simply said, 'That is all right, be firm, and so shall I.'[24]

Her thoughts after she left him and returned home were dashed breathlessly into her journal:

> . . . Truly we never know from one half-hour to another what will happen. Life is like travelling in an open carriage with one's back to the horses – you see the path, you have an indistinct notion of the sides, but none whatever of where you are going . . . I have gained half the desire of my life; he loves me. But the other half remains unfulfilled; he wants to marry me!
>
> Perhaps I must not regret the misery that has spoilt the six best years of my life. But must I wait again? What can I do to gain the end? Nothing! My whole heart and mind is fixed on this marriage. If I cared less I could plan some course of action; but my heart and head are not cool enough . . . I feel all my own weakness and nothingness . . . I have at last met the master who can subdue me . . . In one sense I have no more reason to fear for my future, now that the load of shame and wounded pride, and unrequited affection is lifted . . . He loves me – that is enough for today.[25]

If these comments of Isabel's betray her longing for a dominant male to subdue her and sweep her off her feet, what can we make of Richard's motivations? Why did he propose to Isabel? And especially at a time when he was about to leave for Africa, for some three years, on a journey fraught with potentially lethal dangers from disease alone not to mention wild animals, reportedly murderous tribesmen and other, unknown, factors. She had little to offer a bachelor who needed to marry money. She had a small 'pin money' allowance, but otherwise her dowry consisted of good breeding and connections. Richard's motivation could *only* have been a strong physical and emotional attraction to an intelligent young woman who though not conventionally pretty was certainly striking.

Perhaps what initially attracted Richard was the apparent ease with which he could dominate the brilliance of this unusual girl. And dominate he did, for one entry in Isabel's journal reads:

> . . . when I am in his presence I am not myself – he makes me for the time see things with his own eyes, like a fever, or a momentary madness; and when I am alone again I . . . am frightened at my weak wavering and his dangerous but irresistible society . . .[26]

Immediately after the meeting during which he proposed to Isabel, Richard dropped a note to Shaw explaining that he was making a short trip to Baden-Baden and that when he returned to England he would make the final arrangements for his departure. The purpose of his brief visit to Germany is not known, but he was back in London on 21 September.

Following his return to England, Isabel wrote that, 'Richard and I had one brief fortnight of uninterrupted happiness, and were all in all to each other.' Because of his impending trip and the imminent parting they decided not to announce their engagement or seek permission from her parents, fearing that Isabel might have been prevented from even seeing him during their short remaining time. He told her that he would write from his ports of call, but once he left Zanzibar for the interior he could not guarantee she would receive any letters at all. He hoped to get post-bags back to the coast and Zanzibar by means of any coast-bound caravans he might meet on his journey, in which case she would hear news of him through the R.G.S. Any letters he wrote to her must be suitable for her to share with her family, so he would have to be 'most cautious'. Isabel could write to him as often as she wished, he said, only she had to accept the fact that it might sometimes be months before post-bags caught up with him, and again the safe receipt of these was uncertain.

In order to provide some excuse for writing, Richard then called at the Arundells' house in Russell Square. He introduced himself as a friend of Mrs Buckley and Mrs Segrave, reminding Isabel's parents that they had met at Boulogne several years earlier. 'He fascinated, amused and pleasantly shocked my mother, but completely magnetised my father and all my brothers and sisters,' Isabel recalled. 'My father used to say, "I do not know what it is about that man but I cannot get him out of my head; I dream about him every night."'[27]

Isabel's joy, so long in putting in its appearance, was both marred and heightened by the knowledge that their time together was so limited. And although Richard hoped to remain until mid-October there was a matter brewing which, if he was not careful, could adversely affect his exploration plans. He told her all about it; a former officer of Beatson's Cavalry, Colonel Shirley, was under detention pending court-martial in London, and Richard had been privately notified that he was to be called as a witness. While he had no objection to appearing as a witness, *per se*, there was a real danger that the case might drag on for many weeks, causing him to miss the monsoon he counted on to carry him to Zanzibar from Bombay. He therefore intended (with the help of a confidant who was watching out for a subpoena in Richard's name), to slip away before it could be served on him. If this happened, he warned Isabel, he would have to leave within 24 hours.[28]

This was not Isabel's only worry. She knew that her future happiness, i.e. marriage to Richard, depended on 'willing parents and a grateful country', and both of these looked so unlikely as to make the dream an almost impossible one. 'Richard too was exercised about how I should be able to support his hard life, and whether a woman could really do it,' she wrote. It was natural that he should give some thought to this; Isabel's background and her present manner of living was far removed from the peripatetic lifestyle that suited Richard. She did not, however, take his concern lightly and later would do what she could to prepare herself in a practical manner for the sort of life he offered.

They met for a few hours each day. For her the rest of the time was interminable. Richard was fully occupied with last-minute preparations, with his circle of men friends, or with the geographers at the R.G.S. rooms. On 1 October he received the drafts of the remaining three-quarters of the R.G.S. funding; he had already been given (and spent) £250, the second £250 was to be paid to him at Bombay, the third instalment on arrival at Zanzibar and the fourth 'to be kept by Colonel Hamerton until called up by Captain Burton'.[29] It was the final outstanding item of his preparations. On the evening of 2

October he dined with his old friend from Oxford University, Alfred Bate Richards, and confided that he was leaving on the following evening for Ostend. Travelling overland via Berlin to Trieste, he would 'ship to Alexandria,' he said, asking A.B. Richards 'to see him off, as before'.[30] Because of Burton's horror of leave-taking from those to whom he was emotionally attached, no one else – not Isabel, and no member of his family – was told of the imminent departure.

On the morning of 3 October Isabel went to meet Richard as usual in the park. She took with her, to show him, the horoscope written for her in Romany by Hagar Burton so many years before. Richard, always fascinated by magic, the occult and general hocus pocus, was delighted by Isabel's story of how this had been obtained.[31] They exchanged gifts; he had drawn for her a sketch map of the lakes he expected to find in Africa:

Sketch map drawn by Richard Burton for Isabel before he left for Africa.

and gave her a curiously apposite poem that he had written concerning his ambitions:

I wore thine image, Fame
Within a heart well fit to be thy shrine!
Others a thousand boons may gain,
    One wish was mine . . .

The hope to gain one smile,
To dwell one moment cradled on thy breast,
Then close my eyes, bid life farewell,
    And take my rest.[32]

Knowing that their remaining time was growing short, Isabel placed around his neck a medal of the Virgin Mary upon a steel chain which she hoped would protect him, in the way that many people place faith in St Christopher charms. She had originally offered this object on a gold chain but he had asked her not to give him a gold chain, saying that 'they will cut my throat for it out there'. Both Richard and Isabel had a regard for such talismans and, as they arranged to meet on the following day, he promised her he would wear it throughout his journey. He kept his promise and made a similar one to his sister Maria. She gave him a star-sapphire ring, to replace the gold snake ring with a diamond head which he had worn in India, and had given her.

That afternoon Richard called at the Arundell home, ostensibly to visit Mrs Arundell. 'We met of course before my mother only as friends . . . [and] talked formally . . . It chanced that we were going to the play that night. I begged him to come, and he said he would if he could, but that if he did not I would know he had some heavy business to transact . . . He appeared to me to be agitated, and I could not account for his agitation. He stayed about an hour.' As he left she shook hands with him and said, gravely serious for her mother's benefit, but in the happy and secret knowledge that she would see him as usual on the following morning, 'I hope we shall see you on your return from Africa.'

That night she dreamed he had departed for Africa leaving a letter of explanation. She woke in a panic and ran downstairs in tears. The post had not arrived and one of her brothers, to whom she confided her fear, suggested she had had a nightmare after having eaten too much lobster at supper. But when the post arrived there was a letter for Blanche from Richard (as an engaged woman Blanche was able to receive private letters), and inside was a note for Isabel saying that he had found it too painful to part and that he thought they would suffer less this way. He told her that they would be reunited in 1859. She wore his note in a little bag on a chain around her neck until his return. Distraught, Isabel retired to her bedroom for three days in deep depression. Her only consolation was the knowledge that at least she 'was not unloved . . . now the shame of loving unasked was taken from me.'

Ten days later (by then she had 'got into a state of listening for every post'), she received her first letter from him, presumably through Blanche. He had written from Bruges on 9 October, hoping she was not offended at his abrupt departure. He asked her to write to him at Trieste and Bombay, and promised that he would write from both those places. She did not know, then, that almost all their partings in the future would be equally abrupt, nor that Richard's family felt as bereft as she did at the only manner in which Richard could contemplate leaving those he loved. As the days wore on, knowing he was travelling across Europe to Italy she wrote him three letters, pouring into them all her thoughts, 'everything, just as it enters my head, as I would if I were with him . . . a mixture of love, trust, anger, faith, sarcasm, tenderness, bullying, melancholy, all mixed up'. Her letters to him were cathartic and eased her depression.

There was no immediate reply; she did not expect one for some weeks but in early November Isabel received, via an unknown hand – possibly Louisa's – a copy of Richard's book *Falconry in the Valley of the Indus*. He had initialled it. Isabel wrote her name under his, and dated the gift.[33] By now she had rallied from the blow of Richard's leaving, as her journal entries show.

> A woman feels raised by the love of a man to whom she has given her heart . . . It is true I was captured at first sight; but his immense talents and adventurous life compelled interest, and a master mind like his exercises influence on all around it. But I *love* him, because I find in him a depth of feeling, a generous heart, and because, though brave as a lion, he is yet a gentle, delicate, sensitive nature, and the soul of honour . . . he unites the wild, lawless creature and the gentleman . . .

She also respected Richard's ambitions; and was awed by his desire to make discoveries, his will and power to change the face of scientific knowledge:

> . . . Fancy achieving a good which affects millions, making your name a household name! . . . half the men in the world live and die, and are never missed and, like a woman, leave nothing behind them but a tombstone . . . I would at this moment sacrifice and leave all to follow his fortunes, were it his wish or for his good . . .[34]

Then, with her customary energy she busied herself making early plans for Blanche's forthcoming marriage, drawing up guest lists, writing the invitations, helping to prepare the trousseau, and plan and order the wedding carriages.[35] She marvelled at her sister's contentment in her decision to marry for position and financial security rather than love, and though she was happy for the younger girl, in her journal Isabel exulted:

> I love and I am loved . . . no gilded misery for me. I was born for love, and require it as light and air. Whatever harshness the future may bring, he has loved me, and my future is bound up in him with all consequences . . . he thinks he is sacrificing me; but I want pain, privations, danger with him . . . Where I could not so follow him, I would not be a clog to him, for I am tolerably independent.[36]

She might have been less sanguine had she known that Richard had also given a copy of his poem 'Fame' to her cousin, *and* named his portable metal boat the *Louisa*.[37] Previous biographers have made much of this, inferring that because he did not name the vessel the *Isabel*, Richard's true feelings lay with his former love. This is to neglect the rules of play in Victorian England in the mid-nineteenth century. Even had he wished to do so Richard could not have called his boat after Isabel, a young unmarried woman, without impossibly compromising her reputation. Significantly, Louisa's name and address did not appear in the short list of those to whom Richard had promised to write, which he copied into the back of the letter-book that was his daily companion in Africa. There, along with his closest friends Alfred Bate Richards, Henry Murray and Richard Monckton Milnes, were a few geographers and influential supporters, his sister, and Isabel Arundell. Also on the list was Isabel's friend, Miss

Providence Cooper, to be addressed care of a firm of solicitors. Her inclusion was a route by which Richard could occasionally contact Isabel without the risk of his letter being intercepted by Mrs Arundell.[38]

From Alexandria, Burton and Speke travelled overland to Suez, where they shipped for Aden and, eventually, Bombay. On Richard's first visit to India the journey had taken four months. Now, overland, with luck and good management of timetables it could be done in half that time. Burton grew more expansive and light-hearted as they travelled east. Speke gave no indication of it at the time, but he was nursing a deep resentment of Richard.

Shortly before Richard left England, his book *First Footsteps in East Africa* had been published. An edited version of his daily journals and logs, this was Richard's two-volume account of his successful trip to Harar. The main part of the book contained some 317 pages of narrative, the final eleven pages being given over to an explanation of the Berbera incident. Following this were some 250 pages of appendices, glossaries and assorted information, of which 40 pages were entitled 'Lieutenant Speke's Diaries'.

Richard considered that the journals kept by his team, and any discoveries made during the expedition, were available to him, as Commander, to write about. Doubtless, had Speke wished to write his own book from his journals, Richard would have been the first to offer encouragement. Indeed he had already done so, for when Speke returned to Aden after his unsuccessful Somalia venture he showed Richard his journals. Richard stated:

> He had recorded his misadventures in a diary whose style, to say nothing of sentiments and geographical assertions, rendered it, in my opinion, unfit for publication, and I took the trouble of re-writing the whole. Published as an appendix to 'First Footsteps in East Africa', it was in the third person, without the least intention of giving offence, but simply because I did not wish to palm upon the reader my own composition as that of another person.[39]

Speke did not mention his irritation about Richard's use of his diaries at the time. Nor, apparently, did he discuss with Richard his annoyance when a review of *First Footsteps* – which appeared in *Blackwood's Magazine*[40] after the two men left England – was

forwarded to Trieste by Isabel.[41] The reviewer in this instance was
Lawrence Oliphant whom Richard had known for some years, having
met him at Henry Murray's apartments. Oliphant also knew Speke,
having met him briefly in Constantinople when Speke told him of his
travels in the Himalayas and Somalia. With his penchant for, indeed –
according to his biographer – his delight in causing mischief, Oliphant
mentioned in his review the short appendix containing Burton's edited
version of Speke's observations:

> . . . it lacks the interest of a personal narrative; and we much regret
> that the experiences of one whose extensive wanderings had already
> so well qualified him for the task, and who has shown himself so
> able an explorer, should not have been chronicled at greater length,
> and thrown into a form which would have rendered them more
> interesting to the general reader.[42]

With hindsight Richard recognised this statement as 'a brand, not
foolishly thrown'. It fostered in Speke's mind the conviction that
Burton had not only plagiarised his work, but had deliberately damaged by rewriting what had originally been a good piece of
penmanship. A more rational man might have realised that there was
an obvious solution; Richard had used only 40 pages (it comprised
less than 10 per cent of *First Footsteps*), so there was no reason why –
had it indeed been publishable – Speke should not still publish. But
Speke was not a rational thinker. Along with his feelings of injured
authorship went the theme that Richard had unfairly profited by his
(Speke's) work which had cost him so much in financial terms
through his losses at Berbera. He was unaware that Richard made no
profit from this book.

Another cause for resentment was the fact that Richard had forwarded the entire collection of fauna specimens, shot by Speke during
his Somali journey, to the Calcutta Museum of Natural History. Later,
Richard would state several times that he did this on instructions
from Speke given before the latter left Aden for sick leave in England;
that the collection was forwarded to India fully acknowledged as 'the
work of Captain Speke' and was mentioned in the book (and in the
Bombay Times) as being wholly Speke's work. In fact one of the
small rats sent as a specimen was new to science, and was named
Pectinator Spekii. He said he assumed Speke had kept duplicates of

his expedition specimens for himself, as he was well aware of the younger man's ambition to build up a 'natural history museum' in his parents' home.[43]

At the time, however, as the two men travelled as quickly as possible towards India, Richard knew nothing of the sore festering secretly in his companion's mind. It was only with hindsight that he identified Speke's inward-looking nature, his tendency to hoard memories of incidents and dwell on them, 'till brought to light by a sudden impulse. He would brood, perhaps for years, over a chance word, which a single outspoken sentence of explanation could have satisfactorily settled. The inevitable result was the exaggeration of fact into fiction, the distortion of the true to the false.'[44]

Speke was not by nature a diary-keeper when Richard met him; he relied on his own recollections of events, and it was only after firm instructions from Richard that he began a regular journal on his travels. Consequently, as Richard pointed out, Speke had few notes to refer back to, to remind himself of factual sequences of events or his own on-the-spot reactions, and therefore when recalling events at a distance in time he spoke with all the conviction of an honest man. Richard once pointed out to him the difference between what he had written some time earlier and what he now said, 'and he looked at me in absolute incredulity'.[45]

All the constituents of what he regarded as ill-usage, and other grievances as yet unidentified, were quietly coalescing in Speke's subconsciousness, disguised by the fact that he still stood in semi-awe of Burton, and in Burton's ability to get things done. At the time Richard saw only the quiet charm of his tall, fair companion. Why else should he invite him to join the most important project he had ever undertaken?

Nearly twenty years would pass before Richard could write sadly that the literary firebrand mischievously thrown by Lawrence Oliphant had 'kindled a fire which did not consume the less fiercely because it was smothered'. Indeed, the resulting conflagration would have an epic effect on both their lives. But far more complex than Richard's decision to take Speke were Speke's motives in joining Richard.

13

THE SCENT OF CLOVES
1856–1857

Richard began the published record of his most famous journey with the words, 'Of the gladdest moments, methinks in human life, is the departing upon a distant journey into unknown lands . . .'[1]

He wrote of the relief of leaving behind daily routine and the constraints of civilisation, of the lure of the unknown to the imagination and memory, and the welling up of hope. This is one of the keys to Burton's personality. Unwilling, and perhaps unable, to cope with the tedious demands of everyday life, his intellect required the constant stimulation of new challenges which he found in travel. Richard chose to call this characteristic the 'gipsy' element of his nature. He began identifying himself with gipsies very early in life, his physiognomy and colouring lending itself to the fantasy, as well as the fact that one of the foremost gipsy tribes in England bore the surname Burton. This self-delusion was bolstered by his fascination with, and research into, mystical practices and beliefs, and his conviction that he could read not only the future but, using hypnosis, certain people's minds. There is, however, far more evidence in his antecedents to support the Burton family's belief in an illegitimate descent from Louis XIV than his theory that in some respect he was a gipsy.

Burton and Speke reached Shepheard's Hotel, Cairo at noon on 6 November, and were met by the British Consul who handed Richard an official letter. It demanded his 'instant return' to London to attend the court-martial of Colonel Shirley, and stated that as Chief of Staff of the Bashi-Bazouks during the time in question he was a vital witness. 'You are directed to proceed not through France but by the steamer direct from Alexandria to Southampton.'[2]

The curt tone of the letter may have been provoked by critical remarks made by Richard in the Preface of *First Footsteps* which had gone on sale about the time of his departure from England. Here, he commented on the manner in which the once-great Indian Navy had been 'crushed by neglect and routine into a mere transport service, remarkable for little beyond constant quarrels between . . . officers and their [army] passengers . . .'[3] He was also frankly dismissive of British policy at Aden, and attacked what he saw as weakness in dealing with the Arabs who dwelt in the neighbourhood of the British fort there. He appears to have forgotten that in seeking permission to publish the journal of his Harar adventure, he had assured the Company 'that all political allusions would be carefully avoided'.

He decided to ignore the command to return. Fortunately, the steamship on which he arrived had already left Alexandria at 10 a.m. that morning. The next ship to England would not depart for another three weeks. Pausing only one night, the two men rushed across the desert to Suez and sailed for Aden; there, as they boarded the first ship bound for Bombay, Richard handed his official response to Dr Steinhaueser to be sent through the Company's overland mail. He knew it could not arrive in England for nearly three weeks, and that a reply would take a further six weeks to arrive in Bombay.

> . . . It is therefore evident that I could not possibly obey the order within the limits specified [and] no mention was made about my returning to England by the next steamer. Probably, however, the Ct. Martial now pending . . . will before that time have come to a close. I need hardly say that should I on arrival at Bombay find an order to that effect it shall be instantly and implicitly obeyed.
>
> Considering, however that I have already stated all I know upon the subject . . . that I was not subpoenaed in England and that I am under directions of the RGS and employed . . . under the patronage of the Foreign Office . . . I venture respectfully to hope that I have taken the proper course . . . by the loss of a few weeks a whole year's exploration must be allowed to pass by . . . As a servant of the Hon'ble EIC in whose interests I have conscientiously and energetically exerted myself for . . . 14 years I request . . . the

Directors to use their powerful influence on my behalf. Private
interests cannot be weighed against public duty. I remained long
enough in London to enable the War Office to call for my presence . . .[4]

In England, Norton Shaw – having been advised that Burton had
been recalled – did his best to have the summons squashed, but in
answer to Shaw's observation that Richard was heading a highly
important expedition he was haughtily informed by a staff secretary
from India House that Speke was 'a most intelligent superior officer
and, as I understand it, is second in command in Captain Burton's
party . . .' Speke therefore, Shaw was told, could take command of the
expedition until after the trial when Captain Burton would be 'able to
follow and overtake him'.[5] Shaw bridled at this and wrote to the
Earl of Clarendon that he could not, under the circumstances, 'advise
the substitution of another leader to the Expedition'.[6]

Richard had originally intended to spend some days in Aden with
Dr John Steinhaueser, discussing his old friend's projected participa-
tion in the expedition. It now became expedient to push on for
Bombay and make for East Africa before the English mail caught up
with him. The strategem worked. He arrived in Bombay on 23
November and on 1 December he embarked for Zanzibar. In a single
week of frenzied activity he outfitted the expedition with a mountain
of stores, and hired two Goanese butlers. With the assistance of James
Lumsden he persuaded Lord Elphinstone to release Speke and
Steinhaueser to his command; to send the expedition to Zanzibar in
grand style aboard the Indian Navy sloop of war, *Elphinstone*, so that
there might be no doubt in the minds of Zanzibar's inhabitants as to
the status of the explorers; and to officially instruct and personally
request the British Consul there to afford Burton 'every assistance'.[7]

Richard's final action before he sailed was to write to London
advising that as he had found no instruction awaiting him at Bombay,
and having been allotted passage on an Indian Navy vessel due to
depart imminently, he was proceeding for East Africa as planned. 'If
I have mistaken the intentions of the Company, I venture to hope that
an error of judgment may not be confounded with intentional disrespect,' he wrote piously.[8] The *Elphinstone* sailed on the following
morning after Lumsden had been rowed out to wish them God-speed.

London's response to Richard's Aden letter arrived in Bombay in late December, still shrilly demanding his recall. In January the Directors insisted that on his return to Bombay his behaviour be thoroughly investigated.[9] He received this demand two years later on his return journey. But as though this were not enough tweaking of the official noses, Richard raised the temperature of the senior staff of London's India House to steam heat, by a long letter written during his passage to Zanzibar. This outlined what he saw as the present unsettled state of affairs in the environs of the Red Sea and Arabia, resulting from 'the mismanagement of the Anglo-Indian government' and the hot temper of the Arabs. His keen observation processes and his interrogation of knowledgeable local people during his journey made it obvious to him that trouble was brewing; the Company would need to act quickly and firmly, he concluded, if almost inevitable bloodshed was to be avoided. He could not resist recording his observations in minute detail and sending his recommendations on how the matter should be dealt with; '. . . The next step should be to provide ourselves with a more efficient naval force at Aden, the head-quarters of the Red Sea Squadron. I may briefly quote here as proof of the necessity for protection, the number of British protégés in the neighbouring ports and the present value of Jeddah trade . . .'[10]

The tenor of this letter would probably have been perfectly accept-able as the intelligence report of an officer sent on a specific mission. But this was not the case, and the report was not read by men like Charles Napier but by civil servants. So it was regarded as rank impertinence from a junior officer, and later even Richard recognised this, writing wryly, 'Again, that zeal!' and realising that he should have written in rose-coloured terms.[11] His fears were eventually proved correct. The Company's response, a sharp rebuke which took two years to reach its unrepentant addressee, arrived in the same post as a newspaper report of a massacre at the port of Jeddah in which fourteen Christians were butchered.

While Richard was being carried across the Indian Ocean by a brisk north-easterly wind, thrilled at the clean efficiency under which the *Ephinstone* operated in direct contrast to the confusion, noise, smells and sea-sick passengers he had recently experienced on the Red Sea packet, Isabel was at home beginning yet another of her large scrapbooks devoted to his exploits, and working out the time in East Africa: 'I have made out that at 10 p.m. it is midnight there, and the morning star shines on him two hours before it does on me.'[12] He had written to her, as promised, from Trieste, and she prepared for Christmas eagerly awaiting his promised letter from Bombay – not knowing of his hasty departure from there – which should arrive with the India mail in mid-January. After that, as she wrote sadly in her scrapbook, '[I] can only hear of him . . . through such scraps as these, doled out quarterly in the *Times*.'[13]

Isabel's life that winter was made of small joys, duly entered into her journal: Venus, her morning star, shining brightly at dawn through frost-covered windows at her Aunt Monica's (Lady Gerard's), house 'Porto Bello', in Mortlake. Here she met Wilfred Scawen Blunt who described her as 'fair-haired and rather pretty . . . quiet . . . of the convent type'.[14] A report in *The Times* about Richard's progress eastwards brought his name into family discussion. 'I was delighted to hear father and mother praising Richard today; mother said he was clever and agreeable and she liked him so much, and they both seemed so interested about him. They little know how much they gratified me.' She was pretending to read a book, 'but when . . . I came to put it away I found it had been upside down all the time.'[15] Each night she prayed for his safety, and that he would return to her 'with changed religious feelings', so that her parents would give their consent and she could be married.

On the evening of 18 December the *Elphinstone* dropped anchor off a reef near the Islands. Next morning Richard was on deck at dawn to drench his delighted senses in the sights and smells of the archipelago. The warm breeze laden with the scent of cloves wafted from the white coral-sand beaches of the tranquil islands, which he described as the lands of 'the Lotus Eaters'. Zanzibar lay 'soft and smiling' in a luscious mysterious beauty he described in wholly feminine terms:

> . . . the swelling line of the Zanzibar coast . . . wrapped in a soft and
> sensuous repose. The sea of purest sapphire . . . lay basking, lazy . . .
> under a blaze of sunshine which touched every object with a dull
> burnish of gold . . . The island itself . . . voluptuous with gentle
> swellings, with the rounded contours of the girl-negress, and the
> brown-red tintage of its warm skin showed through its gauzy attire
> of green . . . whilst every feature was hazy and mellow, as if viewed
> through 'woven air'.[16]

Later that morning the ship 'glided S. by E. along the shore' to the harbour of Zanzibar. They passed dozens of vessels, some of whom hailed them. They could not understand what was being shouted, and became increasingly puzzled at the lack of bunting and flags which were customarily hoisted when a foreign cruiser entered a harbour. As well as Arab dhows which had run before the monsoon winds, as the *Elphinstone* had done, there were some half-dozen European and American merchantmen who had rounded the Cape and sailed north to the only trading point on the East African coast. Here, they loaded with 'cargoes of copal, coconuts, ivory, hides, tortoiseshell, red pepper, ambergris, beeswax, hippopotamus teeth, rhinoceros horn [and] cowrie shells' from the Zanzibar markets.[17] These, too, were devoid of any signs of welcome. In the absence of any obvious problem, Captain Frushard ordered the cannon cast loose and loaded, and with the Sultan's ensign on the mainmast and 'the union jack at the fore', the *Elphinstone* dropped her anchor with a loud rattle, and began a smart 21-gun salute. 'Whereupon a gay bunting flew up every [mast] . . . ashore and afloat, while the . . . Muscat navy roared a response of 22.'[18]

Once ashore the British Consul, Colonel Atkins Hamerton, received them 'like sons rather than passing visitors',[19] explaining the reason for the initial lack of civilities. The Sultan Sayyid Said, staunch ally of the British, had died. Fortuitously, the *Elphinstone* had arrived just as the statutory period of mourning was ending, at noon on the fortieth day. But though welcoming Richard and his party warmly, Hamerton had depressing news. The late Sultan's elder son refused to accept as heir to the throne the younger son appointed by his father, and was threatening to attack Zanzibar. As a result the mainland of East Africa was 'in a state of anarchy', added to which an exceptionally severe drought (they had arrived in the dry season) had reduced the coastal areas to a state of famine. In short, Richard deduced, Hamerton's advice to him was 'that I had better return to Bombay. But rather than return to Bombay I would have gone to Hades.'[20]

Painfully aware that, 'after the disaster in Somali-land, I was pledged at all risks and under all circumstances to succeed', Richard prudently decided to delay the main expedition until after the rains when food and water should be readily available. Meanwhile, at Hamerton's invitation he and Speke made their base in the beach-side Consulate, a large dun-coloured building 'shaped like a claret case'.[21]

From there Richard explored the island over the next weeks, making copious notes and observations. These notes would eventually make a book[22] which is still regarded as a standard work on Zanzibar from which Burton's comments are extensively quoted by present-day historians and anthropologists.

From his book, it is obvious that the exotic promise Richard glimpsed from the deck of the *Elphinstone* on that serene morning was not always reflected in the reality of Zanzibar. Certainly the scented island was fascinating. Colourful birds nested in the chandeliers of the Residency, and Burton could lie in bed listening to the murmur of soft African voices. But over the island's natural beauty, humanity had cast its usual detritus. A colourful multi-ethnic population of 100,000 lived for the most part in the crowded Stonetown, and Richard was interested to note that some effort had been made to take away the monsoon rains with the first street gutters he had seen in the east. The narrow and often befouled streets wound between tall, overhanging shuttered buildings and teemed with a constant procession of residents going about their daily business and marketing. Chain-gangs of slaves were driven under the whip from one holding point to another, cattle and beasts of burden moved slowly through the crowds, beggars and pariah dogs hugged the walls and doorways. Musky, spicy scents fought with a pervasive stench of copra and decaying fish. Cowries (still a form of currency in parts of the Orient) were piled in great heaps on the harbour beach; in the deeply oppressive heat the revolting smell of decomposing molluscs was overpowering.

Diseases of all kinds flourished, from tropical fevers and cholera to smallpox and malaria. Wide and varied insect life and water organisms led to unpleasant bowel and pulmonary complaints, indeed Richard noted with glee that in Zanzibar heavy consumers of alcohol usually outlived water drinkers. Venereal diseases were rampant, he noticed, probably out of personal interest. His engagement to Isabel did not, apparently, prevent him from seeking sexual partners during his African journey. 'Arab women . . . fearing scandal and its consequences . . . deny themselves to Europeans . . . [but] girls who work for hire are always procurable.'[23]

But far, far worse than all the other ills, to Richard's mind, was the misery and degradation of the slave trade. Some 40,000 slaves a year passed through Zanzibar in the mid-nineteenth century, and a poll tax was payable to the Sultan on every one landed. They were transported crammed into dhows 'with eighteen inches between the decks', Richard wrote, '[and] given a pint of water a day'. One third died of disease and malnutrition. Slave masters would toss a sick captive overboard rather than pay to take him or her ashore to die. As a result, decaying human corpses being picked over by cur dogs were a common sight on the beaches. Speke recalled how he was horrified to see the treatment of a divorced woman who had been returned to the slave market by her husband for suspected inconstancy. When some would-be buyers began an intimate inspection of her, Speke saw that 'she had learned a sense of decency during her conjugal life, and the blushes on her face now clearly showed how her heart was mortified at this unseemly exposure, made worse because she could not help it . . .'[24]

Richard witnessed what appears to be the same incident at a slave auction and wrote it in his diary:

Lines of negroes stood like beasts . . . some appeared hardly human . . . all were horribly thin, with ribs protruding like the circles of a cask, and not a few squatted sick on the ground. The most interesting were the young boys who grinned as if somewhat pleased by the degrading and hardly decent inspection to which both sexes and all ages were subjected . . . there was only one decent looking girl, with carefully blacked eyebrows. She seemed modest, and had probably been exposed for sale in consequence of some inexcusable offence against decorum . . . The dealers smiled at us and were in a good humour . . .[25]

But shocked as Speke was when he and Richard were in Zanzibar in 1857, Atkins Hamerton had spent 16 years of his life, sacrificing his health and any possibility of marriage, to achieve the state of affairs which then prevailed. Slavery was an economic fact of life, but many improvements had been achieved by Hamerton's representations to the late Sultan. Due to him, confiscations from, and floggings of, slave-owners for excessive cruelties were made law. During his years on Zanzibar Hamerton had become a highly respected figure, regarded second only to the Sultan in stature.

Like Burton and Speke, he had first seen service in the Indian Army where he had shown an aptitude for native languages, especially

Hindustani and Persian, and he qualified as an interpreter. His rise to the position of Company Agent was halted briefly when he was formally admonished for acting as second in a duel in which one of the protagonists lost his life.[26] Speke wrote of Hamerton's vivacity and fund of uproarious anecdotes with which he kept them entertained after supper, but Richard saw plainly that the 50-year-old Irishman was seriously weakened by the effects of constant attacks of malaria and dysentery: 'The worse symptom . . . was his unwillingness to quit the place which was slowly killing him. At night he would chat merrily . . . about a return to Ireland; he loathed the subject in the morning.'[27] It seemed easier, to Hamerton, to stay where he was than face the long journey home, but he lulled Richard's anxiety by promising to return to Ireland after he had seen the expedition off into the interior.

Hamerton and Burton got on well together, they shared a similar robust sense of humour and Richard's part-Irish heritage undoubtedly helped. Richard also found the Consul highly intelligent and unexpectedly knowledgeable on the subject of Oriental scholarship in the long conversations they shared each evening after dinner. But he was startled to hear from the strongly Catholic Hamerton a firm recommendation to distance himself from the Christian missionaries who had made themselves unpopular.[28]

Richard learned that there was deep mistrust of the expedition by the Arabs both on the island and along the coast; they feared that it was an excuse to gain a British toehold in East Africa which would end their own trading monopoly and damage the lucrative slave trade. The danger to the members of the expedition, should the tribes in the interior be encouraged to be obstructive, was obvious. Hamerton believed he had been successful in 'obscuring the old prejudices, [and] fears . . . long entertained of foreigners penetrating into Africa . . .',[29] but he cautioned Richard to proceed with utmost care. He also advised him to delay the main expedition until after the rains.

Although Richard wrote to Norton Shaw that he did not believe half of what he had been told about the dangers and difficulties of the journey,[30] he decided that the best way to ascertain the true situation on the mainland was to make a few 'excursions', exploring and surveying the mainland coast, returning to Zanzibar between times to prepare for the main expedition.[31] After all, the nearest point on the mainland was only 20 miles away and could be seen quite clearly on most days. This plan had the added advantage of allowing more time for Steinhaueser to join them.

At the Consul's request Richard met the new Sultan, a mild and amiable youth who was recovering from smallpox. Richard needed the Sultan's *firman* as protection during their travels. This was granted on two conditions; first that those involved in the expedition were all sound men for whose goodwill Hamerton could personally vouch; and second that no attempt would be made to gain Christian converts along the way. Having agreed to these conditions, Richard was provided with a document signed by the Sultan. He added it to the two 'passports' he already wore in a leather pouch, the illuminated letter from Cardinal Wiseman, and the diploma of the Sheikh of Mecca certifying his *haj*. As a further sign of patronage, the Sultan furnished Richard with a small force of thirteen Beluchi *askaris* (gun-carrying guards) and ten slaves, to whom he promised an appropriate reward if the expedition was successful.

In order to visit the mainland, he chartered a vessel for 32 dollars a month. It was a ripe old dhow with a single mast, patched and baggy lateen sail, a bowsprit almost as long as the boat itself, a full complement of cockroaches and an alarming tendency to fill with bilge-water. On 10 January they sailed for the island of Pemba, which Richard combed and recorded with his usual diligence. For Richard, Pemba's chief attraction was the legend that it was here, in 1698, that the infamous pirate Captain Kidd had buried the treasures he had plundered throughout the Orient. After Pemba they made for Mombasa, not only to see the land-locked harbour with its famed ancient citadel but to visit Mr and Mrs Rebmann at the Christian Mission of Kisulodiny, 15 miles up-river.

He had initially intended to persuade Rebmann to join him and make a fourth team member (with Steinhaueser), and indeed he carried with him a letter from the Church Missionary Society advising Rebmann that the Society had no objection to his joining the expedition.[32] However, following Hamerton's strongly expressed remarks about missionaries, Richard changed his mind. Rebmann made things easy for him by stating that he would only agree to join if he could continue his missionary work during the expedition. Richard explained how he had given his word to the Sultan that no attempt would be made to gain converts as they travelled, and therefore, ('reluctantly') he could not allow it.

Nevertheless, Rebmann and his English wife received them hospitably. Mrs Rebmann, especially, liked Richard, and he appears to have made a special attempt to charm this woman for whom he felt a great sympathy in her comfortless home.[33] Rebmann insisted that, at all cost, the expedition should avoid the Masai plains lying between Mombasa and 'the inland sea'. The Masai tribesmen were the fiercest warriors in East Africa, 'life is valueless amongst them', he warned. Any Europeans travelling through their territory would do so at their peril.[34] Krapf, too, had reported to the R.G.S. that Arab caravans venturing into the Masai country always took with them 600–1,000 men armed with muskets.

So, although the northern route inland from Mombasa looked to be an easier one, Richard could not afford to ignore advice on dangers from men well used to travelling in the country. The memory of the barbarous murder of the first European explorer to venture beyond the coast, a young French naval officer named Maizan, was still fresh in men's minds. Maizan, who had prepared well for the expedition, had been captured in 1844 after becoming separated from his armed escort. His captors hog-tied him to a spit and hacked off various parts of his body. Finally, having lifted his axe to perform the *coup de grâce*, the executioner had cruelly paused and sharpened his blade in front of the victim before decapitating him.[35] The murderer was never apprehended, but the man who beat the drum during this grisly incident was captured. When Richard first arrived in Zanzibar he was shown this prisoner, chained like a dog in a small container in which he could neither fully stand up nor properly lie down. He had been there for ten years.

Richard had proposed, during his short exploration of the East African coast around Mombasa, to travel inland to see the ice-capped mountain which natives called Kilim n'jaro (Kilimanjaro). Thus he could have sent an appealing 'appetiser' report back to London, before departing on the main expedition. However, his negotiations with potential guides were complicated by the wrangling of men of different tribes, each vying to route the party through his own village, a privilege which Richard guessed would prove too costly in gifts. Added to this, the drought had made it difficult to procure adequate provisions, and parties of armed plunderers were raiding villages and caravans for food, making it a dangerous time to travel. Eventually, on Rebmann's assuring him that they would see the mountain from their 'safer' proposed southern route to the lake, following a recognised slaver track, Richard abandoned the idea, to Speke's 'undisguised relief'.[36]

Years later Speke would claim airily (to Richard's astonishment) that he had always favoured the Northern Route, and saw 'no cause for alarm, for I thought we could have easily walked around the Masai party'. He also claimed that Richard had been nervous of taking some supplies from the mission to a beleaguered village on their route, 'because . . . of the shock his nerves had received since the Somali encounter . . . and this appeared to affect him during the whole of the journey . . .' In his own copy of Speke's book, in which he scribbled his private comments on Speke's statements, Richard denied this vehemently, recalling that it was Speke who was afraid. His 'silly laugh' and nervousness was so pronounced that 'he almost refused to go', Richard wrote.[37] It was, apparently, only the promise of some hippopotamus hunting which resolved the situation.

They marched inland along the banks of the Ruvu River as far as Fuga, where Richard occupied much of his time compiling a grammar of Swahili words and phrases to add to the work he had done on this language in Zanzibar. The march in hot sun, with limited availability of fresh water, was hard on morale and their feet. Their luggage shrank alarmingly from nightly depredations, and the porters defected pro rata to the losses. It was a portent of what was to come later. The best thing to emerge from this trip was a man recruited along with a few dozen sundry porters and guides who quickly proved himself a 'gem' amongst a group of otherwise unsatisfactory employees. He was Sidi Mubarak, a man who liked to be called by his nickname 'Bombay'; in time, the industrious and honest Bombay was destined to become the most renowned guide in Africa.

By now it was February and the rains were at their height as the party tracked down the coast, landing at regular intervals in the *Louisa* which did sterling work. Being towed astern of the old dhow while at sea, the portable tender caused mayhem by an annoying tendency to break free, due to the quality of rope securing her. On these occasions the dhow's inability to sail to windward made recovery a lengthy and difficult process. During their tour Richard and Speke called on anyone of importance, such as the *Wali* of Tanga, sending their letter of introduction ahead and waiting for a dignified period before they followed. They were usually received civilly and often with celebration, but it was not all straightforward. The elder son of the late Sultan demanded they carry back gifts to Zanzibar, and as persons of consequence they suddenly found themselves besieged by natives begging *bakshish*. They were stared at by Africans who had never seen a white skin, and the term *m'zungu* (white man) called after them was used derisorily, for it was the Portuguese who, in the sixteenth and seventeenth centuries, had introduced slavery to East Africa in the name of Christianity.

Speke was eager for some shooting but although they saw plenty of spoor, and heard of man-eating leopards and lions as well as boar, buffalo and antelope, they saw little game because they tended to land close to habitation. To Speke's irritation Richard vetoed his requests to venture further inland to look for elephant herds where, they were told, there were bulls with tusks in excess of 175 lbs. He wrote sulkily in his journal that, 'Captain Burton being no sportsman would not stop for shooting.'[38] Hamerton had warned them against going into the thick vegetation because of the risk of 'jungle-fever', but eventually Richard gave in and agreed to a hippopotamus shoot. Speke described what he called his 'first flirtation with the hippopotami' at Tanga in his book (alongside this remark in his copy Burton has written, 'A failure; it rankled.'). The next encounter was at the Pangani River where Speke was rather more successful. Burton, as usual, viewed the incident objectively:

> A hippopotamus, called by the Sawahilis *kiboko* resembles a mammoth pig . . . rather than a horse or cow . . . when undisturbed he may be seen plunging porpoise-like against the stream, or basking in shallow water, or cooling himself under the dense mangroves singly and in groups, with his heavy box head upon a friend's broad stern. He is easily killed by the puny arrow on *terra firma*; in the water he is difficult to shoot.

One morning at dawn, directed by Bombay, Burton and Speke dropped downstream in a 40-foot-long canoe looking for the quarry. Having located a herd, they poled up towards it through the rippling and swirling water created by the animals swimming beneath them. 'The smooth water undulates, swells and breaches a way for the large black head. Eight ounces of lead fly in the right direction. There is a splash, a struggle. The surface foams and the [animal] with mouth

bleeding like a gutterspout rears and plunges beneath the stream.'
They recovered this beast and delivered it to the delighted natives for
whom it provided an unexpected feast. Speke stripped to the waist in
anticipation of hot work and helped to paddle the canoe, but the herd
had become wary. 'Whenever a head appears an inch above water,'
Richard observed, 'a heavy bullet "puds" into or near it; crimson
patches adorn the stream, some die and disappear, others plunge in
crippled state . . . or splash and scurry about with puzzled snorts.'

The distasteful record of slaughter is, however, chiefly interesting
to the biographer for Richard's statement that even during an attack
by one of the animals, when the canoe was almost overturned and
Speke lost his balance, '[because] I ever make a point of ascertaining
fellow-traveller's habits in that matter . . . I observed that . . . he
[Speke] never allowed his gun to look at himself or at others.'[39]
When Richard and Lieutenant Herne first met Speke at Aden in
1854, they each noted that he was not an accurate shot, but at least
his gun manners were beyond reproach. Years later Richard would
recall this hippo incident with startling clarity.

Their march inland and the Pangani River excursion were a waste of
effort; they learned nothing of any value and Burton and Speke went
down with 'a violent bilious fever'. Both men and one of their
Portuguese boys were stricken for weeks with alternate chills and
sweats, headaches, vomiting, fits and delirium. Richard's consolation
for the misery of this attack lay in the fact that he had been warned by
Hamerton and Rebmann that no European could visit East Africa without being affected; '. . . the traveller is advised to undergo this seasoning
upon the coast before marching into the interior; but after recovery he
must wait a second attack, otherwise he will expend in preparation the
strength . . . required for the execution of his journey . . .'[40]

Although he carried quinine in the medical chest, he appears to
have been uncertain about its efficacy, fearing to take it on the
grounds that an overdose might induce fatal apoplexy. This drug,
which had been isolated from the bark of the cinchona by a French
pharmacist in the 1820s, was just beginning to be used in India with
great success. Later, in West Africa Burton would rely heavily upon
quinine and write of his regret that he had not appreciated its pro-
phylactic properties while he was in East Africa. He relied instead on
the quack compound of quinine, bitter aloes and opium much
favoured by Colonel Hamerton, called 'Warburg's Drops'.

All thoughts of cruising further south along the coast were now at an end, and Burton decided to return to Zanzibar. Speke, who had the fever less severely, managed to walk unaided to the beach, Burton 'alas for manliness, was obliged to be supported like a bedridden old woman'. In Zanzibar the men were nursed slowly back to health and Richard noted with interest that 'as proof that the negro enjoys no immunity [to the fever] Bombay is at this moment . . . suffering severely.'[41] Burton and Speke made a further brief foray to the coast for commercial reasons. The East India Company had asked Richard to look for supplies of copal, a tree resin used in the manufacture of 'camaque' coach varnishes which was becoming expensive through scarcity. Richard's letter-book contains a draft to the R.G.S. which shows that in late May he was still hoping that Steinhaueser would arrive; 'I have . . . shaken off the miasmatic fever of the brain and am eager to set off again when the rains show any sign of halting. Dr Steinhaueser has not yet joined us but we are in daily hopes of this welcome event. His presence will be no small subject in a sickly climate.'[42]

In England, Isabel was desperate for any news of Richard; a few brief reports clipped from *The Times*, and a short letter from him notifying the Arundells of his arrival in Zanzibar, were all she had. From somewhere she learned that the R.G.S. had received a longer letter from him, but she was taxed as to how to find out what it said for she could hardly approach the Society personally. She resolved the dilemma cleverly. Knowing that one of their neighbours in Montagu Place, a Mr Charles Fellowes, was a member of the R.G.S., she persuaded a woman friend, Mrs Nicholls (who knew Fellowes) to write and ask him for information. Mr Fellowes recalled hearing of a letter from Burton some weeks earlier: '. . . I forget the exact district he writes from but he is in East Africa. I will enquire as to the mode of communication with him.' A few weeks later, in March, Fellowes duly sent a hand-copied version of the letter to Mrs Nicholls, which Isabel stuck into her album though it was three months out of date by then:

Zanzibar 28 December [1856]

My dear Balfour,
    I arrived here a week ago. Imman just dead and war impending. Season bad for our entrance into the country so Jack Speke and I

are going in a pattimar to the coast, Mombasa . . . and other places . . . We shall be away about a couple of months . . . then we return and prepare for our start into the interior . . . Hamerton has been very kind . . . he has been very ill, but is recovering. Rebmann is still at Mombasa. We are in excellent health and spirits, so adieu with Speke's compliments. Yours ever, RFB

By May the rains eased and it became increasingly obvious to Richard that Steinhaueser was not going to join them at Zanzibar. Official acknowledgement of the doctor's leave had been held back for months. When he eventually received sanction in April it was too late; the south-westerly monsoons had begun and no ships could sail against them to Zanzibar. Undaunted, Steinhaueser gathered a small party of bearers and sailed across the Red Sea to Berbera, from where he proposed to march south to Mombasa. But it proved hopeless; illness and the effects of the heavy rains upon the country made his progress so slow that he was forced to accept he would never reach his destination in time, and reluctantly he made the decision to return to Aden.

'The loss of Dr Steinhaueser lost the East African Expedition more than can be succinctly told,' Richard wrote later. Steinhaueser was an experienced traveller, a well-read graduate whose cheerful mien was appreciated by both Burton and Speke so that he might have created a balance between the two. Furthermore, he might have been able to treat the devastating illnesses from which both men subsequently suffered, and which blighted the expedition. But with no word from Aden by early June, Richard could not afford to delay any longer. He had already used up six months, and more than half of his budget. The little rains would begin again in October and last two months; he decided that he and Speke would have to make the journey alone, while the weather was most favourable.

During their final weeks in Zanzibar, Richard concentrated on finishing his two writing projects. In the six months between his arrival and departure from Zanzibar, he was on the mainland for two months, and seriously ill with malaria for another three weeks or so. Yet he managed to research and write some 1,000 printed pages. He also wrote several long letters; to the R.G.S. detailing his progress, and to the East India Company on the subject of recompense for the losses suffered by his party at Berbera: 'Some months ago the Somal,

I am informed, offered to pay a sum far exceeding the amount plundered and, if this was refused we now look to the Gov't for compensation of our losses . . .'[43]

Speke spent his time 'especially the evenings . . . rating chronometers and getting all the surveying instruments into working order . . . Captain Burton, besides book-making busied himself in making all the other arrangements for the journey.'[44] To Richard's approval, Speke also made himself thoroughly conversant with the use of all the instruments including the sextant. Burton had his writing to occupy him through the hot and humid days of physical inactivity, but Speke was often bored and suffered after-effects of the fever contracted on the mainland. He revealed in his book that he suffered from 'a nervous sensibility I never knew before, of being startled at any sudden accident. A pen dropping from the table would make me jump . . .'

The relationship between Speke and Hamerton was not as close as that between Burton and Hamerton.[45] Instead, Speke found congenial companionship in the company of Mr Frost, an apothecary who acted as the Medical Officer to the British Consulate in Zanzibar. Frost did not like Burton. Possibly he was jealous of Burton's easy relationship with Hamerton; formerly Mr and Mrs Frost had been among Hamerton's closest confidants. Frost encouraged Speke's gossipy complaints about Burton, especially the shabby way Speke felt he had been treated with regard to his Somalia journal.

With Frost's support Speke's grudges crystallised and he began to feel vindicated in his resentment; he resolved that Burton would not be allowed to treat him so badly a second time. Hints of this are already evident in the note Speke sent on 20 May 1857 to Norton Shaw:

20 May 1857

. . . Burton tells me it is requisite for anyone wishing to become a member of your admirable institution the R.G. Society to pay a donation of £30. If this sum be the limit, and there be no further annual or other subscriptions required I should feel extremely grateful by your proposing me to the committee in the usual form. Led on from shooting, collecting, mapping and wandering the world generally, I feel myself gradually wedded with, and instinctively impelled to the prosecution of Geographical research, the same way as formerly the attainment of sport was the culminating point of my ambition.

This note is forwarded by my mother . . . Burton painted in and despatched *the* map along with his report many days ago, probably you received them, but in case any accident should befall their transmission I have taken the precautionary measure of enclosing a duplicate . . . for my own satisfaction, I being its sole constructor . . . Burton tells me he sent from Aden in 1855 my sketch map route of the Somali country to the R.G.S., but no notes having accompanied it . . . I fear you have laid it aside as useless lumber . . .

Yours ever truly

J.H. Speke[46]

And in a surviving fragment of a badly written and somewhat puzzling letter to his mother (not previously available to Burton biographers), Speke revealed for the first time his true feelings about Burton:

. . . He preaches to me in the evening what I say to the colonel [Hamerton] in the morning, it is truly laughable to watch the progress of this circular communication. I now have analogous proof that B. never went to Mecca and Harar in the common acceptation of that word but got artful natives to take him to those places, & I won't swear he did many a trick at their instigation . . . Wishing I could find something more amusing to communicate [than] such rot about a rotten person . . .[47]

His 'analogous proof' appears to have consisted of his observation that on the march to Fuga Richard had left it to Bombay, who knew the country, to lead the way instead of himself mapping out the route and directing the marches. Also Speke was convinced, undoubtedly from Burton's stories of his Arabian adventure (often told self-deprecatingly to raise laughter), that 'Lieutenant Burton received £100 from the Royal Geographical Society to cross Africa [sic] from west to east, and whilst attempting that journey he got drifted off with the flood of pilgrims to Mecca.'[48] This immature malice was somewhat dangerous considering it was directed against a man with whom Speke proposed travelling for some eighteen months through unknown and hostile territory. And furthermore, the man he regarded as 'a rotter' was – with the single exception of the bearer, Bombay – the only person in the party with whom he could converse.

It was still not too late for Speke to pull out of the expedition; he certainly considered it, for he asked Hamerton if he thought he could mount his own expedition and was told, 'For God's sake, no!' Clearly, at some point during their time in Zanzibar, Speke made a positive decision to continue as second-in-command to the man he already disliked intensely. And all the evidence points to a calculated plan by Speke to work on his own behalf, from within Burton's expedition.

14

THE LONG SAFARI
1856—1857

Present-day visitors to East Africa, with health secured by antibiotics, anti-malarial prophylactics and injections against cholera and yellow fever, are whisked there by jet in a matter of hours. From the safety of four-wheeled vehicles they can view, effortlessly, unique quantities of animals that are peculiar to Africa. At the end of a *safari*,[1] pleasantly tired and coated in East Africa's red dust, today's traveller retires to air-conditioned clubs and hotels, hot baths, iced drinks, good food, clean sheets and – if required – instant satellite communications with home.

Picture a different scenario. East Africa long before refrigerators, tinned foods and telephones. The route taken by Burton lay through present-day Tanzania; then a creeper-strewn Eden, with few beaten tracks other than those made by animals, hunting tribesmen or slave-traders. Indeterminate, as they wound through forests of strange trees dripping with grey, whiskery lichen, these trails were usually no more than a few feet wide. In rain they turned to a glutinous morass through which bearers struggled with heavy, wide loads against snatching bushes and branches. Overhead troops of white and black Colobus monkeys watched and played, screaming as they darted about on the lianas, thick as coir-cables, that hung from the deep green canopy. Gaily coloured butterflies flitted between patches of sunlight slanting through branches. Only bird calls, and sudden unidentified cries and roars – the sounds of Africa – broke the silence.

The first Europeans to travel there had no idea of what might lurk behind the dense high screen of luxuriant foliage. Wild animals of an unknown species perhaps? Venomous snakes and spiders? The coastal dwellers told them that savage tribes with poisoned arrows routinely attacked travellers. But the jungle-like forests were not the only problem; there was thorny scrubland, unremitting desert, mountains with ground too hard to hold a tent-peg, tsetse-fly infested swamps, and plains with spear grasses higher than a man's head; all bringing different but no less difficult challenges, and their own variety of terrors to snag the days and haunt the nights. It was a beautiful primeval but brutal environment, where nature held sway and only the strongest survived.

This was the world that Burton and Speke proposed to penetrate. Without maps. Without the comfort of guides who had travelled the route before. Without any knowledge of what lay beyond the next range of hills, without even knowing whether they could communicate with the nomadic tribes they might meet along the way. Without any access to assistance, or communication of any kind, for a year or more, apart from the dubious advantages of meeting an occasional slave caravan, and for part of the way the use of paths beaten by the slave-traders. Every item needed to sustain life during that time must be manhandled by superstitious, fearful porters who spent most of their waking hours planning larceny and desertion. And all this to reach a lake which might, or might not, be a myth.

Before he left Zanzibar in mid-June 1857 aboard the old frigate, H.M.S. *Artemise*, Richard had almost finished his lengthy report on Zanzibar,[2] as well as a magazine article entitled 'Zanzibar, and Two Months in East Africa'. He put the finishing touches to both manuscripts during the voyage to the coast, the first addressed to Norton Shaw at the R.G.S. The second was for the publisher John Blackwood in Edinburgh: '. . . If you think it fitted for *The Magazine* by all means insert it. If not I will trouble you to keep it for me till my return, should that comfortable event ever occur . . . It is useless to write to me . . . [but] I would send all salaams to Lawrie Oliphant if there be any chance of their finding him. He was starting to do the Yankee when we parted. Good luck to his inclinations if they be virtuous! . . .'[3]

Richard intended to give both packages to Colonel Hamerton, for forwarding to England by the next British ship to call at Zanzibar, but

Hamerton became unwell during the voyage. Despite his illness, the Consul insisted that the *Artemise* remained at anchor off the beach for the two weeks or so needed for preparations, so that the two explorers could live on board in reasonable comfort. And, he decreed, following their departure the ship would remain a further week, firing her cannon each evening to make her presence known along the coast.[4] To Richard's anxious entreaties that he should waste no time but return as soon as possible to the healthy climate of Europe, Hamerton gave the evasive response that as a Catholic he had no fear of a physical death.

Following Rebmann's warnings, and Hamerton's strong recommendations that they should avoid the dangers of the Masai Plains, Richard chose the longer southern route, known to traders.[5] Accordingly, the expedition began at Wale Point, Kaoli, south of Bagamoyo on the Tanganyika coast opposite Zanzibar. Having landed the mountain of supplies, Burton and Speke set about trying to engage 170 porters. The schedule of personnel and supplies, which covers three closely-packed typed pages of detail, had been drawn up by Francis Galton, who had previously travelled in South Africa. Richard added a few items to Galton's schedule but otherwise accepted it as sensible.[6]

Said bin Salim, a nervous Afro-Arab, had been ordered – much against his will – by the Sultan, to act as Caravan Guide to the expedition. He had been sent in early June, from Zanzibar to the mainland, to hire porters. Hamerton warned Richard against putting too much trust in Salim, but he had apparently done his best. He hired a gang and paid them an advance. On subsequently learning that their employers were *m'zungu* (white men) the porters disappeared, 'forgetting,' Richard said wryly, 'to return their deposits'. As a consequence, apart from the financial loss, Richard was obliged to recruit expedition personnel from the small garrison town of Kaole before he could set out.[7] All the best men had been hired already by Arab traders, and taken off into the hinterland so that they could not be seduced by the high wages of the white men. Only 36 men were available, all insisting that an escort of a hundred armed *askaris* would be necessary to protect the caravan from attacks by raiding tribesmen said to lurk along the route.

The bazaars of Zanzibar and the mainland had already been combed for animals and some 30 asses, 'good, bad and indifferent', procured. The shortfall in human and animal porterage was a serious setback and the only solution was to leave half of the supplies behind (including the portable boat) to follow them. A trading caravan travelling in the same direction was due to leave ten days later, and Richard paid its sheikh 150 dollars to provide 22 men to bring up whatever they could carry. It was seven months before they appeared.

Burton and Speke rehearsed loading the porters and animals with about half of the 70 huge bales of cotton cloth, brass and copper wire and beads that were indispensable for trading and gifts; and half of the 40 heavy boxes of ammunition and gunpowder – the wherewithal for providing meat for the expedition personnel. Also carried were dry provisions such as rice, dates, coffee, flour, ghee, grain and salt. There was a medical chest, and other essential equipment such as a large stock of writing paper, sealing-wax and ink, books, maps, surveying instruments, rifles and ammunition, fishing hooks and line. Burton's and Speke's domestic arrangements consisted of a tent with matting as carpet, camp-beds with air pillows, blankets and mosquito nets, a collapsible table and chairs, oil lamps and a full canteen of cooking utensils and cutlery. A few cases of good brandy were considered part of the necessary provisions. Despite the economies, men and beasts were overloaded – each man carried a 70 lb load besides his own travel baggage and a variety of weapons. It was not a good start, but Richard anticipated recruiting more men as they marched. Furthermore, as the party would be eating their way through the food supplies and doling out gifts as it travelled, theoretically things should improve.

In the event the expedition departed abruptly on 27 June after the apothecary, Mr Frost, visited Richard with a grave demeanour and an officious manner guaranteed to irritate. He said that in his opinion the Consul was too ill to remain any longer at the coast, but refused to depart until Richard was on his way.[8] Frost therefore recommended that the expedition got away sharply. Richard had not taken to Frost on the occasions they had met in Zanzibar (though he was unaware of Speke's disloyalty). He regarded the apothecary as a narrow-minded charlatan, a 'Eurasian chemist' masquerading as a doctor, who was not treating his friend Hamerton appropriately. This opinion was reflected in his response to Frost's approach. 'I contented myself,' Richard wrote, 'with remarking once more that morphia appeared a curious cure for a confirmed liver complaint, and I made preparations for landing at once.' Bristling with resentment, Frost retorted that the doses of morphia he prescribed for Hamerton were 'very little ones'.[9]

Richard could hardly bother Hamerton with commissions at such a time and had no option but to place the two manuscripts, packed and addressed care of the Foreign Office, in Frost's unsympathetic hands. In the circumstances it is hardly surprising that Frost treated the task with a lack of reverence. The smaller package to Blackwood arrived safely (and to Isabel's joy was published). The more important and larger manuscript, 'a detailed report concerning the commerce and capabilities of Zanzibar', failed to arrive at its destination and, as Richard wrote accusingly on his arrival back in England, 'I fear it came to an untimely end.' It would transpire that Frost had opened and read the report, and – since it was written with Richard's usual incisive observation but lack of diplomacy – was duly affronted. He forwarded it to the Government at Bombay, where it lay in the desk drawer of an unknown official for a decade.[10]

By his arrogant dismissal of Frost, Richard made another enemy, and it is one of the few occasions when we know precisely why and how he acquired an addition to the circle of men who held him in such dislike that they were prepared to band together and work against him. Frost was not a major player, but still managed to inject his share of poison into the Burton legend. Later he would relate how when Hamerton parted from Speke and Burton he wished them good luck, and said to Speke, 'Good luck, Speke; you know I would not travel with that man under any condition.' In fact, Hamerton made this comment facetiously, in Burton's presence, not behind his back as Frost implied; it was exactly the sort of humour that appealed to Richard. But Frost's malicious misquote was later used by Speke and Rigby as evidence of Burton's general unsoundness.[11]

Yet Hamerton *was* concerned about the relationship between Burton and Speke. He told Richard that although he had encouraged them in their mission he was now sorry they were going, for he was anxious about what might befall them. Probably he had learned of Speke's grudge against Burton from Frost, for on parting he apparently made the peculiar remark: '. . . I hope you get on well together.'[12] But it is equally likely that Hamerton had recognised the basic personality differences in the two men and knew that it would be difficult for them ever to work together.

Burton was mercurial, unconventional, intellectually and sexually curious. Speke was conservative, socially correct and prudish. The English expression 'he was very pleased with himself' fitted Speke well; he regarded himself as *a leader* and expected others to judge him on his own terms. There was a good deal about Speke that made him worthy of respect and admiration, but he was also weak, vain and obstinate. Two qualities that these two exceptional men shared in abundance, however, were bravery and arrogance; had their differences been leavened by a third party, Steinhaueser for example, history might have been very different.

Burton quickly became irritated at Speke's constant requests for a halt so that he could shoot specimens. He was also scornful of the younger man's desultory efforts at journal-keeping. Burton's own compulsion to record would provide material for several books, and articles of scholarship with brilliant leaps of thought. Speke, in turn, was jealous of Burton's authoritarian hold on the leadership of the expedition. However, for the moment an adherence to social politeness, allied with personal ambition and the remnants of their original friendship, enabled them to work together.

The expedition marched inland to the monotonous note of the kettle-drum to warn of their coming, led by the red ensign of the Sultan to warn anyone they met that they were from Zanzibar and travelled under his protection. For five days Burton and Speke heard the comforting report of the *Artemise*'s cannon each evening, but on the sixth day there was no sound and they concluded that she had sailed. In fact, the diarrhoea from which Hamerton had suffered prior to their departure had turned to dysentery, and as his patient became dehydrated and comatose Frost countermanded the Consul's orders, sensibly directing an immediate return to Zanzibar. Hamerton, too far gone even to know he had returned to the island, and too ill to be carried ashore, died shortly afterwards, still aboard the *Artemise* on 5 July.

It was some months before the news caught up with Richard and even then he was unsure whether to believe it. Said bin Salim eagerly offered to return to the coast to discover the truth of the verbal report, but Richard forbade this, suspecting that the man wished to return only to see if Hamerton's death had prompted a change of heart by the Sultan towards the expedition.

At a village called Zungamero (no longer identifiable) they hired more porters bringing their personnel up to strength, 132 in all. The marching day for the caravan began at 4 a.m., with coffee or tea and porridge for Burton and Speke to warm the dark, pre-dawn chill. While they breakfasted the Muslims of the party turned towards Mecca for the first of their daily prayers. After a delay around the camp-fire haggling about this or that, the camp would be struck, men and beasts loaded and as soon as practicable after daybreak, the signal given to move off.

> There was a rough and ready order in the long procession when it finally got under way. In the lead went the guide, wearing a ceremonial head-dress and carrying the red flag of the Sultan of Zanzibar, and behind him marched the drummer. The cloth and bead porters came next with their bolster-like bundles on their heads, then the men carrying the camp equipment, and their women, children and cattle. The armed guard [askaris] was dispersed along the line, each man carrying a muzzle-loaded 'Tower musket', a German cavalry sabre, a small leather box strapped to the waist and a large cow-horn filled with ammunition. Many of them were accompanied by their women and personal slaves . . . Almost every male member of the expedition had a weapon of some kind together with an assortment of pots and pans and a three-legged wooden stool strapped to his back. A continuous and violent uproar of chanting, singing . . . and shouting accompanied the march, for it was thought important to make as much noise as possible so as to impress the local tribes. If a hare chanced to run across the track all downed burdens at once to go in pursuit of the animal which, if caught, was eaten raw.[13]

Burton and Speke generally drew up the rear, walking, riding a donkey, or when incapacitated being carried on litters. They marched through the morning until the sun became too hot, usually about 11 a.m. when a final halt was called. The tent would be erected, a *boma* or kraal made of thorn-tree branches for the cattle and a fire built for the evening. During the afternoon Burton and Speke worked on sketches, their 'observations' and journals, and dealing with the problems brought to them by one or another of the personnel. If they had halted near a village Bombay would be sent to bargain for poultry, grain, butter, eggs and milk with lengths of cloth or beads. Supper

of goat, fowl or game, with rice, was served as soon as the sun began
to go down, at about 5 p.m. The evening scene by the camp-fire
where the porters and *askaris* gathered to sing and dance, was captured by Richard in his journal:

> The dull red fires flickering and forming a circle of ruddy light in
> the depth of the black forest, flaming against the tall trunks and
> defining the foliage of nearer trees, illuminate lurid groups of savage
> men, in every variety of shape and posture. Above, the dark purple
> sky, studded with golden points . . . in the western horizon, a
> resplendent crescent with a dim, ash-coloured globe in its arms, and
> crowned by Hesperus sparkling like a diamond . . .[14]

A month into its journey, the expedition halted for a week to allow
Richard and Speke to recover from marsh fevers. Even so, when they
moved on Speke was too weak to march and had to ride an already
overburdened ass which threw him heavily on several occasions. All
personnel suffered from a poor diet. Richard had incorrectly anticipated there would be ample game along the entire route, whereas for
the first few months it was sparse. They were therefore often con-
strained to live on their supplies of dry goods. Several porters had
already tried to desert and had been brought back at gun-point; the
sore-backed pack animals showed a depressing tendency to lie down,
and the more delicate of the fine, light Zanzibari riding asses began to
chafe, sicken and die almost as soon as they left the coast:

> On 18th July we resumed our march over a tract which caused
> sinking of the heart . . . near Kiruru the thick grass and humid veg-
> etation, dripping till mid-day with dew, rendered the black earth
> greasy and slippery . . . we advanced over deep thick mire interlaced
> with tree-roots through a dense jungle and forest . . . In three places
> we crossed bogs from 100 yards to a mile in length and admitting
> a man up to the knee; the porters plunged through them like laden
> animals . . . this 'yegea mud' caused by want of water-shed after
> rain, is sometimes neck deep . . . the only redeeming feature was a
> foreground of lovely hill, the highlands of Dut'humi, plum coloured
> in the distance, and at times gilt by a sudden outburst of sunshine.[15]

When Verney Lovett Cameron travelled the same route almost two decades later, he had not only a better equipped and financed expedition but Burton's instructive *Lake Regions* as a guide. It was, he said, 'a work which for minuteness of detail, must ever stand foremost amongst books of descriptive geography'.[16] Even so, Cameron would write in his diary that 'this bothersome little journey to Ugigi is giving more trouble than a march of a thousand miles.'[17] And he experienced the same ills, travelling through the long dark, boggy valleys which acted as a drain for the Useghara mountains. Rain and mud; sick bearers and lame animals; constant fevers; tsetse flies and mosquito bites which caused abscesses; larceny by the bearers for which there were constant floggings; and desertions; all these combined to hinder progress.

From the start both Speke and Burton suffered from racking malarial fevers. Richard's mouth became infected with mouth ulcers, and he frequently suffered delirium, during which he believed he could fly, and felt himself to be, 'a divided identity, never ceasing to be two persons, who generally thwarted and opposed each other'.[18] Speke was hardly better; 'he had a fainting fit which strongly resembled a sunstroke, and it seemed to affect him more or less throughout our journey.'[19] With their donkeys dying they had to walk on swollen feet, stumbling along 'through sun, rain, mud and miasmic putridities'. As they forded rivers, sometimes breast-high, there were inevitable accidents when vital supplies of food and valuable equipment – including Richard's elephant gun and some precious journals – were swept away. Everything became soaked. Their 'best quality Lucifers' (matches) were ruined and they had to rely on phosphorus and oil for lighting fires.

In the small settlement of Dut'humi, they rested and were treated with kindness. Richard moved into a thatched hut, revelling in the cosy atmosphere of warm, sweet wood-smoke; Speke, however, refused to leave their damp and miry, but British, tent. Feeling marginally better, and in order to repay the kindness of his hosts, Richard led a small force against a neighbouring tribe who had previously raided the village, and carried off five prisoners as slaves.

> I had the satisfaction of restoring the stolen wretches to their hearths and homes, and two decrepit old women that had been rescued from slavery thanked me with tears of joy. This easy good deed done, I was able, though with swimming head and trembling

hands, to prepare accounts and a brief report for the Royal
Geographical Society. These, together with other papers, especially
an urgent request for medical comforts and drugs, especially quinine and narcotics . . . were intrusted to Jemedar Yaruk . . . The
escort from Kaole, reduced in number by three desertions, was dismissed. All the volunteers had been clamouring to return, and I
could no longer afford to keep them.

Besides the . . . supplies of cloth, wire and beads, which preceded,
and which were left to follow us, I had been provided by Ladha
Damha with a stock of white and blue cotton, some handsome
articles of dress, 20,000 strings of white and black, pink, blue, and
green, red and brown porcelain beads, needles and other items of
hardware to defray transit charges through Uzarama. This provision, valued at 295 dollars should have carried us to the end of the
third month; it lasted about three weeks.[20]

Richard was appalled to discover that the timid Said bin Salim,
'through fear', had disbursed beads to 'every wretch that held out his
hand' demanding *hongo* (tax) or *bakshish* (gift). Whenever they
passed a collection of huts the chief would demand a gift, and Said
had been over-generous with his employers' property.

Richard and Speke had been too ill to superintend the handing over
of these 'gifts', and the disbursements to porters, by Said. Now they
discovered that he had allowed the more aggressive expedition personnel to help themselves to stores and, Richard suspected, had also
helped himself liberally, secreting his booty. With hindsight Richard
realised he would have been better advised to have travelled as a
trader. 'It explains the traveller's motives, which are always suspected
to be bad ones. Thus the Explorer can push forward into unknown
countries, will be civilly received and lightly fined [taxed], because the
host expects to see him and his friends again. To go without any
motive only induces suspicion . . . nobody believes him to be so stupid
as to go through such danger and discomfort for exploring or science,
which they simply do not understand . . .'[21]

Having dismissed bearers proved guilty of theft, Richard persuaded
the slaves provided by the Sultan to take over their loads, offering to
pay them a bonus at the end of the expedition. Knowing that the
expedition funds were already overspent, Speke queried their ability
to fulfil this commitment. He claimed Burton told him that Arabs

often made such promises and never kept them. 'Moreover', Speke declared in his book (but it is not mentioned in his limited journal), Burton told him mildly that 'slaves of this sort never expected to be paid'.[22] Speke claims to have been scandalised at this remark, but it is worth noting that in Burton's own copy of Speke's book he wrote against Speke's statement that it was 'not true'.[23] Assuming Speke did not completely invent the conversation, Richard – who had refused in Zanzibar to accept the slaves as outright gifts to him by the Sultan, and had paid them an advance exactly as the free men – may have felt justified in making some sort of offer in order to save the expedition. Having done this, he sidelined Said bin Salim and placed Sidi Mubarak ('Bombay') in charge of logistics. But even Bombay could not prevent the theft and desertions. By the time the expedition returned to the coast almost two years later, every single man with the exception of Bombay and the two Goanese boys Richard recruited as personal servants had attempted to desert on at least one occasion.

Bombay, an African of the Yao tribe, had been captured by slavers as a 12-year-old boy, and taken to Zanzibar where he was sold in the market to an Arab merchant who was visiting from India. He served this master for several years and on the merchant's death obtained his freedom.[24] He worked his passage back to Africa, where he made no attempt to hide contempt for his ignorant countrymen (whom he dismissed as 'jungly'). His industry and a smattering of Hindustani made him an ideal member of the expedition. He was a powerful, ugly man and his appearance was made more singular by virtue of his teeth which he had filed into sharp points. He could be surly and violent, but Richard had identified him from their first meeting as honest and reliable, and had paid off Bombay's debts in order to persuade him to join them. 'He works on principle, and works like a horse, openly declaring that not love of us, but attachment to his stomach, makes him industrious,' Richard wrote, adding that he was 'a gem' among his associates.

Bombay managed the bearers and *askaris* with more expertise than Said bin Salim, but naturally the latter was sullen about his demotion and encouraged constant quarrels and petty differences among the men. Bombay had been Speke's gun-bearer from the start of the expedition (as Mabruki was Burton's). Apart from Burton he was the only person with whom, because they both spoke limited Hindustani, Speke could converse; and he was also the means whereby Speke could interrogate Africans, albeit in a limited fashion, independent of Burton.

As well as recording their progress and relentless problems, Richard's journals contained detailed lively descriptions of everything from local customs to flora and fauna, to the intoxicants – *pombe* (beer) brewed from grain, and cannabis ('it grows beside every cottage door') – and the eating habits of the local inhabitants. From the 'curious mincing gait' of the women to childbirth and religious practices, from the art of the medicine man to death rites, from native morality to the trading prices of sheep, goats, hens, eggs, rice, all were recorded; nothing escaped his erudite pen and no observation was so sacred that it could not be graced by a lick of sardonic humour. He illustrated his writing with thumb-nail sketches, and sometimes larger sketches which were later turned into illustrations for his book. He spent some time teaching Speke the rudiments of sketching scenery, and shared with him his 'scanty library . . . of Shakespeare, Euclid and so forth which we read together again and again'.[25] Throughout his life Richard never travelled anywhere without his basic library: 'Shakespeare, the Bible, and Euclid . . . they were bound up together, with three large clasps and went everywhere with him.'[26] At Speke's request he often 'went over' Speke's field notes with him, correcting and making suggestions.

At length they tired of waiting for the balance of their equipment to catch up with them. Richard selected a slave whom Bombay felt was trustworthy and sent him back to the coast with mail advising that they were moving on. He requested medical supplies and asked that these be sent with the recalcitrant porters and baggage, to catch them up. He and Speke were weak from the effects of fever, but Richard was determined to press ahead to the Usagara mountains where he guessed, correctly, that there would be an improvement in climate.

As they gained height and left the swampy river valley behind them, 'health and strength returned as if by magic', depression vanished and the men revelled in the fresh clear air and hot sunshine. Richard wrote that he was so enchanted with this different world that he never wearied of looking at the beauty of the transparent sky with hawks soaring, the peaceful scene broken only by troops of monkeys playing and chattering; stretched out below them under a layer of leaden cloud lay Zungomero, mud-coloured, windswept and deluged. There was a down side to the lovely scenery as they travelled now on a well-trodden slavers' path. 'All along our way,' Richard wrote, 'we were saddened by the sight of clean picked skeletons, and here and there the swollen corpses of porters who had perished in this place by starvation.' Some slave caravans that they crossed on the road contained thousands of captured people; one especially tragic one had just 'lost fifty' due to smallpox. Among the pitiful survivors were many who were clearly already affected. Some, including women with small babies on their backs, staggered on knowing that to stop meant certain death.

Insects often made the journey a torment. Small red ants with cruel stings, and large black ones, the dreaded pismire or *siafu* which marched in columns at night – most often in the rainy season – and were capable of stripping a small animal to the bone within hours. Individually they fastened themselves to the ankles of anyone in their path and their bite, intended to stun a smaller victim, was like 'the pinch of a red-hot needle'. Clouds of mosquitoes filled the air. The tsetse fly which 'when beaten off, will return half a dozen times to the charge . . . cannot be killed except by a smart blow, and its long proboscis draws blood through a canvas hammock.'[27] Its sting left sore and itchy red lumps. Recognising, as Lord Delamere would fifty years later, that the land was potentially perfect for agriculture and cattle farming, Richard also astutely realised that the tsetse would first need to be dealt with; 'perhaps some day it will be exterminated by the introduction of some insectiferous bird, which will be the greatest benefactor Central Africa ever knew.'[28] Richard thought that in some way the tsetse was responsible for the recurrent fevers from which they suffered, but did not make the connection with the mosquito, though he unfailingly slept under a mosquito net. Ironically, he had been told in Zayla, prior to his journey to Harar, that 'the mosquito bite brings on . . . deadly fevers'. But he wrote this information off as superstition arising 'from the fact that mosquitoes and fevers become formidable about the same time'.[29] The mosquito nets may have been effective against the mosquitoes, but it was ticks which carried relapsing-fever.

A physician who recently studied Speke's medical history wrote:

The rest houses where they stayed were infested with ticks, which lived in the mud walls, emerging at night to feed on man. Although a differential diagnosis between malaria and relapsing fever cannot now be ascertained, the latter must certainly have been responsible for at least some of their fever episodes. Cerebral manifestations were common; they presented as schizophrenic episodes in the case of Burton, and as delirium with aggressive behaviour in Speke.[30]

On one occasion an attack by killer bees dispersed the entire caravan. Livingstone wrote that he reckoned to lose a dozen porters from the stings of these tiny creatures on a long march, and when Burton's caravan was attacked, baggage and livestock was abandoned willy-nilly as every man fled to his own safety. Later, to Richard's distress it was found that in the total confusion one of the bearers had deserted, taking with him 'the most valuable of our packages; a portmanteau containing the *Nautical Almanac* for 1858, the surveying books and most of our paper, pens and ink'.[31] Amazingly, some weeks later this loss was restored (though at a price) by some porters of another caravan who had found the portmanteau in the long grass close to where the bees attacked. On another occasion, 'all our bullet moulds and three boxes of ammunition were lost'; these were never recovered.[32]

In the mountains they marched under a fiery sun, buffeted by furious hot winds, but at night the temperature dropped to a damp and 'chill 48 degrees, . . . a killing temperature in these latitudes to half-naked and houseless men', Richard commented. Sometimes they were fortunate enough to come upon friendly villagers who fed them with milk and butter and honey, 'a great treat', but generally they eked out their poor diet with the occasional gazelle. In hunting for the pot, Speke revealed a curious partiality which Richard found distasteful. Whenever he shot a pregnant female animal, Speke ordered the foetus cooked for himself, dismissing the unease with which the Africans viewed this practice as 'native superstition'. He recorded loftily how his 'native huntsman . . . shrank from the work with horror . . . fearing lest [it] should have an influence on his wife's future bearing'.[33]

When he was well enough to shoot, Speke greatly deprecated Burton's refusal to allow him to shoot other than for food, but this was not often, for both men were in appalling physical condition. Richard wrote in his journal, 'When we were ill our followers often mutinied . . . stole and lost our goods, and would not work. Sometimes, though they carried the water they would refuse us any. Jack was as ill as I was.'[34] When he was too ill to exert his authority the only way Richard could get the men to work was to offer huge bribes of beads and wire, which depressed him greatly.

By a lucky chance when things looked blackest, they met a caravan under the leadership of four Arabs who befriended Richard. 'I was always at home when I got amongst Arabs,' Richard wrote. 'They always treat me as practically one of themselves.' They gave him useful information about the trail to Ujiji, a town said to be on the shores of the inland sea. They placed at Richard's disposal their own house at Unyanyembe, a principal staging post for traders on his route. They reprimanded the bearers for neglecting their duties and for not caring for Burton and Speke when they were ill. And before departing they superintended the ongoing arrangements. A few days and evenings spent among courteous men with civilised manners, with whom he could discuss news, who recognised him as a *hajji* and who fed them as honoured guests gave a lift to Richard's spirits. More importantly they loaned him three reliable bearers to travel with them as far as Unyanyembe, and took a mail-bag down to the coast with a second request that the missing equipment be sent up with the next trading caravan to Unyanyembe. 'When they went away I charged them not to spread reports of our illness. I saw them go with regret. It had really been a relief to hear once more the voice of civility and sympathy.'[35]

Richard was not the only one to gain by this meeting. Said bin Salim acquired a slave girl who, for an appropriate consideration, he soon married off to one of the donkey men, who 'was palpably guilty of such cruelty that I felt compelled to issue a dissolution of the marriage', Richard wrote. The woman was eventually returned to Zanzibar with a passing caravan. Other female slaves made brief appearances during their journey, and were usually the cause of quarrels among the men.

On the plains approaching Ugogo they began to see a great abundance of big game, all the species that Speke wanted to add to his collections; but he was too ill to hunt. At night they often heard the roar of lions though they did not see any. Still, a major obstacle lay ahead of them, the ascent of a great mountain range that would have been a gruelling climb for fit men and beasts. Speke was so ill that he was supported by three men, and even Richard needed the assistance of one of the Goanese. He could not ride for all the beasts were needed to carry baggage. At the summit, 'poor Jack was seized with a fever fit and dangerous delirium; he became so violent that I had to remove his weapons, and to judge from certain symptoms the attack had a permanent cerebral effect. Death appeared stamped on his features, and yet our followers clamoured to advance *because it was cold*. This lasted two nights, when he was restored and came to himself and proposed to advance. I had a hammock rigged for him and the whole caravan broke ground.'[36]

It was during this episode that Burton first became vaguely aware of Speke's resentment against him, dating from what Speke saw as his ill-treatment by Burton. He dismissed the delirious ramblings as due to the illness, but he could not avoid noticing how Speke's 'former alacrity had vanished':

> He was habitually discontented with what had been done. He left to me the whole work of management, and then complained about not being consulted . . . unaccustomed to sickness he could not endure it himself nor feel for it in others; and he seemed to take pleasure in saying unpleasant things – an Anglo-Indian peculiarity. Much of the change he explained to me by confessing that he could not take an interest in an exploration of which he was not the commander. On the other hand he taught himself the use of the sextant and other instruments, with a resolution and pertinacity which formed his characteristic merits. Night after night, at the end of a burning march, he sat for hours in the chilling dews, practising lunars and timing chronometers.[37]

The expedition equipment included a full set of surveying instruments: two chronometers, a lever-action watch, two prismatic compasses, a sundial and rain gauge, a barometer, a pedometer, two boiling thermometers, two bath thermometers and two sextants. Unfortunately, all the instruments except a sextant, thermometer and compass were damaged by accidents while fording rivers, and were useless long before they reached their destination. The two men were obliged to guess altitude by measuring the time water took to reach boiling point.

When 15 porters deserted with their baggage as the expedition neared the half-way point of their outward march, Richard began to think light-headedly that it was pointless to worry about the supplies. Another passing caravan going down to the coast took pity on their plight and loaned Richard a good riding animal which, after they had gone, he handed over to Speke who was the weaker of the two.

Isabel Arundell was at this point touring Europe. Blanche, now Mrs John Smyth Piggott, knowing her sister's desperate urge to travel had invited Isabel to accompany her and her husband on their extended honeymoon tour which was expected to last six months. Among the trivia of Isabel's packing list (her riding outfit alone comprised: 'little boots, stockings, chemise, stays, trowsers, plain simple dash, blue habit; tight body and sleeves and full long skirt, small standup collar, and button gauntleted gloves; pocket handkerchief, whip.') in her memoranda book, is a note that would be sad news for Richard: 'Colonel Burton, Richard's father, died on Sunday, 6th September 1857 buried on Thursday 10th'.[38]

> October 3rd 1857. [Paris.] This day last year how wretched and truly miserable I was! On the evening of this day Richard left.
> . . . After dinner we strolled along the principal boulevards. I can easily understand a Parisian not liking to live out of Paris. We saw it to great advantage . . . a beautiful moon and clear sharp air . . . If Richard be living, he will remember me now; [on] the night of my parting with him a year ago when he went to Africa for three years.[39]

Her wistful comment 'if Richard be living' underlines what travel and separation really meant in those days of poor communication. Richard would not learn of his father's death for another nine months.

The honeymooners travelled slowly south to Marseilles where they took a steamer to Nice. The sea was anything but blue and the rough passage was the first of many such journeys that Isabel would subsequently endure in the Mediterranean. Many passengers were sick and screamed every time the ship took a big wave, 'I slept till we were in Nice Harbour. My sister and her husband went off to find a house; I cleared the baggage and drove to the Hotel Victoria where we dined and then went to our new lodging.'

> November 1857. Nice is a very pretty town . . . I am told there is no land between us and Tunis – three hundred miles! . . . We have an African tree in our garden. And Richard is over there, in Africa. My

favourite occupation . . . [is] sitting on the shingle with my face to the sea and Africa. I hate myself because I cannot sketch. If I could only change my musical talent for that, I should be happy . . .

November 14th 1857 . . . We left Nice for Genoa at 5.30 . . . my sister, her husband and self, in the *coupé*, which was very much like being packed as sardines – no room for legs. However we were very jolly, only we got rather stiff in the 24 hours' journey for we only stopped twice – once for ten minutes at Oniglia at 4 a.m. for coffee, and once at noon for half an hour . . . to dine. However, I was too happy to grumble having received a letter saying that Richard would be home in next June [1858] . . .

[December 1857]. I have been abroad now two months. I have had one unsatisfactory note from Richard; he is coming back in June or July. Oh what a happiness and what anxiety! In a few short months, please God, this dreadful separation will be over . . . Monsieur Pernay spent an evening with me; and on seeing the picture on the wall of Richard in Meccan costume, he asked me what it was . . . On my telling him he composed a valse on the spot, and called it 'Richard in the Desert' . . . How I wish Richard were here. It makes me quite envious when I see my sister and her husband. I am all alone and Richard's place is vacant in the opera box, in the carriage, and everywhere. Sometimes I dream he came back and would not speak to me and I wake up with my pillow wet with tears . . .[40]

The letter Isabel refers to in this entry was incorrect; it would be June 1859 before she saw Richard again, but the origin of the letter is interesting. It came from Richard's sister Maria Stisted, who had written to Isabel on his instructions because he dared not write directly to her himself.[41]

He and Speke were still marching towards Ujiji. Each day seemed much like another, relieved occasionally by meeting a caravan of ivory traders, or the business of finding replacements for deserters. It was only through Richard's forceful personality and determination to succeed that they were able to continue at all. He was not above threatening '*dawaa*' (magic) on the superstitious Africans to keep them working. Their inclination was to spend all day gorging on meat, or supping *pombe* beer, acquired from a village on their way.

Though suffering the effects of fever and trembling with ague, he was determined to average at least 4 miles a day and he kept up the pace with relentless purpose. For most of this section of the journey Speke was carried in a hammock, and was a burden rather than of any assistance. Fortunately, many of the tribes spoke a version of the Kiswahili spoken at the coast, so Richard and Bombay were able to trade for sheep and goats when Richard could not hunt for the pot.

Not only were the men habitually indolent and greedy, Richard wrote, but often cowardly and fearful:

> At 8p.m. I was roused by my gun-bearer, Mabruki, who handed me my Ferrara, and by the Baloch, Riza, who reported that the palisade was surrounded by a host of raging blacks. I went out . . . [to find] the guard was running about in a state of excitement which robbed them of their wits, and I saw a long dark line of men sitting silently and peaceably, though armed for fight, outside the strong stockade . . .

Richard never learned to like Africans, regarding his men in the main as lazy, ignorant and sometimes malicious children thwarting his desire to reach his objective. He deprecated the behaviour of his porters and guides throughout his book, except where he took up a few pages to provide detail on the more important members of the team when he also noted good or entertaining characteristics about each man. He knew that when they composed songs about him they referred to him as the *Mazungu M'baya*, (the wicked white man); 'To have called me a *good* white man would mean that one was . . . an innocent who would be plucked and flayed without flinching; moreover, despite my wickedness, it was always to *me* they came for justice and redress if anyone bullied or ill-treated them.'[42]

Richard sanctioned occasional beatings as punishment for misdemeanours such as theft, desertion and fighting; but unlike Speke, who claimed to love Africans, he did not administer the punishments personally. Subsequently Speke would beat Bombay, a man he claimed to love 'like a brother', so badly that he knocked out his front teeth. 'He had violent quarrels with the Baloch,' Burton wrote, 'and on one occasion the Jemadar returned to him [Speke] an insult which, if we had not wanted the man, he would have noticed with the sword-cut . . .' Presumably, since Speke did not speak Swahili, these quarrels were conducted through Bombay.

Speke believed Africans – indeed all Negroes – to be racially inferior. Questioned about this by Bombay, Speke resorted to the Bible,
'related the history of Noah . . . and showed him that he was of the
black or Hametic stock, [who] by the common order of nature . . .
had to submit to their superiors . . .'[43] Richard's comment on this
statement was, 'Humbug!'[44]

A story about Richard's relationship with the bearers, which he
told a literary connection (W.F. Kirby) many years later, may or may
not be rooted in truth. He often exaggerated to shock or stimulate his
audience but in old age he would state, unequivocally, that he had
never killed a man. During the first part of the journey to Lake
Tanganyika, he told Kirby, several *askaris* who had attempted to
desert had been brought back but not chastised. Kirby takes up the
story:

> Mistaking his forbearance for weakness, [they] became daily bolder
> and more insolent, and now only awaited a convenient opportunity
> to kill him. One day as he was marching . . . gun over shoulder and
> dagger in hand, he became conscious that two of his men were
> unpleasantly near, and after a while one of them, unaware that
> Burton understood his language, urged the other to strike. Burton
> did not hesitate a moment. Without looking round, he thrust back
> his dagger, and stabbed the man dead on the spot . . .[45]

Despite his illness, Burton was an active collector of anthropological
data. He certainly possessed a more than passing knowledge of the
sexuality of African women, in particular those of the Wagogo tribe.
'[They] are well disposed towards strangers of fair complexion,' he
wrote, 'apparently with the permission of their husbands.' Nor did he
confine his 'sexological' research to women; 'I measured one man . . .'
he wrote in a footnote to *The Arabian Nights* 'who, when quiescent,
numbered nearly six inches. This is a characteristic of the Negro race
and of African animals . . . the "deed of kind" takes a much longer
time and adds greatly to the women's enjoyment . . . Debauched
women prefer Negroes on account of the size of their parts . . . In my
time no honest Hindi Moslem would take his women-folk to
Zanzibar on account of the huge attractions and enormous temptations there, and thereby offered to them.'[46]

'It will be seen,' wrote Fawn Brodie in her fine biography of

Burton,[47] 'that Burton with all his note-taking, measuring, and endless questioning, was in every way *involved* with the Africans. Speke on the other hand, recoiled with distaste from such involvement. Unable because he knew no Arabic to talk to anyone save Burton and Seedy Bombay, he was shut out of many decisions and all of Burton's ethnological research. One can begin to see him, increasingly lonely and suspicious, harbouring a growing conviction that Burton was "going to the devil", and quietly storing evidence on the subject to report back in England . . . Burton was like a sponge, Speke a stone.'[48] Involved Richard certainly was, but he did not belong; as usual he was the outsider looking on.

One hundred and thirty-four days out from the coast they reached Kazeh, an Arab settlement of substantial single-storey houses.[49] The 25 Arab residents having been warned of Richard's arrival rode out to greet the visiting *hajji* with a gratifying show of civility. And though Richard carried a letter of introduction to an Indian merchant from the Sultan, it was left to the Arabs to provide hospitality to the two weary men. Their hosts lived 'comfortably, and even splendidly . . . their gardens are extensive . . . they receive regular supplies of merchandise, comforts and luxuries from the coast.' They had their harems containing 200–300 women, and their slaves.[50] The only drawback appeared to be the effect of climate on their health; a man who escaped fever for two months boasted of the fact. 'What a contrast between the open-handed hospitality and the hearty good-will of this truly noble race (Arabs), and the niggardliness of the savage and selfish African . . . They warehoused my goods . . . and made all arrangements for my down march on return,' Richard wrote. 'During two long halts at Kazeh, Snay bin Amir never failed to pass the evening with me and, as he thoroughly knew the country all round, I derived immense information from his instructive and varied conversation.'[51]

Here were the times when Jack was at a disadvantage from want of language; he could join in none of these things and this made him, I think, a little sour . . . Snay bin Amir was familiar with the language, the religion and the ethnology of all the tribes. He was of a quixotic appearance, tall, gaunt and large limbed. He was well read, had a wonderful memory, fine perceptions and a passing power of languages. He was the stuff of which I could make a friend, brave as all his race, prudent, ready to perish for honour, and as honest as he was honourable.[52]

The admiration Burton felt for Snay was reciprocated by the Arabs of Kazeh towards Burton. Here was a man, a *hajji*, who could speak and read their own language to perfection, who understood and respected their customs and manners. He could entertain them with stories from the *Arabian Nights* and speak at length on matters that interested them. Housed comfortably among such friends, Richard halted at Kazeh for a month during the 'short rains' of November while Speke recovered his health. Whatever their personal feelings might have been regarding slavery, neither man felt obliged to disapprove of the source of their hosts' income.

Richard and Snay bin Amir quickly struck up a friendship. Snay had made the arduous journey between Kazeh and the coast three times, and visited Uganda. During their long conversations Richard questioned him closely and was grateful to have confirmation of what he had long suspected, the existence of more than one lake. Snay knew of four lakes, two of which were of great size. He had actually sailed across one of these (Lake Tanganyika) which lay due west. The other, he said, was north of Kazeh. Speke was obviously party to some of these discussions, but in his book, *What Led to the Discovery of the Source of the Nile*, he made the incredible claim that it was he, not Burton, who extracted the vital information from Snay:

> . . . On my opening Messieurs Rebmann and Erhardt's map and asking him where Nyassa was, he said it was a distinct lake from Ujiji lying to the Southward. This opened our eyes to a most interesting fact, for the first time discovered . . . the missionaries had run three lakes into one. In great glee I asked Snay through Captain Burton whether a river ran out of that lake.[53]

In his own copy of Speke's book, Burton has annotated this paragraph with the handwritten comment, 'A lie!', as well as several other succinct editorial remarks indicating his contempt for Speke's claims. The report of a series of lakes may well have been news to Speke, but Richard had stated his belief that there were probably three lakes in his written report to the R.G.S. before leaving Zanzibar. Indeed, he had drawn three large lakes on the map he sketched for Isabel before leaving London. Speke's incredible statement that it was *he* who had questioned Snay, *through Burton*, as though Richard was a disinterested interpreter, is heavily underlined by Burton, and an exclamation mark denotes his irritated amusement. To the equally ludicrous remark which Speke added as a footnote, 'I may as well mention the fact that neither Captain Burton nor myself were able to converse in any African language until we were close to the coast on the return journey,' Burton simply remarks tiredly, 'untrue!'[54]

Snay told the two men that the northern lake lay due north of Kazeh, 'at 15 marches distant'. He himself had never travelled this route, he told them, it being too dangerous, but had followed the shores of the western lake and crossed the mountains, 'from which he could see over its expansive waters and from which, together with his enquiries, he considered it to be a larger lake than the Tanganyika.'[55] Speke would subsequently claim that at this point Burton became desperately ill, leaving him in virtual charge of the expedition, 'I picked up all the information I could gather from the Arabs, with Bombay as interpreter,' Speke stated. Yet even though he implied that he alone had been given the information about the northern lake, Speke admitted elsewhere that he and Burton had discussed, at great length, the information given by Snay. 'We . . . argued that we thought the lake in question . . . would more likely prove to be the source of the Nile, from the simple fact of our knowing the Jub[56] to be separated from the interior plateau by the East Coast Range . . .'[57]

We know that Burton was never so desperately ill at Kazeh that he handed over control. He certainly suffered from the same fevers and chills, aching eyes, 'liver derangement', and general debility which afflicted the entire party except, that is, Speke, who had now regained almost full health after having been carried for the past few months. For the most part when he was at his lowest ebb, Richard lay on a day-bed on the east-facing verandah of Snay's house to catch any breeze. But he was far from idle as his journal and observations log show.[58] At Snay's request Richard submitted himself to the Bedouin cure-all of the cauterising iron (red hot iron applied to the skin at strategic points),[59] and when this failed an old medicine woman was called in. She gave him some green powder to take as snuff which produced a paroxysm of sneezing, when she shouted for joy, predicted an immediate recovery, and demanded *pombe* as payment.

Her prophecy was not fulfilled. It was, however, only after he left Kazeh, as his impressively detailed journal reveals, that Burton became so unwell that he could not keep his journals and logs written up. At this time Speke wrote to the Royal Geographical Society enclosing Burton's field-book, and reported that Burton was suffering from 'a fever which attacks all newcomers'. Speke later claimed that it was he who organised the expedition's departure from Kazeh in early December. He persuaded the armed slaves to march with them by paying the wages that had been promised to them by Burton earlier on the journey. The slaves had demanded to return to Zanzibar, saying that they had been ordered by the Sultan in January to serve with the expedition for a year, and that had now almost expired. Richard was amused rather than annoyed that they had twisted a period of less than six months' actual service into a year, and ignored their demands. Speke, who obtained a garbled version of the complaints through Bombay, chose to regard the grievances more seriously and later used the incident against Burton.

Notably, despite Speke's subsequent claims that he had assumed leadership of the expedition, the route taken from Kazeh was westward; a route selected by Richard on Snay's recommendation, 'in direct opposition to Speke's wish' to strike north for 'the northern lake'.[60] Snay strongly warned against taking the northern route saying that the relatively small size of their caravan would make them vulnerable to attack by hostile tribes. Although confirming that the northern lake was a much greater sheet of water, he firmly advised that it was safer to travel west, to the Tanganyika. With Snay's generous assistance Richard was able to restock with vital supplies, and with his detailed instruction on how to reach the lake the expedition set off once more. Had Speke really been in command at this point, as he claims, the expedition would surely have taken the northerly route. However, these technical arguments lay in the future.

From extant papers it is clear that both Richard and Speke were aware, at this point, that there were four lakes; also that they were convinced that the source of the Nile, which had for so long eluded geographers, lay somewhere in this region of lakes. Richard gambled on the Tanganyika being the most likely feeder of the more northerly lakes, and therefore the Nile's ultimate source. Speke, with far less scholarly knowledge and information than Burton, made what can only have been a lucky guess that the northerly lake was the more likely source. And, since Burton rejected his suggestion, it became in Speke's mind his property alone. Henceforward he protected it with a jealousy that was almost maternal in ferocity. After Kazeh, Burton noted that Speke became more morose and argumentative; operating alone and keeping his journal entries secretly.

In fact, as Burton's journals show, Speke did 'lead the Expedition' after a fashion. After 'much murmuring', he followed Burton's order to take an advance party to set up a camp at Zimbili, leaving Burton to follow in a week or so, when he thought that he might be better able to face the rigours of travel. They met up as planned, Burton having been carried there in a hammock. During the two-week journey his only log entry reads shakily: 'Unyanyembe and Kapunde. Too sick to observe. Climate precisely the same.' He then despatched Speke back to Kazeh, having received word that the long-awaited supplies and the twenty-two porters had finally arrived there, seven months late. Burton used this period to convalesce. He was well enough to recruit another twenty bearers and, clearly, to appreciate feminine beauty:

> On the 15th we went to Yombo, where I remarked three beauties who would be deemed beautiful in any part of the world. Their faces were purely Grecian, they had laughing eyes, their figures were models for an artist . . . cast in bronze. These beautiful domestic animals smiled graciously when, in my best Kinyamezi, I did my *devoir* to the sex, and a little tobacco always secured for me a seat in the 'undress circle'.[61]

On 22 December Speke returned with the missing porters, and the heavily pilfered stores they brought with them. No mail had been forwarded and the much-needed quinine and other medication, that Richard had several times requested from Frost, had not been sent. Speke reported that he had paid off a number of porters and sent them back to the coast as they now appeared superfluous, an action he would come to regret bitterly. The two men separated again, taking different routes so that Speke could do some hunting and Richard could travel at an easy pace, but when Richard reached their agreed rendezvous he found Speke prostrate in the hut of a poor villager looking 'very poorly'.

They halted a few days for Speke to recover, and marched through Christmas Day to make up for lost time. They celebrated instead on

New Year's Day with roast beef, and a Christmas pudding that 'knew neither flour nor currants'. Speke relates distastefully how the porters and bearers were permitted to relax with the inhabitants of a friendly village, 'giving themselves up to dancing, pombe-drinking and other related pleasures . . . even Bombay became so *love-sick* we could hardly tear him away.'

On 10 January Burton collapsed with the worst illness that was to affect him during the journey. It caused severe pain and a complete paralysis of all his limbs. Fearing he might not survive he instructed Speke, in the event of his death, to carry home the results of the journey, before sinking into agonised oblivion. 'I had done my best, and now nothing appeared to remain for me but to die,' he wrote. He believed he was suffering from recurrent malaria, but the locals diagnosed mushroom poisoning and said he would be able to ride in ten days. Though Burton never accepted the diagnosis, ten days later he was shakily able to mount his donkey and go on. Eleven months would pass before he could walk properly again, due to a lingering partial paralysis and numbness in both legs. During that time he rode when possible, or was carried.

But Burton's letter-book reveals that even while stricken he was actively working, and writing, on all but five days – the only time he actually relinquished leadership to Speke. The entries during those five days of Speke's administration provide an interesting comparison of styles. Whereas Richard wrote a complete draft copy of all his letters, even when they might be pages long, Speke provided only a brief summary of what he wrote:

> Mesinay Jan'y 15, 1858
>
> To Ludhgen [Zanzibar],
> A letter ordering the medical stores, Amerikan [cotton], and coloured stuffs up, sharp.
> J.H. Speke

It was this practice of Speke's, of not providing himself with adequate notes and memoranda, which Burton believed led to Speke's subsequent gross exaggeration and distortion of what took place on the expedition between the two men.

Meanwhile, still beset by continuous personnel problems and illness – Burton's mouth was ulcerated to an extent where he could scarcely eat or drink – they came to the fast and deep river at Wanyika where they had reluctantly to pay a *hongo* (tax), the equivalent of £50 in London, to be ferried across in bark canoes. While sitting waiting, Burton was fascinated to see an entire herd of elephant disappear into the tall reed-beds on the banks. Beyond the river though, the countryside was depressingly bare of any habitation. Once well-populated, in recent years it had been laid waste by tribal wars.

Speke was in better physical condition than Burton except for an inflammation of the eyes. It was a weakness from which he had suffered since childhood, and at this point it had rendered him temporarily almost totally blind. But both men were in extremely poor physical condition when, as the long caravan snaked and straggled through screens of head-high grass, the expedition finally reached its goal on 13 February 1858 after a journey of 950 miles. Richard was also suffering from an eye infection, though it was mild compared with Speke's affliction. He could at least see, whereas Speke's donkey had to be led by a bearer.

The first thing out of the ordinary that Richard noticed was that the guide, hired at Unyanyembe, had run ahead and was changing the direction of the caravan. Puzzled that the man should take this responsibility upon himself, he urged his donkey after him up a steep and stony hill sparsely clad with thorny trees. At the summit the exhausted beasts refused to proceed any further (in fact Speke's donkey collapsed and died shortly afterwards), and they halted to recover breath. Looking around from the advantage of height, Richard saw a streak of light in the distance and he asked Bombay what it was. 'I am of the opinion,' Bombay told him gravely and without any show of emotion, 'that that is *the* water.'

Burton was shocked. Could this small patch of bright water really be the much vaunted 'inland sea'?

I gazed in dismay . . . [and] began to lament my folly in having risked life and lost health for so poor a prize, to curse Arab exaggeration, and to propose an immediate return, with the view of exploring the Nyanza or Northern Lake.[62]

However, on moving forward a few yards he realised that what they had first seen was merely an inlet, and as he rounded the contours of the hill the splendour of the huge lake itself, the longest (and second deepest) freshwater lake in the world, lay before his awed gaze, filling him with 'admiration, wonder and delight . . . Nothing could be more picturesque than this first view of the Tanganyika Lake as it lay in the lap of the mountains, basking in the gorgeous tropical sunshine.'[63]

> Beyond . . . a narrow strip of emerald green . . . shelves towards a ribbon of glistening yellow sand . . . the waters [are] . . . an expanse of the lightest and softest blue, in breadth varying from thirty to thirty-five miles . . . Truly it was a revel for soul and sight. Forgetting the toils, dangers, and the doubtfulness of return, I felt willing to endure double what I had endured; and all the party seemed to join with me in joy . . .[64]

Speke, blind and understandably frustrated by his exclusion of this supreme moment, would write:

> You may picture . . . my bitter disappointment when after toiling through so many miles of savage life, all the time emaciated by divers sicknesses and weakened by great privations of food and rest, I found, on approaching the zenith of my ambition, the Great Lake in question nothing but mist and glare before my eyes . . . The lovely Tanganyika lake could be seen in all its glory by everybody but myself . . . The fevers and . . . inflammation, caught by sleeping on the ground during this rainy season . . . rendered every object before me enclouded as by a misty veil.[65]

Later the two would coldly argue the precise altitude of the lake, which they gauged by the boiling water method – Speke stating that it was 1,800 feet, Richard, pedantically, insisting on 1,844 ft. In fact it is some 700 feet higher than either estimate. Nevertheless, it was a great discovery. They had proved the existence of the great lake and therefore achieved the main objective of the expedition.

15

THE LAKE REGIONS
1857–1858

Richard had intended to make a base camp at Ujiji. He was disappointed to find it consisted of only a few scattered beehive-shaped huts near a gently shelving beach suitable as a landing place. Far from the well-established port he had expected, it was little more than a camping ground. A short distance inland, however, was Kawele, 'a small village . . . whose mushroom huts barely protruded their summits above the dense vegetation'. It was here and not on the lake shore at Ujiji that the two officers, bottomed by fatigue and inherent ill-health, thankfully took a period of rest. After more than seven months of successful endeavour, they might have been justified in experiencing a certain euphoria, but neither man mentions any rejoicing.

Among the huts was 'a deserted house that had been left to decay by some Arab merchants'. The rent demanded for this luxury, together with the so-called 'protection' of the local chief, made heavy inroads into their trading stocks of beads and cloth,[1] but they were too exhausted and too short of supplies to wander about seeking a less expensive base and paid the exorbitant price. Arab traders had first visited Ujiji in 1840. By 1858 three or four caravans called each summer to collect slaves and ivory from the tribes along the banks of the lakes, and there was a thriving spirit of entrepreneurialism among the inhabitants.

The abundance of fat lake fish and fresh produce tempted the men 'to commit excesses' for which they paid in gastric upsets which, as Burton's journal reflects, further affected their already fragile health:

> I lay for a fortnight upon the earth too blind to read or write, too weak to ride, too ill to converse. Jack was almost as groggy on his legs as I was, suffering from a painful ophthalmia, and a curious contortion of the face, which made him chew sideways, like an animal that chews the cud . . .[2]

The Nile source still beckoned. Richard wrote, 'I was determined to explore the northern extremity of the lake, whence everyone said, issued a large river [the Rusizi] flowing northwards.' Could this be the Nile? Clearly the easiest way to investigate the reports was to travel on the lake, but the only native craft were shallow dug-out canoes. These were not only easily capsized in heavy weather, but hardly capable of carrying sufficient supplies for the month-long survey that Burton anticipated. Furthermore, in open canoes they would be vulnerable near the banks to attacks from the reported hostile tribes along the northern shore. Snay had told them of a large dhow belonging to a wealthy Arab trader, Sheikh Hamed bin Sulayim,[3] and Burton decided to try to hire this vessel. However, his physical condition remained extremely poor; his legs were semi-paralysed and he was not capable of moving from his bed without help.

Speke's eye infection improved, and with it his general health. Posting a watch for hippos or crocodiles he bathed each day in the lake, took a gentle stroll in the cool of the mornings and evenings, and rested during the heat of the afternoons. By the end of a fortnight he was able to wander about the market place, with strings of beads as currency slung over his arm, 'protected by an umbrella and fortified with stained-glass spectacles . . . to purchase daily supplies'. His 'French grey' sunglasses were a traffic-stopper in the market place, and at times he had to remove them to make onlookers disperse. Shopping trips aside, he became increasingly bored and he wrote of 'longing for a change of scenery'. He was not unimpressed by the landscape but he felt it would benefit by civilisation, 'with white-washed houses, well-trained gardens, and the like [to] vary the unceasing monotony of . . . green trees, green grass – green grass, green trees, so wearisome in their luxuriance – what a paradise of beauty would this place present!'[4] It was his suggestion that he should take Bombay across to the island of Kasenge, off the opposite shore of the lake, where Sheikh Hamed lived, to arrange the hire of the dhow.[5] Burton at first demurred. He had been told that it was too dangerous to cross the lake by canoe during the rains because of sudden storms, but Speke convinced him otherwise and despite a heavy downpour set off on 3 March.

Two weeks after Speke's departure a messenger called Khamis called on Burton with a letter from Sheikh Hamed. Having heard of the expedition, and unaware that Speke was on his way to meet him, the Sheikh had written offering to lend them the dhow. With this assurance that Speke could not fail (though his mission appeared almost superfluous since they could have dealt with Khamis), Richard gave himself up to his illness. Speke was away for almost a month during which time Richard was capable of little except directing the daily routine of the expedition personnel through Said bin Salim and the Jemadar (head porter). Most of the time, he said, 'I lay like a log upon my cot, smoking, *dreaming of things past, visioning things present* and indulging in a few lines of reading and writing.'[6] Along with unusually rhapsodic descriptions of the scenery, Richard's reports of smoking, dreaming and envisioning reveries suggest frequent use of narcotics as medication.

To Richard's relief, as his journal shows:

On the 29th March, the rattling of matchlocks announced Jack's return. He was moist, mildewed and wet to the bone, and all his things were in a similar state; his guns grained with rust, his fireproof powder magazine full of rain and, worse than that he had not been able to gain anything but a promise that, *after three months* the dhow should be let to us for five hundred dollars . . .

Since this was no more than the promise already given through Khamis, Richard – whose health was marginally improving – was quietly resentful of Speke's failure, because of the time and supplies wasted. 'He had done literally nothing,' he wrote bitterly in his journal, believing, probably accurately, that he himself could have achieved more had he dealt directly with Khamis from his bed. It was a repeat of the Somalia mission where Speke had returned with nothing to show for his journey but excuses. And there was further mortification for Speke during their debriefing discussion; 'Bombay now thought, when it was too late, that if I had offered to give him [Hamed] 500 dollars' worth of cloth, landed at his house, he could not have resisted the offer.'[7] In fact it might be argued that Speke had achieved something, the first crossing of Lake Tanganyika by a European, thereby defining its width.

Richard must accept some of the blame for Speke's lack of success in this mission. Once again Speke's lack of languages made him a poor envoy. Richard should have recognised this and, despite Speke's badgering, ought not to have consented to his going if the outcome was so vital. The negotiators had no common language. Speke's only point of contact had been through Bombay, speaking Hindustani to one of the Sheikh's slaves who in turn acted as his master's interpreter. Had Richard been able to make the journey, with his fluent Arabic and understanding of Arab culture, the result might well have been different. But language had not been the only problem Speke encountered.

On 8 March while off the western banks of the lake, Speke's expedition ran into a storm which threatened to capsize the canoe. His escort, consisting of Bombay, one of the Goanese cook-boys, two Belochi guards and the captain and crew of the canoe (twenty 'stark-naked natives'), beached the dug-out on Kivera island and they spent the day there sheltering from the rain.

> At night a violent storm of rain and wind beat on my tent with such fury that its nether parts were torn away from the pegs . . . on the wind's abating, a candle was lighted to rearrange the kit, and in a moment, as though by magic, the whole interior became covered with a host of small black beetles, evidently attracted by the glimmer of the candle.

Speke spent some time trying to clear the insects out of his clothes and equipment but in the end gave up, extinguished his candle and settled down to sleep despite the annoyance of the 'intruders crawling up my sleeves and into my hair, or down my back and legs'. Some time later he was awakened by an intense irritation as one of the beetles crawled into his ear. Nothing he did dislodged the tiny creature; shaking and banging his head only served to make it burrow deeper until eventually it came up against the ear-drum. 'This impediment evidently enraged him, for he began with an exceeding vigour, like a rabbit at a hole, to dig violently away at my tympanum. The queer sensation

this amusing measure excited in me is past description.'[8] Seeing
Speke's excusable panic, his escort made several suggestions including
blowing tobacco smoke into the ear and the application of hot oil or
salt. Unfortunately none of these commodities was available.

> I therefore tried melted butter; that failing, I applied the point of my
> penknife to his back, which did more harm than good for though a
> few thrusts quieted him, the point also wounded my ear so badly
> that inflammation set in, severe supporation took place, and all the
> facial glands extending from that point down to the point of the
> shoulder became contorted and drawn aside, and a string of boils
> decorated the whole length of that region. It was the most painful
> thing I ever remembered to have endured, but more annoying still,
> I could not masticate for several days and had to feed on broth
> alone. For many months the tumour made me almost deaf and ate
> a hole between the ear and the nose, so that when I blew it, my ear
> whistled so audibly that those who heard it laughed. Six or seven
> months after this accident happened, a bit of the beetle – a leg, a
> wing, or parts of its body – came away in the wax.[9]

Several days after this incident, Speke's party reached Kasenge island.
He was given a 'hearty welcome' by Sheikh Hamed and made comfortable as an honoured guest, but the negotiations were not
straightforward. The dhow was engaged picking up supplies from the
eastern shore of the lake. Hamed was willing to hire it out, but said
that the vessel's size made it unlikely that any local crew could be
found capable of sailing it. He could not lend his own crew as he was
about to depart for three months' ivory trading, and needed all his
men.[10] It was too large to be propelled by paddles and local men did
not understand the art of rowing. If he waited a week, Hamed told
Speke, his men would try to recruit a suitable crew. To Speke's irritation, Bombay then reminded him of the porters he had insisted on
paying off at Kazeh as surplus. Being coastal men, Bombay said helpfully, they would have been perfectly capable of crewing the dhow.

From this point, Speke was more interested in the geography of the
lake than negotiating the hire of the boat. He questioned Hamed
about the reports he and Burton had been given by the tribes on the
western shore and, *through the interpreters*, Hamed confirmed he
had visited all parts of the lake and was certain that a large river

flowed out of the lake at the northern end. 'Although I did not venture on it,' he told Speke, 'in consequence of its banks being occupied by desperately savage Negroes . . . I went so near its outlet that I could see and feel the outward drift of the water.'[11]

These words, written in his report, thrilled Speke; if a river indeed flowed northwards out of the lake, there was a strong possibility that it was the Nile. Later he would say that he was always unconvinced about the river because he had also heard that the northern end of the lake was 'encircled by high hills – the concave of the Mountains of the Moon . . .', but there is little doubt that at the time he was carried along by an acute attack of find-the-Nile fever. Subsequently he would change his reports about what Hamed told him.[12]

For Speke the time dragged. Unlike Burton, he could not occupy his time by long gossipy conversations with Hamed. He did not trust Arabs and was faintly repelled by Africans. He sourly watched his host sitting under a canopy, 'surrounded by a group of swarthy blacks, gossiping for hours together, or transacting his worldly business, in purchasing ivory, slaves, or any commodities worthy of his notice.' Whereas Burton would have been among the group making notes about customs and mores at tedious length, and was likely – in good health – to have slept with the women, Speke was totally alienated. His attempts at describing the local peoples perhaps say more about the writer than his subject.

> . . .They are extremely filthy in their habits . . . In appearance not unlike the kaffir, resembling that tribe in height, and general bearing, having enlarged lips, flattish noses and frizzly woolly hair. They are very easily amused and generally wear smiling faces . . . they lie about their huts like swine, with little more animation than a pig has when basking in a summer's sun.
>
> The mothers of these savage people have infinitely less affection than many savage beasts of my acquaintance. I have seen a mother bear, galled by frequent shots, obstinately meet her death by repeatedly returning under fire whilst endeavouring to rescue her young from the grasp of intruding men. But here, for a simple loin-cloth or two, human mothers eagerly exchange their little offspring, delivering them into perpetual bondage to my Beluch soldiers.' [13]

After ten days the dhow returned to the island. 'She looked very graceful in contrast to the wretched little canoes, and came moving slowly up the smooth waters of the channel decked in her white sails,' Speke wrote, 'like a swan upon a garden reach.'[14] He saw himself returning in triumph to Ujiji aboard the lovely vessel, but when the dhow was unloaded – a task which occupied several days – the Sheikh reported that he had had no success in the hunt for an alternative crew. After a further two days he reported that the vessel needed some repairs, and pressed Speke to stay while he extended his search for crew. Speke, thoroughly frustrated after two weeks of idleness, eventually lost his temper with Hamed. 'We had a little tiff,' he wrote in his journal. 'I accused him of detaining me in the hopes of getting powder . . . which I knew he wanted . . . I could see no other cause for his desiring my further stay there . . . Hamed, however, very quietly denied the imputation, declaring that he desired nothing but what I might frankly give . . .'[15]

Following this, despite a specific visit to Hamed by Bombay to discuss the hire fee, and the fact that Speke was rendered every courtesy as a guest, Hamed refused to re-open discussions on the matter. He made it clear that the dhow would be available to the expedition on his return in three months if they could wait. His withdrawal of cooperation appears to have completely baffled both Speke and Bombay. Burton would have understood how implicitly offensive was Speke's accusation – warranted or not; also he would not have ignored Hamed's open invitation to rectify the discourtesy with a generous gift, which Speke did not even recognise.

Eventually, the hapless Speke decided nothing could be achieved by further delay and he ordered the return of the party to the Ujiji base camp. He fully realised that the only result of his 4-week trip was a few shells he had picked up on the western shores of the lake (which, fortunately for his pride, subsequently turned out to be new to science), and he was truculent and mortified at having to return unsuccessful. Although he did not say so in his published accounts, in his first report to the Royal Geographical Society he openly admitted that 'as far as the dhow was concerned, my trip was a signal failure. But in other respects it was highly satisfactory for it enabled me to measure the lake in its centre and gain some information . . . about its southern extremity.'[16]

Following Richard's instructions, he had kept a diary of his journey and a few days after his return he asked Richard to help him put the manuscript into a suitable state for publication. Never a jealous author, Richard complied. Bearing in mind Speke's resentment stemming from the previous occasion when this had happened, it may seem curious that he sought Burton's help. Perhaps it was his way of indicating that he intended to publish the journals. Speke had yet to achieve his later status as a leading explorer, and his report mixed fact with conjecture. Richard was startled to note the inclusion, on a map designed to accompany a serious paper, of a fantastic feature for which there was no evidence but inexact native reports. He wrote:

> I was immensely surprised to find, amongst many other things, a vast horseshoe of lofty mountains that Jack placed, in a map attached to the paper . . . I had seen the mountains growing upon paper under Jack's hand, from a thin ridge of hills fringing the Tanganyika until they grew to the size printed in Blackwoods, and Jack gravely printed in the largest capitals, 'This mountain range I consider to be the Mountains of the Moon;' thus men *do* geography, and thus discovery is stultified.[17]

Richard's superior attitude regarding this, allied to his only partially concealed irritation over the failure to secure the dhow, was immensely galling to Speke who, it must be remembered, already harboured antagonism before he left Zanzibar. Now, in the face of Richard's continued incapacity, Speke conveniently forgot his own bouts of illness and began to believe that he was carrying Burton and, in fact, it was he who was in command of the expedition in all but name.

The failure to secure the dhow left the men with no option but to explore the northern end of the lake in canoes. They could not afford to wait three months for Hamed because their supplies were dwindling dangerously low. Burton set about acquiring the largest canoes in the area. He had heard they were about to depart for trading purposes to Uvira, the northernmost station to which the Arabs had penetrated. Speke attempted to seize the initiative and make the exploration alone on the grounds of concern for Burton's health: 'my companion was still suffering so severely that anybody seeing him attempt to go would have despaired of his ever returning. Yet he could not endure to be left behind.'[18] But Burton wrote that he was 'resolved at all costs, even if we were reduced to actual want, to visit the mysterious stream. I threw over [the chief's] shoulders a six-foot length of scarlet broadcloth which made him tremble with joy, and all the people concerned . . . received a great deal more than [their] worth.' By dint of this generous gift, he wrote, 'I secured two large canoes and fifty-five men.'[19]

Even so, to ensure that the chief did not break his promise and leave without them, Richard slept on the beach near the canoes sheltering from the heavy rain under a mackintosh. Finally, 'at 7.0 on the 12th April 1858, my canoe . . . followed by Jack's . . . made for the cloudy and storm-vexed north.' They zig-zagged up the lake calling at small villages on both banks; a voyage of nine days. Both men made notes as they travelled. The crowded open boats provided an acme of discomfort; they were alternately soaked by heavy downpour or baked by the sun, and for the invalid Burton there was no way even of resting the back or lying down. At Uvira 'all my hopes were dashed', Richard wrote. First the crew refused to take them to the north shore as promised, because the tribes there were implacable enemies. Second, everyone Richard questioned insisted that the river flowed *into*, not *out of* the Tanganyika. 'I felt sick at heart,' he wrote. When he interrogated Bombay as to exactly what had been said by Sheikh Hamed, Bombay declared that Speke had misunderstood him; his informer had always spoken of 'a river falling into, not issuing *from* the lake'. Bombay then added his own conviction that 'the Arabs had never sailed north of Uvira . . .'[20] To add to Richard's misery, his tongue became so ulcerated that he could not speak.

Apart from the danger on several occasions of being upset among crocodiles in storms, the only incident of any note during the return voyage was a disturbance one night when Mabruki rushed into their makeshift tent (a sail draped over a ridge-pole), thrust Richard's sword into his hands and shouted that they were being attacked. Memories of Berbera must have struck both men. The fracas had begun as a drunken squabble, during which a local chief was badly wounded by one of the Goanese cook-boys. Richard doctored the man and after 24 hours of nursing 'he was able to rise . . . This did not prevent the report at home that I had killed the man.'[21]

Their arrival back at Kawele a month after their departure saw them both improved in health: 'Jack was still deaf, but cured of his blindness; the ulcerated mouth, which compelled me to live on milk for seventeen days returned to its normal state, my strength increased.

My feet were still swollen, but my hands lost their numbness and I could again read and write.'

Richard now reviewed his position and seemed to realise for the first time that they had actually met the written objectives of the expedition. They had found the 250-mile-long lake, had navigated a good part of it, and had surveyed and mapped large areas of the East African hinterland, pinpointing the mountains Kilimanjaro and Kenya with their glacial summer snows. Although he had not been able to visit the north shore of the lake, all evidence pointed to the fact that they were very close to finding that elusive Source of the Nile. He believed that when he returned home with this information he was virtually guaranteed sponsorship, and paid leave, for a further expedition. This would inevitably be a better financed and equipped one, since he had proved it was possible to travel safely. He knew now the mistakes to avoid. Having accepted that 'the object of my mission was effected . . . I threw off the burden of grinding care, with which the imminent prospect of a failure had before sorely laden me . . .'[22]

Speke would later claim that he wanted to remain longer at the lake to make a trip around the southern parts, thereby completing a circumnavigation, but that Burton had refused to allow him to do so, saying he 'had had enough of canoe travelling'. Burton denied this, writing against the paragraph in his copy of Speke's book, 'untrue'.[23] Indeed, Burton's journal establishes beyond any doubt *his* reluctance at leaving the lake incompletely surveyed, but he was compelled to do so by lack of supplies. The expedition left Lake Tanganyika on 26 May and backtracked to Unyanyembe, which they reached on 17 June after a 'toilsome trudge'.

Here a mail-bag, brought up by a passing caravan on the instructions of the French Consul in Zanzibar, awaited them. It was only the second mail they had received since setting out a year earlier. 'Everyone had lost some friend or relation dear to him,' Richard grieved. 'My father had died on the 6th of last September, after a six week illness at Bath, and was buried on the 10th, and I only knew it on the 18th of June in the following year.' With this mail came their first news of the Indian Mutiny. Richard's brother Edward, having apparently recovered from his beating, had survived the fighting but Speke's brother, also named Edward, had died. Grimly Richard recalled the warnings he had given, both in correspondence with his superiors and in his book, *Pilgrimage to El-Medinah and Meccah*. Isabel had written faithfully, twice a month; each letter full of chatty information, each envelope packed with cuttings and news that she thought Richard would like to have. This, he would later tell her, lifted his spirits tremendously.

On the following day the expedition reached Kazeh, where the entire party was treated for fever with the 'Warburg's Drops' so highly recommended by Colonel Hamerton. In the drier climate and civilised surroundings, there was an instant improvement in health and well-being. The few supplies that had been sent up from the coast, in response to the repeated requests he had sent down with passing caravans, were disappointing. Only a portion of the cloth he ordered had been forwarded, and the ammunition was the wrong size for their weapons.

What should have been a period of rest at Kazeh was marred by further disagreement between Speke and Burton. Richard was undecided about the best course of action. On one hand the northern lake – which Snay called Ukewere – was temptingly close and Richard 'had not given up the project of returning to the seaboard via . . . the lake – lying fifteen or sixteen marches to the north'. On the other hand, he knew it was sensible to return rapidly to the coast while the good weather lasted in an attempt to minimise further cost. He could then organise another, better-funded expedition specifically to seek the Nile source. But Speke was frantic to go to the Ukewere. He had drawn up a map of the lake, based upon the information provided to Burton by Arab merchants and Sheikh Snay during their previous visit to Kazeh. From their descriptions it seemed that the Ukewere was even larger than the Tanganyika, and Speke was convinced that it must be the source of the Nile.

Burton purchased further stores, compromising his personal finances by issuing promissory notes which he would have to meet on their return to Zanzibar. Even so, there were insufficient supplies to enable the entire expedition to go to the Ukewere. The only possibility of investigating the reports was for one man to go north, travelling fast and light with a small party, while the other remained at Kazeh preparing for the return journey to the coast. Hence the disagreement. Speke's account – that he *instigated* the side-trip because Burton was too ill to go – appears to have been accepted without question by most previous biographers. Richard was certainly in poorer condition than Speke, but the entry in his journal detailing why Speke made the all-important trip also deserves consideration:

> I saw . . . that the existence of this hitherto unknown basin would explain many discrepancies promulgated by speculative geographers . . . [but it] remained to ascertain if the Arabs had not with usual Oriental hyperbole, exaggerated the dimensions of the northern lake. My companion who had recovered strength appeared to be a fit person to be detached upon this duty; moreover his presence at Kazeh was by no means desirable . . .

Just as he had offended Sheikh Hamed, Speke had now provoked their courteous hosts at Kazeh by taking offence when it was least intended, expecting servility as his due, and treating 'all skins a shade darker than his own as "niggers"'. Richard found himself 'between two friends who have quarrelled with each other . . . [and] the difficulty was exaggerated by [Speke's] complete ignorance of Eastern manners and customs and of any Oriental language beyond, at least, a few words of the debased Anglo-Indian jargon.'[24] In short, 'there was no need for two of us going, and I was afraid to leave him behind in Kazeh.'[25]

That the Nile source lay thereabouts was now beyond dispute; it was merely a matter of time before someone gained the glory. Speke must have known that Richard would never include him in a second expedition to the area – their relationship was too fractious, and his record of achievement was pitiful. If he was ever to prove himself, this was his best chance. All the same, it seems unlikely that at this point Speke deliberately intended to *damage* Burton; he merely wished to make his own reputation by achieving something significant. Eventually, Speke's arguments that he should be the one to go wore Richard down and he agreed, in his own exasperated words, 'to get rid of him'.[26] Under normal circumstances, as leader, Richard had nothing to lose; the results of an expedition – whichever team member makes the discoveries – are, after all, a group achievement.

A year later, Speke would claim that *he had decided* to make the trip because Burton 'was most unfortunately quite done up, and most graciously consented to wait with the Arabs and recruit his health'. But on 2 July 1858, *writing on the spot* he wrote to Norton Shaw, 'To diminish the disappointment, caused by the shortcomings of our [sup-

plies of] cloth, in not seeing the whole of the sea of Ujiji, I have proposed to take a flying trip to the Ukewere lake, while Captain Burton
prepares for our return homewards . . .'[27]

Yet even as he reported on Burton's health Speke managed to place
a spin on his apparent concern, untruthfully hinting that Burton had
been a passenger all along, with Speke carrying the main burdens of
command: '. . . only fancy what a time he has had of it,' he wrote,
'eleven months [sic] in a bed-ridden state and being obliged to travel
the whole time . . . What torments me most is the inability to take
Lunars . . . I have failed . . . simply from the want of an assistant to
take the time, for Burton has always been ill . . . I took only one at
Ugigi and then my eyesight was very bad . . .'[28] He explained that the
lack of factual information in his letter was due to the fact that there
was 'nothing to write about in this uninteresting country, nothing
could surpass these tracks, jungles, plains etc for dull sameness. The
people are the same everywhere, in fact the whole country is one vast
senseless map of sameness.'[29]

While Speke made preparations to leave, Richard also wrote to
Norton Shaw. The letters of the two men, written in the same week,
are in marked contrast. Burton's lengthy epistle enclosed a copy of his
field book, and maps: his own and Speke's. These were not for publication before their return, he stressed, but were sent 'in case of
accidents'. He packs his letter with information and data, including
details of their plans:

> . . .We left the lake of Ugigi about a month ago, and are now halted
> in this main depot of Arab traders. Captain Speke has volunteered
> to visit the unknown lake of which the Arabs give grand accounts.
> It lies nearly due N of Unyanyembe at a distance of some 12 to 15
> marches. On his return we shall lose no time in returning to the
> coast which if we pass safely through dangerous Ugogo we may
> hope, DV, to reach about Dec next.[30]

Because the expedition had taken longer than anticipated, he wrote,
the state of his exchequer was desperate. He had already committed
the final £250 of the expedition funds, held in Zanzibar against his
requirement, and had also spent 'at least £500' of his own money to
buy further supplies which, among other things, would enable Speke
to visit the Ukewere. He was not only worried about their ability to

reach the coast within the limit of their supplies, but also concerned that on their return to Zanzibar he would be unable to meet the financial obligations promised by Hamerton to their escort, which amounted to nearly $1,000 (local currency).

He had just learned that Hamerton's replacement was none other than his old rival C.P. Rigby who, he thought, would not be eager to pay the expedition debts 'unless ordered to do so'. In view of accusations that would later be made by both Speke and Rigby, it is significant that Burton had advised the Expedition Committee of the impending problem well in advance, and asked for help. 'I venture to lay the subject before the Expedition Committee of the RGS, as unless Col. Hamerton's promises be fulfilled by his successor we shall be placed in a most disagreeable position at Zanzibar.'

Among the letters waiting for him, he told Shaw, had been an 'official wigging' from the 'Hon. Gov. in Bombay', because of the remarks he had made about British policy in the Red Sea area. He had sent the document (via Shaw) for the private information of the Directors in London, but it had been leaked and consequently he had been 'rebuked for "want of discretion and due respect for the authorities to whom I am subordinate" . . . I have extended my regret for having offended the Government to which I am so indebted, at the same time I am at a loss to know how I have offended . . .' The rebuke was dated 1 July 1857, almost a year earlier. As well as his apology, he undoubtedly hoped that Shaw might help to dig him out of this latest brush with his superiors; he would need their cooperation to mount his next expedition. He concluded his letter to Shaw with a request 'that this account of our health may be kept from our families and friends'.[31]

Speke departed on 10 July and expected to be away six weeks. This was the extreme extent of supplies that they could afford to expend on the project while remaining reasonably sure of having sufficient for the journey to the coast. Furthermore, Speke wrote, they had been told that the Arabs ceased travelling to the coast at this season, 'from fear of being caught up by droughts in the deserts between this place and the East Coast Range, where, if the ponds and puddles dry up, there is so little water in the wells that travelling becomes precarious'.[32] If Speke was late they would lose the weather slot.

Richard occupied the first three weeks compiling a vocabulary of local dialects, variants of Kiswahili, for future travellers. The remainder of his time he devoted to preparations for the return caravan and some necessary mending to the tent, to his clothes and to the umbrellas. From time to time he heard disturbing reports of tribal wars in the area into which Speke had travelled, which made him anxious for his companion's safety.[33]

By the last week in August he had completed all outstanding tasks, and being in reasonable physical condition began making preparations for a short surveying expedition to the south of Kazeh. At dawn on 25 August he heard the sound of cries and gunshots that heralded the arrival of a caravan. To his gratification it was Speke, returning somewhat earlier than he had expected, in triumphant mood. 'At length,' Burton wrote in his journal, 'Jack had been successful. His "flying trip" had led him to the northern water, and he had found its dimensions surpassing our most sanguine expectations.'[34] Burton was delighted at the news and pleased for Speke, too.

> We had scarcely, however, breakfasted before he announced to me the startling fact that 'he had discovered the sources of the White Nile.' . . . The moment he sighted the Nyanza, he felt at once no doubt but that the 'lake at his feet gave birth to that interesting river, which has been the subject of so much speculation and the object of so many explorers.' The fortunate discoverer's conviction was strong. His reasons were weak . . . of the category alluded to by the damsel Lucetta, when justifying her penchant in favour of 'the lovely gentleman', Sir Proteus;
>
> > I have no other but a woman's reason –
> > I think him so because I think him so.[35]

In the face of close questioning, Speke presented his arguments with a bluster guaranteed to provoke Burton's incredulity. It was to Speke's great credit that he had returned to Kazeh at a spanking pace, arriving well within the allotted time. But equally, his tight timetable had allowed him to spend only three days at the lake. He had not been able to sail on the lake, and had physically seen only a small area of the south-east bank. Why then, Richard asked, was he so sure that the Nile flowed out from its northern limits?

Speke's 'evidence' consisted of a conversation with a man whom he described as 'the greatest traveller in the place' who began by nodding his head towards the north 'and by hand signals to indicate that the extent of the lake to the north was immeasurable'. Subsequently Speke (i.e. through Bombay) understood the traveller to say that he thought the lake 'probably extended to the world's end'.[36] Based on this meagre information, Speke arbitrarily placed the northern limit of the lake at about 4° N lat., but his unscholarly deductions and unshakable conviction without substantiated evidence irritated Burton: 'What tended to make me more skeptical was the substantial incorrectness of the geographical and other details brought back by Jack.'[37]

The fact that 'Jack was wholly reliant upon Bombay' raised further doubts. Speke's claim relied entirely upon Bombay's correct interpretation, but a year's hard experience had taught Richard that Bombay spoke 'an even more debased dialect than his master'. He frequently 'misunderstood Jack's bad Hindustani . . . [and] mis-translated the words in Kiswahili to the best African, who in his turn passed it on in a still wider dialect to the noble savages under cross-examination.' Also, Richard said, he knew only too well how 'words in journeys to and fro are liable to the severest accidents'. He cited as an example of this their disappointment at Lake Tanganyika when they discovered that the river Speke had understood from Bombay to be an effluent was in fact an influent.

When Richard attempted to point this out the younger man truculently changed the subject, criticising 'the falsehood of the Arabs at Kazeh' who, he claimed, had given him deliberately misleading information. Even before he left for the lake they had annoyed him, he said, by advising him to wear Arab clothing 'in order to attract less attention'. This was an insult, Speke said, born from their wish to see '*an Englishman lower himself to their position*' (the italics are Burton's), rather than concern for his safety.[38] That Richard was taken aback by this attitude is obvious from the exclamation marks he inserts as he records it. 'Jack changed his manner to me from this date,' he wrote. 'His difference of opinion was allowed to alter companionship. After a few days it became evident to me that not a word could be uttered on the subject of the Lake, the Nile, and his *trouvaille* generally without offence. By a tacit agreement it was, therefore, avoided.'[39]

In the hostile atmosphere that now existed between the two men, Richard began to wish that he had made his expedition alone, or with Arabs, 'or at least with a less crooked-minded, cantankerous Englishman. He is energetic, he is courageous and persevering. He distinguished himself in the Punjaub [sic] Campaign . . . You would now think to see his conduct . . . that he had taken me, not I him; whereas I can confidently say that, except his shooting and his rags of Anglo-Hindostani, I have taught him everything he knows . . .'[40]

Richard knew that the ideal solution would be for them both to return to the lake immediately, so that a more detailed survey could be conducted, but the lack of adequate provisions was an insurmountable problem. In addition their furlough was running out fast. If they failed to return within the two-year period they were liable at the least to forfeit a year's salary, and possibly risked their commissions. Any future explorations would be made more difficult without the 'pay and expenses' of a serving officer. He felt he had little choice than to return to the coast in the shortest time possible. He presented the case to Speke, saying, 'we will go home, recruit our health, report what we have done, get some money, return together, and finish our whole journey . . .' Apparently, Speke agreed, but later he would write that he had wanted to return to the Nyanza, only to be roughly told by Richard that he (Burton) had done enough, and did not wish to see any more Lakes.[41]

To the further disappointment of both men, their advisors told them that the quickest route down to the coast was the way they had come up. Richard spent the last few days of their time at Kazeh questioning travellers from several caravans that arrived close together. On 6 September they were ready to move off:

> The hospitable Snay bin Amir came personally . . . to superintend our departure, provided us with his own slaves and a charming Arab breakfast . . . nay he did more – he followed us to the next station . . . and he helped us to put the finishing touches to the journals.[42]

The return trek was as troublesome and difficult as before; theft, desertions, quarrels, and fighting among the men were rife. Richard alternately, drove, cajoled, bullied his team, but – recalling his experience with the Bashi-Bazouks – refused to become actively involved in disputes. He paid some men off and chastised others, deciding that he would have to live with the problems.

On 10 October, a little over a month into the journey, Speke became extremely ill with pleurisy and pneumonia. As his fever increased he began hallucinating. 'At dawn,' Richard wrote, 'he woke with a horrible dream of tigers, leopards, and other beasts, harnessed with a network of iron hooks, dragging him, like the rush of a whirlwind, over the ground. He sat up on the side of his bed, forcibly clasping both sides with his hands. Half stupefied with pain he called for Bombay.' Bombay had already suffered a similar illness (he called it *kichyomachyoma*, 'the little irons') and knew what to do to make Speke as comfortable as possible.

For forty-eight hours Speke was delirious, staggering about the camp supported by two men. He experienced two further acute attacks of what appeared to Burton, 'like hydrophobia or severe epileptic fits'. Between these he raved incessantly about 'crowds of devils, giants, lion-headed demons who were wrenching with super-human force, and stripping the sinews and tendons of his legs down to his ankles'. With his face and features contorted by cramp, his eyes glazed and glassy, 'he began to bark with a peculiar chopping motion of the mouth and tongue, with lips protruding, the effect of difficulty of breathing, which so altered his appearance that he was not recognisable, and terrified all beholders.'[43] After the third attack, Speke called for pen and paper and wrote an incoherent letter of farewell to his family. 'That was the crisis,' said Richard. 'I never left him, taking all possible precautions, never letting him move without my assistance . . .' At last the pain eased and he whispered, 'Dick, the knives are sheathed!' It is difficult to know from this remark whether he meant the pain, or his feeling for Burton.

During Speke's ravings, Richard wrote, 'he let out all his . . . grievances of fancied wrongs, of which I had not even the remotest idea';

> . . . He was vexed that his diary (which I had edited so carefully and put into the Appendix of 'First Footsteps in Eastern Africa') had not been printed *as* he wrote it – geographical blunders and all; also because he had not been paid for it, I having lost money over the book myself. He [had] asked me to send his collections to the Calcutta Museum of Natural History; now he was hurt because I had done so . . .

But to Speke, the worst injustice concerned the Berbera fiasco. Until he published his book on Zanzibar in 1872 (years after Speke's death), Burton never revealed the *entire* sequence of events at Berbera.

Indeed, it was Speke himself who first put the matter in print.[44]

It will be recalled that when they were attacked at Berbera, Speke had rushed into Burton and Herne's tent to ask what was happening. As the attack intensified, he was nearest the entrance; peering through the flaps, he must have inadvertently stepped back as the first rush came. Ever since, Speke had brooded over what happened next. In his delirium he spat out the cause of his bitterest resentment: the implied charge of cowardice. Burton finally explained, '. . . in the thick of the fight at Berbera, three years before, I had said to him, "Don't step back or they will think we are running."'[45]

> I cannot tell how many more things I had unconsciously done, and I had crowned it by not accepting immediately his loud assertion *that he had discovered the Sources of the Nile.*

Richard had identified a previously unknown sullenness in his companion from the start of the journey; a lack of cooperation, a habit of 'saying unkind and unpleasant things', and Speke's unhelpful statement that 'he could not take an interest in any exploration if he did not command it.' But had Speke not voiced his grievances during his illness, Burton wrote, he could never have guessed at the level of antagonism harboured by his companion. This had even spilled over to the personnel. For several months Bombay, too, had been difficult, uncooperative and careless of Richard's property. He had broken one of Richard's guns (Speke was responsible for the loss of two more), killed Richard's riding ass by lack of care, and lost his bridle among other irritations. However, during Speke's illness Bombay returned to his 'former attitude, that of a respectful and most ready servant'.[46]

Richard sent back to Snay for medications for Speke: 'powdered myrrh with yolk of egg and flour of *mung* for poultices'. From a passing caravan he hired an extra thirteen porters to help carry himself and Speke and, as soon as the patient was fit to be moved on a stretcher, Richard ordered the march onwards, to a higher – and healthier – climate. Richard himself could still only walk with difficulty and was mostly carried, but with increasing vigour he took to one of their few donkeys. As before, the higher ground proved a tonic, and gradually Speke also recovered sufficiently to be able to ride a donkey, though for the remainder of the journey he would suffer from headaches, nausea and biliousness.

On 6 December 1858, they met a caravan carrying letters and papers up for them. Having devoured his letters (there were always some from Isabel), Richard was riveted to read in a Bombay newspaper of an incident that had taken place in Jeddah six months earlier. On 30 June 1858 the Muslim population of the port had slaughtered more than two dozen Christians there, including the British and French Consuls and members of their families. The leading editorial warned of great fear that 'the Arab population of Suez might be excited to commit similar outrages.' There would have been a certain grim satisfaction for Richard, both in the vindication of his warnings and the fact that the official rebuke he had formerly received for daring to raise the subject was dated almost a year prior to the uprising. But as Richard had known the British Consul personally, there was merely a cold acceptance at the stupidity of his superiors.[47] Further unpleasant news lay in a firm official refusal to pay any compensation for the losses incurred at Berbera to the officers involved.

On being offered the services of a messenger who was returning to the coast, Richard scribbled one hasty letter to the Government on another subject that had been causing him concern, the fact that he and Speke were now 'Absent without Leave'. Their furlough, two years from the date of their departure from Bombay on 2 December 1856, had now expired. Their situation must be well known through his reports to the Royal Geographical Society, but he had learned to expect no consideration and formally requested an extension of six months for them both.[48]

'On Christmas Day 1858, at dawn, we toiled along the Kikaboga river, which we forded four times. Jack and I had a fat capon . . . and a mess of ground nuts sweetened with sugar cane which did duty for plum pudding.' Knowing that they could now reach the coast in about 6 weeks they were both able to rejoice in the knowledge that '. . . We might now *see* Christmas Day of 1859, whereas on Christmas Day 1857 we saw no chance of that of 1858.'[49] Even at this stage he was plagued with personnel problems and was driven to offering liberal rewards to make the men do any work. 'There was some intrigue about the pay afterwards which I never understood, which was annoying to me,' was a typical journal entry.

Burton and Speke communicated, now, under a pretence of polite camaraderie. In a letter drafted on 1 January 1859 to the R.G.S., Richard enclosed 'Speke's . . . road map and field book to the Nyanza district which he has been successful in discovering . . . These however demand further enquiry, and he particularly requests that all the documents now forwarded be not submitted to the public until they have received revision at Zanzibar . . .'[50] Burton always freely acknowledged Speke's solo journey to, and discovery of, the Northern Lake in the most generous terms, notwithstanding his reservations concerning Speke's claim that the Lake was the source of the Nile.

As he wrote this letter, they had been halted for more than a fortnight by further trouble with porters. The coast now lay only 13 marches away. Kilwa, which Burton wished to survey before returning to Zanzibar, and Kaole, the nearest port to the homes of one gang of men, were equidistant. Burton noted in his journal, 'our refractory porters refused to march on any port but Kaole, and I refuse to provision them for any port but Kilwa, which we would insist for the purpose of inspecting the lower course of the . . . Rufiji River. The most obstinate will win the day, but I cannot exactly, at the moment, decide which party is in that predicament.'

He warned the men that if they refused to work they would forfeit pay for the entire downward march. When this had no effect he summarily dismissed them. Some days later he was able to recruit nine men from a caravan to carry their equipment to Konduchi, the nearest coastal town. In a gesture deliberately aimed at convincing both local natives and the remaining porters that his object in dismissing the original gang was not to avoid paying their wages, he offered the new men 'seventy-two cloths, as much as if they had carried packs from Unyamwezi'.

On 14 January 1859 the drugs and medical supplies which Richard had requested in July 1857, a month after setting out, reached them. Improving health now made the medications almost unnecessary, but a supply of citric acid proved a useful ingredient for making refreshing sherbets and lemonade. Richard incorrectly blamed Frost and Consul Rigby for the delays. In fact a year elapsed between Hamerton's death and Rigby's appointment, during which time there was no formal British presence on the island and Richard's requests had been simply ignored.

'On 2nd February 1859, Jack and I caught sight of the sea. We lifted our caps, and gave "three times three and one more",' Burton wrote. Their entrance to Konduchi was an excuse for unbridled rejoicing by the inhabitants. The men danced, shot and shouted, the children mobbed the travellers, the women shrieked a joy cry, drums throbbed. They were taken in triumph to the chief's hut, amazingly clean, swept and 'garnished for us'. Burton immediately sent a note to Consul Rigby at Zanzibar, advising him of their safe return and enclosing a short official report.

Even now, Burton had not finished; though they reached the coast almost destitute, when the boat arrived from Zanzibar to take them off he did not return directly to the island. Part of his mission had been a survey of the coast as far as Kilwa, and he thought to use the vessel to complete this outstanding item. Only when the crew began to fall ill with cholera did he abandon his resolve to visit the mighty Rufiji river which might, he thought, 'become a highway . . . into Eastern Equatorial Africa'.

The men returned to Zanzibar on 4 March, and as so often happened to Burton the moment he completed a major project he succumbed to exhaustion, illness and despondency. 'Even the labour of talking was too great,' he said.

His revised plan was to remain in Zanzibar and recuperate while he applied by mail for 'fresh leave of absence and additional funds'. In this way he could minimise the time before he could practically return to the northern lake. But 'Mr. Apothecary Frost . . . advised a temporary return to Europe' to enable him to recover strength.[51] 'I was unwilling to go,' Richard wrote, 'because so much remained to be done.' But depression robbed him of determination to resist and the Consulate, with its pleasant memories of Hamerton whom he had liked immensely, was no longer welcoming to him under the regime of its new Consul.[52]

Christopher Palmer Rigby was an intelligent man and a brilliant linguist. His subsequent work in helping to eliminate the slave trade in East Africa is remarkable. But he had apparently never forgiven Burton for several times beating him out of his accustomed first place in the language examinations in Bombay. Severely beaten as a boy whenever he failed an examination, Rigby had grown up obsessive about success; this 'professional jealousy' was not confined to Burton, for as a young man he had apparently earned himself a good deal of unpopularity for it at Addiscombe House, the East India Company's military college in England.[53] Like Speke he was self-opinionated and ultra-conservative. He found Burton's intimacy with Africans and Asians extremely distasteful, and was squarely in the camp of Burton's 'unfriends', Playfair and Coghlan. Beyond any shadow of doubt, he subsequently used his official position to cause as much harm to Burton's reputation as he could wreak. To the end of his days the mention of Burton's name would provoke him to fury.

Richard now found himself as isolated as Speke had been on their previous visit to Zanzibar. Rigby immediately took to Speke and, as Speke's biographer put it, the pair 'fell on each other's necks like Greeks'.[54] As much as anything, they were allied by a mutual animosity towards Burton. Rigby actively encouraged Speke to speak against his commander and listened with sympathy to claims that Speke had been the 'true leader' of the expedition.

In fairness to Speke there must be some doubt whether Burton, in his state of health, could have accomplished alone the things Speke had done; crossing Lake Tanganyika, for example. Burton was in far worse health than Speke, and furthermore there are good grounds for supposing him clinically depressed for part of the time they were at Ujiji. But it must not be forgotten that Speke had been a virtual passenger for a large part of the journey up country and also on the return; indeed, but for Burton's nursing he would probably have died on the latter one. Speke's subsequent frantic manoeuvring suggests a resolve to make his own reputation at any cost. Nor was his jealous and self-protective attitude confined to Burton. On his next expedition, Speke would send Grant away on an unimportant errand as they neared their goal, enabling him to be able to claim to have made the discovery of the Nile source alone.

While Richard and Speke remained in Zanzibar, Said bin Salim (their erstwhile expedition guide), often called on them. All three discussed the expedition in detail with Rigby. At the time, Speke and Salim agreed that everything possible had been done to meet the payment obligations to 'those who had fairly earned their reward'. Accompanied by Rigby, Burton visited the Sultan to explain that he was unable to reward the Belochi escort. As a result the Sultan made the 'magnificent sum of $2300–£460' available as a reward for them.[55] By the time he sailed Richard had either spent or otherwise committed himself to the tune of £1,400 in extra expenses. He hoped that when they laid the results of their expedition before the Government this excess might be reimbursed. Speke was well aware of this, and would subsequently write, 'I made a compact with Captain Burton that in the event of the government not paying the excess of our expenditure I would pay him half of those expenses . . .'[56] Later, Speke, Rigby and Said bin Salim would change their recollection of events, to Burton's discredit.

Within days news was received that H.M.S. *Furious* had newly arrived at Aden. Aboard were Lord Elgin and his private secretary Laurence Oliphant, en route to England from the Far East. Hearing of the expedition's safe return, Elgin offered to wait at Aden in order to convey Burton and Speke home. Richard was fully aware of 'the evident anxiety of Consul Rigby to get rid of me, and Jack's nervous impatience to go on'.[57] Against his better judgment he agreed to return home, and make arrangements for a new expedition from there.

Richard had not forgotten Isabel, though how he intended to explain his new plan to spend another two years exploring Africa – in the light of their understanding – is not clear. He wrote to her from Zanzibar; not a letter but a six-line poem, unaccompanied by any explanation. Perhaps he was unsure that she had waited for him, despite her frequent letters. Perhaps he was concerned that her parents would intercept a letter:

> To Isabel
> That brow which rose before my sight
> As on the palmer's holy shrine;
> Those eyes – my life was in their light;
> Those lips – my sacrificial wine;
> That voice whose flow was wont to seem
> The music of an exile's dream.[58]

Rigby made his disapproval of Richard patently obvious by failing to see the ship off when they sailed from Zanzibar on 23 March. It was a marked incivility, not wholly explained away by rumours of an invasion of the island by the Sultan's rival brother. Among the mail-bags on board the Yankee clipper, *Dragon of Salem*, was a letter from Rigby to a friend which confirms his opinion and hints at the conversations he had enjoyed with Speke:

> . . . Speke is a right, jolly, resolute fellow. Burton is not fit to hold a candle to him and has done nothing in comparison with what Speke has, but Speke is a modest unassuming man, not very ready

with his pen. Burton will blow his trumpet very loud, and get all the credit of the discoveries. Speke works, Burton lies on his back all day and picks other people's brains . . .[59]

Richard was touched that at the last moment, 'Bombay's honest face turned up and seemed peculiarly attractive.' As he watched the cocoa palms and clove shrubs of Zanzibar fade out of sight, he was wholly confident he would be returning within the year.

The journey to Aden aboard the *Dragon of Salem* was tediously longer than anticipated. Although it was the season of south-westerly monsoons, light and veering winds forced them to tack back and forth across the Equator three times. By the time they arrived at Aden on 16 April Richard was acutely ill with another bout of malarial fever.

Elgin and his party had waited for them as promised, but they were now impatient to leave. Also awaiting their arrival at Aden was Dr John 'Styggins' Steinhaueser, who had invited both men to stay at his home. On seeing Richard's condition he refused to give him a medical certificate to travel further, recommending immediate rest and nursing. A P. & O. steamer was due to leave Aden for London only twelve days later, but Speke decided not to wait. He went directly aboard the *Furious*, after a hurried farewell with Burton who recorded their final conversation. Speke, he stated, 'voluntarily promised, when reaching England, to visit his family in the country, and to wait my arrival that we might appear together before the Royal Geographical Society'.

Confident that he would be able to persuade Steinhaueser to give him a medical certificate in time for the next ship, Richard told Speke: 'I shall hurry up, Jack, as soon as I can.' To which Speke replied, 'Goodbye old fellow; you may be sure I shall not go up to the Royal Geographical Society until you come to the fore and we appear together. Make your mind quite easy about that.'[60]

Steinhaueser was puzzled. Speke, whom he regarded as a friend, boarded *Furious* without even saying goodbye to him. From what he saw, Speke had a highly agitated demeanour. He told Richard he suspected that 'all was not right', and warned him to be cautious of Speke.[61] Richard was not sanguine about Speke's behaviour either, but in the circumstances he could do little more than accept the promise of a gentleman. Speke's verbal undertaking was reinforced by a letter he wrote from Cairo. It was, said Richard, 'a long letter, reiterating his engagement, and urging me to take all the time and rest that broken health required'.[62] All the same, when the next steamer left Aden for Suez on 28 April, Richard was aboard it.

In the meantime he had written to Norton Shaw explaining his short medical detention at Aden. The letter went by the 'overland' route, and therefore reached England before Speke:

> Captain Speke . . . will lay before you his maps and observation and two papers, one a diary of his passage of Lake Tanganyika between Ugigi and Kasenge, and the other the exploration of the Nyanza Ukewere or Northern Lake to which I most respectfully direct the serious attentions of the Committee as there are grave reasons for believing it to be the source of the principal feeder of the White Nile . . .[63]

Throughout, Richard behaved honourably, fully acknowledging Speke's achievement, and his discovery, at every stage. At no point did he rule out Speke's claim, querying its validity only in the light of the other's lack of adequate geographical evidence, and only then privately with Speke. He returned home with every reason to suppose that his arrival in London would be greeted by acclaim. After all, he had led the first expedition into a completely unknown land and was returning successful, though in broken health, after more than two years of incredible hardship and at considerable personal cost in financial terms.

Though he did not know it yet, and despite the fact that he would continue to travel indefatigably for the remainder of his life, it was the end of Burton's career as an explorer. Speke made sure of that. Speke's first success – not undeserved, for it, too, involved great personal hardship and determination – was the springboard for his undeniably meritorious career as one of the foremost African explorers. Yet, arguably, it was achieved in a singularly cold-blooded manner at Burton's expense.

In six years Burton had successfully undertaken three major expeditions, any one of which should have been sufficient to establish his fame and fortune. Yet through his own uncompromising nature, the accidents of mistiming and choice of companion, he would find that he had achieved 'more notoriety than fame'.[64]

16

THE BETRAYAL

SUMMER 1859

Despite having given his word to Richard that he would not approach the Royal Geographical Society until they could do so together, the first thing Speke did when the *Furious* reached London on 8 May 1859 was to contact Norton Shaw. His letter, written on the very day of his arrival, stated that he wished to speak privately with Shaw on various matters of geography. 'I believe most firmly that the Nyanza is one source of the Nile, if not the principal one.'[1]

In those days London mail was delivered within hours of being posted. The same evening Speke received a reply from Sir Roderick Murchison, President of the R.G.S., inviting him to call at Murchison's home on the following morning to talk about his discovery. Murchison entertained none of Burton's geographical reservations; 'Sir Roderick,' Speke wrote, 'at once accepted my views; and knowing of my ardent desire to prove to the world by actual inspection of the exit, that the Victoria Nyanza was the source of the Nile, seized the enlightened view that such a discovery should not be lost to the glory of England and the society of which he was President.' Aglow with enthusiasm, Murchison had declared, 'Speke, we must send you there again.'[2]

He did not, it will be noticed, say, 'Speke, we must send you *both* there again!', which would surely have been the obvious comment had Speke not deliberately appropriated all the credit for himself. Speke was then persuaded – 'much against my inclination', he said, somewhat sanctimoniously in the circumstances – to give a lecture before the fellows of the Society at Burlington House. Even here, however, his famous sensitivities did not prevent him from presenting himself as the key figure in the expedition.

Richard arrived in London on the morning of 22 May, having disembarked at the coast late on the previous evening. His first call, not surprisingly, was the R.G.S. He was too late, Speke had left for the country on the previous day, having used his two-week head start to the utmost. Richard found his role had been relegated almost to that of a sick colleague, struggling along in the valiant Speke's wake. His ravaged appearance even gave apparent credence to Speke's story. The years of research and planning prior to the expedition, the hardships of the two years in Africa, and the solid achievement of Burton's geographical and ethnological work in a previously unknown country, were all eclipsed beside the brilliance of Speke's discovery, despite the lack of any real evidence to support the latter's Nile claims.

With hindsight we know that Speke *had* discovered the source of the Nile; even though he was unable to prove it. Indeed, it would not be proved in Speke's lifetime. It was suggested to Richard in Aden, probably by Steinhaueser, that when he reached London, 'you should boldly assert that *you* have discovered the source of the Nile – if you are right, *tant mieux*, if wrong you will have made your game before the mistake is found out . . .' At that point there was at least as much geographical evidence for Tanganyika being the source of the Nile. But Richard could not bring himself to take the advice, even though later he would grunt that in this case, 'Honesty . . . has not proved the best policy.'[3]

Although warmly welcomed and congratulated by Murchison, and his friends at the Society's rooms, it was clear to Richard that the discovery of Lake Tanganyika, the existence of which had for so long been the subject of controversy, was yesterday's news. Speke was the lion of the hour; indeed a second expedition, with Speke as the leader and with generous funding of £2,500, had already been proposed by Murchison. Tired and ill, Richard felt totally defeated. 'My companion,' he wrote subsequently, 'now stood forth in his true colours, an angry rival.'

These true colours were succinctly summed up some years later by Richard, with the benefit of hindsight. Speke was, he wrote:

uncommonly hard to manage . . . having been for years his own master, he had a way as well as a will of his own. To a peculiarly quiet and modest aspect – aided by blue eyes and blonde hair – to a gentleness of demeanour, and an almost childlike simplicity of manner which at once attracted attention, he united an immense and abnormal fund of self-esteem, so carefully concealed, however, that none but his intimates suspected its existence. He ever held, not only that he had done his best on all occasions, but that no living man could do better. These were his own words . . .[4]

In the light of this description, it is not difficult to understand how much easier it was for the geographers to accept Speke's word – given his apparently gentle and modest attitude, and boyish appearance – rather than Richard's intellectual, and often cutting, cynicism. It was some comfort to Richard that a handful of experienced travellers, men who had actually travelled as opposed to what Burton termed 'armchair geographers', remained wary of Speke's claims. Even Livingstone, who disliked Burton intensely because of the sexual aura that clung to his reputation, regarded Speke as 'a poor misguided thing . . . who gave the best example I know of the eager pursuit of a foregone conclusion'.[5] But of course Livingstone had his own agenda; he also wanted to be the discoverer of the Nile's source.

Speke's epic betrayal of Burton has been explained by most historians as not being entirely his fault. Speke's travelling companion on the *Furious*, Laurence Oliphant, is widely credited with persuading a reluctant Speke to stake his claim immediately to the discovery of the northern lake, before Burton did so. In part this is true, but all the surviving evidence shows that rather than suggesting the act of betrayal, Oliphant merely needed to encourage Speke's own inclinations.

Previous biographies state that Burton and Speke were good friends when they began the expedition. In fact, most recent biographers surmise that their relationship was 'fraternal', with Speke taking the place of Edward or an admiring 'younger brother', and that the relationship only began to sour on the journey when Speke found it impossible to impress the older man. There is even the surprising – serious – claim (based on psychoanalytical deduction), that their relationship was homosexual.[6]

The facts are that Speke had been nurturing resentment of Burton ever since the Berbera incident. As stated earlier, it was in Constantinople while he was serving in the Crimea that Speke first met Oliphant. Still smarting from his failure in Somalia, which he blamed on Burton's recruitment of the corrupt *abban* Sumuntar, Speke was already bragging of his intention of going to Africa under his own steam 'to find the source of the Nile'. At that time, with the exception of Somalia, the only expeditions Speke had made were shooting trips. He was not even a member of the R.G.S. until Richard introduced him after he agreed to join the East Africa expedition. But Speke's letter to his mother, written even before they left Zanzibar for the coast, in which he described Burton as 'a rotter', adequately demonstrates that there can have been no real friendship between the two men when they began the expedition. Burton took Speke (believing that Steinhaueser would also join them) because there was no alternative suitable candidate. Speke went along as Burton's second man because there was no other way for him to explore Africa which fascinated him, and held the promise of fame and fortune. The problem was, Speke was not prepared to share these.

From this unstable platform the relationship deteriorated further while they were thrown together in mutual reliance. Jealousy caused Speke's hostility to spiral. He could never overcome Burton's dominance of the expedition, to take command, even when the leader was incapacitated. We have his own evidence that the 'private letters' sent to his family and friends from Africa describe Burton unfavourably:[7] 'Is Burton so vain that he thinks no-one can dislike him?' he asked Rigby on one occasion. 'I can only say that I did not desert him out of consideration for the Expedition as all my letters to my friends confidentially written can testify.'[8]

Speke even confirmed his malice towards Burton publicly, in a deposition in which he admitted that he 'told Captain Rigby about their disagreements at Zanzibar'. Apparently, Rigby had initially accepted Burton's explanations concerning the non-payment of the guard on the grounds of bad behaviour and constructive desertion. This did not suit Speke. He wrote how he told Rigby, 'that I was sorry he did not seem to consider the matter in the same important light as I did, and urged him to use his able ingenuity in bringing the case to its proper conclusions . . . sparing me the pain of appearing as an informer against him [Burton].'[9] It will be seen, therefore, that Oliphant's role was a supporting rather than leading one.

What did Laurence Oliphant gain by encouraging Speke against Burton? Oliphant was one of those strange mixtures of eccentric and brilliant men thrown up by the Victorian tide. Like Richard, he had been reared and educated for the most part out of England. Later, instead of going to Cambridge he acted as private secretary to his father (chief justice in Ceylon) until called to the colonial bar. By the time he returned to England aged 23, to (successfully) study law at Lincoln's Inn, Oliphant had already been engaged in twenty-three murder cases. He would become successively journalist, author, and brilliant economist; like Burton, he crammed enough into the first thirty-five years of his life to fill the lives of two or three men.[10] Also like Burton he was a restless character, happiest when travelling. His early travel articles were published in *Blackwood's Magazine*, and the book he wrote about a trip to the Crimea shortly before war broke out there was fortuitously 'the right book at the right time'. It required four reprints to satisfy public demand, and evident knowledge of the area prompted Raglan to offer him a position. However, he had already accepted an appointment as private secretary to Lord Elgin, with whom he travelled to America and Canada on a diplomatic mission.

On his return to England, Oliphant 'put forward a recommendation . . . to be sent as an envoy to Schamyl, with a view to a diversion against the Russians'. His visit to Constantinople was made in the hope of furthering this plan. To his great disappointment he learned that Burton had turned down a similar mission as impractical (see p.193). Possibly this was the source of his rancour towards Burton for previously, Oliphant and Burton had been on the friendliest terms, referring to each other in correspondence as 'Lawry' and 'Dick'.[11] The first hint that Richard had of any change in the relationship was Oliphant's review of *First Footsteps*, in which he criticised the use of Speke's diaries.

In 1857 Oliphant accompanied Elgin on a two-year mission to China, and the party was returning to England via Aden when they heard the news that Burton and Speke had just returned, after their long journey into Africa's interior. On the passage from Aden to London, it was inevitable that as well as describing his undeniably meritorious solo feats, Speke would recount his self-aggrandised version of what had occurred on that long and awkward expedition, just as he had done to Rigby and Frost in Zanzibar. And it was possibly because of his own earlier disappointment concerning Burton that Oliphant sympathised with Speke's clear concern that Burton would take the credit for all the discoveries.

Isabel was a distant kinswoman of Speke's, by marriage. Some months later she arranged to meet him and asked him to explain why he had treated Richard so shabbily. Speke blamed Oliphant, telling her, 'He [Oliphant] said that Burton was a jealous man, and being Chief of the Expedition he would take all the glory of the Nyanza, which he [Oliphant] said was undoubtedly the true source of the Nile, for himself.' Oliphant advised him to go to the Royal Geographical Society at once, to secure command of a new expedition, and said that not only would he back Speke in this but would get others to do so. We know this is partially true because Isabel next confronted Oliphant, who apologised saying, 'Forgive me – I am sorry – I did not know what I was doing.'[12]

As a young man Oliphant's life was exciting, but exemplary, and he played by the establishment rules. But while he was on that fateful voyage in 1859 from China to England, his beloved father died in England. Oliphant dreamed of the death on the very night it happened. He told his companions about it, weeks before the news reached the ship. In a sense, this experience ruined his life. During his next visit to America he came under the malign influence of Thomas Lake Harris, the charismatic, homosexual leader of an obscure religious sect whose beliefs were based on spiritualism. The obsessed Oliphant became a 'spiritual slave', and not only gave away his fortune to the community, but persuaded his widowed mother to join. He worked as a labourer on the sect's land while living in poverty, and 'proved' his obedience and self-control by sleeping alongside his lovely wife (the former Alice le Strange) for twelve years without making love to her. His behaviour became increasingly bizarre, but when he gave his wife's dowry away her family, not surprisingly, accused him of insanity. He blamed 'malicious spirit controls'. Only late in life did he realise that he had been duped; a sad finale to early promise.[13]

Yet from Speke's correspondence and actions before, during and long after the expedition, it is evident that it had always been his intention to wrest glory for himself given the opportunity. And that Oliphant, charming and popular as he was in those days, had little work to do on very fertile ground to persuade Speke to act as he did.

Isabel Arundell had heard nothing from Richard for eighteen months when *Furious* docked in London. Prior to that she had received only four letters written by him between London and Bombay. She had just returned home after a Lenten retreat at her old convent school when she heard a rumour that Speke had returned alone and Richard had stayed on in Zanzibar, intending to return into the interior. She said she almost decided to take the veil. But ten days later, on 19 May an envelope arrived addressed to her, postmarked Zanzibar. Inside was a scrap of paper containing Richard's six-line poem, 'To Isabel'. There was no note and no signature, but it didn't matter. 'I knew then,' she said, 'it was all right.' Richard was safe, and he still loved her.

At this point, she had been home from the Continental tour she had made with the Smyth-Piggots for a year. While travelling she had been constantly diverted by new sights and experiences; freedom from the tiresome restrictions of chaperones gave her vivid personality opportunity to expand. She also improved her knowledge of languages; her French was already fluent, but she took Italian lessons while in Italy, and German instruction while in Switzerland and Austria. She delighted in visiting the places where Richard had spent his childhood. From Nice the honeymoon party travelled to Italy. At Pisa Isabel climbed to the top of the tower to find the place where, 'Richard had chiselled his name . . . The man who shows the Campanile remembered Richard, and it was he who told me where he had cut his name at the top of the tower . . . so I did the same.'[14] In Florence she met many friends of Richard's who 'finding I knew his sister in England were very kind to us'. Venice was her favourite place; it 'fulfils all the exigencies of romance,' she wrote in her journal. 'It is the only thing that has never disappointed me. I am so happy at Venice. Except for Richard's absence, I have not another wish ungratified; and I also like it because this and Trieste were the last places he was in near home, when he started for Africa. . . . How heavenly Venice would have been with Richard, we two floating about in these gondolas!'[15]

Accounts of her experiences jostled for space in her journal between her continuous thoughts about Richard. 'I so love and care for him that I should never have the courage to take upon myself the duties of married life with any other man. I have seen so much of married life; have seen men so unjust, selfish and provoking; [I] never could receive an injury from any man but him without everlasting resentment . . . if he should come home and have changed, it would break my heart!' Yet despite her obsession with Richard she made a number of romantic conquests during her tour. She was introduced to

the Chevalier de St Cheron on the night of the famous Carnival Ball
in Venice by some mutual friends, and wrote that he 'is a perfect
French gentleman of noble family, good looking, fascinating, brilliant in conversation; has much heart, *esprit* and *delicatesse*'.[16]

St Cheron was, in fact, just the sort of man that Mrs Arundell
hoped Isabel would marry. He was a trusted aide-de-camp of the so-
called Henri V (known as the Comte de Chambord) at the Bourbon
court-in-exile in Venice. After the night of the Masked Ball St Cheron
spent many evenings with Isabel, and although they always met
within a party he obviously took pains to find ways of pleasing her.
'One night we rowed in gondolas by moonlight to the Lido; we took
the guitar. I never saw Venice look so beautiful. The water was like
glass, and there was not a sound but the oars' splashing. We sang
glees . . . at the Lido we had tea and walked the whole length of the
sands.' They went sightseeing together, read Byron together, and as
proof of his regard he even arranged an audience with his master.

Isabel's party sailed to the royal villa in 'a very smart gondola
covered in our flags, the white one uppermost for the Bourbons';
Smyth-Piggot was dressed in his Royal Yacht Squadron uniform,
Blanche wore her bridal gown and Isabel wore her pastel silk brides-
maid outfit.[17] Fashion in 1858 decreed the tiniest waists and widest
crinolined skirts; beautiful and elegant especially on a young woman
as tall as Isabel. Boarding, travelling in and disembarking with appropriate modesty from a gondola in these confections must, however,
have been an experience to remember. Isabel's French was better than
anyone else's, so she was seated next to Henri and chatted away with
ease, telling him that he had once danced with her mother. The Comte
was charmed and it proved an evening to remember for Isabel.

But despite his many assets St Cheron stood no chance. Isabel compared him with Richard and, though she liked the Frenchman, she
could not help noticing some foppish mannerisms. She made a dispensation because of his nationality, but, she wrote in her journal,
'were he an Englishman, I should think him vain and ignorant.' The
Chevalier continued to escort Isabel until the party left Venice for
Switzerland, and they corresponded a few times until the relationship
gently faded away.

In Switzerland she rowed and swam every day and even tried her
hand at painting landscapes.[18] Wearing thick boots, and with a red
petticoat under her substantial brown climbing skirt (so as to be seen

from a distance in case of accident) she went mountaineering. She learned to ride astride 'like a man'. Once, while sailing she almost drowned when a storm capsized her dinghy and she was in the water for several hours. But Richard was always with her; on a desolate mountain plateau she thought she would rather spend a hundred years there, with him, than a life of luxury elsewhere with another man; on her balcony in the evening as the evening stars appeared and glow-worms shone in the grass, 'I thought of Richard in that far-away swamp in Central Africa ... I wonder if he too is thinking of me at this time.'[19]

At Geneva Isabel attracted two further suitors, each of whom proposed marriage. The first was 'an American, polished, handsome, fifty years of age, a widower with £300,000 made in California; but,' she wrote on the evening she refused his proposal, 'there is only one man in the world who could be master of such a spirit as mine. People may love (as it is called) a thousand times, but the real *feu sacré* only burns once in one's life.'[20]

Besides the 'American Croesus' (as she afterwards gaily referred to him) there was a 40-year-old General from the Russian court, spangled with military decorations. He was charming and multi-lingual, 'is a musician, and writes, and has made me an offer,' she wrote. Her beau sprang from a distinguished family; he worshipped the Tsar, owned nine castles and had an income of half a million francs a year. 'He saw me at the altar of the Madonna, Genoa, two months ago. He tells me he fell as much in love with me as if he were a boy of fifteen. He followed me here, changed his hotel to come here, came to dinner and took the room next to me.' The lovelorn Russian serenaded Isabel at 6 a.m. and 11 p.m. on the violin (he must have been tiresome to the other guests). When she ignored him he sent her baskets of fruit, and flowers accompanied by a six-page letter saying that if she would be his he would make her a '*déesse*' (goddess) in his country. None of these blandishments tempted Isabel, 'I refused him of course,' she wrote in her journal.[21]

On one occasion she lost her treasured photograph of Richard to a pickpocket. It was returned after she had 200 posters printed and distributed, and paragraphs placed in the local papers, shamelessly offering a reward for the return of the photo of a 'beloved brother killed in the Crimea', in order to protect her reputation.[22] On another she made herself ill by jumping over the side of her rowing boat for a

swim in the icy waters while overheated after a long row across the
lake. When the hotel they were staying in caught fire, Isabel only
made her way to safety after pausing to save Richard's picture, her
dog and her pet bullfinch. At Lausanne she became seriously ill with
a form of rheumatic fever, and when she recovered was sent home
ahead of her sister and brother-in-law who were also ill.

For part of her journey she was alone in a railway carriage with an
unknown male passenger. A short time after the train set off he said
to her, 'I am very sorry but I am going to have an epileptic fit', and
immediately suffered a convulsion, which frightened her considerably. It was not a corridor train and she had no means of summoning
help, so she had no option other than to assist him. 'I pulled the man
down on the ground, undid his cravat and loosened all about the
neck. I had no medicine with me, except a quarter of a bottle of
sweet spirits of nitre [potassium nitrate] which I was taking for
rheumatic fever.' Pouring the lot down his throat, she covered his face
with her black silk scarf so that she could not see his frightening
expressions, and squeezed herself into the corner of the carriage to
await developments. Presently he recovered and they chatted and she
told him what had happened. 'I think it is my duty to tell you,' she
confessed boldly, 'that I have poured about three ounces of nitre
down your throat.'[23]

So the 28-year-old Isabel who waited in London for further news of
Richard was a far more worldly woman than the one who had taken
to her bed in a swoon when he left for Africa. Even so, she suffered
strong emotions when on 21 May 1859 she read in the papers that
Richard was expected to arrive in London imminently, and her diary
entry for that evening reads:

> May 21 . . . I feel strange, frightened, sick, stupefied, dying to see
> him, and yet inclined to run away, lest, after all I have suffered and
> longed for, I should have to bear more.

On the following afternoon she called upon a friend (probably Alice
Bird).[24] The friend was out but was expected to return shortly for
tea, and Isabel was invited to wait in the upstairs drawing room.
After a few minutes she heard the doorbell ring and the sounds of
another visitor being shown upstairs and invited in to wait.
Suddenly she heard a familiar 'deep, sweet' voice saying, 'I want

Miss Arundell's address.' Even as her body thrilled to the sound, the door of the drawing room opened and Richard stood at the threshold. 'For an instant we both stood dazed,' Isabel wrote. 'I felt so intensely that I fancied he must hear my heart beat, and see how every nerve was overtaxed. We rushed into each other's arms. I cannot attempt to describe the joy of that moment.' He had come straight from the Royal Geographical Society, to find out where she was now living.

> . . . We forgot all about my hostess and her tea. We went down-stairs, and Richard called a cab, and he put me in and told the man to drive about – anywhere. He put his arm round my waist, and I put my head on his shoulder . . . When we were a little recovered, we mutually drew each other's pictures from our respective pockets at the same moment, to show how carefully we had kept them . . .[25]

When she could tear herself out of his embrace to look at him, she was shocked at his appearance. 'He was a mere skeleton,' she wrote, 'his brown-yellow skin hanging in bags, his eyes protruding, and his lips drawn away from his teeth.' In all, he told her, he had suffered twenty-one attacks of fever, in addition to being partially paralysed for some months and partially blind for others; '. . . his youth, health, spirits and beauty were all gone for the time . . . never did I feel the strength of my love as then.'[26]

He told her that her letters – packed with cuttings on public and private news, reviews of books and newspaper cuttings – had been a huge consolation to him. She had written twice a month for the entire duration of his trip, giving him all her news, so she had little to tell him.

Wrapped in ecstasy, Isabel returned home and told her mother about her love for Richard and that he had proposed to her. She hoped that her own happiness would change her mother's mind. It was a supreme misjudgement; Mrs Arundell told her coldly that Captain Burton was the *only* man she would never consent to her daughter marrying, and that she would rather see Isabel 'in her coffin'.[27] Her reasons were all those Isabel had recognised before Richard went away. His religion, or professed lack of it; his inability to support Isabel;[28] and thirdly, but hardly least, his dubious reputation. 'At this time,' writes a contemporary, 'there were some unpleasant rumours flying about concerning Burton, and some echo of them had reached Mrs Arundell's ears.'[29]

After that the couple were reduced once again to covert meetings, at the houses of Isabel's friends, Prudence and Providence Cooper and Alice Bird, 'who allowed and encouraged our meetings', or at the Botanical Gardens, where Richard would take her arm for support as they walked. They were both 'most anxious' that their marriage should take place so that they could be together, and Isabel felt strongly that her place was at his side to nurse and help him. But she refused Richard's suggestion that they should simply marry without consent because it would damage his chances of obtaining a position in the Consular Service, which was his main hope of an acceptable career.

Two days after his arrival, on 23 May, at a specially convened meeting of the Royal Geographical Society, Richard was presented with the Society's supreme award, the Founder's Gold Medal, by Murchison. The decision to present this award to Richard had been taken in the general elation of hearing that the expedition had been successful, months before Speke's return. It could hardly be rescinded now, without controversy. But Murchison, who was firmly behind Speke, made it clear in his speech that his protégé was equally deserving:

> . . . I must also take this opportunity of expressing to you my hearty approbation of the very important part which your colleague, Captain Speke has played in the course of the African expedition headed by yourself . . . the discovery of the vast interior Lake of Nyanza, made by your associate when you were prostrated by illness – a discovery which in itself is also, in my opinion, well worthy of the highest honour this society can bestow . . .[30]

Richard's reply was a generous and honest acknowledgement of Speke's contribution, with no hint of justifiable indignation or anger:

> I thank you, Sir, most sincerely for this honour, and for the kind and flattering expressions by which you have enhanced its value . . . Justice compels me to state the circumstances under which [the expedition] attained that success. To Captain John Hanning Speke are due those geographical results to which you have alluded in such flattering terms. Whilst I undertook the history, ethnography,

languages and the peculiarities of the people, to Captain Speke fell the arduous task of delineating an exact topography, and of laying down our positions by astronomical observations – a labour to which at times even the undaunted Livingstone found himself unequal . . .[31]

With the exception of his relationship with Isabel there seemed no area of Richard's life untouched by misfortune in that spring of 1859; even his home-coming was marred by an appalling family tragedy. Edward Burton, Richard's closest confidant during his childhood and youth, had been shipped home from India having been discharged on medical grounds. The family believed he had never entirely recovered from the severe beating administered by enraged Singalese villagers in 1856. However, Edward had been sufficiently able during the fighting of the Mutiny, a year after the incident, to give such a valiant account of himself that it led to a commendation and offer of 'a valuable appointment in Lucknow'. During the fighting he suffered an acute sunstroke from which he emerged with a psychiatric disorder; probably, it was diagnosed, due to belated effects of the battering. Between the time he returned home in 1858, at the age of 35, and his death in the autumn of 1895, Edward Burton never spoke, except on one occasion when he quietly denied a humorous imputation that he had not repaid a debt to a cousin. The clarity with which he articulated his denial suggests a psychotic rather than physiological condition.[32] Edward would spend many of those 37 years in the Surrey County Lunatic Asylum, a grim fate indeed in the Victorian era.

Richard's own poor physical condition, combined with Speke's perfidy, Edward's illness and the lack of resolution in his relationship with Isabel, precipitated a depression. There are many surviving notes written in poor handwriting, cancelling engagements because he was too unwell or could not face society. Isabel felt resentful that her mother's attitude prevented her from nursing Richard, and was deeply anxious about his emotional well-being when his poetry became increasingly introspective:

> I hear the sounds I used to hear
> The laugh of joy, the cry of pain
> The sounds of childhood sound again.
> Death must be near!

A lovely sprite of smiling cheer,
Sits by my side in form of light;
Sits on my left a darker sprite.
Sure, Death is near . . .[33]

It was an anxious time for Speke, too. His expedition remained to be ratified and until he received his back pay he was short of money. Recognising that Richard would shortly expect him to reimburse half of the excess expenditure (which Richard had met immediately on his return home) he wrote to Norton Shaw on 5 June 1859:

Mind you don't show this to anyone.
My dear Shaw,
. . . I hope there will be no difficulty in the refundment of monies because I left a private exploratory party to join Burton at his invitation 'free of all expenses'. He at that time thought he had sufficient money coming from the Gov[ernment]. Expecting according to Colonel Sykes statement that the India Gov would have furnished him with £1,000. This you know proved otherwise and as the Gov funds did not hold out I told Burton that I would hold myself responsible for the half of any advances that he might make for carrying out the object of the RGS. Whatever happens I shall stand by him. I further trust that these monies will be refunded to me as *his title* of Commandant over me, precluded my making any private use of the countries [sic] resources, or my time . . .
J.H. Speke[34]

Speke's claim that he abandoned a 'private exploratory party' to join Richard is an exaggeration; the project between himself and Edmund Smyth had never progressed beyond the stage of a proposal, and demonstrably stood no chance of being given necessary permissions nor any outside funding.

On 13 June the Society met to hear Speke's paper. Murchison hoped that the occasion would be used to agree to conferring the Gold Medal on him, 'equally with Burton'. Speke wrote in high spirits to ask for tickets for his mother and sister; 'I hope the petticoats won't take up all the house,' he said, alluding to the latest fashion in crinolines. He went on to say he would not, in his speech, refer to ethnological matters 'out of fairness to Burton, who has been very industrious' about collecting this sort of information. In the main he read from his notebooks, giving permission for these to be printed in the Society's *Journal*. But to the disappointment of Murchison, Speke's claim regarding the discovery of the source of the Nile was not wholly accepted by experienced geographers. James MacQueen, whose work Richard admired and quoted (and who would later become, on his own account, a bitter enemy of Speke), in particular queried the evidence. He rose to his feet 'with great reluctance,' he said, for he considered Speke's paper interesting and valuable, 'to express a contrary view to that of Captain Speke as to the sources of the Nile.'

MacQueen pointed out that the Nile in lower Egypt rose in June, and continued to rise until September. Speke and Burton had said that the monsoons in the Lake regions did not commence until the autumn; a monsoon beginning in September could not account for the rise of the Nile in the previous June. Furthermore he doubted the latitudes quoted by Captain Speke and asked for further evidence for his deductions. Speke could only bluster unconvincingly that as he had visited the lake during the dry season the vegetation was mostly burned off. With this somewhat puzzling response to his questions Mr MacQueen sat down, apparently far from satisfied. Other geographers, too, found Speke's case 'not proven', and there was no recommendation that he should be awarded a Gold Medal. Richard also spoke on this occasion but his speech was limited to matters of ethnology and he did not refer to the Nile sources.[35] Noticeably, he and Speke had no private conversation.

Richard's health improved only slowly. He suffered from recurrent fevers and debility and he spent weeks trying various treatments at Spas such as Norwood – taking the 'cold water cure' which was said to 'cleanse the system' – and Harwich.[36] But with the support of his family and friends, including Isabel, to boost his confidence, he fought against Speke's appropriation of the laurels. The geographers' reaction to Speke's paper gave him hope that he might yet obtain sufficient backing for a second expedition of his own. Speke's project had not been formally adopted, either by the geographers or the Government. The R.G.S., faced with two plans and the obvious enmity of the two protagonists feebly suggested that 'considering the vastness of the field of enquiry and the respective qualifications of Captains Burton and Speke, the preferable course would be that they should proceed . . . by two distinct and independent routes . . .' But everyone knew there was funding for only one expedition.

A few days after the June meeting Richard wrote asking Speke for his share of the money that had been spent in excess of the government funding, as agreed. 'The sooner this affair is settled the better,' he said. It was the first in a series of remarkable letters between the two, and formed their only manner of communication. Speke reacted angrily, spilling out in writing what he had raved in delirium and what – undoubtedly – he had been telling anyone who would listen to him:

My dear Burton,
   . . . I am fully aware of my liabilities to you. The agreement between us was this. I said to you 'as soon as the Gov't money was all expended that . . . I would be answerable for the half of any sums that might be legitimately expended in prosecution of the travels before us, and would pay it provided that the Gov't should refuse to admit our advancement'. At present the Gov't have had no opportunity of refusing any refundment . . . I must say your importunate demand has rather surprised me. Especially when I reflect to former relations between us. I mean the Somali affair. Then I spent *everything*, ready money, and received *nothing* in return. You, in virtue of your position as Commandant took my diaries from me, published them and never offered me even half returns for your book in which they were contained. My specimens also which I had industriously collected, together with my notices of their habits etc, you took from me and presented to the Bengal Museum . . .

   I must beg you to be more moderate, at least until I get my pay from the Gov't for the time of which I have been serving with you. As yet I have not been able to draw one penny.

Yours truly
J.H. Speke[37]

Richard's reply, stating that he had not intended to be importunate and expressing surprise that Speke claimed 50% of the royalties when he had contributed less than 10%, did little to mollify Speke, and he wrote again regretting that he had taken 'the two letters you sent in rapid succession as indicative on your part of immediate nastiness . . .';

In the first place . . . I never wanted 'half returns', but only thought it rather odd that you did not offer to pay me anything when, on the last expedition I understood you to say you had made some 2 or 3 hundreds by your work. I put the question to you purposely and thought it singular that so much matter could be produced, returning only so insignificant a sum, and felt wonderfully astonished in considering how scribblers could make a living . . .

> Yours truly,
> J.H. Speke[38]

Following this exchange there was a strained silence between the two men for some months during which time Speke made contact with John Blackwood of *Blackwood's Magazine*. 'I have just returned from Central Africa,' he wrote, 'having mapped the whole of those regions and discovered what I consider to be, as stated in my late lecture at the Royal Geographical Society, the true source of the Nile and I have fixed the true Mountains of the Moon . . . Whilst engaged above I kept diaries which both Captain Burton and Mr Laurence Oliphant have read . . . the latter gentleman has advised my applying to you to publish them . . .'[39] He explained that he had been approached by a London publisher to write a book at once and bring it out before Captain Burton published his account. But, he confessed, he was 'no writer', and therefore thought that publishing his diaries, in letter form, 'before or during the coming Autumn', would be a better way of handling the matter. He realised that Burton was a *Blackwood's* contributor, but since his own diaries covered only the two journeys he had made alone, on Lake Tanganyika and to the Nyanza, he thought there should be no 'clashing of interests'.

Blackwood asked for a sight of the material, and said he would let Captain Burton know as a matter of courtesy that they were in communication. In reply to this note Speke explained a lacuna in his journals: 'I have omitted to mention Captain Burton's name as far as possible; this is because I have not communicated with him about it, and also because, I was at the time of keeping these journals, *nominally* under his command and therefore reflections about him by myself would be out of place . . .'[40] Richard retaliated in kind. While he had mentioned Speke by name in *First Footsteps*, in *Lake Regions* he referred to Speke throughout as 'my companion'.

Speke was still under attack from MacQueen for a number of

technical blunders in his address, causing him to write nervously to Norton Shaw with edits for the paper which was being typeset for the Society's house *Journal*.

> ... I think it is in my third paper that I remarked upon the mode of expression used by the Africans when talking of the flow of a river, 'they always describing them to flow up instead of downstream', to which I unfortunately added 'which is not surprising, when we see so many instances of the same thing occurring in the Bible'. I wrote that from hearsay but now I investigate the Bible I find that I was incorrectly informed so would you kindly draw your pen across the words in allusion to the Bible.[41]

The summer of 1859 was unusually hot, and all the protagonists left London. Speke and Oliphant went north. Isabel went to Wardour with her family, and Richard went to stay with his sister on Marine Parade at Dover which he found 'a wilderness of bathers'. He spent a month there working on his book. 'I was driven out of town by an intense longing for cool air and a weight upon the mind – something like what *conscience* must be – upon the subject of writing a book,' he wrote to his friend Richard Monckton Milnes who had invited him to stay at his country home, Fryston Hall. 'I will do my best to be with you during the last week in August . . . The prospect of a book which will produce horripilation [gooseflesh] is refreshing but I cannot believe it till the operation takes place.'[42]

Burton's friendship with Richard Monckton Milnes was a long and important one. Milnes was a rich and influential older man; he inherited Fryston Hall and his London house at 16 Upper Brook Street on his father's death in 1858. But there was nothing self-seeking in Richard's regard for him; the two shared the same obsession for acquiring knowledge in a diverse range of subjects, a quirky – often bawdy – sense of humour, and a love of travel.

Fryston Hall was a lavishly appointed mansion,[43] with 'prairies of park and miles of larch and beechen woods', situated within easy driving distance of Pontefract, which constituency Milnes represented as Member of Parliament for twenty-five years.[44] With its magnificent silver, wine cellars and art collection, and squads of liveried servants, Thackeray said, Milnes' hospitality 'combined the graces of the chateau and the tavern'.[45] What Richard most loved about his visits was the famous library. Among the massed classics and general works one would expect to find in a well-stocked country-house library, Milnes (who was a published poet), 'owned what was probably the largest collection of erotica ever assembled by a private collector or for that matter ever likely to be; he employed agents on the Continent who were always on the lookout for "curious" books and pictures to enrich his library.'[46] These included books which were banned in England, on the subjects of sado-masochism, witchcraft and the occult.[47] Milnes was extremely proud of his collection and would genially (and surely mischievously) point out particular items of interest to his weekend guests, on Sunday morning before they went off to church.[48]

Richard did not attend church and could easily lose himself for hours in the library, but equally he revelled in the erudite discussions that were the mark of Fryston house-parties. Travel, archaeology, politics, theology, science, poetry and literature; the criterion for invitation to Fryston was a proved knowledge of any subject. Women, however, needed only to be well-bred or beautiful. Since his earliest youth Milnes had 'collected' interesting personalities – Beau Brummel and Wordsworth, to name but two in a vast and disparate throng who were recipients of Milnes' lavish hospitality.[49] Among his fellow house guests during the last week in August 1859, Richard found a group of men well-known for their interest in travel and geography, among them 'Mansfield Parkyns of Abyssinia; Robert Curzon of The Monasteries; Petherick of Khartoum; Sir Charles MacCarthy, who rose from a friendless student of theology in the English College at Rome to be Governor of Ceylon; W.E. Forster [traveller and statesman] . . .'[50] During subsequent visits he would be part of a glittering pageant of extraordinary personalities such as Swinburne, Vambery, Palmerston, Thomas Carlyle, Sir Samuel and Lady Baker, Leigh Hunt and others of the pre-Raphaelite brotherhood. Fryston enjoyed the same reputation in the nineteenth century as did Cliveden in its heyday under the Astors, a hundred years later.

Milnes was an enigmatic man of whom his biographer, James Pope-Hennessy, commented, 'he was . . . incapable of passionate love,' but equally, 'incapable of real evil'. Milnes himself wrote, during a period of deep depression, 'there are moments when I feel that nothing is real but evil, nothing true but pain.'[51] He was an active flagellant, and one of Burton's biographers pointed out that while Milnes' wife 'radiated a light-hearted innocence and irresistible zest for living' she suffered secretly from headaches and melancholia.[52] Milnes was certainly not an evil man,[53] but it appears doubtful that his wife ever enjoyed a normal sex life and his periodic depressions are said to have been caused by his consequent guilt.

Speke and Oliphant met again in Aberdeen in early September. There, Speke gave a talk to Section E of the British Association at its annual meeting, and Oliphant read a paper on his travels in the Far East. Murchison, who was the Director of Section E, had arranged the prestigious event for his protégé, Speke, upon whose behalf he worked unceasingly among men of influence throughout the summer.

Speke's main purpose in travelling north was for the August shooting. From Ross he advised John Blackwood gleefully that he had had 'a glorious time . . . killing all sorts of game . . . the first day after my arrival the largest stag that has been killed save one, in this Forest, fell a victim to my rifle.' He was working at 'rewriting' his diaries and asked Blackwood to send him a copy of Richard's articles, 'I should then be able to enter dates etc from them,' he wrote ingenuously.[54]

Speke was still in regular correspondence with Rigby who, since the departure of the explorers, had written on a number of occasions to the Foreign Office, and the Indian Government, praising Speke and denigrating Burton. And since in the same month Lords Russell and Palmerston at the Foreign Office received a formal recommendation in respect of Speke from Lord Ripon (President of the R.G.S),[55] Rigby's letters were well-timed to effect damage. Speke wrote to Rigby that he was 'giddy from being hauled from right to left and back again', but that Lord Elgin was now pushing his planned expedition, so he had magnanimously invited Burton to join his own expedition:

> I mentioned to Burton that he might have a fair chance which I am happy to say he took advantage of by sending the following day his papers proposing himself for my scheme . . . Well, I say I am glad because in the Elections of the council the preference was given to me in consequence of my having done the scientific part of the last one. Although he, Burton, had many powerful friends contesting his rights for him, Sir R. Murchison is patron this time. I hope you have made Ramji[56] complain [about Burton] and will assist him in getting his rightful dues. If he is not paid by any other means I must do

it on return to Zanzibar. Tell Bombay I was swelling him all over
the world and I have created so much here that next time I must
bring him home with me. You will see by my map in Blackwoods
that I have christened the Nyanza after the Queen and a little island
on it after the Majid . . .[57]

Rigby had indeed told Ramji to complain, as well as anyone else
with half a grudge against Burton – in particular those porters whom
Burton dismissed without pay for refusing to obey his orders. But
Speke niggled away at this matter, encouraging Rigby to take the
matter further and raise it at an official level. Subsequently Rigby contacted the Principal Secretary of State for India; Lord Stanley; the
Foreign Office; and the Government at Bombay, until it finally
became a political issue and Lord Elphinstone and the Bombay
Government authorised Rigby 'to pay to the men who accompanied
Captain Burton whatever may be due on their agreements. The claims
of Ramjee [sic] and Said bin Salem should also be liberally satisfied . . .' Further, Elphinstone continued, Rigby should present a gold
watch to Luddah Damha, the Customs Manager, 'as a recognition of
his disinterested services in aid of the Expedition'. In the meantime,
'Captain Burton should be required to explain why he neither paid
these men nor brought their services and his debts to them to the
notice of the Government.'[58]

In the event Speke was unable to trace a single one of the unpaid
porters, but the fact that he was empowered to reimburse them, without any further recourse to Burton, was extremely damaging in a day
when a man's honour and reputation was a precious commodity.
Richard was perceived as having behaved dishonourably, slinking
away from Africa without paying men who – according to Speke –
had served them loyally. Burton's surviving journal, written-up daily
throughout the expedition, demonstrates that the reverse was true.
But Speke was always aware that there were no funds to make a payment even had Burton felt the men warranted one. Burton had
notified the Royal Geographical Society and the Foreign Office of
their financial predicament during the final stages of the expedition,
advising that they would meet difficulties in Zanzibar.

And even now, Speke had still not paid Richard his proportion of
the expedition costs, though it was he who had reaped all the rewards
of the expedition: fame, glory, the promise of a well-funded and

supported second expedition, and financial gain from the sale of his story to *Blackwood's*. Yet it was Speke, actively pursuing the claims of the recalcitrant porters, who was seen as acting honourably. One cannot avoid wondering whether he would have pursued the matter so assiduously had it not proved an effective weapon with which to attack Richard.

With the assistance of Murchison and Oliphant, Speke gained access to influential men, including Lord Russell – with whom Oliphant was staying, and to whom Speke wrote: 'The Consul of Zanzibar has been writing very kind letters to the Bombay Gov't as well as to myself advocating that I should go again and absolutely to render every assistance he can to me. His first reason for advocating my being sent again is that he thinks from Native report there, that I am better able to do the work than anybody else could be, and, from the men whom I commanded on the last expedition having stated to him their willingness to go with me again to any place that I might direct.'[59]

There is no doubt that Speke conducted a well-orchestrated campaign against Burton, in order to further his ambitions. Surviving examples of his correspondence, too voluminous to include here in full, demonstrate that his campaign was not so much straightforward rivalry as passionate dislike, almost certainly rooted in jealousy. He was determined to make trouble for Burton, and where possible even reduce him to a figure of ridicule and pathos, as this letter from Speke to Rigby illustrates:

My dear Rigby,
    . . . your letter has gone the rounds of the family circle and been much chuckled over, especially that part descriptive of Burton and his big boots. The boots were worn day and night until he arrived at Aden . . . and then he took to quiet slippers – an article much better adapted to the miserable constitution of his weak legs and rotten gut.
    Poor devil, what will not vanity inflict on a weak mind devoted to flattery . . . he must have been in agonies of pain all the time that he was wearing them but won't own it out of sheer conceit. Burton is now employed in washing his hair out at the hydropathic Institution of Norwood. I hope those cleansing waters may wash him clean. He tried to cripple my chance of going out again by

sending in a counter application to the Gov't., when I volunteered
to revisit the Nyanza and connect it with the Blue Nile (see map in
Blackwood) from Kazeh to Kibuya and thence to Gonderoko on the
Nile. But he did not succeed for the matter came before the
Geographical council at the same time and I was elected in conse-
quence of my having done all the work last time.

The RGS and the Br. Assoc have both been working at the Gov't
to let me go again in the most urgent manner but as yet I have had
no reply. Confound these slow-coaches, during the time that they
make their debating about the trifling matter of fourteen hundred
pounds the Bombay Gov't, I hear, have completely organised a
party of explorers from that quarter . . .[60]

Speke was incensed to read, on the publication of Playfair's book *A
History of Arabia Felix*, that he judged all four officers equally negli-
gent in the Berbera fiasco. Writing to exonerate himself, Speke added
the following waspish comment, '. . . I cannot answer for Burton, all
I saw about him in that respect . . . from the outset until I last saw
him, he was engaged in loading his pistol *within* his tent. I never for
one moment saw him out of it, but, that Herne was ready, is proved
by his having advanced, at Burton's order I believe, to check the
advance of plunderers. I *was* ready, having placed my pistol and
sword handily by me in case of an emergency. Stroyan, I imagine, was
killed whilst lying in his bed.'[61] This is not only at odds with Herne's
statement but also with Speke's 'on-the-spot' declaration, signed by
him in the Somali expedition letter-book. It is typical of the many contradictions he made almost every time he put pen to paper.

Playfair replied pointing out some of the differences between
Speke's statement at the time and his later claims (the inevitable result,
said Richard, of not keeping a diary), to which Speke blustered: 'I
think I said I had placed four sentries on that occasion, this may be an
error for if the usual number was only two, then I placed only two
. . . I still maintain that the guard could not have been better disposed
of than it was that night and so far I did my duty. If there was any
error at all, except Burton's confessed [sic] unpreparedness, it was that
no officer was on watch. . . . Burton's defying danger, and bragging
I regard as so much claptrap.'[62]

But Speke's campaign to damage Burton was not confined to his
correspondence. He repeated the same sentiments to any sympathetic

ear and also reminded his listeners of the old rumours about Richard
from India. The writer W.H. Wilkins – who not only had access to
both Richard's and Isabel's personal diaries while helping Isabel to
write her autobiography, but the first-hand witness of Isabel, and her
sister Dilly (who personally approved everything Wilkins wrote about
the Burton/Speke feud) – wrote, '. . . Speke had spread all sorts of
ugly – and I believe untrue – reports about Burton. These coming on
top of certain other rumours – also, I believe untrue – which had originated in India, were only too readily believed.' A footnote on the
word 'rumours' in this statement, refers the reader to Richard's
account in *The Arabian Nights* of his investigation into the Karachi
homosexual brothels. In his various papers Speke also made broad
disapproving hints about Burton's sexual activities with African
women.

The harm Speke did Burton that summer was incalculable. One
wonders why it was necessary since Speke had already secured his
position as the sole discoverer of the Northern Lake, and his leadership of the second East African expedition. Reading the accounts of
the expedition by the two men leaves one in little doubt which is the
more accurate and informative in every field; anthropology, geography, readability, and in superior intellect. Burton must have seemed a
massive threat to Speke's hopes and ambitions. This partially explains
why he seemed prepared to go to any lengths to utterly destroy
Burton's reputation. He even claimed (to his family, to friends, and to
officials such as the traveller and archaeologist Austen H. Layard
who was then Under-Secretary for Foreign Affairs) that Burton had
attempted to murder him by ordering Bombay to add poison to his
medicine during his illness on the return journey to the coast.[63]

According to Speke's sister, Speke learned of this attempted murder
from Bombay, who 'being too much attached to Speke, never administered it'. She told Grant, 'that it caused her brother great distress for
some time'. Grant concluded that, 'Burton felt so sore at Speke's discovery of the Vic. Nyanza that he tried to get rid of him by poison and
claim the discovery for himself.' Grant was so convinced of the truth
of this story that he refused to be introduced to Burton and never
spoke to him.[64]

The portrait of Burton as a calculating would-be poisoner, patently
ludicrous to anyone who had made an in-depth study of his character, poses a question. Was Speke an unblushing liar who would say

anything to achieve his ends; was he simply guilty of Walter Mitty-like fantasies; or was he suffering from the obsessive after-effects of a psychotic illness?

Given the mass of contradictions and errors in Speke's surviving papers, it is likely that he bolstered vestiges of truth into versions which 'convinced himself', as Burton observed, so that he was able to speak with an air of innocent conviction. I could find no further material on this accusation of attempted murder, but a clue to its conception may lie in an incident that took place some years later on an expedition through the same tract of country in East Africa, under the leadership of Verney Lovett Cameron. Cameron's team included one Dr Dillon R.N., who became seriously ill. His symptoms, including manic raving, were remarkably similar to those which Burton graphically described in Speke, during the latter's serious illness on the journey down to the coast. Cameron wrote:

> I got him quiet again but presently he commenced afresh, 'Fraser tells an infernal lie in saying I divulged the secrets of Masonry, I never told a soul a Masonic secret in my life;' adding plaintively, 'how could I when I know so little?' He talked of me wanting to poison him and turned on me saying, 'How can you sit there looking down on your victim . . .'[65]

Shortly afterwards Dillon shot himself. 'Blood was streaming from the tent,' a shocked Cameron wrote, '. . . he had taken the gun from the tent pole and, loading it with a bullet, tied a string to the trigger which, as he had fallen across the bed backwards, he had pulled apparently with his toe . . . the upper part of his head was completely blown off.'[66]

Cameron's diaries and private letters, which I obtained unique permission to examine, show how Dillon – a sane and reliable man prior to the expedition – was psychiatrically changed by the illness. He 'remembered' things that had not happened other than in his imagination, such as Cameron walking into his tent and threatening to sell his guns. Dillon's paranoid fear that his companions planned to kill him was so great, and so real to him, that he killed himself to prevent it. Did something like this permanently affect Speke, as Richard suspected? Probably we shall never know, but it is at least a possible explanation of his subsequent behaviour.

What other reason could there be for Speke's bizarre conduct when he first returned to England? Although there was no trace of any impediment during his talks with Murchison, Speke was said to have 'astonished his friends ... by speaking in a sort of broken English, as if he had forgotten his vernacular in the presence of strange tongues'.[67] Richard was generous enough to regard this as a sort of 'whimsical affectation' of Speke's. Today's historians must form their own opinions.

17

TURNING POINT
1859–1860

Both men worked on their respective publications during the autumn of 1859; Speke on numerous corrections and edits for a series of articles for *Blackwood's Magazine*. The tenor of these is made evident by the concluding statement; 'If what I have written . . . may appear harsh to one with whom I have travelled I trust it will be understood that I have done so not in any consideration for myself but merely to vindicate the honour of those who befriended me in carrying to a successful issue our late explorations . . .'[1]

Richard meanwhile worked on his detailed paper for the Royal Geographical Society's *Journal*. Every day when he was in London he spent hours at his Club working at his fact-filled account that would eventually fill an entire issue. Subsequently, it would also form the basis of his book on the subject, *The Lake Regions of Central Africa*, regarded for over a century by travellers in East Africa as the standard guide. Although Isabel would not have accepted it, and Burton would not have admitted it, he would never entirely regain his former vigour. For too many years he had drawn on reserves of strength while working in inhospitable environments; suffering the effects of sunstroke, dysentery, malaria, fevers, agues, lameness and blindness, not to mention syphilis. He was far from being a broken man, but he had passed his physical prime, his body had been traumatised, and for the remainder of his life he would pay the price.

The R.G.S. expected explorer members to provide accounts of

their travels in the house *Journal*, for the benefit of other members, prior to any general publication for personal gain. But although the text of his initial speech to the Society appeared in the *Journal*, Speke withdrew the written account of his journeys across Tanganyika and to the Northern Lake, at Oliphant's suggestion. This resulted – after the October publication of Speke's article in *Blackwood's* – in a reduction in his popularity among some members of the Society who felt he had behaved badly. Asked to comment on this, Richard noticeably ignored the moral issue and concentrated on the many errors in Speke's papers, especially three serious inconsistencies.

First, he pointed out, Speke's claim that the northern shores of the lake extended to latitude '4° or 5° north' was demonstrably specious. Some twenty years earlier an Egyptian expedition (often referred to by geographers as 'The Navigators'), had followed the Nile upstream beyond Gonderoko, as far as 3° 22' north, and had still not reached a lake. Speke had drawn the northern boundary of the lake so wide on his map, Richard said, that it 'drowned' Gonderoko.*

Second, Speke claimed that the river – called Kivira by the natives – flowed out of the lake and was, in all probability, the Nile. He said he had heard about it first at Kazeh, though he had never seen the river. But Burton had heard from Bombay, and the Arabs at Kazeh, that the Kivira flowed from the west *into* the lake; Speke had even got the name of the local tribe wrong, calling them, apparently incorrectly, 'the Bari'.

The third main point of contention was Speke's assertion that the range of hills at the northern end of Lake Tanganyika was the fabled 'Mountains of the Moon'. He had considerably elevated their height on his map to support this claim; but Burton knew that mythology described these mountains as being always snow-covered, and suggested that the true Mountains of the Moon probably lay north-east of the lake. In fact he was not correct; they were situated to the north-west, as Henry Morton Stanley discovered thirty years later when he first saw the great Ruwenzori Range bestriding the Equator with snow-covered peaks reaching 18,000 feet.

In sending in his own paper to the R.G.S. for publication Richard apologised for its length, stating pointedly, 'A detailed account is the

---

*A town almost 400 miles north of Lake Victoria.

more necessary as of late some erroneous opinions concerning the country have found their way into print.'[2] He too, had received an offer from a publisher, for the piece he published in the *Journal*, but this would need considerable work for as it stood, he told Shaw, 'it is too geographical for a general book'.[3] However, on 8 October he wrote to *The Times* on the subject of the Lake regions. His letter did not specifically mention Speke's inconsistencies, but it contained enough supported facts to enable the *cognoscenti* to recognise that the latter's claims warranted some query.

Speke's early reaction to Burton's criticisms was contained in a letter to Shaw, ostensibly written to advise that his old shooting friend Edmund Smyth wished to accompany him to Africa. Accordingly, Speke wrote, he had invited John Petherick (British Vice-Consul in Khartoum, who had surveyed 'the upper Nile') and Smyth down to Jordan's for the following weekend, 'that we might make arrangements for *ripping* open Africa together.' He added that he had received a letter from Burton and was

> . . . much amused to hear that he differs from me in his accounts of Africa and that part relating to the north end of the Nyanza. I thought he would for he used to snub me so unpleasantly when talking about anything that I used to keep my own council. Burton is one of those men who never *can* be wrong, and will never acknowledge an error so that when only two are together, talking becomes more of a bore than a pleasure . . .[4]

And he cleverly hinted (not without some foundation) that had he been leader of the previous expedition there might have been no need for a second:

> . . . I cannot help thinking what a green thing it was of Burton not remarking that when at Kazeh, we were due south of Gonderoko with a sea, according to everybodies account, stretching clear up to it. Its a devil of a bore having to go all over the same stale ground again . . . I would not attempt doing it on any account if I did not feel quite certain of being able to connect my lake with the Nile for there is no shooting in the country or any other inducement. We ought never to have gone westward from Kazeh . . . the distance that took us to Ujiji and back would have landed us at Gonderoko.[5]

But in fact, Speke was far from being 'amused'. He was furious at
Richard's mainly valid criticisms, and in particular his sneers at the
English names that Speke sprinkled across his maps. Speke's decision
to name the northern lake after the Queen was merely the sort of
opportunism employed by many explorers (Livingstone's Victoria
Falls for example), and occurred soon after his return. 'I told Lord
Elgin that I christened the Lake after the Queen because she asked so
politely after my health on my return,' he wrote. But Burton strongly
objected to Speke naming places they had visited together on the
Tanganyika 'Speke Channel' and 'Burton Point'. MacQueen also
complained, 'nothing can be so absurd as to impose English names
on . . . places in the remote interior of Africa. What nonsense it is calling a part of Lake Nyanza the Bengal Archipelago, or a stagnant
puddle with water in it only during the rains . . . "the Jordans"'.[6]

In a rambling ten-page letter to the Society, Speke attempted to
explain away his mistakes.[7] Here, his tone is far from the studied
amusement of his previous correspondence; he knows he is on uncertain ground and appears highly agitated, a recurring mannerism of
Speke's when placed under pressure by Burton.

> . . . I wrote the word 'Bari' . . . from information which I obtained
> from the Shaykh Abdullah, at the time that our camp was pitched
> under a Búgú tree in the Ugigi district. Burton at that time was
> unwell, sitting in one tent whilst I at his command was engaged in
> another tent, purchasing cloth from Abdullah for the use of the
> Expedition as I was . . . general manager of the conduct of the expe-
> dition . . . I enquired if he knew anything about the Northern
> countries . . . He then told me that he had been in Uganda, had
> heard of the Ruvira River from the reports of the natives living to
> the Northward of the [Olat?] country and . . . told me of the
> Navigators but in a more lucid manner than anything I had ever
> heard before. He said that of all the tribes living near the Kiveri R
> the largest was the Bari people, I [assumed therefore that] . . . they
> must be called the WaBari in the same manner as the people of
> Uganda are called WaGanda, but he said no, They were only called
> Bari and at that same moment I wrote the word Bari on the map . . .
> I was distrustful of this information, and intended enquiring more
> about it . . .
> . . . When I went to discover the Nyanza, I asked Burton to give

me any hints he could about the Lake and he gave me some, but *strange* to say only with regard to some districts and tribes on the west flank of the Nyanza . . . *now* he tells me that before going to Africa he had read Werne's book . . . had it in his possession at that time, and *ought* to have known that the Nyanza . . . was very close to Gonderoko. Indeed he ought never to have allowed my map to go home without remark or telling me that I had flooded the mission station with my Lake . . .[8]

Later he would ask Murchison to correct his maps in line with the errors Richard pointed out, 'not only for my credit's sake, but to save young men who have read my Blackwood, and mapped it, distrusting me for the future . . .'[9]

Notwithstanding Richard's criticisms and pointed queries, the edition of *Blackwood's Magazine* containing Speke's article sold out. Subsequently Speke was delighted to receive a cheque which exceeded his expectations, together with a request for further material. He had already told Blackwood that he had kept no other diaries of his travels, but Blackwood had noticed, 'When we were talking the other day you said there was at home an immense collection of your letters from Thibet etc to your mother and other members of the family. It has frequently occurred to me that something very interesting about Thibet might be made from these letters. Could you ask your mother to select a few which you might not object to my seeing and send them to me? . . .'[10] For reasons best known to himself, Speke refused this request.

I do not think you or anyone else save myself could make head or tail of my letters written from Thibet for they are not connected nor do they give any lively stories . . . I hate writing, but hate to be bothered to write still more . . . I think as soon as Burton has come out, which he will do shortly through Longman, I might make a clean sweep of all my experiences in foreign parts by giving a short pithy account, as for instance, 'Experiences in the Life of a Vagabond', embracing all the time between this and the date at which I left the Mammy strings . . .[11]

Speke's biographer contrasted Blackwood's eagerness to publish extracts from the letters with 'Speke's grim determination to withhold their contents from the public', and deduced as the reason the 'intro-spective nature of these letters, which have since either been lost or destroyed'.[12]

On 31 October, Burton wrote to Speke complaining that not only did the series in *Blackwell's* contain material extracted from his [Burton's] journals, but that Speke had altered it to support his inac-curate statements. Speke's response was not promising:

> Lypiat Park
> Nov'r 3rd [1859]
>
> My dear Burton,
>
> I have just received yours of the 31st ultimo, with its insinua-tions. I have given all my knowledge of African matters in the three numbers of Blackwood which I have desired him to send you . . . You can contradict anything that *you* do not think truthful in my diaries. I dont want to be bothered anymore with writing now that I have told my tale and published it for everybody to criticise as they may please.
>
> Yours truly,
> J.H. Speke[13]

At the end of October Richard spent a few weeks in France. Maria and Edward were staying in Paris where Edward was being treated by a leading neurologist. Richard went on to Vichy for treatment of an attack of gout,[14] a condition which would afflict him for the remain-der of his life. In Paris he also met Frederick Hankey, by a letter of introduction from Monckton Milnes. Hankey was a bizarre acquain-tance of Milnes; a gentleman by birth (he was the son of Sir Frederick Hankey the Governor of Malta), he had resigned his commission in the Guards in 1847 to settle in Paris and pursue his chief interest in life: obscene, pornographic, sadistic and masochistic literature, and aberrant sexual practices. Characteristically, Richard was instantly attracted. Hankey interested and amused him, and had many anec-dotes to add to Richard's fund of information on sexual matters. By 1857 Hankey was functioning as a book runner for Milnes, finding and smuggling into England unusual books, and objects, for Fryston's famous library.[15]

Richard returned to London in November. All the elements of

dissension between him and Speke, confined by social politeness during the previous months, erupted when Richard received a curt official letter from India regarding the non-payment of the expedition guards. The letter referred him to a statement by Rigby and demanded an explanation.

Richard replied in a strongly worded 11-point epistle (too long to reproduce), giving his version of events; 'the men alluded to rendered me no service and . . . I could not report favourably of them.' He had not recruited them; they were hired by Lieut. Colonel Hamerton who had offered to defray their expenses and reward them liberally 'from public funds' for a successful outcome. The amounts offered by Hamerton were, in Richard's opinion, 'exorbitant'. But even so, Hamerton's offer was conditional on good behaviour (a fact omitted by Rigby), and the men concerned had been guilty of 'notorious misconduct'. Rigby 'understood' that they had been promised a salary, said Richard, but 'this was not the case'. Rather, they were given $20 each at the start, and it was agreed that the expedition should provide them with daily rations. He pointed out that conversations referred to in Rigby's letter, which had taken place between Hamerton, Burton and Speke, were written 'in a distorted form, and improperly represented'.

He was not astonished, he said, 'That Said bin Salem, and Ramjee . . . should have appealed to Captain Rigby, according to the fashion of Orientals after my departure from Zanzibar . . .':

> But I must express my extreme surprise that Captain Speke should have written two private letters, forcibly pointing out the claims of these men to Captain Rigby, without having communicated the circumstance in any way to me, the chief of the Expedition. I have been in continued correspondence with that officer since my departure from Zanzibar, and until this moment have been impressed with the conviction that Captain Speke's opinion, as to the claims of the guide and escort above alluded to, was identical with my own.

He concluded by expressing surprise that Consul Rigby should have forwarded the complaints of those who had appealed to him without checking the validity of the claims with the leader of the expedition.[16]

When Burton next met Speke, on 25 November at the R.G.S., he pointedly cut Speke dead, a studied insult not lost on those present. Speke soon discovered that there was more; Richard had left copies of all the correspondence concerning their dispute on the reading-room table for members to read. These papers were accompanied by an open letter to Shaw:

My dear Shaw,

I don't wish to have any further private or direct communication with Speke. At the same time I am anxious that no mention of his name by me should be made without his being cognizant of it.

I must request that you would as soon as you can let him know that a complaint as regards certain non payment of the Expedition has been received by me from the Indian Gov, that his name occurs in them and that in my reply I have been obliged to take notice of the private letters said to have been written by him.

I presume that without reference to the Council the whole of the correspondence will be open to him if he calls to see it. Excuse bother, and believe me,

Yours ever Truly
R.F. Burton

There was also a note for Speke himself, in which Richard stated, 'Your impression of occurrences is so often totally opposed to my convictions on those points that no profitable good can come from the discussion of them. And as the only effect can be an unseemly dispute, I hope that you will agree with me that all points of difference should be simply communicated to the RGS to be used by them as they think fit.' In other words, he was content to leave it to the geographers to decide whose version was the true one.

Clearly upset by what had transpired, Speke wrote that evening to Rigby to tell him about the latest developments and protest that he believed the men ought to have been paid.

I wanted to do so but Burton would not . . . In all Burton's answers I see the same avoidance of the naked truth; it is that sort of thing that has always made me feel raised against him and although I felt obliged to travel with him I entertained a loathing for him. I know that I ought to have hauled him up long before I did but felt compunctions about doing it as he is my senior . . . I was almost afraid to say such things of him as I know that he is likely to deny me, judging from the way that he has sometimes denied me to my own face . . . and there is no evidence to prove my assertions . . .[17]

The private letters he had sent home from Africa, Speke thought, might help, for he had often told his family how much he disliked Burton; 'being private . . . they were never meant to act in any way against him. But never mind . . .' Two weeks later he wrote again to Rigby, thanking him for his second letter to the Government castigating Burton and praising Speke's behaviour in the affair.

In December the Government 'accepted' Richard's statement of accounts for the expedition at £2,494; almost £1,500 more than the funding provided. Ironically, it was due to these meticulously detailed accounts of Richard's that Speke's expedition was subsequently guaranteed £2,500, on the personal approval of Lord John Russell. But the Government refused to repay the excess expenditure of Richard's expedition. Instead, in January, Richard was sternly informed of the official opinion that he had acted wrongly in not bringing the matter of the dismissed men 'properly to the attention' of Rigby so that their claims could be 'adjudicated on their own merits'. It had now been decided that the amounts claimed by the escort were justified. These would be paid by the Bombay Government, who were presently considering 'whether you shall be held pecuniarily responsible . . .'[18]

Game, set and match to Speke, who wrote at once to Rigby: 'I have driven the fox to earth at last and now only require a little drawing to get him in the bag . . .' Nor was Burton's reprimand the only good news he had to impart; 'Lord Elphinstone in a letter to Sir C. Wood expresses his regret that the Gold Medal was not given to me instead of to Burton . . . [who] has got into the dumps and is cutting himself at every turn . . .'[19] He went on to outline his expedition plans; he and Grant intended to trek up the west side of the Victoria Nyanza, and 'sail down the Nile' to meet Petherick.

Isabel had been dutiful to her parents' wishes all summer. She had accompanied them into the country, though resenting the passing of time which she could have spent with Richard, and the fact that she was unable to give him the level of support she should. She also recognised the possibility that if she did not marry him soon he would return to India, and from there to other expeditions, and that next time he might not come back.

While Richard was in France Mrs Arundell was away visiting her brother, Lord Gerard; Isabel wrote her a long, impassioned letter hoping to win her over:

October 1859

My dearest Mother,

I feel quite grateful to you for inviting my confidence. It is the first time you have ever done so, and the occasion shall not be neglected . . . I fell in love with Captain Burton at Boulougne . . . and determined that he was the only man I would ever marry, but he never knew it until three years ago before he went to Africa . . . you may remember he came to see us . . . he fell in love with me and asked me to be his wife and was . . . amazed to find that I had cared for him all that time . . .

It surprises me that you should consider mine an infatuation, you who worship talent, and my father bravery and adventure, and here they are both united! Look at his military services – India and the Crimea. Look at his writings, his travels, his poetry, his languages and dialects. Now Mezzofanti is dead he stands first in Europe; he is the best horseman, swordsman and pistol shot. He has been presented with the gold medal, is an F.R.G.S. and you must see in the newspapers of his glory and fame . . . where he is called 'the Crichton of the day,' 'one of the Paladins of the age,' 'the most interesting figure of the nineteenth century'. In his wonderful explorings he goes where none but natives have ever trod, in hourly peril of his life . . . one day he is a doctor, one day a priest, another he keeps a stall in the bazaar, sometimes he is a blacksmith. I could tell you adventures of him . . . that would delight you, were you unprejudiced . . . He is not at all the man . . . that people take him to be, or that he sometimes, for fun, pretends to be . . . Any evil opinions you may have heard . . . arise from his recklessly setting at defiance conventional people talking nonsense about religion and heart and principle . . .

You and my father are immensely proud of your families, and we are taught to be the same; but I believe our proudest record will be our alliance with Richard Burton. I want . . . I *want* a wild, roving, vagabond life. I am young, strong and hardy . . . I wonder that you do not see the magnitude of the position offered to me. His immense talent and adventurous life must command interest . . . but

I love him because I find in him . . . a generous heart . . . There is a touching forgetfulness of himself and his fame . . . he is proud, fiery, satirical, ambitious; how could I help looking up to him . . .?

I wish I were a man. If I were I would be Richard Burton; but, being only a woman, I would be Richard Burton's wife . . . I love him purely, passionately and respectfully . . . It is part of my nature, part of my religion . . . I have given my every feeling to him and kept nothing back for myself. I would at this moment sacrifice and leave *all* to follow his fortunes, even if you all cast me out – if the world *tabooed* me . . . No compensation could be given to me for his loss . . . he is perfect to me and I would not have him otherwise than he is.

You have said 'you do not know who he is, that you do not meet him anywhere.' . . . Considering the particular sort of Society you seek with a view to marrying your daughters, you are not likely to meet him there . . . Most great houses are only too glad to get him . . . the only two occasions he came out last season it was because I begged him to, and he was bored to death . . . As to birth he is just as good as we are; all his people belong to good families. With regard to . . . [religion] he says there is nothing between Agnosticism and Catholicity. He wishes to be married in the Catholic Church, says that I must practise my own religion, and that our children will be brought up Catholics, and will give such a promise in writing . . .

No.3 point is money. And here I am before *you*, terribly crest-fallen – there is nothing except his pay. As Captain that is, I believe, £600 a year in India and £300 in England. We want to try and get the Consulship of Damascus where we would have a life after both our hearts and where the vulgarity of poverty would not make itself apparent . . .

Dearest mother . . . let him go to my father and ask for me properly . . . We shall never marry anyone else and never give each other up . . . do not accuse me of deception, because I shall see him and write to him whenever I get a chance, and if you drive me to it I shall marry him in defiance . . . I have got to live with him night and day for the rest of my life . . . Do not embitter my whole future life, for God's sake. I would rather die a thousand times than go through what I have borne for the last five years . . . I will not allude to the marriages that you *have* consented to, but you should rejoice

that I have got a man who knows how to protect me . . . Do think
it all over in earnest and if you love me as you say you do . . . be
generous and kind . . .

Your fondly attached child
Isabel Arundell.[20]

But Isabel's appeal made little impression on Mrs Arundell, whose
declared aim was to make grand matches for her daughters. In fact
two of them did marry well in financial terms, but neither were happy
unions and it is doubtful that Mrs Arundell was happy to be reminded
of this in Isabel's letter. She answered Isabel negatively with a long,
'solemn sermon . . . that Richard was not a Christian and had no
money'. As far as she was concerned, that was the end of the matter.[21]

In January, after appearing as a witness in the long delayed law-suit
brought by Beatson against Consul Skene, Richard left London for
several months in Boulougne where he wrote to Milnes that he was
there because of 'the conviction that here I can work'. He had a
pressing financial necessity 'to produce . . . something more popular
than a geographical report, and upon this I am engaged', he wrote,
before turning from serious matters to the usual ribald humour with
which he and Milnes addressed each other:

> . . . Since we met I saw Hankey. The 'sisters' are a humbug – Swiss
> women. Cold as frogs and thorough mountaineers. A breed as unfit
> for debauchery as exists in this world. I told Hankey so and he
> remarked philosophically enough that they were quite sufficiently
> good enough for the public of *paillards*.
>
> He showed me also a little poem entitled the 'Betuliad'. I liked
> much every part except the name – you are writing for a very very
> small section who combine the enjoyment of verse with the practice
> of flagellation and the remembrance that betulo is a birch, why not
> call it the 'Birchiad'? If you want it corrected here I can do so.
> Hankey and I looked over the copy made at Paris and corrected the
> several errors . . .[22]

The sophisticated humour of Richard's letters to Milnes hardly
reflects the broken man of Speke's wishful imaginings, and indeed
Richard had hit back strongly at the Company's letter to him. Having
not seen Speke's deposition he was, he wrote, 'not in a position to

understand on what grounds the Secretary of State for India should have arrived at so unexpected a decision as regards the alleged non-payment of certain claims . . . Although impaired health prevented me from proceeding . . . to the adjudication . . . in the presence of Consular authority, I represented the whole question to Captain Rigby who, had he at that time, deemed it his duty to interfere, might have insisted upon [doing so] . . . before we left Zanzibar':

> . . . In conclusion I venture to express my surprise, that all my labours and long services in the cause of African exploration should have won for me no other reward than the prospect of being mulcted in a pecuniary liability incurred by my late lamented friend, Lieutenant Colonel Hamerton, and settled without reference to me by his successor, Captain Rigby.[23]

And Rigby was not pleased to receive the following Burton-at-his-best letter, reminding him of the intellectual drubbing Burton had given him in the Gujerati language exams in India.

January 16th 1860

Sir,

I have been indebted to the kindness and consideration of my friend Dr Shaw, for a sight of your letter addressed to him the 10th of October last from Zanzibar. I shall not attempt to characterise it in the terms that best befit it. To do so, indeed, I should be compelled to resort to language 'vile' and unseemly as your own . . . A person who could act as you must be held by everyone to be beneath the notice of any honourable man.

You have addressed a virulent attack on me to a quarter in which you had hoped it would prove deeply injurious to me; and this not in the discharge of public duty, but for the gratification of a long-standing private pique. You gave me no copy of this attack, you gave me no opportunity of meeting it; the slander was propagated, as slanders generally are, in secret and behind my back . . . [while] your distance from England puts you in a position to be perfectly secure from any consequences of a nature personal to yourself.

Such being the case, there remains to me but one manner of treating your letter, and that is with the contempt it merits. My qualifications as a traveller are, I hope, sufficiently established to render your criticisms innocuous, and the medals of the English and French Geographical Societies may console me for the non-appreciation of my labours by so eminent an authority as yourself . . . I can hardy think that your statements will have much weight with those who are aware of the cogomen* acquired by you at Addiscombe, and which, to judge from your letter now under notice, I think you most entirely, richly deserve. . . . I shall forward a copy of this letter to Dr Shaw and . . . shall at all times, in all companies, even in print if it suits me, use the same freedom in discussing your character and conduct, that you have presumed to exercise in discussing mine.

> I am, Sir, your obedient servant.
> Richard F. Burton[24]

The barrage of angry letters swept to and fro with the Royal Geographical Society caught in the crossfire. By this time Speke was well aware that anything he wrote to Richard was liable to end up on public display at the R.G.S., so he chose his words carefully in reply to yet another request from Burton, sent through Norton Shaw, for payment of his expedition debt. He would pay his share, he said 'when your agreement to ask the Gov't (the Indian one which we both belong to) for refundment, shall on your part have been fulfilled and, as is possible may be the case, they shall have *refused* to requite you . . .'

Addressing Speke curtly as 'Sir', Burton replied from Paris on 3 February 1860. The subject of their monetary transactions was distasteful to him in the extreme, he said with deliberate insult, but Speke had forced him into the situation. 'The debt was contracted unconditionally by you in Africa. Since your return home you have remembered an "agreement" which never existed and you propose conditions which, allow me to say, are not exactly your affair. It is for me to decide if I choose to [ask] the Gov't for refundment. Had I known you then as well as I do now I should have required receipts for what was left a debt of *honour*. I must be contented to pay the penalty of ignorance . . .'

---

* Rigby's nickname, which the tone of the above letter suggests is not flattering to him, is not known.

There was further irritation for Richard when he received a note from Shaw, still a close friend and ardent supporter of his, asking if it was 'by your permission that Speke has published in Peterman's Journal every full map of the proceedings of the Expedition under your command'. These maps, he wrote, contained significant alterations by Speke.[25] To which Burton retorted, 'Captain Speke has published nothing with my permission . . . I know nothing of his proceedings . . . [and] with respect to the map I object to any alteration.'[26]

Burton's appeal, with Shaw's support, regarding the Government's refusal to refund the excess expenses of his expedition had received a frosty response. In effect, all the money the Government was prepared to expend on African exploration was already being channelled into Speke's expedition. But Speke stubbornly insisted that Burton had not gone through the appropriate channels. At this point Burton decided he was wasting his time trying to effect a refund, and gave it up. But he was determined that Speke must pay his half-share of the £1,494 excess expenditure, according to their agreement. Having made this decision, he decided to enjoy himself in Boulogne with his old friend 'Styggins', while he worked on his manuscript.

Despite technical criticisms by Richard and MacQueen, the public reception of Speke's Somalia articles in *Blackwood's Magazine* was heartening to him. He was delighted to receive a cheque for £60 for the final one in the spring of 1860 (Speke earned more for his three articles than Richard earned from his two-volume book *First Footsteps*). Once again encouraged by Oliphant, Speke next began work on a book beginning, he said, from the time he 'first contemplated an attack upon . . . Africa'.[27] His letters on the subject to John Blackwood show that not only did he feel free to use the materials lodged by Richard at the Royal Geographical Society, but that he also borrowed writing techniques which he learned from Richard.

He knew, for instance, that when Richard described 'risqué' subjects, such as circumcision in *Pilgrimage*, and female genitalia and clitoridectomy in *First Footsteps*, he wrote in Latin, so as not to offend 'the general [non Latin speaking] readership'.[28] Speke, uncharacteristically, now insisted that there were 'certain things in Africa that must be told'. He included details of how in certain tribes the *labia* of young girls was sewn up until their marriage, to ensure virginity. When Blackwood protested about the material submitted, Speke advised him to translate the 'delicate' text into Latin or Greek; 'the persons who are interested will like it even more if they have to work at it,' he said, echoing a well-used sentiment of Richard's.

Richard's book on the expedition, *Lake Regions of Central Africa*, was advertised for publication in the early summer of 1860. Two months beforehand, he informed the Royal Geographical Society that it included a detailed account of the contentious 'non-payment of porters' matter, in order to give the Society time to present the last of his technical papers before publication occurred.

It would be surprising if Speke was not apprehensive of what Burton might say in his book about him, and about the claims made in his *Blackwood's* articles. His letter, though, shows a lack of concern: 'Burton's [book] will be very different from mine. I wish it was already out, for although I might be in his way he could not run foul of me,' he wrote to Blackwood. But he knew that Burton's material was more accurate than his own. 'I shall have to alter a good bit of the [material in the] numbers already printed in the magazine . . .' John Blackwood, however, was more concerned that Speke's diaries might contain libelous material. Speke reassured him, 'there is nothing in my diaries but honest truth . . . in no way do they show Burton in a false light.'[29] And in respect of the subject matter the publisher considered 'too delicate' for publication, Speke attempted levity: 'if you persist in gelding me I shall think you more barbarous than the Somali who after all did spare the knife work.'[30]

But Blackwood, who liked Speke immensely, would have none of it; the laws on pornography were too severe for him to risk printing the offending material. The piece on virginity was edited out.[31] Richard's publishers also, despite having initially printed an Appendix (describing clitoridectomy) entitled, 'A Brief Description of Certain Peculiar Customs', written in Latin, suddenly realised what it represented, and censored the material at the binding stage. A page was substituted bearing the words: 'It has been found necessary to omit this Appendix.'[32] Richard apparently experienced similar problems with the first edition of his *Pilgrimage*. Stanley Lane Poole observed in his introduction to a later edition that the book was 'only saved from the top shelf (with bookseller's "curious items") by the absence of its author from England; for Sir Gardner Wilkinson, to whom the manuscript was entrusted, remarked that the amount of unpleasant garbage which he took upon himself to reject would have rendered the book unfit for publication', The only 'garbage' that escaped Sir Gardner's censorious eye was a Latin excerpt on circumcision translated by Richard from an old Arabic manuscript.[33]

Following his return from Africa, whenever they were both in London Richard and Isabel met regularly. When Isabel told him of her mother's unbending attitude, he said they 'would have to take the law into [their] own hands'.[34] But she still hoped to win her parents over, and begged him to be patient for a little longer. Richard was in love, but he was not a man to brook opposition. Though we have no record of his specific reaction, he could hardly have relished the prospect of a long-term relationship consisting of *ad nauseam* stolen moments. He had few family ties to keep him in England; Maria was happily married and had her two daughters, Edward had become a mute and gentle 'idiot'. Perhaps Richard became uneasy that this romance, like a number of previous ones, was also doomed to failure because of parental disapproval despite Isabel's unquestionable love for him. He became restless. He was 38 years old and Isabel was 28; they had declared their love for each other more than three years earlier.

He did not warn her of his plan to visit America with John Steinhaueser in the spring of 1860. Perhaps he jibed at hurting her, or perhaps he hoped that his absence would provoke her to make a decision. The idea was initially conceived during a supper that Burton had with Steinhaueser in 'M. Paschal's excellent bistro' in Boulogne. With respect to alcoholic drinks, 'Styggins,' said Burton, had 'that kind of attraction which the . . . Magnetic Mount had upon the iron-work of Sinbad's ship.' By the end of the meal both men were pleasantly drunk and discussions turned to the merits, or otherwise, of that recent import to Europe, the American cocktail. And then Steinhaueser gurgled tipsily, 'I'll tell you what . . . I'll go to America . . . Will you come with me and eat and drink through America? Hmmm?'

Richard, who felt 'light and ethereal and pleased with myself', after an excellent dinner followed by his favourite brandy and cigarettes, decided, 'I could not say no . . . after drinking with him on and off for fifteen years.' Besides, he wrote, he was weary of the 'nimglow gorgeousness of the East' and the 'monotonous savagery' of Africa. Why not explore the New World? 'We resolved to leave without delay and to hurry on the necessary preparations. £300 each was considered sufficient – "if we take more," said my friend, "we shall only throw it away."'[35] They planned to leave in early May.

Speke had eventually fixed on James Grant as second-in-command. Edmund Smyth dropped out in the early stages of discussions, and Petherick was mounting his own plans to approach the lake by tracking up the Nile to meet Speke's party, taking fresh supplies, after which they would 'sail down the Nile together'. This was a logical, and apparently simple, strategy to prove Speke's claims once and for all. As part of his preparations to leave, Speke wrote to Richard through the R.G.S., requesting permission to use extracts and maps in a further article he was leaving with Blackwood on Tanganyika. He would have liked to settle his debt, he wrote, but for the fact that 'the Geographical Society is shut up and I cannot get at the exact amount for which I am liable to you, whatever it is I shall be happy to pay as I've said before, and have now asked my brother the Reverend Ben Speke to arrange for me whilst I am away . . . I expect to leave England at the end of this week.'[36] Burton replied by return.

Sir,
    Mr Wheeler, the Chairman of the R.G.S. has shown me your letters and I have authorised him to inform you that your request respecting various items met with opposition on my part. As regards your communication of the 10th April which I have just received I shall place it in the hands of Messrs Grindlay as I also am on the point of leaving England and shall direct them to receive the money at your earliest convenience.
                                    I am, sir, Yr Ob't Servant
                                    R.F.B[urton]

The chilly formality of the above note wounded Speke and he wrote again. In the light of his behaviour towards Burton, it is an astonishing example of hypocrisy; not least because he had received, a few days earlier, a letter formally advising him that the India Office 'was unlikely' to refund the claim for excess expenditure on the Tanganyika Expedition.[37]

Jordans
Illminster
Somerset
16th April [1860]

My dear Burton,

I cannot leave England addressing you so coldly as you have hitherto been corresponding, the more especially as you have condescended to make an amicable arrangement with me about the debt I owe to you . . . I am happy to say I have succeeded in accumulating money sufficient to meet my debt to you and have therefore authorised my brother (Rev'd Ben. Speke) to pay you the money into Mssrs Grindlays hands, as you proposed, immediately after the refusal has been received to refund you from the Gov't Treasury.

Hoping this meets your wishes as I anticipate it might do.

Believe me yours faithfully,
J.H. Speke[38]

Anyone who has researched this feud in depth will sympathise with Richard's response that while he accepted the financial terms he could not 'accept your offer concerning our corresponding less coldly. Any other tone would be extremely distasteful to me.'[39]

Within days of this exchange both men set off on their respective journeys. Having served a short 'apprenticeship' with a blacksmith, so that he could make horseshoes and shoe his own horse if necessary, Richard's last act was to consign all his worldly goods, including his valuable library of Oriental manuscripts (especially those purchased from the library of the Emir of Sindh), and his private papers, to his agents Messrs Grindlay for safekeeping in their warehouse. Speke's last chores included a letter to Blackwood confiding how much he now regretted not having kept diaries during the previous expedition, for although he had been a party to many interesting conversations and events, he did not recall them 'sufficiently well to be justified in publishing . . . May this be a warning to others who travel,' he wrote, 'and a caution to be precise in recording everything they see and hear . . .'[40] His admitted lack of accurate recollection did not, however (years after the events) prevent him from providing – in sworn statements to the Government – word-for-word accounts of lengthy conversations he said had taken place with Richard and others during the expedition.

In the four years that followed, even as unchallenged leader of his own expedition Speke continued to be haunted by Burton. He rarely wrote a letter without making some pejorative comment about Burton, and the claims grew more incongruous with time. 'I am sure everyone at Zanzibar knows,' he wrote on one occasion to Rigby regarding the first exploration, 'that I was the leader and Burton the second of the Expedition.'[41] In another letter he wrote that 'he [Burton] did not come out here to open up the country but to make a book and astonish the world with his powers. He never learned observing until we returned to the coast when finally ashamed of his ignorance he asked me to teach him and I did so.'[42] Presumably Speke was not aware that Burton had learned surveying and observation as part of a Government team in India and had been officially commended for the maps and reports he produced of Sindh.

But no failure was ever Speke's fault; he continued to blame Burton even for incidents that occurred in the second expedition. In December 1860, when Speke's porters deserted him 'en masse', he placed the blame squarely on his former companion. The problem was due to Burton's 'blackguard treatment,' he wrote to the R.G.S. 'in cheating the first men of the moon who had dealings with our race.' In letters written to Blackwood from Africa he described Burton as 'a vile, dastardly wretch',[43] who had made the Royal Geographical Society 'dupes to his insane vanity'.[44]

Undeniably, Speke deserves recognition for his bravery and stoicism, and for the discoveries that he made in Africa in the name of science. But there was some defect in his character as far as Burton was concerned. I believe that Speke's relationship with Grant succeeded because Grant was content to travel in Speke's shadow, both during the expedition and on their return to England. Even so, matters were not always as smooth as both men afterwards presented them. Grant's private papers reveal that during their expedition, whenever they approached a place of importance, Speke would send him off on spurious errands, so that there could be no doubt that Speke was the discoverer and might therefore claim the entire credit.[45]

Before he left England with Grant, Speke wrote, 'I fondly hope there will be no jealousies on this expedition which will lead to unseemly ruptures and I have the fullest confidence in Grant's integrity.'[46] Behind this remark lay an extraordinary contract (extra-ordinary given Speke's own behaviour to Burton) that he had made Grant sign on the eve of their departure from England:

> I hereby agree to accompany Captain J.H. Speke in his expedition to Eastern Central Africa on the following conditions: That I shall be no expense to the Expedition throughout its whole journey and that I devote my entire services and abilities to the Expedition and renounce all my rights to publishing or collections of any sort on my own account until approved of by Captain Speke or the R. G. S.
>
> On the other hand Capt Speke agrees to make Captain Grant a part of the Expedition upon the conditions above stated.
>   [signed] J.A. Grant
>   J.H. Speke[47]
>
> Jordans
> 16th April 1860

Speke took no chance that Grant might behave to him, as he himself had done to Burton.

18

THE PRAIRIE TRAVELLER
1860

One evening in mid-April 1860 a letter addressed to Isabel was delivered to the Arundells' house in Montagu Place. The envelope bore Richard's well-known handwriting and as she had experienced a presentiment on the previous evening she guessed its contents even before she opened it. 'He had left;' she confirmed, bleakly, 'could not bear the pain of saying good-bye; would be absent for nine months, on a journey to Salt Lake City. He would then come back and see whether I had made up my mind to choose between him and my mother, to marry me if I *would*; and if I had not the courage to risk it he would return to India . . . I was to take nine months to think about it.'[1]

A few days later she became ill with influenza and mumps. The infection was persistent and she was in bed for six weeks. Privately, she thought that her inability to recover her health was because she was heartsick at the inevitability of what lay before her. There was never any real doubt that in a straight choice she would choose Richard, but she continued to hope that she could win her mother's approval. She could not regard filial disobedience lightly, nor the possibility of being ostracised from her beloved family. Mrs Arundell appears to us in the late twentieth century as an austere and forbidding woman, yet her children adored her and found excuses for her even when she meddled inexcusably in their lives. There must, surely, have been some hidden sweetness in her nature to win such affection?

By the time Isabel emerged from the sick-room she had made her decision. If her mother had not come round by the time Richard returned she would marry him come what may. Under the guise of convalescence in good, country air she spent the summer on a farm, this would not have been difficult since both sides of her family were major landowners. But it was not the air and healthy food that dictated her choice of venue. Since she was going to marry 'a poor man' (Isabel's words), she decided she must learn to be independent of servants; she needed to learn how to clean and cook for Richard, and how to run a home, not merely direct how it was to be run. Her hostess was no doubt surprised when Isabel, a young lady from the big house, insisted on enthusiastically sharing all the domestic duties, heavy and light, about the farmhouse. In addition to indoor chores she learned how to make cheese, keep poultry, groom and feed the horses and milk the cows; essential skills, Isabel felt, for the adventurous life she was to lead as Richard's wife.

On her return to London Isabel's first call was on her friends 'Lallah' Bird and her brother George, an eminent physician at 49 Welbeck Street.[2] The Bird and Arundell families were old friends, but Dr Bird had come to know Richard through Isabel and liked him a good deal. The two men fenced together, and shared the same sense of humour. The doctor's laugh was so hearty, apparently, that it turned heads in the street. Isabel had a favour to ask; she wanted George Bird to teach her to fence. When he asked her why, she replied, 'Why? To defend Richard when he and I are attacked in the wilderness together.'[3] But there was probably also an element of wanting to impress Richard, who had told her on numerous occasions that fencing was the pastime he enjoyed most. While Richard toured the United States Isabel made it her business to become a proficient swordswoman. She also filled several scrapbooks with reviews on his *Lake Regions of Central Africa*.[4]

It is not the purpose of this book to draw attention to specific inaccuracies contained in previous biographies of Burton, but an exception must be made at this point for an important instance. The late Fawn Brodie, in her otherwise excellent 1967 biography *The Devil Drives* (arguably the finest modern work on Burton to date) used three and a half pages of text[5] to quote from, and expand, what she referred to as the 'intimate journal' of Richard's passage to Newfoundland aboard the S.S. *Canada*. A page of the faded manuscript is reproduced in her book, where it is captioned incorrectly as 'the only known surviving extracts from Burton's forty-year collection of daily journals'.[6]

A thorough examination of this document (in the British Museum's Manuscript Department) reveals that although it was certainly written by Burton, it is not a journal. It is a satire; a 'spoof' diary, entitled, 'Leaves from Miss A—— B——'s diary'. Composed as the supposed intimate, daily revelations of a flirtatious and silly young lady on the look-out for a husband during a passage on the S.S. *Canada* (the ship on which Burton and Steinhaueser sailed to Newfoundland), it is full of pungently witty references to the two men and their fellow-passengers. This in itself makes the document important biographically, for it reveals Burton's sense of fun. Its *raison d'être* was probably to amuse Steinhaueser (or perhaps Isabel on his return), much as he had written satirical pieces in India to amuse his mess companions:

21st April 1860. Went on Board the B&NA Steamship *Canada* – walked over a plank – crinoline is very inconvenient at times – I hoped that I did show my ankles.

22nd April 1860. Awoke early – a terrific noise upstairs – saw beautiful face opposite me, with hair dishevelled and a lovely glow upon her cheek. Told by the stewardess that it was the looking-glass . . .

30th April 1860. In the evening played backgammon with Mr R[ichard] . . . who is going to be married . . . [he] asked me if I had ever been mesmerised. Said no. We then walked on deck; Mr R said something very pretty about the water . . . when a horrid person whom the gentlemen called Mr Stiggins said loud enough for me to hear 'Bosh'. Memo to ask the Captain what 'Bosh' means . . .

Ms Brodie clearly did not have time to transcribe the document properly in the British Library; she spent only a few weeks in England and time was not on her side.[7] But she used some of the more readable extracts from the manuscript (which she described with feeling as 'so illegible it was almost a code'), to illustrate aspects of Burton's character. Convinced that his comments were his private thoughts, she postulated that it demonstrated his 'responsiveness to strangers, and his frequent fluctuation from interest and quick affection to momentary hatred'. Because Brodie considered the source to be so important, it is the use she made of the material which is crucial here, not the error itself. For example she patently misinterpreted the overt feminine tone of the entries as this short extract from her book, misquoting Burton, shows:

> 'My poplin *did* look so ridiculous,' he [Burton] wrote, like any blushing adolescent . . . 'only imagine that wretch R is a widower with 3 children, one nearly grown up – how could I have thought him handsome. I refused to walk with him this morning and I thought he looked very disappointed.'[8]

Brodie used such material to support her conclusion, which was based on psychoanalytical techniques (*there is no historical evidence*), that Burton had homosexual tendencies. And since subsequent biographers have not only accepted her opinion in this respect but have subsequently quoted it as fact, it should be recognised that – at least in this important instance – her reasoning was flawed in that it was based on a misconception.

Burton's *genuine* journal of the trip, some 34 pages of which are now known to have survived,[9] also begins with the sea voyage on 21 April:

> Having passed over a plank onto the large heavy *Canada*, conspicuous from afar by a vermilion coloured chimney – the distinctive mark of Cunard – we steamed past the 5 miles of docks which line the right bank of the Mersey estuary; past Black Rock . . . and finally with the sun-streaked Welsh Mountains, a distant reproduction of the Spanish Sierra Nevada, bounding the horizon on the left, she stood out with a goodly breeze, into a sea which wanted but little of their incidence . . .[10]

He kept a daily record of distance run, described his fellow-passengers, the crew, food and water rationing. And when he disembarked at Halifax, Nova Scotia, he maintained the same observant record of population, commerce, customs, transport and personalities that are found in all his books. Nor does he neglect personal anecdotes. When invited by a backwoodsman to join him in a drink, Burton responded enigmatically, 'Willingly sir. There are four D's which I never refuse.'

Asked to elaborate, he replied to the delight of his host. 'A Dinner, a Duel, a Drink and a fair Dame!'

Steinhaueser is mentioned often; usually in connection with the practical jokes the two men played upon each other. When they boarded the *Canada*, for example, Richard 'could not but remark that my stature and height were significantly scrutinised by those on the quarterdeck'. He soon discovered the reason, 'it was Stiggins'* first coup – he had been privately insinuating that his companion was the "Tipton Slasher" who was proceeding for a fistic tour to the United States.'[11] He describes how he and Steinhaueser bid for, and purchased, a black Newfoundland puppy, then the principal export of Halifax. And on the subject of sensual pleasures he observes pithily:

> It's all very well the copy-book wisdom which I say talks nonsense, 'A man must eat to live, not live to eat' . . . A youngster may have something better to do. After 40 a man should eat *and* live. After 60 he hasn't a pleasure in life *but* to eat his food; as for that other excitement:
>
> > Twixt sixty and eighty
> > It's all a dead weight t' ye.[12]

He and Steinhaueser spent May, June and July travelling down through 'lower Canada' and on to Boston, New York, and Washington where Richard was 'courteously received by John B. Floyd, Secretary of War'. Floyd warned him that he risked running into an Indian war by his plan to travel to the west coast. A subsequent tour of the Southern states by the two men culminated in a visit to New Orleans.[13]

By the first week in August Richard was alone, contentedly comparing the refreshing air of the mid-west city of St Joseph, Missouri (the western terminus of the railroads) with briskly chilled *Veuve Clicquot*. For the sum of $175 he purchased a ticket aboard a stagecoach bound for Salt Lake City. After a visit there he intended to travel on to the embryo cities of Sacramento and San Francisco before returning to England by sea, via Panama and the Caribbean. Steinhaueser had already left him to return to Europe, and their parting was to be final; he died suddenly, like Dr Stocks, of an embolism. Richard would write:

---

* Elsewhere he spells this Styggins.

It is my comfort, now that he also is gone, to think that no unkind thought, much less an unfriendly word, ever broke our fair companionship . . . He was one of the very few who, through evil as well as through good report, disdained to abate an iota of his friendship, and whose regard was never warmer than when all the . . . world looked its coldest . . . He died suddenly of apoplexy at Berne, when crossing Switzerland to visit his native land . . . I well remember dreaming, on what proved to be the date of his death, that a tooth suddenly fell to the ground, followed by a crash of blood. Such a friend indeed becomes a part of oneself. I still feel a pang as my hand traces these lines.[14]

Although he found enough material about the pioneer territories to fill a book, Richard's three-week stage-coach journey was lacking in any real excitement. Much to his disappointment he never became involved in the Indian wars; his nearest brush was when the stage-coach arrived at Fort Kearney within hours of an action fought there, between the U.S. Cavalry and 'a considerable body of . . . Comanches, Kiowas, and Cheyannes'.[15] Among his fellow passengers were U.S. Cavalry Officer Lieut. James Jackson Dana, his (Dana's) wife Thesta, and their two-year-old daughter. A Federal judge, the judge's son and a U.S. Marshal comprised Burton's fellow-travellers and for the men at least, on that journey, a night spent on clean straw in a barn 'hardly fit for a decently brought-up pig'[16] would become a small luxury.

For travelling Richard dressed in a dark flannel shirt and buckskin reinforced trousers tucked into the top of his leather Wellington-style riding boots. In his broad leather belt nestled a pair of pearl-handled Colt .45 revolvers and a long clasp-knife, and his 'good English tweed shooting jacket' was provided with capacious poacher pockets. A large brown felt hat completed the ensemble, but he also carried a specialised, recommended garment: 'an india-rubber blanket pierced in the centre for a poncho' which with buttons and elastic straps converted itself into a carpet bag.[17] The Danas could not help but be intrigued to learn that in Burton's luggage was a top hat in a tin hat-box, a frock-coat, a silk umbrella and all the accoutrements an Englishman regarded as necessary for visits to VIPs; indeed, he wore them to visit the Mormon leaders in Salt Lake City. Besides this, his luggage included several books, sketching materials, a pocket sextant, tea, sugar, tobacco and cognac, opium and quinine, the latter two he

regarded as 'invaluable when one expects five consecutive days and
nights in a prairie wagon'.[18]

His purpose in visiting Salt Lake was, he said, to add the name of
the 'young rival' to the Holy Cities of the old world that he had
already seen; 'Benares, Rome, Meccah, Medinah'. The Mormons
were not well-regarded by fellow citizens, particularly because of
their practice of polygamy, 'a bestial and barbarous thing' said popular opinion; but although he did not visit as a believer, Richard said,
it was not his purpose 'to make light in others of certain finer sentiments . . . which Nature has perhaps debarred me from enjoying'.[19]
As Brodie points out (she was herself raised as a member of the
Church of Latter-day Saints), Burton was not the only writer to make
the trip to Utah and write about it; two accounts preceded his, in
1855 and 1857 respectively. Half a dozen more, including Mark
Twain ('Mormon religion is singular and their wives plural') would
follow him, but none of the others made the same serious attempt at
examining the theology. And none, says Brodie, 'wrote as sagacious,
and thorough a study as Burton', which was:

> . . . interlarded with lively descriptions of Indian ethnology, includ-
> ing a clinical essay on scalping . . . a detailed account of Indian sign
> language. Along with detailed descriptions of the Sioux and Dakota
> villages are botanical and geological notes, and ironic asides on the
> nature of man.[20]

He concluded that the 'red indian' ('not red at all', Burton wrote,
'more like a Tartar or an Afghan after a summer march') had suffered
rather than gained through contact with the white man; those living
nearest the stage-coach routes had become horse-thieves, liars, drunk-
ards and prostitutes. As a result the race had lost public esteem.
Nevertheless he was as fascinated by the ethnology of the indigenous
people of the Western prairie as he had been of those of Africa and
India. Indeed, he found many similarities with the people of the East.
The American Indian was 'as fond of talking nonsense as the African';
rode bareback, without the cruel ring bit of the Arabs, 'like the
Abyssinian eunuch, as if born upon and bred to become part of the
animal';[21] and when he learned that the Sioux bit off the tips of the
noses of adulterous women he remarked that he had seen the same
custom in Hindustan.[22]

Although he was unable to converse with the Indians he met, he made initial contact by sketching one or two and showing them his work and, not surprisingly, made an attempt to compile a vocabulary. In an essay written in 1930, a nephew of Lieut. Dana claimed that Richard's sketch of an Arapahoe provoked an attack by 'enraged Kiowas' who had to be fought off by Burton and his party aided by 'Wild Bill Hickock' and the gunslinger outlaw Joseph Slade.[23] There was nothing Richard wanted more than to see action of this sort. His guns were daily unloaded, cleaned and primed, so as to be ready when needed. However, since he neglected to mention any event even remotely resembling this engagement in his book, I agree with Fawn Brodie that the story was probably 'greatly exaggerated in the retelling by Dana's descendants'.[24]

Characteristically Richard did not neglect his study of the women he met on the journey, as usual observed in great detail, the favourable recorded with the unfavourable. One woman who wore bloomers (after the style of Amelia Bloomer) was dismissed as 'uncouth . . . with haunches which would only be admired in venison'; another, the inevitable result of the interaction of races was praised; '. . . how comes it that here, as in Hindostan . . . the half-caste is pretty, graceful, amiable, coquette, while the Anglo-Saxon is plain, coarse, gauche and ill-tempered?'[25]

It was with some relief that on 19 August, a few days out of Laramie, that they reached the Sweetwater Valley. Here the weary travellers were invited to 'stay-a-piece' with an English settler, Mrs Moore, whose 'little ranch was neatly swept and garnished, papered and ornamented . . . the table cloth was clean, so was the cooking, so were the children; and I was reminded of Europe by the way in which she insisted upon washing my shirt . . . which since leaving Missouri, had fallen to my lot.'[26] The first shave in a fortnight, followed by a bathe in the Sweetwater River, treading with care to avoid rattlesnakes (on the instructions of the redoubtable Mrs Moore), were not the only events noted in his diary that day. He also wrote of experiencing a 'novel' concept that seemed widespread in the United States: the feeling 'that all men are equal; that you are no man's superior, and that no man is yours.'[27] As they left the little homestead Mrs Dana could not resist pointing out to him one sign of 'demoralisation' in their hostess, however. 'It was so remote that only a woman's acute eye could detect it,' Richard explained, savouring the humour of the moment, 'she [Mrs Moore] was teaching her children to say, "Yes surr!" to every [stage-coach] driver.'[28]

In the late afternoon sunshine of 25 August, he experienced a moment of *déjà vu* when the coach rumbled through the final mountain pass, and the valley containing the Great Salt Lake lay unfolded beneath them. Just as on his pilgrimage in Arabia, Richard was able to stand gazing down upon the city he had travelled so far to see. And just as at Medina he was moved by what he saw; a 'lovely panorama of green and azure and gold, fresh as it were from the hands of God . . . Switzerland and Italy lay side by side . . . touched with a dreamy haze . . . a little bank of rose-coloured clouds edged with flames of purple and gold, floated in the upper air . . . and bounding the far horizon lay, like a band of burnished silver, the Great Salt Lake.'[29]

Richard had researched his subject and, according to contemporary accounts, appeared well-briefed in meetings with Elders. He requested, and was granted, an interview with the Mormon leader Brigham Young. He expected an old man, but he found that the tall and strapping president – looking more like a 45-year-old than his 59 years – was well-preserved and with hardly a grey hair in his thick, light-coloured hair which he wore, 'below the ears with a curl'. He found Brigham Young so lacking in pretension that he could not help contrasting him favourably with certain 'pseudo prophets' he had met, and yet the man exuded a sense of power to which he had obviously become so accustomed that he cared nothing for its display. He was 'affable and impressive, simple and courteous . . . he shows no signs of dogmatism, bigotry, or fanaticism and never once [spoke] . . . of religion . . . His manner is cold, in fact, like his face, somewhat bloodless but he is neither morose nor Methodistic and where occasion requires he can use all the weapons of ridicule to direful effect. He has been called hypocrite, swindler, forger, murderer – no one looks it less.'[30]

They discussed trade, transport, the India question and spoke of the expedition to the African lakes. As the meeting drew to an end, Burton lightened the tone by complaining that he had come all the way to Salt Lake City without a wife, only to find that all the women were married. Waving his hand towards the Lake he chanted, 'water, water, everywhere'; and then turned towards the City saying with mock sorrow, 'and not a drop to drink'. The Prophet laughed, and to Richard's suggestion that he might embrace the Mormon faith, he answered with quiet humour that he thought not, 'I think you've done that sort of thing before, Captain.'[31]

As he wandered about the neat town, Burton sought in vain the 'outhouse harems' he had been told of, 'where wives are kept like stock. I presently found this but one of a multitude of delusions.'[32] To his old friend Norton Shaw he wrote a characteristic letter which, read aloud at the R.G.S., 'gave rise to much laughter'.[33]

Salt Lake City, Utah, September 7 [1860]

My dear Shaw,
    . . . I reached this place about a week ago, and am living in the odour of sanctity – a pretty strong one it is too – apostles, prophets, *et hoc genus omne*. In about another week I expect to start for Carson City and San Francisco. The road is full of Indians and other scoundrels, but I've had my hair cropped so short that my scalp is not worth having . . . I hope to be in San Francisco in October and in England in November next. Can you put my whereabouts in some paper or other, and thus save me the bother of writing to all my friends? . . . I'm travelling for my health which has suffered in Africa, enjoying the pure air of the prairies, and expecting to return in a state of renovation . . .[34]

In his book *City of the Saints* Richard referred to heavy drinking bouts throughout the trip; they usually occurred when he was tired or in low spirits, but sometimes in celebration or friendship.[35] He had begun to drink heavily, but the fact that he wrote about it so openly probably discounts any unhealthy dependence on alcohol. He seems to have regarded it as a manly pursuit, and unselfconsciously discussed the merits of various liquors such as Mexican brandy, and whisky – the strength of which was measured, he said, by the distance a man could walk after drinking it.

The local newspaper declared as Richard left town: 'As far as we have heard Captain Burton is one of the few gentlemen who have passed through Utah without leaving behind him a disagreeable souvenir. The Captain has seen Utah without goggles.'[36] He was, in fact, one of very few who would write objectively about Mormonism:

There is a prevailing idea, especially in England, and even the

educated are labouring under it, that the Mormons are Communists
or Socialists . . . that the wives are in public and that a woman can
have as many husbands as the husbands can have wives – in fact, to
speak colloquially, that they all 'pig together'. The contrary is
notably the case.[37]

In fact, he pointed out, the Mormons regarded adultery as a mortal
sin, and the man who seduced his neighbour's wife was liable to the
ultimate penalty, death at the hand of the injured party, just as in
Somalia.[38]

The rationality of his arguments escaped the reviewers of his *City of
the Saints*; he was severely criticised for his liberal views and accused
of being in favour of a 'disgusting' tradition. In fact, several years
earlier in *First Footsteps*, Richard had made his position on polygamy
quite clear; although he recognised that the practice was 'indispensable
in a country where children are the principal wealth . . . I would not
advise polygamy amongst the highly civilised races, where the sexes are
nearly equal, and where reproduction becomes a minor duty.
Monogamy is the growth of civilisation; [but] a plurality of wives is the
natural condition of man in thinly-populated countries, where he who
has the largest family is the greatest benefactor of his kind.'[39]

For the settlers in Utah, too, he could see a certain logic in
polygamy, 'life in the wilds of America is a course of severe toil; a
single woman cannot perform the manifold duties of house-keeping,
cooking, scrubbing, washing, darning, child-bearing and raising a
family. A division of labour is necessary, and she finds it by acquiring
a sisterhood.'[40] This argument is flawed, of course, since so many
women pioneers *did* manage to do all those things within the frame-
work of a conventional monogamous marriage. But there is no
gainsaying Richard's conclusion that in the final analysis, polygamy
among the Mormons flourished by virtue of the fact that the ethic had
the approval of the women. 'Were they to oppose it, nothing could
preserve the institution,' he wrote.[41] Yet, though women were well
aware of the rules of sharing a man under Mormonism, he continued,
'many converts are attracted by the prospect of becoming wives, especially from places like Clifton,* where there are sixty-four females to

---

*Presumably Clifton near Bristol, in England.

thirty-six males.' One huge advantage of Mormonism was, he said, 'the old maid is, as she ought to be, unknown.'[42]

In fact, stated Burton, the *chief* objection to the polygamy practised by the Latter-day Saints was, in his opinion, its effect on the supreme emotion: romantic love. Where multi-parties were involved, he said, 'Love, that is to say the propensity elevated by sentiment, and not undirected by reason; subsides into a calm and unimpassioned domestic attachment. Romance and reverence are transferred from Love and Liberty to Religion and the Church.'[43]

When he left Salt Lake City he was not travelling alone; he travelled as far as Carson City 'with my old *compagnons de voyage* the judge and the marshal'. There was a brief excitement during their passage through extremely hostile Indian territory, when the driver spotted smoke signals and dashed on to the next station which they found burned down to its chimney-stack. It had been fired in revenge for the killing of seventeen Indians during a skirmish in the previous week. As they drove on, Burton and his companions saw the grim evidence of this battle; Indian corpses dug out of the snow, and partially eaten, by wolves.

In Carson City – then a wild cowboy town where, said Burton, the rule was 'a dead man for breakfast' – he visited the silver mines, watched the huge cattle drives and replaced his stocks of tobacco at three times the prices of those 'back East'. On the evening of 24 October he enjoyed a 'last "liquor up"' and posted out of town on the following day, with the judge's son in his care, bound for the West coast. There was a fast mail-coach to Sacramento which took only two days, but although the high passes were already covered in snow, Richard wanted to cross the Sierra Nevada so he took a week to savour the experience, calling on several gold-mining towns en route.

From Sacramento, 'a mass of shops and stores, groggeries and hotels', he sailed down the river, an eight-hour voyage, to San Francisco 'where a tolerable opera, a superior supper, and the society of friends made the arrival exceptionally comfortable.' He had intended to see the great Redwoods at Yosemite, the Alamaden cinnabar mines, the island at Vancouver and 'Los Angelos'. All these attractions were 'temptingly near. But . . . I was aweary of the way. For eight months I had lived on board steamers and railroad cars, coaches and mules; my eyes were full of sight-seeing, my pockets empty, and my brain stuffed with all manner of useful knowledge.' In the end, faced with the discomfort of further travel in the winter months, he opted to remain for 'ten pleasant days at San Francisco', and was 'grateful to flanner* about the stirring streets, to admire the charming faces, [and] to enjoy the delicious climate'. He spent a lot of time paying social calls, and relishing 'the quiet picture of old Spanish happiness, fast fading from California'.[44]

There are obscure hints that he spent time in the company of women. In San Francisco he became, he said, a 'ladies man'. Later in the trip he would mention a Mrs Seacole who made his stay memorable. Clearly, though he was eager to return home where Isabel awaited him, Richard was not above being attracted to a winsome personality, but nor did he make any attempt to hide his weakness for pretty women; similar understated encounters pepper his other early books. 'The bachelor,' he apologised, 'is prone to backsliding.'[45]

Although the trip across the United States could not be compared with his great expeditions in terms of discomfort and endurance, nevertheless, in those pioneering days it was no picnic either and he was exhausted. So much so that when his host (the British Consul) to whom he was deeply grateful, asked him to give a lecture on his former adventures, he was obliged to refuse. On 15 November, 'I bade my adieux to San Francisco . . . with regret.'

The ship made a brief stop at Acapulco, 'the city of Cortez and Doña Marina, where any lurking project of passing through ill-conditioned Mexico was finally dispelled'. To overcome the disappointment of having to bypass Mexico he found 'philosophical consolation . . . in Mezcal-brandy, the Mexican national drink'.[46] He disembarked at Panama on 5 December. It was dull, dirty and wet, and his hotel reminded him of the Parsee Hotel in Bombay, but he managed to pass the time pleasantly due to the hospitality of the Spanish Consul who also introduced Richard to 'a charming countrywoman, whose fascinating society made me regret my stay there could not be protracted'.[47]

On 8 December he travelled across the isthmus by rail, where he took passage 'across the Spanish Main' to the Caribbean island of St Thomas where he boarded the Royal Mail steamship *Seine* bound for Southampton. The weather, for once, was reasonably kind and during

* saunter (?)

the first nineteen days, as the ship tramped comfortably across the Atlantic, Richard was able to work on his manuscript and sketches. On Christmas Day they were almost within sight of Land's End, but 'Britannia received us with a characteristic welcome, a gale and a pea soup fog which kept us cruising about for three days in the unpleasant Solent and Southampton Water'.[48] He had hoped to be home at Christmas, but the ship did not dock until New Year's Eve.

Isabel, meanwhile, continued her course of preparation for marriage to an explorer. In addition to the practical subjects, she had widened her range of reading in order 'to be able to discuss things with Richard'. But the emotional predicament facing her took its toll and according to her sisters and friends she often looked thin and wretched.[49] Rigid fasting during novenas while she prayed earnestly for divine guidance could not have helped in this respect.

Like her parents, Isabel was a devout Catholic. On both sides of her aristocratic family there were countless examples of how her forebears had suffered for 'the old religion'. It was how she had been raised; her faith was of enormous importance in her life and she believed strongly in the power of prayer. In several biographies of Richard Burton, Isabel has been alternately mocked and traduced for this, as though her faith in some way diminished her as a person. It should be borne in mind by late twentieth-century readers that Christian faith of some persuasion – Anglican, Methodist, Catholic etc. – was intensely important to the *majority* of Victorians. One only has to see the size of churches built during Victoria's reign, and compare them with those built at other times, to recognise that this was an era of dedicated churchgoers. The majority of contemporary pictures of Victorian domestic scenes contain the inevitable crucifix over the bed. Isabel was only unusual in that despite her unusual faith in the Roman Catholic church she married out of it. Again, like the majority of Victorians including Richard, she was also superstitiously credulous. Some biographers have married her religious faith, and her readiness to believe in dreams, omens and sundry incomprehensible experiences, to bolster the image of a silly and ill-educated woman, which patently she was not.

Isabel would never have made the mistake of combining these two canons. Her faith was her bedrock, simple and never questioned. But her interest in the supernatural, like Richard's, was enjoyed and researched in an attempt to understand the inexplicable. She *was*

superstitious, as was Richard. In Isabel's writings she often quoted
dreams and psychic occurrences which appeared to have some physical relevance, or which she regarded as portents. She was certainly
not alone in this. Victorian memoirs and contemporary magazines are
full of similar attitudes to the subject; Richard, for example, took seriously the fact that he dreamed his tooth fell out at the time of Steinhaueser's death. Laurence Oliphant's 'vision' at sea of his father's
death in England ruined Oliphant's life, so convinced was he that his
dream was some kind of mystical portent.[50]

It is fair to state, however, that Isabel was lacking in tact where her
faith was concerned. Even when in company that was patently
Anglican Protestant (that is to say most of English society), she sprinkled her conversation with phrases such as 'the Blessed Virgin' or 'the
Holy Father', as unselfconsciously as she did at home. She placed
huge importance on her 'holy' relics and talismans, and worried if she
mislaid one; she kept candles burning before images of saints. All
these things were (and are) almost guaranteed to create a feeling of
nausea in a conventionally Anglican audience. Richard viewed this
characteristic in Isabel with amused complacency, saying that she
was like someone 'who had strayed from the middle ages'.[51] But he,
also, became deeply upset if he mislaid one of his own talismans, his
star sapphire ring or the medal Isabel had given him, for example.

There was nothing superstitious about Isabel's raw panic when she
read in the newspapers that a Captain Burton had been murdered at
sea. Lacking details, she was in such a state of anguish that even her
mother took pity on her, and took her to interview the clerk at the
mail office where the story originated. 'My life seemed to hang on a
thread until he answered,' Isabel wrote, 'and then my face beamed so
that the poor man was quite startled. It *was* a Captain Burton; murdered by his crew. I could scarcely feel sorry – how selfish . . . and yet
he too, doubtless, had someone to love him.'[52]

Richard had told Norton Shaw that he would be home in
November, but as Christmas loomed there was still no news of him.
Isabel and her half-brother, Theo, were invited to stay with some rel-
atives, Sir Thomas and Lady Clifford-Constable* ('his *first* wife, née

---

* Theo's mother (Henry Arundell's first wife) was formerly Miss Mary Isabel
Clifford-Constable. The two families maintained very close contact after her
death and Henry's second marriage.

Chichester', Isabel was at pains to point out, to distinguish her from the much-married Rosina whom Sir Thomas subsequently married).[53]

On Christmas Day 1860 the whole of the country lay under a seasonal deep blanket of snow which had begun falling on 20 December. The northern counties were particularly hard hit, *The Times* reported, with temperatures down to −12°.[54] Burton Constable, near Hull in Yorkshire, where the Clifford-Constables had one of their country seats, was no exception and the large house-party of twenty-five friends and relatives, including Isabel, found themselves marooned for a week. Clearly things had begun to improve by New Year's Day, for although the snow still lay so thickly that there were many accounts of trains and coaches being stranded in drifts, the London newspapers had started to get through again.

There was a jolly New Year's Day party on the evening of 1 January 1861. Isabel was singing with a group round the piano when she caught sight of that day's *Times* which had been used to prop up the sheet music. She could hardly miss it. The newspaper had been folded at page 7 and in a heart-stopping moment her eye lighted on a report at the very top of the right-hand column:

> The Royal Mail Co's steamship *Seine*, Captain Richard Rivett, arrived in Southampton yesterday. 79 passengers were aboard, among whom were Commander H.T. Evans R.N. from Jamaica, and Captain R.F. Burton from California etc.[55]

She wrote that it was only with the greatest resolution that she was able to continue what she was doing. As soon as she could decently do so she made an excuse and retired to her room, where she spent the remainder of the night packing a large number of cases and 'conjecturing how I should get away – all my numerous plans tending to a "bolt" next morning should I get a letter from him. I received two; one had been opened and read by somebody else, and one, as it afterwards turned out, had been burked [intercepted] at home before forwarding.'[56]

Still, it was no easy matter to bolt. Between the house and railway station lay nine miles of snow-covered lanes; and then there was the matter of her 'heaps of luggage'. She could hardly expect her relatives (and especially not her half-brother) to assist her in rushing to join a lover of whom her parents strongly disapproved. On reflection she decided that precipitous flight was out of the question; she needed a more practical plan. Early on the morning of 2 January, only twelve hours after having seen the newspaper, she 'managed to get a telegram ordering me to London, under the impression that it was of the most vital importance'.[57] How did she contrive this? There were no telephones and there had been no time to contact a sympathetic friend in London by letter. Probably she persuaded a servant to travel to the telegraph office in Hull from where a telegram could be delivered to the house within hours. At any rate she reached London late on 2 January, and was immediately reunited with Richard who had been advised by wire of the time of her train.[58]

At that romantic meeting all her patience, courage, prayer and suffering were repaid when she found his feelings for her had remained constant. Richard opened the conversation at once, speaking firmly, not giving her time to explain that she had already won her battle with family obligation. 'I have waited for five years', he said:

> The first three were inevitable on account of my journey to Africa, but the last two were not. Our lives are being spoiled by the unjust prejudices of your mother, and it is for you to consider whether you have not already done your duty in sacrificing two of the best years of your life out of respect to her . . . you must make up your mind to choose between your mother and me. If you choose me, we marry and I stay; if not, I go back to India and on other Explorations, and I return no more. Is your answer ready?

Her answer was quite ready, she told him without hesitation. '. . . I marry you this day three weeks, let who will say nay.'[59] Isabel wanted to be married on 23 January, because in the Roman Catholic calendar it marked the day of the betrothal of Mary and Joseph. Richard, however, would not agree to this because, he told her, Wednesday the 23rd and Friday the 18th were unlucky for them. So they settled upon 22 January which he regarded as more auspicious.

With the business element of their tryst out of the way, they were free to speculate on the happy domestic scene that now lay ahead of them. They had no money but they had 'youth, health, courage and talent to win honour, name and position'. They also had 'the same tastes and perfect confidence in each other'. Buoyed with this happiness, Isabel completed her journey home on that snowy January night.

'I went straight to my father and mother, and told them what had occurred. My father said, "I consent with all my heart, if your mother consents."' But Mrs Arundell would not be moved. Her answer was 'Never.' It was the moment Isabel had been dreading, but she would not retreat: 'Very well then, mother!' she said defiantly, 'I cannot sacrifice our two lives to a mere whim, and you ought not to expect it, so I am going to marry him, whether you will or not.'[60]

Despite her resolution, the parental opposition spoiled what should have been a very happy period for her. Her brothers and sisters all liked Richard and supported the union, but Mrs Arundell decreed that if the marriage went ahead neither she nor any of Isabel's sisters would attend the wedding; she could not, of course, answer for Mr Arundell or his sons. Isabel saw that this would not only be the cause of a major family schism but an insult to Richard, which his family would be justified in taking to heart. Also – for social reasons and the sake of Richard's future career – even though it might be conducted discreetly, it was important there must be no suggestion of the wedding being seen as a 'hole-in-the-corner' affair. Isabel asked George and Lallah Bird, who were after all old friends of her family, if she could be married from their house 'to throw a cloak of respectability over the affair'. The Queen and the Prince Consort took morality to absurd lengths, refusing even to receive the wife of the Lord Chancellor, Lady St Leonard, because her marriage to Lord St Leonard, *nearly fifty years earlier*, had been an elopement. The Birds willingly agreed and offered to provide a wedding breakfast.

The Arundells were close friends of Cardinal Wiseman, who had once given Richard a letter of introduction to Colonel Hamerton (before he and Isabel declared their love for each other).[61] Isabel called on Wiseman to put the matter before him, telling him that her mind was made up but asking for his advice. 'Leave the matter with me,' said the Cardinal. He asked Richard to call on him, as a result of which Richard gave him a signed agreement that Isabel would be allowed to freely practise her religion, that they would be married in the Catholic Church, and that their children would be raised as Catholics. The Cardinal later told the family that Richard had retorted, 'Practise her religion indeed! I should rather think she *shall*. A man without religion may be excused, but a woman without religion is not the woman for me.'[62] Burton's old college friend, A.B. Richards, would recall that, 'Wiseman, with his large intelligence, said he clearly saw the hand of God in favour of these two people being united and himself procured the dispensation from Rome.'[63]

Henry Arundell, caught unhappily between the wishes of the two strong-minded women he loved, welcomed Wiseman's subsequent visit to his home. He agreed that although he and everyone else in the family approved of the match, his wife was bitterly opposed, but that as she suffered from a tendency to embolism and had been warned to avoid shocks or agitation which might lead to paralysis, she must not be placed in any danger. It is difficult to know how the diagnosis of Mrs Arundell's condition was arrived at; possibly she had already suffered a mild stroke and this would explain Isabel's reluctance to disobey her.

With the Cardinal's approval, Mr Arundell agreed that the best solution was for the marriage to take place quietly without Mrs Arundell's knowledge; with no family from either side present, in fact, and with just a few friends as supporters. In order to avert a family quarrel Isabel would say quite truthfully, but vaguely, that she was going to spend a few weeks with friends. Henry Arundell would break the news to his wife at a time he considered suitable. 'Mind,' he cautioned Isabel, 'you must never bring a misunderstanding between mother and me.'[64] Wiseman undertook not only to obtain papal dispensation for the lack of parental consent, but also to perform the marriage service himself.

Richard's sister Maria were also deeply religious. Her grandfather had been an Anglican clergyman and there was a number of practising clergymen in the Burton family. Indeed, it will be recalled that Richard and Edward had been educated with the intention of their making a career in the Anglican church. Richard told his sister about the forthcoming marriage a few days before the ceremony. Maria Stisted was as dismayed at Richard's marriage to a Catholic as if he had married a woman of a lower class, but since no family from either side were invited she had no opportunity to show any disapproval by refusing.[65]

Isabel's 'Memoranda Book' shows how enthusiastically she had thrown herself into the organisation of the weddings of her sisters, compiling innumerable lists of bridal clothes and trousseau, guests and seating plans. She was a superb organiser and feminine enough to relish every part of the preparations. But in her own wedding arrangements, 'Gowns, presents and wedding pageants . . . had no place.' In order not to give her mother any reason for concern Isabel spent the week previous to her marriage at home, described as 'a prisoner' by Richard who could not even meet his bride-to-be. Isabel spent her time solemnly defining her new course in life:

1. Get Richard a good place
2. Keep him out of debt
3. Don't worry yourself or him
4. Show affection always
5. Keep yourself healthy[66]

She also kept a devotional book which she called *Lamed*[67] into which she wrote her philosophical and theological reasoning, her hopes and dreams. After her death W.H. Wilkins, who completed Isabel's unfinished autobiography, quoted extracts from *Lamed* written by her in the week before her marriage where she outlined her principal hopes: 'Marriage with Richard; My parents' blessing and pardon; A manchild; An appointment; Money earned by literature and publishing; A little society; Doing a great deal of good; Much travelling . . .' Richard was ambitious, she wrote. And though 'some [i.e. her mother] understand Ambition as Title, Wealth, Estates; I understand Ambition as Fame, Name, Power. I have undertaken a very peculiar man . . . we must lead a good, useful, active, noble life . . . and if we have children bring them up in the fear of God . . . [I] pray for a child to comfort me when he is absent and cannot take me . . .'[68]

She also compiled a personal code for herself in her marriage, a revealing document to which she adhered throughout her life with her husband. These reflections show that though she adored him and believed herself loved in return, she recognised less-than-perfect traits in Richard. It also reveals an acceptance that if she did not work at it the marriage might not succeed. Written by a woman who would prove herself to be strong, intelligent and independently resourceful, it is an extraordinary statement of love.

Rules for my Guidance as a Wife

1. Let your husband find in you a companion, friend and advisor and *confidante* that he may miss nothing at home; and let him find in the wife what he and many other men fancy is only to be found in a mistress, that he may seek nothing out of his home.

2. Be a careful nurse when he is ailing, that he may never be in low spirits about his health without a serious cause.

3. Make his home snug. If it be ever so small and poor there can always be a certain *chic* about it. Men are always ashamed of a poverty-stricken home, and therefore prefer the club. Attend to his creature comforts; allow smoking or anything else; for if you do not *somebody else will*. Make it cheerful and attractive, and draw relations and intimates about him, and the style of society (*literati*) that suits him, marking who are real friends and who are not.

4. Improve and educate yourself in every way, that you may enter into his pursuits and keep pace with the times, that he may not weary of you.

5. Be prepared at any moment to follow him at an hour's notice and rough it like a man.

6. Do not try to hide your affection for him, but let him see and feel it in every action. Observe a certain amount of reserve and delicacy before him; keep up the honeymoon romance, whether at home or in the desert. At the same time do not make prudish bothers, which only disgust, and are not true modesty. Do not make the mistake of neglecting your personal appearance, but try to look well and dress well to please his eye.

7. Perpetually work up his interests with the world, whether for publishing or for appointments. Let him feel, when he has to go away, that he leaves a *second self* in charge of his affairs at home; so that if he is obliged to leave you behind, he may have nothing of anxiety on his mind. Take an interest in everything that interests him . . . and if that is only planting turnips . . . try to understand turnips.

8. Never confide your domestic affairs to your female friends.

9. Hide his faults from *everyone*, and back him up through every difficulty and trouble; but with his peculiar temperament advocate peace whenever it is consistent with his honour before the world.

10. Never permit anyone to speak disrespectfully of him before you; and if anyone does, no matter how difficult, leave the room. Never permit anyone to tell you anything about him, especially of his conduct with regard to other women. Never hurt his feelings by a rude jest or remark. Never answer when he finds fault; and never reproach him when he is in the wrong, *especially when he tells you of it*, nor take advantage of him when he is angry; and always keep his heart up when he has made a failure.

11. Keep all your disagreements for your own room, and never let others find them out.

12. Never ask him *not* to do anything – for instance, with regard to visiting other women, or anyone you particularly dislike; trust him, and tell him everything, except another person's secret.

13. Do not bother him with religious talk, be religious yourself and give good example, take life seriously and earnestly . . . do all you can for him without his knowing it, and let your life be something that will win mercy from God for him.

14. Cultivate your own good health, spirits and nerves, to counteract his naturally melancholic turn and to enable you to carry out your mission.

15. Never open his letters, nor appear inquisitive about anything he does not volunteer to tell you.

16. Never interfere between him and his family. Encourage their being with him, and forward everything he wishes to do for them, and treat them in every respect (as far as they will let you) as if they were your own.

17. Keep everything going and let nothing ever be at a standstill: nothing would weary him like stagnation.

Isabel was now 29 years old. Were it not for the fact that she was known to have turned down a number of proposals from men of position and wealth, she would have been regarded by society as having been left 'on the shelf'. But nothing in her attitude suggested fear of being 'an old maid'. She was driven by a love that transcended every other emotion or attachment, except perhaps (though it was never put to the test) her powerful faith.

That she was aware of what marriage to Burton involved is obvious from a correction she made to some notes she had written years earlier. It was a list of the virtues that as a teenager she had striven to cultivate: 'Chastity, Charity, Prudence, Truth, Gratitude (to Christ for joy), Endurance . . .' In the same ink as that used in her pre-marital philosophising she scored through the word 'Chastity'.[69]

On Tuesday 22 January 1861, Isabel was up early and dressed in drab travelling clothes. At 9 o'clock the hackney cab arrived at the front door and she watched her box being loaded on to it. She had sent four trunks to Richard, secretly, in the previous week. It only remained for her to see her parents and wish them goodbye before leaving, but the thought of what she was about to do made her so nervous her legs would hardly support her. Before she left her own room for the last time she knelt and prayed for her parents, 'that they might bless me'. If they blessed her, she told herself, she would take it as a favourable sign that all would come right.

Her parents were still in bed. She kissed her mother first who innocently said, 'Good-bye child; God bless you.' She then went to her father, and knelt down beside him and whispered her farewell. Henry Arundell, knowing all, placed his hand on her head and said, 'God bless you, my darling.' With silent tears coursing down her cheeks Isabel kissed their bedroom door as she closed it. Then she ran downstairs and out into her new life.

19

MARRIAGE
1861

The cab took Isabel to the Birds' house, where she had arranged to change from her travelling clothes. She had no bridal finery; she dressed in a quiet fawn-coloured dress over which she threw a lace cloak, and a white bonnet. Then, composed, and accompanied by the doctor and his sister – 'always our best friends' – Isabel would say of them, she drove to the Church of Our Lady of the Assumption[1] on Warwick Street. Richard, also wearing 'ordinary dress',[2] was waiting for her on the church steps with his best man, Thomas Watson.[3] Three friends (one of whom was Alfred Bate Richards) brought the wedding party to eight. Also waiting was a Registrar, at that time mandatory for ceremonies in mixed marriages.

As they entered the church Richard dipped his hand in the bowl of holy water and made an ostentatious sign of the cross, an act he had presumably learned at the Catholic church in India. The doors were open and the church was full of parishioners at the 10.30 mass, many of whom knew both Isabel and Richard so they were ushered into the sacristy. Here they were informed that Cardinal Wiseman had been taken seriously ill during the night, with the medical condition which would subsequently claim his life, but he had deputed his Vicar-General Dr Edward Hearne to conduct the ceremony as his proxy.

Twenty-six years later Burton's authorized biographer, Francis Hitchman, would use Richard's own words to describe the wedding;

These two people, without any joyful meeting of friends or

relatives, without any bride's trousseau, or presents, or cards, or
cake, or congratulations, with no appointment, nor prospects, nor
fortune, but with true, strong hearts and the consolation of her
father's blessing and her four brothers' approval, were launched
into the world hand-in-hand, to work, to win their way and to live
their lives . . .[4]

A.B. Richards, friend of the groom since their days at Oxford, recalled
that the wedding was 'so romantic . . . destined to be one of the happiest as it was one of the most opposed. The bride's mother was
inveterately prejudiced against her daughter marrying out of the
Catholic pale. No Catholic girl had ever yet done it . . .'* Afterwards
there was a small wedding breakfast at the Birds' house during which
Doctor Bird began teasing Richard about the rumours of his having
killed a man in Arabia, and another in Africa. 'Now Burton, tell me,'
he said quizzically, 'how do you feel when you kill a man?' Richard
looked up and grinned at the physician who had invited such an
obvious answer. 'Oh, quite jolly!' he drawled. 'How do you?'[5]

Richard had a bachelor apartment in the heart of Clubland; Bury
Street, near the junction with Jermyn Street. He enjoyed club life
and the camaraderie of intelligent men and he was either a member
of – or had access to through friends – several clubs such as the
Beefsteak, the Garrick, and the Arundel; the latter was regarded as
'very Bohemian . . . meagerly furnished . . . smoking and drinking . . . shirt sleeves were *de rigeur* in the billiard room, and there
were many Jews.'[6] His great cronies Henry (later Admiral) Murray
and Richard Monckton Milnes lived within a short stroll. A few
days before the wedding Richard had written to Milnes referring to
Isabel. 'By all means,' he said, agreeing to defer a meeting because
Milnes had a minor infection. Their appointment could wait, 'until
I have married the prisoner & settled in the country. I only hope
that you may live till then.'[7] Milnes, in fact, was a champion of
Isabel's, and the two would correspond affectionately until his
death. Her religion seemed no impediment to him; he had always
had the greatest sympathy for Catholics. Not only had he seriously
considered becoming a Catholic in his youth, and studied in Rome

---

*Probably he meant no Catholic girl of the upper classes.

for that purpose, but he numbered Cardinal Wiseman among his greatest long-standing friends.[8]

After the wedding breakfast, Richard and Isabel walked down Bond Street to his apartment in Bury Street; 'a bedroom, dressing room and sitting-room', Isabel noted.[9] Shortly after they arrived, a bachelor friend of Richard's called in unannounced and was taken aback to find Isabel 'seated there, and in every sense mistress of the situation . . . Burton proudly introduced her as "my wife".' They did not send the caller away but invited him to stay and chat and smoke with them. A few days later Richard met his cousin, Dr Edward Burton, in the street. Edward said he was 'surprised to hear the news . . . that you are married.' Richard replied characteristically, 'I am myself even more surprised than you. Isabel is a strong-willed woman . . .'[10] But one of the first things Richard asked of Isabel was an unusual request for a bridegroom. 'There is one thing I cannot do,' he told her, 'and that is, face congratulations. So if you are agreeable, we will pretend we have been married some months.' Isabel was not of a mind to refuse him anything, and for several months Richard continued to convey the impression, whenever asked about it, that they were not newlyweds but had been married for some time.

In the months following their marriage it might be said that, in keeping with her 17-point charter, Isabel held Richard on the lightest of reins. He continued to attend his clubs and visit his friends much as he had done as a bachelor, but this was not an unusual domestic arrangement in their social strata. Many public places were 'men only'. Clubland was one of these and in the previous decade no respectable woman would allow herself to be seen driving through the St James's area. So Richard's enjoyment of male company was not a characteristic that should be viewed out of context. In the mid-nineteenth century, London clubs, learned institutions, universities – all these gathering places were male preserves. Isabel's father and brothers undoubtedly behaved in the same manner.[11]

Richard worked on his book, *The City of the Saints*, every morning. The couple lunched and spent the remainder of each day together, until after dining at 9 p.m. (if they were not dining out), Isabel retired and Richard would go out to meet his friends. She seemed at ease with this arrangement, recognising that he was gregarious and enjoyed male company. Some weeks after the wedding a woman friend asked her in confidence how things were working out; '. . . can you manage him?' 'It works very well indeed,' Isabel replied gaily, 'he always comes home with the milk in the morning.'[12]

Isabel explained why she married Richard; because she loved him, he was her youthful physical ideal, and he personified the adventurous life to which she aspired. For Isabel, her real life did not even begin until after her marriage. But Richard never said why he married Isabel. We know that he enjoyed the company of women, but not abnormally so. He also greatly enjoyed – but again not abnormally so – the camaraderie of men friends and club life, and carousing drinking parties where he could speak openly without the restrictions dictated by female presence. He was a healthy male, in his prime, with a normal libido. He knew the rules of the game; as a bachelor he could sleep with a certain type of woman, but not with one who was suitable to marry.

But he *wanted* a wife and the comforts of a home. We know that he proposed to at least two women before he declared his love for Isabel. Isabel herself acknowledged this; 'as he was between thirty-nine and forty at the time of our marriage it is very natural that it should be so,' she said mildly.[13] His recently discovered unpublished poetry reveals that until his marriage he had a propensity for falling in love with surprising regularity, and even provides the names of some of his inamorata (see Appendix 2). His statement about the drawback to polygamy amongst the Mormons indicates that marriage without romantic love was unacceptable to him. We also have statements from close friends about his behaviour towards Isabel.

'I have never seen a pair,' Justin McCarthy wrote, 'who seemed to be more completely, yet less ostentatiously devoted to each other . . .'[14] And one of their closest friends, Ouida, the novelist, who at the time she wrote it had fallen out with Isabel, stated: 'In the eyes of women he had the unpardonable fault; he loved his wife . . . his love for her was extreme.'[15]

Isabel had no dowry beyond a small dress allowance and some good pieces of inherited jewellery. Her religion, or rather her conspicuous celebration of it, made Richard's marriage to her unpopular with some members of the Burton family, notably his cousin Eliza. And although many contemporary descriptions portray Isabel as an attractive woman with a vivacious personality, she could not be described as a great beauty, nor a seductress. So, if it was not money, outstanding beauty or family pressure, why did Richard marry her?

He could not have been unaffected by her obvious adoration, nor her unswerving support when everyone apart from his family seemed to believe badly of him. She understood him, had always done so according to her instinctive note at their first meeting, 'when he smiled, he smiled as though it hurt him'. In her massive biography of Richard, Isabel would hint at his tendency to depressive melancholy when events overwhelmed him. She, perhaps uniquely, recognised that the physically daring Burton and the brilliant pantologist Burton also encompassed a hypersensitive introvert with strong emotional needs. And that all the planes of this multi-faceted man united to produce an immense drive that would not be denied. Furthermore, she was a practical and active personality; a good communicator, and – as Isabel's authorised biographer succinctly put it – 'the eagle does not mate with the domestic hen.'[16] From surviving, previously unpublished letters we now know that Richard addressed Isabel throughout their thirty years of married life as 'my darling'.[17] When this is added to the testimony of close friends who observed them during that period, it seems, quite simply, that Richard married Isabel because he was in love with her.

His niece, Georgiana Stisted, who in middle age came to dislike Isabel intensely, grudgingly admitted in an error-ridden biography of Burton written after Isabel's death that her uncle's bride was 'a handsome and fascinating woman, then entering her thirtieth year', but she took pains to imply that in marrying Richard, Isabel had not married beneath her. 'Her father, Henry Raymond [Arundell] who with his brother Renfric carried on business as wine merchants in Mount Street was not very prosperous and, as often happens in such case, had a numerous family.'[18] This statement, almost breathtakingly spiteful, was ridiculous of course. Even a junior branch of the Arundell family would have taken precedence over the Burtons and Stisteds in Victorian society, despite the unhappy link with 'trade', and the 'not very prosperous wine merchant' left far more to his heirs than did Richard's father.

Georgiana was not always so sour about Isabel. When Richard and Isabel married, Georgiana was an impressionable 17-year-old, hero-worshipping her famous uncle and viewing his radiant and aristocratic bride as something akin to a princess. A warm correspondence existed between Isabel and Georgiana for many years, in which they called each other by pet-names; Georgiana was 'Dearest

Georgie' and 'Precious child'; Isabel became 'Aunt Puss' and 'Aunt Zoo'. There is even evidence that Richard's sister Maria was inclined to be friendly, but at some point in the first years after the marriage something occurred which set her implacably against her sister-in-law. Georgiana wrote to Isabel, 'imploring me to take her, get her baptised and received into the Catholic Church. I did not do so because it would have been an act of treachery to her mother . . . and dishonourable to take advantage of a girl . . .'[19] Maria presumably considered that Isabel had encouraged Georgiana in the first place, and never forgave her. Isabel wrote that Georgiana was always grateful to her for not taking advantage of her youth. If this was so, her gratitude ended with Isabel's death as we shall see.

On the day after the wedding Richard had thoughtfully written a note to Mr Arundell, which might be shown to Isabel's mother when the news was broken to her. It was carefully composed so as not to compromise members of the family who had been included in the secret:

January 23rd 1861

My dear Father,

I have committed a highway robbery by marrying your daughter Isabel at Warwick St church and before the Registrar – the details she is writing to her mother.

It only remains to me to say that I have no ties or liaisons of any sort, that the marriage was perfectly legal and 'respectable'. I want no money with Isabel: I can work, and it will be my care that time shall bring you nothing to regret. I am, yours sincerely

Richard F. Burton[20]

In fact Isabel did not write to her mother, it was agreed that the news would keep until Mr Arundell's return from a visit to Wardour. However, a few weeks after the wedding, word that Isabel had been seen going in and out of a bachelor lodging in St James became the subject of gossip in matronly circles. When it reached Mortlake and the ear of Monica, Lady Gerard, she and another aunt of Isabel's bowled swiftly into town to inform Mrs Arundell. The result was an agonised letter from Mrs Arundell to her husband in Wiltshire telling him of the 'dreadful misfortune' that had occurred. Isabel could not be at the country house of her friend, as they supposed her to be, she wrote in agitation. Isabel's father, glad of an end to the subterfuge, telegraphed a terse reply: SHE IS MARRIED TO DICK BURTON AND THANK GOD FOR IT.[21] He then wrote a letter of explanation, enclosed the note he had received from Richard, and requested her to send one of their sons to Richard's lodging to invite the couple to visit so that they could be properly received.

Richard and Isabel duly dined with her family at Oxford Terrace. At first the atmosphere was stiff and restrained, with many awkward silences which Isabel attributed to her family's awe of Richard. Over dinner Richard was speaking on some subject and did not notice that the wine had stopped in front of him. One of Isabel's small brothers, allowed as a treat to join the adults for desert, was waiting for his 'doll-tumbler' to be filled. Finally he could not contain himself; 'I say, old bottle-stopper,' he piped, using a family expression, 'pass the wine!' Richard burst out laughing, which caused everyone to laugh and begin talking normally. Mrs Arundell ordered that as a punishment for such appalling behaviour her small son would not take wine, but Richard protested with winning charm, 'Oh, Mother, not on my first night at home!' After that there was a truce and Richard seemed to be accepted. Georgiana Stisted claimed to have heard Mrs Arundell say on the last occasion they met that Dick Burton was 'no relation' of hers.'[22] But Isabel's sister, Dilly, counter-claimed that Mrs Arundell grew to love Richard and even on her death-bed was still relenting her initial unkindness to the couple.[23] Recently-discovered photographs of the Arundell family which include both Mrs Arundell and Richard suggest that at least she tolerated him.[24]

'We had seven months of uninterrupted bliss,' Isabel wrote, and after her long years of unhappiness it must have seemed an enchanted period. But it was not without problems. At first all went well. During the spring months they paid 'bridal visits' to Richard's sister at Dover, and to Richard's aunt, Georgina Bagshaw, and her husband Robert (the M.P.) at their home, Dovercourt, in Essex. They were entertained by Isabel's Arundell cousins at Wardour Castle and her Gerard cousins at Garswood.

Richard Monckton Milnes persuaded Lord Palmerston, who was then Prime Minister, to throw a dinner party in honour of the newly-weds. As the 'bride of the evening' Isabel took precedence over women of all ranks, and when dinner was announced Lord Palmerston gave her his arm and escorted her in, a mark of considerable social significance. This and Isabel's influential connections happily ensured that a cloak of acceptability was thrown over the marriage, enabling her to 'put her name down for a Drawing-room'. To everyone's relief the Queen assented to receive her.

Isabel had already been presented (as a débutante), but it was customary for women of Isabel's class to be presented again shortly after marriage. Isabel's sister, Mrs Dilly Fitzgerald, described how Isabel descended the stairs in full court plumage (feathers were *de rigeur*), 'a beautiful woman, beautifully dressed', she said. Richard, Mr and Mrs Arundell and all their children were gathered in the hall to see her off. If she was expecting fulsome compliments from Richard she was disappointed; he was not a man who wore his heart on his sleeve for anyone to see, though she read approval in his eyes. But as she was going through the door she heard him say softly in French to Mrs Arundell, 'The girl has nothing to worry about!' and she went down to the carriage radiant with pleasure. Lady Russell presented her, and Isabel duly made her curtsy.

There is no way to overstate the value of this type of socialising in respect to Richard's career. Suddenly he was perceived as 'respectable'; suddenly he had influential family connections. Within a month of the wedding Lord John Russell, then Secretary of State for Foreign Affairs, recommended him for a position in the Consular Service. When he attended an interview at the Foreign Office in March, Richard was disappointed to find the position offered was not Damascus as he hoped. Rather, the post was the lowest rung of the Consular ladder, in the 'white man's grave' of West Africa. He was to be Her Britannic Majesty's Consul for the island of Fernando Po in the Bight of Biafra, with responsibility for about 700 miles of the coast of West Africa. He decided to look upon it as a beginning and was quite cheerful about it in his correspondence. Success there should lead to better posts, and meanwhile it would provide opportunities to explore a part of Africa he had not yet seen. One of his cousins, Captain Edward Burton of the Royal Africa Corps, had served in the Gambia in 1840 and had told him about an unusual form of hypnotism that he had witnessed. Richard looked forward to comparing the tribes and customs of Africa's west coast with those of the east.

Isabel was less pleased. The Foreign Office frowned on officials serving in West Africa taking their dependants out there; it was regarded as too dangerous for white women. Few white men, in fact, survived West Africa. A former Consul, Mr George Brand, had died there in the previous June 'after a long and troubled illness called dysentery, very fatal in this climate'.[25] Richard's two successors, one of whom was Charles Livingstone (brother of David), also died of endemic fever. So it was hardly surprising that, though she tried every means she knew to persuade Richard to allow her to accompany him, Isabel's pleading met with his firm refusal. He was consistently scathing of those missionaries he met during his travels in West Africa, who took their wives into intolerable climates.

And suddenly, when everything had appeared to be going reasonably well for them, the Burtons were hit with a series of disasters. First, Richard lost his commission. The administration of the Indian Army was no longer under the control of the old East India Company. Following the Mutiny, the Indian regiments were merged in 1858 with those of the British Army, though in practice the men in control were former senior officers of the old administration. However, new policy dictated a significant weeding-out of malingerers, half-pay officers and the like. Some traditional customs were suspended; the ability of an officer to sell his commission on retirement or resignation was one. Another was the accepted practice that Indian Army officers might accept Foreign Office posts while remaining on the list of their regiment, thus drawing half-pay and maintaining their pension rights. Many Indian Army officers formerly took advantage of this concession; Hamerton and Rigby for example, both of whom received promotions to their army rank while serving as H.B.M. Consuls.

Richard assumed he would be treated in a similar fashion. He had been on the lists of his regiment for almost twenty years and, although less than half of this period had been what might be termed conventional active duty, he had considerably advanced geographical knowledge which the East India Company had traditionally regarded as an acceptable form of Army service.

He was not only wrong in his assumption, but was not even informed of the fact that he had been removed from the Army Lists until he saw in the *London Gazette* that another man had been appointed to his position in the regiment. Incredibly, it seems he had not sought permission of any senior officer before seeking and accepting the post of Consul. By accepting the office of Consul of Fernando Po, he was regarded as having resigned his commission; by definition he therefore forfeited his half-pay and all pension rights. He was, so to speak, starting out all over again, as though he had never served at all and with nothing to show for it but his rank as Captain and a certain fame. The loss of pension seems a gross unfairness and Richard certainly regarded it as such, fighting vigorously but in vain. He sought permission to serve as Consul in a temporary capacity until he might be needed for active service, but this was refused.[26] Officials at the India Office agreed that concessions had been made in a few cases; for Indian Army officers already serving as Consuls in Arabia and in the area of the Indian Ocean. But they felt justified in refusing Richard because West Africa was well beyond the limits of their jurisdiction.

Francis Hitchman, who wrote an authorised biography of Burton with access to many papers that are probably no longer extant, declared, 'his enemies may be congratulated upon their mingled spite and meanness.'[27] But men who made the Army their career, and who served conventionally and consistently, could hardly be relied upon to view with much sympathy the situation of a man who, since 1849, had manipulated Army rules to support long periods of adventure under the guise of paid sick leave and 'expedition furlough'. Especially if those same men also held long-standing grievances against the applicant.

Hoping that Monckton Milnes might be able to speak to some influential contacts on his behalf, Richard wrote from his aunt's house, Dovercourt, where he was recovering from an attack of bronchitis:

20th March [c1861]

Caro Milnes,

Lord J. Russell has offered me the Consulship of Fernando Po – a kind of Juan Fernandez affair off the Bight of Biafra . . . Needless to say that I have gratefully accepted it. The dog that refuses the Governmental crumb shall never be allowed by a retributive destiny to punish with his molars the Governmental loaf.

There is one point however which I have brought to his Lordship's notice. After 19 years service one doesn't like to leave without pension or selling out, so I want to be retained upon the cadre of the Corps. This is the case with Captain Rigby, H.M. Consul at Zanzibar – and was the case with Mr Cole V. Layall at Jeddah – to quote no other names. They may quote against me the obsolete rule that the meridians of the Cape and Egypt are the furthest West points (from India) where an Indian Officer can accept detached employment and yet remain in his regiment – but the objections would be ridiculous in this our day. Only, you see, there is nothing obsolete in official matters. Our camp notes still resemble those of Moses.

The book [*The City of the Saints*] progresses apace – a month will see it among the alumnae of Paternoster Row. Every day brings with it a relief – a little load of matter lifted off my brain ...

> Adieu à bientot (portez vous bien?),
> and believe me ever, Tout à vous
> Hadji Abdullah [in Arabic characters]

Milnes advised Richard to write privately to Lord Russell explaining the matter. He did so, pointing out that there were some officers – still on the lists of Indian regiments – serving in England, which was as distant as West Africa. But Russell had done all he could, or would. And even as they came to terms with this shock to their financial planning, the Burtons were hit again.

Grindlays Warehouse, where Richard had stored all his trunks and belongings, burned to the ground in the spring of 1861. He lost everything: all the Oriental manuscripts and books on which he had spent 'every spare rupee' while in India; the journals of his travels, specifically those of his years in India which formed the basis of his books on Sindh and Goa etc; trunks full of Oriental and African costumes and mementoes that he had collected over twenty years of travelling. He was stunned by the magnitude of his loss which he continued to regret until his death. 'As always,' said the loyal Isabel, 'he saw the comic side of a tragedy as well as the pathetic.' She recounted how the clerk at Grindlays, 'when he saw Richard's distress, asked sympathetically if he had lost any plate or jewellery. Hearing the reply, "No", Richard experienced a wry amusement at "the change in his face from sympathy to utter surprise that I should care so much for any other kind of loss".'[28] To make matters worse, Grindlays, who were paid in advance up to the date of the fire, refused to recognise that the items lost had any intrinsic value, and though they themselves were insured they refused to compensate Richard.

The third setback was to learn from Norton Shaw that Speke had written to the R.G.S. and others, still intent on damaging Richard as much as possible. Indeed, now that he had received and read Richard's *Lake Regions*, he was more virulent than ever. 'That wicked book,' Speke's mother wrote, '. . . so cruelly unjust . . . as he is unable to defend himself.'[29] Speke, having received a copy of *Lake Regions* through Rigby, now resolved to write his own book telling 'everything' about the expedition, which Blackwood astutely agreed to publish.

In fact, it might be said that the first and third setbacks experienced by the Burtons at this time were inter-related. Speke's campaign was not a solo affair. In the previous November Rigby wrote a brilliant, and most damaging, 3,000-word letter to the Governor at Bombay, on his own behalf and that of Speke, setting out 24 points of serious contention. '*The Lake Regions of Central Africa*', he said, 'contains so many gross calumnies, and imputes to myself and other persons such improper motives that I trust I may be excused for troubling His Excellency with the following statements . . .'[30]

He stood accused, he said, of misplacing the *Zanzibar* manuscript which Burton had given to Mr Frost before departing on his expedition. 'He [Burton] states that I was actuated by "private malice under the specious semblance of public duty,"' Rigby wrote, 'and deems proper to publish my official letter on the subject . . .' Rigby's defence was strong and well constructed. It was supported by two letters written by Speke aboard the *Dragon of Salem* after he had left Zanzibar in 1860, bound for Aden, in which he requested Rigby to investigate his charges that Burton had cheated their bearers.[31]

Rigby's letter was received at Government House in Bombay at the same time as one from Mr Frost, complaining that in his book Burton had 'distinctly charged him with having caused the death of Colonel Hamerton by improper medical treatment and . . . with having knowingly made away with a packet entrusted to his care.'[32] A further complaint was received from Captain Playfair stating that Burton had grossly misrepresented 'the proceedings of the Authorities at Aden'.[33]

In fact, though the points made in these letters could have been addressed and justified by Richard (the lost manuscript, for example, did turn up after a decade of having been pigeon-holed in Bombay), he was not invited to answer the accusations by either Government

House at Bombay nor the India Office. The reason seems obvious.
Not content with printing correspondence between himself and Rigby
in the appendix of *Lake Regions*, Richard had also published a series
of letters between himself and the Indian Government. This consisted
of his comprehensive report warning of the potential dangers in the
Red Sea, together with the letter of 'severe censure' which this had
earned him, and the details of the subsequent massacre at Jeddah in
which every Christian in the city, including the British Consul, was
murdered. Some highly placed men in the Indian Government were
made to look fools; which was Richard's intention of course. He
never seemed to learn that it was not possible to publicly bait his
superiors without making enemies of them.

Rigby's, Frost's and Playfair's complaints were officially ratified,
just as the question of Richard's consular appointment was being discussed.[34] This matter was harmful enough to Richard's career, even
without the innuendo which always hung around his name. The
Foreign Office had close links with the India Office; both organisations were run by men from an almost incestuous network of public
schools and upper-class families. What was 'known about' in one
organisation was also known about in the other.

Richard's disregard for protocol, and his doubtful reputation,
would hardly have been regarded as assets by the Foreign Office.
However, he *was* given an appointment which, as a friend rightly
says, would surely not have been the case had anything really serious
been known against him:

> Men at the FO . . . used to hint dark horrors about Burton, and cer-
> tainly justly or unjustly he was disliked, feared and suspected in
> English political and social life, not for what he had done, but for
> what he was believed capable of doing, and also for that reserve of
> power and that unspoken sense of superiority which the dullest
> and the vainest could scarcely fail to feel in his presence. Beside him
> most other men looked poor creatures . . . It was impossible for
> those who valued his qualities, . . . ever to discover the secret of the
> black cross which was placed against his name in Downing Street.
> That there was one was never denied. That it could be placed there
> for any grave offence seemed impossible in view of the fact that he
> was retained on active service until the day of his death . . . If he had
> done anything greatly incorrect he should have been dismissed for

the offence and its form declared. If he had done nothing he should not have been subjected to the injury of whispered calumny by the hints of the department that employed him . . .[35]

Whatever the truth behind the hearsay, it seems clear that as soon as the mandarins of the India Office saw an excuse to get rid of Burton, they did so with all possible speed. From a historical perspective few will dispute that to a large extent Burton brought this on himself by his inability to curb his outspoken opinions. The men at the Foreign Office would have realised immediately that they had inherited a difficult personality. In the light of Lord Russell's personal recommendation, Burton had to be found something. With his knowledge of the customs and languages of the East he would have been of incalculable value in Arabia, Egypt or India, but only if he was also reliably conventional. It would not do to have a British Consul making public every petty disagreement he might have with London, or 'going native' in a sensitive arena. Perhaps, in the light of the mortality rates of previous Consuls in West Africa, they hoped that nature would relieve them of the problem.

Speke had by now cobbled together a 'defence' of the tracts in Richard's book to which he took exception, and sent it off to John Blackwood. The letter which accompanied it was typical. He hardly wrote a letter from Africa that did not contain some pejorative paragraph concerning Burton, for example his ludicrous claim to Shaw: 'I don't wish to say anything about Captain Burton. I taught him at his own request the geography of the countries we traversed, and since he has turned my words against me.' With Blackwood he had fewer reservations:[36]

I could stand it no longer so I have let fly at Burton's eye, and I think he has got it as richly as he deserves. I should only like to see your opinion when you read the defence. Old Grant says the man ought to be hung, an opinion I must say I long ago arrived at. What a vile, dastardly wretch he is not to have had it out with me at home when we were there so many months together. But as he has now taken up the pen instead of the pistol we will have it out so – he has brought it on himself. Rigby tells me an amusing story about Burton's first *entré* into Yankee land, when at Salem he met with an editor whose writing Burton had abused in his book and no

sooner did he land than the said Editor called him out and B vanished the same night – how like him!!!*

Whatever the rights and wrongs in the matter of Richard's removal
from the Army Lists, the result was the same. He was left with nothing to show from 19 years of service in the Indian Army which
should, at the least, have provided a pro rata pension for his retirement years. His new appointment brought an income of £700 a year,
of which £500 was salary and £200 was office expenses.[37] He had
inherited a sum from his father from which, after having settled all his
outstanding debts, he was apparently left with some £4,000 which
'prudently invested', said his niece, 'brought in about £200 a year'.[38]
Certainly, the half pay of £300 a year that he had lost would have
been useful. The Bank of England indicates that £1 in 1861 had the
buying power of about £37 in the 1990s. This makes Richard's
earned income of £700 worth some £26,000 in today's terms – the
salary of a junior to middle executive.

There is some doubt as to Richard's worth at the time of his marriage. In her biography of her uncle, Georgiana Stisted stated that he
inherited £16,000 from his father (currently c. £592,000). Joseph
Burton's will, however, reveals that he left nothing to his sons.[39] His
entire estate was placed in trust for his two grand-daughters
Georgiana and Sarah. It is possible that the will was made in expediency; Richard was in East Africa at the time and there was
considerable doubt of his safe return. Possibly there was some deed of
family arrangement involved, whereby the Stisteds made over the
sum of £16,000 following Richard's safe return home. Assuming this
is so, where had it all gone?

We know he paid off the outstanding expedition debts which
totalled almost £1,500. But Speke's brother Benjamin subsequently
reimbursed £600 of that, paying it into Richard's account at
Grindlays while Richard was in Salt Lake City.[40] There was also the
matter of some £400 from the Berbera losses. It is reasonable to
assume he had some debts in London, as did most young officers: bills

---

*I have not been able to reconcile this story with anything in Burton's books
prior to, or during, his trip to North America. It was probably no more than
another rumour. However, the behaviour Speke describes here seems highly
unlike Burton who was always spoiling for a duel.

from tailors, club subscriptions, the cost of carriages, entertaining, books, sundries. But even supposing that these had exceeded his back pay by a generous £2,000, the difference – between his patrimony, his known debts and the sum of £4,000 his niece claimed he retained for investment – is more than £8,000. In fact it is not known how Richard spent the missing money (assuming it ever existed); one modern biographer suggests that he may have lost it gambling while travelling on a Mississippi riverboat.[41] There is no evidence that Richard ever gambled;[42] though there is no evidence to the contrary, either. But it is not surprising that Isabel wrote an important part of her wifely duties was to 'keep Richard out of debt'.

As a couple the Burtons always lived well, consistently in excess of their income. Often during their marriage they were virtually penniless, living from quarter day to quarter day when Richard's salary was paid into his account. When, as happened on a number of occasions, some distant relative of Isabel's died and left her a small legacy, or when her father died and left her a substantial sum, they splurged rather than saved. But there was always money for travel and multi-course meals, and when they lived in London they moved in a high-rolling strata of society. Isabel, who loved beautiful clothes and had to dress appropriately in order to mingle with the country-house set, has been accused of being the extravagant partner.

This charge of extravagance in Isabel is not borne out by historical facts, rather she is to be congratulated on her thriftiness and financial management. During his life Richard was never without his favourite cigars, wines and brandy. His best-selling *Arabian Nights* grossed £16,000, and when he died half a decade later there was less than £200 of that money left. Yet somehow, during the following five years Isabel managed by her own writing and good management of Burton's literary estate to accumulate a personal fortune of £11,766 to hand on to her heirs.[43]

Still, while they were living at the bachelor apartment and being entertained at country houses their expenditure cannot have been exceptional. The important thing was that they were happy, and the marriage was working. Richard completely accepted Isabel's religious obligations; indeed, when one of her brothers died after his horse fell on him, Richard handed her £5 and asked her to have a mass said for the dead youth.

At first Isabel complied unwillingly with Richard's request to be allowed to hypnotise her. 'Richard was a great mesmeriser,' she wrote, explaining how he could put a child into a trance and send it to fetch a book or some object from another part of the house:

> He always preferred women [subjects] and especially of the blue eyed, yellow-haired type . . . he began with me as soon as we married; but I did not like it, and used to resist it, but after a while I consented. At first it was a little difficult, but when once he had complete control, no passes or contact were necessary; he used simply to say, 'Sleep,' and I did. He could also do this at a distance, but with more difficulty if water was between us . . . I could not resist . . . but he never allowed anyone else, nor did I, to mesmerise me. Once mesmerised, he had only to say, 'Talk,' and I used to tell him everything I knew . . . he never took a mean advantage of what he learned in that way, and he used laughingly to tell everybody, 'It is the only way to get a woman to tell you the truth.' I have often told him things I would much rather keep to myself.[44]

The popular name then for hypnosis was 'Zoolectricity'; hence Isabel acquired another nickname. Since childhood she had been known – and generally signed her letters to intimates as – 'Puss Arundell', and later 'Puss Burton'. She even labelled herself 'Puss' in her numerous photo albums, and she was known throughout the Burton family as 'Aunt Puss'. Now Richard gave her his own pet-name, 'Zookins'. She called him Dick, and 'Bird', presumably a corruption of 'dicky bird' from the Victorian music-hall song. In letters to the Burton family, at this point, she began to sign herself 'Zoo' and refer to Richard as 'the bird'.

It is impossible to state with any certainty what their sexual relationship was. In the unlikely event that anything touching on the subject was ever written by Richard or Isabel, we can be sure that it would not have been allowed to survive by Isabel's protective sister and executrix, Dilly Fitzgerald. Some biographers have suggested that there was no sexual relationship. Extensive study of the vast amount of Burtoniana, including previously unseen surviving correspondence between Richard and Isabel and the statements of their closest friends, suggests that they enjoyed a warm and loving relationship.[45] Further, given this close relationship, the intensely intimate dialogue they shared, Isabel's consistent worship and Burton's interest in erotic

techniques, it seems likely that their sex life was both mutually satis-
fying and continuously interesting.

Writing as an older woman, Isabel's comments on the subject of sex
and women echo some of Richard's; and despite her public statements,
written for the sake of her reputation, that she did not read the erotic
sections of his famous works, *The Arabian Nights* and *The Scented
Garden*,[46] in her private papers she admitted that she had done so. In
her published writings she wrote as a sexually content woman, secure
in her marriage, even when other areas of her life – finance, and
Richard's career and health – were doubtful. It is inconceivable that a
man of passion such as Burton, and a passionate woman such as
Isabel, could have lived together so happily as they clearly did if the
most intimate part of their relationship had been unsatisfactory. Isabel
was no prude. In old age she shared Richard's wry amusement, though
perhaps at a different level, at the story of the note a bridegroom
found on the pillow beside his chloroformed bride on her wedding
night: 'Mama says you're to do what you like.' It was probably apocryphal, but it was in wide circulation and is therefore indicative of a
social attitude which Richard chose to address seriously in his writings:

> Moslems and Easterns in general study and intelligently study the
> art and mystery of satisfying the physical woman . . . The mock
> virtue, the most immodest modesty of England and of the United
> States in the 19th century, pronounces the subject foul and ful-
> some . . . Hence it is said abroad that the English have the finest
> women in Europe and least know how to use them.[47]

These are not the words of a man in a celibate marriage.

In the months before he was due to leave for Africa, the couple
paid a succession of visits to grand country houses: Bulstrode, home
of the Duke of Somerset; Broadlands, home of the Prime Minister,
Lord Palmerston; Knowsley, home of Lord Derby, close friend and
neighbour of Isabel's uncle, Lord Gerrard. Their last such invitation
was to Fryston; for Isabel it was to be the first of many visits:

2 August [61], Worthing

My dear Milnes,

Excuse my not having written before, your note has just reached
me. Mrs Burton will be delighted to come down on the 12th and

begs that you will mention it to Mrs Milnes. We shall be with you about 4 p.m. When we meet you shall hear about F. Po. They have run me to grass – I shall shake the Indian dust off my feet. It is impossible to continue in a Service which writes such wonderfully bad English . . . Yours in the haste of correcting proofs,

Very sincerely.

R.F. Burton[48]

The couple were staying with Isabel's family at a seaside villa when this note was written, having given up Richard's bachelor apartment at the end of the spring quarter. During their stay in Worthing Richard decided to pay a visit to one of his cousins, Samuel Burton, who lived at Brighton. He promised to take the last train and return by 9 o'clock and, since his promises were always kept, Isabel worried when he did not arrive. He had in fact caught the last train, but had fallen asleep and not woken until he was 20 miles past Worthing. Unable to find transport so late, and knowing Isabel would be concerned, he set out with the aid of a pocket compass and jogged back, arriving at 1 a.m. She was very touched that out of consideration for her he had not simply taken a room for the night and caught the early train next morning.

On 12 August, with the days of their precious time together fast running out, the couple travelled up to Fryston. Their fellow house-guests were Thomas Carlyle,[49] J.A. Froude (Carlyle's biographer), the Hungarian traveller Vambery, and Algernon Swinburne. All those present recalled the brilliance of that gathering when Richard and Vambery sat cross-legged on cushions swapping stories of their adventures in the East, and Richard, speaking alternately in Persian and English, told tales from *The Arabian Nights*, recited Fitzgerald's lovely rendering of *Omar Khayyám*, and chanted the Islamic call to prayer. Swinburne was enthralled.

This was Swinburne's second meeting with Burton. The first had been on 5 June, shortly after the publication of Swinburne's first book, *The Queen Mother and Rosamund*, when Milnes had invited them both to one of his famous Thursday breakfasts at 16 Upper Brook Street. 'To hear Milnes at his best,' it was said, 'it was necessary to hear him at the breakfast table.'[50] Swinburne would be a lifelong friend of both men, but Milnes would be castigated for the introduction since it was generally held that Richard corrupted the young poet by encouraging his heavy drinking.

Eventually the days that Isabel found so sweet came to an end. Richard delayed his departure as long as possible, sending sick notes, pointing out that it was the 'heart of the unhealthy season' in Biafra. Finally, though, he was ordered by the Foreign Office to 'proceed at once' to his post.[51]

The couple spent a week in London before taking the train to Liverpool. In that time Richard completed his last-minute preparations, polished up the proofs of his latest book, and took his leave of his cronies. From Liverpool's famous Alelphi Hotel, he wrote to Milnes on 23 August:

> I am off tomorrow . . . so this shall not be a long document. The proofs of the 'Saints' have been corrected, and my wife will take them up to town the day after tomorrow . . . My wife is fretting herself into a fever, which as you may imagine greatly adds to the pleasure of departure. I have spent the day calling upon the commercial Princes . . . each received me according to the nature of what he wanted me to do . . . I see that my chums will be Nubies and my friends Fans for some years to come. Du Chaillu showed no end of gratitude,* came up from Scotland P.D.Q. accompanied me to the R.R. [Railroad] and *en partant* thrust into my hand something from which he asks me to drink to his health – when opened it showed up a neat silver mug! . . .

It is not to be wondered at that Isabel was fretting herself into a fever. She had waited so long and now, after only a few months, she was having to part from Richard. Moreover, he was going to a situation where their letters would take up to a month to arrive, where he might be carried off by any number of tropical ailments. And, she wrote, 'knowing he had Africa at his back, [I] was in constant agitation for fear of his doing more Explorations into unknown lands.'[52] Richard was as sentimental as a woman where his family was concerned and had always hated partings. Indeed, his departure for West Africa was the first time since he left for India as a young subaltern that he allowed a loved one to see him off. He gave Isabel permission to come to the ship only after exacting her promise that she would not cry and thus 'unman' him.

---

*Burton had defended Pau du Chaillu's paper on gorillas in a letter to *The Times*, 8 July 1861.

It was a dreadful morning with a strong wind and blustery rain. From the North landing stage the couple boarded a crowded little tender which took them out to the steamer moored to a floating pontoon. The other passengers, about eighteen West African merchants, swirled around the new Consul hoping to make a good impression. One man in particular stuck to Richard's side so that the couple had no opportunity to speak privately ('How I hated him,' Isabel raged in her diary). She went below to see Richard's luggage stowed, unpack his things and make his cabin as comfortable as she could. Before she knew it, all visitors were told to disembark immediately; there was only the briefest of time for a farewell. 'My whole life and soul was in that goodbye,' Isabel wrote, 'and I found myself on board the tug, which flew faster and faster from the steamer.' She had kept her promise not to cry in his presence, but as the waters widened between them she saw Richard put a white handkerchief to his face.[53] As soon as she reached the shore she drove furiously to the last point of land from where she could watch the ship steam out of sight.

Nor was Richard unaffected by the parting. He wrote in his next book, *Wanderings in West Africa*: 'A heart-wrench – and all is over. Unhappily I am not one of those independents who can say, *Ce n'est que le premier pas qui coûte* . . . comes the first nightfall on board outward-bound, the saddest time that the veteran wanderer knows . . . we cut short the day by creeping to our berth, without even a "nightcap", and we do our best to forget ourselves and everything about us.'[54]

For Richard a new challenge lay ahead. Isabel, once she shrugged off her abject misery, also had some consolations. The seven months she had just spent with Richard were an 'oasis . . . the happiest of my life', she wrote in her diary. 'Even if I had no other, it would have been worth living for.'[55] At least during this absence she could help Richard. She could work on his behalf; he had left her in charge of seeing his latest book through the stages of publication, and he had given her several tasks. She could now receive his letters freely, and she was to go out to see him – though not immediately; he would write and tell her when he thought it safe – but she was to go to meet him in Madeira or Tenerife during his first leave.

With these thoughts to assuage her misery she took the train to London, where she was to have her old room at her parents' house, near Hyde Park, in order to save money.

20

CONSUL IN WEST AFRICA
1861–1863

Burton's books of each of his journeys invariably ran to two volumes crammed with details and facts, and in a one-volume biography it is only possible to touch lightly on his wealth of experiences. His published accounts of his three years as Consul in West Africa, for example, ran to nine hefty volumes;[1] and these were in addition to magazine articles, letters, and a number of papers for organisations such as the R.G.S. and other learned bodies.

In his writing about West Africa, his imperialism seems more aggressive than in his other works, possibly because of his official role there. His remarks about black Africans *are* bigoted, but it should be remembered that he was capable of bigotry against members of any race, including his own. It was ignorance he railed against most often, rather than colour or creed, and in this he was unusual for his time. His reviewers nitpicked over his opinions on polygamy and his philosophies; his contemporaries did not call him a bigot, nor a racist, because his views were not perceived as being such. It is impossible to apply the *mores* of the late twentieth century to that of another era with any real relevance.

Wanderings in West Africa, the first of his works during this period, is an edited version of his diary of the voyage to Fernando Po. Writing in the third person (he published the first edition anonymously as 'An FRGS' and referred to himself throughout as 'the Consul'), Burton described the voyage which took just over a month, with stopovers at 24 ports en route. Typically, everywhere the ship visited – Madeira, Tenerife, Bathurst, Sierra Leone, Cape Palmas, the Gold Coast, the Grain Coast, Lagos (in the Bight of Benin) etc., was examined and minutely detailed by him; the geography, inhabitants and customs dissected and set out. He had read all the books available on the route and found them wanting, he said, so he wrote the book he would like to have been able to purchase, with information he considered would be useful to future travellers. Immediately the ship dropped anchor Burton was off exploring, questioning, collecting, sketching. Once his hired horse threw and injured him, but he considered he had 'a pretty escape' for it was a Friday, his unlucky day, and it might have been far worse.

As usual he devotes a good deal of text to the women he saw. In Tenerife, for example, he praised the Spanish women: 'There is nothing more enchanting than the women of Tenerife . . . But,' he said, using the opportunity to pay a compliment in print to his auburn-haired, blue-eyed wife: '. . . I will confess that one soon wearies of black eyes and black hair, and that after a course of such charms one falls back with pleasure upon brown, yellow, or what is better than all, red-auburn locks and eyes of soft limpid blue.'[2] He could never resist sarcasm. Describing how, in Accras, when girls reached marriageable age they were 'taken home, kept from work, highly fed, well dressed and profusely ornamented' before being exhibited in the town with 'the advertisements of finery, dancing and playing,' he could not resist adding 'thus, it is pretty much the same in barbarous . . . Africa as in civilised England.'[3]

The regular steamer service to West Africa had then been established less than five years. In 1857, a mixed expedition – missionary, scientific, naval and commercial – attempted to establish a settlement at what is now Port Harcourt, near the confluence of six rivers: the Niger, New Calabar, Bonny, Old Calabar, Cameroons and Malimba rivers, then known collectively as 'the Oil Rivers'. The first mission failed due to a combination of illness and an inability of the members to work for a common purpose, each organisation working in its own interests. But successive shiploads of optimistic entrepreneurs, mainly Liverpool merchants, had continued to seek their fortunes in the region. Such was the situation when Richard arrived there.

Among the inhabitants he met a Muslim, Selim Aga, whom he instantly hired as his personal servant. Selim had made two expeditions up the Niger as steward to the Captain on the *Day Spring*, one of the merchant ships working out of Lagos; what is more he had once been in the service of Richard's old friend, John Thurburn, in Alexandria. Selim, with his 'lamp-black skin and Semitic features', was an able individual, he could keep accounts, stuff birds and make an excellent turtle soup. He was at Richard's side during all of his travels in West Africa and though he is mentioned only a handful of times in Richard's books, the words, 'I was accompanied by my steward, Selim Aga . . .' occur frequently in his reports to the Foreign Office.[4]

The Bight of Benin, traditionally called 'the Slave Coast', had a good number of missionary stations. The Portuguese had begun the missionary process in the fifteenth century, converting large numbers of the populace to Christianity by the simple expedient of offering the King a European wife in exchange for souls. The volunteer nun who fulfilled the Portuguese half of the bargain 'ought,' said Richard, 'to have been canonised, but it is not known that this deed of self-sacrifice ever received any special notice from the Father of the Church.'[5] Richard's first experience of a Christianised African decided his attitude towards the missionaries. He offered the man sixpence to carry his bag and the man demanded double because it was Sunday and 'he would be breaking the Sabbath'. One can see Burton's lip curling in his account of this transaction. 'I gave it readily,' he wrote scornfully, 'pleased to find that the labours of our missionaries had not been in vain.'

The natural arrogance of the West African irritated Burton; he regarded it as 'insolence', and blamed three centuries of European influence. He was amazed to find that use of the word 'nigger' was illegal.[6] 'How much better is the heart of Africa than its epidermis,' he commented. 'Only the ignorant can boast of the freedom we have given to the African. Freedom, indeed, we should have given, but it ought to have been more qualified to suit their capacities.'[7] He viewed balefully the fact that West Africans were allowed to travel as first-class passengers between ports, and to join white passengers in the dining room. 'What does one think of a dusky belle, after dropping her napkin, saying to her neighbour, "Please Mr Officer-man pick up my towel" . . . And the screaming demands of an African who could not wait his turn to be served with soup? It is a political as well as social mistake to permit these men to dine in the main cabin which they will end by monopolising,' he warned. 'A ruling race cannot be too particular over these matters.'[8]

But 'Christianised' or not, the region produced one of the most cruel and brutal societies Burton ever encountered, anywhere in the world. Human sacrifice was still common. In 1842 a British Parliamentary Report recorded that a small girl was sacrificed annually to placate the rough seas off the mouth of the Bonny River, and in 1861 Burton thought it 'more than probable that the sacrifice is still privately performed'.[9] As the ship prepared to run into the mouth of the river, they had to cross a bar over which 'the breakers – roaring, foaming and bursting everywhere ahead of us and on both sides – looked uncommonly threatening', but the Captain kept to the charts laid down by the Navy and Richard found it, 'not unduly violent: perhaps the annual little girl had just been sacrificed to it.'[10] The port of Bonny had been for three centuries 'the great slave market of the Bights, seldom exporting less than 16,000 souls a year'. This traffic all but ceased during the middle of the nineteenth century after the British blockaded the coast, and when Burton arrived Bonny had become the centre of the palm-oil trade (hence the name 'Oil Rivers') worth over one and a half million pounds sterling a year.[11]

The people of Benin, Burton said, took 'a physical delight in cruelty to beast as well as to man'.[12] He spent only a few days in the area, but the brutality he witnessed or learned of in that short space of time makes difficult reading; a thief could expect to have his hands nailed to a cask, for example. A woman caught in adultery was tied at full stretch to a beam and lashed, with cuts so savage that the 'flesh stripped away as though from a knife wound', but this was a lenient treatment; the more usual punishment was dismemberment, with the pieces thrown to sharks. A woman who gave birth to twins was banished and the children killed. In almost every town he encountered the revolting sight of 'dead and dying animals fastened in some agonising position'. Later, his reports included further incidents such as the day he saw a slave lashed to a keg of dynamite and blown up. 'When he descended,' Burton wrote, 'his brains were beaten out with clubs and sticks, even the women and children joining in the pastime gleefully, as boys killing a rat.'[13]

Almost 140 years after Burton found brutality and a staunch reliance on voodoo and magic spells, 'fetish stalls' are still a part of everyday life in Benin. It is an area where the casual tourist has not yet

penetrated in any numbers, but in 1996 a BBC Television documentary team found that sections of street markets were still given over to
rows of these stalls. Smiling traders were filmed offering a vast and
weird selection of fetish goods ranging from plants and 'magic' carving to hallucinogenic drugs, preserved parts of animals such as
orang-utangs and gorillas, and even desiccated and skeletal human
remains, including those of infants – the latter apparently vital if a
spell is intended against a human enemy.

Apart from the ever-present danger of dysentery, the coastal areas
of the Bights of Benin and Biafra (irrevocably associated in the twentieth century with media pictures of pot-bellied starving children)
were subject to periodic epidemics of typhus and yellow fever which,
said Richard, 'clears off almost all the white population'.[14] Between
March and July 1862, in Burton's first year as Consul, 162 out of
the population of 278 Europeans died in just one of the epidemics.
Burton attributed his own survival to the half-bottle of port he drank
habitually, every day, while in the tropics.

The S.S. *Blackland* departed from Bonny at 4 p.m. on 26
September. She carried a full complement of homeward-bound
passengers collected from ports within the Bights. Fernando Po was
the furthest port of call, and from there the *Blackland* sailed straight
across the Gulf of Guinea to the Ivory Coast, missing the Bights.
Early on the following morning her passengers crowded the ship's
rail to gaze at the huge conical peak which dominates the island of
Fernando Po. This was to be Richard's base for the next few years.
There was no port as such; the ship dropped anchor in a small
semi-circular bay, Clarence Cove. The narrow beach was backed by
steep banks of yellow clay which had to be climbed by ladders. At
the top was a row of buildings, the largest of which was the
Consulate, surrounded by palms, cottonwoods and cedars. From a
distance it looked quite imposing; closer inspection showed the
dwelling to be almost uninhabitable, with leaking roof and rotted
timbers. For the travel-weary Burton it was almost too much to
bear. 'I felt uncommonly suicidal through that first night on
Fernando Po,' he wrote.[15]

Isabel did not have to wait too long before hearing from Richard.
He wrote from Madeira, and again from Sierra Leone; perhaps he
wrote from other ports as well; but we know about these two letters
because she referred to them in her correspondence, and they were the

first of a lifelong avalanche of notes from Richard giving Isabel detailed instructions.[16] Sometimes he included bizarre gifts. When he noticed the silken threads of a large spider hung from tree to tree rather than in webs ('yellow, stronger than silk; a single insect produces more than the largest [silkworm] cocoon,' he wrote), he had some made into skeins and sent them home to Isabel instructing her to have a shawl made of it.[17] Once, a ship on which he was a passenger was caught in a ferocious storm. The mast was struck by lightning which narrowly missed him; afterwards he took a piece of the scorched timber and carved it into a letter-opener for her. And from Dahomey he sent her the gift of an African king; a necklace made from human knuckle-bones.[18]

Throughout his time in West Africa there is evidence from Isabel's surviving papers that she received exhaustive instructions from Richard each month.[19] Sometimes these instructions consisted of tasks he wished her to perform, or the gathering and sending of supplies, books and equipment. In some cases he enclosed drafts of letters purporting to have been written by Isabel, referring to 'my husband', addressed to Government officials, for her to copy out and sign in her name. Examples of these letters in Richard's hand, previously unknown, survive in two major collections.[20] Earlier biographers have castigated Isabel, accusing her of interfering, and of causing harm to Richard's career by her frequent lobbying of officials on his behalf, and wondering why Burton tolerated her behaviour. It is as well to establish, at this early point in their marriage, that – at least on some occasions – we now know she acted under instruction from Richard himself. No wonder he appeared complaisant.

Isabel was only too pleased to be able to do something for her beloved Richard. It gave her a *raison d'être* in his absence. Before he left he had instructed her to pursue his claim for pension rights from the India Office and she lost no time in doing so, using Richard's own arguments but with a verve and enthusiasm that must have startled the recipients.

Richard's book *City of the Saints* was proofed by Monckton Milnes at his request. Some passages were erased. Throughout his life Burton would entrust manuscripts to editors for the final pre-publication editing and proofing stages, usually because by that time he had moved on to a new project or new place. His instructions were simple and consistent; he never objected to cuts in the text; 'You can

take out as much as you wish, but don't add anything!' Milnes found
he had to make some edits, but not for the reason usually responsible
for cuts in Burton's writings: sexual impropriety. 'I think the book
itself delightful,' he wrote to a correspondent after he had condensed
City of the Saints for the *Edinburgh Review*. 'I wish I could have
inserted all Burton's Mormon anecdotes; for example, one person
saying to another, "Sir, if you were Mr Jesus Christ, or Mr Joseph
Smith himself sitting there, with his halo hanging above your head, I
would pull your nose at any rate." But this, alas, the respectability of
the *Edinburgh Review* would not allow.'[21] Once Milnes had made the
manuscript suitable for publication, Isabel nursed it through the pre-
publication stages. She learned quickly, as evidenced by her letters to
various publishers on technical points.

She had so far been unsuccessful in the matter of the Indian Army
pension, but she had not retired from the lists, and when *City of the
Saints* was reviewed less than kindly she sprang into action. Through
her 'warm, kind' friend, James Hain Friswell the journalist, she lob-
bied Lucas, of *The Times*, to review the book favourably. 'Look at the
reviewers,' she pointed out, 'they are making a complete Aunt Sally of
the poor fellow, and he is in Africa and can't stand up for himself. You
will say he deserves it for his polygamous opinions. This is a man who
has married one wife, who is a domestic man when at home and a
home-sick one when away. I want something done and it is this . . .'
She enclosed a favourable review written for her by a friend of
Richard's and asked Lucas to let it head the reviews of Richard's
book in the *The Times* which she described sycophantically as 'a
noble paper'. Using a surprisingly American expression, she said that
Mr Lucas could 'pinch-hit the book' as much as he liked providing he
first gave Richard '5 minutes of praise'.[22]

Isabel's room at her parents' house was now filled with images of
Richard.[23] Her favourite, however, was only slightly larger than a
miniature. It was one of a pair (the other was of Isabel) painted as a
wedding present by Richard's childhood friend from Pisa, Louis
Desanges. Isabel met Desanges at Boulogne around the time she first
met Richard, and the artist apparently painted the two portraits from
memory. Contemporary photographs suggest that the pictures depict
Richard and Isabel as they were a decade earlier in Boulogne, when
they met, not as they were in 1861 when they married.[24]

Shortly after Christmas Isabel carried out one of Richard's most important instructions. His late uncle, Francis Burton,* had been a young officer serving at St Helena in May 1821, when Napoleon died. There is a long family legend detailing how he became involved in taking the plaster death mask, and made a sketch of the dead Emperor. He also obtained some strands of Napoleon's hair, which he preserved in a glass-fronted watch-case. When Francis Burton died in 1860, Richard begged these Bonaparte souvenirs from his cousin Eliza, intending to have them returned to the great man's family in Paris. Eliza was in love with Richard (who was still unmarried at that point) and readily complied. Before he sailed for North America, he arranged to have the hair 'set in a handsome ring with a wreath of laurels and the Bonaparte bees'. He also ordered a complete set of his books expensively bound. One of the tasks he set Isabel when he sailed for West Africa was to take these volumes to Paris, together with the ring and the other artifacts, and present them to Emperor Napoleon III with his compliments. Quite what he hoped to achieve by this gesture is unknown, but interestingly enough in 1864 John Hanning Speke – after returning from Africa in 1863 – would also court the Bonapartes.

Following the tragic death of Prince Albert from typhoid on 14 December 1861, the British nation was plunged into mourning. It was not merely a public observance of grief but 'quite the realest public sorrow I have ever seen', Monckton Milnes wrote to a correspondent. 'The peasants in their cottages talk as if the Queen was one of themselves.'[25] Isabel had already made arrangements to travel to Paris after Christmas to execute Richard's commission, and there seemed no reason to change her plans. She took a maid and stayed in rooms in the Quartier Chaillot. From there she wrote to Norton Shaw, promoting Richard's affairs, particularly his campaign to retain his pension and retire with the rank of Major. 'Do back it up,' she urged him. 'If we can get no one to take our part we are going to try to get some friends to bring the case before Parliament. I will fight for the next ten years if necessary, because it is *unjust*. I simply wish to avoid anything that would be *bad taste* such as publishing the abusive memorandum . . .'[26]

---

* Francis Burton (brother of Richard's father) married Sarah Baker (sister to Richard's mother) and had two daughters, Elizabeth and Sarah. (See Chapter 1.)

A week later she wrote to the journalist James Hain Friswell. It is a long letter, but it contains so much of interest that it is reproduced here almost in entirety. It demonstrates, among other things, that the greater Arundell family was not yet reconciled to her marriage with Richard, even though his immediate family had evidently accepted her.

Paris 4th [1862]

Dear Mr Friswell,

In consequence of Prince Albert's death there are no receptions but I wait quietly till there are. The Empress has received and accepted through the Duc de Bassano all my presents save the 2 principal [ones], the Duke also has received me and I am sure that they cannot deny me an audience.

I am so woefully disappointed about the *Times*.* I enclose you a note . . . as from yourself to Mr Lucas . . . and beg him to work it into it. Put [in] your phrase, 'the most interesting figure of the 19th century' and put 'the Paladin of the age' which, on referring to the newspapers of days gone by, I find was the expression. I want 20 more copies of your [text] and 50 of mine with *that* correction in it.

I am writing to Sir Charles Wood [first Viscount Halifax] to ask for pension & retirement as major. Who could I get to take my case up in Parliament if refused? I think my own relations *not* as they must alter their opinions before I can ask a kindness. I quite forgive your conscientious scruples – of course you [are] . . . an *incipient* British *paterfamilias* and are quite right. Three years of marriage will tone down my husband's writings. He will write from his own clear *understanding* and not from defiance and contempt of *rules* . . .

Not content with her present project, Isabel had stumbled into a fully-fledged gaslight mystery which, containing all the elements of the theft of an oriental jewel by one of Richard's former loves, would not be out of place in the pages of a Wilkie Collins novel. She explained:

---

*Lucas declined to print the favourable review that Isabel had forwarded.

And now to another subject. I am most anxious to speak to you about Mrs Stisted my husband's sister. [She] . . . wore a gold scaly serpent ring with a large diamond in flat head 1853 at the house of Colonel Pryce and Miss [Elizabeth] Burton (1st cousin), [Gunley Hall] nr Welshpool, Wales. Mrs Stisted took her ring off to wash her hands for dinner and the bell ringing in the middle of washing she hurried down leaving the ring, and a common one with an emerald in it, on the table. On returning from dinner they were gone. There was a great fuss – servants suspected – the police and clairvoyants proposed to which Miss Burton thoroughly objected, and accused Mrs Stisted's faithful maid and companion of 16 years standing.

Now the ring in question belonged to my husband. He had gone to Mecca giving it to Mrs Stisted as a keepsake. There was a *historiette* about it and it was admired by all members of the family. Miss Burton, who was in love with my husband, is not a very nice person and is a concealed enemy and mischief maker in the family and it was the first time the ring was seen off my sister's finger . . .

Nine years had passed, said Isabel, but although the matter was never alluded to, it was not forgotten. Shortly after the Burtons' marriage, Maria Stisted confided to Isabel her belief that Eliza Burton had stolen the rings.

She impressed me so strongly with the idea she [Eliza Burton] had got it that I can't shake it off. If I but knew this I would not disgrace her [Eliza] but would stop her evil doings in the family. But I dare not advertise *openly* to find it nor could I let anyone else. It would be the way to lose it. I offered [unreadable name] the detective 10/- to find it but it was not worth his while.

Now I must tell you that the other day I saw a magnificent ring on her hand. A band of gold like my blue [ring], but handsomer with 2 emeralds and 3 diamonds in it. She came to London in April, '54, and Lessier was her jeweller. I said to her 'what a beautiful ring,' and she said quietly, 'Oh yes, that was formerly two rings, an Indian and another. I had them melted together and the stones set.' She could not dare wear the serpent ring as it was.

Do you think you could in any way pretend to Lessier that you forgot whether it is on Messrs Bushells books, and get him to look

for it on his, *since 1853*. I would give anything for the information.
She [Eliza] is however just passing through town and it would be
better to let her start first. It would never do for Lessier to let her
know there had been enquiries. It would simply be whether a serpent ring answering that description has ever been given to him by
Miss Burton to alter or change in any way. But . . . you must never
let him know what the information is for. There is always some
horrid member in every family. I tell you all this quite in confidence . . . Yrs very sincerely, IB.[27]

Regrettably, surviving papers provide no further clues concerning this
entertaining mystery. Probably it was never resolved. What does stand
out in the breathless story, however, is the surprising fact that Maria
Stisted, long thought to be a deadly enemy of Isabel from the start,
confided such a sensitive family secret to her soon after the Burtons'
marriage. However, any goodwill other members of Richard's family
may have entertained vanished when Isabel botched her mission to
the French Emperor; notably on the part of the aggrieved Eliza, who
had entrusted her father's precious Napoleon mementoes to Richard
because she loved him. Isabel and Eliza continued to meet socially and
Isabel was among the guests at Eliza's subsequent wedding to Colonel
Pryce, but there was no love lost between the two women.

Richard's old friend, Alfred Bate Richards, wrote sympathetically
about Isabel's failed assignment:

She was young and inexperienced and had not a single friend in
Paris to help her. She left her letters and presents at the Tuileries.
The audience was not granted. His Imperial Majesty declined the
presents, and she never heard anything more of them. They were
not returned. Frightened and disappointed at this failure of this, her
first little mission, at the outset of her married life she returned to
London directly, where she found the Burton family anything but
pleased at her . . . want of *savoire faire* in the matter, having unwittingly caused their treasure to be utterly unappreciated. She said to
me on her return, 'I never felt so snubbed in my life, and I shall
never like Paris again.'[28]

Isabel set off immediately for her uncle's house at Garswood where
she could be miserable in luxury.

Richard's first two months in West Africa were given over to fact-finding. On arriving at Fernando Po he found that the official Letters confirming his appointment had not been forwarded. Unable to take charge of the Consulate officially, and hearing that a sailing ship was leaving on the following morning for the 'Oil Rivers', he took a passage on it and spent a further week exploring his 'patch' without the burden of administrative duties. He returned to the island on 2 October, and wrote a succinct appreciation of his situation to John Russell:

> When at Lagos I applied to the officer commanding the Bight Division for a gunboat and received the answer that none could be spared . . . The coast under the Consular jurisdiction is 500 miles in length and contains 25 navigable rivers of which six will give me nearly constant employment. But at present I am crippled; there is not a gig at my command. I venture to request that a gunboat may be attached to the Bight of Biafra. The trade is everywhere on the eve of a great change which will require careful superintendence. There is now in the Bonny River a small steamer the 'Eyo Honesty' built by Mr Laird and belonging to Messrs Horsfall which might be purchased for £5000 or £6000. She carries 5 guns, and . . . would be exactly the thing wanted. With her I could greatly extend the traffic of these now important rivers and I doubt not that in the end the measure will prove commercial . . .[29]

He said he intended to use his expenses to purchase a gig for his immediate use. Otherwise, he said, as things stood whenever he required transport he would be obliged to put himself under an obligation to the merchants, which he judged inadvisable.

As a measure of the opposition with which Richard had to contend in the Foreign Office, it is worth recording that his request for a gunboat received the support of the Duke of Somerset, who offered to send a suitable vessel provided the F.O. recommended it. The F.O. official responsible for administration of the Bights was in complete agreement with Richard, and stated that unless Captain Burton had access to a steamer he did not see how he could be expected to carry out his duty of protecting British subjects and property in the area. But his lengthy recommendation was immediately squashed by some higher power:

I have very great doubts as to the discretion of Capt Burton. I believe his character may get us into serious difficulties, and I should scarcely like to see him entrusted with a gunboat. He is utterly reckless.[30]

Richard was consequently advised that there was no case for a gunboat but that instructions had been passed to the Naval Commander at Biafra to make a vessel available to him should he need one.[31] Subsequent requests by Richard for surveying instruments met with a similar fate. At the bottom of one request someone has written, 'Is there any precedence for this at Fernando Po?' And the response, 'No! And I think it would be objectionable to undertake to supply our Consuls with such.'[32]

In fact none of Richard's proposals, which would have enabled him to administer his area with greater efficiency, were accepted. Eventually he got the message, and gave himself over to exploration and writing. Had he been encouraged he might have made a significant mark on a part of the world that is still troubled. When he wrote to Milnes on 1 December however, he was still optimistic;

> Brass River
> 1st December 61
>
> *Caro Amico,*
>   Did you ever hear of the Brass R.? I am almost ashamed to write to you from such place . . . However I must thank you for the trouble you have taken with my Mormons . . . At Lagos I met with a few fellow religionists and we refreshed ourselves greatly with edifying conversation and humble looking-forwards to the day of annihilating all Kafirs in W. Africa. I met there a Sherif (*soi disant*) from Mekkah, a man who had visited El Medinah, a Hausa Iman and some 2,000 Moslems who all call me *Alufa* i.e. one of the *Ulema* . . .
>   The amount of humbug (missionary) concerning Abeokuta [a town in Nigeria] is monstrous! The fact is there is no salvation for Africa but El Islam. At the Chiefs palace – a shed well smeared with moist dung and indigo leaf – I met a young Arab from Burnis and asked him in his own tongue why he had neglected the duty of El Jihad? – of the Holy War? '*Walluh*' replied that excellent youth – whose face may Allah whiten in the next world! – 'wait a

while, have patience and then – *Inshallah*!' To which I replied
'*Inshallah*!'

Abeokuta however is no humbug regarding cotton. The whole of
Yoruba . . . is well adapted to the growth; the people are mostly
slaves (as *you* know a great requisite for industry in Africa and the
chiefs are greedy). At present however there is a dirty little war
which leaves the farms untilled. The people of Ibadan attacked the
people of Ijaga, and the latter claimed the end of Abeokuta.
Abeokuta responded nobly, sent 10,000 or 15,000 troops to the
field in feudal style, and fought several battles in which the dead
and wounded amounted to at least 10. But Abeokuta (being feudal)
had no constraint *il faut vivre*, the consequence is that the warriors
sold off about 20,000 of the Ijagans – their allies.

I have related this thing at some length – it is characteristically
African. We left Abeokuta with a written promise from the chiefs,
that they would abolish human sacrifice. They kept it till we
reached Lagos when they informed us in writing that they had been
compelled by a desire for peace to knock another fellow on the
head . . . Don't let the Niger want an expedition, it is *the* true road,
the main gut (so to speak), that traverses the African interior.

From the . . . Niger I came here and am doing some little details
in the way of exploration. From this to the other Oil Rivers. I have
by this mail volunteered to visit Idahim (Dahomey) and to bring the
King to a sense of his duty . . . I will follow your advice and be 'very
efficient'. Remember me most kindly to Mrs Milnes and with many
hopes of seeing you again believe me ever yrs,

Abdullah[33]

He spent a month aboard H.M.S. *Bloodhound*, touring the entire area
under his jurisdiction, and reported at length on the trade and commercial aspects, geographical facts, outstanding feuds between the
tribes, the display of human skulls in villages, and the 'regrettable' fact
that one African chief numbered two English women among his many
wives. He ended by explaining that on his return to Fernando Po he
found little to do there, 'the whole work of Fernando Po lies in the Oil
Rivers. On 18th December I set out with Rev'd A. Saker of the
Cameroens Mission, Sr Calvo Iturburu the Civil and Criminal Judge
at Fernando Po, and Mr Gustav Mann, Government Botanist in West
Africa, to explore, ascend and survey the Camaroens Mountains – an

admirable site for a sanitarium, a convict station, or a colony of liberated Africans.'[34] What made the area especially delightful, he said, was the absence of sand flies, mosquitoes and prickly heat.

By April he was able to report formally to the F.O. – and triumphantly to the R.G.S. – that he had made two successful ascents of previously unscaled mountains. Two recent attempts had failed, he explained – unable to make a completely serious report even in formal circumstances: 'in 1847 Mr Merrick of the Baptist Mission succeeded in emerging from the forest into the open grassy levels, but pure water failed him . . . and he was compelled to return. Two years afterwards he died of confirmed teetotalism.' Since then another unsuccessful assault on the mountains had been made by F.R.G.S. Sir William Hooker and Gustav Mann. Burton, Saker and Iturburu met Mann on their way to the mountains. He claimed to be returning, having successfully scaled Elephant Mountain, but on checking Mann's notes Richard soon worked out that 'considering the distance and height, it was some mistake on his part; and this was proved to be the case. The enterprising botanist, so far from having scaled the summit had never even seen it.' Mann tagged himself anxiously on to Richard's team.

The entire party started the climb on 18 December and by Christmas Day they had reached a plateau from where they saw two magnificent mountains. The highest, which Mann had called Elephant Mountain, could not possibly have been reached in the time described in his journals. The party re-named the highest mountain 'Victoria' and the smaller neighbour 'Albert'. At the time of this ceremony they had not heard, Burton apologised, 'of the awful event which had destroyed Christmas Merriment in England . . .'[35] Richard's condemnation of Speke for bestowing inappropriate English names on African geographical features seems to have slipped his mind. Nor was this naming ceremony the only one. The party celebrated Christmas merrily, Richard concocting a drink for the occasion: '. . . take mint of sufficient quantity. Soak in Brandy or other liquor for 15 minutes. Sweeten to taste and add smashed ice. Imbibe.' In gratitude to Mrs Helen Saker who had thoughtfully provided a Christmas dinner (complete with a plum pudding, 'which fared badly in the encounter'), they named a smaller cone-shaped peak 'Mount Helen'. Shortly afterwards, Richard wrote, 'we struck a long grassy and rocky reach of mountain slope, separating us from a magnificent mountain [10,590 ft] which I, as a dutiful husband, named Mount Isabel.'

At last came the ascent of Mount Victoria. As they neared the summit the judge sprained his ankle and had to stop. Burton admitted that perhaps there was a 'bit of malice' in his desire to get there ahead of Mann who, presumably erroneously, claimed to have scaled it earlier, but 'to be first in such matters is everything,' Richard said in justification, 'to be second, nothing.' To prove he had been there, he made a cairn of stones and placed in it a note and a few pages of *Punch*. He was so tired when he returned to the base camp that he fell asleep without removing his boots. Next morning he found his feet in 'a sorry state' for the boots had let in water and a fungal infection had resulted. He also had a high fever, so he spent a few days resting up, 'botanising' (to Mann's intense annoyance) and devising a sign language with which he could communicate with tribes whose language he did not speak. 'A hundred words are easily learned in a week. 200 signs and a little facility in sketching, would enable, I believe, a traveller to make his way through any country, even China, a few days after arrival.' A sign language was soon needed. When Burton declined to accept the 12-year-old daughter of a local chief as his wife, the spurned father virtually declared war on the party. It took many presents to pacify him.

After Richard's health recovered, the entire party made a second ascent of Mount Victoria and drank a celebratory bottle of champagne at the peak. They each wrote their names on a slip of paper which they placed in a bottle in the cairn. When Sir Harry Johnson climbed the peak in 1886, he found several bottles inside a cairn, including the one Burton and his party had left.[36]

Naming a mountain after Isabel was not his only tribute to her. During the climb through the bush Burton spotted two hitherto unknown species; the first, a black-olive bird of 6 inches in length with a white spot over its eye which he named after Isabel: '*Cossypha Isabella*' The second a tiny squirrel, 7 inches long with a 5-inch bushy tail, with golden-brown fur with four dark dorsal stripes and underside of pale grey. It is still known as *Sciurus Isabella*. 'I have great pleasure in naming this beautiful new species after Mrs Isabel Burton,' wrote Dr J.R. Gray F.R.S., 'her husband, the discoverer of it requested . . . that it should be so named.'[37] Dr Gray also named a new species of snake, the *Atheris Burtonii*. Richard wrote to Isabel

while on the mountain and she received the letter in early March –
writing with clear pleasure, but some puzzlement, as she advised
Monckton Milnes:

Dear Mr Milnes,
    In a very long letter from dearest Richard he says, 'Tell Mr
Milnes that I have married a fine tall – it looks like – cone, Mr
Milnes. He also says 'the title of my new book is to be *A Flying Visit
to Abeokuta – a reconnaissance of the Cameroon Mountains.*'

Dedication
To my best friend
my wife
These pages are lovingly inscribed

The motto I can't read but it *looks* like this: '*Tui nuili cururun
requies in nocte velastra sumen et in solis tu milu turba licis.*' I am
to ask your advice about this . . . & I hope you will write by return
of post if you can, as the mail goes on the 24th & my letter must
leave on 21st. The A[frican] Mail is only just come in so I am
obliged to write you a line in a hurry. I hope I shall see you all this
season. I am still living with my parents in 13 Oxford Terrace,
Hyde Park but they have taken 14 Montagu Place, Bryanstone Sq.
for some years where we shall remove on 25th of this month. In
May I am going to meet Richard – give my best to dear Mrs Milnes
and the little ones & believe me
                              Yrs always sincerely,
                              Isabel Burton[38]

Isabel was not the only person to find trouble reading Richard's
minute handwriting. On 21 April he was taken to task by his chief at
the Foreign Office over his account of the ascent of the mountains: 'I
doubt not that your report is full of interest, but in consequence of the
illegible characters in which it is written I am unable to make myself
acquainted with its contents. I must beg you for the future to write in
a larger hand and more distinctly.'[39]
    Richard was entitled to an annual leave of one month per annum
which he planned to take in June, and had instructed Isabel to join
him at Madeira. There was no question of her joining him at

Fernando Po, even for a short time. He had made enquiries as soon as he arrived, as he promised her, only to discover that Mrs Hutchinson (wife of Richard's predecessor) was on the island only two months before nearly losing her life to fever, and Mrs Laughland (wife of the leading British merchant) lost her child to a similar illness. During Richard's time on Fernando Po, there were no white women on the island. 'There is no place where a wife is so much wanted as in the Tropics,' he wrote wistfully, 'but then comes the rub – how to keep the wife alive.'[40] But he thought of a solution to their separation, and during his time in the Cameroons he wrote to Lord Russell requesting the same privileges of 3 months annual leave that his predecessor had been granted, in common with other Consuls on the West African mainland such as Lagos. 'The climate of Fernando Po is not less deadly than that of Lagos, in fact it is rather worse,' he pointed out. 'It is impossible to see one's family . . . at a place where the Spanish are compelled to send all their troops to sleep on hulks in the harbour. H.E. the Governor's wife and daughter resided here during the healthy season of 1860, but though they took the precaution of not passing a night on shore they were obliged by sickness after a short time to leave for Tenerife. I have already undergone two attacks of fever . . .'[41] He was sharply advised that he was to take no leave at all until after he had been at his post for at least twelve months.

Compelled to spend the 'unhealthy' season at his post, he spent the summer visiting the mainland coast. There was always some dispute or other between the natives and the traders for him to settle; 'these vindictive cases are endless,' Burton wrote.[42] And he made desultory attempts to make good the Fernando Po Consulate building for which the F.O. stubbornly refused to provide any money for refurbishment, despite Richard's complaints that it leaked like a sieve in the rains and, as a consequence, most of the floor timbers were rotten. When attacked by fevers, as he was frequently, Richard found it best to move up into the hills of the island, where he found a small cottage which he cleaned up and called 'Buena Vista'. From there he sent instructions to the young man who acted as his clerk, Frank Wilson, and the result is a fascinating series of correspondence covering two years, now in the collection of Quentin Keynes. He also wrote to his closest friends of that time, Richard Monckton Milnes, Henry Murray and other drinking cronies, and these letters scintillate with fun and his facetious brand of humour.

To Mr R. Martin of the Gold Coast in May, responding to Martin's advice that he was sailing down to the Bights alone and hoped to see him, Richard wrote cheerfully:

> What have you done with Madam? A pension or divorce? . . . They say I'm to get a Niger expedition and if so there'll be a journey to Kano. No time for authoring here, my work at Fernando Po is laying out a cacao plantation which will probably pay. Bights deadly this year. Two whites just croaked at Bonny; not caring one whitey-brown damn when I croak, I don't croak. Effect of poverty. Old de Ruvigas [Governor of Fernando Po] wants me to apply for Governorship of Gold Coast Castle . . . but I should have to wear socks and stick to their pretensions. *Don't* I remember the 'tigers milk' that morning of my leaving St Mary and the all jolly day before it! I won't ask you to Fernando Po, where my presence is on the whole rare, but let me know where we might meet . . .[43]

His throw-away remarks about the Governorship of the Gold Coast are characteristically jocular. In fact he really *did* want the Governorship of the Gold Coast, and over the next two years made some serious attempts to get it. On his instructions, Isabel approached the Duke of Norfolk at Christmas 1862 and persuaded him to put Richard's name down for the post when it became vacant, and Richard wrote to several friends including Henry Murray asking for his support; 'After all the Governor of the Gold Coast is not expected to set the Atlantic on fire and the appointment is not half so responsible as that of F. Po.'[44] A major advantage was that Isabel might join him in the healthier climate of the Gold Coast. His letters are more characteristic of him than his published work:

Fernando Po. 26th April 1862

Carissimo Milnes,

I feel so much for your me-lan-cho-ly state of mind consequent upon the national loss* that this pen has been taken up *pour divertir vos tristes pensées.*

Imprimés. Many thanks for the article. What Review** does it

*Death of Prince Albert.
**Milnes' review of *City of the Saints* in *Edinburgh Review.*

appear in? I very much admire the way in which – after you have approved polygamy, and thrown St. Jerome & St. Aug. at the Christian's head – you, in your last page, predict its present downfall. It reminds me of a book by the great divine El Siguti. His work is a collection of the most hair-upstanding anecdotes that ever came from mouth of Holy Man – Mullah or Bishop. And in the very ending pages El Siguti remarks, 'these things I remark I have related unto thee, that thou mayest better know what to avoid'. But accept at my humble hands a bit of wisdom polygami. Man is polygamous, woman monogamous; for the time being. A man in love (*un jeune homme*) loves all the sex, a woman generally confines herself to one – which one of course is changed when nature dictates . . .

Greater prostitutes than the Gabon women were never invented. In one day I was offered by those most concerned, a wife, a sister, a daughter-in-law and a daughter! They are rather pretty, small hands and feet, pert faced, not black! The hair however is most grotesque – *à la cockatoo*. I wish that Government would employ me in exploring and informing them about the coast. There are nests of slaves everywhere South of the Corisco Island and I could soon save them £100,000 of African Squadron. At present my work is that of a bailiff to palm oil auditors. *Mais patiente cela is sudra.* The Liberians are scoundrels, they have robbed the whole country from its owners the Krumen. Suspect them of anything.

Remember me with love to the amiable trio Hodgson, Bellamy and Hankey – when shall we all meet again? People die off on this coast like madmen – you would stare at the statistics. I have no such present purpose and therefore keep moving, six weeks settled would kill me. They have not answered my volunteering [to visit] Dahomey, who has just killed off a large town. King Pepple is almost the damnedest scoundrel unhung – but we will soon be even. I am writing very mildly till firmly seated, and then *la patte de velour* will disappear. You will soon hear of me at the Ethnological Society.

Abdullah[45]

June 23rd 1862

To: Admiral Hon. Henry Murray
D4 Albany, London.

Venerable Villain and rulaimer

You are, thank goodness and despite gout, as virulent and as
abusive as ever. Before your letter came I had resolved to send you
a line of respectable espistolary correspondence, sub geographical
and perhaps slightly tinctured with morality. And then comes to
hand a sheet full of the vilest bawdiness and ribaldry. But it *is*
exactly like you . . . do reform your manners . . .

How the devil is it that you don't talk of going out of town this
summer, and why not come and see me next winter? Climate very
fine; I'll cure your old gout in a month by cutting your grog, not
allowing you to dram in secret, and curbing if it is possible your
excessive gourmandising. Let me have a word and a room shall be
built for you. The fact is you are breaking down with regular habits.
You want a little gipsying and sleeping in the bush. You require a
spell of temperance, sobriety and chastity. There's a lot of old sailor
fellows here who will be glad to see you, only mind you, I'll have
nothing stronger than Spartan grog.

I failed to get a Gorilla. They are very wild and timid and their
sharp organs start them at a mile distant. The old males are like all
apes (and Captains R.N.) fierce, crusty, biting, and generally
unamiable. Females, young, are cowardly devils and always bolt.
Better luck next time. I'm not coming out Chailluan[46] or the
reverse. The great 'Nimrod Petherick' is a model ass and fictionist,
and as for that terrible donkey Speke, I hope that by this time he is
decently devoured by jackals. That Court Martial on Crawford
made me laugh – it was Rigby to a T. He never yet could keep his
hands from picking and stealing, and his tongue from evil-speaking,
lying and calumny. I'll settle affairs with him some day.

I'm ordered by Marm [Isabel] to send you a copy of the *Saints*.
Your friend who detected in my original writings lewdness and
pestilence must be a cur after your own heart, one capable like
that blackguard Brooke (ask Strangford) of composing 'Bawdy
Hymns'. Remember me to Stiggins, Singleton, and the big-breasted
Hawkins. Hughes is an earnest jackass, a kind of Tom Brown minus
his hair. What of Spottiswoode? Now he is married, he has I

presume put away such childish things as D4A.* Compliments to Mayo.

You had better try the Clairvoyant; she may do you some good. Mind, I don't believe any of its mysteries, only that it is practised by very clever women with a great knowledge of scruples and a peculiar form of sympathy. My wife sent me a flannel shirt which I was to rub and return it to her. I rubbed it on an old goat in the yard; by return of post came a hundred-weight of medicine and directions about restoring my poor chest. Now that's really too bad. The old goat never coughs, and I'll swear by the Gods that his lungs are as sound as mine . . .

Decency will make me keep this appointment till the end of my 3rd year (one nearly done now) then I shall demand leave. It would be too bad to keep a poor devil in such a place for more than 3 years wouldn't it? Meanwhile I am working like a horse, and putting affairs in order. I wish they would make me Governor of the Gold Coast, I could soon turn out a living worth having. However, *vogue la galère*. Write again and tell me all about yourself, and the habitués of the old haunt. . . I'm now limited to one bottle of claret per diem. Mind your morals and reform in time, says,

Abdullah[47]

Speke, in fact, had not been eaten by jackals and would shortly write confidently to Murchison that, 'I am on the northern slope of Africa, and the Victoria Nyanza is the true and indisputable source of the Nile . . .'[48]

The lack of a vessel was a constant problem to Richard. In July, having experienced considerable difficulties in reaching a trouble spot, he was finally offered the use of a naval vessel and sailed to the 'Oil Rivers' to act officially following a raid by tribesmen on the home and warehouse of some settlers, Dr and Mrs Henry. The couple's servants were wounded in the affray and a few days later Mrs Henry, Richard surprisingly reported, 'died of a fever brought on by fright'.[49] Instructed to try to obtain a workable treaty with the inhabitants, Richard informed the two Kings of Benin that he intended to call on them, and did so, accompanied by a naval officer in full dress

---

* Murray's apartment D4 The Albany, Piccadilly.

to add gravitas. The response of Archibong, King of old Calabar, survives:

> Margesty Consle/ My dear Sir/ I received you note that you send me now I try to fine man who read for me he cannot tell me what you say so I send this note to you Please tell that man what you book say so he can come and tell me what you say I know it well I not hear them good thing book say so I thank you tell that man for you mouth he can come and tell me plen and I hear proper your friend truly Also I send my good complement to you also /King Archibong[50]

'I am here about a sad row . . .' Richard wrote from Benin on 25 August. 'Benin is a place of horrors. The first thing we saw was a man freshly strangled and crucified in honour of our arrival. In "Palace Yard" was a fine young woman slung to a tree-top for rain, she was dead and the vultures had eaten part of the body . . . The roads leading to the palace are strewn with skulls and skeletons. I'm pretty well used to that sort of thing but the first day nearly sickened me. These niggers are the very devils. The King was very civil, and much pleased at the sight of a cocked hat . . .'[51] Richard was still writing articles for the R.G.S. and in September advised Norton Shaw: 'I am going to Madeira by the next mail,' and requested the loan of a book which 'my wife will bring out to me.'[52]

One of his ambitions was to search for the Gabon gorillas so famously described (inaccurately in his first book) by Paul du Chaillu. This region did not come strictly within Richard's consular territory, but he was never overly concerned about stretching a point for the sake of expediency. In *Two Trips to Gorilla-land* Burton describes how in late March 1862 he set out with Selim Aga, a couple of hunting dogs and a boat with a hired crew. He was well stocked with candles, food, cognac and claret. Having reached the area he set off with a guide, Paul, who spoke French and was the son of a local 'king'. They encountered severe storms and everything became soaked as they trekked through the dripping forest. Making a rude camp one night, thoroughly sodden and without the means to make a fire, he was besieged by swarms of mosquitoes and could not rest. Seeing his irritation, Paul asked diffidently whether he should go and get some fire from '*l'habitation*'. Puzzled, Richard asked him what habitation.

'Oh, a little village belonging to Papa.' On learning that this was only half a mile away, Burton asked dumbfounded, 'Why the hell didn't you mention it?' The boy explained that it was on a different road, 'whereas you are bound for M'bata'. Within a twenty-minute walk they found dry huts, warm fires, tea, hot food, quinine and cigars.

Burton was unable to track down the gorillas, but before leaving the area he offered a large reward if one could be trapped and sent to him. Hoping to ensure that an animal was not needlessly killed, he offered to double the sum for a live specimen, but when he reached the coast on his way back to Fernando Po he was sent a dead male gorilla. After examining and sketching it, he had it skinned and dissected, sending specimens of the brain and various other organs preserved in brine, as well as the skin, to the British Museum.[53]

Though he did not yet know it, Richard's account of the ascent of Mount Victoria had brought him under attack from a new quarter, this time from Joseph Dalton Hooker, Assistant Director of Kew Gardens and son of the distinguished botanist Sir William Hooker. Gustav Mann had written to Joseph Hooker complaining about Burton's behaviour and saying that he and not Burton had been first to climb the mountain, but he was reluctant to provoke an open quarrel about it; 'we all know what it is like to touch pitch,' Mann wrote bitterly. Hooker obtained a copy of Richard's paper and took up the complaint.

Writing to the R.G.S., he complained that in Richard's account of the ascent of the Cameroons Mountains, too little credit had been given to Gustav Mann:

Mann is a poor German plant collector sent out by the Admiralty (but under my father's orders) to collect tubers and dig plants on the West coast of Africa. He is a [much] undaunted and adventurous traveller, has three times ascended the peak of Fernando Po . . . and from the first year of his visiting W Africa (5 years ago) set his heart on exploring the Cameroons . . . I am quite aware that Burton is an accomplished geographer and that poor Mann is nothing but an assiduous plant collector and traveller but there is never any need for Burton's being jealous of giving the poor herbalist the credit of his own determination to succeed, and of being in every way indebted . . . I would not have complained of Burton if Burton had coupled Mann's name with his own, which is the very least he should have done.[54]

In fact, it is clear from Hooker's letter that he had only read the paper based on Richard's F.O. report. In his book, aimed at a far wider audience, Richard was properly complimentary about Mann's participation.

However, the importance of this complaint addressed to Sir Roderick Murchison is that it appeared to support Speke's claims that Burton's attitude towards exploration was self-seeking. And looking at the matter from the distance of more than a century, it illustrates yet again Burton's remarkable facility for making bitter enemies by riding roughshod over the sensitivities of other men. Isabel immediately scented danger when advised by Shaw that Hooker had appeared before the Council of the R.G.S. to voice his complaint.

'I don't quite understand,' she wrote anxiously, explaining that Richard regarded Mann as 'a nice person and good friend'. Did Shaw think Mann was another Speke, she asked, 'pretending to be friends . . . but writing privately against him?' She counselled Shaw against writing to Richard about it. 'It would be very dangerous . . . Richard is so *hot tempered* and makes himself *so* disagreeable to anyone if he takes a dislike . . . that I would not, without serious cause say a word.' Fernando Po was a small place, she pointed out, 'it would be made rather hot if these two were at variance.' She thought a better solution would be for her to watch Mann during her forthcoming visit to her husband. 'A woman has great instinct as to who are her husband's *real* friends.' But while she was concerned that Mann might endanger Richard's position in the Consular Service, 'as others have worked him out of the Army', she wished if possible to handle the matter 'without a row'.[55] This is a far cry from the projected image of Isabel by some Burton biographers as a tactless meddler on her husband's behalf.

In fact she was not to make her projected journey after all. Richard wrote on 1 November instructing Isabel to 'leave London on December 8th' and go to stay with her uncle, Lord Gerard, at Garswood, 'to be handy for sailing'. Garswood was less than an hour's drive from Liverpool; she was to wait there until she heard from him that he had arrived at Madeira and cleared it for fever, then she was to join him as quickly as possible.[56] But on 12 December, instead of going to Liverpool to board a ship, Isabel went there to meet Richard. 'I shall never forget the joy of our meeting,' she wrote.[57]

Having obtained the approval of the F.O., Richard had sailed as planned for Tenerife, but found the island in quarantine from an outbreak of yellow fever. The ship sailed on to Madeira where – because they had come from an area where 'yellow jack' was known to be raging – supplies were provided but the passengers were again prohibited from landing. 'I was therefore compelled,' Richard explained to Lord Russell, 'most unwillingly to come back to England. The next steamer departs 24th December. I am prepared to return by this opportunity if your Lordship desires it. At the same time it is the dead season in the oil rivers [and] . . . I venture to hope that your Lordship will allow me to stay over . . . returning in January.' It was most unusual for a Consul to return to England without permission, but the explanation of *un fait accompli* was accepted, and no one at the F.O. was so heartless as to insist on Burton's immediate return before Christmas. However, he was instructed to return in January to his intended leave base, Madeira, and reminded that he was to be back in Fernando Po at the end of his leave in April.

14 Montagu Place, London
22 December 1862

Frank Wilson,
Fernando Po

My dear Mr Wilson,
    Yellow Fever at Teneriffe – obliged to come in to this hole [London] – very much disgusted – hope to leave by 24th Jan. prox. I have proposed you to the F.O. as Vice Consul and want to get you some pay. They have approved of *all* my proceedings in the Benin River and [Dr] Henry will probably get redress . . . My going home may do some good in explaining things about the coast and talking to the African Ass'n. I am asking for a 2nd Vice Consul in the Gabon and to have the place included under my jurisdiction. Just drop me a line to Madeira and tell me how you are – Poste Restante, to be kept till called for . . .
    All my people are in the country doing their Xmas; occupations compel me to remain in town without other company than Lord

Dundreary.* The cold is awful, rain and frost, no snow yet. At the F.O. they had the impudence to congratulate me upon my return home – speechless I pointed at the window, through which appeared a peasoup fog defiling the face of Earth and Heaven – and when voice returned I asked what they *could* mean. To make matters more pleasant I shall be dragged to 'midnight mass' the day after tomorrow . . . It is ever on the board that my stomach may be stuffed with plum pudding, and aching reprovals for not eating mince pie have been showered upon my head. After all there are worse places than West Africa.

Excuse this dull note. All are making Fetish around me, which deadens my monotheistic spirit. A rank idolatry crops out everywhere; the devils come again in mistletoe and holly which daily persecutes Regent Street. On the 25th there will be a big 'chop' and the rest of the week will be devoted to *Nyan'g'a* . . . Remember me to all our friends – the Governor, the Major if he be there, the Viscount etc etc. How is Lorisand? You will see me back soon . . .

P.S. Mr Mann has been writing some complaint about me to that ass Hooker who has been circulating it. Of course you do as you like but when I return Mr Mann does not show his nose within the Consulate. A cursed German snob! – Just like the rest of the breed.[58]

The body of this letter was without doubt intended to amuse Wilson, who recognised that Richard's grumblings about Christmas were facetious and not intended to be taken seriously. In fact Richard enjoyed the seasonal trappings, and he was certainly not as dull as he made out, as witnessed by surviving letters to Murray and Milnes. He did not see Murray during his time in London, but they corresponded several times. In Richard's last letter, written shortly before he left England again, he was still pressing his friend to visit Madeira, while refusing to allow Isabel to risk herself there: 'I'm very sorry old friend, to miss you, but this is our first leave so we must not ask for more but start on 24th instant. My wife goes with me as far as Teneriffe – thus far but no further. She will return about April . . . why don't you come to Madeira for a month? It would quite set you up. You are not

*Probably Lord Russell.

beastly rich like poor Milnes who can no more get out of England than a rich man into the eye of needle. *Do* think of it ... Madam sends all sorts of kind regards and is with me.'[59] He also asked Murray to lobby the Duke of Norfolk regarding the Governorship of the Gold Coast which he thought would soon become available again. He deserved to get this position, he said, 'after some three years in the damnedest hole ever created ... Moreover my work in Africa this year has been a trifle more important than that of all the other Africans put together.'[60]

He was able to meet Milnes, however:

23rd [December 1862]

Caro Milnes,

I'll keep Monday, Tuesday and Wed. intact. When shall we meet? I want to consult you about a new religion which is about to start. *Adieu pour le moment, portez vous bien*

Ever yrs,
Abdullah[61]

His remark about 'a new religion' referred to his proposal to form a new organisation, similar in style to the R.G.S. but which would publish papers of a more ethnological and anthropological nature. Thus came about *The Anthropological Society*, which Richard set up with Dr James Hunt. A dining club within the Society was known as 'the Cannibal Club', to which Richard invited his closest cohorts such as Milnes, Henry Murray and Algernon Swinburne. Dr Hunt was the Chairman and Sir Edward Brabrooke, Thomas Bendyshe and Charles Bradlaugh were also among 'the initiates' and presumably belonged to the more raffish circles in which Richard mixed. The Cannibal Club, which was basically an excuse for the stag revelries which Richard called 'orgies',[62] met at Bartolini's dining rooms. No topic of conversation was barred, and the Chairman maintained order by banging on the floor with a mace carved with the figure of an African gnawing on a human thigh-bone. Richard had always been interested in cannibalism but was never, he said to his regret, to witness it. Swinburne obligingly wrote a charter called 'the Cannibal catechism' which was read out at meetings.

Still Burton had not given up trying to get his pension restored and, equally important to him, a promotion in rank. He wrote to Lord

Russell, 'I should feel deeply grateful if your Lordship would enable me to obtain the local rank of Lt. Colonel. Placed in a Spanish Colony . . . and thrown much amongst British naval officers some of whom rank with me and are much my juniors in years, I feel my position to be somewhat anomalous. For the same reason Captain Rigby . . . was allowed to rank as Lt. Col . . . and there are other precedents . . .'[63] This request, passed down to an official for consideration without comment was once again curtly refused.[64]

Richard should have learned from this experience. He did not. For the remainder of his life he continued to irritate his superiors, and sometimes even his peers, with unthinking requests.

21

ISLAND HONEYMOON
1863–1864

Richard and Isabel left Liverpool, bound for Tenerife, on 24 January 1863 in one of the worst storms recorded during the last century. Several ships were wrecked in the Mersey Estuary on that day. Mrs Arundell, who accompanied them to Liverpool from Garswood, braved the little tender in the heaving sea to board the S.S. *Athenian* with the two travellers. She was still aboard the steamer when it was 'grazed' by a passing ironclad. After they parted she returned to Garswood, her childhood home, and later that day she suffered a stroke.

Isabel, knowing nothing of this, was already enjoying her first trip abroad with Richard. Apart from yachting and the cross-Channel steamer it was her first experience of being at sea and she was in high spirits. Long before they cleared the Skerries rocks where the Irish Sea was whipped into a fury, the ship was in trouble. By then, however, the Captain dared not put about despite the entreaties of his passengers; the mountainous seas broke over the ship so constantly that by nightfall the hold was 7 ft deep in water and the steering was badly affected. All male passengers were called to man the pumps: two men were washed overboard and never seen again. Isabel was sea-sick; Richard never was. Returning from his turn at the pump, he kicked the door shut behind him in their cabin and told her not to worry, '. . . the Captain says we can't live more than two hours in this sea.' When she replied miserably that she was pleased to hear her travail would be over so soon, he was angry with her for being so cowardly. She thought that if he had been able to work out a way of not spilling his ink he would have continued to write throughout the storm.

The usual 8-day passage took 13 days, but Isabel had found her sea legs long before they reached Madeira and was never sea-sick again in her life. One morning she woke, looked through the porthole and saw to her delight a verdant and luxuriant shoreline. They spent 6 weeks there entertained lavishly by friends of Richard Monckton Milnes: Lady Marion Alford and Lord Brownlow. Isabel regarded these weeks as their honeymoon; she lapped up the hot sunshine and the tropical scenery, but her real joy came from sharing it all with Richard. There were ponies to ride, sailing boats to hire; and so many invitations that there was hardly any chance of breakfasting, lunching or dining alone. Fortunately, Lord Brownlow had taken an interest in photography and we have him to thank for a series of early photographs of the couple, published in this book for the first time. The shots of them in a garden are conventional enough, but the one of their contribution to an evening's entertainment, a 'tableau', is bizarre. It shows Isabel seated, dressed in widow's weeds and looking dejected, and behind her, dressed in pale loose draperies, stands Richard. 'Richard Burton's ghost appears to his afflicted widow,' Isabel captioned it in her photograph album. Tastes in after-dinner entertainment change. As usual the ladies, including Isabel, played the piano and sang after dinner. But no evening in Madeira was complete without its Ouija board, Richard mesmerising Isabel, or a fortune-teller.

Isabel was not alone in enjoying the 'honeymoon'. The island was 'a little *Elysium*', Richard advised Monckton Milnes:

Would you believe that I have not yet heard the voice of a scolding woman or a crying child? There is, however, an admirable institution, the Brothers Jesus, where by paying $10 a month, you can place a refractory wife under the best of surveillance. So complete is the fire of life extinct that in proposing a little orgie I was looked at as Sathanas might be. The priests, of course, monopolise all that sort of thing . . . my wife is too busy running about the churches and chapels and convents and other places of idolatrous abominations to do anything else . . . However on the 2nd March I am off to Teneriffe and Madame insists upon going though Yellow Fever is still there.'[1]

By now Isabel had delivered her famous edict that she was no longer content to live as she had done for the past year, never seeing him, 'neither a wife, nor maid, nor widow', and she had won her argument.[2]

They travelled on to Tenerife where the quarantine had been lifted, but within a few days of their arrival another yellow fever epidemic broke out in Santa Cruz, the island's capital. Three thousand people died during the next three weeks. The hotel in which the Burtons found accommodation in Laguna was dismal and depressing, and Richard thought they would be better elsewhere. They set off with knapsacks to walk the 20-odd miles across the island. Isabel's journal of this period survives in the Edwards Metcalf collection in California, part of the text she used in *The Life*, but most of it is unpublished. In it she describes their arrival at the small town of Orotava and the shabby old inn which was the only accommodation available. The landlord 'made his appearance and much to our chagrin conducted us to a room very much like the one we had left at Laguna. I will not say our spirits fell, for we looked at each other and burst out laughing; it was evident that the Canaries contained no better accommodation.' The room offered, 'the salon', was 'the size of a riding school'.

Despite having just walked 20-odd miles, Isabel took charge. She borrowed an apron, and sent Richard out to survey the town. Meanwhile she cleared everything out of the room, swept it clean, ordered the hangings washed and had a few of the better items of furniture, including some screens, carried back in. By the time Richard returned, the room had been screened into four separate areas. One corner of the room had become the bedroom, one the dressing room, one the living room and the other the dining area. It was clean and smelled sweet with the windows cast open to the sea breezes. It was never going to be a palace, but Isabel had made a home of it with characteristic energy, resilience and enthusiasm. Without a doubt, she made Richard happy. It was surely these qualities in her which caused him to dedicate his book, *Abeokuta*, 'to my best friend, my wife', and write beneath it four lines in Latin from one of the elegies of Tibullus, which the *London Review* translated as:

> Oh, I could live with thee in the wild wood,
> Where human foot hath never worn a way:
> With thee; my city, and my solitude,
> Light of my night, sweet rest from cares by day.[3]

On the other hand, he may have felt he had to atone to her for passages in *Abeokuta* such as the one where he described 'a right merry evening' where he and the party of mountaineers were entertained by a local chief on the veranda of a fetish house surrounded by women with lovely bodies ('*superbae formae*'):[4]

> Beautiful women – that is in body, not face – formed up to watch . . . a drum soon made its appearance and after we had passed round a social glass of toast, rum and gin, the merriment waxed fast and furious . . . singing, feasting and dancing . . . Our hosts were perfectly civil and obliging, and so were our hostesses – rather too much so I could prove, if privileged to whisper into the reader's ear. But what would Mrs Grundy* say? . . .

Richard's facetious brand of humour was not appreciated in London. To Isabel's annoyance the *London Review* openly asked, 'We should like to know what Mrs Burton, to whom as his "best friend" the book is dedicated, thinks of these portions of the book so lovingly inscribed to her.'[5] But the verse was not an isolated compliment. He sent the first copy of his next book, *A Mission to Gelele*, to Isabel, inscribed, 'To my darling wife'; beside which Isabel scrawled, 'Thank you, sweet love.'

While they were in Tenerife Richard decided he wished to climb the highest peak, Pico de Teide (12,198 ft). At that time of year the top was covered in snow, and the round trip took several days. Locals shook their heads and said it could not be done in the winter, but Richard recruited a guide and a team of half a dozen porters, muleteers and a cook and – laughing and chattering – they went anyway. They had reached the snow line, above the cloud level, after an eight-hour ride and Isabel was glad to dismount.

> . . . we read and wrote till about 7 o'clock and then it grew darker and colder and I rolled myself in my rugs with my feet to the camp fire and did not sleep but watched. The good humoured guides lay around the fire in their blankets and black velvet

* 'Mrs Grundy': prudish and narrow-minded mythical arbiter of public morals, originating from Thomas Morton's play *Speed the Plough*, c.1798.

sombreros in careless attitudes. I did not know a blanket could look so picturesque. With their dark hair and skins, white teeth, flashing eyes and straight features lit up by the lurid glare of the fire, animated by the conversation . . . they formed a picturesque bivouac scene, a brigand-like group. I listened until the Great Bear sank behind the mountain side, and then fell fast asleep. The men in turns kept up the fire while all but the watcher slept around it . . . the silence was profound. The pleasant reminiscences of that night will live in my memory forever, when most other things are forgotten, or when trials and sorrows make me for the time being, forget to be grateful for past happiness . . .[6]

They set out before dawn and reached the top just as the sun rose. 'At 6 a.m. the guides told us to turn around. A golden gleam was on the sea – the first of the sun; and gradually its edge appeared and rose majestically in pure golden glory. And we were hanging between heaven and earth in solitude and silence – permitted to enjoy this beautiful moment,' Isabel wrote.[7] They spent the morning wandering about at the top of the mountain and began the descent in the afternoon. As they set off Richard called her and pointed out an eagle riding the air currents above them. As darkness fell the steeper parts of the descent became difficult and dangerous, Isabel was sometimes frightened but she was determined not to cry out. She buried her hands in the horse's mane and sat tight. Richard's mule disappeared into a snowdrift at one point but got out without unseating him, and once they got below the snow line the going became easy.

This account by Isabel was written with an eye to publication but Richard read it, made a few edits, then told her it was not good enough to publish. 'He was right in this, and in not letting me share with him the climate of West Africa,' she later wrote. 'But I thought both very hard at the time.'[8]

When Richard returned to Fernando Po he found two things that pleased him. First, the F.O. had finally supplied him with a boat, a large gig reported as having been 'formerly used in West Africa so it should be suitable', he was informed. Richard on seeing it, however, snorted that 'it ought to last another year.'[9] Second, orders to 'proceed as Her Majesty's Commissioner' on a friendly mission to King Gelele of Dahome. The object of this mission was to impress the ruler with the British abhorrence of the slave trade, human sacrifice and certain other obnoxious customs, and to sign a treaty of friendship. Horrific stories of the bloodthirsty regime spread by missionaries had proliferated in the British press during the preceding twelve months.[10] A few years earlier one 'Captain Hopkins saw in Bonny, 17 men killed, boiled and eaten.'[11] The Dahomean armies were reputed to be massing to attack Abeokuta, and it was considered an extremely dangerous place.

Richard himself had suggested this mission, probably after hearing stories that the King's armies included the regiments of beautiful warrior maidens which formed his personal bodyguard. Jules Gérard, the French traveller, put the number at 12,000 Amazons.[12] The report that Richard gave Isabel about these feminine troops during their honeymoon made her 'madly jealous', she wrote, 'I imagined lovely women in flowing robes, armed and riding thoroughbred Arabs.'[13]

Richard also expected something spectacular, but he was doomed to disappointment. Tales brought back by the missionaries were wildly exaggerated on all counts, as he found when he visited there in formal dress and tricorn hat accompanied by his servant Selim Aga, and a Naval officer also wearing full dress uniform. This seemed to impress African tribal chiefs.

> Kanna of Dahome
> 31st May 1863

Caro Milnes,

I have been here 3 days and am generally disappointed. Not a man killed, or a fellow tortured. The canoe floating in blood is a myth of myths. Poor Hankey must still wait for his *peau de femme*.[14] Not a skull have I been able to attest. The victims are between 100 and 200 a year instead of thousands. At Benin *au moins* they crucified a fellow in honour of my coming – here nothing! And this is the bloodstained land of Dahome!! The 'monster' as your papers call the King is a jolly looking party about 45 with a pleasant face, a frank smile and a shake of the fist like a British shopkeeper. He made me Captain of his 'Fanti' Corps of Amazons.

About these individuals a fearful amount of bosh has been talked and written. I was looking forward with prodigious curiosity to see 5000 African adult virgins – never yet having met with a single specimen. I found that most of them were women taken in adultery, and given to the King as food for powder instead of being killed. They were mostly elderly and all of them were hideous. The officers are decidedly chosen for the size of their bottoms. Yesterday the King gave a grand review and I saw the whole army pass by. Nothing could be more contemptible. The women were 2038 in number but of these at least 1/3rd had no arms and were simply carriers. There could not have been more than 10,000 men with muskets and I would rather set it down at 8,000. Carriers of arms are about 2 to 1 fighting men and many carry only a stick or lasso to catch prisoners.

The King gave me a large cloth and a small boy by way of dash. I took up a few presents of cloth, several boxes of liquors which he seems from his blear eyes to like consumedly – malt whisky being the decided favourite – and (keep this quiet) three very *dégagé* coloured prints of white women in a state of Eve-ical toilette. This charmed him and he enquired whether such articles can be procured alive. I told him (Heaven forgive me) a fearful fib, and said that in my country the women are of a *farouche* chastity.

. . . Disgusted with the tameness of the place – the King will not be back for a month – I return this afternoon to Whydah on the coast and shall run about a little before going back to Lagos. The Yellow Fever is so bad in the Bight of Biafra that I daren't take a cruizer there. So most probably I shall go up the Niger and attempt Timbuctoo in a canoe. Really it will be a curious spectacle for the immortal Gods to look down upon, a chap starting in a hollowed log of wood for some thousand miles up a river with an infinitesimal prospect of returning! I ask myself 'why?' And the only echo is 'damned fool!'. *Enfin*; needs must when the devil drives.

African proverbs nearly ready. I shall send them to Tinsley, Catherine Street, Strand. Do you think that the father of proverbs, Stirling of Keir[15], would object to cast his eye over them and emit a few words by way of prologuism. Do you know him well enough to speak to him about it? . . .

Abdullah[16]

Gelele kept Richard waiting for a private audience, at which Richard intended to deliver the message from the British Government. When they did meet the King said he could not interfere with the customs to which the British objected, as his people would rise up and overthrow him. He accepted Richard's presents haughtily, saying that what he most wanted was English horses. Advised that English horses could not thrive in the climate, the King replied that his father had earned great kudos by having English horses, and he did not wish to be less than his father no matter if the horses died the same day they landed. This visit, and a second one in December that year when Richard made a study of the language, provided him with sufficient material for a book,[17] and earned him a flurry of favourable publicity in London newspapers.

In July that year Monckton Milnes was created a peer following the change of government. He assumed the title Baron Houghton of Great Houghton; Houghton Hall being a family property, said to have been passed down from the time of the Conqueror.[18] He left the House of Commons with regret, but as he said to his friend MacCarthy, 'We are a lord-loving people'; he thought he might achieve more in the Upper House. So it was as Lord Houghton that he wrote to complain that Richard, in his last letter, had provided him with insufficient information 'concerning the officers' bottoms'. In reply Richard told him dryly to have patience; that there was a great deal of 'original information' which he would reveal to his friends that he could not include in his forthcoming book; 'I could not insert a description of how the *nymphie* [labia] are artificially enlarged by way of affording pleasant amusement in the way of pulling them . . .[19] [or] the queer infidel circumcision with two semi-circular cuts, one above the other below. The horrid form of making eunuchs by evulsion after 20 years of age . . . Could you hint how to explain these things?'[20]

But ribaldry plays little part in the wealth of ethnological and botanical information provided in Richard's book. Ironically one of his observations, had he only realised the potential of it, might have made him the fortune he was always seeking from gold. He was given a handful of 'kola nuts' (also written as cola, he said), which he described as 'the local "chaw" . . . the nut is easily broken into several, generally four, sections . . . The taste is a pleasant bitter, and somewhat astringent. Water drunk "upon it" becomes . . . exceptionally sweet. It must be a fine tonic in these relaxing climates. I am not aware of an extract being made from it; if not it would be as well to try . . . it quiets the sensation of hunger and obviates thirst . . . [and] it is held to be an aphrodisiac.'[21] It was his misfortune that someone else recognised the commercial properties and manufactured a drink called Coca-Cola. Some years later, in 1875, Richard did attempt to manufacture and launch a soft drink which he called 'Captain Burton's Tonic Bitters', using a recipe which he said dated from 1565 that he had been given by a Catholic monk in India. 'Many people have made a fortune with less,' commented Isabel. 'But we were not moneymakers . . .'[22]

In his book on Dahomey, written after his second visit, his descriptions show no sign of the light-hearted humour evident in his letter to Houghton; here, his disgust at the cruelty of the Dahomeans is self-evident. On one night, which he called the 'Evil Night', twenty-three men were beheaded. Since the punishment for breaking an imposed curfew was death, Burton was neither able to interfere nor witness the executions, but on the following day he saw some of the corpses hanging on gallows around the compound, and noted 'fresh heads . . . at the palace gate'. In all, during his stay he reckoned some 78 or 80 people were executed. On the fifth day of his visit the King commanded Burton to dance. No dancer at the best of times, he performed an energetic hornpipe, to the amazement and delight of the King and his retinue; presently the commander-in-chief of the Amazons joined in. Richard's sketch of this woman cooled any jealousy Isabel might have felt on hearing of the incident, but, he said, the authorities at the F.O. were 'in an awful rage with me as Her Majesty's Commissioner, for dancing'. Some years later when he related this story to the Emperor of Brazil he added, 'I should like to have seen *them* refuse when [in] a single moment of irritability . . . he had only . . . to give a sign, to have fifty spears run into me.'[23]

By the time he returned to his Consulate, Richard was seriously ill with fever. The condition kept him bedridden for nearly a month in 'Buena Vista', during which time he wrote few letters and those written tended to be of half a dozen lines. In London there had been great excitement when Murchison received a letter from Speke, briefly informing him, 'we are now in the latitude 14° 30' upon the Nile, and that the Nile is settled.' Isabel immediately reported to Richard who wrote, generously in the circumstances, to the Secretary of the R.G.S. 'Please let me hear all the details of Captain Speke's discovery. He has performed a magnificent feat and now rises at once to the first rank amongst explorers of the day . . . I hope Dr Shaw's reported retirement is not true.'[24] Isabel's letter accompanied a copy of Speke's second book, *What Led to the Discovery of The Source of the Nile*, in which he gave his version of what occurred between himself and Burton at Berbera, and on the Lakes expedition.[25] From 'Buena Vista' Richard wrote to Frank Wilson that he was 'a little sleepy', having stayed up till 2 a.m. reading it. The book survives in his library;[26] characteristically he annotated the pages as he read and his pencilled remarks are intensely revealing of his very personal reactions to Speke's claims.

p.3. . . . Having shot over three quarters of the Globe . . .
[Burton: 'England, India and a bit of East Africa'].

p.6. Burton received £100 from the RGS to cross Africa [sic]* and while attempting that journey got drifted off with the flood of pilgrims to Mecca . . .
[Burton: 'No. Rot!']

p.112. Lt Burton now conceived the idea of suppressing the system of Abbanship . . .
[Burton: 'Not a word true!']

p.116. Whilst waiting here [Berbera] I heard of the existence of Victoria Nyanza . . .
[Burton: 'Not true. Probably another lake. I heard at Harrar.']

do. Col. Rigby . . . tells me he also heard of this lake when he was travelling in this country some years previously.
[Burton: 'The liar!!']

p.132. Lt Burton now said 'Don't step back or they'll think we're retiring.' Chagrined by this rebuke . . . I stepped boldly to the front and fired . . .
[Burton: 'Brooded two years.']

---

*Speke must have meant Arabia.

p.133. . . . not knowing a word of . . . Arabic, I spoke in broken Somali . . .
[Burton: 'Could not speak a word.']

p.168. . . . Taga where I had my first flirtations with the hippopotami . . .
[Burton: 'A failure; it rankled.']

p.185. Captain Burton being no sportsman would not stop for shooting . . .
[Burton: 'Good. Forgets his eye sickness; poor shot and so risk. Men gone with guns at the time.'][27]

These extracts are only a handful of the comments Burton wrote in the margins of almost every page of Speke's book, which is peppered throughout with exclamations: 'rot!', 'all rot', 'absolute rot!', 'not true', 'not the case', 'silly egotist', 'untrue', 'a lie', 'humbug'. It is sufficient to say, here, that Burton was at variance with almost everything that Speke had to say about the expedition and that since his edits were private notes for himself, not for publication, they have a singular importance. In fact he never stated in public, or in his writings, his objections at this level. His published comments were controlled, and far more damning:

I bring no charge against Jack of asserting what he does not believe . . . His peculiar habit of long brooding over thoughts and memories, [and] secreting them until some sudden impulse brought them forth, may explain . . . [why] he could not grasp a fact; hence his partial eclipse of the moon on the 5th and 6th of January 1863, which did not occur. A 'luxurious village' was a mass of dirty huts, a 'king of kings' is a petty chief, a 'splendid port' is a display of savagery. . . . Jack's 'Mountains of the Moon' . . . published in *Blackwood's Magazine*, September and October 1859, which showed a huge range estimated to rise six to eight thousand feet high . . . he owns in his book, p.263, to having built up . . . solely on geographical *reasoning*. Now Captain Grant said afterwards that these mountains were the work of an engraver, and that Jack was amused by them; but if he had looked into the map-room of the Royal Geographical Society he would have found Jack's own

map . . . in all its hideousness . . . he altered their position, and
inserted them around the western north-sides of the more northern
Lake Rusizi, which was manifestly a widening of the river . . . [28]

When Isabel learned how ill Richard had been, she immediately wrote
to Lord Russell complaining about his being kept so long in such an
unhealthy climate. Russell agreed with her, '. . . but it is not true to say
that he is the smallest of consuls in the worst part of the world. Many
have inferior salaries, and some are in more unhealthy places.
However, if I find a vacancy . . . with an equal salary and a better
position I will not forget his services . . . He has performed his mission
to Dahome very creditably, to my entire satisfaction.'[29]

On this occasion Richard did not recover quickly, and he was still
trembling with ague and suffering severe neuralgia when H.M.S
Zebra arrived at Fernando Po on 29 July. They offered to take him
with them to 'St Paul de Loanda on the southern coast' and, hoping
that the sea air would help his recovery, he accepted. A month later
when the *Zebra* returned, although still not completely well he was set
down at Banana, at the mouth of the Congo. Here, with a team of
eight officers and men from H.M.S. *Griffon* whom he had infected
with enthusiasm, he set out on 14 August to navigate up the Congo as
far as possible.

As usual, he sent a finely detailed report to the F.O. on the survey,
on how suitable the region was for trade. By dint of hand-hauling
their boat over rapids, the party were able to travel almost 120 miles
up-river. Away from the coastal zone, and in a higher altitude Richard
reported the countryside to be 'charming, quite a sanitarium'. With
regular doses of quinine and dryer air, his health rapidly improved
and his notes become more illustrative:

> The slaves are brought from many and distant countries, the most
> prized are the Mundingos, a fine tall race each equal to three
> Congonese arguing high and healthy climate . . . With respect to
> the . . . dialect here spoken, I may remark its wonderful resemblance
> to the Kisawahili of the Zanzibar coast . . . sentences heard for the
> first time, were intelligible to me . . . One of these Mundingos told
> me that at the head of the Congo River, or rather its north-eastern
> branch, there is 'a water where men in canoes do not see land', and
> this agrees with local tradition . . . I need hardly say that if your

Lordship deems the subject worthy of investigation, I should feel highly honoured by being chosen to carry it out . . .'[30]

At the F.O. his report was admired, but this did not prevent the usual adverse remarks that the journey up the Congo 'was undertaken without permission . . . the excuse being impaired health', and therefore his expenses were being disallowed. His immediate chief, however, seems to have got Burton's measure: 'I believe . . . that as long as there is a river unexplored, or a mountain unascended within Captain Burton's reach, his health will always be impaired, until he has accomplished the one and the other, though it may be to the detriment of his Consular duties.'[31]

In fact, somewhat to his surprise, Richard had begun to like West Africa despite the disadvantages; the first chapter of his book on Dahome is entitled 'I fall in love with Fernando Po'. But there were some things he detested – Christianised Africans, and the missionaries who taught them English, dressed them in travesties of English clothing and broke up polygamous marriages. He was also wary of mulattoes (except those who had embraced Islam), and wrote scathingly of their morals. One, William Rainey, a mulatto who had received an education in England and practised in Lagos as a lawyer, exacted a potent revenge by suing Richard through the Foreign Office on behalf of clients.

The subject of the affair was the brig *Harriet*, which was brought into Fernando Po damaged after the death of her owner. The three heirs wrote to Richard asking for it to be sold and the money remitted to them. Richard arranged with one of the Bonny River merchants that the ship be advertised for auction, and a crew put aboard her in the meantime. In the event, the ship was bought by the same merchant (Richard's friend, Laughland) at a knock-down price of £280. But the expenses of the watch-keeping crew, minutely detailed by Laughland down to every bottle of brandy, came to £251. The heirs were therefore sent a cheque for £29. On their behalf, Rainey successfully applied for the difference, producing a printed pamphlet entitled 'The Censor Censored, or The Calumnies of Richard Burton on the African of Sierra Leone'.[32] It looked bad for Richard and the Foreign Office viewed the matter so seriously that, months later, a Naval officer was despatched to investigate. He found that there had been no corruption, but that Burton had been 'plainly careless . . . the charges [levied] were extortionate.' The amount in question was subsequently deducted from Richard's salary.[33]

This took months to unfold. Long beforehand, in August 1864, Richard had returned to London where he was told that he was going to be offered another Consulate.[34] Isabel had begun to lobby for a home leave for him in February on the grounds that 'a very urgent domestic affair' required her husband's presence, and that it took almost three months to get a reply from a letter sent in either direction. 'I hope your Lordship will accept this as an official application, because a refusal would prevent our meeting for six months and our private affairs are really very urgent.' This letter was passed down from Lord Russell and had a number of notes appended to it. 'Captain Burton was absent on leave from 7th November to 28th June 1863, nearly eight months and he has really not been present *at* his post for more than 3 months in the whole of 1863 . . .' said one. 'If leave be given again we shall have repetition of complaints from the mercantile community that Captain Burton's continued absences from his post are injurious to their interests.' Underneath this, written in a different hand is the reasonable statement, given his missions to Dahome: 'Captain Burton must remain at his post for the present, but the F.O. are partly responsible for his absences!'[35]

What the urgent private affair was, to which Isabel referred, is not known. Earlier, she had written to Richard's publishers Tinsley Brothers, having just received three letters from Richard – he wrote each week and they arrived together on the monthly steamer. 'We are in a nice scrape,' she said, 'the box containing the manuscript of *Dahome* which we returned has been lost or stolen and he has never received it, little thinking his two Mss. are in it! I now have the business of 3 letters to transact with you, and want to get the *Proverbs* and my own book off.'[36] But these literary matters could hardly be regarded as sufficiently serious to warrant leave. In her biography of Richard, Isabel wrote that she was 'ill with diphtheria for ten weeks' that spring, which left her weak and depressed. 'One afternoon,' she said, 'I took myself to the Foreign Office, and I cried my heart out to Mr. (afterwards Sir) Henry Layard. He seemed very sorry for me and he asked me to wait awhile whilst he went upstairs; and when he came back he told me he had got four months leave for my husband and had ordered the despatch to be sent off that afternoon. I could have thrown my arms around him and kissed him, but I did not; he might have been rather surprised. Instead I had to go and sit in Green Park till the excitement wore off.'[37]

At about this time Isabel wrote some puzzling statements in her devotional journal: 'As I asked ardently for this mission – none other than to be Richard's wife – let me not forget as ardently for grace to carry it out . . . *I have bought bitter experiences*, but much has, I hope, been forgiven me . . .'[38] Shortly after this, in September 1864, she would write that she had managed to adhere to all her prenuptial promises, 'with God's help, with the only exception that He saw it was not good to give us children, for which we are now most grateful.'[39]

The question of the couple's childlessness has often been raised, and sometimes offered (though not convincingly) as evidence that the marriage was a celibate one. It may be that his attack of mumps and orchitis had left him infertile, but there is another possibility. Could Isabel's 'bitter experiences' be that she was a victim of Richard's early sexual adventures? We know that he suffered from syphilis in 1854 and was advised to refrain from sexual relationships for three years. When he married Isabel seven years later he must have believed, since he had experienced no further symptoms, that he was clear of infection. Pelvic Inflammatory Disease (PID) is a common reason for female infertility. It can result from widespread infection of an adjacent organ, such as an inflamed appendix, or tuberculosis for example; but a frequent cause of this condition is intercourse with a man infected with syphilis. It causes permanent scarring of the fallopian tubes and was, inevitably, far more difficult to treat before the advent of antibiotics.

Isabel's remarks written in the summer of 1864 already indicate her acceptance that she was never to have children. Yet up to that stage she had several times referred to 'any children I might have' in correspondence. Given the couple's long periods of absence from each other up to this point, surely Isabel would not have been so *suddenly* sure of permanent childlessness if it had not been medically diagnosed? It is possible that her description of her illness as diphtheria masked an attack of PID (which is extremely painful), and that this was the 'really very urgent' matter for which, she told Lord Russell, she needed Richard's presence. This is only supposition, of course. There is no extant evidence either way. However, there was no history of infertility in Isabel's family. Her sisters all produced children, and

as one of these children commented, Isabel's religion would not have
allowed her to prevent conception, even had she wished to do so;
'their childlessness was not Isabel's fault.'[40]

Richard sailed immediately he received notice of his leave, but was
detained for over a month in Tenerife because of quarantine. There
was 'a joyous second meeting at Liverpool,' Isabel wrote. And a few
days later, from the Foreign Office, he wrote a long letter to Frank
Wilson. It was mainly Consular business, but he also congratulated
the younger man on his engagement, while warning of 'the big disadvantage' that he had himself experienced, 'namely, that your wife
cannot live at Fernando Po or in Western Africa . . .'[41]

He did not know immediately, but he had sailed back into one of
the most dramatic episodes in his extraordinary life.

22

SOURCE OF THE NILE
1861–1864

Richard arrived in London in August 1864. Fourteen months earlier, in June 1863, John Hanning Speke and James Grant had returned from Africa. It was a triumphal occasion, and there was a civic welcome at Southampton. Colonel Rigby, who was home on leave, met them there; their luggage was waved through customs on the personal orders of Lord Russell. The newspapers informed readers that through these two explorers, Great Britain had 'solved one of geography's most persistent enigmas'. As a result, the public mobbed Burlington House in Piccadilly where Speke was to address members of the Royal Geographical Society and several windows were shattered in the crush.[1]

In the euphoria of these first days Speke was congratulated by the Queen and the Prince of Wales, and the India Office paid off the excess expenditure of the Expedition, some £1,000 more than the original grant of £2,500. He was fêted by Murchison who could hardly dredge up enough superlatives. In Taunton, a dozen miles from Speke's home near Ilminster, church bells pealed, brass bands played and the inhabitants turned out to cheer him. There were bonfires and fireworks displays and bunting and flags. Only a few people noted, said his biographer, that beneath the sun-tanned skin and sun-bleached eyebrows and hair there was 'a strange, haunted look about the eyes'.[2]

Quite soon, it all turned sour. Writing to Houghton in October

1863 after reading the text of Speke's address in the R.G.S. *Journal*, Richard noted succinctly, 'I see Speke is beginning to feel the reaction. He has claimed too much and will therefore get too little. The sources of the lakes will, of course, be the sources of the Nile. His original error was in taking the wrong road, and [having achieved] grand success he will be pronounced a failure – merely another step en route.'[3]

It is directly relevant to Burton's story to back-track here over Speke's expedition. Although we now know that Speke *had* found the main reservoir for the Nile in Lake Victoria, he was still unable to *prove* it, despite the long and expensive second expedition. The geographers were quick to realise that he had failed in his mission objective, which was to circumnavigate the western shore of the Lake travelling northwards to the outlet of the Nile, and then follow the river to Gonderoko. Since Petherick was to travel to Gonderoko from Khartoum, their meeting should have provided indisputable evidence of Speke's claim. The Speke/Grant expedition followed the route of the Burton/Speke expedition as far as Kazeh, and then struck out north-north-west, travelling parallel to the Lake but without ever seeing it for 200 miles.

Whatever may be said here about Speke's behaviour towards Burton, no one can deny that his expedition with Grant was one of the greatest of modern times.[4] It involved a great deal of hardship for both men. They escaped few of the general misfortunes of the first East African expedition; they were delayed by a dictatorial king (M'tesa) for four months; and finally, when they learned from local intelligence that a great river which flowed from the lake lay some two or three marches east, Grant was suffering from an acutely ulcerated and horribly swollen leg which affected his mobility. At this point, within sight of their goal and having shared equally all the misery of an exhausting expedition, Speke decided arbitrarily to split the caravan in two on the grounds that Grant's incapacity would slow them up. In a replay of his behaviour during the Burton expedition, he decided that he would go on alone to find the Nile, ordering his invalid companion to 'remain with the property, cattle, and women'.[5]

Grant, who was a gentle, placid and above all loyal companion, 'yielded reluctantly' to the order from his leader, but the measure of his disappointment at being excluded from the first sight of the great geographical prize is illustrated by the fact that 'a matter of days after Speke had turned away towards the Nile, Grant had his favourite goat-boy tied to a tree and lashed twenty times for temporarily relinquishing care of his flock, a punishment of unusual severity delivered by one whose temperament was customarily so gentle.'[6]

The crowning moment of Speke's life came when he first sighted the Nile at Urondogani. He was unable to procure a vessel and had to work his way back up the river on foot. After four days of weary plodding, he reached some falls where, he said, 'a line of low rocks . . . divided the flow of water out of the Victoria Nyanza and marked the birthplace of the Victoria Nile.'[7] Having named the falls after Lord Ripon, President of the R.G.S.* He returned to Grant to give him the good news.

Bombay was sent ahead to Gonderoko to get news of Petherick. He returned saying the Vice-Consul was not there, but had gone off to trade some 70 miles to the west. Supplies were now low and it became necessary to rendezvous with Petherick as rapidly as possible. At the place where the Nile meets the Kuffo, the party took to dug-out canoes and sailed down the river, an experience Grant later described, inexplicably, as 'not dignified'. At this point the river headed in a westerly direction, so they abandoned the canoes to march for Gonderoko, which they knew lay almost due north. Their route cut across a huge bow in the Nile, so that on the march they saw the river only twice, at Jaifa and Apuddo. Consequently they had no idea that between those points the Nile flowed into, and out of, another great lake.**

John Petherick and his wife Kate (who had shared her husband's hardships) had arrived at Gonderoko some months earlier. Finding that there was no news of Speke and Grant in the area, they went off to do some ivory trading. Like all Vice-Consuls, Petherick's work for the British Government was only part-time and he earned a living by trading. When Speke and Grant reached the agreed meeting point, more than a year behind their projected timetable, the Pethericks were still absent. However, the handsome *dahabiah* they sent up the

---

*   The Ripon Falls; now called Owen Falls.
** Discovered shortly afterwards by Samuel Baker and named Lake Albert.

river from Khartoum a year earlier was moored nearby. It was await-ing Speke's arrival, so that the two groups could unite and sail triumphantly down the Nile to Khartoum, according to Speke's plan.

Petherick's agent was not prepared to break into his client's stores without permission, but sent a runner to the Pethericks with the news. Speke, unable to get at the much-needed supplies, took the strongest exception to the fact that Petherick had not waited for him. Casting around for information, he was told by two informants that Petherick's trading activities included slaves, as well as ivory. Frustrated and angry, he was only too willing to believe that the Vice-Consul was up to no good and returned to his camp to tell Grant what he had learned. Grant was dutifully shocked to hear how poor Speke – yet again – had been deceived. It would later transpire that the two informants had every reason to bear Petherick ill-will since he had previously gaoled them for slaving. But Speke did not need to hear Petherick's defence to pronounce him guilty.

When the Pethericks arrived at Gonderoko some days later, they were too late. By a cruel quirk of fate the north and south routes of the Nile had already been linked. The explorer Samuel Baker had arrived three days previously, with an extravagantly equipped expedition from which he re-supplied Speke. He even loaned them his boats.

John and Kate Petherick had endured many hardships and dangers in their journey. Unlike Speke, they had not been wholly supported by public funding. They received only £1,000 (of more than £4,000 expended by them) from public sources, and £100 from Speke's father; the remainder they found themselves, intending to offset the cost by trading. Speke knew all this in England. It was not Petherick's fault that Speke was so late in arriving at their rendezvous, nor that Speke had been unable to get word to them of his whereabouts. After all, they returned only a few days behind Speke, as soon as word reached them. It was a pure fluke that, in the meantime, Baker arrived and was able to provide supplies. Speke took none of these facts into consideration, however. Believing that he had been abused and cheated by Petherick, he became 'implacably hostile', refusing to accept Petherick's supplies apart from a few bolts of cloth for which he scornfully offered to pay.

On hearing of Speke's arrival the Pethericks had hurried to meet him, expecting a celebration. They were taken aback to find him utterly changed from the man they had parted from so warmly in England two years earlier. He greeted them distantly, and accepted their invitation to dine with chilly disdain. During dinner Mrs Petherick attempted to persuade him to accept at least some of the supplies and equipment they had hauled so painstakingly to Gonderoko. Speke refused everything, including boats, drawling offensively, '. . . I do not wish to recognise the succour-dodge.'[8] Realising from his conversation and insulting demeanour that Speke intended to ruin her husband's reputation Mrs Petherick pointedly got up and left the table.

Speke and Grant then embarked in the boats loaned them by Baker, and sailed down the Nile to Khartoum. From there Speke sent his historic telegram to Murchison triumphantly advising that 'the Nile is settled'. And in yet another echo of his behaviour towards Burton, he attempted to lull Petherick's anxieties by writing from there in a friendly manner: 'Grant's best wishes, conjointly with my own, to Mrs Petherick and yourself, for your health and safety in the far interior.'[9]

Before their voyage to England, Speke and Grant stayed in Cairo where Speke lost no time in taking his complaints about Petherick to Sir Robert Colquhoun, the British Consul-General in Egypt. He accused Petherick of misappropriating public money and of trading in slaves. In a formal report of their conversations to Henry Layard (then Permanent Under Secretary at the Foreign Office), Colquhoun stated that what Speke had told him made Petherick unsuitable to remain as Vice-Consul at Khartoum. 'The Consulate . . . will require some attention . . . perhaps a total reforming. If we are to have a Consulate there the Consul should be above the reach of anything approaching to a suspicion of tampering in such scenes as Captain Speke describes . . . the slave trade demoralises everyone, apparently, who sets foot in it.' [10]

In London, Speke's much-heralded oration before the R.G.S was disappointing. He was not a good speaker, did not satisfy his listeners on geographical points, and could not help using the occasion to denigrate Burton to the annoyance of Burton's supporters. Of John Petherick, whose most recent letter reported truthfully that he had been ill, Speke remarked with spiteful innuendo that Petherick 'was trading energetically when I last heard of him', and he insisted on providing an increasingly unhappy Murchison with evidence which purportedly connected Petherick with the slave trade.

A shock also awaited Murchison when Speke – still smarting from the criticism by MacQueen *et al* of his previous geographical paper – announced that he would not allow his findings to be released through the Society's *Journal*. He intended to publish them through Blackwell, 'for general consumption'. At the end of September, Lord Russell contacted Speke regarding his report 'connecting Mr Petherick with the slave trade'. Speke's reply cannot be found in Foreign Office archives, but a month later John Petherick – despite a previously unblemished record and the lack of any proof of Speke's accusations – was given three months' notice of his dismissal and the Consulate at Khartoum was closed down.

Petherick wrote to the Foreign Office and to Murchison detailing Speke's bewildering behaviour, but absolving Grant of any part in it. By the time he received this letter, Murchison had already observed a side of Speke he did not admire. He replied sympathetically to Petherick, assuring him that the affair would be fully investigated by a committee. But without waiting for the opinion of this committee, Speke gave a public speech at Taunton on Christmas Eve in which he openly accused Petherick both of cheating him and of being involved in the slave trade.

Speke's letters to Playfair, Rigby and Blackwood now carried invective against 'that blackguard Petherick', but he did not let up his splenetic, increasingly ridiculous, threats against Burton: 'Don't be afraid of what I have written for it only rests between Burton and myself whether we fight it out with the quill or the fist . . . He was cut by his Regiment once for not accepting a challenge[11] and now my Regiment expects me to tackle him some way or other . . . [my book may] save me the pain of inflicting the kick I have in store for him should our match not end on paper . . . How I wish I had that blackguard Burton's nose between my fingers and thumb.' And even the loyal Grant was not entirely in his favour; 'I shall *never* travel with a male companion again in a wild country . . .' Speke told Blackwood.[12]

Blackwood was deeply unhappy about some of the things Speke had to say in his draft manuscript, particularly concerning Petherick. He wrote recommending a number of cuts, among them Speke's use of the expressions 'succouring dodge' and 'Turk' to describe Petherick's alleged duplicity. 'Substantially, your statement comes to this,' Blackwood pointed out, 'that you met and dined with him, not quarrelling or showing you were offended, and then when you come home you publish a statement . . . which is infinitely more cutting than if you had cut him on the spot. Consult your brothers or anyone about this and I am sure they will agree with me.'[13]

Meanwhile, Isabel – who could see no end to the bitter and damaging feud between Speke and her husband – tried to effect a *rapprochement*. Through a mutual connection, Kitty, Countess Dormer, Isabel met Speke to discuss ending the quarrel. For a while she had hopes of success, but Speke was too vulnerable to the influence of those who had no love for Richard. At their second meeting he said to her, 'I am sorry . . . I don't know how it all came about. Dick was so kind to me; nursed me . . . taught me such a lot . . .; but it would be too difficult for me to go back now.'[14]

The geographical errors in his accounts and maps of his two journeys, coupled with his continued attacks on Burton at every opportunity, his current attack against Petherick and his 'ungenerous attitude' towards Grant, gradually began to tell on Speke's popularity. Led by MacQueen, a group which included Charles Beke, Galton and even Livingstone openly questioned Speke's claim to have resolved the Nile question. Furthermore, there were a number of passages in the written accounts of his journey, referring to his relationship with African women during his sojourn with King M'tesa, about which the public were uneasy. Attacked from so many sides as Burton had once been, Speke became depressed though still convinced he was right. 'I have answered Galton in full and shown him he is wrong in *all* his conclusions,' he wrote to a friend about just one of his detractors. 'Moreover I have asked him to reconsider his resolution of not attending the meeting, as I wish to have all the pros and cons fairly argued out . . . and I think no man more capable of finding cons.'[15]

Not recognising the growing sympathy for Petherick, Speke next wrote a hysterical letter to the R.G.S. requesting them formally to enquire what 'Consul Petherick has done with the money entrusted to him for the purpose of assisting my late expedition, and also what steps he took to render me assistance dating from the time that he first received [instructions] from the society until he met me in Gonderoko.' At the root of this attack seems to be the sum of £100 donated to Petherick by Speke's father. Speke accused Petherick of affording him no aid whatsoever. He scoffed at Petherick's claims of poor health, pointing out that when he and Grant first saw him, Petherick was with a party of Africans carrying ivory. He claimed Petherick did not tell him at Gonderoko that he had any supplies for him; and he had learned that Petherick had sold some supplies, telling buyers that they were Speke's but that Speke did not want them.[16]

At this point Murchison began to distance himself from his position as Speke's patron. The R.G.S. had heavily sponsored Speke's expedition as a scientific project; but Speke refused to allow the account of the journey to be published first in the Society's *Journal*. Instead he was writing a book, for which he received an advance of £2,000 from Blackwood. So when Speke wrote Murchison a letter on the eve of his departure to Paris with Laurence Oliphant, Murchison regarded it wryly. It requested him to send materials and a letter of endorsement to the Government, to support an enquiry into giving Speke a knighthood: 'In fact to show that I was not a mere adventurer looking for a fortune, but a Government Officer who was bound to give up all the results of his work for the benefit of his country.'[17]

Speke spent a month in France attempting to persuade the Empress Eugénie to back him in leading a Christian mission across Africa from East to West, gathering converts en route. He had arrogantly declared several times in public that if *he* did not do so, Africa would not be crossed 'in this century', for he believed no one else was capable of making the journey. His letters written from Paris had an hysterical, excitable tone. Even Speke's most enduring supporters became concerned by his behaviour. 'My dear Grant,' Murchison wrote in May 1864:

> Our friend Speke is out of favour (*between ourselves*) in the estimate of geographers by having entered into what we all consider a wild and impractical scheme of regimentizing niggers and proselytising Africa as a new plan . . . he seems to have set his face against an exploration *up* the Nile to reach the Equatorial Kingdoms and finish off and complete much of what you *necessarily* left in an uncertain state . . . [and] meanwhile is gallivanting with Louis Napoleon and stimulating his Imperial Highness to expenditure for the Gabon.
>
> Being so occupied Speke could not be present when Petherick's

mention was read, but he sent me a most *violent* telegram. So violent that if I had made it public he could have been very injured. In it he '*denounced*' Petherick as a false man etc., etc. However there is a *very* friendly letter from Speke to Petherick after the meeting at Gonderoko which is inexplicable!

Fortunately, you are clear of this row! Everyone says that your name should have been inscribed with that of Speke in the pages of his book. Now it is lucky that he left you out, indicating that you are not responsible for any indiscretions of his. Again the Council are displeased with him for barring all his papers and giving us nothing for our journal. Could you not get up something for us to show your appreciation of the honour bestowed on you . . .

Yrs sincerely
Roderick Murchison[18]

Rigby, who had returned to India after relinquishing his post at Zanzibar to Playfair, also wrote in less than flattering terms:

Kattywar
30th July 64

My dear Grant,

. . . I am very glad to hear that you are writing an account of the Expedition. Speke tells far too much of his disputes . . . and not enough about the country, and his account is so vague that you cannot follow him. This is particularly so in the description of the Nyanza and its connection with the Nile. Still with all its drawbacks of style it is interesting . . . every copy in Bombay was bought up for 18 rupees each, directly it was advertised . . . I wonder how much Speke is in pocket by it?[19]

Both Murchison and Consul-General Sir Robert Colquhoun now wrote to the Foreign Office in Petherick's favour, contradicting Speke's claims. But despite a valiant fight lasting several years, Petherick received no compensation. Speke ruined Petherick's career just as he had previously severely damaged Burton. The F.O. would never admit to having made an error, and it looked as though the matter was simply ignored, but the archives show that those in the highest positions were closely involved. Lord Russell, for example, wrote:

11th June 1864

My dear Layard,

It is difficult to get at the truth between Captain Speke and Mr Petherick . . . Captain Speke has now written several times on the subject of employment on the Upper Nile – he seems under the impression that you are willing to avail yourself of his advice. Is that so? . . . I infer from your memorandum on Captain Speke's last letter that he is not supported by the R.G. Society. I understand from Murchison that . . . the Geographical Society are anxious to break off all connections with Captain Speke.

Russell,

Murchison's correspondence, also, clearly indicates his disquiet.

16 Belgravia Sq
July 1, 1864

PRIVATE

Dear Layard,

Reference to our conversation . . . relating to Captain Speke . . . As I saw that some people thought that Speke's Expedition Appeal came from *us* [the R.G.S.], I thought it my duty to undeceive his Lordship. What 'liaison' he may have with the Empress of the French I know not, except that he proposed to that potentate an interior expedition from the Gabon – one in fact that Chaillé* is now carrying out at his own cost.

Speke sent me telegrams from Paris denouncing Petherick, but which I could not read or produce so intemperate were they. They are tied up and docketed with others as 'Speke's visions'! I have deeply regretted these aberrations as Speke has, in other respects, the qualities required to ensure success as a bold explorer. Please to return the copy of my letter and believe me to be.

Yours sincerely
Roderick Murchison[20]

Speke was subsequently advised by Layard that, for the present, the

---

* C. Chaillé-Long

Government did not require his further services in Africa. Nothing came of his appeal to the French Emperor. In August Burton heralded his arrival in London by writing a flurry of letters to national newspapers, questioning the claims made by Speke.

He pointed out that Speke had experienced two sightings of a great sheet of water. At Mwanza, while on the first expedition, he saw a lake which he called Victoria. At Ripon Falls, on the second expedition, he saw a major river which he identified as the Nile, issuing from a large lake several hundred miles north of Mwanza. This, Speke assumed – without any geographical evidence – to be the northern boundary of Lake Victoria. He had not circumnavigated the lake shore as he set out to do, yet he claimed a lake almost as large as England. How did Speke know that what he saw was not, in fact, two lakes? He showed several rivers flowing into and out of his lake without any reasonable explanations as to their place in the scheme of things. With regard to Speke's so-called navigation of the Nile, this was a serious error, said Burton. Having lost sight of the river after Karuma Falls, he could not prove that the river at Gonderoko was the same river he saw issuing from Lake Victoria at Ripon Falls. In any case, the sources of rivers did not lie in lakes, but in highlands.

Four decades later, when the area had been thoroughly surveyed and it was known that Speke's intuition (and that was all it could have been) had been correct, Sir Harry Johnson summarised:

> . . . As it was Speke's theories have been shown subsequently to have been very near the whole truth. The Victoria Nyanza is the main source of the Nile, though that river finds another reservoir in the great swampy lakes of Kioga and Kwania . . . and a most important contribution from [Lake] Albert; for this last lake is the receptacle of the Ruwenzori range [the Mountains of the Moon] . . . At that time, however, Speke's theory was not sufficiently supported by evidence, and was certainly open to attack . . . because he had blundered by giving the Victoria Nyanza so many outlets.[21]

Dr Charles Beke wrote to the press strongly supporting Burton's statements.[22] Nor were Burton and Beke alone, for other geographers had been harrying Speke since the publication of his book: Hume, Greenfield,[23] Professor Jukes of Dublin and Colonel Greenwood to name a few. And not content with writing to the press, almost as soon as he returned home Burton began work, in partnership with Speke's adversary, James MacQueen, on a small book called *The Nile Basin*. In this work Burton presented a scholarly technical argument against Speke's claim, while MacQueen specifically charged Speke with immoral behaviour. MacQueen was a friend of Kate Petherick's father and had his own score to settle with Speke.

Speke's sexual morality had been publicly questioned prior to this by a reviewer in the *Athenaeum*, who supposed that a young unmarried officer must have found himself awkwardly placed at having two pretty virgins staying with him in his hut (as Speke described) during his time as solo guest of Chief M'tesa. Speke's account of how he 'measured' various parts of the Queen's anatomy (she presented herself naked for the exercise), lacked the academic touch of Burton's anthropological accounts and made Speke's readers fidgety. MacQueen went further than the *Athenaeum*, wondering whether new explorers would find Ugandan people who were 'half-black and half-white . . . with hair like Speke's'.

Speke would never read this book; it was still in the press when he died. But MacQueen was merely writing what was being openly discussed at the Society's rooms that summer, and Speke was aware of what was being said about him.[24] Such rumours, alone, would have been sufficient to destroy any hopes of the knighthood for which he had campaigned since his return.

23

THE DUEL

September 1864

As soon as he learned that Burton and Speke were to be in England at the time of the British Association* conference, Murchison invited both men to address the geographers in what came to be advertised as 'the great Nile debate'. Richard welcomed the opportunity to argue his corner and travelled back from Scotland for the occasion. He was confident of coming off best and he knew that Speke could not honourably back down from the verbal duel. Furthermore, no matter how loud and long Speke claimed that he had found the Nile, Burton knew that he could not geographically *prove* his case.

Whether Murchison had any ulterior motive in arranging this debate is not known since, surprisingly, there is little regarding the matter in his surviving papers. However, his correspondence leading up to that date indicates that he was disappointed and irritated that having backed Speke financially, and arranged for the Society to bestow its highest honour, the Gold Medal, all Speke gave the R.G.S. was a hastily written, slipshod, error-ridden paper for the *Journal*, after his book was published. It was, Murchison said, brief, imperfect and inadequate. An official history of the Society describes it as 'rank ingratitude'.

Murchison knew that Burton was an accomplished public performer and a brilliant debater. It was generally accepted, even by his

*An organisation dedicated to scientific and geographical exploration.

enemies, that he had 'the best mind of his generation', and this agile brain was crammed with history, geography, poetry and philosophy with which he bolstered technical arguments delivered in his pleasant *basso profundo* voice. He was able to marshal the salient points and direct the course of an argument, moving in to finish off his opponent with an unanswerable statement. So polished was he that he could break off in mid-argument to make a facetious joke, his sarcastic laughter skittering 'like pebbles on a frozen lake', and return to the attack while his opponent was still smirking.[1]

Equally, Murchison knew that Speke was a poor, nervous speaker, who sometimes adopted an Anglo-Indian sing-song accent to cover his anxiety. The *Spectator* once said he was so inarticulate that he was brave to even consider addressing an audience. He was deaf in one ear as a legacy of the burrowing beetle on Lake Tanganyika, making it difficult for him to catch all the nuances of an opponent's argument. And, not least, Speke was intellectually inferior to Burton; he frequently made impulsive contentious statements, which made both Blackwood and Speke's family uneasy.[2] Speke had returned from Africa with the world at his feet. A year later he was at odds with a considerable body of dissenters, and had made a number of enemies in addition to his personal *bête noir*, Burton. It was another R.G.S. member, not Burton, who plotted the expedition log and, seeing that according to Speke's calculations the Nile ran uphill for about 90 miles, humorously pointed this out at a packed meeting.

That Speke was depressed about the welling antagonism and ridicule is evident from his surviving correspondence. He said he would certainly 'never again think of writing a personal narrative since it only leads to getting abused'.[3] His solution was to return to India in October, for '6 months shooting and then . . . return on Furlough for 3 years'. First, though, he had to get the Nile debate over. The measure of his anxiety regarding this ordeal is best demonstrated by frequent characteristic boasts that he intended to physically 'punish' Burton. Ever since their expedition together, whenever he felt threatened by something Burton had said or done Speke had resorted to similar ineffective fulminations; much as he had taken to slaughtering Africa's fauna whenever Richard upset him there.

Enter Laurence Oliphant, who possessed an evil genius for propelling the relationship between Speke and Burton into episodes of high drama. On this occasion, a matter of days before the Bath meeting, Oliphant told Burton what Speke was saying about the forthcoming debate; that if Burton dared to appear on the stage at Bath he would kick him. Richard reacted with irritation. '*That* settles it,' he declared. 'By God, he *shall* kick me.'[4]

According to newspaper reports, more than 2,500 people (nearly half were women) attended during the course of the conference. In practice they were spread throughout seven sections, defined by a letter; 'A'–'G', and each covering a specific branch of science and geography. Murchison was in charge of Section E, which dealt with geographical and ethnological matters. The President of the Association, Sir Charles Lyell, formally inaugurated the conference in the Bath Theatre on the evening of Wednesday 14 September 1864 before an estimated audience of some 2,000. Those present on the platform included Dr David Livingstone, newly returned from his calamitous expedition to the Zambezi, Sir Henry Rawlinson, Sir John Richardson,[5] and Lord Milton who spoke on a journey in the Rocky Mountains.

This massive public interest in the sciences may appear surprising, but has to be taken in the context of the times. The mid-nineteenth century heralded a virtually unparalleled flowering of genius.[6] The pace of new discoveries and scientific advancements, the scale and design of building projects – bridges, railway stations, great hospitals and houses – are breathtaking. The penny press made the names of a glittering phalanx of scientists, engineers, physicians, writers, architects, biologists and explorers as popular as today's screen and pop stars.

The best-known explorers during Burton's time were Burton himself, Speke, Grant, Stanley and Livingstone. Of these, David Livingstone was almost in a class of his own. The masses revered him as a saintly missionary, who converted the heathen by the thousand while he explored Africa. In reality, during his years as a missionary under the auspices of the London Missionary Society (L.M.S.), Livingstone converted just one African, who, according to a recent biographical study, soon recanted. 'Neither Livingstone himself, nor the L.M.S. who were nursing a £13,000 overdraft, felt inclined to breathe a word about the solitary convert who had lapsed.'[7] The general public were also largely unaware that by 1858 Livingstone had resigned his post as a missionary, and accepted employment with the Foreign Office as Consul with a roving commission that extended through Mozambique and westwards, in order to fund his explorations. This was an astute move, for he suffered none of Richard's sponsorship problems; the House of Commons voted £5,000 to Livingstone so that he could embark on his 'voyage of discovery upon the Zambesi'. So in addition to the well-publicised debate between Burton and Speke at the Conference, there was massive public desire to see Livingstone.

On Thursday 15 September, the first full day of the meeting, Section E began its programme at the old Mineral Waters Hospital where there was again a capacity audience for the preliminaries leading up to the great debate, which had been well advertised in *The Times* and the *Bath Chronicle*. Speke was staying nearby with his brother, William, at Monk's Park, Corsham, in Wiltshire, and had driven in for the meeting. He rode into Bath just after 10 a.m., and joined the morning throng in the Pump Room where his presence was noted by the *Bath Chronicle* and others. He walked from there to the meeting. As the principals filed on to the platform the Burtons had to pass Speke, seated on Murchison's right, to reach their reserved seats which were near to but not next to his. They could not avoid eye contact. Isabel recalled: 'He looked at Richard, and at me, and we at him. I shall never forget his face. It was full of sorrow, of yearning, of perplexity. Then he seemed to turn to stone.'[8] Richard, who had not seen Speke for some years, noted: 'I could not but remark the immense change of feature, of expression, and of general appearance which his severe labours, complicated perhaps by deafness, and dimness of sight, had wrought in him. We looked at each other, of course, without signs of recognition . . .'[9]

Burton and Speke were not expected to say anything that morning. The following day, Friday 16 September, had been set aside for their debate, and Livingstone was to arbitrate. Murchison opened the programme promptly as the clock struck 11 a.m., and gave a long speech on exploration in general before he got round to talking of Africa and 'the three gallant captains, Burton, Speke and Grant'. Clement Markham next read a long paper on China, and Colonel Sykes thanked him and instituted a question-and-answer session. By now it was past 1 p.m. and Speke had become irritated. He fidgeted noticeably for a while and eventually exclaimed, 'Oh, I cannot stand this any longer,' and rose to leave. The man nearest him asked, 'Shall you want your chair again, Sir? may I have it, are you coming back?', to which Speke answered, 'I hope not,' and left the hall. It was then about 1.30 p.m. Members of the audience noted that at no time was there 'any mutual greeting' between Burton and Speke.[10] This was the last time he was seen in public.

One witness, Mrs Andrew Crosse who wrote of the dramatic events of the following morning, recounted how, 'on Friday 16th, knowing the rush there would be for places we took care to be . . . in good time. The members flocked in, but strange to say the platform remained vacant . . . even when the hour for business had struck. There were signs of impatience in the waiting crowd; but this was quickly subdued by a growing sense that all was not well.' At that point, she said she could not see any of the three men she had come to see: Burton, Speke and Livingstone. The *Bath Chronicle* also reported that, 'when eleven o'clock came and departed . . . and the platform was still vacant . . . the meeting became impatient.'

The Burtons were standing to one side of the platform. Richard noted that the room was 'crowded to suffocation' as he waited with his debate notes in his hand.[11] Francis Galton, who was also present, explained how, 'each morning, a little before the President and Committee take their seats, they meet in a separate room to discuss matters that require immediate settlement and to select the papers that are to be read on the following day.' Richard was not a committee member and, though distinguished visitors were usually invited to sit in, on 16 September Sir James Alexander had proposed to the Section E committee that they 'urge the Council of the Association to bring Captain Speke's services to the notice of the Government'. It was therefore decided, tactfully and in no sense maliciously, to leave Burton out of the discussion; there were, in any case, several of Speke's detractors present and it was obvious that the motion would not go unopposed.[12]

Sir James was still speaking when a message was brought into the room and quietly handed to Sir Roderick Murchison, who read it. He did not interrupt the speaker but passed the message round the room to those present.[13] Galton was the last to see it, but he already knew it contained bad news from the faces of the others as they read it. 'It was to say,' he wrote in his diary, 'that Speke had accidentally shot himself dead, by drawing his gun after him while getting over a hedge [sic].'[14] Richard was invited in, and was facing Galton when he was handed the note by A.G. Findlay, Honary Secretary of the R.G.S., who was a Burton supporter.[15]

Isabel was standing outside the open door and could not see the contents of the note, but she saw Richard sink back into a chair in a daze. Later she wrote, 'I saw by the workings of his face the terrible emotion he was controlling, and the shock he had received.'[16] 'I was so shocked, so pained, I could not speak,' Richard said. The last time Speke had addressed him directly had been when they parted in Aden in 1859: 'Goodbye, old fellow; you may be quite sure I will not go to the Royal Geographical Society until you come to the fore and we appear together. Make your mind easy about that.' Clement Markham was among those present and he stated that everyone looked at Burton, who expressed a few words of regret and left the room to go to Isabel. 'No one could have behaved better or more naturally,' said Markham.[17]

By now it was almost 11.20 a.m., and the *Bath Chronicle* noted that the audience, who on the previous evening had signalled appreciation with cheers and hats thrown in the air, was becoming impatient; there was even ('regrettably') some booing and catcalling. 'Immediately after, Sir Roderick Murchison took his seat, but the only one of the three faces looked for . . . was that of Captain Burton, bearing like Mr. Murchison [sic], a mournful look. "I have to apologise," Murchison began, "but when I explain to you the cause . . . you will pardon me. We have been in our Committee so profoundly affected by the dreadful calamity that has . . . befallen Captain Speke by which he has lost his life."' This caused a sensational outburst of exclamations. When it grew quiet, Murchison explained the circumstances to further gasps of horror. He went on to say that as they might suppose Captain Burton had been greatly affected, to the extent that he felt unable to speak on the matter and had written a short statement which he had asked to be read out for him. This was read out by Clement Markham: '. . . the differences of opinion that are known to have lain between us while he was alive make it more incumbent on me to publicly express my sincere feeling of admiration for his character and enterprise, and my deep sense of loss . . .'[18]

After a short time, at Murchison's request, Richard read from a paper on Dahome originally intended for another session. He had regained only minimal composure and his voice trembled noticeably during the twenty minute lecture. When they returned to their room at the Royal Hotel he wept, 'long and bitterly', said Isabel, and she was several days trying to comfort him.

Speke had been a hostile rival for the past five years. Burton was more likely to have suffered shock, frustration and pity at the news, rather than great sorrow. And he was not alone in his suspicion that Speke had shot himself rather than face almost inevitable public humiliation in the debate. There was an unsubstantiated but persistent story that on hearing the news Richard said, 'By God, he's killed himself!' as he sank back into the chair.

The cause of Speke's death has since become one of history's great unsolved mysteries, and the query, 'Well, did Speke shoot himself or not?' is well known to any Burton researcher. Speke's connections insisted that his death was accidental. This is hardly surprising since suicide implied in his case cowardice, because of the impending Nile debate. But one must also take into account how self-murder was viewed by Victorians. Like T.B., madness or illegitimacy, suicide was something to be ashamed of and concealed; clinical depression was neither understood, nor was it treatable. So the protective attitude of Speke's family, and the confusing and self-contradictory statements subsequently made by them, should be regarded in this light. This is what happened on the afternoon of Thursday 15 September 1864.

A short distance from the property of Speke's brother William was Neston Park, the home of an uncle, Mr J. Fuller. Both properties were 10 miles or so from Bath, and at 2.30 p.m., an hour after Speke walked out of the British Association meeting, he was setting out from the Palladian villa at Neston with his cousin George Fuller and a gamekeeper, Daniel Davis, for some partridge shooting in the coverts and fields near Wormwood Farm.

At about 4 o'clock while he was climbing over a dry-stone wall, a short distance from the other two men, Speke's gun went off and he fell mortally wounded. Fuller rushed to him and saw that his cousin was bleeding freely from a wound in his chest. Davis soon joined them and saw that Fuller had his hand over the wound, trying to stop the bleeding. Speke was conscious and murmured feebly, 'Don't move me.' Fuller, younger and faster than the gamekeeper, ran for assistance, leaving Davis with the wounded man. Speke died about 15 minutes later without speaking. He was 37 years old and his death occurred on the seventh anniversary of the death of his brother, Edward, in the Indian Mutiny.*

* Edward Speke died at the battle for Delhi in September 1857.

He was already dead when Mr Snow, a surgeon from Box (less than two miles from Neston), arrived on the scene. The body was taken to William Speke's house, Monk's Park. On the following morning, at much the same time as news of the tragic event was being broken in Bath, an inquest was held at Monk's Park House by the Coroner of Corsham. Acting on his recommendation, the jury of 'respectable inhabitants' unanimously declared their verdict: 'Accidental Death by explosion of his own gun.'[19]

This is George Pargiter Fuller's sworn statement:

About half-past two o'clock I left my house, in company with the deceased, to shoot partridges. Deceased carried his own gun. About four o'clock I got over a low part of a loose stone wall, at that place about two feet high. I was about sixty yards from that place when I heard the report of a gun, and looked round thinking to see some birds. I saw the deceased standing on the same part of the wall which I had previously got over. He was without his gun and shortly afterwards fell into the field which I was then in. I immediately ran to his assistance, and found a wound in his chest. It was bleeding and I endeavoured to stop it. He was sensible and spoke to me, but did not remain so. I stayed with him about five minutes and then left him in charge of my keeper, Daniel Davis, and went for assistance. I observed the gun lying in the field that I and the deceased were in. One barrel – the right – was then at the half cock; the left hand barrel had been discharged. I heard very little report, and I should suppose the muzzle of the gun was very near the body of deceased when it went off.

Daniel Davis testified as follows:

I am keeper to Mr Fuller. Yesterday a little before four o'clock, I was marking birds for my master and the deceased who were shooting. I was about 200 yards to their right standing in a field. At this time I saw the deceased go to the low part of a wall he had to get over. He had then his gun in his hand. Almost immediately afterwards, I heard the report of a gun and I looked towards my master, and on seeing him running towards the deceased I went there also. He was then lying beside the wall he had just got over. I found him with a wound in his side and Mr Fuller had his hand over the

wound trying to stop the blood. I heard the deceased groan once or
twice, but cannot say whether he was actually sensible. I stayed
with him until he died, about a quarter of an hour after the gun
went off. The gun was a Lancaster breech-loader without a safety
guard; but I should think the gun was quite safe and in the same
state that Gentlemen's guns usually are.

Mr Thomas Fitzherbert Snow, the surgeon from Box, stated:

Yesterday, about four o'clock, a messenger from Mr Brown of
Wormwood came for me to see a gentleman who, he said, had shot
himself. I went immediately and found the deceased lying in a field
near Wormwood, with a wound in the left side, near the breast,
about an inch long. The appearance of it was such as a cartridge
might make if the muzzle of the gun were close to the body. There
was no other wound beside that in the chest, which I found on
examination, to lead in a direction upwards towards the spine, and
passing through the lungs, dividing all the large vessels near the
heart. Such a wound was likely to cause death; the deceased was
dead when I reached the spot, but seemed to have died only a short
time previously.

No other evidence was given. It was assumed that a twig or loose
stone had caught in the trigger, causing the hammer to strike as Speke
was holding the muzzle close to his chest.[20] The gun – or one like it –
was, according to Speke's correspondence with Grant a decade earlier,
an old favourite.[21]

There are minor anomalies in the evidence. George Fuller said that
as he heard the report he turned (surely an instantaneous reaction)
and saw Speke on the wall without his gun. Davis testified that Speke
was carrying his gun. But Fuller's evidence must be regarded as compromised by a letter he wrote some years later to *The Times*. In this
he argued that as, 'the only surviving eye-witness . . . I can testify that
Burton could not have seen Speke on that day, and that the death
occurred before 1.30 p.m.'[22] It contradicts nearly every important
point of the evidence he had given at the inquest:

It was on the 1st September 1864 that Hanning Speke – my first
cousin – met his tragic end when shooting partridges with me in

[Wormwood] Farm near here . . . The Geographical Society was holding its annual meeting at Bath on the day of his death. In consequence of his deafness Hanning Speke did not attend that meeting . . . I well remember . . . the reasons he gave for not accepting the invitation urged upon him. His natural modesty led him to avoid appearing as a sort of hero . . . He also knew that Burton was to be present . . . It was no secret that Burton had no scruples in putting Hanning in the shade . . . by exaggerating his own exploits . . . Hanning therefore preferred a day's partridge shooting with me to a possible wrangle with Burton . . . Hanning's gun was made by one of the best makers of the day, a double-barrelled muzzle-loading one, with an extremely light pull to the trigger.

While shooting with him on that day, the only day I ever shot with him, I was apprehensive of an accident because he used the gun in the same way that he was accustomed to use a rifle, which as you know has a heavy pull on the trigger and is [not] usually kept broken for safety. I do not think that Hanning for many years before that day had shot with anything but a rifle. He did not seem to have acquired the usual precautions exercised by sportsmen accustomed to the use of muzzle-loading double-barrelled guns. My game-keeper . . . and I, both noticed this carelessness in the use of the gun . . . we therefore avoided being very close to him when walking in the fields . . . The game-keeper saw Hanning on the top of the wall holding the gun in his left hand at the muzzle, supporting himself on the wall with the stock of the gun on the wall. At that moment I was not looking at Hanning but on hearing the report of a gun I immediately looked round . . . On seeing Hanning on the wall with his hand clasping the muzzle end of the gun, and observing him in a falling attitude I knew that something serious had happened and went immediately to his assistance.

Hanning cannot possibly have pulled the trigger of the gun himself. The trigger must have been touched by the butt of a stone . . . or some other force . . . the shot entered his left side below the armpit in an upward direction . . . the hammer of the lock on the other barrel was at full cock when the gun was picked up. These facts correspond with the evidence taken at the inquest and should be an answer to the report, or rather innuendoes made by Burton . . . that Hanning committed suicide . . .[23]

There are a number of obvious errors and contradictions of his sworn evidence here. He has the time of the accident wrong, and even the date. We know Speke *was* in Bath until 1.30 p.m. on the morning of his death because of newspaper accounts written that day, and the eye-witness reports and journals of members of the audience and fellow-geographers. We also know from Speke's letters to Blackwood and Grant that far from never having shot 'for many years before that day . . . with anything but a rifle', he shot birds and small game regularly, and that his shotgun was in regular, if not constant, use. At the inquest, less than 24 hours after the incident, Fuller stated that after the shot he saw Speke on the wall without his gun. In his later statement he recalled 'seeing Hanning on the wall with his hand clasping the muzzle end of the gun'. At the inquest he stated that the right barrel of the gun was at half-cock; evidence not contradicted by Davis. Davis, in turn, stated that the gun was a breech-loader. In the *Times* letter, Fuller describes the gun as a muzzle-loader, with the hammer 'on the other barrel at full cock'.

No one has satisfactorily explained what Speke was *doing*, with his vast experience of gun handling, holding his loaded gun by the muzzle, and apparently using it as a crutch; a gun with no safety catch and with the hammers set at half-cock. And this was a man, remember, who regarded shooting as his *raison d'être*.

Anyone who learns to shoot as a child has gun manners drilled into them as surely as the traffic code. By adulthood the early training has become habit, and is so ingrained as to be automatic reaction. With the traffic code one instinctively looks in the direction of oncoming traffic in the country of one's upbringing – even in a foreign country where different rules apply. It is the same with guns. Modern shotguns have no external hammers, as Speke's gun had, but 'breaking' them as a safety precaution, when not actually shooting, is an *instinctive* reaction; muzzles are pointed at the ground. Only people who take up shooting late in life tend to be careless in this respect; they are usually obvious, and seasoned sportsmen give them a wide berth. Burton particularly observed Speke's gun manners in Africa. Speke, he said, made sure that his gun 'did not look at himself or anyone else'. So that even if Speke was preoccupied, thinking of the debate on the following day, it seems curious that he would be careless enough to forget all his training.

Another oddity is a letter written by William Speke, the brother with whom Hanning Speke was staying when the incident occurred. Two weeks after the event, on 29 September , he wrote to Blackwood;

> . . . I never experienced such a blow in my life as we were together and shooting partridges shortly before the accident in the best of health and spirits.[24]

Although the word 'shortly' is somewhat loose, it tends to indicate that William Speke was with his brother and cousin, at least for part of the time, on the afternoon of Speke's death. He does not say 'the day before the accident' or 'in the early morning before the accident', but 'shortly before the accident'. But if William Speke was with the shooting party, why was he not mentioned by Fuller and Davis in evidence? Davis, as an employee, would almost certainly have been prepared to leave out of his testimony the fact that another person had been present, provided he did not have to perjure himself. Did William Speke perhaps see something which made it impossible for him to give evidence under oath? We can only speculate.

None of this proves Speke committed suicide, of course. But it does suggest that his family were desperate enough to manufacture (or withhold) evidence to prove otherwise. Speke left a letter to a friend unfinished. In it he described his anxieties for Baker, about whom nothing had been heard for some time; but it was apparently quite normal in its wording and did not indicate any depression.

Speke's abrupt and impatient behaviour at the meeting at Bath *does* indicate, however, that he was under considerable stress that day. And the looming debate was not the only cause of this. Upset and depressed by the antagonism directed at him from many sources throughout that summer, he could not see where his future lay for, although he wrote confidently to his correspondents of a new African expedition, he had not received any offers of support; and he had lost the backing of the Royal Geographical Society, Murchison, and the F.O. And, as we have seen, some of his letters in the weeks immediately preceding his death indicate a degree of emotional disturbance. Moreover it cannot be denied that, with his pride, Speke would have found it impossible to bear humiliation by Burton in public debate.

Speke's own considerable correspondence, and memoirs about him relating to the preceding months and weeks, show that his frame of mind was consistent with that sometimes encountered in cases of suicide. Still, it seems unlikely that Speke killed himself. The muzzle of his Lancaster, like other contemporary shotguns, would have been a minimum 28 inches long; probably it was longer. The entry wound on his body was below and to the left of his heart, and the shot angled upwards through the arteries over the heart and towards the upper spine. Even with Speke's height and arm length, it would be extremely difficult to set up a shot where he could physically pull the trigger. Shotgun suicides tend to be aimed at the head rather than the heart, for practical reasons. The only way Speke could have contrived to shoot himself, therefore, would be to place the trigger against a butt of stone and press down. That this is what happened is almost certain, but whether he did it deliberately or it occurred accidentally in a moment of negligence, cannot be proved one way or the other given the surviving evidence. Why, if he wished to kill himself, choose that place, and that difficult shot, with little real guarantee of success?

The British Association went on with its programme more or less as planned. On Monday 19 September Richard was scheduled to present his paper on the Congo River and the audience, if anything, was even more 'vast and very uncomfortable', so crowded was it that even some ladies had to stand. They faced another disappointment.

> Captain Burton's paper . . . was today . . . necessarily postponed, because the map necessary to describe the route was at the theatre, where it would have to be put up for Dr Livingstone's lecture tonight. The audience had a great notion of being angry when Sir Roderick made the announcement; but when, after Captain Burton explained . . . and Mrs Burton, by his side, looked an appeal, the audience became smiling and applauded.[25]

A member of the audience later told Thomas Wright, one of Burton's early biographers, that Isabel dominated the platform. She had two fresh roses tucked into the bodice of her gown; 'from the time I went in to the time I came out, I could do nothing but admire her. I was dazed by her beauty.'[26]

The Times ran a leader article that day eulogising Speke, upon which Richard felt obliged to comment through the correspondence columns: 'The sad event to which your excellent article refers must seal my mouth concerning many things. But . . . I may say that . . . the "settlement of the Nile sources" is in advance of fact.'[27] On the same day he wrote to Frank Wilson that:

> . . . Captain Speke came to a bad end but no one knows anything about it. The F.O. has now transferred me to Santos, Brazil . . . I have applied for 6 months to discover Niger sources and of course shall try to see you. Propose to leave by 24 October . . . but nothing as yet settled . . . You will probably have to keep the Consulship for many months . . . My *Dahome* will be out soon . . . Earl R[ussell] read over my proofs and struck out some, I wonder he did not erase more. The Bath-ites have made much of me and I met Livingstone here for the first time . . . Brazil attracts me – I want to see S. America. Plenty of travel there.[28]

Of all the geographers staying in the West Country that week, only two, Murchison and Livingstone, attended Speke's funeral at the village church near Jordans. Grant came down from Scotland and, as he placed a wreath of laurel leaves on the coffin, his sobs were 'audible throughout the sacred building'.[29]

Three weeks later Richard heard that he was not to be allowed to return to West Africa to explore the Niger to its reported source in a lake deep in the interior. He complained to Lord Houghton that it was 'very hard after three years of preparation. I suppose nothing can be done?'[30] Nothing could be done, and Richard spent the next two months working at his writing projects and preparing to leave for his new post in South America. At the R.G.S. quarterly meeting on 14 November, he gave the speech he was to have given at the Bath debate and which later appeared in print, expanded, as *The Nile Basin*.

He pointed out Speke's obvious errors – such as the Nile flowing uphill – and other inexplicable claims, suggesting that many of Speke's inaccuracies were the result of his inability to understand the language and his reliance upon his interpreters. But why, asked Richard, did Speke send Grant away from the lake on 18 July 1862, 'unless Jack was determined to do the work *alone* and have no one to contradict him . . . I was the first to give flattering opinions of the expedition, until the personal account told me how little had been done . . . a lake, seen for only twenty miles was prolonged by mere guesswork to two hundred and forty miles to the north . . . Had we met at Bath, the discussion . . . would have brought forth a searching scrutiny . . . as it is I am obliged to remain dumb on many points upon which, had Jack been alive, I should certainly have spoken.'[31]

Despite the huge surge of sympathy for Speke following his death, and a memorial paid for by the public (to which the Burtons subscribed),[32] Richard found himself well supported by most leading geographers who no longer considered the Nile 'settled' on Speke's evidence. Even Livingstone, who privately disliked Burton and alternately referred to him as a 'ruffian', 'scoundrel' and 'blackguard', agreed. He apologised for his criticism of Speke but, as he pointed out, members had not previously had access to material that made it possible to query data which had all been kept by Speke for writing his book. Whereas Burton's claims for the first expedition, he said, had all been borne out by detail in Speke's journal of the second expedition.

Livingstone expressed serious doubts at that meeting in a speech longer than Burton's. Could the Nile, which flowed for 4,000 miles, mostly through desert, he asked, really be fed through the relatively insignificant Ripon Falls described by Speke? Privately, he suspected that the true source might lie further south, even further south than Burton's Tanganyika, and he wanted to be the discoverer. Livingstone's most recent biography states, 'the Speke versus Burton Nile controversy marked the beginning of his [Livingstone's] own passionate interest in the source of that river.'[33]

Grant, who was ever loyal to Speke and the Speke family, was furious when he heard about the tenor of the meeting and Francis Galton had to write soothingly but firmly to him:

> I should earnestly recommend your not burning your fingers with meteorological theorising. Poor Speke's notions on these things were so crude and ignorant that his frequent allusions to them did great harm to his reputation. What he could have done and what you can do, is to state accurately what you saw – leaving the stay-at-home men of science to collate the data.[34]

However, Speke's intuition, or lucky guess, about the Victoria Nyanza would in time be proved *virtually* correct.[35] His mistake was in presenting hunches, which he could not support, as geographical facts. This robbed him of ultimate achievement during his lifetime, as well as a knighthood. His indefensible behaviour towards Burton and Petherick rebounded on him and brought him a great deal of misery.

Eventually, after further important discoveries by Baker and Livingstone but most importantly by Stanley, the Lake region gave up its secrets. Lake Victoria was proved to be the head water of the Nile, and Lake Tanganyika a reservoir for the Congo. Richard, for all his brilliance, was forced to accept that he had been wrong and Speke, inexplicably, right; but it was not until 1881 that he admitted it in writing, in the *Athenaeum*. Few modern historians would deny that Speke's claim to fame sprang from what was initially a lucky guess, and that Burton was the trail-blazer whose perseverance and work made it possible for all who followed. Most especially, he made Speke's discovery possible.

As 1864 drew to a close Richard's intense relationship with Africa, and his days as an explorer, came to an end. He would make several trips to the west coast many years later, but inexorably now he moved towards a new phase. Life in Brazil, with Isabel.

24

SOUTH AMERICAN INTERLUDE
1865–1868

Although Richard and Isabel had been married for four years by January 1865, they had spent less than twelve months together. Following their marriage, the first signs of Isabel's strong and independent character began to emerge, and because Burton was a confident and powerful force and was not threatened by this, he actively encouraged her to grow by heaping responsibilities on her. In turn, she took her duty to promote Richard's interests very seriously.

The couple spent December 1864 and early January 1865 visiting family and friends. From Garswood in Lancashire, at Christmas, Isabel wrote to Lord Houghton that they were to go on to Lady Egerton at Tatton Park in the neighbouring county of Cheshire, and then to Alderley, home of Lord Stanley, to Lady Beaumont at Bretton Park and finally to Lord Fitzwilliam before making a two-month tour of Ireland. Isabel was particularly anxious to cultivate the Stanley relationship since his father, Lord Derby, had already been twice Prime Minister (and would later form a third government), while Henry Stanley was tipped to lead the party in future administrations. Richard had been introduced to Lord Stanley through Isabel's uncle, Lord Gerard, a friend and neighbour of Lord Derby's. Richard complained in India that his lack of promotion was due to his having no influential family connections; he could never claim this again. Isabel was a superb 'networker'.

Though it is difficult to picture Richard Burton the hardened explorer enjoying the frivolous-sounding circuit of house-parties, his correspondence indicates that, largely, he relished the lifestyle. It enabled him to meet people of real influence – which his father had always impressed upon him as being essential. Some, such as Lord Stanley and William Winford Reade, another African traveller, would become real friends.[1] Nor were such gatherings all tea and buns with the ladies; Victorian men reserved large chunks of the day to themselves for manly sport and discussions, and for smoking and drinking.

Isabel was confident that when people met her husband they would see for themselves that the stigma attached to his reputation was without foundation. Her dowry, her gift to him, was her casual access to influential contacts whom she used without hesitation in what she believed were Richard's interests. 'I began to feel,' she said, 'that he was a glorious ship in full sail, commanding all attention and admiration and sometimes, if the wind drops, she still sails gallantly, and no one sees the humble little steam-tug hidden on the other side, with her strong heart and faithful arms working forth, and glorying in her proud and stately ship.'[2]

The country-house set was Isabel's milieu. Her entire education had been aimed at it; she had the right wardrobe, the right jewellery (mostly presents from her mother, but a few treasured gifts from Richard).[3] She rode well, was an animated talker, knew her way around the complicated web of aristocracy and high society, and she could entertain the company after dinner. But her after-dinner repertoire was no longer confined to accompanying herself on the piano or guitar while she sang. Kate, Lady Amberley (sister of Lord Stanley), who had met Isabel in London at several parties, noted their arrival at Alderley in January in her diary:

> . . . the Burtons came here. Capt. Burton . . . calls himself openly a Mussulman – a very amusing and clever man . . . His wife was an Arundell a R. Cat. clever sensible woman, much in love with her husband. He mesmerises her constantly and then asks her questions about the future. She does not like it all, as it tires her very much.[4]

Lord Amberley also recorded their arrival:

> . . . He is a very dark man, with a fierce and scowling eye, & a repulsive hard face; but exceedingly clever & amusing in

conversation . . . His wife is a pleasant lively woman, talks much and fast . . . This afternoon while several of us were sitting in the library after lunch she began telling us about her mesmeric experiences of which she has had many. Her husband frequently mesmerises her and . . . consults her while in a trance about what is going to happen . . . of course one cannot know how far she may be deceived but it is impossible on hearing her speak to doubt her honesty . . .[5]

Over breakfast Isabel told the Amberleys about her secret courtship, and marriage in defiance of her parents' wishes. Asked how their 'mixed' marriage worked, she answered that she took great care not to 'disgust Burton with Religion', Amberley wrote. 'Consequently she does not fast or go often to church.' She told them she thought that 'anyone might be saved by his own form of religion', and that she did not care to convert anyone. Richard's response to this chatter was not recorded. Subsequent diary entries reveal Isabel's anger when she learned that Richard had hypnotised one of the Amberley ladies.

> Saturday 7th: Blanche was very anxious indeed to be mesmerised & a sort of attempt was made . . . but she did not go far enough to be in a trance. Airlie & I were in the room. Mrs B. was kept in ignorance . . . but afterwards found out. After dinner . . . Blanche was actually mesmerised, Maude and Airlie being present. Mrs Burton was in a state of rage (as was natural) because she was not admitted.

> Sunday 8th: We heard this morning there had been an awful row after we had gone to bed between Burton and his wife, because she was so angry at his mesmerising without her. She said now he would be doing it with women who were not so nice. He was angry at this & affected to think it folly; that he himself had said that if any man mesmerised *her* he would kill the man and her too. A threat I daresay he is quite capable of executing . . . [6]

The quarrel was soon forgotten as the Burtons travelled to Ireland and went from one large castle and country house to another. Isabel had secured introductions from Lord Houghton, in return for her light-hearted promise to take care that Richard's garish dressing-gown never appeared in public.[7] They travelled about in a smart

pony cart with an Irish maid to take care of Isabel. Richard had
wanted her to take on a woman who had just been released from
prison after serving fifteen years for having, at the age of 19, murdered her baby. 'Well, I would do anything to oblige you,' Isabel
refused sweetly, 'but . . . I daresay I would often be left alone with her,
and at thirty-four she might like larger game.' It rained and sleeted
most of the time, but they dressed for it, and travelled wrapped up in
warm rugs. Tuam, the childhood home of Richard's father, came as a
shock to them. Hundreds of poor, hearing that the grandson of the
late Bishop was visiting, flocked to see Richard, 'most with out-
stretched hands'. Some of Richard's aunts were still living in the damp
and crumbling old Rectory that Richard's father had bequeathed to
his sisters; 'and I was very glad of it,' said Isabel with shivery distaste,
'as I should have been very sorry to have had to stop there.'[8] Richard's
feelings on the country of his father's birth were summed up in a succinct comment that it was 'like a fair wife embraced by a husband
abhorred'.[9] This trip did not result in a book by Richard, only a long
unpublished poem which survives in the collection of Quentin Keynes.
But Richard's pen was never idle for long.

By mid-March the Burtons were back in England and on board a
train when Richard handed Isabel a gift. It was a small, slim book of
poetry, nicely bound in dark blue with gold embellishments, which
she assumed he had just purchased at a book stand. It was called
Stone Talk; written by one 'Frank Baker D.O.N.' and dedicated to
'the author of *The Gentle Life*' (the Burtons' friend Hain Friswell who
incidentally nursed the book through the press). Isabel settled down
to read it and was highly amused by the fact that so much of it
reflected the indiscreet and unorthodox opinions of her husband. She
kept laughing delightedly at the wickedly clever humour, and reading
out to him passages that she knew he would appreciate. At one point
she said, calling him by one of her pet names, 'Jemmy, I wish you
would not go about talking as you do. I am sure this man has been
associating with you at the club, picked up all your ideas and has
written this book, and won't he just catch it!'

She read on until she came to an incident she must have recognised
as having occurred in Burton's own life (in Boulogne), where the
storyteller meets the gross mother of a slender inamorata called
Louise, and beats a hasty retreat. Suddenly, the suspicion that had
been half-forming in her mind crystallised. Burton must have watched

the dawning realisation on his wife's face with great pleasure. Frank Baker? Richard's mother's maiden name was Baker, his middle name was Francis. 'You wrote it yourself!' she accused. 'I did,' he admitted.[10]

Stone Talk is one of Burton's rarest, and cleverest, books. It is a satirical poem in 8-line stanzas (the same style used by Byron in his *Don Juan*) maligning what he regarded as the many-faceted British hypocrisy. It is difficult to know at whom the book was aimed, for it was so unflattering to his countrymen, the Government and large segments of society that, despite its witty sagacity, it was bound to offend almost everyone who read it.

The bitter story-teller, Dr Polyglot, gets drunk and sits down in the road to talk to a stone upon his philosophy of life. He discourses upon many themes in a highly critical manner, echoing Richard's written and frequent verbal condemnation of politics and society, and with equally bigoted theological and anti-racial sentiments. He dismisses the Victorian military heroes Clive, Hastings and Napier as 'bandits', and deplores the policy of knighting Indians. Nothing is sacred, from Mrs Grundy to women's fashions, to over-protective and selfish mothers, to book reviewers. He refers to the United States as 'Uncle Sham', berates Wilberforce and bemoans the fact that without money it was impossible to 'get on' in England. He criticises everything about the Government, from the Crimean débâcle to its policy in Tasmania. Some of the couplets are coarse:

> I felt as if a corking pin
> Were thrust my *os coccygis* in.

When she had time to think about all this, Isabel was appalled and concerned. Richard regarded *Stone Talk* as a piece of semi-serious fun and seemed to assume that others would accept the offensive things he wrote, lightly, because he had veiled them in humour. Isabel saw it with clearer eyes, as an instrument that might easily complete the work begun by Speke. Lord Houghton, too, when she showed him the book, saw at once that it would ruin Richard at the Foreign Office if it got out that he was the author. He strongly advised her to try to buy up every copy she could.[11] Only 200 copies were printed, of which – fortunately for Isabel's finances – Richard reserved 128 for himself and the press.[12] Most of the remaining 72 copies she tracked down with Hain Friswell's help, and bought back at the publishers' price of 3s 7d, or in a few cases at the retail price of 5 shillings.[13] She ordered them destroyed, except for a handful which she kept back for their own library and to give to selected friends.

It is clear from this episode that, although she loved his 'keen sense of humour and ready wit',[14] she had already become wary on Richard's behalf quite early in their marriage. At dinner parties she watched his listeners rather than him, sending him discreet wifely signals to behave when 'in an ecstasy of glee' he set out to scandalise, shock and horrify his audience with absurd versions of his adventures. It is difficult to imagine that this would have had any effect other than to goad him on; he was constantly surprised and amused by the gullibility of his listeners, and could not resist drawing gasps of astonishment from them by wild exaggeration and wicked laughter. He told Isabel that he found it bizarre to be believed when he chaffed people yet not believed when he told the truth. Isabel's resolute loyalty to Richard was total, however, even when she thought him in the wrong. When one woman reported to her his Chaucerian humour at a function to which Isabel did not accompany Richard, complaining that she had been 'inexpressibly shocked' at Richard's conversation, Isabel responded sweetly, 'I can quite believe that on an occasion when no lady was present Richard's conversation was quite startling.'

Before Richard left to take up his second Consulship in South America he had a pleasant engagement in London. On 4 April the membership of the Anthropological Society – which he had set up two years earlier with Dr Hunt – reached 500, among whom were two of Isabel's brothers and many of Richard's closest friends such as George Bird, Swinburne, Lord Houghton and A.B. Richards.[15] A Farewell Dinner was held for Richard, at which Lord Stanley made a highly complimentary speech regarding his travels and achievements and, mentioning the Nile controversy, was warmly applauded by Dr Livingstone, Lord Russell, Viscount Strangford and Laurence Oliphant – to name a few surprising diners. Richard had arranged for Isabel to be present, hidden behind a screen in a gallery. He spoke, touching briefly on the famous debate in a sparkling response: 'I did not consider myself bound to bury my opinions in Speke's grave: to me, living, they are of importance. I adhere to all I have stated regarding the Nile sources.'[16] The evening ended with a flattering toast to Isabel, which Richard said he hoped she wouldn't get to hear about.

Dr Hunt rose and said that since Richard had failed to respond properly he must speak for Mrs Burton. To the delight and cheers of his audience, and no doubt to Isabel hiding behind her screen, Hunt said Mrs Burton begged him to say that she had great difficulty in keeping her husband in order, but she would do what she could to take care of him, and to make him as innocent a man as they all believed him to be.[17]

For once Richard was *persona grata* with his superiors.[18] Yet almost his last action in London was to leave one of his cards on the table at the Royal Geographical Society, with a typically Burtonian epigram written on the reverse as a riposte to the latest promotions listed in the *London Gazette*:

> Two loves the Row of Savile haunt,
> Who both by nature big be;
> The fool is Colonel (Barren) Grant,
> The rogue is General Rigby.[19]

When Rigby heard of this insult he was furious; his letters to Grant and Livingstone, shortly afterwards reached an apogee of vindictive malice, and in some cases contained demonstrable untruths.[20] A few days later the Burtons set out for Portugal together. Isabel was to see Richard off at Lisbon and return to London alone to settle their affairs before joining him a few months later. This time she did not fret at the parting, for she knew it was to be brief. It was, in fact, the start of the 'pay, pack and follow' routine that the couple employed throughout their life together. Whenever they were to make a long journey, Isabel explained, 'he used to like to start *at once* in light marching order, go forward and prospect the place, and leave me behind to settle up our affairs, pay and pack, bringing up the heavy baggage in the rear. It saved time, as double the work got done.'[21]

They stayed at the Braganza Hotel in Lisbon and when they went to their room and lit the lamp they found the walls, floor and the yellow satin hangings swarming with three-inch-long cockroaches. Isabel did what most women wearing sweeping skirts would do, instinctively. She jumped on to a chair and screamed. Richard did not appreciate this behaviour in a travelling companion. 'I suppose you think you look very pretty and interesting, standing on that chair and howling at those innocent creatures,' he drawled witheringly.

Isabel stopped screaming. After a while she got down off the chair with her skirts securely hitched and fetched a bowl of water. It took her 'two hours, by the watch', using a slipper, to knock ninety-seven of them into the bowl. She wrote that the incident cured her of ever again being afraid of insects, 'which is just as well'; she would frequently encounter similar incidents in her travelling life with Burton. She had a minor compensation, however. After a few days another room became free and at Isabel's request the Burtons moved into it. A short time later Lord and Lady Lytton arrived and were given the Burtons' old room. To Isabel's smug satisfaction Lady Lytton's screams rang throughout the hotel.[22]

Having seen Richard on his way, Isabel returned to London to complete his outstanding commissions.[23] A month later, on 9 September 1865, she set off on her lone journey to South America via Lisbon, the Canaries and St Vincent, which must in itself have been a considerable adventure. When the ship touched land at Pernambuco, Brazil, after four weeks at sea, there still remained a coastal voyage of over 1,000 miles before she might expect to see Richard at Rio. Ashore, everything was new and fascinating to her, not least the fact that she was offered 'small black babies' at two shillings each in the market. But when she went to the post office to collect her *poste restante* mail, she found every one of the letters she had written Richard since he left held up there. Therefore he could not know when she was to arrive; she had no news of him, and did not even know whether he was safe and well. She sent a telegram to Rio hoping it would find him, and that evening amid splendid tropical scenery, when the band played and her fellow passengers waltzed on deck in the moonlight, she sat by the ship's wheel and cried.[24]

But Richard got her wire and when the ship reached Rio 'he came on board at half past eight in the morning and we had a joyful reunion'.[25] He had, in fact, written to the Foreign Office the day he arrived in Brazil, seeking permission to go to Pernambuco to meet Isabel when she arrived there. But someone at the F.O. realised that a reply to him could only go by the same ship as Isabel herself, and decided that it was pointless to answer him.[26] We cannot know what they said to each other, but Isabel's long and chatty letters home stated that Richard liked Brazil; 'for the first time in his life he has only pleasant things to say – he likes the Brazilians,' she informed Houghton.[27]

Probably he told her that he had already acquired some mining concessions and would shortly make a trip to the interior to view the sites. It was a lifelong dream of his to achieve wealth through a gold strike, but in Brazil he acquired concessions to mine minerals, coal, lead and precious stones as well. 'I am collecting details about the yield of gold,' he wrote to a geologist friend within days of Isabel's arrival, advising that as soon as he had completed some Consular business, 'I will be off to the Headquarters personally and there enter into details. There are many mines abandoned because the yield was not sufficient and these may probably yield again.'[28] He had already planned his research programme for the next few years, as he outlined to Findlay at the R.G.S. 'My great hope is to throw off the Government and become free man. Then, if rich I go to the South Pole, if poor, to Africa.' He thought he would need two or three years to complete his work, 'and then I hope to return to England for a few months, via Australia, in fact, round the world.' And he did not forget to add, 'My wife likes Brazil very much.'[29]

The harbour at Rio, Isabel said, was the most glorious sight that a human being can behold; Richard told her it beat 'all the scenery he had ever seen in his life'. She never tired of talking about it in her letters to England. They stayed for five weeks in Rio, where Isabel fitted well into the diplomatic and consular set and quickly made some useful friends. 'We liked her from the first,' said the wife of one official there, 'and we were always glad when she came up to Rio or Petropolis from Sao Paulo. She was a handsome, fascinating woman, full of fun and high spirits and the very best of good company. It was impossible to be dull with her for she was a brilliant talker . . . She was a great help to [her husband] . . . for he by no means shared her popularity.'[30]

Richard had hardly helped his cause by observing to a Brazilian minister that the President dressed 'like a French cook', and he was still capable of gratuitous arrogance; 'one booby told me how comfortable were white clothes; I told him I had worn them before he was born.'[31]

The Burtons repaid generous hospitality by throwing a party at their hotel, the Estrangeiros, shortly before they were due to leave for Santos. After dinner Richard proposed a moonlight walk in the Botanical Gardens which were closed, but everyone scrambled over the gate. Since she had gone from a hot room into the damp, chilly night air wearing only a light evening gown, Isabel was not surprised when she awoke next day with a high fever and sickness. However, she soon became ill and delirious. Richard nursed her, dosing her with quinine and applying the conventional treatment of hot baths, emetics and ice. He also hypnotised her until her temperature dropped. As soon as she was able to be moved she was carried on the naval vessel H.M.S. *Triton* for the voyage to Santos, a harbour 200 miles to the south. She recovered quickly in the sea air and by the time they reached their destination was taking lessons from the ship's captain on how to handle a revolver.

Having surveyed his territory before Isabel's arrival, Richard had decided that he needed two bases; one at the coast in Santos, and one in the more wholesome air of the mountains at Sao Paulo. Travelling between the two would enable him to do the job properly and remain healthy. As they went ashore Richard, formally dressed in his braided uniform and tricorn hat,[32] was given a gun-salute and met by local dignitaries. After lunch a large party of twenty well-wishers including officers from the *Triton* accompanied them the forty miles or so to Sao Paulo – by trolley as far as the new railway line went, and then by mules and finally on foot. When they reached the top of the *Serra*, a one-in-nine incline, they came to a huge chasm 180 feet deep, over which the railway bridge was going to be built. At the time, however, there were just a few planks thrown across a scaffold for the workmen. Isabel wrote:

> As I was out in front, supposing that was what we had to cross, I walked right across it, about two hundred yards. When I got to the other side I turned round to speak but nobody answered me, and facing round I saw the whole company standing on the other side not daring to breathe, and my husband looking ghastly . . . I was going to walk back again, but they motioned me off with signs, and all began to file round another way.[33]

On the following day two workmen fell off the same planks and were killed.[34] After dinner Richard and the welcoming party departed back to hot and steamy Santos, leaving Isabel in an hotel in rural Sao Paulo, 'a pretty, white, straggling town on a hill . . . which is well wooded and watered', she wrote home. It was 3,000 feet above sea level, 'too hot from nine till four in summer but cool all the other hours . . . No cockroaches, fleas, bugs and sand-flies, but mosquitoes and jiggers . . . in the country there are snakes, monkeys, jaguars and wild cats, scorpion centipedes and spiders . . .'[35] It was, she said, 'five miles on the temperate side of Capricorn' and surrounded by mountains and forests. She was to stay at Sao Paulo while she searched for a suitable house for them.

After two weeks without any success, and missing Richard, she took the diligence down to Santos, where her 'fresh English blood' provided a treat for mosquitoes and sand flies. Richard joked that at least it kept them away from him. He took her bathing from a narrow strip of sand which locals called the Barra, and they changed into ungainly woollen swimming costumes in a small hut with wooden shutters. 'He taught me to swim without my arms,' Isabel wrote, 'and afterwards without my legs, using either one or the other, in case of my falling out of a steamer and becoming entangled.'[36]

After fifteen days at the coast Isabel began to feel feverish again, so Richard ordered her back to the heights of Sao Paulo. On the way up she engaged a 35-year-old slave 'as black as the grate', who had just gained his freedom. He was called Chico, and was a 4-ft-tall dwarf, but 'in perfect proportion' Isabel said. He was her *major-domo* all the time she remained in Brazil, and she also recruited a maid called Kier.

Eventually she found a suitable property being offered for rent by a French couple. It was a roomy two-storey rustic building; 'a kind of farmhouse' that had previously been used as a convent, furnished with 'rough wooden furniture'. The front door opened on to the street, Rua do Carmo, and the table land at the back ended abruptly, so that their first-floor verandah commanded a wonderful view of the surrounding countryside and mountains.[37] 'Kier and I, and Chico, with the assistance of a friend's servant are painting, white-washing and papering it ourselves,' she wrote home. 'The Brazilians are shocked at me for working!' The walls were rough and coarse with holes and chinks, and she had to nail planks of wood over rat-holes in the floor and cover them with rugs, but when it was finished she was pleased, it looked 'pretty, and comfortable in a barn-like way'. She had already come a long way from the marble halls of Wardour Castle.

One woman caller – a 'notorious person' whom Isabel wished to discourage from calling – finding her with her sleeves rolled up and splattered in paint, commented on this quaint manner of economising:

'Yes, I am economical,' Isabel responded forthrightly, 'but I spend all I have and do not save; I pay my debts and make my husband comfortable; and we are always well-fed and well-dressed and clean . . . That's the English way.'[38] To her family she wrote that, 'I want honestly to live within £700 a year, and have as much comfort as that will allow us.' But the Brazilian currency was unstable even then and inflation meant, 'it will only go as far as £300 in England.'[39]

She selected the best pieces of furniture, stored what she did not want and bought some divans and hammocks. She unpacked the 59 trunks she had brought with her from England, washed them out and stored them. Then she set up a study for Richard with a number of plain deal tables made by a local carpenter. Because he ran several projects at the same time Richard liked to have a table for every subject, each piled with the relevant papers, books and manuscripts. As he worked he simply moved from table to table. The room was 40 ft long, running out on 'an eminence', and had a dual purpose. It was also their 'gallery' where they fenced together each day, practised pistol shooting at targets, and juggled Indian clubs for exercise. 'It opens onto a . . . verandah,' Isabel wrote Lord Houghton, 'where we read, write, study, and Richard smokes on his divan.' They also set up a telescope out there, so that Burton could watch the skies and make his observations.[40]

Once Richard had settled his duties, he came up from Santos and joined her, and for the first time since their marriage they were together in a home of their own. They fell easily into a pattern which suited them both, rising at dawn and quietly going about their separate work until the meal they called breakfast at 11 o'clock. During this period Richard produced a phenomenal amount of written material. He began working on his translations of Camoens' *Lusiads*, a collection of Hindu fairy tales later published as *Vikram and the Vampire* ('They are not without a quaintish merit,' Richard said, offering them to his publisher),[41] and some verses from *The Arabian Nights*. Quoting Victor Hugo, he prefaced one of his translations with the words 'To translate a foreign poet is to enrich the national literature.'[42] He also wrote several articles for *Frasers Magazine*,[43] and a few months later he was working at three major books on South America.[44] Somehow he also found time for several lengthy expeditions, his Consular work, and to be tutored in mathematics, 'It feels odd going to school near 50,' he commented to a friend.[45]

Isabel took great care that he should be made comfortable and saw that he was never disturbed when he was working. She got on with her own affairs, running the house and taking Portuguese lessons from a local woman; 'Richard speaks it perfectly, I only so-so,' she wrote to Lord Houghton after a year, 'but I can say everything I want and be understood.'[46] She also practised at the piano for several hours a day and learned the music and songs of the country and of Spain and Portugal. In Rio the couple had made friends with Albert Tootal, a young clerk at the Consulate, who purchased sheet music for Isabel in Rio and sent it to her. 'You very kindly told me I might ask you for anything,' she wrote, requesting him to get for her 'any of those gay little Andalusian songs – Bull Fight, Contrabandista, or gypsy things I should be so grateful . . . I am spoony on anything Spanish.'[47] She began a fern collection; 'there are three or four hundred varieties in Brazil,' she told friends, 'some 40 feet high.'

Then there were her animals. The period she spent at the farmhouse in England while Richard was in the United States stood her in good stead; she kept two 'not very good' horses, strapping (grooming) and exercising them herself every day, and even acted as vet to them. She kept poultry and goats (no cows or sheep as she was told they would not flourish in Sao Paulo), and a terrier puppy 'Nellie' who 'steals like a magpie and is afraid of nothing'. Nellie came to a sad end after rushing through the open front door one day (it happened to be Friday the 13th), straight under the wheels of a carriage.[48] 'I am getting very well up in all that concerns stables and horses, and ride every day,' she reported home. 'You cannot imagine how beautiful the forests are. The trees are all interlaced with beautiful creepers . . . all wild, tangled and luxuriant . . . you must force your horse through these to make your way . . . The other day I went off to ride and lost myself for four and a half hours in a forest . . . I met two bulls and a large snake (cobra); I rode away from the two former and the latter wriggled away under my horse's stomach; he was frightened at it.'[49] Sometimes she gathered orchids which she packed in damp moss and sent home to her mother and sisters.[50] During one of her solitary rides she was attacked by a brigand but she easily outran him on her fitter horse. Unfortunately, during her flight the horse stumbled, throwing her against the high front of her saddle, causing her considerable bruising and discomfort which lasted some weeks.

Sometimes in the afternoons the couple rode out together, 'fly[ing] over the Pampas . . . like the wind',[51] or went on long walks. 'One day,' she wrote, 'we walked six miles . . . up the mountains . . . there we had Sao Paulo like a map at our feet, and all the glorious mountains around us. We sat under a banana tree and spread our lunch and ate it and stayed all day and walked back in the cool of the evening . . . these South American evening scenes are very lovely and on a magnificent scale. The canoes paddling down the river, the sun setting on the mountains, the large foliage and big insects, the cool, sweet-scented atmosphere and a sort of evening hum in the air.'[52]

Given the chance, Isabel would always have gone with Richard on his frequent travels, but she did not make a fuss or complain to her family when he went off 'gipsying' alone. She understood his need for occasional solitude, but also that this need did not conflict with his feelings for her. The Burtons' marriage worked because Richard was not confined or chafed. No other man could have given Isabel the adventure and freedom that came in abundance in her life with Richard; conversely, few women of her station would have found the life acceptable, let alone revelled in it. Small things can often illustrate the tenor of a relationship better than reams of words; the message he left for her on the back of an old envelope, on an occasion when they had arranged to meet but missed each other, for example:

> Once Venus made a tryst
> With a man of her affection
> Man once made a tryst
> With Venus his affection
> But his charmer missed
> By losing her direction![53]

When Richard went down to the coast she accompanied him, but the rain bucketed down so strongly that it broke her umbrella. When it stopped raining, the ground and vegetation vaporised in the hot sun and the steamy heat made her feverish, and Richard made her return to Sao Paulo. 'I hate Santos,' she wrote crossly.[54] In December 1866 there was an outbreak of cholera. 'I have had a very mild attack,' she wrote to her mother, but some of her 'namby pamby' South American women acquaintances were badly affected. 'If I did not fence, do gymnastics, ride and bathe in the sea, eat and drink but little, attend to my internal arrangements and occupy myself from early to late to keep my mind free from the depression that comes . . . in these latitudes . . . I could not live six months. When I got the cholera it was three in the morning. I thought I was dying so I got up, went to my desk and settled all my worldly affairs . . .'[55]

At home in England Richard had left behind some problems. He had openly criticised the missionaries in Sierra Leone and his comments were now the subject of a House of Commons debate; he had been cross-examined by a committee for four hours the day before he left for Brazil. Livingstone spoke against Burton and carried the day. William Rainey, the mulatto lawyer from Lagos, received compensation for his clients from the F.O. in the matter of the brig *Harriet*; he had a pamphlet printed giving his one-sided version of the case and left a copy at the R.G.S. Rigby saw it there and was elated: 'the agents are going to sue Burton in a Civil Court,' he wrote to Grant, 'and he will have to come home!'[56] Baker was on his way home with his theories about the Lake region. 'I wonder what Baker will say?' Richard mused to Houghton. 'The Anthropological must be very savage.'[57]

Fortunately for the Burtons, during their time in South America their supporter and friend, Lord Stanley, became Foreign Secretary, so enemies like Rigby made little headway when they tried to make trouble for Richard. When the British Ambassador in Brazil, Sir Edward Thornton, made an official complaint about Richard's mining activities in 1866, for example, Stanley replied that he hardly thought an interest in mineral production could be regarded as trading.[58] Isabel, realising that the 'round the world via Australia' plan was beyond their finances and therefore a pipe-dream, was confident that if Richard worked quietly for three or four years Stanley could be persuaded to give him the Consulate he *really* wanted, Damascus.

So she covered for him, copying out lengthy, tedious reports on harbour movements, while he went off to explore the country or visit his mining concessions, or even – on one occasion – to look for a reported 160-ft-long sea serpent. 'Do not tell this as it might get him into trouble at the F.O.,' she wrote to her family.[59] On another, 'I am at present engaged with the F.O. reports: I have to copy (1) thirty-two pages on Cotton report; (2) one hundred and twenty-five pages on Geographical report; and (3) eighty pages on General Trade report. This is for Lord Stanley so I do it cheerfully.'[60]

Among Isabel's papers, and in the Public Record Office at Kew, the

practical results of Burton's period as Consul in South America survive in the form of lengthy reports on towns, people, flora, fauna,
political implications etc. Some are written in Burton's hand, some in
Isabel's and some in an unidentified hand – presumably a hired clerk.
It has been said, correctly, that Richard was 'hardly ever at his post'.
But he achieved far more in the weeks when he did work than most
of his contemporaries did in full-time effort.

By the following summer the railway from Santos reached Sao
Paulo making possible daily commuting between the two bases.
'Richard is as happy as possible,' Isabel reported to Lord Houghton.
'He leads a domestic life to the letter for three or four months and
then suddenly tells me to pack up the saddle bags. Sometimes I go.
Sometimes I am left in charge. I am "Vice Consul", and we have an
acting one, too.' Richard was still avidly following up his mining
interests and Isabel had a chance to see the gold and diamond diggings at Minas Geraes at first hand, as the couple set out on an
exciting expedition which was to culminate in a 1,500-mile journey
by raft and canoe down the San Francisco River to the Atlantic
Ocean. 'We, that is to say my wife and I – and a negret answering to
the name of Chico . . . after exhausting the excitements of the Rio
"season" left that charming but drowsy, dreamy and do-little capital
on June 12, 1867,' Richard wrote in his book *Highlands of the Brazil*.
'Affectionate acquaintances bade us goodbye. I was looked upon as a
murderer . . . because Mrs Burton chose to accompany me.'[61]

Surprisingly it is Richard's account, not Isabel's, which tells of the
difficulties of the journey: the heat and dust, tiredness, ticks, extreme
cold at altitude, difficult mules which threw their riders etc. He speaks
of Isabel with amused affection throughout his book; how, when they
travelled over rough country in a coach, he 'packed . . . my wife in
between us [Richard and the coachman] in case of spills'; 'my wife
was allowed to swing in a hammock inside, while we slept on the
verandah'; 'It was Saturday – begging day by ancient usage in the
Brazil. We were strangers and therefore fair game.' He would have
ignored beggars, but Isabel, he said, 'still believes in knightly and
middle-aged legends about alms . . . all, therefore, received coppers.'

On 24 June they stayed in an inn at Campapuao where, Isabel
recalled, the accommodation given their animals was more luxurious
than their own. Unable to sleep, she overheard the hoarse whispering
of the inn-keeper and his wife through the paper-thin walls of their

room. 'I heard the man say distinctly, "Don't bother me any more: it will be quite easy for me to kill them both and I mean to do it."' In his version of the same incident, Richard wrote that Isabel woke him and he opened his eyes to see 'a bowie knife and repeating pistol make their appearance'. Leaning close, Isabel whispered what she had heard the man say, 'in Portuguese' said Richard meaningfully (Isabel was still learning the language). The couple spent the remainder of the night watching the door. 'If it opens,' Richard instructed, 'I'll let fly at the door; and if a second comes in, then you fire.' No one came and they lay awake till dawn with their pistols in their hands. At breakfast their host brought them a pair of hot roast chickens for which they thanked him. He told them that he and his wife had argued during the night about the chickens, for they were the only two they had and she had not wanted them killed. '"But we had nothing else and I was determined you should have them both."' They were glad when he left the room so that they could give way to laughter.[62]

A month later they were at Morro Velho mine, in which Richard had acquired some shares. The workings were three-quarters of a mile deep. 'We dressed in miner's dresses with the usual candle in our caps, and we got into a basket like a cauldron hanging to the end of a long chain, and we began to descend,' said Isabel. 'It seemed like an eternity, going down, down, down, and of all the things we have ever done, it seemed to me that it was the one which required the most pluck . . . After an interminable distance we began to see lights below, at a great distance like you see a seaport town from a mountain . . . They gave us a hearty cheer . . . I must say I think Dante must have seen a similar place to make his inferno.'[63] Isabel's apprehension cannot have been helped by the fact that a short time earlier the chain had snapped, 'and we saw the poor smashed [bodies] brought up'. The chain also broke on the following day and Isabel was given the broken links as a souvenir.

She was determined to undergo any dangers or discomfort to accompany Richard, but her hopes of being his companion on his white-water rafting expedition were thwarted when she fell and sprained her ankle. That Richard minded about losing Isabel's company is apparent from his book; he speaks with admiration of her fortitude, capability and willingness to live roughly. The account of this first part of his journey is different from his other travel writings. Here he is enjoying his travelling, sharing the pleasures and difficulties with a companion who, he knew, would never be disloyal to him. Sometimes, when there were too many things to see in one area and time was limited, he would confidently despatch Isabel to observe and make notes while he did the same at another site.

However, Isabel's injury made it impossible for her to move about without crutches, and even then in a most limited manner with considerable pain. Knowing that Richard's time was strictly limited, and though she 'would have given worlds to accompany him', Isabel unselfishly made the decision to return to Rio, so as not to hinder his plans. He was full of admiration for her unhesitating decision, 'to travel accompanied by unarmed blacks. There are few places where this can be done with perfect safety,' he pointed out, 'even in civilised America.'[64] On 7 August, Richard recorded that as they walked down to the river where he was to embark alone on his voyage, 'the animals were waiting to carry home . . . my wife – who was [prevented] from accompanying me by a bad fall and serious sprain . . . I felt an unusual sense of loneliness as the kindly faces faded in the distance.'

Isabel wrote and told Lord Houghton about their trip:

> We have had a charming three month journey . . . with mules and horses and went about 25 miles a day on average as the countryside is so difficult . . . The scenery is stupendous, splendid mountains wooded to the tops; valleys with broad rivers sweeping through them to an occasional cataract; long tracts of virgin forests and glorious tropical foliage . . . I accompanied Richard to the big river & went part of the way in his canoe but having hurt myself and being on crutches I was too dependent and a bore, so I was carried back to an Englishman's house who lent me some good animals and I rode back to Rio with two slaves . . .[65]

Her letter merely touched on her first really adventurous journey. She had travelled with only an unserviceable revolver for protection, on the assumption that the threat alone would be enough to discourage anyone. Richard took their guns, his need being considered greater. Chico, Isabel insisted, would protect her. Chico was not much help on the occasion when, on coming across a man thrashing a bundle which turned out to be a groaning slave, Isabel rushed in and tried to hold his hands, calling for Chico to help her. The man laughed, threw Isabel aside and carried on thrashing. 'I very nearly

fainted. I expected the poor wretch to have been pounded to an ointment, but to my surprise when he gave it a kick and told it to get up,
up rose a fine young woman, gave herself a shake, and walked off.'[66]
Her chief concern was to remain free of leprosy and for this reason
she preferred to sleep in her own hammock, slung wherever it was
possible, rather than in hotel or inn beds.

By the time she arrived in Rio, Isabel's appearance would have
shocked her mother. Rather daringly she had ridden the entire return
journey, some 400 miles, astride 'like a man', and her appearance had
suffered in the process. She wrote elatedly that she had 'never enjoyed
anything more'. Without a major change of clothes for three months
she was dirty, dishevelled, and tanned to 'the colour of mahogany'.
Kier had been instructed to bring her luggage to Rio, but Isabel had
not located her maid when she tried to check in to the city's grandest
hotel. There she was taken for 'a sailor's wife' and coolly referred to
a shabby inn on the other side of the street. She stood her ground and
was begrudgingly shown to a room. Later, rested, bathed and changed
into the fresh clothes brought to her by Kier, Isabel opened her door
to find the puzzled manager asking, 'Did that woman come to take
the apartment for you, Madam? I do beg your pardon, I'm afraid I
was rather rude to her.' Isabel explained that she was the woman, but
no apology was necessary. 'I saw myself in the glass,' she told him,
adding that she wasn't surprised at his trying to turn her away.[67]

After a few weeks she went to Santos to bring Richard's Consular
returns up to date. Ten weeks later she returned to Rio at the time
appointed by Richard and met every steamer that came down the
coast in hopes of his being on it. While waiting, she wrote to
Houghton, 'Richard has now been [away] . . . four months and I am
getting anxious as I do not hear any news of him. He will emerge on
the coast . . . [at] Alagoas and steam down to Rio, where I am waiting for him.'[68]

But she was not bored. Under normal circumstances Isabel managed to visit Rio about three or four times a year. The couple had been
introduced to the Emperor and Empress soon after their arrival and
appear to have made a hit with them, for they were on regular calling
terms 'without ceremony'; a privilege not shared by the other English
residents. On one notable occasion at a reception the Burtons were
called out of an ante-room to sit in private conversation with the
Imperial family, while Richard's direct superior, Mr (later Sir Edward)

Thornton, was kept cooling his heels with other ministers outside.* So
Isabel did not lack for company while she waited for Richard. There
were ministers and *attachés* from every civilised country and she was
very much at home among a small coterie of about 25 people who
called themselves 'the Rio Club'; they dined, danced, rode, swam,
sailed, picnicked and went to concerts together. On one of their excursions she was invited by the train driver to drive the engine.

Sometimes she was asked to visit and entertain the Imperial family
in the evenings. 'I am reported to have gone to Court with a magnificent tiara of diamonds (you remember my crystals!),' she wrote
merrily to her mother.[69] On another occasion she told her family of a
frightening experience while swimming off a lonely beach. She left
Kier sitting with her dress and shoes, and in her underclothes went
swimming out to a log she saw floating in the water. As she
approached it the log moved and she turned and swam for her life
back to the beach to find her maid in hysterics. When Isabel scrambled out of the water and looked back she saw that her 'log' was a
shark, 'and a good big one, too'.[70]

The down-side of life in Rio was its unhealthy climate. Isabel suffered recurrent fevers, and acute attacks of boils that were sometimes
so bad that she could neither sit, kneel nor lie down but had to be
'slung up' to get any rest. 'I am very thin, and my nose is like a cut-
water,' she reported to her family. 'People who saw me on my arrival
from England say I look very delicate; but I feel very well when I have
no boils.' She soon found that the topical application of a ring of lau-
danum (opium) cleared them up quickly.

Isabel met Wilfred Scawen Blunt and his sister Alice while she was
waiting in Rio. They had last met when Isabel was a schoolgirl staying with her aunt in Mortlake when Blunt had been an occasional
visitor and, he recalled, she was then a quiet and pretty convent girl.
By 1867, he wrote in his diary, 'She had developed into a sociable . . .
talkative woman . . . overflowing with stories of which her husband
was always the hero. Her devotion to him was very real, and she
was . . . entirely under his domination, an hypnotic domination
Burton used to boast of. I have heard him say that at a distance of

---

*This incident may well have provoked Thornton's complaint about Richard's
  mining interests.

many hundred miles he could will her to do anything he chose as completely as if he were with her in the same room. Burton's sayings, however . . . were not to be altogether depended upon and he probably exaggerated his power.'[71]

One of Isabel's closest friends in Rio was young Albert Tootal who often performed commissions for her while she was in Sao Paulo, such as sending sheet music or books that she needed. She developed a close affection for him which was almost flirtatious. In a remarkable tranche of letters in the Huntington Library, which detail her home life in Brazil far more colourfully than her published writings, she alternately teased, challenged and confided in Tootal who would later become one of Richard's literary associates.

'I am glad to see you *appreciated* my "amiable half dozen lines",' she wrote, typically, to him, 'otherwise you would have been severely punished by a long silence and the withdrawal of the light of my countenance until you showed some signs of feeling the pain of loss.'[72] Other letters teased: 'My dear Mr Tootal, I got your scrubby note this morning. It was the dullest thing I ever read and did not repay me for the labour. But I think I shall be able to repay you in kind as there is positively nothing to say.' At the end of a letter which tells of her riding, her neighbours, and Richard having found diamonds in his diggings, she admonishes coquettishly, 'Mind you write to keep me in a good temper. I had intended to pay you out with a terribly senseless note like your own, but you see I can't contract my wit and intelligence, and you can't expand yours, so it is not fair to make odious comparisons . . .'[73]

She could never have behaved in this flippant manner with a single man outside her family, had she not been safe and confident in her marriage to Richard and aware that he would not take such behaviour amiss. None the less, it would have been frowned upon in England for a woman left alone so often to write to a bachelor friend so intimately, and this correspondence presumably reflected the relationship the two friends enjoyed in person when Isabel was in Rio.

Having met every steamer for a month, she missed the arrival of one only to find that Richard, 'clad in scanty rags',[74] was on it, and was very aggrieved to find she had not bothered to come and meet him. They returned to Santos (which Richard flippantly referred to as 'Wapping in the Far West') and Sao Paulo, to find a novel situation. An Englishman who wished to be married in Sao Paulo had asked

Richard to conduct a civil ceremony in his capacity as Registrar. 'Fancy him doing parson!' Isabel wrote, highly amused. 'I shall wear my poplin, black and white lace and crystal coronet . . . Richard says, "I won't say *Let us pray*." He is going to do with, "Do any of you know any reason why this man and this woman should not be married? Have any of you got anything to say?" Then, shaking his finger at them in a threatening way, he is going to plunge into it. I know I shall burst out laughing.'[75]

They seemed to spend a great deal of their time together laughing, but throughout their joint writings it is clear that at times they also had noisy disagreements such as the one about hypnotism overheard by the Amberleys. This could only be regarded as normal between two intelligent and self-opinionated people, but it belies any implication that Isabel was subjugated by her obsessional love for her husband. Certainly, she stuck to the letter of her private pre-marital vow always to support him in public, but she was more than capable of arguing her opinions with him in private.

During the hottest weeks of December and January the couple spent a good deal of the time at the beach hut, alone. Isabel did not even take Kier, which enabled them 'to sit in the water and let it roll over us,' and walk about barefoot in flimsy nightshirts, 'for there was not a soul to see us.' It was so hot, she wrote home, that 'if one could take off one's flesh and sit about in one's bones, one would be too glad.' They slept in hammocks, with the door and shutters wide open to the ocean winds and the sound of surf.

Sometimes, when Richard had to return to duty, she sent for Chico so that she could remain at the beach hut. Invited to dine with friends who lived about a mile and a half along the coast, she would pack her shoes, stockings and evening dress in oilskin and ride barefoot along the narrow beaches through the surf to her engagement, on a borrowed pony. 'I used to have to get down and lead him through the streams that were rushing to the sea, to which he had a dislike . . . and when we reached the hospitable door I was conducted to a room to put on my shoes and stockings and my dinner dress. However, we were not *décolleté* nor did we wear flowers or diamonds on that lonely coast.'[76]

One of the things that Isabel had come to love about Brazil was the personal freedom it allowed her. Tanned and fit, she was able to behave in a manner that she could never adopt at home. She was not one of those intrepid Victorian women who travelled in stays carrying parasols. She often rode astride, and sometimes in the wilds she even took to wearing gaucho-type trousers for comfort (probably at Richard's prompting). 'People here think me shockingly independent because I ride with Chico behind me. So what do you think I did the other day?' she wrote to her family from Sao Paulo describing an incident which seems at odds with her usual concern for animals.

> They have at last something to talk about now. I rode out about a league and a half, where I met four fine geese. I . . . have never seen a goose; they do not eat them here only use them as an ornamental bird. Well, Chico and I caught them and slung one at each side of my saddle, and one at each side of his, and rode with them cackling and squawking all the way through the town . . . whenever I met any woman I thought would be ashamed of me, I stopped and was ever so civil to her. When I got to our house, Richard, hearing the noise, ran out on the balcony; and seeing what was the matter, he laughed and shook his fist, and said, 'Oh, you delightful blackguard – how like you!'[77]

The spring weather in 1868 was appalling, with ceaseless torrential downpours and high winds that kept them tied to the house. 'You are doubtless very dull at Rio,' Richard wrote to Albert Tootal in February. 'Here it is a chronic state of death. I have finished my translation of *Uruguay* and am copying it out for print. My daily work begins at 6 a.m. and ends at 10 p.m.; there is an immensity of reading to be done before one can write about the Brazil.' To keep his spirits up Richard had planned another long expedition into the interior of the Continent, beginning in April. He intended to journey through Paraguay (to report on the war there), cross the Andes into Peru, track down the coast of Chile to Valparaiso and Santiago and then sail round the Horn to Buenos Aries. He confided in Tootal that he expected this journey to take 'at least eight months', but cautioned him not to speak of it to anyone else.[78]

Isabel was to accompany him part of the way, until he came across a tribe of South American Indians, when she would return home. He thought he would learn more about them if he was alone. Meanwhile, Tootal was to continue working on the translation of a bizarre book about cannibalism (work he began at Richard's suggestion) which would eventually be published as *The Captivity of Hans Stade in AD 1547–1555*. Richard had agreed to act as editor and to arrange for the work to be published, and was unsure who he would use for this specialised subject; 'I am not quite certain about putting Stad [sic] into the hands of the Hakluyt [Society] – it will be like burying the book alive . . . we have time to think it over.'[79]

Isabel had her own plans after she parted from Richard. 'I shall then ride down the coast and embark for England, remain six months, see all my friends, civilise myself a little, buy some new clothes and be back before his return,' she advised Lord Houghton. In the event their departure had to be delayed for, while Isabel was writing this lengthy letter to Houghton over a period of days in mid-April 1868, Richard became seriously ill. Houghton had previously written to say that there had been some unpleasant rumours circulating in London clubs about Richard, after Speke's brother had been missing for a time; Richard was rumoured to have had something to do with his disappearance.

> We laughed heartily at the idea of Richard spiriting away Speke's brother – I just read that he is found again. Now that could only have been done for notoriety – very mad indeed. Had he gone to Timbuctoo well and good – but to throw one's hat into Birdcage Walk and lose oneself in the inhuman wilds of Margate or Broadstairs . . .

Abruptly, the tone of the letter changes:

> [Richard] is now lying ill of fever and ague and can't turn round in the bed and I who have a bad cold and cough and neuralgia am nursing him. He blasphemes every two minutes and then wants to know if he is not behaving like a cherub . . .

> [Later]: I am sorry to say Richard is much worse. We have no doctors out here & I am quite alone & have come to the end of all my domestic practice. I have tried calomel blisters, hot baths & all I know and am very frightened and unhappy. He can't speak nor turn and can hardly breathe and I am now watching and hoping for some favourable turn.[80]

When she had tried all the remedies in their medical chest, including

Richard's self-prescription of massive doses of chlorodyne, he hypnotised Isabel to see if she knew what they should do. But instead of
answering his question about his illness, she became very troubled
and foretold (accurately as it turned out) the murder by poison of
their cook by a jealous rival in love, which occurred some weeks
later. Then she warned him not to trust 'the man that you are going
to take with you, because he is a scoundrel'. Since Richard intended
to travel alone they could not make sense of this.

His condition became worse and Richard concluded that his illness
was a 'Brazilian disease' requiring Brazilian treatment and told Isabel
to get a doctor. The doctor diagnosed hepatitis combined with pneumonia.[81]

Sao Paulo, May 3, 1868

My dearest Mother,

I have been in the greatest trouble since I last wrote. You may
remember Richard was very ill with a pain in the side. At last he
took to incessant paroxysms of screaming, and seemed to be dying.
Fortunately, a doctor came from Rio on the eighth day of his illness . . . and took up quarters in our house . . . he said he did not
know if he could save him, but would do his best. He put twelve
leeches on, and cupped in on the right breast, lanced him in thirty-
eight places, and put on a powerful blister on that side. He lost an
immense amount [thirty-six glasses] of black, clotted blood . . .
This is the tenth day the doctor has had him in hand, and the seventeenth of his illness . . . It was congestion of the liver, combined
with an inflammation of the lung, where they join. The agony was
fearful and poor Richard could not move hand or foot, nor speak,
swallow, or breathe without a paroxysm of pain that made him
scream for about a quarter of an hour . . .[82]

At the climax of his illness, she said, when he could not even move his
head without appalling pain, she thought he was dying. She bathed
his head with holy water and prayed beside his bed. After some hours
he stirred and 'said in a whisper, "Zoo, I think I'm a little better."' He
began to improve then, but Isabel never left his side, day or night:

I begin to feel very nervous, as I am quite alone; he won't let anyone
do anything for him but me. Now, thank God . . . he is out of

danger. He can speak better, swallow and turn a little in bed with
my help . . . [but] he is awfully thin and grey, and looks about
sixty . . . it is sad to look at him . . . His breathing is still
impeded . . . [and] he cannot go to England because of the cold, but
if he is well enough in three months [for me to leave him] I am to go
and remain till Easter. He has given up his expedition (I am afraid
he will never make another), but will take a quiet trip down to the
River Plate and Paraguay (a civilised trip) . . . I tried to go out in the
garden yesterday, but I nearly fainted and had to come back. Don't
mention my fatigue or health in writing back.[83]

Five weeks after he became ill, Isabel was able to have Richard moved
to the beach hut where he could lie with the door open on to the sand
and feel the cool breezes off the ocean. He convalesced by walking up
and down the beach with Isabel gathering shells and catching butterflies, until he was well enough to return to their mountain home at
Sao Paulo. Here, he told Isabel he could not face Santos and Sao
Paulo any longer. 'It had given him the illness, it was far away from
the world, it was no advancement, it led to nothing,' Isabel recalled,
adding, 'He was quite right.'[84]

Isabel loved her home and life in South America, but she recognised, and was frightened by, what was obviously a state of
post-illness depression in her husband and, it seems, an increasing
dependence on alcohol. She agreed at once that they would sell up
and revise their plans, she would return to England and lobby Lord
Stanley, with the help of her family and friends such as Lord
Houghton, to try to obtain the Consulate of Damascus. She would
also edit and publish as many of his South American writings as possible.

Richard, meanwhile – advised not to risk a winter in England until
he had regained his health and strength – had written requesting an
extended sick leave to be combined with a tour of South America
'beginning August 1st 1868 and ending in May 1869'.[85] The F.O.
were sympathetic and granted the request, noting in the file that medical reports said, 'he has been dangerously ill.'[86] Nevertheless, he
anticipated permission by some weeks when, after Isabel embarked on
24 July for England, he set off southwards.

By 6 August he had reached Montevideo, where he spent eight or
nine days. He was surprised that there was no English Club, usually

'the first sign of civilisation', he wrote. He was also surprised to note that women in the city outnumbered men by four to one and 'yet polygamy was not practised'. He then crossed the River Plate to Buenos Aires, spending a day or two there in mid-August writing a critical sketch of the city. At his next stop, Rosario, he spent three days, then made a two-week voyage north on the *Yi*, a 'yankee river-boat', sailing up the Parana River to Humaita, on the Paraguayan bank, where he was to gather information on the war which was then in its fourth year.

The fanatical Paraguayan defence of the fortress at Humaita in 1868, prior to its capture by the Allied forces (Argentina and Brazil, with financial support from Great Britain), made the battle one of the most significant of the war. It had been generally held to be the 'key-stone of Paraguay'. Led by the dictator Francisco Solano Lopez, with the support of the United States (who were opposed to the Brazilian Empire's policy of slavery), the Paraguayan army fought with a passionate commitment pitting their inferior weapons (flintlock muskets) against the Allies with their modern rifles, ironclad gunboats and greater numbers.

As Her Britannic Majesty's representative, Richard ought of course to have openly sided with the Allies against the protectionist policies of Lopez. He spent almost three weeks in what would be his first of two visits to the war zone, noting details of the Allied Forces merchant fleet (270 hulls) assembled in the great bend in the river to supply the 3000 'booth-tents' and up to 40,000 troops. He spent his time walking among and questioning the officers and men, who were protected by armoured Navy ships carrying 8- and 10-inch guns. And after a clear-eyed examination of the history of the war he concluded that Argentina was the villain of the piece. When he wrote to Isabel, he told her that the 'real leader' of the Paraguayans was now 'an Irish girl called Lynch, the unmarried wife of Lopez'. Since so many men had been killed, Isabel wrote, passing on Richard's news to Houghton, Lynch was buying in munitions from England and 'drills the women . . . herself!'[87]

Having obtained as much information as he could Richard retired to Corrientes, the Argentinian town on the opposite bank of the Parana River. It was a typical border town, but its position within viewing distance of the theatre of war had made it the haunt of a lawless and dangerous population. Richard spent a week there, working on his notes and a report to the F.O. recommending that he be allowed to make an attempt to persuade Lopez to free his English prisoners. In the event this was considered to be work for a diplomat rather than a consul, even though the diplomat concerned, 'Mr Gould', had made an enemy of Lopez in previous encounters and therefore could not hope to succeed.[88] Among the more colourful passages in Richard's book *Letters from the Battlefields of Paraguay* is his description of Corrientes and its shifting and shiftless inhabitants. He said that as he walked about the town at night he found a revolver was as necessary as his shoes. 'If an unknown [person] asks for a light, you stick your cigar in the barrel and politely offer it to him, without offence being given or taken.' From Corrientes he travelled south again, to the capital.

Wilfred Scawen Blunt was in Buenos Aires on 5 September 1868 when the newspapers announced Richard's arrival there. *The Standard* welcomed him with the statement that the famous explorer was visiting the city prior to making a major expedition in Patagonia, including an attempt on the then unconquered Mount Aconcagua. 'On his arrival, however,' Blunt wrote in his diary, 'it was soon abundantly clear that there was nothing very serious in the plan':

> Burton, in spite of his naturally iron constitution, was no longer in physical condition for serious work . . . I remember my first meeting with him in the autumn of 1868 . . . we had both been asked to dinner . . . with . . . the notorious Sir Roger Tichborne, in whose company Burton had arrived and with whom he chiefly consorted during his . . . stay in Buenos Aries. They were a strange and disreputable couple. Burton was at that time . . . in point of respectability at his very worst. His consular life at Santos, without any interesting work . . . or proper vent for his energies, had thrown him into a habit of drink he afterwards cured himself of.
>
> He seldom went to bed sober. His dress and appearance suggesting a released convict . . . He wore, habitually a rusty black coat with a crumpled black silk stock . . . a costume which his muscular frame and immense chest made . . . incongruously hideous; above it a countenance the most hideous I have ever seen, dark, cruel, treacherous, with eyes like a wild beast's. He reminded me of a black leopard, caged but unforgiving . . . Of the two Tichborne was distinctly the less criminal in appearance. I came to know them

well . . . and sat up many nights . . . listening while he [Burton] talked till he grew dangerous in his cups, and revolver in hand would stagger home to bed.[89]

Richard met the man who called himself Roger Tichborne – or as history now remembers him, the 'Tichborne Claimant' – at Villa Nueva or Villa Maria.[90] Later, under oath in an English court-room, he stated that Tichborne told him he had come there from Cordova. Perhaps he should have recalled the words Isabel spoke under hypnosis, that his travelling companion was 'not to be trusted'.

Never having set eyes on the real Roger Tichborne – and as he 'seemed very gentlemanly and when he gambled, lost . . . and won . . . without any emotion' – Richard accepted the man, literally, at face value. In fact his new companion had begun life as Arthur Orton, an English sailor who deserted in Australia where he settled down in Wagga Wagga under the alias Thomas Castro, earning his living as a butcher. The authentic Roger Tichborne had sailed from Rio de Janeiro in February 1854 on the sailing ship *Bella*, which sank with all hands in a storm off the South American coast. When his family heard nothing for some years he was presumed to have perished, until a man claiming to be him surfaced in Argentina in 1860. Richard knew the story because Lady Tichborne (a relative of Isabel's) had given him a small gift to take out to South America in case he happened to meet her son.

One wonders whether Isabel, had she been with Richard, would have accepted the impostor. 'Tichborne' told Richard, untruthfully, that he had met Isabel at Rio before she sailed, and she had recognised him as her long-lost cousin. In fairness to Richard, it must be stated that the Claimant also fooled Wilfred Blunt, then a young *attaché* with the British Legation at Buenos Aires. Blunt had been at school with Roger Tichborne's younger brother, Alfred, and one feature that Blunt remembered about Alfred was his thick, bushy eyebrows. When he met the Claimant and saw his similarly thick, bushy eyebrows it never occurred to him to doubt that he was in the company of Roger Tichborne. 'I treated him therefore,' said Blunt, 'as Burton did, [as] a young man of decent birth gone woefully to seed. His huge frame and coarse manner seemed to conceal reminiscences of aristocratic breeding as authentic, perhaps it was not saying much, as Alfred's.'[91]

Blunt spent a good deal of time with Richard. 'My talks with

Burton were of a most intimate kind, religion, philosophy, travel, politics. Eastern travel . . . interested me . . . and Burton was fond of reciting his Arabian adventures. In his talk he affected an extreme brutality, and if one could believe the whole of what he said he had indulged in every vice and committed every crime.' Blunt soon worked out for himself what Isabel was always insisting; that Burton was 'a sheep in wolf's clothing', and that 'his inhumanity was more pretended than real.' The disguise, however, said Blunt, was a complete one and, 'he was not a man to play with, sitting alone with him far into the night, especially in such an atmosphere of violence such as Buenos Aires then could boast, when men were shot almost nightly in the streets. Burton was a grim being to be with at the end of his second bottle with a gaucho's navaja handy to his hand.'

> Even the ferocity of his countenance gave place at times to more agreeable expressions, and I can just understand the infatuated fancy of his wife that in spite of his ugliness he was the most beautiful man alive. He had, however, a power of assuming the abominable which cannot be exaggerated. I remember . . . his insisting that I should allow him to try his mesmeric power over me, and his expression as he gazed into my eyes was nothing less than atrocious. If I had submitted to his gaze for any length of time – and he held me by my thumbs – I have no doubt he would have succeeded in dominating me. But my will also is strong, and once I had met his eyes of a wild beast . . . I broke away and would have no more.'[92]

According to Blunt, Richard spent two months in Buenos Aires. After that only the vaguest outline of his itinerary can be ascertained from several sources. It is the only journey he ever made without recording it in detail, which probably reflects the depressed and drunken state which Blunt witnessed. From Buenos Aires he set out west, riding almost 800 miles across northern Argentina via Cordoba and the Sierra de San Luiz, to Mendoza on the east side of the Andes. Given the magnificence of the scenery alone on this journey, let alone the indigenous peoples he would have encountered, the lack of literary description is a surprising lacuna in his output.[93]

Richard did not travel alone during this period. We know from a long letter written to Isabel from Humaita (which will be quoted later) that on his way there he had met an Englishman, William

Maxwell; there was a mutual liking, and he told her that they had agreed to rendezvous later in the year to make a transcontinental journey together.[94] Any intention that Richard ever entertained of attempting to scale the 28,800-ft Mount Aconcagua was clearly abandoned; as Blunt suspected, Richard's physical condition made this an impossibility. During December Richard and his companion crossed the Andes via the Uspallata Pass (La Combre) to Los Andes. A year later Richard told the journalist Luke Ionides (Dr George Bird's son-in-law) that he spent that Christmas Day in a running battle with Araucanian Indians in which he was wounded four times and killed his four assailants.'[95] Neither Richard nor Isabel ever wrote of this incident, but while under cross-examination in the Tichborne case in December 1871 Richard said under oath that 'it had been a very near thing. We passed Christmas Day in a very disagreeable manner.' 'With the natives?' 'Not with them, fortunately: running away from them.'[96] The killing of four men had been a characteristic make-weight, tossed in to add colour to his story.

Burton and Maxwell headed south and spent a week recuperating at Santiago, and then travelled west to the coast at Valparaiso. In mid-January they began a 1,000-mile, slow voyage northwards up the coast of Chile to Arica, a town just inside the Chilean border with Peru. After wandering on horseback through Peru for some weeks, Richard ended up at Lima in early March.

At this point, although he had written regularly to Isabel, because of the nature of his journey he had not received any mail from her. She had written, of course, but none of her letters ever caught up with him. Richard therefore had no idea that she had been singularly successful in her campaign to obtain a transfer and promotion for him.

25

HOME AGAIN
1868–1869

Before she sailed from Santos in July 1868, Isabel had the sad task of packing up their chattels, selling off their large items of furniture and her animals, and paying off her loyal servants Chico and Kier. At one point she thought of taking Chico back to London with them. There were some light-hearted exchanges between Isabel and one of her brothers, who offered to pay for a 'livery' for Chico so that he could act as her 'tiger' as she drove about town. There was no denying that the move was a wrench for her. Not only had she been happy in South America, her first home with Richard, but she had developed into a confident and independent individual who acted for herself without deference to anyone but her beloved Richard.

She had learned a great deal from Richard; above all a desire to learn more. But she also developed an arrogance regarding her thoughts and work, so once she had formulated an idea it never occurred to her that she might be wrong. This trait earned Isabel many detractors. Had her unswerving loyalty to Richard been confined to parlour prattle it might have earned admiration. But her assertive nature, outspoken views, determination to make others see Richard in the same uncritical light as she did, and her lobbying to obtain advancement for him (sometimes at his secret instigation) would make her unpopular in many quarters.

Isabel's positive nature is illustrated by an incident which occurred during her journey to England, when she called on a friend of

Richard's, Charles Williams, in Bahia.[1] Williams kept a private menagerie on his property and his hall contained cages of snakes. As he was showing these to Isabel he took a rattlesnake out of a cage, his hand slipped and the snake sank its fangs into his wrist. 'He had just time to dash it back into the cage and lock it, and staggered back against the wall,' Isabel recalled. Few women would have known how to handle such an incident, but Richard had 'prepared' Isabel in case this sort of emergency occurred while they were travelling alone together. Seeing a box of wooden Lucifer matches on the table, she snatched these up and striking them one after another, used the flares to burn a hole at the puncture site. Then she made a ligament with her handkerchief, while calling loudly for the servants to bring a bottle of whisky. 'By degrees I got the whole bottle down his throat,' and then with the help of servants she kept her patient walking for about three hours. She then allowed him to be put to bed, and when he rose next morning he was in perfect health. Isabel thought that probably the bite had not been very deep, but Williams was convinced that her rough-and-ready first aid had saved his life. As a mark of appreciation, he had a riding whip made for her with a handle of solid silver 'up to the lash'. It was still among her possessions when she died.[2]

She landed in England during a heat-wave on 1 September, but still found it necessary to light a fire and have extra blankets while she acclimatised. Her mother, paralyzed and bedridden since her stroke, wanted her to stay with them, but Isabel quickly found lodgings. She set about her tasks for Richard, finding time also to lunch with old friends such as John Larking (of Alexandria), Samuel and Florence Baker (now Sir Samuel and Lady Baker by virtue of his discoveries in Africa), and John and Kate Petherick. The Nile's ultimate source, she learned to her satisfaction, was still very much an open question.

Among other commissions Richard had instructed her to have his *Pilgrimage to Mecca* republished, by Longmans. 'I think the subject is worn out but must obey orders.' Isabel wrote to Lord Houghton:

I am editing his book on Brazil . . . and 5 other small things, so shall be tied to London for a time.[3] . . . I must have offended Swinburne. He called twice and I did not happen to be in; I can't get him to call again and I have so much to say to him . . .[4] You see Dick is going to be *the* Nile man after all. I shall go in for a KCB; won't you back me up? I had a long letter from him today from Humaita. He was going to cross the Andes with Wm Maxwell (one of the Yorkshire ones). Humaita is a mere entrench camp. He himself is as strong as a horse and shay, to use his own language; he sends best love to you and says he will be here about May or June.'⁵

So busy was Isabel editing, dealing with publishers (Longmans and Tinsley) and meetings with F.O. officials, she continued, that she had to refuse tempting invitations such as one from Lady Marion Alford (a woman Richard described as 'enchanting') and could not spare the time to come to Fryston as he suggested. She admitted that she had allowed herself a few days at Wardour, but now she wanted to remain available should Lord Stanley be free to see her and anyway, dared not 'leave the accumulation of work' for fear that 'it would throw Richard back.'⁶ By mid-November she was better placed, and with Mr Tinsley's blessing she was able to accept Houghton's invitation to spend a long weekend at Fryston.⁷ She warned that she was obliged to come dressed in deep mourning, for she had recently lost two much-loved members of her family (her half-brother Theo, and an aunt who was her godmother), and that she would arrive laden with a stack of proofs for *Highlands of the Brazil*, but hoped that Lady Houghton would be understanding on both counts.

There was a general election looming and Stanley was busy 'addressing constituents at Kings Lynn'. Isabel hoped that if the Tories were defeated, Stanley would give Richard a place as his parting shot. But at present, she advised Houghton, there was little more that she could do to advance the matter. 'Besides, I have bothered him pretty well and if Richard does not get well served it will not be the fault of his hard working wife. It will be a shame if he [Stanley] goes out and gives me nothing. Every relation I have, and they are legion, the entire old Roman Catholic clan, are red hot Conservatives so that when *your* side comes in, I can expect no quarter and can't ask it.'⁸

That weekend was notable not only for the fact that Isabel played music from her new South American repertoire, as an accompaniment to Houghton's readings of his poetry, but also that she was able to ask his advice about her proposed Preface for *Highlands of the Brazil*, which referred critically to certain passages within the book. Houghton and Isabel were invariably in agreement about what was good for Richard; in this case they both thought that his repeated championship of polygamy was liable to be detrimental to his career prospects. Richard knew of Isabel's disapproval (not of his views but his writing about them), and had advised her to say so in her Preface.[9]

To Tinsley, Isabel explained, 'You will see my few words soften off what offends different classes of people [about] Captain Burton and explains him to the public. A man's own wife may do this . . . I mean Captain Burton to take a much higher stand in the world than he has ever done. I have got the wedge in now, and I shall din it in. You know how his writings have kept him back from place or power . . .'[10]

Her Preface was short and to the point.

Before the reader dives into the interior of Brazil with my husband . . . let me address two words to him. I have returned home after three years in Brazil . . . to see the following pages through the press. It has been my privilege, during those three years, to have been his almost constant companion, and I consider that to travel, write, read and study under such a master is no small boon to any one desirous of seeing and learning . . . Although he frequently informs me, in a certain Oriental way that 'the Moslems can permit no equality with women,' yet he has chosen me, his pupil, for this distinction, in preference to a more competent stranger . . .

Although I . . . pledge myself not to avail myself of my discretionary powers to alter one word of the original text, I protest vehemently against his religious and moral sentiments, which belie a good and chivalrous life. I point the finger of indignation . . . at what upholds the unnatural and repulsive law, Polygamy, which the author is careful not to practice himself, but from a high moral pedestal he preaches to the ignorant as a means of population in young countries.

I am compelled to differ with him on many subjects; but be it understood, not in the common spirit of domestic jar, but with a mutual agreement to differ and enjoy our differences, whence points of interest never flag. Having . . . given a friendly warning to . . . the reader . . . I leave him or her to steer through these anthropological sandbanks and hidden rocks as best he or she may.[11]

Tinsley was deeply unhappy about this Preface; it seemed to him to undermine the book's authorship, and he strongly recommended it should not be included for fear of affecting sales. Isabel had paid half the cost of publication of the book. Tinsley believed it had a limited market at best, and warned that the Preface placed her own and his investment at risk.[12]

The publisher's letter advising caution arrived at much the same time as Isabel was celebrating a significant triumph. Lord Stanley's fears for the Tory party had been substantiated and in November Disraeli's first short administration was defeated in the polls by the Liberals, led by Gladstone. Stanley advised Isabel that one of his final acts before resigning as Foreign Secretary was to offer the Consulate of Damascus to Richard; a position which carried a salary of £950 a year plus expenses.[13] She was thrilled. Stanley also hinted that if he made a success of Damascus the Foreign Office plum of Constantinople was within Richard's grasp. She wrote immediately to tell Richard the news but her letter never reached him, nor did two letters from Lord Stanley ordering him to 'proceed at once' to his new posting.[14] These letters would have arrived in Santos in early January – by then he was in Santiago, Chile, and about to sail for Peru.

When Isabel replied to Tinsley she made the position on her Preface abundantly clear; no matter how much she had invested in the book, it was of secondary importance to Richard's long-term prospects.

Dec 4th 1868

Dear Mr Tinsley,

   . . . It would be more profitable to smash up the book than *not* to let my preface stand as it is. The Queen *hates* polygamy, and *I am acting under orders*. The British Public hates polygamy. Captain Burton has chaffed the public long enough. I now intend to make it my business that it shall understand him.

   The Brazilian Government is Catholic. The Empress Ultra-papist. Do you think that the Emperor would order three or four thousand copies to be distributed in his Empire if Capt. Burton's animus were not somewhat annulled . . .? The men in your office who set you against my preface are underhand enemies to my husband. Believe me if I could only publish anything like a difference between us all London would buy it – so it won't damage you! . . .

   We cannot well risk an appointment of £950 a year for the sake of one £250. Please *be quiet* about this and let it be.

Yrs etc
Isabel Burton

The book itself received the usual mixture of praise and brickbats in the literary columns, but Isabel's Preface and the suggestion of domestic badinage fascinated the reviewers, who had enormous fun at her expense. 'One of the most magnificent efforts of self-assertion ever made by a weak woman', said the *Pall Mall Gazette* ('Oh!' Isabel wrote in the column of this press cutting).[15] 'No doubt Mr & Mrs Burton have a happy and amiable connubial understanding,' but, said the *Daily News*, picking up on Isabel's analogy of sand banks and hidden rocks (and referring to her as 'amiable and estimable'), 'the very perils of this moral navigation will attract a multitude of readers . . . [so] she might have spared herself the trouble of writing any preface at all, and have let her gallant and adventurous husband tell his own tale, as the lawyers say, "Without Prejudice".'[16] The *Athenaeum*, to which Richard was a frequent contributor, considered that, 'the mere fact that a man who is not dissatisfied with slavery, finds good in cannibalism, advocates polygamy and is a brother anthropologist of Lord Stanley, should travel with a Roman Catholic wife, and should depute her the task of seeing his work through the press is deliciously suggestive . . .'[17] The *Sunday Observer*, however, found the Preface 'a model of good taste and just feeling . . .'[18]

Stung, Isabel wrote to Houghton,

> I'm so glad you like my preface . . . but I am smarting under the lash of the *Pall Mall* and *Athenaeum*. I have never stood before the public yet and am too thin-skinned and feel quite ill about it all . . .[19]

But she was too intelligent (and so was Richard) not to recognise that the small controversy raised the profile of the book, and that the additional publicity – whilst it made her momentarily uncomfortable – helped to sell more copies. It was a lesson well learned and her skin became thicker. She wrote to thank every reviewer. 'I cannot resist the temptation of writing to you and thanking you for your kind and able review,' she said typically to those who had written favourably.[20] To the unfavourable, such as the editor of the *Academy* she wrote, 'Dear Mr Cotton, I am not so stupid as to be offended, and shall *always* be glad to see you. I think my paragraphs prettier than yours, that is all. I will try to get [others] . . . to think so too. Ever yours truly . . .'[21]

News of Richard's appointment was now widespread throughout the Foreign Office. The new Foreign Secretary, Lord Clarendon, found himself on the receiving end of a number of complaints about it. The most important of these came from Henry Elliot (later Sir Henry), British Ambassador at Constantinople to whom the Consul of Damascus reported. Henry Elliot's sister was married to Lord John Russell, and his own appointment by Russell in 1860 had been the source of much controversy in the House and in the press. *The Times* openly accused Russell of 'jobbery' in the matter.[22] This did not prevent Elliot – who also had many close connections with senior administrators in India, and was friendly with Laurence Oliphant – from 'representing very strong objections to Burton's appointment':

> I was astounded when I heard that [Lord Stanley] had named Burton, whose character was so well known in the East as to make it a certainty that trouble would come from it . . . The fact of the matter is that Eastern Travellers are for the most part exactly the people the least fitted to fill the responsible position of Consuls in Turkey. They have got accustomed to overbearing exercise of authority and to a neglect of anything like sense in dealing with the people about them. Which may be necessary in the wilds, but which cannot be tolerated at or near the seat of administration.[23]

Lord Clarendon was not unsympathetic to Elliot's objections but said he was unwilling to cancel his predecessor's nomination.[24] Isabel heard from Stanley, that the appointment had been criticised, and immediately cabled and wrote to Richard. Although in her correspondence with Lord Houghton she mentioned receiving letters from her husband on a regular basis, she had no way of knowing where Richard might be a month hence, when her letter reached South America. But she knew he was headed for Chile, so she despatched copies to him, *poste restante* Rio, Buenos Aires and Valparaiso:

London, January 7,1869
My darling,
    If you get this, come home at once by shortest way. Telegraph from Lisbon and Southampton, and I will meet you at latter and have all snug.
    Strictly Private. The new government have tried to upset some of

the appointments made by the last [one]. There is no little jealousy about yours. Others wanted it even at £700 a year, and were refused. Lord Stanley thinks, and so do I, that you may as well be on the ground as soon as possible.

Richard was still living the vaguely dissolute life described by Blunt, as he wandered about South America. He was in a café in Lima, Peru, when he met a Foreign Office colleague who had heard the news and congratulated him on the transfer to Damascus.

He shrugged off his depression like a damp overcoat and caught a ship that was just departing from Lima on a 5,500-mile coastal journey to Buenos Aires, rounding the southern tip of the continent via the Straits of Magellan. It was twice the overland distance, but Richard rationalised that it would take no longer, would be less taxing, and would give him a final chance to see parts of South America he had not yet been able to visit, in particular the wild and magnificent scenery described by Darwin during the *Beagle* voyage. He arrived in Buenos Aires on 29 March 1869, where he found Isabel's letters.

According to his formal letter of acceptance written on 30 March (some two months later than the F.O. might have reasonably expected), he had already missed the monthly Royal Mail steamer by a week. He therefore proposed to return to the war zone to update his information, before travelling to Rio in time to catch the 23 April sailing of the next fast ship to England.[25] He spent about two weeks in early April in and around Paraguay's capital, Asunción, which had recently been taken by the Allies, and where he was granted interviews by political and military leaders on both sides of the conflict. Then he rode to Santos and took a steamer to Rio where he boarded the Royal Mail S.S. *Douro* bound for Southampton via Lisbon.

From Lisbon Richard telegraphed Isabel to meet him at Southampton at the end of May. And when he looked over the ship's rail as the vessel docked at 4 a.m. on 1 June, the first person he saw was Isabel waiting for him on the quay. His appearance, she said, was pretty much what hers had been when she returned from the mines. He bathed and changed into some clothes she had brought with her, so that they could pay some local calls and visit the flower show at Netley Abbey that afternoon. But when they reached London next day she drove him straight to 'a haberdasher, tailor and hatter'.

On 3 June he presented himself, bathed, clipped and shorn, to Lord Clarendon who confirmed what Isabel already knew: that he had received a number of objections to Richard's appointment, some of which he regarded as 'very serious'. These appeared to consist mainly of a belief that Richard's well-known Moslem sympathies would inevitably lead him to act in a prejudiced manner in what was 'the most fanatical town in the [Turkish] Empire . . . and would be likely to produce very undesirable consequences.' Ambassador Henry Elliot, who was still agitating to have the appointment annulled, warned in a despatch dated 3 May 1869 (received by Clarendon two days before this interview): 'By the Mussulman population Captain Burton is regarded either as having insulted their religion by taking part in their most sacred rites, or else as having, at that time, been a Mohammedan and having become a renegade. It is my duty to draw your Lordship's attention to a consideration which was probably lost sight of when Captain Burton was selected for the post.'[26]

Richard refuted the allegations as being totally without foundation, and assured Clarendon that he had only ever received the most courteous welcome from Moslems. The Minister accepted this, but warned him that if it was found that his sympathies were shown to adversely affect the performance of his office, he would be 'recalled forthwith'. Richard gave him an undertaking to act with 'unusual prudence' (afterwards repeated in writing)[27] and left with permission to take a further period of six weeks' sick leave to try to shake off the lingering effects of his attack of hepatitis. Two weeks later Richard received a letter from the F.O. reiterating what had been said at the interview: 'Although Lord Clarendon has allowed the appointment to go forward on receiving your assurances . . . his Lordship has warned you that if feelings stated to exist . . . should prevent the proper performance of your official duties it would be his Lordship's duty . . . to recall you.'[28]

Precisely what lay at the bottom of Elliot's antipathy towards Burton cannot be ascertained. It might have been the old rumours passed on by one of his Anglo-Indian relatives, or possibly something he was told by his brother-in-law, Lord Russell. It could not have been personal, for Elliot and Burton had never met and Richard never realised – even with hindsight – how much harm this man did to him. But Henry Elliot's private papers, now in the National Library of Scotland, reveal that for two years he worked assiduously to get

Burton replaced, and that this campaign caused as much damage to the latter's reputation as Speke's had done. Richard could never have succeeded in Damascus given this attitude in the man to whom he reported.

When Elliot learned that Clarendon was sending Burton to Damascus in spite of his warnings, he went to work immediately. He met Rashid Pasha, the Turkish Governor in Damascus, on 19 July 1869, and assured him that although Captain Burton's appointment was going ahead, Lord Clarendon had 'laid strict injunctions on his head . . . to be extremely careful to avoid doing anything calculated to give offence.' This was diplomatic parlance; it meant that Burton was without any official backing or power. And not only that, it indicated to the wily Rashid Pasha that in any dispute with Burton, he could rely on Elliot as an ally.

Fortunately, Richard was not aware of the treachery going on in the corridors of diplomacy. When not engaged in a busy social round of a London Season, Foreign Office and Admiralty parties, country-house visits and a royal levée, he spent most of his six weeks of sick leave finishing his outstanding writing projects and dealing with publishers. He also dined with Sir Roderick Murchison and attended a meeting of the Royal Geographical Society, but found it 'slow' and was disgruntled at his reception there. He was also able to renew friendships which he valued, notably Houghton and Swinburne. The latter's friends and family always blamed Houghton for introducing Swinburne to the works of Le Marquis de Sade which afterwards so dominated his psyche, and for introducing him to Burton who was in turn widely credited with leading the poet into drinking dens. Neither charge stands up to examination of the facts but by whatever route the decline occurred, in 1869 it had become virtually impossible for any London hostess to invite Swinburne to dine.

An alcoholic, each day he rapidly drank himself into a violent and abusive state. Many people such as Lord Houghton and the Rossettis felt sorry for him; he looked so slight and boyish, but his still-cherubic appearance belied his increasingly bizarre behaviour; for even when not drunk he was capable of disrupting a party by 'dancing and skipping about the room reciting his poetry'.[29] Luke Ionides, the son-in-law of Dr George Bird, met Richard for the first time in June 1869. He recalled seeing Richard pick up the bantam poet and carry him under his arm, kicking and shouting, down a steep flight of stairs.

Swinburne was so drunk, Ionides recalled, that he could not find the steps of the cab and complained that they were becoming higher each year.[30]

Richard, who appears to have curbed his own massive alcohol intake, now proposed to help Swinburne to do the same by inviting him to join him taking the waters at Vichy in August while he was en route to Damascus. Richard planned to take the cure for the 'liverishness' from which he had suffered since his bout of hepatitis. The heavy drinking described by Blunt cannot have helped Richard's recovery from the illness, but now he was determined to get fit. As a young man he had mocked his parents for their non-stop round of spas; ironically, as an adult, he became an ardent disciple himself. 'I go on Thursday next, July 15th,' he wrote to Albert Tootal. 'I have done the London Season for the last time and shall never return except in Autumn or Winter [he did of course]. It has been a life of bed at 8am, no breakfast, lunch at 2pm, dine at 830 pm and then soirée. Not so tiring when one is broken to it but deadly monotonous . . . As soon as I get my library from Hunt I intend to publish *The Lowlands of Brazil*. My book on Paraguay still hangs fire; Lt. Col. George Thompson has his ready and I want to give him a few months. This is only fair . . .'[31]

Houghton had written advising Richard to drop his work on the *Lusiads*, as he considered there would be little demand for such a book. 'Thank you for your excellent advice about Camoens,' Richard replied lightly. 'I love him and your forbeodan invests the affair with [heightened] interest. Why should not people read the *Lusiads* when the other morning you received a translation of Tazo? Please don't explain . . . the first Canto is nearly finished. Your note will lift me through it!'[32] He also wrote to his old friend of his pilgrimage days, John Larking, to ask for introductions to important people in Egypt, since all his old friends were dead. 'I go [from here] to Paris, Vichy, Brindizi, Alexandria, Suez Canal, Beyrout and Damascus, then I return to Alexandria to fetch my wife.'[33]

The Burtons set out together in July and spent a few days in Boulogne, the scene of their first meeting seventeen years earlier. Their plan was that he would rendezvous in Paris with Swinburne and take the train to Vichy. Isabel would return to London to nurse various books through publication, and complete her usual 'Pay, Pack and Follow' routine, before meeting him in Alexandria in November. But by the time Isabel reached England she was already missing Richard acutely. They had been parted ten months while he toured South America, and he had been home only six weeks. When she thought about the work she had to get through, she decided she could have the month at Vichy with him and still get the necessary tasks completed before leaving for Syria at the end of the year. She turned round immediately and went to Paris where she met an old friend and Sao Paulo neighbour, Mr Aubertin, the railroad engineer, and travelled to Vichy with him, arriving on 6 August a week after Richard.

Richard and Swinburne enjoyed a healthy, reasonably teetotal life in Vichy, walking most afternoons in the mountains, or visiting nearby sights such as the Cathedral at Clermont-Ferrand. 'This place is doing me good,' Swinburne wrote to his sister, enclosing some flowers he had gathered for her at the top of Puy de Dôme.

> Coming here from Paris on a broiling day with my back to the engine I got to feel as sick as anything and you cannot think how kind and careful of me he was . . . I knew for the first time what it was to have an elder brother. He is the most cordial, helpful, sympathetic friend to me . . . and it is a treat at last to have him to myself instead of having in London to share him with all the world and his wife and children, from Lords Clarendon and Stanley, to Col this and Captain that. I rather grudge Mrs Burton's arrival here on Monday, though we are excellent friends, and I dare say I shall see none the less of him . . . in our ascent of Puy de Dôme he began at once gathering flowers to press for her . . .[34]

Richard and Swinburne met Isabel's train and the trio were joined later that day by the artist Frederick Leighton and his mistress, the *diva* Adelaide Kemble (Mrs Sartoris), who were on a touring holiday.[35] 'Vichy is a small dull place, full of sickly people with liver complaints,' Isabel wrote. 'The drinking fountains are the principal rendezvous. There is the usual band, promenade under the trees, casino, garden, and theatre. They were very happy days. We made excursions in the day and in the evenings the conversation . . . was brilliant; everybody contributed something that made him or her valuable. Swinburne recited poetry, Mrs Sartoris sang to us, without accompaniment.'[36]

They spent a week exploring nearby towns, and châteaux and

fortresses, picnicking by waterfalls, walking in the moonlight.[37] They
were all sorry when the time came to leave, especially Swinburne for
whom the month had been one of the happiest periods of his life.
Before they said farewell, Richard and Swinburne drank a toast to
each other in warm Vichy water, each pledging to dedicate a work to
the other.[38] The trio parted at Lyons station. Swinburne returned to
Paris, Richard and Isabel went on to Turin where they spent a few
days exploring the city. On the evening of 1 September Richard left
for Brindisi to catch the next P. & O. ship for Alexandria. Next
morning Isabel caught the train to Paris; the first leg of her journey to
London.[39]

In November Isabel attended a meeting at the Royal Geographical
Society where the still-open question of the Nile's source was being
debated following a report from Livingstone that he had discovered a
new lake, south of Lake Tanganyika. She came away incensed, and
wrote immediately to *The Times* and *Telegraph*. 'Five African explorers have pined for the honour of discovering the sources of the
Nile and each one in his turn has believed himself to be that fortunate
person, until now that Livingstone . . . has discovered waters more
southerly still. Judge my mortification . . . on Monday night to hear
all the papers read and discussed almost without reference to Captain
Burton. His lake, which lies nearest to Livingstone's new discovery
was almost skipped over and my revered friend, Sir Roderick
Murchison, spoke of "Central, or Equatorial Africa, in which lie
those great water basins which, thanks to the labours of Speke, Grant
and Baker, are known to feed the Nile".'[40] She stated that she asked
Murchison why he had left Burton's name out of this list, and he
replied that it had been 'an oversight' which would be rectified in the
published reports of the meeting. This, she said, had not been done
and she was writing to set the record straight. 'He [Burton] was the
first to conceive the idea twenty years ago, the first to enter and penetrate that country . . . bringing back sufficient information to smooth
the path to all who chose to follow him . . .'

This sparked off a controversy in the correspondence columns
which lasted some days and produced a satisfactory amount of publicity for both Richard and Isabel; 'a wifely and spirited letter . . . from
the accomplished wife of the Consul at Damascus . . . unlike some of
her sex (and of mine), that lady can think as well as write,' wrote one
appreciative contributor. Murchison was furious, writing icily to

Isabel that he was sorry she had not called on him instead of writing to *The Times*. 'No change in the wording of the address could have been made when you appealed to me for the printed report was in the hands of several reporters. Nor can I, in looking at the address, see why you should be offended . . . I was under the necessity of coupling Speke with Burton as *joint discoverers of the Lake Tanganyika* inasmuch as they worked together until prostrated by illness; and whilst your husband was blind or almost so, Speke made all the astronomical observations which fixed the real position of places near the lake.' He pointed out that when he had presented her husband with the Gold Medal, Burton had admitted this in his acceptance speech.[41]

Isabel replied in a firm, but light and friendly tone saying she had felt, 'nettled . . . [to hear] Captain Burton mentioned only once, and the other *twenty* times.' Even so, had it not been for the complaints of her husband's supporters she would have let the matter lie. But they had pointed out to her that calling on Murchison, and a correction in the printed address, would not put right the incorrect impression gained by those in the audience at the R.G.S. But, she went on, 'I am glad you mentioned Speke . . . Speke was a brave man, and full of fine qualities. I grudge his memory no honour that can be paid; I never wish to detract from any of the great merits of the other four. I only ask to maintain my husband's right place amongst them, which is only second to Livingstone. I hope I shall see you in a few days.'[42] She was justified; no one would dare to try leaving Burton out of discussions on the subject again, but Murchison never forgave her for embarrassing him in public and thereafter always regarded her as a meddlesome woman. Like Richard, Isabel was adept at gathering detractors.

Having taken a month off work to join Richard in Vichy she now found herself under considerable pressure, with hardly enough time to finish editing *Letters from the Battlefields of Paraguay* and complete all the outstanding tasks. She had not only to organise maps for the book (which she did with the assistance of Captain George of the R.G.S.), but to proof the manuscript written in execrable handwriting by Richard while he was ill.[43] 'Dear Mr Tinsley, . . . you don't know how hard it is to read that vile manuscript and compare with every word of proof,' she wrote in considerable irritation to the publisher. 'Find me an intelligent Devil, a boy reader – I will make him read the Ms. and I will correct the proof.'[44]

And books were not the end of it. Richard had designed a gun, a carbine pistol, which he claimed was capable of killing a man at 500 yards.* One of Isabel's tasks was to see arms manufacturers in an attempt to get the design taken up. She also travelled to Essex to see how some tube-wells worked, because Richard thought that the engineering principle might be useful for producing water in the desert. She acquired a pony cart and learned how to take off the wheels and axles, oil them and put them back together; and she bought some suitable guns and took lessons in taking them apart, cleaning and reassembling them. Her uncle, Lord Gerard, sent a huge old chariot which he thought she might find useful, but when Lord Houghton roared with laughter and teased her with jokes about her tearing round the desert in it, drawn by camels, she decided to leave it in England. The more mundane arrangements included a wine and spirits order, for shipping to Damascus, which included '25 cases each 12 bottles best Claret', as well as smaller orders of Richard's favourite brandy, port and 'pale-dry sherry'.[45]

It was 16 December before she left London by train bound for Dover. Her brother, Roddy, escorted Isabel, her English maid and 'a large St. Bernard dog' as far as the port, where a violent storm delayed the entourage at Dover for 24 hours. The delay necessitated a mad dash south to Marseille where she lost two trunks, one of which contained nearly all her money and the other her overnight things and 'creature comforts'. It was six months before she saw them again, but the difficulties did not bother her. As the steamer left Marseille she was only too delighted to have exchanged the dreary, damp, cold of an English winter for the mother-of-pearl sea and the balmy air of the Mediterranean. She was on her way to Richard, and romance. 'I had shaken the dust off my feet of . . . respectability – the harness of European society. My destination was Damascus, the dream of my childhood and girlhood. I am to live amongst Bedouin Arab chiefs; I shall smell the desert air; I shall have tents, horses, weapons, and be free . . .'[46]

Her fellow-passengers were all Anglo-Indians on their way to the subcontinent. They were amused at her ignorance of their jargon: *tiffin, griffin, punkah.* Isabel was equally amused that several newly-wed couples were 'evidently not used to steamers'; their conversations

---

* Now housed at Orleans House Gallery.

and passionate responses were clearly audible through the ventilators over their cabin doors.[47] As they sailed past the coast of Sicily and the Straits of Messina, the others lined the deck to marvel; Isabel thought it a lovely sight, but she had been 'spoiled by South America' and felt 'a sort of secret superiority'.

She spent Christmas Day at Alexandria, and cabled Richard at Damascus. It never reached him, for she had not been told to write 'El Shám' for Damascus, and it was directed to Beirut where it was held up. 'It was a strange Christmas Night, spent all alone, in a small room . . . passed writing letters home and thinking of the merry family parties and festivities . . .'[48] On the following day she caught a Russian ship for the three-day voyage to Sa'id, Jaffa and Beirut. Most of the other passengers were pilgrims making their *Haj*. At each port she sent a cable to Richard, but he received none of them.

On the early morning of 29 December Isabel reached Beirut. There was no harbour or quay; ships anchored in the open roadstead and flew the appropriate signal or sent a message ashore. As she waited patiently for someone from the British Consulate to come on board to collect her, Isabel stood by the rail drinking in the view. The cobalt sea washed gently on to yellow sand. Whitewashed villas crawled up the verdant hillsides towards dark green pine forests, and all this was set under a startling, cloudless turquoise sky. 'The air is redolent with a smell of pine-wood;' she noted, 'every town in the East has its peculiar odour and once you have been in one you can tell where you are blind-folded.'[49]

Isabel was now 38 years old. She was physically and mentally prepared for adventure following her experiences in South America, and she was about to embark upon the most fulfilling period of her life.

DESTINY IN DAMASCUS
1869–1870

Isabel was met by Vice-Consul Thomas S. Jago, who took her ashore and gave her breakfast before introducing her to Consul-General Eldridge, a man who would play a major, and fateful, role in the Burtons' life in Syria. She was not to know how much she would come to hate him; her first impressions were only of his consideration.

She wanted to leave for Damascus at once, but found she had missed the diligence (public stage coach) which left at dawn each day. Eldridge was unhappy for her to use the public transport as a few days earlier, a woman missionary on the coach had been 'kissed all the way to Damascus, by a Persian scamp'.[1] He offered to hire a private carriage for her, and she telegraphed Richard accordingly. This was the third cable she had sent to Damascus; all three arrived after she did. Isabel spent the evening with the Duchesse de Persigny (wife of the French Ambassador in London), who had heard of her arrival and sent a note suggesting they dine together at her hotel.

The promise of a 'private carriage' was misleading. On the following morning, 'a shabby little omnibus' drawn by three thin and tired-looking horses made its appearance. Isabel and her maid, a mountain of luggage and St Bernard dog were squeezed into and on to it. Together with a splendidly attired *kavas* (armed servant) provided by Eldridge, they set off from Beirut, Isabel's last connection with European languages and customs, on the 78-mile journey to Damascus.[2] For the first few hours they bowled along on the smooth tarmac toll-road built by two French brothers across valley, hill and plain; after that they made poor time on roads churned into deep mud by winter rains. The diligence (one left Damascus at the same time each day and they met half-way) had several changes of horses along the route, and could thus perform the journey in around 12 hours. Isabel's omnibus took two days over the journey, which was a gradual ascent of 2,500 feet. After the rampant luxuriance of South America she was initially disappointed at the bleakness of the Anti-Lebanon in winter, but she was thrilled by the sight of a Bedouin sleeping against a rock with his carbine to hand, and his horse grazing next to him.

Suddenly, at sunset on the second day when she was cold, tired and 'least prepared for it', the vehicle emerged from a gully in the rocks above Salahiyeh, 500 feet above the plains, to reveal a scene which profoundly moved every traveller fortunate enough to experience it. Surrounded by desert and backed by distant mountains coloured red and purple in the misty glow of the setting sun, lay Damascus. The Bedouins say it was 'founded by Uz, son of Aram, son of Shem, son of Noah. It existed before Abraham and is the oldest inhabited city in the world.'[3] The Prophet Muhammad is said to have turned away at this spot, declining to proceed into the city on the premise that man could only enter one paradise and he preferred to wait for Allah's. For Isabel it was the beginning of a love affair with the city she called:

> . . . my pearl, the Garden of Eden, the Promised Land. My beautiful white City with her swelling domes and tapering minarets, her glittering golden crescents set in green of every shade, sparkling with fountains and streams, the [River] Abana rushing through and watering the oasis. The river valley spreads its green carpet almost thirty miles around the city and is dotted with white villages. All around that again, like another or outside frame, and as if nature had drawn the line between green and yellow like a ruler, are the reeking sands of the sunburnt Desert.[4]

She never tired of this view, and later she often went there at dawn, standing among the camomile-covered and scented sloping meadows near her hill-side home. Around her, the usual bird-song and faint chime of bells from grazing animals were obliterated by the haunting first call to prayer as the *Muezzin*'s voice, echoing from the minaret of the great mosque, was taken up and repeated from smaller minarets all over the city: *God is great. There is no God but Allah, and Mohammed is his prophet! Let us kneel before him, and to him alone be the glory! Come to prayer, there is no God but Allah . . . God is great . . .!* But on that evening of the last day of 1869 as she rode into the city, Damascus itself proved a disappointment. At close quarters, in the damp chill of a December dusk, its fabled gardens were seasonally shriven, its minarets were hidden in gloomy skies, and the buildings that gleamed so purely at a distance rose grimy and scabrous from muddy streets.

Richard had been staying since October at Demetri's, the city's only inn which was 'called by courtesy a hotel', said Isabel. The establishment's squalor was thinly disguised under an Oriental veneer of ornate grilles, tiles and a courtyard with fountains and citrus trees. Isabel went straight there, having not stopped on her 15-day dash eastwards. 'After an hour Richard came in,' she recalled, 'and I was glad that I had waited for nothing but necessity as I found him looking very old and ill.'[5] Until he came close to her she did not recognise him. He was suffering from neuralgia and, since the last communication he received from Isabel had been an almost indecipherable cable sent before she left London, he was depressed at hearing nothing from her. It was a pleasant surprise for him to find her comfortably ensconced in his room, having ordered two charcoal braziers to warm it up. He told her he had been several times to Beirut to meet steamers, hoping she would arrive, but had missed the Russian pilgrim boat just as she had missed him at Rio. 'Though he greeted me in that matter-of-fact way with which he was wont to repress his emotions, I could *feel* that he was both surprised and overjoyed,' Isabel wrote. 'The climate and loneliness had had a bad effect on him, both mentally and physically.'[6]

Early next morning Isabel, of whom Richard said that she could 'make a home of a coal hole', was up and about. Sightseeing could wait, she said. Her first task was to make a comfortable home for Richard. The previous Consul had lived in a large house in the city belonging to a rich Jew. They could not afford accommodation on a similar scale, but in any case Isabel considered the old walled city an unhealthy situation in which to live and sleep. The city's eight gates were closed at dusk each night and she felt that to live there, behind tightly shuttered windows, would feel like imprisonment. There were pleasant suburbs of large villas outside the gates, but these too were beyond their finances, so she rode back to Salahiyeh, a Kurdish village of 15,000 inhabitants. It was on the hills over which she had approached the city; 'just beyond it was the desert sand, and in the background a saffron-hued mountain known as Camomile Mountain.'[7] From here, on horseback, they could be in the city in minutes, and in the same time they could be in the desert.

The house she chose overhung the road, opposite gardens and apricot orchards and was, she admitted cheerfully, 'quite second-class'. It was flanked on one side by an old mosque and on the other by the local *hammam* (baths). Behind it was a garden through which wended a river. It had the ubiquitous courtyard with *liwan*, splashing fountains and trees for shade. There was a large reception and dining room on the ground floor, and a living room on the first floor which like the bedrooms faced on to the balcony that ran round two sides of the inner courtyard. The other two sides of the building were occupied by a long rooftop terrace. On warm evenings, 'we used to spread it with mats and divans and sit among the flowers and shrubs, and look over Damascus and sniff the desert air beyond.'[8] Alternatively, they sprawled on a divan and smoked and chatted in a shady arbor that Isabel made from citrus bushes and supported vines, overlooking the river.

In the apricot orchard opposite the house, she was able to rent a stable for twelve horses and accommodation for *syces* (grooms). Not that she ever owned twelve horses, but she usually had four or five half-breeds purchased inexpensively and 'improved'. Richard never interfered with her stable management and she filled empty stalls with a menagerie of camels, asses, goats, rescued cats and dogs – in addition to the St Bernard and two bull-terriers, Fuss and Fidget, that she and Richard had brought with them from England – and a collection of turkeys, ducks, geese, hens and guinea-fowl. She loved all animals with the passion that is often characteristic in a childless matron, and when she noticed that the horses and donkeys shied at her crinolined skirts, it amused her. 'Fancy being so queer that the animals take fright at one!' she wrote.

Once she had the domestic arrangements secure, Isabel took time to go about the old city, exploring the famous *souks* and visiting the sights: the 'street called Straight' mentioned in the Bible; the house of Ananias where Paul lodged after his divine revelation blinded him, and the window in the city walls from which he had been lowered in a basket to escape his pursuers; the great mosque; the labyrinth of narrow winding streets enclosed by buildings whose grilled and latticed windows almost met overhead. All around her the cosmopolitan throng of Arabs, Turks, Bedouins, Persians, Kurds, Circassians, Anatolians and African slaves, each wearing their own costume, went about their business. Water sellers dispensed cool drinks, milk-sellers rang a bell and shouted, '*Leben, le-ben*', while donkeys and camels laden with produce jostled with pedestrians as they were led through the narrow thoroughfares. In winter the streets were full of muddy holes, in summer choking dust; pariah dogs picked at and fought over offal thrown into the street. Squalid and noisome though it could be, Damascus was still romantic and alluring.

At Richard's request Isabel visited the women's *hammam* (baths) to give him a description. She found it such a refreshing experience that she became addicted. Whenever she could she visited the *harems* of important citizens; her problem was that she spoke no Arabic or Turkish and unless one of the women spoke French she had to get permission to take her *kavas* (blindfolded) with her to interpret. Eventually she acquired an Arab maid who spoke English, which made such visits a lot easier. It was important for Richard to know what local gossip said, and the *harem* was a good place to hear gossip for the women in wealthy houses had little else to do.

Within days Isabel made the acquaintance of 'the only other English person of note in the city'. As a 17-year-old débutante, Jane Digby had married Lord Ellenborough (who was Governor-General of India during Richard's service there). He divorced her after she ran off with an Austrian prince who subsequently deserted her. When the Burtons met her in Damascus she was happily married to a handsome Bedouin sheikh who was young enough to be her son. Like Isabel she had an impeccable aristocratic lineage; unlike Isabel she was rich enough to live luxuriously in exile. She spent six months of the year living in the palatial villa she had built at Damascus; the remaining six months she spent in the desert, sharing the famous black tents of Arabia with her husband's people.

Jane, who now styled herself Jane Digby el Mezrab (though Isabel always referred to her as Lady Ellenborough), was 63. A great beauty in her youth, she still retained her legendary power to dazzle and charm. On her latest marriage she had adopted the dress of a Bedouin princess, and with her slender figure and lithe movements, Isabel said, she looked more like a 30-year-old as she went about the city. Most members of major English aristocratic families are related through marriage in some manner and, sure enough, when Isabel looked into the branches of her mother's family tree, she found that the 4th Lord Gerard had married a Jane Digby at the time of the Restoration. This distant kinship cemented a friendship between the two women. Jane was multi-lingual and had friends among the European diplomatic legations, but she was delighted to meet an Englishwoman of her own class who knew families in England known to her. Whenever she went into Damascus, Isabel called at the Mezrab villa, and often the two women exercised their horses together. A good deal of what Isabel wrote about Syria she learned from Jane Digby, but her attitude towards the inhabitants she learned from Richard.

Despite his chivalristic ideals, and access – through linguistics – to greater understanding of his host country, Burton was a gun-boat diplomatist. He believed that in order to command the respect of a 'native' population it was necessary to speak and act firmly. Disobedience always merited rebuke or punishment (or dismissal in the case of his servants), so that word would spread that he was not to be trifled with; he meant what he said. It was inevitable that Isabel would adopt this attitude; if Richard said that was how to behave, that was how she behaved. In Salahiyeh she often went about unaccompanied as Jane did; but in Damascus she regarded herself as 'on duty' as the wife of the British Consul, and – since she wore European clothes and was unveiled – she was liable to being spat at or otherwise abused. Consequently, like the wives of other European Consuls, she was always accompanied by four *kavasses*, splendidly dressed in the Consular livery. Whether she was on foot or riding her favourite white donkey, it was their task to clear a way for her through crowds, but she was not entirely comfortable about this; 'it was far more pain than pleasure to me to see mules, horses, donkeys, camels, little children and poor old men thrust out of the way as if I was sacred and they were dirt. How they must have cursed me!'[9] She felt she could do little more than order her escort not to be more officious than was absolutely necessary.

Almost from the start, the fascinating Jane Digby began to confide odd snippets of her history during their meetings. She had borne two children to Prince Felix Schwarzenberg, but he deserted her in Paris and she subsequently became the lover of King Ludwig I of Bavaria. When she became pregnant, she made a marriage of convenience to a Bavarian baron, but left him to elope with a Greek count. The baron chased the lovers and fought a roadside duel to keep his wife, but Jane divorced him anyway and left their two children with him. Later she divorced the count for infidelity (her third divorce) and became the mistress of a charismatic Albanian general. For a time she lived as his partner like a *banditti* Queen, in the wild mountains of Northern Greece, until discovering him in a compromising situation with her trusted maid of twenty years. Swearing never to trust another man (but keeping the maid), the still bewitching Jane travelled to Syria, where the Bedouin sheikh hired to guide her to the ruined desert city of Palmyra fell madly in love with her. She married him in Muslim law, and was blissfully happy. She had had to overcome many cultural prejudices but, by the time Isabel met her, Jane had been accepted by the tribe as matriarch.[10]

Mesmerised by Jane's stories, Isabel encouraged her confidences and was full of sympathy for her new friend whom she regarded as 'more sinned against than sinning'. That Jane habitually divulged more than she intended to, and usually regretted having shared her secrets, is witnessed by her diary. She castigated herself for having spoken in an uncomplimentary manner of men she had truly loved; 'I was vexed with myself for speaking of . . . bygone days. *Why?* neither did the noble-minded Baron justice nor the love I bear to the dear Sheikh.'[11] But she liked Isabel enormously and admired the younger woman's drive. She wrote in her diary that Isabel's enthusiasm, energy and horsemanship reminded her of herself at the same age.[12]

Richard, too, had made a new friend in Damascus who was as celebrated and fascinating as Jane Digby. The princely Algerine earned Richard's respect, for His Highness Emir Abd el-Khader was not only a master-Sufi but studied languages, Oriental history and literature. Indeed, they had so much in common that it was inevitable that they would become friends. Born in the same year as Jane Digby, as a young man el-Khader had been elected by the combined tribes of Oran to lead them in the fight against the French. This had given him virtual sovereignty of two-thirds of Algeria for fifteen years. Eventually he was forced to surrender, and was imprisoned for five years in the Château D'Amboise. In 1852, after pleas for clemency by the British, Louis Napoleon released him with an annual pension (equivalent to £200,000 today), on condition that he never returned to Algeria and did not involve himself in politics. Usually el-Khader did not intervene in politics but during the 1860 massacre of Christians in Damascus he saved hundreds if not thousands of Christians from certain slaughter, a deed for which he was decorated by both the French and the British.

When Richard met him – 'a dark, and a splendid-looking man with stately bearing and perfectly self-possessed' – the emir was living a quiet, almost academic life, with his five wives and private army of 500 faithful Algerines. He was reputed to divorce one wife each year in order to add a fresh young beauty to his harem; but his first wife, the love of his youth and unchallenged chatelaine of his palace, was irreplaceable to him. Though now aged and ugly, she had great wisdom and he regarded her as his most trusted counsellor. She was jealous and miserable, Isabel said sympathetically. 'Her woman's heart wanted more,' and only pride in her lineage eased her grief, for she alone was *Bint el Naas*' (daughter of a good house) while the young and pretty wives were *surrayeh* (bought ones). Of el-Khader, Isabel wrote:

> He dresses purely in white . . . enveloped in the usual snowy *burnous* . . . if you see him on horseback without knowing him to be Abd el Kadir, you would single him out . . . he has the seat of a gentleman and a soldier. His mind is as beautiful as his face; he is every inch a Sultan.[13]

A rewarding find for Richard in Damascus was the wonderful Ommayad Library containing rich collections of Arabic papyri and other literary treasures. His reputation as the traveller who went to Mecca in disguise had gone before him, as his enemies had warned Clarendon, but by and large his appearance in Syria as British Consul was welcomed. His predecessor, Richard Rogers, had not been liked, Jane Digby told Isabel; he had been open to bribes.[14]

The couple rose at dawn and Richard took advantage of the coolest part of the day to work at his writing. He was working on *The Lowlands of Brazil*: 'a kind of make-weight for the highlands . . . same style but with fewer notes,' he wrote to Albert Tootal. As well, he was editing Tootal's translation of Hans Stade, and had begun writing about Syria and the Lebanon. 'I have done a good bit of the old Phoenicia and am gradually doing Syria and Palestine. No intention of publishing for 2 or 3 years. The absence of ten years has made me rusty in Eastern matters and I am only just getting back into the swing . . . I have just finished one about Zanzibar . . .'[15]

Isabel quickly settled down to a busy life similar to that she had lived in Brazil, in which a twenty-four-hour day seemed hardly sufficient. As before she looked after the house, the servants, the stables, the animals, the garden. She also acted as Richard's confidential secretary, dealing with any correspondence that he could not trust to his Consular staff. She had a few servants – maid, cook, man-of-all-work, house boy and a few *syces* (grooms) – but compared with that of other Europeans in Damascus their household was a small one, run thriftily by Isabel on a limited budget. She had set herself several reading and writing projects, in addition to the long epistles she wrote about her daily life to send home each month, and she took lessons in Arabic (Richard had set her to learn ten words each day and to use them in conversation; 'Don't be like the Irishman who would not go into the water until he could swim,' he told her).[16] She supervised the feeding and grooming of the horses daily (she trained the *syces* herself) and exercised them in the desert. Her notebook on stable routines and veterinary information reveals a sound and sensible approach to horse management, except perhaps for one slightly bizarre piece of advice given her by an unnamed friend: 'How to tame a wild horse; go twice a day, each time rub on his nose a little aniseed, 16 drops mixed with oil of rhodium 8 drops, oil of juniper 8 drops, oil asp. 8 drops. Put a little in the mouth and make him an oatmeal cake of it.'[17]

With a white apron and cuffs over the dark blue riding habit which she wore for chores, she treated any sick villagers who knocked on her door asking for help. Like Jane Digby, Isabel was referred to as the *sitt* (lady or noblewoman) and such duties came with the title. Usually she saw about fifteen patients a day. Later she would dress formally and pay and receive visits from the wives of notable citizens. Any spare time in the evenings she spent practising her music on the 'pianette' she had shipped to Damascus, and writing her journal which eventually provided the basis for her best-selling two-volume work *The Inner Life of Syria*.

Richard, whose health improved dramatically after they moved out to the dry fresh air at Salahiyeh, was busy and absorbed in his role as Consul for the first time. His role in Damascus was more diplomatic than consular, for there was a limited amount of commercial work. The largest set of British residents in Syria were missionaries who had been only too aware of his scathing comments on the missionaries in Sierra Leone which had resulted in a Parliamentary Committee in 1864. 'When it became known that Burton was destined for Damascus,' said leading missionary the Reverend William Wright, 'there was a kind of panic among the missionaries in Syria and active steps were taken to prevent the appointment being carried out.'[18]

Richard learned of this unease from Clarendon, and consequently one of his first acts was to visit William Wright to smooth things over. He was shown into the drawing room by an Arab servant and Wright, working in his study, wrote how he was irritated to hear the Consul command the man 'to fetch me, in harsh, peremptory tones, which were meant to be obeyed'. As the servant went away to find his master in another part of the house, Wright walked to the door of his study which adjoined the drawing room. In his soft Persian slippers his footsteps could not be heard, and he related how, as he reached the door, he came upon an unforgettable scene:

> At one side of the room stood my curly-headed, rosy-cheeked little boy of five; on the other side stood Burton. The two were staring at each other. Neither was aware of my presence. Burton had twisted his face into the most fiendish aspect. His eyes rolled, exposing the whites in a most alarming manner. The features were drawn to one side, so as to make the gashes on his jaw and brow appear more ghastly. The two cheeks were blown out, and Burton, raising a pocket handkerchief to his left cheek, struck his right with the flat of his right hand, producing an explosion, and making the pocket handkerchief fly to the left as if he had shot it through his two cheeks. The explosion was followed by a suppressed howl, something between the bark of a hyena and a jackal . . . The child stood riveted to the floor as if spell-bound and fascinated like a creature about to be devoured.
>
> Suddenly a very wonderful thing happened. The little boy, with a wild shout of delight, sprang into the monster's arms, and the black beard was instantly mingled with the fair curls, and Burton

was planting kisses all over the flaxen pate. The whole pantomime was gone through as quick as lightning and Burton, disentangling himself, caught sight of my Arab returning without me and instead of waiting for an explanation, hurled at him a volley of exasperating epithets, culled from the rich stores of spicy and stinging words which garnish Arab literature. Burton had revealed himself to me fully before he saw me. The big, rough monster had a big child's heart behind the hideous grimaces.[19]

After that, Wright said, 'the more I saw him alone the better I liked him . . . he was a brave, strong man in a blatant land. When you got down through the crusts you found a fearless and honest friend.' He had heard all the stories that preceded the new Consul and quickly concluded that, 'Burton was incapable of either monstrous cruelty or gross immorality . . . I knew him well, in sickness, in trouble . . . in his home, in the saddle, under fire . . . and I have noticed that acts of cruelty and immorality always drove him into a white heat of passion . . . Shielding the weak from cruelty, and protecting the poor from oppression, constituted Captain Burton's chief work at Damascus.'[20]

Within two weeks of his arrival, Richard had received the leaders of all the factions which made Damascus a notable flash-point: the Chief *Mufti* of the Moslem community, the Patriarchs of the Greek and Syrian Orthodox Christians, and the senior Rabbis. Far from the uprisings against him by orthodox Moslems which had been predicted by Elliot and Rashid Pasha, 'he became a great favourite with them,' Wright testified.[21] With the Christians, too, he maintained an excellent working relationship and they frequently referred to him in difficulties. But Elliot's warnings were not completely wrong. Richard did encounter problems, though not from either of the directions anticipated.

Before he went to Syria his opinions on Jews were conventional enough, afterwards his anti-Semitism was pronounced. Damascus was home to a colony of 4,000 Jews, some of whom were 'men of great wealth and affluence'. Twenty-six of the richest men among them, originally from Russia and various eastern European countries, had been granted British citizenship.[22] By contrast, Jane Digby had been stripped of her British citizenship during the time of Richard's predecessor, ostensibly because her marriage to an Arab made it difficult for him to pursue her claims. Notably, she offered no costly gifts.

Richard wrote how, shortly after his arrival in Damascus, one of the Jewish moneylenders had come to him and, 'patting me patronisingly on the back, told me he had three hundred cases for me, relative to collecting £60,000 worth of debts'. Richard, deeply affronted, told him he had better hire himself a debt-collector, for he was not there to do so. 'He then threatened me with the British Government. I replied, "It is by far the best thing you can do."'[23] This was the start of war between Richard and the moneylenders, and though he worked happily with other British Jews and pursued their interests, in his subsequent writing he would always dismissively refer to the moneylenders at Damascus as 'Shylocks'.

For a while attempts were made to curry favour. 'He might have seen his beautiful wife flashing in brilliants, roped in pearls, and riding the best blood Arabs of the desert,' Wright stated, writing with first-hand knowledge of the situation. Isabel in fact cared nothing for the caskets of jewels she politely returned, though 'I like diamonds as much as most any woman,' she said. But she 'would have given worlds' for the thoroughbred Arab mares she had to reject, five in all. The last of these, offered as a gift, was 'a beautiful white mare . . . I had to look hard the other way to refuse the temptation . . . because I knew there must be something not altogether right . . . to be done for it.'[24]

It was immediately evident to Richard that the moneylenders, of whom as British Consul he found himself the official protector, were making their fortunes by usury, charging interest rates between 30 and 60 per cent or even more. In the past, when a debt remained unpaid, one of these 'British' moneylenders had only to apply to the British Consul to have the debtor thrown into prison until his relatives paid his debt 'down to the last farthing'. Technically, it was Richard's official duty, also, to urge the recognition of these British claims and insist on their being paid. But when he began to investigate some of the cases brought before him by the moneylenders, he discovered to his fury that entire peasant families had been turned out of their homes to starve, and breadwinners of families had been cast into prison for years on the word of his predecessor, without any hope of release. Interest continued to compound on the original debts while the offender was in gaol, and in one instance he found that a loan of 2,420 Napoleons made in 1857 had become by 1870 a claim by the lender for 35,000 Napoleons. 'Throughout the country,' Richard wrote to the F.O., 'the villagers had been impressed with the idea that the usurer's word was law to the British Consulate; even the Bedouins shunned us, as though they expected harm at our hands.'[25]

Before he had been in Syria six months Richard had publicly announced that he would not be a 'bumbailiff to a parcel of blood-suckers', and indeed caused the release of several pauper debtors including an old man of 90 years who had spent the entire winter in an unheated cell for a debt of one Napoleon (less than £1: current-day value £34). He pinned a notice to the door of the Consulate which read in part:

> Her Britannic Majesty's Consul hereby warns British subjects and protégés that he will not assist them to recover debts from the Government or from the people of Syria, unless the debts are such as between British subjects [and] could be recovered through H.M.'s Consular Courts . . . HBM's Consul feels bound to protest strongly against the system adopted by British subjects and protected persons at Damascus who habitually induce the Ottoman authorities to imprison peasants and pauper debtors for simple debt, or upon charges which have not been previously produced for examination at this Consulate . . .

'In this case,' said William Wright, who watched the matter unfolding, 'I am inclined to think that Burton's impatience led him into doing the right thing in the wrong way. He was indignant, his blood was up, and on being asked what was the use of a Consul at Damascus if he did not enforce British claims, he lost the composure befitting the Diplomatic Service.'[26] His protagonists appealed to the *Alliance Israelite** who contacted 'noble, humane and generous Jews in England', asking them to aid their persecuted brethren in Damascus. Thus, quite soon after Richard's arrival in Syria the Foreign Office began to receive the first complaints against him from influential quarters of the City of London.

As usual he took time to conduct detailed surveys of the surrounding country, investigating remote villages, ancient ruins, and

---

*An international organisation linking members of the Jewish faith.

unusual ethnic groups. He made a point of visiting missionary schools and examined the children, always making some 'valuable suggestions . . . as to the perfecting of their educational organisation'.[27] Two weeks after Isabel's arrival the great caravan of the *Haj* assembled at Damascus, and the Burtons were invited to accompany Abd el-Khader to watch its departure from a balcony in the citadel. There were two days of celebration as the colourful and exotic procession wound its way through the city, out of the gate and south into the desert.

Few people in Damascus were unaware of Richard's pilgrimage to Mecca, and he was everywhere respectfully saluted as a *hajji* to his undisguised pleasure. He reported this seal of approval to the Foreign Office in validation of his initial statements to Clarendon: 'even the Mueyzins (Prayer-Callers) of the great Amawi Mosque led by a Shaykh in brown cloak and black hood . . . the most fanatical, smiled at me as I looked down upon them.'[28] He accompanied his report with a lengthy and lively description of the *Haj* procession and this memorandum – with some editorial changes to the person, spelling of Arabic words, and a few domestic asides to make it more palatable – appears almost *in toto* as a chapter in Isabel's book *The Inner Life of Syria*.[29] From this point onwards the couple worked in partnership, to some degree, on all their literary projects.

The southern suburb of Damascus, known as Maydan, was the headquarters of an obscure esoteric sect called the Shazlis who attempted to spiritualise the material aspects of Islam. They were Sufis and therefore immediately attracted Richard's interest. 'The mystic side of their faith especially appealed to him,' Isabel wrote. 'He thought he saw in it a connection between Sufiism* and Catholicism . . . he followed it up unofficially, disguised as a Shazli, unknown to any mortal except myself. He used to mix with them, and passed much of his time in the Maydan at Damascus with them.'[30]

Many of these Shazlis were converted to Christianity in the spring of 1870, a process which began, according to William Wright, two years earlier after a large number of the sect experienced a vision.

---

*Sufiism: Isabel habitually used the word Sufiism in her writing. I am advised that more correctly the word is Sufism.

Despite Isabel's belief that she was the only person who knew of Richard's disguise it is clear that the Rashid Pasha learned of it also. Incorrectly, he connected Richard's presence with the conversions and this increased his deep suspicions of the English Consul. Steeped in political intrigue himself, Rashid placed the worst interpretation on the Consul's constant journeys about the country, believing that Richard's interest in archaeology and anthropology was a cover for more sinister work. He hid his hostility very well, accepting Isabel's invitations to their house and in every way affecting to regard them as friends. Isabel was taken in, at least at first; Richard was not. Later Jane Digby and el-Khader told him of Rashid's corruption and venality.

Isabel began to love Damascus as she had once loved South America. When they were not entertaining, the couple 'lived like natives', but every Wednesday she held an all-day reception for which she dressed 'as for visiting in London' and invited anyone of note in and around the city, so that there was a real gathering of cultures. At first she made an attempt to integrate her guests, the women sitting uneasily with their husbands. 'I used to get up as a matter of course, make tea and coffee, and carry them around.' When she asked the Consular dragomans (male secretaries) to help her hand the drinks round,

> they were pleased to do so and willingly handed it to any European man or woman, but not to their own ladies who blushed, begged pardon and were altogether confused. They looked appealingly at me, and stood up, praying not to be served. And when one, who was really in love with his wife, a beautiful creature, gave her the tea-cup he did it as if it were a rather good joke . . . she bent and kissed his hand and humbly begged his pardon.

One of the men said to her in English: 'Pray Mrs Burton do not teach our women things they don't know and never saw.' After that she did not try to change things again and always set a room aside for Moslem women, where she greeted them and removed their veils and izzars personally, performing her duties as hostess in both reception areas.

Jane Digby, when she was in Damascus and not travelling with her husband, often helped her to receive, and interpreted for her. Jane told

Isabel hundreds of insignificant details of Arab life, for example how Arab men liked to have little incense burners placed about the divan so they could waft the rising smoke through their beards to perfume them. The Franco-Prussian conflict was raging, so Isabel frowned on political discussions, and because Damascus housed so many fanatical coteries she also barred religion as a topic of conversation at her receptions. Sometimes, she wrote, Richard would flash a look at her in warning, or approval, or indicating that she should do something; they had long ago evolved a secret sign language that was as meaningful to her as conversation; 'we could almost talk before outsiders in this way, without speaking a word out loud.'[31] Isabel invariably acted as he indicated, except once in Brazil. On that occasion, despite the fact that, 'Richard stared very hard at me over the top of his newspaper', she brazenly told a white lie to an irate husband, to protect a woman friend she knew to be in an adulterous relationship.

When everybody else left them, usually in the late afternoon so as to be back inside the city gates before they closed at sunset, two guests habitually remained. Jane Digby, who lived outside the city and who had no qualms about riding home alone after dark (though she was twice attacked); and Abd el-Khader who owned a summer villa in Salahiyeh. These two joined Isabel and Richard for supper. Afterwards the quartet retired to the rooftop logia to sit under the stars and smoke and talk. These conversations had no limits; all and any subject was open for dissection in a multilingual forum on philosophy, politics, history, travel, theology, magic.[32]

These evenings were 'my great intellectual treat,' Isabel wrote. Although she spoke only a few words of Arabic she was fluent in French, and had conversational German, Italian and Portuguese. Jane Digby spoke nine languages fluently, and el-Khader, like Richard, had studied languages intensively. 'I shall never forget the scene on the housetop,' Isabel wrote: 'backed as it was by the sublime mountain, a strip of sand between it and us, and on the other three sides was the view over Damascus and beyond the desert. It was all wild, romantic and solemn; and sometimes we would pause in our conversation to listen to the sounds around us; the last call to prayer on the minaret-top, the soughing of wind through the mountain gorges, and the noise of the water-wheel in the neighbouring orchard.'[33]

Richard said that Jane was 'out and out the cleverest woman he ever met'. Isabel agreed. 'There was nothing she could not do. She spoke nine languages perfectly, and could read and write in them. She painted, sculpted, was musical and her letters were splendid. And if on business there was never a word too much, or too little.'[34]

It was from Jane that Isabel (and through her, Richard) learned a good deal of her knowledge of harem life, about which she wrote. This was necessarily abridged, she explained coyly, in *The Inner Life of Syria*, because 'the minute detail would not be suitable for English girls.'[35]

But despite her affection for, and admiration of Jane Digby (neither ever enjoyed a really close relationship with other women other than their maid-servants) Isabel had some reservations. She found Medjuel el Mezrab a likeable man and respected his intelligence (he could speak Turkish and a little French, and unusually for a Bedouin, could read and write); yet she found it incomprehensible that her beautiful and fastidious friend could have sacrificed life in England with her family to live with a black husband. The first time Isabel called at the Mezrab villa, Medjuel opened the door to her. Like most true Bedouins he was short and slight, unlike some of the tall and imposing Arab chiefs Isabel had already met. 'I thought at first he was a native servant. I could understand her leaving a coarse cruel husband, much older than herself, whom she never loved;[36] I could understand her running away with Schwarzenberg; but the contact with that black skin I could not understand.'[37]

The most important point of dissension between the two women, however, was in respect of the unmarked thoroughfare through the desert between Damascus and the ruins of the ancient and romantic city of Palmyra (still called by the Bedouins by its old name, Tadmor).[38] According to the Bible, it was built by King Solomon beside the great oasis as a safe halt for the caravans on the important trade routes from India and Persia. The Mezrab tribe had held territorial rights over the section of the desert around Tadmor for centuries and Medjuel, whose elder brother was their leader, had special responsibility for the revenue earned by escorting travellers. Although the Mezrabis were virtually self-sufficient, there were commodities they needed to buy in; material for clothing, metals for cooking implements, weapons and jewelry, flour and grain, and guns, for example. European tourists were a relatively new – and important – source of income. In addition to knowing the positions of the few wells along the 150-mile route, Medjuel commanded an armed escort to protect travellers from attack by marauding gangs of Arabs. When Jane made her first, romantic journey to Palmyra with Medjuel in 1853 she was only the second European woman to have done so in modern times; Hester Stanhope was the first. The then British Consul (Mr Wood), was so concerned at the risk involved, and the implications of an Englishwoman travelling alone in the desert with an Arab, that he did everything in his power to prevent Jane making the trip. Consul Wood was right to be worried; they were attacked and Medjuel had to shield Jane with his own body while he fought off the intruders in vicious hand-to-hand fighting.[39] That was when she fell in love with him.

Since that time, small parties of European visitors had arrived in Damascus every few months hoping to persuade Medjuel to take them to Palmyra. But it was an arduous journey and he would not take everyone; only those he considered fit enough to make the journey safely. Jane was very protective of this enterprise since rival tribes, noting the flow of rich foreigners, were lobbying Rashid Pasha in an attempt to have him refute the claims of the Mezrabis to exclusive rights to the route. The Mezrabis' case was not helped by the fact that they had recently been defeated in a major battle by the combined force of their enemies, the Wuld Ali, the Mowali and Hadiden tribes. In some of these battles Jane had ridden at her husband's side; but bravery was not enough against overwhelming odds and the Mezrabis lost many horses, camels, sheep and tents in the series of encounters. They were therefore in a poor position to guarantee the safety of travellers under their protection.

Richard told Isabel shortly after her arrival that he intended to make the journey to Palmyra without a Bedouin guide. They could not have afforded Medjuel's normal fee of £240; but it is difficult to picture Richard Burton ever travelling to Palmyra as a paying tourist. Several books written by travellers who had made the journey with Medjuel gave some information about the route and stopping places.[40] In addition he made his own extensive enquiries about the position of *khans* and known wells on the route, and was able to justify his plan officially by informing Jane and Medjuel that because of the tribal in-fighting which was especially savage that year (Jane described the desert as being 'in an uproar'), it was his duty to open the road for travellers. He gave Isabel the choice of accompanying him, or staying behind. She unhesitatingly chose to go; 'I said as I always said, "I will follow you to the death."[41] Subsequently, she received so many warnings from people she regarded as trustworthy that she suspected they might indeed be marching to their deaths.

When Richard was first planning the journey, about a dozen Europeans asked to be included in the party; in 1870 Palmyra had been seen by fewer than a hundred non-Arab visitors. But one by one they sent in their apologies until only the Russian Consul and a French count who was visiting Damascus remained. As if to underline the warnings, a few days before their departure an English couple, Mr and Lady Adelaide Law, arrived in the city almost destitute, their party having been attacked by a gang of Bedouins. Their dragoman was seriously wounded and their escort had run off, leaving them at the mercy of the attackers. They were not hurt but robbed of everything, except Lady Adelaide's engagement ring which she saved by putting it in her mouth before capture.

In the week prior to the Burtons' departure, Jane Digby tried everything she could think of to dissuade them from making the journey without Medjuel and an escort. But even had they been inclined to go with Medjuel the timing was unfavourable, for he had gone to his distressed tribe and no one knew when he might return. Jane had spent the years since her marriage to Medjuel actively working on the tribe's behalf; endowing them with large flocks, the best breeding mares and the newest guns from the West. She was now, said Isabel, 'more Bedouin than the Bedouin' and knew that if the Burtons were successful it would demonstrate that the protection of the Mezrabis was no longer necessary. When the Burtons called on her to say *au revoir*, her great blue eyes filled with tears as she warned that they were placing themselves in great danger and might never return. Jane's genuine affection for the couple created a dilemma for her. She suggested a compromise, if it could be seen that they had taken a member of the tribe with them, it could still be demonstrated that the Burtons had Mezrabi assistance. 'She offered us the escort of one of her Mezrabs,' Isabel wrote, 'that we might steer clear of the Bedawi raids and be conducted to water quicker *if it existed*. Richard made me a sign to accept the escort, and we did.'[42]

The Burtons left Damascus on 7 April. Later, Isabel would take to wearing Arab clothes, but when they first set out she wore an English riding habit. Over this she wore an Eastern belt containing a revolver, cartridges and a dagger, and round her neck Richard slung 'a whistle and compass, in case of my being lost'. She tucked her hair away under an Arab headdress, and wore a short 'face veil' of gold and brown.[43] Isabel was horsemaster and had provided her best horses. Richard preferred *rahwans*, sturdy little Kurdish ponies with a high trotting action, but Isabel took her two half-breed stallions to ride herself and hired useful horses for their retinue. They used camels as pack animals; 17 were laden simply with water-skins – enough, Richard hoped, to get them through the long and difficult final stage if they could not locate the two wells he believed to exist.

Their eight-day ride was hard, even for the men. And at the end of each day, camp was a busy time rather than a restful one for Isabel. Although there were *syces* to care for the pack animals, she looked after her own and Richard's horses herself. 'I think I may say without flattery,' she wrote as an old woman, 'that I had a good many capabilities for being a traveller's wife. I could ride, walk, swim, shoot and defend myself if attacked, so that I was not dependent on my husband, and I could also make myself generally useful – that is to say I could make the bed, arrange the tent, cook the dinner, if necessary wash the clothes by the river-side, mend them and spread them to dry, nurse the sick, bind and dress wounds, pick up a smattering of the language, make the natives respect and obey me, groom my own horse, saddle him, wade through rivers, sleep on the ground with a saddle for a pillow, and generally rough it.'[44] It was Richard's task to 'take all the notes and sketches, observations and maps, and to gather information'.

During the first part of the journey they stayed at *khans* beside desert settlements, at one, the Burtons were invited to stay at the home of Da'as Agha, a wily and cruel border chief who proposed that he should join them with ten of his armed guards.[45] Isabel spent the evening with the Agha's *harem*, who shrieked with laughter at her undergarments and kept her awake all night by peering through her window and rattling at her locked door. Next morning she found one of the chief's sons swinging round his head a swallow tied by one leg to a long string. She begged his father to give her the bird as a gift, knowing he could not refuse the request of his guest, and as she released it she tried to explain to the child about cruelty to animals. She thought her words had had some effect, but shortly afterwards she saw the boy spearing pariah dogs with his father's lance; 'a chip off the old block', she commented angrily.

After they reached the desert proper there were no more settlements or *khans*. They made their own camp each night, sleeping fully dressed with weapons by their sides, ready to mount and fly if attacked. On Richard's instructions they always doused the fire after cooking and took off the camels' bells so as not to draw anyone to them in the silence of the desert nights. Isabel never forgot the romance of her first night in the desert under a bright moon and an endless canopy of stars: the black tents, the camels resting, the horses picketed all about grazing on scrub, the exotically dressed men lying here and there in the moonlight, which glinted on their tripod and kettle. Even the howling of jackals was attractive to her; 'it was the prettiest thing to see them gambolling in the moonlight,' she said. But the first time a pack of jackals swept past in full cry she jumped to her feet in fear thinking it was a *ghazu* (raid) bearing down on them.

They rose in the freezing dawn, shook as much dust out of their clothes as possible, boiled water for tea, struck the camp, and saw the animals fed, watered and packed. Those with the tents were sent off first, otherwise they loitered and the tents were not on site at the end of a day. It was a late spring that year. Sometimes the midday sun burned down on them as they trekked across the inhospitable landscape; but at others they experienced gales and hailstorms. On one occasion a sandstorm blew up. 'Once you have been in a sandstorm . . . will never forget,' Isabel wrote. She turned and looked to Richard who motioned her to fall in behind him, which she did, and with *keffiyehs* drawn across their faces they galloped into the teeth of the storm 'as if we were riding for a doctor'. This lasted three hours; unable to see anything, Isabel threw down her reins and left it to her horse who was desert-bred and seemed to know what to do. At one point he cleared a huge pit with a massive leap; Isabel had not even seen it.

Sometimes, when the ground was firm they could gallop the horses and make good time. At others, deep shifting sand alternated with desolate plains of sharp flints and loose slabs of rock through which the animals had to pick their way slowly. Away from wells, water was strictly rationed. Isabel always made a point of personally ensuring the animals were adequately watered, but she found the thirst terrible, 'the throat seems to close and lightheadedness soon sets in,' she recalled.[46] They constantly experienced mirages, but Richard was wise to these visions and would not deviate from his compass course. They were shadowed the entire time by Bedouins; often they heard

1 & 2
Portraits of Isabel and Richard by Richard's boyhood friend, the painter Louis Desanges,
presented in 1861 as a wedding gift.

3 The Old Ramparts at Boulogne where Isabel and Richard first met. For Isabel it was love at first sight.

4 An amateur painting of the Burton children before the family left for France in 1825. *l. to r.* Edward, Richard and Maria.

5 Lieut. Edward Burton, Richard's younger brother; a beating by Indian bearers left him brain-damaged for life. He died aged 70 in a mental institution.

6 Barham House, Elstree, the home of Richard Burton's maternal grandparents, where he spent the first few years of his life.

7 Lieut. Richard Francis Burton (aged 30), painted with his sister Maria (Mrs Stisted) at Boulogne; by Jaquand in 1851.

8 'Miss Isabella Arundell aged 4'.
An engraving of a miniature.

9 Isabel aged about 14 with her father and the inevitable
small dogs she always had around her.

10 Wardour Castle, ancestral home of the Arundells, where Isabel spent much of her childhood.

11 'Mirza Abdullah the Bushiri'; Richard Burton in disguise c. 1849. Artist unknown c. 1850.

12 Isabel's favourite painting of Richard, by Wilhelm Lehman, remained in the hands of the Arundells until 1997.

13 'Sir Charles Napier', a caricature used in Isabel's best selling book *A.E.I: Arabia, Egypt, India*. The caption in Richard's writing (top l.h. corner) confirms his close involvement in her works.

14 John Hanning Speke c. 1861. Burton did not recognise
the deep animosity that Speke harboured towards him even
before they set out to explore East Africa together.
A rare signed photograph from Isabel's photo album.

15 Photo of Richard in 1854 prior to the
Somalia expedition.

16 Speke flees for his life at Berbera, Somalia 1854. The horrific attack on Burton's party left Speke and Burton badly injured.
Lucky to escape court martial for negligence, Burton was 'severely censured'.

17 Engraving of Burton's sketch of Zanzibar.

18 *Sidi* Mubarak, 'Bombay', guide to the East African expedition. Speke later claimed that Burton ordered Bombay to poison him while he slept.

19 Burton in Cairo, December 1853, after returning from his *Haj*. One of two watercolour portraits of Burton by Edward Lear.

20 An idealised contemporary cartoon of the Burton/Speke expedition in East Africa.

21 Mrs Arundell. Isabel's mother disapproved of Richard, regarding him as unsuitable for her strictly reared daughter.

22 'Puss Arundell', taken in Venice c. 1858.

23 & 24 Photograph of the letter Richard wrote to Isabel's father after their 'secret marriage' in January 1861. Now in the Richmond Library. 'I want no money with Isabel; I can work and it will be my care that time shall bring you nothing to regret.'

25 Madeira 1863. Although taken two years after their marriage, the couple regarded this trip as their real honeymoon. Previously unpublished, this photograph, 'taken by Lord B.', is from Isabel's photo album.

26 Richard and Isabel Burton 'at home' with the Arundells at their Wardour Castle apartment in January 1863. One of several taken in a session, this previously unpublished picture from Isabel's album is annotated by her; 'Back row l to r: Rudolph, Emmaline, Richard, Papa, Puss. Front: Blanche, Mama, Uncle Renfric, Jack'.

27 Richard and Isabel provided unusual after-dinner entertainment for fellow guests. Sometimes he hypnotised her, but in this eerie tableau in Madeira 1863, Isabel acts as a grief stricken widow with the ghost of Richard appearing to her. A rare, previously unpublished picture from Isabel's photo album.

28 Frederick Foster Arbuthnot, 'Bunny', who collaborated with Richard in the translation, and publication into English, of the erotic classic *The Kama Sutra*.

29 This affectionate caricature of Isabel by Burton (c. 1871) hints at her intrepid nature: but his self portrait forming the Lion's face suggests that at times even he may have found her overwhelming.

30 'Richard Burton in his tent in West Africa.'
The caption is taken from Isabel's photo album. c. 1862.

31 'My dear Boy'; Mr Frank Wilson, Richard's assistant in West Africa. An entertaining series of letters to him from Burton survives.

32 One of the photographs of the Consulate at Fernando Po which Richard sent home to Isabel.

33 Burton shooting the rapids on the Rio das Velhas, Brazil, c. 1868.

35 Richard Burton as HBM Consul of Santos, Brazil c. 1867 (aged 46).

34 Isabel with a group of friends in Rio de Janeiro, 1866. Her vivacity and musical ability made her a popular member of society. The handwritten caption is hers.

36 Isabel in 1868 in Santos, Brazil. Her little dog, 'Nellie', was killed on Friday 13th when it ran into the path of a passing carriage. Both Burtons were superstitious.

37 A uniquely informal picture of Burton, taken by Isabel in Santos c. 1865. She captioned it 'Her Majesty's Consul in Santos'.

38 Albert Tootal, of the British Legation in Rio. Isabel was able to flirt with Tootal from the safety of her impregnable relationship with Burton.

39 Chico, the Burtons' dwarf manservant; Isabel described him as 'our right-hand man in Brazil'.

40 S. Jackson Eldridge, H.B.M. Consul-General of Syria, who connived, from the moment of Burton's arrival there, to have him dismissed.

41 Khamoon, Isabel's maid at Damascus. Isabel recruited her as a 15-year-old from a mission school. Subsequently she treated her 'almost as a daughter', bringing her home to England in 1873 to the irritation of Burton's family, who thought the striking foreign maid 'a silly affectation'.

42 Isabel in 1869, taken before she left for Damascus.

43 Burton dressed for fencing in Trieste. A life-size portrait (probably copied from an 1876 photograph by Barrand) painted c. 1889 by Albert Letchford.

44 View of Damascus from Salahiyeh where the Burtons lived. c. 1869.

46 Charles 'Charlie' Tyrwhitt-Drake. Young enough to be the Burton's son he moved into their home and was loved by them 'as a brother'. His death at the age of 28 was a tremendous blow to them.

45 The enigmatic Jane Digby el Mezrab, formerly Lady Ellenborough and latterly a Bedouin matriarch. She was Isabel's best woman friend in Damascus and her adventurous life was the stuff of legends.

47 The 'cool summer consulate', in the mountains at Bludan, where Burton received the telegram which dismissed him from his post. The drawing is by Tyrwhitt-Drake. The building was only recently demolished.

48 The Burtons in their dining room at Trieste in 1890. One of a series of photographs detailing their home. Some of their furniture belongs to the present British Consul there.

49 Richard in his study while working on *The Arabian Nights*. Trieste 1886.

51 Frederick Leighton's masterly portrait of Burton, 1872. 'Don't make me ugly, don't, there's a good fellow,' Burton begged him.

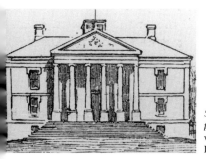

50 Contemporary sketch of the Burtons' *palazzo* in Trieste. Its elevation and glorious views from every side appealed to the couple. It is now converted into luxury apartments.

52 Richard aged 69 a few weeks before his death, photographed by Dr Baker.

53 The exotic tomb that Isabel designed for Richard. It still draws sightseers to the Mortlake churchyard.

54 Isabel, two years after Richard's death. Although suffering from cancer she filled her last years with literary achievement.

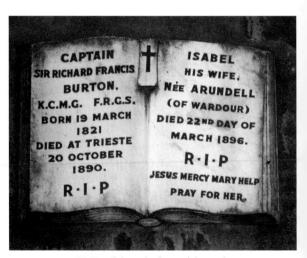

55 Detail from the front of the tomb.

gunshots in the mountains beside their track. Richard suspected that the tribesman mounted on a thoroughbred Arab mare, provided by Jane Digby, was not so much an escort as an agent placed among them to give away their position and bring members of his tribe down upon them, thus proving that the journey could not be made without Mezrab escort. Isabel confided her unease about the man to Richard, who smiled grimly 'under his moustache'.[47] Later he instructed Mohammed the Afghan, 'in his own language so as not to be understood by anyone else', that their 'guide' was to be shown every courtesy and comfort but he was to be disarmed, remounted on a mule and never left without two guards, day or night. In the desert, whenever they heard gunshots the Mezrabi was brought to the front of the cavalcade alongside Isabel, to demonstrate they had a Bedouin escort. Richard always brought up the rear, to prevent stragglers.

Their numbers had swelled to 160. As they stopped at *khans* and wells in the first days, they had gathered up groups of travellers waiting for a caravan to pass by. It was not unknown for *ghazus* to number several hundred, however, so size alone did not guarantee safety. On the eighth day they struck camp before dawn so as to travel as far as possible in the coolest part of the day. Lack of water in this desolate section of the desert was the chief obstacle to travellers, but Richard had heard that there was a well called *Ayn el Wu'úl* and was determined to find and chart it. He found it, 'full of the purest water', in the lower slopes of the mountains, but as they filled their water-skins and watered the animals they heard gunshots echoing 'like thunder through the rocky peaks'. Richard steadied the nervous travellers by saying that if they were to be attacked, they were in a good position, at a height and with cover; they could defend themselves easily. When no attack came they descended to the plains for the final leg of the journey. At about 11 a.m. outriders spotted a small lake; it was the legacy of a rainstorm during the night and would have sunk into the sand by nightfall. As they approached they saw that a party of about 150 Bedouins had got there before them. The French count and the border chief, Da'as Agha, took an escort of men and rode off at a wide angle to reconnoitre.

Richard, Isabel and the Russian Consul led the caravan in a straight line towards the Bedouins. Behind them some of their escort curvetted their horses, which Richard knew was preparatory to their bolting, and he called out loudly, 'The first man who bolts I will shoot him in the back.' There was a small rise in the ground between them and the lake and the trio rode to it. Richard tied a Union Jack to his spear and planted it in the sand. In the clear desert air, Isabel said, it could be seen for miles.[48] At Richard's command they dismounted, and their followers came to them and spread out the usual breakfast arrangements. The reconnaissance party returned saying that the Bedouins were 150 Seba'ah (a tribe closely related to the Mezrabs), but that they appeared to be only watering their animals and probably would not attack unless their numbers were reinforced.

Isabel suggested a *tír* (shooting contest) as a noisy diversion, and Richard set up an orange on a lance point. She was first to shoot. 'By good luck I hit it, and by better luck they did not ask me for a second shot so that I came off with a great reputation, hardly deserved,' she recalled.[49] Though everyone took a turn, only Da'as Agha and one Turkish soldier equalled Isabel's feat, so she was being modest. When they remounted they rode along in lines abreast cheering and singing, to look as impressive as possible. This is how they came upon Palmyra, with its pink limestone glowing rosily in the setting sun. It took Isabel's breath away; 'a more imposing sight I never looked upon,' she said. 'So gigantic, so extensive, so bare, so desolate . . . this splendid City of the dead . . . in its solitary grandeur. You feel as if you are wandering in some forgotten world.'[50] She was probably only the fifth or six European woman to reach the city, although the redoubtable Jane Digby had made the journey on many occasions, several times alone with only two Bedouins as escort.

They were welcomed by horsemen from the nearby town of Palmyra with a *jerid* (traditional fantasia) in which many of their own men joined, galloping about wildly at full speed firing their guns, each screaming his own war-cry. It was an occasion for celebration and demonstrating horsemanship. Some hung to one side of the horses, or under the horses' bellies with the reins held in their mouths, others lofted long quivering lances, the shining tips of which were decorated with ostrich feathers, 'throwing them into the air and catching them at the full gallop'. Some dashed up to Isabel and Richard with lances poised as though about to spear them, wheeling away sharply when they were mere feet away. The many colours of the horsemen's clothes, their splendid mares, the noise and sheer extravagance of the spectacle were breathtaking; 'but you have to be a good rider yourself,' Isabel warned, 'as the horses simply go wild.'

In contrast to this exciting and barbaric scene she found the people of the town, the *fellahin*, 'hideous, poor, dirty, ragged and diseased. Everybody has ophthalmia and you feel to catch it by looking at them . . . they look born to misery.' The travellers made their camp inside the ruins, among the remains of villas, palaces, theatres, triumphal arches and colonnades that lined ancient stone roads still bearing deep grooves scored by the wheels of Roman chariots.[51] Streams and water culverts ran everywhere, accounting for the success of the old city. They camped beside two wells, one to drink from and the other – which was fed with continuous lukewarm water from a sulphurous spring – to bathe in. Here, in 1854, Jane Digby had bathed naked in the moonlight for her sheikh on their honeymoon but Isabel was not to know that, of course. 'Sometimes there were some snakes in it,' said the woman who had once screamed at the sight of a cockroach, 'but they were quite harmless.' Like Jane, her first tour of the ruins was made by moonlight. The limestone which appears pink in the dawn light, bone-white in hot sun and a fabled rose-colour at sunset, gleams ghost-like and silvery-white under the moon. It remains one of the world's unforgettable experiences.

Isabel has often been incorrectly described by biographers of Richard as corpulent, presumably because until now the only photographs of her that were known were taken in late middle age, when she *was* overweight. A niece who saw her regularly in her old age described 'Aunt Puss' as 'a mountain of a woman'.[52] But as younger photographs and the diaries of contemporaries such as Jane Digby show, in Brazil and in Syria Isabel was fit, active and slender. Tall for a woman, when she adopted the dress of an Arab at Palmyra she was mistaken by the townspeople for a youth.

When she saw the success of her costume Isabel happily adopted it, for even a youth was shown far greater respect than a woman – wife of a Consul or not. 'All I had to do towards maintaining my character was to show great respect to my father [Richard], to be very silent before him and my elders, and to look after my horses.' At the end of each day when they rode back to camp, Richard's divan was always ready for his return, 'before the tent door, a sherbet, or cup of coffee, a narghileh, and very often an ovation of Shayks and villagers. I, in my character of son, run up and hold his stirrup to dismount, and salute him, and leaving him to do the *grand seigneur* I walk off with the horses which is what I like best.'[53] After Palmyra, whenever they travelled in Syria and the Lebanon she went as Richard's son, or his groom. Often as they travelled Richard received important visitors, sheikhs and civic leaders;

> ... one day, at a halt, we were sitting a divan ... and all were paying attention to my husband. Suddenly the village priest (Greek Orthodox) looked over and pointing at me said ... 'Is that your son my Lord Beg?' My husband, with the gravest face in the world, answered, 'Yes, O Reverend Father.' I saluted him in the usual fashion, and my husband quickly turned to another subject.[54]

Later, in Damascus she would adopt the dress of an Arab woman cloaked and hidden behind a full *izzar*, to go into the *souks* with her Arab maid to learn the gossip. Isabel wrote that from that time on, both she and Richard always wore Arab clothing in the desert. So blasé did she become that on one occasion she forgot and walked into a *harem*, setting the women screaming and the guards running with their hands on their swords. She pointed to her beardless chin to illustrate her extreme youth and ignorance, and fortunately the difficult situation was diffused.

The Burtons spent five days in Palmyra; writing up journals, sketching, mapping, deciphering Palmyrene inscriptions, exploring the unique tower tombs. The count was shocked, one day, to come across Isabel happily assisting Richard to sort and catalogue human bones. The flora and fauna were not neglected: all the spring flowers, the insects and beetles, butterflies and bird life; the flash of a roller, a flight of storks, a passing hoopoe, a meandering dung-beetle. Richard wanted everything noted, for they might never return (in fact they never did). Anything portable – coins, tesserae etc. – was carefully labelled and packed to be sent to the Anthropological Institute in London. At night they sat in a ring on the sand and were entertained with music and singing by the soldiers and muleteers before the camp fire, 'they danced the sword dance with wild grace, to their ... barbarous musical accompaniments and weird songs.'

This truly was the crest of Isabel's life. This is what she had always dreamed of, always longed for. All the danger, all the adventure, all the spice, all the romance. And alongside her – sharing it all – was the man she worshipped.

27

A SWEET UNREST
1870–1871

The return journey to Damascus was made in four days, since Richard needed to be there in time to receive the monthly English mails due on 23 April. On the second night, Isabel became ill with a malarial fever and Richard treated her with quinine. She refused to be left behind to follow on slowly as he suggested, and rode with the rear of the group, sometimes crying quietly with sickness and tiredness. She wrote graphically of their arrival among the orchards and gardens of Damascus, always a welcome sight, she said, 'no matter how you love the desert and camp life,'

> . . . you smell the water from afar, and you hear its gurgling long before you come to the rills and fountains; you scent and then you see the fruit – the limes, figs, citron, water-melon; you feel a madness to jump into the water . . . to go to sleep in the delicious shade . . . you wonder if your blinded eyes are seeing a mirage. Your tired, drooping horse tells you it is true; he pricks up his ears, he wants to break into a mild trot; done up as he is he stops to drink at every rill, and with a low whinny of joy gathers a mouthful of grass at every crop.[1]

Their home seemed 'like a palace of comfort' after the arduous journey but she was not allowed to rest for long. Cholera and scarlet fever

broke out in Salahiyeh and within days she was busy nursing the
sick, whose families called her out in desperation.

> Several people died in great agony . . . I did what I could . . . I made
> the peasants wash and fumigate their houses and burn the bed-
> ding, and send to me for medicine the moment a person was taken
> ill . . . I secured the services of a kind-hearted French surgeon Dr
> Nicora[2] who attended the patients and I myself nursed them. I
> wore an old woollen dress when attending cases, and this I hung in
> a tree and never let it enter my house.[3]

Here there is a sharp divergence between Isabel and Jane Digby.
Physically courageous as Digby was, she had a paranoid fear of infection and during outbreaks of cholera or typhoid would isolate herself
or leave the city. Isabel felt it was her duty to minister to the poor
despite the risks. But she still found time to write a long account of the
Palmyra journey, which was subsequently published by both *The
Times* and *Morning Post*. Thus began for her a long period as a newspaper correspondent. During the remainder of her time in Syria she
regularly sent lengthy tracts about life in Syria to English newspapers,
and to the *Levant Herald* and *Galligani*, newspapers printed in
English and circulated in the Levant and Middle East.

While Isabel was so preoccupied, Richard was writing gloomily to
Albert Tootal: 'I have a presentiment that my stay at Damascus won't
be long and I am quite prepared for a move. If here till next autumn
I shall dress as a Bedouin, get camels and ride off into the Nejd – part
not yet visited by any European. But that must be when the
Conservatives come in. I see they will soon. The Libs are sure to get
beaten on the Irish question.'[4] After a few weeks of nursing others
Isabel herself contracted cholera. It was a mild dose, but even after the
worst symptoms passed she 'could not move without fainting'.
Richard took her to Beirut for some sea-bathing and within a week
she was able to join him at the Queen's Birthday ball at the Consulate-
General. Later the couple made several excursions along the coast, but
Richard made the further journeys to Tyre, Sidon and Carmel alone,
for Isabel was not strong enough.

They returned in June, riding together without servants or escort
across the spectacular mountains of the Anti-Lebanon. One night a
blizzard threatened to blow away their tent. 'We passed the dark

hours in holding [on to] our tent pole . . . and digging trenches outside to let the water off. There were no dry clothes to be had, and the various vermin would not let one rest. We were like that three days; so we piled up the trunks and sat on top of them, and read "Lothair" by Disraeli . . . the description of the great houses of England read so funnily sitting in this black mud in the centre of desolation . . .'[5]

During the Burtons' absence, Mr Mentor Mott, whose wife Augusta ran the British Syrian School in Beirut, was in Damascus. Described by the Reverend William Wright, witheringly, as 'an amateur missionary', Mott visited seventy Moslem prisoners and gave them soft drinks and 'small religious books to read'. The *Wali*, Rashid Pasha, was in Constantinople, but awaiting Richard's return was a strong complaint from the Deputy Governor, Holo Pasha. Mott's proselytising, he said, had 'excited the Mussulman population'. With the massacre of 1860 in mind, Richard wrote to Mott and did not mince his words. 'It is my duty to inform you that those living in security at Beirut will not suffer by displays of indiscreet zeal; they may, however, imperil the whole Christian population of Damascus, who live among fanatical Mussulmen communities.'[6]

Stung, Mott complained to Consul-General Eldridge that Burton was up to his old tricks, persecuting missionaries. Eldridge always felt threatened by Richard's overwhelming presence in his region. Instead of supporting his colleague, he immediately sent Mott's complaint to the British Ambassador in Constantinople. Henry Elliot had been waiting for an opportunity like this and made the matter part of his official despatch,

> . . . It is undoubtedly his [Burton's] duty to set his face against any attempt to proselytise the Moslem population, but . . . I agree with . . . Mr Eldridge that any indiscretion committed by Mr Mott has been unnecessarily exaggerated, and commented on in terms which were not called for towards a gentleman who is rendering valuable service in the cause of education in Syria . . . Captain Burton's antecedents, the fact of his still, as I understand, professing Mahomedanism, renders his position as representing a Christian, one of peculiar delicacy and difficulty.[7]

He added that he had asked for a translation of the tract given by Mott to prisoners and had been informed that it contained nothing of 'an offensive nature'. This is a remarkable attitude for a diplomat to take when Richard's reaction was in response to a serious and formal complaint from the Deputy Governor of their host country.

A few weeks later the Burtons moved to the cooler climate of Bludan (now spelled Bloudan) a village in the Anti-Lebanon mountains. Their house, shaped like 'a large claret-case' with a deep-covered verandah, had been acquired by a former Consul, Richard Wood, and had since become summer quarters for British Consuls and their dependants during the hottest months.[8] It was five or six hours' ride from Damascus and 'very basic', but its wonderful setting in a wild garden with rushing streams and waterfalls and views across the mountains made up for any deficiencies in comfort. The couple were out walking shortly after dawn each day dressed in Arab clothes and carrying their guns. The mountains supported a varied wild-life, bears, gazelles, wolves, wild boar and a small leopard (*nimr*) but Richard's attitude towards killing had never changed; 'he only wanted to kill a beast that would kill us if we did not kill it . . . the smaller game partridges, quails, woodcock, hares and wild duck we never shot unless we were hungry, and we would not have the gazelles hunted.'[9]

During the hotter part of the day they worked indoors or entertained the numerous visitors such as the sheiks of the local villages: Bludan, Ma'arabun, Madaya and Sarghayam. English tourists and residents of Beirut or Damascus sometimes called to see them, and Isabel had her 'pianette' to provide entertainment.[10] Here, too, she was the local doctor, and spent most late afternoons running a clinic. Her book of remedies, medicines and treatments survives; it is a fascinating mixture of her own knowledge, press cuttings on various illnesses, and the written opinions and prescribed remedies of top London doctors to whom she wrote for advice.[11]

From their 'eagle's nest', as their friends called it, Richard rode into Damascus once a week to deal with Consular matters. On 7 July they received news of the death of Lord Clarendon. Richard decided to return to the Consulate to send condolences and catch up with his mail. Isabel rode half-way with him, down the mountains until he reached the plains, then she returned to Bludan alone.[12] She disliked being left behind, but accepted that it was sometimes unavoidable and kept busy to assuage her disappointment.

While Richard was in Damascus on this occasion he met two Englishmen who were working with the Palestine Exploration Fund.

'On a red hot morning in July 1870,' said Richard, 'I rode from Damascus to Bludan and said to my wife, "I have fallen in with two such nice fellows . . . Drake and Palmer, who have been doing Sinai and Tih."'[13] He had been at their house in Salahiyeh when the two men appeared in the garden, 'sunburnt, "hard as nails" [and] in the finest travelling condition'. The 24-year-old Charles Tyrwhitt Drake, a giant of a man, would become like a younger brother to Richard and Isabel; Professor E.H. Palmer, then aged 30, would become a Professor in Arabic at Cambridge, and would figure largely in Richard's life at a much later date. Richard invited them to Bludan and they followed him there a few days later, camping out in the Burtons' garden.

Richard and Isabel were about to depart on a month-long expedition and agreed to invite their two visitors to join them. After a few days' rest Drake and Palmer were ready, and the foursome set off 'at the head of a small caravan of horses, servants, tents and light baggage'.[14] The first week was spent at Baalbak, whose ruins Isabel found smaller but as beautiful as those of Palmyra. Palmyra was more romantic, picturesque and startling, she said, but, 'Baalbak can be seen without danger, Palmyra can not.'[15] One night Isabel and Professor Palmer illuminated the ruins with magnesium flares. 'The effect was very beautiful . . . a gigantic transformation scene in a desert plain.' Her accounts of this (which included a plea for help in preserving the remains) and other journeys were published in the English newspapers and, as her confidence grew, she began to introduce comments on the local political situation. These were not always her own views. Richard found Isabel's unexpected success in getting her work published under the guise of 'Our Correspondent in Damascus' an ideal forum for voicing opinions he could not otherwise put forward in his official capacity.[16]

After Baalbak the quartet 'rode up the fertile and malarious Coelesyrian plain as far as El Ká'a', from where the town of Homs could be seen shimmering in the hot pellucid air, and then 'we galloped across the valley . . . camping in a Maronite stronghold at Ayn Urghush.' From there they rode to the Cedars of Lebanon where they camped among 'banks and wreaths of snow, even in July'. Here the friends had to part; Drake and Palmer riding off to Beirut, where they were to sail for home. 'I cannot say,' Richard wrote, 'which of the four [of us] felt the parting most.'

Richard and Isabel made a long, slow journey homewards doing what they both liked best: 'gypsying'; camping in the mountains, stopping here and there to visit anyone of interest such as the Patriarch of the Maronites, 'who is a sort of Prince, or Pope, in the Lebanon', Isabel wrote to her family.[17] A few days later at Zahleh they called on a Miss Wilson who ran a missionary school; too late they discovered that many of the girls were ill with Syrian fever. Richard contracted it overnight and in nursing him Isabel caught it. They were both in bed for a week. Isabel was eventually carried back to Bludan in a litter, so still and pale that the villagers thought she was dead and set up loud lamentations for her.[18]

While nursing Richard, Isabel was assisted by a beautiful 17-year-old girl called Khamour (the Moon). Miss Wilson suggested that Khamour would make a good addition to Isabel's household, and the girl returned with them. It was just as well. In early October the weather began to turn cold in the mountains; Isabel was packing to return to Damascus when her English maid was badly injured; she was at the top of the stairs at the side of the house when a strong wind caught under her crinoline and threw her from top to bottom. During the woman's convalescence, Khamour was hardly an ideal replacement. She was 'a thorough child of nature' and just at that time, Isabel said 'when a girl needs careful guiding'.[19] With her long black hair, 'round baby face, large eyes, long lashes, small nose and pouting lips [and] white teeth', she was remarkably pretty, said Isabel, by turns amused and exasperated by the girl whose entire *raison d'être* seemed to be the captivation of men. Her temperament was 'all sunshine or thunder and lightning in ten minutes', and despite her missionary schooling she had a stock of 'fearful oaths' to rival Richard's. One day she came to Isabel and complained that the chief dragoman at the Consulate, Mr Hannah Misk (a married man of considerable importance in Damascus) had importuned her. 'O Lady,' she told Isabel in distress, 'all the men want my lip and my breast.' Isabel told her that if it happened again she was to slap Misk's face and scream, '. . . and I will come and ask him what he takes my house to be.'[20]

It had been intended that Isabel should return home in August to visit her mother, but Richard pressed her to stay on for another few months in the hope that he might be able to get sick leave, enabling them to return together.[21] The Mott affair refused to die, carefully kept alive by Elliot's despatches to Lord Granville who took over the Foreign Office on Clarendon's death. In one communication he reported his discussions with Rashid Pasha, as a result of which Richard was asked to explain why he had over-reacted to what both his Ambassador and Consul-General regarded as 'an insignificant affair' which had been fully resolved by Mott's letter of apology. From Damascus on 4 October, Richard replied tersely:

> . . . I am not aware that any letter of apology had been addressed by Mr Mentor Mott to the acting Governor . . . or that it had been accepted as satisfactory . . . Nor do I believe that anything of the kind took place. Moreover . . . Rashid Pasha was far distant from Damascus at the time, and I am better acquainted with the state of the capital than he could be. The [acting] Governor of Damascus at once closed three Protestant schools, one of 13 or 14 years standing and was persuaded to reopen them only by the influence of this Consulate . . .[22]

It is fair to state that leading Christians in Damascus, including Jane Digby and William Wright, were deeply fearful in the weeks that followed. There were frequent incidents in which Christians were spat at and generally abused, a pattern frighteningly similar to that which preceded the 1860 riots and massacre which both had experienced. Rumours of growing malevolence among fanatics in the city even reached the desert and Medjuel galloped in to protect Jane,[23] indicating a momentum far exceeding Henry Elliot's appreciation of the matter.

Late on the evening of 26 August, two letters were delivered to Richard in Bludan by messenger. One was from the secretary left in charge of the Consulate; one was from William Wright. Both advised him of the unrest in Damascus; a situation not helped by the fact that, following the example of the Russian Consul, all the European Consuls had left the city.[24] Wright said that the following day, the 27th, was the day rumoured to be 'slaughter day'.

Richard was ready to leave in ten minutes and refused to take Isabel, telling her she must remain to defend Bludan with half their attendants. He insisted they said their personal goodbyes indoors. Afterwards, she rode with him down to the plains as usual, and when they parted it was as he instructed; 'we shall shake hands like two brothers . . . tears or any display of affection will tell the secret to our men.'[25] She had accepted soon after her arrival that any public demonstration of affection, such as taking the arm of one's husband when walking, was unacceptable in Syria; 'the woman does not raise herself but lowers her husband.'[26]

In the 1860 massacre it was the passive stance of the Turkish troops that allowed, indeed encouraged, initial skirmishes to escalate into riots which concluded with the burning and sacking of the Christian quarter. Arriving at 6 a.m., Richard went directly to the *Serai* and insisted that Holo Pasha order the Turkish forces on full alert. He reminded the Acting Governor that after the 1860 riots the Governor was hanged for negligence of his duty. 'It will cost you Syria, and if you do not take these measures at once I shall telegraph Constantinople,' he warned. By 10 a.m. guards were posted on every street and all-night patrols were activated. Jews and Christians were confined to their homes. For three days Richard and Holo Pasha regularly did the rounds of the city. By the end of that time the message had gone home that any attempt at rioting would be quelled by force, and Damascus had become quiet again. William Wright and Jane Digby wrote independently that, had Richard's recommendations not been carried out, there would almost certainly have been a repeat atrocity.[27]

Isabel, growing up on legends of her heroic ancestress Blanche Arundell, was somewhat disappointed not to be called upon to prove herself at Bludan. She had hoisted the Union Jack over her house, armed all her men and placed them strategically. She locked up Khamour (who was hysterical), and sent word to local Christians that they would find refuge in her house. Then she positioned herself on the roof armed with Richard's elephant guns, her own pistols and some soft drink bottles filled with gunpowder and fuses ready to hurl on any aggressors.

When the danger was over she sent a clear (if somewhat less than diplomatic) account of the affair and its antecedents to the *Levant Herald* as their 'Correspondent in Damascus'. Mott was not mentioned by name, but Augusta Mott bridled on her husband's behalf and wrote complaining to Henry Elliot (now Sir Henry) that Richard had written the piece to belittle her husband. Asked to comment, Richard replied: 'I have done my duty in reporting the danger of this gentleman's visits . . . in times of excitement; after this I can no longer hold myself responsible for what may occur in case his visits are repeated.' He stated that he had been shown a copy of a letter sent by Mrs Mott to the Ambassador:

> . . . the letter contains the following words: 'Captain Burton has thought to publish a most injudicious and insulting article in the *Levant Herald* which our Consul-General advises should be submitted to you.' Mr Eldridge has distinctly denied that he advised anything of the sort. I published nothing of the kind. Mrs Augusta M. Mott alludes to an anonymous news letter . . . attributed by her to me . . . What I publish in the *Levant Herald* is signed with my own name, and that paper has other correspondents in Beyrout and Damascus besides myself.[28]

But Eldridge continued to support the Motts, and he in turn was supported by the Ambassador. In a chain of letters and reports, in which he refuted any connection between Mott's proselytising and the subsequent unrest in Damascus, Elliot continuously voiced his concerns about Richard. 'The quarrel between him and Mr Mott is of such trifling importance that Eldridge is right in saying it need not have been reported at all. But what makes me anxious is Burton . . . trying to be in favour with the more intolerant section of Damascus – and this may . . . lead to serious trouble . . .'[29] On another occasion he commented, 'Damascus ought, I think, to be under the direct management of the Consul General at Beyrout with a Vice, instead of a full Consul . . .'[30]

As if this was not enough, several highly respected London Jews made serious formal complaints against Richard directly to the Foreign Secretary. Sir Moses Montefiore wrote to Granville enclosing letters from the Jews in Damascus: 'Your Lordship will perceive that the Jews complain that the attitude affected towards them by Captain Burton, is such as to occasion them much injury and considerable anxiety.' Sir Francis Goldsmid also wrote: 'I hear from another quarter that the lady whom Captain Burton has married is believed to be a bigoted Roman Catholic, and to be likely to influence him against the Jews.'[31]

As well as sending Richard copies of all these letters for comment, Granville asked Mr C.M. Kennedy, a Foreign Office official, who was about to depart for Syria on an unrelated mission, to investigate the matter thoroughly. Shortly after Kennedy's arrival in Beirut, where the Burtons and the Motts were present at a reception for him, Augusta Mott called on William Wright in Damascus. She told him that in the presence of a large gathering, Kennedy had read out his instructions from the Foreign Office which, she alleged, were 'to force an apology out of Burton or compel him to resign'. Wright had previously found Mrs Mott untruthful, and said cautiously that he had heard Kennedy's mission was a commercial one involving the three Syrian ports, but she insisted that 'he has been sent out expressly with reference to the British Syrian School.' She also said that when Isabel denied to Mr Kennedy Richard's authorship of the *Levant Herald* articles, she had challenged her with the words, 'Do not tell a falsehood, Mrs Burton. Captain Burton told me himself he wrote the letters, and you added, "and I put in the spice".' Whereupon, Augusta Mott told Wright, Isabel had kissed her by way of apology.[32]

Mrs Mott repeated this to members of the Damascus mission, and also to Jane Digby. Wright took up the matter with Kennedy in Damascus some weeks later, and was therefore as astonished as his colleagues to hear from Kennedy that when he questioned Mrs Mott as he returned through Beirut, she had denied all knowledge of the story. In a letter to her, Wright asked for an explanation: 'Will you enable me to say whether or not . . . you made these statements . . . and I shall place these questions and answers before the several members of our colony who heard the words.'[33] Caught out in a blatant lie, Augusta Mott replied with all the guile of a modern politician in a television interview: 'I am at a loss to understand the drift of your letter. I have fully replied to Mrs Burton on this subject. "In a multitude of words there wanteth not sin." I believe you will agree with me that the Christian missionaries have something better to do than stir up strife.'[34]

Wright now dispensed with diplomacy. 'Those stories which you told . . . with such zest, were entirely of your own invention,' he accused. 'I am no advocate of Captain Burton for he needs not my advocacy . . . but he has never . . . said or done . . . anything disrespectful to Christianity.' She had accused the Burtons of lying, he continued, and yet in this and other instances it was clearly she who was guilty of 'malignant untruths . . . I fear your sense of right and wrong is too indistinct to enable you to profit by any advice of mine [but] . . . it is curious that every one at Damascus speaks well of

Captain Burton, while those at Beyrout speak evilly of him behind his back.'[35] The leading missionaries who had once been so afraid of Richard's appointment were now afraid of losing him, and rallied round. Several wrote to apologise for Augusta Mott's mischief-making lies:

> It distresses me to have to expose the self-contradiction and pre-varications of one who claims to be considered a Christian lady [one wrote] but I feel I will ill-deserve the position of missionary in Damascus, and forfeit all right to the name of gentleman if I remain silent. Had Mrs Mott's words been mere idle gossip, or . . . unfriendly criticisms of character, I should never have referred to them. Such things one expects . . . but I have been in Syria long enough to know that an attack on the Consul's character concerns us all . . . I feel it doubly incumbent . . . to defend the good name of a Consul who has . . . brought to his office the two essential . . . qualities of integrity and energy. Use this letter in any way you think fit.[36]

But Wright's accusations did not stop Augusta Mott from pursuing her vendetta against the Burtons, for she was confident of Eldridge's support. Finding an old letter from Richard to her husband, she realised that if she changed a few words it could be made to read in an entirely different light. She had no hesitation in making the alter-ation and sending it to the Missionary Society in England, as evidence of Captain Burton's anti-missionary attitude.

When Richard sent his lucid denial of all the charges against him to Lord Granville, including copies of all the letters of support that he had received, his first thought was for the attack on his wife. 'The uncalled for assertions touching "the bigoted Roman Catholic" . . . insinuations which should, I venture to remark, never have been pro-duced in official correspondence . . . I shall leave to be dealt with by the person whom it most concerns. I will merely remark that my offi-cial proceedings are not influenced by domestic interference.'[37] Isabel wrote, 'I have always understood that it is a rule amongst gentlemen never to drag a lady's name into public affairs, but I accept with plea-sure the compliment Sir Moses Montefiore pays me in treating me like a man as it enables me the privilege of writing to you . . . I have [no] . . . prejudice . . . except against hypocrisy.' She was surprised, she

said, that Sir Moses and Sir Charles were prepared to protect a usurer
simply because he was a Jew; 'if three Catholics were to do one half
of what the Jews [here] have done, I would not rest until I had
brought them to justice.'[38]

Isabel also followed Augusta Mott's example and wrote her complaints to the Ambassador. She used the public mail, explaining
pointedly that she did not trust the Consular post in Beirut. Elliot
replied in a kindly tone many weeks later, explaining (with doubtful
veracity) that her letter had only just reached him:

> I quite agree with you in thinking that more has been made of the
> Mott incident than there was occasion for, and it may be allowed to
> drop if possible. He has always been represented to me as a well-
> intentioned man but like many other well-intentioned persons, he
> may possibly be more zealous than discreet, and I will have a note
> conveyed to him to be more cautious to avoid giving offence espe-
> cially in such a ticklish place as Damascus. The recent excitement in
> which Damascus seems to have been for a short time was attributed
> here entirely to the proceedings of the Russian Consul who evi-
> dently did his best to spread alarm of an impending menace. The
> Russian Ambassador fully recognises the extravagance of his con-
> duct and caused him to be removed . . .
>
> With reference to the articles in the *Levant Herald* to which you
> allude I can assure you that I never assumed that Captain Burton
> would write anonymously to newspapers upon what passes in his
> Consular district, but a very general impression prevails here and –
> I am told – in Athens that the letters were written by someone con-
> nected with the Consulate; and I will also add that once or twice I
> was myself so much startled by the similarity of the letters to some
> of Captain Burton's Dispatches that I was on the point of writing to
> him privately to put him on his guard, and to ask if he was quite
> sure that there was no one who had access to his correspon-
> dence . . . I certainly am not blind or indifferent to the good that is
> done by wholesome newspaper criticism but I should be very sorry
> to see the position of any of HBM Consuls lowered, as it would be
> if it were known to carry our sanction of a correspondence, with the
> papers on the public affairs of his Consulate.
>
> I shall always be glad to hear from you privately, or Captain
> Burton but I am afraid I cannot so far break through the system of

correspondence as to keep the Consul-General in the dark on matters connected with his district. I hope that . . . at any time you may
take this route we may have an opportunity of making your
acquaintance.[39]

Reading this, it is hardly surprising that the Burtons never suspected
that their most dangerous enemy in Damascus was not Eldridge or
Mrs Mott, but their Ambassador. Within days of writing the above
letter to Isabel, Elliot wrote nastily to London:

> You know that I have been anxious about Damascus ever since
> Burton's unfortunate nomination there. I inclose extracts of a
> couple of letters from Eldridge from which you will see that I have
> not much encouragement in taking a more satisfactory view than I
> did at first. Burton wrote to me that he wanted leave of absence in
> order to undergo a surgical operation. I thought he had long ago
> undergone the only operation necessary to complete his qualifica-
> tion as Mohammedan or Arab . . .[40]

Problems seemed to follow them everywhere. Invited to attend the
wedding of the *Wali*'s daughter among the women – the men had separate receptions – Isabel went with Jane Digby and the wife of the
Italian Consul. At the request of their hostess all three women wore
European ball gowns, with hooped skirts, tiny nipped-in waists and
off-the-shoulder sleeves (Isabel's was blue trimmed with tulle, and tiny
pink rosebuds). The women of the *harem* were entranced but deliciously shocked by their naked shoulders. 'Are you not cold being
thus uncovered?' they asked, and, 'Is it true that strange men dance
with you one after the other, and put their arms about your waist? Do
you not feel dreadfully ashamed?' By popular request Isabel entertained the women's gathering, speaking in French, with an account of
an English ball; she chose her coming-out ball at Almack's, which
brought back old memories for Jane Digby. But it was Isabel's turn to
be fascinated when she learned that it was not until after the end of
the marriage ceremony (which followed the receptions) that the
bridegroom was allowed to lift the veil of the woman and see his
bride. 'This was the first time they had really seen one another,' she
wrote. 'What an anxious moment for a Moslem woman!'[41]

During the reception the wife of one of the Jews who had

complained about Richard cornered Isabel, and tried to persuade her to change Richard's mind. Isabel tried to brush her off, 'Pray do not let us discuss this now,' she said. But the woman protested that it was the sole reason for her attending the wedding. The same woman called at Salahiyeh a few days later and Isabel sent down the message that she was 'not at home'; the accepted euphemism for avoiding inconvenient callers. Subsequently Jane Digby, who had been at Isabel's side throughout the reception, heard the preposterous rumour that Isabel had not only refused to speak to the woman there, but had torn her diamond headdress from her hair and stamped on it. This story was repeated to Isabel and Richard over Christmas lunch with the Eldridges, with Kennedy present. 'What a pleasant person I must be to invite to a party,' Isabel responded.

There were other rumours: that Burton had tortured a seven-year-old Jewish boy to obtain a confession to painting crosses on the walls of the mosque to incite riots; that Isabel had drawn her revolver and shot and killed one Arab beggar, and injured another, at her gate because they did not rise to salute her. These reports, easily spread in the tight, disparate communities which thrived on intrigue and hearsay, both reached Eldridge and, through him, Ambassador Elliot. However Elliot repeated only one item of gossip in his monthly dispatch to London: that Isabel had struck a Moslem boy in the face with her whip. This was true, but he neglected to explain that the youth had spat at her and tried to pull her from her horse in a mêlée. Nor that the *Wali* subsequently sent armed *kavasses* to take the culprit and sack his village, which was only saved by Isabel's intervention. When the boy emerged from prison he apologised to her, and became one of her most trusted servants.[42]

Garbled versions of these malicious stories, and others, were widely circulated in Damascus. Jane Digby became so anxious for her friends that she sent a warning letter to Salahiyeh. On the previous day, she wrote, while visiting a house in the city she had overheard some fellow guests, Jewish moneylenders, boasting that they had arranged for Burton to be recalled, and for the reinstatement of Richard Rogers as Consul because he was open to bribery. 'You know,' Jane wrote urgently in her distinctive bold handwriting, 'that Sheikh Mohammed ebn Dhuki and Faris el Meziad openly say in the desert to those who ask them that they owed having won the camel law suit I had with them, to the considerable sum they gave *Mr Rogers*, after he told me that I had won it. And this affair – as you know – involved the loss of my British Protection which is such a serious misfortune . . .'[43]

Jane and Medjuel had good reason to be grateful to Richard, despite his solo journey to Palmyra in the previous year. The Mezrab tribe had been badly affected by damaging losses through raids, and Richard tried hard to negotiate compensation for them. On one occasion, while on a hunting trip in the desert with William Wright, Richard and Isabel visited the tents of the dreaded and feared Sheikh Mohammed ebn Dhuki of the Wuld Ali tribe to negotiate for the Mezrabs. 'Dhuki . . . is a curious mixture of savagery and civilisation,' Isabel commented, '[but] he has progressed far enough to become a Freemason.'[44] One by one their timid attendants dropped back; even Richard's faithful Afghan pretended his horse had cast a shoe and stopped to replace it. By the time they came within sight of the encampment the couple were completely alone.

Richard warned Isabel what would happen next. A company of Bedouins would gallop wildly towards them, screaming war-cries and with lances couched. She must stand perfectly still and not allow her horse to move, but face the charge as if a statue. If she did this they would not be harmed, but if she ran they would both be killed. Just as he predicted the frightening charge swept down on them, wheeling away within a few feet. It is a tribute to Isabel's blind trust in her husband, her own courage and also her horsemanship, that she was able to curb her urge to bolt. 'I was glad he put me up to it,' she wrote simply. Some of the Bedouins dismounted, came towards them grinning and – calling a welcome to 'Aak-hu Sebbah' (Brother of the Lion) – held on to their stirrups and kissed their hands.[45]

They were officially welcomed at the tents by ebn Dhuki's deputy, Sheikh Salih, who told Richard that the chief was away on a raid. Richard doubted this, believing him more likely to be hiding somewhere, having suspected their mission regarding the Mezrabis. He left an invitation for Dhuki to attend a *divan* in Damascus to discuss the matter and when the couple left, Sheikh Salih and a group of his Bedouins offered to escort them to their camp as a courtesy. As he and Isabel mounted, Richard said quietly to her, 'Let's show these fellows the English can ride; they think that nobody but themselves can ride and that nothing can beat their mares.' Isabel wrote that she looked doubtfully at the lean flanks of the fabled thoroughbred desert horses as he spoke. But though their own half-breeds were not as fast, she knew they were at least in first-rate condition, 'full of corn, and mad with spirits. So I gave my usual answer, "All right! Wherever you lead I'll follow."'

As soon as the 'Yallah' was uttered for starting, we simply laid our reins on our horses' necks and neither used whip nor spur, nor spoke to them – they went as though we had long odds on our ride. We reached our camp in one hour and a half. Salih and his men came up . . . later . . . their mares were broken down, and the men . . . scarlet and perspiring. 'Ya Sitti!' [Oh Lady!] said Salih . . . 'el Shaitan [Satan] himself could not follow you.' 'I am so sorry,' I replied, 'but our Kaddishes would go . . . we wanted to ride with you.' This was all [due] to food and condition, for there is no question of the advantage of 'blood' that their mares had over our horses.[46]

Because Richard had called at his tents, ebn Dhuki was obliged to return the visit, and the requested council-of-war was duly arranged on 4 February 1871. It took place at Jane's villa because Medjuel had been seriously ill and was still too unwell to travel.

The two chiefs were present with several followers. There had been a fight, and El Dhuki had robbed the Mezrabs of camels, horses and everything. Captain Burton wanted, if possible, to obtain a part restoration but El Dhuki was too slippery, and though everything was promised nothing was done. One point of honour, however, he religiously kept: when the time came to eat bread and salt together, he sprang into his saddle and rode away. By that we knew he did not mean friendship with the Mezrabs . . .[47]

Isabel was now in her second year at Damascus and felt very much at home there. Even during Richard's absences her diary was filled with invitations. Perhaps the strangest compliment paid her was an invitation to act as a sponsor for a boy about to undergo the ceremony to mark his passage from childhood to manhood. Circumcision ceremonies were 'quite public'; as common as weddings and funerals, nevertheless the first one she attended with Richard startled Isabel. 'Singing, dancing and feasting went on for about three days . . . there was a loud clang of music and firing of guns to drown the boy's cries, and with one stroke of a circular knife the operation was finished in a second. The part cut off was then handed round on a silver salver . . . to attest that the rite had been performed. I felt quite sick . . . English modesty overpowered curiosity, and I could not look.'[48] She had attended many similar ceremonies since, but even so found it 'curious' to be invited to be the boy's sponsor, as one might be invited to be a godparent at a christening in England. Knowing it involved holding the boy in her arms while the cut was made, she was inclined to refuse but instead recognised the immense compliment, unusually paid to a woman let alone a Christian.

Another tribute to Isabel was an unusual gift from Holo Pasha for her menagerie. Since it had no intrinsic value and was offered in recognition of Richard's part in preventing the threatened riot, she felt able to accept it; it was a panther cub which had been trapped in the desert. She treated him like a domestic cat, keeping him well fed so that he would not attack the other animals. Her Persian cat was frightened of him, but he was frightened of the bull terriers, Fuss and Fidget. 'He had bold bad eyes that seemed to say "be afraid of me",' Isabel wrote (she could have written the same thing of Richard); 'he used to sleep by our bedside . . . and hunt me round the garden, playing hide and seek . . . When he bit too hard I used to box his ears.' Richard and Isabel loved the animal, but when he grew to his full height and strength the neighbours became concerned and eventually someone fed him with poisoned meat.

> He withered away and nothing we could do did him any good, and one day when I went to look for him round the stables, he put his paw up to me. I sat down on the ground, and took him in my arms like a child. He put his head on my shoulder, and his paws around my waist, and he died in half an hour. Richard and I were terribly grieved.[49]

Her sole regret in her marriage, she confided to Jane Digby at this time, was her lack of children. She said that she and Richard had both hoped for a family, but had long ago resigned themselves to the fact that there would be none. The women in the *harems* visited by Isabel saw this as a great tragedy after ten years of marriage and not only pitied her but gave her advice on how to conceive.[50] They asked if Isabel did not fear her husband would 'put thee away and take a second wife', and she replied with a confident smile that her husband would not divorce her. 'I feel quite secure of my place. The *Sidi Beg* may marry after my death but not before.' But if the Moslem women were fascinated by her attitude to childlessness, she was equally intrigued by their capacity to cope with sharing a husband; something she felt she could never tolerate.

In March Richard returned from a 17-day archaeological trip to northern Syria and the Ansari Mountains, taking in Homs and Hamah. As often happened on his solo trips he returned ill, and this time he was affected by frostbite in his fingers and toes. Isabel, who seems to have known how to deal with all eventualities, calmly set about nursing him, keeping the affected places 'saturated with arnica' for several days. Richard was not the only invalid in the house and his homecoming provided him with a pleasant surprise. On a cold damp evening a few nights earlier, Isabel had been surprised and delighted at the unexpected appearance at her door of 'Charley' Tyrwhitt Drake. This young man, whom the Burtons both loved and regarded as 'a member of the family', was ill with bronchitis when he arrived, a condition serious to Drake who was a chronic asthmatic. Isabel nursed them both, and the men convalesced by working at transcriptions, for Richard had brought back with him 'in the absence of squeeze paper . . . a native copy of [the inscriptions on] the Hamath Stones'.[51] Drake subsequently wrote a tract on the stones, stating that the inscription might provide 'the opening page of a new chapter in history'.[52]

For the next few months the trio were inseparable:

> We all three visited almost every known part of Syria [Richard wrote], either for the first time or over again, taking observations, making sketches and skeleton maps, and writing diaries and accounts of our journeys. We divided the work each taking what was best suited. My wife had charge of the camp generally . . . especially the horses and the sick or wounded, and visited harems to note things hidden from mankind.[53] Drake copied inscriptions, mapped the country . . . collected geological specimens . . . the time was passed most joyfully. Our companion was one of the few who can make a pleasant third in a ménage . . . a true friend to us both in an honest way, and that is high praise.[54]

One of Drake's greatest assets was an ability to perform 'magic' tricks with which he delighted poor villagers. He also sketched and painted; Isabel later used some of his work to illustrate her books.[55]

In the early spring of 1871 two English visitors arrived in Damascus for a short stay: Lord Stafford and Mr 'Barty' Mitford. Mitford, who regarded Burton as 'one of the most notable men of my time', was working in the Slave Trade Department at the Foreign Office when Richard was made Consul at Fernando Po and, through correspondence, the two men became friends.[56] Richard and Isabel spent several days showing them round the city and introducing them to notables such as Jane Digby and Abd el-Khader. Mitford recalled Burton in Damascus as 'if not a great man . . . at any rate a remarkable one. His personality was striking; as he strode through the streets with his crisp staccato walk no one could help noticing him'

> . . . his frame was that of a Titan. His broad shoulders and highly developed chest indicated strength above the common . . . he was the only man I ever knew who could fire the old-fashioned elephant gun from the shoulder without a rest. His powers of endurance were simply marvellous and he could drink brandy with a heroism that would have satisfied Dr Johnson. [He] would have been handsome but for the lower jaw, which was too strong for beauty, and indeed almost tigerish, with a ferocious expression belying his really kind nature.[57]

However, 'as an official,' Mitford said, 'Burton was a failure . . . He was impatient of control, had no idea of discipline, and as for all conventionalities he simply scattered them to the winds . . . at Damascus he was continually in hot water.' Yet Mitford could not find it in his heart to blame his old friend for this; rather he blamed Isabel. 'His wife was not the woman to make diplomatic relations easier. Her manner with the Mohammedans among whom she lived, and whom it was her business to conciliate so far as in her lay, was detestable. On one occasion I was with her and one or two others in a very sacred mosque; a pious Moslem was prostrate before the tomb of a holy saint. She did not actually strike him with her riding-whip, but she made as though she were going to do so, and insisted on the poor man making way for her to go up to the tomb . . . I left the mosque in disgust.'[58]

Mitford, or Lord Redesdale as he was when he wrote this passage many years later, had no reason to fabricate this incident. Yet it is difficult to equate his reminiscence with more sympathetic descriptions of Isabel in Damascus, written contemporaneously by Jane Digby, William Wright and Charles Tyrwhitt Drake, all of whom knew her intimately. Isabel made it clear that she adopted her husband's 'firmness of manner' with nationals, some of whom were abusive to an unveiled woman. Apart from the time when she beat the youth who attempted to pull her from her horse, we know of several other occasions when Isabel attacked men with her riding-whip. However, on each occasion this was to defend animals being treated cruelly. When her *kavasses* rudely pushed people out of her path it caused her anguish, not satisfaction, so it is difficult to explain this alleged behaviour in the mosque. It is even more inexplicable in consideration of the fact that throughout her time in Damascus, Isabel was a frequent and welcome visitor in the houses of many devout and leading Moslems who would have had greater cause than Mitford to take exception to behaviour such as that he described.

Mitford went on to declare that in his opinion Isabel was responsible 'for all the trouble which led to Burton's removal a few months later from the romance of the Damascus he loved'. This statement, I believe, owes more to a book written by Richard's niece, Georgiana Stisted, than to Mitford's personal experience. Georgiana would say in December 1896, eight months after Isabel's death, in an error-strewn hagiography of Burton that, 'thanks to his wife's imprudence and passion for proselytising all further promotion was hopeless . . . his career was blighted.'[59] A wealth of documents and correspondence, only a few of which can be extracted here, proves this allegation to be totally incorrect. The legend that Isabel was in some manner responsible for his recall was also fed by a contribution to a missionary paper five days after Richard's death in 1890. A letter initiated by Augusta Mott claimed that Burton's recall was due to the fact that his wife had shot two men because they refused to salute her.[60]

Previous Burton biographers appear to have taken Mitford's statements at face value, and some have adopted his assessment of Isabel. It is fair to say that the wealth of new material in her surviving papers was not then available, but in querying the accuracy of Mitford's recollections one does not have to look far to find flaws in his memory. The introduction of Burton in his memoirs, alone, reveals his fallibility:

> In 1861 a fight . . . was raging around Du Chaillu's recently published book . . . upon the question whether the gorilla was a reality or only a fabulous animal . . . Burton always eager for a fray, whether with pen or sword, was on fire to go and ascertain the truth. He was however a Captain in the Indian Army, and so long as he remained a soldier the thing was impossible; so he contrived to be appointed Consul at Fernando Po, severing his connection with the India Office, who never forgave him . . .[61]

Here, too, the reminiscence is built around a grain of truth. Richard was certainly interested in the gorilla, and purposely met du Chaillu to discuss his findings – but only *after* his appointment to West Africa. He neither actively sought to go there nor 'contrived' at his severance from the Indian Army. Richard's pained correspondence at the time, some quoted in earlier chapters, is evidence that Redesdale's entertaining recollections were at odds with reality. It suggests that he did not keep a detailed journal but relied on a doubtful memory at a distance of 40 years and more.

Probably his recollection of Isabel at Damascus was coloured by a vague remembrance of rumours about both Burtons which were widely spread in Syria at the time of his visit there. William Wright recognised this possibility long before Mitford wrote his memoirs: 'Many influential travellers pass yearly through Syria, deeply interested in the educational and religious efforts being made to elevate that land.' Everywhere these visitors went, Wright stated, they heard malicious rumours about Richard and Isabel, especially in Beirut, 'and the constant drip made a deep impression.'[62]

Like that of many others, Mitford's main memory of Burton was his predilection for entertaining with exaggerated anecdotes invented to shock a gullible audience. For the sake of a good yarn, Mitford said, 'he would not hesitate to assault the virtue of the pure maiden who dwells in the well.' He told how, illustrated with fiendish expressions and gestures, Richard once described to him an occasion when he had cut an Arab almost in two; '. . . "Unfortunately I did not cut through the last bit of skin, so the horse galloped off with half the man's body hanging over the saddle." . . . Burton had done more than almost any man living,' Mitford said, 'that, however, was not enough for him. He was compelled to invent more. But his little inventions were almost childlike in their transparent simplicity.'[63]

As soon as Stafford and Mitford left, the Burtons and Drake departed on a long and eventful journey. Isabel had long yearned to visit the early sites of Christianity, and Richard had acquired nine weeks of sick leave. As a treat for her, he suggested they spend Holy Week in Jerusalem so that she could provide 'a good Catholic's account' of it, and return via many of the other places mentioned in the Bible.[64] It was agreed that Richard should ride to Jerusalem with the horses, entourage and equipment, and Isabel and Drake would take the diligence to Beirut, sail from there to Jaffa, and then take public transport for the short distance from there to Jerusalem. The Burtons pretended that this arrangement was for Isabel's sake but, given the far more difficult journeys she habitually made with the greatest enjoyment, it was more likely to have been a way of ensuring Drake did not relapse.

Isabel immersed herself in religious observances and visiting locations associated with Christ's ministry, while Richard and Charles Drake explored the area as archaeologists. From Jerusalem they went on to Bethlehem and Nazareth, stopping en route to bathe in the Dead Sea and explore Jericho and the sites of Sodom and Gomorrah. Richard thought that it would not have needed an act of God to set the cities on fire for the land was covered with lumps of pure sulphur; he suspected an unusual atmospheric influence might have produced spontaneous combustion.[65] They had intended to visit the ancient village of Libnah, but it was there that Isabel, wearing the clothes of a man, enraged the villagers by forgetfully entering a *harem*. Though Richard and Drake found the incident amusing, they decided to leave the area for diplomacy's sake.

Isabel arrived at Nazareth alone, some hours behind the men. She had travelled separately that day, as she was suffering from fever and wished to go at her own pace. She found that Richard and Drake had erected the camp on a hillside outside the town and gone off exploring. Four groups of English, American and German travellers, whom they had met elsewhere on the road from Jerusalem, were camped nearby on the other side of a small rise on the hillside. Shortly after Isabel arrived, some Copt pilgrims came round the tents begging and she gave them a handful of small silver, 'as did also my fellow travellers'. Still feeling unwell Isabel retired early, while the two men dined and sat talking. Richard moved his bedding roll to Drake's tent to avoid disturbing her. She woke at sunrise and shortly afterwards heard a commotion:

> . . . a Copt wanted to enter my tent, either for curiosity or stealing, or perhaps for the more innocent purpose of asking for bakshísh. At all events to intrude upon *harím* in the East is an outrage. I was still in bed half awake, and I heard the servants tell him to go. He refused and was very insolent; he took up stones and threw them and struck the men. No one knows what a weapon the stone is in Syrian hands; it is their natural defence . . . I got up and watched the proceedings through the top of my tent wall. I called to the servants to leave him alone but by this time they were angry and began to beat the Copt.[66]

Some 150 parishioners leaving a nearby Greek Orthodox church became involved, siding with the Copt who took the first opportunity to escape. The scrap escalated and some of the Greeks began to hurl stones. By now Richard and Drake had emerged to investigate the disturbance. Richard tried to restore calm but his words were received, Isabel recalled, with 'a hailstorm of stones. A rich and respectable Greek called out, "Kill them all. I will pay the blood money!"' One of the servants cried that this was the English Consul. The remark only inflamed matters, for the church was built on the site of a synagogue bought from Rashid Pasha; the British Jews claimed that it had been stolen from them, and Richard had been suing the Greeks for compensation.

Isabel threw on her desert clothes, anxiously watching over the tent flap as she dressed. 'As an old soldier, accustomed to fire he [Richard] stood perfectly calm, collected and self-contained though the stones hit him right and left,' she said. He was unarmed; all his things were in their tent. She picked up his two revolvers and ran out to give them to him, but he saw her from the corner of his eye and waved her away. 'I understood that I should embarrass his movements; so I kept near enough to carry him off if he were badly wounded, and put the revolvers in my belt,' she said resolutely, 'meaning to have twelve lives for his one if he were killed.'[67]

Three of their servants were badly injured, a fourth was knocked unconscious, and when the attackers began jumping on him Richard drew a pistol from another man's belt and fired a warning shot into the air. Isabel leapt up and ran to summon the other European travellers from across the hill. When the Greeks saw ten armed men running over the rise, they fled. 'The whole thing did not last ten minutes,' Isabel said.

Richard reported the incident to the local Turkish official, demanding reparation for their damaged equipment and a thorough investigation. He got a 'trial' after five days, but it was a farce. The official had a dozen men to keep the peace in a population of 7,000; some 2,500 of these were Greeks and he was not prepared to antagonise them. After a party of the Greeks involved came to the Burtons and apologised, Richard decided to leave the matter there. Unfortunately, while he had been waiting for the trial, the Greek leaders sent an untruthful account of the incident to the Turkish Government at Damascus and Beirut, and with a copy to Constantinople. Henry Elliot therefore heard about it from the Turkish *Porte*.

The Greeks' case was that Burton's party had instigated the fight by shouting abusive and insulting remarks about their religion. They claimed that those who threw the stones were 'a group of innocent children playing at games, and that Captain Burton had fired into them several times'. The report claimed that none of the Burton party was injured, and that following the incident Mrs Burton entered their church in her nightgown with a sword in her hand, and in an act of revenge tore down sacred objects, hangings and pictures, and then jumped upon the debris. This document was verified by the Greek bishop who was not present at the incident, but whose signature carried as much weight as that of a viceroy.

Richard made a serious mistake in not reporting his version of the incident to his superiors immediately. Instead, his party packed up and moved on to Cana in Galilee, as planned. Their equipment was damaged and four of their men were in various states of disablement. Richard's right arm had been badly injured as he fended off the huge stones, and it was two years before he was able to fence properly. Some months after the incident, the British Consul from Jerusalem was sent to follow up the matter. As a result of his inquiry, the bishop withdrew his support of the statement, and several perpetrators were fined and imprisoned (the fines were subsequently distributed among the Burtons' injured servants).

The Burtons and Drake made their way via Tiberias and Bethsaida to Mount Hermon, and then back to Damascus. It was a splendid journey which took seven weeks and was extraordinarily well documented by all three writers.[68] Nevertheless Isabel was pleased, as always, to be back in her own home. On the following day they paid and dispersed the men, returned the hired animals and cleaned the weapons and saddlery. Later, she would write sadly. 'I did not know it then, but it was my last happy day. We found all manner of official troubles waiting for us.'[69]

28

PAY, PACK AND FOLLOW!
1871–1873

After his return Richard worked quickly to clear his backlog of tasks, but for some reason he did not think it necessary to report the Nazareth incident in any detail. Having – as he thought – cleared the decks, and with two weeks of unused sick leave, he took off for the Hauran Desert with Charles Drake to copy Greek inscriptions, investigate extinct volcanoes and visit some Druze chiefs with whom he and Isabel had become friendly in the previous autumn. Isabel did not accompany them, he wrote, because she had not yet recovered from a series of fevers and 'she was in no state for hard riding at the time.'[1] A shrewder man might have concluded that he had been away from his post for long enough.

Although Richard and Mohammed Rashid Pasha* had always maintained an outward appearance of sociability, neither man liked nor trusted the other. To Rashid, Burton was a thorn in his side; a man who could damage his reputation and retirement plans. Some days after Richard's departure Rashid wrote to Isabel; it was, she said, an extraordinary letter. 'He accused Richard of having made a political meeting with the Druze chief in the Hauran and of having done great harm to the Turkish Government.' The Turks had never been able to subdue these fierce mountain people and Rashid had

*Sometimes spelled Reschid; the Turkish *wali*, Governor of Syria.

spent months stirring sedition among them, in order to excuse an attack by his troops. Richard counselled the chiefs to submit to the Turkish Government, a stratagem he had discussed with Consul-General Eldridge some months earlier. Thus, knowingly or otherwise, he thwarted Rashid's game plan, causing the Governor to report furiously to the *Porte* that Richard had 'meddled with Turkish affairs'.[2] Eldridge instantly distanced himself, saying he was unaware that Richard had gone to see the Druze, having received only a courtesy note that Captain Burton had gone on a short visit to the Hauran Desert.

When a great favourite of Rashid's asked Isabel on what day her husband would return, giving a flimsy excuse for wishing to know, she was wary. They had been ambushed inexplicably on their way to Beirut for Christmas, which Richard suspected was Rashid's doing. Scenting fresh danger, Isabel immediately sent a coded message to Richard concealed in a water bottle (they had been communicating in this fashion for some months), explaining her suspicions and urging him to return by a circuitous route. Accordingly he took a mountain road from where he and Charles Drake, looking down on the plain, clearly saw a *ghazu* of three hundred horsemen and camel riders, riding up and down the road he would have taken. It was obvious they were waiting for someone, he told her; 'I was never more flattered in my life, than to think it would take three hundred men to kill me.'[3] When the couple pointedly attended an official reception later that evening; Rashid was shocked and 'white with rage'.

Several messages awaited Richard's return to office. Rashid formally complained that Richard had endangered the 'peaceful conditions in Syria', which Rashid claimed to have created. 'I do not know what object you had in mind in making this journey but certainly the Druze in the Hauran have seen quite a different meaning from that which you had in view . . . I received a report that you visited the Druze to reconcile them. If this is true it is a very serious matter . . . I feel I must express formally my regrets to you about this matter.'[4]

There was also a telegram dated 5 June 1871: 'REPORT TO ME IMMEDIATELY . . . PARTICULARS OF THE AFFRAY AT NAZARETH. HENRY ELLIOT.'[5] Richard replied: 'MY SERVANTS UNPROVOKEDLY ATTACKED BY GREEK ORTHODOX AT NAZARETH ON ACCOUNT OF SLIGHT QUARREL WITH INSOLENT NEGRO. THREE OF MINE SEVERALLY HURT. HAVE APPLIED TO LOCAL AUTHORITIES FOR

REDRESS. GREAT OPPOSITION AT FIRST FROM GREEK CLERGY WHO NOW OWN
THEMSELVES MISTAKEN AND WISH FOR AMIABLE SETTLEMENT. DETAILS BY POST.
BURTON.' Elliot sent a copy to Granville on the day he received it, 9
June. 'What is going on in Damascus makes me particularly anx-
ious . . . Which may be the most wrong in the late row with the
Greeks I cannot yet say, but it is certain that Burton's general pro-
ceedings are of a nature to make rows inevitable . . .'[6]

The next English mail brought a letter from Odo Russell at the
Foreign Office (nicknamed by his friends 'O don't', he was a nephew
of the former Premier, Earl Russell). He enclosed a copy of Rashid's
formal indictment, and stated gravely, 'serious complaints about you
have been made by the Porte to H.M. Government . . . His Lordship
[Granville] wishes that from the time of receipt of this despatch until
further instructions reach you, you should not quit the seat of your
Consulate in the city of Damascus.'[7]

At the end of June Isabel again became ill with Syrian fever, which
left her 20 lb lighter, weak and trembling with ague. Richard insisted
she retire to the cooler air of Bludan without him. After her departure
he settled down to report on the Nazareth row to London and
Constantinople. His account, backed up by signed statements of cor-
roboration, was unemotional and restrained. But Sir Henry Elliot
regarded the matter as the best opportunity yet for ridding himself of
a man to whom he was unrelentingly hostile. Ignoring Richard's evidence, he wrote to Granville:

> I am constantly getting further driblets or complaints or explana-
> tions about Burton . . . with which it is not necessary to inflict you.
> He has got an inconvenient way of making his wife write to me on
> public matters and it is difficult to snub a lady beyond certain
> limits . . . They carry the system so far that last night I got a
> telegram from her asking leave for him to go to some place four
> hours distance from Damascus on account of the heat . . .[8]

Richard next turned his attention to answering all the complaints
made against him in a series of five reports. He denied Rashid's
charges against him and counter-attacked, accusing Rashid of maladministration, duplicity, avarice and deeds of peculation. He set out
individual cases of severe hardships inflicted by the Jewish moneylenders, and examples of Rashid's prejudice against the English in

Syria. He defended his own frequent absences which were necessary, he said, for observing the situations prevailing in his consular province. Explaining that the journey to the Druze had been proposed by Eldridge himself a year earlier, he apologised for his inability to provide evidence of this – caused, he said pointedly, by the fact that Eldridge never wrote officially to him, only communicated verbally or by private note.[9]

During this same period, several hard-hitting letters from 'Our Correspondent in Damascus' appeared in the *Levant Herald*, referring to the *Wali*'s maladministration and its effects. Rashid Pasha had had enough. In the previous January he had written a long letter to Henry Elliot complaining of Richard's frequent absences on hunting trips with his wife; stating that he habitually lived at Bludan and could never be found at the Consulate; that he continuously spread rumours of Christian massacre, and that he was responsible for the critical articles in the *Levant Herald*. Now he wrote a letter to the Turkish Government formally advising that if Burton was not replaced, 'I will find it extremely difficult to govern the country with authority . . . I have a bitterly hostile enemy in Mr Burton.' The tone of this letter, which survives in the British Library, is not a confident one. Rather it is frightened, angry and abject; the *Levant Herald* article had obviously hurt.[10]

When he received no reply from Elliot after ten days to his request for leave, Richard decided to join Isabel in Bludan anyway. His letter to Constantinople, copied to London, said that he was sure no one would object to his moving from the stifling and fetid heat of Damascus. The temperature was regularly 120°,[11] he explained and it had long been the practice for British Consuls at Damascus to operate from Bludan in the summer months. Furthermore he was moving there under advice from his doctor that if he remained he would become seriously ill. He could provide an appropriate medical certificate if required. 'I trust that the step will not be viewed in any other light but as an act of necessity, and that the explanations forwarded to your Lordship will explain the surprise and mortification felt by me when I found the transparent machinations of the Governor-General of Syria had been successful.'[12]

Few men in Burton's position would have ignored a direct instruction from the Foreign Secretary, and coupled this with a complaint against their immediate superior officer.[13] But this was probably the least of Granville's concerns in respect of Burton. He had received complaints from Elliot, from Eldridge, from Mott, from the Jews, from Turkish diplomatic channels, and missionaries in London. The Foreign Office can hardly be blamed for concluding that, whatever the rights and wrongs of the various affairs, at the very least Burton was the right man in the wrong place. Elliot's personal vendetta – which began before the Burtons set foot in Syria – made success in Damascus impossible. But Elliot was probably correct in alleging that Richard's nature invited controversy and, inasmuch, he was not an ideal diplomat.

Nor was Kennedy's report favourable to Richard. Since Kennedy was a friend of Eldridge and spent most of his time in Syria living at the Consulate-General at Beirut, with only a brief excursion to Damascus, this is not surprising. He recommended that Damascus be reduced to a Vice-Consulate, and Elliot heartily endorsed this:

> I have not been satisfied with the manner in which Her Majesty's Consulate at Damascus has been conducted . . . I cannot with-hold the opinion that he [Burton] is not well suited to the post which he occupies . . . it would be very desirable that he should be removed whenever an opportunity for it might offer.[14]

At the same time Elliot's close friend and regular correspondent, Foreign Office Permanent Under-Secretary Edmund Hammond, began urging that Burton be dismissed from the Service. Odo Russell (also an Under Secretary) wrote a reasoned response to Hammond's recommendations. He knew both Burton and Elliot, and said that while it was 'clearly impossible' to leave Captain Burton any longer at Damascus and essential to recall him immediately, 'I do not think he can be dismissed . . . A man of Captain Burton's ability should not be lost to the Public and he should be re-employed in some post unconnected with the Mohammedan faith.'[15]

On 22 July 1871, Lord Granville wrote a letter recalling Richard; it would take three weeks to reach Damascus, but Henry Elliot received notification of the official decision almost immediately. He wrote gratefully:

> My dear Granville,
>   Thank you for what you have done about Burton, whose

removal will be a weight off my mind as we should certainly have had serious difficulties in Syria if he had been allowed to remain; as it is he has been long enough to leave the seeds of mischief, tho' I hope they won't come to maturity.[16]

It all seems tediously familiar – this ganging up against Burton by disparate factions; his clear explanations which, although vindicated by time, were somehow always too late to remedy unfairness; his superiors unsure of what to make of it all and eventually coming down against him simply because of the weight of complaints against him; the official dislike of admitting errors. It is a virtual replay of what happened in India, in the Crimea and with Speke, Rigby, Frost, Coghlan, Playfair et al. The fact was that though undeniably brilliant, Richard Burton had a blind spot in his social skills. While adept at spinning yarns to entertain and amuse, he could not dissemble in his personal relationships. He either lacked the patience, or he could not be bothered to pretend to like, or work with, people he did not like or respect, no matter what their station or influence. And to these individuals he gave deep offence without hesitation, frequently intentionally.

Those final few weeks which the couple and Charles Drake spent in Bludan, before Granville's letter arrived, were especially pleasant. They rode out most days on excursions and sent out invitations to sheiks and leading inhabitants to meet them. 'We would choose a spot near water, or near Badawin tents, or a melon plantation; and arriving at the appointed place we would eat and drink, make a fire, roast and prepare our coffee, and have a siesta,' Isabel wrote. 'These impromptu picnics were very pleasant, and we always found the Bedawin charming . . . our lives were peaceful, useful and happy.'[17] One day while they were galloping along in the company of a good friend, Sheikh Hasan of the nearby village of Madaya, the sheikh was *jeriding* and lofting his lance when the blunt end caught in the deep sand, slipped from his grasp and stood at an angle with the spear end quivering. Isabel, who was close behind him, saw the point 'glitter between my eyes'. Only the miraculous instinctive swerve of her horse prevented her being impaled; 'he saved my life by the breadth of a wafer,' she recalled. The sheikh made abject apologies and everyone fussed about his carelessness and the danger. 'Never mind this time, Shayk,' Isabel remarked briskly. 'Only when I want a

dentist I will tell you.'[18] Some of the trips were very arduous and on
one fifteen-hour journey Richard noted in his diary that they were all
exhausted; 'my wife jogged along sobbing in her saddle.'[19]

On the morning of Wednesday 16 August, the trio were about to
leave home for a day riding in the mountains when a messenger came
to Richard with a letter. It was from Thomas Jago, the man who had
welcomed Isabel to Syria eighteen months earlier:

> Sir, . . . I have this morning, Tuesday, arrived here to take over from
> you the charge of HM Consulate in this city and to carry out the
> duties of that office temporarily as Acting Consul until some other
> arrangements can be made. I am also the bearer of a sealed
> despatch . . . which I am requested to deliver personally to you. I
> have the honour to request . . . you come to Damascus . . . without
> delay . . .[20]

Richard and Charles Drake were in the saddle in five minutes, Isabel
said, 'and galloped into Damascus without drawing rein. Richard
would not let me go with him . . . later a mounted messenger came
back to Bludan with these few written words: "Do not be afraid. I am
recalled. Pay, pack and follow at convenience." I was not frightened,
but I shall never forget what my feelings were when I received that
note. Perhaps it is best not to try to remember them . . . I went about
trying to realise what it all meant.'[21] That afternoon a distressed
Thomas Jago had presented Richard with the sealed despatch from
the Foreign Secretary.

> You were informed by a despatch written to you on the 19th
> January 1869 by direction of the late Earl of Clarendon, that very
> serious objections had been made to your appointment as Her
> Majesty's Consul at Damascus, and that though His Lordship was
> willing to allow you to proceed to that Post on receiving your assur-
> ance that the objections were unfounded, you were warned that it
> would be necessary that you should be recalled if the feeling stated
> to exist against you, on the part of the Authorities and people of
> Damascus, should prevent the proper discharge of your Official
> Duties.
>
> I regret to have to inform you that the complaint which I have
> now received from the Turkish Government in regard to your recent

conduct and proceedings render it impossible that I should allow you to perform any Consular function in Syria, and I have accordingly to desire that you will, on receipt of this Dispatch, hand over the Archives of Her Majesty's Consulate at Damascus to the person whom Mr Consul General Eldridge will appoint to carry on the duties of the Consulate until further orders. You will therefore make your preparations for returning to this country with as little delay as possible . . .

GRANVILLE

Subsequently, Richard would refer to his period in Damascus as the happiest time of his life so that the recall was a crushing blow. In the twentieth century we recognise the trauma and depression experienced by redundant middle-aged executives, and Richard presented classic symptoms over the succeeding months. He spent the following day clearing his office and collecting some personal items from the house at Salahiyeh. Having found that there was a ship sailing from Beirut on the evening of the 20th, he determined to leave by the 4 a.m. diligence. 'Drake's kind heart was greatly grieved by the loss of our happy home,' Richard wrote some years later, 'he advised me to await at Damascus the result of my explanatory report . . . But I knew better; the greater the right in such cases the greater the wrong.'[22] On the following day he wrote in his journal:

August 18th. Left Damascus for ever; started at three a.m. in the dark, with a big lantern; all my men crying; alone in a *coupé* of diligence . . . Excitement of seeing all for the last time. All seemed sorry; a few groans. The sight of Bludan in the distance at sunrise, where I have left my wife. *Ever again?* Felt soft. Dismissal ignominious, at the age of fifty, without a month's notice, or wages, or character.[23]

He asked Drake to take care of Isabel while she settled their affairs, and to see her safely off to England. As soon as he saw the diligence away Drake returned to Bludan where he knew Isabel would be anxiously waiting for news. She listened resignedly, for there seemed nothing she could do. That night she was understandably restless and in the early hours, somewhere between waking and sleeping, she thought she heard a voice saying, 'your husband needs you.' She turned over and tried to sleep but it happened again, twice. Isabel did not claim this as an example of Richard controlling her from afar, but the occurrence convinced her that he was in trouble.

Without waking Drake, she sprang out of bed and dressed. Then she tacked up her best horse and, ignoring the protests of her sleepy servants, she set off at a wild gallop across the mountains towards the Beirut road. There was no road to the south-west, but a faint lightening in the eastern skies gave her an indication of direction. The diligence stopped mid-morning at Shtora for half an hour to change horses. If she could reach this half-way station between Damascus and Beirut in time to intercept the coach, she would be in Beirut that evening. She knew that if she missed it, by even five minutes, she would not see Richard until she could return to England. Neither she nor her horse would be able to go on beyond Shtora.

> I rode for five hours across country, as though it were a matter of life and death, over rock and through swamps, making for Shtora . . . I shall never forget that night's ride. Those who know the ground well will understand what it meant to tear over slippery boulders and black swamps in the darkness . . . My little horse did it all, for I scarcely knew where I was going half the time.[24]

As she came in sight of the diligence station the passengers had already taken their places in the coach and it was just about to set off. Fortunately, the coachman turned his head and saw Isabel galloping in.

> I was hot, torn, and covered with mud and dust from head to foot; but he knew me. I was too exhausted to shout, but I dropped my reins on my horses neck, and held up both my arms as they do to stop a train. The coachman saw the signal, pulled in his horses and took me into the diligence and told the osler to lead my dead-beat horse to the stable.

What the other passengers thought of the spectacle of the wife of the British Consul appearing in such a dishevelled condition is, unfortunately, not divulged to us. As the diligence approached its terminus at 4 o'clock that afternoon she spotted Richard walking alone in the street, 'looking sad and serious'. Previously, whenever he visited

Beirut he had been accorded the full courtesies of his rank, with accommodation, transport and an escort of *kavasses* provided by the Consulate-General. This time, in a studied insult, the Consulate had not officially recognised him; he reminded Isabel of a sick old lion. 'He was so surprised and rejoiced when he greeted me that his whole face was illuminated. But he only said, "Thank you. *Bon sang ne peut mentir.*"'[25]

Her account of this restrained greeting, after her desperate journey across territory described by modern-day journalists as 'lunar', has in it the ring of a woman totally confident in the love of her husband. She wrote it several years after Richard's death and, had she felt the need to prove anything, could have exaggerated his response.[26] Richard had avoided emotional farewells and greetings since childhood, but Isabel did not need effusive praise. She knew he was fully aware what her ride had entailed. His obvious need of her, together with his allusion that she had lived up to her illustrious ancestry,* was sufficient reward. Richard wrote that he 'made' Isabel remain in Syria after his recall, to prove that what Rashid said about his unpopularity was untrue. She could not have done so, he said, 'had not both of us been sure of our native friends. She slept with open windows and doors in Salahiyeh . . . a quarter which once had so lawless a reputation that at night none would venture into it.'[27] We can assume from this statement that Isabel would rather not have been left alone in Syria but followed orders.

'We had twenty-four hours to take comfort and counsel together,' Isabel wrote. Her first act in Beirut was to send a message to the French Consul, who unhesitatingly invited them to stay with him. Many acquaintances called on them there and Richard was brisk and cheerful, fending off sympathy by stating that he was returning to London to vindicate himself in person with the Foreign Secretary. Most callers were from the various European Consulates, but no one from the British Consulate put in an appearance. 'I do not know whether Richard felt the neglect or not,' Isabel mused. 'I only know that I felt it terribly.'[28] Twenty-four hours after her arrival, she boarded the ship to say goodbye to him. Later, as she stood watching

---

* '*Bon sang ne peut meutir*', loosely translated to mean 'Good breeding will always show', or 'Blood will out'.

him sail away, one of Richard's servants, Habib, rushed up. He had somehow made the journey to Beirut only to miss Richard by minutes. 'He flung himself down on the quay in a passion of tears.'

Isabel took the night diligence to Shtora, where she collected her horse. She was weary, cold and uncomfortable, her clothes were stiff and dry from her mad ride two nights earlier, and she had nothing to change into. As she rode along she saw the Damascus Consulate dragoman, Hannah Misk, riding towards Beirut and called out a greeting. 'He quickly reminded me that I had no official position now, for he turned his head the other way and passed me by. I sent a peasant after him, but he shook his head and rode on. It was one of my reminders that "Le roi est mort." I suppose the King's widow feels it most. I wonder how old one has to grow before learning the . . . rules of life, instead of allowing every shock . . . to disturb one, as if one were newly born?'[29] Exhausted, she called at the missionary school of Miss Wilson, who insisted that Isabel spend the day with her. A message was sent to Bludan while she rested, and Charles Drake came with fresh clothes, servants and another horse. On the way back, however, 'we lost our way in the mountains, and had a nine-hour scramble,' Isabel wrote tiredly.[30]

Over the next few weeks while she packed up their establishment, Isabel was touched by the massive support demonstrated by Moslem villagers who 'poured in' to the house at Bludan. Every day she received letters of support. One man offered to assassinate the *Wali*; another offered to put poison in his coffee. But it was a painful period. She packed up their extensive library and shipped it back to England. Two pets – a donkey which had lost a foot, and a sick Kurdish dog that she had rescued in her first days in Damascus – she could not give to anyone or sell. She shot and buried both because she could not bear the thought of their being starved or tormented by village boys; this upset her more than anything else about that dreadful time.

Her final act at Bludan has made some biographers uncomfortable. One of Isabel's many patients was a Bedouin boy whom she had treated for rheumatic fever, but whose grandmother had taken him back to the tribe against Isabel's advice. On her last full day in the mountains the child was much in her mind so she rode off towards the tents. After about three hours she saw the old woman struggling towards her, carrying her grandson in a sling over her back. The boy had asked to be taken to Isabel's clinic. Isabel dismounted and helped to lay him on the sand under a tree, but examination revealed that the end was close. 'Is it too late?' he asked. Isabel told him it was. 'Would you like to see Allah?' she asked. He said he would. She took out her water flask and baptised him, using the Roman Catholic liturgy. 'What is that?' asked the grandmother. 'It is a blessing and may do him good,' Isabel answered. 'I remained with him until he seemed to become insensible,' she wrote. 'I could not wait longer, as night was coming on; so I rode back for I could do no good. I felt sure he would not see the sun rise.'[31] In view of the fact that Isabel has been accused of proselytising for the Catholic Church, to Burton's disadvantage, it is worth noting that her 'conversions' consisted of this boy and two dying babies.

Between the time of Richard's departure and her own, she wrote several letters on Syria which were published in *The Times* (one on a potential route for the Euphrates Valley railway). They are interesting, not only for their common-sense grasp of Syrian affairs but for the fact that although Isabel and Richard had undoubtedly researched the subject together, these letters could have had no input or editing by Richard.

She rode to Damascus numb from the emotional turmoil of leaving Bludan for the last time. Hundreds of villagers and patients turned out to say farewell to her, and many rode and ran behind her entourage as she rode down the mountains to the plain of Zebedani. As she reached Damascus, she met Rashid and his suite riding out in state towards her. Radiant with satisfaction, he saluted her gaily. 'I did not return his salute,' Isabel said.

She had less work to do at Damascus for, convinced that British justice would prevail, Charles Drake offered to take over the house and much of the furniture as well as Isabel's two best horses and her dogs and cat, pending their return. Jane Digby helped her to pack and ship valued belongings in case they should not return. 'She was as much grieved as I and wept with me,' Isabel said. Jane had a lot to lose by Burton's recall; he had been an important ally in her interminable fights for fair treatment of her tribe by the Turkish Government. Isabel, pretending a confidence she did not feel, insisted that Richard would return to Damascus as Consul-General. But she did not fool Jane, who was deeply distressed to lose them; 'This is very bad news for me,' she wrote in her diary, 'for they were most

kind and sincere friends and many a pleasant hour have I passed in
their society which I shall always remember.'[32] When Jane and
Medjuel asked Isabel if they could do anything to help Richard, she
suggested Medjuel write a letter of support to disprove allegations
that Richard was not trusted by the Moslem community.

Again there was a constant stream of visitors offering support,
making tearful farewells. Isabel's surviving papers contain dozens of
letters from supporters and well-wishers, written at that time, testify-
ing to Burton's honesty, integrity, ability and energy. Some of these
were from important personalities such as Sheikh Medjuel, leaders of
the Moslem community and sects such as the Druzes, sheiks of
Bedouin tribes, British residents, missionaries and clergymen, leaders of
the Greek Orthodox and Russian Churches, F.O. officials from neighbouring districts, and – notably – a Rabbi. Later they were published,
along with many others from unimportant residents, reflecting the
general esteem which Burton earned in Syria. If only he had combined
his enormous ability with a modicum of tact, he might have survived
with honour, as did men of inferior competence such as Eldridge.

By September Isabel was ready to leave. Her uncle, Lord Gerard,
telegraphed money to the Imperial Ottoman Bank to enable her to
meet their outstanding commitments: rent, servants' wages, and other
bills. Her animals were sold: some horses, a camel, her goats, sheep
and donkeys along with unwanted furniture. Knowing how distressed
Isabel was to part with her stock (many of them had been purchased
from cruel or neglectful owners), Charles Drake supervised the sale
while Jane Digby rode with Isabel up the camomile mountain. It was
Isabel's final opportunity to witness a sunset over Damascus and she
was understandably emotional. 'How I regret their departure and
how I shall miss her lively, friendly society,' Jane wrote later, in her
diary.[33]

The two women spent the last two days together and on 12
September, 'at night we parted,' Jane wrote, 'probably never to meet
again, notwithstanding her hopes of his return here as Consul-
General.' Isabel decided to slip away quietly before dawn on the
13th, to avoid a rumoured demonstration of support for Richard.
Prayers had been said in the mosque for his return, and she feared that
a demonstration might lead to violence for which he would be
blamed. Abd el-Khader and Jane Digby said their farewells on the eve
of her departure, riding with her out of the city through Bab Tuma

(one of the city's main gates) as she returned to Salahiyeh for the last time. As Jane wrung her hand, Isabel said, her parting words were, '"Do not forget your promise if I die and we should never meet again." I replied, "Inshallah, I shall soon return." She [Jane] rode a black thoroughbred mare . . . in the moonlight her large sorrowful blue eyes glistening with tears, haunted me.'[34] This 'last promise' would cause embarrassment for Isabel some years later.

In the meantime, at 3 a.m., accompanied by her English and Arab maids, Charles Tyrwhitt Drake and several *kavasses*, Isabel set out for Beirut. She found the journey difficult, and by the time they reached the last range of hills, from which they had their first sight of the sea, the reason for her unusual lethargy became obvious. Isabel was very ill with yet another attack of fever, the worst she had experienced. Fortunately they were close to Khamour's family home and Isabel was carried there and nursed for ten days, emerging hollow-eyed and wraith-like. As she recovered she wrote a long letter to Lord Derby who, although out of office, was still a power in the land, and then she took the first ship out of Beirut. Even before Isabel sailed, Jane was noting in her diary: 'The Grand Vizier is dead and the Wali [Rashid Pasha] is recalled.' She hoped that a new regime might be less corrupt, yet had this only occurred a month earlier, she wrote, 'the Burtons might have staid!'[35]

It was 14 October 1871 when Isabel landed in England, having been away just under two years. As the lights of Portland hove in sight, 'all the English rushed on deck and cheered.' Isabel remained on deck then, watching the coast as the ship slipped past the Isle of Wight, 'the Needles looked lovely in the moonlight,' she wrote. At Southampton she caught the express train to London where Richard met her. And only then, in the happiness of their reunion, was she able to temporarily forget her overwhelming misery.

Richard had been depressed, too. He spent a few days at the Stisteds' house in Norwood. His sister and brother-in-law were absent, but his two unmarried nieces, Georgiana and 'Minnie' (Maria), aged 25 and 23 respectively, were there. Georgiana recalled some years later that her uncle had been wretched and unnerved. 'His hands shook, his temper was strangely irritable, all that appreciation of fun and humour . . . had vanished. He could settle to nothing . . . he was restless but would not leave the house; ailing, but would not take advice. It was a melancholy spectacle.'[36] In fact Richard did not, as

Georgiana Stisted recalled in her biography of her uncle, make his home with them until Isabel returned. Neither, according to his surviving correspondence, was he quite as beaten as her description suggests. Extant correspondence reveals that he quickly fell into his old routines; visiting old friends such as the Birds, calling in at the Geographical, Anthropological and Scientific institutions, and writing to authors of papers on abstruse subjects.[37] Certainly his first attempt to reach Houghton on 20 September was subdued:

> *Mi querido Amigo,*
>   *Eccomi qua.** Having done my duty a trifle too well the Government has thought proper to recall me. I mention this to you as you are one of my oldest and best friends, but pray don't think that I have any grievance or that you are going to be bored about it. When shall I see you? I have dropped as it were from the clouds and find all London abroad. With proffered salaams to my lady I am ever, Yr. Affec'te
>   R.F. Burton[38]

But his subsequent letters indicate that he was in good form:

>   Sept 26th '71
> *Mon cher Ami,*
>   I have received two notes from you; 20th and 24th. Please direct to Athenaeum or 14 St James. I walked on Sunday with old Hodgson – as jolly as ever . . . Where can Swinburne be? Even Mrs Thompson does not know. My story is too long to tell you in a note. When my wife arrives (5th or 6th prox.) I shall do it all up in form of print so that you can run your eye over it at once. Many thanks for all your kindness. On the 28th inst. I must run down for a few days and see my sister, returning here on the 2nd. I hope that all your family are flourishing. Have you any news of Fred Hankey? Trojan fruit indeed.
>   Ever yours sincerely,
>   R.F. Burton

> PS: . . . Swinburne has just walked in looking well.[39]

*Italian: 'Here I am.'

There is a possible explanation for his misery when he stayed with his nieces; he had just come from visiting his brother Edward in the Surrey County Lunatic Asylum at Wandsworth Common. Isabel accompanied him on a subsequent visit and wrote of her own distress at the haunting faces of the inmates.

Although Richard had called at the Foreign Office and was interviewed, it is worth noting that he did not attempt to commit his defence to paper before Isabel's return, indicating his reliance on her. In fact, to Isabel's dismay when she arrived, he had done nothing further to defend his recall and was treating the matter as beneath his contempt. He was sick of the whole affair, he told her, and wanted nothing more to do with it.

'I applied myself for three months to putting his case clearly before the Foreign Office in his name,' Isabel recalled. She knew, or had access to, thirteen of the most important men in the F.O. and she visited them all, asking them to tell her frankly the reason for her husband's recall. In respect of accusations made against herself by the Jews, she commented, 'I am proud to say that I have never in my life tried to influence my husband to do anything wrong, and I am prouder still to say that had I tried I should not have succeeded.' Formally she was advised that 'Lord Granville did not think it necessary to enter into any review of his [Burton's] conduct.'[40] A lesser woman would have accepted this as the final word, but Isabel had not been educated to accept a put-down; she insisted on an interview with Granville. She got it, too, and he told her he would be happy to consider anything she might lay before him on the subject of Richard's recall.

As a result she compiled the famous Blue Book for the Foreign Office entitled, '*The Case of Captain Burton, late H.B.M's. Consulate Damascus.*' Among Isabel's papers at the Wiltshire Record Office are the drafts and manuscript of this document, in her handwriting, with some edits and a 7-page concluding statement by Richard. It is a fascinating record of the problems encountered by Burton, of the support he earned from the various local factions, the deviousness of Rashid, the lies of Augusta Mott.[41] In that it answered every accusation against Richard with documentary evidence collected from independent witnesses, it is a brilliant defence.

But even before he read the Blue Book, Lord Granville had digested a specially commissioned report on Burton's case (the complicated issues ably summarised by William Owen and Odo Russell)[42] which concluded that the serious charges against Richard were flimsy to say the least. Granville wrote to tell Elliot this, intimating that Burton's defence was impressive and that his influential friends might cause trouble. Elliot replied that he was sorry, but not surprised, that Burton might cause trouble:

> You may, however, be certain that if you had not removed him it would have been far more serious . . . there cannot be the shadow of a doubt that Burton assumed a position utterly incompatible with that of a Consular Agent. The tone which he takes up about maintaining British influence may tell with people who are caught with words . . . but we have nothing to gain by our Consulates becoming rallying points for the disaffected . . .[43]

In Granville's reply to Richard, on 25 October, he acknowledged that the F.O. accepted that the charges made against him had been unfounded. Richard would never receive an apology, but as Isabel said it was '*the nearest thing* to an apology that one could accept out of a Government office'.[44] But despite official absolution, and his record of proved ability and achievement, there still remained the problem that Burton was simply too volatile a character for a high-profile Foreign Office post. Elliot had been clever; he never made a personal accusation in his formal reports, and merely passed on rumours. One of his many ploys to remove Richard had been the recommendation that Damascus could be operated by a Vice-Consul; a measure, not surprisingly, favoured by Eldridge. Granville now used this to excuse Richard's recall:

> I am willing to give you credit for having endeavoured to the best of your ability and judgment, to carry on the duties which were entrusted to you. But having come to the conclusion, on a review of the Consular establishments in Syria, that it was no longer necessary to maintain a full Consul at Damascus . . . your withdrawal from that residence necessarily followed on the appointment of an officer of lower rank and at a lower rate of salary, to perform the Consular duties of that place.[45]

Richard replied somewhat wryly, with the memory of his ignominious removal – and Eldridge's behaviour to himself and Isabel in Beirut – which bore all the hallmarks of disgrace, still searing:

> It is gratifying to me to find that the cause of my recall from Damascus is not on account of any erroneous impression that ill feeling existed against me on the part of the authorities or the people of Syria. This circumstance will render it unnecessary to trouble your Lordship with any other testimonials recently forwarded to me from the British protected Jews of Tiberias and Safed, from the Druze, from the villagers about Damascus and from other sections of the community.
>
> In my Despatch of July 24th, 1871 ('Consular Changes – Suggestions') I had the honour to point out the serious detriment . . . resulting from Her Majesty's Consul-General being placed at Beyrut; whilst in Damascus, the Head Quarters of the province, the Residence of the Governor General, and of the High Court of Appeal, Her Majesty's Government is only represented by an officer of lower rank. I should be deservedly subject to blame did I neglect to lay before you the state of affairs in Syria . . . With respect to my own future employment, it only remains for me to place myself at your Lordship's commands, in the assured hope that such employment will be of a nature to mark that I have not forfeited the approbation of Her Majesty's Government . . .[46]

Prior to Isabel's return to England, Richard had been busy with an old project. Indeed, he was so absorbed in it when she arrived home that it occurred to her that he had already forgotten all about Damascus.[47] The large manuscript on Zanzibar, which he had entrusted to Apothecary Frost on the morning he and Speke set out on their long safari to the Central Lakes, and of whose suspected 'untimely end' he had publicly accused Rigby in his *Lake Regions*, had resurfaced while Richard was in Syria. Bartle Frere, yet another old adversary of Richard's from India days, wrote to Rigby that he had read Burton's remarks upon its loss: 'You will be glad to hear that when searching the strong box of the Bombay Branch of the Royal Asiatic Society two days ago I found a parcel, apparently a book, directed to the Royal Geographical Society with R.F. Burton in the corner . . . I sent it to the Chief Secretary of the Government who will by the next mail forward it to its destination. You will probably be glad to have this information as it shows the parcel got beyond Zanzibar and out of your hands.'[48]

Between his visit to his Stisted nieces, his calls on his friends and a renewal of his vigorous public denials that Speke had solved the Nile question (brought into the public domain again by obituaries written for Murchison who died on 22 October 1871),[49] Richard worked at preparing the Zanzibar manuscript for typesetting. However, he did not exonerate Rigby of responsibility for its long disappearance, indeed he repeated the charge. 'The white population in those days had a great horror of publication, and thus it is easily explained how a parcel legibly addressed to the R.G.S. had the honour of passing eight years in the strong box [at] Bombay.'[50] Rigby was incandescent when he read it.[51]

But the greatest problem facing the Burtons was financial. Richard's salary had ended on 18 August. Pride would not allow him to ask for help from their relatives and, together with Khamour, they were now incurring the rental of several rooms at Howlett's Hotel in Manchester Square. Richard viewed their future prospects with utmost gloom. 'Are you not afraid?' he asked Isabel curiously.' 'Afraid?' She replied airily, 'What, when I have you?'[52] The books he had produced during the last few years brought in very small returns; even so, within two days of her return Isabel wrote to Mr Tinsley explaining their desperate plight and asking that any monies due to Richard be paid immediately.[53] Meanwhile it was important, she felt, that they were seen holding up their heads in public. They were not short of dinner invitations, and they were able to live inexpensively by spending long weekends with friends.

Meanwhile she kept up a lively correspondence with Houghton; 'Richard is offered Pará [in the north of Brazil]; £750 a year and yellow fever. Perhaps tomorrow he may be offered the Fiji Islands. May Allah burn their houses . . .' While Richard was treated so unfairly, she complained, Mr Eldridge, the Consul-General in Syria, neglected his work, played with his barometer and drew his pay which – since Richard's return – had been increased by £150. Eldridge was 'a very bad man', she said, obviously hoping her remarks would be repeated by Houghton where they might count. 'His Russian wife is the paid spy for Igroalieff at Constantinople . . . Damascus is now in his power.'[54]

There was obviously some exchange between the couple in which

Richard said that as he was not appreciated he was no longer interested in a career in the Foreign Office. She had acquiesced when he turned down Pará ('Too small a place for me after Damascus,' he wrote in his diary), but he was over fifty and had no prospects outside the Foreign Office. Isabel recognised that under his professed indifference Richard was simply a deeply hurt man. Wisely, she avoided confrontation which she knew would harden his attitude, instead she wrote him a note and placed it in a book he was reading at the time:

> You tell me you have no wish to re-enter official life. Putting my own interests quite out of the question, when there are so few able men, and still fewer gentlemen left in England, and one cannot help forseeing bad times coming, it makes one anxious and nervous to think that the one man whom I and others regard as a born leader should retire into private life when he is most wanted.
>
> Now you are not going to be angry with me; you must be scolded. You have fairly earned the right to five or six months of domestic happiness, but not the right to be selfish . . . you are smarting under a sense of injustice now, and talk accordingly. If I know anything of men in general, and you in particular, you will grow dissatisfied with yourself, if your present state of inaction lasts longer . . .[55]

As the fateful year drew to its end Richard was called as a witness at the Tichborne trial. It was a *cause célèbre* and was in its sixty-fourth day when he appeared on 13 December as a witness for the Tichborne family (relatives of Isabel's). It will be recalled that Richard met the man who called himself Sir Roger Tichborne in South America in 1868. According to Wilfred Blunt, the two 'disreputable' men had spent all their time in Buenos Aires together. Extracts from his diary read by Richard at the trial show that they actually spent only one week in each other's company, at the 'Hotel Orientale' in Buenos Aires. Reading the transcript of the case, it appears that Richard was careful to say nothing that could harm the case of either side. Perhaps he had something to hide in this somewhat shadowy episode in his life.[56] He assumed his habitual* cynical arrogance when cross-examined:

---

* He had acted in exactly this manner at the Beatson trial. It offended people and reflected badly on him.

Q: I understand that you are the Central African Traveller.
A: I have been to Africa.
Q: Weren't you badly wounded?
A: Yes, in the back, running away.

His testimony consisted of a statement that he had taken a gift with him from Lady Tichborne to give to her son if he met him; 'being unable to find him I sent the present back. When returning from South America, I met the claimant, and I recognise him simply as the man I met. That is all.'

By now the Burtons' exchequer was in a serious state. They were reduced to 15 sovereigns when they received an invitation (and return rail fares) from Lord Gerard, inviting them to spend Christmas at Garswood. They travelled on Christmas Eve and as Isabel opened her purse one of the sovereigns rolled out and fell on open planking near the door. She swooped after it but 'it slid between the boards of the carriage and the door, reducing us to £14. I sat on the floor and cried, and he sat down by me with his arm round my waist, trying to comfort me.'[57]

This was the nadir of their lives together. Richard's only prospect of bringing their fortunes about was *Zanzibar*, and a hope that Tinsley would stand the cost of reprinting *Highlands of the Brazil* in Portuguese. He believed that if he presented a well-bound copy to the Emperor, the book would be bought by the thousand in Brazil. That evening, shortly after they arrived at Garswood, Richard wrote to James Hunt, his co-founder of the Anthropological Society, 'I hope that the idea of presenting the work to the Emperor of Brazil will not come to grief. It will enable me to muster all kinds of members and deal a neat little blow at the R.G.S.' He added sourly, 'The country does not amuse me in the least. Merry Xmas. *Tout à vous*'.[58]

Lord Gerard came to the rescue with a Christmas gift of £25, after which things began to improve slowly. Tinsley sent a small royalty cheque and they sold some of Richard's writings. *Zanzibar* was rushed into print. All the same, Isabel was greatly moved to see a note in Richard's journal that he had seen some oysters, 'and looked at them long' but 'they were three shillings a dozen – awful, forbidden luxury!'[59] He was humiliated by his poverty, writing that 'it is not so much that it renders man ridiculous, as that it brings him in contact with a life-form of which only *Mr Punch* can make fun.' He envied the rich man, he said, 'because . . . his wealth removes him from all knowledge of what is going on within a few yards of him, the mean jealousies, the causeless hatreds, the utter malice and uncharitableness which compose "life below stairs".' The word poverty is a relative one, of course. Richard was in an unhappy position, but he still had his clubs, such as the Athenaeum, Isabel had her Arabian maid, and the couple were still socially in demand.

My dear Houghton,

We ran up north on December 24th and on Thursday next go to Knowsley[60] for a short visit, shortened by Lady May Cecil's marriage in London. After a long visit I go to Edinboro' and stay a month with my sister whom I have not seen for years. We shall much regret missing dear old Fryston . . . One naturally thinks of friends today. How is your health now? Has the change done you good. Don't trouble yourself with writing but perhaps someone about you will let us have a line. B.

[p.s.] Mathews wants me to do a 'good action' to write down the Nicaraguan war in the *Times*. But just at present I can't afford good actions and to tell the truth my humour does not lie that way . . . I think you will sympathise with me. Isabel joins me in best love to you and yours.[61]

Richard's visit to his sister was one he had to make alone, as Isabel wrote to Georgiana: 'I hope you are taking care of yourself. Good people are scarce and I don't want to lose my little pet . . . I hope you all understand that no animosity keeps me from Edinburgh. I should have been quite pleased to go if Richard had been willing, but I think he still fancies that Maria would rather not see me, and I am quite for each one doing as he or she likes . . . The Bird [Richard] sends his fond love and a chirrup . . . Your affectionate, Zoo.'[62]

At Knowsley they planted a cedar of Lebanon, and a cutting from Abraham's oak which they had especially brought back from Syria for their host, Lord Derby. They also visited his extensive coal mines. At dinner one evening, the Duke of Edinburgh was the guest of honour. The talk turned to Livingstone and on an impulse the Duke offered Richard £500 towards the cost of an expedition to Africa to find him. Isabel lifted her head eagerly; Richard went on spooning up his soup. He was, Isabel said, in one of his contrary moods. 'I'll save your Royal

Highness that expense,' he said. Isabel nearly fainted. But it was not mere moodiness of the moment, for he had already been asked by Henry Walter Bates at the R.G.S. to lead a similar expedition and had turned it down. The Society then chose Verney Lovett Cameron. 'I am very pleased you have a good man,' Richard wrote:

> Please suggest to him that he may do good work by returning north (especially) or south of the beaten track. Of course, his first object is to find Livingstone. I would not go for three reasons:
> 1st: Rather *infra dig* to recover a miss[ionary].
> 2nd: Had F.O. asked me I should, of course, have gone. But I won't let them get rid of me quietly.
> 3rd: I look to W. Africa, the Congo and Gaboons for my next venture. East Africa is waxing trite and stale.[63]

Lord Derby advised Richard to 'play a waiting game' with the F.O., and find something to occupy himself in the meantime. Isabel's work on Richard's behalf had succeeded in gaining him a great deal of public sympathy, and it could only be a matter of time before a suitable position became available.[64] 'I think we can get employment that would suit us,' Isabel wrote to Houghton from Garswood after Richard left for Edinburgh, 'but, Oh please, not Bolivia which would be a life of banishment on a shelf far from kith or kin.' Henry Elliot was returning home on extended sick leave, she said, and if Buckley Mathews (an old acquaintance) replaced Elliot in Constantinople it ought to be possible to place Richard in the East once more. 'I don't say Syria, but I say the East; Morocco or Teheran.'[65]

Before Richard left for Scotland the first copies of his *Zanzibar: City, Island and Coast*, were delivered to Garswood. Only submitted in November, it had been rushed out by Tinsley's at Isabel's urging. A copy was immediately inscribed and presented to Lord Gerard, who had been such a supporter: 'To dear Uncle Robert, with the best love of Richard and Puss Burton, January 22, 1872.'[66] On the following morning Richard travelled up to Scotland:

Edinbo' Jan 24

My darling,[67]

Stinking train delayed, got here about 10, comfortably housed and to bed sharp . . . Can hardly see the hands in front of me.

Georgie makes many enquiries about you. I have promised her that you will . . . write to her.[68] I begin my Campaign today, hair cutter, Museum, Library, Philosophy Institute. Object of lecture to bring girls forward. Of course you found [your] mother far better than you expected. Give her my best love and don't sit with her too much. Kisses to the sisters, and love to Winfric and Rudy, [unreadable foreign phrase]

RFB

[*Enclosure*]

Notes

1. Don't forget to send me my crest[ed] paper this is wanted at once.
2. They want me to lecture here. Get from Anthrop. Soc. my biggest sketch, the prettiest notes in my hand, all my flint implements and photos of Zenobia. Send by parcels delivery company.
3. You will see by enclosed what to do with Tinsley.
4. Ditto with Mr Friswell.
5. Ditto Club etc
6. Don't bother Rudy, or overwork yourself. It will be all in good time.
7. You of course will call on B. Mathew and sound him well.
8. What do you think of transferring our wills and papers from Styan to Mobert . . . Dr Bird can perhaps give you the name of some decent man to supersede Styan.
9. Before Lord Derby or Houghton (both I think should be told that you are in town) bring up my name in the house, they should see *Levant Herald* upon effects of turning Dam[ascus] into Vice Consulate. Also my report to the F.O. (Copy was sent to Lord Derby).
10. Enclosed can pay Cunliffe costs.[69]

This letter, not available to previous biographers, is one of very few of the couple's letters to each other which survive. Though appearing trivial, it is an important document. It demonstrates Richard's love and care for Isabel, and also his affection for her family, especially Mrs Arundell – previously refuted in varying degrees by Burton's biographers.[70] The instructions to Isabel reveal perfectly the manner in which Richard directed and utilised her energy and ability. All too often she has been accused, particularly at this critical point in Burton's life, of interfering in his career to his detriment. Richard's notes here prove that he was very much the driving force behind her activities.

Despite the enmity of Maria, Isabel's relationship with Georgiana Stisted resulted in a series of warm letters between 'Georgie' and 'Zoo'. 'My time is divided between [my mother's] and Richard's concerns,' Isabel wrote to Georgiana on 29 February. 'She did rally a little and I took advantage to go out to . . . dinner and the Thanksgiving Day[71] . . . I am working tooth and nail at the Bird's case, and have got our Ambassador (Elliot) to see me at twelve next Saturday.'[72] By now, though, even Isabel had recognised that they were not returning to Damascus. She wrote to tell Jane Digby and Charles Tyrwhitt Drake and both replied sympathetically; Drake confessing that he had not been a very successful pet-sitter, for one dog died and the cat ran away.[73]

While Richard was in Edinburgh, Henry Stisted introduced him to Alfred Lock, a Southampton businessman who had recently purchased from the Danish Government an interest in some sulphur mines at Myvatn, in the north of Iceland. He planned to visit the site and, on learning of Richard's interest in mining and minerals, offered to pay Richard's expenses if he would accompany him and produce a survey. Furthermore, said Lock, if his survey proved good, he would pay a further £2,000. The need for a new project, the opportunity to visit a new country and the chance of a large sum which would resolve the Burtons' immediate financial problems was too good to turn down, and Richard impetuously agreed to Lock's proposals. Isabel was slightly annoyed to hear that Lock would not cover her fare as well, but she recognised the venture would be good for Richard. It was arranged for the coming June.

In response to his request for compensation for expenses incurred in their recall from Syria, Richard appeared before a Foreign Office committee, 'and made them all laugh', Isabel wrote. Arguing that Consuls' salaries were inadequate to the position, he complained that in Santos he had been obliged to use up his own small capital to maintain the dignity of the Consulate. When asked how his predecessor (a baronet) had managed, he retorted, '"By living in one room over a shop and washing his own stockings."'[74]

He gave a series of lectures on South America, on Syria, and on East Africa. At one of these, at the Royal Geographical Society, his old rival Colonel Christopher Palmer Rigby was in the audience. Richard wrote how Rigby and another man '[both] began to contradict me':

> . . . so I made it very lively, for I was angry, and proved my point, showing that my opponents had spoken falsely. My wife laughed, because I moved from one side of the table to the other unconsciously, with the stick that points to the maps in my hand, and she said that the audience on the benches looked as if a tiger was going to spring in amongst them, or that I was going to use the stick like a spear upon my adversary, who stood up from the benches.

Isabel wrote of this incident, 'I never saw Richard so angry in my life; his lips puffed out with rage.'[75] But his anger quickly turned to laughter:

> . . . my wife's brothers and sisters were struggling in the corner to hold down their father, who had never been used to public speaking, and who rose up in speechless indignation at hearing me accused of making a mis-statement, and was going to address a long peroration to the public about his son-in-law Richard Burton. As he was slow and very prolix he would never have sat down again, and God only knows what he *would* have said; they held onto his coat tails, and were preparing, in the event of failure, some to dive under the benches, and some to bolt out of the nearest door.[76]

It was now generally accepted at the F.O. that Richard had been treated unfairly and, thanks to Isabel's determined campaign, that something would have to be done for him. Just at this point the Consulate of Teheran became vacant, and for a heady few days the Burtons hoped it might be offered since Richard's name was listed. Then they learned that it had already been promised to a close friend of Edmund Hammond and Henry Elliot. Richard was bitterly disappointed; as usual he had been ousted by 'interest'.

In April he sat for a half-length portrait by Frederick Leighton, a work proposed by the artist during their meeting at Vichy in 1869.[77] 'Richard was so anxious that he should paint his necktie and his pin, and kept saying to him every now and then, "Don't make me ugly, don't, there's a good fellow,"' Isabel wrote, 'and Sir Frederick kept chaffing him about his vanity, and appealing to me to know if he was not making him pretty enough . . .'[78] The result was one of Leighton's masterpieces and remained in the artist's personal collection until he died, when he left it to the nation.[79] The lack of background detail and the foreshortened perspective of the subject emphasise the power of Richard's compelling personality, yet it also exposes – with almost shocking candour – his vulnerability. Leighton's biographer states:

> It is not only the glinting eye, and jagged scar that express Burton's demonic and electrifying personality, but the drama of light against dark, the severity and cohesion of the forms as a whole, and the firm, inquisitive brush strokes. There can be no doubt that Burton inspired this tour-de-force. A portrait of May Sartoris's husband . . . [completed some months later] showing him in an almost identical pose, is dull and feeble in comparison.[80]

Leighton subsequently visited Damascus and stayed with Drake at the Burtons' former home at Salahiyeh. He painted the house and sent it to them as a gift;[81] shortly afterwards Drake gave up the property and sold what was left of the Burtons' possessions there.

Between preparing for his trip to Iceland, working on his Syrian manuscript, attempting to set up an association for 'diffusing useful knowledge', making '*good* literature more available' to the general public and supporting struggling young authors,[82] as well as his many social engagements, Richard kept busy. The reviews of *Zanzibar* which were being published at about this time were generally complimentary about the book, but some took exception to Burton's explanations of his relationship with Speke. 'We could wish that the author's unkind remarks had been omitted,' one reviewer wrote.[83]

On 15 May Richard travelled to Edinburgh again, spending two weeks with the Stisteds while he made the final arrangements for his Icelandic trip. Maria's husband (now General Sir Henry Stisted, following conspicuous bravery during the relief of Lucknow), had just returned from Canada. When the family attended a reception at Holyrood the women wore their most splendid gowns, there were many officers of the 93rd Highlanders present and, like Sir Henry, they wore full regalia and decorations. Among this glorious throng, Burton in his plain evening suit 'looked almost conspicuous in unadorned simplicity'.[84] On 4 June he set off for Grantham to sail for Iceland. As usual on parting – though it was only for a few months – 'his hands turned cold and his eyes filled with tears,' his niece recalled.

Isabel spent the first week of Richard's absence correcting the proofs of *Unexplored Syria*, a book she cobbled together. It is effectively an anthology of papers – some written by Richard, some by Charles Tyrwhitt Drake and some by Isabel – on a variety of subjects whose only link is Syria and the Lebanon. Richard described the work as a *pot pourri*, and the lack of cohesion between one chapter and another makes this a good description of a book which is not aimed at any particular audience, though it contains a great deal of solid information for scholars of the Middle East. Richard had begun work on this book aboard ship while returning to England, but had dropped it in favour of the *Zanzibar* project which merely needed editing. Some 281 (of 757) pages of *Unexplored Syria* are appendices, which Richard admitted in the preface ought to have been 'worked into the text' but he had not been able to find the time to do so. He states in the introduction his intention to write a book on his personal experiences in Syria at some point in the future. He never did so, but Isabel did, launching herself into a successful literary career in her own right with her *Inner Life of Syria*. Mr Tinsley told Richard that *Unexplored Syria* had 'ruined him'; Richard's reaction was that he had 'long ago proposed "lying like publisher" as a proverb.'[85] He dedicated the book: 'To my father, Henry Raymond Arundell, these pages are affectionately inscribed.'

On 5 June, the day after Richard sailed from Grantham for Iceland, Mrs Arundell died suddenly, having been an invalid for nine years. 'My darling child,' Isabel wrote to Georgiana Stisted,

> My dear mother died in my arms at midnight on Wednesday . . . I need not tell you who know the love that existed between her and me, that my loss is bitter and irreparable . . . May *you* never know it. I have written pages full of family detail to Nana [their current pet name for Richard], and I intended to enclose it to you to read en route, but I thought perhaps our religious views . . . might seem absurd to the others and I felt ashamed to do so . . . Your dear little letter was truly welcome with its kind and comforting messages. I am glad that our darling [Richard] was spared all the sorrow we have gone through, and yet sorry he did not see the beauty and

happiness of her holy death. She called for Richard twice before her
death. Do write again, and often, dear child . . . Your loving
Zooey[86]

An unexpected vacancy now occurred in the Consular Service.
Charles Lever, the Anglo-Irish novelist who was Consul at Trieste,
died suddenly on 1 June. As far as the Foreign Office was concerned,
Trieste was a sinecure. In appointing Lever in 1867, Lord Derby commented, 'Here is six hundred a year for doing nothing and you are
just the man to do it.'[87] Lever took the Minister at his word and subsequently produced some of his best literary work, though he blamed
the climate for the death of his beloved wife. To the F.O., Trieste –
with its reasonable proximity to London, low workload, minimal
responsibility and lack of controversy – seemed the perfect solution to
the Burton problem.

It is perhaps a measure of Isabel's strength of character that Lord
Granville wrote to her, asking if she thought Richard would accept the
post, adding that he strongly advised acceptance since it might be a
long time before another position became available. The salary was
£600 plus £100 for expenses and an *ex gratia* payment of £100 for a
new Consular uniform.[88]

It was a demotion, and Isabel knew that Richard would regard it as
such, but they were not in a strong bargaining position. She had
already resorted to selling some of the better items she had collected
on her travels in order to raise cash. 'I am very glad you got the
thurible and I am sure you must be the best judge of its price,' she
wrote to a collector who purchased a number of items. 'Of course one
is glad to turn the largest "honest penny" one can in these times. It is
very kind of you.'[89] She wrote to Richard with a copy of Granville's
letter and several copies of *Unexplored Syria*, which was published on
21 June. Then she went down to Wardour for ten days to mourn for
her mother.[90]

Richard arrived in Reykjavik on 8 June 1872 and spent seven
weeks travelling and exploring, by canoe, on foot and riding one of
the sturdy little Icelandic ponies. The result was several articles[91] and
the inevitable two-volume comprehensive treatise, *Ultima Thule*; or *A
Summer in Iceland*.[91] It makes dry reading for the researcher seeking
some insight into Burton the man, but it is still used by students of
Icelandic history, geography and geology. Richard's preparation had

included reading every book on Iceland that he could lay his hands on. And, just as he had criticised existing accounts in his works on India and the United States, *Ultima Thule* criticised and debunked all previous books on Iceland. Nothing was as grand or interesting as he had been led to believe. The 'giddy, rapid rivers' proved to be only three-foot deep; 'stupendous precipices' were easily scaled by the ponies, the 'fierce and dangerous polar bears' appeared starved, rangy specimens who bolted at the first sight of man, and the geysers merely bubbled and hiccuped with no fiery display. Almost everything he saw reminded him of a sight he had seen previously in another country, and failed miserably to come up to his first experience; a desert plain is compared unfavourably with the Arabian desert, the southerly wind with the warm winds of India, his night spent in the open at the foot of Mount Heccla with the night he spent at the foot of the Fernando Po peak; a rock formation reminds him of a Moslem grave. Nothing pleases or entertains him, for he does not want to be pleased or entertained. Disillusioned by life in general, the lively enthusiasm of his early writing so evident in *Sindh*, *Goa* and *Pilgrimage* was gone for ever in his work.

When it was published a few years later, the reviewers were not kind; most of them regarded *Ultima Thule* as dry-as-dust and deprecated the wealth of foreign expressions used throughout the book. In a preface written for an intended second edition which was never published, Richard wrote defensively: 'It is not my fault if I am better educated than my fellows. I appear to them pedantic because I speak according to my nature. I would lower it in speaking to those whom it offends if I knew how.'[93]

But he worked hard and with interest at the mining survey. The sulphur was there in large quantities, and Richard considered that only the logistics of extraction and transport needed to be overcome to make Mr Lock's speculation very promising. He also located and identified a new site, some way from the first, with large deposits of the element.

My Pet, [Isabel wrote to Georgiana Stisted on 5 July] I have neither cried nor slept since mother died a month tomorrow. I go to my convent for ten days . . . then back to town in hopes of Nana in August about the 7th. Then we shall go to Spain, and to Trieste, our new appointment if he will take it, as all our friends . . . wish, as a stop-gap for the present. Arundell has done an awfully kind thing. There is a large Austrian honour in the family with some privileges, and he has desired me to assume all the family honours on arriving [in Trieste] and given me copies of the Patent with all the old signatures and attested by himself . . . to be presented to the Herald's College at Vienna . . . my cards [are] to be printed Mrs Richard Burton, née Countess Isabel Arundell of Wardour of the most sacred Roman Empire. This would give us an almost royal position at Vienna . . . and with Nana's own importance and fame we shall (barring salary) cut out the Ambassador . . . I want a quiet year to learn German and finish some writing . . . Your loving, Zoo.[94]

A week later she heard from Richard, telling her to accept the Trieste job: they should regard it, he told her, as a waiting room to the Consulate of Morocco. On 15 July she wrote on his behalf to Lord Granville accepting the post.[95] Despite being in full mourning, and suffering from neuralgia, she set out on a round of country-house visits, arriving at Garswood at 10 p.m. one night in late August to be greeted with the distressing news that her youngest brother, a Navy captain aged 31, had died as the result of an overdose of an opiate administered in error during a fever.[96] It would have been tragic at any time, but coming so close on the heels of her mother's death it was a devastating blow to Isabel.

Richard arrived back in Edinburgh on 5 September. Although he delivered a good report on the sulphur mines, his sponsor's reluctance to stump up the promised £2,000 put him out of temper with the world.[97] The matter would rumble on for several years and there are good grounds for believing that had he received this money at the time Richard would have used it to fund an expedition to West Africa, and refused the Trieste post. Now he had no option. He returned to London, arriving just before midnight on 14 September.

On the following day he wrote to the F.O.: 'I venture to request that, as I am obliged to have a slight operation performed, I may delay my departure till early October, and that I may be allowed to travel by steamer to Trieste.'[98] The operation was one that he had put off for over a year: the removal of a carbuncle, or large cyst, on the back of his shoulders. It had formed as the result of a blow from a single-stick during a practice bout some years earlier and periodically became infected, causing him a good deal of pain. The Burtons' old friend,

George Bird, performed the operation without anaesthetic. 'I assisted Dr Bird,' Isabel wrote. '[The cut] was two inches in diameter and from first to last occupied about twelve minutes . . . He sat astride on a chair, smoking a cigar and talking all the time.'[99]

Richard admitted to Houghton that Trieste was 'a fall after Damascus', but said he was obliged to accept the post, 'in order not to sacrifice the results of 30 years public service. Otherwise I could get $30,000 by 100 lectures in the United States, and that would enable me to explore the Congo and Mwata'ja, etc.' The loss of Isabel's favourite brother there would inevitably influence her against a return to West Africa, he wrote, 'but [she] would yield in time.'[100] The spark of adventure was not yet dead in Richard, it appears, it was merely defeated by financial necessity and domestic responsibility. But he would never again return to the enthusiastic adventuring of his youth; Damascus had been a watershed in that respect.

Before he set off for Trieste Richard met Henry Morton Stanley and Verney Lovett Cameron (the young officer who was to lead an expedition to relieve Livingstone) at a dinner at Clement Markham's house. Burton had previously been somewhat scathing of Stanley and his expensively supported, though successful, search for Livingstone. But on meeting the younger man he was favourably impressed and became a staunch supporter. Stanley wrote in his diary that he was struck by Burton's 'keen, audacious look . . . he spoke well and avoided jarring my nerves.' He recognised Burton's perverse pleasure in drawing shocked opprobrium on himself by barbed and cynical observations, many of which were 'libels upon himself . . . He is brilliant in conversation – and upon any subject not connected with himself, his tastes and prejudices, he exhibits sound judgment and penetration. I am sorry he is so misguided – for his talents deserve a wider recognition than he is likely to obtain.'[101]

Of the two explorers, however, it was Cameron who would subsequently become one of the Burtons' closest friends. Like most people meeting Richard for the first time, Cameron was struck by the savagery of his physical appearance and the cynical remarks which punctuated his speech, though he was 'patient and kind' answering the young man's queries about Africa which the latter realised must have appeared very simplistic to an experienced traveller. Later, when Cameron got to know Richard well he saw how easily the piercing dark eyes 'would beam upon his friends; advice and information would take the place of . . . sarcasm, and his heart was as tender as that of a woman. Witty remarks . . . were always at his own expense. When I asked him to tell me about [his] African expedition he refused to say anything detrimental about Speke . . .'[102]

Richard's departure for Trieste was delayed because of his shoulder. The gaping wound had to be kept open, with cotton stuffing and a probe, to enable deep-seated infection to drain before the tissue was allowed to heal over. As a consequence he was ordered to rest, though he ignored this instruction in order to visit his brother who was now in a mental institution near Brighton. Some days earlier Edward had been visited by his cousin Dr Edward J. Burton and his wife Bessie. Dr Burton was teasing Edward about the repayment of a small sum of money he had loaned him many years earlier in Margate. He was astonished when Edward suddenly announced with great effort: 'Cousin, I did pay you, you must remember that I gave you a cheque.' But in the twenty years until his death, Edward never spoke again; even Richard could not tempt him to break his silence.

Richard sailed on 24 October, with his wound still open, and against doctor's orders. On the 31st Isabel received a telegram from Gibraltar advising that he had arrived safely through terrible gales. She knew that a rough journey inevitably meant a good deal of discomfort for him, and worried about the competence of the ship's surgeon. She was to follow, overland, as soon as she had paid and packed. 'Excuse me if I am rather incoherent,' she told one correspondent, typically, 'for I have 68 letters to answer for him, and four newspaper articles [to edit] and I have to go on Tuesday, to pack and to see dozens of friends who come to say goodbye.'[103]

Isabel left England in early November and travelled in easy stages through Cologne, Frankfurt, Wurzburg and Innsbruck, arriving in Venice on 5 December 1872. It was the first time she had been there since 1857, after Blanche's marriage, and she was delighted to find it unchanged. She sent a telegram to Trieste, advising Richard that she would join him in a few days, and then hired a gondola to take her to all the places she remembered. In the evening, as a courtesy, she called on the British Consul, introducing herself as 'the wife of Captain Burton at Trieste'. 'Captain Burton? Trieste? No, he has just left me,' muttered Sir William Perry, who was elderly and deaf. Isabel assumed from his response that he was also becoming senile and had misunderstood her. She leaned close and shouted into his ear, 'I am

Mrs Burton . . . just arrived from London . . . on my way to join my husband at Trieste.' 'I know that,' said the old man impatiently. 'You had better come with me in my gondola; I am going to the *Morocco* now, a ship that will sail for Trieste.' Totally at a loss, Isabel followed him aboard the Cunard steamship *Morocco*. To her astonishment when she went into the saloon she found Richard sitting at a table. 'Halloo!' he said, looking up from his writing. 'What the devil are you doing here?' 'Halloo!' she returned with amusement. 'What are *you* doing here?' Perry dined out on this story for years.

Richard's wound had forced him to rest at Gibraltar for two weeks, and then a temporary quarantine order had kept the *Morocco* at Venice. Each therefore assumed the other was already at Trieste. Since the ship was still unable to sail, the Burtons returned to Isabel's room at the Hotel Europa. During her secret engagement in 1857, she had written wistfully, 'How heavenly Venice would have been with Richard, we two floating about in these gondolas!'[104] At last the dream became a reality.

The couple arrived in Trieste on 6 December. It was rumoured in the town that he had disembarked with a game-cock under his arm, that she had a bull-terrier under hers, and that they had gone straight to the Hôtel de la Ville where they had taken up quarters. It all sounded faintly raffish. Richard's first report to the Foreign Office, however, states that their arrival was conventional and that they were officially received, 'with every cordiality'.[105]

29

TRIESTE — THE EARLY YEARS
1873–1875

The Burtons went to Trieste determined to dislike it; 'commercial work in a small, civilised, European seaport, under-ranked and under-paid . . . cannot be considered compensation for the loss of wild Oriental diplomatic life,' Isabel sniffed. '[It] might be considered a waste of such material as Captain Burton.'

The city, with its polyglot society of Austrians, Italians, Slavs, Greeks and Jews, had at one time or another owed allegiance to each of the three powers on its doorstep. In 1873 it was part of the Austro-Hungarian Empire. The received religion was Roman Catholic so Isabel's credo could not be used against her as it had been in Syria. Its climate would have been ideal, said the Burtons, had it not been for the three winds which seasonally affect the city. The southerly summer *sirocco* was humid, noisy and debilitating; the winter *bora* howling down from the mountains with hurricane strength had been known to sweep pedestrians, and even horses and donkeys, off the promenades into the sea. And between these extremes were occasions when both winds blew together, which the inhabitants called the *contraste*.

After six months at the Hotel de Ville, Isabel was telling friends that she thought she could be happy in Trieste for another year, but that she craved a home of her own. With no suggestion of an imminent transfer she began searching for accommodation that would appeal to Richard and suit her own needs; 'four or five first class rooms with good views, and 3 second class rooms' plus utilities, work-rooms, storage and servants quarters.[1] Richard actually enjoyed living in the hotel, incidentally the best in town; 'It saves the bore (not to speak of the expense) of housekeeping,' he wrote to Houghton. 'It allows one no end of time, it is, in fact, freedom.'[2]

They still rose at dawn and worked until mid-day at their literary projects, and at a voluminous correspondence which ran to hundreds of letters a month.[3] Determined not to go to seed like so many expatriates, they crammed their days with activity. Isabel at once engaged tutors to improve her languages, German, Italian and Arabic. She was also kept busy 'writing [my] Syria book, and keeping up singing,' Isabel informed Houghton, three months after their arrival. 'Richard is learning Russian and modern Greek and writing his Iceland book and going through a fresh course of Chemistry and Botany.'[4] They lunched lightly and rested before taking daily exercise, 'we go to the fencing school for an hour's fencing and drill every day for our health because we can't afford horses.' They fenced with each other, and with a 'first rate broadsword man and fencing master, a retired soldier' who, Isabel said, gave them a 'set-to . . . this prevents us getting fat and sofa bound and keeps me in good condition.'[5]

When the weather became warmer they would also swim each day in the sea baths, an acre of sea outside the harbour entrance, enclosed by floating pontoons above the surface and weighted nets below 'to keep out the sharks'. The *camerino* who ran the booth where bathers changed provided Isabel with a swimming costume: 'short trousers with bodice or belt, of blue serge or white alpaca trimmed with red'. Richard and Isabel were strong and adept swimmers and swam energetically for two hours at a time. 'We . . . plunged in head first from a sort of trapeze, or from the roofs of the dressing rooms, making a somersault on the way . . .'[6]

From 4 until 6 p.m. Richard worked in the Consulate, attending to his duties which, since there was an efficient Vice-Consul, were minimal. Isabel meanwhile went house-hunting or paid visits. Unless they were invited out they dined *table d'hôte*, and sat on the hotel terrace when weather allowed, smoking and chatting, to finish their day. The couple clearly allowed themselves to daydream of great success, for in Isabel's memoranda book she details what they hoped to achieve when their fortunes turned around: 'a flat in London as a *pied à terre*, a flat in Trieste (for a while), a property in Damascus (*or* look at Morocco'). She also made elaborate notes of their 'dream boat', a 250-ton yacht to be called the *Stella Maris*, in which they could travel anywhere in the world. It would carry guns, three tenders, and eleven crew in uniform. The figure-head would be a carved Madonna. Among the list of fittings Richard's influence is seen: pikes, cutlass, revolvers and Bowies and telescopes, compasses and sextant, a writing and sketching study with work benches. But Isabel must surely be responsible for stipulating a piano, guitar, musical box, sofas and fireplace, refrigerator, and a divan awning.[7]

Richard kept up his spirits by writing to influential contacts suggesting where he might best serve the country. At the time Persian and Russian influences on fiefdoms along India's north-west borders were causing increasing concern to the British Government. To Houghton Richard wrote, 'The key of our position is Afghanistan and we are allowing it to rust in the wards. Why does not the F.O. make me resident at Cabul and find out what Russia is doing there? . . . I can ride, outwalk my mare here, speak Puktu (Afghan), Persian, Hindustani and so forth. However, strong men can wait; my day will come.'[8] A week later he wrote on the same subject to Lieut.-General William Wylde:

My dear Wylde,

Why don't you send me as Commissioner or Resident or something of the kind to Afghanistan? Within six months you shall know everything about Andakhstan north of the Oxus – its most valuable part – about Wakhan and about Kafiristan (now mere names) and about the actual state of Russia in that part of the world.

You are aware that I am well up in Persian Hindostani and Punjabi, the languages spoken all round Afghanistan, but perhaps you do not know that as early as 1846 I learned Pushtoo and by the by had to get my books from St Petersburg. I am working at Slavonic Jaghatic; Turkish will take me only a couple of months and Arabic brings one in no end of Kudos as far as Samarkand. I could survey the frontier and send home specimens of every -ology known. Trieste is very nice for a comfort loving old Gen'l but – what am *I* doing in this galley.

Do put in a word for me and send me rejoicing Eastward Ho! Everybody will say . . . [a] round man is the right place for [a] round hole, and you will gladden somebody's soul by stationing him at the classical Turgiste. My wife asks to be kindly remembered to you and is quite ready to follow where her devoted husband leads,

Ever yours sincerely,
R.F. Burton[9]

This letter, unknown to previous biographers' is something of a mystery, for it points to an acquaintance that has never been explored. General Wylde was A.D.C. and long-time secret envoy to Queen Victoria. Why should Richard write to this man – who had no previously recorded interest in the area – about Afghanistan, unless somehow he had been advised of Intelligence missions which turned out then to be under discussion? Burton's light-hearted, 'My dear Wylde . . . Do put in a word for me and send me rejoicing Eastward Ho!', appears to ask Wylde to speak to the Queen on his behalf. The informal tone also implies that the two were on very friendly terms, yet neither Isabel nor Richard ever mentioned the relationship with William Wylde in their memoirs. Given Wylde's important position this is surely a surprising omission? The only evidence amongst surviving correspondence appears in a letter from Isabel to Henry Wylde in 1883 when she refers to 'your father and . . . your brother William who were (and are still, I hope) great friends of ours.'[10]

Richard must have placed considerable importance on this contact for shortly afterwards, when writing to the geographer A.G. Findlay, he commented: 'Now that there is a chance of my leaving Trieste we find we like it. I shall be in no hurry to go, as my next change will be to something wild – may it only be savage enough.'[11] Trieste's howling winter *boras* had, by now, been replaced by balmy spring temperatures. Heavily wooded hillsides around the city became lush with new growth. The deep blue of the sea was suddenly dotted with multi-coloured lateen sails. Gaily dressed peasants, warm sunshine, flowers, bird-song, the hum of insects and fresh sea air made the couple re-evaluate their first impressions.

In early March the Burtons were shocked to read the announcement of Jane Digby's death in the *Morning Post*. Under the headline, 'A Remarkable Career', it was a farrago of absurd exaggerations:

> . . . [As] Lady Ellenborough . . . her name was once known throughout Europe . . . [she] eloped with Prince Schwarzenberg from the

residence of her first husband. She then went to Italy where she was married six times in succession . . . In 1848 she concluded an eighth marriage with an old Palikare chieftain . . . During a journey from Beirut to Damascus she got pleased with the camel driver Sheik Abdul and selected him for her ninth husband . . .[12]

Isabel was genuinely distressed. She had been in regular correspondence with Jane since she had left Damascus and her first thought was to set the record straight. At the same time, one cannot help suspecting she realised that here was a subject for a potential best-selling biography:

Trieste
19th March 1873

Sir,

Will you allow me to contradict the correspondent at Beyrout who writes concerning the late Lady Ellenborough? I scarcely know where to begin, but I must do it to keep my promise to her.

I lived for two years at Damascus while my husband, Captain Burton was Consul there and in daily intercourse with the subject of this paragraph. Knowing that after her death all sorts of untruths would appear in the papers, very painful to her family, she wished me to write her biography, and gave me an hour a day until it was accomplished. She did not spare herself, dictating the bad with the same frankness as the good. I was pledged not to publish this until after her death and that of certain new relatives . . . I left Damascus just a year and a half ago, in the middle of the night and she was the last friend to see me out of the city . . . her last words were 'Do not forget your promise if I die and we never meet again'. I cannot meddle with the past without infringing on the biography confided to me, but I can say a few words concerning her life dating from her arrival in the East about sixteen years ago, as told me by herself and those living there . . .

Lady Ellenborough arrived at Beyrout and went to Damascus, where she arranged to go to Bagdad across the desert. A Bedouin escort for this journey was necessary and as the Mezrab tribe occupied the ground the duty of commanding the escort devolved upon Sheikh Medjuel, a younger brother of Sheikh Mohammed . . . on the journey the young sheikh fell in love with this beautiful woman who possessed all the qualities that could fire the Arab imagination. Even two years ago she was more attractive than half the young girls of our time. It ended by his proposing to divorce his Moslem wives and to marry her; to pass half the year in Damascus (which to him was like London or Paris would be to us) for her pleasure, and half in the desert to lead his natural life.

. . . She was married in spite of all opposition made by her friends and the British Consulate . . . according to Mohammedan law, changed her name to the Honourable Mrs Digby el Mezrab and was horrified when she found she had lost her nationality by her marriage and had become a Turkish subject . . . In Damascus we Europeans all flocked around her with affection and friendship. The natives the same. She only received those who brought a letter of introduction . . . but this did not stop every ill conditioned passer by from boasting of his intimacy with the House of Mezrab . . . to sell his book or newspaper at a better profit.

She understood friendship in its best and fullest sense and . . . it was a treat to pass the hours with her. She spoke French, Italian, German, Slav, Spanish, Arabic, Turkish and Greek as she spoke her native tongue . . . Her heart was noble, she was charitable to the poor . . . she fulfilled all the duties of a good Christian lady and an Englishwoman . . . She had but one fault (and who knows if it was hers?) washed out by fifteen years of goodness and repentance. She is dead . . . let us shame those who seek to drag up the adventures of her wild youth to tarnish so good a memory . . .

Isabel Burton[13]

In early April Isabel received a letter from Jane, who was not only very much alive, but wanted an explanation of Isabel's letter and the return of the notes Isabel claimed to have written. 'I received [a letter] from Mrs Burton from Trieste,' Jane wrote to her sister-in-law on 1 May, 'explaining the *reasons* for her "Defence"; the keeping people at bay by telling them *she* possessed the real biography, and to prevent any more being said on the subject.' She continued:

I certainly *always* deprecated every idea of publishing anything relating to myself or my former existence, as you can easily believe, and I never spoke to her at all on the subject except to answer some of her general queries as to what the world of that day knew, positively denying some other histories that people have forged. As to *begging* her to remember my promise after my death *justifying* me, it is pure error; she knew the horror and aversion I have to this kind of thing.[14]

Several weeks later a letter appeared in the *Pall Mall Gazette* from the Reverend William Wright, who had been one of Richard's most ardent supporters in Damascus. Wright stated that Jane was alive and denied wanting anyone to write her biography.

It is very difficult to get at the truth here. Jane's diaries confirm that she often gossiped about her scandalous early life. Apparently she could not help herself, as a typical entry after a tea party with casual acquaintances shows; 'I was vexed with myself for speaking to them of bygone days,' she wrote. '*Why?* I neither did the noble-minded Baron justice, nor the love I bear to the dear Sheikh.'[15] Furthermore, there is evidence in Jane's surviving letters to her family that she was less than truthful about certain aspects of her life. When Isabel wrote about the matter in her memoirs, she stated that the very fact that she had been asked to *return* the notes was evidence that Jane knew of their existence. Jane had denied the story to save embarrassing her relatives and Isabel declined to return the notes as requested, she said, because she needed them to prove her account.[16]

Yet her précis of Jane's life, eventually published as part of Isabel's memoirs, offered no information that was not generally known to most of Jane's acquaintances. It did not contain rumours, but Isabel had the number of Jane's children wrong. Surely if she were telling Isabel her whole story, even with her complete lack of maternal obligation, Jane would have got this fact right?[17] Isabel was in general a truthful woman, but when writing about Richard's dismissal in her memoirs, she had no qualms about changing the ending of Jane's letter to her about the Jews, to read, 'your affectionate cousin', when the original actually reads, 'yours most affectionately'.[18] Still, it seems doubtful that Isabel (convinced of divine retribution for sin) would have deliberately invented the entire story and continued to lie about it. Surviving letters, diaries and papers in a number of disparate archives and private collections demonstrate that Isabel's written accounts of her life, and that of Richard, are extremely accurate.

Perhaps both women were telling the truth as each remembered it, several years on. It is almost certain that Jane told parts of her story to Isabel, just as she recounted it to people with whom she was far less intimate. Probably Isabel recorded these conversations in her diary, and to these entries would have been added information about Jane from other trustworthy sources. Perhaps Isabel believed Jane would not object to a biography written by a sympathetic friend; even convinced herself that Jane understood her motives in asking questions. It is curious too that Jane, herself a dedicated diarist, should not have recognised that her words might be written down and used by Isabel, who made no secret of the fact that she intended to write a book about her experiences in Syria. In the end it is simply one woman's word against another's. Both felt humiliated by the affair and their friendship cooled.

Fortunately, just at this time Richard was given two weeks of approved leave, ostensibly to convalesce after an infection, and he suggested they visit Rome and Vienna. The two weeks expanded into two months because Isabel became ill in Italy, and when they went on to Vienna Richard accepted a commission to report on the Great Exhibition there.[19] Rome was well known to Richard from his youth, and he acted as enthusiastic guide to Isabel and two cousins of hers whom they met there.[20] But, as Isabel wrote to her cousin, Lord Arundell, 'we were unlucky for it was that fortnight the Pope was ill in bed and there was no hope of an audience . . . I saw Rome as much as anyone could in that time but took fever and with difficulty got to Florence where I was in bed a week, and thence to Boloougne and Venice, again laid up, and by Trieste to Vienna for 24 days. I never saw such a scene of gaiety and dissipation which began daily at 12 noon and lasted till 3 in the morning';

I was presented at the Imperial Court as Mrs Burton, née Countess Arundell without any difficulty. I made every type of enquiry whether I ought to report myself at the College of Heralds but the Grand Master de la Cous assured me it was [unnecessary] being a recognised fact. The Crown Prince sent for me . . . [and] I saw the Prince of Wales who spoke to me for about half an hour . . . The expense . . . was fearful. Poor me. I ran through £140 in 24 days without being aware of it and am paying for it now . . . with the greatest economy.[21]

The extortionate prices commanded during the Great Exhibition in

Vienna are legendary; even one of the Rothschilds complained at the cost of accommodation.[22] One night at dinner Richard asked for a 'beefsteak'. He was served a plate on which reposed a small sliver of meat. Richard turned it over with his fork and examined it. 'Yes, yes, [he pronounced it 'yaas, yaas']²³ that's it,' he said to the hovering waiter. 'Bring me some.'[24]

Isabel wrote home about her presentation at the Austrian Court. Of its glitter and style, its bewitchingly beautiful Empress clothed in silver with roses in her hair, the bejewelled women in light frothy ball gowns, the men in evening dress with diplomatic sashes and decorations, the blaze of candles in crystal chandeliers, the mingled scents of perfume and cigars, the fabled Strauss waltz music. Her delight was marred when she found that although, as the bearer of a Holy Roman Empire title, she was welcomed at Court it appeared that Richard could not be admitted; the position of Consul carrying with it an unfortunate aura of trade.[25] Isabel took up the matter with the British Ambassador to the Austrian Court (Lord Houghton had provided Isabel with a personal introduction to Sir Augustus and Lady Paget while they were in Rome). The matter eventually reached the ears of the Emperor who had no objection – indeed, he wanted to meet the famous traveller – but it was a matter of etiquette. 'Has Captain Burton no other profession?' he asked in an attempt to resolve the perplexing question. On being told Burton was a retired Army officer, 'Oh, tell him to come as an Army man,' he said, 'not as a Consul.'

Shortly after their return to Trieste Isabel found an apartment. She took a lease, unpacked their things and furnished it, hoping she might economise on the high cost of living at the hotel. It was opposite the railway station on the sea front, and the rent was low because it was on the fourth floor at the top of a flight of 120 stairs. Considering it good exercise, the Burtons did not mind the climb, and they loved the views out over the harbour. They had six rooms initially, but Isabel steadily acquired others as they became vacant and eventually they were leasing the entire floor (27 rooms). It would be their home for ten years.

An hour's drive or 90-minute walk away, on a steep wooded hillside of the Karso 1,200 feet above Trieste, was a Slav village called Opcina. Richard soon discovered this idyllic spot and the couple took furnished rooms at an inn there, Daneu's, using them as a *pied à terre*. The old inn is closed now, but from its crumbling terrace the stunning views of this underestimated city surrounded by woodland, cobalt sea and distant mountains are dramatically displayed, just as Isabel wrote, 'like a map at your feet'.[26] Here the Burtons spent long weekends when the summer heat of Trieste became too oppressive, or during periodic outbreaks of cholera and typhoid. At other times they retired there, among the cool pine woods and chestnut trees, for up to six weeks at a time. It was their private 'sanatorium', just as they had enjoyed Bludan as a break from Damascus, and Sao Paulo from Santos. It made a good base for long, healthy walks across the hills when Richard always carried a heavy iron walking-stick, swinging it or carrying it over his massive shoulders to keep his muscles hard. He was a great believer in the maxim *mens sana in corpore sano*, and apparently it worked for one acquaintance wrote that 'a blow from his fist was like [a] kick from a horse.'[27]

Amongst the many visitors to Trieste that summer was one of Richard's oldest friends, Alfred Bate Richards. He was openly doubtful of their situation; 'a quarter of a hundred languages are scarcely needed for the entry of cargoes at a third-rate seaport,' he argued. '"What can anyone find to do here?" "Stay and see,"' said Richard, 'with a slap on the shoulder to enforce the invitation.'[28] Richards, under the pseudonym 'Old Oxonian', wrote three biographical sketches of Richard Burton; the first of these, compiled at the time of this visit, included a description of the Burtons' apartment.

The reception rooms were 'bright with oriental hangings, with trays and dishes of gold and silver, brass trays and goblets, chibouques with great amber mouthpieces, and all kinds of Eastern treasures mingled with family souvenirs.'[29] There were no carpets or sofas, but brilliantly coloured Bedouin rugs and divans covered in Damascene silks vied for attention with Persian enamels and good pieces of English and French porcelain. Somewhat out of place amidst this oriental setting was Isabel's grand piano, and large collections of books – a complete set of Richard's published works (then about fifty volumes), given pride of place in the main drawing room along with his honours and diplomas such as the R.G.S. Gold Medal and the *Brevet de pointe*. Next to this hung the Leighton painting of their home at Salahiyeh.

As well as 'feminine touches' such as mirrors, flowers and photographs, Isabel's bedroom and dressing room were predictably decorated with crucifixes and statuettes. In stark contrast Richard's small room, off these, was as simple as a monk's cell. The bedside table bore the three books which travelled with him throughout his life: Shakespeare, Euclid and Breviary. His bed was a simple iron bedstead and mattress without sheets – which he did not like – but plenty of soft, white, warm English blankets. Over the bed hung a map of Africa, and an Arabic proverb which read 'All things pass'. From time to time Isabel tried to introduce touches of comfort, but as soon as she did so her additions were removed to the passage without comment.[30]

Every room in the apartment, including three work-rooms containing a dozen deal tables for writing projects, was lined with bookshelves housing the Burtons' library: 'eight thousand or more volumes in every Western language, as well as in Arabic, Persian, and Hindustani'. In every corner lurked collections of weapons, guns, pistols, spears, swords of every type, oils and masks, and scientific instruments such as barometers, chronometers and sextants. One huge cupboard contained Isabel's extensive collection of medicines and was labelled 'The Pharmacy', and there were reminders of India in the statues of the elephant God and Vishnu.

Richards asked the Burtons why they lived so high up. 'We are in good condition,' Richard told him, 'and run up and down like squirrels. We live on the fourth storey because there is no fifth. If I had a campagna, and gardens and servants, and horses and carriages, I should feel tied, weighed down in fact. With a flat and two or three maid servants one only has to lock the door and go. It feels like "light marching order", as if we were always ready for an expedition.'[31] Furthermore, he explained, the climb of 120 steps protected them from 'old women of both sexes'. They had no cook, as such. Isabel always prepared tea, bread and fruit at about 5 a.m. Her maid prepared a light lunch such as soup. They generally dined out, even when entertaining.

Isabel once likened their routine at Trieste to living 'like two brothers', and this echoes Richard's casual remark to Alfred Bate Richards, 'my wife and I are like an elder and younger brother living en garçon. We divide the work. I take all the hard and scientific part, and make her do all the rest.' It was an acknowledgement, by Richard, of how involved Isabel had become in his work, but the phraseology has caused some modern biographers to theorise that the Burtons' relationship was always a celibate one.

Surely, an equally likely explanation is that the completeness of their relationship on every level enabled Isabel to satisfy at least part of Richard's liking for fraternal companionship. Without sacrificing any femininity throughout their previous fourteen years of marriage, she had wholeheartedly participated in activities considered 'manly' by most of their contemporaries; what they called 'camp-life', for example, smoking, fencing and to a certain extent his reading matter.

By now they were totally dependent upon each other. When questioned on their relationship by a friend Richard replied, 'I am a spoilt twin, and she is the missing fragment.'[32] This was a man who prided himself on calling a spade a spade, yet he habitually addressed his wife as 'my darling' (as we have seen), and spoke affectionately of her to male friends. There is hardly a letter to his intimates in his last twenty years in which he does not mention her, and it would have been deeply inconsistent behaviour in him had their lives lacked romance and sexuality. Even their bantering exchanges in company demonstrate the depth of understanding in their relationship. Offence is never taken because the humour is a fond and understanding one. This exchange was recorded by A.B. Richards while the couple were at work together:

[Richard]: Bless (sic) you, hold your tongue. Who wants your opinion?
[Isabel]: (in a smaller voice) . . . It's all very well but you know you are like an iron machine, and I do all the wit and sparkle.
[Richard]: Oh, I dare say – the sparkle of a superannuated glow-worm.

(Then both roar . . . with laughter, and writing is suspended for several minutes).

[Isabel]: Now then, go on old iron-works, and have the first say.[33]

As in all marriages there were arguments, and Richard's temper was formidable; roused, he was capable of sweeping the carefully placed ornaments, so beloved of Victorian interior decorators, from their tables, and overturning furniture. As described, in the rooms which Isabel had appropriated for her personal belongings she had pictures and statues of significance to a devout Roman Catholic, and in the entrance hall she had votive lights burning.[34] 'Mrs Burton's joss house,' Richard referred to it facetiously, and during one disagreement he apparently threatened to 'throw her joss house out of the window'.[35] But the love and shared humour between them always triumphed, and though some of their partings suggest that Richard needed periods away from domesticity, Isabel stuck to her girlish vow to be an understanding wife and never to nag, behaviour she considered 'ungenerous and unbecoming' in a gentlewoman. Even their partings tended to strengthen rather than diminish the bond between them.

She was probably understating the facts, however, when she said in old age, 'We never had a quarrel in our lives, or even cross words . . .' Most people reflecting on a long and happy marriage tend to remember the good times rather than what Isabel called, 'the cab-shafts of domestic life'. Richard was simply too large-minded to prolong their disagreements. One statement of Isabel's reveals a good deal about their relationship: 'If I ever saw him getting put out about anything, and felt myself getting irritable I used to go out of the room till it had passed, and then come back, and by that time we would begin to chaff about it, and it was all gone. I remember once slamming the door when I went out, and I heard him roaring with laughter.'[36] There was a good deal of laughter in their marriage. This semi-submissive behaviour by Isabel might well be regarded by feminists as a denial of her own identity. But her marriage worked. What is more it worked wonderfully. 'He was a man,' she continued, 'with whom it was possible to . . . keep up all the little refinements of the honeymoon.'

The F.O. had ignored all Richard's suggestions regarding transfers, and by autumn he had resigned himself to a further two years at Trieste. He was particularly annoyed that his request to be returned to West Africa as Governor was turned down. He attributed the Ashanti Wars to mishandling by the Colonial Office. 'Had I been sent [there],' he wrote to Houghton:

the whole Western Coast would not have been up in arms against us . . . How many years have I been writing and warning my dumb brained fellow countrymen . . .? The F.O. is completely silent. Like orthodoxy, Red Tape never forgives nor forgets . . . This affair, which a mission and £1,000 would have settled any time between 1862–1870 will now cost the country millions. In 1872 I offered . . .

to settle the business . . . I ask myself if the Colonial Office ever really wanted to make peace with the Ashanti, [who are] thoroughly in the right whilst we are utterly in the wrong. By taking Elnissa we closed their only port [and all access to the sea] and left them at the mercy of our local protégés the Fantes who admirably combine all the worst qualities of white and black. And if Wolsley depends upon these curs he will come to grief.[37]

Debates about the source of the Nile still rumbled on in London (amazingly, Stanley's evidence was disbelieved by the R.G.S.) and Richard's written responses ranged from mild to choleric. 'Exploring, like campaigning,' he wrote on one occasion, 'is a series of mistakes, and he is greatest who makes least.'[38] He watched for news of Verney Lovett Cameron, the young explorer he had met in London, who had gone to East Africa but missed meeting Livingstone. The great man had died and his preserved body was brought down to the coast even as Cameron's party marched up-country. Instead, Cameron went on to make the first march across the continent from the east to west coasts, and obtained his first sight of Lake Tanganyika in February 1874, sixteen years to the day after Burton first saw it. 'Going over ground [Burton] explored, with his *Lake Regions of Africa* in my hand,' Cameron said, 'I was astonished at the acuteness of his perception and the correctness of his descriptions. One was tempted to apply the phrase *verbal photographs* to his records of travel, but though equalling photographs in minuteness and faithfulness, they far exceeded photographs.'[39]

In the spring of 1874 Disraeli's party scraped to victory in a general election. Lord Derby (the former Henry Stanley) once again headed the Foreign Office and Richard lost no time in confidently representing his claim for expenses due to loss of office. Derby regretfully refused to open the matter because too much time had elapsed, but by the time his response arrived in Trieste Richard was seriously ill. He joined a mountaineering expedition up the Schneeburg, and to prove his hardiness wore only very light clothing and slept out in the snow, while his companions were warmly clad and took shelter in mountain huts. When he returned home and complained of being ill, Isabel – irritated that he still felt it necessary to subject himself to juvenile tests – thought he had merely taken a chill.

However, after a few days it was evident that he had a bad

infection. Eventually, an 'inflammation settled in the groin . . . a tumour formed, and he suffered tortures. The doctor told me it was going to be a long illness,' she wrote. 'So I telegraphed home for good port wine and all sorts of luxuries, and put two beds on rollers, so as to be able easily to change him from one to the other, and a couch for myself, so that I might sleep when he slept. We had seventy-eight days and nights of it.' The massive *staphylococcus aureas* infection Isabel describes in her letters was probably the consequence of improper healing of the excised carbuncle on his shoulder in the previous autumn. A serious feature of such deep-seated infections is the tendency to migrate to other areas of the body. Usually associated with poor general health, in pre-antibiotic nursing the condition often proved fatal. Isabel kept up Richard's strength with brandy, cream and fresh eggs. 'He was in such pain, as weak as a child, and unable to turn in bed without assistance,' she wrote to Lord Houghton. 'Besides he seemed to have a complication of things all at once, fever, gout, rheumatism, deafness, sore throat etc. He had two bad operations performed [to remove the tumour], the last one under chloroform. It took two bottles and 40 minutes to put him under. The physician held one pulse and I the other and the surgeon . . . cut a hole about a finger deep and three inches wide . . . happily he was unconscious (I thought I should have died).'[40]

An hour later he was sitting up, insisting on smoking a cigar and drinking brandy and soda; but this was an act of pure bravado and distressing news about their young friend Charles Drake a few days later caused a serious relapse. The Burtons believed Drake was in Bludan at their old summer home, having a holiday, and when a letter arrived with a Palestine postmark Isabel thought it must be from another friend, Walter Besant,[41] whom she knew to be working in Palestine. She handed it to Richard unopened, thinking it would be a treat for him to hear from an old friend. To her consternation he dropped the letter and fell back on the pillows looking pale and shocked, and his wound burst open. When she had dealt with the crisis, she picked up the letter and read it.

While working in Palestine Drake had contracted a fever which led to a bronchial infection. An attack of the asthma that had plagued him all his life subsequently proved fatal. He died on the day of Richard's operation, and asked that his mother be told that he had died 'in the love of Jesus'. Since 'Charley' had always spoken 'as agnostically as Richard', this news gave Isabel great comfort but she, too, was upset.[42] 'Despite all my care to give him [Richard] only pleasant news I had handed him the worst letter I could possibly have done,' she wrote later. '[We] loved him like a younger brother; he repaid us in kind.'[43]

As soon as Lord Derby heard of Richard's condition, he sent a personal telegram granting extended leave of absence 'without waiting for a formal application'. And when she thought he was well enough Isabel had her impatient patient conveyed to Opcina. He was so weak he could hardly tolerate the thought of leaving his bed. 'Do you know I am shaking with funk,' he told Isabel as they waited for the carriage. But the cooler air had a bracing effect and within a few weeks she was able to arrange for them to make the much longer journey to a Tyrolean spa for the prescribed warm mineral baths. During Richard's illness she had written regularly to Swinburne:[44]

Poor Burton has been at death's door at Trieste [the poet told a friend], but I hope his best of all wives . . . has pulled him through . . . her account of his suffering and danger was terrible; however it seems he has now been able to read and enjoy Bothwell . . . His loss would have been one of the heaviest that either his friends or England could have sustained; and it is enraging to reflect how he has been neglected and thrown away with all his marvellous and unequalled powers, and qualities as a soldier, scholar, thinker, ruler, leader, by a country in whose service he might have done wonders and earned honours even higher than he has . . .[45]

In October, when Richard wrote to Albert Tootal to congratulate him on his recent marriage, he was still convalescing at Opcina. Yet, despite his four-month illness he had not wasted much time. He had edited and written an Introduction for *Hans Stade*, the proofs of which (he advised Tootal) had been forwarded to Clement Markham 'who promises to add a few lines about the various editions and translation', before an imminent publication by the Hakluyt Society (of which Markham was Honorary Secretary). But this was not all; his literary output, 8 volumes completed during his first eighteen months at Trieste, had been phenomenal ('by this time next year 15 will be ready,' he advised Houghton, 'of course not to be printed at once').[46]

It was Richard's idea that Isabel should go ahead of him to London
to sell his books, and nurse them through the various stages of publishing, and this is an important point. It demonstrates that, despite
her contradictory preface to *Highlands of the Brazil*, he still trusted
her ability to edit and proof his work to his satisfaction. Anyone who
believes that Isabel was merely a pseudo-secretary and amanuensis to
Richard is in serious danger of overlooking the extent of her intelligence and independence. She certainly fulfilled both these roles, but
she had also become a first-class literary agent and editor. Before
leaving for London she parted with Khamour. Genuinely fond of the
girl, Isabel had treated her more as a petted foster-daughter than
maid, and as a result Khamour had become spoiled and imperious
with the other staff. Georgiana Stisted compared her behaviour with
that of Richard's former servant, Allahdad, who had been returned to
India in 1850 for much the same reason. Khamour was provided
with a small dowry and loaded down with gifts, and soon after arriving in Syria she wrote to Isabel that she was to be married.

Isabel arrived in London on 8 December 1874 and within the next
three months sold *Ultima Thule, A New System of Sword Exercise*,
and *Lands of the Cazembe. Two Trips to Gorilla Land* and *Etruscan
Bologna* were harder to place and would not be published for some
years, though she tried playing off one publisher against another in an
attempt to have them taken up.[47] The nature of the subject materials,
which would now be termed 'limited interest works', meant that
there was little she could do to make the works palatable to the specialist or non-academic by adding what she called 'sparkle'. Her
emphasis on the need to lighten his style was not a specious desire to
interfere with Burton's literary technique, but rather a desperate
attempt to earn some much-needed money for the Burton exchequer.

Isabel was well aware that the potential earning power of the books
was small, but she promoted them positively. *Sword Exercise*, she
wrote, would 'be pushed at the Horse guards . . . [and would] do for
broadsword exercise what a score of years ago he did for bayonet
exercise . . . A thousand writers have been at this subject for three
hundred and fifty years, and yet Richard has found lots of new things
to say about it.' Besides the lengthy book manuscripts there were
specialist papers and pamphlets: on *Rome*;[48] *Volcanic Eruptions in
Iceland*;[49] *Castillieri of Istria*;[50] *The Long Wall of Salona and the
Ruined Cities of Phatia and Gelsa di Lesina*;[51] *The Port of Trieste*

Ancient and Modern;[52] *Human Remains and other Articles from Iceland;*[53] and a translation of Gerber's *Province of Minas Geraes.*[54]

She fussed endlessly over presentation and technical details. 'Captain Burton's portrait as a fencing master is to be used as the fronticepiece; the negative is with Mr Barrand, 96 Gloucester Place for that purpose;' 'More illustrations can be had if required'; ' . . . Reduce space by printing these notices [list of books] in light small type . . . as small as possible please.' 'Dear Sir, I accept your last offer "to purchase the absolute copyright of the *Ultima Thule* . . . at the price of £150 guineas to be paid on publication"'; 'I would prefer [galley] slips if possible – two sets.'[55]

Her own 2-volume work, *Inner Life of Syria*, written for women, was nervously handed over to her publisher on Christmas Eve, having taken Isabel sixteen months to write. Previously, three books had been required reading for any visitors to Syria: Murray's *Handbook for Travellers*, Emily Beaufort's *Egyptian Sepulchres and Syrian Shrines*, and – Isabel's own favourite – Mark Twain's hilarious account of a boatload of earnest Americans travelling in the Holy Land, *Innocents Abroad*. In the *Inner Life*, as elsewhere, the literary collaboration between the couple is evident. Although the bulk of it is lifted straight from Isabel's journals, surviving manuscripts in the Public Record Office and Isabel's surviving papers show that parts were from Richard's pen.[56] He also made editorial corrections, without in any way attempting to alter Isabel's gossipy matter-of-fact style.

Agenting books was not Isabel's only commission. Working thirteen hours at a stretch, at what Burton described with affectionate pride as '250 women-power', she had other projects too.[57] Richard proposed to make money by patenting and marketing a soft drink, the recipe of which had been given to him in India by a Franciscan prior. The details of this project, 'Captain Burton's Tonic Bitters,' including Richard's design for the label and advertising copy, survive at the Wiltshire Record Office, Trowbridge. 'Extensively used by the monks for three centuries . . . one tablespoon in a glass of water or sherry . . .' the label recommended. She located a manufacturer willing to take on the recipe (possibly a trade contact of her father's), a Messieurs Corbyn of 86 New Bond Street, but nothing ever came of the venture.

Two other assignments also came to grief. She attempted unsuccessfully to make Mr Lock pay Richard the £2,000 for the Icelandic survey, and she tried to obtain an honour for Richard, or 'my dear old man' as she had begun to refer to him to their most intimate friends.[58] 'Dear friend,' she wrote to Lord Houghton on 11 February 1875:

> Richard is pining at being passed over and wants to be made a KCB. I enclose you a little resume of his innumerable services which I have printed for private friends to save my bad writing. You will, I know, agree that no [other] candidate can show such an honest list of services without a shadow of reward . . . Mr Disraeli and Lord Derby both know like and think highly of Dick & have each a copy of the enclosed . . . I think it would be a very popular act and after all is [not a] party question. I know I need not ask you if any opportunity occurs to say a good word, for though on the other side you must have lots of private friends in the Ministry . . . Ever yrs affectionately,
>
> Isabel[59]

Houghton was only one of 171 'friends in both houses, on both sides', contacted either personally or in writing by Isabel. Each received a well-presented printed statement of Richard's accomplishments, accompanied by a private note from Isabel. Houghton's mild response that Richard's name hardly needed honours stung her to reply vigorously from her hotel in Manchester Square.

> My dear Friend,
>   You are quite right. This plain hero is grander than all the lilies, and decorations that adorn commoner men. But after 32 years a hero cannot, however philosophical he may be *outside*, bear to sit forgotten by his distant fireside: nor to read in the papers of little men culling the credit and good opinion of others for the deeds that were done by him, for words that have been spoken, or written, by him long ago . . . To stand on a pedestal unadorned before the world is one thing, but to live for England's approbation, credit, honour, and praise, and to see that England does not remember one is alive, is another thing. What comforted him under his toils, dangers, fevers, starvation, thirsts and burning suns, but the hopes of England's praise?
>   You think him foolish from your pedestal . . . but I *understand* him . . . the thought of being Lady Burton has *never once* crossed

my thoughts but the world will say so . . . if my poor darling could only think as I do he would not care two pence for this honour. But he has not got that comfort, and so long as we both live I will cry for justice from the house tops till he gets it.

Thanks dear friend for saying that we 'are beloved'. Those are the sort of things that warm my heart with a flush of happiness, & I suppose it is because our foreign lives are not passed among English *gentlemen* that makes him value this empty title . . . Dizzy . . . I believe, wishes to give it him. I have had a very kind letter from that quarter through Montagu Corry, and dine with Lady Derby on 3rd. I am living in hopes of getting Dick home for a month in end of March, but have not yet asked. My book will be out mid-March . . . This, and hoping to get a good Eastern place . . . and seeing 6 books of Richard's through the press, are my only reasons for not doing what I wanted to do; run down to Fryston when you asked me. Ever yrs affectionately,
Isabel[60]

Isabel was correct in predicting that people would assume she was working for her own elevation. But her contemporaries were not the main offenders; many of Burton's biographers have accused her of self-interest. However, the drafts for the documents used in the attempt to obtain a knighthood for Burton, together with a list of important names for Isabel to contact, survive among Isabel's papers,[61] and they are in Richard's handwriting, not hers, proving that Richard himself was behind the campaign. But who can blame him for feeling that he had *earned* recognition and reward, as others such as Grant, Baker and Markham etc. had?

Never happy in one place for any length of time, he was stuck in Trieste where, he said, he knew every stick and stone for ten miles around. When he wrote to Houghton on 2 March 1875 he headed his letter 'Purgatory' and asked him, if Houghton met Disraeli, to tell the Premier, 'that Trieste is not half large enough to hold me, but that I should be contented with central Asia or even Africa.' He had applied for home leave to join Isabel, he said, but until his application was approved, he was amusing himself by collaborating with 'Bunny' Arbuthnot in 'the study, pure and simply, of Hindú erotic literature'. He mentions a book by 'the Holy Sage Vatsyayana Muni . . . translated . . . into our cleanly English language by two ruffians who sign themselves A.F.F. & B.F.R.* . . . One of his chapters treats of courtesans, another of managing one's own wife and a 3rd of managing other men's wives. It is *the* standard book.'[62]

Richard's letter is light-hearted and bantering. He appeared to have no premonition that he had embarked upon a new and important phase in his life; the one for which he is now largely remembered. The allusion to Vatsyayana is his first reference to the *Kama Sutra*, a Sanskrit book of about the third century A.D., one of the earliest Indian studies in the science and art of love-making and now, arguably, one of the most famous books in the world.

In fact, the *Kama Sutra* was the second erotic work upon which Burton and Arbuthnot worked together. As early as 1869, before the Burtons departed for Damascus, the two men had begun their collaboration, apparently conducted by post. When Arbuthnot visited England on leave in 1872 he brought with him a translation of a book well known in India and Arabia; a sixteenth-century work called *Ananga Ranga*. Written by the poet Kalyan Mall, its declared aim was to promote sexual ecstasy in marriage. 'I have shown in this book,' the author states, 'how the husband, by varying the enjoyment of his wife, may live with her as with thirty-two different women . . . rendering satiety impossible.'

The text of the *Ananga Ranga* was translated, literally, by Arbuthnot's friend, the Hungarian scholar Edward Rehatsek (of whom more later). Arbuthnot, who made no claims to literary accomplishment, then 'smoothed' Rehatsek's translation so that it read easily in English. But there is more than a mere 'Englishing' in the published work. The translation is subtly elegant, and deftly avoids any suspicion of grossness. Although we do not know *precisely* to what extent Burton worked on the manuscript, the style, the eloquence and the inevitable explanatory notes, as well as the strong preface, are unmistakably his work. We know he considered Arbuthnot's initial draft to be pedestrian from his remark to Houghton. It was 'rather dull', he wrote, '. . . curious to see the deadening effect of Indian air, even upon that merriest of boys. He actually talks [in it] of early history!'[63]

---

*The initials A.F.F. and B.F.R. are those (reversed) of F.F. Arbuthnot and R.F. Burton; a veneer of anonymity made necessary by the Obscene Publications Act, also known as 'Lord Campbell's Act', passed in 1857.

Arbuthnot (still a bachelor at that time) regarded the *Ananga Ranga* in a sensitive manner, as an instructive manual of serious social significance. Writing to the bibliographer and erotologist, Henry Spencer Ashbee (pseud: *Pisanus Fraxi*),[64] who was also a friend of Houghton and Burton, he said:

> The first impression on roughly running through the writings of the old Indian Sages is that Europeans and modern society generally would be greatly benefited by some such treatises. It is difficult to get Englishmen to acknowledge that matrimonial happiness may in some cases be attained by a careful study of the passions of a wife, that is to say admitting that a wife be allowed to feel passion. Many a life has been wasted and the best feelings of a young woman outraged by the rough exercise of what truly become the husband's 'rights', and all the innate delicate sentiments and illusions of the virgin bride are ruthlessly trampled on when the curtains close around the couch on what is vulgarly called the 'first night' . . .[65]

In 1873, before he returned to India, Arbuthnot arranged to have the *Ananga Ranga* printed for private circulation. However, after a few proof copies[66] had been run off, the printer realised what the book contained and withdrew from the commission. Arbuthnot made no further attempt at that time to print the book, but neither he nor Burton were deterred from their ultimate aim of bringing the ancient erotic lore of the East into English for 'a small portion of the British Public which takes enlightened interest in studying the manners and customs of the olden East'.[67]

In the *Ananga Ranga* there were frequent references to the 'sage' Vatsya. Further investigations by Arbuthnot revealed that, 'Vatsya was the author of the standard work on love in the Sanscrit literature, that no Sanscrit library was complete without his work, and that it was now most difficult to obtain in its entire state.' The first copy of the ancient *Kama Sutra* manuscript obtained by Arbuthnot in Bombay was 'defective' (presumably meaning incomplete), but further copies were obtained from Benares, Calcutta and Jaipur and with the help of 'learned Commentary . . . a revised copy of the entire manuscript was made'.[68] When Richard wrote to Houghton in March 1875, mentioning Vatsyayana, the first English translation of the *Kama Sutra* was well under way.

By the time Richard arrived in London in June, there was general agreement, in society and in the press, that he deserved a knighthood. He wrote at once to Lord Derby, enclosing the printed petition and its c.v. which referred to the unfairness of his treatment over his enforced resignation from the Army in 1861. Drafted by Burton himself, this charged that he was 'compelled to leave [the Army] without a pension by Sir Charles Wood', that his service in the Crimea, and his summary recall from Damascus was 'under a misapprehension . . . my conduct eventually formally approved by the Government, but no compensation allowed'.

> I have the honour to request that your Lordship will be kind enough, should no other officer have been chosen, to place my name on your list as candidate for the Consulate General, Tiflis, which I hear is to be established as soon as the Russian Government shall permit. I have lately been studying the Slovene dialect of Slav; it is cognate with Russian and a few months will make me perfect in the latter tongue which I formerly spoke. Your Lordship well knows that I am acquainted with Turkish and Persian. A military man being wanted, my nineteen years service may be in my favour.
>
> I beg also to forward the enclosed and to request that if your Lordship thinks it a fair petition that it may be presented and supported . . .[69]

On the same day he wrote to Lord Houghton complaining that he was 'sick of being marooned in Trieste . . . I want to be up and doing . . . do lend me a hand and send an *elderly* gentleman to Trieste.'[70] It is clear from his correspondence that his objective in visiting England was to arrange a transfer. This was not to be. Derby replied diplomatically that he would bear 'both requests' in mind, but pointed out that the question of honours 'rests with the Prime Minister', and furthermore that there were 'many considerations affecting the appointment to Tiflis', which overruled his personal inclinations.[71]

Houghton's party was out of power but he made his support known. A huge number of favourable testimonials, from prestigious friends and from organisations such as the R.G.S., were – according to Isabel's files – sent directly to the Government in support of the petition. However, officials in the Army in India and in the Foreign

Office were canvassed, and from each of these sources there was official deprecation of a knighthood for Burton. The proposal was
'referred'. [72] For the first time Richard began to understand that the
Trieste appointment was regarded as a permanent one. Henceforward
he would use the system to the utmost. Though for the next fifteen
years Burton never ceased to lobby for a transfer to a more exciting
post, he spent only five months out of every twelve at his official
work. He passed the remaining time in London in his traditional
manner, calling on friends, working on his literary projects at the
Athenaeum Club, lecturing at the institutions. That summer, 1875, he
began his famous Sunday evening smoking parties; the equivalent,
perhaps, of Houghton's 'Thursday breakfasts' which had been dis-
continued since the death of Lady Houghton in the previous year. As
well as old friends such as Houghton, Swinburne and Alfred Bate
Richards, Burton's 'divans' attracted a wide circle of politicians and
academics, geographers and travellers, artists, publishers and writers.
All the invitations were written by Isabel on postcards: '*Hadji
Abdullah's divàn from 9.30 to 12. Sunday evening. 36 Manchester St.
Isabel Burton.*' They rarely broke up before the small hours,[73] and
although they were confined to male guests Richard insisted that
Isabel preside as hostess. Her confident, bantering letters to Richard's
friends reflect the position she enjoyed within this otherwise masculine circle. And Swinburne's letters to his correspondents, in which he
referred to Isabel as 'the best of wives' among other fulsome compliments, indicate that she was genuinely admired and respected by
them.

The couple met the Gladstones, and often dined with members of
the royal family; Lord Houghton presented Isabel to the Queen of
Holland. As usual the Burtons spent weekends in the country and
once, when Richard was obliged to make a short visit with his sister's
family to his Aunt Georgina, Isabel remained at Fryston with a host
of interesting fellow guests. Richard made his personal preferences
plain in a note to Houghton: 'Doverscourt is so slow after Fryston,' he
said.[74] The Stisteds blamed Isabel for Richard's infrequent visits to
them, but they were probably wrong to do so.

In August the Burtons made a second visit to Ireland, staying with
Isabel's cousin Lord Talbot of Malahide at Malahide Castle. Before
they left, Richard received the first of a series of long letters from
General Charles G. Gordon (also known as 'Chinese' Gordon, and

Gordon of Khartoum). In 1875 Gordon was employed by the Khedive of Egypt, and was conducting a survey of the unexplored stretches of the Nile. He wrote that he was navigating the river in a small steamer and had got to a point 23 miles south of Gonderoko (previously the Nile was thought unnavigable beyond 18 miles south of Gonderoko), and expected to reach Kerri, a further 23 miles south, on the high waters of the rainy season. 'When I contrast the comparative comfort of my work with the miseries you [suffered] I have reason to be thankful,' he wrote to Richard. It was the start of a long and mutually rewarding relationship between the two men.

Isabel had every reason that midsummer to feel pleased with herself. Her book, *The Inner Life of Syria*, was published, reviewed sympathetically and sold well and she was especially gratified to receive 'warmest congratulations' from Swinburne on its 'general triumph . . . [to] judge from reviews'.[75] Isabel made a point of writing to thank every reviewer, even those who inevitably used the opportunity to demonstrate their own knowledge at the author's expense. It is not strictly a travel book, but it is gossipy, entertaining and informative on its subject, and provides the best portrait of Damascus and Syrian social customs at that period in the English language. Her intimate portrait of Jane Digby, the aristocratic black sheep – unnamed but easily identified – may have helped sales for Jane's activities were never long out of the British newspapers.

Emulating Richard, Isabel used her books to promote their ambitions. Throughout *Inner Life* she shamelessly championed Richard; his work, his thoughts, his ideology. Lady Anne Blunt (wife of Wilfred Scawen Blunt) read the book on her way to visit Jane Digby and commented in her diary that while it contained a great deal of valuable and interesting detail on Syria, 'it is all coloured by the constant fulsome praise of Captain Burton, his wisdom and courage, which must have done his prospects harm rather than good.'[76] Anne Blunt was in the minority. 'The few who have been against it,' Isabel replied to one of the hundreds of appreciative readers who wrote to her, 'do not like the Romanism, but that is not my fault. Being a Roman [Catholic] I cannot change my spots . . . I quite agree with all you say . . . I am a disciple of Newman's, who enters *really* into the *Catholic* spirit as if he were born [to it].'[77]

The chief curiosity, which puzzled but did not especially antagonise reviewers, is chapter 27 which is given over to a vivid dream Isabel claims to have had while taking a siesta in a cave during their tour of Jerusalem. She wrote down the details at the time and took 51 breath-less pages to record how, in her dream, she had been given a divine mandate to redress evil and sent off flying round the world accom-panied by an angel. Apart from addressing some factual horrors (which she claims occurred after the dream but before the book was written), she ordered a palace built at Jerusalem for the Pope as an early attempt at ecumenism; she had an audience with the Queen in which she begged for restoration of Richard's military status and an appointment as an Envoy Extraordinary somewhere in the East. She also took the liberty of pointing out defects in administration in India and warned the Queen of the dangers attached to wearing the fabled Koh'i'nor diamond which Richard believed carried bad luck. The dream in fact enabled her to synopsise her own (and partially, Richard's) religious and political ideology. Her readers (whose letters are preserved at the Wiltshire Record Office, Trowbridge) wrote to applaud her for such a 'natural, frank and truthful' appraisal. 'Your dream,' one wrote, 'I am so pleased with. It was so good, and suited to the times.'[78]

Today such a naïve device to promote a personal credo would be (rightly) sneered at by reviewers. In the mid-nineteenth century, even tutored minds were receptive to unexplained phenomena and clair-voyant dream sequences in literature were not unusual. Wilkie Collins, for example, famously used one as a serious component of the plot in his epic *The Woman in White*. And perhaps because of Richard's firm belief in dreams and portents, Isabel expected her almost visionary experience to be taken seriously, despite its patently obvious promotional elements. Writing subsequently to Houghton she said:

> You promised to love me privately you know, even if you cut me publicly. However you ought *not*, for my book is a success which I never anticipated in my wildest dreams and you *ought* to be very proud of me. I shall produce another in the spring, but no dream this time, unfortunately. Do you see how my dream is coming about? The Queen . . . talks of the Pope going to Jerusalem and *many* other things. Do you see that the Queen would open Parliament with the Koh'i'nor on her forehead, and what a mess this session has left us in with Russia . . .?[79]

Whatever reservations the 'dream' invoked, however, Isabel's income from the unexpected success of her first literary venture, together with yet another small legacy from an unnamed Arundell relative, put the Burtons temporarily in funds. But while Richard was predictably proud of Isabel, her success may not have helped his masculine pride as provider.

Shortly after their return from Ireland, Richard made a second brief visit to Iceland with a 'witness' (another surveyor) to establish the co-ordinates of the new mine he had discovered, and in order to gather evidence for a legal action against Lock. When he returned from this trip he was unwell with backache, gout and general debilitation. As soon as he felt able to travel he decided to go to Vichy (visiting his old childhood home at Tours *en route*), from where he wrote officially to Lord Derby of a relapse, stating that he had been advised 'to avoid passing the approaching winter in the rigorous climate of Trieste'. He requested that his sick leave be extended for a further six months. This was accompanied by a medical certificate from his London doctor who, presumably by coincidence, was also in Vichy:

Vichy September 21st 1875

I have known Captain Burton for the last sixteen years, when I began to treat him after his return from Africa. He is now suffering from a restriction of the urethra and functional derangement of the liver. The former is the result of an orchitis which attacked him in 1874 and the latter has been increased by the unwholesome climate of Trieste. There is no objection to his returning to the Consulship at the latter place at the end of its rigorous winter, but I have strongly advised him to pass the cold season in a milder climate such as Egypt, or if he prefers it, in the tropics.

L.A. Ritterbrand MD
54 Manchester St, Manchester Sq[80]

During his absences in Iceland and Vichy, Isabel made a final great series of visits to twenty-two country houses. These included the homes of the great and the good; Badminton, Bowood and Knowsley – in short, anyone who could push Richard's interests in parliament or at court. The year was a triumph for Isabel all round;

she met so many well-known people that her list reads like a *Who's Who* of Victorian society and the arts, from the Princess of Wales to Henry Irving and Frederick Leighton. One intriguing meeting she had was with Laurence Oliphant. He was no longer the arrogant, assertive mischief-maker of 15 years earlier. He had now left the religious sect in America, through which he lost his wife and his fortune. He apologised simply to her for the trouble he had caused between Burton and Speke.

The fact that Isabel did not accompany Richard to Vichy in 1875 caused an early biographer to suggest a coolness between the couple.[81] However, it is clear from her papers that she remained in London to represent Richard in the Lock case. In the end she settled out of court, unhappily but on Richard's instructions, for £500.[82]

Richard arrived back in London on 6 October, and shortly afterwards Rigby overheard his conversation with a friend at the R.G.S. rooms. 'He talks of going to Zanzibar & Arabia etc. I suppose from this he is no longer Consul at Trieste,' Rigby wrote to James Grant.[83] Richard's surviving correspondence shows that he did consider visiting Egypt and Africa. He told Isabel he needed to go somewhere warm for the winter; his former iron constitution had not recovered wholly from the major illness of the previous year, and in fact he would never wholly regain fitness. It was Isabel who suggested they go to India. She knew a return visit would please Richard. He had many friends there, and because over the years she had heard him tell so many stories of the subcontinent she longed to see it for herself. It was decided that they would return to Trieste for Christmas and sail from there via Egypt and through the new canal at Suez.

London lay under deep snow when they left on 4 December. It was a dark, foggy day and the candles and gas lamps had been lit all day, epitomising everything that Burton hated about English winters. The weather created inevitable travelling difficulties, and they were three days getting to Boulogne. Members of Isabel's family, knowing they would not see the couple for at least another two years, accompanied them through 8-foot snow-drifts to Folkestone. This parting would be Isabel's final goodbye to the last remaining of her four brothers: Rudolph ('Rudy') who was well placed at the Admiralty and closest to Richard out of all her family. He died a year later of smallpox, believed to have been contracted in an infected hackney carriage.

The couple spent some days at Boulogne, visiting the 'old' places they recalled from their first meeting; the Ramparts – site of that romantic first glance – and the house where they had first danced together. For Isabel there was also an opportunity to visit the grave of her infant brother to plant a small rose-bush; to call on her old friend Caroline, 'Queen of the *poissardes*', old now but still as majestic and dominant in her community. Long ago she had asked Isabel to 'bring her a rosary from Jerusalem'. At the time it had seemed unlikely that Isabel would ever visit Jerusalem, but now it pleased her to fulfil the singular request. The sand dunes brought back memories of days when she accompanied her father and brothers on rabbit-shooting expeditions. For Richard there was a chance to call in at the fencing school of the celebrated swordsman, Constantin, where the 'Burton *une-deux* and *manchette*' which had earned Richard his *Brevet de pointe* were still being taught.

A leisurely journey through France and Italy reads like a gourmet's tour,[84] and culminated at 'dear old Venice', where the quiet plash of oars in the wintry canals was balm to the home-sickness Isabel always experienced on leaving England and especially her ageing father. They left Venice on 23 December and arrived at their apartment in Trieste on Christmas Eve. Isabel had been away over a year; Richard nine months.

Isabel immediately gave the servants a holiday, so that they could spend Christmas Day with their families.[85] She and Richard planned to accept one of numerous invitations to Christmas Dinner with friends. However, during the day Richard became ill and had to retire to bed. That Christmas night all Isabel could find in her kitchen was bread, olives and wine, which she prepared on a tray and they shared at his bedside. It was, she wrote, 'our greatest feast . . . how happy we were!'[86]

30

A CHARMING DAY
AND NO ONE DIED
1876–1879

They began their journey with the New Year (1876). Accompanied by their favourite fox terrier 'Nip' and Isabel's German maid, Richard and Isabel embarked on the P. & O. steamship *Calypso* at Trieste for Bombay. At last Isabel was able to see some of the places she had heard Richard speak of in his romantic past, for they made short stops at Yambu, Jeddah and Aden, and everywhere they went they met friends; friends of Richard's from his bachelor days, and friends and connections from their life together in Syria, Brazil, London and Trieste. To pass the time on board ship they began working on a new book, Richard's autobiography. Richard dictated, Isabel wrote, Richard edited. This (never completed) manuscript survives in the collection of Quentin Keynes and parts were used word for word by Isabel in the early part of her posthumous biography of Richard.

It was not an uneventful voyage. They had a serious collision with an iron-clad, and at Suez they took on board 800 homeward-bound Mecca pilgrims, many of them dressed only in loin-cloths and dependent for even the most basic needs upon the charity of their fellow-passengers. Storms in the Indian Ocean took an inevitable toll of men already suffering dysentery and fever and there were 23 deaths, mostly resulting from privations. Their plight moved Isabel greatly and she did what she could to help. 'During my short snatches of sleep I dreamed of the horrors . . . several came to me daily to wash, clean, anoint and tie up their feet.' On one occasion shortly after leaving Aden, Richard protectively lost his temper when he found his exhausted wife tending a patient who was not ill, as she assumed, but drunk. But he too was sensitive to the needs of the poorer pilgrims, and when they were not working on the biography Isabel and Richard both went round the shuddering vessel with medicines, food and drinks. Isabel once asked her German maid to help them, but the woman refused on the grounds that the stench offended her. They sighted the coast of the subcontinent on 31 January, a month after leaving Trieste. 'Thousands of dolphins playing leap-frog under our bows, and keeping up with the ship,' Isabel wrote in her diary. 'A charming day and no-one died.'[1]

If India was for Isabel the coming to life of Richard's early books, for him it was a re-evaluation of youthful experiences, an examination of the changes, and a farewell, for he knew he would never see it again. Not being obliged to live there, he could view Bombay with affection and nostalgia, he told Isabel. They were met by 'Bunny' Arbuthnot who during the next days drove them about in his four-in-hand, a dashing style of driving at which he was an acknowledged expert.[2] Arbuthnot was now the 'Collector' of Bombay, a significant and responsible position in the days of the Raj. For Isabel's sake the trio 'did' all the tourist sites: the Bhendi Bazaar, the elephant caves and the temples, and Richard's pleasure was in Isabel's reactions. But he was happier simply relaxing in the cool and refreshing beach house at Bandra on Salsette Island, where Arbuthnot stabled his horses. Here the two men engaged in lively discussions which would have far-reaching effects on the Burtons.

Forster Fitzgerald Arbuthnot was twelve years younger than Richard. Born in India, he was the son of Sir Robert Arbuthnot of the Bombay Civil Service, his mother being the daughter of Field-Marshal Sir John Forster Fitzgerald. In 1851 he went to Haileybury School to train for the India Civil Service, and apart from three lengthy home leaves he spent his entire working life in India, from 1853 until his retirement in 1879. He then married and settled near Guildford. He was evidently a 'sweet-natured' man who, though never brazenly unconventional like Richard, was quietly purposeful about taking his own line.[3]

The two men had known each other since at least 1854 when Richard went to Bombay prior to his Somalia expedition. Arbuthnot was 20 when they met and the then 32-year-old Burton awed and fascinated him. When Arbuthnot was on leave in 1859–60 Richard introduced him to Henry Murray's circle in the Albany, and to Houghton. Probably as a result of these introductions, Arbuthnot developed a scholarly interest in Eastern erotica.

Arbuthnot could hardly wait to introduce Richard to Edward Rehatsek. An Austro-Hungarian, Rehatsek was two years older than Richard and had spent 25 years in India teaching Latin and Mathematics. When he retired in 1871 at the age of 53, it was to work on ancient manuscripts for his own intellectual fulfilment. Living the life of a *fakir*, dressed in threadbare clothes, Rehatsek's austere and unpretentious appearance masked a brilliant mind which, Arbuthnot knew, would appeal to Richard. No record survives of Burton's discussions with Arbuthnot and Rehatsek, but we know that one of the subjects was the translation of the *Kama Sutra*, a work then unknown in the Western world. As previously stated, Rehatsek had been primarily responsible for the literal translation of the *Ananga Ranga*.

On his return to India in 1874 following the abortive first attempt to publish *Ananga Ranga*,[4] Arbuthnot had concentrated on acquiring copies of the *Kama Sutra* manuscript. This was beyond Rehatsek's ability, and through Dr Buhler (a Sanskrit professor in Vienna who was a correspondent of Richard's), two scholars, Bhugwuntlal Indraji and Shivaram Parshuram Bhide, were recruited as translators. Neither was particularly fluent in English and it is probable that they translated the ancient Sanscrit into a modern Indian language, for in 1876 when Richard arrived in India Rehatsek was translating their work into English. They agreed that, as with *Ananga Ranga*, after he had corrected the English and accuracy of the 'matter', Arbuthnot would forward the mss. to Richard for a general polishing, annotation and preface.

Publication was, in fact, the chief problem facing them. The Obscene Publications Act of 1857 was a well-intentioned attempt to stem the proliferation of pornographic literature. It was never intended to apply to works of literary or artistic merit, nor to scholastic works, but in practice it turned every country magistrate into an arbiter and censor of literary morals. Of the first 159 prosecutions brought by The Society for the Suppression of Vice (or 'Mrs Grundy' as Burton referred collectively to its followers), 155 convictions were obtained. The usual punishment was a hefty fine or prison sentence but, as in the case of Oscar Wilde at a later date, permanent social ostracism was also the inevitable aftermath.

This law applied only to those who published and sold obscene works; possession of suspect material was not in itself a criminal offence. Material circulated privately between individuals was arguably beyond the scope of the Act and – one step up from this – a closed society, with material printed privately for distribution to members only, was a grey area. Richard was very much in favour of using this grey area as a device to publish. Thus was born the bogus 'Kama Shastra Society' of Benares and London; bogus in that it consisted only of Burton and Arbuthnot. In an unpublished document amongst her papers, Isabel explains the rationale of the Society and states that she was present at its conception at Arbuthnot's house. There had been much laughter at the idea, she said.[5] It is easy to see why the scheme appealed to Richard. He did not view it as breaking the law, rather as using intelligence to circumvent what he regarded as stupidity. His intention was to personally contact potential subscribers, thus controlling the distribution.

When the couple left Bombay to tour Sindh, the extent to which Richard had shared his early experiences with his wife was obvious. Isabel wrote how he pointed out to her the sites of his three shops in Karachi, where he had operated in many disguises and written messages in phosphorus on the walls for his Intelligence contacts; here, he told her, was the place where he and Beresford had larked about on the backs of crocodiles; here was where he had lived with little Núr Ján and where he had temporarily 'buried her' when the head of police gave orders to search the house ('a very romantic affair', Isabel commented without giving any further details), and where the roof had fallen in and injured him. Here was where he had buried Bhujang, his fighting cock.[6] Here was 'the place where he had a serious flirtation with a Persian girl'; here was the convent where he had tried to kidnap a young inmate.[7] Richard wrote only briefly of his private reactions to the scenes of his youthful adventures, 'how very unpleasant to meet one's Self, one's Dead Self, thirty years younger!'[8]

Richard called on the Agha Khan, who invited the couple to the Festival of *Ashúra* celebrations as his guests. They met Mirza Ali Akbar, Richard's old *munshi*, and John MacClean and Grattan Geary, editors of the two big Bombay papers, and Richard published several articles in *The Times of India* under the pseudonym 'R.F. Baker'.[9]

They dined at Government House, met the Prince of Wales who was on a State Visit, and attended a dizzying round of garden parties, balls, races, teas, theatricals and parades. This was the height of the Raj; 'there is so much hospitality,' Isabel wrote, 'that we dined out every night, and the drives out to dinner and back were delicious on the balmy Indian nights.'

In Sindh they visited Residencies and diamond mines, the famous caves and carved temples, and dined with the Nizam. They attended the Protestant Cathedral, a Hindu burning of the dead, mass at the convent of Misericordia, and were welcomed (when Richard told the janissary that he had been admitted to the Brahminical thread) into one of the sacred Brahmin temples. Isabel collected photographs everywhere they went. Sadly they are of landscapes and not people, but they survive in her scrapbooks at Trowbridge in Wiltshire, a remarkable record of India in 1876.

They toured Hyderabad on elephants, and 'Ooty' on horseback where Isabel worried about overtaxing the small horses, but Richard weighed more than she did; at 11 stones (154 lbs) she was hardly seriously overweight for her height. Richard's description of Ootacamund on this trip was certainly unsentimental. It was, he said, 'a rotten hole full of middle class, respectably pious and water swilling pratts! A race that disagrees with me.'[10]

The voyage home was hot and humid. There was no awning on the ship, and crossing the Indian Ocean and Red Sea the seventeen European passengers 'fried alive'. Early in the voyage Isabel gathered the women together and persuaded them to sleep on deck, and to dress simply in light, loose tea-gowns for dinner. They spent a short time in Cairo, Alexandria and Ramleh before catching a Lloyds boat home, steaming into Trieste harbour on 18 June almost six months after leaving it. 'The beautiful little City, nestled in its corner in the mountains,' Isabel wrote. '[It] seemed to us the most beautiful spot we had ever beheld after hot India and barren Egypt.'[11]

Initially, Richard had no time to feel stifled by returning to Trieste. The summer weather was idyllic and the distant alps were still covered in snow. They arrived back to a mountain of interesting mail. Charles Gordon had written from Central Africa, 'these lakes and rivers are very trying to a man, you never can get to the end of the tangle.'

Verney Lovett Cameron – who, after marching across the African

Continent from the east coast had walked into a west coast
Consulate, saluted and said to the startled official, 'Cameron reporting, from Zanzibar overland' – had written to thank Richard 'for
fighting my battles while I was away. Anything I may have said about
your Lake Regions cannot half express how much I was indebted to
you whilst in Africa,' he said. He also mentioned the forthcoming
African Conference in Brussels in September. 'I wish you could be
there as Grant is going to be one of the representatives of the RGS and
he is nearly as big a fool as Galton, which is saying a good deal.' They
had wanted him to change his maps to agree with their theories, he
reported incredulously. 'I value your appreciation of my journey more
than that of any other [man] in the world, . . . as you know what it is
like to have to get along with a crowd of unwilling devils when one is
ill and lame and all the rest of it.'[12]

There was distressing personal news. Alfred Bate Richards had
died, like Steinhaueser, of apoplexy. Richard's brother-in-law, Sir
Henry Stisted, had also died, of consumption. 'What an end to a successful life,' Richard wrote to their cousin Edward. 'A great loss to
Maria and the chicks.'[13] But who could blame Richard and Isabel for
being pleased to hear that their old enemy, Rashid Pasha, had been
assassinated in Constantinople? Richard is said to have 'howled' in
triumph at the news. 'Serve the scoundrel right!' he wrote to a number
of correspondents. He had never liked or trusted the man, or his
countrymen, as revealed in his letter to Grattan Geary, the Bombay
newspaper editor: 'This is an exciting moment. The move of the
English Fleet to the Bosphorous may very probably bring the Russians
out of the Danube, in which case Turkey in Europe bursts up. We
should be ashamed to support a Power whose only policy is sheer
rank murder . . .'[14]

His replies over the next few weeks to numerous correspondents
about the couple's schedule reveal that his holiday had rejuvenated
him. Both had begun working on books about their journey to India,
but Richard had several ideas for making some serious money. He
mentions a plan to use modern extraction techniques on the 'enormous' diamond fields in India which had so far 'only been scratched';
in Arabia he had 'heard about a new gold mine . . . and I know
where plenty of Guano is to be had'.[15] Despite the long absence from
his post he hoped to be able to attend the African Conference in
Belgium, and to one correspondent's suggestion that he must be

'horribly sick of travelling' he rejoined vigorously, 'Good Allah!!! When old, I intend to take a permanent passage in some old steamer and go round and round the world till I die.'[16]

This is the key to Burton, in a sense. He needed the stimulation of constant travel almost to keep him stable; without it he became depressed and bitter. Had he been born a wealthy man – like Houghton, for example – he could have indulged this hunger for change. He had chosen the Foreign Service because it appeared to offer the opportunity for paid travel. That it did not work out quite as he hoped was partially due to the enemies he made in other sectors of his life. It was chiefly, however, lack of money that made him dependent on his paid employment. The novelist Ouida, one of the couple's closest friends, believed that Burton remained in the Foreign Office for Isabel's sake. To some extent this is probably correct, but it overlooks the fact that Richard had no other source of income. Despite his huge literary output, income from his writing alone could not have supported him and, no matter how dismal he sometimes thought his life was in Trieste, the fact remains that the Burtons lived a relatively ritzy lifestyle on the salary of a minor Consul. Had they been able to leave the Foreign Office and travel more extensively, no one would have been happier than Isabel.

Throughout the summer and autumn Richard occupied himself writing long, right-wing appreciations of the turmoil affecting eastern Europe. It had begun in 1875 as an insurrection in Herzegovina which quickly spread to Bosnia. In 1876 Serbia and Montenegro declared war against Turkey and fighting began in Bulgaria. Turkey bolstered its troops with irregulars such as the Bashi-Bazouks who resorted to a series of massacres which became known as 'the Bulgarian atrocities'. Escalating tensions subsequently led to a declaration of war between Turkey and Russia (in April 1877). The British Embassy at Constantinople was much criticised for its delay in reporting the massacres, but an official inquiry exonerated Richard's old enemy. A secret despatch from the British Consul at Adrianople communicating the news to the terminally-ill Consul-General at Constantinople was not passed on to Sir Henry Elliot.

Meanwhile Burton's articles appeared in various newspapers. Political historians agree that his criticisms were sensible, though they ran counter to political views of the day. 'My partition plan which (if I remember right) you chaffed, has been bodily accepted by the *Post* newspaper of Berlin – so you see the Prussians don't complain of it,' he wrote to one correspondent. 'The Liberals in England are against Turkey to a man, and the Gov't would never dare propose another Crimean War. I find myself herding with a strange lot, Shaftsbury, Bright [etc.], but men who prefer *patria* to party must expect strange company.'[17]

The political landscape of eastern Europe at this critical point was largely responsible for Disraeli's decision to resign the premiership in August 1876 (he was over 70 by that time, and could not take the continued stress). That Richard had a first-class grasp of the complicated issues is evident from his long series of letters on the subject to the celebrated Oxbridge political historian Edward Augustus Freeman (whom he had known since they were freshmen together at Trinity College, Oxford).[18]

Richard felt so strongly about the Government's appeasement policy towards Turkey (in which Lord Derby played a significant part) that he was prepared to disregard the problems his letters to newspapers in Syria had caused, and he fired off a chain of strongly worded epistles defining the role of the Turks in the recent troubles and in particular the Bulgarian atrocities. He wrote under pseudonyms; in the *Daily News* he was 'Conscience',[19] and elsewhere he was 'Pantillaria'.[20] To one editor he wrote, 'Please keep the authorship a complete secret. F.O. and I are not very good friends just now.'[21] But even though he persuaded friends to mail the missives from addresses in England, he knew the F.O. suspected him of being the author. 'I dare not go to Belgrade,' he wrote to Freeman, 'or F.O. would pay me out for letters in the *Daily News* (August 15th and 24th). Still, I strongly sympathise with Serbia and hope firmly to see Turkey fall.'[22]

He was correct in believing that he was suspected of authorship. Freeman had urged him to 'bring some of the important points of the case privately before Lord Salisbury now he is to be the Plenipotentiary? Your knowledge . . . would get you a hearing . . .'[23] Salisbury's train halted a few miles from Trieste on the night of 27 November 1876 on his way, during an armistice, to the international conference between the great powers. He pointedly ignored Burton's telegraph of official greeting and proposed meeting, and answered with a curt instruction to forward any mail for him to Rome. 'The reason is,' Richard wrote to Grattan Geary, 'I am a suspect, especially after the letter of March 7 in the Daily Telegraph, reprinted by

Maclean and commented on by you. Yet it is going to prove true. Men fear Lord Salisbury's fiery temper. I don't. He will be mild enough at Istanbul . . . the Turks will probably just drift into war.'[24]

That winter Isabel received news of a series of deaths in her family. Throughout her life her father's two bachelor brothers* had made their home with them, and to Isabel and her siblings these two men had acted as 'second fathers'. They died within weeks of each other in December 1876, and hardly had she recovered from this shock when in January she had word that Rudolph, her only surviving brother, had died from smallpox. 'We have been in great distress,' Richard wrote to friends. He was as much affected by Isabel's inconsolable grief as by the loss of his brother-in-law, though the latter had been a favourite companion.[25]

Deeply depressed, Isabel went into retreat at a convent at Gorizia. While there, the Comte de Chambord (Henri V of France) and his family and small court arrived to stay nearby. Hearing that Isabel was in the area, and remembering their meeting in Venice 16 years earlier, they sent a message inviting her to dine with them. She explained that having nothing but a sombre travelling dress she was obliged to refuse, but they asked her to wear this and join them anyway 'en famille'. She dined twice with them, sitting in the place of honour next to her host, and she appreciated the act of kindness greatly, 'more than if they had come into their own and received her royally at the Tuileries'.[26] This was not petty snobbishness on Isabel's part; her upbringing in the old aristocracy, legitimists to the end, had instilled in her – as with most of her contemporaries – a deep respect for royalty.

But apart from the grief caused by the loss of much-loved members of her family, Isabel was increasingly bothered by her belief that as matters stood, she and Richard could not be together in an afterlife (Richard being a non-Catholic and thus, according to the Roman Catholic teaching, ineligible for heaven). She wrote to her cousin Lord Arundell that she wanted nothing more in life than Richard's conversion, though she knew better than to ask or press him. 'I would think good appointments, and money or title, *dirt* in comparison,' she wrote.[27] She evidently had some grounds for believing it a possibility

---

*Renfric and Raymond.

that Richard might one day accept the Catholic Church; but the recent sudden deaths in her family gave rise to the haunting fear that he might leave it too late to act. It is easy to dismiss this apprehension as irrational, but Richard understood its importance to her. Why else would he sign the short statement she wrote out?

Gorizia, 15th February 1877

> Should my husband Richard Burton be on *his* death-bed unable to speak – I perhaps already dead – and that he may wish, and have the grace, to retract and recant his former errors and to join the Catholic Church, and also receive the Sacraments of Penance, Extreme Unction and Holy Eucharist, he might perhaps be able to sign this paper, or make the sign of the cross to show his need.
>
> Richard F. Burton[28]

Although the signature appended to this document is undoubtedly Richard Burton's, it is not evidence that he really wished to join the Catholic Church, or any Christian church. It could be argued that he researched numerous theologies with the fervour of a man seeking spiritual answers, but he never wrote about his personal belief, only once remarking in a speech that his religious opinions were his own business. His signing of this document was, rather, a demonstration of his love for Isabel, an attempt to quell her overwhelming dread that they would be parted in a hereafter in which she believed but he did not.

During the previous year Richard had spent a considerable amount of time and effort investigating the Burton pedigree. Using Isabel to do the legwork through a publication called *Notes and Queries*, and by writing to his numerous relations in Ireland and to experts in lineage, Richard proved to his satisfaction his illegitimate descent from the French Sun King Louis XIV and Countess Montmorency.[29] There was also a defunct title in the Burton family and for a while he investigated this, with a view to claiming it, but he eventually dropped the idea, writing to 'Bessie' (wife of his cousin Dr Edward Burton):

> . . . Had the old man left me his money . . . I should have applied for permission to take up the old baronetcy. But now I shall not. Your husband is *the* baronet and he can if he likes assume the 'Sir' at once. Why the devil doesn't he? . . . Neither he nor you may care for

it, but think of the advantage it will be to your children . . . the British public are such snobs that a baronet, even in the matrimonial market, is always worth £50,000, and it is one of the oldest baronetcies in the kingdom. Do take my advice and get it for your son.[30]

Previous biographers have attributed the research to Isabel's yearning for a title.[31] Once again the papers at Trowbridge prove otherwise; Richard was behind the research. Isabel already had a title and was everywhere addressed as 'Countess' in Europe,[32] but both Burtons believed that a title would benefit Richard's career.

In March, Isabel wrote to Houghton and to Ouida that Richard had been given a month's leave to go to the Middle East.[33] At the bottom of her letters Richard scribbled his glee at being able to break away from 'pestilent Trieste'.[34] The talk of a new gold discovery in Arabia, overheard by Richard while in Cairo on their return journey from India, had stirred his gold fever which was never far from the surface; his trip would be the first of two expeditions that Burton made to the Midian, an area of land on the eastern shore of the gulf of Aqaba (now part of Saudi Arabia).

During his *Haj* in 1853, Richard's sometime companion Haji Wali Alioghlú the Persian had showed him some rocks containing traces of gold and told him he knew where to find more. Richard now became fired with enthusiasm to capitalise on this old information. With the help of Hugh Thorburn, he traced Haji Wali who was now an old man. Nevertheless, he remembered the occasion, was adamant that the gold existed and that he could pinpoint the site. Typically Richard overstayed his month of authorised leave, writing to Lord Derby that he could not return to his duty until the end of May. He had been preparing to return to Trieste at the end of his month's visit, he said:

> . . . when H.M. the Viceroy favoured me with a special invitation to proceed in the frigate *Sirmá* with a guard of three officers and twenty men to visit a neighbouring part of the Arabian coast where I had ascertained the existence of gold about twenty years ago . . . we returned here [Port Suez] today having discovered, during our 16 days of travel, the ruins of 6 large mining cities, and fine specimens of gold, silver and other metals. The Land of Midian is in fact another California.[35]

Although Isabel had by now resumed her busy life – she had five pro-
fessors coaching her in languages and music, and was patron of
numerous charitable institutions caring for the aged, children and
abused animals – the loss of her uncles and brother had a lasting
effect. During Richard's absence in Arabia she was honoured by the
city for her achievements, but 'in one sense I regret [the gold medal],'
she wrote to Houghton, 'as I do not wish to have any reward here
below. I am quite changed. I have no ambition. I want only for
Richard to become a good Catholic, I want no honours or rewards of
any kind . . . We are no longer young . . . what do we want with a few
empty baubles for our remaining years?'[36] But she took her responsibilities seriously, speaking at fund-raising fêtes and dinners, and
offering inducements in the form of prizes for well-cared-for animals.
'I made my speech in Italian and spoke for nearly three-quarters of an
hour,' she recorded on one occasion.

Her doldrums vanished for a while when the young couple who
had taken over the running of the inn at Opcina (from the husband's
parents) produced a baby. The mother was only 16, knew little about
child care, and the baby became seriously ill. The child's weak crying
alerted Isabel and she took over its full-time care; 'I passed three
weeks with that child in my arms. I dressed it in English baby clothes,
fed it and doctored it till it got quite well.'[37] Isabel would have made
a good mother. After 18 years of childless marriage, she could say
equably that it was probably a blessing that they had no children ('I
have twelve nephews and nieces 6 Arundells and 6 Piggots. Quite
enough. Thank God *we* have none'),[38] for it enabled them to travel
without hindrance. But there are several extant letters in which she
bemoans the fact, especially during Richard's absences, that her home
is childless. Her affectionate letters to her many nieces and nephews,
and their testimonies after her death, reveal that she genuinely liked
children; it appears that she submerged strong maternal urges in an
extreme, protective love of animals. Richard, too, loved children. His
nephews and nieces recalled how he willingly provided 'horse-rides'
on his back; a friend remembered how he could never resist patting
the head of any small child.[39]

As Isabel's health improved, she began to worry about Richard's
continued absence (without leave), and she wrote to Houghton that
she regretted not having accompanied him 'just to smell the desert
air', but at the time of his departure she had been too depressed and

they were short of money. She agreed to Houghton's suggestion that she should write an article about Fryston for the press. The great house was no more by this time, having been destroyed in a fire the previous year, to the immense regret of the Burtons who had come to regard it almost as a second home.[40]

During his voyage Richard reviewed Cameron's book *Across Africa*;[41] he praised Cameron unreservedly, openly gratified by Cameron's paeans of praise for *Lake Regions* (a view shared, incidentally, by Charles Gordon).[42] In thanking Cameron, Richard could not resist the opportunity to rake a few public shots across the bows of James Grant and several others; 'For the last seventeen years explorers have made indiscriminate use of *Lake Regions of Central Africa*,' he wrote. 'Captain Grant, who now claims to have discovered the Victoria Nyanza, coolly took what he wanted from the book, without acknowledging its very existence. Mr Stanley ably converted it into a popular and imaginative account of the regions through which his trip lay; moreover by way of showing independence, he criticised instead of thanking its author; Mr Cooley opened a regular campaign against it.'

As Speke presciently observed, though Burton was adept at hurting others he was extremely sensitive, himself, to criticism. His nine-page response to a poor review of his *Ultima Thule* in the *Saturday Review* was brilliant, but hurt lurks beneath the cynical humour. 'There are few literary occasions more unpleasant,' he began, 'than when a friend looks up from reading his review and says to the author reviewed, "You must answer this!" We all know what to expect from those whose trade it is to throw soot from the safety of a dark corner . . . the Saturday Reviewer who on February 3, honoured me with his fierceness, has ably preserved all the traditions of a paper which rarely pretends to be written by gentlemen for gentlemen.'[43]

On his return to Trieste in June, he received a surprising letter from Charles Gordon. The two men had become regular correspondents while Gordon conducted his Nile survey, during which he opened 'the whole of the Victoria Lake to Egypt'. The Khedive, loath to lose him, had now made him Governor-General of the three territories of Sudan, Darfur and Equatorial Africa. He needed, in turn, 'to appoint an autonomous Governor to administer each area', he told Richard, particularly in Darfur where the inhabitants were mainly Islamic and spoke Arabic, 'which I do not.'

You now, I see, have £600 a year, a good climate, quiet life, good food etc, and are engaged in literary enquiries etc etc. I have no doubt that you are very comfortable, but I cannot think entirely satisfied with your present small sphere. I have therefore written to the Khedive to ask him to give you Darfur, as Governor-General, with £1,600 a year and a couple of secretaries at £300 a year each.

Darfur is *l'enfer*. The country is a vast sand plain, with but little water; the heat is very great; there is little shooting. The people consist of huge Bedawin tribes and of a settled population in the larger villages. Their previous history under the Sultan would show them fanatical . . . if you got two year's leave from H.M.'s Government you would lose nothing. You know the position of Darfur; its frontier through Wadi is only fifteen days from Lake Tchad. On the other side of Lake Tchad you come on another Sultanate, that of Bowmon, and then you near the Gulf of Guinea . . . You will do a mint of good and benefit these poor people . . . Now is the time for you to make your indelible mark in the world . . . you will be remembered in the literary world, but I would sooner be remembered in Egypt as having made Darfur . . . You [would be] Commander of Civil and Military and Finance, and have very little to do with me beyond demanding what you may want.[44]

Had this offer come from the Foreign Office, Richard almost certainly would have accepted it. But he turned down Gordon's proposal which, on the face of it, appeared to offer a well-paid opportunity for travel and further exploration. Primarily he felt the Midian gold project offered a more rewarding and independent future, but also, 'you and I are too much alike,' he wrote to Gordon. 'I could not serve under you, nor you under me. I do not look upon the Sudan as a lasting thing. I have nothing to depend upon but my salary; and I have a wife, and you have not.'[45]

Gordon did not take any long-term offence, but he was disappointed. '£1,600 or indeed £16,000, would never compensate a man for a year spent actively in Darfur,' he agreed. 'But I considered you, from your independence, one of Nature's nobility, who did not serve for money . . . "Men now seek honours, not honour." You wrote that in one of your books. Do you remember it? How true it is! I have often pirated it, and not acknowledged the author, though I believe *you* stole it.'[46]

When Gordon's offer was echoed by the Khedive on 16 September, Richard replied that while the development of Africa would always be close to his heart, he was more interested in conducting another mining expedition to the Midian to open up the gold fields for Egypt.[47] He suggested that he return to the Midian for a three-month expedition to carry out 'an exploration which will . . . promote the power and prosperity of the country'.[48]

It appears he took the Khedive's agreement for granted, for even before he sent off his reply to Egypt he had written to the F.O. advising that the Khedive had invited him to spend three months there. The work of his Consulate would not be affected, he said, for his able Vice-Consul Mr Edward Brock would take over in his absence. With Lord Salisbury's sanction the F.O. agreed, but stipulated that Brock's salary must be deducted from Richard's own. A note attached to Richard's file, when he subsequently extended the three-months authorised period to six, reads resignedly: 'There is no use asking him when he will return to Trieste – Captain Burton has always had as much leave as he liked and he is much better employed where he is than at his post.'[49]

Richard was confident that the Khedive would accept. Ismael I had overstretched his resources in his grand plan to reform Egypt educationally, culturally and economically. Under his rule Egypt had annexed the Sudan, pushed into Africa and had embarked on an ambitious civic building programme which included the Cairo Opera House (for which he commissioned Verdi to write *Aida*). Ostensibly, at least, he deplored the slave trade and therefore had the support of Great Britain. When Ismael received Burton's letter suggesting that the Midian could provide Egypt with the riches of the Californian gold fields, the Khedive saw a solution to his burgeoning economic crisis. One of his advisors subsequently replied to Richard that a sage in Egypt had experienced a vision, in which the prophet instructed him to tell the Khedive that Burton's project would bring 'great victory and glory against his enemies'.[50] Richard took this as a 'Yes'.

Since Richard was convinced that the gold fields of the Midian would make him rich, Isabel naturally believed him. She wrote to Houghton and other close friends advising them to hold on to any Egyptian investments. To Luke Ionides, the banker son-in-law of Dr Bird and a close friend of the Burtons, Richard suggested that as well as finding gold, early knowledge of a major find could enable them to make a killing in the stock market. What is now regarded as Insider Trading was not then considered a criminal act, and many commercial fortunes were built on the foundation of privileged information. Ionides agreed; Isabel was to keep him informed of progress.

> Richard left 19th October and reports well of the expedition for which he sails on November 15th. He will not get back . . . until March 15th. I go out . . . February.
>
> You will, of course, be the first to know, and before the Khedive knows. Richard thinks that Egyptian [funds] are 33 or 34 – the discovery will raise them to 40 or even 50 . . . if it is really what he expects it must be done on a large scale . . . it is your business to keep the secret of the funds, and to watch out for and catch the moment we will give you notice of, and the instant there is a rise to make use of it, and to give him a share of what you and Fitz make *by this means*. There would be lots ready to do it . . . but we want to put the profit into the hands of friends and relatives.[51]

Prior to his departure Richard had spent money with casual abandon. His personal account at the Consulate shows that in addition to a large quantity of purchases for his expedition, he bought opera glasses and a fur coat for Isabel, and sanctioned a subscription of £100 to her church. There was a bill for £468 for sundries alone; a large sum from an income of £600 per annum.[52] But he was convinced he was going to be a rich man; what did such trifles matter? He finished off a new book, *The Gold Mines of Midian*, leaving Isabel to proof it as usual, before he departed. His agreement with the Khedive was that he would be reimbursed for the expenses of the expedition, and receive 5 per cent of gross profits on the mining venture.

Isabel followed on 2 January, a day after she completed proofing and a preface for the book.[53] It was a few weeks earlier than she planned, but Houghton wrote to say it was rumoured that Richard was seriously ill in Cairo. In fact he had suffered no more than a case of the usual diarrhoea, as had most members of the expedition, and when Isabel arrived he had already gone to the Midian. She found only an instruction that she was not to join him, 'unless I could do so in proper order,' she said, finishing with a rare touch of asperity: 'It remained to be seen what *proper order* meant.'[54] But there was no way she could follow him. 'To have crossed the Red Sea in an open *sambuk* with head winds blowing, and then to fight my way across the desert alone on a camel, would have been dangerous to me and *infra-dig* for my husband's position.' She decided to wait at Suez and from there wrote to Georgiana Stisted: 'I have taken a room over-looking the Red Sea and desert towards Midian, and hope to finish my own book. What on earth Paul* is doing with Richard's *Midian* God only knows. I have written and telegraphed till I am blue in the face and telegrams cost 2s. 6d. a word . . .Your loving Aunt Zoo.'55

During her 10-week wait she visited Cairo at the personal invita-tion of the Khedive, and was received there with gratifying pomp and graciousness. She also met Richard Lyon Mitchell who was a mutual friend of Edgar Larking (son of Richard's old friend John Larking). The two young men had spent time with Richard before the expedition departed and Mitchell escorted Isabel about the city. The two corresponded for some time afterwards, but it is probable that Mitchell did not share with her the incident described in his diary when Richard had taken him on a tour of what he called 'his old haunts', the stews in the north-east parts of Cairo between Babel Sharifeh and the old ruined Mosque of El Hakim. Mitchell recorded that Burton carried as protection against attack 'an iron bar which looked like a walking stick without a handle. He said [it] kept his biceps and arms in good order.'

One evening the conversation turned to the *Arabian Nights* and Mitchell asked Richard about his translation. Richard had evidently let it be known for some years that he was translating the stories into English and would one day publish them privately. This conversation, dated in Mitchell's diary, proves that Richard was already working on the *Nights* (an important point which will become relevant later). 'People had begun to think that this work might not appear at all – even if privately printed. Years had passed and it was rumoured that Burton had given up the idea. In reply he told me that it would most certainly appear and that it was well advanced but that he could say no more at present.'56

On her return from Cairo Isabel made the acquaintance of Charles Gordon who, having heard of her presence in Suez, went there espe-cially to meet her. In the week that followed, the two became firm

*Kegan Paul, Publisher.

friends and Gordon became one of Isabel's greatest admirers; she thought him 'very eccentric but very charming'. He did his best to persuade her that Richard was wasting his time in the Midian looking for gold, and that he should accept the position of Governor of Darfur. He said he would increase his offer to £3,000. Isabel 'scoffed' at him, saying that after Richard found gold he would spend that sum on gloves, alone.[57] At last, on 20 April, a week after Gordon's departure, she received a note from Richard who was in sight of the port. She hurried to meet him, finding him ill and tired, and immensely disappointed to have missed meeting Gordon.

The Khedive, expecting good news, sent a special train to meet Richard. It was stocked with champagne and delicious delicacies. Their departure from Suez was reported as having caused a sensation:

> His name is as well known among the Egyptians as if he had passed all his days amongst them. Pashas and other great personages from Europe are continually passing to and fro almost unheeded. How different . . . when it became known that Haji Abdullah was leaving for Cairo! The platform was crowded with Europeans and natives . . . 'that wonderful man' was at Suez on his return from the exploring trip to Midian . . .[58]

Burton's expedition had explored, surveyed and mapped a 600-mile stretch of northern Midian. Many important archaeological sites, the remains of 18 cities and 20 settlements were identified, and all of the 40 ancient sites known about by mediaeval geographers. They brought back ancient artifacts and bones, and prehistoric shells, and flora, fauna and insect specimens. They proved the existence of valuable minerals: sulphur, salt and saltpetre and 'vast deposits of gypsum' (had Burton being prospecting for oil he would have earned the fortune he was seeking).[59] They found agates and turquoise. But they did not find gold, at least not in the quantities that Richard was convinced existed in the alluvial sands. The expedition brought back 25 tons of sample rocks for metallurgical analysis, selected by George Marie, the French geologist and mining engineer appointed to the project by the Egyptian Government. Marie was confident they would prove the existence of silver.

The presence of silver rather than gold would, incidentally, have been most pleasing to Richard. He had a curious passion for the metal, declaring that it had some unexplained influence on him. He would 'put florins on his eyes if they ached from over reading or study; he would apply them to his pains where he had gout.' Later, when he made money from the *Arabian Nights*, 'everything he bought was silver,' Isabel said. 'A heavy six-guinea knob of silver to a huge stick, his *toilette* box, his pencil case, his snuff box, his roll to put his pens and pencils in, everything was silver. His theory was that every man has some metal which affects his illness, and [he] had found his.'[60]

The couple returned to Trieste on 10 May. Richard was tired after the heat and hard work of his expedition, and weary of 'Cairo's intrigues, [and] silly reports of the envious'. Though he professed to dislike Trieste he wrote that he was grateful for the calm, cool and peaceful home in which 'friendly faces smiled a welcome.'[61]

He began his first Midian explorations with almost boyish enthusiasm. 'At last! Once more it is my fate to escape the prison-life of Europe, and to refresh body and mind by studying Nature in her noblest and most admirable form – the Nude . . . to enjoy a glimpse of the glorious Desert, to inhale the sweet pure breath of translucent skies . . .'[62] By the end of his second expedition, sickness, tiredness and a subconscious sense of failure had reduced his euphoric descriptions of the desert to a jaundiced appraisal. The sand dunes now became 'huge rubbish heaps', the valleys 'mere dust-shunts that shoot out their rubbish, stones, gravel and sand in a solid flow, like discharges of lava.' This he said, was the harsh reality of what at first 'appears a scene in fairyland'.[63]

Despite the increasing likelihood of war in Eastern Europe, he wrote within weeks to the F.O. requesting two months' leave to return to London to have his rock samples analysed and to attend to urgent private affairs. The couple left for London on July 7 before receiving a reply, evidently still convinced that Richard's work in the Midian would make their fortune and that they no longer needed to placate the minions at the Foreign Office.

31

LENGTHENING SHADOWS
1879–1880

They lived as they always did in London, staying initially with Isabel's father in Montagu Place, and drawing on their huge circle of friends for entertainment. In August they paid a third visit to Ireland. Having spent a week at Malahide Castle, they then went to Dublin where Richard gave three lectures on the Midian to the British Association. While there he heard again from Charles Gordon, who wrote to increase his offer of £1,600 to £5,000.[1] 'Do something to help me,' Gordon pleaded, 'you would lift a burden off my shoulders . . . I am in a deplorable state. I have a nasty revolt of Slandralus at Bahr Gazelle . . . I am hard at work against the slave caravans; we have caught fifteen in two months and I hope by a few judicious hangings to stop their work. I hanged a man the other day for making a eunuch without HH's leave.'[2] Richard was still convinced that his discoveries in the Midian would make them rich; therefore he refused, saying that his reasons had not changed and that he felt the existing state of affairs in the Sudan 'could not last'.

On 13 August as the Burtons left Dublin on the Belfast train, they found they were sharing a compartment with Henry Irving and Bram Stoker. Irving was already acquainted with Richard and Isabel; mistakenly he assumed Stoker also knew them and neglected to introduce them. Stoker was fascinated with this unusual couple. 'The lady was a big, handsome, blonde woman, clever-looking and capable. But the man riveted my attention. He was dark and forceful, and masterful, and ruthless. I have never seen so iron a countenance.' After they left the train, Stoker asked Irving. 'Who was that man?' Hesitating for a minute, Irving asked, 'Tell me why you want to know?' 'Because I never saw anyone like him. He is steel and would go through you like a sword.' 'You are right!' was the answer. 'That is Burton – Captain Burton who went to Mecca.'[3]

Back in England the Burtons embarked on a round of visits, spending time at the homes of Lord Derby, Lord Gerard, Lord Beaumont, Lord Houghton and (through an introduction by Houghton) Lord Salisbury, where they met Disraeli.[4] When they returned to London both were unwell, Richard suffering from 'flying gout' and Isabel 'inflammation of one kidney and womb', but they settled down to work on their respective literary projects and to prepare for a return to Egypt and the Midian once the results of the assays became available.

Richard had almost completed his second book on the Midian (*The Land of Midian (Revisited)*), and was working to complete the first canto of his epic translation of Camoens' *Os Lusiads*, and what was arguably his finest poetry, *The Kasìdah of Haji Abdul El-Ynezdi*, haunting and often self-revealing:

> The hour is nigh; the waning queen walks forth to rule the later night,
> Crowned with the sparkle of a star, and throned on orb of ashen light,
> The wolf-tail sweeps the paling East to leave a deeper gloom behind.
> And dawn uprears her shining head, sighing with semblance of a wind . . .
>
> Do what thy manhood bids thee do, from none but self expect applause,
> He noblest lives and noblest dies who makes and keeps his self-made laws
> All other life is living death, a world where none but phantoms dwell,
> A breath, a wind, a sound, a voice, a tinkling of the camel-bell.

The Kasìdah, which has been compared with Edward Fitzgerald's

Rubaiyat of Omar Khayyám, made a slow start and sold only 100 copies before the remainder were returned to him by its publisher.[5] Some years later it became sought after and went through many reprints. Although it never achieved the success of Fitzgerald's poem, it is still in print in a number of editions.

For the first time in almost three years they met Swinburne, after Isabel badgered him into attending a dinner party later described by Alice Bird. Those present, she wrote, included 'Swinburne, Captain Richard Burton and his wife Isabel, four other friends, my brother Dr George Bird and myself. Swinburne talked brilliantly on a variety of subjects but he looked ill and worn and older . . . he had a haggard expression as if his nerves were out of tune.'[6]

'What is the matter with Swinburne?' Isabel asked Houghton afterwards in a letter, continuing:

> I don't think that when we are millionaires, as we are going to be you know in about 2 years, that I shall ever court the fashionable world. We shall lead the same life, with a steam yacht, and a pied-a-terre in London . . . we shall collect around us an entourage which will be perfection; old friends, and everybody will be somebody worth knowing. I mean to have a *divàn* . . . where you will be one of the cherished *intimes* . . . It is a pleasant dream to look forward to. Dick has worked 36 years and I have helped him now 18 years. It is time we had something for it, & I think these Midian Mines are going to prove our reward.[7]

The assay report, however, was disappointing; the samples submitted for analysis contained evidence of minerals, but at best only 2 oz of silver per ton, with minute traces of gold. It was too low to make the cost of extraction a viable proposition, the assayist thought, but enough to justify further exploration.[8] He suggested that the samples brought back were probably those rejected by ancient miners, and left lying about.[9]

Bitterly disappointed, and fuming at the wasted time and expense, Richard lashed out at George Marie. 'An engineer is not supposed to be a mineralogist,' he wrote, 'all the same it is regrettable to the last degree . . . during the two Khedive Expeditions it was your duty to collect up the specimens not mine.'[10] In his report to the F.O. Richard again blamed Marie who, he said, had acted with 'marvellous carelessness' in searching for 'tailings' instead of alluvial gold as Californian prospectors did.[11] An objective reader might be forgiven for enquiring why, if Richard was aware of this, he did not collect his own samples. But he was reluctant to let go of a dream and wrote to the Khedive, pointing out that the ancient miners had worked only 40 feet deep; 'with modern appliances 1,000 or 1,200 would be feasible,' he said.[12] He proposed mining the area himself, as a concession, in return for 12 per cent of the profits.

He then wrote to Salisbury requesting another six months' leave to go to Midian during the winter of 1878–79. 'As regards the winter of 1879–80, I will again apply to your Lordship, in case my services are, as I expect they will be, required by the Mines.' It is hardly surprising that this request raised hackles at the F.O. At the beginning of his present leave it had been noted that in the previous four years, 'Captain Burton has been at his post about sixteen months.' This is where the time the couple spent socialising paid off. Lord Salisbury, who a few years earlier had pointedly 'cut' Richard at Trieste, was now an ally. 'Grant this extension but add that Lord Salisbury trusts he will be able to return to his post at the end of that time,' was the laconic response. Memoranda continued to fly about. 'I hardly see why the Midian gold digging business should be made an excuse for a perpetual absence from his posts. If it is true, as he says with characteristic modesty, that he is the only man who can do what is required there, there are many men more fitted than he is to be Consul at Trieste,' one official noted.[13] One document in Burton's file reads:

The reason why Captain B has always had so much leave is that successive Secs. of State have always granted as much as he asked for, but I have never known the reason for this unvarying compliance. I can suggest the following reasons for again granting the application.
1. That he is of no particular use at Trieste.
2. That the V. Consul Mr Brock always does the work very well during [Burton's] absence, and also I believe when he is at Trieste.
3. That the discovery of the mines would be of great value to Egypt at the moment and that Captn B's services wd. doubtless be specially useful for that purpose.
4. That Captn B. and Mrs B. are so well known to a great many

people in this country, and have the ear of the Press and the Public, and they would make a tremendous outcry if the request were refused.
[In a different hand]
For all which excellent reasons, grant the request. Salisbury.

In the event the Khedive ignored Richard's proposals, and his chancellor refused to reimburse his claim for £525-worth of expenses incurred during the previous expedition. Representing almost a year's salary, this might have been a financial disaster for the Burtons, who lived very much up to and beyond their annual income. However, fate extended a helping hand when Richard's uncle by marriage (to Aunt Georgina), Robert Bagshaw, died and left him some money.[14]

Bagshaw was not the only death at that time. Richard's 30-year-old niece Maria 'Minnie' Stisted died suddenly, of what was thought to be only a minor illness. Isabel was in Brighton when she heard, having travelled there at the request of Ouida to deliver a lecture to the Anti-Vivisection League. 'My poor darling Georgie,' she wrote to Georgiana, 'I grieve for you with all my heart . . . Dick feels Minnie's death fearfully . . . He telegraphed [the news] and writes every day about it. I don't think he is in a state of health to bear many shocks just now, he is so frightfully nervous. He so little expected it . . . so it has come like a sledge-hammer upon him.'

This letter, intended only to offer sympathy and comfort, caused deep offence in a staunchly Protestant household. 'I can only pray for you with all my heart,' Isabel continued, 'as I did at communion this morning, and have masses said to create another gem upon Minnie's crown. God . . . has taken the angel of your house, as He always does . . . there is some change about to take place and some work or new thing you have to do in which Minnie was not to be . . . I feel what a poor letter this is but my heart is full, and I do not know how to express myself. Your attached and sympathising Aunt Zoo.'[15]

Maria Stisted, who had been cold towards Isabel for many years because of her manifest Catholicism, was outraged that Isabel would dare to have Catholic masses said for her dead daughter. All the natural anger she felt about young Maria's death was henceforward directed at Isabel. And from this date onwards it appears that Georgiana, too, was alienated. Richard dedicated his next book, *The Land of the Midian*, to the memory of Maria, his 'much loved niece'.

Isabel also lost a relative. One evening an owl flew in the window and perched on a table in front of Lord Arundell. 'There's an Arundell dead,' he said. 'I'm afraid it's Henry [Isabel's father].'[16] Within the hour his wife Theresa was found dead in her bed. Both Richard and Isabel were fascinated with incidents of this sort. A few weeks later Isabel discarded her deep mourning clothes for the grand wedding of a Gerard cousin, when her uncle presented her with a sweeping blue velvet gown and coronet for the occasion. From there the Burtons were to go on to Arundell Castle for Christmas, but first Richard had to address the National Association of Spiritualists.

This engagement had come about after Richard's letter to *The Times* in November 1876 during a spate of correspondence regarding mediums. He wrote then that his observations over twenty years had convinced him that extra-sensory perception was possible. He had personally experienced on numerous occasions a force or power which he could not understand, he said. But he did not believe that humans could summon spirits at will, or that the dead could be communicated with at all. 'I know nothing of what is absurdly called Spiritualism,' he concluded, 'I must therefore be content to be a Spiritualist without the spirits.'

In his speech he said he accepted that inexplicable phenomena occurred, but felt that such experiences resulted from some as yet unexplained natural sense; 'a force of will', which enabled humans to sense what they could not feel, hear, see and taste, not a supernatural force. 'St Paul introduced into Christendom the threefold idea of a natural body, which could become a glorified body, of a soul and of a spirit. Personally,' he said, 'I ignore the existence of soul and spirit, feeling no want of a self within a self, an I within an I.' He was a follower of Darwin, 'I cannot but hold to the Apes.'

He discussed the spiritualism practised in the East which, he said, he had explained in his book *Vikram and the Vampire, or Tales of Hindu Devilry*. These 'so-called supernaturalisms . . . show the terrible "training", the ascetic tortures, whereby men lose their senses, or attain the highest powers of "magic" . . . commanding nature by mastering the force, whatever it may be, here called zoo-electric, which conquers and controls . . . matter.'[17]

When he sat down the audience were asked to comment. They were momentarily stunned, trying to connect Burton's brilliant and wide-roving rhetoric with the spiritualism of table-rapping and hugely

popular Ouija-board parties. Since there were no immediate
responses, Isabel asked to be allowed to comment. Speaking off the
cuff from notes she had made during Richard's ovation, she reminded
the audience good-naturedly that her husband's beliefs in 'the force'
did not make him a spiritualist in the generally accepted sense.
Spiritualism as practised in England was quite different, she pointed
out, 'to that practised in the East'. She too had experienced strange
phenomena, she said, but though it was new to England, 'it is as old
as time in the Eastern countries, I think we are receiving it wrongly.
When handled by men of science . . . it will rank very high. Hailed
. . . as a new religion by people who are not organised for it, by
people who are wildly, earnestly seeking the truth [about God] . . . it
can only act as a decoy to a crowd of sensation seekers, who yearn to
see a ghost as they would go to a pantomime. This can only weaken
and degrade it, and distract attention from its true object; Science.'
Ironically, though Isabel disparaged spiritualism, she believed she had
a guardian angel who helped her at such times as her night-time
gallop through the Anti-Lebanon.[18]

Richard responded humorously, saying, 'A man's wife knows, perhaps, too much about him.' And encouraged by this, the audience
began a vigorous debate in which Richard had the final word.
'Spiritualism . . . seems to have let in a hurricane of swindling. It has
done . . . good work; it has proved that the spirit is essentially material i.e. subject to the five (or six) senses . . . [but] the ghost business
is shown to be a peculiarity of mediumistic organisation . . . Soul is
not a thing but a state of things.'[19]

In February 1879 Isabel's second book, *A.E.I.: Arabia, Egypt and
India,* was published. In essence an account of their tour of India,
it includes long political dialogues, written by Richard[20] but purporting to be Isabel's views, on the 'partition of Turkey'. The
publisher threw a glitzy launch party attended by Lord Houghton,
Henry Irving and Bram Stoker which lasted until 5 a.m. Bram Stoker
recalled Richard talking about three projects upon which he was
working, 'the translation of *Arabian Nights*, the metrical translation
of *Camoens*, and the *Book of the Sword* . . . all works of vast magnitude and requiring endless research.' Stoker wrote his recollections
from his diary entries and was quite specific about his conversation
with Burton that night. Later, enemies would accuse Richard of
having only begun working on his version of the *Nights* in 1884, and

of cribbing some of his translations. Along with Mitchell's testimony in Cairo, Stoker's evidence proves that Burton was working on the *Nights* many years earlier.

Stoker also recalled how, at Isabel's launch party, Burton spoke vividly and thrillingly about his adventures, 'to this day I can seem to hear the deep vibration of his voice,' Stoker wrote a quarter of a century later:

> As he talked, fancy seemed to run riot in its alluring power and the whole world of thought seemed to flame with gorgeous colour. Burton *knew* the east. Its brilliant dawns and sunsets; its rich tropic vegetation and its arid fiery deserts; its cool dark mosques and temples; its crowded bazaars; its narrow streets; its windows guarded for outlooking and from in-looking eyes; the swagger and pride of its passionate men; the mysteries of its veiled women; its romances; its beauty; its horrors.

Richard's strong sense of humour and readiness to laugh impressed him, 'Burton's face seemed to lengthen when he laughed; the upper lip rising instinctively and showing the right canine tooth. This was always characteristic of his enjoyment.' Stoker saw the canine appear on another occasion when over dinner he queried – as so many others had done – the rumoured murder during the pilgrimage to Mecca. Richard smiled, the scar twisting the symmetry of his features. 'He said it was quite true, "The desert has its own laws, and there . . . to kill is a small offence. In any case what could I do? it had to be his life or mine!". As he spoke the upper lip rose and his canine tooth showed its full length like the gleam of a dagger.'[21]

The Burtons rounded off their visit to England with a great flurry of parties and visits. Isabel attended a 'drawing room' at the Palace and they threw dinner parties for all their friends, one of which was a masquerade dinner at which Richard dressed as 'an Austrian miner' and Isabel was 'Carmen'. It is easy to see how Richard had become the subject of rumour and conjecture. A fellow-guest at one of the Burtons' dinner parties recalled how Richard held the large table spellbound with a tale of how he was once 'shipwrecked in the Red Sea . . . remote from all human habitation'.

After describing how they had all suffered from pangs of hunger and the wolfish glances they began to cast on each other . . . as the days wore on . . . dropping his voice to a whisper, almost under his breath, he added: 'The cabin boy was young and fat, and looked very tender, and on him more than any other such looks were cast, until ——' Here he paused, looked around at the strained and startled faces of his audience in which horror was depicted, and then abruptly concluded as though dismissing a disagreeable memory; 'But these are not stories to be told at a cheerful dinner party in a Christian country, and I had best say no more.' . . . Burton told me he was thoroughly convinced by the looks cast upon him by the younger ladies, that they believed he and his tough comrades . . . had roasted and eaten that cabin boy . . .[22]

This need to shock never left Richard. He told an American journalist, G.W. Smalley, that he received his facial scar 'from the hand of a jealous husband'. 'On this occasion,' said Smalley, Isabel was 'frankly delighted'. On another evening Smalley arrived late at a noisy stag 'smoking party' and almost fell over Richard who was sitting on the stairs with a book and pencil in his hand, 'indifferent to everything around him'.

When I spoke to him he woke up as if from a dream with the dazed air of one not quite sure where he is. I asked him what he was reading. It proved to be Camoens and he told me he was translating [it]. It seemed an odd place for such work and I said so. 'Oh', answered Burton, 'I can read or write anywhere . . . I always carry Camoens about with me . . .' He added with a kind of cynical grin . . ., 'You will find plenty of dull people in the rooms above . . . I can't waste time . . .'[23]

In mid-April 1879 Richard left to travel to Trieste via Hamburg where he had arranged to meet a Mr Schweinfurther, a metallurgist and mining expert.[24] He planned to take three weeks over the journey and Isabel, who was unwell, decided to stay in London until the end of April and return to Trieste directly, via Paris. They agreed to meet in Trieste on 5 May. Richard arrived early; 'I expect my wife from Paris tomorrow,' he wrote to Grattan Geary.[25] Isabel, however, was late. While rushing to carry out a commission for Richard in Paris, the high heels of her boots slipped on some polished stairs and she fell from top to bottom with one leg doubled up under her. She was picked up unconscious and put to bed. Her first words were, 'Don't send the carriage away. I must get my work done . . .' As she attempted to rise she fainted again. Her boot had to be cut off, for the leg was so black and swollen that the doctor thought it was broken, but it turned out to be a badly sprained leg and a back injury.

Advised to spend six weeks in bed, she had her leg bound up and four days later in great pain set off for Trieste on a slow train with no sleeping compartments. A concerned Richard met her train at Trieste and she was carried home and put to bed. His sweetness helped her to bear the distress of a long convalescence, but she was never to make a permanent recovery. Isabel had always taken robust good health and strong nerves for granted 'and supposed everybody had them . . . but I began to learn what suffering was from this date.' [26] Richard too was experiencing a good deal of painful gout which prevented him walking for any distance. As soon as she was able to travel they went to Baden-Baden, where they spent a month at the spa receiving treatment. The parallel between their lives and those of Richard's parents, a lifestyle he had mocked mercilessly as a youth, is inescapable.

Sometimes they visited Graz and nearby Vienna where Richard conducted research for his treatise on the Sword, and Römerbad where an early form of *jacuzzi* was used to treat back injuries. Despite ill-health, it was a tender and happy time for them at a personal level. Richard made a number of sketches, often including himself and Isabel as two tiny figures against panoramic backgrounds. One, which shows them picnicking on a lake shore promontory amidst spectacular mountain scenery, he titled: 'Músavík Bay from Össur (Hungry Hounds Head)'.[27]

While on this journey they met and became friends with a couple who later moved to Trieste, M. and Mme Gutmanstal de Benvenuti. Madame was an amateur portrait artist and began work on a portrait of Richard which was later exhibited at the Grosvenor Gallery in London. By the time they returned to Trieste Isabel was mobile, but she was never again entirely free from pain. Richard was fit enough to resume fencing and long walks. 'Perhaps [I] have now got over what the feminines call "Change of Life",' he wrote to Clement Markham. 'At any rate I can now walk a whole day long.'[28]

In December 1879 Richard took advantage of the postponed six-month leave he had been granted and sailed for Egypt, where he hoped to talk the Khedive into granting the mining concession and reimbursing his £525. It was agreed that if Isabel thought they could afford it, and felt well enough, she was to follow him. On both counts this appeared doubtful, and she did not look forward to the prospect of waking up alone on Christmas morning. 'Darling Dick started on Friday 5th., in high spirits,' Isabel wrote to Georgiana Stisted. 'My position is singular, no child, no relative, and all new servants.' She had just sent off her latest manuscript, she said; it was a book on adventures in India, called *Aunt Puss's Christmas Book for Boys*.[29] It is for boys from 12 to 16, culled from ten volumes: Dick's three books on Sind, his *Goa, Vikram, Bayonet and Sword Exercise*, and my *A.E.I.*' Apart from earning some money, she hoped it might revive interest in Richard's earlier works. *The Christmas Book* was never published.[30]

Isabel was still experiencing pain and was generally unwell, but her London doctor (consulted by mail), clearly believed stress to be responsible for some of her symptoms. He prescribed a course of medication (the ingredients of which included zinc, quinine, nut reomic, acid and belladonna) but strongly recommended:

> exercise without fatigue, amusement without excitement; absence of worry, and *absence of work which has to be done against time* will do more to restore your overworked nervous system than all the medicines in the Pharmacophia. Plain simple food . . . only light wines . . . early to bed. I am sorry you have to go to Egypt so soon. The heat and fatigue are not good for you. Delay departure as long as you can, and do all you can in the meantime to restore your strength.[31]

By February she could not move without pain, and could not sleep, even with drugs. Her local doctor advised her to consult a chiropractor, which suggests that the pain was due to sciatica resulting from her fall in Paris. She cabled Richard and he replied by return ordering her to cancel plans to join him in Egypt: 'go at once to Hutton the bonesetter in London.'

Richard had been in Egypt over two months by this time and had made no progress. Indeed, he would come away empty-handed after almost six months. Ismael Pasha abdicated in June 1879; he left in his private yacht for a palace on the Bosphorus after stripping the

Egyptian treasury of £3 million. His son Tewfik, inheriting the title and a bankrupt exchequer, felt no obligation to carry out his father's promises and ignored Richard's requests for a personal audience, to the latter's 'impotent rage and disgust'.

As one might expect, Richard did not spend all his time waiting at the palace kicking his heels. He made friends with William Robertson Smith, the Scottish biblical-archaeologist and philologist, who was in Egypt researching ancient texts.[32] In April the two men made an exploration of the ruins around the El Faiyum oasis and Wadi Natrun, north-west of Cairo, and while doing so stumbled upon incontrovertible evidence of a flourishing trade in slaves. The British Government believed the slave trade had been stamped out in Egypt by Gordon's determined efforts, especially following the fall in demand occasioned by the American Civil War. But in a report to the Foreign Office, Richard estimated that some two-thirds of the population of Darfur had been carried off into slavery. 'Men, women, children and babes in arms forming regular caravans . . . are driven to the Natron Lakes. If the adults refuse to walk they are beaten; and as a last resource in sickness, they are tied on the camels' backs . . . we were shown the sweet-water pools . . . where they are halted to rest and recruit [strength] before being smuggled one by one into the capital . . . we heard that the last convoy of 1,880 had passed in March.'

As well as the general trade in black slaves from the Sudan, Richard advised, there was a thriving luxury trade in white Circassian and also Nubian girls, destined for *harems*. A 'beauty' commanded £40–£50, others £12–£15. But perhaps even worse than this was the detestable trade in eunuchs. 'Not less than eight thousand of these unfortunates are annually imported into Arabia, Egypt and Turkey.' He explained that because of the official nature of his report he had censored the most explicit descriptions of his findings for the sake of decency, but even so, 'it makes the blood run cold. The subjects range between four and ten; if this operation be performed on older boys, they seldom survive. At the age of ten the loss may be seventy per cent, and even in the case of younger children about one-fourth, to state a low figure, die from the razor. By this murderous operation, boys who would fetch £5 to £10 rise in value to £25 and £80.'[33]

In a footnote to his great treatise on sex in *Supplemental Nights*, printed in 1886 for private circulation, Richard described the operation suppressed in his report. 'The parts are swept off by a single cut of the razor, a tube (tin or wooden) is set in the urethra, the wound is cauterised with boiling oil, and the patient is put in a fresh dung hill. His diet is milk and if under puberty, he often survives.'[34]

His letter accompanying the report suggests he should be given 'a temporary appointment in the Red Sea as Slave Commissioner':

> I want a salary of from £1600 to £2000 a year (£1600 would do if allowed to keep Trieste on half-pay, £350 per annum), the use of a gun boat, and a roving commission independent of the Consul-General of Egypt, but to act in concert with a consul (such as young Wylde) appointed to the Soudan . . . Gordon Pasha has long wished to recommend me for this work . . . I should like to keep Trieste to fall back on when my work is done, and as a home for my wife when she cannot be with me.[35]

On the evening of the day Richard wrote this, he was viciously mugged by a gang of nine men while returning to his hotel after dining out. Struck over the head with a heavy weapon from behind, he was dazed but managed to inflict some damage with his fists and iron bar before his assailants ran off. The motive was not robbery; his watch, chain and purse were untouched. Injured and ill, he took the first steamer for Trieste.

Isabel's long course of treatment by Dr Sutton succeeded in giving her some relief from the pain in her back and legs. Sutton referred her to a gynaecologist for severe menstrual pain and menorrhagia, and a non-malignant fibroid tumour in the right ovary was diagnosed.[36] Her convalescence in London was enlivened by regular visits from Charles Gordon, who not only wrote her regular, erudite and amusing letters[37] but visited her bedside to amuse the invalid. On the last of these visits, which was on 15 April 1880, she recalled thirteen years later,

> he asked me if I knew the origin of the 'Union Jack', and he sat down on my hearth-rug before the fire, cross-legged, with a bit of paper and a pair of scissors, and he made me three or four Union-Jacks, of which I pasted one into my journal of that day . . . I never saw him again.[38]

Until his horrific and heroic death in Khartoum in 1885 Gordon (by then General Gordon) continued to write regularly to Richard. But he also wrote long letters, quite separately, to Isabel. She maintained a lively personal correspondence with statesmen, academics, historians and writers, in addition to personalities already mentioned. The Lords Salisbury, Clarendon, Beaconsfield and Derby, and the statesman and entrepreneur W.H. Smith are only a few of the men who recognised in Isabel an ability which, since her death, it has became fashionable to disclaim. This came about following Burton's death when members of the Bohemian movement turned against her almost to a man, after she made it known that she had burned some of her husband's unpublished manuscripts. Even Swinburne, who for years was a devoted and admiring friend,[39] joined the wolf-pack. Subsequently, Burton biographers have painted her as an essentially irresponsible, prim and foolish woman. But the letters among her papers are not those which men of character and influence write to a woman merely out of social obligation. They are erudite discussions on important political subjects, which appear to invite, and respect, her opinions.

Isabel left England dispirited by an unusually cold spring, and disappointed at having failed to get Richard's name on the retirement honours list when Beaconsfield's government fell.[40] She arrived in Trieste literally hours before Richard's return from Egypt on 29 May 1879. He had not told her about the mugging and she was shocked, when he disembarked, to see his condition. He was not only still suffering severe headaches (he feared he might have meningitis), cuts and bruises, but his gout had flared up and he could hardly walk. She had him carried up to Opcina where she nursed him back to health. In July they went to the spa at Malfalcone, and then on through the Tyrol to Munich, and to Oberammergau for the Passion Play in August.[41]

Even in serious descriptions, one finds evidence of the laughter always present between the Burtons, it was the lubricating oil to the machinery of their marriage. In her book on the Passion Play Isabel describes how, because Oberammergau was crowded with tourists, they were lucky to find two rooms in a private house kept by an old woman. 'She always had some excuse for not making our beds, so we used to have to do our rooms ourselves. The second day I came in tired and scolded her, and she replied that "she was not used to people who required so much luxury," which set us laughing.'[42]

Isabel produced a small book on the play which included

surprisingly good descriptions of scenery, travel details and costs. Richard also wrote about his impressions. 'I'm writing a realistic account for the Spiritualists and comparing it with Meccah drama,'[43] he told Houghton. Richard's essay was turned into a pamphlet, *A Glance at the Passion Play*, in 1881; he initially wanted the two accounts to be published together as *Ober-Ammergau as Seen by Four Eyes*, but Isabel's manuscript remained unpublished until 1900.

Knowing that Houghton also planned to visit Oberammergau, the Burtons had been disappointed to miss him by only a few days in Munich. 'I wanted so much to speak to you about the Lusiads,' Richard mourned. The first canto, and the episode 'Ignez de Castro' (Richard's favourite) was almost ready for publication. 'I wish . . . that you would review it, as you are one of the half dozen capable of understanding it. Far ahead of the unhappy British Public.'[44] This offhand statement underlines what is already obvious. Burton wrote for pleasure as an academic; he was not commercially motivated as was Isabel. The scholarship he devoted to his translations of Camoens was immense, even though he knew that its likely readership was at best a limited one.

The *Lusiads* was a project on which Richard had worked, intermittently, since 1847. He had adopted Camoens as a role-model and even referred to him as 'my Master', having become enchanted by the romance of the story as a young subaltern in Goa. Camoens lived c.1524–1579 and had an exuberant, carefree youth at the brilliant Portuguese court. A great doomed love affair with the Queen's maid of honour, Caterina de Ataide, made it necessary for him to leave home to seek his fortune, and twenty years of adventurous wanderings in the East Indies – which included perilous voyages, shipwrecks, debts, fights, imprisonment, and a passionate affair with a beautiful Chinese girl – followed. News of Caterina's death caused a great depression which put an end to his ambitions, but his poem based on the life of Vasco da Gama, vibrant with patriotic pride, became the national epic of Portugal. He died a pauper, from plague, in his mother's arms.

'As soon as the world gets home and snuggled down for the winter,' Richard continued, to Houghton,[45] 'I'll send you [a] printed account of my last visit to Egypt and the proceedings of that poxy little Jew Riaz Pasha . . . A highly literate person is writing to you, so I shut up.' In Burton's letters every word counts, and one feels the intellectual and physical power of the man in the construction of his sentences. He writes as he speaks. His microscopic and often crabbed writing is extraordinarily difficult to read until familiarity enables one to break the code. The inability to decipher – or the mistranscription of – a single word will often change the sense of an entire letter.

Isabel was more verbose, chattier, more revealing of their lifestyle and relationship. Her handwriting is large, strong, confident, well formed. Her affection and open friendship for Houghton are clearly evident in the letter which accompanied Richard's on this occasion. 'We have had a bad run of luck for two years . . . I had a model publisher [for *Book for Boys*] and Dick a model miner [George Marie] who has turned out equally bad. We spoiled them by inviting them to dinner and now if we write on business the first threatens to have brain fever, and the latter threatens Dick to have a fit.' She suspected them both, she said, of being alcoholics.[46]

But there is no denying that Isabel's natural exuberance often led her to act impulsively without thinking things through. Like Richard she was sensitive to criticism of her literary work, yet she could not resist criticising others and when Georgiana Stisted published a 3-volume novel called *A Fireside King*[47] (which sank without trace, having been published by Tinsley as a favour to Richard),[48] Isabel was the first to offer advice. Her own two highly successful books were non-fiction, but she was working on a 'gothic' novel of her own and had worked on the translation of *Irecema* with Richard.[49] Richard's amused, but fond, referral to her as 'a highly literate person' was probably how Isabel had come to regard herself. 'Of course I recognised your father, Minnie and many others,' she wrote helpfully to Georgiana,

but you should never let your heroine die so miserably, because your reader goes away with a void in his heart, and you must *never* put all your repugnance in the first volume, for you choke off your reader . . . You don't mind me telling you the truth, do you, because I hope you will write another, and if you like you may stand in the first class of novelists and make money . . . I read all the reviews that fell in my way, but though some were spiteful that need not discourage . . . Believe me, your affectionate, Zookins.[50]

Georgiana, as it happens, did mind. In fact her book had been much admired by her friends and she deeply resented 'Zookins' patronising comments. The small goodwill she had left for Isabel disintegrated, and she went over entirely to her mother's camp.

By 1880 the Burtons appear to have reached some form of haven. They had always been happy together, but previously Richard had relentlessly placed his travel and work before domestic considerations. Isabel accepted this, but she wrote of the years 1880–1882:

> I can never remember to have had a more peaceful and happy time . . . we led a Darby and Joan life . . . We did all the six volumes of Camoens. He translating, I helping him and correcting. I wrote the little sonnet for him,[51] my preface, and the Glossary, and his *Reviewers Reviewed*. He was quite upset about the Glossary . . . He had used archaic words, which belonged to Chaucer and Spencer [and] said, 'Do you mean to say that they won't understand me?' [And] when I produced my glossary of three hundred and fourteen words, he said, 'You are never going to insult the English Public with that?'

Richard published the Camoens series with the by-line 'Englished by Richard F. Burton'. He stated in the Preface that he had followed Camoens' own eclectic style, which seemed to him 'necessary when translating a poet older than Shakespeare'.[52] Isabel said that only a handful of people would understand his use of Chaucerian English (by which she meant his use of words such as *fere, hythe, targe, shend* and *wox*). And she argued that while reviewers might pretend they did understand, and would deprecate the glossary, nevertheless they would use it and be grateful for it. She was right. Even with the glossary Richard was criticised for his use of archaic terminology, and a welter of foreign phrases, both in his Camoens publications and in his *Kasìdah*.

One reviewer thought the work 'very prolix, and often exceedingly dull, the epithets tiresome and the machinery cumbrous'.[53] Even his friends complained; one wrote, '"Wox" made me shudder! If you give more specimens do be good and sparing of the "pights", "ceres" and "woxes".'[54] But Lallah Bird was more flattering about the two volumes that followed, in December 1884.

> I found them one afternoon when I came home pining for something nice to read . . . they look so pretty and their green covers

make a spring time in the room [pale green covers with gilded impress]. How mortally sad Camoens is, '*Ah me! How long the longsome lengthens year by year*' . . . How wonderfully you have done the three lines: *Who hath what he may tyne?/He only fear can feel/But histe the mortal soul can tyne no more . . .*' Perhaps Shakespeare knew this when he wrote: '*I joy to have what I so fear to lose.*' At any rate they had the same idea. All women must like Camoens as a lover. He understood the meaning of real surren-der . . . the language is as sweet as the thoughts . . . I can't think how you could preserve so much truth grace and force and simple beauty.[55]

Richard had been determined to write for posterity, what he regarded as a 'faithful rendition' of the *Lusiads*, and he defended the ethos of his translation by quoting Byron: 'The things given to the public as poems of Camoens are no more to be found in the original Portuguese than they are in the song of Solomon.'[56] This is a typical example of Burton's literal translation;

> 'Twas the glad season when the God of Day
>   into Europa's rav'sher 'gan return;
> When warmèd ether point his genial ray
>   and Flora scatter'd Amalthéa's horn.

A translator less faithful to sixteenth-century idiom might have ren-dered this as: 'It was early April, the season when flowers abound.'[57] In his more accessible introduction, however, Richard's précis of his subject unmistakably invites an analogy between Camoens' life and his own: 'The Student, the Soldier, the Traveller, the Patriot, the Poet, the mighty Man of Genius, thus crowded into a single career the efforts, the purposes, the events of half-a-dozen.' And, he stated, 'The most pleasing labour of my life has been to translate the Lusiads . . . of my master Camoens.'

He dedicated the first volume of *Lusiads* to Swinburne, whom he called 'the Prince of Lyric Poets of his day', fulfilling his part of their joint pledge to dedicate a work to each other. 'My dear Swinburne,' he wrote:

Accept the unequal exchange – my brass for your gold. Your 'Poems and Ballads' began to teach the Philister what might there is in the music of language, and what the marvel of lyric inspiration, far subtler, and more ethereal than mere poetry, means to the mind of man . . .

Swinburne was equally flattering when he wrote to acknowledge receipt of his presentation copy, inexplicably inscribed in Richard's handwriting, 'To my dear Swinburne with joint love from Frances and Richard F. Burton.'[58] Swinburne clearly understood the inscription however, and wrote:

> Thanks to you both – and notably to Frances for her letter (or rather your joint one) . . . The learning and research of your work are in many points beyond all praise of mine, but not more notable than the strength and skill that wield them. I am hungrily anticipating the 'Arabian Nights' . . . just after a favourable review of my book in the *Times* I got a pathetically pressing invitation to luncheon from . . . Houghton. I'm afraid . . . [he] is getting very shaky . . . You both know how we look forward to our next meeting . . .[59]

In the copy inscribed to Isabel, Richard wrote, 'To my darling wife, Pet.'[60] It seems he had as many nicknames for her – 'Puss', 'Zoo', 'Belle', 'Pet', 'Blackguard' – as she had for him – 'Jemmy', 'Bird', 'Dick', 'Nana', 'darling love'. On several occasions she signed herself tantalisingly 'KTT', which, like 'Frances', no Burton scholar has yet been able to explain.[61]

However, the domestic happiness that Isabel described was overshadowed by a curious series of events which occurred over a period of several years and which perplexed the Burtons. They began receiving a number of anonymous letters which attempted, ineffectively, to set them against each other. They each showed the other their missives and, unable to explain them, brushed them aside with laughter, referring to the mystery perpetrator as 'It'. Occasionally over a long period Isabel would find 'love-letters' to Richard among the usual litter in the pockets of clothes he had left out for cleaning or brushing, work she tended to do herself when he was unwell 'in order not to have servants in the room'. Because she felt secure in his love for her Isabel always took these letters straight to Richard; but the matter was as much a mystery as the disappearance of papers and letters, which would suddenly reappear weeks later. On one occasion Richard found a copy-book on the floor in which there were examples of forgeries of their handwriting.

Although neither doubted the other, it was natural for Isabel to feel disquiet. 'It' apparently had casual access to their home and knew a great deal about their affairs. Richard realised her unease and prior to his second trip to Midian had cautioned her not to allow herself to become worried. He felt sure that 'It' was a woman intriguing to separate them, and he thought the matter might be concerned with money, for they had made no secret of the fact that they expected the Midian project to make them rich. 'Believe nothing, and nor shall I,' he said, 'one day or another it is bound to ooze out.'

It did, eventually. A year after Richard's death, Isabel was called to the deathbed in England of a woman whom the Burtons – and Isabel in particular – had regarded as a close friend in Trieste, one indeed with whom they had frequently joked about the likely identity of 'It'. Isabel went to her friend in great distress at the news. But her sympathy turned to consternation when the dying woman said she had a confession to make, but needed Isabel's promise of confidentiality before she could explain it, for the sake of her husband and daughters and their position in society. She then confessed that she was 'It' and asked forgiveness. She had been 'much attracted to Richard', and though she liked and admired Isabel she was jealous of their close relationship and of the talk of the riches they expected to earn from the Midian mines: '£100,000 in six months, you said . . . I was surprised you never suspected [me] . . . towards the end I could see that your husband disliked and distrusted me, but he could not fix in his own mind why it was.'

A terrifying catalogue of mischief-making 'oozed' out of the dying woman. Isabel had asked her on occasions to help her with her correspondence; 'Sometimes I wrote gushing letters so as to make you seem silly . . . I gave your opinions, to make you seem impertinent.' In return for giving her words of forgiveness, Isabel promised anonymity and extracted the names of people who had received such letters. She then wrote an account of what she had been told and sent a copy to every person involved. With one exception they all answered her. The woman died and Isabel kept her secret.[62]

In the spring of 1880 Isabel's health was still causing them concern, although she was able to walk out most days with Richard and she writes of attending dinners and parties. She and Richard loved to dress up and she describes several fancy dress parties, where he dressed as 'a roudy goldminer' to Isabel's 'Hagar, the old gypsy matriarch' and 'Richard, coeur de lion' to her 'Berengaria'. Nevertheless she was clearly below par and having difficulty coming to terms with the fact that she could no longer ride, climb and fence. She blamed the menopause for a number of irritating symptoms ranging from irregular menstruation to intestinal pain, depression, weight gain and an increasing tendency to panic attacks.

She wrote to an English consultant that before her fall in Paris, 'I was quite fearless, like a man.' Like her husband, she said, she had had 'a hard life . . . over energetic' in both physical and mental undertakings, but ever since her fall, she said,

> I began to get frightened in the streets, and feel as though I were going to tumble down . . . I have days when I am worn out with struggling against fainting or hysteria, or whatever it is . . . (I never in my life had hysteria) . . . the least agitation brings it on. I get it worse in the streets and have now arrived at that pitch that I cannot go out without my husband or my maid, and carry restoratives in my pocket.

This is a very different Isabel from the sparkling and vivacious woman described by friends of the Burtons only two years earlier. 'I must plainly state,' she went on, 'that I am at the change of life . . . My husband says all my ailments come from the liver, or that I am full of gout or rheumatism, likely enough as it is in my family and my bones ache and are stiff . . . My head is often full and woolly. I am languid and hate work, yet I cannot keep from it and am always tired . . .'[63] It is possible that Isabel's unaccustomed weakness was responsible for bringing out a protective and gentle side of Richard which created the 'haven' Isabel wrote of.

In July the couple played host to a visit by the British Fleet, but a storm wrecked the ambitious *fête champêtre* that Isabel had worked so hard to produce at Opcina at which more than 800 people sat down to supper in the gardens of the old inn. After a week of monster picnics, excursions, teas and balls thrown as reciprocal gestures by the officers, the Burtons escorted the Fleet out of the Gulf of Trieste in a borrowed yacht, and received the salutes of each ship while a band played 'Auld Lang Syne' and popular ballads such as 'Goodbye, Sweetheart, Goodbye'. 'It was the prettiest sight,' said Isabel. The gaiety had restored her spirits and they took a few weeks unauthorised leave and went touring in the Tyrol, ending up at Salzburg. Here they separated; Isabel went to Marienbad for the 'electric spa' treatment, Richard to Vienna and an interview with Sir Henry Elliot.

They met again after a week and went directly to Venice for the International Geographical Conference which opened on 15 September. There they found Verney Lovett Cameron, with whom Richard had been in regular correspondence for some years following the younger man's great transcontinental achievement in Africa. Neither Richard nor Cameron had been invited to address the conference, or take any part in it, a slight which the two men – arguably two of the greatest living explorers of their day – felt deeply. It was perhaps the more insulting to Richard, since the conference was being held on the doorstep of his Consulate, so to speak.

Initially Richard 'held himself aloof' from the geographers, but Cameron was 'wild with spirits', said Isabel. The two men egged each other on in schoolboy pranks such as an incident on the Lido beach. The Burtons and Cameron were on the beach one morning when they saw the British delegation under the leadership of Lord Aberdare (President of the R.G.S.) heading towards them. Cameron and Richard took off their shoes and stockings, rolled up their trousers and began frolicking about in the sand, pretending they were two children (Dick and Cammy) under the guardianship of their nurse. This was punctuated by shouts to Isabel such as 'Please tell Dick not to touch my spade,' and 'Look, nurse, we have made such a beautiful pie.' It was pure mischief and Isabel was so helpless with laughter that she could not speak to the delegates who formed a prim audience. From that point on Cameron was always 'Cammy', 'Boy No. 2', or 'that other boy' in his correspondence. Isabel was 'Nursie', or 'the nurse', and Richard was invariably 'Boy No. 1'.[64]

Later that day, Richard vented his hurt in an old ploy; a verse designed to give offence to the R.G.S. representatives (none of whom was especially notable for achievement in geography). He wrote it on the back of his visiting card so that there would be no doubt as to its origin, and left it on a table in the room where the conference was to meet.

> We're Savile Row's selected few
> Let all the rest be dammed
> The pit is good enough for you,
> We won't have boxes crammed.

Richard's real purpose in visiting Venice without an invitation to the conference was the presence there of a large number of foreign delegates, some who were well known to him and some he wanted to meet. One day when Richard and Cameron were out walking they met Dr Gerson da Cunah, a Camoens student and enthusiast whom Richard had met in Goa in 1876. Cameron recounted how Burton and the man had launched into a learned discussion in which Burton demolished his protagonist's argument; 'the entire conversation was conducted in Portuguese'. Almost immediately after parting from da Cunah they bumped into an Egyptian officer who had just returned from Mecca with a series of photographs. Richard spoke to him in Arabic. 'Burton was superior in many matters of detail,' Cameron observed, 'to say nothing of far-reaching knowledge of the doctrines of el-Islam. [He] actually explained to this Mohammedan the meaning of much of the ritual of the pilgrimage of which he had previously known nothing.'[65] For the remainder of that week Cameron was dazzled as Richard drew around him the 'brightest and best of all those assembled at Venice'; to each Burton spoke on the man's own subject in his own language, understanding even the *patois*, slang and spirit, said Cameron.[66] And when they toured the city in gondolas Richard was able to tell him something of the history of almost every building.

A sparkling if caustic account of the conference, written by Richard, subsequently appeared in the *Academy* and H.W. Bates of the R.G.S. wrote from the Society's Savile Row address to say he had been amused by it, but assuring him that no insult was intended. The Society had not deemed the conference important enough even to cover the event in their house *Journal*, he said, nor had they sent anything for exhibition. 'Lord Aberdare represented us there, but there was no intention . . . of British geographical science being represented there for serious purposes. Notwithstanding this I cannot understand why you and Cameron were not asked to take the active part that was your due . . . We shall perhaps give a page about it in November . . . can you supply it, i.e. a dry, serious, *compte-rendu*, professionally?'[67]

Throughout the year, despite the frequent excursions, Burton worked steadily at his literary projects. One can imagine him going from table to table – each with a red handkerchief tied to a table leg as pen-wiper – as each mail delivery brought in relevant correspondence from a formidable number of expert correspondents. *The Book of the Sword*, a work of stupendous scholarship,[68] was the most immediate undertaking that summer. He conceived it as three large volumes covering weaponry up to the Middle Ages in the first, the Mediaeval period in the second, and the Modern schools in the third, but only the first volume was ever published. He dedicated it to the late Alfred Bate Richards, his old fencing partner at Oxford. He also continued work on the later cantos of the *Lusiads* and, periodically, translating his versions of the stories of *Arabian Nights*.

There were already a number of English versions of the *Nights*, most notably that of Edward W. Lane in 1840, which Richard called 'a sorry performance at best'.[69] But the sanitised fairy stories that found a place in the libraries and drawing rooms of middle-class Victorian families were all based on an early French translation by Antoine Galland (1646–1715), which bore little resemblance to the rollicking and bawdy chronicles so appreciated by male audiences across the Orient where the traditional fables of Sinbad, Sheherazade and Aladdin provided popular entertainment in coffee-houses and by camp firesides.

Some of these stories, the folk-lore of the East dating back as far as the 8th century AD, were written down in ancient manuscripts; some had simply been handed on orally from century to century. For years, on and off, ever since his earliest collaboration with his close friend John Steinhaueser, Richard had been collecting them, translating them, identifying their sources and making explanatory footnotes from his own experiences. He had no doubt from observation of his spellbound male audiences in London that a printed edition of the unexpurgated stories of the *Nights* would be well received. Earlier his problem had been how to publish such a work without risking prosecution and possible imprisonment under the Obscene Publications Act of 1857. The advent of the Kama Shastra Society resolved the problem. We do not know for sure how much actual work he had done on the *Nights* prior to this point, although Lord Redesdale claimed Richard had shown him 'a roll of MSS' at Damascus in 1871. 'It was the first two or three chapters of his translation of the *Arabian*

Nights. He assured me he had shown the translation to nobody [else].'[70]

In June 1881 Richard was disappointed to learn that the writer (and Arabic speaker) John Payne had the same idea and was bringing out a privately printed, unexpurgated translation of 'all the stories'. This, unlike Lane's work, was a serious work of scholarship and as Richard still needed time to complete his own book he must have wondered if Payne's publication would make his own project redundant. 'I wonder what he'll make of the "1001 Nights" (*Arabian* be damned!),' Richard wrote to the poet Gerald Massey. 'I intend to publish (at Brussels) some day all the excised parts in plain English. It will be nice reading for babes and sucklings.'[71] In another letter, some weeks later he states, 'I am working as hard as ever . . . at the 'Arabian Nights.'[72] Richard was not a jealous writer. There is evidence that on several previous occasions he held back a publication for a year or more to allow a rival author on the same subject to have a fair crack at the marketplace. When a notice of Payne's impending book appeared in the *Athenaeum* in November he replied through the correspondence columns, advising how he had also been working on the *Thousand Nights and a Night* project for many years.[73]

> . . . mutilated in Europe to a collection of fairy tales, and miscalled the *Arabian Nights* [it] is unique as a study of anthropology . . . a marvellous picture of Oriental life; its shiftings are those of the kaleidoscope. Its alteration of pathos and bathos – of the boldest poetry (the diction of Job) and the baldest prose (the Egyptian of today) and finally, its contrast of the highest and purest morality with the orgies of Apulenius and Petronius Arbiter, take away the readers breath . . . Although a host of friends has been eager to subscribe, my work is still unfinished, nor could it be finished without year's hard labour . . . I rejoice, therefore, to see that Mr John Payne . . . had addressed himself to a realistic translation without 'abridgements or suppressions' . . .[74]

He added the rider that if Mr Payne did not do justice to the stories he himself would have to do so. As a result of this letter Payne (already a well-regarded author) contacted Richard and suggested a collaboration. When Richard replied stating that he intended to be in

London in the following April when he hoped they would meet and discuss the matter, he was already embarked upon his latest attempt to make his fortune through mining, this time on West Africa's Gold Coast.

32

ARABIAN NIGHTS
1881–1883

Isabel wrote that she was always sorry when Richard took up a new mining interest. Although he worked in a scientific and knowledgeable way, she said, he had no head for business and was inevitably exploited by men who merely wanted to use his name for publicity purposes. Nevertheless she always helped him, because she knew how passionately interested he was in the subject. In 1881 Richard began corresponding with James Irvine, a Liverpool businessman who owned six mining concessions in Guinea. Richard knew Irvine from his West Africa days, twenty years earlier. Then, Irvine had worked for one of the West African Oil Rivers merchants; now, he invited Richard to conduct a survey of each mine and prepare a report for potential investors. Richard was keen to go, still convinced that mining was the route to fabulous riches for himself and Isabel, and he particularly remembered seeing African women sluicing black sand for gold, 'within shot' of the walls of the Gold Coast Castle.[1]

For some time the Foreign Office had frowned on its Consuls 'promoting any specific commercial or industrial undertaking, in a foreign country'. Because of this Richard could not negotiate in person, so he drafted letters, as if written by Isabel, for her to copy out and send. His drafts survive among Isabel's private papers; 'I think this arrangement perfectly fair,' he wrote, 'and if you agree to it my husband shall at once take the work in hand.'[2]

When he had completed this project, Richard informed Ouida that before his departure he intended to apply for early retirement and a pension so that he could write without interruption, but this would not be in England. 'Between Mrs Grundy, widow Brown* and Mr Gladstone, England is no place for an English man.'[3]

By this time Isabel's health had improved and she could walk, fence and swim a little, but even had Burton thought her capable of withstanding the climate of West Africa, they could not afford for her to go. The syndicate provided Richard's fare only; other expenses for the four-month expedition were to be met by Richard and reimbursed from future profits. She accompanied him for the first ten days of the voyage, in November, and returned alone. Prior to this journey, she wrote to Miss E.H. Bishop (niece of Dr George Bird, who had spent a summer with them at Trieste), that they had spent 'two charming, quiet, delicious months together; and to my joy he gave up dining out and we dined at home *tête-à-tête*, but of course it was overshadowed by the coming parting, which I feel terribly this time, as I go on getting older.'

He has to change ship four times, and this is a great anxiety to me in the stormy weather . . . The mines are all round the coast, and then I dread fever for him. He wishes to make a little trip to the Kong Mountains, and then I fear natives and beasts. Perhaps Cameron will be with him, but *entre nous* Cameron is not very solid, and requires a leading hand . . .

If all goes well . . . we are to meet in London in March [1882]. I am fearfully sad . . . I neither visit, nor receive, nor go out . . . but I must fight the battle [and] learn to live alone and work. I feared my empty home without children or relatives; but I have braved the worst now.[4]

Cameron – or 'Boy No. 2', as he signed himself – worried Isabel further when he wrote to advise that he was unable to get a passage until mid-December, 'but', he wrote winningly, 'as the other boy's wire has [still] not arrived I expect to be out there as soon as he [is]. I'll look

---

*'Widow Brown' is a reference to Queen Victoria's relationship with John Brown, her Scottish gillie.

after your little pet as well as I can [and] give him his gruel and hot water bottle.'[5]

As usual Richard's experiences in West Africa provided the basis for a book, *To the Gold Coast for Gold*, but a good deal of the text appears to have been taken from his earlier work, *Wanderings in West Africa*. He surveyed the mine properties, interviewed the managers, summarised their problems, and made suggestions as to how to resolve them. Though hard work came naturally to him, he was now over 60 years of age and the climate took a heavy toll. He was frequently ill, but in letters to Irvine he instructed that Isabel was not to be worried.

All communications between the couple went through James Irvine because the only ships regularly visiting the area were out of Liverpool. 'I have today received a letter from Mrs Burton,' Irvine wrote to Richard on January 19th, 'she asks me to get ready a large Ulster [overcoat], and a number of other comforts for you, to await your pleasure at Madeira; of course I shall do it with pleasure.'[6] 'Captain Burton is well,' Irvine informed Isabel on 14 April. 'He will leave Axim positively on 23rd April and be home in Liverpool on 18th May . . . I have posted his letters to you and have no doubt he will convey these facts to you himself in his letters.' On one occasion when the fortnightly steamer brought no letter from him, Isabel knew something was wrong and splashed out on a cable: 'DEAREST LOVE MOST ANXIOUS, LAST LETTER MONTH OLD, IF ILL COME BACK, TELEGRAPH WHERE TO MEET.'[7] He had, in fact, been ill with fever and dysentery and unable to write, but his next one-page report on the mines, to Irvine, contained a message for her: 'Please let my wife know I am greatly improved in health. I shall write to her by the usual Liverpool mail.'[8]

Isabel, however, was also ill. During March and April of 1882 she felt increasingly weak and faint. Her fencing master pointed out that her proficiency with the broadsword had diminished; 'What is the matter with you?' he asked.[9] As a result she consulted Professor Liebman, a gynaecologist who diagnosed a cancerous tumour in her right ovary. He suggested that the condition had been initiated by a severe shock or physical trauma. Isabel blamed the fall in Paris, but later she began to wonder if the severe bruising she received in Brazil, as a result of her horse's stumble during the flight through the forest from the brigand, was to blame.

As soon as she arrived in London on 3 May 1882, she consulted a top specialist who confirmed the diagnosis and, since the tumour was in a very early stage, he recommended a hysterectomy. On learning that the tumour was slow-growing, Isabel made a decision not to have the operation. First, she was afraid of the knife and of anaesthetics; second, the convalescence for such major surgery might take up to a year during which she 'would not be able to look after Richard', and third, she did not wish to worry him and therefore would not have him told. One can sympathise with the first reason; the mortality rates for surgery were terrifying and anaesthesia as a branch of medicine was still in its infancy. Her second and third reasons, however, appear to owe more to the muddled thinking that she experienced after the menopause than to the old decisive Isabel.

Richard arrived home to a mixed reception in the press. 'Every two or three years Captain Burton appears like a meteor in London, and in that City of four millions he invariably succeeds in creating a stir,' one journalist wrote. 'However hurried his visitations his presence is keenly felt. He wakes up the learned Societies, startles the Geographers, is the hero of banquets, and drops a new book in his wake. He comes this time in his familiar character of Gold-finder.'[10] Another writer was less flattering, reminding readers of the frequency of Richard's leaves and accusing him of being 'an amateur Consul'.

Once again, Richard believed he had found enough gold to make the couple rich. 'Samples of surface soil [contain] between 3 & 4 ounces per ton – an enormous proportion when in California 2 ounces was looked upon as rich enough to make the fortune of a digging,' he told Irvine. 'When the dirt is exhausted the quartz reef will stand up like a wall and require neither shafting nor tunnelling.'[11] All the problems were practical ones; the method of extracting the ore was difficult and costly, involving hydraulic sluicing processes. West Africans were lazy and arrogant, and he recommended shipping in a Chinese labour force.[12] Nevertheless he regarded the expedition as successful and on his return asked Irvine (through Isabel) for an advance of £200 against his anticipated 'profits' to offset his personal expenses. Irvine refused on the grounds that it could be '12 or 18 months [before] the mines actually begin to pay', 'so far all my profits have been on paper, otherwise I wd. offer straight off to do it,' he said. Meanwhile, he said, he hoped to float three further concessions based on Richard's surveys, and if stocks in these sold quickly, as he expected, within the next few weeks, 'I will be delighted to advance that amount.' In this connection, however, he was concerned that Richard had decided not to address the shareholders' meeting held on the previous evening. 'Anything he says carries twenty times the weight Cameron does – who has spoilt himself – *this most confidential* – his failing is well known.'

Cameron had upset potential investors by stating in his speech that the climate of the mine-sites was an unhealthy one.[13] Hardly surprising when he and Richard had suffered constant attacks of fever during the trip. Richard was still unwell when he arrived home, and suffered from intermittent fevers and a form of dysentery for months afterwards. Cameron hid his genuine concern about Richard's health under banter, chiding 'nurse' for getting into a fuss. 'Boy No. 1' would recover pretty quickly, he said, if she fed him *only* invalid food. 'If slops don't do it, take away the clothes and confine to bed with no books except *religious* ones!'[14]

The long-term outcome of this venture was disastrous. The '200 ft gold reef' identified by Richard certainly existed, indeed the area is still being mined over a century later, but it proved difficult to extract the ore with nineteenth-century technology. Costs escalated after a series of blunders caused by poor on-site management, and rumours began to circulate in the City that the area was a swamp and that no gold existed there. Despite Richard's vehement public denial of these rumours, investors became wary and withdrew before the reef could be properly exploited.[15] Irvine lost everything,[16] as did numerous small investors, some of whom had been tempted to speculate because of Richard's involvement. Cameron took a good deal of the blame. His loss of credibility began shortly after he returned from West Africa in July 1882, when he was arrested for drunkenness in the middle of the morning. In the existing moral climate, this was sufficient to cause investors to think again about backing West African Gold Fields Company Limited.[17]

But the failure of the project was in the future. For the moment investors were interested, and the optimistic Burtons enjoyed two months in London seeing many old friends, following which Richard talked Lord Granville into giving him an extra week of compassionate leave to take Isabel to Marienbad because she was too nervous to travel there alone. A second Vice-Consul, Mr Cautley, had been appointed to Trieste and Richard suggested that the wages of both Vice-Consuls (Brock and Cautley), should be taken from his salary during his extended leave. Although several officials believed Isabel's illness was merely a ploy, Granville granted the request but there was a 'quid pro quo' in a gently couched, but firm, suggestion that Richard resign as director of the mining company.[18] This, he said, was in line with new policy, the rules of which had already been sent to all Consuls. The changes concerned look suspiciously aimed at Burton. In future, the circular stated, the Foreign Office would,

> decline to give letters of introduction or recommendation to Her Majesty's Diplomatic or Consular Agents . . . in favour of gentle-men proceeding to foreign countries, for the purpose of promoting any specific commercial or industrial undertaking, or of obtaining concessions from a foreign Government.[19]

In the event they did not go to Marienbad. Richard left for Paris on 15 July, taking a discountenanced Cameron with him. Isabel followed them on the 22nd, taking her niece Blanche Piggott with her. They spent four days in Paris where Richard again became ill with 'African ailments', then Cameron left for London and the other three travelled directly to Trieste, arriving there on 31 July.[20] Blanche had just left New Hall convent and was to live with them for a year or so, 'Richard and I, having no children, thought it rather fun having a daughter,' Isabel wrote.

Soon after their return, Isabel went with Blanche to Marienbad and Richard began corresponding with John Payne whom he had met in London following his return from the Gold Coast. As mentioned, Payne was also working on a translation of the *Arabian Nights* and, having heard of Richard's interest, made an appointment to see him. As a result, Richard agreed to 'look over' the proofs of the first volume. In September, hearing of fighting between Moslem sects in India, he thought the trouble might spread throughout the East and wrote to Granville offering to organise a force of the men of Zanzibar and East Africa, 'sturdy labourers and stokers, popularly known in Bombay as *Seedy-boys*'*, who had proved combative powers and would not sympathise with either of the fanatical wings. 'If H.M. Government think proper I could proceed to Zanzibar . . .

---

* Sometimes spelled Sidi, e.g.: Sidi Bombay.

and organise a levy of one thousand men. Commander Cameron R.N. C.B. etc, who is also a good Kisawahili scholar, would willingly accompany me.'[21] Cameron had learned his lesson, he said, and was now 'one of the blue ribbon brigade'. That is to say he had become a teetotaller, indicated by the wearing of a blue ribbon in the buttonhole.[22]

The tenor of Richard's correspondence is that of a man bored with the prospect of another year in Trieste with no adventures to look forward to. 'I am very much amused at your remark that "the domestic quiet of home has laid you up",' Irvine wrote. 'It is quite on a par with a remark you made to me nearly twenty years ago when you were . . . going out [to West Africa] after three or four months at home . . . I congratulated you on your healthy look and you said, "I cannot help it. You see what I suffer by civilisation."'[23]

In addition to helping John Payne, Richard was still working at his own, unexpurgated, version of the *Nights*. On 24 September he wrote to John Tinsley, enclosing some specimen pages, advising that it was 'more than half already done. It will be a marvellous repertory of Eastern wisdom; how eunuchs are made, how Easterners are married, what they do in marriage, female [techniques?] etc . . . Mrs Grundy will howl until she almost bursts and will read every word I write with intense enjoyment.'[24] At this stage he hoped to interest a publisher and obtain an advance. When Tinsley turned down the project, Richard wrote to Quaritch:

> As regards the Nights I leave all business matters to my wife; but I may tell you that the work will be a wonder. Payne was obliged to 'draw it mild' and it was not in his place to explain by means of notes. I have done the contrary . . . the tone of the book will be one of extreme delicacy and decency, now and then broken by the most startling horrors like 'The Lady Who Would be Rogered by the Bear.' It will make you roar with laughter; some parts beat Rabelais hollow. What *will* Mrs Grundy say? I predict read every word of it and call the translator very ugly names . . .

Quaritch wrote at once to express interest. By now Isabel had returned and she took over the negotiations. She replied that they were now thinking of publishing the book privately, but that they would sell the manuscripts with all rights for £10,000. Across the bottom of this letter Quaritch scribbled, 'Mrs Burton gone mad!!'[25] Later, he would write in the *Bookman*: 'It was the biggest mistake I ever made in my life'.[26]

Richard's literary activities were dropped with alacrity the instant he received a cable from the Foreign Office which promised action:

October 27th, 1882 4.40pm

H.M.'S GOVERNMENT WISH TO AVAIL THEMSELVES OF YOUR KNOWLEDGE OF BEDOUINS AND THE SINAI COUNTRY TO ASSIST IN SEARCH FOR PROFESSOR PALMER STOP THERE IS A CHANCE OF HIS STILL BEING ALIVE THOUGH BODIES OF HIS COMPANIONS CHARRINGTON AND GILL HAVE BEEN FOUND STOP PRO-CEED AT ONCE TO GHAZA AND PLACE YOURSELF IN COMMUNICATION WITH CONSUL MOORE WHO HAS GONE THITHER FROM JERUSALEM TO INSTITUTE ENQUIRIES.[27]

Richard replied instantly, and eagerly:

READY TO START BY FIRST STEAMER STOP WILL DRAW £100 WANT GUNBOAT FROM ALEXANDRIA TO GHAZZEH OR SINAI LETTER FOLLOWS.

It was twelve years since he had first met Edward Palmer in Damascus when Palmer had been travelling with Charles Tyrwhitt Drake while they worked for the Palestine Exploration Fund. The instant respect and liking Richard felt for the two younger men had never wavered and he had last seen Palmer eighteen months earlier, while in the Midian. Then, Palmer was engaged in gathering intelligence for the British Army, and as a result of this meeting Richard began noting appropriate information. Among his Midian expedition papers on mining, geography and archaeology are 70 pages of notes and jot-tings, collected during his journey, marked 'to send to Palmer', demonstrating nicely how his natural powers of observation and multi-lingual contacts enabled him to gather valuable information of a more political nature.[28] When Isabel voiced her concern at the dan-gers of following Palmer into the desert, Burton reminded her how, when they had been recalled from Damascus, the young man had publicly supported them. 'If there is any chance of saving dear old Palmer,' he told her, 'I will go anywhere and do anything.'

In many ways Palmer was a young Burton who had not made

Burton's mistakes. He was an academic (a Cambridge don), a traveller and a linguist (he spoke Arabic, Persian and Hindu fluently as well as many European languages).[29] He was also a writer, archaeologist, translator, draughtsman and caricaturist. Among his multitudinous interests were spiritualism, magic and mesmerism. No wonder Burton was drawn to him! After the death of his first wife in 1878, Palmer tired of University life and, even though he remarried after a year, he did not return to academia but accepted Secret Service work in Egypt.

The Suez Canal gave fast access to India and the Far East, and Disraeli's sensational purchase of Khedive Ismael's shares in 1875 made Britain the largest shareholder in the Suez Canal Company.[30] This did not please either the French or the Egyptians, and in 1882 a rebellion led by Arabi Pasha made it necessary for the British to defend the Canal against repeated attacks. Palmer's mission in 1882 was to raise the wild Arab tribes of the Sinai peninsula against the Egyptian rebels, to secure the safety of the Canal.[31] Arriving in Alexandria on 5 July 1882, he assumed the identity of 'Abdullah El Shami', a rich Syrian, and spent three weeks travelling round the desert calling on the most important sheiks, with many of whom he was already acquainted from his previous wanderings in the Tíh desert. He then managed to evade Egyptian sentries in order to rejoin the English fleet which had bombarded Alexandria in his absence. On 2 August he was in the first boat that landed during the British occupation of Suez.

Palmer believed that with £20,000 or £30,000 in gold he could suborn a Bedouin army to guard the Canal. The sum of £20,000 was subsequently placed at his disposal and he was given a secondary assignment to sabotage the telegraph wire between Cairo and Constantinople. He accepted his mission in the full knowledge that capture as a British spy carried the death penalty. He spent a few days buying camels for transport and on 8 August, in an uncanny preview of T.E. Lawrence's adventures, he set out in Arab clothes carrying £3,000 in gold to attend a *divan* of the most powerful sheiks. He took with him two volunteer officers: Lieutenant Harold Charrington and Captain R.E. Gill. The entire party, including two servants, a guide and a number of camel men, then vanished. At first their disappearance caused no undue alarm; after all, Palmer had been out of contact for three weeks in July. But in late September the remains of

Charrington's and Gill's bodies were discovered. Widespread rumours of a white man captured by the Bedouin gave rise to the hope that Palmer had escaped the fate of his companions.

Even before Richard arrived in Cairo the F.O. had cabled several times aborting his mission, but these instructions somehow always missed him. It was 28 November before he had to admit to receiving further instructions. While he was travelling, an investigation team had discovered all the bodies. It was surmised that Palmer's party had been attacked by an Arab *ghazu* (raid), and all five men were captured and executed. Rumours had reached the English papers that, given the choice of a firing squad or leaping off a cliff, Palmer chose the latter. In fact all the men were shot and their bodies thrown into a gully; three had been washed a considerable distance away by a flash flood. Theft was said to be the motive, but Richard was dubious of this theory, saying that the cold-blooded murders were uncharacteristic of the Bedouins accused of the outrage. He believed the Egyptians were behind it and was setting out to find the murderers when ordered home. His lucid official report ended with a sting: 'I have the honour to express my gratitude to your Lordship for proving that there is not (as has been reported) any objection to my being officially employed in the Ottoman dominions.'[32]

Curiously, in his paper on the Palmer affair written for the *Cornhill*, Richard used the opportunity to air Isabel's animal welfare crusade. The manuscript is in his hand,[33] not Isabel's, which discounts any suggestion that it was her doing. In recommending a Police Force be set up to patrol the Canal, he suggested that part of its duties should be 'to suppress that cruelty to animals which is one of Egypt's many abominations. The want of such a measure has long been felt, and during the last ten years a succession of dilettante has attempted to take the matter in hand . . . but the work is too serious, too continuous for amateurs.'[34] His polite statements to Lord Granville mask the aggravation he felt at being recalled when he believed he might have apprehended the murderers. Writing to friends, such as Ouida, he was less inhibited. Having been invited to go by the Government, he said,

> I started at once, ran to Alexandria, Cairo and Suez, saw Tel el-Keb [where the British routed Arabi Pasha] and Colonel Warren (an old acquaintance) who was leading the search and leading it well.

We agreed that I should go to Ghazzah and search the northern
road for the 21 fugitive murderers. I did so; made all my arrangements and was ready to start when I received at Jaffa another
tel[egram] inviting me to return to Trieste. So I damned them all
and did. This is simply making a fool of me. They wanted my name
while the House of Commons was sitting and then – nothing.
However I hope soon to throw up their rotten Consulate & to
start in life free . . . Isabel joins in best love, Yrs etc.[35]

In fact the Palmer affair marked the end of Richard's physical adventures. His body was winding down, the result of a life spent in hostile
environments subjected to almost constant parasitic, fungal and bac-
terial infections. But as his health declined, his literary output
increased. He told John Payne that he planned to go to the Greek
Islands in the spring to brush up his modern Greek, but meanwhile he
threw himself into work upon *Camoens: the Lyricks*; *A Thousand
Nights and a Night*; *To the Gold Coast for Gold*; and *The Book of
the Sword*. Other work tables housed manuscript volumes of Payne's
Arabian Nights, and he was revising the Kama Shastra Society's
Ananga Ranga of Vatsyayana. His papers, pamphlets and contributions to journals and newspapers are too numerous to list, and besides
all this he maintained a constant and ongoing revision of all his previous publications.[36]

The last phase of Richard Burton's life was destined to be, despite
ill-health, an extraordinarily prolific and fruitful one, bringing him at
last a measure of financial success and public honour. The gold he had
always sought lay not in the ground, but in his own inkwell.

33

KAMA SHASTRA — PARADIGMS OF PASSION
1883–1886

By 1883 the Burtons had spent almost a decade in their rambling apartment when Richard suddenly took a violent dislike to it, saying the drains were bad. Their declining health must have made access difficult for they were no longer fit enough to 'run up and down like squirrels', as he once bragged to A.B. Richards.[1] So Isabel went house-hunting again.

There was only one house in Trieste that they both admired. *Palazzo Gossleth* was a substantial stuccoed villa with a Palladian façade, built in the previous century by a rich Englishman and situated at the summit of a wooded promontory which divides the older parts of the city from the Bay of Muggia. Its elevation meant that during the summer months it was cooler than at sea level, and the views were superb. The Burtons thought that had the same views been in England, tourists would have come in train-loads to see them. 'I know nothing finer, except Rio at sunrise,' Isabel would tell Albert Tootal. The entrance was large enough to allow a carriage to be driven into the hall, and a polished marble staircase gave access to the living accommodation. Although there were fewer rooms than the apartment, 20 as opposed to 27, the largest of these were magnificent with lofty ceilings. And there were gardens with tall shady trees for hot summer days.

The Burtons had never aspired to the property for it was occupied by a local family, but that spring of 1883 Isabel learned that a

substantial part of the house was being offered for lease.² The décor
had become shabby but it was grander altogether than their apartment, and although the rent was not appreciably greater the running
costs must have been significant. Today the *palazzo* is subdivided
into half a dozen luxurious and spacious apartments and its façade
has been slightly altered at ground-floor level, but it is easy to understand why Isabel and Richard were prepared to stretch their limited
resources to live there.

The move coincided with a number of changes in their lives. As
usual they had taken up sea bathing when the weather began to warm
up, but neither enjoyed it, so they gave it up for good. Isabel had not
been able to fence properly for a year, and Richard had been away so
much that he had done little either. They were both deeply shocked
when their Bohemian fencing-master committed suicide that spring.
'Richard said he was the finest broad-swordsman he had ever seen,'
Isabel wrote. One of his favorite demonstrations involved her standing motionless while he made a *moulinet* (circular swing) at her head.

> You could hear the sword swish in the air, and he has touched my
> face like a fly in the act of doing it. He did it frequently to show
> what he *could* do, but he used to say that he could not do it to any
> of his men pupils, for fear they would flinch . . . but he knew I
> should stand steady. I liked that.³

Isabel's pride in her staunch reliance on the old man's skill was a form
of heroism which would not have been lost on Richard with his
schoolboy ideals of valour. But by the date of their joint birthday
party in March (Richard was 62 on the 19th March and Isabel was 52
on the 20th), they had put aside fencing bouts. They celebrated with
a meal which had become traditional for all their wedding anniver-
saries and birthdays, Richard's favourite: a roast suckling pig, 'three
weeks old . . . with the crackle, stuffing and apple-sauce'. His usual
drink was port. Also he always enjoyed a whisky every evening, 'three
ounces' (a good 'double' measure) in water; and a medicinal 'grog' of
rum and water before retiring.

Apart from entertaining the Navy Squadron again for thirteen days
in an orgy of *fêtes* and balls, the couple spent the early summer writing. For Richard one of the early highlights of his year was
notification from Arbuthnot that the *Kama Sutra* was about to be

printed ('printed, not "published"', Burton used to say) under the auspices, or guise, of the Kama Shastra Society.

As with the *Ananga Ranga*, the precise amount of Richard Burton's involvement in the translation of this work is not known. The late W.G. Archer (Archivist of the Indian Section of the Victoria and Albert) wrote that there are touches of Burton and Arbuthnot everywhere in the English version of *Kama Sutra*.[4] The work is still in print; indeed it is probably – by repute at least – one of the most famous books of all time. In most modern editions, title pages credit Richard Burton as the translator. Clearly, since he did not speak ancient Sanskit, this is incorrect. He interpreted and revised Arbuthnot's manuscript, which – in turn – was based on the original translation of the two 'pundits' mentioned earlier.

Professor Archer made a study of the literary styles of both Burton and Arbuthnot. 'The English, at least in draft, was Arbuthnot's,' he stated. However, 'left to himself, Arbuthnot could not have given it rhythmical vigour and assured style. These are Burton's contribution . . . Using Arbuthnot's plain and simple language, he made it read well . . . without Burton's aid, Arbuthnot's version would have lacked brilliance.'[5] We know that the extensive explanatory footnotes and an epilogue, called 'Concluding Remarks', are wholly Burton's, and there is a good deal to be learned about him from these alone.

A basic precept of the *Kama Sutra* is that in order to promote joy and stability in marriage, a wife must derive equal satisfaction with her husband from the act of sex. This was a far cry from the 'lie back and think of England, dear' school of thought which prevailed in Britain in the nineteenth century. In addition to explicit technical instructions on various positions, descriptions of sexual organs, different types of men and women and aphrodisiacs, the book promotes love-making techniques (and several medical prescriptions) which delay orgasm for the man and hasten it for the woman.

In his added Preface, Richard describes 'the ideal woman':

Her face is pleasing as the full moon: her body, well clothed with flesh, is soft . . . Her bosom is hard, full and high. Her eyes are bright and beautiful as the orbs of a fawn . . . her nose is straight and lovely . . . her *yoni*[6] resembles the opening of a lotus bud and her love-seed is perfumed like the lily which is newly burst . . . her voice is low and musical as the note of the Kokila bird . . . she is respectful and religious as she is clever and courteous . . . ever anxious to worship the gods, and to enjoy the conversation of the Brahmans.[7]

Contemporary descriptions of Isabel as a young woman show that she fulfilled at least some of the criteria of this physical blueprint: large clear eyes, straight Grecian nose, a low and musical voice. But his notes also suggest that Richard, assuming he practised the substance of his writings, was a skilled and sympathetic lover. And perhaps this goes a long way to explaining why the marriage of these two extraordinary people was so successful that it was commented upon by their contemporaries. Ouida, one of Richard's closest women friends, wrote, 'his love for her was extreme; it was a source of weakness, as most warm emotions are in the lives of strong men. Their marriage was romantic . . . a love-marriage in the most absolute sense of the words . . . on each side impassioned. She adored him . . .'[8]

Richard Burton's lively style and his contagious delight in his subject, so apparent in his contributions to *Kama Sutra*, in his subsequent *Perfumed Garden* and throughout the *Nights*, hide the fact that they were written by a man not only in physical decline but often in acute pain. The great hard body that his contemporaries spoke of with respect; 'a shade under six foot' . . . 'massive shoulders' . . . 'enormous frame' . . . 'muscled like a bull' . . . 'a blow like the kick of horse'; yet which, at the same time, had been so disciplined, so agile, that he had been able to match world-class swordsmen, was finally succumbing to age and the physical effects of harsh treatment and illness.

'For the first twenty-two years of my married life,' Isabel wrote, 'I made our early [morning] tea at any time between three to half past five, according to the seasons (and if I happened to go to a ball I did not find it worthwhile to go to bed); we had tea and bread and butter and fruit.' From 1883 the pace was more relaxed; Richard began to suffer from insomnia, so he worked or read into the small hours and rose at 6 or 6.30 a.m. In early October Isabel's niece Blanche Piggott returned to England after her eighteen months' residence with the Burtons, and Miss Bishop was staying with them. One morning Isabel and Miss Bishop returned from a walk to find Richard almost fainting from the pain of an acute attack of gout. The agonies of gout and arthritis can be controlled to a great degree by modern pain-killers, but it was not an illness that a patient could take lightly in the nineteenth century.

When the Burtons first took on the *palazzo*, Richard appropriated the largest room in the house as his own. It made a vast self-contained apartment of bedroom, dressing-room, breakfasting area and work room; it was large enough to take a number of work tables, and had windows on two sides with good views. In the summer it was cool and ideal for his long periods of work, but as winter set in, with the howling *boras* winds that he loathed, it was damp and chilly despite being heated by a stove. Isabel fussed because the metal arms of his chairs rusted, and she was sure the dampness was responsible for his poor health. Richard stubbornly refused to move and took to wearing a fur-lined coat during the day and throwing a buffalo skin over his bedclothes at night. He had a room off this which he called his 'den', which he could lock. For whatever reason Richard suffered a second serious attack of gout at the end of November and on 6 December, a week after the attack began, a week in which he had learned of the deaths of several old friends, he wrote irritably in his journal, 'Today, eleven years ago, I came here; what a shame!!!'[9]

'When he was free from pain,' Isabel wrote, 'he was immensely cheerful and used to laugh like a schoolboy at his doctor, who *would* speak English for the sake of learning and practising it. "What him eat today?" "Pheasant, doctor." He plunged his hands into his hair as if he were going to tear it all out. "What for you give him the wild?" . . . "You shall give him ten drops of rum in a tumbler of water for his dinner!" Peals of laughter came from the sick-bed. "Ach! Das ist gut to hear him laugh like dat. Vat for he laugh?" I answered, "Because he gets a brandy grog fit for a sailor every night, or he would have been a dead man long ago." More tearing of the hair, and real displeasure.'[10]

Fortunately, Isabel had been able to lavish comforts on the invalid for she was unexpectedly left a legacy of £500* by an old aunt. This also helped to pay for an amanuensis, Mrs Victoria Maylor, a widow in reduced circumstances. Mrs Maylor fair-copied the sheafs of text Richard turned out every day, which left Isabel free to nurse and to deal with his correspondence and business affairs. 'When he got over that illness he was a veritable skeleton; his legs were like two sticks of sealing wax,' Isabel wrote.[11] For a while he completely lost the use of

*1997 equivalent = c. £19,000.

his legs and lay on a sofa in the drawing room with his work to
hand; it was early March before he was allowed up. On the 14th a
servant came rushing to tell Isabel that Richard had fainted. She
found him 'very bad' and sent for two doctors who diagnosed a mild
heart attack and treated him with digitalis.

A month later he was back at work, writing to Payne for advice on
self-publication. Payne also privately printed and distributed his
Nights and had filled his subscription list of 500 copies.

> I am just beginning . . . to hobble about (with a stick). A hard time
> since Jan 31st! . . . Now that your 1001 is nearly complete I am
> working up my translation and hereupon I have two little requests
> to make. They are somewhat indiscreet but you must have no cer-
> emony in the matter of refusing.
>
> > 1. I want the loan of your Collector and Brazil editions: the
> > volumes shall be punctually returned to you.
> > 2. For my guidance with that ticklish animal the publisher it
> > would be a great kindness to me to know what arrangements
> > you made. I understand you printed 9 vols at £1.1.0 each, 500
> > = 4,500. What concerns me is the cost of each volume before
> > it was delivered to the subscribers. Whatever you tell me will
> > be kept secret, no-one shall know it but ourselves.
>
> My illness has thrown all my work into arrears but a few weeks will
> fill in the hole . . .

Isabel had written to the F.O. and obtained a two months' leave of
absence for convalescence purposes, but he was too ill to take advantage of it until June when the couple travelled to Marienbad.[12] They
stopped frequently to allow him to spend a day in bed in order to
build up strength for the next stage. 'On getting out [of the train at
Graz],' Isabel wrote, 'he could hardly stand, and his head was
whirling. The Hotel Daniele was only just across the road and, leaning on me, he managed to get there; I left the baggage at the station till
afterwards . . .'[13] Under the 'cure' he improved rapidly and began to
take walks, taking a great enjoyment in the pure air and lush flora;
Isabel made sure that a bath-chair always followed them about. Later
on, 'we drove out, made excursions, and read and wrote under the

trees. Despite these distractions Richard found it easy to work there and made good progress.'[14]

He wrote to tell Payne that his corrections to Payne's edition had reached vol. iv, but his own manuscript would not be ready until January. 'I am going in for notes,' he stated, 'where they did not suit your scheme and [this] will make the book a perfect repertoire of Eastern knowledge in its most esoteric form, including the habit of the Egyptian fellahs of copulating with the crocodile, a treatise on the geographical limits of sodomy and other excerpts from my note books . . .'[15]

Previously, he had stated to Payne his theory that homosexuality was geographically confined. Now he explained it:

> . . . Unfortunately, it is these 'offences against nature' (which come so naturally in Greece and Persia and which belong strictly to their fervid age) that give the book so much of its ethnological value. I should put it into the hands of every cadet going to the East. I don't know if I ever mentioned to you a paper (unpublished) of mine showing the geographical limits of sodomy. A broad band across Europe and Asia widening out into China and embracing all of S. America.

Port. Spain   S. France Italy Greece Turkey Persia   China America
N. Africa   Cashmere

Behring

Magellan

Curious, is it not? Beyond the limits the practice is purely sporadic, within them endemic. I shall publish it some day and surprise the world. I don't live in England and don't care a damn for the Public Opinion. I would rather tread on Mrs Grundy's pet corn than not. She may howl on her big bum to her heart's content.[16]

Isabel was deeply involved in the production of Richard's *Nights*. From Opcina (where they spent every weekend) in October, she sent out 'thirty-four thousand' advertising circulars. There were three separate fliers. The first described the work: an edition limited to 1,000 sets of 10 volumes, each volume costing a guinea payable on delivery. Subscribers were invited to apply directly to 'Captain Burton, Trieste,

Austria'. The second tabled the contents of the volumes. The third
was a reproduction of a favourable article from an American newspaper, welcoming news of Burton's edition of the *Nights*.

Payne had told Richard that his edition of *Nights* had been 100
per cent over-subscribed and at Isabel's request he provided a list of
the disappointed subscribers. Eventually Burton's edition, too, was
100 per cent over-subscribed, but when sending out the first prospectus neither he nor Isabel apparently had the confidence to float an
edition of 2,000. They were, after all, bearing the costs of the project
themselves. 'It will cost £2,000 to £3,000 to bring out,' Isabel
explained to Albert Tootal, who subscribed to four copies including
one for the Emperor of Brazil. '. . . it would never do to let the
public be able to buy it . . . from all Dick says it would make one's
hair stand on end.'[17]

Quaritch subscribed, and – probably based on something Richard
or Isabel had told him – advertised the edition in his catalogue as 'the
only absolute true translation of the *One Thousand and One Nights*'.
Realising that this would annoy Payne, Richard wrote immediately
of his 'horror' on reading the advertisement. 'My wife telegraphed to
him [Quaritch] and followed with a letter ordering it not to be
printed. All in vain. I notice this only to let you know that the impertinence [by Quaritch] is wholly against my will.'[18]

Richard was touched that Payne dedicated one of the later volumes
to him, but offered his frank opinions on Payne's expurgations. 'You
know your own affairs best but I am sorry to see the [original] style
altered. The *Nights* were by no means literal but [were] very readable . . .'[19] Payne later wrote: 'Burton allowed that in all other
respects my translation was thoroughly literal, but I never could get
him to understand my objection to filth for filth's sake, altogether
apart from all question of prudery. He himself had a "romantic passion" for it.'[20] Richard's response to Payne's reservations was, 'You
are applying to 1750 the morality of 1890.' From these small irritations, Payne began to dislike Burton.

Isabel dealt with all other aspects of Richard's work to leave him
free to write, but it was not easy in that autumn of 1884 with the
problems erupting in Egypt in which Charles Gordon was deeply
involved. The Burtons were kept busy meeting VIPs at the station, and
acting as hosts to the 'great flow of English going to Egypt beginning
with Lord Northbrook'. Isabel wrote to Ouida: 'I am so *thankful* that

Dick is not in that mess – luck! We are very hard at work on *Arabian Nights* – and me with my various projects. Dick does all the translation and except consulting me on a word or passage, I am not allowed to read it. It will be a wonderful work – but I do all the financial part and it keeps my hands full.'[21]

Four months later 'that mess', as Isabel called it, led to the death of General Gordon on 26 January 1885, at Khartoum, when he was overwhelmed in a charge. His severed head was carried back to the Mahdi as a trophy. In the six months prior to this Gordon had already acquired the status of hero in England. In the media of the day he was depicted as an ageing patriot, a Christian soldier, abandoned by the British Government, single-handedly holding back the heathen forces of the Mahdi. Public outcry, a parliamentary defeat and the direct intervention of the Queen led to the mobilisation of a relief force, but it arrived too late to save him. Before Gordon's death was confirmed, one of the illustrated London papers depicted him lying deserted in the desert with his Bible in one hand and revolver in the other, vultures hovering near. This upset Richard greatly, 'Take it away!' he told Isabel sharply. 'I can't bear to look at it. I have had to feel like that myself; I know what it is.'[22]

News of the massacre at Khartoum reached England on 5 February, provoking an outburst of national and international grief only paralleled in our century by the death of Diana, Princess of Wales. Richard and Isabel were devastated, the more so because it had been mooted that Richard be sent out to assist Gordon. Isabel said that she wrote to the Foreign Office at the time (without Richard's knowledge), advising them that he was not fit enough to spend any time in the Sudan, and his name was dropped from consideration. 'We are feeling perfectly miserable about the war publicly and privately,' Isabel told Albert Tootal before the news of the tragedy broke. 'Gordon is a great friend of ours.'[23] No two accounts of his death agreed, which led Richard to believe for some years that Gordon had not perished but had escaped into the desert, and would eventually turn up from the direction of the Congo.

Richard was seriously ill again over Christmas 1884 and Isabel, who loved Trieste, began to get very nervous that another winter there would kill him. She wanted him to resign the Service, and move to a place of his choice, even though this inevitably meant they would have to live very simply. It was Richard who, though he regarded

Trieste as a hated symbol of the waste of his life, refused: 'I won't throw up the Service until I either get Morocco, or they let me retire on a full pension.' He was coming up to 64, but full retirement age then was 70. Having obtained a six-month leave on grounds of their joint ill-health, it was their intention to travel to London where Richard would see the first volumes of the *Nights* published,[24] and Isabel was to lobby their contacts for his early retirement on full pension. Meanwhile, he concentrated on trying to complete two extra volumes so that he could bring out 'five volumes instead of three' during the summer of 1885.[25]

Fortuitously, Isabel was left another £500 by an obscure relative; these timely legacies which occurred half a dozen times or so, together with loans from Isabel's father, saved the Burtons from financial embarrassment. They travelled separately to London, for Richard had been ordered to travel by sea (which he loved), and because of her condition Isabel had been advised to go quietly over-land. She carried with her the manuscript of the first three volumes of the *Nights* and one of her first appointments was with Oliver Notcutt, of the Waterlow Publishing Company, who had provisionally agreed to print the work.

The directors of the company, hearing rumours of what Burton's *Nights* contained, had become nervous. The Obscene Publications Act was vigorously applied, and an accusation by a member of the Society for the Suppression of Vice that a company had published obscene literature was enough to cause the police to search the premises. Conviction meant a substantial fine that could close them down. Notcutt asked Isabel to send the manuscript to him so that it could be examined. She replied confidently that she was unable to do this as she had made her husband two promises: first 'not to read the manuscript', and second, 'not to let it out of my hands.' She would call on them as arranged, 'on Monday after ten . . . a room should be placed at my disposal.' The directors could examine the manuscript for as long as they wished, she said, but only in her presence.[26]

As a result of examination of the manuscript the company drew up a highly protective contract, making Burton liable for any legal actions which arose from their printing the matter, and requiring the entire costs of the project to be paid up front. Isabel, the literary agent, bridled; publication was to take place over a number of years. They did not have that amount of money, but even if they had she would not have agreed to tie it up over such a long period. As for the protective clause, it was one 'which a man ought not to sign to save his life! It binds him body and soul, and all the property he has or ever might have, at the caprice or religious calls of every body on your premises whose sister or aunt may be made a confidant of, and who thinks it her duty to make it known. We honourably pledge ourselves never to divulge your name . . . Mr Payne's printers make no such difficulties for him and . . . they [the Society for the Suppression of Vice] would have to be unpleasant to Mr Payne *first*, else one could prove *animus*.'[27]

That week a top gynaecologist, Mr Spencer Wells, confirmed that Isabel had a malignant tumour in the right ovary, and if that was not sufficient distress her father, now 86 years old, suffered a second stroke.[28] It was a relief when the novelist Elizabeth Lynn Lynton, a neighbour of the Arundells in Montagu Place, introduced Isabel to the famous criminal lawyer George Lewis who specialised in the Obscene Publications Act law. 'Thank you a thousand times, you dear, kind, and deliciously shocking woman,' Isabel wrote to Mrs Lynton, 'in procuring for Dick and me, who are sort of "Babes in the Wood" in business . . . the friendly and strong protecting wing of George Lewis. I shall go and cower under it tomorrow . . . and feel safe from the den of thieves, the "Trade", as they call themselves – more villainous than dealers in horse flesh – also from that hideous humbug The Society for the Suppression of Vice.'[29]

Waterlows accepted Isabel's terms. As an agent she was first class; nothing escaped her from the weight of paper, the size of type, the leading and typeface, to the page and cover design. Naturally she expected to pay for changes to proofs that Richard was constantly polishing, but she was careful to identify typesetting errors for which the printer was responsible: 'your men have left out one sentence, apostrophes and in all there are 11 *little* faults . . .'; '. . . you get dearer and dearer, and more difficult about trifles . . .'; 'use Captain Burton's portrait as fencing master . . . for that purpose . . .'; 'Reduce space by printing these in a small light type . . .'; 'the bibliography is imperfect . . .'; 'I want to reprint . . . in French, Italian, German & modern Greek and wish to retain all rights . . .'[30] The quantity and detail of her correspondence with his various publishers alone is evidence of the major role Isabel played in Richard's literary career.[31]

Richard arrived on 14 June 1885, twelve days after Isabel and two days after a general election put the Conservatives back in power with Lord Salisbury as premier. Because of his expertise in that field, Salisbury decided to keep the Foreign Office himself. Having the sympathetic ear of the most powerful man in the country put Richard in a better position than he had ever been, to further his ambitions to be transferred. Furthermore, Isabel had made a point of becoming friendly with Lady Salisbury, as a result of which the couple received invitations to the Salisburys' home, Hatfield House. Here, Richard was able to voice his trenchant opinions on the two most pressing foreign affairs problems of the day: the disastrous conduct of Gladstone's government in the Sudan, Egypt and Afghanistan, and the ever-present Irish question.

When Swinburne met the couple he found they both looked 'younger than ever – friendlier and pleasanter they could not be', and could not resist commenting on Isabel's golden (but unfashionable) tan.[32] They dined with Cameron, who wanted to marry despite having no position and no immediate prospects. He had previously written to advise them that he had fallen passionately in love and become engaged: '. . . you will say it is not wise as there are no shekels – but I cannot help myself. It is one of those things which no one can understand.'[33] They also lunched with Houghton prior to his departure for some treatment at Vichy, and were deeply upset a few weeks later to learn of his death there of a heart attack on 11 August. Richard devoted a whole page of his journal to recording this; it had become a regular thing now, this recording of the deaths of the friends of his youth. But the loss of Houghton, like that of Alfred Bate Richards and Steinhaeuser, was an especially heavy blow.

Although he occasionally travelled to Oxford to work at the Bodleian Library on the Wortley Montagu Arabian manuscripts, Richard spent most of his days at the Athenaeum on Pall Mall. The Secretary there, Tedder, recalled how Richard 'would work at the round table in the library for hours and hours with nothing for refreshment except a cup of coffee and a box of snuff, which always stood at his side.' He always wore the same white outfit: white trousers, white linen jacket and a shabby old white beaver hat. His tie-pin was shaped like a sword. He was a compound, said Tedder, 'of a Benedictine monk, a Crusader and a Buccaneer'.

Sometimes amid the bustle of London he would remind Isabel of their garden in Trieste, which would now be at its summer best. They had a favourite spot under a magnificent lime tree where they had a table and benches. They referred to the tree as 'our tree', and on one hot day when they were driving in a stuffy cab to see a publisher he said to her, 'Our tree is out beautifully now. Are you regretting it?' 'No,' Isabel answered. '*My* tree is wherever you are.' And the part of him that Richard liked to keep hidden from the world replied, 'That is awfully sweet of you.'[34]

The first volumes of Burton's *Book of the Thousand Nights and a Night* were published on 12 September, but a few days earlier Isabel collected an advance copy and wrote in it:

> Richard Francis Burton
> with the congratulations of
> the one most interested in
> its success – his best friend
> September 10, 1885
> London[35]

No one knew more than Isabel how much of Richard Burton went into his *Nights*, with its fascinating and jewel-like procession of caliphs and houris, *jinns*, eunuchs and slaves, fishermen and porters. The stories were told through a conceit: a woman, the beautiful Sheherazade, who must entertain her King with stories or die (she was so successful that he made her his Queen). Throughout the fascinating progress of tales within tales, the personalities come to life with their passions, wit, cruelties and kindnesses. The underlying theme is simple: love, and the pursuit of love. Who can forget characters such as the sweet, tender, beautiful and pious slave girl Zumurrud who became a Queen and thought nothing of flaying a couple of men alive before lunch; Sinbad and 'the Old Man of the Sea'? The *Edinburgh Review* suggested a moral for the *Nights*: 'Nothing is impossible to him who loves, provided he is not cursed with the spirit of curiosity.'

But as well as his fascinating and extravagant translation of the classic stories, told in his pseudo-Renaissance English, it is the notes in Burton's *Nights* which, more than anything, distinguish it from the versions by Galland, Lane and Payne. Here, among the kaleidoscope of human triumphs and failings, lie the fruits of his lifetime's research. His knowledge of anthropology, ethnology, geography,

geology, metallurgy, mining, botany, biology, linguistics and astrology, and his overriding, inquisitive interest in sexual mores, all come
together here in an intriguing eclectic harvest of information, ranging from the position of stars in the heavens to female circumcision
and sodomy.

There was criticism, as he knew there would be. Henry Reeve in the
Edinburgh Review wrote: 'Probably no European has ever gathered
such an appalling collection of degrading customs and statistics of
vice. It is a work which no decent gentleman will long permit to
stand upon his shelves . . . Galland is for the nursery, Lane for the
study and Burton for the sewers.'

Richard regarded such reviewers as ignorant and humourless. In a
later volume he explained:

> the naïve indecencies of the text are rather *gaudisserie* than prurient,
> and when delivered with mirth and humour, they are rather the
> 'excrements of wit' than designed for debauching the mind . . .
> they cannot be accused of corrupting suggestiveness . . . theirs is a
> coarseness of language, not of idea, they are indecent, not
> depraved . . . the childish indecencies and unnatural vice of the orig-
> inal cannot deprave any mind save that which is prepared to be
> depraved.[36]

Isabel, however, would live in fear of the Society for the Suppression
of Vice for the rest of her life. Within days of the issue of the first
volume (the remainder were despatched to subscribers at monthly
intervals), she had her first alarm regarding some proofs of the *Nights*
which were couriered to their apartment. 'My landlord thinks the
house is being watched; he has seen two or three strangers hovering
about . . .' she wrote to Notcutt. 'Send [proofs] by post as they might
ask the messenger where he came from, or follow him . . .'[37] When
she voiced her fears to Richard he told her not to concern herself, 'I
don't care a button about being prosecuted,' he said, 'if it comes to a
fight, I will walk into court with my Bible and my Shakespeare and
my Rabelais under my arm and prove to them that, before they condemn me, they must cut half of *them* out, and not allow them to be
circulated in public.'[38] But the book also received a healthy share of
rave reviews, and the overall result was a huge success. No one
returned books asking for a return of their subscription – one of the

terms offered to subscribers – and within a short time copies were changing hands at grossly inflated prices.

Richard decided to add six volumes to the original set of 10, making 16 to the complete set. These were called the *Supplemental Volumes*. Like the first volumes they sold at 1 guinea each, bringing the gross income from the whole project to just over £16,000. The costs were approximately £6,000, leaving a net profit of some £10,000.* This was more money than Richard had ever had in his life and he responded cynically: 'I have struggled for forty-seven years, distinguishing myself honourably in every way that I possibly could. I never had a compliment, nor a "thank you," nor a single farthing,' he said to Isabel. 'I translate a doubtful book in my old age, and I immediately make sixteen thousand guineas. Now that I know the tastes of England, we need never be without money.'[39]

The financial worries that had always dogged the Burtons had thus been lifted as he embarked upon his celebrated Terminal Essay in volume ten, and the six 'Supplementals'. Nor was there a need to find publishers for their joint translation of *Irecema*, or Richard's translation of *Manoel de Moraes*; they simply paid all the costs themselves.

On 19 October Lord Salisbury, still combining the office of Prime Minister with that of Foreign Secretary, approved Richard's request to be allowed to spend the winter in Morocco for health reasons.[40] Two days later Richard wrote to him:

> My Lord,
> Having been informed that [Ambassador] Sir John Drummond-Hay proposes retiring from Morocco, I venture to think that your Lordship will consider that my knowledge of Arabic, and of the East, perhaps would make me a suitable successor to him. I need hardly remind you that, during a term of twenty-five years in the Consular Service, I have never received a single step of promotion, nor, indeed, have I ever applied for it.

Richard had hankered after Morocco for a number of years and it was the only career ambition he retained. Isabel rounded up fifty 'names' in a petition supporting the request and sent it to the F.O.

---

*1997 equivalent = c. £380,000.

Almost immediately the Burtons were invited by the Salisburys to spend the last weekend in October at Hatfield House, which led Richard to conclude that Morocco was to be offered to him. In fact the matter was never raised, though he continued to believe for many months that he would get the post; the subject under discussion that weekend was Egypt and the beleaguered premier actively sought Richard's opinion.

During one conversation Salisbury asked Richard to write down his recommendations. Richard retired into the library and emerged a few minutes later. One word appeared on the single sheet of paper: 'Annex'. At Salisbury's look of enquiry Richard told him, 'If I were to write for a month I could not say more.'[41] However, having made this wholly characteristic dramatic gesture, he consented to provide a serious assessment. This advised, primarily, the annexation of Egypt and all its territories, the installation of the former Khedive, Ismael, as English Viceroy with a guard of honour *only*, and the recall of Arabi Pasha and Wilfred Blunt from Cairo with subsequent transfer to the Sudan and Darfur respectively.[42] Recommended tactics for dealing with the army of occupation, taxes, slavery, roads, education, settlement, trade, and religion followed. Some of his recommendations were subsequently adopted.[43]

Rumour said that Richard irritated the Prime Minister by addressing him as 'Salisbury' during their conversations.[44] This seems unlikely, given his impeccable courtesy in surviving correspondence with Lord Salisbury. However, there was also a story going the rounds that summer that he offended the leader of the opposition, former Prime Minister Gladstone. The two men were at a dinner at which Gladstone was the guest of honour, and when he pronounced his opinion on the Egyptian situation everyone listened in respectful silence. Except Richard. 'I can assure you, Mr Gladstone,' he is alleged to have said, 'that everything you have said is absolutely and entirely opposite to fact.' Their fellow diners were aghast and presently someone passed Richard a card on which was written, 'Please do not contradict Mr Gladstone. Nobody ever does.'[45]

Henry Arundell's stroke had left him paralysed but lucid. According to medical opinion he was in no danger of imminent death, but he required round-the-clock nursing. Isabel was therefore in a quandary about the imminent departure for Morocco. Despite her heavy literary workload, she insisted on sharing the daily nursing duties equally with her three sisters (a nun took the night shifts). On 12 November, Isabel sent a hasty, typically worded note to Ouida: 'Dear Ouida, I'm up to my eyes in work; sail at end of month. So you, an *idle* woman, must come and see *me* – before 1 if you can. Yours etc.'[46]

Since Richard planned to work and travel about in Morocco, the couple subsequently decided that Isabel would stay on to bring out volumes 7–10 of *Nights* and join him there in early January 1886 in time for their Silver Wedding Anniversary. By then they hoped to have news of the Morocco appointment. Richard sailed on 21 November after an emotional leave-taking of his father-in-law. Contrary to the statements by modern biographers that Richard did not get on well with Isabel's family, all the surviving evidence (his unpublished – handwritten – autobiography, and affectionate inscriptions in books presented by him to Henry Arundell addressed to 'my dear father') points to a sympathetic and affectionate relationship.

After Richard's departure, Isabel was constantly aware of being watched and followed. This was no mere paranoia; contemporary correspondence demonstrates that Notcutt and other members of the production team of the *Nights* experienced the same shadowing. When she found that a member of the Society for the Suppression of Vice had taken rooms in her building, she insisted that either the new tenant went or she did. But the situation demanded evasive techniques, and notes between Isabel and Oliver Notcutt reveal that they began meeting at 'neutral' venues such as Isabel's bank, to hand over manuscripts.[47]

Richard arrived in Tangiers in December and at first was delighted with the dry and balmy air. The euphoria soon wore off. Although he was walking 5 miles a day, 'and soon hope to walk ten', he was 'much scandalised by the filth and horrors of the place'.[48] In his autobiography he elaborated, 'The capabilities of the country were enormous; a luxuriant waste awaited only cultivation and all manner of metals noble and ignoble abounded in the mountains . . . [but] the foul and filthy harbour-town reflected Suez during the first quarter of the 19th Century. The streets were sewers, the houses "native" and half ruins; the Suks were ankle deep in mud or dust and the Jewish slaughter houses polluted the land breeze . . . the winter climate was atrocious . . . more than once, unremitting rain lasted for three consecutive days.'[49] The cold humidity brought on his gout and British residents who believed he was to be the next Ambassador showered him with complaints. He became disgruntled and testy, realising that his longed-for transfer could easily turn out to be a poisoned chalice.

In January he went to Gibraltar to meet Isabel, but an outbreak of typhoid and cholera caused the imposition of a quarantine order. He cabled her not to sail as planned, for she would not be allowed to disembark. 'You will be glad to hear,' he wrote to Payne from Gibraltar on 15 January 1886, 'that today I finished my translation [of the first ten volumes] and tomorrow begin my Terminal Essay, so that happen what may the subscribers are safe. Tangiers is beastly but not bad for work . . . it is a place of absolute rascality and large fortunes are made by selling Europeans protection – a regular Augean stable. When you have time send me news of yourself. My wife is still in London where she is detained by these abominable quarantines.'[50]

Isabel was not in London, as it happened. Determined to join Richard by 22 January for their wedding anniversary, she ignored his warning and sailed after cabling Sir John Ayde, Commander-in-Chief at Gibraltar, asking if he could provide a naval vessel to transfer her from the P. & O. steamer direct to the Tangiers boat. Richard went to meet her in the tender. He was wearing a fez, and she thought he looked 'very puffy' in the face and depressed, but he soon - recovered, she said, 'as he always did when he was with me'.[51]

Imagining that Morocco would be a second Damascus, Isabel was very disappointed. She found the Embassy squalid and mean: 'a miserable little house after the Palazzone at Trieste,' she wrote. Still, she intended to make a home of it, if it was offered to Richard. She quickly discovered that Richard was the target of local children who had only to present themselves before him, and beg, to be given the entire contents of his pockets. A friend, who called on him one day to go for a walk, was present when Richard asked Isabel for some money. Isabel handed him 'the equivalent of half-a-crown.[52] "Is this all I am to have, Belle?" he queried somewhat ruefully. "Yes, Dick, and quite enough too, for you know you will come back without a penny and nothing to show for it either." And the great man pocketed the coins, laughing at his wife's sage remarks and went out as happy as a schoolboy in receipt of a tip.'[53]

After three weeks they left what Burton referred to as 'this North African Home of Dullness' for Gibraltar. In the meantime, on 5

February, they had received a cable from England. They had been expecting to hear about the posting to Morocco but, inexplicably, it was addressed to Sir Richard Burton. Richard declined to open it, thinking that either a mistake had been made (there was another Sir Richard Burton in India at the time), or that someone was playing a practical joke. Isabel opened it, to find that it was from Salisbury advising that his government had been defeated and he had resigned on 28 January. Among the Resignation Honours list was a K.C.M.G. (Knight Commander of St Michael and St George) for Richard, which the Queen had approved.

Richard's first inclination was to refuse it; a reaction perhaps best explained by his subsequent sour comment on the subject to Ouida, '. . . "Half gives who late gives"'; though it must be said that when he wrote this he knew that Morocco had been given to W. Kirby Green, who had succeeded him at Damascus.[54] Isabel was alarmed that all her years of lobbying for public recognition for Richard were likely to be thrown away on a sulky whim. It would have been characteristic of him to make an impulsive public gesture which, she believed, he would come to regret. But she had not been married to him for 25 years without learning something. 'You had better accept it, Jemmy,' she told him, 'because it is a certain sign they are going to give you the place.'[55] It can be assumed, since he accepted the honour, that his adverse reaction to Tangiers had not changed his desire to be transferred there. Perhaps he saw the squalor and corruption as opportunities to show his abilities in the last few years of his working life.

Lady Salisbury wrote privately to tell Isabel that the Queen had specifically stated her pleasure in being able to make an award that they could both 'share' to mark the anniversary of their Silver Wedding, which Isabel felt was 'sweetly done'.[56] Previous biographers have commented on Isabel's triumph that she was at last entitled to call herself Lady Burton. For the record, although Richard began using his title immediately in correspondence, Isabel did not, continuing to write her return address as 'Isabel Burton, Continental Hotel, etc . . .'[57]

Their return to Trieste in April was one of the most uncomfortable voyages Richard ever remembered in the Mediterranean. Approaching Naples, the ladder between decks was carried away by a massive wave; Isabel was in the way and was knocked from the upper deck to the lower one. She 'hurt herself terribly', Richard wrote anxiously in a scrap of surviving diary.[58] 'She was already not well enough to risk any shaking . . . I saw something which I took to be a large feather pillow roll lightly into the timbers below. I saw several people rush to pick it up, and to my horror, found it was my wife.' He rushed down to her and she 'seemed stunned for a minute'. He saw through the act she assumed for his behalf, however 'She was so frightened that I should be uneasy, that she just shook herself and said she was all right; but at Naples it was evident that she had damaged herself.' He ordered her to go to Trieste comfortably by train, whilst he continued by sea.

Isabel found 120 letters awaiting her in Trieste.[59] Also waiting were three cables. The first said, 'Father very ill; can you come?' The second, 'Father died today.' And the third informed, 'Father buried today at Mortlake.' Local news was also upsetting. At Opcina the child Andrino, whom as a baby Isabel had nursed for three weeks, had died; the dog, Fazan, had been given away. On learning of this Richard noted in his diary, 'I shall not now care so much to go to Opcina; all my amusements are taken away.'[60]

Learning of Henry Arundell's death, Richard requested a further home leave, 'for urgent private affairs connected chiefly with the decease of my father-in-law'. The F.O. minions were livid; he had hardly been back a month, after a year's leave. One official noted that in the past eight years he had had leave of '3 years 9 months and 4 days (although this included the period spent on Government business looking for Professor Palmer). It is a scandal . . . embarrassing to the Service . . . On one sick leave he went on a mining expedition.' The request was, nevertheless, granted.[61]

While the bereavement was undeniably distressing to both Burtons,[62] its effect on their lives was significant for another reason. Henry Arundell's estate was more than £44,000. Isabel's quarter-share in this was reduced by £1,800 being the total of two sums of £1,000 and £800, advanced as loans to the couple some years earlier (which partly explains how the Burtons maintained their lifestyle),[63] and she thus inherited approximately £10,550 to add to the £10,000 earned from the sale of the *Nights*.

This was in addition to the unknown income which Richard earned through sales of the Kama Shastra Society publications, for the Society had not been dormant since the issue of the *Kama Sutra* in

1883. The *Ananga Ranga* was successfully printed between 1883 and 1885 (not to be confused with the very limited print run in 1873), but the numbers are unknown. Before he left Trieste for London on 4 June 1886, Richard received a note from Robson & Kerslake in the Haymarket, a bookseller who dealt in erotic literature.

> Sir, A book has recently appeared in Paris which we think will probably interest you i.e. *Le Jardin Parfumé* – and thinking so, we have ventured to send a copy by book post today and beg your acceptance of it.[64]

Richard was just completing his Terminal Essay, which he told William Forrell Kirby had been 'awful hard work'. Professionally, Kirby was a noted entomologist. Privately he had collected a fine library on the subject of European versions of the *Nights* and, having become something of an expert, had published a book on the subject titled *The New Arabian Nights* (1883). Richard's knowledge of the *Nights* was all based on the Oriental originals, and in the early spring of 1885 he contacted Kirby with a query. Kirby promptly offered to provide him with a bibliography. 'I do not think my readers will want an exhaustive bibliography,' Burton responded, 'but a tabular arrangement of the principal tales will be extremely useful.'[65] There were other men too, mainly Arabists and linguists, whom Richard used to garner information and check various parts of his manuscript: A.G. Ellis, Dr F. Steingass, Justin Huntly McCarthy, George Percy Badger, to name a few.

The Terminal Essay is Burton's own famous treatise on sex, as opposed to his translations and annotations of the works of others; in it he strikes back at the critics of the earlier volumes of his *Nights* who had called his translation 'vulgar, puerile, coarse', and worse. 'I can reply only by quoting the words . . . of Dr. Johnson to the lady who complained of the naughty words in his dictionary – "Madam, you must have been looking for them!"'[66] It was not difficult, however, to find words that the average Victorian would consider 'naughty'. In the Terminal Essay he chose, deliberately, to comment on the more erotic, racist and grosser passages of the *Nights*, so bringing them into sharper focus. He compounded this with detailed observations and theories on sexual lore culled from his own experiences and research. These, under the section headings of 'Women', 'Pornography' and his infamous though often misquoted section 'Pederasty', also covered subjects such as incest, sodomy, group sex, lesbianism and masturbation.

Curiously, it was the section on homosexuality that caused deepest offence,[67] indeed was deleted from subsequent editions with the printer's note: 'It has been deemed necessary to omit from this volume the article on Pederasty.' Burton wrote this essay almost clinically, detailing the history from the earliest times of what he called 'the love of boys', rather than the act itself:

> There is another element in the *Nights*, and that is one of absolute obscenity utterly repugnant to English readers, even the least prudish . . . *le vice contre nature*. Upon this subject I must offer details, as it does not enter into my plan to ignore any theme which is interesting to the Orientalist and the Anthropologist . . . Before entering into topographical details concerning Pederasty, which I hold to be geographical and climatic, not racial, I must offer a few considerations of its cause and origin. We must not forget that the love of boys has its noble sentimental side . . . Among the Greeks . . . the system of boy-favourites was advocated on considerations of morals and politics.

Moving through the ancient world into the modern he pointed out that:

> In [Morocco] Moslems, even of saintly houses [monasteries] are permitted . . . to keep catamites, nor do their disciples think worse of their sanctity for such licence . . . Yet Pederasty is forbidden by the Koran . . . At Damascus I found some noteworthy cases amongst the religious of the great Amawi Mosque. As for the Druses we have Burkhardt's authority, 'unnatural practices are very common amongst them' . . . The Kurd population [of Asiatic Turkey] is of Iranian origin, which means that the evil is very deeply rooted: I have noted in the Nights that the great and glorious Saladin was a habitual pederast . . . whatever may be its origin, the corruption is . . . bred in the bone.

He explained a favourite Persian punishment for strangers caught in the *harem*. They were stripped and sodomised:

I once asked a Shirazi how penetration was possible if the patient resisted with all the force of the sphincter muscle: he smiled and said, 'Ah, we Persians know a trick or two to get over that; we apply a sharpened tent peg to the crupper bone (*os coccygis*) and knock till he opens.' A well-known missionary . . . was subjected to this gross insult by one of the Persian Prince Governors; in his memoirs he alludes to it by mentioning his 'dishonoured person' but English readers cannot comprehend the significance of the confession.[68]

The Bedouins and the negro race were free of sodomy, he said. Conversely he had noted during his time in Dahomey that a corps of male prostitutes 'were kept for the use of Amazonian soldieresses'. After 48 pages he concludes with an argument that while the *Nights* included some objectionable passages, this did not make the work itself objectionable. 'Those who have read through these ten volumes will agree with me that the proportion of offensive matter bears a very small ratio to the mass of the work.'

The same argument might easily be applied to several recent biographical characterisations of Burton himself, which quote his writing on homosexual practices as being indicative that he was a repressed homosexual.[69] But by far the mass of his sexological writing was on heterosexual love; he was simply fascinated by all aspects of sexual anthropology, and the more bizarre the act the greater was his interest. Although, for example, he writes of his disgust at 'the perversion' of Egyptians copulating with crocodiles, he is nevertheless fascinated, and feels obliged to provide graphic details.

It was as he put the finishing touches to his Terminal Essay that *Le Jardin Parfumé* arrived in Richard's postbag. This work, a French translation of an ancient Arabic manuscript entitled *Al Raud al atir wa nuzhat al Khatir*, had been discovered in Algeria by a French army officer about 1850.[70] In 1876 a group of French army officers in Algiers produced 35 copies of the 283-page translation by a lithographic process.*

The book sent to Richard by his Haymarket booksellers was a

---

*This process was called the autographic process, hence the description of this edition as 'the autograph edition'.

revised version of the 'autograph edition'. It was conventionally printed and bound in Paris in 1886 by the bookseller Isidore Liseux, as an edition of 220 copies, and distributed privately to scholars and collectors. Richard immediately recognised it as a potential publication for the Kama Shastra imprint, and translated it from French to English. Two editions of his translation were published under the imprint, as *The Perfumed Garden of the Cheikh Nefzaoui* in 1886; the first, probably in September, in a series of parts[71] (opinions vary as to whether seven or ten) housed within paper covers.[72] The second edition issued a few months later was bound (like the Kama Shastra Society's edition of *Kama Sutra*) in white vellum with a narrow gold border and lettering.

As far as Richard could ascertain from rumours, the French translation consisted of only the first half of the original manuscript which had been discovered at Algiers. Several copies of the original were said to exist at Paris, Copenhagen and Gotha and he was keen to produce a translation of the entire manuscript from the original Arabic. Particularly tantalising was the generally held belief that the missing half of the work was so obscene that the French had balked at including it.

During that summer the Conservatives defeated Gladstone's government and Salisbury took the premiership again, this time appointing Lord Iddesleigh as Foreign Secretary under his supervision. By now Richard knew that Morocco had been given to Kirby Green; he told friends that he was able to bear the disappointment because it had been given to a good man, but Isabel was furious that he had been hurt. She wrote of their disappointment to a friend in the Cabinet who replied disarmingly, 'We don't want to annex Morocco, and we know that you two would be Emperor and Empress in two weeks.'[73] It was his reputation for indiscretion, which clung to Burton all his life, that was responsible for his lack of promotion in the Foreign Office. Many theories have been put forward, stemming from his brothel report in Karachi, that 'something [unpleasant] was known about him', to explain this. But it is far more likely that his own undiplomatic behaviour – sending controversial letters to the press opposing official policy, and championing sections of native communities such as the Shazlis in Damascus – made him a bad risk even in old age, quite apart from his breathtaking ability to make enemies. Added to this was the fact that he had 'no background'. When a mutual friend asked Lord Lytton (a former Viceroy of India) why

Burton had not been used in a top position there, the reply was, 'They'd never send him. He's got no title or position; besides he'd be too independent. My God, how he'd kick over the traces and upset the cart.'[74]

Richard, accepting at last that it was intended he should finish his days in the Service in Trieste, embarked on a campaign to 'get his freedom' with a pension. 'My Lord,' he wrote to Iddesleigh,

> . . . I have not had that promotion which would encourage me to hope for more, nor do I see a prospect of any post which I could accept with pleasure and satisfaction. I have therefore come to a determination, after-forty five years in the Public Service, nineteen years in the Army and twenty-five and a half years in the consular service to beg to be allowed five years grace, as compensation, and to retire now, at the age of sixty-five, on full pension.[75]

Officials at the Foreign Office regarded this letter as a form of resignation and accepted it. However, they declined to top up his earned pension by the deficit of £300 per annum and offered a part-pension only. This was not what Richard wanted at all; he had already forfeited 19 years of Indian Army pension and was not about to lose the one he had worked for in the service of the Foreign Office. Acting on Salisbury's advice, he wrote to Iddesleigh withdrawing the resignation and asking to be allowed to remain at Trieste until some arrangements could be made regarding his pension. 'If there is a deficiency from the Treasury to make up full consular pension, your Lordship might recommend my services to the Civil List, on the grounds of literary and linguistic labours,' he suggested.[76] Privately, Salisbury told him that he need not do the work of Consul, since this could be adequately covered by the Vice-Consuls. He was to think 'only of recovering [his] health'.[77] This followed a third attack of gout which put him in bed for six weeks in the autumn of 1886.

Despite Richard's argument that he could quote a number of previous cases where early retirement under full pension had been allowed, the F.O. still feared such a concession might create a precedent. Perhaps, he wrote to Iddesleigh, a way might be found around the problem. 'The [suggested] Literary Pension might be put in my wife's name, she also being an authoress and my coadjutor.'

Richard spent a good deal of time that year working on the

Wortley Montagu manuscripts of the *Arabian Nights* at the Bodleian Library in Oxford. Letters between the two survive and show that in London, Isabel was busily campaigning on his behalf. 'My darling,' she wrote, enclosing a list of the people to whom she had written.[78] 'Today I call on Lady Iddesleigh and the three [Alston, Anderson and Lister] at the F.O., & Lady Dorothy Neville . . . tomorrow Lady Hardman. Tomorrow I dine with Lessing. Feel seedy – a little over-work and *cold* weather . . . Your loving Puss and KTT.' She added as a postscript that she would make her real 'push' two days later on the 23rd, which he had advised her was 'a propitious day'.[79]

Despite Isabel's hard work, nothing came of the campaign, though Salisbury supported Burton in every other way. When an Englishman in Trieste wrote taking exception to the Consul's continued long absence and recommended that Sir Richard be relieved of his duties, Salisbury replied that he regarded 'the consulship of Trieste as a gift to Sir Richard Burton for his services to the nation, and must decline to interfere with him in any way.'[80]

Successively issued volumes of the *Nights* continued to provide subject matter for literary reviewers all that year. 'Wonderful leader in the *Standard*,' Richard wrote to Kirby, 'followed by abuse in the *Pall Mall*.' Constant controversial exposure ensured that interest in the work was not confined to subscribers and literary critics. 'I have come across a young woman friend greedily reading it in open draw-ing-room,' Richard wrote, 'and, when I warned another [woman] against it she answered, "Very well – Billy (her husband) has a copy and I shall read it at once!"'[81]

Richard's belief that women would read the book secretly and enjoy it, despite what they might say, was echoed in verse in the newspapers:

> What did he say to you, dear aunt?
> That's what I want to know.
> What did he say to you, dear aunt?
> That man at Waterloo!
>
> An Arabian old man, a Nights old man,
> As Burton, as Burton can be;
> Will you ask my papa to tell my mama
> The exact words and tell them to me?[82]

Such episodes, far from isolated, convinced Isabel that a revised expurgated edition, 'suitable for the drawing room', was a commercially viable proposition. Richard agreed and it was decided that she should bring it out in her name. There was a problem: Isabel could hardly edit a book which she claimed, staunchly, never to have read. 'Richard forbade me to read these pages until he blotted out with ink the worst words,' she was fond of saying. Even Richard went along with this fiction: 'Mr Justin Huntly McCarthy converted the "grand old barbarian" into a family man to be received by the "best circles",' he wrote. 'His proofs, after due expurgation, were passed on to my wife, who I may say has never read the original, and she struck out all that seemed over-free . . .'[83]

Justin Huntly McCarthy M.P.,[84] one of the men with whom Richard had corresponded during the gestation of his *Nights*, was recruited to edit the text for words that might be considered too obscene for 'Lady Burton's edition of her husband's Arabian Nights' (also known as 'The Household Edition'), which was dedicated 'To the Women of England'.[85] In a statement made by Isabel which survives among her papers, however, she admits that McCarthy played only a minor role; 'We found his erasures were chiefly on Christianity, and that he had left in stories that were not fit for general use, my husband did it himself and then passed it on to me to re-read.'[86] Richard himself culled the material most obviously unfit for Isabel's audience – the Terminal Essay, for instance;[87] he knew very well which material was not suitable for general distribution – hence his insistence, corroborated by Georgiana Stisted, that his sister and his other female relatives should never read it.

Despite the Burtons' public statements that Isabel had never read the original, indisputable evidence exists that she did. The Burtons' own copy of the original *Nights*, now at the Huntington Library, was used to produce the manuscript of the 'The Household Edition'. It is annotated not only by Richard but also in Isabel's handwriting. Some of her annotations have even been corrected by Richard. There are no words 'inked out', to make it suitable for her to read, as they both claimed. After Richard's death, when his reputation mattered more to her than her own, Isabel admitted this. She could not afford to be particular, she said, nor could words do her any harm; 'Richard wished his men friends should think I did not know what he was engaged upon, and had he lived one would have carried that idea out.'[88]

Working together, Richard and Isabel excised many notes and translated material regarded as too objectionable. For example, 'So saying she opened her clothes and introduced the singer's prickle, and fell to tooing and froing';[89] and 'taking the woman by the legs he fell to shagging her,'[90] were simply scored through with no indication of who was responsible for the edit. But other material such as, 'Oh my Lady, and my beloved . . . give me possession of thy person and satisfy my need in the presence of thy husband,' was corrected in Isabel's handwriting to 'Give me possession of thyself'.[91] Likewise, she scored through, 'The King arose and did away with his bride's maidenhead' and wrote, 'The King arose and embraced his bride.' These are only a few of hundreds of examples. 'I managed my editing by making young Justin McCarthy *sweep it first* and I pruned the rest,' Isabel wrote for publication, 'but not more than absolutely necessary, and we have taken off between us 250 pages of crudities.'[92]

The Burtons also spent some time with the father of Justin Huntly McCarthy. Justin McCarthy (senior) was an old acquaintance of Richard's dating back to the days when they both belonged to the set of writers and artists who met in a Fleet Street club, who were known as the Bohemians, and whose chief members were George Sala and Hain Friswell. Then, McCarthy 'bumped into Burton' frequently, but they had not seen each other for years when they met again at the Birds' house in Welbeck Street in 1886. McCarthy's earliest memory of the younger Richard was of his 'domineering presence and almost overbearing manner':

> Dark, swarthy, loud voiced, self-asserting, bearing down all argument with a vehement self-reliance . . . the Richard Burton of those days [was] . . . the very type of a romantic young lady's ideal pirate, or captain of a robber band . . . The sense of power . . . was borne out in every glance . . . It was impossible not to admire him . . . and yet I found it, at the same time, impossible to get rid of a certain feeling of dislike.

When they met again, however, McCarthy saw a change:

> I met a man strangely soberised and calmed down in temperament and manner from the Richard Burton of my earlier acquaintance . . . he had become quiet, even gentle in demeanour, willing to

listen to anyone's views . . . patient of contradiction, even on subjects of which he had made himself a master.

What had brought about this remarkable change? I . . . have no hesitation is ascribing it . . . to the influence of the gentle true-hearted woman whom he had made his wife and his companion. I have never seen a pair more ostentatiously devoted to each other.

All the . . . dogmatic self-assertion, the desire to startle and shock . . . had passed away . . . and left . . . the truest and brightest parts of his nature . . . the quiet courage, patience and moderation of a genuine hero. I am glad and proud to have known the earlier Richard Burton, but I should not have known him . . . truly, if I had not known the later Richard Burton as well.[93]

At about this time Richard began to sit for the artist G.F. Watts at his studio near Arbuthnot's house near Guildford. The work survives today as part of the artist's collection at Compton in Surrey,[94] but it is incomplete, and largely unknown. Watts wrote in his diary that Burton's sinister expression upset him too much to allow him to finish it.

The Burtons had hoped to 'flit' to the sun in November, but their work and Richard's condition kept them in England for a while longer while he underwent treatment which he described as 'simply horrible. The gouty limb which can hardly bear the noise of a person passing over the carpet . . . is twisted and pumped . . . till the patient is in absolute agony, and as soon as he is able to stand on it he is driven round the room like a wild beast.'[95]

They spent Christmas at Garswood, which they had now come to regard as the family base in England. Isabel's uncle (Lord Gerard) welcomed them warmly. 'He had ever been to [Isabel] a second father,' Richard noted. 'It was with hearty sorrow that [we][96] saw him fast declining and felt sadly that [we] should not see him again.'[97]

34

BID THE WINTER COME
1887–1890

The Burtons left London in January 1887 to return to Trieste via Paris. Having obtained rooms at the Hotel Meurice in the rue Rivoli, Richard's first call was the Bibliothèque Nationale where one of his correspondents, Monsieur Zotenberg, had discovered Arabic manuscripts of 'Aladdin and the Wonderful Lamp' and 'Zayn As-Asnam'. These stories were not part of the original '1001 Nights', having evolved at a later date. As Payne had not used them, Richard was keen to include them in his *Supplemental Nights*.

Isabel spent most of her time in Paris helping to nurse her friend Anna Kingsford who was dying of consumption and, Richard wrote, 'suffering in mind and soul . . . at the signs and sounds connected with Parisian vivisection'.[1] In his last years Richard was as tormented as Isabel at animal abuse. When he became ill with the complications of a heavy cold, Isabel had two invalids to care for and consequently became unwell herself. She was very relieved when Dr George Bird appeared providentially, prescribed medication and ordered them to travel south to the warm weather. When Richard protested that his work in Paris was important, Bird insisted he obtain transcripts to work from.

They arrived in Cannes, exhausted, on the morning of their 26th wedding anniversary, after an eighteen-hour train journey. However, a comfortable hotel, clear blue skies and crisp breeze, combined with 'friends without number', soon had a positive effect and the couple joined in the social life which was especially lively due to the presence of the Prince of Wales and his party. While participating whole-heartedly in these activities, Richard still worked every morning at *Aladdin*, and often into the small hours, Isabel said, 'throwing his used quills about like a porcupine'. But he had not forgotten *The Perfumed Garden*. To Isadore Liseux, on whom he had called while in Paris, he wrote, 'I have just bought a fine copy of the *Jardin Parfumé* for 50 francs and I shall not want any other or bother my friends any more in the matter. But you would do me a favour if you could find for me the name of the Officer of the French staff who produced the autograph [edition].'[2]

The pleasant sojourn in Cannes ended with the famous earthquake of 23 February. The Burtons were woken a little before 6 a.m. by a rumbling of what seemed, Richard wrote in his autobiography, 'like the rumbling and shaking of a thousand express trains hissing and rolling along, and in a few moments followed the shock, making the hotel reel and wave. The duration was about one minute.' Isabel told him the hotel was being evacuated and asked whether they should dress and leave; 'I said, "No, my girl; you and I have been in too many earthquakes to show the white feather at our age." "All right," she answered; and I turned round and went to sleep again.'[3]

Isabel rose anyway and began to dress; seven minutes later the area was hit by a second shock. There was great devastation and many casualties and fatalities (mostly from heart attacks), but the Burtons made a leisurely *toilette*. The Prince, he noted in his diary, showed 'his accustomed *sang-froid*', but for the most part panic was widespread. Half-dressed mobs with half-packed luggage headed for the railway station to escape the continuous tremors. The Burtons, who had planned to leave on the 26th anyway, remained quietly in their hotel, working and receiving calls from friends who had remained behind despite the continuing after-shocks.

'I enjoyed it as much as a schoolboy,' Richard wrote.[4] However, on the following morning Isabel became very concerned when she noticed him behaving oddly. He kept 'dipping his pen anywhere except into the ink'.[5] When he talked he could not always find the right words, and he bumped into the furniture. Clearly he had suf-fered a mild stroke during the 24 hours following the earthquake, and though Isabel suspected as much she was afraid to put her fear into words. Eventually, she called in a doctor who pronounced Richard fit and sound, and suggested to Isabel that her anxiety was due to 'an understandable nervousness' caused by the earthquake. But the unusual clumsiness continued for a further two days and even Richard began to notice, for he said to her, 'Do you know I think that earthquake must have shaken me up more than I was aware of.'[6] But he refused to allow her to call the doctor again until, on the day they were due to depart, Isabel announced that she would not leave until he was examined. The doctor did not hurry and called in after his rounds.

While his pulse was being taken, Richard suffered a major heart attack and seizure which lasted half an hour, during which there were several periods of epileptic convulsions. 'I never saw anything so dreadful,' Isabel said. 'Dr. Franks assured me he did not suffer . . . [but] seemed doubtful as to whether he would recover.' Isabel's distress was exacerbated by her profound faith in the teaching of the Roman Catholic Church, which taught that an unbaptised soul could not enter Heaven. Since he had previously signified his willingness to be baptised in such circumstances (by the signed statement), she asked the doctor if she might baptise him. 'He said, "You may do anything you like." I got some water and knelt down and saying some prayers, I baptised him. A short time later he opened his eyes and said, "Hallo! there's the luncheon bell; I want my luncheon."'

Dr Franks later confirmed Isabel's recollection of this event, but Richard recalled nothing of the incident that marked the beginning of his life as a semi-invalid. Isabel wrote that when she told him, later that day, about the baptism he was amused. 'Now that was superfluous if only you knew; the world will be very much surprised when I come to die.' It was a curious statement, but it was even more curious that Isabel did not query its meaning. Perhaps he was simply too ill to be quizzed; we know that it was some days before he was able to get out of bed. Later, she took his remark to mean that he had been baptised by the priest in Goa when he worshipped at the Catholic Church there. Whether or not she was correct we do not know. But it is unlikely that in her statements on this subject, Isabel would have lied. She would not have jeopardised her immortal soul; her childlike fear of divine retribution was too ingrained.

Two local doctors were called in for second opinions, and were persuaded to provide round-the-clock care with the help of an English doctor, Dr Grenfell Baker,[7] who was himself convalescing at the hotel.

As assistant nurses Isabel had her maid, Lisa, and a nun from the nearby Bon Secours convent. Isabel gave Dr Baker permission to be frank with Richard about his condition. Later he wrote:

> I recall Sir Richard's wonderful eyes intensely gazing at me with that extraordinary faculty of his appearing to look not only at but through and over and around one . . . when I had finished speaking [he] asked quietly if I believed he was going to die . . . I felt bound to tell him that was the general consensus. 'Ah well, what must be must be,' he said, shrugged his shoulders and proceeded to chat quite cheerfully, and finally told me a story from the Arabian Nights.[8]

Two doctors, consulted during the writing of this book, independently suggested that the cause of Burton's cardiac problems in old age probably lay in the syphilis he had contracted thirty years earlier.[9] The symptoms described by Isabel and Dr Baker, and his condition during the last three years of his life, are consistent with that of patients suffering from tertiary syphilis. Burton must have lived with the knowledge that this was a possibility ever since the primary infection was diagnosed in 1854. However, the greatest fear of all syphilis patients was madness; perhaps he was able to regard cardiovascular problems, and an inevitable prognosis that he had five years at the most, as the lesser of two evils. His doctors would have known this and almost certainly, despite the fact that she and Richard referred to his condition as 'gout', so did Isabel. 'I shall never have a really happy, peaceful moment again,' she wrote to Lallah Bird. 'He will always require *great care and watching* all his life . . . as his heart is weak.'[10]

As Richard began to recover he talked of returning to Trieste, but medical opinion was that he should not travel without a doctor in the party. He complained to Isabel that he disliked the idea of a stranger always with them – who would inevitably be party to their private affairs and might not be discreet – and of the cost involved. Isabel argued that they had to take the risk, a resident doctor, she said, was no more of a 'disagreeable luxury' than any other servant. She proposed that they used £2,000 of the *Nights* money to provide a live-in doctor until May 1891 – the date of his official retirement. And recognising the validity of Isabel's argument that her skill was as a nurse, not in treating a potentially life-threatening heart attack, Richard allowed her to telegraph to London for a young Canadian physician, Dr Ralph Leslie, who had been highly recommended.

By mid-March Richard was able to travel short distances, and with Dr Leslie in attendance they set off along the Riviera for Italy, stopping at Nice and Monte Carlo where the couple paid a visit to the Casino; Richard wrote that the play was, 'very slow. My better-half lost eighty five francs in ten minutes.'[11] The journey took 28 days by carriage and train. At Milan Isabel opened an English newspaper and learned of the death of her uncle, Lord Gerard. Richard was as distressed as she was; the old man had always been a support to them both and he had died on the first anniversary of her father's death. They had been away ten months when they reached Trieste on 5 April 1887, and both were grateful to be home.

Desperate to complete the final two volumes of *Supplemental Nights*, Richard immediately began work on *Aladdin*. 'You must not be alarmed about his overworking himself,' Isabel wrote to Bernard Quaritch, 'I have tried it all round, & it does him more harm to take his books away from him than to let him work. But I draw him off gently whenever it ought to be done. These *Arabian Nights* are to him "as easy as drinking water" to use his own phrase.' In May Richard wrote to a subscriber that his proposed new version of *Perfumed Garden* would not be available 'for six months . . . My old version may be had at Robson and Kerslake, 23 Coventry Street, Haymarket. The *Supplemental Nights* may be had from the agent, Oliver Notcutt, Farleigh Road, Stoke Newington.' In fact he did not begin serious work on the contentious revised version of *The Perfumed Garden* until at least eighteen months later.[12]

They spent the heat of the summer of 1887 in the Tyrol, but when they returned to Trieste in October Dr Leslie – whom Richard and Isabel both liked a good deal – was offered a permanent position in the Far East, his long-term ambition, and so regretfully gave in his notice. Richard 'clamoured' not to have a replacement, but Isabel could now walk only with difficulty and had long spells of secret discomfort due to the growing tumour in her ovary, so she could not adequately care for him on her own. Sometimes during their short walks she had to take alternate spells with him in the wheelchair, and she could no longer help him in and out of the bath-tub each morning. Dr Grenfell Baker the young Englishman who had come to their aid in Cannes, had retired from his London practice and was seeking a position in the Mediterranean. Hearing of Dr Leslie's resignation, he proposed himself as replacement and took up the appointment on 15 October. It was agreed, Isabel wrote to a correspondent in England, that Dr Baker 'will bring us home to England [next spring] when I hope [Richard] will be quite out of danger . . . The Government is still haggling over his paltry little pension. Richard is very good to me and gives me wonderful energy, so I am never depressed but hope, as ever.'[13] In the same letter she answers a query about a rumoured biography of Richard. 'Yes, a life of R. is coming out . . . We dread it as the editor is not competent. I did contribute a great deal, in fact his early life to about 29 years of age, but the editor has picked and chosen, and not put it as I meant.'

While the Burtons were in London in 1886, Isabel had been interviewed several times by Frances Hitchman, in respect of his proposed biography of Burton. She thought that a book detailing Richard's career might help his chances of obtaining an early retirement with pension and, having read and approved of Hitchman's previous biography of Disraeli, she thought she could trust him. Subsequently, she provided him with Richard's unpublished autobiography, as well as access to their books and papers. Her clear understanding was that Hitchman would do the job that she herself would have liked to do, but had no time to undertake. The title was to be *Richard F. Burton – his early life and private life, his public life, and an abridgement of his travels and explorations*, edited by Francis Hitchman. This is what Hitchman proposed, and what was agreed by both Richard and Isabel.[14] As time went on, however, the biographer broke his promise to allow them to see what he had written and ignored Isabel's requests to approve the proofs. As the date of publication drew near, she became increasingly anxious and asked Oliver Notcutt to get hold of an advance copy and give her an opinion. 'About Hitchman's book,' he responded:

I do not think [it] will be a popular one . . . I do not think the author emphasises the great services [Sir Richard] rendered the country as he should. He *refers* to them, but does not keep them before the reader. This is particularly noticeable in the mission to Dahome . . . As to how it will help your interests with the Government I really can hardly answer . . . but I do think the

author has made one fatal mistake and that is to constantly and per-
sistently abuse the officials of the Foreign Office. Sir Richard
fearlessly spoke *his* mind and lost favour accordingly, but that is no
reason why his biographer should have done so too. It would not
have mattered . . . had Sir Richard required nothing more from the
Government. But it is sheer folly to hit a man one moment and to
ask a favour of him the next.[15]

Notcutt's views proved sound. Reviewers concluded that Richard
was guilty of disrespect to his superior officers; 'ungrateful with his lot
and perpetually whining after more rewards and honours and better
paid posts', said one. 'We wonder what Consul or other servant of the
Foreign Office ever had such long and frequent leaves of absence, and
spent so little time at his post (drawing salary all the time, it may be
presumed),' said another.

A good deal of Hitchman's first volume is simply a transcript of
part of Richard's autobiography, and elsewhere text is lifted straight
from Burton's published works. The title page credited Hitchman as
author, instead of editor as originally agreed. It was, in fact, blatant
plagiarism.[16] Worse, Hitchman told the press that he had been obliged
to excise part of the material offered to him by the Burtons because of
its 'unsuitability'. The clear implication, picked up by journalists,
was that the excised material (marked by Isabel, 'nb: Do not quote
this') was in some way improper.

Isabel refuted Hitchman's allegations, of course, writing to the
newspapers that her notes had been intended merely to protect third
parties from identification. 'I am not on quarrelling terms with the
author – there have been no "daily battles by telegraph",' she
insisted.[17] But to her solicitor she wrote angrily: 'Just look what a
dreadful mess I have got into with this cad Hitchman, who whined to
me about his sickness and poverty till I gave him my notes and 25
guineas . . . He wouldn't dare do this to a man, nor yet a woman of
his own class; but because I am a lady he knows he has me at his
mercy . . . Can you threaten Hitchman that if there is a word more of
this kind in the newspapers that you will [sue] him for libel?'[18]

One of many correspondents who wrote sympathetically to the
couple over this affair was Leonard Smithers, a young Yorkshire
solicitor. Smithers was a subscriber to Richard's *Nights* and had
already written a couple of times to him about a literary venture of his

own, a list of books to be printed under the imprint of Erotika Biblion.[19] The relationship deepened over the Hitchman affair and, henceforward, Smithers would play a major part in the Burtons' lives.

For eighteen months after his heart attack at Cannes Richard remained a desperately sick man, but – in a classic case of 'cry wolf' – officials at the F.O. refused to believe it. 'It seems peculiar that [immediately after the heart attack] he was strong enough to make the journey [to Trieste],' one official noted, 'but that now convalescent he is not sufficiently strong enough to undertake the duties of Consul.' It was left to H.T. Anderson (a friend of the couple) to ask, amid a welter of other internal memoranda on the subject. 'Might we not now leave it alone? Burton is going to do the right thing.' Eventually the sick leave was extended because, as one official pointed out, failure to do so would 'inevitably beget another circular to the crowned heads of Europe and the nobility of Great Britain, Scotland and Ireland, full of allusion to unrequited services and the base ingratitude of a thankless country.'[20]

By the end of November 1887 Richard had almost completed volume 5 and wrote to Kirby, the *Nights* expert, asking if he would let him have some observations, 'such as those Mr Clouston has done so ably for vols II & III. But I want a change of tone and . . . no one could do this better than yourself. Of course I do not expect this work to be done for "Love", but that is a question we can afterwards settle. What I want to know is whether your work will allow you to write say 20-30 pages of remarks by the end of May next, as appendix to vol. five?'[21]

Two weeks later an evidently stressed Isabel confirmed the above letter. Using the same 'businesslike' tone she habitually adopted in her dealings with publishers, she asked if he would do the work requested by Richard in return for a complete set of Richard's *Nights*, and a set of her own 'Household Edition'; 'you will then have received 21 volumes gratis, worth 18 guineas . . . [which I] consider fair remuneration for your assistance. Vol. 4 shall go home in January. Number 5 shall go home with us in May . . . My husband advises you to read the Wortley Montagu manuscript as that will compose his 4th vol and half his 5th.'[22]

But Kirby was not a publisher, and though he was not of Isabel's class he was a gentleman. In a chilly reply he made it clear that he had taken deep offence at the suggestion that his assistance was regarded as 'a matter of business'.[23] Isabel, it seemed, had as great a facility for making enemies as did Richard. Her reply from Abbazio in Austria was breezily apologetic: 'My husband has desired me to answer your letter and to say he thinks it very kind . . . of you to propose not to make a matter of business of your work, although he himself felt bound to offer it and hence my last letter . . . Sir Richard is very pleased that you care to have the books and exchange mutual tokens of regard, but it would not have done for him to propose it – it had to come from *you*.'[24] But Kirby was not placated, henceforward, though he called Richard his friend, he was Isabel's foe.

The Burtons returned to Trieste in the spring of 1888. Their days began gently at 7 a.m. now, with a light breakfast which Richard always shared with the garden birds who lined up on a branch of an almond tree that brushed his bedroom window; 'then he wrote his journals – two sets, one private, which was kept in a drawer in my room,' Isabel wrote, 'and one public ephemeris of notes, quotations, remarks, news and weather memoranda; then he would fall to his literature.'[25] At mid-morning Dr Baker would help him in and out of the bath, and while he bathed he often read aloud from his morning's work. Then he would shave and dress himself.

For a period every day the couple used to sit under 'our tree', the great lime tree in their garden, and receive visitors. Richard enjoyed this enormously, for anyone of note passing through the port was sure to make their way up the steep narrow hill to the *palazzo*. Men of scientific stature from all over Europe such as Heinrich Schliemann ('of Troy') went out of their way to call on the couple, and friends such as Arbuthnot and George Bird came and stayed with them. Richard's ability as a raconteur was unchanged and Baker noted how some of his younger callers were often left open-mouthed at his hair-raising stories: '"Another moment," he would say, "and I should have been a dead man, but I was too quick for my gentleman. I turned round with my sword and sliced him up like a lemon."' He advised Baker that in the event he were 'called out' by an Austrian, '"Never attack a man, but if he attacks you, kill him."' And on one occasion when asked the usual question by a young curate, '"Is it true you shot a man near Mecca?"'; "Sir" replied Burton tossing his head haughtily, "I'm proud to say that I have committed every sin in the Decalogue."'[26]

The small boy showing off before his adoring and admiring family had never quite died in Burton, even though he was now an old man who retired to bed exhausted at 9 p.m. Isabel habitually sat beside his bed and said her prayers (which he liked to hear) and chatted to him a while before going through to her room, leaving him with some light reading, 'chow-chow' he called it, to send him to sleep. The two rooms were linked by an electric buzzer so that he could call her day or night in the event of sudden illness.

On 19 March 1888, his 67th birthday, Richard completed the last volume of the six *Supplemental Nights* in Trieste, heartily relieved to be free of further obligations to the subscribers. Modern scholars contend that the six supplemental volumes are not as brilliant as the first ten, and this is hardly surprising given the marked decline in his health following completion of his Terminal Essay. Isabel's 'Household Edition' had been a flop, and sold fewer than 500 copies. She had been convinced that the general public would flock to read the stories for themselves, and that an expurgated edition was a way of increasing their income without compromising Richard's promise to the subscribers that the first edition would be limited to 1,000 and not reprinted. To Ouida he wrote, 'for me the *Nights* are finished, all but the printing. As the idiot public has despised my wife's Household (much chastened) Edition, I go to England (July 15th) and print (not publish) "The Black Book of the Arabian Nights" with all the horror between two pasteboards. Aha!'[27] But in a sense he felt vindicated by the failure of Isabel's version, for he wrote in the last of the *Supplemental* volumes; 'even innocent girlhood tossed aside the chaste volumes in utter contempt, and would not condescend to aught save the thing, the whole thing and nothing but the thing, unexpurgated and uncastrated.'[28]

With the *Nights* completed Isabel noted a new gentleness in Richard, although increasingly he found it hard to concentrate and locate the papers he needed for his ongoing work, and this inevitably made him irritable at times, like a sick child. She was often summoned with an agitated demand that she find a lost paper. They left Trieste in June – accompanied by Isabel's maid, Lisa, and Dr Baker – for a leisurely journey to England through Austria, Switzerland and France. Isabel and Baker planned that she and Lisa would always go ahead of the two men when they left a hotel, to organise the luggage and tickets of trains and steamers so as to make transfers smooth for Richard. Invariably he circumvented this arrangement. 'He would not let me go away a single instant before him,' she wrote, 'and used to jump into the same carriage.'

They reached England in mid-June, spending a day at Folkestone with Maria and Georgiana Stisted. The two women were shocked at the change in Richard's appearance. 'We knew of course that he had been ill,' Georgiana said, but this knowledge had not prepared them for the 'utter breakdown in [his] health'.

Burton biographers have always queried and speculated on Burton's motivation in producing a second version of *The Perfumed Garden*. In his scholarly introduction to a reprint of the Kama Shastra version in 1963, Alan Hull Walton repeated the query:

> Why, it may be asked, was this new version necessary? The answer, I think lies in that . . . letter of Guy de Maupassant which stated that the original French translator had not 'dared to translate a chapter concerning a vice very common in this country – that of Pederasty'.[29]

Undoubtedly Richard was intrigued by the missing material, rumoured to consist of one chapter in the original manuscript, but this lacuna – Chapter 21 – was almost as long as the previous twenty chapters. Isabel's papers in the Wiltshire Record Office provide a further answer.

Hardly had the Burtons arrived at the St James Hotel in London when Arbuthnot called on them to tell Richard that a pirated edition of their *Ananga Ranga* was being sold in a Soho bookshop. Furthermore, the printers had just announced that they were bringing out an edition of *The Perfumed Garden*. It did not take Richard long to find out that the offender was Edward Avery, printer and bookseller of 145 Great College Street, Camden Town, and he wrote demanding an explanation. Avery – knowing that Burton and Arbuthnot could hardly seek legal redress – sent a prospectus of his *Ananga Ranga* and answered unblushingly:

> . . . I have laid your claim before the parties who reprinted the A.R. [*Ananga Ranga*] and in consideration of your interest in the translations they have requested me to make you the following offer. 4 copies of A.R. and 6 of Perfumed Garden, the latter when ready for delivery which will be in about 4 weeks. At the same time I am

requested to point out to you that the work would not have been reprinted had your publisher been satisfied to supply the work at the original cost of 30/- which allowed a reasonable profit on the sale.[30]

'Avery is a most unedifying rogue,' Burton wrote to Smithers, 'who pirated my friend Arbuthnot's book, and our joint work . . . in order to make more money.'[31]

Burton's first *Perfumed Garden* was his translation from the French, *Le Jardin Parfumé*, as explained earlier. But he had long wanted to make his own translation of the original Arabic; particularly in view of the rumoured unpublished Chapter 21, which he had not yet been able to trace. Avery's plagiarism determined him to begin work on a new translation, which he stated would be superior to his earlier one. It would be more extensively annotated, and he hoped to add material from the intriguing missing chapter. The copy of the Arabic manuscript in the Bibliothèque Nationale, which he had ordered to be hand-copied in Paris prior to his heart attack, had been sent to him some months prior to the Avery incident. Having read it, he said, he now preferred the translation 'Scented Garden' to 'Perfumed Garden'. However, it is just as likely that he changed the name in order to distinguish the new translation from his earlier version.

His health continued to give cause for concern. Ten days after arriving in England he suffered an attack which alarmed Isabel and Dr Baker, but on the following day he insisted on being taken to the Athenaeum as usual. Loving him as she did, Isabel fully understood that the regime imposed by his illness was onerous to a man whose world had previously known no boundaries. 'What a delight it was to him to return to the club,' she wrote.

> He used to be dropped there at about half-past eleven . . . lunch there, take a siesta after, and read and write and see his men friends . . . Dr Baker or I used to call for him at six. It was the only free time he had from our surveillance the whole three and a half years of his illness, and it was an immense relief for him. I do not mean to say that he could not be alone in his room as much as ever he liked, but we never let him walk or drive out by himself lest a return of the attack should occur.[32]

On the days when he did not visit his club, Isabel gave lunches for their old friends Du Chaillu, F.F. Arbuthnot, Henry Irving, Swinburne – with his ever-present companion Theodore Watts Dunton – John Payne, Laurence Oliphant, Verney Lovett Cameron and his young wife. Occasionally, the couple held dinner parties when, invariably, Richard retired exhausted at 9 p.m. leaving his guests to smoking and banter – and Isabel. She remained because Richard decreed it, but his friends were not universally pleased about her presence in their male coterie. 'She had a clumsy zeal for Burton's supposed interests,' said John Payne (whose own wife was dutifully 'seen but not heard', until her early death). 'Her devotion to him was a great nuisance, still it was her only redeeming feature. She told me life would have no interest for her without him. Women in all ages have mistaken *vox uteri* for *vox Dei*.'[33]

In September they spent a fortnight in an hotel at Norwood, so that they could visit the Crystal Palace. Members of his family, staying nearby at Aunt Georgina's house, Dovercourt, joked that he explored the exhibition as exhaustively as he had once explored Tanganyika and Harrar.[34] One day they met a clairvoyant who, among other things, accurately described Richard's heart problems. Turning to Isabel, she told her she had cancer. This made Richard very unhappy, 'till he saw how little I believed it', Isabel said briskly.[35]

At the end of October the Burtons stayed ten days at Folkestone so that Richard could spend time with Maria before they returned to Trieste. Georgiana had seen him only 6 weeks earlier in Norwood, but she saw in him a further deterioration. 'His eyes wore that strained look which accompanies difficult respiration, his lips were bluish-white, his cheeks livid,' she wrote in her biography of him. 'The least exertion made him short of breath and sometimes he would pant even when quietly seated in his chair . . . he seemed to live by sheer force of will.' Every morning, brother and sister took a walk together; to Maria's unease she found that his memory of childhood events was often faulty. Afterwards they joined Isabel and Dr Baker for lunch, but this daily routine soon palled for him. 'By degrees,' Georgiana Stisted wrote in one of her more reliable statements, 'the longing for change seized him, . . . it seemed he must travel or die.' It was less than three years from Richard's retirement and, as he took his leave of his sister, he spoke of his permanent return to England. After he had gone, however, Maria tearfully told her daughter that she would never see him again.[36]

Conversely, Isabel thought that the holiday had done Richard so much good that she had high hopes for him. In Switzerland he gave a lecture at the Geneva Geographical Society, researched and produced a paper on Edward Gibbon's house at Lausanne, and wrote a letter to *The Times* deploring the fact that British soldiers were engaged in protecting Egyptian and Turkish rights in the Sudan. Since his Victorian bigotry regarding ethnic races has been pointed out earlier in this book, it seems appropriate now to notice another, fairer, side of Burton:

> . . . The grievance of the Soudanese Tribes is most reasonable . . . To my countrymen I would say '. . . at least be humane. The Soudanese tribes never had any quarrel with you. They knew you only as the folk who came among them to shoot big game. They entertained you hospitably . . . With indescribable levity you attacked these gallant and noble Negroids, who were doing battle for liberty, for their hearths and homes, and for freedom from the Egyptian taxgatherer and the Turkish despoiler . . . Unlike your forefathers who dearly loved fair play . . . you aided in oppressing the weak by a most unholy war . . . with your breech-loading rifles and Gatling guns . . . Your errors were those of ignorance. Do not persist in them now that you have learned the truth . . . seize the earliest opportunity of showing your magnanimity and come to terms with a gallant enemy . . . And if this step fails (but it will not fail) to restore peace, you will at least have offered the best atonement for the bloody misdeeds of the past.[37]

Other letters at this time demonstrate high spirits. 'Today has been glorious – all sun and blue with Mont Blanc clear as crystal,' he wrote from the Hotel National in Geneva. 'Hotel first-rate, the best known to me.'[38] While in London he had taken up several classical projects: *Catullus, Ausonius, Pentamerone*, which he hoped eventually to translate, publish and distribute through Smithers' own imprint, Erotika Biblion.[39] But these must wait, he wrote to Smithers, 'until the *Scented Garden* is finished, say about next autumn'. As to other titles suggested by Smithers, 'I shall have nothing to do with *Liseux* and *Justine*. The French of Dr Sade is monstrous enough and a few pages choke me off. But what bile it would be in brutal Anglo-Saxon . . . as Fanny Hill shows, one language is not fit for everything.'[40]

The voluminous correspondence with Smithers is valuable to Burton researchers.[41] Although it is principally about their mutual interest in erotic literature, there are also illuminating snatches of Richard in the closing stages of his life. In one, for example, he complains about the quality of work and speed of the printers, finishing, 'but I can pity the poor beast. Life in England for the poor and the working man is pure purgatory. So, by the way, is the English country-house life for women, and it is a standing marvel to me how they stand it. What would French or Italian women do under the circumstances?'[42]

In January 1889 the couple spent their wedding anniversary at Montreux, where Baker tipped off the hotel manager and a surprise celebration was sprung on them with flowers, presents and speeches. 'I got quite choky,' Isabel wrote. Richard, who had a very English dislike of public displays of affection, was embarrassed; he 'ran away and locked himself in his room'.[43]

When Smithers pressed him about his plans for *The Scented Garden* he replied that he had 'done so little work with the Garden it hurts when I expected so much . . . I shall print 1,000 and might expect my old subscribers to take them up. But the public is a fickle collector and a manual of erotology cannot have the interest of the *Nights*. It is, however, giving me the devil's own botherment and putting me to all manner of expense. The manuscripts* are so vile . . . errors in every page.' Anxious to locate a complete manuscript with the missing chapter, he added, 'I begin to see that a visit to Algeria will be necessary.'[44]

Their return to Trieste found Isabel unwell and in constant pain. Richard apparently had no suspicion of its true cause, but it concerned him for he mentioned her poor health in several letters during April. As for himself, he told Smithers, he was 'somewhat out of condition', but well advanced in the edits and revision of the *Priapeia* (a canto of verses by Catullus). 'Nearly half the first volume is ready for the copyist. I must be careful about sending the ms. home or it will come to grief in the post office. I envy you your facilities and arrangements for over-riding these miserable obstacles.'[45] He asked if Smithers could 'suggest . . . a list of Latin names applied to the *yoni*

---

*Presumably those he had had copied from the copy in the Paris Bibliothèque. He paid £80 for this work to Professor M.O. Houdas of the Ecole de Langues.

as a pendant to the latin *phallus*. The *Scented Garden* has reached a point where these are necessary to complete the Foreword . . .'

Every letter from Smithers reveals the dangers they ran in producing literature which contravened the Obscene Publications Act. Prompted by the Society for the Suppression of Vice, a question regarding the proliferation of 'Soho publishers' had recently been asked in the House of Commons and this precipitated a purge by the police. Smithers was uncertain about the security of his mail and his printer, H.S. Nichols, who operated in Soho, was also sure he was being watched. Richard was concerned enough to begin leaving his signature and address off letters, or signing his letters with the pseudonym he had chosen for the Smithers imprint, 'Outidanos' (Good for nothing), but not enough to withdraw from the project; after all, he told Smithers, 'Catullus is openly published and never prosecuted.' Smithers subsequently adopted the pseudonym 'Neaniskos'.[46]

Writing to Kirby in May 1889, Richard said that he could not return to England that year:

> I cannot remove myself so far from my books, and beside, I want a summer in Austria . . . We had a ten months holiday and must make up for time lost. *The Garden* is very hard work and I have to pay large sums to copyists and so forth. Yet I think it will repay the reader if the National Vigilance Society permit it to be, or become. What a national disgrace is this revival of Puritanism with its rampant cant and ignoble hypocrisy! I would most willingly fight about it but don't see my way . . . Do you know of a book by Peter Dens, the Roman Catholic Priest? I want it very much.[47]

The couple duly toured Austria as Richard wished. He spent a good deal of the time working. 'Many thanks for the sheets [proofs] of *Priapeia*,' he wrote to Smithers, 'it is delicate and artistic; we must avoid anything bawdy. The volume must be large and handsome.'[48] In August Isabel somehow learned of the risks that Richard was running. Her resulting lengthy letter to Smithers, requesting that all future letters to Richard be sent registered and through Notcutt, rather than direct, makes it obvious that she was aware of the nature of Richard's work:

> . . . my husband's service ends in '91 and I do not want him mixed

up in anything till he is a free man. He must take a course which must be kept secret – if he *must* [continue]! How foolish to sacrifice a better post and good pension for a little amusement. I have induced him to postpone *all his own* works. Think of this – you are your own master. He did not tell me to say this, however. Burn this letter directly. Yrs Isabel Burton.[49]

Even though she did not approve, Isabel accepted Richard's involvement. He had always enjoyed the highly erotic writings of the Latin world; one of the works to which he frequently referred in his correspondence to men friends, over the years, was Ovid's *Ars Amatoria* (*The Art of Love*). 'Pleasure given as a duty has no charms for me,' the author states, 'for me let no woman be dutiful. I like to hear her words confess rapture, that beg to hold me back and stay awhile. May I see my mistress in frenzy, with eyes that confess defeat, or, languishing with love, keep me for long at arm's length . . .' Burton regarded the printing and distribution of such work, privately, between educated *gentlemen*, to be something entirely divorced from sales of cheap works of pornography sold at outrageously high prices in specialist bookshops along Holywell Street in Soho. His translations were works of scholarship, extremely well produced books that he considered any gentleman would be proud to have in his library. Isabel, however, recognised that not everyone could appreciate the finer points of this distinction.

With the retirement date fast approaching she decided, that winter, that it would be nice to have a permanent record of the *palazzo* to take with them to the mythical 'our cottage', where they were to make their final home. Accordingly, she commissioned an impoverished young artist, Albert Letchford, to produce a series of paintings for her of the splendid views from the windows of the *palazzo*. She was so pleased with these that she subsequently asked him to paint nine of the main rooms of their home. Later, he produced a painting of Richard working in his study, and a full-length portrait of him in his pose as fencing-master.

Letchford spent months working at the *palazzo* on this project; he did not paint from life, but from photographs of the *palazzo* which Baker had taken earlier.[50] Isabel was so pleased with the full-length portrait of Richard as fencing master that she later arranged to have it exhibited in London. Letchford specialized in landscapes and still-life. Though he claimed to have several commissions for portraits the maquette he painted from life is coarse and a poor representation of Burton. The finished portrait, copied from an 1876 photograph by Barrand, is a considerable improvement. To him, however, working at the Burtons' house meant exposure to a constant stream of potential buyers. He came from a respectable but poor family and he had few contacts, so he strung out his work so that he and his pretty sister, Daisy, were constantly to be found at the *palazzo*. Letchford recalled how one day the Princess of Thurm und Taxis (one of Isabel's regular callers) brought a companion who was also a princess. When the unnamed princess was introduced to Richard, she held out her hand imperiously, with the elbow held very high, for a submissive tribute. Without speaking he took the proffered hand and shook it, while quietly lowering her elbow and arm with his other hand.

Richard's journal was increasingly filled with entries of the deaths of their old friends. He told Isabel there would be no one left when they retired to England. This was a mellowed Burton, who had time to stop and care for birds and animals, who had developed a tremendous affection for kittens and always had one round his shoulders, and who appeared to suspect that there might be something in the oriental belief in *karma*. In a neighbouring property, a pet monkey was kept in a small barred room and boys used to poke sticks through the bars or throw pebbles at the animal. The Burtons would stop by on their walks and Isabel would feed it fruit and cake. Richard used to ask, 'What crime did you commit in some other world, Jocko, that you are caged for now, and tormented, and going through your purgatory?' And Isabel heard him muttering as he walked away, 'I wonder what he did – I wonder what he did?'

By September Richard was staggering under a huge workload. Although he intended to complete an autobiography, to counteract Hitchman's work, 'it would have to wait,' he informed Smithers, 'till the present load is off my head; *Catullus, Ausonius, Scented Garden, Pentamerone.*' The *Priapeia* was at last completed; he suggested the title page should state that it was 'for the first time Englished in prose (the new version by the translator of the "Book of the Thousand Nights and a Night"), with introductory notes.'[51]

I should like to see this in print. We must not hurry this affair but allow Mr Nichols plenty of time to kick off. When this is done I

must find a new lot of subscribers . . . Let us say 500 copies at
£3.3.0 – 320pp; an outlay of £150–£200, which we* must share . . .
I shall winter in Malta, Tunis and Algiers returning to Trieste at the
end of April.[52]

The trip was ambitious considering their health, but Isabel went along
with the plan knowing that such travelling would be out of the question after they retired to England. Richard's primary purpose in
visiting Algiers, of course, despite his letters to friends that he was
sun-seeking, was his search for an original Arabic manuscript of what
he now referred to as *The Scented Garden*. He had been told that the
Museum in Algiers owned a complete manuscript. In the meantime,
pending their departure on 15 November, he worked at *Catullus*.

Despite several mild attacks of gout, which Baker referred to as
'healthy gout' to distinguish it from the 'suppressed gout' which
brought on cardiac pain and convulsions, Richard enjoyed the
voyage. Indeed it was Isabel, suffering in secret from abdominal pain,
who found travelling irksome. Once when they were due to leave a
port a great storm blew up and even Richard declined to embark on
the steamer. 'I shall never forget the joy with which I bolted back into
bed,' Isabel wrote.[53]

Tunis was not as grand as Damascus, but the couple agreed that
despite a strong French influence, it was not as 'spoiled' as Morocco.
Isabel enjoyed it and Richard wrote that 'being amongst Moslems
again is a kind of repose to me. The atmosphere of Christendom
dominates and distresses me.'[54] Their next call, Carthage, provided
him with welcome opportunities for research upon which he produced several papers which Isabel later reproduced in the *Life*. When
they arrived at Algiers, with its famous *kasbah* and citadel and
labyrinthian alleyways, Richard was delighted. 'He thought he would
end his days there,' Isabel wrote; 'but in about three weeks he began
to change his mind, and he said nothing would induce him to have
"our cottage" there.'[55] This was possibly connected with the fact
that his old Anglo-Indian adversary Robert Lambert Playfair (now Sir
Robert) was British Consul there; the two couples met socially on a
number of occasions.

*Arbuthnot, Quaritsch, Robson and Kerslake, Burton and Smithers.

Richard said that one of the reasons he disliked Algiers was the 'intense cruelty to animals'. The majority of English visitors deplored the distressing sights of overworked, abused animals. Unlike most, however, Isabel did not try to avoid seeing them. Just as she had done in Damascus, but this time in collaboration with the Reverend Colin Campbell (a local Protestant minister), she set out in a practical manner to alleviate the worst cases. She badgered donations from English visitors to buy, feed and treat ill-used beasts. And she tried to educate owners that a well-fed and cared-for animal would do more work.

So far, Richard wrote, he had been frustrated in his search for a complete Arabic manuscript of *The Scented Garden*. He combed bazaars and bookshops in Tunis and Algiers in vain, 'French friends . . . offer to lend me mss. galore,' he complained to A.G. Ellis (a scholar of Arabic manuscripts). 'I accept them and hear nothing more of them . . . After a month's hard work I came upon only a single copy, the merest compendium, lacking also Chapter 21, my chief want.' He was allowed to see the manuscript belonging to the Algiers Bibliothèque Musée, but, he wrote to Smithers, 'no native was available . . . to assist me so I have had to work entirely alone on a [rotten] manuscript, also full of errors. That hurts my workman's conscience but needs must when the devil drives.'[56] Eventually, he realised that the elusive Chapter 21 in the Algerian manuscript was incomplete.[57]

A week after their return to Trieste on 19 March 1890 (Richard's 69th birthday), he wrote again to Ellis, 'It is very kind and friendly of you to write about the *Scented Garden* . . . I know the two Paris MSS . . . they are the merest abridgements, both compressing Chapter 21 of 500 pages (Arabic) into a few lines. I must now write to Gotha and Copenhagen in order to find out if those there be in full. Can you tell me what pages they contain? You will see me in England some-time after March 19th 1891.'[58] Twelve days later he wrote in his diary, 'Began, or rather resumed *Scented Garden*, don't care much about it, but it is a good pot boiler.'[59]

In fact Richard was never able to locate a complete copy of Chapter 21, and his completed manuscript of *The Scented Garden – Man's Heart to Gladden* consisted of a revised version of his earlier *Perfumed Garden* (i.e. the first twenty chapters), with some changes to the transliteration following his examination of the incomplete

Arabic manuscript at Algiers. But although he was disappointed about this, in the absence of an original complete Chapter 21, he told John Payne, he had collected 'all manner of tales and learned material of Arab origin bearing on my special study and I have been so successful that I have thus trebled the original manuscript.'[60]

Letters from Smithers were becoming increasingly agitated. A package sent to Richard disappeared (it transpired that it had been intercepted at the Post Office), and a detective had been making enquiries at Nichols' print shop where the *Priapeia* was about to be printed. Smithers, too, felt he was under surveillance, and as he had several manuscripts at his home 'any one of which might have led to arrest', he was understandably nervous. 'You are the best judge about the probability of a search warrant but you should be perfectly prepared,' Richard wrote, taking the precaution of leaving his letter unsigned and without any address. 'I suspect Vigilance Society . . . who clearly had scent of the book some time ago . . . As I told you, [it is] impossible for me to appear clearly as long as I hold Consulate.'[61]

> . . . The thing is a misfortune and nobody's fault. But there is one precaution absolutely necessary. All the copies at the printer should be packed up and forwarded/stored. We must then have patience and delay till times are quiet. Of course no-one can complain of translations from the classics, but the notes and discourses will bring me under the act.[62]

Over the next few weeks he sent a series of unsigned notes showing concern and offering advice.

> Do not send out copies. This venture has come to grief and we must get rid of it as fast as we best can. If I were you I would see Quaritsch and the others and find out what they will pay for the 500 copies en bloc . . . No news, good news. I therefore hope that nothing fatal has happened . . . I leave the matter wholly in your hands as advice from this distance is a farce . . . I am much annoyed[?] at leaving you after this fashion but I must regard the advise of my friends. Hence forward you will act as you please taking every precaution for your own safety and keeping me au courant . . . Everyone will see my hand in the book not to speak of the first prospectus which we sent out. In those to follow you

should send just one, not mentioning the names of 'Outidanos' and 'Neaniskos' . . . I don't want to write anything in any of the copies until I return home pensioned.[63]

Shortly after their return, Dr Baker diagnosed Isabel's pain as due to 'recurring peritonitis'; it seems that he was not aware of the true nature of her condition any more than Richard. But her health was not helped by constant worry that Smithers would be arrested and implicate Richard. During a visit by Arbuthnot in May 1890, she wrote secretly to Smithers begging him to gather together any dubious materials, 'pack in boxes and hide secretly in a warehouse, and insure if you like'. If he would only be patient until Richard's retirement, she wrote, she would then have nothing more to say about the matter.

> You are quite aware of *your own* dangers, which is evidently [why you are] concealing your name . . . but my husband is doing *a most quixotic thing* . . . His best friend for the past 40 years, Mr Arbuthnot, is staying with us and I have asked him to go down to Sheffield in June on his return to England, to see you and to tell you exactly what he and I think. You see you do not know my husband and cannot care for him. He is all I have, and Mr Arbuthnot loves him too. This is his last year's service. In March he becomes a free man – his official career is ended, and between March and August the question of his pension will be settled and we transfer ourselves from Trieste to London and shall be able to go to Sheffield to see you. Meanwhile you seem to be his evil genius. If there is a row, the pension which is to keep him for the remainder of his days, after an honourable career of 49 years, will most likely be withheld or reduced to a minimum. And for what? What madness possesses him I cannot think – to risk a whole future for a miserable £500 *possible gain* . . . You must not write my husband of this letter, but you may show it to Mr. Arbuthnot when you see him (who you will like immensely) . . . I deliver your letters faithfully, unopened, to my husband. You need not be afraid to trust me.[64]

Smithers replied, assuring her that he had done as she asked, and she wrote to thank him, saying that they had experienced similar problems during the printing of the *Nights*. 'We had the greatest risks

and difficulty . . . it was only *Benares* that saved us,' she wrote. 'All
my life has been spent . . . restraining him to suit his interests . . .'

> Sir Richard has warm friends and popular honour everywhere but
> a few bitter enemies he had quizzed and criticised in early days; and
> those are near the throne and always setting the Queen against
> him. Hence, instead of being General Sir Richard Burton KCB;
> HM's Ambassador at Constantinople, he is Captain, and Consul of
> an obscure port, shortly to retire on £400 a quarter, after 57 years
> service (49 actual) . . . To give you some idea of the fix I was in, Sir
> Richard wanted to throw up the Consulate . . . because he could not
> keep his engagements with you otherwise.[65]

By July that year (1890) when the couple made their annual summer
trip, this time to Zurich via Innsbruck and Feldkirch, Richard had
temporarily abandoned *The Scented Garden* and was working obses-
sively at his *Catullus* translations. He even took his Latin copy to the
dinner table to scribble notes as they occurred to him. He bolted his
food in order to return to work, and appeared to regard meals as a
waste of time. Perhaps it is not surprising that amid her descriptions
of scenery and their calls on English Consuls and old friends, Isabel
wrote that Richard was increasingly affected by attacks of indigestion
and painful flatulence 'around the heart'.

She noticed in him a new, nervous insistence on moving from place
to place. His brain was so quick, she said, that he absorbed all there
was to know about each new location, 'scenery, people or facts;
before the rest of us had settled down.' He then became bored and
wanted to move on. Latterly, she said, 'this restlessness became
absolutely part of his complaint.'[66] One day he said to her, 'Do you
know I am in a very bad way; I have got to hate everybody except you
and myself, and it frightens me, because I know perfectly well that
next year I shall get to hate you, and the year after that I shall get to
hate myself, and then I don't know what will become of me. We are
always wandering, and the places that delight you I say to myself,
"Dry rot", and the next place I say "dry rotter", and the third place
I say "dry rottest", and then *da cappo*.'[67] Isabel was very disturbed.

During their return journey via St Moritz and Maloja[68] Richard
raised the possibility that he might die suddenly, though he lightened
the mood by assuring Isabel that he had every intention of not doing

so. In the discussion which followed they talked of his literary estate and Isabel suggested four people who she thought would expect to be made literary executors: his sister, his niece, F.F. Arbuthnot and Dr Edward Burton. 'He absolutely declined to let *anybody* but myself search into his papers,' Isabel wrote. Later he dictated and signed in her presence three documents. These contained his instructions concerning his money and mining interests, religion, and his private papers and manuscripts. The latter made her sole literary executrix in the event of his death.[69]

> In the event of my death, I bequeath especially to my wife Isabel Burton, every book, paper, or manuscript, to be overhauled and examined by her only, and to be dealt with entirely at her discretion and in the manner she thinks best, having been my sole helper for thirty years.
>
> [signed] R.F. Burton[70]

Because of accusations that would be made against Isabel at a later date, the fact that Burton signed this document while he was still mentally alert, during the time when he was translating *Catullus* and *Perfumed Garden*, is important. The couple had worked together for 35 years and he affirmed her role as his literary collaborator, on more than one occasion, to the Foreign Office. He was well aware of her religious views and moral opinions, and her likely reaction towards any material with which she disagreed. From their earliest time together Isabel had never been afraid to take her own line, as demonstrated by her controversial preface to his *Highlands of the Brazil*. Knowing all this, he appointed her, *unconditionally*, his sole literary executrix.

While at Maloja they met the Henry Morton Stanleys. Richard had liked Stanley ever since their first meeting at a party at Clement Markham's house in 1872. When the fellows of the R.G.S. ridiculed Stanley's reports he had stood up for him, and he once accused the publisher, Quaritch, 'You are not fair to Stanley, he is at least the Prince of Pioneers. His 1st descent of the Congo River was an epoch to Africa.'[71] The two couples spent several enjoyable days together, during which Richard told Lady Stanley he intended to write his autobiography as soon as he finished the work in hand. Isabel was delighted. She had urged him for some time to counteract Hitchman's biography, but she also had an intensive dislike of Richard's increasing involvement with men who 'dealt in' erotic literature. Stanley wrote that Richard's appearance was very worrying, and described his sunken eyes, emaciated frame, shortness of breath and transparent skin.

For a month after their return to Trieste on 8 September, the couple were fully occupied replying to a huge postbag and working at their various projects. The most active of Richard's work tables at this time contained *Catullus*, and *Scented Garden*. In addition he was working at odd moments on 'Ausonious', 'Apuleius or the Golden Ass', the 'Autobiography', and 'chow-chow' – various papers and articles for journals. Mrs Maylor, his amanuensis, called in several times a week for drafts which she typed out for him. His minute writing, never easy to understand, was now execrable so it was no easy task. Isabel made a start at packing the items that were not in everyday use, in readiness for their ultimate departure in the following spring.

They had made plans to spend the winter months from 15 November in Greece, where they had arranged to return the visit of Heinrich Schliemann and his wife,[72] and round off the trip at Constantinople prior to returning on 15 March. Finally, after they had moved out of the *palazzo*, Richard wanted to spend the summer at Engadine, 'before returning to England for good, at last,' he wrote to Kirby. 'But the time [till then] is long, and fate is malignant.'[73] Isabel was also corresponding about their return to England. 'In one sense I am glad, because he yearns for a little flat in London,' she wrote, 'on the other it is a wrench to give up my nice home . . . I don't know how I shall concentrate myself and belongings into a vulgar little flat – on small means. If you see a little flat likely to suit us, let me know.' Dr Baker indulged in his favourite hobby, photography, and took a series of photographs of the couple in their garden.

During one of their daily walks along the 'Largo del Promontorie' in front of their house, the couple visited the grave of Richard's predecessor, Charles Lever, in the Protestant burial ground. Some months earlier Richard had told the Protestant chaplain – in the presence of the Vice-Consul, P.P. Cautley – that he was an atheist. However, he said, he had been brought up in the Church of England, 'and that is now officially my church.'[74] Cautley thought Burton might have said this to shock the clergyman rather than make a declaration of faith.

But Richard knew that in the absence of a positive declaration to the contrary, in the event of his death he would be considered as an Anglican. Lever's grave was situated in a damp and melancholy corner which habitually collected bits of paper and rubbish blown in by the wind. Isabel recalled that Richard had shuddered as he looked at Lever's grave, and said to her, 'If I die here, don't bury me there. They will insist . . . will you be strong and fight against it?' When she asked where he wanted to be buried he said he would prefer a burial at sea, for he hated the idea of being underground. Regarding cremation, she said, 'He made his usual joke at a serious thing, "I do not want to burn before I have got to."' Isabel told him she would not be able to cope with a burial at sea and asked, '"Won't anything else do?" "Yes," he said, "I should like us to lie in a tent, side by side."' She let the matter rest here. She did not want to face the possibility of Richard's death, and she was distressed by his recent attitude whenever the subject of religion arose in conversation. There seemed to be some conflict within him, she said, for he spoke 'more than ever agnostically . . . He said to me once, after an unusual outburst at tea, which had made me sad, "Do I hurt you when I talk like that?" And I said . . . "Well, yes; it always appears to me like speaking against our best friend."' He told her that once he was free from the Government and Trieste he would not talk in that manner. '"How I long for that time," Isabel said. "So do I," he replied.'[75]

Dr Baker stated that during this time Richard worked 'sedulously' at *The Scented Garden* despite his feeble health, 'begrudging himself the hour or two required for meals and exercise . . .' He claimed that one day, when the two men were walking together in the garden, Richard suddenly said to him, 'I have put my whole life and all my life blood into the *Scented Garden*, and it is my great hope that I shall live by it. It is the crown of my life.'

This hearsay is at odds with Richard's (surviving) statement to Smithers that he regarded the work as 'a manual of erotology' which could not have 'the interest of the *Nights*', and his diary entry which called it a pot-boiler. However, there is no reason at this stage specifically to doubt the accuracy of Dr Baker's testimony, even though it was written fifteen years later. Baker continued his recollection with his response: 'Has it ever occurred to you,' he asked, 'that in the event of your death the manuscript might be burned?' 'Do you think so?' Richard is said to have replied (without, apparently, querying the implications of this enigmatic statement). 'Then I will write at once to Arbuthnot and tell him that in the event of my death it is to be his.'[76]

In October Richard noted the swallows flocking round the house prior to their departure for Africa. He asked Isabel to call him when they 'form a dado round the house [and] are crowding on the windows in thousands'. When she did so, he watched them 'long and sadly' as though he knew something about them that she did not. One day, after the birds had begun to depart, he told her that a swallow had been tapping at his window all morning and that it was 'a bad omen'. Isabel pooh-poohed the remark, saying it was hardly surprising since he fed the birds at the window every morning. 'Ah, it was not that window,' he said sadly. Later, he wrote a verse in the margin of his journal for that day.

> Swallow, pilgrim swallow,
> Beautiful bird with purple plume,
> That, sitting upon my window-sill,
> Repeating each morn at the dawn of day
> That mournful ditty so wild and shrill –
> Swallow, lovely swallow, what wouldst thou say,
> On my casement-sill at the break of day?[77]

On 18 October he complained of pains in his back and legs and said that the climate of Trieste was beginning to undo the good of their Swiss holiday. He was counting the hours, he told her, till the 15th of November.

The following day was a Sunday; 'the last happy day of my life,' Isabel said. Returning from church, she went to his study to report back and deliver her habitual kiss of greeting. She found him 'engaged on the last page of "Scented Garden" which had occupied him seriously for about six months . . . He said to me, "Tomorrow I shall have finished this, and I promise you I shall never write another book on this subject. I will take to our biography."'[78] This pleased her; she was only reconciled to his work by Dr Baker's statement that Richard was fortunate to have something which so fully occupied his time and interest. Richard said then that *The Scented Garden* would 'make a great row in England'. The *Nights* was tame by comparison. However, he thought it would earn a lot of money. 'This is to be your jointure,' he said, 'and the proceeds are to be set apart for an annuity for you.' Isabel replied, 'I hope not; I hope you will live to spend it like the other.'[79]

That afternoon Mrs Maylor called in, bringing with her some typed pages of the manuscript of *The Scented Garden* upon which she had been working, together with a copy which she had made for the printer, as instructed by Richard.[80] The couple spent the afternoon writing letters*, and sitting and walking in the garden where Richard found a robin drowning in the water tank. Having rescued it, he warmed it between his hands and placed it inside his fur coat. 'He made a great fuss till it was quite restored,' said Isabel.

In the evening he abandoned his usual insistence on pedantically sitting down to dinner at precisely 7.30, and dawdled about tidying up his tables. Seeing Isabel waiting, he said to her, 'You'd better go in.' She replied, 'No, darling, I will wait for you.' Every word they spoke was etched on her memory, and recorded in her journal. 'He dined well, but sparingly . . . he laughed, talked and joked . . . We discussed our future plans and preparations. We talked of our future life in London.' They retired at 9 p.m. as usual and he heard her say her prayers, as he had done for many years. Then she kissed him, handed him a novel by Robert Buchanan and went through to her own room.

> At twelve o'clock he began to grow uneasy. I asked him what ailed him and he said 'I have a gouty pain in my foot. When did I have my last attack?' I referred to our journals and found it was three months previously . . . though he moaned and was restless he tried to sleep, and I sat by him [massaging] the foot . . . to soothe the pain. He dozed a little, and said, 'I dreamt I saw our little flat in London, and it had quite a nice large room in it.' Between times he laughed and talked . . . and even joked.

At 4 a.m. he became very uneasy, but protested when Isabel rose to summon Dr Baker. 'Don't disturb him,' he said. 'He can't do anything.' But she insisted and Baker came, examined Richard, gave him some medication and returned to bed. At 4.30 while they were 'laughing and talking',[81] Richard suddenly complained that there was no air in the room and she became frightened at his demeanour. She flew

---

* Richard wrote to Smithers and Quaritch that day.

along to wake Baker, and the servants hearing the commotion came and hovered at the door. Baker found Richard in the early stages of a heart attack.

Every day for the rest of her life, Isabel would relive what followed. She and Lisa, working under Baker's instruction, 'tried every remedy and restorative'. It was hopeless. At the end, she wrote,

> ... for a minute or two he kept on crying, 'Oh, Puss, chloroform – ether – or I am a dead man!' My God! I would have given him the blood out of my veins if it would have saved him, but I had to answer, 'My darling, the doctor says it will kill you; he is doing all he knows.' I was holding him in my arms, when he got heavier and heavier, and more insensible, and we laid him on the bed. The doctor said he was quite insensible and assured me he did not suffer. I trust not, I believe it was a clot of blood to the heart.

During the fight for Burton's life Isabel had asked the servants to send for the priest at the church where she worshipped. He was Father Pietro; young, newly ordained, and new to the parish. Understanding that Burton was Protestant, he went first to see his superior who advised him to act as seemed appropriate. When he arrived at the Burtons' home at 6 a.m., some 90 minutes had elapsed since the onset of Burton's heart attack. 'I found him in bed,' he said, 'with the doctor and Lady Burton beside him.'[82]

To Father Pietro it appeared at first that Burton was already dead, but Isabel told him that he was deeply unconscious. She pointed out that his eyes were still bright, and she said his brain still lived for she could feel the trickle of his blood under her fingers. Later, the priest would state that he believed Burton was still alive chiefly because the doctor was still treating him by alternately attempting to stimulate the heart with an electric battery, administering injections, and feeling the pulse; 'these are things one would not do to a corpse, but only to a person still living.'

Isabel asked the priest to administer extreme unction, but he called her aside to say he could not do so because Captain Burton was not a Catholic. Isabel told him that two years earlier, 'at Cannes . . . he had abjured his heresy and professed himself as belonging to the church . . . she begged me to carry out fully the prescribed ceremony of Extreme Unction.'[83] The priest asked Dr Baker and Lisa if they thought Burton was dead, and they both replied '"No."' Later, he would state that, 'the doctor in charge . . . with a single word, or even a sign given secretly . . . would have been able to prevent the administration of the Holy Sacrament of Extreme Unction.'[84] Father Pietro therefore went ahead with the rites and prayers for the dying, and left. At 7 a.m. Dr Baker declared Richard dead. Determined to do everything she could for him, Isabel insisted on drafting the short formal announcement of the Consul's death 'at 7 o'clock am, 20th October 1890 at Palazzo Gossleth, Largo del Promontorio,' she wrote.[85] Despite this, she believed that Richard remained in a deep coma until the evening of that day. Then, she said, 'his soul went forth with the setting sun.' She said she sensed the moment he died in a flash of his happiness, and immediately offered a prayer of thanksgiving, before misery swamped her.

Baker was a trained doctor who knew his patient intimately. Isabel wanted desperately to believe that Richard was not dead. One naturally tends towards the professional opinion, but coma was not understood by Victorian doctors. Even today, with technology that can detect faint signs of life long after the pulses can be determined, coma patients occasionally confound medical declarations of death. No one who has stood over a loved one in intensive care, watching electronic blips when there are no apparent vital signs, would argue this. Nor can the testimony of countless medical staff be ignored, that a partner or parent of a coma victim is frequently the first to know when death actually occurs.

After she accepted that Richard was dead Isabel had his ulnar nerve exposed and electricity applied, as she had promised him, to ensure that no life-sign remained. This stemmed from a long-ago conversation with Jane Digby and Abd el-Khader on the roof-top terrace in Damascus. One evening they had discussed the terrible incident of a man who had been inadvertently buried alive. Many people heard screams all that night, but were too afraid to go to the graveyard. Next morning they investigated and found the body behind the stone door, his winding sheet trailing from the original resting place at the back of the tomb. Richard recommended electrical stimulation of the ulnar nerve to unequivocally confirm death.[86]

We know what motivated Isabel to have the sacrament of extreme unction administered to Richard. Ten days prior to his death, she wrote to a recently widowed friend, 'My heart is grieving for you, and with you, in this greatest trial a woman can know [and] . . . before which my own head is ever bowed, and my heart shrink[s] in terror. But you have such consolations. He was a religious man, and died with the Sacraments, and you are sure of a happy meeting, just as if he had gone on a journey to wait for you, but *more surely to meet* than if he had gone on an earthly journey.'[87]

From her own profound faith, Isabel acted to ensure an after-life for Richard, but also, as she told St George Burton some months later,[88] so that they could eventually be buried together.* Georgiana Stisted would later accuse Isabel of proselytising the corpse of her husband, whom she could not convert in life; 'Isabel had been too well-trained by the Society of Jesus not to see that a chance yet remained of glorifying her Church,' she wrote bitterly in her biography of her uncle.

This is to misunderstand Isabel entirely. Her motivation was not to gain another Catholic soul for the Church, but so that the soul of the man she loved more than her own life did not perish in the eternal flames of her religious teaching. She did it to ensure that he would be waiting for her in an after-life of which she was utterly, and enviably, convinced. And, as a secondary consideration, she did it so that their bodies could lie side by side in death. Any other conclusion is unconvincing. The matter was of supreme importance to her and she believed the truth could not be hidden from God. Unless she *really* believed that Richard had accepted the emergency Catholic baptism she had conducted in Cannes, there would have been no point in having the sacrament of Extreme Unction administered.[89]

Most likely, however, Richard Burton died an agnostic: an open-minded searcher who was never convinced by any religious dogma despite – or perhaps as a result of – his thorough research. His signature on the paper mentioned in a previous chapter,[90] signifying his wish to be received into the Catholic Church on his death-bed, is a physical fact. But it was probably nothing more than a desire to afford comfort to Isabel in the event of his sudden death. Clearly, he had none of his family's Protestant horror of Catholicism *per se*. He admitted to attending the Catholic church in Goa; he married Isabel

---

*Had Richard died a member of the Anglican Church, their bodies could not have shared the same burial place.

in a Catholic church; he often attended Catholic services with the family in the chapel at Arundell; he boasted of his friendship with Cardinals Newman and Wiseman and Atkin Hamerton. But if he seriously wished to become a Catholic, why did he not convert during his lifetime and thus give Isabel the single gift that would have made her happier than all the riches in the Orient? And if, as Isabel later hinted, Richard had been baptised in Goa, why was there any need to have had the Registrar present at their Catholic marriage in 1861? This was only necessary for legal reasons in mixed marriages.

Surely he made his feelings perfectly clear when he wrote to Smithers in 1888, 'Being amongst Moslems again is a kind of repose to me. The atmosphere of Christendom dominates and distresses me.' This does not suggest a closet Christian, nor any major change in his ideology from his address to the Spiritualists in 1876: 'Personally I ignore the existence of soul and spirit, feeling no want of a self within a self, an I within an I.' He once told John Payne that Islam was 'the only practical ethical religion and almost free from the two great demoralising elements – dogma and priestcraft. Christianity . . . has no practical value as a moral agent.'[91]

Conversely, as an agnostic, the fact that his dead body might be baptised would have been an irrelevance to him, and if it afforded Isabel comfort, why not? He knew perfectly well, when signing the document, what her most likely action would be in the event of his near death. He had heard her praying for his conversion often enough. When he learned of the 'emergency baptism' at Cannes he reacted with equanimity, which perhaps is hardly surprising. After all, he had undergone other 'conversions' as a young man in the pursuit of knowledge, to Islam, to Sufism (perhaps even to Catholicism). We know, from his own pen, that he would have become a Mormon in the interests of research, had Brigham Young agreed to it. But – as with his earlier 'conversions' – if he had no religious faith he had nothing to lose; a man cannot fear retribution from a deity he believes does not exist. Had Richard come to believe in God, as Isabel hoped, he would not have been the first atheist or agnostic to reverse former fervently expressed dialectic against religion. It is certainly true that Isabel knew him better than anyone, but there is no evidence of a conversion, and she did not prove her case.

At the last, both Richard and Isabel acted according to their own beliefs, but also in the interests of each other. This is wholly consistent with the behaviour of two ageing people who have shared a long and loving relationship.

35

ACTIONS AND REACTIONS
1890–1891

Isabel's conduct over the next days, weeks and months should be viewed in the light of her extreme distress. For the previous three and a half years, she wrote, she had lived 'every moment in fear'. When the thing she most dreaded occurred, she thought she too must die soon from the sense of loss and desolation; indeed she prayed for it. She could not envisage, nor did she want, life without Richard. All she could do was go through the motions of what seemed to be expected of her.

A photograph taken by Dr Baker shows Burton's body clothed in checked pyjamas, wearing the medal on a steel chain which Isabel had given him before he went to Africa with Speke, and which he had worn ever since. Behind the bed a huge map of Africa dominates the wall. A crucifix which Isabel had placed on the chest of the corpse provides an incongruous note. The Anglican chaplain called in and Isabel asked him if he 'would like to do anything'. He told her there was nothing to be done, but he said a prayer with her beside the body before he left. When her old confessor called to comfort her she asked him, too, to pray with her over the body. The Triestienne Catholic machine took over; that day eight masses were said for Richard and a choir from the orphanage of St Joseph, which Richard and Isabel had supported, and other 'pious people', came in to sing hymns and say rosaries.

The laws governing expeditious burial of the dead were strict in a city which enjoyed hot summers and suffered regular outbreaks of typhoid and cholera, but Isabel obtained permission to circumvent regulations. She was given a stay of sixty hours, during which time she commissioned Letchford to take plaster casts of his head, hands and feet,[1] and to paint the scene from Baker's photographs. But the weather was inclement, and Letchford, 'being rather delicate . . . could not go . . . night and morning back to his house about half an hour away,' so she allowed him to stay and work in the *palazzo*. 'Miss Daisy Letchford, his sister who teaches English, came . . . to keep her brother company, and Mr Peter Jones [the Letchfords' uncle; he was also Mrs Maylor's cousin-in-law], also moved in.'

The body lay in a candle-lit room filled with flowers, while scores of friends and local people called to pay respects. In that predominantly Catholic environment, such an occasion called for the chanting of appropriate Latin prayers while holy water was sprinkled over the corpse; noisy displays of passion were considered complimentary. The Letchfords – born and bred Triestiennes – wholeheartedly participated in this; 'the whole house resounds with the passionate grief and importunate position of Dr Baker and Miss Letchford,' one visitor observed. 'The poor widow, who is like a stone in her grief, might as well not be in the house.'[2]

The British reserve of Consular staff and the Burtons' Anglican friends was severely affronted, but Isabel, who could not cry (that would come later) said that as they were living in a foreign country they were obliged to observe local customs. Day and night, alone or in the presence of others Isabel sat quietly by the body, sometimes praying, sometimes simply gazing numbly at the face of the man she had worshipped from the age of nineteen. 'I find something so horrible, so repulsive, in the people who abandon their dead . . . in winding sheet, in a darkened chamber,' she said. After three days, the body was embalmed for eventual shipment to England and dressed in the official uniform of a British Consul. At Isabel's request Dr Baker assisted at the embalming and somewhat surprisingly – he had been Richard's personal physician for three years after all – he professed to be surprised by the number of scars, 'the witness of a hundred fights', which covered the body.

Baker supported Isabel sympathetically in the first weeks following Richard's death. Later he would say that he was uncomfortable at what he regarded as an orgy of Roman Catholic fetishism over the body of a man whose contrary views on such matters were hardly a secret, but that he had been in a difficult position. He had lived with the couple for three years, was still technically in Isabel's employ, and he appreciated and was sympathetic with the depth of her grief. He adopted what was probably Richard's attitude: 'if it helps her what does it matter?' When a member of the small English community called to protest on behalf of Anglicans who were refusing to attend the funeral if it were to be a Catholic one, Dr Baker refused to have Isabel disturbed, and 'told him in very plain terms that they had better stay away'.

On the fourth day, the morning of the funeral, Isabel watched as Richard's embalmed body was 'deposited in a zinc coffin, hermetically closed with metallic solder'. This leaden inner coffin, which had a plate-glass 'window' over the face, was then placed in an outer coffin of steel and gilt, and 'the whole in a deal case, closed with four seals . . .' A certificate was then issued that 'the body in the coffin may be transported anywhere without danger for public health.'[3]

Trieste gave Richard a full military funeral 'such as is only accorded to Royalty'. All the flags in the city were lowered to half mast and most of the 150,000 inhabitants turned out to watch as the coffin, 'covered in the Union Jack' and bearing his court sword, was escorted down the hill away from *Palazzo Gossleth* by the Consular corps wearing full uniform. The officers and cadets of a visiting English warship formed a conspicuous part of the cortège, and a wagon heaped with flowers and wreaths clip-clopped slowly behind. A long procession of carriages bearing mourners followed. At the service in St Mary's Church, Dr Ortis – the Town Librarian, who had been a particular friend of Richard's – gave the oration above the occasional sound of sobs. 'I alone was tearless,' Isabel recalled, 'I felt turned to stone.' The coffin was placed in a consecrated room at the small burial ground behind the church, and Isabel remained there alone with it for a few hours. Here the body would remain awaiting shipment to England, as before, surrounded by flowers and tall candles.

Returning to the empty house which previously had been filled with Richard's personality, a deeply traumatised Isabel faced a daunting task: the breaking up of their large home. Photographs of the principal rooms, alone, show that they were crammed with furniture and items collected on the couple's travels. In every space not covered in bookshelves the walls were lined with pictures, maps and photographs. According to A.B. Richards, the library consisted of some 8,000 books. Everything had to be packed for shipping to England or disposed of. As well, she had to find positions for her staff, and people to take over the positions she herself had held on the Boards of the charities for orphans, animals and 'the poor', for which she had raised thousands of pounds.

All this had to be done without family support, and without money. Richard's salary ceased on the day of his death and his pension died with him. It is probable that Isabel was in possession of about £250 at this point. Richard's estate was subsequently proved at £188.15s 1d.[4] Her accounts show that the funeral and related expenses, including embalming, the special coffins, 'obligatory' press notices, cables, shipping of the body and settling his small personal debts in the Consular accounts, totalled £410.13.8d.

The income from the *Nights* and other Kama Shastra editions, and Isabel's inheritance from her father, had all been spent. Dr Baker, who had been a witness to, and beneficiary of, the Burtons' extravagance in those last three years – 'private trains, the best rooms at the best hotels, a large staff' – can hardly be blamed for assuming that there was some solid foundation to their lifestyle. Isabel had lavished treats, luxuries and care on Richard. 'He never knew how much he had, [or] if he had debts,' she wrote indulgently. 'I managed all that, and used to show him once a month a total of what was spent and what there was to go on with. He liked money for what it would bring, but he was very generous; he never gave it a thought, and spent it as fast as he got it. He gave freely. He was born to be rich, and he liked to be thought rich.'

Since she controlled the finances she knew only too well the desperate nature of her situation. There were no older men left in her family, upon whom she could lean or ask for financial or practical support. While Richard lived, it had not mattered. They had muddled along for so many years on the income from their writing and his salary that it was second nature. The only assets left to her were a small annuity to which they had contributed for some years, the knowledge she had gained of the publishing world during that time, her own literary reputation and Richard's books and papers.

Isabel spent the night of Richard's funeral writing letters to their closest relatives and friends in England. She used the same format in every letter, and in the weeks that followed she would use the same phrases time after time, referring to Richard as 'my earthly god'. To

Richard's sister she wrote a more detailed description. 'I did not have him buried, but had a private room in the cemetery consecrated . . . above ground where I can go and sit with him every day.'

What made her imagine that Maria Stisted would have welcomed the following statement? 'He had three church services performed over him and 1,100 masses said for the repose of his soul.' (One acquaintance dryly suggested that 1001 might have been more than enough.)[5] She estimated that she would need a minimum of eight weeks to put their affairs in order, but she could not bear the thought of arriving at Christmas when everyone would be celebrating; 'but in early January, I shall arrive, if I live, and pass through Folkestone on my way to Mortlake . . . to make a tomb there for us two; and you must let me know whether you wish to see me or not.'

> I should like to live very quietly in a retired way in London till God show[s] me what to do, or, *as I hope*, will *take me also* . . . my belief that I shall go in a couple of months is my only consolation . . . I do not know how anyone can suffer so much and live . . . I had a supernatural strength of soul and body but I cannot cry a tear. My throat is closed, and I sometimes cannot swallow. My heart is swelled to bursting. It must go snap soon, I think. I have not forgotten you, and what it means to you who loved each other so much. I shall save many little treasures for you. His and your father's watch etc. There are hundreds of telegrams and letters and cards by every post from all parts of the world, and the newspapers are full. The whole civilised world is ringing with his praise, and appreciative of his merits – every one deeming it an honour to have known him. Now it must be felt what we have lost . . . Your affectionate and desolate, Isabel.[6]

Isabel filled two huge albums with the reams of obituaries that appeared; the combination of adventurer, scholar, iconoclast and writer providing rich seams of interest for journalists.[7] Universally, he was praised as one of the most distinguished personalities of the century, which should have been some form of consolation to Isabel. 'No man of action – Sir Walter Raleigh alone excepted – has equalled Burton in purely intellectual and scholastic gifts,' was a typical statement. 'With the exception of Australia . . . he added to our geographical knowledge of *every* continent in the world,' reads a

more perceptive analysis.[8] Perhaps the one which would have pleased
Burton most was that of the R.G.S., who at last admitted what they
had neglected to say in his lifetime: 'His permanent fame as an
explorer will rest on his journey to Lake Tanganyika, which takes
rank among the greatest deeds in the history of African discovery; he
pioneered the way into the heart of Africa.'[9]

For Isabel, the pleasure of seeing Richard acclaimed in the manner
she felt he always ought to have been was made bitter by the fact that
it had all come too late. 'How I wish he could have known,' she
wrote.[10] Perhaps Cameron's letter to the *Daily Graphic* about his
dead friend gave her some comfort. 'In one thing above all was he fortunate – his wife, who was the one woman in the world who would
have suited him, and whose devotion to him, her hero and her husband, has been above praise . . .'[11]

Most accounts mentioned Isabel's staunch lifetime support and latter
care of Richard, and if Isabel had left matters like this she would have
been regarded in an almost saintly fashion. But for too long she and
Richard had regarded the newspapers as their personal broadcasting
system. In an attempt to buy time, she wrote a long letter to the English
press describing Richard's last hours and advising the 2,000 or so
people who had written letters of condolence that she would eventually
answer every letter, but that it might be some months before all were
dealt with.[12] She included a frank account of the administration of
Catholic last rites to the unconscious (or, arguably, dead) body. This
shocked his family and many of his friends, particularly Swinburne.

We can only speculate on the precise nature of Swinburne's feelings
for Burton. With the exception of the period in Vichy, the two men had
seen very little of each other for eighteen years, and even during
Richard's visits to England one could count the known meetings in
single figures. But Swinburne's anger, immortalised in his work, infers
an emotion hardly reflected by the number of their recent meetings and
extant correspondence. To Swinburne, as well as Isabel apparently,
Richard had been 'an earthly god'. Since Swinburne's youth, Richard
had been a major presence in his life, the charismatic, powerful elder
brother who never censored but laughed at and even encouraged his
excesses when the polite world stood scandalised. Swinburne did not
possess Burton's will-power or physical resilience and his excesses had
almost destroyed him; Richard had realised this too late, and tried to
make amends at Vichy. When Richard died Swinburne had been for

some years under the benign but nevertheless stifling dominance of his solicitor Theodore Watts Dunton*, who practically abducted him to Putney where they lived in their famous house 'The Pines'.[13] Swinburne would never forgive Isabel for 'Romanising' Richard's body. Formerly, he had regarded her as an ideal consort for his hero; for years he had referred to her in correspondence as 'the best of wives', and his published letters show that they often met when Richard was not present and that he frankly enjoyed her company. Now, he considered that Caesar's wife had betrayed Caesar, and the full force of the anger born of his grief was directed at her.

On the morning after the funeral, Isabel called Dr Baker and told him the truth about her financial situation. Baker was paid weekly at the rate of 2 guineas a day, with all food and accommodation provided. At the date of Richard's death he was owed 10 guineas. Isabel offered him £5, all she could spare, saying that she wished him to remain with her if he would, and accompany her to London in late January. She would pay his fare to England, she said, but it would be some time before she could remunerate him for his duties, for she hoped to sell some of Richard's works to raise money on which to live. Baker refused the £5, telling her that 'some things had no price' and he would accept payment when she could do so. 'That was kindly done, kindly meant,' Isabel wrote to him later.[14]

Over the following days she leaned heavily on Baker, and on Albert Letchford. Her severely shocked state made her unusually absent-minded and she feared her brain might become permanently 'affected by grief', making her incapable of acting for herself. Albert and Daisy Letchford and their uncle, Peter Jones, were not the class of people, she later wrote, that she would normally have had living in her home on equal terms. They belonged to the respectable but poorer professional classes in Trieste, but Albert Letchford had the manners of a gentleman and was talented, and had dined with her and Richard occasionally in the past year.[15] Also the Letchfords were solicitous towards her in those first terrible days when she was hardly able to think coherently. 'I was so touched by the kindness shown me by these people, and thinking to have protectors till I should reach my friends [in England], I sent for a lawyer and signed a [power of attorney] appointing Dr

* Also well known subsequently as a writer. See D.N.B. d.1914.

Baker and Mr Letchford . . . with full power over me, my house, my effects, my money . . . and gave the papers to Dr Baker.'

She also made Baker and Letchford her executors, providing a portfolio of precise instructions on what to do with the bodies of herself and Richard and their effects in the event of her death.[16] Under no circumstances, she directed, were they to be buried in Trieste. It appears she copied out the wording of documents left by Richard which gave her his power of attorney and made her sole executrix.[17]

Both Richard and Isabel had written explicit instructions as to what the survivor should do with personal papers and property. These were contained in 'a Portfolio and 6 blue copy books marked 1, 2, 3 and A.B.C.'[18] Although some were subsequently destroyed by Isabel's sister, Dilly, all these documents were seen over a period of six years by Dr Baker, Albert Letchford, Isabel's two secretaries in England, two of her sisters, and her biographer W.H. Wilkins. Instructions as to what was to be burned, and what was to be saved, were precise. Having made the necessary arrangements in the event of her death, she retired into Richard's room and began sorting and classifying his papers.

The popularly accepted version of the story at this point, begun during Isabel's own lifetime and strenuously denied by her, but nevertheless accepted by virtually every Burton biographer in this century, is that on the day after Richard's death she locked herself in the room and systematically burned all of his personal papers, diaries and erotic manuscripts, beginning with *The Scented Garden*. It is claimed or suggested that her motive for this was sheer prudery and ignorance, and in the case of his diaries her discovery that Richard had written derogatively of their relationship and/or of his own homosexual proclivities. Most of this is, demonstrably, myth.

Isabel says she worked alone 'for sixteen days, sorting and classifying his manuscripts, packing and arranging his books, and carrying out his last wishes and written instructions. What a terrible time it was . . . in solitude and refusing all offers of assistance.' Years later Daisy Letchford, who was barely 18 years old at the time of Richard's death, claimed she had been asked to assist in the so-called holocaust, 'she [Isabel] would have no-one but me.' In fact she did assist but in a minor way, and not until three weeks or so after Burton's death. We know Isabel did not labour exclusively at her lone sorting and classifying task, even during those first sixteen days; she responded to a huge number of letters during the same period and spent several hours a day praying beside Richard's coffin. But it was a massive chore simply to sort and pack the library of 8,000 volumes. 'I have so much to do with his books and MSS,' she wrote to Arbuthnot.[19]

Daisy Letchford would state, to the biographer Thomas Wright fifteen years later:

> I helped Lady Burton to sort his books, papers and manuscripts. She thought me too young and innocent to understand anything. She did not suspect that often when she was not near I looked through and read many of those MSS. which I bitterly regret not having taken . . . I remember one poem . . . the biting sarcasm of which, the ironical finesse – is beyond anything I ever read. Many great people found their way into these verses. I begged Lady Burton to keep it but her peasant confessor [Father Pietro Martelani] said 'Destroy it' so it was burnt along with a hundred other beautiful things.[20]

Long before Daisy Letchford wrote this, Isabel had sworn that she did not show any of Richard's papers to her priest; 'although a Catholic, I do not consult priests about my temporal matters, nor yet about my spiritual [ones], unless I doubt whether I am right or wrong, and in this instance I needed no guidance.' Father Martelani quite independently (after Isabel's death) denied any knowledge of being asked about, or of the burning of documents or manuscripts. Daisy went on to state that Isabel had burned all Richard's 'diaries and valuable papers, while she carefully preserved and docketed as priceless treasures mere waste paper.'[21]

Daisy was no more 'an educated woman' than was Isabel. If anything, in formal terms she was far less so, for her education was simply that afforded by a respectable but poor English-speaking family. She taught English to help support her large family who, it seems from extant correspondence, were constantly in financial difficulty.* It would have been scarcely possible for Daisy to have evaluated which of Burton's papers were 'priceless treasures' or 'mere waste paper', and her claims to have been a better judge than Isabel

---

* A year after Isabel left, the family fled from Trieste to escape their creditors.

are simply ludicrous. Isabel had spent more than thirty years working alongside Burton as his agent/editor/assistant and was, unquestionably, the person to whom he was closest in his life. The accuracy of Daisy's statement may be judged by evidence that Richard's diaries were still extant among Isabel's papers six years later on her death. They were certainly not destroyed in Trieste, nor was the bulk of Burton's collection of erotic literature.

Daisy, however, could not have known this; her attention-seeking account (made and published a decade after Isabel's death) was accepted by the credulous as proof of the widely believed stories that Isabel, in a fury of outraged Catholic virtue, had engaged in a 'holocaust' in Trieste. According to Isabel's unpublished papers, the girl was invited in occasionally to assist after Isabel and her maid/companion, Lisa, quarrelled. About three weeks after Richard's death, Isabel found Lisa rifling through private papers and as a result of the ensuing argument the woman departed – having been, the unpaid Dr Baker asserted, 'over-generously rewarded'.[22] This left Isabel, who had never been without a lady's maid from her childhood, to fend for herself at the very moment when she most needed support. Since Daisy always seemed to be hanging around with her brother at the *palazzo*, and continuously begged to be allowed to serve, Isabel said that 'occasionally . . . I asked her to run errands' and generally assist her with packing. In a flush of gratitude, she invited the girl to accompany her back to England in Lisa's place.

It requires little imagination to appreciate the amount of practical work involved in Isabel's leaving Trieste. She could not bring herself to sell the furniture; 'it would be like selling one's friends,' she said. She gave most of the items to the orphanage and the hospital, while the better pieces went to friends (including Lisa) as keepsakes.[23] A few treasured pieces were packed to send home, including Richard's favourite chair and the deal table with the red pen-wiper still tied to the leg, upon which he had written *The Book of the Thousand Nights and a Night*.

So what did Isabel burn in Trieste? We know for sure that she burned two copies of *The Scented Garden*; the one that Mrs Maylor called 'the manuscript', and a carbon copy she had made on Richard's instruction. Later Isabel would say that Richard himself had already burned the original manuscript 'he burnt all his original manuscripts concerning it, and I helped him.'[24] Apart from this, we know that

Isabel burned the huge unwanted accumulated paperwork of an eigh-
teen-year residence in Trieste; paperwork which she thought not
important enough to warrant being shipped home, just as she had
burned unwanted papers in Santos and on leaving Damascus. But she
shipped back to England, eventually, 200 packing cases which contained the books and papers from Trieste, that she believed warranted
preserving. She also destroyed a few erotic books which appeared on
a list for burning left by Richard, but some of the titles on this list
were shipped home for burning at a later date, when she had time.[25]
At the same time Isabel also had her own accumulated papers, books
and mss. to sort and pack. Again, some of these she burned because
she considered them to be of no value, such as her unpublished manuscript, 'The Sixth Sense'.[26]

Probably the only accurate piece of information in Daisy
Letchford's entire story concerns the bitingly sarcastic poem which
mentioned 'many well-known people'. Any work which caused
offence to the living, and might therefore have been potentially damaging to Richard's memory, would have inevitably found its way on to
the fire. But why should Isabel have needed to ask a 'peasant priest'
about this? Father Martelani was a young man who had been
appointed to the church in Trieste only a few weeks before Richard's
death. He spoke no English, only the languages of his country, and the
names of famous personalities, especially English ones, would have
meant nothing to him. Isabel knew what needed to be done without
consulting anyone, for the same reason that Lord Houghton had considered *Stone Talk* dangerous to Richard during his life. It is
noticeable that apart from *The Scented Garden* (the ashes of which
Daisy claimed to have recognised), the poem was the only piece of
Richard's work actually identified in Daisy's statement. For the rest
her description was broad, 'diaries and valuable papers . . . and a hundred other beautiful things'. By then, of course, Isabel was dead and
no longer able to refute the accusation.

Isabel did in fact confide in a clergyman – not her 'peasant priest'
but her cousin, Canon Waterman, who had been in Rome and went
to stay with her during January, some ten weeks after *The Scented
Garden* was burned. Significantly, despite Waterman's visit, we know
that all the erotic papers upon which Richard had been working in the
months prior to his death were subsequently packed and shipped to
England.[27] It should also be noted that the fire of Daisy Letchford's

memory was the small grate in Richard's bedroom-cum-study – not a
huge garden bonfire. Undoubtedly there was a good deal of burning
of paperwork, we already know this from Isabel's own account. Apart
from receipts and domestic detritus, there were 'a lot of private papers
which I knew nobody ought to see but myself, and much that he particularly desired me to burn if anything happened to him,' she said.
But there was no great burning of Burton's manuscripts as such, with
the exception of *The Scented Garden*.

There *was* a burning of Richard's papers, but it took place much
later, and not at Isabel's hands. We can be sure of this because she
painstakingly wrote out an inventory of the contents of the boxes
she packed at Trieste, and this surviving document can be compared with a similar inventory made six years later, after Isabel's
death, by her secretary.[28] Meanwhile there were other matters to see
to, and the most important of these was the resting place for
Richard's body in England. Friends wrote suggesting Westminster
Abbey and made enquiries of the Dean, who replied that it was
impossible to bury any more people at the Abbey. Isabel's reaction
was off-hand, 'nor can I say that I was very sorry.'

> Neither did St Paul's offer. I saved our dignity by taking the initia-
> tive, following a line of our own, and refused before I was asked . . .
> In these churches a showman could . . . earn . . . a sixpence by
> pointing out a cold, dark slab to trippers and saying, 'There lies
> Burton, Speke,[29] Livingstone' . . . and many others, *some* of whom
> were not fit to tie the latchet of his shoe.[30]

She was desperately anxious to accede to the wishes Richard had
expressed during their walk a few months earlier; 'he hated darkness
so much that he would never have the blind down lest he might lose
a glimpse of light from twilight to dawn.' But she could not think how
to enable them to lie 'side by side in a tent' until she thought of the Taj
Mahal and conceived the idea of a small mausoleum. She would build
'an Arab tent . . . made of dark Forest of Dean stone and white
Carrara marble',[31] where filtered light could be admitted and where
Richard's coffin could lie above ground on a bier. Her letter in
November to Messrs Dyke, Stonemasons of Highgate, commissioned
a structure based on the tent the Burtons had used in Syria. It was
not – as some have written – a Bedouin tent (i.e. the low black

traditional tent of the desert) but a tall white structure, designed by Richard and made in Damascus, in which he was not obliged to stoop and which they used on many journeys.

In England there was talk in the press of forming a national committee to decide where Burton's remains were to rest but Isabel wrote to the *Morning Post*, explaining her plans and inviting instead donations for the stone tent which would enable her to fulfil what she regarded as his wish. In return, she said, she would leave to the nation after her death a library of all his works, a number of paintings of him, and memorabilia concerning his major expeditions.[32] The resulting public subscription eventually raised £665 towards the total cost of £674 for the tomb and the English funeral.[33] Her appeal also alerted the press and others to the fact that she had been left in straitened circumstances. A group which included Francis Galton, Lord Salisbury, W.H. Smith, Lady Stanley and Lord Northbrook subsequently petitioned the Queen to provide Isabel with a small pension from the Civil List. To Isabel's grateful surprise, she learned in January that an annual pension of £150 had been granted to her for life.[34]

Prior to this, she had no idea how she was to meet even the most basic of her needs in the future; she considered entering a convent, but concluded she would not be accepted because of her age and lack of 'dowry'. One possible source of income had been brought to her attention in a letter from Leonard Smithers, dated a week after Richard's death, offering £3,000 for *The Scented Garden*.[35] Isabel replied on 31 October: 'As to the business part of your letter I cannot at present feel any interest in worldly affairs, and Dr Baker seeing I am very poor asks me to appoint him to look after my worldly concerns . . . I told him to do whatever he thought right, whatever Richard would have liked him to do, and not to tell me about it as I cannot care.'[36]

Later Isabel stated that she had not at this point read the manuscript, though she knew its likely subject matter. But when she received a rival offer of £6,000 from a total stranger, she felt obliged to do so. 'It was only on getting the double offer from the unknown man which was more than I could ever have hoped for . . . that I sat down to read it.' She never revealed the source of this second offer, but there are good reasons (which will be explained later) to believe that it was made through the Letchfords' uncle, Peter Jones, who had somewhat unaccountably taken up residence in the house 'to help'.

We know Isabel was no prude by the standards of her day; 'she knew that ignorance was not necessarily innocence,' as her biographer put it.[37] We know that she had read and defended Burton's *Nights*, which is not for the narrow-minded. Nevertheless, Victorians had very fixed ideas about homosexuality and Burton had written comprehensively and – judging from his other works – scientifically on the subject.

'It treated of a certain passion,' Isabel wrote carefully.[38] 'Do not let anyone suppose for a moment that Richard Burton ever wrote a thing from the impure point of view. He dissected a passion . . . as a doctor may dissect a body, showing its source, its origin, its evil, its good,' (and, she might have added, its humour). Summarised, her reasoning was that it would have been acceptable to publish this work when Richard was alive to justify himself (she had no doubt that he could do so), but, as things stood, undefended, it could only misrepresent him. 'He always wrote . . . sixty years in advance of his time,' Isabel wrote. 'I think that about fifteen people would have possibly understood it . . . two thousand or more . . . would buy the book and in course of time would tire of it and sell it . . . It would, by degrees, descend amongst the populace of Holywell Street.'[39]

There was another justification in her argument. *The Scented Garden* had been produced during Burton's final illness. '[It] was not up to the standard of his former works,' she said. 'Turner's executors burnt a few of his last pictures under similar circumstances to leave his reputation as a painter at its zenith.' If true, this is a valid point. Even the *Supplemental Volumes* of *Nights* are held to be inferior to the original ten volumes produced before his heart attack in Cannes. *The Scented Garden* was written much later when he was far frailer, although his final correspondence shows no deterioration in his thought processes.

Isabel decided, after considerable heart-searching, to burn the manuscript. It could not have been an easy decision for her to make; this was, after all, the work upon which her 'earthly god' had spent his last days. Furthermore, he had told her it would replenish their finances, and from the offers now received he was proved correct. Despite these two important considerations she decided to burn it, probably about two weeks after Burton's death. She kept some pages of the manuscript, and she copied out all his explanatory notes. She also copied out the first and last line of each page, with the page numbers, as she burned it. A summary page was made for purely practical reasons; the amanuensis, Mrs Maylor, had yet to be paid, and she was paid 'by the page':

Scented Garden	882 pages +
Preface	100
Parody of Sermons	50
Excursions	200
Law & Prophets	50
	———
Total	1282

Not Paid[40]

In addition, Isabel preserved all the correspondence on the subject between Richard and Mrs Maylor. She eventually paid off the debt to Mrs Maylor and thought the matter ended there. In fact it was to haunt her remaining days, but for a while her attention became engaged elsewhere.

In late October, a letter had appeared in *The Times* written by James Grant in response to that paper's glowing obituary of Burton, which referred to him as '*the* pioneer in a region where subsequently splendid work was done by Livingstone, Cameron and Stanley'. The only mention of Speke was a brief allusion to his dispute with Burton. It was too much for Grant, perhaps smarting because he was not cited at all. 'Speke was too generous to publish what occurred,' he wrote angrily. 'But he communicated grave charges against Burton to his relatives and to the Geographical Society, and the judgment of the Society was shown in the fact of their selecting Speke, and not Burton, to complete his discoveries.'[41] Some weeks later this letter was brought to Isabel's attention and she flew to Richard's defence, inferring that Speke had been a sick man after the expedition with Richard, and that Grant was a coward for never raising the subject during Richard's lifetime:

> 'He had not dared to do it,
> Except he surely knew my Lord was dead'

. . . I regret that he had not written this letter any time within the last thirty-one years, that my husband may have heard and answered the 'grave charges' of which Colonel Grant speaks now,* but of which Richard Burton never heard . . . If I live, my future work will be to write my husband's life; but as that will take some time I cannot have the public misled until then. I know I am right in saying that whatever the Royal Geographical Society may have thought then, they have since learned the truth . . . no one can speak so truly as I can because I possess all Richard Burton's private journals; I know all the secrets of his life for the past thirty-five years. I have all Speke's letters and copies of my husband's to him. Men do not tell everything to their men-friends . . . the world knows what a terrible journey they had . . . no money, no comforts, no support or protection . . . There was no picnicking on champagne and truffles then; no 'riding to Tanganyika in a bath-chair'. It was work for men. They were both fearfully ill . . .[42]

Leonard Smithers had now written to Isabel four times in eight weeks,[43] each letter asking after the manuscripts about which he and Richard had recently corresponded; *Catullus*, *Juvenal* and *Ausonius*. He told her that £35 was due to her from sales of *Priapeia*, and was at pains to assure her that on her return to England he could show her detailed accounts to support this amount. When she finally answered him, she made it clear that she expected nothing less.

By this time, January 1891, *Palazzo Gossleth* had become stiff with discord. Dr Baker – to whom Isabel had given her power of attorney – had been in favour of selling *The Scented Garden* to Smithers and had probably already intimated he would do so, to either Smithers or the unknown bidder. His discovery that Isabel had burned it 'wounded his vanity', Isabel said.[44] His behaviour towards her changed overnight from that of kind protector to bullying tormentor, 'and from having been treated with the greatest consideration and kindness as resident physician to Sir Richard Burton for 3 years,' she wrote, ' he became my most bitter enemy.' It was from Baker that Maria Stisted learned the distorted version of her brother's death-bed, which later appeared in Georgiana Stisted's biography of her uncle. But before that, Isabel wrote, he made her life a misery:

---

*Presumably the story that Burton had tried to have Speke poisoned.

He induced Mr Letchford . . . to follow his lead, also the painter's sister [Daisy], the painter's uncle, Mr Peter Jones, and one of my housemaids named Ursula, whom they set to spy on all my actions; also my husband's copyist Mrs Maylor, . . . she was on *both* sides, and consequently kept me informed, and kept them informed . . . She told me they had begun to conspire against me the night after my husband died . . . I ought to have cleared out my house (of them) then, but I was too dazed and miserable to care . . . Dr Baker . . . has since occupied his time in going round to all the people to whom we introduced him during his 3 years with us, to speak ill of me, most of which I have heard back.[45]

The unfolding events were fully detailed by Isabel in a dramatic sworn statement prepared at the office of her solicitor, for her family's use in the event of her death. This document has only recently been discovered among her private papers.

Baker, Letchford and Jones were convinced that both copies of *The Scented Garden* manuscript had not been destroyed as Isabel had told them. When she heard the men discussing the manuscript, Daisy told them that she had seen Mrs Maylor's 'clean copy', hidden behind the altar in Isabel's chapel, and undoubtedly they found it easy to believe that no one would destroy such a valuable property (Isabel stated that what Daisy saw was her summary and scraps of the typescript that she saved). From that point Isabel's house guests concentrated their efforts on finding the manuscript. 'Everything was resorted to, of treachery, to frighten me,' Isabel stated. 'Dr Baker used to come into my husband's room, and to make frightful quarrels with me; they had visions of my husband walking about (without his hat) in the streets and under the house.'* Isabel took to locking herself in Richard's 'den', which infuriated Baker who declared himself affronted and insulted. Nor did the behaviour of Isabel's tormenters stop at *The Scented Garden*:

When they had got all the little I had to give, of remembrances of my husband, and presents, and what I had agreed to pay Mr Letchford, he suddenly asked for [another] £40, and Miss Letchford proposed that he should go to England with us. [That meant] that I should have to pay for Dr. Baker, Mr. Letchford, Miss Letchford,

---

* A hall into which carriages could drive.

myself, and a maid during the journey home, and at the Langham Hotel on arrival.

Although she did not agree that she owed Letchford the extra money, Isabel felt isolated and intimidated and agreed to both demands. She sat down and wrote out a post-dated cheque for 500 florins, for Dr Baker to give to Letchford on the due date, and said that Letchford might go to England on the ship that was transporting Richard's body. One morning she noticed that some of Richard's diaries were missing; '1859, 1860 and 1861 . . . fortunately not the private ones, which were always kept under lock and key.' Subsequently, she told Mrs Maylor that she suspected Daisy of having taken them.* Things got very bad after that. Every time Isabel emerged from Richard's room she found the others whispering together. She felt increasingly terrorised and one morning, at Christmas, she found that Daisy had packed and fled from the house without a word. Letchford claimed that his sister had been forced to leave because Isabel inferred to Mrs Maylor that Daisy had taken the missing diaries.

The intimidation subsided dramatically after the arrival of Isabel's cousin, Canon Waterman, in January. Isabel spent hours closeted with him, and with his support her own strong personality – submerged since Richard's death – reasserted itself; 'my eyes began to open,' she said. Two days before Richard's body was to leave Trieste for England, she sent for Baker and demanded the return of the power of attorney, and other documents. He still had the post-dated cheque she had written in favour of Letchford and she took it from him and tore it up. Then she rescinded the arrangement whereby Letchford was to travel with the coffin aboard the (aptly named) S.S. *Palmyra*.[46]

Letchford had already moved out of the *palazzo*, but informed by Baker of the latest developments he wrote an aggressive and abusive letter demanding a written apology on his sister's behalf, and a further 500 florins for the painting of Richard on his death-bed and the plaster casts, all of which were still in his possession. Failing her

---

* Daisy Letchford certainly had parts of these diaries. Many years later, using her married name, Madame Nicastro, she showed some pages to the bibliographer Norman F. Penzer, saying that she had 'saved them' from the fire. Later she donated them to the British Museum where they can be seen in the Manuscripts Department. They include the 'spoof' diary of his passage to Halifax, quoted in an earlier chapter.

compliance with this demand, he said, he intended to keep everything, and to sue her through the courts for the monies she owed him. She took advice and was told that, as the law was structured, Letchford would win such an action if she was not present at the hearing. Knowing that she would have left Trieste before this could take place, she was confounded. But more important to her was the thought of losing the precious mementos that were a physical embodiment of her grief. Uncharacteristically, she compromised. She promised to pay Letchford when she could raise sufficient money in England, and she wrote an apology regarding Daisy.

> Dear Mr Letchford, I solemnly swear that I have never said anything detrimental about Miss Letchford's character which of course would only have been downright scandal on my part. Miss Letchford came to me as a friend in time of need and I deeply regret she does not accompany me to England as I had hoped she would.

But in her private correspondence Isabel would write that the fables about her burning all Richard's papers and books were, 'the result of the mischief-making and misrepresentations of Miss Letchford . . . who was my companion for 11 weeks and whom God mercifully preserved me from bringing to England amongst my relations and friends.'[47] Later she wrote to many influential people to whom she had introduced Letchford as an artist, detailing his extortion and warning them not to be too trusting.[48]

Even more than its immediate effect on Isabel, the importance of this episode is not who said what, or even who was right, but the fact that it reveals Daisy Letchford and Dr Baker in a different light from that in which they have always been portrayed by Burton biographers. Previously, details supplied by these two informants ten years after Isabel's death, to the biographer Thomas Wright (and much later, Daisy's testimony to Norman Penzer), have been accepted without question. They were regarded as objective, first-hand witnesses of what occurred at Trieste after Burton's death. Based on their testimony, Wright began the destruction of Isabel's reputation and character which has continued remorselessly ever since.

Isabel's sworn statement, made after she returned to London, and other documents in her private papers, show that their evidence and opinions should no longer be regarded as objective. The true character

of Albert Letchford, whose only claim to fame lies through his connection with the Burtons, is revealed through his surviving letters in Isabel's
papers. Far from being the upright, struggling, talented young man
Isabel and Richard believed him to be, he was a deeply unpleasant personality, willing to virtually blackmail his former benefactress when she
was most vulnerable and becoming – for the remainder of Isabel's life –
a whining apologetic sycophant, endlessly begging favours of her.[49]

On 27 January Isabel left for England. She took with her 25
packing cases of the most valuable and essential belongings, but the
mass of books, papers and heavy luggage (housed in 175 cases) had
to remain in storage with friends, for she could not afford to ship
them at that time. Dr Baker accompanied her and Canon Waterman
travelled part of the way with them. Without the power of attorney,
and without Letchford and Jones to lend him support, Baker reverted
to the role of inoffensive, concerned protector.

Apparently Maria had agreed to see her sister-in-law, for Isabel's
first call on reaching England was the Stisted home, Newgarden
Lodge in Folkestone, 'to acquaint them with all the circumstances and
my intentions'. Maria was coldly polite; as far as she was concerned,
Isabel had long ago shown her true colours when she encouraged
Georgiana to convert to Catholicism. Thanks to Baker's account of
her brother's death, she believed that – unable to gain Richard for her
Church in his lifetime – Isabel had behaved disgracefully over his
helpless body. Whether Maria actually voiced her opinions to Isabel
is not known, but she apparently made it clear that she would not
attend the Catholic funeral service at Mortlake; nor, she said, would
any other Burton relative attend it.

Having done what she considered her duty, Isabel went straight to
London where her three sisters were waiting for her at the Langham
Hotel in Piccadilly. Baker left her at this point, to go and live with his
mother. Isabel could hardly have been surprised at Maria's attitude; it
was not new. She was obviously sad that even after Richard's death
they could not be friends, but she was far more upset to learn that
because of adverse weather it had proved impossible to quarry the
stone for the tented mausoleum. The earliest anticipated completion
date, she was told, was May – three months away. She went next day
to the cemetery at Mortlake where many of her family were buried.
Her last visit had been with Richard; he had looked at the head-
stones of her mother, brothers and uncles, and commented that it was

'like a private club'. She chose a plot near the boundary wall and had the area pegged out so that a base could be laid down to take the structure. On the following day she went north to meet the S.S. *Palmyra* at Liverpool, and accompanied the coffin as it was conveyed by train to Euston, and by hearse to Mortlake. She had arranged for it to lie in the crypt under the altar, until the marble and stone tent was ready.

Isabel had now done everything there was to do. She had brought Richard safely home, she had worked without pause since his death, packing and leaving the life she had built up and loved over eighteen years, and she had been travelling continually for the past two weeks. Suddenly, there were no immediate calls on her courage. She collapsed, exhausted, and at last gave way to the tears she had previously been unable to cry, and to the pain of her cancer which was always threatening to overwhelm her.

She spent the next month in her rooms at the Langham Hotel, grieving and ill, never going out. When she could she made a desultory start at answering the massive backlog of condolence letters which sat in a large box on the floor beside her desk. To all her correspondents she spoke of the impossibility of facing up to the magnitude of her loss; she felt as though she had suffered a 'severe blow to the head . . . I was completely stunned.' To a few, very close friends, she confided the ordeal of the weeks in Trieste when she was working furiously to clear and pack the house and settle their affairs; and of her fear when those upon whom she most relied had turned on her; 'during that time I swam through a sea of small horrors – wickedness, treachery, threats; but . . . I pulled through.'[50]

Meanwhile, she had to consider her financial position. Her Civil List pension, small enough for her needs, would begin in July and she had an annuity of £204. Having made a conscious decision to destroy the most valuable property in Richard's estate, she was totally reliant on the small sums which trickled in from various publishers from previous works. Leonard Smithers was also ill, so the two had not yet been able to meet. But he wrote often, constantly excusing the fact that there was so little money due to her from sales of *Priapiea*. The copies sold added up to £240, he told her; '. . . I have received about £190 in cash and enclose a cheque for £25 and hope to send another for £25 speedily. Immediately the money comes in I shall remit to you . . . I should like to call on you and explain my accounts and also my suggestions as to the disposal of the edition . . . Sir Richard had practically finished *Catullus* and was engaged on *Juvenal* and *Ausonius*, to be followed by the Greek anthology.'[51]

Smithers also detailed some of the measures he had been obliged to take in respect of *Priapeia* to evade detection: 'On the death of my friend Mr Black I moved the agency to the country again to Wakefield in the name of Morton . . . when I see your ladyship I will give you full details.' While these stratagems might have amused Richard, with his delight in tweaking the nose of the Establishment, they served only to fill Isabel with deep unease. During Richard's lifetime she had been terrified that he would be discovered as part of a pornographic publishing organisation, and thus be publicly shamed with all the attendant effects on his career and pension. After his death Richard's reputation became in a sense like her child, to be guarded and nurtured at all costs. The difficulty was that she could not turn back the clock. The *Priapeia* was already in circulation, indeed it formed a source of regular income, in dribbles of £25. Sometimes these cheques were not honoured when she presented them at the bank, but Smithers always had some plausible explanation: he/his wife/his child was ill and he had been unable to see to his affairs; a cheque he had presented had been returned; he was waiting on the sale of property, or subscribers had not paid up.

Isabel's unusually spindly and weak writing during this time is a testament to her ill-health. She was also grieving and ageing; but she was not fooled. 'I had no trouble with the *A. Nights*,' she wrote on one occasion when Smithers complained that sales were poor. She reminded him that if the entire edition of 500 copies of *Priapeia* sold at £3 each, as he forecast it would, she was entitled to half the £1,500 income. 'I am very glad to have the £25 . . . but you have sold for £240 about 80 copies . . . as you have collected £240 I am entitled to £120 already. [I hope] you will be able to let me have the remainder soon . . . to bridge over this awful time until about July.'[52]

It was June before the tent was completed at Mortlake. The press were intrigued: 'The appearance of a tent is well maintained . . . lighted from . . . a small stained glass window. Within, the Oriental style . . . is maintained by a number of beautiful lamps . . . Four are suspended from the ceiling and shed a dim . . . light through jewel-shaped facets of coloured glass . . . the floor is of white Carrara

Marble and on each side are coffin bearers about six inches high for the coffins of Sir Richard, and eventually Lady Burton.'[53]

Any suggestion that the Oriental structure with its crescents and fringes and stars was alien in a Catholic churchyard was overcome by a crucifix and other symbols of Christianity inside and out. Isabel was pleased with it, and was at last able to send out announcements of the funeral service on thick, black-edged cards: '. . . It will take place on the 15th of June at St Mary Magdalene's Church, Mortlake at eleven o'clock. Train [from London] leaves Waterloo at 10.00 a.m. and reaches Mortlake at 10.47. The station is a few yards from the church.'[54]

Five hundred people attended; four hundred declined, many of whom – as in the case of Lord and Lady Salisbury – intended to accept but were subsequently unable to do so when a late outbreak of Asiatic influenza infected thousands in the capital during May and June. Maria Stisted and Georgiana were notable absentees, but despite Maria's assertion that no member of the Burton family would attend, Richard's two closest cousins – Dr Edward Burton (and his wife Bessie) and Captain St George Burton – and Mr Mostyn Pryce (son of Richard's old girl-friend and cousin, Eliza Burton), along with a few other nephews and nieces, represented the Burton family. Isabel's family attended in force – the Arundells, Smyth-Piggots, Van Zellers, Gerards; following these came Arbuthnot and McCarthy, Doctors Bird, Leslie and Baker, Verney Lovett Cameron, Lord Northbrook and Francis Galton ('It was a ceremony quite alien to anything I could conceive him to care for,' Galton wrote), and representatives of the many societies to which Burton belonged. The occasion was widely reported in the press, and Isabel's appearance was covered with almost modern-day media intrusiveness:

Her palpably great sorrow was blended with a dignity that was almost majesty. Her mien was upright, her step firm, her glance straight before her . . . the long semi-aquiline nose would have made the face hard but for the large soft eyes, the rounded cheek, and the tender yet firm mouth, tremulous now with suffering . . . There was a respectful curiosity to gaze upon the features of this woman as she moved slowly . . . towards the mausoleum . . [carrying] a simple bunch of forget-me-nots . . . [which she] placed on the coffin.[55]

A few days before this dignified display Isabel had done a foolish thing. One might have thought that she would have learned some discretion from the controversy caused by injudicious letters to the press from her and Richard in Syria, and over her Jane Digby obituary. Apparently not. Gossip clearly originating from Baker – that she had burned Richard's manuscripts and papers – reached her, and she acted with characteristic impulsiveness, writing her answer to the *Morning Post*. She had already alienated a number of Richard's friends by mentioning the Catholic rites at his death-bed in the press. Now she proceeded to acquire the condemnation of a good many of the remainder. She justified the letter because, she said, some 1,500 potential subscribers had been expecting to receive *The Scented Garden* and she was unable to cope with the correspondence. There had also been, she said, 'a great deal of talk and excitement as to what manuscripts he [Richard] might have left behind.'

She had received, she said, many exhortations 'not to burn them, not to lose them, not to bury the MSS. in my husband's coffin . . . asking me to put them at the disposal of this society or that, or from individuals writing on a certain subject . . . I have guarded every scrap of his writing as jealously as if it were the Holy Grail. After [his death] . . . I locked up his rooms, knowing there were many things which . . . should be private between ourselves. Some took exception to that, but one cannot please everybody and I had only to think of him.' She explained how she took sixteen days to sift and classify the papers and manuscripts; 'I know them as a shepherd knows his sheep. I have worked with him for 30 years and have been told everything . . . I know all his plans and only in one incidence have I not cooperated:

> I now have a terrible confession to make . . . one which I know will close a great many houses against me and deprive me of friends whom I value . . . but I want to sail under no false colours . . . My husband had been collecting for fourteen years information and materials on a certain subject . . . Some days [after he died] I read this . . . No promise had been exacted from me and I remained for three days in a state of perfect torture as to what I ought to do about it. 'Bury it' said one advisor . . .'Get a man to do it for you,' said No.2 . . . I tested one man who was very earnest about

it . . .'don't let my name get mixed up in it, but it is a very beautiful book I know.'

   . . . I sat down before the fire at dark . . . My heart said 'You can
have 6000 guineas; your husband worked for you, kept you in a
happy home, with honour and respect for thirty years. How are you
going to reward him? That your wretched body may be fed and
clothed and warmed for a few miserable months or years' . . . it
would be just parallel with the original 30 pieces of silver. I fetched
the MS, two large volumes . . . Still my thoughts were 'was it a sacrifice?' Will he rise up in his grave and curse me or bless me? The
thought will haunt me to death . . . And then I said, not for 6,000
gns [nor] 6,000,000 gns will I risk it. Sorrowfully . . . in fear and
trembling I burnt sheet after sheet until the whole of the volumes
was consumed.[56]

She was certainly right in one respect. The doors of many former
friends were henceforward closed to her. The press took up the story
and sizzled with innuendo about the subject matter of the burned
papers. Too late Isabel realised the value of the maxim, 'never explain
and never apologise'. She had condemned herself and would come to
bitterly regret her confession (though, she said, never the act itself). In
vain did she protest, 'he had 35 years experience of me, as a fiancé
and as a wife, and he knew right well what I should do with that particular manuscript. He meant to bring it out had he lived, but he
never meant anyone else to bring it out.'[57]

   Not everyone criticised her, of course. This was the era of virtuous
morality; upright and respectable people approved of her actions.
But they were not necessarily the people that Richard would have
wished to please, nor those amongst whom the Burtons had found
their friends for 30 years: the Bohemians, the *literati*, the chattering
classes of the day. In February 1891, when Swinburne had published
his 14-verse poem, *Verses on the Death of Richard Burton*, comparing his subject with England's heroes such as Raleigh, he referred
obliquely to Isabel's religious beliefs;

> . . . Souls there are that for soul's affright
> Bow down and cower in the sun's glad sight,
> Clothed round with faith that is one with fear,
> And dark with doubt of the live word's light.

But him we hailed from afar or near
As boldest born of his kinsfolk here
And loved as brightest of souls that eyed
Life, time, and death with unchangeful cheer.

A wider soul than the world was wide,
Whose praise made love of him one with pride,
What part has death or has time in him,
Who rode life's list as a god might ride?[58]

But in the *Elegy*, published two weeks after Isabel's confession of the destruction of the manuscript, the full force of Swinburne's anger was unleashed in execration of the scenes said to have been enacted around Richard's death-bed. He wrote to a friend that he had added a few lines to the Elegy, 'the sentiments will hardly be grateful to Lady B. and her fellow conspirators against a deathbed on behalf of the 'Oly Catholic Church.'[59]

. . . Priests and soulless serfs of priests may swarm
With vuturous acclamation, loud in lies,
About his dust while yet his dust is warm
Who mocked as sunlight mocks their base blind eyes.

Their godless ghost of godhead, false and foul
As fear his dam, or hell his throne: but we
Scarce hearing, heed no carrion church-kites howl:
The corpse be theirs to mock; the soul is free . . .[60]

Swinburne's bitter eloquence proved a rallying cry for some disparate groups: those such as Maria Stisted who regarded the Roman Catholic Church as an anathema; those of the 'Bohemian' arts movement (some of whom belonged to both groups, of course) who regarded the burning of *The Scented Garden* as a crime akin to sacrilege; and those subscribers who collected erotica, who had been eagerly awaiting the book. Smithers was obviously disappointed about the fate of the *Scented Garden* manuscript, but dared not be critical for fear of antagonising Isabel and destroying any chance of winkling out of her the surviving unpublished manuscripts, over which he was patiently negotiating.

Some of her critics said she was simply 'an uneducated woman'. 'I am not going to deny it,' she responded. 'But my husband found that I had quite sufficient common sense to trust me unreservedly with the whole of his business of whatever nature for thirty years, and never had cause to regret it, nor did he ever do the slightest thing without consulting me.'[61] Isabel would publish further justifications of her behaviour, hoping to correct the colourful but generally inaccurate perceptions of events in Trieste, but the damage was done. The exaggerated story of the 'death-bed conversion' (implying baptism rather than the administration of last rites to an existing member of the Church), along with the 'book-burning holocaust', was already firmly rooted.

Ironically, the effect was to propel Isabel into the shadowy world inhabited by purveyors and publishers of pornography.

36

'HERMAPHRODITE' AND THE PORNOGRAPHERS

1891–1894

Thanks to loans from her sisters, Isabel was able to pay off Letchford and bring back the belongings she had left stored in Trieste. The 175 packing-cases arrived in July and were delivered to 67 Baker Street where Isabel had taken 'a little apartment of nine rooms and a kitchen. My favourite sister [the recently widowed 'Dilly' Fitzgerald] who is also alone in the world is going to live with me.' A major consideration in her choice of the Baker Street apartment was its large loft. Here Isabel housed the bulk of Richard's papers and manuscripts, on bookshelves that she had built, and in dozens of packing-cases, which lined three sides of the room. Almost daily for two years, whenever she had a few spare hours, she used to clamber up the ladder to sit and read, and unpack, and remember.[1]

As soon as she could do so, in July, she sent to Dr Baker part of his outstanding bill, but he returned her cheque. She assumed it was because she had paid Letchford a few months earlier, and wrote again explaining that she had borrowed from her family on that occasion because Letchford had been so unpleasant to her. She was still unable to send more than half Dr Baker's fee because, 'I am unable to do more . . . I am so poor . . . I cannot furnish my rooms yet.' But she hoped to sell some books and find the remainder soon. She was bewildered by his behaviour she said, after

your 3 years care and attention to my beloved husband: your

kindness and consideration to me at his death bed and 3 weeks afterwards – then followed eleven weeks during which you were anything but kind – the why is known only to God and yourself – [and] that was followed by another period of kindness from January 27 [date of leaving Trieste] till about 20th April when you paid me your last voluntary visit . . . I have seen you once in these three last months . . . Your conduct is so unusual in a young man who has lived in a person's house for three years on good terms; no quarrel, no offence given, that I must remark it and *wonder* at it.

. . .You are a professional man, and you have no excuse for treating me like a 'bad debt' which I shall be able one day, I hope, to make good.[2]

Baker cashed her cheque, but they met only rarely after this. She heard some time later that he had contacted publishers with a view to writing a book about his time as Sir Richard's doctor. She asked Smithers to speak to him about it. 'I saw Dr Baker yesterday,' Smithers reported back. 'He tells he has no work in hand in any way touching on Sir Richard's life.'[3] She was relieved, but the incident jolted her into starting work on her own seminal biography of Richard.

Georgiana Stisted, now a middle-aged spinster, anxious to overcome the recent adverse publicity given her uncle's death and his erotic manuscripts, produced a series of articles under the title, 'Reminiscences of Sir Richard Burton'. These were later used as the basis for her biography of him, but apart from a few family stories they contained virtually nothing that was not culled from Hitchman's book, or Richard and Isabel's published works. In view of her subsequent attitude to Isabel, the few references to her uncle's wife are hardly surprising. 'In January 1861,' she said, 'he married the handsome, fascinating Isabel Arundell. A great surprise to us as he had become such an inveterate traveller that we had come to think of him as a confirmed bachelor . . . there were some difficulties in the way of this marriage. Mrs Arundell, a very strict Romanist, objected to a Protestant son-in-law . . . Isabel very wisely [did not allow this] . . . to prevent her from marrying the man of her choice, and she never had reason to regret it – a better husband never lived.' Georgiana carefully neglected to mention the fact that Richard's family had also strongly opposed the match on religious grounds. For the moment claws were sheathed.

Isabel wrote kindly that she had read the 'clever . . . article on my darling . . . I congratulate you on it, and on being able to write again. I was very sorry you and Maria would not come to the funeral. When you come [to London] in August I shall give you a photo of the monument and a list of the people invited . . . Your loving, Zoo.'[4]

Apart from the biography, Isabel's strategy for earning her living was to edit and sell Richard's unpublished manuscripts, and to reprint and sell his older published works in a 'Memorial Edition'. She was now in almost daily contact with Smithers, who was working on the prose element of the proposed edition of *Catullus*, 'which I am confident will prove a great success, and I find the amount of gross lines in the work very small indeed,' he wrote to her. She had shown him the *Catullus* manuscript at their first meeting and given him a few pages to take away to work on. In her letters to Smithers on this subject, and on other works such as *Priapeia* and *Pentamerone*, she adopted a pseudonym 'Hermaphrodite', presumably in case the letters fell into the wrong hands.[5]

Meanwhile her public confession concerning *The Scented Garden* continued to cause her problems. She received offensive and obscene anonymous letters on a regular basis. At first she had been deeply upset by them, but eventually came to regard them as a justification of her decision to destroy the manuscript; 'when I reflect . . . the class of people who would have received the manuscript with joy, I know how right I was to burn it,' she wrote to a friend. 'It was not the *learned* people, as you imagine, who regret this, because there was no learning to be gained in it. My dear husband did it simply to fill our purse again . . . I was astonished to find myself either praised or blamed; it seemed to me to be the natural thing for a woman to do. But I see how mistaken I was to have confessed, and to imagine it was my duty to confess.'[6]

In August Smithers brought to her notice an advertisement which had appeared in the *Sporting Times*. Taking advantage of recent press coverage of her confession, it purported to be selling a version of the *Garden* with the insinuation that it was Burton's last work. But, Smithers wrote:

the volume advertised is called the *Perfumed Garden*. It is a poor and rubbishy translation. I cannot but lament the destruction of Sir Richard's translation, but I am confident you took the right course, although many people who have written to me hold a different view.'[7]

'Be sure you have the pluck to tell people that you know I took the right course,' Isabel replied. 'I find lots of people who tell me *privately* I am right, run with the hounds as well. And they are hounds, and no mistake.'[8] As far as the advertisement was concerned, 'the para you sent me is only written to draw me out, or sell some translation of his own. *Burton's* "Scented Garden" is *burnt* and if *anyone* brings it out and calls it *his* I will bring an action.'[9] But on another occasion she made it clear to him: 'I do not want damages, I want honour intact!'

Smithers now suggested that Isabel allow the publication of a revised edition of Burton's *A Thousand Nights and a Night*. Copies of the original were changing hands at £30 a set, almost twice the original price; if the demand was there, he asked her, why not republish it? He could have it printed at a lower price than she had originally had to pay Waterlows. His friend, the printer H.S. Nichols, would produce it 'very tastefully', which would overcome any promises Sir Richard had given to subscribers about not publishing a subsequent 'cheap edition'. Isabel replied that he had misinterpreted Richard's promise to the subscribers. Richard had not 'only guarded against a *cheaper* edition,' she wrote, 'he guarded against an unexpurgated edition, and when I wanted to bring out another, *at the same price*, he forbad it then and forever . . . All the 1,000 subscribers know it. He did not understand an "expurgated" version to go as near to the wind as would copyright – he was simply honest.'[10]

She reminded Smithers of a letter he had written to Richard, about Mr Nichols,[11] 'in which you say . . . that he is a very unsafe man to deal with, that he is unscrupulous, has no commercial honesty and in addition is a really magnificent liar, and you describe his methods of shady business . . . Whilst you were away Mr Nichols spoke very openly to Mr Curtis [her solicitor]. He told him you were not going to have the thing "petticoated" [and said] "She may make the revisions but we need not attend to them."' Mr Curtis had also warned her that if she sold the copyright to Smithers, there was nothing to prevent him selling it on again.[12]

In four years of a close business relationship, the manipulative Smithers never got the better of Isabel in a straight fight. He and Nichols only finally defeated her by subterfuge. To an extent she needed him because of his former collaboration with Richard; she used his good contacts with printers, and his willingness to run errands such as tracking down ownership of Richard's early copyrights (some had been sold outright to the publishers), but she was – in modern parlance – 'on his case'. Having inherited some money on his father's death, Smithers had given up his law practice in Sheffield to move to London and set up a publishing company.[13] He stuck to Isabel because he wanted Burton's manuscripts; furthermore his correspondence with Peter Jones in Trieste, and contacts with Dr Baker, led him to believe she had not, as she claimed, destroyed both copies of *The Scented Garden*.

The death of her sister, 'poor little Blanche', in September and the first anniversary of Richard's death set Isabel back a good deal. Blanche was the small, fair-haired bride whom Isabel had accompanied on her year-long honeymoon. As Mrs Smyth-Piggot, Blanche had been chatelaine of a magnificent West-Country home, had six healthy children and no financial worries, but she had shared her ageing husband with a succession of mistresses and her chief pleasure in life had been her garden. Despite her lack of material wealth, Isabel had always felt herself better off than Blanche. The subsequent deaths of her two remaining brothers-in-law (including Blanche's widower), within a few months of each other, also affected Isabel for she valued the ties of her extended family. Nevertheless, her clear-sighted notes on the administration of the Smyth-Piggott estate and trusts of her orphaned nephews and nieces demonstrate a remarkably efficient and businesslike grasp of legal practicalities.[14]

Unable to face the thought of Christmas celebrations, Isabel went into a convent for a few days, travelling through streets that were 'sheets of ice', as she wrote to her friend Miss Bishop:

Late on Christmas Eve . . . I went in my cab . . . [with] two flambeaux each side. In Regent's Park the fog was black and thick . . . Midnight [Mass] . . . was too lovely: in the dead silence a little before midnight you heard the shepherd's pipe or reed in the distance, and echo nearer and nearer, and then the soft, clear voices burst into 'Glory be to God in the Highest,' and this was the refrain all through the service. I passed the time with our Lord and my darling . . . I am better and have stronger nerves and am perhaps more peaceful.[15]

In the early months of 1892 she struggled on with her plan to reprint all of Richard's books ('I dream always of my books and the pile of work,' she wrote),[16] slipping easily into her old routine of working from dawn until late into the evening. So many letters survive of this period that it is easy to gauge what a whirlwind of energy Isabel was, even as an ageing widow. No publisher was a match for her shrewd and perceptive analysis of their politely worded notes; she said she recalled Richard once saying that 'publishers and politicians will find the gates of heaven very narrow,' and acted accordingly. Smithers wrote to say that Kegan and Paul claimed, for example, that she had sold them the copyright of her best-selling *Inner Life*, and Mullans likewise claimed *A.E.I.* though the contract of the latter had apparently perished in a fire. 'I do not think Messrs Kegan & Paul have any contract,' she responded. 'They would not have given me £100 for the second [single volume] edition if I had sold the copyright at first,' she pointed out. The fire was, she thought, a rather convenient excuse.

Mrs Maylor wrote from Trieste to ask for help because her father had died, and she was having to care full-time for her mother who was suffering from senile dementia. 'My duty enforces me to sell all the furniture and with part of the money put her somewhere . . . whilst I work and try to earn money to keep her . . . If it would go on thus I would be prevented working . . . and we would both be out on the streets . . .' Isabel responded by sending part of the edited *Catullus* manuscript to copy out and a few months later, to her surprise, Mrs Maylor arrived in London to deliver the work personally. 'She seemed to think that I should keep her,' said Isabel, and she did find Maylor some work to do for a while, but she became suspicious for the woman was always 'tidying' piles of paper in the attic. When she wrote about Mrs Maylor in her published writing, Isabel described her as 'a good Catholic lady' who was adept at deciphering Richard's writing and who was never offended by the bawdiness of his manuscripts. But privately her opinion was far less flattering and, as things turned out, she was right to mistrust the woman,[17] who almost certainly had travelled to England at the suggestion of Jones and Letchford in an attempt to find the manuscript of *The Scented Garden*.

Letchford also began writing to Isabel again, admitting she had good reason 'to think very hard things' about him. He apologised for his offensive behaviour in Trieste, and begged her help; 'I trust that the recital of my worries, with which I am now going to inflict you, will go a long way to exculpate me,' he wrote.[18] Surprisingly, for she had been genuinely frightened of him in Trieste, Isabel forgave him and subsequently helped him by writing on his behalf to Lord Leighton, and by arranging to have some of Letchford's work (notably the full-length fencing picture) exhibited in London. Perhaps Letchford's sycophantic letters convinced her that he had behaved badly because he had been as traumatised by Richard's death as she had been; 'I can but feebly express my admiration [of] a great and noble love which during his life time hung over you both like a shining golden aureole,' he wrote, 'and which now divided, is yet not severed . . . Some day will the Blessed Virgin place your hand once more in his, to leave him no more . . . all our love and admiration, dearest Lady Burton, Albert Letchford.'[19]

Isabel remained in correspondence, too, with some of Richard's former friends such as Kirby and Payne. She occasionally spent a few days with the Arbuthnots at their house near Guildford. No matter what they said of Isabel in private or at a later date, the letters of these men to Isabel were polite and friendly. It was the couple's former women friends who were most antagonistic towards her. Ouida, whom Isabel had supported and comforted over many years through numerous sad love affairs, 'could not bring herself to speak to Isabel' because of the destroyed manuscript. But at least Ouida did not broadcast her opinion in the press; Isabel's friend Elizabeth Lynn Linton, who had met Richard 'only six or seven times' according to Isabel, assumed for herself the role of Burton's literary champion. In an article which was actually an attack on feminist women, whom she called 'the swaggering wild women of the present craze', Linton – somewhat inappropriately for her argument – targeted Isabel:

> The truth is simply this – the unsexed woman pleases the unsexed man . . . domineering women choose effeminate men who they can rule at will . . . such conditions of the masculine life as they did not care to adopt they would forbid men to practice.
>
> We have had a notable instance of this mental absolutism of late, at the death of one of our most learned scholars and frank agnostics. He was no sooner dead than his widow surrounded him with the emblems and rites of her own faith – which was not his. She did not shrink from inflicting this dishonour on the memory of

the man who had systematically preached a doctrine so adverse to her own. She cared nothing for the integrity of the man she thus stultified – nothing for the grandeur of the intellect she thus belittled . . . she would not see the pitiful discredit she thus cast on the name of the man she professed to love.[20]

The two women had a reunion shortly after Isabel's arrival in England. Mrs Linton had already seen Isabel's account of the death-bed episode in the newspapers, but 'she visited me as a friend, kissed me and assured me of her friendship,' Isabel said, puzzled, and deeply upset at the attack. The true explanation appears to lie in the fact that in attacking Isabel, Linton earned the gratitude of a literary coterie – including Swinburne and Ouida – to which she had long aspired but from which she had previously been excluded. Later that year, Linton wrote to Swinburne asking him to write to the press 'to expose . . . the popish mendacities of that poor liar Lady Burton', for she could hardly do so herself. 'My dear friend,' Swinburne replied,

Of course she has befouled Richard Burton's memory like a harpy – and of course it might have been expected. But I can't hit harder or straighter than I did in my Elegy. If you thought fit (as Mr Watts [Dunton] agrees with me . . . in thinking no one else could do it nearly so well), to expose and chastise her treacherous profanation of his name and fame, it would not be like 'two cats spitting at each other' but like one of the noblest and loveliest of creatures springing and setting her paw – with all the incomparable grace which beautifies and glorifies her strength and fierceness – on a furtive though audacious rat.[21]

Meanwhile articles about *The Scented Garden* continued to appear in the press and Isabel continued to answer her critics publicly. Writing to Smithers, with whom she was working on *Catullus*, she said about the matter:

I wish you could assure me on one point. Why did he wish the subject of unnatural crime to be largely aired and expounded. He had such an unbounded contempt for the vice and its votaries. I never asked him this question *unfortunately* . . . Though it may be a safe dissection for a live man to undertake, I think it such a dangerous one for a dead man's memory, who, if his motives be *once misunderstood* cannot defend himself.

I do not know if you can enter into my feelings but the world and I are at daggers drawn, evidently because the world takes the public and scientific standpoint, and I on a nice island in a surging and boiling ocean take the standpoint only of Richard Burton; how it will affect *him* . . . I have no public spirit in the matter. I feel that if a rotten carcass has to be dissected for the public good, let some other living man, with a living tongue and pen, bring in his knife and scalpel, not my dead husband.[22]

Isabel made regular pilgrimages to Mortlake to visit the tomb and on one of these visits she noticed that a small cottage close to the churchyard was available for rent. The thought of living so close to Richard was irresistible. She justified the expense to herself on the grounds that she often visited the churchyard at weekends, and needed an inexpensive pied-à-terre outside London for the summer months. Her first action was to have a name-plate made for the gate – 'Our Cottage' – and to plant ivy, roses and honeysuckle at the front door.

She knew, now, that her own time was limited by the cancer which increasingly often required injections of morphia to enable her to cope with pain.[23] She had no fear of death *per se*, but there were several objectives she wanted to achieve first. Commuting between the Baker Street flat and 'Our Cottage' that year, she worked to a punishing schedule.

Apart from setting in motion the Memorial Edition whereby she hoped to republish 34 works by Burton, she also completed in only eight months her massive two-volume biography, *The Life of Captain Sir Richard Francis Burton*.[24] Undoubtedly, the *Life* (as it is known to Burton researchers and collectors) contains some minor errors in spelling (she spelled Oscar Wilde, Wylde, for example),[25] and grammar, as her critics are anxious to point out. Nevertheless it is an invaluable compendium of accurate and generally unique information.[26] She covered every event in Burton's life, including the contentious issues such as his 'conversion' and *The Scented Garden*,

. . . Was it a classic? No! It was not a classic; it was a translation from Arabic manuscripts very difficult to get in the original, with copious notes and explanations of his own. But it is very difficult for me, as a woman, to tell you exactly what it was . . . Had we lived to come home together I should have talked him off printing it, as I did another manuscript . . . and he knew that if I had my will I would burn it.

. . . I am by no means going to tell you that his Catholicity was a life-long, fixed and steady thing, like mine. It was not. He had long and wild fits of Eastern Mysticism, but not the Agnosticism that I have seen in England since my widowhood. It was the mysticism of the East – Sufiism. Periodically he had Catholic fits, and practised it, hiding it sometimes even from me, though I knew it . . . Most of his intimate friends are dead but there are still a few left . . . who might possibly write sections of his life . . . One would describe him as a Deist [Maria Stisted], one as an Agnostic, and one as an Atheist and Freethinker, but I can only describe the Richard that I knew, not the Richard they knew. I, his wife, who lived with him day and night for thirty years, believed him to be half-Sufi, half Catholic . . .

. . . I was wife, and mother, and comrade, and secretary, and aide-de-camp, and agent to him; and I was proud and happy to do it all, and never tired . . . I would rather have had a crust of bread with him, than be a Queen elsewhere. At the moment of his death I had done all I could for [his] body, and then I tried to follow his soul. I *am* following his soul and *shall* reach it before long. Agnostics! 'Burnt manuscript' readers! Where were *you* all then? Hail-fellow-well-met, when the world went well; running away when it pursed its stupid lips . . . He said always, 'I am gone, Pay, Pack, and follow.' . . . I am waiting to join his Caravan. I am waiting for a welcome sound. The tinkling of his Camel-Bell.[27]

One-third of the second volume consists of material she did not wish to leave out, but which she could not place chronologically in a work already so bulging with extraneous information that – like Burton's own works – it is sometimes difficult to follow. Considering her other projects and huge amount of correspondence, it is astonishing that she was able to complete the work in the time she did; in part she managed by simply dumping unedited tracts of text from letters and articles throughout the book. It would have been a better read (though perhaps less valuable to the modern-day biographer) had she allowed her publishers to edit it. But she would not permit this, setting her face against any interference. 'No – Mr. Chapman is not mangling your preface,' her editor, George Etheridge, wrote placatingly, 'and has not altered a word of it. I would not let him.'[28] All the knowledge she had gained in thirty years was used to produce and design the book. She allowed Chapman very little say and wrote daily instructions to Etheridge, often more than once daily.[29]

The book was published on 11 July 1893. The first reviews in the major literary organs were critical, but the general mass of newspaper reviews (there are many hundreds in Isabel's press cutting albums) delighted, as the obituary writers had done, in a meaty story. They were neatly summarised by the *Edinburgh Review*'s, 'this is a very extraordinary book, by a very extraordinary woman about a very extraordinary man.' Isabel replied spiritedly, as usual, to those reviewers who were speciously critical, but she had grown inured to genuine criticism, recognising that even harsh reviews were better than no reviews, and that a little controversy often contributed more to sales of a book than did praise.

'I have had my head quite turned by the great success of my book,' she wrote to a friend.

> With my earnings I am embellishing his mausoleum, and am putting up in honour of his poem *Kasidah*, festoons of camel bells from the desert, in the roof of the tent where he lies, so that when I open or shut the door . . . the tinkling of the camel bells will sound just as it does in the desert. On January 22 I am going down to pass the day in it as it is my thirty-third wedding day, and the bells will ring for the first time.
>
> I am also . . . bringing out by degrees all his works hitherto published or unpublished, as of the former only small quantities were published and these are mostly extinct. If God gives me two years I shall be content.[30]

As well as the Memorial Edition, she was involved in the proposed reprinting of the *Nights* and, she wrote, she had 'several unpublished manuscripts. When the Biography begins to pall I [shall] bring out a popular edition. I will then collect his pamphlets, correspondence with the Press, any interesting letters and the pith of his labours for England, in two volumes called the Wit & Wisdom of Sir Richard

Burton. If I live long enough I will write my own Autobiography.'[31]

Although to an extent Isabel never recovered from losing Richard, following the example of the Queen she gloried even in being his widow, and it is evident from her papers that after the second anniversary of his death she began to make a life for herself. From the proceeds of the *Life*, approximately £2,000 in the first year after publication, she was not only able to purchase the leasehold of 'Our Cottage' but to realise a measure of financial security for the first time since Richard's death. Her lifestyle and physical needs were limited; she dressed simply and comfortably, discarding the stays and tight-waisted gowns she had worn while Richard was alive for dark loose-flowing gowns which caused her less abdominal discomfort. Her bank accounts show that she habitually saved more than she spent.

As she regained something of her old self-confidence, Smithers found Isabel increasingly difficult to deal with; she had never entirely trusted him and was wary of everything he told her. She spent weeks in consultation with her solicitors, about whether a 'Library Edition' of the *Nights* (that is an edited version, but without the total emasculations of her own unsuccessful 'Household Edition'), would contravene the spirit of the original prospectus. The conclusion was that it was a different book, rather than a cheaper edition, and therefore would not affect the value of the first edition.

When she had made her decision to proceed with the work, Smithers and his financial partner in the deal, Mr Jeffcock, balked at Isabel's terms hoping to beat her down. After a few weeks of this she wrote to Smithers, telling him the deal was off because she had received a better offer. He replied that he was astounded, after their lengthy friendship, that she could do such a thing to him. He had always dealt fairly with her, trusted her, and even at her request gave up selling *Priapeia* (after she finally got around to reading it), which had cost him a good deal of money.

By May, however, Smithers and Jeffcock had agreed to all Isabel's terms; she was to receive £1,000 on signature, and a further £2,000 in monthly instalments of £200.[32] The first print run was to consist of 10,000 copies; royalties of 6d per copy were to be paid to her or her heirs for any subsequent editions. Any obscene material (which she called 'black') was to be excised. There was to be 'no black . . . of any kind, tolerated in any way', she insisted; no coarse or immodest words were to be introduced, and all proofs were to be delivered to her for correction and approval. Finally, it was agreed that Smithers would return to her all unsold copies of *Priapeia* in exchange for being allowed to publish *Catullus*.[33]

One of her solicitors checked the agreement and said she might sign it, but warned her on no account to give it to Smithers to obtain Jeffcock's signature. She must keep her own signed original by her and give him signed copies for himself and Jeffcock. 'I'm not sure that he [Jeffcock] is the innocent individual he appears,' he cautioned her, 'though at present he is playing the part to perfection.' In June the same solicitor told her that the 'game of bluff' was almost over. In fact it had hardly begun.

Isabel received all the money contractually due to her. After a good deal of effort, she also received the unsold copies of *Priapeia*, which she burned on a bonfire in the garden at Mortlake. As for the proof sheets for *Nights*, Nichols sent her these as they came off the presses for editing. They were always delivered to her by messenger. Isabel dictated the changes to her secretary, Alice Quarry, who corrected the sheets and then returned them personally. It involved a lot of work for both women but when Isabel opened the first volume after publication, she found to her consternation that her corrections had been completely ignored. She wrote angrily to Nichols, who replied that he had not been able to understand Alice Quarry's handwriting. Miss Quarry was dumbfounded. 'I stood beside him as he turned the leaves, examined and expressed himself satisfied,' she wrote, 'He never said he could not understand my markings.'[34]

Isabel was equally astonished when she attempted to have the book stopped; her lawyers, whom she had consulted at every stage of the agreement, now advised that legally she had no case; Nichols' response – 'we agreed to let you correct the proofs, but we did not contract to observe your corrections' – was incontrovertible.[35] She had to be content with the knowledge that it was a handsome production and that at least the more objectionable parts (such as the famous section 'Pederasty' in the Terminal Essay), had been omitted. She even gave some copies as gifts to selected friends; 'I have sent you as a New Year's Gift, my husband's "Arabian Nights" (the new one compressing his sixteen volumes into twelve) which will be, it is thought, the future Standard Library Edition.'

It was hardly surprising that Isabel was so wary of Smithers and his collaborators. At the time of the publication of the *Nights*, *The Scented Garden* issue flared again following a visit by Smithers to Mortlake. He visited Isabel almost weekly to see parts of the *Catullus* manuscript and work on it. She would never allow him to take the entire manuscript away – doling out a few pages at a time, edited by her, which caused him a good deal of frustration. Sometimes he challenged her edits, saying that certain words must stand; 'one could find them in any bible, and scholars will be offended if the translation is not literal.'[36] In some cases she would not allow him to see the original manuscript pages, substituting instead a 'clean copy' of her edited version so that he could not even see what Burton had originally written.

After one of these weekly visits by Smithers, she found on the floor a packet containing a number of letters to him which had evidently fallen out of his pocket. The letters were postmarked Trieste. She opened one, and found that it was from Peter Jones and mentioned her; so she had no hesitation in reading the entire package. What she read confirmed that she had been right to mistrust Smithers, even though she quite liked him as a person and had come to enjoy his visits. She typed out copies of the letters and sent the originals back to him at once without saying she had read them.

Peter Jones was employed as a clerk but occasionally earned money writing for magazines. The son of an English engineer who worked for the Lloyds Steamship Company in Trieste, his parents were 'respectable and humble people'. Isabel had first met him when, after making his mother's housemaid pregnant, he had married the girl and, being homeless, applied for Isabel's help and influence in achieving a reconciliation with his parents. He was related to both Mrs Maylor and the Letchfords by marriage. It is clear from the package of letters that there was a scheme involving himself and the Letchfords, and Dr Baker, either to produce and publish a spurious *Scented Garden* as Burton's work, or to force Isabel to admit that she had not destroyed all copies of Burton's manuscript and to obtain and publish it.

He had been told by a relative, Jones explained to Smithers, that Isabel had destroyed only 'the original MSS of the *Scented Garden* . . . together with many of Zola's novels and some rarer books'. The 'clean copy', delivered to Sir Richard by Mrs Maylor on the day before his death, had been seen some weeks after the original manuscript was burned, hidden behind the altar in Isabel's chapel. On her typewritten copy of this letter, against this accusation, Isabel has written, 'This is quite false.'

She sent for Mrs Maylor and questioned her closely, worried that the woman had kept back some notes or papers which would lend credence to an attempt to bring out a version of *The Scented Garden*. Mrs Maylor assured her that she had not kept any notes or copies; indeed, she said, she was willing to solemnly swear under notarised oath that if any copy did appear, 'it would be a spurious one.' A few days after this Mrs Maylor vanished, emerging some weeks later in Trieste. Before she left she had persuaded Isabel to order a typewriter from the Bar Lock Company; the new machine (still in its packing case) and Mrs Maylor disappeared together, leaving Isabel to pay the bill.

Isabel now tackled Smithers, admitting she had read the letters from Jones. He claimed he had merely been attempting 'to draw Jones out' to find out the truth of the matter. As evidence of his good faith he offered to continue to do so (he and Jones were also genuinely corresponding on other literary matters), and share the correspondence with her. In July he reported, 'I have had a long letter from Jones, full of disgust about my declining his book ['Petronius']. Mrs M.[Maylor] did type it. I don't know, but I infer, that there is a good deal of undercurrent from her, against you, with the Triestines she knows.'[37]

Smithers wrote again, asking for further details, and Jones replied:

> . . . Mrs Maylor's copy was however hidden for some time in the altar of the chapel Lady B. had in her house. Then it was packed in a packing case with many valuables. This box did not go by sea like the books and heavy luggage, but was taken by land. That copy was not, therefore, burnt in Trieste. Moreover – as you doubtless know – priests hide, bury, build up books; they as a rule will never burn a precious manuscript . . . nor does it stand to reason that an object so jealously preserved in Trieste will be destroyed in London. Lady Burton will of course deny these facts and act under due guidance of her confessor and Compagnie de Jesus . . .[38]

In September Smithers wrote to Jones that Lady Burton was deeply anxious about the possibility of a *Scented Garden* being published;

she insisted she had burned all copies, keeping only a skeleton of the contents, and it would be impossible to publish it. Jones replied that he was sure 'Lady B. was living in mortal dread about the S.G. I am equally sure that with a little well-managed pressure she could be made to find it and publish it. She may call it a skeleton or a plan, or whatever she likes. Of course it would not be an impossible task to bring it out. Its style was that of the *Nights* and that can be imitated, and the notes are the same. What might prove even more interesting,' he wrote, with an unmistakable hint of menace, 'can be a preface with the story of the conversion two hours after death, and many other interesting details . . .'[39]

After reading this Isabel went to her solicitors and swore a deposition setting out the facts of the affair.[40] The 10-page typed statement is a dramatic document which sets out full details of the scam and its proponents. Jones and his three accomplices had spent an 'immense time' concocting a spurious manuscript using the original Kama Shastra version of *Perfumed Garden*, 'strewn about with sentences out of the "Arabian Nights", in order to give a colouring of Sir Richard's style.' Despite her statement sworn under oath, Mrs Maylor was clearly involved, Isabel said, for she was adept at 'imitating my husband's style, adapting words and phrases'. Through Smithers, Isabel had learned that the production was to be fully illustrated, 'which my husband shrank from . . . [I] hope it is not true . . . if it is, it will be by Mr Albert Letchford, nephew of Mr. Jones, a very clever artist.' Dr Baker was also implicated in this intrigue, for the proposed work was apparently to include two chapters of a Burton manuscript which she had given Baker as 'a keepsake', shortly after Burton's death.

She had learned that 2,000 copies were to be printed. 'When it arrives in England I do not believe any *scholar* will be taken in by it,' she said, 'but it may be largely bought by the Great Uneducated unless they are warned.' She listed the names of bookshops where the book would be distributed, Avery of Soho, and Robson and Kerr of Holywell Street, and 'Mr Smithers, 3 Soho Square will doubtless be able to *procure* information,' she wrote. 'The four conspirators, and the bookseller who receives it, have nothing to fear from me, unless there is a pretence of it's being Sir Richard's translation . . . It is shameful to obtain money on false pretences . . . money I have sacrificed . . . I have been sworn in before a commissioner, and have

placed my Deposition and that of my copyist [Maylor] and all of her
letters to Sir Richard and me, in the hands of my lawyer, and also a
skeleton plan of Sir Richard's [mss.] with a list of all his annotations,
the pages they belong to, and the first and last line of the page.'

Despite everything she did, the *Scented Garden* row refused to go
away. Subsequently she learned that Jones had visited Tunis and
Algeria, to obtain copies of the original manuscripts as Richard had
done[41] and, Smithers told her, he believed Justin Huntly McCarthy
had agreed to translate it.

This last information was a severe blow to Isabel, who had last
seen Justin McCarthy at the funeral in Mortlake. Then, he had been
gratified that his sonnet to Burton[42] had been carved on the front of
the tent, but she had been told since that he was angry at her burning
The Scented Garden. He had not replied to her, even when she sent
Richard's gold shirt-studs to him as a memento a few weeks after the
funeral. She wrote angrily, demanding to know whether it was true
that he had agreed to translate *The Scented Garden* for Jones and his
cohorts. McCarthy, equally angrily, denied the story. He was
astounded that she could believe him capable of doing anything to
harm the reputation of a man he had honoured and loved. The reason
for his recent lack of contact was work and ill-health but, he admitted, he strongly disapproved of her burning Richard's manuscript.

He could hardly blame her for thinking he was unfriendly and
'might do an unfriendly act', Isabel replied, only marginally mollified.
'Although you were more than pleased to meet me, or write to me,
and to have literary dealings with me when my husband was alive . . .
[after his death] you never called, you never wrote . . . You cannot
suppose, that had Sir Richard been alive he would, in the face of this
treatment of me, have kept up your acquaintance? I did not know you
well enough to know you would not do this [translation], and I measured your love for my husband in your treatment of the wife he
loved and honoured, and would have defended.'

> You cannot *possibly*, whether you approve or not, judge the course
> I pursued about Sir Richard's translation, but I have reason to
> know that I did *what he wanted me to do*, what he wished himself.
> The only thing in which I erred, and which I shall regret till the day
> of my death, was in confessing it . . . not a soul on earth *really*
> understood Sir Richard but myself, and everybody else's love is a

pale painted flame in comparison to mine . . . And now . . . as far
as I am concerned this misunderstanding is cleared up for ever and
I trust we shall always be good friends.[43]

Her comment, 'I have reason to know . . .' may or may not confirm
a claim that Isabel told friends in Trieste that Richard's ghost had
appeared to her and ordered her to burn the manuscript.[44] There
seem to have been several ghostly apparitions in Trieste. Daisy
Letchford swore that Richard Burton appeared to her (half a mile
away) at the very moment of his death, and that she had flown, sobbing, to the *palazzo*, only to have her worst fears confirmed. We
know that Isabel was taking pain-killing drugs at that time, and may
even have been prescribed other drugs by Baker. Assuming she did
have a vision, it could be explained as drug-induced hallucination. But
what can be made of Daisy Letchford's claims?

It is fair to say that Isabel spent every day of the last productive
part of her life working at some aspect of Richard Burton's literary
estate, and whether one agrees with her decisions and actions or not,
she was a protective guardian. It is hardly surprising that she felt the
need to keep unpublished work out of the hands of men such as
Nichols, Jeffcock and Smithers, who attempted to circumvent her
good intentions at every turn, and succeeded in doing so in the case of
the Library Edition of the *Nights*.

Isabel was genuinely upset at the death of Maria Stisted in
December 1893,[45] despite the fact that for almost thirty years
Richard's sister had been cold to her. 'You would be surprised to
know,' she wrote to St George Burton, 'and I am surprised myself,
how much I feel it . . . I wish nothing had come between us.'[46] Isabel
had sent the Stisted women a presentation copy of the *Life* six months
before Maria's death. No account of Maria's reaction survives, but
neither she nor Georgiana could have been happy about Isabel's
obscure reference to them in a paragraph defending her Catholicism:

> . . . My Burtons mostly have Catholic-phobia; they hate it without
> knowing what it is because their ancestors seceded from it at the
> time of the Reformation; but one of the most anti-Catholic of them,
> at the age of seventeen, wrote me more than one beautiful letter
> imploring me to take her, and get her baptised, and received into the
> Catholic church. I have them among my treasures now; but I did

not do so, because it would have been an act of treachery to her mother, and dishonourable to take advantage of a girl, and she has since been very grateful for it . . .[47]

A few weeks after Maria's death, Isabel heard through Smithers that Nichols intended to publish a hitherto unknown erotic manuscript by Richard, called *Elephantis*, which he had purchased from Arbuthnot. Isabel had never heard of the work and wrote immediately to ask to be allowed to see the manuscript. 'With regard to . . . Elephantis,' Nichols replied, 'this volume is packed away somewhere, and I could not, without a great deal of inconvenience, get at it at the present moment. As soon as it is unpacked I will let you know.'[48] Isabel wrote agitatedly to Arbuthnot, who replied that there had obviously been some misunderstanding; the book Nichols referred to was *Instructions Libertine*, formerly written by a French lawyer and lithographed for circulation.

Burton knew all about it and suggested [a translation] should be called 'Elephantis' and wrote two or three pages as a sample but had no intention of bringing it out himself . . . it would have to be printed for private circulation only and would be a sequel to the *Ananga Ranga* and *Kama Sutra*, but much shorter than either of these works . . . a sort of *vade mecum* for men, maidens and young married couples. As for being offered £300 for the few pages in B's handwriting that is absurd. I fancy he wanted to see if you would offer money for it . . .

He was currently very busy with his work for the Oriental Translation Fund, Arbuthnot said kindly, but as soon as he had time, he would call on Smithers and resolve the matter.[49]

In the meantime I can tell you that I did *not* sell the two or three pages of notes to Smithers. I sold him the *Instructions Libertine* with some 90 or 100 plates; nine volumes of *Le Diable au Corps*; six volumes of *Faubles* and some other books I wanted to get rid of for a few sovereigns, £14 or £15 if I recollect right, and far below their value. I did not sell him the few notes of Burton's but *gave* them to him with *Instructions Libertine*, and there was not any idea of using his name in any way in connection with the book. There is no such work as 'Elephantis' . . . I will come and see you after I have seen Smithers.[50]

Arbuthnot resolved this affair satisfactorily, but Isabel felt over-whelmed; the fight against so many, much younger men, on so many fronts over such a long period of time, was simply too much for her. She worried that after her death Smithers, Nichols, Jones or someone she had never heard of, would publish erotic books, claiming them to be by Burton. As a consequence she drew up detailed instructions to her executors to burn *all* unpublished manuscripts of Richard's, and to pass relevant material to the National Vigilance Society to enable them to have any books purporting to be Burton's investigated and stopped. At the end of her life she added the name of W.A. Coote, a leading member of this Society, to the list of her executors to ensure that her wishes were carried out.

One biographer wrote that Isabel 'had, in truth, gone over to the enemy.'[51] In a sense she had, of course. Like Richard, she had spent years publicly and privately traducing and ridiculing Mrs Grundy; 'how sick the creator must be of these goody-goody shams – this 19th century would-be virtue,' she once mocked in a letter to the *Liverpool Mercury* in 1884.[52] Now, in order to protect Richard's reputation, she had patently joined their ranks. In mitigation, her surviving papers show that she had not simply 'gone over' to the enemy. Rather, she was driven there by the greed of unscrupulous men.

LAST TINKLE OF
THE CAMEL BELL
1894–1896

Despite her illness and the stresses of managing and protecting Richard's literary estate, Isabel was able to travel about a good deal during 1894. She visited the Arundells at Wardour, and the Somersets at Bulstrode. She even travelled to Carlisle to spend a short holiday with Canon Waterton. These visits were pale reflections of the country-house visits she had made in her prime, where she had always been welcomed for her stimulating and lively company.

By 1895 she found travel difficult. She could not walk far and special arrangements had to be made for her, so she began to spend her time between Baker Street and Mortlake where her numerous nieces and nephews, and their children, often visited her. One of Blanche's grand-daughters remembered that, 'Great Aunt Puss was a mountain of a woman . . .':

We used to visit her in [her] little house not far from the tomb . . . her conversation was punctuated by the words 'Dearest Richard' . . . I had to sit like a good Victorian child and keep my little bare legs still even when Aunt Puss's pug dog came and sniffed and snuffled . . . in the room was Uncle Richard's top hat and gold-topped cane, also in a case his Consul's uniform and hat. There were photographs of him everywhere. Afterwards we used to visit the tomb and kneel down on the grass and say a 'de Profundis' for his naughty old soul.

This, her mother told her, was quite different from visits during Richard's lifetime. Then, apparently, 'Great Uncle Richard used to tell rude stories to Isabel's sisters, who were rather prim – however my mother had a great sense of humour and refused to be shocked.'[1]

Isabel maintained her close links with children and animal charities. Sometimes she hired large open-top carts and took groups of orphans and 'poor Catholic children' off to Wimbledon Common for picnics and games. At Christmas she bought toys in wholesale quantities, stopping her cab in Regent Street and Oxford Street to haggle with street vendors over 'job-lot' prices. This always drew a small appreciative crowd, and on completion of formalities any children present were invariably rewarded by her with a smile and a toy.

The abuse of animals, in any form, made her incandescent with rage; she could still bring an anti-vivisection meeting to its feet, would readily tackle any politician on the subject, and wrote indefatigably to the press. When she hired a cab she always inspected the condition of the horse and tack, and kept her window down so that she could watch the driver. The merest flick of the whip brought a lunging prod from her umbrella and the comment, 'Well, and how do you like it?' She also spoke out on women's rights and – while she believed that in general a woman should defer to a husband – she thought that women should take more responsibility for their own lives. She was an active supporter of the move to give knighthoods to women such as Florence Nightingale, and wrote to the press on the subject.

Meanwhile she continued to work for at least eight hours a day, through bouts of increasing pain, to publish all she could of Richard's works. She succeeded with *Pentamerone* and *Catullus*, and *The Jew, The Gypsy and El Islam* was completed ready for publication.* In an attempt to speed up progress and make some incomplete manuscripts publishable, she contacted several men with whom Richard had corresponded and whom she trusted implicitly; Edward Sieveking, for example, who she asked to work on the two incomplete volumes of *The Sword*, and Edgar Prestage, the Camoens expert, who wrote a Preface to a manuscript Richard had abandoned after realising that the work was probably not that of Camoens after all. 'He gave it up after turning 60 stanzas into English,' she told him. But, she warned

---

* But not published until 1898, see Bibliography.

Prestage on one occasion when he wanted to make a point to which she objected, 'you see our present object is less Camoens . . . than Richard Burton and his work. Now I am afraid that you will not like my idea, but you must remember that you are a disciple of Braga* and I of Richard Burton.'[2]

During the summer of 1895 she began work on her autobiography but a bad attack of influenza, followed by a longer than usual attack of abdominal pain and nausea, prevented her from progressing very far with this project. From Baker Street in July she sent for W.H. Wilkins, a writer she had met a few months earlier, and asked him if he would help her with this book when she returned to work on it. 'I was grieved to see the change which a few months had worked in her,' he said. 'She was lying on a couch in an upper room. Her face was of waxen whiteness, and her voice weak, but the brave indomitable spirit shone from her eyes still, and she talked cheerfully for a long time about her literary labours and plans and arrangements for some time ahead.'[3]

Taking her doctor's advice, she decided to convalesce on the South Coast. Taking her secretary, Miss ('Minnie') Plowman, a nurse to administer morphia injections and deal with medical emergencies, and her maid, she went to Boscombe – paying calls on the Arbuthnots and Mrs Thomas Huxley (who had been recently widowed) *en route*. She chose a respectable and comfortable guest-house but found it unedifying: 'always chock full of Plymouth Brethren and tract-giving old maids,' she wrote to a friend. 'We got very tired of it.'

In September she moved to Holywell Lodge, Eastbourne, which she rented for the winter from a friend. Dilly went down to join her, taking the house parlourmaid and cook from Baker Street. The servants bothered her with incessant quarrels. 'They have too much to eat and too little to do,' Isabel wrote to Georgiana Stisted in December. Despite the sea air she seemed unable to rally, and was now in constant pain. 'As to myself, I am so thin and weak that I cannot help thinking there must be atrophy . . . I may be able to last till March.' She still signed herself 'your loving aunt, Zoo', as she always had to Richard's niece.

On good days she did some work on her autobiography, and her visitors were pleased to note that she retained her quick intellect and

---

*Theophilo Braga; biographer and bibliographer of Camoens.

ready sense of humour. She also still enjoyed smoking her narghileh, or a small cigar after dinner, but she knew that time was running out. By March she was desperate to return home to die among the things which had belonged to her and Richard. 'I am very bad,' she wrote to Madame de Gutmansthal-Benvenuti, 'and my one prayer is to get home to London. The Doctor is going to move me on the first possible day. I work every moment I am free from pain.'[4]

Ten days later, on 21 March, she was moved on an invalid bed by train, and then by carriage. At Victoria Station she thought she felt well enough to stand and walk along the platform, but as soon as she stood up she fainted. That evening as she lay in her room, beneath the last picture painted of Richard, she kept repeating to her sister, 'Thank God I am home again!' and she appeared stronger. Next morning, however, it was evident to Dilly that her sister was dying and she asked if she should send for the priest. Isabel weakly told her she must make the decision. Dilly sent for the priest immediately, and he came and administered extreme unction, and worked through the detailed programme of prayers which Isabel had long ago specified she wanted at the end.

She remained conscious throughout the service and when it was all over, she bowed her head and whispered, 'Thank God.' She died a few moments later.

A week later Isabel's funeral was held on a 'bright spring afternoon when nature seemed to be waking from its winter sleep', reported the local newspaper, listing a large number of family and friends who attended. Next to Richard's name, on the stone 'book of life' where his deeds and honours were proudly recorded, she had ordered to be added the words, 'and Isabel, his wife.'

After the church service, her simple brown coffin was carried into the stone tent and placed on its stand beside – but slightly lower than – Burton's splendid black and gilded one. Again, there was a list of prayers she had stipulated for the occasion, and the door of the tent stood open so that the mourners could hear them being intoned, with the committal hymn.

Above the voices of the priest and the choir, creating an exotic alien sound in the quiet English churchyard, strings of camel-bells tinkled gaily in the brisk spring breeze.

EPILOGUE
1896 ET SEQ

Isabel's probated will shows that she left an estate of £11,766. Considering that she was almost penniless after she had paid Richard's funeral expenses, and that her two pensions amounted to £354 a year, the fact that she managed to live well *and* amass this sum in only five years is a tribute to her administrative ability. Because of her fear of being buried alive she directed that a post mortem be carried out to ensure death had genuinely occurred, that the tumour be removed from her body, and that a needle be passed through her heart.[1]

In a series of fascinating documents entitled 'Last Wishes' and 'Private Instructions to my Sister', she left precise instructions about the disposal of her chattels.[2] The list of what was to be burned proves that the stories of wholesale burning of diaries and letters in Trieste were fallacious. This list includes;

> 5 Blank books of Sir Richard's early journals (tied together)
> His journals from 1862 to 1890 bound in green or yellow calf
>   (Letts)
> 4 of my girl's journals *at once and without reading*
> My private journals . . . in green or calf.
> All the journals copied by Mrs Maylor in writing or type . . .
> A very large packet of Richard's letters to me, and some of mine to
>   him

A few books that are not very creditable: . . .[3]
All the Arabian Nights [subscribers] lists.
All the letters to Sir Richard in packets, except those marked 'not to
    be burned'[4]

Some unpublished and unfinished manuscripts were to be destroyed;
'such as "Lowlands of Brazil, North and South America, Personal
Experiences in Syria".' Not because they were contentious but
because she did not want them 'finished', and brought out by someone who might not understand Richard Burton as she did. Likewise,
with the diaries and letters, 'I will not have another biography
brought out.' She already had ample proof that unscrupulous men,
pretending to be friends, would publish anything to make money.

> Also such Manuscripts as I have not had time to look over, and
> which Richard himself had no idea of bringing out. [These] will
> probably be found in the loft in boxes labelled 'to be overhauled
> and burnt, . . . a few pages on Polygamy – An envelope full of odd
> pages (very large) . . . Also a Manuscript about the Jews – Richard's
> fair copy and rough copy must be burnt . . .

A number of manuscripts were complete and the executors were to
have these published if possible (see Bibliography). 'As to the rest,' she
wrote, 'for instance the books, novels, music, maps . . . [Richard's]
pictures, table, chair and other things,' most of these things were
already bequeathed to the Nation (see Appendix 1).

It was 'the rest' which caused a problem, however, for when the
executors met to discuss carrying out Isabel's instructions, they
found that Dilly Fitzgerald wanted to err on the safe side by burning everything not specifically mentioned: papers, manuscripts and
books. Minnie Plowman, who had been Isabel's secretary for some
years, knew that this was not Isabel's intention. Mrs Fitzgerald had
lived a very closeted life and had never travelled; she was an affectionate but rather simple woman who was intensely loyal, but in
awe of her elder sister. As a consequence, Miss Plowman quickly
contacted a friend, Herbert Jones,[5] who was Librarian at the
Central Library in Kensington, to ask if he could accept the collection in order that scholars could consult it.[6] Jones was able to set
aside a room at the Library and he accepted the offer, however, as

the transfer took place, it was found that there was insufficient space and the Library was able to accept only the main collection of books, afterwards known as 'Sir Richard Burton's Library'. At one point we know that this Library had numbered 6,000 to 8,000 books (see Appendix 1).

There remained the items which Isabel had promised to leave to the nation at the time when she invited donations for the tomb at Mortlake, as well as her own complete collection of Richard's works, and all their papers. With the exception of the material specifically mentioned to be burned, and Isabel's private papers, the second part of the collection eventually found a home at Camberwell Library, where the Librarian, Mr Foskett, promised to house and display everything in one room, again in accordance 'with Lady Burton's wishes'.[7]

In the event, it was decided to burn nothing until after W.H. Wilkins completed Isabel's autobiography, begun over a year before her death. Wilkins had access to Isabel's papers, through Dilly Fitzgerald and Minnie Plowman, throughout the period of his work, which was eventually completed and published as *The Romance of Isabel Burton*.

If proof were needed that Isabel's precautions were necessary to protect Richard's reputation, it was quickly provided. The manuscript 'about the Jews', that Isabel specifically directed was to be burned, was an essay about a Jewish sect in the Middle East said to practise human sacrifice. Wilkins decided to include it in Burton's *The Jew, The Gypsy and El Islam*, which he edited for publication by the executors.[8] Jewish leaders in London having been shown galley proofs of the book brought an action to prevent its publication; 'such a book would revive a cruel and absurd mediaeval legend which has been refuted over and over again,' a representative wrote to the executors.[9] The book was subsequently amended prior to publication in 1898.

Wilkins was implicitly trusted by Isabel and the executors; after *The Jew, The Gypsy and El Islam*, he compiled a book entitled *Wanderings in Three Continents* from papers and lectures which Burton had delivered at learned societies. It was badly edited and appears to have been the last work he did for the executors. Some years later, Wilkins fell on hard times and subsequently a number of Burton manuscripts appeared on the market which the executors traced back to him. They included the essay concerning Jewish human sacrifices, which he had sold to a publisher,[10] and the Estate had to bring an action to prevent publication.[11]

Isabel's obsession with protecting Richard's name by destroying any publications which contained 'coarse' material might also be considered justified in view of what happened to his contemporaries who fell foul of the Obscene Publications Act. Havelock Ellis, for example, who wrote his famous book on sexual inversions in 1898, was prosecuted, as was his printer. Oscar Wilde's fate needs no elaboration, and H.S. Nichols (shortly after he published Georgiana's book) was arrested and charged with producing hard-core pornography. Granted bail, Nichols fled the country, carrying on his profitable business from Paris for another decade until France also became too hot for him and he moved on to America.

The casual reader might be forgiven, at this point, for wondering if it really matters whether Isabel burned Burton's diaries and private papers in Trieste, or ordered them burned in London after her death. However, it matters for two reasons.

First, it proves that the burning was not so mindless and comprehensive as is generally believed. Isabel burned in Trieste those documents liable to damage his reputation, i.e. *The Scented Garden*, and probably his notebooks on the subject of homosexual love, as well as 'one or two' of the books and papers on a list of items he wished burned which she claims Richard left. Burton was not a fool; his letters to Smithers illustrate that he knew perfectly well the risks he was running, probably he enjoyed the element of danger, and was as confident as Oscar Wilde that he could talk himself out of trouble in court if necessary. But if he were not there to answer in person? Isabel's list of instructions that Richard's diaries and letters be destroyed after her death contained the words, 'as Dick instructed'. Presumably, she could not bring herself to destroy them; indeed, she even paid Mrs Maylor to decipher and type out some of his diaries so that she could read them more easily. She could hardly have done so if they had been burned in Trieste.[12]

Second, the fact that the diaries, letters and a number of 'dubious' manuscripts and books survived until Isabel's death, proves that Dr Baker and Daisy Letchford lied about the material Isabel burned at Trieste. They were not present at the event, and did not know what she burned. She told them she had burned the *Scented Garden* mss. (which they never entirely believed), and notebooks, and they simply surmised that she had also burned Richard's diaries and other manuscripts. And if they lied about, embroidered or invented the details of the burning, what credence can be given to the other statements they made about her actions following Burton's death?

We know that Georgiana Stisted's version of the death-bed scene, and the burning of papers in Trieste, was based on information given to Lady Stisted by Dr Baker. Some years later, both Baker and Daisy Letchford were interviewed and quoted at length on the subject by the author of the first major biography to follow Isabel's *Life*. Thomas Wright's two-volume *Life of Sir Richard Burton* was published in 1906 and this biography, together with one of lesser importance by Georgiana Stisted, provide the roots of the present inaccurate perception of Isabel. As late as 1926 Dr Baker was still writing about the 'ruthless holocaust', he insisted had taken place in Trieste, and was still exaggerating his role in Burton's life, always to Isabel's detriment.[13]

Georgiana began work on a 'popular' biography of her uncle as soon as her mother Maria, Lady Stisted, died.[14] Two months after Isabel's death, Georgiana contacted the novelist Lynn Linton (who had publicly denounced Isabel's burning of the *Scented Garden* manuscript), to ask if Linton would help her to edit the book. It was intended 'to repair the tarnished memory . . . of one of the greatest men of our century,' perpetrated by his 'vain and bigoted wife,' she said. 'My views on almost every subject are identical with Dick Burton's . . . I understood him thoroughly,' she wrote. 'I have tried to keep her out of it as much as possible . . . it contains a full account of the burning of the MS. and the horrible farce around the deathbed.'[15] Besides her biography, Georgiana said, she intended to set up a subscription for a Memorial to Burton in Westminster Abbey. 'That idiotic tomb in Mortlake was subscribed to by just a few Roman Catholic friends of Lady Burton's. Mine will be the *National* Monument . . . Hatred of shams and lies must be my excuse.'[16]

In the series of letters between the two women[17] that followed, Georgiana constantly expressed her hostility towards Roman Catholicism. Her book, she declared, 'will be useful for the masses, rather than the classes, and may warn Protestants that Romanists are better off outside the house than in.' Stisted's version of her uncle's life, *The True Life of Captain Sir Richard Burton*, published in

December 1896 by H.S. Nichols,* was received indifferently. Most reviewers asked the same question: 'How could she know more about what happened at Burton's deathbed than Lady Burton, who was present?' Georgiana blamed the book's reception on 'the Romanists who are doing their very utmost to damn it',[18] and requested Dr Baker to write to *The Times* corroborating what he had told her mother. Baker neither replied to her letter nor wrote to *The Times*, which put Georgiana out. 'It is very necessary Dr Baker come forward,' she explained to Linton, but if he did not, she hoped Mrs Linton would help her to deal with the criticisms; 'it seems scarcely fair to ask you to interfere in a disagreeable controversy, for disagreeable, of course, it is.'[19]

There is insufficient space here to detail the Stisted biography. Its value to the Burton researcher lies in a few isolated family anecdotes which do not appear elsewhere, and as an illustration of the bitterness that existed between Isabel and Maria. The major part of the book is easily identifiable as having been taken from Richard's and Isabel's published works. Having so roundly condemned Isabel for burning her uncle's manuscripts, diaries and papers after his death, it is curious that Georgiana not only burned her parents' papers, but stipulated that her own be burned after her death. She did, however, preserve Richard's and Isabel's letters and the journal that Richard kept during his trip to America.[20] She totally believed Burton's claim to her mother and herself that his *Nights* had been published in Benares. And the promise Burton extracted from his sister and niece, that they would never read *Nights*,[21] did not prevent Georgiana from writing a well-meant but somewhat ludicrous 'defence' of the contents of both the *Nights*, and also *The Scented Garden* which, she claimed, Isabel had destroyed 'in a fit of hysteria or bigotry'.[22] She described the *Nights* and its Terminal Essay as 'an ideal book for young men' studying for the Indian Civil Service, F.O. officials, 'or even our cleverest soldiers'.[23]

What most upset Maria and her daughter was Isabel's confession that she had destroyed *The Scented Garden* because it was indecent. By doing so, she conveyed 'a wrong impression concerning the character of

---

*It is tempting to wonder what Georgiana's reaction was when she learned, shortly afterwards, that Nichols was one of the most notorious publishers of pornography at the time.

the book', said Georgiana, who had no idea of the book's subject material but imagined it was similar to the 'library edition' of Burton's *Nights* published by Leonard Smithers and H.S. Nichols, which Nichols had shown her. Thomas Wright aptly summed up her protests by stating that 'Miss Stisted's . . . innocent remarks on *The Scented Garden* must have made the anthropological sides of Ashbee, Arbuthnot and Burton's other old friends shake with uncontrollable laughter.'[24]

Meanwhile, using Isabel's papers and with the assistance of her sisters and her former secretaries, Minnie Plowman and Alice Quarry,[25] W.H. Wilkins had sympathetically completed Isabel's unfinished autobiography. In *The Romance of Isabel, Lady Burton* (published 1897), he defended his subject:

> Last December, when this book was almost completed, a volume was published calling itself 'The True Life of Captain Sir Richard Burton', written by his niece, Miss Georgiana M. Stisted, stated to be 'issued with the authority and approval of the Burton family.' This statement is not correct – at any rate not wholly so; for several of the relatives of the late Sir Richard Burton have written to Lady Burton's sister to say that they altogether disapprove of it. The book contained a number of cruel and unjust charges against Lady Burton, which were rendered worse by the fact that they were not made until she was dead and could no longer defend herself . . .

The *Romance* adds a good deal of early material on Isabel, some of the more personal aspects of the couple's relationship and their travels. It also includes some interesting correspondence which has not survived, and an account of Burton's last hours from Isabel's papers and diaries. But although Wilkins wrote a highly readable account of Isabel's life, he never captured the innate sense of humour, and the ability to laugh at herself, which never deserted her, and which shines through so many of her letters. Take the one she wrote to 'Ally Sloper' for example, the pseudonym of an anonymous character who began a spoof journal called *The Sloperite* through which he conveyed 'certificates of honour' to many well-known personalities. In 1886, Isabel found herself one of the 'chosen', and her response sparkles with a sense of fun:[26]

> I was quite overcome . . . I felt that I had really 'awoke' and found

myself famous . . . and that my poor husband who has spent 32 years translating and perfecting the Arabian Nights wasn't in it at all. I did not feel at *all* like the bellows to the organ, or the fly on the wheel . . . since I have received the diploma I give myself such dreadful airs that no one can live with me. When I have calmed down and grown used to my new honours I will strive always to deserve the good opinion and confidence of the Sloperies by emulating all that is best and noblest . . . for my remaining years.[27]

The publishing company of H.S. Nichols closed when he was arrested, so there was no second edition of *The True Life*, corrected and edited by Lynn Lynton, as Georgiana hoped there would be; and both women were dead when the next major treatment of Burton was published in 1906. Thomas Wright's book was so popular that it was reprinted three times in twelve months. Its importance lies in the fact that he was able to interview surviving contemporaries of the Burtons, although the last major figure in Burton's life, F.F. Arbuthnot, had died, and neither the Birds nor Isabel's two secretaries (Minnie Plowman and Alice Quarry – the latter had worked for Richard in London) would consent to be interviewed.[28]

Thomas Wright's style is more readable than that of the previous Burton biographies, but even before he began writing the Burton biography he had in his sights the subject of his next book: John Payne, who had published his translation of the *Nights* immediately prior to Burton's version. Despite the fact that Burton and Payne corresponded for half a decade and collaborated over their respective editions of the *Nights*, and that Payne was a frequent visitor to 'Haji Abdullah's Divan' during Burton's final visit to London, it would be incorrect to call them friends. Burton respected Payne's scholarship, but he regarded him as narrow-minded. Payne believed that Burton had plagiarised his manuscripts when he sent them to Trieste for checking, and disapproved of what he regarded as the coarser side of Burton's nature. With no close living relatives to upset, Wright felt able to be critical of Burton.

He made a comparison of the respective versions of the *Nights* by Burton and Payne. We know, not only from Richard's and Isabel's writings but from the statements of people who met him through the years, that Burton had been engaged in collecting manuscripts of the *Nights*' stories and translating them, on and off, for over twenty-five years before he met Payne.[29] So Wright's claim that Burton had not done his own translation, but had 'taken from Payne at least three-quarters of his entire work',[30] is extraordinary.*

The remaining members of Burton's family, mostly cousins who had given unstinting assistance to Wright,[31] were furious. Especially Edward Mostyn Pryce, who was Georgiana's heir and inherited from her the collection of Burton letters which dated from Richard's time in India, and Isabel's letters to Georgiana for thirty years. Pryce had allowed Wright to quote from some of these, and also provided family photographs and pictures as illustrations, so when the biography was published he was mortified to find it questioned Burton's literary accomplishments. Writing in the *Times Literary Supplement* on 16 March 1906, he angrily refuted Wright's claim that Burton had plagiarised Payne's work: '. . . He had no need to do so, being one of the most learned Arabists of his day,' he pointed out. Burton learned and used his Arabic in situations where, had he been revealed as an impostor, his life would have been in jeopardy. 'Had Burton's fame as an Arabist been attacked in his lifetime,' he said, 'by someone who does not even speak Arabic [Wright] he would have shaken the dust off his boots upon such a miserable insect.' In answer to Wright's insinuations that Burton's mental faculties had been failing in his latter years, Pryce ended with a recollection that even during his last visit to England when he had been physically frail, Burton was still able to play four simultaneous games of chess, blindfolded, 'and win!'[32]

Wright did not stop at disparaging Burton's literary reputation, however; he also effectively destroyed Isabel's character. While magnanimously declaring that in respect of the destruction of *The Scented Garden*, 'she was justified . . . in doing so,' (Payne had told him it was a 'vile' work), he drew his portrait of her on information provided by those who had already proved that they disliked her for one reason or another: Dr Baker, Daisy Letchford (who had become Madame Nicastro by this time), and Messrs Kirby, Payne and Swinburne. None of Isabel's surviving friends and admirers were approached; it was a thorough hatchet job, and as a result Isabel was depicted as a foolish,

---

*This episode has been admirably covered by Fawn Brodie in her excellent biography of Burton, *The Devil Drives*, and by N.S. Penzer in his *Annotated Bibliography* (see Bibliography for details). Both books are in print at this time (1998).

uneducated, prudish and scheming woman, tolerated rather than loved by Burton, and who placed proselytising for the Catholic Church above all other considerations. With the exception of Daisy Letchford Nicastro, Wright's contributors were all men. He was a widower and, apparently, something of a misogynist for he openly stated his opinion that 'the wives of nearly all his principal friends tormented their husbands . . . [and] nearly all the miseries that have befallen empires have resulted from intemperate love of some woman.'[33]

The next major work on Burton was published in 1923; a bibliography by Norman Mosley Penzer, whose technical approach would have undoubtedly appealed to Burton. Penzer refers to Wright's book as one 'to be regretted . . . owing to its large number of mistakes, continual repetition, bad arrangement and incompleteness of references . . . it appears convincing and complete, but a little closer observation will show how utterly unreliable and full of blunders (to say the least) the work really is.'[34] Penzer also made a few mistakes (not in his technical bibliographical data, but in his biographical coverage), but these errors are minor. More importantly, Penzer also totally believed Baker and Nicastro, both of whom were major contributors to his book. Nicastro provided a touching fable of how in spite of her 'many vigorous appeals' to Isabel, she was ignored as 'the bonfire' was stoked in Trieste. Baker provided a preface as 'the last of that small body of devoted friends who were with him [Burton] when on October 20, 1890, he fearlessly met his death at Trieste'.[35] Nicastro now admitted having 'saved' a notebook and parts of a diary (presumably some of the items which Isabel accused her of stealing). She gave the notebook to Penzer and he used it as an illustration.* Unfortunately, this notebook also, apparently, perished in flames when Penzer's house was blitzed during the Second World War. The fragments of diary, part of which were the spoof journal of the transatlantic voyage, were presented by Madame Nicastro to the British Library where they now are. It is not known what happened to the remaining parts of the stolen diaries.

After Penzer's bibliography, major biographical treatments of

---

* Penzer mistakenly believed it to be the 'only remaining Burton notebook', but Isabel preserved many pages of illustrated notebooks in albums which survive at the Wiltshire Record Office, in Trowbridge.

Burton followed at an average of roughly one per decade (see Bibliography). Each has added something new to what is known about the Burton saga, although none until now had the advantage of Isabel's private papers which, among other things, throws new light on the Baker/Letchford involvement. Like all Burton biographers, I can only regret the fact that the Burtons' diaries were destroyed. However, this was fairly typical for the time. Most historians could provide a list off the top of their heads of important diaries which perished in the same manner; Queen Victoria's daughter, for example, produced a book from her mother's journals before burning them. Even comparatively recently there was an incident where a major literary figure directed that his diaries be burned; the matter was hotly disputed in the newspapers when his executors disobeyed his last instructions. However, it is important to remember that in respect of other materials about Burton (see Appendix 1) the documentation that has survived constitutes almost an embarrassment of riches.

Even though I have managed to research the known collections, and locate a significant amount of new material, I know of more that has eluded me. Some of this is of relatively minor importance. Sifting through the archived catalogues of leading London auction houses dating from 1896, it appears that a large number of surviving A.L.S (autographed letters) and a few manuscripts of both Richard and Isabel have disappeared into unknown private hands.

But there are also some major finds still to be made. Those letters from Burton to his parents and his sister, for example, that Mostyn Pryce owned when Wright was working on his biography, and the journal notebooks kept by Burton during his journey to the U.S.A. in 1860. These items survived two World Wars, and I managed to trace them through several owners as far as 1958, when the person who owned them at the time died in a nursing home. I cannot be more specific about this because my research to find them is ongoing.

Shortly before finishing this book, it occurred to me to try to find out what happened to the 'skeleton copy' of Burton's *Scented Garden* made by Isabel and lodged with her solicitor, Mr Curtis of Bedford Row, Russell Square, in 'a large packet'. Somewhat to my surprise, when I investigated, I found that the firm was still operating from the same address. There were an exciting few days while their Archivist, Ms Trottnow, searched through their oldest client archives. Sadly she was unable to find the item described. Perhaps it was misfiled;

perhaps one of the executors withdrew it. But the possibility remains that this document still exists, somewhere. Quentin Keynes has Isabel's summary of it.

According to Dr Baker, who says Burton showed him the *Scented Garden* manuscript as he worked on it, this second version 'was merely a greatly annotated edition of that published in 1886 . . . a good opportunity for putting on record what remained in Burton's private note-books and partly in his great brain.'[36] Isabel swore in a notarised deposition that she copied *all* Burton's annotations in the 'Skeleton Copy' that she made before she burned the original.

Who knows? Perhaps at some point in the future this unique record of Burton's *Scented Garden* will re-surface and provide the basis for yet another book on Burton. It seems a tantalising note on which to end.

Appendix 1

The Burton Papers

The surviving private papers and memorabilia of the Burtons are held in five main collections, two of which are in private hands: Quentin Keynes and Edwards Metcalf. The other three are the Huntington Library, the Borough of Richmond, and Wiltshire Record Office.

About the Huntington Library Collection

This main part of this collection consists of the library of books, manuscripts and papers originally deposited at the Central Library, Kensington, in 1896, after Lady Burton's death. In 1955 the Royal Borough of Kensington reorganised its library facilities and the Burton Library was handed over to the Royal Anthropological Institute for safe-keeping when a group of Fellows made it financially possible for the Institute to house the collection.

This was an appropriate home, for Richard Burton was associated with the organisation from its conception in 1862 until his death when he still held the office of Vice-President. There had been some damage to the collection in the intervening years, due to bomb damage and flooding, and it is not known whether the collection was precisely intact since there are a few significant works missing, which were noted by Penzer as being at Kensington in the 1920s. A detailed catalogue of the holding, as inherited by the Royal Anthropological Institute, was produced by Miss B.J. Kirkpatrick, who was the Librarian. It comprises 2,552 lots of books, pamphlets, periodicals, press cuttings, catalogues, manuscripts, maps, and sundry papers. The majority of the books (Burton's own copies of his and Isabel's works and the works of others), contain annotations in his handwriting (some very extensive), plus letters and press cuttings.

Burton's friend A.B. Richards stated that the library at Trieste contained some 6,000 books, but many unimportant ones were given away by Isabel in Trieste because she could not afford to ship them to England. Later, in London, she sold a number of very valuable ones to Bernard Quaritch to raise money. A few which she considered unimportant or not worthy of keeping, were burned. In her private papers she stated that some of these were burned on Richard's instructions, and some she burned after reading them.

This entire collection is now owned by the Huntington Library in California who purchased it from the Royal Anthropological Society which needed to raise money for a new building. Some flood damage still remains to be repaired and a number of volumes are in fragile condition, but it is now held in secure and controlled conditions where it is freely available to bone-fide researchers. There has been a certain amount of criticism that the collection was allowed to leave the United Kingdom, thus making it difficult for British scholars to access it; however, there is at least as much interest in Burton in the United States as in the U.K. During the six weeks I spent at the Huntington Library I was given unparalleled assistance by the library staff there (see acknowledgement section), and the working conditions are luxurious compared with those of similar facilities in England.

Borough of Richmond Collection
This collection, housed in two locations, comprises the items which were originally presented to the Central Library, Camberwell.

1) At Richmond Central Library (Special Collections):
Consists of Isabel Burton's collection of books and pamphlets written by Burton and herself. Most are inscribed by him, or her. There are a number of letters, including the one written by Burton to Isabel's father after Richard and Isabel's wedding, and photographs and ephemera.

2) At Orleans House Gallery:
This part of the collection comprises the paintings and memorabilia which Isabel promised to leave to the nation in return for the public subscription to Burton's tomb. The paintings include the 'wedding portraits' by Desange, a portrait of Burton en route to Mecca, the Burtons' house at Salahiyeh, Damascus, by Leighton, and the paintings of the Trieste house by Albert Letchford. The memorabilia includes many items mentioned in the *Life*, some of which are mentioned in this book also: the paper-knife made by Burton from the lightning-scorched mast of his ship, the *Haj* diploma, necklet of human bones from the King of Dahome, the 'housewife' made by Eliza Stisted which Burton carried on his *Haj*, flowers picked by him on the day before his death (the envelope reads, 'The last flowers my darling culled the day before his death'), and the plaster casts made after Burton's death, by Letchford, etc., etc.

About the Trowbridge Collection
There are only a handful of books in this collection which has never been accessed by previous Burton biographers. Its seven large boxes largely contain unpublished personal documents, letters, manuscripts, and albums containing press cuttings, reviews, and photographs and scraps of Burton's notebooks and sketchbooks.

Although larger than either of the private document collections of Quentin Keynes and Edwards Metcalf, the papers at Trowbridge dovetail neatly into each of them. Indeed, some of the papers at Trowbridge are actually part of documents held in one of the other two collections. It was quite clear, therefore, that in total these three collections comprise almost all of Richard and Isabel's surviving papers. How had they come to be separated?

Following Isabel's death, and after the executors had disposed of the library, and bequeathed items, and burned materials destined to be destroyed, Elizabeth 'Dilly' Fitzgerald and the other executors were left with a large quantity of private papers.

Mrs Fitzgerald eventually placed these papers in a facility she regarded as completely safe for the succeeding centuries, the attics of Wardour Castle. She could not have anticipated that two World Wars and punitive death duties would eventually pitch the contents of the attic into the public domain. The death in rapid succession of two senior members of the Arundell family between 1939 and 1946 led to the eventual sale of Wardour. A number of books and papers identified at the time as being items of considerable interest to Burton collectors, were disposed of at an important sale in London. Although some lots went to smaller collectors, most of the important items went to two main, anonymous bidders who were in fact representatives of Edwards Metcalf and Quentin Keynes. Fortunately, the estimable Miss Plowman (Isabel's secretary) compiled an inventory of all the papers that were sent to Wardour, which survives at the WRO, and this, together with catalogues of sales since the 1920s, details the full extent of the Burton papers.

Some time later, the County of Wiltshire bid for and acquired the Arundell Papers. The Arundells had been a powerful family, involved in the highest Court circles, especially during the reigns of the Tudors, so it was an important collection for the county. In the main the accession was unsorted and contained in several hundred archive boxes. When cataloguing began (it is not yet completed), it was found that seven boxes contained papers belonging to Lady Burton, the former Isabel Arundell. Not only do these provide the basis of Isabel's mammoth *Life of Captain Sir Richard Burton*, but considerable new insight into the Burtons' lives and particularly their financial circumstances. When I first saw these papers no attempt had been made to catalogue them and even the boxes were unnumbered. It was a 'once in a lifetime' find for a biographer.

I made a rough catalogue, for my own purposes, identifying and indexing the more important items. I was also allowed to photocopy hundreds of documents, so that I could transcribe them in my own time. Together with photocopies from the other collections around the world, this 'copy archive' makes up a collection of thousands of documents filed in chronological order stored in some thirty crammed Lever-Arch files.

Throughout my work I have been struck by how closely Isabel stuck to facts in the *Life*. Several biographers have called her account into question, and I myself doubted some of the things she wrote about Jane Digby* With more information I now feel I owe Isabel an apology.

---

* In my biography of Jane Digby, *A Scandalous Life*, published 1995.

APPENDIX 2

The following poem, 'Past Loves', which appears to be autobiographical since Caterina and Núr Ján are known to be part of Burton's life, was written by Richard Burton in a notebook of (unpublished) poetry, c.1847–48 in India. It is in the collection of Quentin Keynes with whose kind permission it is printed here.

1. I cannot tell the Christian names
   Of all my past and present flames
       but *en revanche* will try
   To collect a few details
   Of adventures with fair females
       that filled my history . . .

2. First, Caterina came, her eyes
   Redoubtable artilleries
       Soon struck my heart
   But little came of that amour
   I was a pauper, she was poor
       And so we met to part.

3. Next was a little girl who stole
   Most artlessly my heart and soul
       And has she not them yet?
   Here again poverty and pride
   Combined to drive me from her side
       And so to part we met.

4. Years, weary years of wandering passed
   In toil and trouble till at last
       I saw her face once more
   But Ah her face was changed to me
   It was not as it used to be
       In the dear days of Yore.

5. . . . But that is by the by. Meanwhile
   I flirted with about a mile
       of Whites, Browns and Reds
   Yellows and browns of every race
   Tawny Body and sooty face
       full bred and [sometimes] half bred

6. One was the flower of Isfahan
   A princess and a courtesan
       yet a most charming dame . . .
   Another a Bush woman fair
   With greasy hair and quarters bare
       Short, squat and rather lame

7. One came from far Bokháráa walls
   Another from Gandoppa's falls
       A fourth from hot Muskat
   Bagdad gave me a dozen at least
   And Aden many a pretty beast
       Strong as full-grown muskrat

8. The Nubians and the Abyssinians
   Sent me at least a score of minions
       Cashmere was not behind
   But of them all the fair Núr Ján
   The Venus of Belochistan
       Was most to my mind.

9. So passed my youth, soon age crept on
   And stole my vigor, looks, bon ton,
       With all my will of love
   Dress soon became a sad, sad pest
   Permanently courting lost its zest
       Beauty its power to move

10. Yet still excitement wanted I
    To live without it & to die
        were equal, so I drank
    Brandies and waters, wines and gins
    By casks and bottles, bins and skins
        enough to fill a tank.

11. That vanity soon passed away
    My next resource, of course, was play
        by ennui haunted still
    She played so well and I so ill
    Soon I was beaten to my fill
        cursed cards & paid the bill

12. And now my life draws to an end
    Wine, women, dinner, card and friend
        now yield me scant delight
    Yet am I not content? I am.
    I've had my day, I've lived my life
        ~~and now expect my night~~.*

* After their marriage Isabel scored through the last line and changed it to:
'*and given the debris to a wife.*'

APPENDIX 3

CHRONOLOGY

RFB's age on 19/4	Year	Events
	1821	Richard Francis Burton born 19 March, at Torquay. Baptised Elstree 2 September. Family live with Baker grandparents in Hertfordshire.
2	1823	Maria Catherine Eliza (sister) born.
3	1824	Edward Joseph (brother) born. Death of Mr Richard Baker (grandfather).
5	1826	Burton family move to Tours, France.
6	1827	RFB begins day school.
8	1829	Burtons return to England; RFB attends school at Richmond.
10	1831	Burtons return to France; Blois. Isabel Arundell born 20 March.
11	1832	Burtons tour Sienna/Perugia/Florence/Rome/Pisa.
12	1833	Burtons settle in Naples.
15	1836	Burtons leave Naples for Pau, S. France.
16	1837	Queen Victoria ascends throne. Burtons return to Italy, settle in Lucca.
19	1840	RFB enrolled at Trinity College, Oxford.
20	1841	RFB at Oxford University. Begins to study Arabic; summer vacation in Weisbaden.
21	1842	RFB leaves Oxford. June: RFB embarks for India. October: RFB arrives Bombay, serves under Charles Napier.
22	1843	Regiment stationed at Baroda. Passes language exams in Hindustani (1st of 12 entrants), and Gujarati.
23	1844	Stationed at Karachi and later Gharra (Sindh); passes language exam. in Mahratta; sent to Hyderabad with Survey Dept.; begins to learn Persian language.
24	1845	Appointed Assistant Surveyor and given intelligence missions including secret brothel report for Napier (precise date uncertain). Passes exam. in Persian (1st of 30 entrants). Isabel Arundell attends New Hall School, age 14.
25	1846	RFB returns to Hyderabad; appointed Regimental Interpreter; resigns from Survey Dept. contrary to direct order, and marches with regiment, but battle aborted and he returns to reprimand; begins lifelong study of Camoens; given two years' sick leave.
26	1847	Proceeds to Goa and Neilgherries for convalescence; spends summer in hill stations (Ootacamund). Returns to Bombay in October, sits Persian exam., passes 1st in class with honours.

27	1848	Following Napier's return to England, RFB's secret brothel report is found. RFB returns to regiment in Sindh; too ill to work at Survey, studies Arabic and Sindi. Becomes Master Sufi. Passes language exams in Sindi and Punji. Writes comprehensive reports: *Grammar of Játaki or Mulltani Language*; *Remarks on Dr Dorn's Chrestomathy of the Afghan tongue*; *General Notes on Sind*; *Notes on the Population of Sind*; (all published internally by H.E.I.C.).
28	1849	RFB's application to serve as Chief Interpreter to C.O. in Mooltan campaign refused. He obtains home leave on medical grounds.
29	1850	Returns to England; visits parents in Italy.
30	1851	Stays in London and Dover, then goes to Boulogne where his parents and family join him. **Meets Isabel Arundell.** Publishes: *Sinde or the Unhappy Valley*; *Sinde and the Races . . .*; *Goa and the Blue Mountains.*
31	1852	Plans solo expedition to Mecca. Pub: *Falconry in the Valley of the Indus.*
32	1853	Visits Mecca and Medina as bone-fide pilgrim. Pub: *Complete System of Bayonet Exercise.*
33	1854	Plans African expedition. Meets Speke. RFB's mother dies on 18 December.
34	1855	April: Burton and Speke attacked and wounded at Berbera; return to Aden. RFB diagnosed with syphilis and sent home for treatment. Pub: *Personal Narrative of a Pilgrimage to Meccah & Medinah.*
35	1856	RFB serves in Crimea with Beatson's Horse (irregular cavalry regiment); meets Isabel at Kew and becomes unofficially engaged; returns to Bombay, sails for Zanzibar. Pub: *First Footsteps in East Africa.*
36	1857	June: Burton/Speke Expedition sets out from coast for Central Lake regions of East Africa. September: RFB's father dies.
37	1858	Expedition successfully locates Lake Tanganyika. During return journey Speke makes side expedition and finds Lake Victoria. Isabel Arundell spends the year touring Europe with sister and brother-in-law.
38	1859	Expedition returns to E. African coast and Zanzibar. While RFB recovers from fever Speke returns to England alone and is given most of the credit for the expedition's success. Richard returns to find he has been sidelined. Meets Isabel again but finds her parents still opposed to him.
39	1860	RFB feud with Speke; leaves for U.S.A. tour. Speke returns to Africa to find source of Nile with Grant. Pub: *The Lake Regions of Central Africa.*
40	1861	January: **RFB and IB marry**. Fire at Grindlay's warehouse. RFB accepts position as H.B.M. Consul Fernando Po, W. Africa and thereby inadvertently resigns commission in Army. Sails for West Africa. Pub: *The City of Saints.*
41	1862	IB goes to Paris with Napoleon memorabilia. RFB makes first tour of West African coast and interior including expedition to search for gorillas and cannibal tribes. December: first home leave; Christmas at Wardour Castle.
42	1863	RFB co-founds Anthropological Society. Couple sail for Madeira

and spend several months 'honeymooning' there before RFB returns
to his post. Explores Congo as far as Yalalla rapids. Acts as Foreign
Office emissary on mission to Gelele, King of Dahomey. Pub:
Abeokuta and the Cameroons Mountains; *Wanderings in West
Africa*.

43	1864	August: RFB returns to London. September: Bath meeting and Speke's death. RFB appointed Consul in Santos, Brazil. Pub: *Mission to Gelele, King of Dahome*; *The Nile Basin*.
44	1865	August: Couple go to Lisbon where RFB sails for Brazil; IB returns to London to pay, pack and follow. Pub: *Wit & Wisdom*; *Stone Talk*.
45	1866	HBM Consul Santos.
46	1867	RFB makes several expeditions into Brazilian interior, one with IB, terminated by her accident. RFB goes on alone, sails/canoes 1,500 miles (much whitewater rapids) down S. Francisco River to coast while IB returns alone to Rio.
47	1868	May: RFB critically ill with pneumonia and hepatitis, sends in resignation. IB returns to England to lobby for Syrian posting, while RFB makes S. American tour including Paraguay and Chile.
48	1869	RFB appointed H.B.M. Consul in Damascus, proceeds there via Vichy; IB follows later (in December). Pub: *Highlands of Brazil*.
49	1870	Damascus. Desert excursions including Palmyra. Pub: *Vikram and the Vampire*; *Letters from the Battlefields of Paraguay*.
50	1871	Damascus. Attack at Nazareth; RFB recalled, returns to London to answer unfair charges. IB sells up and follows some months later. Pub: *Unexplored Syria* (with Charles Tyrwhitt-Drake).
51	1872	RFB twice visits Stisteds in Edinburgh; first visit to Iceland. Death of Isabel's mother and brother. RFB offered Trieste; operation to remove carbuncle. Pub: *Zanzibar*.
52	1873	H.B.M. Consul Trieste. Couple visit Rome and Florence. Vienna (Great Exhibition). Pub: *Lands of Cazembe* (translation).
53	1874	RFB seriously ill after op. to remove tumour. September: tour of N. Italy; December: IB to London to publish books.
54	1875	May: RFB joins IB in England; makes second visit to Iceland. 'Captain Burton's Tonic Bitters'; Leighton's portrait of RFB exhibited in RA. December: couple return to Trieste for Christmas. Pub: *Ultima Thule*.
55	1876	Couple spend six months' holiday in India revisiting scenes of RFB's service there. Plans bogus 'Kama Shastra Society' as device for publishing erotica. Pub: *Etruscan Bologna*; *A New System of Sword Exercise*. IB pub: *Inner Life of Syria*.
56	1877	Trieste. RFB goes to Egypt; from Cairo makes 3-week 'reconnaissance' expedition in Midian, to look for gold. Pub: *Sind Revisited*.
57	1878	Second Midian expedition – 4 months supported by Khedive. RFB mugged in Alexandria. Couple return to England; RFB lectures at Spiritualist Association. Pub: *Gold Mines of Midian*.
58	1879	April: couple return to Trieste separately. IB badly injured in fall in Paris. October: tour of N. Italy. Pub: *The Land of Midian*. IB pub: *A.E.I. Arabia, Egypt India*.
59	1880	Trieste. Couple visit Oberammergau. IB writes *Passion Play at*

		Ommerammergau (published posthumously in 1900). Pub: *Kasidah*; *Os Lusiads*.
60	1881	RFB to West Africa for Guinea Coast Gold Mines Co. Joins Isabel in London before returning to Trieste. Pub: *Camoens – His Life and Lusiads*, a commentary; *A Glance at the Passion Play*.
61	1882	Trieste. RFB ordered to Egypt to search for Palmer.
62	1883	Trieste. Burtons move into *Palazzo Gossleth*; RFB working on 'Arabian Nights' translations; suffers first heart attack. Pub: *To the Gold Coast for Gold*; *The Kama Sutra*.
63	1884	Trieste. RFB very ill all spring. F.O. refuse to allow early retirement. Pub: *The Book of the Sword*; *Camoens – The Lyricks*.
64	1885	Begins to publish his translations of the *Arabian Nights*. Pub: *Ananga Ranga* (with F.F. Arbuthnot); *The Book of the Thousand Nights and A Night* (first vols published of set of 16).
65	1886	Tangiers and Gibralter; knighthood conferred on 25th Wedding Anniversary. Storm during return to Trieste, Isabel injured. Death of Isabel's father. Home leave. Pub: *Supplemental Volumes of 1001 Nights*; *Iracéma, The Honey Lips* (with IB); *The Perfumed Garden* (from the French).
66	1887	RFB taken ill with second heart attack in Cannes. Dr Leslie replaced by Dr Baker as permanent private physician. Winter in Abbazia – snowed-in for 2 months. Edits and annotates: *The Behâristân* and *The Gulistan* for Kama Shastra Society (translated by Edward Rehatsek). IB learns she has ovarian cancer.
67	1888	RFB's last trip to England. Winter in Switzerland. IB publishes 'Household Edition' of *Nights*.
68	1889	RFB works on translations of erotic mss. all year. Winter in North Africa to search for original Arabic manuscript of *Scented Garden*.
69	1890	RFB translates and annotates *Scented Garden*. October 19: **Death of RFB**. IB burns ms. of *Scented Garden*. Pub: *The Priapeia* (with Leonard Smithers).
	1891	June; RFB buried at Mortlake.
	1892	IB publishes seminal 2-vol. biography of RFB: *Life of Captain Sir Richard F. Burton*.
	1896	March 22nd: **Death of IB**.

Posthumous publications:
Il Pentamerone (translated by RFB, 1893).
The Carmina of Gaius Valerius Catullus (translated and annotated by RFB, with introduction etc. by Leonard Smithers, 1894).
The Jew, The Gypsy and El Islam (RFB, 1898).
Wanderings on Three Continents (RFB, 1901).
The Passion Play at Ober-Ammergau (IB, 1900).

SOURCE NOTES

The following abbreviations have been used in the notes:

Richard F. Burton = RFB
Isabel Burton = IB

Bodleian Library, Oxford – Dept. of Western MS (Fahie) = BOD
British Library Manuscripts Dept = BL
Edwards Metcalf (Private: stored at the Huntington Library) = EM
Foreign Office Records at PRO = FO
Huntington Library, San Marino, California = HL
India Office Records = IOR
National Archives of Zanzibar = ZA
National Library of Scotland = NLS
(Relevant Collections of Papers at NLS: Blackwood; Grant; MacKenzie; Scott; Roseberry)
National Archives of Scotland = NAS
Orleans House Gallery, Surrey = OHG
Public Record Office = PRO
Quentin Keynes (Private) = QK
Royal Geographic Society = RGS
The Royal Anthropological Institute = RAI
Borough of Richmond Library, Surrey = RL
University of London – School of Oriental & African Studies = SOAS
Trinity College Library, Cambridge – Houghton Library = TCC
University of Edinburgh = UE
Wiltshire County Records Office = WRO

Researchers might like to know that smaller collections are held by:
Syracuse University, NY, USA; E.S. Bird Library (Special Collections), Yale University; Harvard University, Brigitte and Harry Spiro (Private Collection) Library of the Boston Athenaeum; The Royal Archives, Windsor; University College – Galton Collection, Royal Commonwealth Society – Ms: *An African Odyssey* by Dr Edwin Smith; Royal Asiatic Society – C.E.J. Whitting papers and others and a comprehensive collection of Burton's published works, The Earl of Halifax; Huddleton Papers, Fitzwilliam Museum – Papers of Wilfred Scawen Blunt.

Introduction
1 Brodie, Fawn: *The Devil Drives,* and McLynn, Frank: *Snow Upon the Desert.* See Bibliography for full details.
2 QK. Burton to Gerald Massey, 30 July 1881.

Chapter 1 (1821–1840)

1 Burton, Richard F. Unpublished manuscript in the Quentin Keynes collection. Uncatalogued. Hereafter called Autobiography. Parts of this manuscript were used verbatim by Francis Hitchman in the first biography. It was later used more extensively by Isabel in her informative, rambling biography *The Life of Captain Sir Richard F. Burton* (hereafter referred to as *Life*) which remains the first point of reference for any Burton scholar.

2 The Autobiography (op. cit.) is written in Isabel's handwriting, and extensively corrected in Richard's handwriting. Together with other autobiographical manuscripts of specific adventures it provides the Memoir Burton would have written for himself up to his time in Damascus.

3 Trinity College, Oxford, archives.

4 Elstree parish church baptismal register; p. 19. Date of baptism, 2 September 1821. A certified copy of the certificate of baptism is also attached to Richard Burton's Cadet Records L/Mil/9/206 at the India Office Library, London.

5 Ibid; and letter from a subsequent incumbent to the librarian in the Torquay Library Archives.

6 WRO: Burton Genealogy. Eight children survived to adulthood.

7 QK. Autobiography by Richard F. Burton in ms.

8 WRO: Printed 'Notes on Burton Genealogy'.

9 *Voyages and Travels of H.M. Caroline, Queen of Great Britain* by one of her suite (Jones & Co., 1821), p. 328.

10 Fraser, Flora, *The Unruly Queen* (Macmillan, 1996), p. 273.

11 PRO: Army Lists under entry, Burton, Richard Netterville.

12 Autobiography; also *Life*, vol. I: p. 5 and p. 41.

13 Richard Burton related the story of his father and the Queen in his 'Autobiography' (included in Isabel Burton's *Life,* op. cit.) Burton's niece, Elizabeth Stisted, also included it in her biography of Burton which infers that she may have heard it from her mother, Burton's sister Maria, but no hard evidence exists that this was the reason for Joseph's early retirement. Against this family legend one must balance the facts that Joseph had been responsible for crippling (in a duel, itself a criminal offence) a brother-officer, and that he was a chronic asthma sufferer. Either of these could have caused his being placed on half-pay.

14 Torquay Reference Library archives. Dymond and White, *Torquay Directory* 1823, p. 258.

15 QK. Autobiography; also *Life*, vol. I: p. 15.

16 WRO: Burton Genealogy; notes by IB.

17 WRO: Burton Genealogy p. 8.

18 NLS: MS3867 f.121.

19 QK. Autobiography: Also *Life*, vol. I: pp. 17, 20.

20 Ralph Steadman's interview by Danziger: *Daily Mail*, 17 Aug. 1996, relates a similar experience. '. . . He was, I would say, a sadist. It destroyed me . . . I began to live in fear of authority and that's stayed with me ever since . . . We lived in fear of this man. He loved using the cane for the smallest offences . . . [he] seemed intent on crushing the spirit in children and bending them to his will through fear. This fear has damaged me psychologically . . .'

21 WRO: Burton Genealogy.

22 Autobiography; also *Life*, vol. I: p. 30.

23 Ibid. *Life*, vol. I: p. 28.

24 Autobiography; *Life*, vol. I: p. 32.
25 Autobiography; also letter from Mr Mostyn Pryce, *Times Literary Supplement*, 16 March 1906, p. 91.
26 QK. See Appendix 2 for complete poem.
27 *Life*, p. 62.
28 Ibid., p. 63.

Chapter 2 (1840–1842)

1 *Sketch by an Old Oxonian*, p. 33. Published anonymously but known to be by A.B. Richards.
2 Trinity College Archives: Letter from Mrs C. J. Hopkins, Archivist to the author, dated 10 Oct. 1996.
3 Greenhill was a Hertfordshire man and it is possible that there was some old family connection with the Bakers. Apart from his role at Oxford he is also famous for having been one of the major contributors to the massive first edition of the *Dictionary of National Biography* (hereinafter *D.N.B.*).
4 Trinity College Archives: Bursar's 'Broad Book' 1840–42. This book details the weekly accounts for students' meals and beverages. The lack of buttery bills for Richard Burton during his first three terms (though his tuition fees and charitable contributions were paid up) indicates that he was not 'in residence' in the College until Sept. 1841. From September 1841 his bills prove he lived in college and his expenditure was 'average'.
5 QK. In his Autobiography, RFB mentions 'a few friends at "Exeter"' [college] including A.B. Richards, three 'at "Brasenose" then famous for drinking heavy beers . . . but I delighted in "Oriel" . . . the nicest college of my day. There I spent the chief part of my time with Wilberforce, Foster and a little knot amongst whom was Tom Hughes (afterwards Tom Brown).' See also *Life*, vol. I. pp. 79–80.
6 Autobiography and *Life*, vol. I: p. 72; Here Richard says he spent a small part of his day at lectures. However in *Falconry in the Valley of the Indus*, written in 1852, Burton states that he studied hard for 12 hours a day and failed at everything.
7 This must have been in 1842, for which year Trinity College does not have the names of the Torpid crew.
8 Autobiography; also *Life*, vol. I: p. 73.
9 Usually misprinted as Alfred Bates Richards because in his mini-biography of Burton the printer mistakenly added 's' to the middle name. With one exception – Edward Rice – every biographer, and Norman Penzer who wrote the standard bibliography, has since used it incorrectly. See *D.N.B.*; Burton's dedication to Alfred Bate Richards; and other contemporary reference books such as his Oxford registration; A.B. Richards' own publications.
10 Richards, Alfred Bate; *Oxford Unmasked* by a graduate (Effingham Wilson, 1842), p. 38; also Brock, M.G., *History of the University of Oxford* (Clarendon Press, 1977) p. 280; and Burton, *Falconry in the Valley of the Indus*, pp. 93–107.
11 *D.N.B.*, vol. 40.
12 Obituary of Dr W.A. Greenhill in *The Academy*, September 1894.
13 Autobiography; also *Life*, vol. I: p. 77.
14 Autobiography; also *Life*, vol. I: p. 78.
15 Ibid. IB in a letter to *Epsomian*, 22 November 1893, wrote, 'My husband told me he was laughed at – nay hissed – for making his first speech in real Latin . . .'

16 Burton, *Falconry in the Valley of the Indus*, pp. 93–107.
17 Ibid.
18 Ibid; also *Life*, vol. 1: p. 90.
19 Trinity College archives: Caution Book 1840–42. Students paid £30 and a £5 non-returnable fee for utensils.
20 HL: BL 355 p. 2, *A Sketch of the Career of Richard F. Burton.*
21 Hopkirk, Peter, *The Great Game* (OUP, 1990), p. 261.
22 Law, Sir Algernon, *India under Lord Ellenborough* (John Murray, 1926), p. 23.
23 Hopkirk, *The Great Game*, pp. 263–4.
24 Morris, Jan, *Stones of Empire* (Penguin, 1994) p. 144.
25 Law; *India Under Lord Ellenborough*, p. 20.
26 Burton, *Falconry in the Valley of the Indus*, pp. 93–107.
27 See India Office Cadet Service Record L/MIL/12/73; dated 1 June 1842.
28 Ibid., p. 3.
29 The British traded opium for tea. See Leask, Nigel, *British Romantic Writers in the East* (Cambridge University Press, New Delhi 1993), p. 217.
30 *Life*, vol. I: p. 141.
31 Morris, *Stones of Empire*, p. 194.
32 Ibid., p. 94.
33 *Life*, vol. I: p. 99.
34 Ibid., p. 99.
35 Ibid., p. 100.
36 It was Catherine of Braganza's dowry, rather than her person, that initially won the heart of the impoverished newly restored monarch. It consisted of $30,000 in gold, the island of Bombay, the port of Tangier, and valuable trading rights for English seamen in the New World. See *Charles II*, Christopher Falkus (Weidenfeld & Nicholson, 1972).
37 *Life*, vol. I: pp. 100–101.
38 Ibid., vol. I: p. 101.
39 Ibid., p. 104.
40 Autobiography; also *Life*, vol. I: p. 102.
41 *Life*, vol. I: p. 130.
42 Ibid., p. 102.
43 IOR: L/Mil/12/73.
44 Autobiography; also *Life*, vol. I: p. 103.
45 Ibid., vol. I: p. 115.
46 Ibid., vol. I: p. 100.
47 *Scinde*, vol. I: p. 42.

Chapter 3 (1843–1845)

1 *Life*, vol. I: p. 105.
2 *Scinde*, vol. I: p. 34.
3 This list, the names of which are spelled incorrectly in *Life*, vol. I: pp. 106–7, is verified in the Company Registers for Bombay 18th B.N.I. in the years 1842–49.
4 Unpublished MSS: 'An Anglo-India Glossary'. QK collection.
5 Autobiography; also *Life*, vol. I: p. 135.
6 Autobiography; also *Life*, vol. I: p. 109.
7 Autobiography; also *Life*, vol. I: p. 135.
8 Baker, Frank (a pseudonym of Richard F Burton); *Stone Talk* (Robert Hardwicke, 1865), p. 10.

9 *Life*, vol. I: p. 136.
10 Rice, Edward, *Captain Sir Richard Burton* (Charles Scribner, N.Y., 1990), p. 46.
11 The title of Gaikwar or Gaekwar was unique to Baroda and has now fallen out of use.
12 IOR: L/MIL/12/73 folio 115.
13 *Life*, vol. I: p. 123.
14 Rice, *Captain Sir Richard Burton*, pp. 62–3.
15 Ibid.
16 Anglo-Indian expression for accommodation shared by several bachelor officers.
17 *Sindh and the Races that inhabit the Valley of the Indus*; H.T. Lamrick's introduction (OUP, 1973), pp. xi & xii.
18 Burton, *Scinde or the Unhappy Valley* (Richard Bentley, 1851), pp. 1–20.
19 *Life*, vol. I: pp. 126–7.
20 In March 1856 after Lord Dalhousie annexed Oudh, the following couplet appeared in *Punch* attributing the famous quip to Lord Ellenborough:
    Peccavi – 'I've Scinde', wrote Lord Ellen so proud,
    More briefly Dalhousie wrote Vovi, 'I've Oude'.
    nb. *Vovi* = Latin: I vowed.
21 In 1843 there were 13 rupees to the £ sterling. The amount of £6,500 per year is taken from the Bank of England sterling equivalent tables.
22 *Scinde*, vol. I: p. 62.
23 IOR: L/MIL/0/201/ ff.46–9.
24 Ibid.
25 The most famous spymaster Colonel Thomas Montgomerie of the Survey of India Office recruited Indians who posed as Buddist monks mapping the areas beyond the troubled northern frontiers. He is believed to be the model upon which Kipling based his character 'Colonel Creighton'. See Hopkirk, Peter, *The Great Game*.
26 *Sindh and the Races that inhabit the Valley of the Indus* (OUP, Karachi 1973). Introduction by H.T. Lambrick, p. vi.
27 Burton, *Falconry in the Valley of the Indus* (Van Voorst MDCCCLII), p. 1.
28 *Scinde*, vol. I: p. 92 & vol. II: p. 110.
29 *Scinde*, vol. I: pp. 247, 273.
30 Ibid., pp. 276–7.
31 *Nights*, vol. V: p. 77.
32 *Kama Sutra* (George Allen & Unwin 1963), p. 132n.
33 *Arabian Nights*, Terminal Essay.
34 *Scinde*, vol. I: p. 58.

Chapter 4 (1845–1846)
1 Hopkirk, Peter, *The Great Game*, pp. 123–6.
2 Conolly, Arthur, *Journey to the North of India . . . through Russia, Persia and Affghaunistaun*, 2 vols, 1834.
3 Hopkirk, Peter, *The Great Game*, p. 279.
4 Ibid., p. 119.
5 'A Sketch of the Career of Richard F. Burton', an anonymous pamphlet (published initially in 1880 and republished in 1886), known to have been compiled by three of Burton's friends: Alfred Bate Richards (to 1876); Andrew Wilson (to 1879); and St Clair Baddeley (to 1886), p. 4.

6   *Scinde*, vol. II: p. 34.

7   Ibid., p. 38.

8   EM: Box 11, Envelope 6/10. Letter to Hain Friswell, 4 Jan 1862.

9   *Scinde*, vol. II: p. 35.

10 *Scinde*, vol. I: pp. 95–6

11 *Life*, vol. I: pp. 147–8.

12 Burton, *Falconry in the Valley of the Indus*, pp. 100–102.

13 *Scinde*; and *Personal Narrative of a Pilgrimage to Al-Madinah and Meccah* (hereafter, the *Pilgrimage*), vol. I: p. 40.

14 *The little Autobiography*, 'Who would believe the things [I] saw' quoted in *Falconry in the Indus*; A.B. Richards' short biography and *Life*, vol. I: p. 157.

15 Letters Napier to Simpson. BL: Napier Papers MSS54520.

16 William MacMurdo distinguished himself at Meeanee in February 1843 when he killed three men in hand-to-hand fighting, and a further three a month later, before he himself was severely wounded. Subsequently, Napier appointed him ADC and later he married Napier's daughter, Susan. The *DNB* states: 'He took part in the operations of the hillmen on the right bank of the Indus in 1844–45, when he again distinguished himself by his intrepidity.'

17 Not to be confused with Mohammed Akbar Khan, the treacherous Afghan leader responsible for the deaths of agents MacNaughten, Trevor and MacKenzie before the Kabul massacre.

18 Autobiography; also *Life*, vol. I: p. 141.

19 *Life*, vol. I: p. 142.

20 Ibid., p. 162

21 *Arabian Nights*, Terminal Essay, pp. 205–6.

22 Ibid.

23 Ibid., p. 237.

24 *Life*, p. 160, but see also *Romance*, p. 50; Autobiography (no page numbers); *Life*: vol. I: pp. 144–5; scrap of CV in Richard's handwriting in QK collection for other references to his Intelligence work.

25 Rice, Edw., *Captain Sir Richard Burton* (see Bibliography).

26 *Life*, vol. I: p. 159. Gordon Waterfield in his 'Introduction' to *First Footsteps* states: 'Burton is probably the inspiration for Kipling's character of Strickland.' p. 10.

27 *Life*, vol. I: p. 160.

28 *Scinde*, vol. I: p. 77D.

29 Ibid., p. 72. Note that although he repeats this story in *Scind Revisited*, he did not alter these words except to change the spelling of the town to the modern one, Karachi.

30 This is an amalgamated version of the story taken from *Scinde* (vol. I: pp. 71 et seq), *Scind Revisited* (vol. I: pp. 70 et seq), and the handwritten amendments made by Burton in his own copies of these books (the latter now housed at The Huntington Library, California).

31 *Scinde*, vol. I: p. 73.

32 Burton, *Sindh, and the Races that inhabit the Valley of the Indus* (Bentley, 1851), p. 249.

33 Burton, *Love, War & Fancy*, ed. Kenneth Walker (Wm. Kinber, 1964), p. 268.

34 Bank of England, Historical Research section: 'Equivalent Contemporary Values of the Pound' (1994).

35 Stisted, Georgiana, *The True Life of Captain Sir Richard Burton* (H.S. Nichols, 1896), p. 44.

36 Only one of whom, Fawn Brodie, actually saw Burton's manuscript which is in QK's collection. Ms Brodie had insufficient time to spend transcribing the notebook and quoted a short extract which has been since taken up by subsequent biographers from her book, *The Devil Drives*.

37 QK; *idem*.

38 QK collection. The notebook is foolscap size with a hard cover. The final third of the book has had the pages cut out, apparently with scissors, near the margin so that only a word or tantalising part-word is visible on each line. Fawn Brodie conjectured that this was done by Isabel after Burton's death as part of an orgy of destruction. But why should she do this and leave evidence in poetry of Burton's attraction to other women? The pages could equally have been removed by Isabel's literary executor, her sister 'Dilly' (Fitzgerald). But there is a more reasonable alternative. As in some earlier pieces the lines of text on these pages contain numbers which do not coincide with the actual number of lines in the work, a device employed by Burton when he was translating material from another language. Bearing in mind the probable date of the work in those missing pages, it is entirely possible that they contained early translations of Camoens' *Os Lusiads* and were removed by Burton himself as the basis for that work which he completed in middle age.

39 *Scinde*, vol. II: pp. 231 et seq.

40 *Goa and the Blue Mountains* (Bentley, 1851), pp. 73–4.

41 Ibid., pp. 81 et seq.

42 *Life*, vol. II: pp. 109–10.

43 Fawn Brodie, in *The Devil Drives*, p. 55. Ms Brodie, however, had only a short amount of time to review the Quentin Keynes collection during her limited time in London and only transcribes parts of the poetry book. In revealing the full extent of the poem I wish to stress that I am not deprecating Ms Brodie's fine biography of Burton.

44 QK collection. Burton's poetry book. This extract is taken from a 16-verse poem in five parts, each part covering the course of the love affair and titled, 1: 'Terpsichore' (Muse of dancing); 2: 'Eros' (Muse of love); 3: 'Clio' (Muse of History); 4: 'Calliope' (Muse of epic poetry), and 5: 'Melpomene' (Muse of tragedy).

45 The importance of the mighty River Indus with its tributaries rising beyond the north-west frontiers cannot be overstated.

46 NLS: MS3867 f. 109 Napier to Scott, 7 July 1845.

47 IOR: Richard F. Burton: Service Record L/MIL/12/73.

48 QK collection. Sir Charles Napier to Lady Bunbury, 28 Dec. 1845.

49 Quoted in *Life*, vol. I: p. 146.

50 IOR: Richard F. Burton: Service Record (op. cit.).

51 *Life*, vol. I: p. 146.

52 J.L. Blagrave to Lt. Richard F. Burton; 18th Regiment, Sukkur. 13 February 1846. NLS: Mss 3867 f. 119.

53 *Love, War and Fancy* op. cit., p. 163.

54 *Life*, vol. II: p. 65; also *Scind Revisited*, vol. I, p. 256.

55 Ibid.

56 As a matter of interest this town is Benazir Bhutto's home town; see *Sindh Revisited*, Christopher Ondaatje (Harper Collins, 1996), p. 245.

57 See Appendix II to this book.

58 QK collection. Poetry book page 3, 'Past Loves', reprinted in Appendix 2.

59 *Life*, vol. II: p. 65.
60 BL: Napier Papers MSS54520 (iii).
61 A number of these caricatures survive in Isabel's albums at the WRO, and in the QK collection. The couplets, including the one about Corsellis, survive in Richard Burton's poetry book in the QK collection.
62 QK. The Indian notebook.
63 *Life*, vol. I: p. 148.

Chapter 5 (1846–1849)

1 Mohammed Hosayn died of cholera shortly after his arrival in Shiraz.
2 NLS: MS3867 f. 121. The letter is headed by permission to show the letter to Richard.
3 Scott papers. NLS: MSS 7178 f. 96. Napier's personal staff at this time consisted of his two remaining nephews William Napier and Lieutenant Byng.
4 Burton, *Scinde*, vol. I: p. 93.
5 QK collection.
6 Ditto.
7 IOR. Service Record L/MIL/12/73.
8 *Goa*, p. 4.
9 IOR: Dr Bird to Court of Directors 1850.
10 This practice is still employed by intruders; several friends of the writer have experienced it in various parts of Africa, India and the Caribbean. The greased intruder cannot be grasped firmly.
11 *Goa*, p. 258.
12 Ibid., p. 308.
13 Ibid., p. 301.
14 *Life*, vol. I: p. 105.
15 IOR. Service Record L/MIL/12/73.
16 *Life*, vol. I: p. 150.
17 Dated 'Bombay 1847' the bound ms. in RFB's hand is part of Burton's own library, now housed at the Huntington Library in California. Ref: BL 104.
18 IOR. Service Record L/MIL/12/173.
19 Later, critics suggested Burton had claimed he was the first European to enter the sacred birthplace, but he made it quite clear that he was following these early explorers, even providing extracts from their works in his appendix. See Pilgrimage and Lecture notes: *Visitation at El Medinah*, Huntington Library.
20 *Life*, vol. I: p. 150.
21 *First Footsteps*, vol. II: p. 40 fn: 2.
22 A.B. Richards' article is reproduced in *Life*, vol. II: p. 13. Published in an unidentified newspaper c. 1864, an original is contained in one of Isabel Burton's cutting albums at WRO.
23 *Pilgrimage* vol. II: pp. 391–2. Here Burton quoted a Mr Bankes who had translated the account of Giovanni Finati, who had travelled to Mecca as a Mameluke in 1805. Finati did not enter the city as a born believer but the account of his experiences – occurring only 50 years earlier – played a major part in Burton's decision to go there.
24 Ibid.
25 *Life*, vol. II: p. 35.
26 1. 'Notes relative to the Population of Sind, and the Customs, Language and

Literature of the People'; and 2. 'Remarks on the Division of Time, and the modes of Intoxication in Sind'.

Written in collaboration with Dr John Ellerton Stocks, these reports were submitted to the Government on 31 Dec. 1847 and 2 March 1848 respectively, they were printed in 'Selections from the Records of the Government of India', (pub: Bombay, 1855) New Series, No: xvii part 2. Also: Edward Metcalf collection, Box 5; env. 6, p. 1. They also formed the nucleus for Burton's monumental published work *Sindh and the Races that inhabit the Valley of the Indus* (see Bibliography).

27   *Grammar of the Jakarti or Mulltani Language* and *Remarks on Dr Dorn's Chrestomathy of the Afghan Tongue*; now at the HL.

28   *Life*, vol. I: p. 151.

29   *The Times of India*, letter to the editor from Walter Abraham 31 Oct. 1890.

30   Ibid.

31   RFB to Sarah Burton (later Mrs Pryce Harrison) dated Kurrachee, 14/11/48. Quoted in Wright's biography (see Bibliography).

32   It was either Pringle or a senior member of his staff; no one else would have had access to such high-level archives. Burton declined to give a name when he told the story for the offender was dead, he said, and could not answer the accusation. It was almost certainly Pringle himself.

33   The fate of this report is not known. Many Burton scholars have sought it both in England and India, but so far it has eluded its searchers. This has prompted several scholars to doubt that it ever existed. For what it is worth, I believe that it did exist; and that if it was not destroyed in a fit of moral outrage (perfectly possible given the accepted morals of the day) it will be found among the papers of the East India Company, or possibly within the private papers of an official. In my research I have discovered many papers that were previously not known to Burton scholars. With a finite date on my researches I felt very strongly that given another two years I might have discovered a great deal more.

Isabel Burton knew of the existence of this report and it is probable that during his visit to India in 1876 Richard Burton himself unsuccessfully attempted to locate it.

34   *Life*, vol. I: p. 102.

35   Stisted, *The True Life*, p. 55.

Chapter 6 (1831–1852)

1   *The Romance of Isabel, Lady Burton* by Isabel Burton and W.H. Wilkins (Dodd Mead, N.Y. 1897), p. 14. Hereafter called *The Romance*. The first half of this book was dictated by Isabel herself and edited by her sister, 'Dilly'. The remainder, written from Isabel's notes and papers after her death by W.H. Wilkins, was also edited by Dilly.

2   William D'Aubigny, son of William the Conqueror's cup-bearer, married the fair young widow of King Henry I (the Conqueror's son) Queen Adelicia. Arundel Castle had been left to her by Henry but it was not until some years later that D'Aubigny was created the 1st Earl of Arundel after he arbitrated peace between King Stephen and the subsequent Henry II, and successfully negotiated the Wallingford Treaty.

3   Isabel was the direct descendant of the first Lord Arundell. He married his cousin, who was sister of Queen Catherine Howard. His mother was the sister

of the Duke of Suffolk, husband of Henry VIII's sister, Mary (Queen Dowager of France).

4   Details of Isabel's lineage are extracted from *Debrett's Peerage* (1893 edition).

5   The house is now developed into luxury apartments. The old castle ruins are open to the public.

6   New Hall School archives.

7   *The Romance*, p. 16.

8   *The Times*, 9 December 1996, p. 23.

9   *The Romance*, p. 17.

10 *Life*, vol. II: p. 414.

11 New Hall archives.

12 Ibid., booklet in French on the history of the school. (This passage (p. 15) translated by Bernadette Rivett.)

13 Ibid., specifically School Accounts registers 1841–46.

14 IB to the *Epsomian*, 16 Dec. 1893.

15 It is now a hotel, but still recognisable from Isabel's descriptions.

16 *The Romance*, p. 1. Despite her claim that even as a child she had been attracted to 'the east', I am not sure about the date when she developed her interest in the East; it may not have occurred until after she met Richard and although she mentions that Disraeli's *Tancred* was always her favourite book she did not obtain this until 1853 when Richard was on his way to Mecca. It was inscribed to her by her mother in 1853; see Huntington Library, Burton collection.

17 Meggs, N.B., 'The Gypsy's Words Came True', unpublished article in New Hall archives.

18 *The Romance*, p. 21,

19 RFB to J. Pincherle. Quoted in Wright, vol. II: pp. 178–9.

20 Ibid., pp. 21–2.

21 *The Vegetarian* (27 January 1894), p. 45.

22 *The Romance*, p. 27.

23 Ibid., p. 28.

24 Sala, Mrs G.A.: 'Famous People I have known' (published in *The Gentlewoman*, 1893).

25 *The Romance*, pp. 30, 36.

26 Margetson, Stella, *Leisure and Pleasure in the Nineteenth Century* (Cassell, 1969), p. 29.

27 *The Romance*, p. 37.

28 Ibid., pp. 37–8. This extract was said by Isabel to be an entry made some two or three years prior to her first sight of Burton. Given the physical similarity between her 'ideal' and Burton, one is tempted to question its authenticity. However, according to documentary evidence at the WRO, Isabel's diaries were extant at her death, and destroyed later by her sister. Prior to that they were available to Isabel's biographer W.H. Wilkins. It should be noted, too, that other statements Isabel made about Burton, which also seemed unlikely, proved factual in surviving documents – for example her scrapbooks of his progress in Arabia before he became well known.

29 Ibid., p. 33.

30 Wright, *Life of Sir Richard Burton*, vol. I: p. 92.

31 Burton, Isabel, *A.E.I.* (Mullan, 1879), p. 7.

32 *The Romance*, p. 52.

33 Ibid., Richard Burton fully endorsed this memory.

34 This incident has been written about in many sources, especially in *Life*, vol. I: p. 167, and *The Romance*, p. 53.
35 Louisa Segrave, née Buckley. See Isabel's Album at WRO; uncatalogued.
36 *The Romance*, pp. 55–6.
37 Ibid., p. 60.
38 Ibid., pp. 56–7.
39 Extracts from Isabel's diary quoted in *The Romance*, pp. 66–9.

Chapter 7 (1849–1853)
1 'Reminiscences of Sir Richard Burton' by his niece Georgiana M. Stisted. Published in *Temple Bar*, July 1891, No. 368: pp. 335–42.
2 HL: IB to Hain Friswell, Paris, 4 Jan. c.1862. 'Miss Burton was in love with my husband, is not a very nice person and is a concealed enemy and mischief-maker in the family . . . There is always some horrid member in every family.'
3 *Life*, vol. I: p.164.
4 Henry A. Murray (1810–1865) was the 3rd son of Baron Dunmore. He later became a Rear-Admiral.
5 IOR: Directors' Court Minutes Bombay B221: 13 Nov. 1850 and 25 Feb. 1851.
6 IOR: Directors' Court Minutes Bombay B222: 6 Aug. 1851 and 27 Aug. 1851.
7 Lambrick, H.T. in Introduction to 1973 reprint of *Sindh and the Races that inhabit the Valley of the Indus* (OUP, Karachi 1973). The traveller Christopher Ondaatje, in his *Sindh Revisited* op. cit., p. 149, records a recent interview with Dr G.A. Allana, Vice-Chancellor of the University of Sindh. Dr Allana stated that not only had Burton studied the people of Sindh very minutely to provide information which is still relevant in today's educational establishments but he had made a profoundly important contribution to the country's progress in that he recommended the Arabic script for uniform use in Sindh. 'When the British came there were about twenty different scripts in use,' he explained. 'Every Hindu caste had its own script, and sometimes more than one script . . . The Muslims, too, had more than one . . . Burton's greatest legacy . . . is our Sindhi language script . . . that is why he is so well known in Sindh. Ask any primary school teacher in Sindh and he or she will acknowledge that . . . his name crops up, even today.' Ondaatje continues, 'Burton's case for using the Arabic script for Sindhi was laid out in a detailed memo to the [British] Commissioner, dated 2 May 1848. He gave, in effect a summary of his arguments in *Sindh, and the Races that Inhabit the Valley of the Indus*. Burton had left Sindh by May of 1849. But the language controversy continued. . . . Burton's memo [was used] to convince the East India Company in Bombay to agree to the Arabic script, which it did in the early 1850s . . .' He states that when Burton's *Sindh and the Races* was republished, unedited, in Karachi in 1973, 'it was an instant best-seller . . . now it is part of the curriculum for undergraduates and graduate students of history'.
8 Stisted, *The True Life*, p. 58.
9 Lieut.-Colonel Arthur Shuldham to Georgiana Stisted, quoted in Stisted, *The True Life*, p. 67.
10 *Temple Bar*, July 1891, Stisted, 'Reminiscences'.
11 Stisted, *The True Life*, p. 58. Also IOR: L/MIL/2/450, 22 Oct. 1852.
12 *Life*, p. 166.
13 Stisted, p. 59.
14 Ibid., p. 58.

15 Burton, *Pilgrimage*, vol. I: p. 24.

16 QK collection. See also travel journal of Elizabeth Stisted.

17 Stisted, *The True Life*, p. 70.

18 RGS: Burton correspondence 1854. When Francis Galton FRGS, the traveller and author, married in 1853, RFB wrote to Norton Shaw, 'So Galton is married and the world has lost a right good traveller'.

19 Stisted, *The True Life*, p. 59.

20 Burton, R.F., *Stone Talk*, pp. 4–5. This is one of the rarest of Burton's books. After Lord Houghton advised that the work rendered Burton liable to prosecution for libel by a senior politician, Isabel bought up every copy she could find and burned them.

21 Stisted, *The True Life*, p. 63.

22 IOR: L/Mil/2/436 Military Home Corresp. April and October 1852.

23 Ibid.

24 IOR: Court Minutes, Bombay B225 F.53.

25 Stisted, Georgiana, 'Reminiscences of Sir Richard Burton' in *Temple Bar*, No. 368, July 1891,

26 FO: 7/942 (1878) IB to Grandville letter from Trieste; re Richard's attack of orchitis. See also p. 638.

27 'Literature of the Month', Aug. 1852. The reviewer of *Falconry in the Valley of the Indus* says: 'The book is written in an easy, agreeable style, and . . . will add to the good repute of rising young author. Mr. Burton has (as we think injudiciously) defended himself, in a monster preface, against certain criticisms, levelled chiefly against his style, by the *Athenaeum* and other journals . . . we advise him to . . . leave criticisms on his writings to establish, or refute themselves.'

28 George A. Wallin (1811–1852). Performed the *Haj* in 1845. See his paper, RGS *Journal* vol. 20, 1850, pp. 293–344, and his *Travels in Arabia 1845 and 1848* (Falcon Oleander Press, 1979) which originally appeared (posthumously) in the *Journal* of the RGS (vol. 24, 1854, pp. 115–207).

29 Ibid.

30 *Pilgrimage*, vol. I: p. 1.

31 QK collection. RFB's unpublished memoir of Outram. James Lumsden was Director of the Company and a supporter of Burton who dedicated *First Footsteps* to him. That Outram gave a favourable report regarding Burton's suitability to make the trip is covered in IOR: L/MIL/P & J/1/62.

32 RGS Archives, Correspondence Block 1851–60: RF Burton. Burton correspondence 1852.

33 WRO. Article by W.H. Harrison in *The Spiritualist* 1880: 'Physic Facts' p. 75. Also see Burton's speech to the Spiritualists in Dec. 1878 (reproduced in *Life*, vol. II: pp. 138–51) where he describes how the 'black mirror' is used in the East as part of the tools of a magician (p. 146).

34 IOR: L/P & J/1/62 f.318 1852.

35 Burton reiterated his warning that a general uprising by Indians was spoken of and planned in the *Pilgrimage*, vol. I, p. 38, published three years before the Mutiny.

36 Ibid. Added by Burton to his 1879 edition of *Pilgrimage*. He refers to this 'report' elsewhere in his writings at a later date.

37 RGS: East India Co. to Sir Roderick Murchison, Jan. 1853.

38 IOR: Court Minutes B225 f.511–2 and f.611. Also *Pilgrimage*, vol. I: p. 1 and L/Mil/2/458 Home Correspondence/Military papers, 1–9 Feb. 1853.

39 RGS Archive, Correspondence Block 1851–60: RFB to Shaw 'Friday night', u/d, rec'd Jan. 1853.
40 IOR: L/MIL/P & J/1/62 Revenue, Judicial and Legislative Committee 1852. Richard Burton, 2 rue Neuve Chausee, Boulogne to HEIC, India House London. 6 Nov. 1852.
41 RGS: Committee Minute Book vol. I, 1841–1865. 10 March 1853.
42 RGS: G.E. Renouard to Norton Shaw, 23 March 1853.
43 IOR: Court Minutes B225, 2 February and 8 March 1853.
44 UCL: Greenhough Papers. Norton Shaw to Dr Greenhough, 1853.
45 UCL: RFB to Frances Galton, u/d, rec'd March 1853. In this letter Burton also uses another alias: 'Alias Il Conte Birtone'.
46 Quoted in Life, vol. II: p. 13. Original in Isabel Burton's cutting album. WRO.
47 See Burton/Shaw correspondence in RGS archives.
48 It is not known how Burton and Arbuthnot met, but Wright is emphatic that they were already intimate friends by 1853 (see Wright, p. 99). It is probable they met at Leadenhall Street, since many members of Arbuthnot's family were senior executives of the HEIC.
49 The Royal Geographical Society moved to its present famous location in Kensington Gore in 1914. From 1870–1914 its address was 1 Savile Row, and prior to that 15 Whitehall Place.
50 UCL: See Burton correspondence in Galton and Greenhough papers.
51 Stisted, The True Life, p. 72. Here Stisted incorrectly states that Burton left Bath and went directly to Southampton. In fact we know from several authorities that he went to London first. This fact is mentioned only because it is illustrative of many errors in Stisted's biography, which will be important later.
52 Stisted, The True Life, p. 72.
53 HL: IB to Mr Hain Friswell, Paris, 4 Jan. c.1862. The incident occurred shortly after Burton's departure for Mecca, in 1853. 'Mrs Stisted took her ring off to wash her hands for dinner and the bell ringing . . . she hurried down leaving the ring, and a common one with an emerald in it, on the table. When she returned they were gone.' All the servants having been accused and exonerated, Miss Elizabeth Burton was suspected by Maria Stisted of having taken the rings and the matter was quietly dropped.

Chapter 8 (1853)
1 Burton, Richard, Travels in Arabia and Africa (edited by John Heyman for Huntington Library, 1990), p. 20.
2 Butler, A.J., Court Life in Egypt, pp. 55–6. Note: Burton was still a second-lieutenant when this incident occurred. He had been promoted to Captain when Butler wrote about it.
3 Richard Burton's memoir of his entire trip, the 2-volume Personal Narrative of a Pilgrimage to Al-Medinah & Meccah, containing some 1,000 pages of text, is still in print almost 150 years later. Clearly, a biographer can only briefly summarise this epic work since each page is packed with information and anecdotes. See Dover Publications edition, published in 1964, reprinted in paperback (Constable, London, 1994).
4 Pilgrimage, vol. I: pp. 14–15.
5 Ibid., p. 19.
6 Ibid., p. 24.
7 Ibid., p. 28.

8 Ibid., p. 3.
9 Ibid., p. 3. Also see *Journal of Royal Asiatic Society*, 1931, 'Burton Memorial lecture', where Mr Bertram Thomas theorises that four Arabian languages are actually nearer to the Semitic languages of Ethiopia than to Arabic.
10 Ibid., p. 23.
11 Pathan: generally taken to mean a Hindi (Muslim) born in Afghan who has settled in India.
12 An obsolete dress of the ancient Arabs but still worn today by *Haj* pilgrims. It consists of two lengths of white cotton, six feet long by three or four feet wide. As worn by men, one cloth is wound around the torso and one is draped over one shoulder and gathered at the back, the arm is left bare. The women's dress revealed only the eyes: 'we could not help laughing when these queer ghostly creatures first met our sight,' Burton wrote, 'and, to judge from the shaking of their shoulders, they were as much amused as we were.' In the event of death during the pilgrimage the victim was wrapped in the garment which was essentially a shroud. See *Travels*, op. cit. pp. 40–41.
13 *Pilgrimage*, vol. I: p. 141.
14 Ibid., p. 151.
15 Ibid., p. 159.
16 Burton was told this by Omar Effendi some time after the completion of his *Haj* when they met in Cairo. See *Pilgrimage*, p. 167.
17 Ibid.
18 *Life*, vol. I: p. 173.
19 *Travels in Arabia & Africa*, p. 25.
20 *Pilgrimage*; 1: 240n. Von Wrede died in 1861 but his book was brought out almost a decade later by his friend Heinrich F. von Maltzan who owned that his own pilgrimage to Mecca in 1860 had been made due to discussions with Richard Burton while they were both staying at Shepheard's Hotel.
21 *Travels in Arabia & Africa*, p. 28.
22 Ibid.
23 Richard Burton summed up the relationship between the two sects with typical dry humour in *Arabian Nights*, vol. IV, p. 44n: 'The feeling between Sunni (the so-called orthodox [majority]), and Shi'ah is much like the Christian love between a Catholic of Cork and a Protestant from the Black North.'
24 RGS *Journal*, 1854, vol. XXIV: p. 209.
25 *Pilgrimage*, vol. I: p. 292.
26 RGS Archives, Correspondence Block 1851–60. Burton correspondence 1853. RFB to Norton Shaw, 16 Sept. 1853.
27 RGS *Journal*, 1854, vol. XXIV: p. 210.
28 *Travels in Arabia & Africa*, p. 35.
29 *Life*, vol. I: p. 175.
30 *Travels in Arabia & Africa*, p. 38.
31 Diary of Jane Digby el Mezrab; property of Lord Digby. See Lovell, *A Scandalous Life*.
32 Richard's *Ihrám* was in the baggage at Berbera when his party were attacked and looted; 'It came to a bad end,' he said. See chapter 10.
33 *Pilgrimage* vol. II: p. 42.
34 Ibid.
35 Ibid., p. 44.
36 *Life*, vol. I: p. 178.

37 *Pilgrimage*, vol. II: p. 257.
38 Ibid., pp. 256–7.
39 Wrapper on box of Harrod's Turkish Delight. Jan. 1997.
40 RGS: Burton correspondence 1853. RFB to Norton Shaw, 16 Sept. 1853.
41 *Pilgrimage*, p. 271.
42 *Life*, vol. I: p. 179 fn.

Chapter 9 (1853–1854)

1 So much so that he appears to have forgotten the date; his letters written to the RGS during this period in 1853 were incorrectly headed 1854.
2 RGS: Burton correspondence 1851–60. RFB to Norton Shaw from Suez. 16 Sept. 1853.
3 Extract from *The Sporting Truth*, quoted in *Life*, vol. I: p. 182.
4 A former fellow-officer of Richard's in India explained that 'nothing offensive was meant by that epithet.' The author recalled two pugilists named 'Old Ruffian' and 'Young Ruffian' purely because of their style of fighting, not because of their character. 'For much the same reason was Burton dubbed "Ruffian Dick" by his pals. He was without doubt, a terrible fighter, and sent to their last account in single combat more enemies than any man of his time . . . A man of peculiar temper . . . and strong individuality . . . No braver man . . . ever lived. He was as cool when his life hung on a hair's breadth, as when he sat smoking in his own snuggery.' See *The Sporting Truth* article in Isabel's Scrapbooks at WRO.
5 Wallin had refused the sum of £200 to make his exploration on the grounds that it was insufficient to cover the anticipated expenses.
6 RGS: Burton correspondence 1851–60. Notes: Murray: Capt Murray FRGS of the Albany, Burton's closest friend at that time; Parkyns: probably Mansfield Parkyns FRGS (1823–94), author of 'Life in Abyssinia' (John Murray), 2 vols, pub 1853.
7 *The Romance*, p. 71.
8 The others are Marco Polo; Charles Doughty; Arminus Vambery (a contemporary of Burton who also travelled as a dervish in Central Asia in 1862–64), and, in this century, T.E. Lawrence.
9 Maitland, *Speke*, p. 6.
10 Johann Ludwig Krapf, missionary in East Africa and the first European to record the snows of Kilimanjaro.
11 In 1848 Lieutenant Cruttenden of the Indian Navy travelled along part of the coast by sea, landing several times. Dr Henry J. Carter, Hon. Sec. of the Bombay branch of the Royal Asiatic Society, who had some years earlier explored the south-east coast of Arabia in the survey ship *Palinurus*, proposed a more detailed exploration of the east coast of Africa using a ship as his base. He recommended avoiding the interior, inhabited – it was generally believed – by fierce savages who wore the dried genitalia of their enemies as war trophies.
12 Mohammed Ali Pasha (1769–1849), founder of the dynasty which ruled Egypt and the Sudan throughout the late nineteenth century.
13 RGS: Burton correspondence 1851–60.
14 HL: *Travels in Arabia & Africa* (hereafter called *Travels*), p. 67. Remarks in square brackets are Burton's. Burton's marked copy of *Claudii Ptolemaei, Geographica* ed. C.F.A. Nobbe (Leipzig, 1843) is now part of the Huntington Library collection. Ref: BL2430. See *Zanzibar*, pp. 4–5.

15 Ibid.

16 See Bibliography.

17 RGS: Burton correspondence 1851–60: RFB to Norton Shaw, Cairo 15 Dec. 1853. Received 1 Feb 1854.

18 John Elphinstone 13th Baron 1807–1860. A Scottish peer by birthright, he was created an English peer in 1859 for his services during the Mutiny of 1857.

19 Mountstuart Elphinstone, 12th Baron, 1779–1859. Governor of Bombay 1819–27.

20 Didier, Charles, *Sojourn with the Grand Sharif of Makkar* (Cambridge University Press, 1985), p. ix.

21 IOR: L/Mil/12/85. He was appointed in March 1853 but did not take up the appointment until 10th July.

22 *Life*, pp. 54–5.

23 Memorandum book belonging to Isabel Arundell Burton; WRO: uncatalogued.

24 Quoted in *The Romance*, pp. 72–73.

25 EM collection. See IB's copy of *Tancred*, inscribed; 'Isabel Arundell from her attached mother, 20th March 1854'.

26 IOR: Service Report of Richard F. Burton, op. cit.

27 Despatched from Belair House, Bombay 13 April 1854, the rough draft is contained in the Greenhough Collection at UCL (file 6/13h); and the corrected draft (published in the *Journal*, 1854 Vol. XXIV) in the RGS archives.

28 Mr Joseph Hume called for a statement on the number of all surveys conducted so far, the accusation having been made from the ranks of officers that Sir Robert Oliver, Superintendent of the Indian Navy, was stifling scientific exploration. It transpired that he had disbanded or refused some twenty expeditions and proposals. These are fully explained in the preface to Richard Burton's *First Footsteps in East Africa*.

29 RGS archives. Sir Charles Malcom, President 17 Aug. 1850 (also quoted in *First Footsteps*, vol. I: xvii).

30 Bernadette Rivett to the author. Private correspondence, 8 Jan. 1997.

31 *The Romance*, p. 73.

32 Thomas Wright, *Life of Sir Richard Burton*, vol. I: p. 125.

33 Letter from Bapoojee Hurree Scindia to Burton in 1876. See Huntington Symposium notes, p. 98. Scindia was a clerk from Hyderabad. He was studying Mahratt when he met Richard; 'You were good enough to give me [in 1854] a number of Mahratta and English books. Your own remarks and notes in the margin of the Mahratta books are very dear to me, and I often read them to think of you . . . it is so seldom that a European can write with so much correctness and ease a language that is entirely a stranger to him.'

34 The first edition of *Pilgrimage* ran to three volumes. Subsequent editions were condensed into two.

35 This favourable testimonial sits oddly with Richard's subsequent statements that his career was blighted by the Bombay Government's reaction five years earlier to his undercover work for Lord Napier, which he claimed caused his departure from India in 1849. Neither is his claim borne out by his Inspection report (in his Service Record, op. cit.) of May 1854 which speaks highly of his 'very good' conduct, and highly creditable zeal for the service. IOR archives.

36 IOR: RFB's Service Record L/mil/12/73, op. cit. Also, Maitland, *Speke*, p. 7.

37 *Journal* of RGS, 22 May 1854.

38 C.P. Rigby; 'Outline of the Somali Language with vocabulary', contained in *Transactions of the Geographical Society of Bombay*, 1854.

39 *Lake Region of Central Africa* (Folio Society edition, 1993), p. 44.

40 Especially Lieut. Cruttenden's report which he singled out for credit in *First Footsteps.*

41 IOR: E/4/1101 f.465 dated 23 Aug. 1854. See also remarks by Gordon Waterfield in his masterly Introduction to the 1966 edition of *First Footsteps in East Africa* (Frederick A. Praeger, N.Y., 1966), 'The Directors could hardly have expected Burton to go into unexplored country, among tribes described in official documents as "savages", without endangering his life. Burton would never have left Zayla for Harar if he had been cautious . . .'

42 Transactions of the Bombay Geographical Society Vol. XII; Dec. 1854–March 1856.

43 QK collection. Uncatalogued.

44 Ibid.

45 Ibid.

46 IOR: *Bombay Times*, 12 May 1855, editorial by Dr Buist, Outram's crony.

47 Transactions of the Bombay Geographical Society vol. XII, pp. xxiv–xxxi.

48 IOR. *Bombay Times*, Saturday 12 May 1855.

49 Maitland, *Speke*, p. 7.

50 NLS: Speke to Grant, 12 Oct. 1854. MSS: 17931:68.

51 QK collection. Burton to Outram. Extract from the Political Resident's letter-book. Uncatalogued photocopy.

52 NLS: Speke to Grant, Aden, 12 Oct. 1854. MSS: 17931:68. Speke arrived in Aden on 26 Sept.

53 *Zanzibar*, vol. II: p. 382.

54 Burton, *Zanzibar* (see Bibliography), p. 373.

55 *Life*, vol. I: p. 315.

56 Maitland, *Speke* pp. 8–9.

57 Speke, *What Led to the Discovery of the Source of the Nile* (William Blackwood & Sons, 1864), p. 4.

58 NLS: Grant papers.

59 *First Footsteps*, vol. I: p. 58.

60 Speke, *What Led to the Discovery of the Source of the Nile*, p. 2.

61 Anton Mifsud, 'Medical History of J.H. Speke' (*The Practitioner,* Jan. 1975 vol. 214) p. 125 et seq. Dr Mifsud states that excessive watering and inflammation could last many years but there was seldom any permanent damage 'and the eye sight remains good'.

62 Speke, *What Led*, p. 149 and *Journal of the Discovery of the Source of the Nile*, p. 408.

63 *Life*, vol. I: p. 315.

64 QK collection. Speke to Captain Hay (Asst. Commissioner at Koolso).

65 NLS: MSS: 17931:68.

66 Ibid.

67 QK collection. Speke to Hay, Aden, 10 Oct. 1854.

68 Speke, *What Led*, p. 126.

69 Robert Lambert Playfair, later General Sir Robert Playfair 1828–1899; see *D.N.B.* for biography.

70 HL: Burton Library, No. 9, Letter in Burton's copy of *Zanzibar*, op. cit. Badger to RFB, 21 Feb. 1872.

71 Ibid.
72 *First Footsteps*, p. 28.

Chapter 10 (1854–1855)
1 *First Footsteps*, p. xxv.
2 Ibid., vol. I: p. 18.
3 This condition is discussed in detail later in the chapter.
4 *First Footsteps*, vol. I: p. 83.
5 Ibid., pp. 19–20.
6 Ibid.
7 Ralph E. Drake-Brockman, *British Somaliland* (Hurst & Blackett, 1912) states that he had met an old man who had been a boy of fifteen when Burton stayed at Zayla. He told Drake-Brockman that not only could Burton read the Koran better than the *mullahs* but was also better versed in the teachings of the Prophet.
8 *First Footsteps*, vol. I: p. 26.
9 Ibid., p. 33.
10 QK collection. According to a note this item is a single sheet of paper covered on two sides with Arabic script in black ink. A note in English (added) explains the contents.
11 *First Footsteps*, vol. I: p. 93.
12 Waterfield, Gordon, in his introduction to the 1966 edition of *First Footsteps*, p. 32.
13 *First Footsteps*, vol. I: p. 137.
14 Ibid., pp. 143, 150, 152–3, 194.
15 *First Footsteps*, vol. I: p. 201.
16 *Life*, vol. I: p. 207.
17 *First Footsteps*, vol. I: p. 206.
18 The QK collection contains a note regarding two pages of Arabic script sold at auction, one of which was purported to be a horoscope with circular diagram, drawn up for Burton by a *mullah* at Harar.
19 *First Footsteps*, vol. II: p. 42.
20 Ibid., p. 151.
21 The 'Harar Grammar' was published by RFB as an appendix in his *First Footsteps* (Longmans, 1856) and later translated into French and published in Belgium.
22 *Life*, vol. I: p. 215.
23 Ibid.
24 *First Footsteps*, p. 70: 'I fell asleep, conscious of having performed a feat which, like a certain ride to York, will live in local annals for many a year.'
25 At Aden he was assisted in the editing of this paper by Lieut. Dansey who wrote out Richard's note and corrected his copy. The entire paper is included as an appendix to *First Footsteps*.
26 RGS archives (Spiro collection): RFB to Political Resident, Aden, 18 Feb. 1855.
27 BL Colindale: *Bombay Gazette*, 14 March 1855.
28 QK collection. RFB to British Asst. Political Resident, Aden, 21 Feb. 1855, Camp Aden.
29 Stisted, *The True Life*, p. 159.
30 RGS: RFB to Shaw, Aden, 25 Feb. 1855,
31 RGS (Spiro collection): RFB to Political Agent (Coghlan), 25 March 1855, Aden.

32 Speke, *What Led*, pp. 115–16.
33 IOR: R/20/A/129 ff. 140–1. This important file also contains hand-written reports by RFB on his Harar expedition, and a 30-page report on Speke's Somalia expedition.
34 IOR: Political & Secret. Series R/20/A/142 f. 114 and 140 f. 175.
35 Ibid.
36 Ibid.
37 *Life*, pp. 221–2. An on-the-spot account of this incident appears in IOR: R/20/A/129 ff.140–152 and in QK: the letterbook.
38 *First Footsteps*, p. 105.
39 Ibid.
40 IOR: R/20/A/129 ff. 149–52.
41 QK collection. Surgeon's report dated Aden, 22 April 1855.
42 Ibid. Note: There are three stages in syphilis. In the first, or primary stage a chancre (hard sore) forms, usually on the genitals, three to four week after infection. Neighbouring lymph nodes enlarge about two weeks afterwards. The secondary stage occurs about two months after infection. Sores are frequently present on the genitals and in the mouth, the central nervous system and the eyes may be affected. Mild illness, headache and a sore or ulcerated throat is common. Fever and kidney dysfunction would be likely to have affected Richard Burton in the tropics. The disease is highly infectious at this stage. The symptoms of early syphilis disappear without any treatment. This is called the latent stage and the male patient is rarely infectious after three years (i.e. will not infect a partner). The third (tertiary) stage can occur at any time but usually some years later and, typically in a man, between 50 and 60 with fatally damaging effects to the heart, arteries and circulatory system, brain and spinal cord. Because its symptoms are extremely varied syphilis has been called 'The Great Imitator'. See Mann & Lessof; *Conybeare's Textbook of Medicine*, 15th edition (Livingstone, 1970) pp. 88–91 and p. 526.
43 IOR: L/MIL/12/85 f. 288.
44 *Life*, vol. I: p. 31.

Chapter 11 (1855–1856)
 1 IOR: L/P&S/9/35: Letters from Aden 1856–57. Also, R/20/A/142 (1854).
 2 *General Rigby, Zanzibar and the Slave Trade*, op. cit., covers many of these points.
 3 Maitland, *Speke*, p. 44.
 4 IOR: L/P&S/9/35 f.5.
 5 IOR: R/20/A 114 et 142. Brigadier Coghlan's official report dated 23 April 1855.
 6 IOR: E/4 1103 f.255–257. EIC London to India, 1 Aug. 1855.
 7 IOR: R20/A/142 f.14. Edmonstone, Secretary of Government, India to H.L. Anderson.
 8 IOR: Bombay Secret Consultations: Minute 307, 26 May 1855 (vol. 34). J.G. Lumsden and A. Malet to Bombay Council.
 9 IOR: L/P&S/9/35 f.6.
10 IOR: R/20/A/14 f.5. Anderson to Coghlan, 15 Jan. 1856.
11 IOR: R20/A/129. Statement from Lt. Herne, 26 April 1856.
12 IOR: R/20/A/f.142. Coghlan to Bombay Council, 19 April 1856. This file, together with R/20/A/129 and R/20/A/140, contains most of the correspondence

concerning the Somali incident. This is a highly important source, but it is beyond the scope of this book to do other than summarise the material.

13 Ibid.

14 Stisted, *The True Life*, p. 160.

15 Dedication reads: 'To the Honourable James Grant Lumsden, Member of Council etc, Bombay. Within your hospitable walls my project of African travel was matured in the fond hope of submitting, on my return, to your friendly criticism, the record of adventure in which you took so warm an interest. Still, I would prove my thoughts are with you.'

16 Ouida (Rameé), *Richard Burton Fortnightly Review*, 1906.

17 SOAS: MS204772 (15). Mitchell, Richard Lyon Nosworthy, 'Reminiscences of Sir Richard Burton'.

18 Some of Isabel's scrapbooks, including some of the earliest, survive at the WRO.

19 Quoted in *The Romance*, p. 74. W.H. Wilkins was shown the quoted extracts from the diary when helping Isabel with her autobiography in the last months of her life. She left instructions for her diaries to be burned after her death.

20 For a full description of Florence Nightingale's work at Scutari and a general summary of the Crimean War read Smith, Cecil Woodham: *Florence Nightingale* (Constable, 1950).

21 Quoted in *The Romance*, pp. 75–6.

22 WRO.

23 Ibid.

24 *The Romance*, pp. 77–80.

25 The 'Monday Evening Lecture' is still being held at the Society's headquarters in Kensington Gore, London.

26 QK collection. Ms of 'Beatson's Horse'.

27 Stisted, *The True Life*, p. 163.

28 Ibid.

29 RGS: RFB to Norton Shaw, 18 Aug. 1855.

30 Unless otherwise stated, all information on Burton's time in the Crimea is taken from an original manuscript in Burton's hand called 'With Beatson's Horse' in the QK collection. In the main this ms. appeared in the *Life*, with some minor edits by Isabel Burton.

31 RGS Burton correspondence 1851–1860. RFB to Shaw; 18 Aug. 1855.

32 Lord Stratford; also known as Stratford Canning, and Lord Stratford de Redcliffe, British Ambassador to the Ottoman Court.

33 Burton, *Zanzibar*, p. 3.

34 'Our Indian Heroes', *Good Words*, June 1851, quoted in *Zanzibar*, p. 15.

35 QK collection. 'With Beatson's Horse'; also *Life*, vol. I: p. 245.

36 *Zanzibar*, p. 3. Skene was later disgraced for similar conduct in Syria after he cheated W.S. Blunt and his wife, Lady Anne, over some transactions involving sales of horses.

37 In unrelated research, some years ago, the author found unequivocal evidence that Mr Skene was not only guilty of long-term professional embezzlement but of cheating several people who purchased horses from him.

38 'With Beatson's Horse', also *Life* and Hitchman, p. 315.

39 As 'O'Reilly Pasha' he caused untold mayhem a decade later in the Middle East. See diaries of Lady Anne Blunt. BL: Mss BL 54146 Wentworth Bequest.

40 Wright, *Life*, vol. I: p. 141.

41 *The Romance*, p. 39.

42   Ibid., p. 83.
43   Wright, *Life*, vol. I: p. 142.
44   UCL: Galton papers. Also Galton, Francis, M*emories of my Life* (see Bibliography), p. 171,
45   Galton: *Memories of my Life*, pp. 171–2. Although he wrote politely of the fellow-traveller in his published works, Burton wrote to Lord Houghton (23 Sept. 1872): '. . . The RGS has as usual put its foot into the wrong hole but what can you expect of a body which owns as one of its heads Mr Galton? The creature is Grundy, knows Grundy and owes all his strength to Grundy. He hates with a harsh and frustrated (almost Xstian) hatred all who take the position that ought to have been, but has not been, taken by himself – Galton. For years he inflicted his corvine voice upon every meeting simply for the same petty vanity . . .' TCC Houghton Library.
46   RGS: Burton correspondence 1851–60. RFB to Norton Shaw, 9 April 1856.
47   RGS: Committee Minute Book, vol. I: 1841–1865. Minutes of the Expedition Committee, 12 April 1856.
48   Anon., *The Periplus of the Erythraean Sea* c.AD 60. Written by a Greek trader living in Egypt, the *Periplus* provides the first detailed record and map of the sea ports and trading areas of the Indian Ocean – called by the writer 'the Erythraean Sea'; comprising the coast of East Africa north from Zanzibar, the Horn of Africa, Arabia, and the west coast of India.
49   RGS: Burton correspondence 1851–60. Burton/Shawe, 19 April 1856.
50   Henderson, Philip, *The Life of Laurence Oliphant* (Robert Hale, 1859), p. 52.
51   Maitland, *Speke*, p. 51.
52   Ibid.
53   Speke, *What Led*, p. 129.
54   Speke, *Journal of the Discovery of the Source of the Nile*, op. cit., p. 13.
55   Quoted in Russell: *General Rigby; Zanzibar and the Slave Trade*, p. 230. Speke to Rigby: 'the Hindu map published by Wilford has turned out to be forgery, so in the second edition it will be left out . . .'

Chapter 12 (1856)

 1   QK collection: Letterbook 31 May 1856; 'Four months will be required to lay in the necessary stock of instruments, maps, equipment and Portuguese works which can be procured only at Lisbon . . .'
 2   PRO: FO2.37, 3 July 1856. In fact the Treasury had only agreed to provide support of £1,000 provided the East India Company also supplied a similar sum. This document notes the 'great interest of Lord Clarendon respecting the expedition, and [his] readiness to promote it in every way'.
 3   *Zanzibar*, p. 7.
 4   RGS: Burton correspondence 1851–60. Burton/Shaw. (Aug.) 1856.
 5   WRO: Letter from IB to publisher (undated), also quoted in Hitchman, vol. I: p. 449.
 6   Robinson, Jane, *Wayward Women* (OUP, 1991), p. 25.
 7   WRO: IB to publisher (undated). Also see this story misquoted in Hitchman, vol. I: p. 449.
 8   Speke, *What Led*, p. 156.
 9   RGS: Erhardt correspondence 1856. Also quoted in *Tanganyika Notes and Records*, Dec. 1957 (No. 49).
10   See the sketch map he drew for Isabel (p. 215) which shows three large lakes and

a network of river tributaries. Also his correspondence about visiting 'the Northern Lake' after he had located the first objective. Also his scribbled note in his own copy of Speke's *What Led*: 'I heard about it at Harar' (p. 116). Original now in the Huntington Library, Burton collection.

11 In his book *What Led* . . . (p. 157) Speke alleged that this cheque had been paid 'out of the public funds', and moreover had bounced after his departure for Africa. Alongside these allegations in his own copy of Speke's book, Burton has written 'private funds', and 'not true'.

12 For Milnes' friendship with Wiseman *see* Wemyss-Reid, T., *The Life of Lord Houghton* (Cassells and Co., 1890), p. 123 et 127 etc. I feel sure that had she been involved in this introduction Isabel would have mentioned it.

13 Quoted in *The Romance*. See also original document in RGS archives dated 1863 to African missionaries, signed by Newman, renewing his 'request of 1856' to protect Burton and provide hospitality on his journeys. In Quentin Keynes' library is a book presented to Wiseman by Richard, inscribed: 'To his Eminence Cardinal Wiseman with the respectful affection of his devoted servant. R.F. Burton.'

14 Stisted, *The True Life*, p. 163; also Wright, *Life*, vol. I: p. 142.

15 *The Romance*, p. 81.

16 New Hall archives: information contained in a letter from Blanche's grand-daughter Mrs Dorothy Fleming.

17 Isabel did not always provide precise dates in her autobiography. However, her comments such as 'we had about two weeks' are verified by extant correspondence in the author's possession which positively places Burton in London for two weeks from mid to late August, visiting Baden Baden and Hamburg between 31 Aug. and approx. 20 Sept., and in London two weeks from 21 Sept. to 3 Oct. when he departed for Bombay.

18 WRO: Burton collection /2667: Louisa is included in the meeting notes on the formation of the club in IB's Memoranda Book.

19 *The Romance*, p. 81.

20 Stisted, 'Reminiscences', p. 338.

21 *See* Tootal Correspondence (Huntington Library) and IB's Memoranda Books (WRO).

22 *The Romance*, pp. 81–3.

23 Ibid., pp. 82–3.

24 Ibid., p. 83.

25 Ibid., p. 84.

26 Ibid., pp. 91–2. Although this journal was destroyed after Isabel's death by her written instruction, it was available to the editor of her autobiography, written but not completed in the last months of her life. See Epilogue.

27 Ibid., p. 84.

28 Ibid., p. 89; and letters between HEIC and Richard Burton in his letterbook; property of QK.

29 QK collection. Burton's Letterbook. 1 Oct. 1856.

30 RGS: Alfred Bate Richards correspondence 22 Nov. 1856 to Colonel Colt.

31 The veracity of Isabel's story about Hagar and the horoscope has been queried by a recent Burton biographer. But Burton certainly saw the paper; he later wrote about it in an article for *Gipsy Lore* and in correspondence to J. Pincherle.

32 *The Life*, pp. 255–6; also *The Romance*, p. 86. The two verses extracted here are the first two of six.

33 This book is part of the HL's Burton Collection. BL4.
34 *The Romance*, pp. 91–2.
35 WRO: Arundell 2667/26 IB's Memoranda Book
36 *The Romance*, p. 93.
37 A revolutionary idea. Richard first learned about it at a lecture at the United
    Services Club given by Lt. Lynch of the U.S. Navy of his descent of rapids in the
    Jordan. Richard noted in his letterbook (QK collection) that the portable boat
    was made of 'thin sheets of copper or iron, thick as sixpence, strengthened by
    corrugations on longitudinal plaitings (material used in railway stations for
    roofing). They are fireproof, wormproof, waterproof, buoyant and cannot
    become water-soaked . . .' The 20-ft craft was constructed for him in seven
    pieces by Marshall Lifferts of New York in galvanised iron, each piece numbered
    for easy construction, 'copper is too soft . . . you suggest a flat keel; this would
    not survive in river flow . . . while the cork fender would be so much additional
    bother.' Subsequently, Livingstone would write imperiously to Murchison, 'I
    want a collapsible metal boat like Burton's!'
38 QK collection. Burton's Letterbook, 1853–1860.
39 *Zanzibar*, vol. II:p. 384.
40 Blackwood's Magazine; vol. 80; Oct. 1856; pp. 489–502.
41 QK collection: see also *Westminster Review* for the same month which includes
    a review of a book by South African traveller C.J. Anderson, *Anderson's Lake
    Ngami*, in which Anderson claims the East African Lake is 'a mirage' (pp.
    562–3). Isabel kept duplicates of these reviews in her scrapbooks which are now
    in the WRO.
42 Blackwood's Magazine; vol. 80; Oct. 1856; pp. 489–502.
43 QK collection; undated extract. 'As. Soc. Bombay xxiv p. 294'.
44 *Zanzibar*, p. 385.
45 Ibid., p. 386.

Chapter 13 (1856–1857)
 1 *Blackwood's Magazine*, Feb. 1958: pp. 200 et seq. Burton's 'Zanzibar and Two
    Months in East Africa'.
 2 PRO: FO2/37 ff.52–53.
 3 *First Footsteps*, p.i:xxii. Note, however, that these criticisms were endorsed by
    O.R. Law in his masterful *History of the Indian Navy*.
 4 QK collection. Burton's Letterbook, Aden, 14 Nov.
 5 PRO: FO1/37 ff.52–53. G.L. Graham to Norton Shaw, 1 Nov. 1956.
 6 PRO: FO2/37 f.65. 3 Jan. 1857.
 7 QK collection. Burton's Letterbook, 30 Nov. 1856.
 8 Ibid., 1 Dec. 1856.
 9 IOR: E4 1106–1232 London to Bombay, 7 Jan. 1857.
10 QK collection. Burton's Letterbook written 15 Dec. aboard H.M.S.
    Elphinstone.
11 *Zanzibar*, p. 11.
12 *The Romance*, p. 94.
13 WRO: IB's scrapbooks.
14 Blunt, Wilfred Scawen, *My Diaries* (Alfred Knopf, N.Y., 1921),vol.II: p. 128.
15 *The Romance*, p. 94.
16 *Zanzibar*, p. 29.
17 Moorehead, Alan, *White Nile*, p. 24.

18 *Zanzibar*, p. 34.
19 *Lake Regions*, p. 64.
20 *Zanzibar*, p. 37.
21 The building is extant and is one of the main tourist features of the island. Today it is pointed out by guides as 'the house where Dr Livingstone stayed'.
22 *Zanzibar, City, Island and Coast*; 2 vols. Published 1872.
23 *Zanzibar*, p. 380.
24 Speke, *Journal of the Discovery of the Source of the Nile*, p. 361.
25 *Zanzibar*, vol. I: pp. 351–2.
26 IOR: Hamerton cadet papers: L/MIL series: 9.156 ff.97–9 and 12.69 f.373.
27 *Zanzibar*,vol. I: p. 35.
28 QK collection. Burton's Letterbook, RFB to Norton Shaw, c. June 1857.
29 Zanzibar Archives. Hamerton to Anderson, 26 Dec. 1856.
30 QK collection. Letterbook, RFB to RGS, 5 Jan. 1857.
31 Zanzibar Archives. Hamerton to Anderson, 26 Dec. 1856.
32 QK collection. Letterbook, 30 Sept. 1856.
33 Ibid. Letter from Rebmann to RFB, 21 March 1859. Richard is often accused of facetiousness towards missionaries in Africa. In fact, though he regarded their work as wasted effort he was unfailingly kind to the wives of these men, for example Mrs Saker, *Wanderings*, Chapter XX on Fernando Po. Also FO84/1176 f. 75–79.
34 'Zanzibar and two months in East Africa' by R.F. Burton (*Blackwood's Magazine*), p. 224, Feb. 1858.
35 In *Journal of the Discovery of the Sources of the Nile* (pp. 29–30), Speke states that he was told by the chief who had murdered Maizan that it was done on written instructions of the Diwan of the Coast. This could not be corroborated however, and robbery is generally thought to be a more likely explanation.
36 Maitland, *Speke*, p .61.
37 HL: Burton collection: *What Led*, pp. 164–6.
38 Quoted in Maitland's *Speke*, p. 61.
39 *Zanzibar*, p. 398.
40 *Life*, vol. I: p. 277.
41 Ibid.
42 QK collection. Letterbook, undated entry c. May 1857.
43 Ibid., 1 May 1857.
44 Speke,*What Led*, p. 189.
45 Telephone conversation between the author and Dr C.S. Nicholls (Oxford), 1 Oct. 1995.
46 RGS: Speke, J.H., LibrMS(a) Correspondence with RGS 1857–64(3).
47 QK collection: J.H. Speke to his mother Mrs Georgina Speke, c. late May 1857. See also: *In Search of Sir Richard Burton*, Jutzi, op. cit., pp. 15–16.
48 Speke, *What Led*, p. 6n.

Chapter 14 (1856–1857)
1 Burton is generally credited with the introduction of the word *safari* into the English language.
2 This report was published many years later as *Zanzibar, City Island and Coast*.
3 NLS: MS4122 f.48. RFB to Blackwood, 10 June 1857. Burton considered Oliphant a friend at this point; had he not been planning the African trip he would have accompanied Oliphant to the U.S.A.

4   PRO: FO54/17 ff.71-76. Death of Colonel Hamerton and report on the depar-
    ture of the E.A. expedition.
5   *Lake Regions*, vol. I: p. 22–5.
6   Ibid., pp. 116–19.
7   A centennial pillar was erected by the Town Council on the site of the expedi-
    tion camp at Kaole. The inscription reads: 'On the 27th June 1857, Burton and
    Speke set off from Kaole near this site on their expedition to Lake Tanganyika.'
8   *Lake Regions*, vol. I: p. 33.
9   Ibid.
10 Ibid., pp. ix–xii.
11 Letter from Speke to Rigby, 6 Oct. 1860, quoted in *General Rigby* op. cit., p.
    235. In this letter Speke described Hamerton's parting conversation, claiming he
    told Burton: 'I must say you are lucky having Speke with you, and I hope you get
    on well together,'; and said to Speke, 'Do you know I would not go with that
    man Burton on any account.' Speke changed the exact wording of this remark
    on at least three occasions. Rigby subsequently wrote a statement about Burton
    in which he stated: 'When Colonel Hamerton bid farewell to Speke on board the
    Artemesa his last words to him were: "Speke, I would not travel with that man
    for any consideration, I feel for you with such a companion." Mr Frost . . . was
    present at this scene and related it to me.' NLS: Mss 17922 Rigby papers. f.107.
12 Speke to Rigby, quoted in *General Rigby*, p. 25. See also NLS.
13 Moorehead, Alan, *The White Nile* (Penguin, 1963), p. 42.
14 *Life*, p. 292.
15 *Lake Regions*, p. 73.
16 Cameron, Verney Lovett; *Across Africa* (George Philip & Son, 1885), p. 503.
17 NLS: MS101120 (1) VLC 'Livingstone Journals', vols 1–4.
18 *Life*, vol. I: p. 281.
19 Ibid.
20 *Lake Regions*, p. 77.
21 *Life*, vol. I: p. 300.
22 Speke, *What Led*, p. 197.
23 Burton's copy of Speke's *What Led*, p. 197. This copy is at HL. Burton's hand-
    written annotations refuting many of Speke's claims appear throughout the
    book.
24 Speke, *What Led*, p. 212.
25 *Zanzibar*, vol. II: p. 389.
26 *Life*, vol. I: p. 499.
27 Ibid., p. 286.
28 Ibid., p. 286.
29 *First Footsteps*, vol. I: p. 17n.
30 Mifsud, Anton, 'Medical History of J.H. Speke', in *The Practitioner*, Jan. 1957,
    pp. 125–30.
31 *Lake Regions*, p. 179.
32 Ibid., p. 201.
33 *Blackwood's Magazine*, Nov. 1859, p. 575.
34 *Life*, vol. I: p. 287.
35 Ibid., p. 286.
36 Ibid., p. 287.
37 *Zanzibar*, vol. II: p. 388.
38 WRO. IB's memoranda book.

39 *The Romance*, p. 98.
40 Ibid., p. 101–4.
41 *The Romance*, p. 120–21.
42 *Life*, p. 292.
43 Speke, *What Led,* p. 340.
44 Handwritten comment by Burton in his own copy of Speke's *What Led to the Discovery of the Source of the Nile*, p. 340. This volume is part of the Burton collection in Huntington Library.
45 Wright, *Captain Sir Richard Burton*, pp. i: 153–4.
46 *Nights*, vol. I: p. 6*n*.
47 *The Devil Drives*, p. 152.
48 Ibid., pp. 152–3.
49 Henry Morton Stanley, famous for his meeting with Livingstone, travelled these regions and wrote that Burton and Speke must have been mistaken in the location of the town for none of the local people he spoke to had ever heard of Kazeh. However, Verney Lovett Cameron, the first European to traverse the continent from East to West, explained that Kazeh was latterly known to Africans as Tabora.
50 *Zanzibar*, vol. II: pp. 183–4.
51 *Life*, vol. I: p. 290.
52 Ibid.
53 Speke, *What Led*, p. 198.
54 Burton's comments are in his copy of *What Led*, see Burton Collection at the Huntington Library. That Burton could not speak the African dialects of the Lake regions is probably correct. However he spoke Kiswahili, which was readily understood all over East Africa and was the *lingua franca* used by Arab merchants to trade in the Lake Regions. He also compiled and published a Swahili Grammar.
55 RGS: 'Explorations in Eastern Africa' by Captains Burton and Speke. Corrected printed draft of the Burton and Speke journals, p. 2.
56 I am unable to explain what Speke meant by 'the Jub', but quote it as written.
57 Speke, *What Led*, p. 198.
58 RGS archives; see also *Zanzibar*, vol. I: Appendix C pp. 442–3.
59 *A Scandalous Life*, p. 268. Jane Digby's description of treatment of her sick husband: 'I committed him to the curing of the Bedouins who burned four *misamar* in his head with a hot iron which hissed as it touched him . . . shortly after he broke out in a profuse perspiration, which I trust has spared him.'
60 Maitland, *Speke*, p. 69.
61 *Life*, vol. I: p. 293.
62 *Lake Regions*, p. 307.
63 Ibid.
64 Ibid.
65 Speke, *What Led*, pp. 202–3.

Chapter 15 (1857–1858)
 1 Speke, *What Led*, p. 204.
 2 *Life*, vol. I: p. 300.
 3 Probably Ahmed bin Sleyyim. See *Tanganyika Notes and Records*, Issue No. 49, p. 235 (Government printer Dar es Salaam, Dec. 1957).

4 Speke, *What Led*, p. 218.
5 Ibid., p. 207.
6 *Life*, vol. 1: p. 300. The italics in this extract are Richard's though it is not clear why. There is a strong impression that he was using narcotics.
7 Speke, *What Led*, p. 245.
8 Ibid., pp. 324–5.
9 Ibid.
10 Hamed and all his slaves were murdered at Uruwa during this expedition. See Speke, *What Led*, p. 241.
11 Speke, *What Led*, p. 231.
12 Ibid., pp. 231–2.
13 Ibid., pp. 234–5.
14 Ibid., p. 239.
15 Ibid., pp. 239–40.
16 RGS archives: Speke J.H., Journal Mss Africa (Nile) 1859.
17 *Life*, vol. I: p. 301.
18 Speke, *What Led*, p. 246.
19 *Life*, p. 302.
20 *Lake Regions*, p. 353.
21 *Life*, vol. I: p. 303. Livingstone heard this rumour and believed it.
22 Ibid., p. 304.
23 HL: Burton's own annotated copy of *What Led*.
24 *Lake Regions*, p. 390.
25 *Life*, vol. I: p. 309.
26 HL: Burton's own annotated copy of *What Led*, p. 265.
27 RGS: Speke correspondence 1857–64 (3) 1857–58. Speke to Shaw (one of two letters written on the same date), 2 July 1858.
28 Ibid.
29 Ibid.
30 QK collection. Letterbook. RFB to Shaw from Unyanyembe, 24 June 1858. See also RGS archives: Burton correspondence.
31 QK collection. the Letterbook entry 24 June 1858; also RGS; Burton correspondence 1851–1870.
32 Speke, *What Led*, p. 262.
33 Ibid., p. 370.
34 *Life*, vol. I: p. 312.
35 Ibid.
36 Ibid., p. 313.
37 Ibid., p. 314.
38 Ibid., p. 315.
39 Ibid., p. 315.
40 Quoted in *Life*, vol. I: p. 316.
41 *Life*, vol. II: p. 424.
42 *Life.*, vol. I: p. 321.
43 Ibid., p. 322.
44 Speke, *What Led*, p. 132. 'Lieutenant Burton now said, "Don't step back or they will think we are retiring." Chagrined by this rebuke at my management in fighting, and imagining by the remark that I was expected to defend the camp, I stepped boldly to the front, and fired at close quarters into the first man before me.'

45 *Life*, vol. I: p. 323.
46 Ibid.
47 Richard liked to say that he received the rebuke and the news of the massacre by the same post. This could not be so for he mentioned the rebuke in his letter of 24 June 1858, written 6 days *before* the massacre occurred. This is typical of the way in which he (and most raconteurs) would exaggerate facts to make a good story.
48 QK. Letterbook, RFB to Andrews, 7 Dec. 1858.
49 *Life*, vol. I: p. 325.
50 RGS: Burton correspondence, 1851–1860. 1 Jan. 1859.
51 *Lake Regions*, p. 526.
52 See: *DNB Missing Persons*; ed: C.S. Nicholls (OUP, 1993), p. 555; also Russell, Mrs Charles; *General Rigby, Zanzibar and the Slave Trade* (George Unwin, 1935).
53 *Lake Regions*, p. 525, Burton hints at the rumours of Rigby's unpopularity in the baiting taunt, 'perhaps he remembers the cognomen by which he was known in days of yore among his juvenile *confrères* at Addiscombe.'
54 Maitland, *Speke*, p. 92.
55 QK. Letterbook. Camp Aden, April 1859. RFB to the Political Secretary, Bombay.
56 Speke, *What Led*, p. 193.
57 *Life*, vol. I: p. 327.
58 *The Romance*, p. 148.
59 *General Rigby*, p. 43.
60 *Life*, vol. I: p. 328.
61 Maitland, *Speke*, p. 94.
62 *Zanzibar*, vol. II: p. 390.
63 RGS: Burton correspondence. RFB to Shaw, Aden, 19 April 1859.
64 *Burton; an Appreciation* by R.G.H. Risley (see Bibliography).

Chapter 16 (1859)

1 RGS: Speke to Norton Shaw, 8 May 1859. Speke correspondence file 1859. Addressed from 'Hatchets, Piccadilly'.
2 Speke, John H, *Journal of the Discovery of the Source of the Nile* (Blackwoods, 1863), p. 31.
3 *Zanzibar*, vol. II: p. 321.
4 Ibid., p. 380.
5 BL: Addl MSS 50184. David Livingstone to his wife.
6 Both Fawn Brodie and Frank MacLynn (op. cit.) in their respective biographies of Burton, examine the relationship using psychoanalytical methods, and conclude a homosexual relationship.
7 NLS: MSS17910 f.88. Speke to Rigby, 25 Nov. 1859.
8 NLS: MSS17910 f.82. [Aug.] 1860.
9 Speke's letter to the Government at Bombay, 12 Dec. 1859. The original is in the India Office archives, but it has been reproduced in *General Rigby* pp. 250–55.
10 Henderson, *Life of Laurence Oliphant*, op. cit., p. 124.
11 See Blackwell archives in NLS.
12 *Life*, vol. II: pp. 424–5.
13 *D.N.B.* vol. 42, pp. 133–137.
14 *The Romance*, p. 109. The famous Leaning Tower has been closed to visitors for restoration during my research. I have therefore not been able to discover

whether these *graffiti* survive.

15 Ibid., pp. 112–3.
16 Ibid., p. 115.
17 IB's Memoranda Book at WRO contains descriptions of her wardrobe.
18 Quentin Keynes has a watercolour by Isabel which she has entitled 'my first attempt at painting'.
19 *The Romance*, p. 133.
20 Ibid., p. 121.
21 Ibid.
22 Ibid., pp. 104–5.
23 Ibid., pp. 134–5.
24 IB's Memoranda Book. WRO. Richard counted George and Alice Bird, whom he met through Isabel, among his closest friends.
25 *The Romance*, pp. 149–50.
26 Ibid., p. 151. This was the last thing Isabel wrote in her autobiography, which was subsequently completed from her *still intact* diaries and papers. These were then destroyed by her younger sister Dilly.
27 *Life*, vol. I: p. 333.
28 Georgiana Stisted in her *True Life* states that Burton inherited £16,000 from his father. In fact Joseph Netterville Burton left nothing to either of his sons. In his will made a few weeks before his death he revoked all previous wills and left his entire estate in trust for his two grand-daughters, Georgiana and Maria. It may be that some private arrangement was made in the event that Richard survived his trip to Africa for the Stisteds to make an ex-gratia payment to Richard, but the figure Georgiana mentioned is highly dubious. See PRO: Family Records Centre, London, PROB 11/2258:quire 732, f.255. Last Will and Testament of Joseph Netterville Burton.
29 *The Romance*, pp. 152–3. These comments made by Wilkins who co-authored Isabel's 'autobiography' (i.e. completed it after her death), were checked, and information provided by Dilly, who would have known Mrs Arundell's reservations.
30 RGS archives. Proceedings vol. III Session 1858–1859 ff.217–219 (Presentation of Royal Award to Burton; 23 May 1859).
31 Ibid.
32 Stisted, *The True Life*, pp. 163–4. Wright, *Life of Sir Richard Burton*, vol. II: p. 238. There was a number of identical cases, after the 1914–18 War. This type of trauma is now a recognised syndrome.
33 *Life*, vol. I: p. 332.
34 RGS: Speke correspondence, 1851–60. 5 June 1859.
35 RGS: *Proceedings*, vol. III, Session 1858–59. ff.357 et seq.
36 RGS: Burton correspondence, block 1851–60. RFB to Galton, 7 Sept. 1859, addressed from the Hydraspathic Institution at Upper Norwood.
37 QK collection. Speke/3.
38 QK collection. Speke/4.
39 NLS: MS4143:116. Speke to Blackwood, 10 July 1859.
40 NLS: ditto f.123.
41 RGS: Speke correspondence 1859. Speke to Shaw, 18 July 1859. The extract referred to is Genesis 2:14.
42 TCC Houghton: 228:12 RFB to Milnes n/d [Aug. 1859].
43 Generally believed to be the setting for Thackeray's, *The Virginians*.

44 Burton, Isabel: 'Celebrities at Home' No. XLIV *Lord Houghton at Fryston Hall* (*The World*, 20 June 1877) p. 4 et seq. This article did not carry Isabel's name but correspondence between her and Lord Houghton's agent, now at the Trinity College Library, Cambridge make it clear that she was the author, authorised by Lord Houghton.

45 Wemyss-Reid, *The Life of Lord Houghton*: p. 454.

46 Montgomery-Hyde, H., *A History of Pornography*, p. 14. Hyde continues: 'Next in importance to [Houghton's] collection was probably that of the bibliographer, Henry Spencer Ashbee, who died in 1900 and bequeathed the bulk of his library to the British Museum.' See Ashbee's catalogue published under the pseudonym 'Pisanus Fraxi'.

47 The salacious element in Milnes' character sits strangely with one of the most important relationships in his life. By 1859 Milnes was happily married to Annabelle (younger daughter of Lord Crewe), but earlier in life he had fallen 'violently in love' with one of the purest icons in British history, the young Florence Nightingale. Although she always referred to him in her private journals as 'the man I adored', Nightingale rejected his proposals of marriage, after a seven-year courtship, to pursue what seemed at the time (pre-Crimea) an unlikely destiny. She recognised that Milnes would satisfy her passionate emotional and intellectual needs, but she also saw that as his chatelaine, the moral, active side to her nature would not be satisfied. 'Since I refused him,' she wrote many years later, 'not one day has passed without my thinking of him, . . . life is desolate without his sympathy.'

48 Wemyss-Reid, *Life of Lord Houghton*, op. cit., vol. I: p. 181.

49 Sutherland, James: *Oxford Book of Literary Anecdotes* (Clarendon Press, 1975), p. 235.

50 Ibid.

51 Pope-Hennessy, James, *Monckton Milnes, The Flight of Youth*, pp. 6, 133.

52 *The Devil Drives*, p. 196.

53 There are two excellent biographies of Milnes. the first by his authorised biographer, T. Wemyss Reid, *The Life of Lord Houghton* (Cassells and Co.,), 1890 – two vols; the second by James Pope-Hennessy, *Monckton Milnes* (Constable, 1951). Two vols: *The Years of Promise*; and *The Flight of Youth*. There is no opportunity in a book on Burton to do this interesting man any justice.

54 NLS: MS4143: ff.131–132. Speke to Blackwood, 2 Sept. 1859.

55 FO2/37. Ripon to Palmerston, 16 Aug. 1859.

56 'Ramji the Hindoo', owner of the slaves who accompanied the expedition. In his defence, Richard explained to the RGS that these slaves, 'received on departure the extravagant sum of £300, which would have purchased the whole gang in the bazaar'.

57 NLS: MSS:17910 f.82 Rigby papers. Speke to Rigby, 3 Sept. 1859.

58 IOR: Elphinstone to Rigby, 19 Aug. 1859.

59 PRO:. FO2.37 69/7. Speke to Lord Russell, Oct. 1859.

60 NLS: MSS:17910 f.82. Speke to Rigby, 17 Oct. 1859.

61 Quoted in additional chapter added by Gordon Waterfield, editor of 1966 edition of Burton's *First Footsteps in East Africa* (Praeger, N.Y.), p. 283.

62 Quoted by Waterfield in his additional chapter to the 1966 Praeger edition of *First Footsteps*, p. 254. Speke to Playfair. There is no evidence that Burton ever 'confessed' to being unprepared, merely that he did not panic because 'such inci-

dents are all too common in countries through which I have travelled.'
63   QK. J.G. Grant to S. Baker, 26 June 1890. Stating that Layard, when serving on the Council of the RGS, received a letter from Speke stating that poison was to have been put in his medicine on the orders of Burton – but that 'the native responsible [Bombay] being too much attached to Speke never administered it . . . I have it from the lips of Speke's sister that this is a fact.'
64   QK collection and Baker papers. Grant to Baker, 26 June 1890.
65   NLS: ACC 10120 (20) Cameron papers. Verney L. Cameron to his mother, 24 April 1873
66   Ditto: f.13
67   *Zanzibar*, vol. II: p. 380.

Chapter 17 (1859–1860)
1   NLS: MS4143 f.224 Blackwood papers 1860.
2   RGS: Burton correspondence 1851–60 RFB to Shaw, 17 Oct. 1859.
3   Ditto, 7 Oct. 1859.
4   RGS: Speke correspondence 1857–64. Speke to Shaw postmarked 28 Oct. 1859.
5   Ditto, u/d 'Sunday' Nov. 1859.
6   *Zanzibar*, vol. II: p. 392–3.
7   RGS: Speke correspondence 1857–64. Speke to Shaw, 5 Nov. 1859.
8   Ditto.
9   NLS: Speke to Murchison, 11 May 1860.
10   NLS: Blackwood to Speke (U.D.C. Sept. 1859), Blackwood papers.
11   NLS: MS4143 f.134/5 Blackwood papers. Speke to Blackwood, 5 Nov. 1859.
12   Maitland, *Speke*, p. 19.
13   QK collection. Speke to RFB; folios 2 et 8, Nov. 1859.
14   More likely this was a circulatory disorder, perhaps resulting from his attack of syphilis.
15   *Swinburne's Letters*, vol. II: p. 20 fn.
16   This letter is published in several sources, but it was first published in *Lake Regions* as part of a series of letters explaining the background to the accusation of his conduct in respect of non-payment of debts.
17   NLS: MSS 17910 f.88. Speke to Rigby, 25 Nov. 1859.
18   RGS: Burton correspondence 1851–60. T. Cosmo Melvill, India Office to RFB. 14 Jan. 1860.
19   *Rigby*, pp. 233–5.
20   *Life*, vol. I: p. 332–7.
21   Ibid.
22   TCC Houghton: 228:14. RFB to Milnes, 22 Jan. 1860, addressed from Hotel de Paris, Boulogne.
23   RFB to Government, Bombay, January 1860. Quoted in *Rigby*, p. 262.
24   RGS: Burton correspondence files. RFB to Rigby, 16 Jan. 1860. Also quoted in *Rigby*, p. 274.
25   RGS: Burton correspondence 1851–60. Shaw to RFB, 4 Feb. 1860.
26   Ibid. RFB to Shaw, 9 Feb. 1860.
27   NLS: MS4154 ff.86.
28   *Pilgrimage*, see footnotes vol. II: pp. 110–11.
29   NLS: MSS 4154 f.110 11 April 1860.
30   Ibid., 4154 f.9.
31   A century later, my friend the late Elspeth Huxley, experienced a similar brush

with outraged morality when Macmillan refused to publish her novel *Red Strangers* because they felt that clitoridectomy, though an important part of Kikuyu culture and crucial to her story, 'had no place in a novel'. She changed publishers.

32 A few copies of *First Footsteps* were, however, unwittingly bound with the excluded matter. A century later one was acquired, by accident, by the Burton biographer Fawn Brodie. Until recently this copy was considered unique – even Burton did not have the excised material in his copy – however I have since heard of another copy in a private collection in Hertfordshire.

Fawn Brodie's copy is now the property of Quentin Keynes. The surviving text was translated and appears in the 'additional material' added by Gordon Waterfield to the 1966 edition of *First Footsteps* published by Frederick Praeger, pp. 285–286: 'A female slave . . . cuts out the girl's clitoris and nymphae [then] . . . sews up the lips with a continuous series of large stitches . . . This barbarous guarantee of virginity is preserved until marriage . . . a husband will take great pains to increase and amplify his physical strength . . . and when he goes to bed with his newly-wed bride will strain to break through the blockage with his sword of love . . . The pain is so intense as to cause the woman to shriek; . . . to counteract this . . . musicians drown the cries of the bride by singing . . .' The original manuscript of this material, in Richard's handwriting, can be found in the Houghton Library, TCC. Uncatalogued.

33 *Pilgrimage*, vol. II: p. 110–11.

34 *Life*, vol. I: p. 337.

35 BL: incomplete section of a Burton journal in ms, dated April 1860, page numbered by Burton pp. 54–7. A few odd pages of this manuscript are in the Quentin Keynes collection and some 16 pages (pp. 8–24) were offered for sale at auction some years ago. Previously unpublished, this manuscript must not be confused with excerpts from Burton's satirical sketch, also in the BL; 'Leaves from Miss A—— B——'s diary', mistakenly attributed by biographers Brodie and McLynn as being from his private journal.

36 QK collection. Speke to RFB, 10 April 1860.

37 RGS: Speke correspondence. Speke to Wheeler, Jordans, 12 April 1860.

38 QK collection: Speke/12.

39 Ibid.

40 Letter dated April 1860, quoted as Preface to 'Captain Speke's adventures in Somaliland'; *Blackwood's Magazine*, May 1860, p. 561.

41 Quoted in *Rigby*, p. 240.

42 NLS: MSS17910. Speke to Rigby, 22 Oct. [c.1861].

43 NLS: MSS4731 f.233. Speke to Blackwood, 1 Feb. 1861.

44 NLS: MSS17910. Speke to Rigby, 22 Oct. [c.1861].

45 For example on 19 July 1862 Grant was sent, without any valid reason, to the headquarters of the chief of Unyoro lying in the opposite direction to the one Speke then took. Speke then marched from Urondogani 'to the place where the river, which he believed to be the White Nile, issued from the supposed Nyanza Lake'. After following it for 50 miles to the north from Ripon Falls, he gave up and rejoined Grant.

46 NLS: Speke to Murchison, from Madeira, 11 May 1860.

47 NLS: 17922:2 Grant papers.

Chapter 18 (1860)

1 *Life*, vol. I: p. 337.

2 Dr George Bird was personal physician to most of the great names in the pre-Raphaelite movement. His papers, if they survived, would undoubtedly be fascinating and revealing of Burton since he doctored him for nearly forty years, however I have only been able to trace a few letters from Dr Bird to Frederick Leighton and Holman Hunt.

3 *The Romance*, p. 155.

4 WRO: Arundell Papers 2667.

5 Brodie, *The Devil Drives*, pp. 179–82.

6 Ibid., p. 181.

7 The British Library Manuscripts Department supplied me with good photocopies which took me over 100 hours, using a powerful magnifying glass, to transcribe. Fortunately I had already spent almost two years transcribing Burton's handwriting and was accustomed to it. The transcription was then checked by Bernadette Rivett (see Acknowledgements).

8 Brodie, *The Devil Drives*, pp. 180–81.

9 *Burton's Journal of the American trip 1860*. 18 pages of handwritten text survive at the British Library, Ref: Addl MSS:49.380K, numbered pp. 54–64, including some verso pages. A further 16 pages, part of the same manuscript and numbered 8–21 and 23–24, were offered for sale in recent years by a London auction house and appear to have disappeared into a private collection. The QK collection has a photocopy of several of these pages which I have also transcribed.

10 BL: Manuscripts Dept. Ref: MSS Add:49.380K.

11 Ibid.

12 Ibid.

13 Burton, Richard F., *City of the Saints* (Longman, 1862), pp. 2, 52.

14 *Zanzibar*, vol. I: pp. 14–15.

15 *City of the Saints*, pp. 53–4.

16 Ibid., p. 115.

17 Ibid., p. 11.

18 Ibid., p. 12.

19 Ibid., p. 185.

20 Brodie, *The Devil Drives*, p. 182. In his tribute to Burton 'Memories' printed in *Transatlantic Review* in March 1924, Luke Ionides tells the story that just before Burton left for the USA the wife of a friend asked him flippantly to 'bring her a scalp back . . .' On his return he asked a host to seat him next to her and during dinner, to her horror, he casually handed her a scalp which he had acquired during his journey.

21 *City of the Saints*, p. 69.

22 Ibid., p. 143.

23 Hale, Richard Walden: *Sir Richard Burton, a footnote to History* (Privately printed, Boston, Christmas 1930).

24 *City of the Saints* (Alfred A. Knopf, 1963). This reprint contains an introduction by Fawn Brodie, p. xxi.

25 Ibid., p. 99.

26 Ibid., p. 191.

27 Ibid.

28 Ibid., p. 194.

29 Ibid., pp. 240–4.
30 Ibid., pp. 292–3.
31 Ibid.
32 Ibid., p. 246.
33 This letter also published in *The Times*, 14 Nov. 1860, and the *Athenaeum* as a part of the proceedings of the RGS.
34 RGS: Burton correspondence, 1851–60.
35 *City of the Saints*, p. 605.
36 Library of Congress newspaper archives: *Desert News*, 3 Oct. 1860. Contemporary diary entries quoted by Guy Bishop at Huntington Library Burton Symposium, see *In Search of Sir Richard Burton*; edited by Alan Jutzi (Huntington Library publication) p. 62–70.
37 *City of the Saints*, p. 517.
38 Ibid; and *First Footsteps*, p. 84.
39 *First Footsteps*, vol. I: p. 85.
40 *City of the Saints*, p. 522.
41 *Wanderings*, vol. I: p. 28.
42 *City of the Saints*, p. 523.
43 Ibid.
44 Ibid., p. 604.
45 Ibid., p. 525.
46 Ibid., p. 605.
47 Ibid.
48 Ibid., p. 606.
49 *The Romance*, p. 155.
50 There are numerous incidents which proved Burton's belief in a supernatural force. Thomas Wright reported that while Burton was in Mecca, for example, a young [English] woman psychic 'saw' him in her 'black mirror'. She described what he was doing at the time, his clothes and companions. Her statement was written down and dated. When he returned to England it was shown to Burton, who consulted his journal and confirmed its accuracy by signing it as being a true account.
51 Wright, *The Life of Sir Richard Burton*, vol. I: p. 168.
52 *Life*, p. 338.
53 See *Debretts 1893* on the dowager: 'Rosina (Lady Clifford-Constable) daughter of Charles Brandon Esq, married 1stly 1865, as his 2nd wife, Sir Thomas Aston Clifford-Constable, Baronet who died 1870; 2ndly 1872 Edgar Trelawney Esq who died the same year. 3rdly in 1876, Francis John Hartley who died in 1880. Residences: Staffordshire and Paris.'
54 *The Times*, 20 Dec. et seq, 1860.
55 Bristol City Library; Newspaper archives. *The Times*, 1 Jan. 1861, p. 7. Reports of the adverse weather conditions appear in editions covering 20 Dec. 1860 et seq.
56 *Life*, vol. I: p. 339; *The Romance*, p. 157.
57 Ibid., pp. 339–40; *The Romance*, pp. 157–8.
58 Although Isabel does not give dates in her account of the meeting, she tells Richard that they would be married 'this day three weeks . . . I wanted to be married on the 23rd'. Therefore they met on the 2nd – the same day she left Yorkshire.
59 *Life*, vol. I: p. 340; *The Romance*, pp. 158–9.
60 *Life*, vol. I: p. 340.

61 Wiseman was a close friend of Monckton Milnes. It is much more likely that Richard's introduction to Wiseman prior to the African trip came from Milnes.

62 *Life*, vol. I: p. 341.

63 Richards, A.B., 'Sketch of the career of Richard F. Burton', p. 16.

64 *Life*, vol. I: p. 341.

65 Stisted, *The True Life*, p. 275.

66 IB's Memoranda Book at WRO.

67 She gave titles to her notebooks, i.e. *Alpha*, *Beth*, *Caph*, which survive at the WRO in Trowbridge. W.H. Wilkins quoted at length from *Lamed*, which was apparently destroyed some time after Isabel's death by her sister.

68 Ibid.

69 WRO: IB's Memoranda Book.

Chapter 19 (1861)

1 Also known as the Bavarian Catholic Church.

2 Georgiana Stisted, who inferred that Richard married against his will, stated that he wore a 'rough shooting coat, other garments to match, and a cigar in his mouth' to hide his nervousness. She was not, of course, present. Prior to Stisted's concoction someone who was present, almost certainly one of the Birds, told the biographer Francis Hitchman that Burton and the guests wore 'ordinary morning dress'. See Hitchman, vol. II: p. 98.

3 PRO: Marriage certificate dated 22 Jan. 1861. Richard Francis Burton to Isabella Arundell. Witnesses: Thomas Watson and George Bird.

4 Hitchman, *Sir Richard Burton*, vol. II: p. 98. Note that precisely the same wording is used by A.B. Richards, who also used RFB's 'autobiography' to write his 'Sketch of the Career of Richard F. Burton by an old Oxonian'.

5 *Life*, vol. I: p. 342

6 Burton, Jean, *Sir Richard Burton's Wife* (Alfred Knopf, N.Y., 1941). The author (no relation to Richard or Isabel) quotes Francis Burnand of *Punch* in this description of the Arundel club. p. 111.

7 TCC:228:11. RFB to Houghton, Jan. 1861.

8 Wemyss Reid, *The Life of Lord Houghton*, vol. I: p. 118.

9 *The Romance*, p. 167.

10 Wright, *Burton*, vol. I: p. 166.

11 I have laboured this point since Burton's enjoyment of male company has somewhat speciously (in my opinion) been used to support a charge that he was a misogynist. This is to completely ignore the changes in social mores between then and now.

12 *The Romance*, p. 178.

13 *Life*, vol. I: p. 393.

14 McCarthy, Justin, *Reminiscences* (Chatto & Windus, 1899), vol. II: p. 333.

15 Ouida (Ramée), 'Richard Burton', *Fortnightly Review*, June 1906 (vol. 85), pp. 1039–45.

16 *The Romance*, p. 172.

17 Letters in QK collection, quoted later in this book.

18 Stisted, *The True Life*, p. 274.

19 *Life*, vol. II: pp. 445–6. Although Isabel does not give Georgiana's name it is obvious to whom she refers.

20 This letter is extant and can be seen at Richmond Library, in Special Collections.

21 *Life*, vol. I: p. 343.

22 Stisted, *The True Life*, p. 275

23 *The Romance*, p. 167.

24 See Photo Section.

25 NLS: George Brand Papers; MS2031 letter from Acting Consul Henry Hand to FO. London, Lagos, 16 June 1860, advising Mr Consul Brand's death.

26 PRO: FO files: RFB to Russell 27 March 1861.

27 Quoted in *Life*, vol. I: p. 345. Originally in Hitchman's *Life*, vol. II: p. 102.

28 *Life*, vol. I: p. 345.

29 NLS: Blackwood papers MS4154 ff.82–85.

30 *General Rigby*, pp. 264–71. Dated 16 Nov. from Zanzibar, it would have reached Bombay a month later. A copy was received in London in February.

31 Ibid.

32 Ibid., p. 272.

33 Ibid.

34 IOR: Bombay Governing Council to H.M. Secretary of State for India, 27 March 1861. Quoted in *General Rigby*, pp. 271–2.

35 Ouida, 'Richard Burton'.

36 NLS: Blackwood papers. MS4731 f. 233. Speke to Blackwood dated 21 Feb. 1861, headed 'Kazeh, in the Land of Moon ensconced in Musa's house. "All right and ready to fight".' Copy in QK collection.

37 PRO: FO2/40. FO to Captain Burton. As well as advising the salary it outlined certain rules: 'You are restricted from trading . . . your salary will commence 10 days previous to your embarkation . . . the sum of £165 has been granted towards your outfit and passage'.

38 Stisted, *The True Life*, p. 275. Stisted inaccurately states that Richard's appointment as Consul was worth £350 a year. Copies of Richard's letter of appointment in PRO and WRO, confirm Isabel's statement that it was £700.

39 Somerset House – Wills Division.

40 The Speke family apparently paid this debt rather than Speke himself. See letter in QK collection. Benjamin Speke to Norton Shaw, 21 Aug. 1860: 'I have paid my brother's debt to Burton, £600 and consequently hope that there will be no more said about it. I hear from my mother that there was much talk about it in London, rather derogatory to my brother's honour . . .' Richard subsequently wrote to him pointing out further amounts still outstanding, for which he said Speke was responsible, but Speke refused to pay these and Richard probably wrote them off.

41 McLynn, Frank, *Snow Upon the Desert*, p. 174.

42 He visited the casinos in the South of France occasionally, but found them 'slow'.

43 WRO. Copy of IB's last will and testament, also bank statements and correspondence.

44 *Life*, vol. I: pp. 450–51.

45 It is necessary to address this point since doubt has been cast on Isabel's testimony. In my experience, however, though she was sometimes guilty of exaggeration whenever I have attempted to verify a statement of hers I have been able to do so; a simple example would be her story of seeing the notice in *The Times* while snowed up in the wilds of Yorkshire. A check revealed the notice, just as she said. There are other examples, too numerous to quote here. Isabel's veracity will be examined in a later chapter.

46 *The Perfumed Garden* which Burton translated from the French was published

in 1886. *The Scented Garden*, Burton's translation from the original Arabic, was destroyed by Isabel after Burton's death. See later chapters.

47 *Nights*, vol. X: p. 200. *Supplemental Nights*, vol. VII: p. 438.
48 TCC. HL 228: 116.
49 Monckton Milnes to Thomas Carlyle, 5 August 1861. 'I have a benefit next week.' Milnes wrote urging Carlyle to attend the gathering at Fryston. 'Burton, whom the Indian Government have turned off brutally because he accepted the Consulship of Fernando Po, comes with his wife'. Quoted in Wemyss Reid, *Life of Lord Houghton*, vol. II: p. 72.
50 Wemyss Reid, *Life of Lord Houghton*, vol. I: p.461.
51 PRO: FO2/40 f.11. FO to RFB, 9 July 1861.
52 *Life*, vol. I: p. 348.
53 Ibid.
54 Burton, *Wanderings in West Africa from Liverpool to Fernando Po* (Tinsley Brothers, 1863), p. 1.
55 *The Romance*, p. 179.

Chapter 20 (1861–1863)

1 *Wanderings in West Africa from Liverpool to Fernando Po* [hereafter, *Wanderings in West Africa*] (published 1863); *Abeokuta and the Cameroons Mountains* (also 1863); *A Mission to Gelele, King of Dahome* (1864), *Two Trips to Gorilla Land and the Cataracts of the Congo,* (1864). Each of these works consisted of two volumes. The single volume, *Wit and Wisdom in West Africa*, was published in 1865.
2 *Wanderings in West Africa*, vol. I: p. 107.
3 Ibid., vol. II: p. 168 fn.
4 Selim Aga was killed in Liberia during the Grebo War in 1875.
5 *Wanderings in West Africa*, vol. I: p. 244.
6 Ibid., p. 206.
7 Ibid., p. 223.
8 Ibid., p. 211–12.
9 Ibid., p. 267 fn.
10 Ibid., p. 267.
11 Ibid., p. 234. Palm oil was used for making soap, candles, hair preparations etc., but its major value was as a lubricant in a variety of heavy industrial processes such as the iron and tin plate industries etc. Its use declined sharply with the discovery of petroleum.
12 Ibid., p. 283.
13 PRO: FO2/45 f.49.
14 *Wanderings in West Africa*, vol. I: p. 286.
15 Ibid., vol. II, p. 295.
16 NLS: MS4158 f.118. Blackwood papers. IB to John Blackwood, 17 Oct. 1861. 'My husband . . . writes from Sierra Leone as follows: ". . . Write to Mr John Blackwood and ascertain whether in cases of my sending them articles they could let me have proofs of a single revise. If not I must employ a clerk which will cause delay . . ." . . .'
17 *Wanderings in West Africa,* vol. II: p. 169.
18 The letter-opener and the necklace of human bones are part of the Burton collection at Orleans House Gallery.
19 For example her letters to Norton Shaw, 11 Jan., 12 Feb., 17 March, 13 May,

RGS archives. Others to Milnes and Friswell confirm her receipt of similar instructions.

20 WRO and QK collections. Examples will be quoted in later chapters.

21 Monckton Milnes to C.J. MacCarthy, 20 Jan. 1862.

22 HL: Burton collection. Box 11, Envelope 6, folio 10. IB to Friswell undated, c.October 1861.

23 WRO: See IB's inventory of pictures in Memoranda Book.

24 The exquisite 'wedding portraits' are now the property of the Orleans House Gallery, Richmond and may be viewed by request. Isabel left a record of the images of Richard in her room in the form of one of the innumerable lists in her Memoranda Book; now the property of WRO. Not catalogued.

25 Wemyss Reid, *Life of Lord Houghton*, p. 74. Quotes letter from RMM to J. MacCarthy, 21 Dec. 1861.

26 RGS: Burton correspondence. IB to Norton Shaw. One of two letters dated 11 Jan. 1862. There is no indication of which abusive memorandum Isabel refers to here. Among Fawn Brodie's private papers (in the EM collection at HL) is a note by Brodie suggesting that Isabel might mean the Karachi Brothel Report; but I think Isabel's letter makes it obvious that she is referring to some FO correspondence.

27 HL: Burton collection. Box 11, Envelope 6, folio 111–14. IB to Friswell, dated 4 Jan. [1862].

28 Richards, Alfred Bate, 'A Sketch of Sir Richard Burton by "Oxonian".'

29 PRO: FO84/1117 ff. 97–98, dated Fernando Po, 4 Oct. 1861. 'Eyo Honesty' was the name of a local chief.

30 PRO: FO84/1147 ff. 100–104, dated Nov. 1861.

31 Ibid. ff.27–29.

32 PRO: FO2/40.

33 TCC: Houghton Library 228: 18

34 PRO: FO84/1176 ff. 46–51.

35 i.e. Prince Albert's death in Dec. 1861.

36 Farwell, *Burton*, p. 214.

37 QK collection. Paper for Royal Society, 10 June 1862, Dr J. E. Gray, 'Camaroon Mammals'.

38 TCC: Houghton Library 4:180. 15 March [1862].

39 PRO: FO84/1176 ff. 9–10.

40 *Wanderings in West Africa*, vol. I: p. 296.

41 PRO: FO2/42 ff. 76–77.

42 *Wanderings in West Africa*, vol. II: p. 216.

43 QK collection. RFB to R. Martin [later Sir R. Martin] 4 May 1862.

44 NAS: Edinburgh. Murray: C29796. RFB to Murray 20 Jan. 1863.

45 TCC: Houghton Library. 228: 19.

46 Paul du Chaillu, first European to see and write of gorillas. He was not believed. See his *Explorations and Adventures in Equatorial Africa* (John Murray, 1861).

47 NAS. Edinburgh. Murray C.29796. RFB to Murray 23/6/1862.

48 RGS: Speke correspondence file. Speke to Murchison, 6 July 1862.

49 PRO: FO84/1176 f.249 et seq.

50 From unidentified sales catalogue in QK collection.

51 Magg's Catalogue Christmas 1923. Item number 63. In Burton's handwriting, signed RFB, dated Benin River, 25 Aug. 1862. The addressee is not given.

52 RGS: Burton correspondence 1862. RFB to Shaw, 26 Sept. 1862.

53	The taxidermist, with little to go on to tell him what the animal looked like in life, did the best he could. Burton's description of the animal when he first saw it was, 'a fine specimen . . . when placed in an arm chair he ludicrously suggested a pot-bellied and patriarchal Negro considerably the worse for liquor.' On his next visit to London he was dismayed to find the stuffed skin had become a ghastly caricature of the original animal: 'pigeon-breasted, lean flanked and shrunken-limbed.

54	RGS Correspondence Block 1851–70. Hooker, J.D., Nov. 1862. Noticeably, Mr Mann was not given a great deal of credit in the biography of Alfred Saker either, in which the climb was described from Saker's notes. See Underhill, E.B: *Alfred Saker, a biography* (Alexander & Shepheard, 1884), pp. 110–116.

55	RGS: IB to Norton Shaw, 1 Dec. [1862].

56	Ibid.

57	*Life*, vol. I: p. 376.

58	QK collection. Wilson/7.

59	Scottish Record Office. C29796. Murray correspondence.

60	Ibid.

61	TCC: Houghton collection 228: 20.

62	The relative innocence of these so-called 'orgies' is evidenced by the fact that Isabel's father and brothers often attended them.

63	PRO: FO84/1203 ff. 276–80; and ff. 217–18 abrupt refusal of the request.

64	Ibid. ff. 217–218.

Chapter 21 (1863–1864)

1	TCC: Houghton 228: 21. RFB to RMM, 17 Feb. 1863.

2	*Life*, vol. I: p. 376.

3	*London Review*, 16 Jan. 1864.

4	*Abeokuta*, pp. 11–12.

5	*London Review*, 16 Jan. 1864.

6	HL: B/L #117. Burton, Isabel: 'Scenes in Teneriffe' (unpublished manuscript).

7	Ibid.

8	*Life*, vol. I: p. 381.

9	PRO: FO84/1203. This entire file contains many reports from, and correspondence between the FO and Richard.

10	Mr J.W. Watson, writing in the *North American Review*, claimed to have seen 200 people butchered by a mob of 5,000 in three hours. Modern historians believe that European visitors were always received with intimidating displays of violence in an attempt to protect the lucrative slave markets that still existed away from the coastal areas. See Halladay, Eric, *The Emergent Continent* (Ernest Benn Ltd, 1972), pp. 42–3.

11	*The Times* cutting in IB's scrapbooks, 27 Dec. c.1859.

12	TCC: Houghton 228: 25, 25 Oct. 1863.

13	*Life*, vol. I: p. 383.

14	Frederick Hankey, whose library of erotic literature in Paris was even more compressive than Houghton's, told Burton that his copy of *Marquis de Sade* was bound in human skin, but as it had not been stripped from 'a living victim' the outside did not match the contents of the book. Richard laughingly agreed to bring him back the skin of a young girl from Africa. It was not a promise Burton took seriously. See *Swinburne's Letters*, vol. II: p. 20 fn.

15	William Stirling MP, of Keir. In the event RFB wrote his own preface for *Wit &*

Wisdom and mentions Stirling in it.

16 TCC: Houghton Library 228: 23, 31 May 1863.
17 *A Mission to Gelele, King of Dahomey*. With Notices of the So-called 'Amazons'. (Tinsley Brothers, 1864). 2 vols.
18 Wemyss-Reid, *Life of Lord Houghton*, vol. II: pp. 96–97.
19 TCC: Houghton Library 228:25. RFB to Lord Houghton, 25 Oct. 1863.
20 Ibid., 228:27, 24 March 1864.
21 *Wanderings in West Africa*, vol. I: p. 226–7.
22 *Life*, vol. II: p. 44. At WRO Burton's original artwork for his 'Tonic Bitters' is contained in one of IB's scrapbooks.
23 *Life*, vol. I: p. 438.
24 RGS: Burton correspondence. RFB to J. George Esq., from Bonny River, 27 June 1863.
25 Published by Blackwoods in 1864. Speke dedicated the book to Outram 'who gave me a start in Africa'. He neglects to say that the start consisted of introducing him to Burton.
26 At the Huntington Library.
27 HL: B/L: 1680. Burton's annotations in his own copy of Speke's book, *What Led to the Discovery of the Source of the Nile*.
28 *Life*, vol. I: p. 407.
29 Lord Russell to IB, 6 Oct. 1863. Quoted in *The Romance*, p. 227.
30 PRO: FO84/1221 f.297.
31 Ibid., ff.302–3.
32 The Bodleian Library, Oxford, has an original of this pamphlet. I did not find any others in my research.
33 Isabel's counter-revenge, thirty years later, was to publish an unflattering caricature of Rainey in *Life*, vol. I: p. 353.
34 QK. RFB to Wilson/13, dated Teneriffe, 30 June 1864.
35 PRO: FO2/45 ff.96–98.
36 Maggs Catalogue 1912 301/4353. Undated letter from IB to Tinsley, c. spring 1864.
37 *Life*, vol. I: p. 376. As usual, when it is possible to check Isabel's statement she is accurate in her recollection. See also FO2/45 f.9–12 dated 23 April 1864 in which his four-month leave is granted, and subsequently approved by Lord Russell. Also 16 May 1864 letter to Burton advising him officially.
38 Quoted in *The Romance*, p. 242.
39 Ibid., p. 165 fn.
40 New Hall archives.
41 QK collection. Wilson/14. RFB to Wilson, dated London, 23 August 1864.

Chapter 22 (1861–1864)

1 *Life*, vol. I: p. 406.
2 Maitland, *Speke*, p. 181.
3 TCC: Houghton Library 228:25. RFB to Houghton, dated 25 Oct. 1863.
4 It was not, however, greater than Burton's in terms of endeavour. The first expedition not only explored unmapped territory but involved a long and difficult return journey. Speke and Grant returned by sailing down the Nile, a far less arduous sequel.
5 Speke, *Journal*, p. 458.
6 Maitland, *Speke*, p. 169.

7 Ibid.
8 Petherick, *Travels in Central Africa*, vol. II: p. 130.
9 Ibid., p. 132.
10 BL MSS. Dept. Add'l. MS38990. Layard Papers.
11 I have not been able to discover to what this remark refers.
12 One of a series of letters from Speke to Blackwood abusing Burton. NLS: Blackwood papers. MS4193 f.184: 192 and 194.
13 NLS: MS17909. Blackwood papers. Blackwood to Speke, Nov. 1863.
14 *Life*, vol. I: p. 331.
15 QK collection. Speke to Safford, 14 Feb. 1864.
16 RGS: Speke correspondence files. Speke to RGS dated 19 Feb. 1864.
17 RGS: Speke correspondence. Speke to Murchison, 7 March 1864. This despite the fact that in that month alone Blackwood had sent him a royalty cheque for £1,500 – probably more than Burton had earned in total on all his books at that date.
18 NLS: MSS17909 f.1. Grant papers.
19 Ibid., f.42. Rigby to Grant from India, 30 July 1864. The first print run of Speke's book was 10,000 copies, which sold as the controversy grew. A further 2,500 were printed but not entirely sold.
20 BL Mss dept: Layard Papers Add'l Mss 38990.
21 Sir Harry Johnson, *The Nile Quest*, p. 171.
22 NLS: MSS17910 f.80. Grant papers. Speke to Grant, 4 July 1864.
23 *Athenaeum*, 14 June 1863.
24 NLS: MS4185 19 Dec. 1863. This letter, written by Speke on the day the review was published in the *Athenaeum*, shows that Speke was aware of the unease with which many of his remarks concerning women were regarded. For example, as well as having two pretty maidens living in his hut for some weeks, he had written of intimately measuring a number of women (which hints of something learned from Burton), and on one occasion of agreeing to show the woman part of his own naked body in exchange for permission to do so. Speke responded to the Editor: 'I do not think I deserve the imputations . . . which you have cast at me.' Other statements in the letter, that he had never read Petherick's book and that Petherick never used any navigational instruments, are proved untrue by other correspondence. And although he was at that time still avidly campaigning against Petherick, he stated, '. . . what I have written regarding him I am sorry but I was obliged to.'

Chapter 23 (1864)

1 Sometimes this worked, sometimes not. He used this technique during the Beatson trial, but some thought his act in the witness box demeaned his evidence.
2 Blackwood to Speke, 1 Feb. 1864, following Speke's blunt letter about the Pethericks to *The Times* in January. 'I hope . . . you have not . . . been firing off any more letters to the newspapers'. During these months he even wrote peevishly about Grant, to Blackwood (NLS 4185) and of his old friend from his Himalaya days, Smyth, to the FO (BL MSS 45918).
3 NLS: MS4185. Blackwood papers. Speke to Blackwood, 25 July 1864.
4 *Life*, vol. I: p. 389.
5 The Arctic explorer. After having been compelled to eat human flesh to stay alive, he became a lifelong vegetarian.
6 Not only in Britain, of course: it was the age of discovery in many countries with

Einstein, Eddison and Bell, Morse, Nobel and Pasteur, to name only a few of those nurtured by an age of incredible confidence.

7   *Livingstone*, published by the National Portrait Gallery for the 1996 Livingstone exhibition.

8   *Life*, vol. I: p. 389.

9   *Zanzibar*, vol. II: pp. 397–8.

10 WRO: 2667. Printed article, 'A Twilight Gossip with the Past', by Mrs Andrew Crosse. Undated. In IB's press cuttings book.

11 *Life*, vol. I: p. 405 gives Burton's version of the Bath meeting. Richard and Isabel state that they stood alone on the platform, waiting. But the evidence of eye witnesses is that they waited 'in the wings' and Richard mounted the platform with Murchison and Markham.

12 Sir James Alexander's motion was that Section E recommended that the Government be urged to give Speke a knighthood and Grant a C.B.E. William Speke told Grant this had been ratified by Section E, but Galton's evidence makes it clear that it was still under discussion when the news of Speke's death came through. Agreement after this point was academic – knighthoods are not awarded posthumously.

13 In his book, *Memories of my Life*, p. 202. Galton states that Burton was present in the room when the message was delivered; but this is at odds with two other accounts that he heard the news when it was read out from the platform.

14 Galton, Francis, *Memories of my Life* (Methuen), p. 202.

15 *Zanzibar*, vol. II: p. 398. *Life*, vol. II: pp. 38–40.

16 *Life*, vol. I: p. 389.

17 RGS archives: 'An unpublished history of the RGS' by Markham, p. 381.

18 *Bath Chronicle*, Report of the British Association, 17 Sept. 1864.

19 Information regarding Speke's last hours is taken from *The Times*, 17 Sept. 1864, and the *Bath Chronicle*, 17 Sept. 1864, which carried a transcript of the inquest. The QK collection has an article by H.B. Thomas, 'The Death of Speke in 1864'. *Uganda Journal*, vol. 13, No. 1, March 1949, pp. 105–7, which is also quoted by Maitland in his excellent but difficult to find biography, *Speke*, pp. 210–11.

20 Reports on the inquest in the *Bath Chronicle* for 17 and 22 Sept. 1864 and *The Times*, 17 Sept. 1864.

21 NLS: MSS17931 f.68. Speke to Grant, Oct. 1854 and MSS17910 f.71, March 1855.

22 *The Times*, 20 March 1921.

23 Copy of document in possession of Fuller family; quoted in Maitland, *Speke*, pp. 214–16.

24 NLS: MS4143 f.225. William Speke to John Blackwood, 29 Sept. 1864.

25 WRO: 2667. Unidentified cutting in IB's press cutting books. Also quoted in *The Search for Richard Burton*, papers of the Huntington Symposium, pp. 97–8.

26 Wright, *Life of Sir Richard Burton*, vol. I: p. 192.

27 *The Times*, 22 Sept. 1864.

28 QK. Wilson/15, dated Royal Hotel, Bath, 21 Sept. 1864.

29 *Bath Chronicle*, 29 Sept. 1864. Speke's tomb (and the Papworth bust of Speke) may be seen in the family vault, at the XIVth century church of St Andrew at Dowlish Wake, about 14 miles south-east of Taunton.

30 TCC: Houghton Library 228:28. RFB to Houghton, 12 Oct. 1864.

31 RGS: Proceedings, 14 Nov. 1864.

32 The Speke memorial was erected in Kensington Park. The public subscription

fell short of the costs and the Speke family apparently paid the difference, according to a letter from Grant to Murchison in the QK collection, u/d 'Friday', c. January 1865.

33 NPG: *Livingstone*; book published as part of the Livingstone exhibition in 1996.

34 NLS: MSS17909 f.93. Galton to Grant, from 42 Rutland Gate, 24 Nov. 1864.

35 As Burton wrote to *The Times*, 'the sources of rivers are not in lakes'. In fact the draining Ruenzori mountains (the ancient Mountains of the Moon) which feed the lake might equally be regarded as the 'true' source.

Chapter 24 (1865–1868)

1 In a typical Burtonian exchange, Richard wrote to Winford Reade from Ireland sending their joint regards and saying that when he returned they must meet: '. . . Don't tell anybody, a week must be dedicated to sobriety . . . I shall see none but you. Then for a debauch that must last till sailing [on] April 9th.' Photocopy in QK collection.

2 *The Romance*, p. 173.

3 IB's inventory of her jewel box includes, 'real pearls, rubbish pearls, Turquoise brooch from Richard, Mama's [——], diamond tiara etc etc.' WRO. Box 2.

4 Russell, *The Amberley Papers*, p. 347.

5 Ibid., p. 348.

6 Ibid., p. 350.

7 TCC: Houghton Library 4:161. IB to Houghton, 1 Jan. [1865].

8 *Life*, vol. I: p. 398.

9 QK. RFB's book of poetry. Long unfinished poem includes:
   On to Dublin dear & dirty, dear indeed and very dear
   With its claret at eight shillings little better than small beer . . .
   O thou capital of Oirland what fierce questions roll
   As I am to thee a stranger – o'er my quasi-Irish soul.

10 *Life*, vol. I: p. 393. In the Huntington Library there is a manuscript in Burton's hand entitled *Uruguay*, and signed by him 'Frank Baker'.

11 Ibid., vol. I: pp. 391–3.

12 Quentin Keynes has a review copy which eluded Isabel. Inside the cover is Burton's letter asking a Mr Dixon to review 'a neat article' written by 'a friend' of his: 'Can you not give him, as he deserves, the cut-up proper. How are you off for Nile Basins?' RFB to Dixon, 10 March 1865 from 36 Manchester St, London.

13 HL: BL26. Holograph material in Burton's own copy of *Stone Talk* (1 of 2 copies), lists Gentlemen's Clubs from which Isabel recalled the book: Athenaeum, Arts Club, Oriental, Reform, Carlton, United Services, Junior Service, Conservative, New Athenaeum. There is also a letter and statement from the publisher signed by R. Hardwick, advising that over and above the '128 to Press and Author' only seven copies had been sold. 'people are afraid to tackle it . . . I would advise that somebody pitch it hot and strong in some of the papers and that might, possibly, give it a stir. I am afraid it is too sensible and strong to sell . . .' A second copy of *Stone Talk* in Burton's library has a large number of edits in Isabel's writing. These edits are copied from the more heavily annotated first copy in Burton's handwriting. Clearly he intended an edited reprint at some point.

14 *Life*, vol. I: p. 397.

15   BL: MS10826 bbb 28.

16   The Nile debate ran on for years, but there is insufficient room in this book to take it further. As Richard left for Brazil Livingstone was writing spitefully, and largely incorrectly, to a friend: 'Burton is an awful ruffian; I must keep clear of his spoor for Rigby informs me that he on purpose behaved wickedly, refused payments and did what he could to shut out everybody else from Tanganyika . . . I don't believe Burton was ever at Mecca. Col. Rigby found a book written by an American who ran away and lived among the Sawahilis which Burton copied word for word in those months at Zanzibar. The fellow's wickedness cannot be put on paper and he is upheld by Lords Stanley and Houghton . . . Now imagine Burton and Winwood Reade, a dirty little Jew, inveigling Coleuzo into the Anthropological which consists mainly of West Coast oil traders'. QK. Livingstone to Sir Thomas Maclean, 27 May 1865.

17   Ibid: Programme and report of Farewell Dinner for Burton, 4 April 1965.

18   According to the *Pall Mall Gazette*, 10 Oct. 1890, there was even a bust of him by Papworth exhibited at the Royal Academy that summer of 1865. I think this is probably an error, however, and the Papworth bust was that of Speke.

19   *General Rigby*, p. 274. Grant had been promoted to Colonel and Rigby to General. Burton's reference to Grant as 'barren' doubtless refers to his record of discoveries.

20   Rigby spent a lot of time, for example, promulgating his belief that Richard had never gone to Mecca. When Livingstone repeated what Rigby told him, he used phrases virtually identical to those used by Speke to his mother, 'I do not believe Burton ever went to Mecca . . .' Had he known about it and wished to do so, Richard had only to present the signed document he received in Mecca from the Sheikh, certifying him as a *Hajji*, to refute this silly rumour.

21   *Life*, vol. I: p. 418.

22   Ibid., p. 416.

23   As part of her packing and storage preparations, Isabel made long inventories of the couple's belongings at this time which provide a fascinating glimpse of their domestic arrangements. See WRO: IB's Memorandum Book.

24   *Life*, vol. I: p. 418.

25   Ibid.

26   PRO: FO13/432 f.30-31. Folios 1–55 in this file has a good deal of correspondence between Burton and the FO during his time at Santos.

27   TCC: Houghton Library 4:184. IB to Houghton, 23 Nov. 1867.

28   EM collection at HL: Box 11, Envelope 4/10. RFB to Crookes, 21 Oct. 1865.

29   QK collection. RFB to A.G. Findlay, 'Santos 1/8/67'.

30   *The Romance*, p. 247–8; Wright, *Life of Richard Burton*, pp. 47–8.

31   EM collection at HL: RFB to Tootal, 26 [Jan.] [1866].

32   New Hall School archives: Isabel's great-niece recalled that IB kept this uniform prominently displayed in her cottage at Mortlake after Richard's death.

33   *Life*, vol. I: p. 421. Isabel repeated this story in a letter to her mother, 15 Dec. 1865. Quoted in *The Romance*.

34   IB to Mrs Arundell, 15 Dec. 1865. Quoted in *The Romance*.

35   Ibid.

36   *Life*, vol. I: p. 471.

37   TCC: Houghton Library 4:184. IB to Houghton, 23 Nov. 1867.

38   *The Romance*, p. 255.

39   IB to Mrs Arundell, 3 Jan. 1866. Quoted in *The Romance*, p. 253.

40 TCC: Houghton Library 4:184. IB to Houghton, 23 Nov. 1867.
41 HL: Box 11, Envelope 4/10.
42 HL: See unpublished Ms. entitled 'Uruguay', written in Burton's handwriting and signed 'Frank Baker'; includes biographical notes about Balilio Da Gama.
43 All of these manuscripts are mentioned in Burton's letters to Albert Tootal during the period mentioned. See Edwards Metcalf collection, a private holding housed at the Huntington Library. The series of 3 articles written in Nov. 1865 appeared in *Frasers Magazine* in the following year entitled 'From London to Rio de Janeiro'.
44 QK. RFB to A.G. Findlay, 1 Aug. 1867: 'I am writing a book on the seaboard of Brazil "From Paraguay to the Equator", and another on the province of S. Paulo . . . and finishing off some old scores with Africa.' TCC: Houghton Library 4:184. IB to Houghton 'Richard has four books on Brazil getting ready . . . one is on Sao Paulo, one on the coast, one on the river San Fransisco . . . and the fourth is general Brazil . . .'
45 EM collection: Bound letterbook. RFB to Albert Tootal, [Feb.] 1867.
46 TCC: Houghton Library 4:184. IB to Houghton, 23 Nov. 1867.
47 EM collection: Box 11, Envelope 5/10. IB to Tootal, u/d [autumn 1867].
48 WRO: 2667/ uncatalogued. Caption under photograph of the dog in one of IB's photo albums.
49 IB to Mrs Arundell, 22 Dec. 1866. Quoted in *The Romance*, p. 266.
50 *Life*, vol. I: p. 439.
51 TCC: Houghton Library. IB to Houghton, 23 Nov. 1867.
52 IB to Mrs Arundell 14 May 1866. Quoted in *The Romance*, pp. 256–7.
53 HL: Box 11, Envelope 4/10.
54 *The Romance*, vol. I: p. 250.
55 Ibid., 8 Dec. 1866.
56 NLS: MS17909 f.52. Grant papers. Rigby to Grant, 12 Feb. 1866. FO13/450 ff. 129–144. A major point in Rainey's case was that the ship has been bought in at a knock-down price by Edward Laughland, one of Richard's friends who sometimes stood in as Vice-Consul during Richard's absences. Even though Stanley and others at the FO believed that Burton was 'ignorant of the facts' and innocent 'he is still responsible and therefore owes the estate £280' (folios 129–31).
57 TCC: Houghton Library 228:30. RFB to Houghton, 23 Oct. 1865.
58 *Life*, vol. I: p. 425.
59 IB to Mrs Arundell, 23 July 1866. Quoted in *The Romance*, p. 261. Also WRO: bundle of copies of the reports written by IB for the FO while in S. America. Uncatalogued.
60 IB to Mrs Arundell, 15 Sept. 1866. Quoted in *The Romance*, p. 264.
61 Burton, Richard, *Highlands of the Brazil* (Tinsley Brothers, 1869), p. 20.
62 *Life*, vol. I: p. 441. *Highlands of the Brazil*, vol. I: p. 161.
63 *Life*, vol. I: p. 443. Richard also described this journey, though less personally, in *Highlands of the Brazil*.
64 Ibid., p. 260.
65 TCC: Houghton Library 4:184. IB to Houghton, 23 Nov. 1867. For a detailed account of Isabel's adventurous ride to Rio see *The Romance*, Chapter VIII.
66 *Life*, vol. I: p. 448.
67 Ibid., p. 449.
68 TCC: Houghton Library 4:184. IB to Houghton, 23 Nov. 1867.

69 IB to Mrs Arundell, 22 June 1866. Quoted in *The Romance*, p. 260.
70 *Life*, vol. I: p. 437.
71 Blunt, Wilfred Scawen, *My Diaries*, vol. II: p. 128.
72 HL: Box 11, Envelope 5/10. IB to Tootal, 9 Feb. 1867.
73 Ibid., IB to Tootal, 3 April 1867.
74 TCC: Houghton 4:186. IB to Houghton, 18 April 1868.
75 IB to Mrs Arundell, 2 Sept. 1866. Quoted in *The Romance*.
76 *Life*, vol. I: p. 439.
77 IB to her family, 13 April 1867. Quoted in *The Romance*, pp. 269–70.
78 EM collection at the HL. RFB to Tootal u/d, c. Feb. 1868.
79 Tootal, Albert. *The Captivity of Hans Stade* was eventually published by the Hakluyt Society in 1874, with preface and annotations throughout by Burton.
80 TCC: Houghton 4:186. IB to Houghton, 18 April 1868.
81 PRO: FO13/457 f.189.
82 IB to Mrs Arundell. Quoted in *The Romance*, pp. 344–5.
83 Ibid.
84 *Life*, vol. I: p. 453.
85 PRO: FO13/457 f.189. RFB to FO (in IB's handwriting) dated Santos, 14 June 1868.
86 Ibid.
87 TCC: Houghton 4:190. IB to Houghton u/d 'Sunday', c. late Nov. 1868.
88 Ibid.
89 Blunt, *My Diaries*, vol. II: p. 129. Although this appeared in the author's published 'diaries' he admitted he had written it from memory, as he had not kept journals while in Brazil. Significantly, we know he had previously read Isabel's *Life* of Burton, which contained a note of Richard's criticising Blunt to the Prime Minister.
90 Burton's evidence at the Tichborne trial in London, Dec. 1871.
91 Blunt, *My Diaries*, vol. II: p. 130.
92 Ibid., pp. 130–31.
93 Burton researchers will find many documents relating to Burton's period in South America, including reams of statistics gathered for official reports, among IB's papers at WRO. Uncatalogued.
94 TCC: Houghton 4:188. IB to Houghton, 9 Oct. 1868.
95 *Transatlantic Review*; 'Memories' by Luke Ionides, March 1924, vol. I, No. 3., pp. 22–7.
96 Evidence given by Richard Burton in the Tichborne Trial, quoted in Farwell, *Burton*, pp. 293–5.

Chapter 25 (1868–1869

1 It was 'Charley William' with whom Richard had stayed in Bahia while he waited for a steamer to Rio, following his white-water rafting expedition in 1868. See *Life*, vol. I: p. 449.
2 *Life*, vol. I: p. 454. This whip is mentioned in an inventory of her possessions in her Memoranda book at WRO .
3 TCC: Houghton 4:187. IB to Houghton, 14 Sept. 1868. The manuscripts brought back by her were Burton's: *Highlands of the Brazil*; his translations of *Lacerda's Journey in Cazembe*, *Vikram and the Vampire*, a book of Hindu stories. In addition she had two manuscripts on which she had herself worked, the novel *Iracéma, The Honey Lips; A Legend of Brazil*, and *Manuel de Moraes*;

the latter was a collaboration between the two. Besides these, she had a manuscript entitled; *Guide-book, A Pictorial Pilgrimage to Mecca and Medina, Including some of the More Remarkable Incidents in the Life of Mohammed the Arab Lawgiver.* Her instructions were that this was to be 'brought out' together with a new edition of his *Pilgrimage*. The manuscript of *Iracéma*, in Isabel's handwriting but with a few edits by Richard Burton, is among Isabel's papers at WRO.

 4 In a letter written shortly after this to Houghton by Swinburne, he advises: 'I have seen Mrs Burton and found her very well and bright – pleasant and friendly, of course, but I fear her late family loss will have cut her up much.' *Swinburne's Letters*, vol. I: p. 345 vol. IV: p. 310.
 5 TCC: Houghton 4:188. IB to Houghton, 9 Oct. 1868
 6 TCC: Houghton 4:189. IB to Houghton, 28 Oct. 1868.
 7 See *Swinburne's Letters*, vol. I: p. 345 vol. I: p. 311. Swinburne to Houghton, 16 Nov. 1868. In this letter Swinburne regrets not being able to escort Isabel to Fryston for the weekend; 'I hoped against hope . . . [but] have the usual November influenza so badly I am all nose (weeping) and throat (coughing).'
 8 TCC: Houghton Library 4:190. IB to Houghton, Sunday u/d [Dec. 1868].
 9 TCC: Houghton 4:191. IB to Houghton, 20 Jan. 1869.
10 IB to Tinsley, u/d (c. mid-Nov. 1868). Quoted in Maggs Catalogue 289/1997.
11 IB's preface in RFB's *Highlands of the Brazil*.
12 WRO: Tinsley to IB, [24] Nov. 1868, uncatalogued.
13 The letter of appointment signed by Queen Victoria and Lord Stanley, dated 39 Nov., is among IB's papers at WRO.
14 PRO: FO40612 ff.1-3. Stanley to Burton, 3 and 7 Dec. 1868.
15 *Pall Mall Gazette*, 13 Jan. 1869.
16 *Daily News*, Monday, 11 Jan. 1869. See IB's press cutting albums. WRO. Uncatalogued. Box 3.
17 *Athenaeum*, 16 Jan. 1869, No. 2151; p. 83.
18 *Sunday Observer*, 31 Jan. 1869.
19 TCC: Houghton 4:191. IB to Lord Houghton, 20 Jan. 1869.
20 From IB to unknown correspondent, 7 Sept. 1869. Quoted in Maggs Catalogue 1112/1990 No. 24.
21 EM collection at HL: Box 11, Envelope 5/10 (v). 27 June [1869].
22 *The Times*, 13 March 1860.
23 NLS: MSS13069 f.66, Private letterbook of Sir Henry Elliot. Elliot to the Earl Granville, Therapia, 9 June 1871.
24 Ibid.
25 PRO: FO406/12 ff.1–2. Also WRO, for steamship timetables with marked sailings.
26 PRO: FO78/259. Elliot to Clarendon, 3 May 1869.
27 Burton's letter reads: '. . . I now renew in writing the verbal statement in which I assured you that neither the authorities nor the people of Damascus will show for me any but a friendly feeling; that they will receive me as did the Egyptians and the people of Zanzibar for years after my pilgrimage to Mecca. But as designing persons may have attempted to complicate the situation, I once more undertake to act with unusual prudence and to hold myself . . . answerable for the consequences.'
28 PRO: FO78/259. Murray to Burton, 19 June 1869.
29 *Swinburne's Letters*, vol. VI: p. 240.

30 *Transatlantic Review*, 'Memories' by Luke Ionides, op. cit.

31 EM collection at HL. Albert Tootal letters in red leather binder. RFB to Tootal, 9 July 1869.

32 TCC: Houghton 228:32. From RFB at Garswood to Lord Houghton, u/d (c. June 1869).

33 RFB to (Sir) John Larking, offered for sale and quoted in Maggs Catalogue, Christmas 1921; number 2584.

34 *Swinburne's Letters*, vol. II: p. 23.

35 Richard and Leonée Ormond, *Lord Leighton* (Yale University Press, 1975), p. 70.

36 *Life*, vol. I: p. 459.

37 Swinburne wrote a poem about this holiday in 1892 which was published in the *Fortnightly Review*.

38 Swinburne dedicated his *Poems and Ballads, Second Series* to Burton 'in redemption of an old pledge'. He also wrote a poem which he called 'Dedication' which appears as the last poem in the book. This book is said by many to be Swinburne's finest work. See his letter to Theodore Watts, 16 Feb. 1878: 'I . . . have spent half the morning on . . . some stanzas of dedication to Burton . . .'

Burton dedicated the first volume of his translation of Camoens' *Lusiads*, the 'Lyrics', to Swinburne, 'The Prince of the Lyric poets of his day,' asking him to 'accept the unequal exchange – my brass for your gold. Your *Poems and Ballads* [teaches] . . . what might there is in the music of language, and what marvel of lyric inspiration, far more subtler and more ethereal than mere poetry, means to the mind of man.'

39 TCC: Houghton 228:33. RFB to Houghton from Turin, 1 Sept. 1869.

40 *The Times*, 14 Nov. 1869.

41 Murchison to IB, 14 Nov. 1869. Quoted in *The Romance*, p. 356.

42 IB to Murchison, 15 Nov. 1869. Quoted in *The Romance*, p. 358.

43 IB to Tinsley, u/d c. September 1869, written on RGS writing paper. Letter quoted in Maggs Catalogue 309/1653.

44 IB to Tinsley, u/d c. Oct. 1869. Quoted in Maggs Catalogue 303/103.

45 WRO: 2667/26 Isabel Burton's memoranda book, p. 52.

46 *Inner Life*, vol. I: pp. 4–7.

47 Ibid., p. 9.

48 Ibid., p. 12.

49 Ibid., p. 16.

Chapter 26 (1869–1870)

1 Wright, Rev. William: *Burton at Damascus* (*The Bookman*), October 1891, pp. 23–5. 'A young English lady had been treated rudely . . . by a Persian, and when Burton failed in securing official redress I was in dread for months that he would with his own hands kill the ruffian if he met him. The scoundrel however met his fate at other hands.'

2 The present-day railway line follows the route taken by Isabel almost exactly.

3 Jane Digby's unpublished diary, a copy of which is in the author's private collection. Original in Digby family archives. Information given her by Sheik Medjuel el Mezrab (her fourth and last husband).

4 *Inner Life*, vol. I: p. 25.

5 *Life*, vol. I: p. 468.

6   *The Romance*, p. 373.

7   Ibid., p. 376.

8   Ibid., p. 376.

9   Ibid., p. 388.

10   For Jane Digby's biography see Lovell, Mary S: *A Scandalous Life* (Richard Cohen Books, London); and *Rebel Heart* (Norton, N.Y., 1995).

11   Copy of Jane Digby's diary in the author's possession.

12   Ibid.

13   *Inner Life*, vol. I: p. 126.

14   PRO: FO78/2259. Jane Digby to IB; sent with official report to FO.

15   EM collection at HL: RFB to Tootal in red leather-bound volume of letters, 16 May 1870.

16   *Life*, vol. I: p. 499.

17   WRO: 2667 uncatalogued. This notebook, mostly written in her own hand also contains press clippings and letters of advice from others regarding treatments for various equine ailments.

18   Wright, *Burton at Damascus*.

19   Ibid.

20   Ibid.

21   Ibid., also Jane Digby, diary entries.

22   See: Burton, Richard: *The Jew, the Gypsy and El-Islam* (published 1898). 'On January 26, 1849, an order from the Russian Consulate-General of Beirut obliged [Jews of Russian origin] either to return home biennially in order to renew their passports or give up their nationality. They were then taken under the protecting wing of Great Britain by the immense exertions of their co-religionists in . . . London . . .'

23   *Life*, vol. I: p. 534.

24   *Inner Life*, vol. II: p. 248.

25   RFB to Foreign Secretary, 28 Nov. 1870, printed in the Blue Book of his Damascus case, p. 31. Copies of this rare document may be found in the PRO and WRO.

26   Wright, *Burton at Damascus*.

27   Ibid.

28   PRO: FO78:2150. 14 Jan. 1870.

29   *Inner Life*, vol. I: pp. 54–72.

30   *The Romance*, p. 498.

31   *Life*, vol. I: p. 471.

32   When Lord Redesdale was taken by Richard Burton to visit Abd el-Khadir, he was taken aback to see 'the old warrior' was reading a book 'on Magic!' See Redesdale, *Memories* (Hutchinson, 1915), vol. II: p. 570.

33   *The Romance*, p. 397.

34   *Life*, vol. I: p. 486.

35   Ibid., p. 293.

36   These statements which apparently relate to Jane's first marriage to Lord Ellenborough show that Jane's confidences were not so detailed as Isabel would later claim. In fact Ellenborough was neither coarse nor cruel (though he was adulterous). But Jane was in love with him and was not forced into the marriage.

37   *The Romance*, pp. 394–5.

38   *Bible*: Kings I; ch. 9 vs.17–18. 'And Solomon built . . . Baalath, and Tadmor in the wilderness.' Also Chronicles II; ch. 8 v.4.

39   There was a rumour that the attack which took place during Jane's first visit to

Palmyra was a set piece to impress her and wring more money out of her. Jane's diary makes it clear that this was not so.

40 There are several such books in Richard Burton's surviving library at HL. Specifically, his copy of *Five Years in Damascus* by J.L. Porter in which Richard has written 'NB!' whenever the author mentions a well. In Isabel's *Inner Life*, she declined to include a detailed description of Palmyra because, she said, it had already been well described and she did not wish to bore her readers. See also Beaufort, Emily, *Egyptian Sepulchres and Syrian Shrines* (Longman, 1861).

41 *The Romance*, p. 405.

42 Life, vol. I: p. 471.

43 *The Romance*, p. 405.

44 Ibid., p. 420.

45 Jane Digby related in her diary how Da'as Agha personally beheaded one of his wives for infidelity. In 1871, after Richard had left Syria, Da'as Agha burned alive two Bedouins from a tribe with whom he had a blood feud. He was apprehended and brought to Damascus in chains to be tried for murder. He asked Isabel to intercede for him. Having eaten bread and salt in his house she felt she had no option but to do as he asked, though she did so very unwillingly. He escaped before sentencing.

46 WRO: IB's press cutting. IB to *Liverpool Mercury*, 15 Oct. 1884.

47 *Life*, vol. I: p. 473.

48 *Inner Life*, vol. I: pp. 220–1.

49 Ibid.

50 Ibid., pp. 221–2.

51 As seen by the author in 1993.

52 New Hall archives.

53 *Inner Life*, vol. I: p. 243.

54 Ibid., pp. 224–5.

Chapter 27 (1870–1871)

1 *Life*, vol. I: p. 479.

2 Nicora had been ship's surgeon on the steamer which took Richard out to the Crimea. He was Jane Digby's doctor and was a frequent visitor to the Burtons' house in Salahiyeh.

3 *The Romance*, p.425–6.

4 EM collection at HL: RFB to Albert Tootal, 16 May 1870.

5 *Life*, vol. I: pp. 509–10.

6 WRO: 2667/26.

7 NLS: MSS13089. Private papers of Henry Elliot. Elliot to Granville, 11 Aug. 1870.

8 Letter to the author from Mr Peter Clark of the British Council in Damascus, 23 Nov. 1995: '. . . The Consular building in Bloudan was known to the villagers as "únsuliyyat Wuud", Wood's Consulate. This refers to Richard Wood, a legendary British Consul for many years in the middle of the last century . . . [see *DNB*]. The building was used by the British right up to the 1940s as a summer resort.' Mr Clark photographed the building before it was demolished in 1995; see picture section.

9 *Life*, vol. I: p. 499.

10 *The Romance*, p. 429.

11 WRO: 2667/26. Uncatalogued. This book also contains Isabel's veterinary notes

and opinions on feeding and caring for horses. These are sound and sensible and would not be out of place in a modern hunting stable.

12 *Inner Life of Syria* contains many daily entries from IB's journal. This expedition is described in vol. I: p. 283.

13 Richard F. Burton's introduction to *Literary Remains of Charles F. Tyrwhitt Drake*, p. 14.

14 Besant, Walter; *Literary Remains of Charles F. Tyrwhitt Drake FRGS* (Richard Bentley, 1877). This book contains written appreciations of Drake by both Richard and Isabel.

15 *Inner Life*, vol. I: p. 293.

16 WRO: IB's press cutting books contain copies of all her 'Letters from a Correspondent'.

17 QK collection. IB to her sister 'Dilly' Fitzgerald, 29 Aug. 1870.

18 Ibid., '. . . Syrian fever begins with pain all over the body, particularly in the head and back – freezing and burning alternately, and lethargy, then intense billiousness and low spirits.'

19 *The Romance*, p. 441. Khamour had a sister who was named 'The Sun', apparently because she was very placid compared with Khamour ('The Moon'). The sisters, who were from a very poor family near Beirut, were adopted by a wealthy Protestant Lebanese family, and sent to Miss Wilson's school. This information from Mr Nadim Shehadi who is a descendant of the adoptive family.

20 Ibid., p. 444.

21 QK collection. IB to her sister 'Dilly', 29 Aug. 1870. ' I suppose you are all at Weston? How I wish I were with you! It is not my fault either. Richard rather wanted me to stay till October . . .' NLS: MSS13069 Sir Henry Elliot's private papers. Elliot to IB, 5 Nov. 1870: '. . . Captain Burton wrote that he expected to be leaving for England about the end of this month . . .'

22 WRO: 2667/26 uncatalogued.

23 Jane Digby's diary, op. cit.

24 *Life*, vol. I: p. 538.

25 Ibid., p. 503.

26 *Inner Life*, vol. I: p. 352.

27 Jane Digby's diary, Aug. 1870.

28 RFB to Sir Henry Elliot, 4 Oct. 1870. Quoted in the FO 'Blue Book' of the Damascus affair.

29 NLS: MSS13069 f.66. Private papers of Sir Henry Elliot. Elliot to Hammond, 6 Sept. 1870.

30 Ibid., 7 Oct. 1870. This file has many private letters from Elliot directed against Richard Burton. Space limits further quotation.

31 FO Blue Book, Damascus.

32 PRO: FO78/2660. William Wright to Augusta Mott, 1 March 1871. The original of this letter and those which follow are in the Foreign Office archives with copies of Richard's 'Blue Book' printed to defend his recall from Damascus. Copies exist in IB's papers at WRO: 2667/26 Box (i) ff.25–51.

33 Ibid.

34 Ibid. Augusta Mott to William Wright, 8 March 1871.

35 Ibid. William Wright to Augusta Mott, 15 March 1870.

36 Ibid. James Orr Scott to RFB, 17 March 1871.

37 PRO: FO278/2259. RFB to Granville, 29 Nov. and 6 Dec. 1870.

38 Quoted in *The Romance*, p. 456.
39 NLS: MSS13069 f.129. Minto Papers, private letterbook of Sir Henry Elliot. Elliot to IB, 5 Nov. 1870.
40 NLS: MSS13069 f.104. Minto Papers, private letterbook of Sir Henry Elliott. Elliot to Hammond, 2 Dec. 1870
41 *The Romance*, p. 461.
42 A year after Isabel left Damascus, the same man strangled his mother and buried her in the courtyard of her house.
43 PRO: FO78/2259. Jane Digby to IB, 28 Nov. 1870. The original of this long letter is in the Foreign Office archives, sent by Richard with other corroborative evidence of the plot to remove him. There is a copy in Isabel's papers at WRO. Isabel quotes an abridged version in *Life*; had she not abridged it she could certainly have been sued for slander, since in it Jane openly accused Richard Rogers of corruption.
44 *Inner Life*, vol. II: p. 5.
45 *Life*, vol. I: p. 512.
46 *Inner Life*, vol. II: p. 6.
47 This incident in IB's *Inner Life*, vol. II: p. 12, and many others described by her are verified by Jane Digby's diaries, a copy of which is in the author's possession.
48 *The Romance*, p. 390.
49 *Life*, vol. I: p. 506.
50 *Inner Life*, vol. I: p. 153. Also WRO. In IB's Memorandum Book she has several entries headed 'How to conceive a child' which probably date from this time.
51 The Hamath Stones are five basalt monoliths at Hamah, covered in hieroglyphs.
52 *Literary Remains*.
53 In my biography of Jane Digby I was doubtful of Isabel's ability to learn much from *harems* because of her very limited Arabic. Further research now reveals that she often took her little maid, Moon, with her as interpreter.
54 *Literary Remains*. p. 17.
55 *Inner Life*, vol. II: p. 294.
56 Redesdale, Lord, *Memories* (Hutchinson, 1915), vol. II: p. 562.
57 Ibid.
58 Ibid.
59 Stisted, *The True Life*, p. 363.
60 *Life*, vol. I: p. 600. 'Utter fabrication', Isabel wrote about this, recognising that it was a version of the incident where the youth had tried to pull her from her horse. 'It is monstrous to pretend that my husband was recalled because I defended myself gainst a man who attacked me . . .'
61 Ibid., p. 562.
62 Wright, *Burton at Damascus*.
63 Redesdale, *Memories*, op. cit., vol. III: pp. 562–3.
64 *Literary Remains*, p. 18. See also Isabel's lengthy accounts in *Life* and *Inner Life*. She also sent several pieces to *The Times* which were published in May 1871.
65 *Inner Life*, vol. II. p. 193.
66 Ibid., pp. 220–21.
67 Ibid.
68 Ibid., pp. 18–257. Also *Unexplored Syria* by Richard Burton, Isabel Burton and Charles Tyrwhitt Drake (2 vols), 1871.
69 Ibid., p. 256.

Chapter 28 (1871–1873)

1 *Life*, vol. I: p. 516.
2 *The Romance*, p. 495.
3 *Life*, vol. I: p. 517.
4 WRO: 2667/6 uncatalogued. Copies also exist in the QK collection and Huntington Library.
5 WRO: 2667/26 uncatalogued.
6 NLS: MSS13069 f.66. Elliot to Granville, 9 June 1871.
7 WRO: Also quoted in Blue Book, pp. 88–9.
8 NLS: MSS13069 f.183. Private letterbook of Sir Henry Eliott. Elliot to the Rt. Hon E. Hammond, Therapia, 14 July 1871.
9 PRO: FO78/2259. These reports are dated 5, 11, 17, 21 and 24 July. The notes are among IB's papers at WRO.
10 BL. Add mss 46,698 ff. 230-231. Rashid Pasha to Ali Pasha, 30 July 1871. Written in French.
11 Jane Digby's diary confirms the excessive heat that month which even she found trying.
12 PRO: FO78/2259. RFB to Lord Odo Russell, 21 July 1871.
13 When the matter was investigated some months later the FO gave Richard the benefit of the doubt, agreeing it was possible that he had not received the instruction when he wrote his letter.
14 PRO: FO88/2148 f.41. Elliot to Granville, 22 April 1871.
15 PRO: FO78/2259. Aug. 18, 1871.
16 NLS: MSS13069 f.186. Private letterbook of Sir Henry Elliott, Elliot to the Earl Granville, Therapia, 11 Aug. 1871.
17 *The Romance*, p. 499.
18 *Inner Life*, vol. II: p. 270.
19 *Life*, vol. I: p. 522.
20 WRO: 2667/26 Box 2 (i) 9. Jago to Burton, 15 Aug. 1871
21 *The Romance*, p. 499.
22 *Literary Remains*, pp. 20–1.
23 *Life*, vol I: pp. 568–9. This staccato entry was typical of the manner in which the Burtons kept their journal while travelling. It was an aide-memoire to enable them to make more detailed descriptions when time and circumstances allowed.
24 *The Romance*, p. 500. Later she learned that some of her servants saddled up and followed, but they never caught up with her.
25 Literally: 'Good breeding cannot lie'; figuratively: 'Breeding will tell.' *Life*, vol. I: p. 569.
26 I have drawn attention to this because of the assertions by some recent biographers that Richard was trapped in a loveless marriage. This will be addressed in a later chapter.
27 *Literary Remains*, p. 20.
28 *The Romance*, p. 502.
29 Ibid., p. 502, and *Life*, vol. I: p. 571.
30 *Inner Life*, vol. II: p. 281.
31 Ibid., p. 283.
32 Jane Digby's diary, 18 Aug. 1871.
33 Copy of Jane Digby's diary in the author's personal collection.
34 *The Romance*, p. 507.
35 Jane Digby's diary, Aug./Sept./Oct. 1871.

36 Stisted, *The True Life*, p. 363.

37 HL: Box 11, Envelope 10. 24 Sept. 1871. RFB to William Crookes who was investigating spiritualism. 'Having just returned from Damascus I called upon Miss Bird who kindly lent me your papers upon the new force. Allow me to congratulate you; we of the demi scientific monde always declared it was a new force although "Aura Magnetica" appeared to be rather a name than a substance though I failed to get any results out of electronites . . .'

38 TCC: Houghton 228:34. Written from Howlett's Hotel, Manchester Square.

39 Ibid., 228: 35.

40 FO: 7/803. FO Minute 25 Oct. 1871.

41 Two copies of this document also exist in the Foreign Office archives at the PRO. Ref: FO78/2259. Quentin Keynes also has one.

42 PRO: FO78/2259. Dated 18 Aug. 1871

43 NLS: MSS13069 f.201. Elliot to Granville, 17 Oct. 1871.

44 *Life*, vol. I: p. 591.

45 PRO: FO78/2259. Granville to RFB, 25 Oct. 1871.

46 WRO: 2667/26 Box 2 (ii) 7. RFB to Granville, 1 Nov. 1871.

47 *The Romance*, p. 526.

48 *General Rigby*, p. 276.

49 Richard wrote: ' Sir R.I. Murchison has passed away, full of years and honours, I had not the melancholy satisfaction of seeing for the last time our revered Chief, one of whose latest actions was to oppose my reading a paper about the so-called Victoria Nyanza before the Royal Geographical Society; whilst another was to erase my name from the list of Nile Explorers when revising his own biography. But peace be to his manes! I respect the silence of a newly made grave.' See also *The Times*, 28 Oct. 1871. Letter from Burton protesting that the obituary of Murchison quoted the address to which Isabel had taken exception, and coupled Murchison with Speke, Grant, Livingstone and Baker in the researches of the Nile. This omitted any mention of 'the man who led the first expedition in to the Lake regions which are now known to send forth the Nile.' In his Journal Burton wrote that Murchison hated him, and had 'done me the honour of not honouring me.' *Life*, vol. I: p. 593.

50 *Zanzibar*, vol. II: p. 370.

51 *General Rigby*, op. cit.

52 *The Romance*, p. 526.

53 EM collection at HL: three letters from IB to Tinsley, specifically 16 Oct. 1871. Uncatalogued: file B335.

54 TCC: Houghton 4:214 (1).

55 *The Romance*, p. 527.

56 *The Times*, 18 Dec. 1871.

57 *Life*, vol. I: p. 591.

58 QK collection. Burton to Hunt, Garswood, Christmas Eve 1871.

59 *Life*, vol. I: p. 591.

60 Home of Lord Derby, formerly Lord Stanley, who had given Richard the post at Damascus.

61 TCC: Houghton 228:36. From Garswood, 1 Jan. 1872.

62 Quoted in Wright, *Sir Richard Burton*, vol.I: p. 228. IB to Georgiana Stisted, 4 Jan. 1872.

63 RGS: Burton correspondence. RFB to Bates, Garswood, 18 Jan. 1872

64 TCC: Houghton 4:194. IB to Houghton, 10 Jan. 1872.
65 Ibid.
66 This inscribed copy of *Zanzibar* in original binding was offered for sale in 1996 by Gerald Rilling Books (USA) at $5,800. The cost reflects Tinsley's hasty work on the first edition, Rilling commented that the book is seldom found in its original binding as the book 'was poorly bound by the publisher'.
67 It is obvious that this was their habitual manner of addressing each other. There are half a dozen examples in the Burtons' library where Burton addresses Isabel as 'darling'; and on one occasion as 'my darling wife, Pet'.
68 Isabel did write to Georgiana on 2 Feb.: '. . . Khamour was charming at the theatre. I cried at something touching and she, not knowing why, flung her arms around my neck and howled . . . She was awfully shocked at the rustic swains and girls embracing each other.'
69 QK collection.
70 See also RGS: RFB to Henry Bates, 34 Queen Street, Edinburgh, 26 Jan. 1872. 'My mother-in-law is very ill, so I may be obliged to return to London at once. If not I stay here till the end of February . . .'
71 Public thanksgiving for the recovery of the Prince of Wales from typhoid.
72 Isabel to Georgiana Stisted, 29 Feb. 1872. Quoted in Wright, *Sir Richard Burton*, vol. I: p. 26.
73 *Literary Remains*, p. 39, also letters from Drake to Burton in QK collection.
74 *Life*, vol. I: p. 596.
75 Ibid., pp. 593–4.
76 Ibid.
77 Ormond, Richard and Leonée, *Lord Leighton* (Yale University Press, 1975), p. 121.
78 *Life*, vol. I: p. 596.
79 Now in the National Portrait Gallery.
80 Ormond, *Lord Leighton*, p. 121.
81 In 1876 while visiting India Richard kept a promise to Leighton to 'try to find some beautiful tiles, from an old house being torn down', which the artist wanted to complete the Oriental decor of his house. 'These are taken from the tomb (Moslem) of Sakhar, on the Indus. I can give you analysis of the glaze if you want it,' Richard wrote, 'the yellow colour is by far the rarest and least durable . . . the blues are the favourite and the best.'
82 TCC: Houghton 4:195. IB to Houghton, 12 April 1872.
83 *Blackwood's Magazine: Zanzibar, a review*, April 1872, p. 691 et seq.
84 Stisted, *The True Life*, p. 336.
85 NLS: MSS2031 f.103–5. Burton to Murray, 3 Sept. 1872.
86 Quoted in Wright, *Sir Richard Burton*, vol. I: p. 226.
87 *D.N.B.*: vol. 33 p. 139.
88 PRO: FO7/803 (1872) Trieste. f.1.
89 QK collection. IB to Mrs Franks, 1 Nov. 1872.
90 TCC: Houghton 4:199. IB to Houghton (Sept. 1872).
91 The articles appeared in the *Mining Journal* and the *Morning Standard*. Copies of both are among IB's papers at WRO.
92 *Ultima Thule*. Literally: an unknown land far away.
93 QK collection. Unpublished 8-page manuscript entitled 'Preface to Second Edition'. Uncatalogued.
94 Copies of the Letters Patent referred to here are now in the EM collection at the

HL: Box 11, Envelope 5/10 (b). The title is still used, and highly regarded, in Europe.

95   TCC: Houghton 4:200. IB to Houghton. u/d Sunday. c. 14 July 1872.

96   Captain Arundell had been in command of H.M.S. *Bittern* and contracted rheumatic fever while on a passage between the West Coast of Africa and Ascension Island.

97   Wright, *Sir Richard Burton*, vol. I: p. 237.

98   PRO: FO7/803 Trieste (1872) f.4.

99   *Life*, vol. I: p. 598.

100 TCC: Houghton 228:37. Burton to Houghton, 23 Sept. 1872.

101 Stanley's Journal in the Stanley Family Archives. Quoted in Frank McLynn's *Snow Upon the Desert*, p. 290.

102 Cameron, Verney Lovett, *Burton as I knew him* (*Fortnightly Review*), vol. LIV [878–884] 1890.

103 QK collection. IB to Mrs Franks, 1 Nov. 1872. Uncatalogued.

104 *The Romance*, pp. 112–13.

105 PRO: FO7/803 f.8. Burton to FO, Nov. 1872.

Chapter 29 (1873–1875)

1   WRO: IB's Memoranda Book.

2   TCC: Houghton 228: 38.

3   WRO: Accounts submitted by the Vice-Consul to the Burtons show that their personal (not Consular) postage account averaged £15 or more a month. In those days there were 240 pence to the pound and postage ranged from one penny for inland to sixpence for overseas mail; by any arithmetic this is a minimum of 600 stamps.

4   TCC: Houghton 4:198. IB to Houghton, 18 March 1873.

5   TCC: Houghton 4:207. IB to Houghton, 3 Dec. 1876.

6   *The Romance*, p. 541.

7   WRO: IB's Memoranda Book 2667/26 p. 18a (author's page numbering).

8   TCC: Houghton 228:38. Burton to Houghton, 14 Feb. 1873.

9   Printed in Sotheby Sales catalogue. Now in the QK collection. On mourning paper bearing Burton's crest in Arabic, from Hotel de Ville, Trieste. Uncatalogued.

10   PRO: FO7/1058 (3). IB to Henry Wylde, 8 April 1883. Isabel does however, mention the General's sons, Henry (of the FO) and William, and his grandson, Gustavus, who was Vice-Consul at Jedda in 1876, in *Life*, vol. II. p. 55.

11   QK collection. RFB to Findlay, 14 March 1873 from Trieste.

12   *Morning Post*, 14 March 1873.

13   This letter from IB appeared in *The Times*, the *Pall Mall Gazette* and the *Morning Post* in March 1873.

14   Digby archives. Also *A Scandalous Life*, p. 305.

15   Jane Digby's diary. Original in Digby archives. Copy and transcript in author's collection. See November 1862.

16   *The Romance*, p. 539. Although the Digby correspondence appears not to have survived Dilly Fitzgerald's selective burning of IB's papers, it was apparently available to W.H. Wilkins when he completed Isabel's memoirs.

17   *A Scandalous Life*, p. 331.

18   PRO: FO78/2259. The original letter from Jane Digby was sent to the FO as proof of the support for RFB in Damascus.

19   PRO: FO7/819 7. 25 April 1873. RFB/FO.

20 RFB wrote an article about this visit to Rome; 'Notes on Rome' published in *Macmillan's Magazine* 1873.

21 QK. IB to Lord and Lady Arundell, Trieste, 30 June 1873. Isabel has been called a snob for her quickness to adopt the obscure title of Countess Arundell. However, it was a route by which – without wealth – the Burtons had access to people of influence. Nor was RFB unappreciative of this. In February 1874 in a letter to a cousin, St George Burton, he counselled: 'Assist your mother in drawing up a list of the . . . heirs, should the girls die without a will. As the heir to a baronetcy you would be worth ten times more than heir to an Esquireship – in snobby England.'

22 Rothschild's hotel room cost £100 a month. The Bank of England gives the equivalent value of £1 in 1873 to £33.65 today. Mr Rothschild's room therefore cost him £3,365.

23 Wright, vol. I: p. 255.

24 *Life*, vol II: p. 24.

25 Lady Paget, who presented IB and became a lifelong friend, wrote in her memoirs that in order to be admitted to this proud and exclusive society it was 'absolutely necessary to have irreproachable quarterings'. Ministers might sometimes be presented at Court, but they would never be admitted to mix in society. See *In My Tower*, Lady Walburga Paget (Hutchinson, 1924), p. 220.

26 Burton, Isabel, *A.E.I.* (William Mullan, 1879), p. 30.

27 Article by Edwin de Leon, reproduced by IB in *Life*.

28 *Life*, vol. II: p. 8.

29 Published in *The World*, 1877. Extracted in *The Romance*, p. 605.

30 *Life*, vol. II: p. 263.

31 Ibid.

32 Wright, *Sir Richard Burton*, vol. I: p. 251.

33 *Life*, vol. II: p. 255.

34 I am told that this would have been common in the Roman Catholic homes of their friends in Trieste at that time.

35 Wright, *Sir Richard Burton*, vol. I: p. 250.

36 *Life*, vol. II: p. 259.

37 TCC: Houghton 228:40. RFB to Houghton, 5 Nov. 1873.

38 QK collection. From the manuscript (probably unpublished) of RFB's long draft letter to the editor of *Ocean Highways* 1874, referring to an article by Cooley to whom RFB referred as *serpity humi* [one who crawls]. 'His speciality is to crawl, spit venom and bruise heels . . . there is sadness in the spectacle of white hairs and no wisdom . . . a friend writes to me "Is Mr Cooley a missionary or madman?" No . . . he is only a morose, peevish old man, altogether incapable of contradiction . . .'

39 Cameron, Verney Lovett, *Burton as I knew Him*.

40 TCC: Houghton 4:204. IB to Houghton, 12 Aug. 1874. This letter also referred to the recent death of Lady Houghton.

41 Walter Besant was then Secretary of the Palestine Exploration Fund.

42 Drake's servant, Habib (the same man who had painfully followed Richard to Beirut only to see Richard's ship steaming towards the horizon), was with Drake at the end and had the news relayed to Trieste.

43 *Literary Remains*, pp. 46–8.

44 At least two letters are known, dated, 7 July and 11 Sept. 1874. These were sold by Sotherans in 1930; present whereabouts unknown to the author.

45 Swinburne to George Powell, 1 Sept. 1874. Ms. in National Library of Wales.
46 EM collection at HL. RFB to Tootal, 29 Oct. 1874. Red leather-bound letter-book.
47 Two letters offered for sale by Sotherans in 1930 (the author has copies but the present whereabouts of the originals are unknown). IB to Theodore Watt-Dunton (April 1875) mentioning the interest of Tinsley and Stevens in RFB's works; and another 'to jog your memory about Etruscan book and the Icelandic notes . . .'
48 Two papers by RFB on 'Rome' were printed in *Macmillan's Magazine* in 1874–75.
49 Published by the Royal Society, Edinburgh.
50 Published by the Anthropological Society and later translated into Italian and used in universities there.
51 Published by the Anthropological Society, 1875.
52 *Journal of the Society of Arts*, 29 Oct. and 5 Nov. 1875.
53 RGS.
54 Anthropological Society.
55 From paperwork in the author's collection and at WRO in IB's handwriting. Also QK; IB to Tinsley, 16 Jan. 1875. A large number of unpublished mss. by RFB exist at the PRO and WRO.
56 A good deal of technical information in *Inner Life* was taken from Murray's *Handbook for Travellers in Syria and Palestine*, but IB did not plagiarise; she used the book as an *aide memoire*. Her copy of Murray's handbook, extensively annotated and corrected by both Isabel and Richard, survives in the remnants of the Burtons' library at HL.
57 EM collection at HL. RFB to Tootal, 10 April 1975. Uncatalogued, in red leather-bound letterbook.
58 EM. IB to Mr Friswell, 7 Feb. 1875.
59 TCC: Houghton 4:205.
60 TCC: Houghton 4:206. IB to Houghton, 21 Feb. [1875].
61 WRO. Arundell Papers 2667. Uncatalogued.
62 TCC: Houghton 228:42. 2 March 1875.
63 TCC: Houghton 228:44. 3 April 1875.
64 H.S. Ashbee left his massive library to the British Museum, having published a three-volume catalogue (with extracts) of erotica and the banned books of the world. His pseudonym *Pisanus Fraxi* was derived: *Fraxi* from l. *fraxinus* for 'ash-tree' or 'ash'; *Pisanus* is assumed to be a scatalogical pun.
65 F.F. Arbuthnot to H.S. Ashbee. Quoted by W.G. Archer in his Introduction to the *Kama Sutra*, 1963.
66 H.S. Ashbee in his opus on banned books (*Index Liborum Prohibitorum; Notes on Curious and Uncommon Books*, pub: 1877–1885), identified Arbuthnot and Burton as the authors, and stated that of this first edition, 'only four [proof] copies exist, for the printer, on reading the book, became alarmed at the nature of the book, and refused to print off the edition.' Richard later corrected Ashbee: 'The work . . . contains ten chapters, and has been translated into English, but only six copies were printed for private circulation'. Scholars suggest that, alarmed by the publisher's attitude, Ashburton opted for discretion, 'deeming it better to postpone full publication until later'.
67 RFB's dedication in *Kama Sutra*.
68 RFB's Introduction to *Kama Sutra* (1883), p. 8.

69 PRO: FO7/860 (9). RFB to Derby, 15 June 1875. Petitioning for honours was quite normal in the nineteenth century.

70 TCC: Houghton 228:43. RFB/Houghton, 15 June 1875.

71 Ditto.

72 Houghton advised Burton who was behind this. 'I am glad indeed that Lord G[ranville] was not the author,' Richard responded. 'The Council being Anglo-Indian snobs of a high order have acted with an appropriateness which satisfies my mind – if it does not please it. Indian officials eat abominations through youth . . . the practice of answering one's enemy at the gate is a domestic institution [and] a public difference never fails to become a private grudge. I have the satisfaction of being on the worst possible terms with Hogg (*that* hog as old Charley of Sindh always called him), Vivian, Sir Irksome etc, and they rarely waste an opportunity to make me as they say westward smell par-tik-lar smell.'

73 EM collection at HL. RFB to Albert Tootal, 24 May 1875. Among many guests to the divans were publishers James Friswell and James Cotton; geographers and anthropologists Walter Besant, James Hunt, and Admiral George Back; the artists Lord Leighton and Holman Hunt; the writer Wilkie Collins, and the cartoonist Carlo Pellegrini whose cruel 'Spy' caricature of Burton was, Isabel said, 'his only failure'.

74 TCC: Houghton 228:46.

75 *Swinburne's Letters*, No. 646, 30 Aug. 1875, Swinburne to Theodore Watts.

76 BL: MSS53892 Wentworth Bequest. 5 Dec. 1878.

77 WRO: Arundell 2667/26. Draft letter by IB to unnamed reader, undated, uncatalogued.

78 WRO: Mrs Major to IB, 5 Jan. 1877. Uncataloged.

79 TCC: Houghton 4:207.

80 PRO: FO7/860 (10 and 11). A note attached to RFB's request for extended leave by 'M.W.' states that Burton had already had six months' leave but, 'I am not aware that the service will suffer by the prolonged absence of Capt'n Burton from his post . . .' He suggested leave could be extended to 31 Dec. and then 31 April 'if necessary', which was approved by Derby. When RFB applied for a 2nd extension in Dec., 'M.W.' queried the application, having heard of the expedition to Iceland. Derby cut across the arguments with a firm, 'Give him leave for the time originally asked for – the end of April. D.'

81 Thomas Wright suggests a serious dissension by incorrectly stating that the couple spent the summer of 1875 apart 'from July 6th . . . to October 6th' (vol I: p. 260). This has been picked up and used in several subsequent biographies. However, as surviving correspondence clearly shows the Burtons were together for several weeks in Aug. at Castle Malahide, and visited friends together in Sept.

82 The bulk of the correspondence regarding this affair survives at WRO. Other papers are held in private collections.

83 NLS: MSS17909:61. Rigby to Grant, 26 Oct. 1875.

84 *A.E.I.*, Chapter 1.

85 WRO: Arundell 2667/26. In IB's Memoranda Book her job specification for 'a new maid' reads: 'must do my room, her room, dust the drawing room, feed my birds, Capt'n Burton's clothes, iron a dressing gown or dress of mine, wash lace, do my hair, wash dresses etc. On journeys she must do all for us both, [be] kind if sick and not fail. She must have good health and nerves and have a cheerfull temper, and not fuss and not want to be married. Someone who won't spoil and become rude or infirm.'

86 *Life*, vol. II: p. 52; and *A.E.I.*, p. 28.

Chapter 30 (1876–1879)
1 *Life*, vol. II: p. 61.
2 *Bailey's Magazine*, April 1883.
3 IOR: Papers of W.G. Archer, also *D.N.B.*
4 There is also reason to assume that Lord Houghton was somehow involved in the publication of this first version of *Kama Sutra* for it bore the name of a fictitious printer, Cosmopoli. Thirty years earlier this had been used by a group of 'like-minded men' (i.e. collectors of erotica) under the nominal chairmanship of Richard Monckton Milnes (before he became Lord Houghton).
5 WRO: Statements written and signed by IB regarding *The Perfumed Garden*.
6 *Life*, vol. II: p. 65.
7 IB reveals in *A.E.I.* and in *Life* that RFB had told her of the Persian girl, Núr Ján, and the kidnapped nun.
8 *Sind Revisited*, vol. I: pp. 47 and 257.
9 See for example: *Noted from the Mediterranean* by F.R. Baker, 4 Nov. 1876. The article deals with Richard's views on the troubled state of affairs in Turkey and Algeria.
10 EM collection at HL. RFB to Grattan Geary, 13 July 1877.
11 *Life*, vol. II: p. 117.
12 QK collection. Cameron to Burton, 23 June 1876.
13 EM collection at HL Box 11: 4 (10). RFB to Dr Edward Burton, 24 June 1876.
14 EM: Tan bound letterbook containing 17 letters from RFB to Grattan Geary (1), 20 June 1976.
15 RGS. RFB to H.W. Bates, 2 July 1876.
16 RGS. RFB to H.W. Bates, 27 July 1876.
17 RL. RFB to Freeman, 7 Sept. 1876.
18 Freeman shared Burton's hatred of the Turks and was an early critic of the Crimean War because it upheld them, and also served the purposes of the French. He was deeply moved, as was Burton, by the Turkish atrocities in the Slavonic provinces. The correspondence between these two men can be seen in three main archives: Trinity College (Freeman Papers); Richmond Library (Burton Collection) and WRO (Arundell papers).
19 EM collection at HL. RFB to Grattan Geary, 1 Sept. 1876. 'Do you ever read the Daily News, especially the letters of "Conscience"? I'm Conscience, but don't publish the fact . . .'
20 Ibid., RFB to Grattan Geary, 2 Nov. 1876, re submission of five 'Pantillarias' letters for publication on condition 'you promise me absolutely that this secret will not be told to a soul – Lord Derby is not the only one I want to be kept in the dark! You can't believe a word in the English papers. All are writing Party, none the truth.'
21 Maggs Catalogue 1940 letter 627. RFB/James S. Cotton, editor of the *Athenaeum*, 12 Sept. u/d.
22 RL. RFB to Freeman, 7 Sept. 1876.
23 WRO: Box 2 (iv) 50b. Freeman to RFB, 10 Nov. 1876.
24 EM. 30 Nov. 1876
25 WRO: Among IB's papers are the printed programmes of many functions which RFB attended or addressed. In many of these the name Rudolphe Arundell R.N.

also appears. His presence among Burton's party (with Houghton *et al*) was also frequently noted in newspapers.

26   *The Romance*, p. 610.
27   QK collection. IB to 'John and Lucy' (Lord and Lady Arundell), 27 Aug. 1876.
28   *The Romance*, vol. II: p. 711, where the document is photographically reproduced.
29   WRO: (uncatalogued). There are numerous documents in both IB's and RFB's handwriting on this subject. From the information gathered, IB prepared, and had printed, a Burton 'pedigree'.
30   Ibid., and letter from RFB to Mrs E.J. Burton, 18 Jan. 1877, reproduced in Wright's biography of Burton.
31   Fawn Brodie in *The Devil Drives*, pp. 30 and 345 (n.20). Brodie found IB's attitude here 'amusing', claiming Isabel had altered the pedigree in RF's handwriting in favour of respectability by adding that the King had 'morganatically married the Countess'. Bastardy was a significant social stigma, but the Trowbridge papers demonstrate that RFB wanted to prove that he was a 'legal' descendant of the French King. The most likely explanation is that she did this on RFB's instruction.
32   Many European titles still in use today are those of the Holy Roman Empire. The British tend to regard them as second class.
33   TCC: Houghton 4:208. IB to Houghton, 20 April 1877.
34   QK collection.
35   PRO: FO7/914 (6). RFB to Derby, 21 April 1877.
36   TCC: Houghton 4:208. IB to Houghton, 20 April 1877.
37   *Life*, vol. II: p. 127.
38   EM. Box 11: 5 (10). IB to Albert Tootal, 18 Oct. 1878.
39   Smith, L.A; 'Recollections of Sir Richard Burton', *Paternoster Review*, Dec. 1890.
40   IB, 'Fryston Hall', published in *The World*, Jan. 20, 1877.
41   The review was syndicated; the copy used here is from the *Times of India*, 27 March 1877 in QK collection.
42   Gordon to RFB, 12 Jan. 1877. Reproduced in *The Romance*, 'I may tell you that your book was thought by us all out in Africa as by far the best ever written . . .'
43   EM. Unnumbered Box. File B347 (1). Draft letter from RFB to *Saturday Review*.
44   WRO. Uncatalogued. Gordon to RFB, 21 June 1877. Also reproduced in *The Romance*.
45   Ibid.
46   'Honour not Honours' was Camoens' motto. Richard had come across it when he first began reading Camoens; he had recently started quoting it as his own maxim.
47   Extracted from unidentified sale catalogue in QK collection. RFB to Ismael, Khedive of Egypt, 28 Sept. 1877.
48   PRO: FO7/914 (8). RFB to FO, 20 Sept. 1877.
49   PRO: FO7/942 (9).
50   WRO: uncatalogued. Letter in Arabic to RFB. Translated by Tariq and Jehan Rajab of the New English School in Kuwait.
51   EM. Unnumbered box; file 334. IB to Luke Ionides, 12 Nov. 1877.
52   HL. 'Captain Burton's Private Account for quarter ended 31 Dec. 1877.' Made up by E.W. Brock.
53   Burton, Richard F., *The Gold Mines of Midian and the Ruined Midianite Cities: A Fortnight's Tour in North-Western Arabia* (Kegan Paul, 1878).

54 *Life*, vol. II: p. 128.
55 Wright, *Sir Richard Burton*, vol. II: p. 281.
56 School of Oriental and African Studies, London. MS204772 (15). Papers of Richard Lyon Nosworthy Mitchell.
57 Charles Gordon to RFB, 31 Aug. 1879. Entire letter reproduced in *The Romance*.
58 WRO: Arundell 2667 press cutting. Uncatalogued. Home News, 1 June 1878.
59 PRO: FO7/977 (3). Printed pamphlet by RFB; *Report on the Minerals of Midian* December 1878. Also, EM: RFB's own note and papers from the Midian expeditions Box 8:4 (1–79).
60 *Life*, vol II: p. 191.
61 *Land of the Midian*, vol. II: pp. 259–60.
62 *The Gold Mines of Midian*, p. 1.
63 Burton, Richard F: *Land of Midian* (revisited) (Kegan Paul, 1879), vol. II: p. 260.

Chapter 31 (1879–1880)

 1 Gordon to RFB, 8 Aug. 1878 (unidentified source due to lost research note). The original is either at the Huntington or the RGS. It is largely reproduced in *The Romance*, p. 663.
 2 Ibid.
 3 Stoker, Bram, *Reminiscences of Henry Irving* (Macmillan, 1906), vol. I: pp. 250–51.
 4 EM. Box 11: 5 (10). IB to Albert Tootal, 18 Oct. 1878.
 5 QK collection. RFB to Quaritsch: 'I want you to publish for me a short affair in verse. The MS will be . . . sent to you by a friend in London. Mind for the present it is to be a complete secret. My wife doesn't know about it and that's the test. I want your advice on the poem. . . . the lines are of 16 syllables and despite their length they would fit in without tails below them . . .' QK also owns the original manuscript of the *Kasidah*.
 6 The *Bibliophile*, 3 July 1909, pp. 238–40.
 7 TCC: Houghton 4:209. IB to Houghton, 15 Sept. 1878.
 8 WRO: uncatalogued. The complete Assay Report and related correspondence survive among IB's papers. Also details of archaeological finds.
 9 PRO: FO7/977 (3). John Percy, M.D., F.R.S. (metallurgist at the Royal School of Mines) to RFB, 13 Dec. 1878.
10 Author's collection. RFB to George Marie (in French), 6 Oct. 1878.
11 PRO: FO7/977 (3). *Report on the Minerals of Midian*.
12 'A Sketch of the Career of Richard F. Burton'. Pamphlet by An Oxonian and Others, 1886. p. 23.
13 PRO: FO7977 (3). 27 Jan. 1879.
14 PRO: FO7/942 (16). RFB to FO, 17 Nov. 1878.
15 Reproduced in Wright, *Sir Richard Burton*, vol. I: p. 284.
16 TCC: Houghton 4:210. IB to Houghton, 19 Nov. 1878.
17 *The Spiritualist*, Dec. 1878.
18 *Life*, vol. II: p. 159.
19 QK collection. RFB to Gerald Massey, 28 May 1881.
20 Manuscripts exist of some of these dialogues, in RFB's handwriting but purporting to be written by IB. WRO. Uncatalogued.
21 Stoker, *Reminiscences*, vol. I: 361.

22 De Leon, E: *Thirty Years of my Life*, p. 251.

23 Smalley, G.W., *New York Tribune*, 2 Nov. 1890. 'Sir Richard Burton by "GWS".'

24 WRO: Arundell 2667. Uncatalogued. Schweinfurther to RFB, 9 Feb. 1879.

25 HL: RFB to Grattan Geary (he always addressed him as 'GG'), 5 May 1879. '. . . From time to time I can write you a letter from Pantillarias. You never told me if the dodge was guessed (of course it was); or what people said of them. I suppose none understood – save yourself . . .'

26 *Life*, vol. II: p. 166.

27 WRO: RFB's sketch book. Uncatalogued.

28 RGS: RFB to Markham, 26 Oct. 1879.

29 HL: Parts of this unpublished manuscript survive in EM collection at HL. The opening chapter was also printed as a pamphlet and is contained in the Burtons' own library at the Huntington, see B/L 117 (bound with 219). The contents list includes: '1. The Government Steamer that took us to Sind . . . 3. Mr Burton proposes to show his friend something of India . . . 14. We prepare to quit Hyderabad . . . 20. A ride to Ameer Ibrahim Kan Talpur's village . . .' Other parts were used in *Life*.

30 The book was, in fact, typeset as the *Midsummer Book for Boys* and had already been 'corrected for press,' when – as Isabel advised Lord Houghton (TCC: Houghton 4:212) – the alcoholic publisher collapsed. 'His father had to get him home and close the London house. My book is therefore at the printers hanging fire, and my draft of £100 returned unaccepted.' Subsequently the manuscript was lost, and Isabel recovered only a part which is now in the possession of EM.

31 WRO: 2267/26 Box 4 (uncatalogued letters). Dr F. MacLaghan to IB, 18 Jan. 1880.

32 WRO: Uncatalogued. W.R. Smith to RFB, 25 March 1880.

33 Burton: 'How to deal with the Slave Trade in Egypt.' A report submitted to FO in May 1880. Reproduced in *Life*, vol. II: pp. 195–210.

34 *Supplemental Nights*, vol. I: p. 70 n.2

35 Reproduced in *Life*, vol. II: p. 195. RFB to Granville, 3 May 1880.

36 WRO: Arundell 2667/26 Box 3 (uncatalogued). IB's handwritten summary of her medical condition.

37 Most of these letters survive, scattered among a number of collections. But they are printed virtually in full in *The Romance*, pp. 645–76. My comparisons of the printed letters with the surviving manuscripts show that they are accurately transcribed.

38 *Life*, vol. II: p. 177.

39 *Swinburne's letters*, vol. IV: p. 135. Swinburne to Houghton, 2 April 1880. While Isabel was convalescing during the spring of 1880 she visited Swinburne's home, The Pines, Putney Hill. 'We lunch, smoke a cigarette in Swinburne's charming den and [return] to town,' she said, adding a postscript to one of Swinburne's letters to Houghton. 'Swinburne looking so well and cheerful and we have been very merry.'

40 QK collection. IB to Mrs White-Cooper, 21 July 1880.

41 Ibid. The famous Passion Play is performed at the village every ten years in fulfilment of a vow made by the villagers in 1633 after the plague bypassed them.

42 Burton, Isabel, *The Passion Play at Omer-Ammergau* (Hutchinson, 1900), p. 70.

43 TCC: Houghton 228:39. RFB to Houghton, 3 Sept. 1880.

44 Ibid.

45 Ibid.

46 TCC: Houghton 4:212. IB to Houghton, 3 c. Sept. 1880.

47 Published by Tinsley 1880.

48 EM: RFB to Tinsley, 2 June 1881. 'You have brought it out very nicely, but that you always do.'

49 The outline for IB's untitled novel (in her Memoranda Book), as well as the ms. of *Irecema*, is among her papers at WRO.

50 IB to Georgiana Stisted, 4 Sept. 1880. Extracts printed in Wright, vol. II: p. 19.

51 'To My Master Camoens', see prelim. pages of *Os Lusiads*.

52 WRO: Arundell 2667/26 Box 2. (xiv)/2. RFB to Don Pedro II; draft letter in RFB's hand.

53 *The Scotsman*, 21 Feb. 1881. Richard's reaction was in verse:

> Perpend what curious fate be mine,
> How queer be Fortune's rigs
> That set my sweets before the swine,
> My pearls before the pigs!

54 HL: BL90. This letter is preserved in one of Richard's copies of *Camoens*.

55 HL: B/L 90. Holograph ALS. Lallah Bird to RFB, 4 Dec. 1884.

56 Burton, Richard F., *Camoens: The Lyricks*, vol. 1 frontispiece.

57 Atkinson, William C., *Camoens: The Lusiads* (Penguin, 1952), p. 34.

58 See lot 126 in Sotheby's *Catalogue of the Library of Algernon Charles Swinburne*, 19 June 1916. Also, *Swinburne's letters*, vol. v: p. 88. Isabel identified 'Frances' as 'me' but gave no further explanation.

59 Swinburne to RFB. Reproduced in *Life*, vol. II: p. 183.

60 HL: BL79b.

61 QK collection.

62 *Life*, vol. II: p. 434–6. Although IB does not give the name of this woman, it would probably be possible to identify her from the comprehensive lists IB made of all her friends and acquaintances in Trieste, and the known facts about 'It': i.e. English, married with several daughters, in good society, died in 1891 etc.

63 WRO: Arundell 2667/26 Box 3. Uncatalogued. Summary of IB's medical condition in her handwriting.

64 These were the forms of address used by all three in surviving correspondence in various collections. e.g. HL Burton, Box 2/11, Letter in Cameron's writing to 'Boy No. 1' signed 'Boy No. 2' refers to Isabel; 'love to the nurse'.

65 Cameron, V.L. *Burton as I knew Him*.

66 Ibid.

67 *Life*, vol. II: p. 223.

68 EM: RFB's working notes for *The Sword*.

69 Maggs Catalogue Summer 1920. Letter #1082. RFB to J.S. Cotton of The Academy, 9 Oct. c.1881. Lane's version contained only a third of the known stories, and was written, according to one reviewer 'in the baldest and most prosaic of English'.

70 Redesdale, *Memories*, vol. II: p. 573.

71 QK. RFB to Massey, 30 July 1881.

72 QK. Massey/7. Burton to Gerald Massey, 19 Aug. 1881.

73 Thomas Wright and John Payne claimed that Burton had not started work on the *Nights* prior to his contacting Payne in November 1881. However, there are

several extant letters prior to 1880 in which he mentions to correspondents that he is working on the subject. In addition there is the testimony of Redesdale, Mitchell and Stoker that Burton was already actively working on manuscripts of the *Nights* in the 1870s.

74 *Athenaeum*, 26 Nov. 1881.

Chapter 32 (1881–1883)

1 EM: Box 1/B342 (2). RFB to Irvine, 12 June 1889.
2 WRO: 2667/26 2 (xiv). Draft letter in RFB's handwriting for IB to copy out as though from her, 10 July 1881.
3 QK. RFB to Ouida, 3 Dec. c.1881.
4 IB to Miss E.H. Bishop, 5 Dec. 1881. See also *The Romance*, pp. 632–3.
5 QK. Cameron to IB, 5 Dec. 1881.
6 WRO: 2667/26 uncatalogued. Irvine to RFB, 19 Jan. 1882.
7 QK collection.
8 Ibid. There are several dozen letters between IB, RFB and Irvine at Trowbridge dealing with the West African mining project in Box 2 (iv) 35 (author's own cataloguing).
9 *Life*, vol II: p. 226.
10 Ibid., p. 229.
11 EM: Box 1/B342 (2). RFB to Irvine, 12 June 1889.
12 Frustrated by the 'apathy, drunkenness and dishonesty' of the West Africans at the mine sites, Burton suggested they transport a large force of Chinese workers to West Africa. This involved a trip to China by himself and Isabel, the expenses for which were to be paid by the company.
13 WRO: Arundell 2667/26 (xviii) f.33. James Irvine to IB, 24 May 1882, and f.39 to RFB, 25 May 1882.
14 EM: Box 10 2 (5). Cameron to the Burtons, July 1882.
15 Notice to Shareholders of the Gold Coast Gold Mining Company, 7 April 1884. 'It is an open secret that the new Board . . . are much disappointed at the insufficient response to their recent appeal for additional capital . . .' WRO: 2667/26 (uncatalogued) with Irvine papers.
16 In response to Isabel's request for an advance against profits to cover part of his expenses, Irvine sent Richard £165. In 1888 when Irvine was in desperate circumstances he asked for this money back. Isabel and the Birds were opposed to returning it but Richard insisted upon doing so. See letters in QK collection.
17 WRO: 2667/26 (xviii) f.54/1. Grant (Mine Manager in West Africa) to RFB, 8 Aug. 1882: 'It pains me . . . that after all the ups and downs of Commander Cameron and the esteem he holds, that by one single act he may . . . lose all. An act which if anyone [else] committed, nothing would be thought of further . . . at the regular time.'
18 WRO: 2667/26 2 (xviii) f.58. Irvine to RFB, 5 Sept. 1882; regretting to learn 'Lord Granville requests your resignation of Director . . . you undoubtedly have no choice in the matter, though it is not so long ago since I saw Lord Granville's name . . . as Managing Director of a large colliery . . .'
19 PRO: General FO directive, 9 March 1881.
20 PRO: FO7/1043 (15). FO correspondence regarding RFB's application for extended leave of absence.
21 PRO: FO7/1041 (7). RFB to Lord Granville, 7 Sept. 1882.
22 WRO: 2667/26 (xviii) folio (uncatalogued). Irvine to RFB, 26 Sept. 1882.

23 WRO: Arundell 2667/26 (uncatalogued). Irvine to RFB, 13 Oct. 1882.

24 Maggs Catalogue. This letter from RFB to Tinsley was offered for sale in several editions of the catalogue eg: #270/57. 24 Sept. [1882]. Its present whereabouts are unknown to the author.

25 Quaritsch correspondence is taken from quotations in various sale catalogues in the QK collection.

26 *Bookman and Print Collector*, 21 Jan. 1921.

27 PRO: FO7/1041 (2). Draft order from Lord Granville, 27 Oct. 1882.

28 EM: Box 6. Working papers on Burton's Midian expeditions. RFB used some of these notes in his paper 'Report on the Search for Palmer'. Reproduced in *Life*, vol. II: p. 591.

29 RFB said of Palmer: 'He mastered [languages] as a musical genius learns an instrument; he picked up words, sentences and idioms like a clever child with the least possible study of grammar and syntax. The truth is he was *supra grammaticans* and . . . revelled . . . in his exceptional power of appreciating dialectic differences . . .' *Life*, vol. II: p. 609.

30 Howarth, David and Stephen, *The P. & O. Story* (Weidenfeld & Nicholson, 1986), pp. 105–106.

31 Besant, Sir Walter, *Life & Achievements of E.H. Palmer* (1883), pp. 253–4.

32 PRO: FO7/1042 (11-12). The first in Burton's handwriting, 16 Nov., the second in Isabel's handwriting signed by Burton, dated 11 Dec. 1882 (the day of his return to Trieste).

33 EM: Box 6. Working papers on Burton's Midian expeditions. RFB used some of these notes in his paper 'Report on the Search for Palmer'. Reproduced in *Life*, vol. II: p. 591.

34 Ibid.

35 QK: RFB to Ouida, c. January 1883.

36 Part of Burton's library is housed at HL in California; part at Richmond City Library, England. Many of his books are extensively annotated and in the case of some, *Stone Talk* for example, where he has used an early edition as the basis for a new one, the pages are crammed with unpublished revisions.

Chapter 33 (1883–1886)

1 *Life*, vol. II: p. 246.

2 The Burtons never occupied the entire property. In a letter to J.J. Fahie [Bodleian] 11 Oct. 1887, IB states: 'I have got the whole of the apartment now – almost 20 rooms and I have made it so pretty you would not know it again'.

3 *Life*, vol. II: p. 247.

4 Archer's introduction to the *Kama Sutra* (George Allen & Unwin, 1963).

5 Ibid., p. 36.

6 RFB and Arbuthnot initially debated whether to use Latin to describe male and female sex organs (as Burton had done previously to describe female circumcision). Eventually they decided to retain the original terms: yoni and lingham.

7 Preface; *Kama Sutra* (Kama Shastra Society, 1883), p. 6.

8 Ouida, 'Richard Burton', *Fortnightly Review*, vol. 85, June 1906, pp. 1039–45.

9 *Life*, vol. II: p. 272.

10 Ibid., p. 273

11 Ibid.

12 PRO: FO7/1086 (1–5). '. . . The climate of Trieste never agreed with Burton and

it first made inroads on his health soon after his appointment in 1872. Granted.'

13 *Life*, vol. II: p. 275.
14 EM: RFB to Payne, 1 Oct. 1884.
15 Ibid., 12 Aug. 1884
16 EM: Box 11. RFB to Payne, 22 May 1883.
17 EM: Box 11/5 (10). IB to Albert Tootal, 19 Feb. 1885.
18 EM: RFB to Payne, 1 Oct. 1884.
19 EM: 22 Oct. 1884.
20 Wright, Thomas, *Life of John Payne* (Fisher Unwin, 1919). The British Museum library copy is the author's own copy, annotated interleaved with unpublished revisions, p. 88.
21 QK. IB to Ouida, 23 Oct. 1884.
22 *The Romance* , p. 675.
23 EM: Box 11/5 (10). IB to Albert Tootal, 19 Feb. 1885.
24 PRO: FO7/1086 (5). RFB's doctor certified that 'out of eighteen months he has had only five months free of suffering . . .' Salisbury granted the request asking for permission to winter in Morocco, commenting: 'He is an old man, in his 65th year . . . and has been badly knocked about in his time . . .'
25 Bodleian Library. Fahie Papers MSS. Eng. Mis. d.187 (1919). IB to J.J. Fahie, 3 March 1885.
26 EM: uncatalogued leather-bound volume of correspondence between IB and Mr Notcutt of Waterlow Publishers Ltd. IB to Mr Notcutt, 13 June 1885.
27 EM: Notcutt correspondence. IB to Mr Notcutt, 27 June 1885.
28 EM: Friswell and Lynton Letters. IB to Lynton, 'My dear Friend', 28 July 1885.
29 QK (ex Burke Casari collection). IB to Lynne Lynton, July 1885.
30 The portrait referred to is a photograph by Barrand. It was later copied in oils by Albert Letchford.
31 WRO: drafts of some of IB's correspondence with publishers are scribbled into her Memoranda Book. Collections of her correspondence with other publishers such as Notcutt, Tinsley etc. are referred to elsewhere in the notes.
32 *Swinburne's Letters*, Swinburne to Lady Henrietta Swinburne, 12 Aug. 1885. Also vol. V, p. 208; Swinburne comments that in a recent hot spell his niece, Isabel, had become 'as [dark] as her namesake, Lady Burton'.
33 EM: Cameron correspondence (f.38). VLC to RFB, 18 Nov. 1884.
34 *Life*, vol. II: p. 317.
35 HL. B/l 91a.
36 *Nights*, vol. X: pp. 203–4 and vol. XVI, p. 431.
37 QK. IB to Mr Notcutt, publisher, June 1885.
38 *Life*, vol. II: p. 284.
39 Ibid., p. 442.
40 PRO: FO7/1086 (5).
41 Wright, vol. II: p. 133.
42 Since IB published this document in full after RFB's death (*Life*, vol. II: pp. 294–6) Blunt was aware of Burton's poor opinion of him. Blunt's jaundiced remarks about Burton in his book *My Diaries*, quoted in an earlier chapter, should therefore be viewed in this light. Blunt admitted that they were written from memory (c.1925) as he had not kept a diary in South America.
43 *Life*, vol. II: pp. 294–6.
44 Harris, Frank, *My Life & Loves*, p. 563.
45 Wright, vol. II: p. 94.

46 QK. IB to Ouida, 12 Nov. 18[85].
47 EM: Burton/Notcutt correspondence.
48 QK. RFB to William Forrell Kirby, 12 Dec. 1885.
49 QK collection. This important 17-page document, a continuation in Burton's own hand of the autobiography dictated to Isabel during their Indian trip, may well have been one of the last things Burton wrote since he refers to 'the six ensuing years [from] the end of 1885'.
50 EM: Burton/Payne correspondence, Box 11/2 (10).
51 *Life*, vol. II: p. 311. Isabel gave as a footnote here the answer to why they often travelled apart. Sometimes it was necessary because of work for each to be in a different place, 'but mostly it was lack of money. If there was enough for one, he went; when there was enough for two, we both went.'
52 'Half-a-crown'; for two shillings and sixpence; in 1998 terms, approximately £5.
53 Smith, L.A., 'Recollections of Sir Richard Burton' in *Paternoster Review*, Dec. 1890.
54 QK. RFB to Ouida, 2 April 1886.
55 *Life*, vol. II: p. 311.
56 IB to E.N. Bishop, 16 Feb. 1886.
57 For example see Bodleian Library. Fahie Correspondence Western MSS: Eng Misc. d.187. IB to Fahie 8 Feb. Gives return address as Isabel Burton.
58 QK collection. Isabel reprinted part of this document and referred to it as coming from his Journal. See *Life*, vol. II: p. 311. It forms part of the 17-page addition to his 'Autobiography from 1886' referred to in an earlier note.
59 Bodleian Library. Fahie, 17 April 1886.
60 *Life*, vol. II: p. 316.
61 FO: 7/1105 (7).
62 QK. RFB mentions in his 'autobiography' the fact that his father-in-law's death cast a cloud over their return to England. 'The good old father, Henry Raymond Arundell, had quietly passed away . . . and the house which had formed a *point de reunion* had to be given up. It was the link which held together a large and united household which once separated would never again unite upon the old terms. All will understand how painful are such final breakings up . . .'
63 Somerset House. Last will and testament of Henry Raymond Arundell. Probate granted 18 June 1886.
64 WRO: uncatalogued. 12 May 1886.
65 HL: Kirby/Burton correspondence. See also Burton's *Nights*, Terminal Essay, part II, 'The Nights in Europe'.
66 *Nights*, Terminal Essay, vol. X, pp. 203–5.
67 In 1885 a law was passed, for the first time making acts of homosexuality a criminal offence. Conviction carried a two-year prison term.
68 The Terminal Essay is in volume X, pp. 205 –54.
69 Archer, Brodie, McLynn, op. cit. These three writers all cited Burton's interest in swords (being symbolic of the phallus) as evidence of his homosexuality.
70 Alan Hull Walton says 'sometime prior to 1850' in his introduction to Burton, *The Perfumed Garden* (Panther, 1963), p. 11.
71 WRO: Justin Huntley McCarthy to RFB, 17 Sept. 1886. 'I ought to have returned the "Jardin" long since . . . will send you back the volume today and volume iii will speedily follow . . .'
72 The early history of *The Perfumed Garden* can be summarised briefly as follows:
          1850   Manuscript discovered in Algiers by French Army Staff Officer.

1876 French translation printed on to lithographed sheets by French Army officers (print-run 25–35 copies). This edition is known as the 'Autograph' edition.

1885 Counterfeit 'Autograph' edition; printed, bound and published in Paris.

1886 April: Authorised 'Revised' edition printed, bound and published in Paris anonymously (by Isadore Liseux).
May: Copy of Liseux's revised edition sent to Burton.
June: Burton begins work on English translation.
c. September: First English edition published in London by Kama Shastra Society in parts held in paper covers.
c. October: Kama Shastra Society second edition, bound.

73 *The Romance*, p. 685.
74 Harris, Frank, *Contemporary Portraits*, (Methuen, 1915), p. 175.
75 PRO: FO7/1105 (11). RFB to Iddesleigh, 8 Sept. 1886
76 PRO: FO7/1105 (12). RFB to Salisbury cc. Iddesleigh, 14 Sept. 1886.
77 PRO: FO7/1153 (7). Salisbury to RFB, 19 Aug. 1889.
78 IB writes: 'I sent lithograph with note from self to Lord Derby (and his brother through him), & Lady Iddesleigh. Alston, Anderson, [&] Lister (FO); Lord Wolseley & Sir A. Herbert (Military); W.H. Smith, Mr Mathews, Lord Charles Beresford, Irving for Lord Randolph Churchill, Hon R. Burke (Ministers) . . .' A list of MPs and wives of leading men follows.
79 QK. The first of these two communications is a postcard, postmarked 21 Sept. 1886; the second a letter clearly several days later but undated. Both are signed KTT, the meaning of which is a mystery.
80 Wright, vol. II: p. 1143.
81 HL. Burton/Kirby correspondence f.19, 16 Sept. 1886.
82 *Life*, vol. II: p. 262.
83 *Nights*, vol. XVI: p. 452.
84 Justin Huntly MacCarthy published his *Ghazels from the Divan of Hafiz [Omar-i-Khayam]* in 1893. His father was an old crony of RFB's and in 1886 he corresponded with Burton on *The Perfumed Garden* and other works.
85 IB's dedication continued: 'believing that the majority can appreciate fine language, exquisite poetry and romantic Eastern Life just as well as the thousand students and scholars who secured the original thousand copies.'
86 WRO: IB to 'Writers Club', 15 Jan. 1894.
87 Schroder's sale catalogue, Lot 10. This consists of pages 63–302 of Volume 10, bound in black buckram, and '30-odd additions and corrections in the Author's hand which were for Lady Burton's Household Edition.' Accompanying letters identify the source of the material, and in one Notcutt assures the printer, 'Sir Richard Burton distinctly informed me that these portions are to be lifted bodily out.'
88 HL: Burton correspondence. Box 1. IB to Smithers, 17 July 1892.
89 Burton, *Nights*, vol. I: p. 239.
90 Ibid. p. 40.
91 Burton's own copy of his *Nights* at HL. vol. I: p. 239. Ref B/L 91a.
92 Bodleian Library. J.H. Fahie correspondence, 11 Oct. 1887.
93 McCarthy, Justin, *Reminiscences* (Chatto & Windus, 1899), pp. 330–35.
94 G.F. Watts Studio, Compton, Surrey. Open to the public.
95 QK. Ms in Burton's writing entitled 'Autobiography' MS. Burton later blamed

the treatment mentioned for his subsequent illness: 'the lithic acid expelled from the joint is absorbed in the circulation, and in the protean malady no one can tell where mischief might break out . . .'

96   Burton writes 'they', the entire manuscript being written by him in the third person; e.g. 'Burton did this, Burton did that, the Burtons etc.'

97   QK. Burton's 'Autobiography'. Isabel quoted this passage in *Life*, vol. II: pp. 330–31. Her edits are light and for the most part are confined to changes of person, 'they' to 'we' etc.

Chapter 34 (1887–1890)

 1   QK. RFB's 'Autobiography'.
 2   QK. RFB to Liseux, 20 Jan. 1887. A second letter on 6 Feb. asks for: '1. The name of the Captain who made the translation of 1850. 2. Some details concerning the Society which produced the autograph of 1876. I have no excuse for troubling you with these questions. I can plead only necessity.'
 3   QK. Burton's 'Autobiography' MS.
 4   Ibid.
 5   *Life*, vol. II: p. 337.
 6   Ibid.
 7   Formerly, Dr Baker had served 10 years as House Surgeon of a charitable institution, 'The Poplar Hospital'.
 8   From 'Sir Richard Burton as I Knew Him' by Dr F. Grenfell Baker, in *Cornhill Magazine*, Issue 304, October 1921, pp. 411–23.
 9   Cardiovascular syphilis commonly occurs within 20 or 30 years after the primary infection. It affects the aorta (aortitis), and features aneurysms (balloon-like swellings in the artery walls), which can rupture or tear, causing haemorrhages, heart failure and/or embolisms. Prognosis of death in the nineteenth century was rarely more than five years from diagnosis. Symptoms include degenerating general health.
10   IB to Alice Bird, 10 April 1887. Quoted in *The Romance*, pp. 668–9.
11   QK. Burton's 'Autobiography' MS.
12   EM: Payne correspondence. RFB to Payne from Geneva, 8 Nov. 1888, '*The Scented Garden* now begins in real earnest.'
13   Bodleian Library. J.J. Fahie correspondence. 11 Oct. 1887.
14   WRO: Hitchman documentation in IB's papers. Arundell 2667/26. Uncatalogued.
15   WRO: 2667/26. Box 4. Oct. 1887. Contained in press cuttings album with Hitchman biography reviews.
16   However, the importance of the Hitchman biography lies in the fact that the first chapters are in RFB's own words, not Hitchman's.
17   WRO: See Hitchman correspondence in IB's papers. Also IB's correspondence with editors; i.e *Western Daily Mercury*, 12 Dec. 1887.
18   Ibid., IB to Russell, 12 Dec. 1887.
19   HL: Box 2. Burton/Smithers correspondence, c.1888 et seq.
20   PRO: FO7/1125 (6) April 1877.
21   HL: Kirby correspondence. RFB to Kirby, 24 Nov. 1887.
22   HL: Kirby correspondence f.35. IB to Kirby from Hotel Stephanie, Abbazia, Sudbahn, Austria, 8 D[ec] 1887.
23   Ibid., f.34. Kirby to RFB, 18 Dec. 1887.
24   Ibid., IB to Kirby, 26 Dec. 1887.

25 *Life*, vol. II: p. 353.
26 Wright, vol. II: p. 166.
27 QK. RFB and IB to Ouida, 14 June 1888. QK also owns RFB's Introduction to the 'Black Book' referred to in this letter. The 'Black Book' mentioned by RFB was not published, but in 1964 a volume of material selectively extracted and edited and introduced by Dr Kenneth Walker M.A. from Burton's *Nights* was published under the title *Love, War and Fancy* (William Kimber).
28 *Nights*, vol. XVI: p. 452.
29 Published by Neville Spearman Ltd., Panther paperback edition 1963 and reprinted 1964, pp. 20–21.
30 WRO: Arundell collection (uncatalogued). Avery to Burton, 29 June 1888.
31 HL: Smithers correspondence. Box 1. Burton to Smithers, 20 Oct. 1888.
32 *Life*, vol. II: p. 362.
33 Wright, *Life of John Payne*, vol. I: pp. 144 and 177.
34 Stisted, *Temple Bar*, op. cit.
35 *Life*, vol. II: p. 363.
36 Stisted, *The True Life*, pp. 409–10.
37 *The Times*, 28 Dec. 1888.
38 HL: Kirby correspondence. RFB to Kirby, 4 Nov. 1888.
39 HL: Box 1. RFB to Smithers, 30 Sept. 1888 re. Erotica Biblion imprint. 'Something of the kind is necessary to abate the increasing growth of the "bawdy publisher" who asks guineas for books only worth shillings, and the books are marketed only for his own benefit.'
40 HL: Smithers correspondence. RFB to Smithers, 14 Nov. 1888.
41 Surviving Smithers/Burton correspondence runs into hundreds of letters. It is only possible in this book to quote from a small number of these.
42 Ibid. from Lausanne, 17 Feb. 1889.
43 Dislike of public displays of affection is still prevalent among the traditional upper classes in England.
44 HL: Smithers correspondence. RFB to Smithers, 31 Jan. 1889.
45 Ibid., April 1889
46 Ibid., 4 and 27 Aug.
47 HL: RFB to Payne, 15 May 1889. The book by Peter Dens referred to here was probably his *Theologia moralis et Dogmatica*.
48 HL: Smithers correspondence. Box 1 ff. 42–44, Aug. 1889.
49 Ibid. IB to Smithers. Box 2 f.105, 1 Aug. 1889.
50 These paintings survive today at the Orleans House Gallery, near Richmond. The original photographs from which they are painted are part of the Burton archives at Richmond Central Library.
51 Smithers subsequently chose the pseudonym, 'Rusticus Isidoctus' from Ephesians i: viii.
52 HL: Smithers correspondence. RFB to Smithers, 13 Sept 1889.
53 *Life*, vol. II: p. 386.
54 HL: Smithers correspondence. RFB to Smithers, 20 Dec. 1888.
55 *Life*, vol. II: p. 391.
56 HL: Smithers correspondence. RFB to Smithers, 5 March 1890.
57 Ibid. RFB to Smithers, 20 Dec. 1889.
58 Wright, vol. II: p. 217.
59 *Life*, vol II: p. 441.
60 Wright, vol. II: p. 198. u/d.

61 HL: Smithers correspondence. RFB to Smithers, Box 2 (f.81).
62 Ibid. May 1890. Though unsigned these letters are in RFB's handwriting.
63 Ibid. Burton to Smithers, unsigned.
64 Ibid. f.106. IB to Smithers, 16 May 1890.
65 Ibid. IB to Smithers, 27 May 1890
66 *Life*, vol. II: p. 364.
67 Ibid., p. 401.
68 *Pall Mall Gazette*, Nov. 1890, states that while the Burtons were at Maloja a fellow-guest, Anna Simonsen, made a portrait of Richard in red and black pastels. It was the last known portrait of him; its present whereabouts are unknown.
69 *Life*, vol II: p. 404. WRO: Arundell 2667/26. Uncatalogued.
70 Although the signature is Burton's the text, like so many of Burton's papers in his last years, is written in Isabel's handwriting, presumably dictated by Burton.
71 QK collection. Quote in an unidentified sale catalogue.
72 Heinrich Schliemann died 6 weeks after Richard Burton.
73 HL: Kirby correspondence. RFB to Kirby, 16 Aug 1890 (f.55).
74 Wright, vol. II: p. 146. However, what evidence exists points more towards agnosticism than atheism. Perhaps Cautley's memory was at fault.
75 *Life*, vol. II: p. 409.
76 Wright, vol. II: p. 217.
77 *Life*, vol. II: p. 408.
78 Ibid., p. 410. We have to assume from RFB's statement to IB that he had given up his search for a complete copy of the Arabic ms. and that in finishing the second volume of *Scented Garden* (the first volume having been finished months earlier according to his letter to Smithers), with its copious notes, he regarded the work as being as complete as he could make it. On the other hand it is difficult to believe, in view of his comments to Smithers, that he seriously intending abandoning the other work he had in hand, Catullus, Pentmerone, Ausonius etc.
79 WRO: IB's statement regarding *The Scented Garden*.
80 Statement by P.P. Cautley to Wright, vol. II: p. 239.
81 HL: IB to Smithers (108), 31 Oct. 1890.
82 WRO: Signed statement of the events taking place at the death-bed of Burton, by Father Pietro Martelani, 12 Jan. 1897.
83 WRO: The statement and translation of Father Martelani were obtained after Isabel's death by her biographer, and are included in her papers. Isabel asked the priest to administer the service *si es capax*, a form of the sacrament administered to an unconscious dying person.
84 WRO: Handwritten, sworn statement by Father Pietro Martelani, parish priest of the Church of Blessed Virgin 'del Soccorso', Trieste. Later Prebendary of the Cathedral of Trieste. With translation from the Italian it was obtained by Catherine de Ralli, friend of the Burtons, after Isabel's death.
85 WRO: Those present at the death: IB, Dr Baker, Father Don Martelani and Lisa dell'Abaco.
86 Jane Digby's diaries. IB's statement: 'I have a great fear of being buried alive, but not of dying.'
87 IB to Madame Gutmansthal-Benvenuti. Quoted in *The Romance*, p. 696. The reply to this letter is among IB's papers at WRO.

88 Wright, vol. II: p. 244.
89 The emergency form of baptism IB administered in Cannes became invalid in the eyes of the church after Richard recovered.
90 See also Wright, vol. II: p. 216. Wright includes a letter from Mr T. Douglas Murray dated 24 Sept. 1904, as follows: 'About a year before her death [in 1896] Lady Burton showed me a paper of considerable length, all of it in Sir Richard Burton's handwriting and signed by himself, in which he declared that he had lived and would die a Catholic, adhering to all the rites of the Catholic Church.' This was possibly one of the documents he wrote and signed in her presence at Majola, to which she referred in *Life* (vol. II: pp. 403–404). Curiously she never referred directly to this document in her defence of the actions she carried out after Burton's death, preferring to rely on the shorter one referred to earlier in this book. I have not been able to trace the document referred to by T.D. Murray.
91 Wright: *Life of John Payne*, vol. I: p. 99.

Chapter 35 (1890–1891)
1 Now owned by the Orleans House Gallery.
2 WRO: (xii) A.2. (author's cataloguing).
3 WRO: Signed document by Dr Costantini, Town Physician, dated 24 Oct. 1890, translated by Mr Cautley, Acting Consul.
4 Somerset House. Will of Richard F. Burton; proved at Principal Registry, 23 March 1891.
5 *Life*, vol. II: p. 418. The City had three great funeral requiems . . . one took place at the Cappuchins, one at the parish church, one at the orphanage of St Joseph. Also Wright, vol. II: p. 245.
6 Reproduced in Wright, vol. II: p. 246.
7 WRO: 2667/26.
8 WRO: Unidentified cutting in IB's cuttings book of Obituaries for RFB. Dated '30.10.90.'
9 RGS: Proceedings, Dec. 1890. Burton would also figure to a greater or lesser degree in the memoirs of almost every important Victorian. Lord Salisbury's restrained comment was almost a *mea culpa*: 'Richard Burton . . . prided himself on looking like Satan – as indeed he did . . . an ill-used servant, ill-used because his invaluable services were not put to the greatest use . . . for what services he rendered he received a most inadequate reward.' See Dunraven, Earl of: *Past Times and Pastimes* (London, 1922), vol. II: p. 178.
10 *Life*, vol. II: p. 418.
11 *Daily Graphic*, 23 Oct. 1890. 'Some Personal Reminiscences' by Commander Verney Lovett Cameron, CB; DCL.
12 *Weekly Register*, 3 Jan. 1891, and other newspapers.
13 Theodore Watts had 'looked after' Dante Rosetti in the same manner until his death. In the Kunitz and Haycroft biography of Swinburne, the authors state: 'Undoubtedly he saved Swinburne's life . . . but in rescuing the man he killed the poet.' Watts hyphenated his name in 1897 by adding his mother's maiden name to his own, but I have used Watts Dunton throughout to avoid any confusion with the painter G.F. Watts who moved in the same circles.
14 WRO: IB to Baker, 21 July 1891.
15 WRO: IB's statement: 'The Scented Garden' which forms part of her instructions to her executors.

16 WRO: uncatalogued. Envelope of signed statements dated 25 Oct. and other documents pertaining to IB's estate in the event of her death; 'my husband has left me in his will *everything* and appoints me sole executor, and his Power of Attorney grants me plenary power and embraces every case'. In the case of the power of attorney 'two signatures will be needed for any act or deed.'

17 Baker suggested that RFB may have written to Arbuthnot saying that the *Scented Garden* ms. was to be his after his death. The will, however, had been written some years earlier and was of a few lines only, leaving everything to Isabel and making her sole executrix. He often assisted British residents to write wills and knew precisely what he was doing; in the *Nights* he stated that 'the Briton's right to will property away from his wife' was a 'gross abuse [and] time-honoured scandal'.

18 Document giving Power of Attorney to Baker and Letchford, and setting out her wishes. Witnessed by Dr Cambon, 25 Oct. 1890. See also HL: Box 2 (110), IB to Smithers, 26 Dec. 1890, 'He left me papers of instructions in case I survived him. This we did mutually.'

19 Wright, vol. II: p. 247.

20 Ibid., p. 251.

21 Ibid., p. 252.

22 Ibid., p. 260.

23 When I visited Trieste in 1996 part of the Burtons' dining-room furniture was owned by the present British Consul. His wife's great-grandparents received it from Isabel.

24 *Modern Review*, Dec. 1893, pp. 224–9.

25 See list of 'things to be burned' in IB's book of last wishes.

26 *Life*, vol. II: p. 245.

27 WRO: See Appendix 1.

28 WRO: 2667/26. Papers of Isabel Burton. Uncatalogued. See Appendix 1.

29 Speke was not buried in Westminster Abbey but in the parish church of his home in Somerset.

30 *Life*, vol. II: p. 418.

31 IB to many correspondents; e.g. To Mrs Edward 'Bessie' Burton, 23 March 1891. Reproduced in Wright, vol. II: p. 262. The Forest of Dean stone was chosen for two reasons, first the stonemasons considered it was least liable to be affected by the weather, second it lent itself well to the carving of soft draping fabric for the 'tent'.

32 Cutting from *Morning Post*, u/d, among IB's papers, written 29 Nov. 1890. The items listed form a major part of the Burton collection at Richmond Central Library, some of which is housed at the Orleans House Gallery.

33 WRO: Statement of Accounts: 'expenses regarding Sir Richard Burton from the hour of his death until the day after his funeral'. Isabel's first letter brought in only £140, and she wrote several letters to other papers in April, explaining the difficulty and saying that friends had advised her 'it was not sufficiently advertised'. The balance was reached within six weeks.

34 RGS: Burton correspondence (1880–1910).

35 Since Isabel stated in her account of the *Scented Garden* that she received an offer of £3,000 for the manuscript 'within a few days of Richard's death' it was almost certainly contained in this letter which I have not been able to find. It is not among the known Smithers collections and was probably included in the papers Isabel deposited with her London solicitors (see following chapter).

Isabel's reply, dated 31 refers to Smithers's comments that he received RFB's final letter on the 24th, 'the day of his funeral'.
36 HL: Box 2. IB to Smithers, 31 Dec. 1890.
37 *The Romance*, p. 237.
38 IB's letter to the *Morning Post* in June 1891. Reproduced in part in *Life*, vol. II: pp. 438–43.
39 Holywell Street was the centre of the Victorian pornography trade. It ran parallel with the Strand between the churches of St Mary le Strand and St Clement's. An unsuccessful attempt was later made to change its name to Bookseller's Row.
40 Copies of some of the documentation are owned by QK. IB has written on the envelope: 'Scented Garden. My own copy for my heirs if needed.'
41 Lt.-Col J.A. Grant to *The Times*, 25 Oct. 1890. The charge Grant refers to is that Burton had tried to have Speke poisoned on the return journey from the lakes. See also NLS: (Grant papers) Grant's subsequent letters to others confirm his unsuccessful attempts to obtain proof that Speke actually spoke to anyone at the RGS about this matter; apparently, only Speke's sister had ever heard the story.
42 *Daily Graphic*. Written by IB, 4 Jan. 1891.
43 HL: Box 2 (110). IB to Smithers, 26 Dec. 1890.
44 WRO: IB's statement, 'The Scented Garden'. Uncatalogued.
45 WRO: (xii) A/2. 'Mrs Maylor, more properly Mrs Owen as she married a second time, but keeps her first husband's name . . .'
46 Reports in the English press stated that RFB's coffin was being shipped home in a 'piano case' to avoid alarming superstitious crew who would refuse to sail with a coffin. At Isabel's request V.L. Cameron publicly denied this but it nevertheless gained wide credence.
47 WRO: Letter from IB to Prince and Princess Thurn und Taxis, u/d c. June 1891.
48 WRO: There are several surviving letters from IB to several members of the Austrian Court in this connection.
49 WRO: Series of letters from Albert Letchford 1890–1896. Uncatalogued.
50 IB to Madame Gutmansthal-Benvenuti, 1 March 1891.
51 EM: Box 9. Smithers to IB, 26 Feb. 1891.
52 EM: IB to Smithers, 22 March 1891.
53 *Thames Valley Times*, c. 17 June 1891. Cutting in IB's papers at WRO.
54 HL and WRO: both collections contain examples of this card.
55 *Thames Valley Times*, 17 June 1891.
56 *Morning Post*, 16 June 1890.
57 *Modern Review*, Oct. 1893.
58 Published for the first time in *The New Review*, vol. IV: pp. 97–9, Feb. 1891.
59 *Swinburne's Letters*, vol. VI: p. 10.
60 First published in the *Fortnightly Review*, No:CCCVII, 1 July 1891.
61 *Life*, vol. II: p. 440.

Chapter 36 (1891–1894)
1 *The Romance*, p. 750.
2 QK. IB to Baker, 21 July 1891.
3 EM: Smithers to IB, 11 Feb. 1893.
4 Reproduced in Wright, vol. II: p. 266, u/d [July 1891].

5   EM: There are several letters to Smithers signed Hermaphrodite, 1891–3.

6   IB to Gwendoline Ramsden, daughter of her old friends Duke and Duchess of Somerset, 31 Oct. 1893. Reproduced in *The Romance*, p. 758.

7   The pages of this 2-page letter somehow became separated. I found page 1 in Trowbridge: WRO 2667/26 Box 2 (iv) 28 IB/Smithers, 16 July 1891. Page 2 is in the EM collection. Box 9 (2).

8   HL: Box 2 (121) IB to Smithers, 18 July 1891.

9   Ibid. (124) 8 Aug. 1891.

10 EM. Box 9 (3) 5. IB to Smithers u/d. uncatalogued in envelope of 85 letters.

11 A copy of the letter IB referred to (Smithers to RFB) is in the QK collection. 'I began to see that he [Nichols] was a very unsafe man to deal with. He is unscrupulous, has no commercial honesty, and is in addition a really magnificent liar!'

12 Ibid.

13 Smithers is probably best known for his publication with Nichols of the so-called Library Edition of Burton's *Nights* and, later, of Oscar Wilde's *Ballad of Reading Gaol*, which he published successfully when no other publisher would touch Wilde. He also published a list of beautifully produced books by popular literary figures such as Aubrey Beardsley, Max Beerbohm and Edgar Allan Poe, and even his erotica list, much of it using the imprint 'Cosmopoli', was a high-class production. Wilde called him 'the most learned erotomaniac in Europe . . . he loves first editions, especially women. Little girls are his passion . . .' Smithers went bankrupt in 1900 and died aged 46 from a combination of drugs and alcohol.

14 WRO. Notes in IB's Memoranda Book.

15 IB/E.H. Bishop, 27 Dec. 1891. Reproduced in *The Romance*, p. 751.

16 Ibid.

17 Mrs Maylor's parents, both Italian, were shopkeepers, and had brought their daughter to England as a child. Her first husband (Maylor) was an English engineer who died young, and she married her late husband's cousin (Cole) who went to South Africa to look for work. She returned with her parents to Trieste where she began working for Burton. 'She is repulsive in her appearance, her habits and her manners', Isabel wrote in her private papers, '[but] seeing she was very sharp and clever we made her our copyist.' When Cole eventually turned up in Trieste, he was clearly a bad lot who expected his wife to keep him. With the help of the Burtons she managed to turn him away and resumed the name Mrs Maylor. 'She then tried to bigamise with consumptive patient named Antonio in the hospital,' but the Burtons stopped her.

18 WRO: Albert Letchford, 19 July 1892. IB's papers contain many conciliatory letters from Letchford and his sisters asking for her forgiveness and help in getting his work noticed.

19 WRO: Albert Letchford to IB, 18 Dec. 1892. There are many similar letters among IB's papers.

20 *Nineteenth Century*, 'The Partisans of Wild Women' by Eliza Lynn Linton, March 1892, p. 46.

21 *Swinburne's Letters*, vol. VI: p. 45. Swinburne to Lynn Linton, 24 Nov. 1892.

22 HL: Burton correspondence. Box 1 (68). IB to Smithers, 17 July [1887].

23 QK. IB to Mr Page, 'Our Cottage, Monday', u/d c. June 1893. 'Smithers arrived her today to see ms. (Catullus) and is spending the day here looking quite sane and pleasant for the first time. I have put away my life preserver and am not afraid of the morphia needle . . .'

24 IB to E.H. Bishop, March 1893. Reproduced in *The Romance*, p. 755. 'It has taken me eight months . . . I do not know if I can harden my heart against the curs [i.e. Lynn Linton] but I can put out my tongue and point my pen play pussy cat. I am to have six months rest but you know what that means . . .'

25 Both Thomas Wright and Norman Penzer drew attention to these spelling errors. Penzer also castigated Wright for his errors, and I have noticed errors, not of spelling but of fact, in Penzer. For example, Penzer scornfully dismisses Wright's statement that Isabel used the typewriter, 'Lady Burton never touched a typewriter in her life'; but evidence exists in her papers that Isabel did occasionally type notes and memoranda for herself. It is probably reasonable to say that in any work on Burton, the subject is so colossal that some errors are bound to occur despite the best efforts of authors and editors.

26 Among her papers are letters from old connections of Richard's anxious lest she should mention them by name in the book and begging her not to do so. Isabel dutifully removed names and substituted dashes or in some cases referred to personalities obliquely. WRO: (xviii) 94. For example, James Irvine to IB, 10–14 March 1893. 3 letters.

27 *Life*, vol. II: pp. 448–50.

28 WRO: Box 2 (xvii). George Etheridge (of Chapman Hall Publishers) to IB.

29 WRO: See envelope of Etheridge/IB correspondence, 1892–93.

30 IB to Mde de Gutmanstall-Benvenuti, 10 Jan. 1894. Reproduced in *The Romance*, p. 755. In a similar letter to Georgiana Stisted, Isabel wrote, 'I am so glad you went to Tussaud's and that you admired Dick and his group. I am not quite content with the pose. I have . . . had trouble with Tussaud about a certain stoop which he declares is artistic, but which I say was not natural to him.'

31 WRO: Box 2 (iv) 25.

32 QK, WRO, EM and HL: Contract and correspondence regarding sale of *Nights* is spread between all four collections. Isabel's accounts show that the monthly payments were made regularly, with interest accruing on the outstanding balance, and the last instalment was paid on 8 March 1895.

33 EM: In his letter of 9 May 1893, to IB agreeing to this, Smithers states that '3500 copies will reach you in a day or two'. This must be an error for 350. The original print run was 500 and in February 1891 80 copies had been sold. The title page states that the edition consisted of 500 numbered copies.

34 WRO: Box 2 (iv) 22. Alice Quarry to IB, 22 Feb. 1895.

35 WRO: IB to the Writers' Club, 15 Jan. 1894

36 EM: Box 9 (3) 5. Smithers to IB, u/d.

37 EM: Box 9/2 (5). Smithers to IB, 6 July 1893.

38 QK collection. 24 Aug. 1893.

39 QK. P. Jones to Smithers, 11 Oct. 1893.

40 There is a copy of this statement among IB's papers at WRO. Isabel also wrote another version of the affair, entitled 'My Deposition concerning the Scented Garden' which is in the QK collection. These statements, while not contradicting each other, differ in some details and it is necessary to read both to get the complete story.

41 EM: IB to MacCarthy, 9 Jan. 1895.

42   Farewell dear friend, dead hero! The great life
         Is ended, the great perils, the great joys;
         And he to whom adventures were as toys;
         Who seemed to bear a charm 'gainst spear or knife

> Or bullet, now lies silent from all strife
> Out yonder where the Austrian eagles poise
> On Istrian hills. But England at the noise
> Of that dreadful fall, weeps with the hero's wife.
> Oh last and noblest of the Errant Knights
> The English soldier and the Arab Sheik!
> Oh, singer of the East who loved so well
> The deathless wonder of the 'Arabian Nights,'
> Who touched Camoens' lute and still would seek
> Ever new deeds until the end! farewell!

43 EM: IB to McCarthy, 9 Jan. 1895.
44 Wright, vol. II: p. 253.
45 Richard and Maria's brother, Edward, survived them both. He died in Oct. 1895, having spoken only one short sentence in his 37 years of institutionalised life since leaving India after the Mutiny.
46 HL: Box 11 (2) 10. IB to Bessie (Mrs Edward Burton), 16 Jan. 1894, and similar to St George Burton quoted in *The Romance*, vol. II: p. 275.
47 *Life*, vol. II: p. 446.
48 EM: Nichols to IB, 22 Jan. 1895
49 WRO: Box 2 (iv) 31. Arbuthnot to IB, 18 Dec. 18[94].
50 WRO: Box 2 (iv) 36. Arbuthnot to IB, 4 Jan. 1895.
51 Brodie, p. 331.
52 WRO: Cutting in press cutting album. IB to *Liverpool Mercury*, 15 Oct. 1884.

Chapter 37 (1894–1896)

1 Letter in New Hall Archives.
2 QK: IB to Prestage, 9 July 1894. QK owns an important collection of letters between the Burtons and Edgar Prestage which, owing to its specialist nature, is not useful in a biography but would be invaluable to scholars.
3 *The Romance*, p. 768.
4 Ibid., p. 769, from Holywell Lodge, Eastbourne, 12 March 1896.

Epilogue

1 WRO: 'Last Wishes of Isabel Burton', contained in three notebooks.
2 WRO: 2667/27. Uncatalogued.
3 These books are listed as: *La Bastonade*; *Clerico-Galante*; *Ovid*; *Turkish Secretary*; *Reflections on Polygamy*; *Fisiologia dell 'Odio*; *Extracts from English Classics*; *Demonialite*. These were the books listed by Burton to be burned after his death. Isabel wrote against this list, 'some are already burned.'
4 WRO: Isabel Burton's 'Last Wishes' cited earlier.
5 Herbert Jones later compiled a list of the Burton Library as part of a work entitled *Contribution towards a Dictionary of English Book Collectors*, issued in sections by Bernard Quaritsch in 1898. Quaritsch also participated in this compilation. According to Penzer the list contains a number of errors.
6 Penzer, Norman, *Annotated Bibliography*, 1923, pp. 291–2.
7 QK collection has the correspondence from Minnie Plowman to Mr Foskett.
8 It was published in 1898 by Hutchinson, with a Preface by Wilkins.
9 WRO: 2667/26–2 (iii) ff.23-24.
10 WRO: 2667/26 (iii).
11 Ibid., and *The Times*, 18 March 1911, p. 3.

12   WRO: IB's 'Private Instructions to my sister.'
13   See F. Grenfell Baker's Preface to Penzer's *Annotated Bibliography*, p. x.
14   QK collection. Georgiana Stisted to Lynn Linton, 25 March 1896.
15   The QK collection contains a series of letters between Georgiana Stisted and
     Lynn Linton, dated 25 March; 5th, 8th, 14th, and 17th April; 9 Nov.; and 22
     Dec., all 1896. The statements here are a compilation of remarks taken from
     several of these letters.
16   Ibid. 25 March 1896.
17   QK collection. Georgiana Stisted to Lynn Linton. Stisted acknowledges that
     she has burned Linton's letters to her, 'as requested'.
18   QK. Stisted/Linton letters.
19   QK. Stisted to Linton, 22 Dec. 1896.
20   Her executor was E.S. Mostyn Pryce, son of one of Richard's first loves, his
     cousin Eliza (Burton).
21   Stisted, *The True Life*, p. 402.
22   Ibid.
23   Ibid., p. 400.
24   Wright, *The Life of Sir Richard Burton*, vol. I: p. xvi.
25   WRO: 2667/26. There are a number of letters from both women in this collec-
     tion.
26   As another illustration, see Appendix 2 for the amendment she made to one of
     Burton's poems.
27   QK collection.
28   Apart from Burton cousins, Dr Baker and Daisy Nicastro, Wright's main con-
     tributors were John Payne; Mr Watts Dunton; W.F. Kirby; A.G. Ellis. F.F.
     Arbuthnot's widow provided several of her husband's manuscripts in which
     Burton was mentioned. Mr Cautley (Richard's long-suffering Vice-Consul) also
     wrote from Trieste.
29   In one letter to Payne, Burton mentioned the loss of his early collection in the
     Grindlay's fire in 1861.
30   Wright, *Life of Sir Richard Burton*, vol. I: p. xii.
31   Mrs E.J. 'Bessie' Burton; Frederick Burton (cousin); St George Burton; and E.S.
     Mostyn Pryce.
32   British Library, *Times Literary Supplement*, 16 March 1906.
33   Wright, *Life of John Payne*, vol. I: p. 213.
34   Penzer, M.: *An Annotated Bibliography of Sir Richard Francis Burton*, p. 28. It
     ought to be noted that even Penzer made *some* mistakes. However, until recently
     his was the most comprehensive bibliography of Burton's works, and it is still
     indispensable to Burton bibliophiles for the physical descriptions of early edi-
     tions. A less technical bibliography was produced in 1990 by James A. Casada;
     it contains a more comprehensive list of magazine articles and papers by RFB.
35   Penzer, *Annotated Bibliography*, p. ix.
36   Ibid., p. 176.

BIBLIOGRAPHY

(All books published London unless otherwise stated)

Primary Sources

Books by Richard Burton in chronological order (first edition details):

Goa and the Blue Mountains, or, 'Six Months of Sick Leave' (Richard Bentley, 1851).

Scinde or, The Unhappy Valley (Richard Bentley, 2 vols, 1851).

Sindh, and the Races that Inhabit the Valley of the Indus, 'With Notices of the Topography and History of the Province' (W.H. Allen, 1851).

Falconry in the Valley of the Indus (John Van Voorst, 1852).

A Complete System of Bayonet Exercise (William Clowes, 1853).

Personal Narrative of a Pilgrimage to El-Medinah and Meccah (Longmans, 3 vols: I & II, 1855; III, 1856).

First Footsteps in East Africa, 'or, An Exploration of Harar' (Longmans, 1856).

The Lake Regions of Central Africa (Longmans, 2 vols, 1860).

The City of the Saints 'and Across the Rocky Mountains to California' (Longmans, 1861).

The Prairie Traveller, a Hand-book for Overland Expeditions by Randolph B. Marcy. Edited (with notes) by Richard F. Burton (Trübner, 1863).

Abeokuta and the Cameroons Mountains (Tinsley Bros, 2 vols, 1863).

Wanderings in West Africa, 'From Liverpool to Fernando Po' by an F.R.G.S. (Tinsley Bros, 2 vols, 1863).

A Mission to Gelele, King of Dahome, 'With Notices of the So-called "Amazons", The Grand Customs, the Yearly Customs, the Human Sacrifices, the Present State of the Slave Trade, and the Negro's Place in Nature' (Tinsley Bros, 2 vols, 1864).

The Nile Basin, 'Part I: Showing Tanganyika to be Ptolemy's Western Lake Reservoir. A Memoir read before the Royal Geographical Society, November 14, 1864' . . . by Richard F. Burton. (Part II: 'Discovery of the Source of the Nile. A Review', by James M'Queen) (Tinsley Bros, 1864).

Wit and Wisdom from West Africa, 'or, A Book of Proverbial Philosophy, Idioms, Enigmas, and Laconisms' (Tinsley Bros, 1865).

The Guide-book, 'A Pictorial Pilgrimage to Mecca and Medina, Including Some of the More Remarkable Incidents in the Life of Mohammed, the Arab Lawgiver' (William Clowes, l865).

Stone Talk, 'Being Some of the Marvellous Sayings of a Petral Portion Fleet Street, London, to One Doctor Polyglott, Ph.D.,' by Frank Baker, D.O.N. [one of Burton's known pseudonyms] (Robert Hardwicke, 1865).

Explorations of the Highlands of the Brazil (Tinsley Bros, 2 vols, 1869).

Vikram and the Vampire, or Tales of *Hindu Devilry*, adapted by Richard F. Burton (Ernest Griset, l870).

Letters from the Battle-fields of Paraguay (Tinsley Bros, 1870).

Unexplored Syria, 'Visits to The Libanus, the Tulul el Safa, The Anti-Libanus, The Northern Libanus, and The Alah' (with Charles F. Tyrwhitt-Drake) (Tinsley Bros, 2 vols, 1871).

Zanzibar; City, Island, and Coast (Tinsley Bros, 2 vols, 1872).

Case of Captain Burton, late H.B.,M.'s Consul at Damascus. Blue Book published by Foreign office, 1873.

The Lands of Cazembe, Lacerda's Journey to Cazembe in 1798 (translated and annotated by Captain R.F. Burton), (Royal Geographical Society, 1873).

Ananga Ranga or The Hindu Art of Love (*Ars Amoris Indica*), (with F.F. Arbuthnot). (Privately printed, 1873). NB: Only four or six copies of this edition were printed. First print run 1885.

The Captivity of Hans Stade of Hesse, 'in A.D. 1547–1555, Among the Wild Tribes of Eastern Brazil.' (Translated by Albert Tootal; annotated by Richard F. Burton) (Hakluyt Society, 1874).

Ultima Thule; or A Summer in Iceland (Wm. Nimmo, 2 vols, 1875).

Etruscan Bologna; A Study (Smith Elder & Co., 1876).

A New System of Sword Exercise for Infantry (Wm. Clowes, 1876).

Two Trips to Gorilla Land and the Cataracts of the Congo (Sampson Low, 2 vols, 1876).

Sind Revisited; 'With Notices of the Anglo-Indian Army; Railroads; Past, Present, and Future' (Richard Bentley, 2 vols, 1877).

The Gold-Mines of Midian 'and The Ruined Midianite Cities, A Fortnight's Tour in Northwestern Arabia' (Kegan Paul, 1878).

The Land of Midian (revisited), (Kegan Paul, 2 vols, 1879).

The Kasîdah of Haji Abu El-Yezdi 'a Lay of the Higher Law.' Translated and annotated by His Friend and Pupil F.B. (Frank Baker). (Privately printed, 1880.)

Os Lusiadas (The Lusiads), 'Englished by Richard Francis Burton; edited by His Wife, Isabel Burton' (Bernard Quaritch 2 vols, 1880).

Camoens; His Life and His Lusiads – A Commentary (Bernard Quaritch, 2 vols, 1881).

A Glance at the 'Passion Play' (W.H. Harrison, 1881).

Lord Beaconsfield. A Sketch (1882).

To the Gold Coast for Gold, 'A Personal Narrative' (with Verney Lovett Cameron) (Chatto & Windus, 2 vols, 1883).

The Kama Sutra of Vatsyayana (with F.F. Arbuthnot). (Privately Printed 'for the Hindoo Kama Shastra Society, London and Benares, 1883.)

Camoens, The Lyricks, Parts I & II Sonnets, Canzons, Odes, and Sextines, 'Englished by Richard F. Burton' (Bernard Quaritch, 1884).

The Book of the Sword (Chatto & Windus, 1884).

Ananga Ranga; 'Stage of the Bodiless One or The Hindu Art of Love (Ars Amoris Indica)'. Translated from the Sanskrit, and annotated by A.F.F, and B.F.R. (Arbuthnot and Burton). (Cosmopoli, for the Kama Shastra Society of London and Benares, and for private circulation only, 1885.)

The Book of The Thousand Nights and a Night, 'A Plain and Literal Translation of the Arabian Nights' Entertainments', with Introduction and Explanatory Notes on the Manners and Customs of Moslem Men and a Terminal Essay upon the

History of the Nights. (Printed by the Kama Shastra Society for private subscribers only, 10 vols, 1885.)

The Supplemental Nights to the Book of The Thousand Nights and a Night, 'With Notes Anthropological and Explanatory'. (Printed by the Kama Shastra Society for private subscribers only, 6 vols, 1886 – 1888.)

The Perfumed Garden of the Cheikh Nefzaoui, 'A Manual of Arabian Erotology (xvi Century).' Revised and Corrected Translation (Cosmopoli, for the Kama Shastra Society of London and Benares, and for private circulation only, 1886).

The Behdristan (Abode of Spring) 'By Jami: A Literal Translation from the Persian' (with Edward Rehatsek). (Printed by the Kama Shastra Society for private subscribers only, Benares, 1887.)

The Gulistan or Rose Garden of Sa'di (with Edward Rehatsek). (Printed by the Kama Shastra Society for private subscribers only, Benares, 1887.)

Priapeia 'or the Sportive Epigrams of divers Poets on Priapus, the Latin Text now for the first time Englished in Verse and Prose the Metrical Version by "Outidanos"; with Introduction, Notes Explanatory and Illustrative, and Excursus, by "Neaniskos" (Outidanos and Neaniskos were pseudonyms used by Burton and Smithers). (Privately printed for the Erotika Biblion Society, 1890.)

Works of Richard Burton's published posthumously:

Marocco and the Moors by Arthur Leared, 2nd edition, revised and edited by Sir Richard Burton (RFB did not collaborate in the first edition). (Sampson Low, 1891).

Il Pentamerone, of Giambattista Basile. (Translated by RFB; Introduction and Notes by Leonard C. Smithers). (Privately printed, 1894.)

The Carmina of Caius Valerius Catullus (Verse by RFB; Introduction and Notes by Leonard C. Smithers). (Privately printed, 1894.)

The Jew, The Gypsy, and El Islam, ed: W.H. Wilkins. (Hutchinson, 1898).

Wanderings in Three Continents, ed: W.H. Wilkins (Hutchinson, 1901).

The Sentiment of the Sword, A Country House dialogue, ed: A.F. Sieveking (Cox, 1911).

Travels in Arabia and Africa – Four Lectures from a Huntington Library Manuscript, ed: John Hayman (Huntington Library, 1990).

Selected Papers on Anthropology, Travel and Exploration (ed. Norman M. Penzer). (Philpot, 1924).

Love, War and Fancy, extracts from the Arabian Nights etc. (Wm. Kimber, 1964).

Books by Isabel Burton:

Inner Life of Syria, Palestine and the Holy Land (Henry S. King, 2 vols, 1875).

A.E.I: Arabia, Egypt, India (Wm. Mullan, 1879).

Iracema, The Honey-lips, 'A Legend of Brazil' by J. De Alencar, Translated with the author's permission by Isabel Burton. (Bound with: *Maluel De Moraes*, A Chronicle of the Seventeenth Century, by J. M. Pereira Da Silva, Translated by Richard and Isabel Burton.)

The Passion Play at Ober-Ammergau (Hutchinson, 1900).

The Life of Captain Sir Richard F. Burton K.C.M.G., F.R.G.S. (Chapman and Hall, 1893).

The Romance of Isabel, Lady Burton: The Story of her Life Told in Part by Herself 2 vols (Hutchinson, 1897). 1 vol (Dodd Mead, New York, 1904). See also W.H. Wilkins – editor and biographer.

Primary Sources: *Selected Articles by Contemporaries*

Anon. 'Obituary: Sir Richard Francis Burton', *Proceedings of the Royal Geographical Society*, December 1890.

Baker, Dr Grenfell, 'Sir Richard Burton as I Knew Him', *Cornhill Magazine*, October 1921.

Burton, Isabel, 'Sir Richard Burton; An Explanation and a Defence', *New Review*, November 1892. 'About the "Scented Garden",' *The Modern Review*, 15 October 1893.

Cameron, Verney Lovett, 'Burton as I Knew Him', *Fortnightly Review*, December 1890.

Harris, Frank, 'Sir Richard Burton', *The Academy*, Parts 1 & 2: 16 & 23 September 1921.

Ionides, Luke, 'Memories of Richard Burton', *Transatlantic Review*, March 1924.

Linton, Eliza Lynn, 'The Partisans of Wild Women', *Ninteenth Century*, March 1892.

Ouida, 'Richard Burton', *Fortnightly Review*, June 1906.

Smalley, G.W., 'Sir Richard Burton', *New York Tribune*, 2 November 1890.

Smith, L.A., 'Recollections of Sir Richard Burton', *The Paternoster Review*, December 1890.

Stisted, Georgiana, 'Reminiscences of Sir Richard Burton', *Temple Bar*, July 1891.

Primary Sources: *Books by Contemporary authors*
(I have included here books written by contemporaries of the Burtons or which contain other relevant primary material)

Beaufort, Emily A., *Egyptian Sepulchres & Syrian Shrines* (Longmans, 2 vols, 1862).

Besant, Walter, *Literary Remains of Charles F. Tyrwhitt Drake* (Bentley, 1877).

―――― *Life of Edward Henry Palmer* (John Murray, 1883).

Blunt, Lady Anne, *Bedouin Tribes of the Euphrates* (Cass, 2 vols, 1986).

―――― *Pilgrimage to Nejd* (Darfy, 1984).

Blunt, Wilfred Scawen, *My Diaries* (Martin Secker, 2 vols, 1921).

Friswell, Laura Hain, *In the Sixties and Seventies* (Hutchinson, 1905).

Galton, Francis, *Memories of my Life* (Methuen, 1908).

Hare, Augustus, *Story of my Life* (George Allen, 1901).

Harris Frank, *Contemporary Portraits* (Methuen, 1915).

Hitchman, Francis, *Sir Richard Burton* (Sampson Low, 2 vols, 1887).

Krapf, J. Lewis, *Travels, Researches & Missionary Labours* (Cass, 1860 & 1968).

MacCarthy, Justin, *Reminiscences* (Chatto & Windus, 2 vols, 1899).

―――― *Portraits of the Sixties* (Fisher Unwin, 1903).

―――― *Our Book of Memories* (Chatto & Windus, 1912).

Murray, John, *Handbook for travellers in Syria and Palestine* (John Murray, 1868).

Paget, Lady Walburga, *Embassies of Other Days* (Hutchinson, 2 vols, 1923).

―――― *In My Tower* (Hutchinson, 2 vols, 1924).

―――― *Scenes & Memories* (Hutchinson, 1912).

Rainy, Wm., *The Censor Censored, or The Calumnies of Richard Burton* (1865).

Redesdale, Lord, *Memoirs* (Hutchinson, 2 vols, 1915).

Richards, Alfred Bate, *Oxford Unmasked* by A Graduate [known to be A.B. Richards] (Effingham Wilson 1842).

―――― *A Short Sketch of the Career of Captain Richard F. Burton*, by An Oxonian, first published 1880.

——— with Andrew Wilson & St. Clair Baddeley: *[Revised] Sketch of the Career of Captain Richard F. Burton* (Waterlow, 1886).

Russell, Bertrand, *The Amberley Papers* (Hogarth Press, 2 vols, 1937).

Russell, Mrs Charles E.B., *General Rigby, Zanzibar and the Slave Trade* (Allen & Unwin, 1935).

Rutter, John, *Descriptive Sketch of Wardour Castle* (Longmans, 1822).

Symons, Arthur, *Dramatis Personae* (Faber & Gwyer, 1925).

Speke, John Hanning, *What Led to the Discovery of the Source of the Nile* (Blackwood, 1864).

——— *Journal of the Discovery of the Source of the Nile* (Blackwoods, Harper NY, 1868).

Stisted, Georgina, *The True Life of Captain Sir Richard Burton* (H.S. Nichols, 1896).

Swinburne, Algernon, *The Swinburne Letters* (Edited by Cecil Y. Lang) (OUP, 6 vols, 1959).

——— *Collected Poetical Works* (Heinemann, 1927).

Underhill, Edward B., *Alfred Saker* (B.M.S., 1884).

Wemyss Reid, T., *Life, Letters & Friendships* of *Richard Monckton Milnes* (Cassell, 2 vols, 1890).

Wilkins, W.H., *The Romance* of *Isabel Burton* (Dodd Mead N.Y., 1984).

Wright, Thomas, *Sir Richard Burton* (Everett, 2 vols, 1906).

——— *John Payne* (Fisher Unwin, 1913).

Wright, William, *Burton at Damascus* (The Bookman, October 1890).

Bibliographies:

Casada, James A., Sir *Richard F. Burton: A* bibliographical study (Mansell, 1990).

Kirkpatrick, B.J., *Catalogue of Richard Burton's Library* (Royal Anthrop. Institute, 1978).

Penzer, Norman M., *Annotated Bibliography* (A.M. Philpott, 1923).

(As well as books Burton submitted articles and papers to journals, magazines and newspapers far too numerous to list in this book. No bibliography yet compiled is totally comprehensive but Casada is best from this point of view.)

Secondary Sources: Modern Biographies: (version referred to in notes)

Assad, Thomas J., *Three Victorian Travellers* (Routledge & Kegan Paul, 1964).

Blanch, Lesley, *The Wilder Shores of Love* (Murray, 1974).

Brodie, Fawn, *The Devil Drives* (Eyre & Spottiswoode, 1967).

——— 'Introduction' to *City of the Saints*, op. cit. (1964).

Burton, Jean, *Sir Richard Burton's Wife* (Alfred Knopf, N.Y., 1941).

Cottrell, John, *Richard Burton, A biography* (Barker, 1971).

Dearden, Seton, *The Arabian Knight* (Barker, 1953).

Dodge, Walter, *The Real Sir Richard Burton* (Unwin, 1907).

Downey, Fairfax, *Arabian Nights' Adventurer* (Scribner, 1931).

Farwell, Byron, *Burton* (Longmans, 1990).

Hastings, Michael, *Sir Richard Burton* (Hodder & Stoughton, 1978).

McLynn, Frank, *Snow upon the Desert* (Murray, 1993).

——— *From the Sierras to the Pampas* (Century, 1991).

Schonfield, Hugh, *Richard Burton, Explorer* (Herbert Joseph, 1936).

Rice, Edward, *Captain Sir Richard Burton* (Scribners N.Y., 1990).

Secondary Sources: General Reading List

Archer & Fleming, *Lady Anne Blunt: Journals and Correspondence* (Heriot, 1986).

Archer, W.G., 'Preface' to *The Kama Sutra* (George Allen & Unwin, 1963).

Baldick, Robert (ed.), *Pages from the Goncourt Journal* (OUP, 1962).

Bennett, Norman R., *A History of the Arab State of Zanzibar* (Methuen, 1978).

—— *New England Merchants in Africa* (Boston University Press, 1965).

Bidwell, Robin, *Travellers in Arabia* (Garnett, 1994).

Blunden, Edmund, *Leigh Hunt* (Cobden-Sanderson, 1930).

Blunt, Wilfred S., *Desert Hawk; Abd el Kader* (Methuen, 1947).

Brendon , J.A., *Twelve Great Passions* (Hutchinson, 1912).

Bridges, R.C., *James Augustus Grant* (National Library of Scotland, 1982).

Brock, M.G. and Curthoys, M.C., *The History of the University of Oxford –
    Nineteenth Century Part I* (Clarendon Press 1997).

Brodie, Fawn, *No Man Knows my History* (Joseph Smith, 1963).

Burton, Rosemary, *Journeys of the Great Explorers* (AA, 1992).

Cadell, Sir Patrick, *History of the Bombay Army* (Longmans, 1938).

Cameron, V. L. *Across Africa* (Daldy Ibister, 2 vols, 1877).

Camoens, Luiz vaz de, *The Lusiads* (transl. Wm. C. Atkinson). (Penguin, 1952).

Coupland, R., *The Exploitation of East Africa* (Faber, 1939).

—— *East Africa and Its Invaders* (Clarendon Press, 1938).

Crofton, R.H., *The Old Consulate at Zanzibar* (OUP, 1935).

Debenham, Frank, *The Way to Illala* (Longman, 1955).

Doughty, Charles, *Wanderings in Arabia* (Duckworth, 1926).

Ffrench, Yvonne, *Ouida; A Study in Ostentation* (Appleton-Century, 1938).

Fraser, Flora, *The Unruly Queen* (MacMillan, 1996).

Fuller, Jean Overton, *Swinburne* (Chatto & Windus, 1968).

Glass, Charles, *Tribes with Flags (*Picador, 1994).

Gray, John, *History of Zanzibar* (OUP, 1962).

Gray Richard & Birmingham, David, *Pre-Colonial African Trade* (OUP, 1970).

Gunter, John, *Inside Africa* (Hamish Hamilton, 1957).

Hale Richard Walden, *A Footnote to History* (privately printed, Boston, 1930).

Hall, Richard, *Lovers on the Nile* (Random House, 1980).

Halliday, Eric, *The Emergent Continent: Africa in the 19th Century* (Ernest Benn,
    1972).

Hanbury-Tenison, Robin, *The Oxford Book of Exploration* (OUP, 1994).

Harrison, William, *Burton & Speke* (Wm Allen (fiction), 1984).

Henderson, Philip, *The Life of Laurence Oliphant* (Robert Hale, 1959).

Hibbert, Christopher, *The Great Mutiny: India 1857* (Viking Press, 1978).

Hopkirk, Peter, *The Great Game* (OUP, 1991).

—— *Quest for Kim* (Murray, 1996).

Howarth, David & Stephen, *The Story of the P. & O.* (Weidenfeld & Nicholson,
    1986).

Hyde, H. Montgomery, *A History of Pornography* (Heineman, 1964).

Imlah, Albert H., *Lord Ellenborough* (OUP, 1939).

Irwin, Robert, *A Companion to The Arabian Nights* (Allen Lane, 1994).

Jeal, Tim, *Livingstone* (Heinemann, 1973).

Johnson, Sir Harry, *The Nile Quest* (Lawrence & Bullen, 1903).

Jutzi, Alan (ed), *In Search of Sir Richard Burton* (Huntingdon Library, 1993).

Kingslake, A.W., *Eothen* (Lehmann, 1948).

Law, Sir Algernon, *India under Lord Ellenborough* (John Murray, 1926).

Leask, Nigel, *British Romantic Writers and the East* (Cambridge University Press, New Delhi, 1993).

Longford, Elizabeth, *A Pilgrim of Passion* (Knopf, 1980).

Lovell, Mary S., *A Scandalous Life* (Richard Cohen Books, 1995).

MacCarthy, Desmond, *Portraits* (MacGibbon & Kee, 1949).

McLynn, Frank, *Of No Country; Anthology* (Scribner, 1990).

Maitland, Alex , *Speke* (Constable, 1971).

Margetson, Stella, *Leisure & Pleasure in the 19th Century* (Cassell, 1969).

Marsh & Kingsnorth, *A History of East Africa* (Cambridge University Press, 1957).

Marston, Thomas E., *Britain's Imperial Role in the Red Sea Area* (Shoe String Press, Hamden Connecticut, 1961).

Melman, Billie, *Women's Orients: British Women in the Middle East* (Macmillan, 1992 & 1995).

Middleton, Dorothy, *Baker of the Nile* (Falcon, 1949).

Misra, B.B., *The Central Administration of the East India Company* (Manchester University Press, 1959).

Moorehead, Alan, *The White Nile* (Hamish Hamilton, 1960).

————— *The Blue Nile* (Hamish Hamilton, 1962).

Morris, Jan, *Stones of Empire* (Penguin, 1983).

Munson, Arley, *Kipling's India* (Doubleday NY, 1915).

National Library of Scotland, *Scotland and Africa* (NLS, 1982).

National Portrait Gallery, *Livingstone* (NPG, 1996).

Neville, Lady Dorothy, *Leaves from the Notebooks* (MacMillan, 1907).

Oliver, Roland, & Mathew, Gervase, *A History of East Africa* (Clarendon Press, 1963).

Ondaatje, Christopher, *Sindh Revisited* (HarperCollins, 1996).

Ormond, Leonée & Richard, *Lord Leighton* (Yale University Press, 1975).

Panhwar, M.H., *Source Material on Sind* (University of Sind, Pakistan, 1977).

Penzer, Norman M., *Harem* (Spring Books, 1936).

Pope-Hennessy, James, *Monckton Milnes: The Years of Promise, 1809–1851* (Farrar, Straus & Cudahy, NY, 1940).

————— *The Flight of Youth, 1851–1885* (Ibid., 1951).

Russell, George W.E., *Portraits of the Seventies* (Fisher Unwin, 1912).

Said, Edward W., *Orientalism* (Penguin, 1995).

Searight, Sara, *The British in the Middle East* (Weidenfeld & Nicholson, 1969).

Sheriff, Abdul, *Slaves, Spices & Ivory in Zanzibar* (James Currey, 1987).

Stanley, Henry Morton, *Through the Dark Continent* (Sampson Low, 1980).

Stirling, Monica, *The Fine & the Wicked: Life & Times of Ouida* (Gollancz, 1957).

Stoker, Bram, *Personal Reminiscences (*MacMillan, 1906).

Thesiger, Wilfred, *Arabian Sands* (Penguin, 1991).

Thurston, Anne, *Review of the Zanzibar Archives* (UNESCO, 1984).

Tidrick, Kathryn, *Heart Beguiling Araby* (Tauris, 1981).

Walker, Dr Kenneth, *Love War and Fancy* (Kimber, 1964).

Wallin, G.A., *Travels in Arabia; 1845 & 1848* (Falcon Orleander, 1979).

Waterfield, Gordon, *Sultans of Aden* (John Murray, 1968).

————— 'Introduction' to *First Footsteps in East Africa* op. cit. (Praeger NY, 1966).

Walton, Alan Hull, 'Introduction' to *The Perfumed Garden* (Neville Spearman, 1963).

Welby, T. Earle, *A Study of Swinburne* (Methuen, 1926 & 1969).

Woodruff, Philip, *The Men who Ruled India* (Jonathan Cape, 1965).

Young, Col. Keith, *Scinde in the Forties; Journal*. Edited by Arthur F. Scott (Constable, 1912).

Secondary Sources: Selected Articles and Pamphlets (modern)

Garcia, Frederick C.H., 'Richard Francis Burton & Basílio da Gama', *Luso-Brazilian Review*, Parts 1 & 2, Spring and Summer 1975.

Godsall, Jon R., 'Fact & Fiction in Richard Burton's Personal Narrative of a Pilgrimage to El-Medinah and Meccah', *Royal Asiatic Society.*

Ingrams, Harold, 'Burton Memorial Lecture', *Royal Asiatic Society* 1945.

Mifsud, Anton, 'Medical History of J.H. Speke', *The Practitioner*, January 1975.

Orleans House Gallery, A *Blaze of Light Without a Focus* (Borough of Richmond, 1990).

Wilson, Sir Arnold, *Richard Burton* (Fifth Burton Memorial Lecture before the Royal Asiatic Society) (OUP, 1937).

Various authors in Burton and Speke Centennial Issue of *Tanganyika Notes & Records* December 1957:

Gray, Sir John, 'Trading Expeditions from the Coast to Lakes Tanganyika and Victoria'.

Harlow, Professor Vincent, 'Burton and Speke Expedition Centenary'.

Ingham, M.C., 'John Hanning Speke'.

Pike, A.H., 'Notes on the Exploration of the Source of the Nile'.

Risley, R.G.H., 'Burton: An Appreciation'.

Wenban-Smith, W., 'Diary of the 1857–1858 Expedition to the Great Lakes'.

Newspaper Archives
The Times.
British Library Newspaper Archives at Collindale.
Bodleian Library: Western manuscripts.

ACKNOWLEDGEMENTS

Many people have helped me during the preparation of this book but there are three individuals to whom I owe special thanks.

Edwards Metcalf, who gave me permission to access his Burton collection, and gave his time to guide me through not only his large holding of Burton books and documents, but his even larger and equally fascinating T.E. Lawrence collection (both held at HL under restrictive access). He was also very helpful in the early stages of my work and made many invaluable suggestions as to the direction my research should take. Nor has he lost interest since, telephoning periodically from California to find out how my work was progressing.

Quentin Keynes, to whom this book is dedicated, has become a good friend during its gestation. His collection of Burton books and documents is amazing, and his generosity in making rare books and unique materials available to me – sometimes for months at a time – has been truly noble. I am particularly grateful to him for permission to quote extracts from materials he has collected for his own book of selected letters, to be published privately in late 1998.

Bernadette Rivett was already a friend before I decided to write about Richard and Isabel Burton, and (though I was not aware of it) she was a Burton collector long before we met. When I began research I suggested that although she is now retired from her important work for the WHO, she made her already full life even busier by helping me with some of the more tedious aspects of research. In addition, she accompanied me on several research trips, notably to Trieste where, a hundred years after Mr Consul Burton's death, we were hospitably entertained by the present-day British Consul, whose wife's grandparents knew the Burtons; and the couple still own some of the Burtons' furniture from the old Palazzo.

Bernadette and I evolved a time-consuming but effective system for transcribing Richard Burton's minute, and difficult to read, handwriting. Using the largest possible magnifying glasses (and sometimes enlarging documents on a photocopier) one of us would do a first draft leaving spaces where words proved unreadable; the other would then take over (also with magnifying glass) and attempt to fill in the gaps. Sometimes a document went back and forth, by post, three or four times, before we were both satisfied that it was correct, and there were thousands of documents in the three years spent in full-time research. Bernadette is clearly a born researcher for she is innately curious, and will never drop a lead until she has hounded it to death. Her own genuine interest in Burton and her knowledge of several European languages has been invaluable. I hope she approves of the use to which I have put all her hard work and enthusiasm.

Many others have assisted me, also. Some a great deal, others to a lesser extent. I should like to have detailed the manner in which each helped but, as space does not allow this, I hope that they will accept my simple thanks in the knowledge that everyone in the following list has played a part in the writing of this biography:

In the United Kingdom. Peter Allmond (Bodleian); Jane Baxter (RL); Hugh Bett (Maggs Bros); Dr David M. Bertie (Aberdeen Council); Michael Blair (Custodian, Wardour Castle); Penny Brooke (IOR); Diana Chardin (TCC); Susan Corrigall (NRA, Scotland); Prof. Ron Edwards: Philip Davies (Bank of England Research

Section); Beryl Evans (National Library of Wales); Julia Findlater (Leighton House Museum); Col. Monty Flash; The Hon. Lavinia Fleming; Mick Fox (Archives, WRO); Lady Fuller; Mrs O.M. Geddes (Snr. Research Asst. NLS); Morna Gerrard (Scottish Record Office); Stephen Hobbs (County Archivist, WRO); Clare J. Hopkins (Trinity College, Oxford); D. Jones (RL); Nicholas Labourn (Christie's); Harold Lomax; Paula Lucas (RGS); John Maddicott (Exeter College, Oxford); the Master and Fellows of Trinity College, Cambridge (for permission to use extracts from the Houghton papers); M.A. McNeile; Laura Mitchell (National Archives of Scotland); Antonia Moon (IOR); Doreen Morris; Steven Nicholls (OHG); Dr Christine Nicholls; Christopher Ondaatje; Mared A. Owen (National Library of Wales); Derek Parker (photographer); Sister Mary Peters (Archivist, New Hall School); John Pryce: Deborah Reynolds (Christie's); Fiona Robertson (OHG); Anne Sanderson; Douglas Saville (Spink & Son Ltd); Nadim Shehadi; Bella Stewart (Fitzwilliam Museum); Huw Thomas (Archives Asst. RGS); Rachel Tranter (OHG); the Trustees of the National Library of Scotland; Dr Magnus Williamson.

Overseas. In U.S.A.: Dr. Jim Casada; Burke Casari; Carolyn A. Davis (Syracuse Univ); Sara Hodson (HL); Alan Jutzi (Curator, HL); Gerald Rilling; Frances Rouse (HL);. *In Europe*: Major and Mrs Norman Lister (British Consul, Trieste); John Joly (France); *In Africa*: Khamis S. Khamis (Archivist, ZA); Professor Abdul Sheriff (Principal Curator, ZA); *In the Middle East*: Peter Clark (British Council, Damascus); Hussein Hinnawi (Guide and Interpreter, Damascus); Jehann and Tariq Rajab (Tariq Rajab Museum, Kuwait).

I would like to record my formal thanks to the owners and trustees of the following archives who have kindly permitted me to quote extracts from manuscripts in their collections. In the UK: The British Library; the Trustees of the National Library of Scotland; the Royal Geographical Society; the Master and Fellows of Trinity College, Cambridge; London Borough of Richmond upon Thames; and the Wiltshire Record Office. In the USA: the Huntington Library, San Marino, California.

Finally , I should like to thank the publishing 'production team' at Little, Brown: Richard Beswick (Commissioning Editor); Antonia Hodgson (Desk Editor); Jean Maund (Copy Editor); Charlotte Windsor (Proofreader) and Neil Hyslop (map maker). I am also grateful to Starling Lawrence at Norton Publishers in New York, for his faith in the project, and to Patricia Chui at Norton who liaised generally.

My particular thanks to Robert Ducas, who must be every author's dream Literary Agent. In the twelve years that I have known him he has never given me a single piece of bad advice. During the last few months of this book's gestation he became seriously ill but continued to work on my behalf (much against my wishes) from his sickbed. I regard him as a very special friend.

Picture Credits
Orleans House Gallery: 1, 2; Author's Collection: 3, 4, 5, 6, 8, 20, 28, 35, 42, 44, 47, 50, 55; Royal Anthropological Society: 7; Wiltshire Record Office: 9, 13, 14, 15, 16, 21, 22, 25, 26, 27, 29, 31, 34, 36–41, 43, 46; Huntington Library: 10; Christopher Ondaatje: 12; Royal Geographical Society: 18; Houghton Library, Harvard University: 19; Richmond Public Library: 23, 24, 48, 52; Zanzibar National Archives: 30; Quentin Keynes: 32, 49; Jehan and Tariq Rajab: 45; National Portrait Gallery: 51. **Reproduced from:** *Travels on Three Continents*: 11; *Zanzibar, City, Island and Coast*: 17; *Highlands of the Brazil*: 33; *The Life*: 53, 54.

INDEX